Routledge International Encyclopedia of Women

Global Women's Issues and Knowledge

Volume 3 Identity Politics—Publishing

Editorial Board

Routledge International Encyclopedia of Women

Global Women's Issues and Knowledge

Volume 3 Identity Politics—Publishing

Cheris Kramarae and Dale Spender
General Editors

Routledge
New York • London

NOTICE
Some articles in the *Routledge International Encyclopedia of Women* relate to physical and mental health; nothing in these articles, singly or collectively, is meant to replace the advice and expertise of physicians and other health professionals. Some articles relate to law and legal matters; nothing in any of these articles is meant to replace the advice and expertise of lawyers and other legal professionals.

Published in 2000 by
Routledge
29 West 35 Street
New York, NY 10001

Routledge is an imprint of the Taylor & Francis Group

Published in Great Britain by
Routledge
11 New Fetter Lane
London EC4P 4EE

Library of Congress Cataloging-in-Publication Data
Routledge international encyclopedia of women: global women's issues and knowledge / general editors, Cheris Kramarae, Dale Spender.
p. cm.
Includes bibliographical references and index.
ISBN 0-415-92088-4 (set) — ISBN 0-415-92089-2 (v.1) — ISBN 0-415-92090-6 (v.2) — ISBN 0-415-92091-4 (v.3) — ISBN 0-415-92092-2 (v.4)
1. Women—Encyclopedias. 2. Feminism—Encyclopedias. I. Title: International encyclopedia of women. II. Kramarea, Cheris. III. Spender, Dale.
HQ1115 .R69 2000
305.4'03—dc21 00-045792

10 9 8 7 6 5 4 3 2 1

ISBN 0-415-92088-4 (4-volume set)
ISBN 0-415-92089-2 (volume 1)
ISBN 0-415-92090-6 (volume 2)
ISBN 0-415-92091-4 (volume 3)
ISBN 0-415-92092-2 (volume 4)

Contents

Editorial Board ii
Alphabetical List of Articles vii
The Encyclopedia 1097

Alphabetical List of Articles

Ability
Abortion
Abuse
Activism
Adolescence
Adoption
Adoption: Mental health issues
Adultery
Advertising
Advertising industry
Aesthetics: Black feminist—A debate
Aesthetics: Feminist
Affirmative action
Ageism
Aging
Aging: Japanese case study
Agriculture
AIDS and HIV
AIDS and HIV: Case study—Africa
Alternative energy
Alternative technology: Case study—Africa
Altruism
Anarchism
Anatomy
Ancient indigenous cultures: Women's roles
Ancient nation-states: Women's roles
Androcentrism
Androgyny
Anger
Animal rights
Anorexia nervosa
Anthropology
Antidiscrimination
Antiracist and civil rights movements
Anti-Semitism
Apartheid, segregation, and ghettoization
Archaeology
Archaeology: Northern European case study
Archetype
Architecture
Armament and militarization
Art practice: Feminist
Assertiveness training
Autobiographical criticism
Autobiography
Automation

Battery
Beauty contests and pageants
Bigamy
Bioethics: Feminist
Biography
Biological determinism
Biology
Bisexuality
Blackness and whiteness
Bluestockings
Body
Bookshops
Borders
Breast
Breast feeding
Buddhism
Built environment
Bulimia nervosa
Bureaucracy
Butch/femme

Cancer
Capitalism
Caregivers
Cartoons and comics
Caste
Celibacy: Religious
Celibacy: Secular
Censorship
Census
Charity
Chastity
Childbirth
Child care
Child development
Child labor
Children's literature
Christianity
Christianity: Feminist Christology
Christianity: Status of women in the church
Citizenship
Class
Class and feminism
Cloning
Cohabitation
Colonialism and postcolonialism
Commodity culture
Communications: Overview
Communications: Audience analysis
Communications: Content and discourse analysis
Communications: Speech
Communism
Community
Community politics
Computer science
Computing: Overview
Computing: Participatory and feminist design
Conflict resolution: Mediation and negotiation
Confucianism
Consciousness-raising
Conservatism
Constitutions
Contraception
Contraceptives: Development
Conversation
Cooking
Cosmetic surgery
Cosmetics
Courtship
Crafts
Creation stories
Creativity
Creed
Crime and punishment
Crime and punishment: Case study—Women in prisons in the United States

Criminology
Critical and cultural theory
Cultural criticism
Cultural studies
Culture: Overview
Culture: Women as consumers of culture
Culture: Women as producers of culture
Curriculum transformation movement
Curse
Cyberspace and virtual reality
Cyborg anthropology

Dance: Overview
Dance: Choreography
Dance: Classical
Dance: Modern
Dance: South Asia
Daughter
DAWN movement
Death
Deity
Democracy
Democratization
Demography
Demonization
Depression
Depression: Case study—Chinese medicine
Detective fiction
Determinism: Economic
Development: Overview
Development: Australia and New Zealand
Development: Central and Eastern Europe
Development: Central and South America and the Caribbean
Development: China
Development: Chinese case study—Rural women
Development: Commonwealth of Independent States
Development: Japan
Development: Middle East and the Arab region
Development: North America
Development: South Asia
Development: Sub-Saharan and southern Africa
Development: Western Europe
Diaries and journals
Difference I
Difference II
Digital divide
Disability and feminism
Disability: Elite body
Disability: Health and sexuality
Disability: Quality of life
Disarmament
Discipline in schools
Discrimination
Disease
Division of labor
Divorce
Domestic labor
Domestic technology
Domestic violence
Dowry and brideprice
Drama
Dress
Drug and alcohol abuse
Drumming

Earth
Eating disorders
Ecofeminism
Economic status: Comparative analysis
Economics: Feminist critiques
Economy: Overview
Economy: Global restructuring
Economy: History of women's participation
Economy: Informal
Economy: Welfare and the economy
Ecosystem
Écriture féminine
Education: Achievement
Education: Adult and continuing
Education: Antiracist
Education: Central Pacific and South Pacific Islands
Education: Central and South America and the Caribbean
Education: Chilly climate in the classroom
Education: Commonwealth of Independent States
Education: Curriculum in schools
Education: Distance education
Education: Domestic science and home economics
Education: East Asia
Education: Eastern Europe
Education: Gender equity
Education: Gendered subject choice
Education: Higher education
Education: Mathematics
Education: Middle East and North Africa
Education: Nonsexist
Education: North America
Education: Online
Education: Physical
Education: Political
Education: Preschool
Education: Religious studies
Education: Science
Education: Single-sex and coeducation
Education: South Asia
Education: Southeast Asia
Education: Southern Africa
Education: Special needs
Education: Sub-Saharan Africa
Education: Technology
Education: Vocational
Education: Western Europe
Educators: Higher education
Educators: Preschool
Elderly care: Case study—China
Elderly care: Case study—India
Elderly care: Western world
Emancipation and liberation movements
Empowerment
Endocrine disruption
Energy
Engineering
Entrepreneurship
Environment: Overview
Environment: Australia and New Zealand
Environment: Caribbean
Environment: Central and Eastern Europe

Environment: Central and South America
Environment: Commonwealth of Independent States
Environment: East Asia (China)
Environment: East Asia (Japan)
Environment: Middle East
Environment: North Africa
Environment: North America
Environment: Pacific Islands
Environment: South Asia
Environment: South Asian case study—Forests in India
Environment: Southeast Asia
Environment: Sub-Saharan and southern Africa
Environment: Western Europe
Environmental disasters
Epistemology
Equal opportunities
Equal opportunities: Education
Equality
Equity
Erotica
Essentialism
Estrogen
Ethics: Feminist
Ethics: Medical
Ethics: Scientific
Ethnic cleansing
Ethnic studies I
Ethnic studies II
Ethnicity
Eugenics
Eugenics: African-American case study—Eugenics and family planning
Eurocentrism
Euthanasia
Evolution
Examinations and assessment
Exercise and fitness
Experiments on women

Fairy tales
Faith
Family law
Family law: Case study—India
Family life cycle and work
Family planning
Family: Power relations and power structures
Family: Property relations
Family: Religious and legal systems—Buddhist traditions
Family: Religious and legal systems—Catholic and Orthodox
Family: Religious and legal systems—East Africa
Family: Religious and legal systems—Islamic traditions
Family: Religious and legal systems—Judaic traditions
Family: Religious and legal systems—Native North America
Family: Religious and legal systems—Protestant
Family: Religious and legal systems—Southern Africa
Family: Religious and legal systems—West Africa
Family structures
Family wage
Fascism and Nazism
Fashion
Female circumcision and genital mutilation
Femicide
Feminine mystique
Femininity
Feminism: Overview
Feminism: African-American
Feminism: Anarchist
Feminism: Asian-American
Feminism: Australia and New Zealand
Feminism: Black British
Feminism: British Asian
Feminism: Caribbean
Feminism: Central and South America
Feminism: Chicana
Feminism: China
Feminism: Commonwealth of Independent States
Feminism: Cultural
Feminism: Eastern Europe
Feminism: Eighteenth century
Feminism: Existential
Feminism: First-wave British
Feminism: First-wave North American
Feminism: Japan
Feminism: Jewish
Feminism: Korea
Feminism: Lesbian
Feminism: Liberal British and European
Feminism: Liberal North American
Feminism: Marxist
Feminism: Middle East
Feminism: Militant
Feminism: Nineteenth century
Feminism: North Africa
Feminism: Postmodern
Feminism: Radical
Feminism: Second-wave British
Feminism: Second-wave European
Feminism: Second-wave North American
Feminism: Socialist
Feminism: South Africa
Feminism: South Asia
Feminism: Southeast Asia
Feminism: Sub-Saharan Africa
Feminism: Third-wave
Femocrat
Fertility and fertility treatment
Fetus
Fiction
Film
Film criticism
Film: Lesbian
Film theory
Finance
Fine arts: Overview
Fine arts: Criticism and art history
Fine arts: Painting
Fine arts: Politics of representation
Fine arts: Sculpture and installation
Food and culture
Food, hunger, and famine
Fostering: Case study—Oceania
Friendship
Fundamentalism: Religious
Fundamentalism and public policy
Furs
Future studies

Gaia hypothesis
Gatekeeping

Gay pride
Gaze
Gender
Gender constructions in the family
Gender studies
Gendered play
Genetics and genetic technologies
Genetic screening
Genocide
Genres: Gendered
Geography
Girl child
Girl studies
Girls' subcultures
Global feminism
Global health movement
Global health movement: Resources
Globalization
Globalization of education
Goddess
Government
Grandmother
Green movement
Grrls
Guilt
Gyn/Ecology
Gynecology

Healers
Health: Overview
Health care: Australia, New Zealand, and the Pacific Islands
Health care: Canada
Health care: Central and South America and the Caribbean
Health care: Commonwealth of Independent States
Health care: East Asia
Health care: Eastern Europe
Health care: North Africa and the Middle East
Health care: South Asia
Health care: Southeast Asia
Health care: Southern Africa
Health care: Sub-Saharan Africa
Health care: United States
Health care: Western Europe
Health of the women of Rastafari: Case study
Health careers
Health challenges
Health education
Heresy
Heroine
Heterophobia and homophobia
Heterosexism
Heterosexuality
Hierarchy and bureaucracy
Hinduism
History
Holistic health I
Holistic health II
Holy Spirit
Homelessness
Hormones
Hormone replacement therapy
Household workers
Households and families: Overview
Households and families: Caribbean
Households and families: Central and Eastern Europe
Households and families: Central and South America
Households and families: Commonwealth of Independent States
Households and families: East Asia
Households and families: Melanesia and Aboriginal Australia
Households and families: Micronesia and Polynesia
Households and families: Middle East and North Africa
Households and families: Native North America
Households and families: North America
Households and families: South Asia
Households and families: Southeast Asia
Households and families: Southern Africa
Households and families: Sub-Saharan Africa
Households and families: Western Europe
Households: Domestic consumption
Households: Female-headed and female-supported
Households: Political economy
Households: Resources
Housework
Housing
Human rights
Humanities and social sciences: Feminist critiques
Humor
Humor: Case study—Comedy, United States
Hunting
Hybridity and miscegenation
Hypermasculinity
Hypertension: Case study—Class, race, and gender

Identity politics
Images of women: Overview
Images of women: Africa
Images of women: Asia
Images of women: Australia and New Zealand
Images of women: Caribbean
Images of women: Central and South America
Images of women: Europe
Images of women: Middle East
Images of women: North America
Immigration
Imperialism
Incest
Indigenous women's rights
Industrialization
Infanticide
Infertility
Information revolution
Information technology
Initiation rites
Interests: Strategic and practical
Interior design and decoration
International organizations and agencies
International relations
International Women's Day
Internet politics and states
Inventors
Islam

Journalism
Journalists

Judaism
Justice and rights

Kibbutz
Kinship
Knowledge

Language
Law and sex
Law enforcement
Law: Feminist critiques
Leadership
Legal systems
Leisure
Lesbianism
Lesbian cultural criticism
Lesbian drama
Lesbian popular music
Lesbian sexuality
Lesbian studies
Lesbian writing: Overview
Lesbian writing: Contemporary poetry
Lesbian writing: Crime fiction
Lesbians: HIV prevalence and transmission
Lesbians in science
Liberalism
Liberation
Liberation movements
Libraries
Life cycle
Life expectancy
Linguistics
Literacy
Literary theory and criticism
Literature: Overview
Literature: Arabic
Literature: Australia, New Zealand, and the Pacific Islands
Literature: Central and South America
Literature: China
Literature: Eastern Europe
Literature: Japan
Literature: North America
Literature: North America—Note on African-American, Latina, and Native American poets
Literature: Persian
Literature: Russia
Literature: South Asia
Literature: Southeast Asia
Literature: Southern Africa
Literature: Sub-Saharan Africa
Literature: Ukraine
Literature: Western Europe
Long-term care services

Magazines
Management
Marriage: Overview
Marriage: Interracial and interreligious
Marriage: Lesbian
Marriage: Regional traditions and practices
Marriage: Remarriage
Martyrs
Marxism
Masculinity
Masturbation
Maternal health and morbidity
Maternity leave
Mathematics
Matriarchy
Matrilineal systems
Media: Overview
Media: Alternative
Media: Chinese case study
Media: Grassroots
Media: Mainstream
Media and politics
Medical control of women
Medicine: Internal I
Medicine: Internal II
Men's studies
Menarche
Menopause
Menstruation
Mental health I
Mental health II
Midwives
Migration
Military
Misogyny
Mistress
Modernism
Modernization
Money
Mormons
Mother
Mother Earth
Motherhood
Motherhood: Lesbian
Multiculturalism
Multiculturalism: Arts, literature, and popular culture
Multinational corporations
Music: Anglo-American folk
Music: Composers
Music: East Asia
Music: Education
Music: Latin America
Music: North Africa and Islamic Middle East
Music: Opera
Music: Rock and pop
Music: Soul, jazz, rap, blues, and gospel
Music: South Asia
Music: Sub-Saharan and southern Africa
Music: Western classical
Musicians
Mysticism
Myth

Naming
Nation and nationalism
Natural resources
Nature
Nature-nurture debate
Nature: Philosophy and spirituality
Nepotism
Networking
Networks, electronic
Nongovernmental organizations (NGOs)
Nonviolence
Norplant
Novel
Nuclear weapons
Nuns
Nursing
Nursing homes
Nutrition I
Nutrition II
Nutrition and home economics

Obstetrics
Occupational health and safety

Oral tradition
Organizational theory
Other

Pacifism and peace activism
Parenthood
Part-time and casual work
Patriarchy: Development
Patriarchy: Feminist theory
Peace education
Peacekeeping
Peace movements: Asia
Peace movements: Australia, New Zealand, and the Pacific Islands
Peace movements: Central and South America
Peace movements: Europe
Peace movements: Israel
Peace movements: Middle East and the Arab world
Peace movements: North America
Pedagogy: Feminist I
Pedagogy: Feminist II
Performance art
Performance texts
Personal and customary laws
Phallocentrism
Pharmaceuticals
Philanthropy
Philosophy
Photography
Phototherapy
Physical sciences
Physical strength
Physiology
The Pill
Plagiarism in science
Poetry: Overview
Poetry: Feminist theory and criticism
Political asylum
Political economy
Political leadership
Political participation
Political parties
Political representation
Politics and the state: Overview
Politics and the state: Australia, New Zealand, and the Pacific Islands
Politics and the state: Caribbean
Politics and the state: Central and South America
Politics and the state: Commonwealth of Independent States
Politics and the state: East Asia
Politics and the state: Eastern Europe
Politics and the state: Middle East and North Africa
Politics and the state: North America
Politics and the state: South Asia I
Politics and the state: South Asia II
Politics and the state: Southeast Asia
Politics and the state: Southern Africa
Politics and the state: Sub-Saharan Africa
Politics and the state: Western Europe
Pollution
Pollution: Chemical
Polygyny and polyandry
Popular culture
Population: Overview
Population: Chinese case study
Population control
Pornography in art and literature
Pornography and violence
Postcolonialism: Theory and criticism
Postfeminism
Postmodernism and development
Postmodernism: Feminist critiques
Postmodernism: Literary theory
Poverty
Power
Prayer
Pregnancy and birth
Premenstrual syndrome (PMS)
Press: Feminist alternatives
Primatology
Privatization
Pro-choice movement
Professional societies
Prostitution
Psychiatry
Psychoanalysis
Psychology: Overview
Psychology: Cognitive
Psychology: Developmental
Psychology: Neuroscience and brain research
Psychology: Personality research
Psychology: Psychometrics
Psychology: Psychopathology and psychotherapy
Psychology: Social
Publishing
Publishing: Feminist publishing in the third world
Publishing: Feminist publishing in the western world

Quakers
Queer theory
Quilting

Race
Racism and xenophobia
Radiation
Radio
Rape
Reference sources
Refugees
Religion: Overview
Representation
Reproduction: Overview
Reproductive health
Reproductive physiology
Reproductive rights
Reproductive technologies
Research: On-line
Revolutions
Romance
Romantic fiction
Romantic friendship
RU 486

Sacred texts
Safer sex
Saints
Science: Overview
Science: Ancient and medieval
Science: Early modern to late eighteenth century
Science: Feminism and science studies
Science: Feminist critiques
Science: Feminist philosophy
Science: Nineteenth century
Science: Technological and scientific research
Science: Traditional and indigenous knowledge

Science: Twentieth century
Science fiction
Scientific sexism and racism
Sects and cults
Settler societies
Sex: Beliefs and customs
Sex and culture
Sex education
Sex selection
Sex work
Sexism
Sexology and sex research
Sexual difference
Sexual harassment
Sexual orientation
Sexual slavery
Sexual violence
Sexuality: Overview
Sexuality: Adolescent sexuality
Sexuality in Africa
Sexuality in Hindu culture
Sexuality: Psychology of sexuality in cross-cultural perspectives
Sexuality: Psychology of sexuality in the United States
Shakers
Shakti
Shinto
Short story
Silence
Simultaneous oppressions
Single people
Sister
Sisterhood
Slavery
Slogans: "The personal is the political"
Soap operas
Social movements
Social sciences: Feminist methods
Socialism
Socialization for complementarity
Socialization for inequality
Sociology
Space
Spinster
Spirituality: Overview
Spirituality: Sexuality
Sport
Sports and discrimination
Stepfamilies
Stereotypes
Sterilization
Street harassment
Stress
Suffrage
Suicide
Surgery
Surgery: Case study—Contemporary issues in the United States
Surrogacy
Suttee (Sati)

Taboo
Technology
Technology: Women and development
Television
Teleworking
Terrorism
Textiles
Theater: Overview
Theater: 1500–1900
Theater: Modern and contemporary
Theater: Women in theater
Theologies: Feminist
Third world
Third world women: Selected resources
Torture
Tourism
Toxicology
Traditional healing: Aboriginal Australia
Traditional healing: Africa I
Traditional healing: Africa II
Traditional healing: Central and South America and the Caribbean
Traditional healing: East and southeast Asia
Traditional healing: Herbalists
Traditional healing: India
Traditional healing: Native North America
Trafficking
Transgender
Travel writing

Underemployment
Unemployment
Union movements
Universalism
Utopianism
Utopian writing

Vegetarianism
Veiling
Video
Violence and peace: Overview
Violence: Australia, New Zealand, and the Pacific Islands
Violence: Caribbean
Violence: Central and Eastern Europe
Violence: Central and South America
Violence: Commonwealth of Independent States
Violence: East Asia (China) I
Violence: East Asia (China) II
Violence: Media
Violence: Middle East and the Arab world (Lebanon)
Violence: North America
Violence: South Asia
Violence: Southeast Asia
Violence: Sub-Saharan and southern Africa
Violence: Western Europe
Virginity
Vodou
Volunteerism

War
Water
Weddings
Welfare
Wicca
Widowhood
Wife
Witches: Asia
Witches: Western world
Woman-centeredness
Womanculture
Womanism
Womanist theology
Womanspirit
Women's centers
Women's movement: Early international movement
Women's movement: Modern international movement

Women's movement: United States
Women's studies: Overview
Women's studies: Australia
Women's studies: Backlash
Women's studies: Caribbean
Women's studies: Central and Eastern Europe
Women's studies: Central and South America
Women's studies: Commonwealth of Independent States
Women's studies: East Asia
Women's studies: Funding
Women's studies: Middle East and North Africa
Women's studies: New Zealand
Women's studies: Research centers and institutes
Women's studies: South Asia
Women's studies: Southeast Asia
Women's studies: Southern Africa
Women's studies: Sub-Saharan Africa
Women's studies: United States
Women's studies: Western Europe
Women-church
Women: Terms for women
Work: Equal pay and conditions
Work: Feminist theories
Work: Occupational experiences
Work: Occupational segregation
Work: Patterns

Youth culture

Zen
Zines
Zionism

Routledge International Encyclopedia of Women

Global Women's Issues and Knowledge

Volume 3 Identity Politics—Publishing

I

IDENTITY POLITICS

Identity politics came to prominence in the 1960s and has remained influential. The term refers to an intersection of *group* identity and politics, which can lead to social change. Identity politics arises when oppression becomes the focus of a strong separate group identity around which support, political analysis, and action are developed, and it has thus been associated particularly with less powerful groups such as women, lesbians, gay men, people of color, other ethnic minorities, and religious minorities. Identity politics has been a subject of debate within and beyond feminism, as in the consciousness-raising discussion groups of the 1960s and 1970s, which focused on personal experience and personal identity and reflected the slogan "The personal is political."

Background

Long before the term *identity politics* was coined, identity was used to rally political opposition to the status quo. The early nineteenth-century labor movements were engaged in identity politics, because "worker" was an identity that implied solidarity and rights; women and men in colonized countries used national identity to resist their colonizers; women suffragists organized politically around the identity "woman." Other activists, of course, also used "woman" as an identity; a famous example is Sojourner Truth's question "Ain't I a woman?" in a speech she gave in 1851. Truth, an African-American who was a former slave, represents the ways in which racism excluded blacks from the category of "women"—an identity she and others worked to reclaim.

The term *identity politics* is often used pejoritively to imply a sterile, exclusionary politics that bases group solidarity on the characteristics that lead to oppression and thus precludes any joint political organization with people who do not share those traits—even though they may have other traits in common with the oppressed group. On this view, identity politics fragments political action. In many societies, however, identity politics has empowered marginalized groups and has been progressive at least in the sense of involving collective struggles, discrediting categorization imposed by outsiders, insisting on definitions formulated within the group, and increasing the group's visibility in categories where its members have been obscured.

Thus identity politics is a somewhat contradictory concept. On the one hand, it can perpetuate the status quo by treating social categories as natural, static, and based on characteristics unique to a group—that is, by being essentialist. On the other hand, it can disrupt the status quo by providing a basis for new political definitions and new struggles. Not surprisingly, then, identity politics has generated controversy about whether it is or is not progressive or even theoretically defensible.

Identity Politics and Feminism: Issues and Problems

Identity politics has benefited feminism by providing an impetus for a shift away from the assumption that the concerns of white, heterosexual, middle-class feminists are relevant to all women. This focus on differences among women has inspired theoretical interest in "difference" as such and in questions about subjectivity; as a result, the concerns of feminism have been broadened to include several dimensions of differentiation, and this has been empowering for many women (Brah, 1996; Sudbury, 1998; Walby, 2000). Still, a major problem with identity politics is that it can be progressive only if this shift leads to a shift in power relations. Also, in stressing the group, identity politics tends to omit discourses on the personal or particular and the collective or universal, a tendency that can lead to apolitical relativism.

In identity politics, it is often said, people can become visible only as categories of difference. For example, black women can represent only black women's position, expressed in essentialist terms; and they are considered interchangeable, as if all black women necessarily share the same political opinions and goals. Thus "giving a voice" to one black woman is considered equivalent to giving a voice to all black women, and a woman's identity is considered synonymous with her politics. Identity politics, therefore, is reductionist: that is, it reduces individuals to all-encompassing categories and fails to recognizes commonalities between collectivities. On this view, identity politics, far from being progressive, can become tokenistic and stereotypical—in which case it resembles theories that treat the category "woman" as undifferentiated while actually addressing only white, middle-class, heterosexual women.

Another perceived problem is that identity politics can tend to set up hierarchies of oppression and to use a language of "authentic subjective experience" in which "oppression markers" serve as moral and political currency. This makes feminism more vulnerable to accusations of political correctness. Some critics also argue that although identity politics generates useful models of oppression, it has not provided ways of understanding more than one identity simultaneously: it ignores the complex relationship between identity and difference, treating identity as something unitary, natural, and stable when in fact identity is always plural or multiple, always in process, and constituted within rather than outside representations. The essentialist assertion of homogeneity can result in absolutism—of gender, sexuality, or race or ethnicity—because it tends to deal with only one marker of difference at a time. Similarly, taking a group identity as fundamental and primary, and claiming rights on the basis of group differences, can result in political authoritarianism.

The question thus arises whether identity politics forecloses political action by limiting feminists' understanding of differences and commonalities. Several significant issues are involved here: How is it possible to maintain feminism as politics when oppression and difference splinter feminists' solidarity? Would putting aside differences for the sake of political solidarity entail returning to an earlier situation in which, for example, black and working-class women were invisible? Can feminists afford to ignore identity politics if it continues to operate implicitly in the real world—as it does, say, when white men dominate politics as elected officials and industry as entrepreneurs?

Many feminists have argued that women need new ways to construct their identity; but there is no single answer to the question of how to retain the benefits of identity politics while avoiding essentialism and sterility, especially in a time when claims of group identity are proliferating. These issues, and the debates they have generated, are central to feminist theories of difference—theories that address the concerns that inspired identity politics but try to move beyond simplistic identities and dualistic concepts of difference (Gedalof, 1999; Henwood et al., 1998).

Some feminsts believe that it may be necessary to risk essentialism in order to create new political identities for the purpose of political agency; Spivak (1987), for instance, suggested that "strategic essentialism" could explicitly recognize that claims about "women" are political interventions. A serious problem with this concept is that "strategic essentialism" may provide a rationale for essentialism, and treating social categories as essential—however well-intentioned this may be—often results in exclusionary absolutism, reinforcing some forms of oppression even while challenging other forms (Brah, 1996). This phenomenon is often held to be particularly visible in the growth of fundamentalist religious movements. Generalizations about shared identity, therefore, need to be qualified, to account for the vagueness of boundaries.

"Alliance Politics"

A number of feminists have addressed ways of acknowledging differences among women while forming political alliances and coalitions across groups (Collins, 1990). Such a position was advocated in the 1970s, for instance, by the black lesbian Combahee River Collective in the United States and the Race Today Collective in Great Britain. Such alliances (another example is Women Against Fundamentalism) want to dismantle the "apparatus of difference" without reinstating a false homogeneity. Many black women's organizations in Britain have developed complex, broad-based strategic versions of identity politics (Sudbury, 1998). In Italy, Women in Black uses a concept called "transversalism"—as distinguished from universalism—as a way to be rooted in their own identities and material and political realities while at the same time shifting empathically in order to communicate with women whose identities and realities are different (Yuval-Davis, 1997). Politics of alliance, as a variation of identity politics, has allowed new ways of seeing and produced new political agendas.

See Also

CLASS; COMMUNITY POLITICS; DIFFERENCE, *I and II*; ETHNICITY; RACE; SIMULTANEOUS OPPRESSIONS

References and Further Reading

Brah, Avtar. 1996, *Cartographies of diaspora: Contesting identities.* London: Routledge.

———. 1999. The scent of memory: "Strangers," "our own," and "others." *Feminist Review* 60:4–25.

Collins, Patricia Hill. 1990. *Black feminist thought: Knowledge, consciousness, and the politics of empowerment.* Boston: Unwin Hyman.

Elam, Diane. 1994. *Feminism and deconstruction: Ms en abyme.* London: Routledge.

Gedalof, Irene. 1999. *Against purity: Rethinking identity with Indian and western feminisms.* London: Routledge.

Henwood, Karen, Christine Griffin, and Ann Phoenix, eds. 1998. *Standpoints and differences.* London: Sage.

Hooks, Bell. 1991. *Yearning: Race, gender, and cultural politics.* London: Turnaround.

Lewis, Gail. 2000. *"Race," gender, social welfare: Encounters in a postcolonial society.* Cambridge: Polity.

Spivak, Gayatri Chakravorty. 1987. *In other worlds: Essays in cultural politics.* London: Methuen.

Sudbury, Julia. 1998. *Other kinds of dreams: Black women's organisations and the politics of transformation.* London: Routledge.

Walby, Sylvia. 2000. Beyond the politics of location: The power of argument in a global era. *Feminist Theory* 1(2):173–190. See also three responses: 191–218.

Yuval-Davis, Nira. 1997. *Gender and nation.* London: Sage.

Ann Phoenix

ILLNESS

See DISEASE.

IMAGES OF WOMEN: Overview

The study of images focuses on a combination of textual representations, aural, visual, and written, of women (and men) in the media and other forms of popular culture. At least since Betty Friedan's *The Feminine Mystique* (1963), images have been a major issue within feminist approaches to popular culture. Friedan discussed women's magazines and political and economic factors in changing images of women, highlighting the importance of popular culture in general, and images in particular, to the feminist struggle. Much subsequent work, by both academics and grassroots activists, has been centered on studying the content of popular culture.

"Symbolic Annihilation"

Not surprisingly, such studies of content consistently find a "symbolic annihilation" of women: that is, the popular media tend to underrepresent women; and when women are represented, they are likely to be trivialized, marginalized, victimized, or ridiculed. This has been found in various forms of popular culture from Hollywood, Indian, and Egyptian films to general-interest magazines to advertising to television to newspapers, and so on. Particular media aimed at women, such as women's magazines, romance novels, and much advertising, overrepresent women but still treat women stereotypically. Women are also overrepresented in pornography—movies, magazines, and other media—and in sexually explicitly material in general. "Symbolic annihilation" of women differs from region to region, but it is a global phenomenon in most mainstream popular culture.

Approaches to Improving Women's Image

In response to these findings, there was a call for increased and improved representation of women in the media. The implicit theoretical logic assumed that increased and improved images in the media would lead to more sensitive representations of women in the culture as a whole. This would eventually improve girls' self-esteem and let them visualize themselves in a wider variety of roles. It would also benefit adult women, in at least two ways: their own self-esteem would improve; and men's exposure to increased and improved images would lead them to treat women better and to envision women in less gender-specific—that is, less feminine—ways. For both women and girls, then, there would be better employment opportunities as well as better treatment overall. Clearly, this theory stressed the power of images.

Unfortunately, however, the theory seemed to have flaws and gaps. First, increasing the images of women proved to be a difficult process. It implied either reeducating or changing the workforce; and even when this took place, through extensive efforts—as when more women entered newsrooms and advertising agencies—it did not necessarily result in increased or improved images of women. In some settings—for example, Hollywood filmmaking—the process of including women in the workforce was much slower and had even less influence. This led scholars and activists to focus on the process of production. Rules and conventions at the workplace, which whether written or unwritten largely set the parameters for portrayals of women, did not change with a changing workforce.

Second, not only was increasing images a major obstacle; the few additional images were not necessarily an improvement. Under the guise of more progressive images were some very traditional components. For example, the movie *An Unmarried Woman* (United States, 1978), though centering on a divorcee, portrayed her as somehow incomplete without a male. Similarly, on U.S. television, the *Mary Tyler Moore Show* was touted as the first feminist sitcom, but its narrative structure was very much that of a family; in the newsroom, Moore seemed to play the traditional role of daughter, with her boss as the father. One could make similar observations about Latin American telenovelas and British and Indian romance novels. In all these cultural forms, women's roles have the traditional feminine components that are central to a critique of images. Another aspect of this problem is that "improvement" is a matter of judgment. Who decides whether a particular image is an improvement? Some people might consider an image improved and others might not. (This raises the question of reception, discussed below.)

Third, even when images were increased and could be considered (on some objective measure) improved—for instance, more sensitive—scholars found that these changes did not necessarily lead to mimetic changes. According to the theoretical model, changes in images would lead to cognitive changes, which would lead to attitudinal changes, which would finally lead to behavioral changes. In fact, though, the few attempts to present more or less feminist images (and this has also been true of similar attempts to present African-Americans and other oppressed groups) have yielded inconclusive and sometimes troubling results. On the one hand, people expose themselves selectively to popular culture and other media. This means that bigots will not typically expose themselves to feminist material; nor will progressives usually consume radical right material, except for research purposes. So, leaving aside surprise or sabotage, a changed image tends to be noticed only by those who are already converted. On the other hand, even when a broader range of people are exposed to changed images, the resulting process does not necessarily follow the linear path implied by the theoretical model. Thus a cognitive change, at the level of knowledge, might very well be no more than learning what is socially acceptable; this lesson would not include an attitudinal change, and any behavioral change would be cosmetic, appearing to follow social norms. Individual private behavior, such as voting, would remain the same. Even an attitudinal change does not necessarily translate into a behavioral change. For example, in the United States a show on public television called *Freestyle* demonstrated to adolescents that it was all right for girls to explore nontraditional jobs such as automotive mechanics rather than, say, baby-sitting. The young people in the audience understood this lesson and also expressed attitudinal support for less gendered occupations, but their response to a behavioral question—"Would you apply for a nontraditional job or hire a girl as a car mechanic?"—was negative. In sum, the dynamic process that would follow a change in image is much more complex and less mimetic than was originally theorized.

Fourth, the original work on images had some of the same blind spots as the feminist movement of that time—by and large most research and activism focused on white, middle-class, heterosexual women. Little work included difference as anything other than gender; most work ignored, the interplay of gender, race, class, ethnicity, national origin, and sexual orientation. Also, there was virtually no research on how, for example, a changed image of a white woman would generate a process of change for a woman of color. In a global context, images had to be considered primarily in terms of western femininity.

Fifth, scholars of popular culture argued that images were a rather simplistic way of addressing issues of representation. Popular culture does not merely reflect culture in general but also speaks to it in a complex manner. Thus the underrepresentation of women refers to more than the fact that women are 51 percent of the population. If one considers that, globally, women own very little property, seldom have positions of power, and earn less than men for comparable work, this underrepresentation both reflects and affects a culture in which women are undervalued and slighted symbolically and materially. Similarly, the fact that women of color were underrepresented in feminist literature expresses and influences the reality of racism within the women's movement and within cultures at large; it also serves to document this reality. The concept of representation makes it clear that the production of popular culture involves a process of mediation: in the production of an image a myriad of decisions are made, consciously or subconsciously; these decisions generate a "re-presentation" that includes the values and norms present within the cultural context. Thus the notion of representation encourages us to consider levels of analysis beyond the individual. That is, an individual consciously chooses a portrayal; but the organizational and institutional level must also be considered—the rules and conventions, written and unwritten, at the site of production and the norms and values, explicit and implicit, that are most powerful during a particular era.

Sixth, drawing once more from cultural studies, feminist scholars consider "reception." This theoretical refinement destabilizes the relationship between content and interpretation. Within a range of possibilities, we are beginning to find that interpretation is not homogeneous or easily predictable. In particular, we find that subcultures, such as (among many others) gays and lesbians, women of color, national minorities, and adolescent girls, learn to apply "active reading" to representations in popular culture. As a rule, oppressed groups cannot expect to see themselves represented in popular culture: they are symbolically annihilated. Studies of these subcultures have found instances of resistant or oppositional readings: the audience—evidently in response to this annihilation—either reads between the lines or takes a stance altogether opposited to the intended meaning of the text. This area of study challenges us to expand the scholarship of representation to include issues of reception, especially as these overlap with issues of race, class, age, and sexual orientation.

For all these reasons, representation continues to account for a large part of the work being done in feminist studies of popular culture. Issues of representation have been well accepted in film studies, though perhaps less so in advertising and journalism, where many "image projects" continue to support the original findings, with some additional twists. Representational studies are deceptively simple in terms of methodology; at least partly for this reason, they are one of the early exercises in the career of many media scholars.

See Also

COMMUNICATIONS: AUDIENCE ANALYSIS; COMMUNICATIONS: CONTENT AND DISCOURSE ANALYSIS; COMMUNICATIONS: OVERVIEW; CULTURE: WOMEN AS CONSUMERS OF CULTURE; GAZE; IMAGES OF WOMEN (REGIONAL)

References and Further Reading

Friedan, B. 1963. *The feminine mystique.* New York: Dell.

Gledhill, C. 1988. Plesurable negotiations. In E. D. Pribram, ed., *Female spectators: Looking at film and television,* 45–63. New York: Verso.

Hermes, J. 1995. *Reading women's magazines.* Cambridge, UK: Polity.

Press, A. 1991. *Women watching television: Gender, class and generation in the American television experience.* Philadelphia: University of Pennsylvania Press.

Radway, J. 1984. *Reading the romance: Women, patriarchy and popular literature.* Chapel Hill: University of North Carolina Press.

Tuchman, G., A. K. Daniels, and J. Benet, eds. 1978. *Hearth and home: Images of women in the mass media.* 1st ed. New York: Oxford University Press.

Wartella, E., and B. Reeves. 1985. Historical trends in research on children and the media: 1900–1960. *Journal of Communication,* 35(2): 118–133.

Angharad N. Valdivia

IMAGES OF WOMEN: Africa

From classical times onward, Africa has exerted a powerful hold on the western imagination. Writings of ancient Greeks and Romans; books published about Africa during Europe's Middle Ages; paintings, literature, and travelogues created during European exploration; and imperialist expansion into Africa in the seventeenth, eighteenth, and nineteenth centuries attest to the dramatic and, often distorted images of Africa and Africans. Because the British, French, Dutch, Germans, and Portuguese each had different experiences on the continent, it is somewhat difficult to generalize about European images of Africa and Africans. Yet it can be said that in European imagery Africa was the antithesis of Europe, and Africans were distinct from Europeans.

Africa as Woman in Colonial Imagery

In the process of making Africa and Africans separate and remote from Europe and Europeans, the European popular imagination exaggerated differences and projected onto Africans behaviors that were labeled unnatural (Hammond and Jablow, 1970). The African continent itself was personified as an irresistible but destructive woman, luring (male) European slavers, explorers, and settlers and ultimately destroying them (McEwah, 1994). In much of European colonial travel fiction and adventure stories, Africa, symbolized as a woman, was seen as a fecund womb to be exploited and controlled.

The convergence of female sexuality with Africa as a place allowed for the incorporation of African women into European popular thought and imagination. Because male colonizers typically had little contact with African women and understood little of the complex nature of women's social roles in various African societies, women in Africa were stereotyped as mindless and instinctual, embodying inferior qualities of womanliness compared with their European counterparts. In their portrayals as instinctual beings, women in Africa were rarely shown as whole individuals, with both intellect and body. Rather, they were represented as workers confined to subservient tasks or as sexual objects equated with primal urges. In either case, European colonial literature and art popularized images that tended to devalue women in Africa.

Over time there has been little shift in the portrayals of women in Africa. What has changed is how these images are communicated. During the period of formal European colonization in the mid-to late-1800s, westerners learned about women in Africa largely through novels, memoirs, religious tracts, and art. Today, in Europe as well as in the United States, images of the countries, peoples, and cultures in Africa are shaped and dominated by the powerful news media. Events and issues in Africa deemed worthy of coverage by global news organizations are almost always associated with famine, poverty, and political strife (Fair, 1993a; Hawk, 1992). Moreover, news out of Africa is very often about U.S. or western interests and involvement, and the sources used to provide information for stories are almost always men (Rakow and Kranich, 1991), sometimes African, but more frequently white and western. As in past eras, when the representation of women in Africa was limited, today's consumers of news quite simply do not see, hear, or learn much about the lives and views of women in the many countries on the African continent.

More of the Same: African Women in News Stories Today

The lens through which news audiences view Africa blurs the contexts of colonial legacies, patriarchy, and economic imbalances by focusing coverage on dramatic, often horrifying, events: wars and natural disasters. News, particularly television with its steady stream of words and pictures, entices audiences into a reality in which unequal power relations appear obvious and given. News also can be seen as encoded with gender to the extent that women are made into objects of patriarchy, and issues and activities in which women are involved are treated as secondary. The United States can serve as an example.

Although some of the world's largest media industries are located in the United States, Africa often remains the "dark continent" of Joseph Conrad's novel *Heart of Darkness* (1902). Understanding, or perhaps really misunderstanding, of Africa is based on a long history of explorers', travelers', and missionaries experiences, retold in travelogues, popular magazines, and, later, in film (Hickey and Wylie, 1993). Indeed, in contemporary accounts of African realities, news media draw on these historically based European notions of Africa as a "distant" and "alien" place, where "exotic" peoples live.

Generally, research on U.S. media coverage of Africa suggests that Africa is in general the least covered region of the world. News organizations defend their lack of reporting from the African continent by citing a host of difficulties: for example, reporters must contend with sources reluctant to speak for fear of their own safety, difficult travel conditions, censorship, inadequate communication facilities that make transmission nearly impossible, and the high cost of maintaining a correspondent.

But when news media do cover Africa, stories often portray Africa in a very narrow focus. They are largely event-based and crisis- oriented. Most commonly, media coverage is of an Africa enmeshed in a series of political and military conflicts and ethnic violence, which until the late 1980s were influenced by a cold war framework. Within this framework of what may constitute an acceptable news story, women, women's voices, and women's activities are often neglected.

In terms of news coverage of Africa, the organizational requirement of suitably authoritative and credible stories has translated into reports that are primarily about men, African and western, and men's activities in creating and resolving conflicts or crises. Women in Africa, as elsewhere, are largely invisible as newsmakers. Very often when women in African countries are presented in U.S. news stories, they do not appear as acting subjects or speaking sources. Rather, women's images are used to symbolize the larger issue addressed in the news story.

For example, within the context of U.S. television news coverage of violence among black South Africans from 1986 through 1990, women were represented primarily as visual images (Fair, 1993b). The predominant image was of women weeping. These weeping women were used in news stories as symbols of South Africa's struggle to develop a postapartheid society. Women existed in these stories of violence only in their connection to men. They were daughters, wives, and mothers who were afforded little opportunity to describe how violence affected their lives or their involvement in violent activities. By contrast, men, even young men, were frequently heard and seen in these televised stories. Their views of violence and of society were the grist of journalists' interviews; they were given a voice and credibility. The difficulty with the coverage was that women served as nearly voiceless symbols of the violent terrain in which they lived. The images of mourning daughters, wives, and mothers circumscribed women's roles, cutting women off from the public sphere and confining them to a seemingly depoliticized domestic sphere.

The authority of journalists to create news stories set in Africa rests with their control over the representation and interpretation of Africa and African peoples. To the extent that news circulates images of African women, stories evoke power relations between the first world and the third world, men and women, and whites and blacks. The use of images of black African women certainly must be influenced by controlling or stereotypical images of African-American women, since ideas about "blackness" and gender relations have historically informed scientific, popular, and news discourses about Africans and African-Americans produced by white-dominated U.S. (or western) institutions (Nederveen Pieterse, 1992).

Patricia Collins (1990) argues that stereotypes of African-American women in books, magazines, entertainment television, and film have revolved around the intersection of race and class with female sexuality, playing on racist notions of black people's sexual behavior. What these stereotypes do is to make racism, sexism, and inequality appear to be unchanging and acceptable norms (68). While Collins's ideas about how African-American women are depicted are not completely transferable to news coverage of Africa, her exploration of how gender, race, and class interlock provides a useful way of thinking about how black African women are classified and objectified.

A Brief News Analysis of African Women

In much of popular culture, women in Africa have been sexualized, as in Collins's typology of images of African-American women (Lutz and Collins, 1993; Nederveen Pieterse, 1992). In novels produced during the Victorian era, it was believed that the warm climate, combined with the black skin of Africans, created hypersexuality in African women. While news today does not perpetuate such explicit stereotypes, the sexuality of African women and their relations to men remain a central focus. From the 16 news stories about women in Africa published by the *New York Times* from the conclusion of the United Nations Decade for Women in July 1985 through 1994, stories treat issues of female genital excision and HIV/AIDS (one story each), rape (two stories), and women deciding against marriage for more open relationships with men (one story). Even within stories that deal with women's working lives in the formal and informal economic sectors (five stories) or explore women's rights or efforts to organize politically (six stories), issues such as fertility, the sexual lives of women, birth control, population growth, female genital excision, HIV/AIDS, polygyny, and sexual (as well as domestic) abuse are frequent secondary themes.

This brief discussion of coverage in the *New York Times* is not meant to suggest that such topics are unimportant to the lives of women in Africa or that such themes should not be covered by the news media. No doubt the stories are meant to be and can be read at one level as inspirational, attesting to the strength and endurance of women confronted by political, economic, and social challenges in the six African countries (Kenya, Tanzania, Uganda, Nigeria, Congo, and Togo) from which stories were filed. What is at issue is not simply how women were described or how their images were displayed in news stories but the cultural context in which they appeared (see Mohanty, 1991). That context weaves together notions of gender and race; and it is the context in which U.S. news consumers, who are overwhelmingly white, learn about (and compare themselves with) women in Africa. Thus, as several feminist media analysts have suggested, the focus on the images of women helps to provide a look below the dominant meanings and knowledge contained in news stories to consider how the social construction of gender, combined in this case with race, affects any understanding of Africa.

See Also

BLACKNESS AND WHITENESS; GATEKEEPING; IMAGES OF WOMEN: OVERVIEW; SEXUALITY IN AFRICA

References and Further Reading

Collins, Patricia Hill. 1990. *Black feminist thought: Knowledge, consciousness, and the politics of empowerment.* Boston: Unwin Hyman.

Fair, Jo Ellen. 1993a. War, famine, and poverty: Race in the construction of Africa's media image. *Journal of Communication Inquiry* 17: 5–22.

———. 1993b. The women of South Africa weep: Explorations of gender and race in news discourses. *Howard Journal of Communication* 4: 283–294.

Hammond, Dorothy, and Alta Jablow. 1970. *The Africa that never was: Four centuries of British writing about Africa.* New York: Twayne.

Hawk, Beverly, ed. 1992. *Africa's media image.* New York: Praeger.

Hickey, Dennis, and Kenneth Wylie. 1993. *An enchanting darkness: The American vision of Africa in the twentieth century.* East Lansing: Michigan State University Press.

Lutz, Catherine, and Jane Collins. 1993. *Reading "National Geographic."* Chicago: University of Chicago Press.

McEwan, Cheryl. 1994. Encounters with west African women: Textual representations of difference by white women abroad. In Alison Blunt and Gillian Rose, eds., *Writing women and space: Colonial and postcolonial geographies,* 73–100. New York: Guilford.

Mohanty, Chandra Talpade. 1991. Under western eyes: Feminist scholarship and colonial discourses. In Chandra Talpade Mohanty, Ann Russo, and Lourdes Torres, eds., *Third world women and the politics of feminism,* 51–80. Bloomington: Indiana University Press.

Nederveen Pieterse, Jan. 1992. *White on black: Images of Africa and blacks in western popular culture.* New Haven, Conn.: Yale University Press.

Rakow, Lana, and Kimberlie Kranich. 1991. Woman as sign in television news. *Journal of Communication* 41: 8–23.

Zoonen, Liesbet van. 1994. *Feminist media studies.* London: Sage.

Jo Ellen Fair

IMAGES OF WOMEN: Asia

As in many other regions of the world, the majority of images of women that appear in the popular media in Asia are negative and not representative of women's abilities or accomplishments. Women's presence in the media as workers and producers increased in many Asian countries during the 1980s, but their portrayal within the mainstream media, particularly entertainment programs and advertising, remained restrictive and demeaning. Women are still generally shown in romantic, subordinate, and subservient roles. In most of the region, in fact, women are now depicted as sex objects and victims of violence more often than before. The spread of advertising is partly responsible for this trend. The ready availability of music television (MTV) through the pan-Asian satellite television service STAR TV has also exacerbated the trend toward more violent and sexually explicit programming, with women being objects of uncontrolled and often violent male sexuality in the music videos. Soft- and hard-core pornography is also becoming more prevalent in the region through the wide distribution of magazines, videos, and other media. In pornography in this region, as elsewhere, women are represented as fragmented body parts, devoid of humanity and dignity.

Representations of Women in Entertainment Media

In general, women are depicted as sacrificing, suffering wives and mothers, as scheming "other women," or as sex objects. The tendency to define women in exclusively sexual terms is intensified in countries such as Thailand and the Philippines, and to a lesser extent South Korea, Taiwan, and Malaysia, where women are used as sexual commodities in advertising designed to support the flourishing sex-tourism industry. This situation is exacerbated by the acceptance of advertisements for sex tourism in the mainstream media in these countries. In countries such as Pakistan and Singapore, strict norms governing sexuality make it less likely that women will be portrayed as sex objects, but they are still portrayed in narrowly defined, stereotypical roles.

In Asian soap operas, films, radio dramas, and advertising, women are rarely depicted as independent, rational beings who determine their own destiny. Rather, they are often shown as dependent, as emotional, and as victims of their circumstances. Beauty rather than intellectual capacity is the major criterion by which women are measured. On the rare occasions when women succeed in the public sphere, their success is attributed to circumstances or luck. They are predominantly shown in the domestic sphere, and they are shown as mainly concerned with family and romance. They are almost never shown finding fulfillment in themselves or their own work. In advertising throughout the region, not only are women shown in limited roles, but they are also routinely exploited as sex objects to sell everything from soap to office equipment. This limiting definition of women serves to maintain male supremacy and women's subordination.

A detailed study of the portrayal of women in the media of Pakistan, including advertising, films, television drama, and school textbooks, found that the image of woman is full of contradictions. This mythic woman is both strong and weak, visible and invisible, foolish and wise, hardworking and helpless, asexual and sexually irresistible, desired and feared (UNESCO, 1989).

Some attempts have been made in the mainstream media to challenge these stereotypes. For example, the newer soap operas in India have some nonstereotypical female characters, and the national television station in Bangladesh introduced a series of progressive programs for women in 1985 to commemorate the end of the United Nations Decade for Women. One Korean study published in 1987 found that the number of female characters in television programs had increased since 1983, but men still clearly outnumbered women in major roles, and both men and women continue to be projected in typically stereotyped roles (UNESCO, 1989).

Representation of Women in the Press

The press of the region has been gradually sensitized to the need to cover women's issues. It is not uncommon to find in the newspapers stories concerning issues important to women, such as rape, wife beating, and dowry-related deaths. In general, there is a tendency to publish stories of women as victims, and these stories are often sensationalized. When stories about action by women's groups are published, they are often trivialized.

Most of the data on news coverage are from India. A study from 1983 found that although issues of direct concern to women were widely covered in the mainstream press, social concern was not emphatic enough. Still, the study concluded that the press has played a significant role in highlighting offenses against women (UNESCO, 1989). Other studies indicate a sharp increase in press coverage of women's issues and actions in India during the 1980s. The women in focus are usually elite women, however there is almost no coverage of working-class women and no mention of rural women.

Until the 1980s, women in the Indian press were portrayed as martyred heroines and as vulnerable creatures dependent on males. Today, news stories often show women as victims of rape, dowry-related murders, and other atrocities. These stories are often trivialized, sensationalized, or glamorized. For example, most Indian newspapers used language that glorified an incident of suttee, or widow immolation (the Roop Kanwar case), that took place in 1986 until women journalists protested and took over the issue in the press. In the Indian context, there has also been a tendency to imbue stories about women with the politics of communalism and religion. For example, a story about a Muslim woman's right to spousal support after divorce (the Shah Bano case) was covered extensively as a communal issue in 1986. A study that looked at coverage of women's issues in the English- and Indian-language press from 1979 to 1988 found that the most visible women's issues were dowry-related deaths, rape, sex-determination tests, suttee, and the Shah Bano controversy. Of these, the suttee case and Shah Bano received the most coverage. Very few stories about these two issues dealt with them from a woman's viewpoint. Both issues involved the law, had communal overtones, and were politically sensitive (Joseph and Sharma, 1994). Issues related to women's work, health, position in society, and experiences within the family receive very little coverage.

A study of press coverage in Sri Lanka in 1983 found that it was mainly the English-language press that covered the women's movement, but the movement was almost always ridiculed. The press in the two other major languages, Sinhala and Tamil, covered women's issues more accurately but did not treat the women's movement as politically important. In the Philippines, a study done in 1985 found that women make news only as rape victims or subjects of scandal. Rape was not portrayed as a serious issue; instead, the victims' physical attributes were stressed. A study in 1987 from Thailand reached a similar conclusion, although it found that the inside pages of some publications carried news on women's development and careers (UNESCO, 1989).

A UNESCO-sponsored study on reporting on prostitution in India, Malaysia, and the Philippines found that although prostitution, and with it sexually transmitted disease, is on the rise in these countries, it is relatively invisible in the media. There was some improvement in the 1980s, with the condition of prostitutes and the worst forms of abuse receiving greater coverage. Some good investigative stories have been done, especially in India. For example, a report in 1980 gave the first detailed description of the life of *devadasis,* temple prostitutes, in the states of Maharashtra and Karnataka. A series of investigative reports followed, which created a public outcry, and this in turn led the government to pass a law forbidding such prostitution. The media coverage itself was prompted by concerted action by nongovernmental organizations working on the *devadasi* issue. But even in India, sustained, in-depth coverage of prostitution is rare. The norm in all three countries is to sensationalize stories about prostitution to sell papers. For example, the dismantling of a prostitution syndicate is more likely to be covered than attempts at rehabilitating prostitutes or the complex reasons for the increase in prostitution. In the Philippines, which has the most serious problem of large-scale prostitution of the three countries, coverage was found to be clearly inadequate. It appears that prostitution has become so taken for granted that even many media professionals did not consider it a serious issue. It was found that the media were producing articles on women only to generate advertising, catering to male readers' sexual appetites with sensational pictures, accepting thinly disguised ads for prostitution, sensationalizing the victims in press reports of raids on brothels, and failing to expose those who benefit from the sex industry (Grjebine, n.d.).

Challenging Dominant Representations of Women

The limited range of representation of women can be partly explained by the fact that in Asia, as in other regions of the world, women are a minority in the media as workers. In broadcasting, they rarely have technical or senior management positions. Women most often tend to get on-screen jobs, such as presentation and announcing. When they are found in production at all, it is in educational and children's programs rather than news and current affairs. There are usually no formal regulations discriminating against women. Rather, there are invisible barriers to advancement, such as perceptions of what women can and cannot do, and a lack of organizational flexibility to accommodate women's multiple roles as workers, wives, and mothers.

In various Asian countries, some women have gained visibility as journalists and producers in both broadcast and print media, and they have done so against great odds. In terms of women's presence at top management levels some countries, such as Hong Kong, the Philippines, and Singapore, fare much better than others. In the Philippines, for example, many women journalists took great risks during the period of martial law (1972–1982) under the Marcos regime, becoming an important part of the alternative press. They have maintained their presence since then, serving as pioneers in the press, in community media, and in communication education. In broadcasting as well, Filipinas range from assistant general managers to producers to talk show hosts (Nicolas et al., 1990; Rosario-Braid, 1996). In many Asian countries, the proportion of women journalism students is on the rise. What impact this will have on their presence in the media industries, particularly in decision-making positions, is an open question. Whether women's increased presence in the media as producers and managers has an effect on the content of the mainstream media is also not yet clear.

Women in Asia are challenging limiting media representations through various means. Some women are working for change within mainstream media. Others are creating their own representations through alternative media. There has been a sharp increase in women's alternative publications in Asia in the last decade. Among the notable examples of alternative media in the region are the journal *Manushi* and the women's press Kali for Women in India, and the Women's Feature Service, headquartered in India. There are also women's networks for sharing pertinent information and organizations that train women in the use of media, such as the Center for the Development of Instructional Technology (CENDIT) in India, the HKW Video Workshop in Japan, and the Asia-Pacific Institute for Broadcasting Development, a regional training institute based in Malaysia. Also of note is the Asian Women Workers, Newsletter in Hong Kong and the Women Make Waves Film/Video Festival held every year in Taiwan. These various groups are engaged in expanding the scope of women's presence in the media in the hope that they will create a broader range of representations of women.

See Also

IMAGES OF WOMEN: OVERVIEW; MEDIA: ALTERNATIVE; MEDIA: GRASSROOTS; PROSTITUTION

References and Further Reading

Garcellano, Rosario A. 1991. *Who calls the shots? Proceedings of the 1991 International Conference on Women, Media, and Advertising.* Quezon City, Philippines: Women's Media Circle Foundation.

Grjebine, Lois. n.d. *Reporting on prostitution: The media, women, and prostitution in India, Malaysia, and the Philippines.* Paris: UNESCO.

Cha, Rama. 1992. *Women and the Indian print media: Portrayal and performance.* Delhi: Chanakya.

Joseph, Ammu, and Kalpana Sharma. 1994. *Whose news? The media and women's issues.* New Delhi: Sage.

Luthra, Rashmi. 1999. The women's movement and the press in India: The construction of female foeticide as a social issue. *Women's Studies in Communication* 22(1): 1–25.

Nicolas, Fort Olicia, Jojo De Leon, and M. Juris Aledia Luna. 1990. *Women and media in the Asian context.* Quezon City, Philippines: World Association for Christian Communication, People in Communication.

Pervaiz, Seema. 1982. *Analysis of mass media appealing to women.* Islamabad: Women's Division, Government of Pakistan.

Rosario-Braid, Florangel. 1996. Filipino women in communications: Breaking new ground. In Donna Allen, Ramona R. Rush, and Susan J. Kaufman, eds., *Women transforming communications: Global intersections.* Thousand Oaks, Calif.: Sage.

UNESCO. 1987. *Women and media decision-making: The invisible barriers.* Paris: UNESCO.

———. 1989. *World communication report.* Paris: UNESCO.

Rashmi Luthra

IMAGES OF WOMEN: Australia and New Zealand

Discussions of images of women in the media usually start from the premise that media portrayals and stories are based on sexual stereotypes that demean or oppress women and restrict their identity (Zoonen, 1991). Liberal, radical, and socialist positions have in common a view of the media as a powerful instrument of social control and an effective conveyor of stereotypical, patriarchal, and hegemonic values regarding women. The problem with this position is that it assumes a presocial subject, a unified, identifiable category called "women," and denies women's power and agency as audience members. If, however, it is assumed, as Nead (1992: 72) says, that there is no "perfect type that represents the interests of all women," then images of women in the media cannot be judged in absolute terms but must be considered in relation to the ways they reflect and contribute to an exploration of women's diverse social, cultural, and economic identities.

The assumption that there is no such thing as the essential women, that there is no "real woman" out there who might be accurately represented, demands a reevaluation of most of the studies that have been done on the portrayal of women in the media. For the most part, research in this area has depended on positivist methodology and content analysis within reductionist categories. Petersen (1994) highlights the problem. He points to an Australian study of 1993, which concluded, on the basis of a review of 5,000 television and newspaper print items, that women do not receive a "balanced representation" in the media, and that where representation is achieved it is "contextually negative" (National Working Party on the Portrayal of Women in the Media, 1993). Petersen asks what the description "balanced representation" means and what a contextually positive portrayal might look like. Such research findings naturalize certain political positions and ignore the struggles over issues of representation.

Nevertheless, some of the research into the portrayal of women in the media is useful for gauging the visibility of particular categories of women, even if the reports cannot state with certainty what the images mean to those who consume them. Women have always been highly visible in advertising, where they function as both a target market and an aid to selling, but advertising is only one aspect of Australian and New Zealand popular culture. How visible are women within those domains of culture inhabited and valued by men—the news, sports, and the countryside?

News

An Australian study commissioned by the Office of the Status of Women found that women rarely figure in the main news stories of the day, that they are seldom approached for comment, and that they have markedly less visibility as reporters than men. Women feature most often in human interest, crime, and leisure stories and are usually shown as victims, witnesses, or casual observers and very rarely as protagonists or authority figures (National Working Party on the Portrayal of Women in the Media, 1993).

Although women do not figure prominently in news content, they are beginning to be seen on camera. Both Australian and New Zealand broadcasters have adopted the practice of balancing gender in televised presentations of news and current affairs. Many channels share stories equally between the male and female readers, while some use a male news reader and a female current affairs anchor or vice versa. However, the women presenters are almost without exception younger than their male counterparts, and, while the men are dressed in identical conservative suits every night of the week, the women call attention to issues of gender and style through regular changes of costume and, less often, hairstyle. In Australia women of color are seen reading for the nightly news only on the ethnic broadcasting channel SBS (Special Broadcasting System), although the Australian Broadcasting Corporation also occasionally uses women of non-Anglo Saxon appearance.

Although women have a stronger screen presence in news and current affairs than they did fifteen years ago, their voices are still largely unheard. The voice-over narration on film clips and file footage is still overwhelmingly male, there are significantly fewer female than male reporters, and men are consistently more likely than women to read "hard" news stories (politics, war, and finance). It is in the news media's coverage of sports that the unequal treatment of the sexes is most obvious. Judy McGregor and Phillip Melville's study of three metropolitan, one provincial, and three Sunday papers in New Zealand (1994) found that coverage of women's sports amounted to only 12.36 percent of the total space devoted to sports reporting in the seven papers. The Australian media fare no better. In 1994 a report titled *Invisible Games*, prepared for the Sport and Recreation Ministers' Council, found that women's sports received only 4.2 percent of the coverage in major Australian newspapers; this was only 2 percent more than in 1980. Television gave 1.2 percent coverage, which was a decline from 1980 of 0.1 percent. On Australian television women's sports receive less than 2 percent of sports airtime (Rowe, 1994). The poor media coverage means that although women reach the highest levels in sports, they are still denied the lucrative sponsorships enjoyed by men.

Rural Life

Much has been written about the representation of women in advertising in Australia and New Zealand, and most of the studies agree that images of women in advertisements reinforce sexual stereotypes, define women in relation to others, and place women in a role subordinate to men. Arguably, however, the last 20 years have seen a slow but significant shift away from the image of the woman as housewife and caregiver; women are increasingly represented in a diverse range of occupations, interests, and leisure activities, giving rise to complaints that new stereotypes of the supermother and career woman are replacing the old domestic image. The change in the images of women in advertising is largely restricted to city-based media broadcasting and publication.

Images of women in the rural media have not changed. In both Australia and New Zealand women's contribution to farm labor has been celebrated in prose, poetry, and painting, but this respectful attitude is not reflected in rural advertising. That farm women generally make an important and often crucial contribution to farm labor, especially on family farms, is well known, and yet in the rural media images of men and women conform to traditional gender-role stereotypes. Farming is consistently characterized as men's work and as almost entirely dependent on men's labor. Women in the rural media are usually represented as housewives and depicted in relation to household products, fashion, and recreational services. They are presented as feminine, lacking physical strength, and not technically minded. The manner in which women are depicted denies them acknowledgment and credit for their labor and contributes to their general invisibility as farmworkers. This emphasis on men as farmers and women as housewives is consistent with the prevailing rural patriarchal ideology. This male-generated and male-centered ideology is defended and maintained by the farming industry, by farm men, and, it would seem, by most farm women, even though it is to their disadvantage (Bell and Pandey, 1989).

Entertainment

In the 1970s and 1980s Australian film was dominated by the "male ensemble" configuration of character (Dermody and Jacka, 1988: 65). With the exception of *My Brilliant Career, Caddie,* and *The Getting of Wisdom,* it was groups of men who played, fought, suffered, and rejoiced together. See, for example, such films as *Breaker Morant, Gallipoli, Sunday Too Far Away,* and *Don's Party.* Television led the change in the early 1980s and 1990s, and a number of television miniseries explored women's and girls' histories. *Come In Spinner* and *Brides of Christ* created female ensemble performances and women-centered narratives and offered alternative popular memories for women. *Darlings of the Gods* and *Edens Lost* probed the complexities of adult female sensibilities.

It is on television too that representational spaces usually closed to women have been opened. Despite the description above of the exclusion, marginalization, and devaluation of women in sporting arenas, it was a television sports program that challenged masculine ownership of sports commentary and authority. Starting in 1993 *Live and Sweaty,* a weekly one-hour live Australian sports magazine program, was presented by three knowledgeable and irreverent women who consistently asserted female expertise and challenged the male expert. They used their considerable knowledge to satirize and subvert both the male sports culture and the respect it is accorded by fans. "By playing with the excesses of all the gender codes, *Live and Sweaty* critiqued the apotheosis of the hegemonic male" (Cook and Jennings, 1995). The women were the program's central anchors and authority figures; the men existed only on the margins as news stringers, buffoons, and comic foils. *Live and Sweaty* did not change the face of Australian television. It lasted only two seasons. Other sport comedy programs followed, however, such as the intensely masculine *The Footy Show* and *Club Buggery.*

This partial and selective discussion of images of women in Australian and New Zealand media highlights contradictions and inconsistencies in both the output of the media and research into the portrayal of women in the media. These inconsistencies probably reflect both the struggles within the media between groups that seek to speak of and for women and the different political and philosophical positions of the researchers who seek to analyze the media's output. What is clear, however, is that control over image and narrative, and thus over identity, is never straightforward or absolute. There is scope for resistance and alternative representations and thus hope that women of color, disabled women, aged women, and women on the margins of society will make their presence known.

See Also

MEDIA: OVERVIEW; REPRESENTATION; SPORT; TELEVISION

References and Further Reading

Bell, J. H., and U. S. Pandey. 1989. Gender-role stereotypes in Australian farm advertising. *Media Information Australia,* 51 (Feb.): 45–49.

Cook, Jackie, and Karen Jennings. 1995. Live and sweaty: Australian women re-cast Australian sports television. *Media Information Australia,* 75 (Feb.): 5–12.

Dermody, Susan, and Elizabeth Jacka. 1988. *The screening of Australia: Anatomy of a national cinema.* Sydney: Currency.

McGregor, Judy, and Phillip Melville. 1994. The invisible face of women's sport in the New Zealand press. *Metro,* 96: 35–39.

McKee, Alan. Forthcoming. *Great moments in Australian television: A genealogy.* Oxford: Oxford University Press.

National Working Party on the Portrayal of Women in the Media. 1993. *Women and media.* Canberra, Australia: Department of the Prime Minister and Cabinet (Office of the Status of Women).

Nead, L. 1992. *The female nude: Art, obscenity, and sexuality.* London: Routledge.

Petersen, Alan R. 1994. Governing images: Media constructions of the "normal," "healthy" subject. *Media Information Australia,* 27 (May): 32–40.
Rowe, David. 1994. The spectacle of sport. In Stuart Cunningham and Toby Miller, eds., *Contemporary Australian television,* 64–89. Sydney: University of New South Wales Press.
Zoonen, Liesbet van. 1991. Feminist perspectives on the media. In J. Curran and M. Gurevitch, eds., *Mass media and society,* 40–41. London: Edward Arnold.

Robyn Quin

IMAGES OF WOMEN: Caribbean

Feminist studies of images of women in the mass media focus on how the media materialize and ideologically maintain women's oppression through sexist imagery. Such studies usually try to contextualize this imagery within larger social structures and discourses. Early media studies were primarily concerned with the role of advertising, but today's research on the representation or images of women also encompasses newspapers, magazines, fictional film, and television. Some countries (such as the United States) have a strong tradition of such research; but images of women in the Caribbean mass media remain relatively understudied. The major exception is research on the images, representation, and role of women in Caribbean literature (Acosta-Belén, 1979; Barrat, 1986; Boyce Davies and Savory Fido, 1990; Johnson, 1983; Lourdes, 1987).

Studies of the intersecting roles of race, gender, and class in the Caribbean often pay little attention to images of women in the mass media; and research about the Caribbean mass media often lacks analyses of gender and race (Dunn, 1995 is one example). Much of the existing research about images of women in the Caribbean mass media is in the form of unpublished manuscripts and conference papers (Cabrera, 1988; Forrester, 1987; Johnson, 1988; Rohler, 1986). Thus, this area of study remains a fertile ground for future research on gender, the media's representation of women, and Caribbean popular culture.

The Caribbean was colonized beginning in the late fifteenth century by the British, French, and Spanish, who brought enslaved Africans and Indians to replace the diminishing indigenous populations of the various islands. Thus, each region—the British Caribbean, French Caribbean, or Spanish Caribbean—is defined by language and a distinct ethnically mixed heritage. Because of linguistic and cultural differences among the twenty or so islands of the Caribbean, research often centers on specific islands or areas rather than on the region as a whole, and rarely looks at multiple forms of media.

Despite the Caribbean's ethnically mixed heritage of European, North American, African, and indigenous populations, many dominant representations of women continue to be based on Eurocentric stereotypes: respectable behavior, "whiteness," and "Europeanness." Thus African or Afro-Caribbean images of women are relatively rare; those that do appear are often derogatory (Barrow, 1986:52). This is an example of the "symbolic annihilation" of women (Tuchman et al., 1978). In general, images of Caribbean women in the media reveal several stereotypes. As workers, women are often portrayed as unskilled, exploitable, inexpensive labor; as mothers, they are often portrayed as devious, submissive to their husbands, and authoritarian with regard to their primary responsibility, their children. Upper-class (nonworking) women are predominantly represented as being of European ancestry and European in appearance, but working-class women are predominantly represented as African or Afro-Caribbean in ancestry and physical appearance.

Two studies of the images of women across several islands, regions, and media found pervasive gender-stereotyped representations. One of these, a historical analysis of print media, found that images of women have been mostly Eurocentric and sexist (Broder, 1982). In various print media, women were most often portrayed as the male objects of European beauty. Upper-class women were often portrayed as frail, nervous housewives; lower-class women were often portrayed as uneducated, sexually permissive domestic workers. The second of these studies found that while the social, economic, and political context had changed, images of women in the mass media remained unchanged, and largely stereotyped (Cuthbert, 1989).

Puerto Rican media scholars have found that negative representations of women persist in the media of Puerto Rico despite sociopolitical-economic changes. Serra-Deliz (1989) examined Puerto Rican newspapers and television and concluded that the image of women as a source of social disorder, as less than equal citizens, and as mothers; of feminine behavior as disruptive; and of women as an object of justifiable discrimination continue to dominate representations in these media.

Images of Women in Television and Film

In general, most images of women (as well as of men) on Caribbean television continue to be stereotyped. Women are often depicted in a narrow range of roles typified by subordinate, passive, supportive, and decorative behavior in relationship to their male counterparts (Cuthbert, 1984). Televised news programs rarely cover women's issues, perspectives, or achievements. Almost all films (75 percent) shown in the Caribbean are produced in the United States, Hong Kong, India, and Spain. These films perpetuate stereotypical and often negative images of women current in the producers' cultures, such as women as sexual objects and as victims of violence.

In Puerto Rican television programming, images of women remain stereotyped. Hernandéz (1987) concludes that Puerto Rican television and advertising predominately portray women in one of three ways: as sexual objects of male desire, as emotionally hysterical, or as sexually undesirable wives. Examining the portrayal of working women, Alegría Ortega (1987) found women overrepresented as secretaries and housewives. In sitcom and comic variety shows, 76 percent of women are portrayed as housewives, 20 percent are unemployed, and 4 percent are secretaries. In advertisements, 80 percent of commercial voice-overs are by women and are about cleaning or cooking products; and 50 percent of women are depicted performing some form of housework for their children or husbands. Thus, as in many other Caribbean countries, there is a disparity between the televised or "ideal" images and the actual experiences of working women in Puerto Rico. Most Puerto Rican programming ignores the increased numbers of working women and the social and political context of the Caribbean women's movement.

Media researchers often focus on the representation of women in *telenovelas,* locally produced Spanish-language soap operas. Some scholars argue that the representation of women in *telenovelas* diffuses social action and organization regarding issues relevant to women's lives and reinforces traditional feminine roles such as housewife or domestic servant (Pineda, 1981). One telenovela author, Maria Zarattini (1990), argues that while images of women in *telenovelas* continue to evolve, the form still reinforces a socially conservative image of women as submissive to the nuclear family; that is, the roles and actions of female characters in *telenovelas* are often based on their dependence on their parents, brothers, husbands, and children. Alegría-Ortega found that in Puerto Rican *telenovelas* 55 percent of women are portrayed as secretaries and 45 percent are unemployed or housewives.

Images of Women in Radio and Music

With regard to images of women on Caribbean radio, two forms are predominately analyzed: soap operas and popular music, especially calypso. Like *telenovelas,* most radio soap operas are centered on domestic, private, personal issues—often emotionally shattering—rather than on politically or socially relevant matters. Most of the leading characters are middle-class, and the narratives revolve around conflicts that threaten middle-class values (Cuthbert, 1984). As in the *telenovelas,* the majority of female characters are housewives or domestic servants.

About 50 percent of radio programming is devoted to popular music, and media scholars argue that most of this music continues to convey images of women characterized by sexism and negative sexual stereotypes. In particular, despite the rise of women calypso artists, calypso often portrays women as promiscuous, dangerous schemers and as sexual objects of male desire, and it reinforces the idea that a woman belongs in the home (Cumberbath, 1989; Reyes, 1986; Rohler, 1986).

Images of Women in Newspapers and Magazines

Most scholars argue that the depiction of women in the Caribbean press is inconsistent (Earl, 1986). Social, political, and economic issues pertaining to impoverished women and children, underpaid domestic servants, single women, and women market vendors are rarely covered, but images of the racial and economic female elite abound. Women's pages and lifestyle sections of many Caribbean newspapers devote more space to recipes and fashion than to social or political issues.

Marlene Cuthbert's analysis (1984) of West Indian Caribbean newspapers concludes that images of women, while still negative, have improved slightly. During the rise of the West Indian press in the mid-1800s, images of women were relatively nonexistent. When women were covered, they were often represented simply as mothers and housewives. Most of these representations were of upper-class women, who were often depicted as frail, nervous, and sickly. In the last 50 years, however, the images of women in most West Indian papers are of foreign white women, such as British royalty, movie stars, international models, and wives and families of the political and economic elite. Today, most newspapers in the Caribbean continue to depict a European standard of beauty in advertising and photographs (Cuthbert, 1989).

Cornelia Butler Flora (1980) analyzed the representation of women in another written form, the *fotonovela,* a romantic novel told through photographs and balloon captions, popular among working-class audiences in many Spanish-speaking countries. Flora found that these novels reinforced negative images of middle-class women as consumers and working-class women as passive victims of sexual violence and social disintegration.

Images of Women in Advertising

The representation of women has improved most in advertising. While some scholars argue that many advertisements continue to portray an alien culture, irrelevant to the Caribbean population, through their use of European models (Earl, 1986), others say that beginning in the 1970s, advertising executives responded to calls for change. Cuthbert (1984) argues that advertisers today are making attempts to represent the physical diversity of the Caribbean peoples and to recognize ethnic and cultural differences among the various regions. Thus, at least the physical images of women in advertisements more closely approximate the demographics of many Caribbean countries, even though the roles women play in commercials remain stereotyped: housewives and mothers in the domestic sphere. In general, advertising now reflects the diverse racial and class composition of the Caribbean more accurately, and more ads focus on the family as a unit rather than on women as sexual objects.

Conclusion

The Caribbean is an ethnically and culturally diverse region primarily defined by its history of British, French, and Spanish colonization and the importation of enslaved Africans and Indians. Today, its mass media still focus on Eurocentric representations of "whiteness" and femininity, and on North American and European cultural products that internalize sexist representations of women. Although the social, political, and economic life of women in the Caribbean continues to change, most Caribbean media still represent women as either mothers and nurturers or sexual objects and promiscuous partners. In part because of the ethnic mix in these islands, there may be greater diversity in the images of women in Caribbean media than in, for example, North American or European media. However, images of women continue to be stereotyped by race and class, with upper-class women represented as "white," educated, physically fragile housewives or mothers and working-class women overrepresented as "black" or of African descent, uneducated, and physically healthy, and as domestic workers.

Relatively few critical studies have been conducted on the cultural aspects of Caribbean mass media. There is a tradition of cultural studies, exemplified by the Caribbean Studies Association and the University of the West Indies Women and Development Studies Project; but there is a need to make this work available to North American and European scholars, and a need for further research on ethnicity, race, gender, sexuality, class, and Caribbean popular culture.

See Also

IMAGES OF WOMEN: OVERVIEW; REPRESENTATION

References and Further Reading

Acosta-Belén, Edna. 1979. Ideology and images of women in contemporary Puerto Rican literature. *The Puerto Rican Woman:* 85–109.

Alegría Ortega, Idsa E. 1987. La representación de la mujer trabajadora en la televisión en Puerto Rico. *Homines* 10(2): 282–293.

Barrat, Harold. 1986. Literature and society: The female image in Mendes's fiction. *ACLALS Bulletin* 7(4): 34–39.

Barrow, Christine. 1986. Male images of women in Barbados. *Social and Economic Studies* 35(3): 51–64.

Boyce Davies, Carole, and Elaine Savory Fido, eds. 1990. *Out of the Kumbla: Caribbean women and literature.* Trenton, N.J.: African World.

Broder, E. 1982. *Perceptions of Caribbean women: Towards a documentation of stereotypes.* Cave Hill, Barbados: University of the West Indies, Institute of Social and Economic Research.

Cabrera, Nydia. 1988. *Women's image in continuing television drama: A comparison of Puerto Rico telenovelas and United States soap operas.* M.A. thesis, University of Florida.

Cumberbath, Janice. 1989. Women in Bajan calypsos: How are they portrayed? *Bulletin of Eastern Caribbean Affairs* 14(5/6): 37–58.

Cuthbert, Marlene. 1989. "Woman day a come": Women and communication channels in the Caribbean. In Ramona Rush and Donna Allen, eds., *Communication at the crossroads: The gender gap connection.* Norwood, N.J.: Ablex.

———. 1984. "Woman day a come": Mass media and development in the caribbean. *Media Development* 31(2): 29–31.

Dunn, Hopeton S, ed. 1995. *Globalization, communications, and Caribbean identity.* New York: St. Martin's.

Earl, Claudette. 1986. Media concepts for human development in the Caribbean with special reference to women. In Pat Ellis, ed., *Women of the Caribbean.* London: Zed.

Flora, Cornelia Butler. 1980. Women in Latin American fotonovelas: From Cinderella to Mata Hari. *Women's Studies International Quarterly* 3(1): 95–104.

Forrester, Claire A. 1987. Popular media images of women and men in the Caribbean. Mona, Jamaica: University of West Indies, First Interdisciplinary Seminar: Gender, Culture, and Caribbean Development, June.

Hernandéz Torres, Elizabeth. 1987. Images of women in mass media. *Homines* February: 296–300.

Johnson, Julie Greer. 1983. *Women in colonial Spanish American literature: Literary images.* Westport, Conn.: Greenwood.

Johnson, Karlene Alicia Yvette. 1988. *The portrayal of women in Jamaican magazine and newspaper advertisement.* M.A. thesis, University of Florida.

Lourdes, Casal. 1987. Images of women in pre- and postrevolutionary Cuban novels. *Cuban Studies,* 17: 25–50.

Pineda, Magaly. 1981. Telenovelas: Just entertainment? *Isis International Bulletin* 18: 16–18.

Reyes, Elma. 1986. Women in calypso. In Pat Ellis, ed., *Women of the Caribbean.* London: Zed, 119–121.

Rohler, Gordon. 1986. Images of men and women in the 1930s calypsos: The sociology of food acquisition in a context of survivalism. St. Augustine, Trinidad: University of West Indies, Women and Development Project presented at the Inaugural Seminar of the University of West Indies.

Serra Deliz, Wenceslao. 1989. La construcción social de la imagen de la mujer en el refrenero puertorriqueno. *Caribbean Studies* 22(1/2): 67–100.

Tuchman, Gayle, Arlene Kaplan Daniels, and James Benet, eds. 1978. *Hearth and home: Images of women in the mass media.* New York: Oxford University Press.

Zarattini, Maria. 1993. Las telenovelas y la imagen de la mujer. *Fem* 17(130, December): 18–19.

Isabel Molina Guzmán

IMAGES OF WOMEN: Central and South America

The images and meanings associated with women in Central and South America are constructed, exchanged, and modified in the production and consumption of mass media representations of this region in general, and its women in particular. People, events, and objects become meaningful through the process of representation—the words, stories, images, classifications, and concepts that are associated with them. The media—with their increasingly global reach—play a crucial role in shaping the shared meanings and interpretations that allow their consumers to understand and make sense of the world (Hall, 1997). Representation has always been important for contemporary feminism (van Zoonen, 1994); therefore, a study of the production and consumption of representations of Central and South American women in film, television, and news is essential to understanding their images.

Film

Historically, the Latin American film industry has been dominated by male directors and producers, and most of their films center on male characters. Even the development of the "new Latin American cinema," with its emphasis on social issues, did not significantly change this situation. These films rarely consider gender issues, focusing instead on class as the main factor in social and political oppression. In these films, the presence of women serves only as a catalyst or facilitator for the actions of the male characters. Women's images lack depth and are usually restricted to the erotic or the romantic (Pick, 1993).

However, the last two decades of the twentieth century saw the emergence of a new generation of women filmmakers in Central and South America. Their films introduce a feminist perspective, give a voice to women in the daily struggle to resist oppression, and explore women as subjects, not objects. Some examples are María Luisa Bemberg's *Camila* (1984) and *Yo, la Peor de Todas* ("I, the Worst of Them All," 1990), Betty Kaplan's *Doña Baibara* (1998), and Eduardo Spagnuolo's *Sin Reserva* (2000) in Argentina; Fina Torres's *Oriana* (1985) and Solveig Hoogesteijn's *Macu, la Mujer del Policia* ("Macu, the Policeman's Wife," 1987) in Venezuela; María Novaro's *Lola* (1989) and *Danzón* (1992) in Mexico; and an integration of five short films produced by teams directed by Hector Veitía, Mayra Segura, Mayra Vilasís, Mario Crespo, and Ana Rodríguez in *Mujer Transparente* "Transparent Woman," (1990) in Cuba.

The majority of Central and South American films are consumed only in the country where they were produced, though some are distributed in other Latin American nations. In most of these countries, access to films is based on socioeconomic class. With the exception of specialized festival screenings, very few of these films are seen by worldwide audiences. Some notable exceptions have been *La Historia Oficial* ("The Official Story," 1985), which won an Oscar from the U.S. Academy of Motion Picture Arts and Sciences; *El Beso de la Mujer Araña* ("The Kiss of the Spider Woman," 1985), whose Brazilian director, Héctor Babenco, was nominated for an Oscar; and *Como Agua para Chocolate* ("Like Water for Chocolate," 1993). These three widely distributed films present women in important roles but were produced and directed by men.

Television

Access to television (unlike film) is widespread in Latin America. For instance, the proportion of households with a television set is 94 percent in Argentina, 92 percent in Venezuela, and 90 percent in Cuba (Getino, 1996). Latin American programs present an array of images of Central and South American women. The spicy *vedette,* or Latin bombshell, is perhaps best exemplified by Puerto Rico's Iris Chacón. Celia Cruz in Cuba is a quintessential *salsera.* Talk show hostesses include Cristina Saralegui, a Cuban based in Miami; and the Venezuelan Maite Delgado. News anchors include Norma Suárez Castellote in Mexico. Alicia Machado in Venezuela is an example of a beauty pageant winner turned soap opera actress; Verónica Castro in Mexico is an example of a soap opera actresses turned showwoman. With the exception of *salseras,* the images presented highlight the desirability of young, beautiful, sexy, light-skinned women. Older women are mostly invisible or are relegated to supporting roles in soap operas or to being a laughingstock in comedy shows, which satirize them as ugly and undesirable.

The Latin American soap opera—the *telenovela*—is important in the production, negotiation, and consumption of images of Latin American women. These series are exported to more than 100 countries (Barker, 1997) and command large audiences that cut across class lines and cultures. Although there are significant differences from nation to nation, all the telenovelas share certain traits: melodrama; a struggle between good and evil, represented by characters who are polar opposites; stark contrasts between social classes; and a search for happiness through heterosexual love.

With the exception of Brazilian telenovelas, the titles of most of these series include a woman's name or the word *mujer* ("woman"), underscoring the fact that these dramas are centered on female characters, presenting a story from the woman's point of view. The images depicted, however, are mostly shaped by a traditional vision of women's role in society and by a steroetypical concept of women as emotional, irrational, and unstable. The viewer sees suffering mothers; flirtatious young women; indiscreet maids; envious sisters and girlfriends; frustrated stepmothers; and beautiful, young, naive main characters who—almost always—become blind, crippled, pregnant, or all of these at different points in the plot (Mazziotti et al., 1993). The women presented are unidimensional and serve the main purpose of the plots in this genre: the dichotomy between good and evil. "Good" women are naive and do not usually make intelligent decisions. "Evil" women seem to be smarter, and their ambitions and behavior have no limits. Stereotypical catfights between women are common in telenovelas. There may be a few female characters who exhibit both good and evil traits, but these are rare and undeveloped. Most female characters represent some version of the dichotomy between madonna and whore that is so much a part of patriarchal myths.

Although there have been some attempts (most notably in Brazil) to present female characters who play an important public role, telenovelas still support hegemonic views by portraying female characters as being fulfilled only when they put their strengths at the service of their families. For example, in the Brazilian series *Corpo a Corpo* ("Body to Body," 1984–1985), one female character's professional success brings about the failure of her marriage. Brazilian telenovelas that have tried to break this mold have had problems with the censors (Fadul, 1993).

Great emphasis is placed on the female characters' physical appearance—their clothes and hairdos are fancy and trendy. Venezuelan telenovelas, in particular, use winners of beauty pageants as actresses; the result is often that the female characters have extraordinary physical attributes but lack any depth, partly because the writers concentrate on exploiting the performers' physical beauty, and partly because the acting of many of the former beauty queens is deplorable.

Latin American telenovelas are one of the most widely consumed television genres in the world (Barker, 1997), and Central and South American women are especially captivated by them. It is important to note, however, that in Latin America, watching telenovelas is a family activity—women, men, and children follow them religiously. Moreover, Brazilian, Mexican, Venezuelan, and Argentinean telenovelas are watched worldwide; in particular, they make up a huge portion of the daily programming of Latin-language networks in the United States (López, 1995). As a result of this wide distribution, the image of Central and South American women presented in telenovelas has tended to become the dominant image of Latin American women around the world.

News

There is also another reason for the dominance of the telenovelas' picture of women: Central and South American women are both underepresented and misrepresented in the news, so that journalism offers few counterbalancing images. In general, news produced in Latin American countries presents women in traditional roles, placing them—for the most part—in the social pages or in feature stories. News coverage of women is pervaded by two ideologies: *machismo,* the idea that men are superior to women, have more extensive rights, and belong to the public sphere while women should stay in men's shadow and in the private realm; and *marianismo,* the idea that women are morally superior, with spiritual strength and a capacity for self-sacrifice that make them good mothers. The combination of these ideologies results in coverage that seldom focuses on the few women who hold public office or on women in grassroots organizations that address human rights, the environment, and the plight of poor urban families.

News produced in Latin American countries rarely reaches the rest of the world, which is dominated by large news agencies such as the Associated Press (AP), United Press International (UPI), and Reuters. These agencies and the world's major newspapers seldom present positive images of Central and South American women, who appear, instead, mostly in reports of war and disasters and are usually portrayed as victims. There is some reporting of women's oppression— legal inequality, the illegality of abortion, and issues associated with machismo—but even this coverage tends to reinforce the overall image of women as victims, for several reasons. First, the stories are typically written from a first-world perspective and show little understanding of the cultural nuances of Latin America. Second, the stories usually do not feature the women's own voices. Third, these stories, in general, trivialize and simplify Central and South American women and their activities rather than treating them as legitimate and significant (Acosta-Alzuru, 1998).

It is important to emphasize that the United States dominates worldwide production and distribution of news—and also of films and television. Thus images of Central and South American women are often equated with stereotyped images of Latinas in the United States: accented speech, little education, low social status, immorality, lack of culture, and relegation to background roles. This is also true of images of Central and South American men, and the study of these images is part of Latino studies in general (see Rodríguez, 1997).

In sum, the representation of Central and South American women in their own media and in international media generally lacks depth and complexity: the media offer simplified images, stressing physical appearance; casting women in traditional roles; disregarding women's voice, intellect, and agency; and thus reinforcing established ideologies and myths about women in general.

See Also

FILM; HOUSEHOLDS AND FAMILIES: CENTRAL AND SOUTH AMERICA; IMAGES OF WOMEN: CARIBBEAN; IMAGES OF WOMEN: OVERVIEW; LITERATURE: CENTRAL AND SOUTH AMERICA; JOURNALISM; MEDIA: MAINSTREAM; MEDIA: OVERVIEW; TELEVISION

References and Further Reading

Acosta-Alzuru, Carolina. 1998. Trivializing a cause: Press coverage of the Mothers of Plaza de Mayo. In Joseph R. Dominick, ed., *The dynamics of mass communication,* 503. 6th ed. New York: McGraw-Hill.

Barker, Chris. 1997. *Global television: An introduction.* Oxford: Blackwell.

Fadul, Ann Maria. 1993. *Serial fiction in TV: The Latin American telenovelas.* Sao Paulo, Brazil: Universidad de Sao Paulo.

Getino, Octavio. 1996. *La tercera mirada: Panorama del audiovisual Latinoamericano.* Buenos Aires: Paidós.

Hall, Stuart, ed. 1997. *Representation: Cultural representations and signifying practices.* London: Sage.

King, John. 1990. *Magical reels: A history of cinema in Latin America.* London: Verso.

López, Ana M. 1995. Our welcomed guests: Telenovelas in Latin America. In Robert C. Allen, ed., *To be continued... Soap operas around the world,* 256–275. London: Routledge.

Martín-Barbero, Jesús. 1995. Memory and form in the Latin American Soap Opera. In Robert C. Allen, ed., *To be continued... Soap operas around the world,* 276–284. London: Routledge.

Mazziotti, Nora, Eliseo Verón, Jesús Martín-Barbero, Jorge A. González, María Teresa Quiroz, and Anamaria Fadul. 1993. *El espectáculo de la pasión: Las telenovelas Latinoamericanas.* Buenos Aires: Colihue.

Pick, Zuzana M. 1993. *The new Latin American cinema: A continental project.* Austin: University of Texas Press.

Rodríguez, Clara E., ed. 1997. *Latin looks: Images of Latinas and Latinos in the U.S. media.* Boulder, Colo.: Westview.

Schwartzman, Karen. 1993. A descriptive chronology of films by women in Venezuela, 1952–1992. *Journal of Film and Video* 44(3–4): 33–50.

Zoonen, Lisbeth van. 1994. *Feminist media studies.* London: Sage.

Carolina Acosta-Alzuru

IMAGES OF WOMEN: Europe

In Europe the study of images of women in the media began with the political concerns of the women's movement of the 1970s. Feminist critics of culture and communication saw the mass media as part of a pattern of discrimination against women, because the content of these media ignored, trivialized, or objectified women. This early feminist scholarship typically used quantitative content analysis of sex roles and stereotypes, but since the 1980s the debate in Europe has increasingly involved qualitiative analysis—for example, how the media define gender, how media images generate a range of meanings, and how audiences interpret different types of content. These approaches have illuminated complexities and contradictions in gender images in the contemporary media, and their resistance to change. Policy-oriented research has also been important, and in the 1990s some researchers and media practitioners collaborated to change professional practices that reinforced gender stereotyping.

Women and Media in Europe

Europe's heterogeneity—in terms of languages, media systems, and traditions in women's studies—makes generalizations problematic. Even the volume of research on images of women varies enormously between countries. A review conducted for the European Commission found that most work has been concentrated in Scandinavia, the United Kingdom, Germany, and the Netherlands (Kivikuru et al., 1998). In countries such as Belgium and Ireland, research is limited by a relatively small population and research community. In countries such as France and Italy, research is limited because issues of women and the media are not yet established academic subjects. In central and eastern Europe, women's studies and critiques of the media are just emerging. Thus Europe's diversity is not fully represented in analyses of women and the media.

Stability and Change in Media Images

Research on representation of gender in European media in the 1990s suggests a shift away from the monolithic stereotyping found during the 1970s and 1980s, but this shift is almost impossible to measure quantitatively—and quantitative studies, mainly of news and advertising, actually indicate that, with few exceptions, a general pattern of male dominance and female dependence has persisted. For instance, the Norwegian researcher Birgit Eie (1998), in a rare international comparative survey, found that, overall, of every three people appearing on television, one was female. Dutch and British studies found that women were most likely to appear in children's programs, less likely to appear in news and current affairs programs, and least likely to appear in sports. Differences persist in media images of women and men, in terms of age, marital status, and employment outside the home; and a lack of longitudinal quantitative research makes it difficult to assess the extent to which such images may be changing. One analysis of advertisements on British television from 1978 to 1995, however, concluded that women are now less likely to be portrayed as dependent, and more likely to be portrayed in a workplace or as "authorities" on a product.

Quantitative studies provide baseline statistics but give little insight into nuances of gender representation. Qualitative research indicates that in some respects media images now reflect less rigid definitions of femininity than were found, say, 20 years ago. Studies of women's magazines in Ireland, Italy, the Netherlands, Spain, and the United Kingdom have reached similar conclusions: the traditional wife, mother, and homemaker is much less evident and has been replaced by images of assertive, confident, ambitious women—though these women often have a self-centred lifestyle focused on consumption and relationships. Various analyses have linked this development to changing markets: women's new freedom, in these magazines, is essentially freedom to consume.

Popular drama also appears to have a wider range of both female and male characters, including men who are strong but nurturing and paternal and authoritative women operating in a traditionally male world. Particularly since the 1990s, this genre has grappled—at least to some extent—with previously ignored issues such as sexuality, racial prejudice, and the patriarchal family. However, some researchers (for example, in Britain, France, and Italy) have interpreted such changes as institutionalizing and oversimplifying women's problems.

Images of men and masculinity are changing in many European countries. In this regard, most studies have focused on advertising, and just a few on television entertainment. Because traditionally feminine qualities such as emotionality and caring are included in the new definitions of masculinity and because male sexuality and the male body are emphasized, some scholars describe the change as "feminization." Others, such as the British feminist Angela McRobbie (1994), argue that these images reflect changes in both masculine and feminine identity and a gradual "unfixing" of gender identity in general, in part as a result of feminism.

In contrast to the shifting media images in areas related to private life, gender representation in areas related to the public sphere seems to be relatively static, homogeneous, and stereotypical. When women step outside their accustomed roles, the media often seem reluctant to accept this displacement of expected patterns and therefore focus on these women's traditionally "feminine" traits. This tendency has been found in studies of the representation of women soldiers (in Italy and the United Kingdom), athletes (in Denmark, Finland, France, the Netherlands, and the United Kingdom), and political activists and protesters (in Ireland and the United Kingdom). British and Italian research has found that women politicians are considered less newsworthy than their male counterparts. Studies in Denmark, Finland, France, the Netherlands, Norway, Sweden, and the United Kingdom have found that women and men are treated differently as politicians and as political candidates: the media emphasize men's political record and experience, but women's family situation and appearance.

Both quantitative and qualitative studies of media content suggest that the question whether media images of women have changed or are changing cannot be answered in a straightforward way. In some cases, apparent changes may be merely superficial, or political and economic developments may have reintroduced older stereotypes. For example, studies in Germany after reunification have noted a new emphasis in television on images of women as mothers and housewives, although in the former German Democratic Republic the media generally portrayed women as capable of combining paid employment and family life. Data from central Europe (Poland and Romania) indicate that the political transformations of 1989 and the market orientation of the media have resulted in a new stereotype of women as sexual objects. Perceived changes in gender images in the European media, therefore, can best be evaluated as tentative, ambiguous, and by no means uniform.

The Audience

Research on viewing, listening, or reading practices is not always easy to interpret. Within the family, men are more likely than women to choose the medium, channel, station, or program, so that women may be an audience for material in which they have little interest. However, there are some fairly clear differences women's and men's preferences. For instance, readership surveys find that men are more likely to read newspapers and women are more likely to read magazines. On television, women tend to prefer drama (including serials and soap operas), talk shows, and some comedy programs; men prefer sports, action-oriented programs, and informative programs. Studies in Finland, France, Portugal, Spain, and the United Kingdom have confirmed these preferences, which are linked not only to gender but also to social class, education, employment, ethnicity, and sexuality.

Gender is also a factor in audience members' identification with characters in the media. Research in the Netherlands found (unsurprisingly) that both women and men tend to identify with competent, attractive characters; but such characters are likely to be male, so women have less opportunity to identify with figures of their own gender. This partly explains why media such as soap opera and women's magazines, in which strong female characters are common, are important in women's daily lives.

The findings of research on women's perceptions of media content have been inconsistent. Some studies suggest that women make quite sophisticated interpretations of media texts, and research from Finland, Germany, Italy, Spain, and the United Kingdom has found that they are particularly dissatisfied with exploitative and simplistic media images. Other British research, however, suggests that women, and audiences in general, are relatively uncritical of gender images in the media. In fact, the behavior of audiences is extremely complex. For example, one study in the United Kingdom found that while women may be critical of media content, they may continue to watch, listen to, or read—and enjoy—it.

Research in Germany, the Netherlands, the United Kingdom, and elsewhere finds that women do favor strong, attractive female characters and believe there should be more female journalists and experts. Certain male-oriented genres do not appeal to women: for example, one French study found that the female television audience declined sharply for "erotic" programs, and a British study found that women were unhappy with televised portrayals of violence against women. However, there has been little research on women's response to genres aimed primarily at men.

Much feminist media research in Europe has focused on women's response to female-oriented genres—soap operas, talk shows, and magazines. This approach, though important, is limited: it rarely considers broader economic and political factors affecting these genres and the pleasure they afford; and it tends to assume that white, middle-class heterosexual women represent all women in the audience, although a few studies have investigated the preferences and practices of, for example, lesbians and black women.

The Production of Media Images

Despite its importance, the relationship between producer and content remains the most underresearched aspect of gender and media in Europe. Most studies focus on the numbers and status of women working at newspapers or in broadcasting. Since the 1980s there has been a large increase in women journalists, program presenters, and producers. Studies of Europe as a whole have found that women account for about 27 percent of reporters, subeditors, and editors in the print press, and about 37 percent of producers and directors in radio and television. Little is known about women's employment in advertising, although in 1990 a British study found that women held only 20 percent of creative positions. This study concluded that women's influence on the content of advertisements was limited by a masculine advertising culture, an ethos of aggressiveness and competition, and male chauvinism on the part of agencies' managers and clients.

In Finland, France, the Netherlands, and the United Kingdom, qualitative analyses have highlighted professional, institutional, and commercial pressures that make it difficult for female journalists and producers to challenge established practices and priorities. Other research has linked male norms and values in the media with specifc "gendered" content. For example, in the United Kingdom one study found that female journalists reporting sexual abuse of children encountered opposition from male colleagues and editors, who were reluctant to acknowledge the prevalence of this mainly male crime and were unwilling to publish the stories (this study is included in Carter et al, 1998).

Of course, professional norms and values change over time. For instance, Liesbet van Zoonen (1994) in the Netherlands noted that a shift in the style of news in the 1980s from serious to more lighthearted had coincided with an increase in the number of women news readers (announcers), who were valued not just for their professional expertise but also for their femininity. Studies in Germany and France indicate that changes in contemporary journalism, especially the trend toward "infotainment," may be giving women new ways to influence content.

Early feminist critiques assumed that there would be a direct correlation between women working in the media and the content or images produced. In retrospect, this assumption was oversimplified, but it is clear that there are multiple views or interpretations of reality, and that the predominance of certain voices and viewpoints affects the nature and range of media content. In Europe, various interventions have been undertaken to challenge dominant patterns and diversify media representations of women.

One approach has been to form independent feminist media; little research exists on this subject, but such feminist media face at least two problems. One issue is how to combine engaged political communication with survival in the market; the other is the vexed question of "marginality." For instance, the Danish researcher Birgitte Jallov (1992) analyzed feminist radio in seven European countries and concluded that it was uncertain whether these enterprises "at the margins of the media" had made women more visible, or whether real changes could be achieved only from within the established media.

A second approach has been to negotiate new representations of gender in the mainstream media, but the extent to which this approach can succeed remains relatively unexplored. Specific examples of introducing new versions of female experiences into media content can be found in television drama, comedy, and documentaries in several European countries. Overall, however, these have been exceptional cases and cannot necessarily be interpreted as heralding any radical transformation of media practices or representations. Rigorous multidimensional research would be needed to explore how new women's perspectives find their way into media production processes, how they become modified, and how they affect established practices.

A third approach argues that both women and men working in the media inherit a set of professional routines that embody traditional assumptions about gender, and that these routines must be unlearned if images of gender are to change. This approach—in which trainers and media practitioners work together—is based on findings in the Netherlands that gender patterns are reproduced through professional choices such as interview subjects and techniques, casting, dialogue, commentary, locations, camera angles, and editing. The emphasis is on professional discussion, aimed at demonstrating how attention to gender portrayals can improve media content. One project was launched in 1991 by the Dutch broadcasting company NOS; in 1997 it was extended to include broadcasters in Denmark, Finland, Germany, Norway, and Sweden. This is a pragmatic but radical attempt to change relatively static representations of gender in European media.

See Also

ADVERTISING; ADVERTISING INDUSTRY; CULTURE: WOMEN AS CONSUMERS *and* WOMEN AS PRODUCERS; MEDIA: OVERVIEW; REPRESENTATION; TELEVISION

References and Further Reading

Carter, Cynthia, Gill Branston, and Stuart Allen, eds. 1998. *News, gender, and power.* London, Routledge.

Eie, Birgit. 1998. *Who speaks in television? An international comparative study on female participation in television programmes.* Oslo: Norwegian Broadcasting Corporation.

Gallagher, Margaret. 1994. Velvet revolutions, social upheaval, and European women in media. In Margaret Gallagher and Lilia Quindoza-Santiago, eds., *Women empowering communication: A resource book on women and the globalisation of media,* 94–125. London: WACC/Isis International/IWTC.

Jallov, Birgitte. 1992. Women on the air: Community radio as a tool for feminist messages. In Nick Jankowski, Ole Prehn, and James Stappers, eds., *The people's voice: Local radio and television in Europe,* 215–224. London: John Libby.

Kivikuru, Ullamaija, et al. 1998. *Images of women in the media: Report on existing research in the European Union.* Brussels: European Commission.

McRobbie, Angela. 1994. *Postmodernism and popular culture.* London: Routledge.

Zoonen, Liesbet van. 1994. *Feminist media studies.* London: Sage.

Margaret Gallagher

IMAGES OF WOMEN: Middle East

Contemporary representations of Middle Eastern, Muslim, Arab, or "Oriental" woman are still influenced by eighteenth- and nineteenth-century western literature, travelogues, and commercial visual sources. The image of the Middle Eastern woman, an amalgamation of often contradictory concepts, is often taken to represent a vast area vaguely referred to as "the Orient," stretching from Iran in the east to Morocco in the west, and including Turkey and the entire Arab world. To some westerners, the "Oriental" woman represents the region's "essential characteristics"—oppression, backwardness, superstition, licentiousness, barbarism, and other "foreign" (that is, non-European) attributes. The image of women in the Middle East, like Middle Eastern culture, politics, and economics, is sometimes thought to be explainable in terms of an undifferentiated Islam. The Middle Eastern woman—whether Sunni, Shi'ite, Christian, Jewish, Armenian, Druze, or Baha'i—is imagined as always veiled, recalling the pseudo-religious taboo in Islam against depicting animate forms.

Historical Images

The emergence of photography, along with European imperialism, academic interest in the Middle East (Orientalism), and tension between the Orientalist image of women and changing attitudes toward women in Europe, led to changes in how Middle Eastern women were seen by others and how Europeans saw themselves in relation to the Orient.

One significant influence was the harem as a metaphorical motif in nineteenth-century painting, engraving, photography, and Orientalist literature. This motif suggested psychological, symbolic, and cultural aspects of the Oriental universe. The harem, in which all Oriental women were imagined as dwelling, became a site for imagined frivolous sexual behavior and was linked to images of Arab women in particular.

Malek Alloula (1986) observes of colonial Algeria from about 1910 to 1930 that "history knows of no other society in which women have been photographed on such a large scale to be delivered to public view." But these views of a predominantly secluded life were mostly staged. In studio photography designed for a western audience, and detached from any temporal or spatial reality, Arab women were reduced to an isolated, half-clothed existence of idleness—drinking coffee, smoking the hookah, and dancing. These women's outings from their protected but licentious quarters were, by contrast, depicted as social, collective visits to, for example, cemeteries and aged sorcerers. Such portrayals emphasized the uniformity of Oriental women behind the veil, their backwardness, and their superstition.

Accounts of actual harem life by such women as Huda Shawrawi in Egypt, Halide Edip in Turkey, and Taj al-Saltanih in Iran suggest that life in the harem was more dynamic and less secluded. In their memoirs, these upper-class women describe power structures, relationships, and an uninterrupted engagement with politics, literature, and the world outside the harem. They emphasize that women in harems were not entirely helpless of passive; rather, the limits of a woman's power depended on her age and her status in the household.

Photography during the early and middle twentieth century was inspired by a romantic longing to capture a vision of the pristine Middle East before it disappeared under the spread of modernization. By the beginning of the century, significant changes in clothing, materials, equipment, ownership of property, and commercialization were already affecting rural and urban life in the Middle East, yet western photography continued to reinforce the idea of an unchanging existence, and it did so through images of the Oriental woman. This was, however, a different woman from the one behind the harem wall. Anthropological photographers, for example, sought out women engaged in traditional (though rapidly disappearing) practices and thus perpetuated stereotypical and timeless images. As Julie Peteet (1993) notes, such practices raise questions about the representation of women as symbols of progress or as upholders of traditional values in the face of external powers. Drawing on the example of Palestine, Peteet suggests that representing an "authentic" culture may be a burden or may expand the concept of authenticity.

The widespread influence of such stereotypical images in western cultures is exemplified by the criteria of one early twentieth-century newspaper. The traveler and writer Grace Ellison reported that she sent a photograph of a woman's drawing room in a Turkish harem to a British newspaper just before World War I. The photograph showed striking similarities between the harem and typical English drawing rooms of the same period. The newspaper rejected it, however, claiming that "the British public would not accept this as a picture of a Turkish harem."

North Africa, Lebanon, Turkey, Palestine, Iran, and Egypt were documented visually in the early years of photography, but there were relatively few photographs of the Arabian peninsula before the 1940s. The Dutch Orientalist Snouk Hurgronje photographed Mecca and Medina in the 1880s; T. E. Lawrence (known as Lawrence of Arabia) and his associates photographed the Hijaz from 1914 to 1917; and Gertrude Bell took photographs of northern Arabia during a visit in 1913 and 1914. (Bell spent much of her adult life in the Middle East, but she took very few photographs of women; her interest was mainly in politics and public life.) The English author and photographer Freya Stark, who traveled in the Middle East from the 1920s to the 1950s, left an extensive record, in her writings and photographs, of her contacts with women. Stark's photographs of Yemen, Iraq, and Kuwait in the 1930s gave Middle Eastern women visibility, and an individuality that many other photographers failed to represent.

It should be noted that while many less well-off and rural women were photographed during this period, westerners in the nineteenth and early twentieth century took virtually no photographs of upper-class or middle-class women. Upper-class women lived mostly in seclusion, an arrangement that was and sometimes still is thought to ensure the honor of their fathers, husbands, and brothers. According to Mona al Munajjed (1997), this is especially true of Saudi culture.

Only a handful of Middle Eastern women worked as photographers before the middle of the twentieth century, and they usually were part of a family enterprise. Sarah Graham-Brown (1998) reports that a "Miss Karimeh Aboud" is named as the photographer of a postcard view of Nazareth dating from before World War I, and a portrait of a female professional photographer, Sadiye Yalmiz, from the late 1930s, exists in Ankara.

Contemporary Images

Images of Middle Eastern women in contemporary western films perpetuate many of the stereotypes of nineteenth-century and early twentieth-century photography, but those are combined, sometimes incongruously, with modern details. In the popular Disney version of the Persian tale *Aladdin,* for instance, Oriental women wear transparent face veils and bikinis; they live behind harem walls and yet are in public view. Such scenes and roles for women are often replicated in the national cinema of Middle Eastern countries.

Responses to these depictions of Middle Eastern women in recent times have differed. Iran, for example insisted on a transformation in the portrayal of women after the 1979 revolution: actresses were discouraged from making direct contact with the camera and had to appear in full Islamic garb (the *hijab*) in every scene, regardless of their role or the setting of the action.

By contrast, Shirin Neshat (1997) an Iranian photographer based in New York, used her work to make a programmatic visual attack on the system of veiling, an attack aimed at both indigenous and western portrayals of Middle Eastern women. As Hamid Debashi notes in the introduction to Neshat's collected photographs, "Enduring assumptions of what constitutes an 'Islamic woman' are at once domestic to that culture and colonially crafted on it. With a singular strike of creative genius, Shirin Neshat manages to target both of these divergent yet colliding agents." Guns hide behind dark veils and tattooed words reveal the silence of the unexposed bodies of Islamic women.

Alternative feminist filmmakers in the Middle East have also attempted radical depictions of all-female spaces. Farida Ben Lyazid's feature *Bab Ilsma Maftouh* ("A Door to the Sky," Morocco, 1989), for example, offers a positive interpretation of the harem, counterposing Islamic feminism to both Orientalist fantasy and Islamic fundamentalism. Documentaries such as Atteyat El-Abnoudi's *Ahlam Mumkina* ("Permissible Dreams," Egypt, 1983) examine female agency within Egyptian society and consider individual women's struggles with patriarchy. The director Heiny Srour's *Leila Wal Zi'ab* (Lebanon, 1984) exposes the hidden role of Arab women in the modern history of Palestine and Lebanon.

Although some female filmmakers—such as Joceline Saab (*Ghazi El Banat,* Lebanon, 1985), Maroun Baghdadi (*Houroub Saghira,* Lebanon, 1982), May Masri (*Tahta Al Ankad,* Palestine, 1982), the Israeli Michal Bat Adam (*Moments/Each Other,* United States, 1979), Pouran Derakhshandeh (*Parendeh Kouchake Khoshbakhty,* Iran, 1988), Rakhshan Bani Ehtemad (*Kharej az Mahdoudeh,* Iran, 1987), Assia Djebar (*Al Zerda,* Algeria, 1980), and Farida Bourquia (*Al Jamra,* Morocco, 1984)—have continued to work in their respective countries, most portrayals of the women of this region in both national and international cinemas perpetuate images of licentiousness, helplessness, ignorance, and victimhood.

Bemoaning the continual presence of the fictionalizing western gaze in postindependence images of Arab women, the Algerian filmmaker and writer Assia Djebar writes in *Les Femmes d'Algiers dans leur Appartement.* "For several decades now, as one nationalism after another is successful, one realizes that inside that orient delivered onto itself, the image of woman is no differently perceived: by the father, the husband and, in a way more troubling still, by the brother and the son" (quoted in Alloula, 1986: xxii). It is largely through the hegemonic power of western cultural discourses, disseminated through photography, film, television, and the media, that stereotypes of "Oriental woman" continue to shape the image of women in the Middle East.

See Also

FAMILY: RELIGIOUS AND LEGAL SYSTEMS—ISLAMIC TRADITIONS; GAZE; IMAGES OF WOMEN: OVERVIEW; PHOTOGRAPHY; VEILING

References and Further Reading

Addison, Erin. 1995. Saving other women from other men: Disney's *Aladdin. Camera Obscura* 13 (January/May): 5–25.

Alloula, Malek. 1986. *The colonial harem.* Trans. Myrna Godzich and Wlad Godzich. Introduction by Barbara Harlow. Minneapolis: University of Minnesota Press.

Gendron, Charisse. 1991. Images of Middle-Eastern women in Victorian travel books. *Victorian Newsletter* 79: 18–23.

Graham-Brown, Sarah. 1988. *Images of women: The portrayal of women in photography of the Middle East 1860–1950.* New York: Columbia University Press.

Matar, Nabil. 1996. The representation of Muslim women in Renaissance England. *The Muslim World* 86(1): 50–61.

Mehdid, Malika. 1993. A Western invention of Arab womanhood: The "Oriental Female." In Haleh Afshar, ed., *Women in the Middle East: Perceptions, realities and struggles for liberation,* 18–58. New York: St. Martin's.

al-Munajjed, Mona. 1997. *Women in Saudi Arabia today.* New York: St. Martin's.

Naficy, Hamid. 1994. Veiled vision/powerful presences: Women in post-revolutionary Iranian cinema. In Mahnaz Afkhami and Erika Friedl, eds., *In the eye of the storm: Women in post-revolutionary Iran,* 131–50. Syracuse, N.Y.: Syracuse University Press.

Neshat, Shirin. 1997. *Women of Allah.* Foreword by Hamid Dabashi. Torino, Italy: Marco Noire Editore.

Peteet, Julie M. 1993. Authenticity and gender: The presentation of culture. In Judith Tucker, ed., *Arab women: Old boundaries, new frontiers.* Bloomington: Indiana University Press.

Said, Edward. 1981. *Covering Islam: How the media and the experts determine how we see the rest of the world.* New York: Pantheon.

Shohat, Ella, and Robert Stam. 1994. *Unthinking Eurocentrism: Multiculturalism and the media.* London: Routledge.

Sreberny-Mohammadi, Annabelle, and Ali Mohammadi. 1994. *Small media, big revolution: Communication, culture and the Iranian revolution.* Minneapolis: University of Minnesota Press.

Negar Mottahedeh

IMAGES OF WOMEN: North America

Portrayals of women in the North American popular media have historically been dominated by stereotypes that cast women in traditionally feminine, limited social roles and situations. Generally, the mainstream media depict women as sex objects, victims, wives, girlfriends, mothers, or servants in sexual, violent, or household settings.

Before the 1980s, there were virtually no diverse representations of women in the popular media. This history of "condemnation and trivialization" was described by Gaye Tuchman as the "symbolic annihilation of women by the mass media" (1978: 8). Within the mainstream media's narrow portrayal of women, women of color and marginalized groups have been particularly excluded and degraded (Jewell, 1993; Lont, 1995).

This article focuses solely on images of women in the "dominant" or "mainstream" media—defined here as national television network programs, wide-distribution films, and mass circulation newspapers, magazines, and advertisements—because these are most widely consumed and most influential. In smaller-scale "alternative" media, such as female-directed publishers and music and video production companies (for example, Pleiades Records and Women Make Movies in the United States, and the National Film Board of Canada's Studio D project), the diversity of women's experiences is more frequently portrayed.

News Media

In the print news media, coverage aimed at women dates back to the late nineteenth century, when newspapers created "women's pages" in an effort to attract female readers. Stories featured in the women's pages reinforced traditional sex roles by promoting homemaking and child rearing as the only socially acceptable behaviors for females, and generally ignoring women's roles in the workplace (Tuchman, 1978). With the exception of limited front-page coverage of women's suffrage movements and women's work during World War II, news about women was confined to the lower-status women's pages for much of the twentieth century (Lont, 1995).

Women's movements in the United States in the late 1960s and early 1970s attracted the attention of the print media, and women became front-page newsmakers. But even as news about women moved from women's pages to the "hard news" pages, coverage remained narrow and stereotypes persisted. Surveying front-page stories in 20 major- and minor-market newspapers, the Women, Men, and Media Project (WMM) found that references to women increased in the late 1980s and early 1990s (from 11 percent in 1989 to 25 percent in 1994) before declining in the mid-1990s (19 percent in 1995). The WMM found that women were rarely quoted in front-page news items and were often identified by personal attributes rather than occupation (Bridge, 1995). Media Watch, a feminist organization working against sexism in media, reported similar trends in the coverage of women in Canadian newspapers. Examining stories from 18 newspapers, Media Watch found that women were the subject of only 20 percent of front-page stories from 1990–1998 (Montonen, 1998). Working women received media coverage in the 1990s, but the stories were frequently negative, highlighting the personal and social misery that presumably resulted from paid employment (Faludi, 1991). Moreover, the particular implications for women of such social issues as welfare or health care reform were often obscured in news coverage that ignored female perspectives.

Discussions of welfare in the mass media in the 1980s and 1990s were often punctuated by attacks on women of color, especially single mothers. K. Sue Jewell (1993: 21) argued that the news media in the United States had produced a "negative and distorted" image of African-American women and children by consistently portraying them as welfare recipients mired in poverty who typically used illegal drugs and were contributing to the decline of the two-parent family. For their part, women of color, including Latina American, Asian-Pacific American, and Native American women, have historically received scant attention in the news media. The presence of lesbian and bisexual women in the news has been confined largely to stock butch/femme images pulled from "gay pride" marches and other public events.

Broadcast news coverage of women in North America has been characterized by the same general patterns of exclusion and degradation evident in the print media. For much of the twentieth century, women were rarely presented in expert or decision-making roles, and women's issues received little attention. By the late 1990s, women journalists had achieved unprecedented visibility on U.S. and Canadian news broadcasts, but male reporters continued to outnumber female reporters by a two-to-one margin (Graydon, 1997; Women in Film and Television, 1998; "Women Have Not," 1999).

Entertainment Media

Images of women in the dominant North American entertainment media have shown wide diversity over time. In the 1950s and 1960s in the United States, portrayals of women on television were limited almost entirely to the devoted wives and mothers found in family comedies like *The Adventures of Ozzie and Harriet.* The 1970s introduced more programs with women as central characters, including *The Mary Tyler Moore Show,* which featured a single working woman; but these images were countered with depictions of women as sex objects in such hits of the late 1970s as *Charlie's Angels.* With a few notable exceptions, such as *Cagney and Lacey* and *Roseanne,* programming in the 1980s and 1990s often portrayed "superwomen" who effortlessly balanced successful professional careers with the demands of marriage and family (Lont, 1995).

Portrayals of women on Canadian television have generally mirrored those of U.S. programming, despite the Canadian government's initiatives to improve gender representation. Dramatic series such as *Traders* have depicted women in professional roles, but Canadian feminists argue that more progress is needed (Graydon, 1997; Women in Film and Television, 1998).

Researchers have identified several patterns in depictions of women in U.S. and Canadian television programming and advertising. First, with the exception of daytime programming, fewer female than male characters appear in television programs, and women have fewer speaking roles, particularly in commercials. Women on television are usually younger, more physically attractive, and more nurturing than their male counterparts, and they are more likely to be portrayed as married or as victims of crime. Before the 1980s, employed women on television were generally shown in such traditionally female occupations as nursing, clerical work, and waitressing (Graydon, 1997; Lont, 1995).

African-American women became increasingly visible in U.S. television programming after the 1970s, but they were often limited to stereotypical roles in situation comedies. Black women were initially most often portrayed as desexualized "mammy" figures, strong matriarchs, or highly sexualized "bad girls" (Jewell, 1993). By the year 2000, however, dramatic series such as *City of Angels* were featuring African-American women in professional, authoritative roles.

Few women of color aside from African-American women, and few lesbian or bisexual women have appeared in leading roles in U.S. or Canadian television series (Graydon, 1997; Lont, 1995). However, there have been some high-profile exceptions. A Korean-American, Margaret Cho, starred in the short-lived situation comedy *All-American Girl* in 1994, and lesbian and bisexual characters have gained increased visibility in many series. *Roseanne* featured the first bisexual female character in 1993 and what was perhaps the first televised same-sex kiss in 1994. These forerunners helped pave the way for Ellen DeGeneres to become the first openly lesbian lead, on *Ellen* in 1997.

Like television portrayals, cinematic representations of women have varied over time, ranging from the assertive persona of Marlene Dietrich in the 1930s to the sex-symbol image of Marilyn Monroe in the 1950s to the merciless serial killers portrayed by Juliette Lewis in the 1990s. Male heroes displaced central female characters in the 1950s and 1960s as rebel and action genres gained prominence. The influence of women's movements led to more diverse roles for women in the 1970s, with such films as *Julia* (1977), but the 1980s ushered in "superwomen" and a return to traditional romantic plots. Notable deviations in the cinema of the late 1980s and early 1990s were a string of "female buddy films," including the controversial *Thelma and Louise* (1991).

Hollywood films have historically promoted a range of stereotypical and often degrading images of women of color. In film as in television, African-American women have most frequently been portrayed in roles as servants or entertainers and are often ridiculed or shown as promiscuous (Jewell, 1993). Images of Asian-Pacific American women in mainstream films have been conflicting, ranging from docile yet threatening to untrustworthy, exotic, sexually adept, and ready to serve (Goldstein, in Lont, 1995). Latina American women have been typecast as gang members' girlfriends (in *West Side Story,* 1961, for example) and as brash antagonists (such as Rosie Perez in *White Men Can't Jump,* 1992). In many high-budget films, such as *Basic Instinct* (1992), lesbian or bisexual characters have been portrayed as evil and perverse. However, sympathetic, well-rounded portrayals of lesbians have been presented in low-budget films created by lesbian filmmakers, such as *Go Fish.*

Advertising

Images of women in advertising and their effects on women's lives have stirred vehement debates among feminists. Feminist critics have charged that advertising images promoting youthful, slender beauty as an ideal contribute to low self-esteem, eating disorders, and unnecessary cosmetic surgeries among women (Graydon, 1997; Wolf, 1992). This argument has itself been criticized for assuming that women are helpless victims of an omnipotent and seemingly static advertising industry; but the concept of advertising as a powerful source of cultural imagery has been supported by feminist empirical research.

Feminist analyses of advertising in the United States and Canada have maintained that women were historically portrayed in advertisements as young and subservient, noteworthy mainly for their relationships with men (Graydon, 1997; Simonton, in Lont, 1995). Researchers have also contended that commercial images often reduce women to a collection of fragmented body parts devoid of feeling or expression—an argument that is also made by feminist with regard to pornography. Ann J. Simonton (in Lont, 1995) asserted that the use in advertisements of values, images, and plotlines once associated with hard-core pornography has made pornography more socially acceptable despite its objectification of women and its images of violence against them. This "mainstreaming" of pornography has been furthered by the glut of pornographic images available on the Internet—a trend that concerns many feminists (Graydon, 1997).

By the late 1990s, images of women in advertising were dominated by two types: the tanned, voluptuous "pinup" look and the pale, gaunt "waif" look. Influenced by pornography, the pinup look was most common in advertisements aimed at male consumers, for products such as alcohol. The waif look, on the other hand, was promoted in fashion advertising and was characterized by models whose appearance conjured up images of heroin abuse. The issue of "heroin chic" gained national attention in the United States in 1997, when President Bill Clinton charged the fashion industry with glamorizing addiction (Wren, 1997). The waif look had declined in popularity by about 1998, but the pinup look remained a prevalent advertising image.

In advertising, women of color and women of marginalized groups have been consistently underrepresented and frequently degraded (Graydon, 1997). In a thirty-year analysis of 4,385 advertisements published in the Canadian newsmagazine *Maclean's,* Robert MacGregor (1989) found that people of color has appeared in only 1.2 percent of ads in 1954, a figure that had increased only to 11.5 percent in 1984. Women of color have been devalued by advertising portrayals that cast them as "animals, savage beasts, or sexual servants" (Simonton, in Lont, 1995: 151).

Dominant media images of women often serve to reflect and reinforce women's subordinate social status. Although portrayals of women in the mainstream media remain generally negative, there has been slow but steady progress toward more positive images. As women assume greater positions of power in creating media messages, this trend will be likely to continue.

See Also

ADVERTISING; ADVERTISING INDUSTRY; FILM; MEDIA: MAINSTREAM; MEDIA: OVERVIEW; POPULAR CULTURE; TELEVISION

References and Further Reading

Bridge, M. Junior. 1995. *Slipping from the scene.* Arlington, Va.: Unabridged Communications.

Faludi, Susan. 1991. *Backlash.* New York: Crown.

Graydon, Shari. 1997. *Round table on the portrayal of young women in the media.* Ottawa: Status on Women Canada.
Jewell, K. Sue. 1993. *From mammy to Miss America and beyond.* London: Routledge.
Lont, Cynthia, ed. 1995. *Women and media.* Belmont, Calif.: Wadsworth. See the articles by Ann J. Simonton and Lynda Goldstein.
MacGregor, Robert M. 1989. The distorted mirror. *Atlantis.*
Montonen, S. 1998. But...is it news? *Media Pipe.*
Tuchman, Gaye. 1978. *Hearth and home.* New York: Oxford University Press.
Wolf, Naomi. 1992. *The beauty myth.* New York: Morrow.
Women have not "taken over the news." 1999. *FAIR.*
Women in Film and Television/WIFT. 1998. *CRTC programming policy review submission PN1998-44,* Toronto: WIFT.
Wren, Christopher. 1997, May 22. Clinton calls fashion ads' "heroin chic" deplorable. *New York Times.*

Lisa M. Sanmiguel

IMMIGRATION

The participation of women in population movements throughout the world has been comparable to that of men, in some cases even surpassing it, as in the immigration flows from Central and South America, the Caribbean, and Europe to the United States since World War II. Only relatively recently, however, have researchers begun to consider women immigrants in statistics and as actors in the process. Efforts have been made to assess women's numerical contribution to migration and resettlement, mainly their participation in the labor force of the host society and the consequences of their economic activities for their families and communities. Worldwide, there are some statistical similarities between men and women, but men's and women's experiences of immigration tend to be very different.

Gender Differences

Differences begin with the reasons for migrating. Among people who migrate for economic or other nonpolitical reasons, both men and women seek better-paying jobs and a higher standard of living; but more women than men tend to migrate as an accompanying spouse, to reunite with family members, or on behalf of their children. (For example, more women than men enter the United States for reasons categorized as "family reunification.") Political reasons can also be a source of difference: women's freedom, mobility, security, and well-being may be restricted by cultural practices in their country of origin, and this often makes them prime candidates for migration. Even when their circumstances in their countries of origin are the same, men and women often respond differently.

Refugees are an example of differing experiences of immigration. There are more than 20 million refugees in the world today, and the majority are women and children. Up to 90 percent of these refugees remain in developing countries, so the problems facing them are similar to those facing women in general in the developing world: poverty, high rates of fertility and child mortality, inadequate food and water, and relatively poor health. In addition, refugee women have problems related to persecution, rape, sexual abuse, and other traumatic events (Forbes Martin, 1991). Refugee women who resettle in developed countries may also experience the traumatic consequences of an abrupt flight and a harrowing journey, and often they have to deal with a disrupted lifestyle, culture shock, adaptation to a new economy and a different labor force, and possibly the psychological trauma of other family members. Thus, whereas men and women may confront the same situations, they experience such threats differently, with direct effects on their eventual adjustment in the host country.

The United Nations guidelines on gender have been used to expedite the emigration of women from areas of war and conflict, and some host countries have special policies for women immigrants and refugees—for instance, Australia accepts single women and women with children whose partners have been killed or are missing (Manderson et al., 1998). In general, however, women are negatively affected by immigration policies, particularly by laws covering family reunification, which restrict women's mobility and their prospects of legalization and sometimes result in the separation of mothers and children.

Education and Participation in the Labor Force

Immigrant women tend to have less education than their male counterparts, and this directly affects their position in the labor market. However, the image of the typical immigrant woman as poorly educated and unskilled is no longer the norm. Immigrant women's educational levels range from illiteracy to primary education to high school to college to postgraduate training as engineers, doctors, nurses, and scientists.

Several of the largest receiving countries now have a policy of recruiting skilled professionals, including women; for instance, since the 1970s the United States has actively recruited Filipina hospital nurses. In the United States, the skills and status of Asian professional women are more easily transferable than those of men, but this varies with the region of origin. Thus during the 1980s men who had immigrated to the United States from certain countries—including India, Japan, and Iran—were able to use their education to achieve a higher occupational status, proportionally more than even native-born whites; however, this was not true of their female counterparts (Waldinger and Gilbertson, 1994). Also, in some contexts immigrant women are less likely than either immigrant men or native-born women to be employed and promoted (Goyette and Xie, 1999). As a result, one can easily find women with college degrees—particularly undocmented women and those who find themselves in a legal limbo in the United States—working at unskilled jobs for years after immigration.

The participation of immigrant women in the labor force varies by region and immigrant group, but generally men find higher-status jobs than women. In industrialized countries, where women's participation in the labor force is high, immigrant women find jobs as domestics in middle- and upper-class households and are often employed by working couples who need child care. For instance, many Latin American women, even some who are educated and skilled, work as caregivers for the elderly and children and as house cleaners in cities such as Los Angeles, New York, Barcelona, and Rome. Immigrant women also find other unskilled and semiskilled occupations, such as factory work, especially apparel manufacturing and microelectronics. Better-educated immigrant women find work in the higher echelons of the service sector, often in the health professions. For instance, about two-thirds of the foreign nurses admitted to the United States from 1988 to 1990 were Asian (the largest supplier was the Philippines). Many Nigerian nurses work in Britain, Jamaicans in New York, and Filipinas on the west coast in the United States.

Immigrants' family-owned businesses usually rely on—and succeed because of— family labor (examples include Asian Indians in England and Koreans in the United States), and this practice often conceals immigrant women's real rates of participation in the labor force. In such businesses, the husband (often with other male relatives) usually is the owner and makes the most important decisions, financial and other. Women work long hours in these enterprises, but their labor is often not acknowledged: it tends to be seen as an extension of their domestic responsibilities.

Women are in a vulnerable position as workers, because of legal instability, lack of fluency in the host language, and sometimes cultural practices that reinforce gender inequalities; and they often suffer abuse, such as improper dismissal, sexual abuse and harassment, fraudulent payments, low wages, and dismal working conditions. Evidently, such problems are common among immigrant women who work; they occur in many different immigrant groups in the United States and Europe, as well as in several Middle Eastern and Asian countries. Examples (many more could be cited) include inhumane abuse by employers of Filipina and other east Asian housekeepers in the Middle East, of migrant workers in Malaysia, of Caribbean and Central American women in the United States, and of eastern European women in western Europe. In addition, many women in family businesses suffer at the hands of their own relatives, as when their husbands drink to relieve the pressures of work or earlier immigrants exploit the labor of newly arrived compatriots. Immigrant women, often together with men, have sometimes responded by unionizing and demanding better working conditions, as in the case of janitors in Los Angeles and hotel chambermaids in Minnesota.

Gender Relations and Household Division of Labor

A powerful effect of immigration is that it often leads to observable changes in gender relations; to a lesser extent, immigration may also change the household division of labor, although it is harder to asses what occurs inside the home. There is extensive evidence that women may benefit from immigration, but this does not necessarily imply a linear progression from gender inequality to parity as women settle in the new country. Often, a gain in one area, such as the household, is not observed in other areas, such as the workplace or the community. For instance, immigrant women in Israel are exposed to Israeli social institutions that lead to social mobility, but also to institutions that reinforce disadvantages, such as religious and ethnic networks in which women's status is unequal to men's.

Women's participation in the labor force of the host society and their increased earnings are believed to lead to gender equality in the home, but this effect is not consistent. Some studies have found that immigrant women do not always improve their status in the workplace, at home, or in the community (Morokvasic, 1984). Moreover, when immigrant women raise their status within the family as a result of their increased economic contribution, gender relations may become more egalitarian but also may become more unbalanced in favor of men because women do not want to threaten men's position by upsetting delicate domestic arrangements. Examples of this latter situation include Asian and Latin American women in the United States and north African and Turkish women in western Europe. Among professionals, the household division of labor often does seem to become more equitable because immigration has narrowed the gap between men's and women's earnings, and because women who must meet the demands of their profession have more leverage to persuade their husbands to share household chores. Thus paid work alone may or may not promote changes in gender relations. However, such changes can also be promoted by the social, economic, political, and cultural environment of the host society: information networks and exposure to novel gender relations can serve as a catalyst (Menjívar, 1999).

Often, the occupational status of both men and women declines with immigration, and when the husband's status is lowered, it can lead to marital conflicts and domestic abuse. Some immigrant women learn about new opportunities in education and employment and, in general, about less restrictive lifestyles; when this occurs, particularly when men do not welcome such ideas and when women start to question and resist traditional gender practices, conflict and even family disintegration are not uncommon. When immigrant women are victims of domestic abuse, they face additional structural and cultural constraints—including language barriers and an expectation that women should tolerate abuse—that prevent them from seeking help from mainstream legal and social services.

Immigrant Mothers

Many women emigrate alone and then establish a family in the host society; some emigrate with a family but go on to establish a new family; some arrive alone leaving a family in the country of origin. Immigration entails special challenges for women who are mothers. For instance, a woman's workload may be increased and her adaptation may be made more difficult if the host country does not provide adequate, affordable child care or if there are conflicting cultural expectations regarding the school system. Many immigants live in inner cities where crime rates are high and drugs are ubiquitous; these mothers are concerned about the neighborhoods in which their children must be raised and the schools they attend.

Sometimes an immigrant woman sends her children back to the home country to remove them from the dangers of the inner city. In such cases, relatives in the country of origin care for the children while the mother works in the more developed host country—the United States, say, or Canada or a western European nation—and sends money for school supplies and for the necessities of life. Materially, this improves the lot of the children (and of their relatives), but that improvement does not come without a price—many immigrant women suffer painful consequences of the separation. However, by managing families and households in their places of origin and in their new life, women actively contribute to strengthening and increasing the ties between sending countries and receiving countries.

The Public Domain

There are important public spaces that often give immigrant women a sense of increased status. These include religious institutions: for instance, some churches provide opportunities for women to be heard, acknowledged, and respected and thus to rethink their experiences, and this may counteract oppression in other areas of their lives. Community organizations frequently offer services that immigrant women are likely to seek, such as information about and assistance with education and health care. Public settings give women opportunities to meet other women in similar circumstances; to exchange valuable information about many aspects of their lives, including their rights; and to learn about novel practices that may lessen gender inequity in the home. Immigrant women's participation in such public settings has significant consequences for the well-being of their families and for community building in their immigrant group.

See Also

ETHNICITY; HOUSEHOLD WORKERS; MIGRATION; RACE; REFUGEES; WORK, *specific entries*

References and Further Reading

Forbes Martin, Susan. 1991. *Refugee women*. London: Zed.

Gabaccia, Donna, ed. 1992. *Seeking common ground: Multidisciplinary studies of immigrant women in the United States*. Westport, Conn.: Greenwood.

Goyette, Kimberly, and Yu Xie. 1999. The intersection of immigration and gender: Labor force outcomes of immigrant women scientists. *Social Science Quarterly* 80(2): 395–408.

Hondageneu-Sotelo, Pierrette. 1994. *Gendered transitions: Mexican experiences of immigration*. Berkeley: University of California Press.

———, ed. 1999. Gender and contemporary U.S. immigration (Special Issue). *American Behavioral Scientist* 42 (4).

———, and Ernestine Avila. 1997. I'm here, but I'm there: The meanings of Latina transnational motherhood. *Gender and Society* 11(5): 548–571.

Manderson, Lenore, Margaret Kelaber, Milica Markovic, and Kerrie McManus. 1998. A woman without a man is a woman at risk: Women at risk in Australian humanitarian programs. *Journal of Refugee Studies* 11(3): 267–283.

Menjívar, Cecilia. 2000. *Fragmented ties: Salvadoran immigrant networks in America.* Berkeley: University of California Press.

———. 1999. The intersection of work and gender: Central American immigrant women and employment in California. *American Behavioral Scientist* 42(4): 595–621.

Morokvasic, Mirjana. 1984. Birds of passage are also women. *International Migration Review* 18(4): 886–907.

Waldinger, Roger, and Greta Gilbertson. 1994. Immigrants' progress: Ethnic and gender differences among U.S. immigrants in the 1980s. *Sociological Perspectives* 37(3): 431–444.

Cecilia Menjívar

IMPERIALISM

The terms *imperialism, colonialism,* and *neocolonialism* are used in many senses. *Imperialism* can be used very generally to refer to the domination of one society by another. Marxists emphasize the crucial role played by economic exploitation in imperialism and its links to the capitalist system. *Colonialism* is used more narrowly to describe the formal political control of one society by another, such as in the British empire. Imperialism and colonialism are distinct but related phenomena, and the terms are often used interchangeably. The more contentious term *neocolonialism* has been used to describe continuing domination of third world countries, once formal colonialism has ended, through other mechanisms such as international institutions like the International Monetary Fund (IMF) and World Bank and multinational corporations. The importance of imperialism, colonialism, and neocolonialism in shaping both the first world and the third world—politically, economically, and culturally—is huge. However, there is disagreement as to the nature of that impact, particularly whether it has had an exploitative or modernizing effect on the third world.

The historical sweep under consideration is enormous, and the nature of imperialism and colonialism has changed over time. Having been colonized by Spain and Portugal from the late fifteenth century onward, most Latin American countries had gained their independence before much of Africa was colonized by European powers such as Britain, Portugal, France, Germany, and Belgium in the late nineteenth century. This article will concentrate on the role of European colonialism in the making of the modern world since the fifteenth century and will examine both the "old empires" of trade and mercantilism and the "new empires" associated with the provision of raw materials that were central to the development of industrial capitalism.

Women and Imperialism

For some time, two different views dominated the study of women, colonialism, and imperialism. The first was that colonialism brought modernization to colonized women and was therefore beneficial. The second saw colonized women as passive victims and colonialism as worsening women's subordination. Each of these views is too simplistic. The relationship between women and colonialism is complex and contradictory, and it is hard to generalize about such a broad historical and geographical subject. There is now greater stress on the need to see colonized people as agents in their own right. Different groups of women played a variety of roles both in resisting and in reproducing colonialism, and they affected it and were affected by it in different ways. In certain contexts, a few of the changes brought by colonialism did allow space for some women to resist and challenge both new and existing patterns of gender relations.

Imperial powers imposed alien economic, political, and religious systems on those they colonized, but the nature of the imperial experience varied according to the nature of both the colonial and the precolonial society and the particular interaction between them. Precolonial societies were not static but dynamic and developing. They ranged from peasant-based surplus-producing societies organized into sophisticated kingdoms and empires (for example, the Aztec kingdom in Mexico, the Inca kingdom in Peru, and empires in parts of west Africa) to less hierarchically organized subsistence societies (found, for example, in parts of east Africa and the Atlantic coast of Brazil).

The position of women varied within and between different precolonial societies and over time. For example, caste was important in Inca society, where elite women and poor women led very different lives. The status of women declined as the Aztec empire developed. Feminist scholars examining precolonial Africa have argued that while it was not characterized by equality, gender relations often were characterized by interdependence: men and women had different but complementary roles, and women gained some autonomy through control over economic resources such as agricultural land. This has been noted in Mona Etienne's study (1980) of the Baule in what is now the Ivory coast and the control of trading networks, for example in west Africa. In some societies, women had economic status through their role in production (for example, as farmers), and this gave them certain political rights, often expressed through their own political organizations. Judith Van Allen (1976) studied female "networks of solidarity" among the Igbo of southern Nigeria, which gave women recognized ways of controlling men's behavior ("sitting on a man"). Irene Silverblatt (1987) also found evidence of sexual parallelism, for example in religious organizations in the Inca kingdom.

Colonial rule brought huge changes that affected women and men in very different ways. Most imperial powers were faced with two contradictory tasks: facilitating the accumulation of capital so that their possessions would be at least minimally self-financing if not profitable, and at the same time maintaining social control. The changes in social and economic structures that were made to promote accumulation of capital sometimes worked to undermine strategies for minimizing social dislocation. In the face of these contradictory impulses, the legitimation of colonial rule became imperative. Nineteenth-century colonialism was justified through an ideology of racial superiority epitomized by the "civilizing mission." A colonial discourse emerged in which the "natives" were seen as other and inferior, and the "Orient" as exotic and irrational compared with the rational West. This construction allowed the colonial powers to regulate their subjects more effectively. Colonial discourse was also highly gendered; for example, images of the Orient were often female. As Lata Mani (1990) shows, the debate on suttee, or *sati* (the Hindu practice of burning widows), is one area where the British claimed to have civilizing mission to rescue Indian women from barbarism. Legal channels became a major mechanism of control of colonial peoples.

Most colonies were governed by a bureaucracy administered at the top by a few officials from the "mother country." Many colonial powers favored less expensive systems of indirect rule, governing through preexisting structures of power and authority at lower levels. Colonists in Spanish America used a system of indirect rule over peasants in the Andes; the British used such a system wherever it was practicable in parts of west Africa and India. Women, whether of the colonizing or the colonized race, were generally excluded from participating in colonial rule. In Africa, colonial officials often ignored women's indigenous networks and organizations; instead, they used indigenous male authorities and thereby reduced women's influence.

Despite indirect rule, the major division was between the colonized and the colonizer. Attempts were made to regulate the boundaries between white and nonwhite, often through controls over sexual morality. Many colonial powers initially forbade white women to live in colonies, and concubinage was therefore widespread. In Latin America, Spanish colonists sometimes married indigenous noblewomen to legitimate their claims to territory. White women arrived in the new empires in the late nineteenth century and, according to Ann Stoler (1989), became the bearers of a redefined colonial morality in which much sharper divisions were drawn between the colonized and the colonizers. The majority of white women were present as the wives of colonial officials, mine and plantation owners, and missionaries. They have often been seen as the most reactionary part of the colonial project, but recent feminist work has highlighted white women's resistance to imperial structures, as activists campaigning for reform; as well as their complicity, in their role as wives of colonial officials, traders, and missionaries and later as missionaries themselves (Chaudhuri and Strobel, 1992).

The Impact of Colonial Policies

Different groups of women were affected in different ways by the various policies used by colonial powers to facilitate the accumulation of capital in their possessions, a process that integrated colonies into an international economic system and contributed to the development of capitalism. The nature of production was often altered in terms of both the ownership of factors such as land and the nature of labor. Land was often taken away from the indigenous inhabitants—"alienated"—and most colonies became providers of primary products for export, such as minerals and cash crops (for example, sugar, palm oil, and bananas). In Latin America forced labor was used for mines and haciendas, and particularly in the eighteenth century millions of slaves were forcibly brought to much of the Americas from west Africa to work on plantations. In colonial Latin America, poor and Indian women worked outside the home while elite women were often confined to the domestic sphere. Slave women played particular roles in plantations in the Caribbean, often forming field gangs and domestic staffs while slave men became more skilled craftspeople. Women were often punished in sexualized ways and were raped and sexually abused by their owners and overseers (Bush, 1990).

In Africa, the development of export economies lowered the status of many women, because their access to economic resources was reduced at the same time as their workload increased. Women often lost their right to use land, while efforts to increase cash crops were channeled through men, giving these men access to cash incomes and (where Africans were allowed them) titles to land. As a result, the interdependence that had existed between some men and women broke down. The development of male migratory, labor systems—to supply, for example, the mines of southern Africa and wage workers in towns—meant increased burdens for women remaining in rural areas. The changes had contradictory results. While the position of many women worsened, others took the opportunity to resist patriarchal control—for example, to escape arranged marriages and make new lives for themselves. In the mid-colonial period of the 1920s and 1930s, some women did go to urban areas and mining areas, where, because of a lack of opportunities for paid work, they engaged in illegal or informal work such as brewing beer and prostitution.

In the face of social and economic changes brought by colonialism, new mechanisms of social control (for example, over mobility) were used by colonial authorities to maintain social order. In Africa by the 1920s and 1930s there was a widespread perception of crisis by both the colonial authorities, who saw a threat to social stability, and male elders, who saw a breakdown of patriarchal controls over women. For example, in the early colonial period (around the turn of the century) individual women used the opportunities briefly provided to bring lawsuits, and some courts were swamped with women seeking divorce. The crisis was therefore expressed as a threatened disintegration of traditional forms of marriage and a rising incidence of adultery and sexual indiscipline. Martin Channock (1982) isolates three sets of factors: first; the strain placed on marriages by the migratory labor system; second, the movement of women to urban areas, away from the disciplinary control of their families; and third, the increasing importance of property transactions in marriage (often in the form of bridewealth) in the new cash economies. The 1930s brought an attempt to reassert male control by an alliance between African male leaders and colonial officials, through increased controls over women's mobility and labor, often expressed in terms of regulations over marriage. These controls were often enforced through the institutions of customary law and the native courts and were justified as traditional. In fact, customary law was created by colonial officials and the indigenous male hierarchy to increase their control over women. But these policies were inherently contradictory, and the social and economic changes (which, for example, entailed tacit state approval for women's mobility in Rhodesia) undermined the attempts at social control.

Other attempts were made to construct particular roles for women, since colonizers brought gender ideologies that were reinforced by the activities of Christian churches; for example, the Catholic church brought its ideology of *marianismo* to Latin America. (*Marianismo*—derived from the Virgin Mary—refers to the ideal of womanhood as self-abnegating motherhood.) Education was often limited, whether provided by missionaries or, as later, supplemented by the colonial state, but it provided a domestic education for a small number of girls. State-sponsored women's organizations often concentrated on providing training to make both elite and poor women better wives.

Women's Collective Responses to Colonialism

Individual women were not passive in the face of the changes brought by colonialism, and some women also engaged in collective responses and resistance. In the Caribbean, for example, individual slave women resisted by not having children; and the Jamaican Maroons, one of the most famous examples of organized resistance, were led by a woman—Nanny, or Nana Yah, who was named "Jamaican national hero in 1975." It has been argued that women's activism was most dramatic in Africa, where status differentials between men and women were small enough that it was not unthinkable for women to challenge male authority and where women had an independent economic base.

Three main types of responses by women can be identified. The first type involved using "traditional" methods and organizations for collective activities. For instance, women developed a culture of resistance in the Puna of the high Andes of Peru (Silverblatt, 1987); and in Africa, although women initially withdrew from the state, women's voluntary associations continued to provide support. Some groups of women used whatever precolonial status they had had to protest against the encroachments of colonial rule. One example is the "women's war" of 1929 in southern Nigeria. A rumor circulated that women were about to be taxed, and thousands of Igbo women gathered outside the district offices to "sit on" warrant chiefs. The British misunderstood what was happening (they did not realize that the women were using recognized channels of expression) and so dismissed the action as the "Aba riots" (Van Allen, 1976).

The second type of response involved new women's organizations, which emerged as a result of the social, economic, and political changes brought by colonial rule. The Lagos Market Women's Association was formed in the 1920s in Nigeria; this was the first Lagos-wide mass-based market women's organization, and it received concessions from the colonial authorities over taxation and price controls (Johnson, 1986).

Nationalist movements were a third type of response. Different groups of women were actively involved in these anticolonial movements, campaigning for independence. Jayawardena (1986) has argued that movements fighting for women's emancipation in a number of Asian and African countries in the nineteenth and early twentieth centuries arose from the same conditions that spawned nationalist movements and had important links with those struggles. Early nationalist movements were predominantly elite movements, but they later broadened out to form mass movements, particularly in Africa and the Caribbean in the aftermath of the Second World War. Women participated in both elite and mass nationalist movements in a variety of ways. In India, women's role in the private sphere was elevated by nationalists as an area of resistance where the "new woman" could practice "enlightened motherhood." In the public sphere, women joined nationalist parties, such as the INC in India; and some parties—for example, in Zambia and British Guiana—recognizing the importance of women's support, encouraged the establishment of women's sections. However, few women were in leadership positions. Women also joined mass actions. In India, large numbers of women took part in the boycott of foreign goods and the violation of the salt laws. Where colonial powers, such as the Portuguese and the French, were determined to hang on, other movements—including the MPLA in Angola, Frelimo in Mozambique, and the NLF in Vietnam—became radicalized, waging guerilla warfare to achieve fundamental changes in society. The liberation of women was one of their aims, and a number of these fighters were women.

Neocolonialism

Most Spanish and Portuguese colonies in Latin America gained independence in the nineteenth century, but other colonies did not become independent until the second half of the twentieth century. Many political, social, and economic trends of the colonial period continued after independence. The economies of many former colonies now considered part of the third world have continued to provide primary products and cheap labor to the international economic system, while other newly industrializing countries (NICs) such as Hong Kong, Taiwan, and Singapore now export manufactured goods. The tendency for land ownership to be invested in men continued in many postindependence land reform programs, as did the channeling of agricultural assistance and development programs toward men. Women's labor in both the agricultural and the industrial sector has continued to be important—for example, in electronic and textile manufacturing. Despite their participation in nationalist movements, few women were rewarded with high office in the newly formed governments, and women's sections often became simply mechanisms for mobilizing women in support of the party. Particularly in Asia, many women who became political leaders (such as Benazir Bhutto in Pakistan, Corazon Aquino in the Philippines, and Chandrika Kumarakunga in Sri Lanka) were members of elite political families; often, they were survivors of an important male figure, who might have been martyred.

See Also

COLONIALISM AND POSTCOLONIALISM; NATION AND NATIONALISM

References and Further Reading

Bush, Barbara. 1990. *Slave women in Caribbean society 1650–1838.* London: James Currey.

Channock, Martin. 1982. Making customary law: Men, women and the courts in colonial northern Rhodesia. In Margaret Hay and Marcia Wright, eds., *African women and the law: Historical perspectives,* 53–67. Boston, Mass.: Boston University Papers on Africa.

Chaudhuri, Nupur, and Margaret Strobel, eds. 1992. *Western women and imperialism: Complicity and resistance.* Bloomington: Indiana University Press.

Etienne, Mona. 1980. Women and men: Cloth and colonization. In Mona Etienne and Eleanor Leacock, eds., *Women and colonization: Anthropological perspectives,* 214–238. New York: Praeger.

Jayawardena, Kumari. 1986. *Feminism and nationalism in the third world.* London: Zed.

Johnson, Cheryl. 1986. Class and gender: A consideration of Yoruba women during the colonial period. In Claire Robertson and Iris Berger, eds., *Women and class in Africa,* 237–254. New York: Holmes and Meier.

Lavrin, Asuncion, ed. 1978. *Latin American women: Historical perspectives.* Westport, Conn.: Greenwood.

Mani, Lata. 1990. Contentious traditions: The debate on sati in colonial India. In Kumkum Sangari and Sudesh Vaid, eds. *Recasting women: Essays in Indian colonial history,* 88–126. New Brunswick, N.J.: Rutgers University Press.

Midgely, Clare. 1998. *Gender and imperialism.* Manchester: Manchester University Press.

Silverblatt, Irene. 1987. *Moon, sun and witches: Gender ideologies and class in Inca and colonial Peru.* Princeton, N.J.: Princeton University Press.

Staudt, Kathleen. 1989. The state and gender in colonial Africa. In Sue Ellen Charlton, Jana Everett, and Kathleen Staudt, eds., *Women, state and development,* 66–85. Albany: State University of New York Press.

Stoler, Ann. 1989. Making empire respectable: The politics of race and sexual morality in 20th-century colonial cultures. *American Ethnologist* 16(4): 634–660.

Van Allen, Judith. 1976. "Aba riots" or Igbo "women's war"? Ideology stratification and the invisibility of women. In N. J. Hafkin and Edna Bay, eds., *Women in Africa: Studies in social and economic change,* 59–85. Stanford, Calif.: Stanford University Press.

Women's History Review. 1994. Special issue on 'Feminism,' Imperialism and Race: A dialogue between India and Britain 3(4).

Georgina Waylen

INCEST

Dictionaries define incest as sexual intercourse between persons so closely related that marriage between them is forbidden by law. However, common usage of the term encompasses a wider range of sexual contacts. Social interpretations may also include sexual contact among close relatives who are not forbidden by law to marry each other. Therefore, common concepts of incest are more amorphous than dictionary or legal definitions.

Anthropological research has found that incest is an ancient preoccupation. Artifacts from many cultures express a desire for intercourse with forbidden members of the clan, tribe, or family (Justice, 1979). However, history also reflects a nearly universal attempt to restrain incestuous acts, and sometimes even incestuous thoughts. The scope of kinship varies, but almost all known societies have had stringent taboos, prohibitions, and punishments regarding vertical incest (between parents and children) and horizontal incest (between siblings). Prohibitions range from folktales and myths evoking supernatural forces to tribal ostracism, condemnation, and even torture and death. A few societies have permitted and even celebrated incest; but these are exceptional, and even they tend to tolerate incest only among deities (as in ancient Greek myths) or royalty (as in ancient Egypt). Incest among commoners is almost never accepted or tolerated (Murdock, 1949; Parsons, 1954).

Nevertheless, incest has occurred throughout human history; even prohibitions by the world's major religions (such as Christianity, Islam, and Judaism), have not eradicated incestuous behavior. Incest is a highly secretive act, so its true incidence remains unknown; but it may be quite frequent, affecting perhaps one in ten families (Finkelhor, 1979). A relatively recent estimate for North America, England, and Germany was that one in three girls and one in six boys experience sexual molestation, mostly at the hands of close relatives such as fathers, stepfathers, uncles, brothers, and grandfathers (Guidry, 1995). To repeat, though, it is impossible to know the exact figure; incest is one of the most underreported crimes in the world.

Theories of Incest

Numerous theories seek to explain why societies curb incestuous behavior. Some theories emphasize that inbreeding increases risk of birth defects. However, this may not account for incest taboos among early peoples, who probably lacked even a rudimentary understanding of genetics (Leavitt, 1992). Other theories emphasize kinship: historically, the survival of kin transcends all other roles and relations, including those among family members. Thus societies regulates links that elicit carnal passions and jealousy among people whose survival depends on cooperation. Also, creating children with ambiguous kinship roles tends to be strongly discouraged. For example, the offspring of a father and daughter will be both a child and a grandchild of the father, and both a child and a sibling of the daughter. Such a child would complicate the roles of the actual wife, siblings, and grandparents and create disorder.

Perhaps the most imaginative theory about incest is the Oedipus complex (along with the Electra complex), propounded by Sigmund Freud (1938). Freud saw "man" as raw, animalistic, and basically immoral in nature. Starting from infancy, the transformation of this entity into a moral being required solutions to a series of dilemmas. One dilemma of utmost significance is the sexual desire of a pubescent boy for his mother. This desire is counterbalanced by the fear of punishment (specifically, castration) from his formidable father. Generally, this dilemma is resolved by the son's identification with the father. Through identification, fear is reduced, while the son indirectly possesses the object of his desire by symbolically becoming the father. Giving up incestuous pursuits also frees his energy to pursue an adult love object. The Electra complex is the female version of this situation: a girl desires her father, fears punishment from her mother, and eventually identifies with the mother. Freud (1951) argued that human culture began with the establishment of the incest taboo, without which a fusion of parents with children would stifle growth and accomplishment.

Feminsts see incest as a social ill arising from power imbalances. On this view, incest is men's abuse of power, since most victims are female children. Incest, then, is less a sexual transgression than a matter of subjugation, control, and domination. Feminists argue that although incest initiated by the mother is very rare, it has preoccupied eminent male theorists like Freud. In any case, the Oedipus complex seems a somewhat ironic concept, because in reality older brothers, fathers, and stepfathers are the most typical predators (Browne and Finkelhor, 1989). Unlike Freud, feminists unconditionally place the blame on the perpetrator, rather than on the acts or thoughts of children.

Effects of Incest

Incest harms the victims. Often, it may start as apparently accidental touching and fondling under the guise of "love," but it progresses to premeditated coercive acts (Finkelhor, 1979). These sexual acts can hurt, deform, and even kill victims who are very young. They can also lead to sexually transmitted diseases, and to unwanted births and unsafe abortions when the victims are adolescent girls or women.

The effects of incest also include psychological trauma. When there are vast differences in age, size, and power, the victims are often terrorized into cooperating. Shattered trust, role confusion, fear, disgust, shame, and guilt continue to victimize the survivors of incest long after their physical wounds have healed. Researchers have found a high incidence of substance abuse, compulsive behaviors, poor interpersonal relationships, sexual promiscuity, and even suicide among victims. These effects often span several generations (Russell, 1986; WAC, 1993).

Given these effects, societies have an obligation to curb incest—and the reasons for doing so must transcend arguments of "survival" and encompass the right of women and children to a safe environment. Feminists would add that the patriarchal structures of domination must be dismantled, and that myths shifting the blame away from male perpetrators must be deconstructed. More than anything else, the victims of incest deserve to be told that it was not their fault.

See Also

ABUSE; KINSHIP; PSYCHOANALYSIS; RAPE; TABOO

References and Further Reading

Browne, Angela, and David Finkelhor. 1989. *Child sexual abuse.* Ottawa: Family Violence Prevention.

Champagne, Rosaria. 1996. *The politics of survivorship: Incest, women's literature, and feminist theory.* New York: New York University Press.

DeMilly, Walter. 1999. *In my father's arms: A true story of incest.* Madison: University of Wisconsin Press.

Finkelhor, David. 1979. *Sexually victimized children.* New York: Free Press.

Freud, Sigmund. 1938. *A general introduction to psychoanalysis.* Garden City, N.Y.: Liveright.

———. 1951. *Totem and taboo.* New York: Norton.

Guidry, Harlan M. 1995. Childhood sexual abuse. *American Family Physician* 51: 407–444.

Justice, Blair, and Rita Justice. 1979. *The broken taboo.* New York: H. S. Press.

Leavitt, Gregory C. 1992. Sociobiological explanations of incest avoidance. *American Anthropologist* 94: 446–448.

Lewis, Tanya. 1999. *Living beside: Performing normal after incest memories return.* Toronto: McGillian.

Mullen, P. E., J. L. Martin, J. C. Anderson, S. E. Roman, and G. P. Herbison. 1996. The long impact of the physical, emotional, and sexual abuse of children: A community study. *Child Abuse and Neglect* 20: 7–21.

Murdock, G. P. 1949. *Social structure.* New York: Macmillan.

Parsons, Talcott. 1954. The incest taboo in reaction to social structure and the socialization of children. *British Journal of Sociology* 5(2): 101–117.

Russell, Diana E. M. 1986. The incest legacy. *Sciences* 26: 28–32.

———. 1998. The making of a whore. In R. K. Bergen, ed., *Issues in intimate violence,* 65–77. Thousand Oaks, Calif.: Sage.

Sheffield, C. J. 1995. Sexual terrorism. In J. Freeman, ed., *Women: A feminist perspective,* 5th ed.: 1–21, Mountain View, Calif.: Mayfield.

WAC. 1993. *The facts about women.* New York: New Press.

Aysan Sev'er

INDIGENOUS WOMEN'S RIGHTS

Indigenous women face unique challenges in asserting their rights. These challenges are a result of their compound identity as both indigenous peoples and women and thus are distinct from challenges faced by women generally, or by indigenous people generally.

Defining Indigenous Peoples

To understand the challenges indigenous women face, we must first define "indigenous peoples" and understand their particular experience. The term *indigenous,* meaning literally "originating in an area," refers to those people who were there "before." Before whom, or before what, is the key to determining which peoples are classified as indigenous. In Asia, for example, it is difficult to definitively identify the first peoples, because of a complex history of conquests and civilizations. In the Americas, it is easier to determine a historical moment (1492, for instance) when contact leading to settlement occurred, and to describe those who occupied the Americas before that time as indigenous.

Indigenous peoples (who number between 300 million and 500 million worldwide) are a vast and varied group sharing not only this relational nomenclature but a struggle for survival, autonomy, and recognition. They include, but are not limited to, the Ainu of Japan, the Adivasi of India, the Maya of Guatemala, the Saami of northern Europe, the Maori of New Zealand, the Aborigines and Torres Strait Islanders of Australia, the Navajo (and other Native Americans) of the United States, the Inuit of the circumpolar region, and the Ojibway (and other First Nations) of Canada. Most indigenous peoples have retained social, cultural, economic, and political characteristics clearly distinct from those of the other segments of the national populations.

Oppression of Indigenous Peoples

Indigenous women suffer as part of the worldwide oppression of indigenous peoples. Throughout history, whenever dominant peoples have expanded their territory, indigenous peoples have been threatened. Typically, the contact follows a similar pattern. The first stage is subjugation (as in the enslavement of Mayan peoples by invading conquistadors). This is sometimes complicated by attempts at elimination (as happened to the Beothuks of Canada) or displacement (as in the relocation of the American Cherokee). Subjugation, elimination, and displacement jeopardize the physical survival of indigenous peoples.

The next stage is assimilation, sometimes seen as "civilizing" indigenous peoples. In general, this stage focuses on teaching indigenous peoples to adopt the ways of the dominant society. Early efforts of colonists to turn Native Americans from hunters to farmers and from "heathens" to Christians are among the numerous assimilative practices designed to "civilize" indigenous people. Inherent in these attempts is an ethnocentric belief that the way of the dominant society is the best way. Assimilation threatens the cultural survival of indigenous peoples.

Worldwide, policies toward indigenous peoples still tend to combine subjugation, elimination or displacement, and assimilation. A final stage could be genuine respect for, and cooperation with, indigenous peoples, but this remains an elusive goal and has not yet been accepted as a concept worldwide, let alone achieved. The UN Draft Declaration on the Rights of Indigenous Peoples seeks to work toward the final stage; it recognizes that indigenous peoples have been deprived of their human rights and fundamental freedoms and dispossessed of their lands and resources, yet development continues to encroach upon traditionally indigenous lands. Land is a critical issue. Generally, indigenous people hold their relationship to the land to be sacred. The land itself is holy, and alienation from it undermines the foundations of their material and spiritual life. Indigenous peoples have neither self-government nor the land base to ensure political representation under the dominant society's government. As a result, they are denied the right to develop in a way that would let them meet their own needs and pursue their own interests.

Effects on Indigenous Women

Colonizers' values and policies favoring assimilation have been particularly detrimental to indigenous women. While indigenous peoples have both matriarchal and patriarchal social structures, and variations in between, it is generally recognized that these cultures tend to be less stratified and less hierarchical than nonindigenous communities. Indigenous leaders worldwide insist that, before contact, their societies were truly egalitarian and afforded women significant political and spiritual power. They argue that, for instance, it was the European settlers in the New World who considered women lesser beings, properly subject to the control of their fathers and husbands.

That attitude toward women does seem to have permeated colonial legislation. For example, until 1982 the status of an indigenous Canadian woman depended on whom she married. If she married a "nonstatus" man—that is, a man of European descent or a "nonstatus" Indian—she lost her own status as an Indian and any associated treaty rights. Children of such a marriage were also denied status rights. In *Lovelace* v. *Canada* (1982), Sandra Lovelace, a Maliseet Indian, fought the legislation to regain her Indian status after being divorced from her nonstatus husband. The Human Rights Committee of the International Court of Justice held that Canada had violated the International Covenant on Civil and Political Rights in applying this legislation. *Lovelace* remains a pivotal victory in the ongoing battle for indigenous women's rights.

It is widely held that patriarchy saturated the colonial enterprise worldwide, with devastating effects that have persisted in modern times. On this view, indigenous systems of government, which often gave women a political voice, were replaced by European systems of government, in which males were privileged and females were silenced. Early colonial legislation perpetuated Europeans' acceptance of violence against women as a method of resolving domestic disputes. Notably, the rates of violence against women within indigenous communities today are among the highest anywhere in North America. In developing countries, indigenous women remain responsible for most food production in the subsistence economies typical of indigenous communities, but globalization favors economies of scale and gives export food crops priority over domestic crops. This has led to an erosion of sustainable economic systems developed and nurtured by indigenous women. The resulting poverty has exacerbated gender inequalities.

Because indigenous women experience violations on so many levels, it is difficult to pinpoint the particular rights for which they struggle. However, the problems described above are indicative. Broadly, indigenous women seek rights to political recognition, self-determination, reinstatement of traditional land bases, environmental security, cultural security, and gender equality.

Barriers to Indigenous Women's Rights

Lack of representation is a significant barrier to indigenous women's rights. A few indigenous women activists, like Rigoberta Menchu Tum of Guatemala, who won the Nobel Peace Prize in 1992, have achieved international recognition, and these activists may bring greater public attention to the perils facing indigenous women. However, it is worth noting that the UN Draft Declaration on the Rights of Indigenous Peoples contains only one passing reference to indigenous women, Article 22, which states: "Particular attention shall be paid to the rights and special needs of indigenous elders, women, youth, children, and disabled persons."

Discrimination against indigenous women is not simply the sum of the burden of being indigenous plus the burden of being female. It is not a matter of addition but rather an intersection—a matter of being, simultaneously and at all times, both female and indigenous. Colonialism and patriarchy combine to deprive indigenous women of adequate representation, marginalizing them both locally and internationally, since they cannot be adequately represented by men—whether these men are indigenous or nonindigenous—or by nonindigenous women. Oppressed from both directions, indigenous women can find that their interests as women run counter to their interests as indigenous people; and this conflict can force them into silence for the sake of their people. For example, formal recognition of customary indigenous law would delineate rights and privileges according to cultural tradition and thus, to some degree, ensure cultural survival. Many argue, however, that, as it currently exists, customary indigenous law is merely the twisted wreckage of the colonial encounter, and reflects the patriarchal ideology of colonizers more than authentic indigenous practice. Indigenous women have difficulty making claims of oppression under customary law, because such claims are seen as arguments against cultural practices. "Intersectionality" can thus silence women even further, and become a significant barrier to achieving indigenous women's rights.

Even when indigenous women do speak, intersectionality can impede their rights. A controversy in Australia over the Hindmarsh Bridge (1994–1996) is a striking example. Aborigine Ngarrindjeri women called for a halt to construction of this bridge, which threatened sites they secretly held sacred. Ngarrindjeri men, many of whom favored construction, asserted that they had never heard these lands were sacred and therefore that the women's claim could not be legitimate. The women countered that the fact that the site's power had been kept secret demonstrated its sacredness—and, further, that the continued power of the site depended on the details' being kept from any and all men. Secret-society Ngarrindjeri women found that their interests were fracturing the community. The media and political attention focused on the dissension among the Ngarrindjeri, and on how the Australian government was handling the situation. The resulting cacophony significantly weakened the women's claim.

Conclusion

In the social and political hierarchy of settlers and indigenous peoples, racism, colonialism, and patriarchy combine to place indigenous women at the bottom of the pecking order. However, the fight for autonomy is gaining recognition. Global and regional conferences focusing on political autonomy, development of resources, and cultural security continue to bring activists together, providing opportunities to share strengths and strategies in the ongoing struggle for indigenous women's rights.

See Also

ANCIENT INDIGENOUS CULTURES; COLONIALISM AND POSTCOLONIALISM; ENVIRONMENT: SOUTH ASIAN CASE STUDY—FORESTS IN INDIA; IMPERIALISM

References and Further Reading

Crenshaw, Kimberle. 1991. Women of color at the center. Selections from the Third National Conference on Women of Color and the Law: Mapping the Margins: Intersectionality, Identity Politics, and Violence Against Women of Color. *Stanford Law Review* 43.

Dussias, Allison M. 1999. Squaw drudges, farm wives, and Dann Sisters' last stand: American Indian women's resistance to domestication and the denial of their property rights. *North Carolina Law Review* 77: 637–729.

Lovelace v. *Canada*. 1982. Communication No. R.6/24, 36 UN GAOR Supp. (No. 40).

Medicine, Beatrice. 1993. North American indigenous women and cultural domination. *American Indian Culture and Research Journal* 17(3): 121–130.

Mendelsohn, Oliver, and Upendra Baxi. 1994. *The rights of subordinated peoples*. Delhi: Oxford University Press.

UN Draft Declaration on the Rights of Indigenous People (as Agreed Upon by the Members of the Working Group at its Eleventh Session).

Rashmi Goel

INDUSTRIALIZATION

Industrialization is the process of introducing machinery and factory systems to increase production. In Britain and Europe, industrialization began in the second half of the eighteenth century and accelerated in the nineteenth century. In developing countries, industrialization began in the twentieth century and continues today as part of the globalization of the world economy. Currently, there is a greater proportion of women in the industrial labor forces of developing nations, where they are concentrated in labor-intensive sections of light industry, than there is in industrialised countries.

Industrialization has brought about a redefinition of sex roles in accordance with reshaped ideologies of masculinity and femininity, and a separation between home and workplace (Lown, 1990). In factories and workshops a rigid sexual division of labor developed. Women, stereotyped as being "less technological" but as having "nimble fingers," typically have been relegated to older machines, assembly lines, and repetitive work while men have held the more skilled and highly paid jobs.

Although women and children were a large proportion of the workforce in the early European industrial period, they were displaced when heavy machinery was introduced. Women's employment in the workforce typically became irregular, episodic, and part-time. Men became producers in the public sphere while women were housewifes and children's social, moral, and physical guardians. This division has been sustained by the idea of a "family wage" and the notion that the husband is the family breadwinner (Tilly and Scott, 1978).

There is much debate regarding the impact of industrialization on women. Pinchbeck (1977) contends that over the long term, women have benefited. Limited work opportunities for women led to pressure for higher education and professional careers for middle-class women, while for working-class women there were improvements in living standards and wages and a chance to escape patriarchal and parental control. However, many writers claim that industrialization has been disadvantageous, that a rigid sexual division of labor persists, and that women have lost out to men in opportunities to participate in the highest-paid and most technical jobs.

See Also

ECONOMY: GLOBAL RESTRUCTURING; FAMILY WAGE; MODERNIZATION

References and Further Reading

Lown, Judy. 1990. *Women and industrialization.* Cambridge: Polity.

Pinchbeck, Ivy. 1977. *Women workers and the industrial revolution 1750–1850.* London: Frank Cass.

Tilly, Louise A., and Joan W. Scott. 1978. *Women, work, and family.* New York: Holt, Rinehart and Winston.

Gaynor Dawson

INFANTICIDE

Infanticide can be defined as actions that result in the death of a young, dependent member of the species. It is found in a number of species, including birds (egrets, skuas) and mammals (ground squirrels, gerbils, Serengeti lions, wild stallions, and primates such as gorillas, langurs, and humans). Among animals in the wild, the general tendency is for an invading male to eliminate the young of a rival male so as to compel the female to mate with him.

Among humans, infanticide may range from deliberate to not fully conscious actions resulting in the death of a young child. Usually, the term *infanticide* is used when the child is under twelve months of age, but this is not a universal criterion: the age may vary from one society to another, depending on cultural concepts of when the actual life of an infant begins. The term is also frequently used to refer to *neonaticide*, the killing of an infant on the day of its birth; and to *filicide*, the killing of child, especially a child below the age of six years, by one or both parents. Common methods of human infanticide are exposure to the elements, withholding of food, drowning, suffocation, and discarding infants in sewers, garbage dumps, or remote areas.

There has been considerable debate among ethicists about the morality of killing a newborn. Some of this debate involves the definition of "personhood." Certain ethicists dismiss the moral argument against infanticide, arguing that it is historically rooted in western culture and is due to the dominant influence of specific theological assumptions (Kuhse, 1987; Tooley, 1983); such theorists sometimes argue, further, that a newborn may not meet the criterion of personhood. Others argue that theories of personhood are problematic if they allow the potential for human beings to actively cause an infant's death; these ethicists maintain, in general, that a moral society must have prohibitions against killing and that the circle of protection and rights must include infants (Post, 1988).

Causal Factors

Infanticide has been explained in terms of various causal factors. It has been seen as an adaptation to scarce resources for subsistence; as a means of regulating the population; as a way to manipulate the sex ratio for personal, ecomonic, or social ends; as a response to different cost-benefit analyses for male and female offspring; as a response to shame and the fear of ostracism when pregnancy and birth have resulted from violating norms of conduct; as a reaction by a mother to postpartum effects; and as an application of cultural views regarding atypical or aberrant situations that are perceived as having possible negative outcomes for the mother, the patrilineal kin, or the community (Dickeman, 1975; Smith and Smith, 1994). On the basis of a review of ethnographic material, Susan Scrimshaw (1984) delineates four major categories of situations in which infanticide is likely to occur: when an infant (1) has some deformity, (2) is illegitimate, (3) is proximate at birth to a sibling, or (4) is of the undesired sex in a society that values males and females (and particularly their labor) differently.

Infanticide in History

Historically, infanticide has always existed, although its form, the motives for it, and the circumstances surrounding it have varied. For example, the Greeks, Romans, French, Brtitish, Indians, Japanese, Chinese, Inuit (Canadian and North American Eskimos), !Kung of the Kalahari, Tikopia of Polynesia, Yanomama of Venezuela, and Bariba of Benin all practiced infanticide.

Infanticide can be traced to the ancient world in the Mediterranean basin. It was a common practice in ancient Greece and Rome. Among the Sabines, Phoenicians, and Carthaginians, it was practiced as a sacrifice to avert evil or calamity or to achieve a wish. The Greek philosopher Plato condoned infanticide and in his *Republic* argued that in a perfect society the quiet extermination of deformed infants and children of inferior people would ensure the quality of the citizenry. Aristotle, in his *Poetics*, argued for a law that would prohibit the survival of deformed children. The Spartans, who were warriors, actually had such a law: according to Lycurgus (the Lawgiver), they were to get rid of deformed babies in the interest of the state. The Roman king Etruscan considered malformed infants monsters and ordered their death. The Greeks effected infanticide mainly through exposure, and the Romans continued this.

The Christians, drawing on some of the principles of Judaism, opposed infanticide, which they saw as a pagan practice. However, certain categories of lives were excluded from their prohibitions, such as deformed babies. In fact, the Christian emperor Justinian, in the fourth table of his legal code, specified that it was a father's duty to dispose of a deformed child (Kuhse and Singer, 1985; Lyon, 1985).

Infanticide persisted in western Europe during the Middle Ages; although in some cases it was defined as a crime, prosecutions were rare and penalties were mild. In the eighteenth and nineteenth centuries, it reached epidemic proportions in England and France: many dead infants were found in the sewers of Paris, and in England infants' corpses were found in streets, ditches, and parks and floating in the river Thames. Historians usually attribute this to oppressive social conditions—female domestic servants and factory workers were often sexually exploited by their male employers and saw no option but to dispose of their illegitimate infants. England eventually addressed infanticide in 1922, when it passed the Infanticide Act; this was replaced by a new act in 1939 (Bourget and Labelle, 1992; Lyon, 1985).

In some cultures, infanticide has been accepted under certain circumstances. For example, the Japanese practiced infanticide as part of the normative order during the eighteenth century and the first half of the nineteenth century. It was most common among the peasants, though not limited to them, and the term for the practice was *mabiki*, "thinning"—an analogy with the thinning of rice seedlings. The primary function of infanticide in Japan was to make family size commensurate with the size of the family's farm, and to achieve what was considered the ideal sex distribution of children, two boys and one girl (Smith, 1977).

The Bariba of Benin in west Africa are another example of a culture that practiced infanticide, although they practiced it secretly because of governmental prohibitions (Sargent, 1988). Among the Bariba in rural areas, infanticide tended to occur in response to cultural perceptions of strange situations, especially at birth, which signified that an infant might be a witch who could jeopardize patrilineal kin. Such signifiers included breech births, premature births, an infant born with teeth, and an infant whose first teeth appeared in the upper rather than the lower jaw.

The !Kung are still another example. They were mainly hunter-gatherers, and they allocated sex roles very clearly: hunting was done by men and the gathering of the family's vegetables and firewood by women. The scarcity of food and water necessitated a nomadic lifestyle and some degree of population control. Therefore, !Kung women practiced infanticide in situations when an infant was seen as a threat to the survival of a sibling or as a serious impediment to the mother's ability to fulfill her labor obligations for the group's economic survival.

In some cultures, the birth of twins has been an occasion for infanticide because twins were considered abnormal or problematic. Gransberg (1973) found twin infanticide—the killing of one member of the pair—in 18 of 70 nonliterate cultures he studied, and he concluded that it was most likely in societies where a mother would not have the means to rear two infants simultaneously while continuing to meet her other obligations.

Female Infanticide

In almost all societies that practice infanticide, the general tendency is to kill female infants. Female infanticide usually occurs in patrilineal, patrilocal, and patriarchal cultures where there is a strong preference for males and thus a devaluation of females. By contrast, in societies where women are important in production processes or in systems of inheritance, female infant mortality rates—often an indicator of infanticide—seem to be very low (Miller, 1981). Examples or apparent examples of female infanticide can be found (among other cultures) in Inuit groups and in India and China.

The Inuit. Census data for the Inuit from 1880 to 1930 show sex ratios that are highly biased toward males and that have been taken to indicate female infanticide. This has been explained as a result of extreme ecological pressures experienced by these groups before the arrival of European mercantilism and government organizations. In the premercantile period, a son was highly valued because as an adult he would be a hunter and the family provider. In a harsh environment, where the family depended mainly on the son, the birth of a daughter could be perceived as endangering its survival. Also, female infanticide may have been used to counterbalance the high rates of mortality among adult males, who were often killed while hunting (Kuhse and Singer, 1985). Smith and Smith (1994: 595) argue that it may be the result of parents' attempts "to match the number of sons with locally prevailing but regionally variable rates of sex-specific mortality and economic productivity."

Among the Netsilik Inuit, a common practice was to place a female infant in the entrance of an igloo, in the hope that another family would adopt her; if none did, she would freeze to death. The other alternative was suffocation. The decision to kill the infant was usually made by the father, although it could also be made by the mother, a grandfather, or a widowed grandmother.

India. A historical review of the sex ratio in India shows a consistent male bias. The exact origin of female infanticide in India is unknown, but the practice was well established in the late eighteenth century and the nineteenth century. Although it was outlawed by the British in 1870, no serious attempts were made to enforce the law. Female infanticide was most pervasive in northern India (Gujarat and Uttar Pradesh), usually among the Kshatriya and Rajput castes (Miller, 1981); it also seems to have been practiced in the south by the Kallars of the Madurai district in the state of Tamil Nadu (Venkatramini, 1986). In India, the strong preference for males and the devaluation of females have been attibuted to various factors: patrilineage; inheritance of property by males; perceptions of males as economic providers for elderly or disabled parents, as vital functionaries in ancestral rituals, and as receivers of dowries; perceptions of females as subordinate to men and as a financial burden because their parents must provide them with a dowry; and the definition of women as property in various religious texts.

Under the present Indian penal code, infanticide is punishable by death. However, in the past two decades or so, an alternative practice seems to have been substituted for it: amniocentesis is used to determine the sex of a fetus, and then female fetuses are selectively aborted. Amniocentesis solely for this purpose has also been prohibited, but it continues to be used in many areas. In the 1990s, India's sex ratio was still biased: 93 females to 100 males. Some states, such as Harayana and Punjab, had districts where the ratio for children from birth to 6 years of age was as low as 85 girls to 100 boys (UNICEF, 1995: 6, 56–61).

China. Systematic female infanticide also occurs in China, though it is not practiced openly. Contributing factors include a strong cultural bias in favor of males; a perception of sons as carrying on the lineage and as a source of support for elderly parents; and the Chinese government's policy of controlling population by limiting each family to one child. The outcome of female infanticide, along with prenatal sex determination and selective abortion, can be seen in China's unbalanced sex ratio: approximately 94 females to 100 males (Tien, 1991; Yi et al., 1993).

Actions Against Infanticide

The past three decades have witnessed considerable protest and action by human rights and women's rights organizations worldwide to end systematic infanticide, especially female infanticide. Pressure has been put on governments—particularly in countries such as India and China—to address the imbalance in sex ratios and to improve the overall status of females. This position was notably articulated in 1995 at the Fourth World Conference on Women in Beijing.

See Also

DISCRIMINATION; DOWRY AND BRIDEPRICE; FEMICIDE; GIRL CHILD; SEX SELECTION

References and Further Reading

Bourget, Dominique, and Alain Labelle. 1992. Homicide, infanticide, and filicide. *Clinical Forensic Psychiatry* 15 (3): 661–673.

Dickeman, Mildred. 1975. Demographic consequences of infanticide in man. *Annual Review of Ecology and Systematics* 6: 107–137.

Gransberg, G. 1973. Twin infanticide. *Ethos* 1: 405–412.

Kuhse, Helga. 1987. *The sanctity-of-life doctrine of medicine.* New York: Oxford University Press.

Kuhse, Helga, and Peter Singer. 1985. *Should the baby live?* Oxford: Oxford University Press.

Lyon, Jeff. 1985. *Playing God in the nursery.* New York: W.W. Norton.

Miller, Barbara D. 1981. *The endangered sex.* Ithaca, N.Y.: Cornell University Press.

Post, S. G. 1988. *History, infanticide, and imperiled newborns.* Hastings Center Report 18 (4): 14–17.

Sargent, Carolyn. 1988. Born to die: Witchcraft and infanticide in Bariba culture. *Ethnology* 27: 79–95.

Scrimshaw, Susan. 1984. Infanticide in human population: Societal and individual concerns. In Sarah B. Hrdy and Glen Hausfater, eds., *Infanticide: Comparative and evolutionary perspectives.* New York: Aldine.

Smith, Eric Alden, and S. Abigail Smith. 1994. Inuit sex-ratio variation. *Current Anthropology* 35 (5): 595–624.

Smith, Thomas C. 1977. *Nakahara: Family farming and population in a Japanese village, 1717–1830.* Stanford, Calif.: Stanford University Press.

Tien, H. Yuan. 1991. The new census of China. *Population Today* 19 (1): 6–8.

Tooley, Michael. 1983. *Abortion and infanticide.* New York: Oxford University Press.

UNICEF. 1995. *The progress of Indian states.* New York: UNICEF. Report by A. K. Shiva Kumar and Jon Rhode. UNICEF House. 73 Lodi Road, New Delhi, India.

Venkatramini, S. H. 1986. Female infanticide: Born to die. *India Today* (15 June): 26–33.

Yi, Zeng, Tu Ping, Gu Baochang, Xu Yi, Li Bohua, and Li Yongping. 1993. Causes and implications of the recent increase in the reported sex-ratio at birth in China. *Population and Development Review* 19 (2): 283–302.

Margaret Abraham

INFERTILITY

Worldwide, infertility affects 8 to 12 percent of couples at some time in their lives (World Health Organization, 1991). However, it is not distributed evenly; instead, it correlates strongly with poverty and social exclusion. In the United States, for instance, infertility rates are at least one and a half times as high among African-Americans as among European Americans (Roberts, 1997). Globally, poor countries have higher rates of infertility than wealthy countries. The highest infertility rates—up to 50 percent—are found in some countries of sub-Saharan Africa (Doyal, 1995). These statistics represent considerable human suffering.

Definitions and Standards of Infertility

The definition of *infertility* is contested, even among feminists. Infertility is variously considered a disease, a disability, and a condition. Medical organizations tend to define it as a disease. Some feminists agree. Others consider it a disability, since it prevents people from participating in the basic human activity of procreation (Rothman, 1989); they argue that, as a disability, infertility should be managed holistically, and medical treatment should be widely available for those who want it. Still other feminists consider infertility simply a condition and decry the "medicalization of childlessness" (Marsh and Ronner, 1996). They argue that, rather than turn to medicine for a "cure," society should promote culturally acceptable alternatives to parenthood and encourage adoption for people who want to raise children.

Criteria for infertility also vary. In some countries, such as France, a couple will be considered infertile after trying to conceive for two years. In others—including, notably, the United States—the standard is only one year. Predictably, rates of infertility are higher in the latter countries, because many couples do conceive in the second year. For couples with health insurance or private means, the standard of infertility has become lower and lower; some physicians now encourage couples to undergo infertility testing even before trying to conceive.

Causes and Consequences

Among heterosexual couples, approximately 35 percent of infertility is due to problems with the woman's fertility, 35 percent to problems with the man's fertility, 20 percent to problems with both partners' fertility, and 10 percent to undiagnosed factors. As these figures show, men and women experience infertility in equal numbers; but the emotional and social consequences are usually more severe for women.

In all countries, women's social status and identity are linked to motherhood; in some cultures, particularly those in which many women are poor and illiterate, motherhood is women's only socially condoned role. In any society, infertility can be devastating to a woman who wants to bear and raise children, but for many women it is also socially and economically calamitous. In cultures that devalue women and girls, an infertile woman (or a woman with an infertile male partner) may be abused or abandoned. For example, in parts of India husbands and extended families have ostracized, maltreated, and even killed women who did not become pregnant (Doyal, 1995: 147). Women who survive such mistreatment may face destitution, despair, and "social death."

Treatment

Globally, reproductive medicine is a high-technology, hugely profitable, but virtually unregulated industry. Middle- and upper-class women face mounting social pressure to undergo treatment. Family members, the clergy, and the state can all promote pronatalist ideologies—often associated with religious fundamentalism—to encourage women's participation in fertility treatments that may last for months or even years.

At the same time, infertility among poor women remains largely untreated. This may be partly due to an implicit notion—which seems both racist and classist—that some potential babies are "priceless" and are worth expensive fertility treatments whereas others are not. Another reason is that in poor countries, governments and ministries of health are often preoccupied with population control, a focus that is sometimes intensified by external influences such as economic incentives. Women's groups have criticized the health services in poor countries for subordinating reproductive care (and primary care as well) to population goals, arguing that population targets dehumanize mothers and families, and that women everywhere should have access to affordable reproductive services that would meet the specific needs of individuals and communities. The legacy of eugenics—a pseudo science that advocated reproduction by the wealthy but curtailed childbearing for the poor and socially marginalized—may still be seen in, for example, the stringent family planning requirements imposed by structural adjustment programs of the World Bank and other international institutions (Stillman and King, 1999). Despite resolutions issued by the women's meetings at Cairo and Beijing, the population control orthodoxy has been slow to change. (A corollary of denying poor women fertility treatments is imposing contraception on them. Coercive and unethical sterilization programs were still being reported at the turn of the twenty-first century; examples included surgical sterilization in Peru in the late 1990s and chemical sterilization with a drug called Quinacrine in Vietnam, Bangladesh, Morocco, and several other countries.)

There are also many problems with infertility treatment itself, which feminist activists and scholars have identified and protested against since the 1980s. Reproductive medicine is often invasive, intimately intrusive, medically risky, physically painful, and emotionally draining, as well as expensive; it frequently exploits surrogate mothers and egg donors; and it is not very effective at producing healthy babies. Many of the drugs and procedures involved have been criticized as experimental rather than therapeutic, and as being conducive to medical control of women. Feminists have also criticized reproductive medicine for promoting a consumerist ideology of childbearing that commercializes babies and children and ultimately dehumanizes motherhood.

Many women find the risks and costs of fertility treatment acceptable, particularly if it results in a healthy baby. Research has found, however, that even the best-informed patients and potential patients consistently underestimate its physical, emotional, and financial burdens.

Prevention

Much infertility is directly preventable; yet while millions of women and men each year seek high-cost, high-technology treatments for infertility, investment in prevention remains grossly inadequate. A significant cause of infertility in women is pelvic inflammatory disease (PID), infections of the reproductive tract that often lead to scarring of the fallopian tubes. A main cause of PID, in turn, is untreated sexually transitted diseases (STDs), including gonorrhea, syphilis, trichomoniasis, and chlamydia. STDs are epidemic in both developing and developed countries; worldwide, the estimated incidence of curable STDs (not including AIDS and other viral STDs) is about 333 million cases (World Health Organization, 1996). STDs also cause male infertility, though not at such dramatically high rates. Much of the infertility caused by these infections could be prevented through health education, sex education, access to condoms, and access to early screening and treatment.

Complications of childbirth are another cause of infertility in women. In poor countries, one woman in four suffers from illness, injury, or disability sustained in childbirth. Women who hemorrhage or develop a fistula or complications from genital mutilation during labor, for example, are at high risk of infertility—as are women who are anemic, women who lack adequate nutrition and health care to begin with, and women who have no access to sanitary medical facilities. Most of these problems are caused by poverty and are almost unknown among wealthy women.

Smoking—of tobacco or marijuana—is a wholly preventable contributor to male and female infertility.

Occupational and environmental hazards also lead to infertility in both women and men. These include exposure to toxic substances such as industrial chemicals, nuclear radiation, and contaminated drinking water, food, and air. Many women are exposed to unsafe concentrations of toxic substances in household products—cleansers, pesticides, and bleaches. Preventing harm from toxic materials involves shifting social and political priorities away from profits and toward protecting humans and the environment; it also involves stricter workplace standards and regulations to protect workers' health and fertility.

Infertility and Women's Status

Empowering women and improving their status overall are crucial to combating infertility. Women whose status is low have little bargaining power to negotiate the terms of their sexuality with male partners and thus protect themselves from infection. Women who are part of trafficking in prostitution usually are even less able to protect themselves. Female genital mutilation (FGM), which affects millions of girls and women, primarily in parts of Africa and the Middle East, also leads to high rates of infertility. At the time of this writing, about 130 million girls and women had undergone FGM, and 2 million more were being subjected to it each year (Seager, 1997). Rape and child sexual abuse also lead to infection, injuries, unwanted pregnancies, and other outcomes that threaten the fertility of survivors.

If one cord ties together the feminist approaches to infertility, it is the assertion that women have a right to be free of needless exploitation, pain, and coercion, whether at the hands of family members, providers of medical care, or the state. Identifying these hazards to reproductive health, and working for collective solutions, continues to be an important focus of feminists internationally.

See Also

ADOPTION; FEMALE CIRCUMCISION AND GENITAL MUTILATION; FERTILITY AND FERTILITY TREATMENT; GYNECOLOGY; MEDICAL CONTROL OF WOMEN; OBSTETRICS; REPRODUCTIVE HEALTH; REPRODUCTIVE RIGHTS; SURROGACY

References and Further Reading

Boston Women's Health Book Collective. 1998. *Our bodies, ourselves for the new century.* New York: Simon and Schuster.

Doyal, Lesley. 1995. *What makes women sick? Gender and the political economy of health.* New Brunswick, N.J.: Rutgers University Press.

Hartmann, Betsy. 1987. *Reproductive rights and wrongs: The global politics of population control and contraceptive choice.* New York: Harper and Row.

Marsh, Margaret, and Wanda Ronner. 1996. *The empty cradle: Infertility in America from colonial times to the present.* Baltimore: Johns Hopkins University Press.

Roberts, Dorothy. 1997. *Killing the black body: Race, reproduction, and the meaning of liberty.* New York: Vintage.

Rothman, Barbara Katz. 1989. *Recreating motherhood: Ideology and technology in a patriarchal society.* New York: W.W. Norton.

Seager, Joni. 1997. *The state of the women in the world atlas.* New York: Penguin.

Silliman, Jael, and Ynestra King, eds. 1999. *Feminist perspectives on population, environment, and development: A project of the Committee on Women, Population, and the Environment.* Boston: South End.

World Health Organization. 1991. *Infertility: A tabulation of available data on prevalence of primary and secondary fertility.* Program on Maternal and Child Health and Family Planning. Geneva: World Health Organization.

World Health Organization. April 1996. *Sexually transmitted diseases (STDs): Fact sheet.* WHO Initiative on HIV/AIDS and Sexually Transmitted Infections. Geneva: World Health Organization.

Internet Sources

<www.desaction.org.>

<www.fertilityplus.org.>

<www.fertilityplus.org/faq/miscarriage/resources.html.>

<www.hsph.harvard.edu/organizations/healthnet/SAsia/suchana/sndtframe.html.>

<www.inciid.org.>

<www.ozemail.com.au/~accessoz/index.html.>

<www.resolve.org.>

Amy Agigian

INFORMAL ECONOMY

See ECONOMY: INFORMAL.

INFORMATION ECONOMY

See DIGITAL DIVIDE.

INFORMATION REVOLUTION

The term *information revolution* refers to the rapid increase in the use of computers, data processing, and the Internet and has come to imply not only information as such but, more significantly, global management and trading, changing economies, consumers' behavior, jobs, and labor markets. Like other revolutions, it is often seen as gendered.

The term *revolution* itself usually refers to a sudden upheaval that results in fundamental changes in the way a society thinks or operates. Often the upheaval is political, involving a change of rulers or other major changes in the system of government, as in the French Revolution and the Russian Revolution. Political revolutions have also occurred in Cuba, Nicaragua, and Iran during the past half-century. There are also conceptual revolutions, such as the changes in popular thinking that followed the widespread acceptance of the ideas of Darwin and Einstein. Technological revolutions involve major changes brought about by new tools that affect, for example, the cultivation and processing of foods, the manufacture of textiles, methods and routes of transportation, the refining and use of fuels, and the treatment of health problems.

These various revolutions can all be analyzed as arising from differing gender and class interests and opportunities, and they have all had a different impact on women and men. For example, the development of the internal combustion engine and electrical engines led to sweatshop industries that used sewing machines to manufacture clothing. The owners and investors were interested in greater per capita production, and indeed work speeded up, production increased, and—for some people—prosperity reached new heights; but at the same time women employees, who worked long hours in unhealthy conditions, were the "cheap fuel" in this revolution.

Certainly the increased use of the computer, which is basically a new tool, is bringing many changes, and these have implications even for the many people who do not have access to a computer or to the Internet. This new tool allows us to accomplish some activities that were not feasible before, and people with access to it have a new, quick form of communication; however, this tool was not initially developed with the interest of the "general public" in mind.

In the 1970s the military of the United States set up a data network, to be used to protect the nation against a nuclear war. In the early days of this network, some educators and researchers were connected to it. Then the Internet (as it had come to be called) spread to engineers in commercial research facilities, and then to many schools, individuals, and businesses. For a short time, many of the people using computers to communicate believed that they were developing a new, collaborative community with rich possibilities for freedom of expression, linking people through common interests rather than by geographical location. Many people now working in education, government, and business, particularly in western countries, still claim that the new tool can be used to provide great amounts of information to individuals, societies, and nations, a process that can result in increased economic growth, increased sharing of information, and new models of participatory politics and community. The movement of information is both a major use of this new tool and a new commodity, to be generated, packaged, and then shipped by global electronic networks.

In the 1990s, popular metaphors for the Internet included "new frontier" and "information superhighway." This terminology led some women to suggest that their role was evidently "occasional frontier mistress" as men occupied the frontier or "roadkill" as men raced along the highway. At the beginning of the 1990s, women were a minority on the Internet, and many of the men on-line, far from supporting a change in concepts of gender relationships, consciously or unconsciously made women feel unwelcome in many of the discussion lists. Now, in the places where computers have become as prevalent as toasters, many women are using them, as part of their jobs or to converse with others or to shop. But access still remains an issue for many women, since even home computers, for example, are not necessarily "owned" equally by all members of the home.

In fact, ownership and its implications represent a much broader issue. Whatever the intent of many individuals and progressive groups eager that these new networks be used for equity and collaborative work, it is increasingly the case that information and the spaces where information is available on-line are owned by individuals and businesses for business purposes. An enormous amount of text, graphics, and entertainment is developed by the western countries not only for their own use but for other cultures and is sent via cable TV and the Internet. Much of this material is in the English language and is created from a western perspective; thus there are barriers facing many users and potential users. For women, particularly, there are also other barriers: educational systems in many areas that foster high rates of illiteracy in females; insufficient resources for the necessary hardware and software and its maintenance; a lack of reliable telephone lines or electricity; inadequate support programs; training materials and methods that are insensitive to women's interests and real-life responsibilities; and computer degree or certificate programs that make expertise in mathematics a prerequisite, rather than welcoming people with a different skills and interests who could bring new approaches.

This exclusionary situation is likely to continue as long as relatively few girls and women, and relatively few men from marginalized groups, are encouraged to help create programs and the strategies for their use. What some businesses present as the latest technological and informational projects, with solutions for some part of almost all problems, may actually operate to reinforce existing inequalities. The new rapid flood of information comes with some old ideologies that are slow to change.

Despite these difficulties, women are using electronic networking successfully in many ways. A survey conducted by the Women's Networking Support Programme of the Association for Progression Communications focused on women's experiences with electronic networking in 30 countries in Africa (Cameroon, Nigeria, Senegal, Tanzania, Zimbabwe), Asia and the Pacific (Australia, India, Japan, Malaysia, the Philippines), eastern Europe (Croatia, Russia Federation, Ukraine), western Europe (Austria, Belgium, France, Ireland, Italy, the Netherlands, Switzerland, United Kingdom), Latin America (Brazil, Colombia, Ecuador, Mexico, Peru, Uruguay), western Asia (Jordan) and North America (Canada and the United States). The survey found that women are increasingly active in using electronic communications and are increasingly experimenting with on-line conferences, mailing lists, and Web sites.

The United Nations Fourth World Conference on Women (FWCW), held in Beijing, China, in September 1995, was organized on the Internet, which was also used to publicize the conference and the NGO (Nongovernmental Organizations) Forum far more widely than any earlier global conferences. In the years preceding these events, much of the conceptual work, such as seeking consensus on issues related to gender and women's human rights, was also done on-line. The Fourth World Conference had nearly 40,000 participants, mostly women who traveled to Beijing; in addition, thousands of women and men in other places were able to follow the daily sessions and forum discussions using computers and telephone lines. Electronic information was also repackaged in different formats, such as newsletters, radio broadcasting, and faxes; was translated into several languages; and was disseminated worldwide.

There are many comparable examples. Flame/Flamme, for instance, is a network of African women, using English and French and new information technologies to lobby, advocate, and participate in the "Beijing Plus 5" (meaning plus five years) review process regionally and globally.

The experiences of the women involved with the Beijing Conference and NGO Forum, and with other advocacy groups, illustrate some of the possibilities that the Internet and related technologies hold for women in many places. However, these new technologies are not in themselves a cure for basic socioeconomic ills, they have not led us into a global village, and they have not revolutionized gender hierarchies—yet.

See Also

COMPUTER SCIENCE; COMPUTING: OVERVIEW; EDUCATION: ON-LINE; INFORMATION TECHNOLOGY; INTERNET POLITICS AND STATES; NETWORKING; NETWORKS, ELECTRONIC; REVOLUTIONS

References and Further Reading

Bromley, Hank. In press. Border skirmishes: A meditation on gender, new technologies, and the persistence of structure. In Ron Eglash, Julian Bleecker, Jennifer L. Croissant, Giovanna Di Chiro, and Rayvon Fouche, eds. forthcoming work. Minneapolis: University of Minnesota Press.

Cherny, Lynn, and Elizabeth Reba Weisse, eds. 1996. *Wired women: Gender and new realities in cyberspace.* Seattle, Wash.: Seal.

Harcourt, Wendy. 1999. *Women@Internet: Creating new cultures in cyberspace.* London and New York: Zed.

Internet Source

APC Women's Networking Support Programme. Association for Progressive Communications. <http://www.apc.org/english/about/apcwomen/index.htm>

Cheris Kramarae

INFORMATION TECHNOLOGY

Definitions

Information technology (IT) is a broad term literally describing hardware that is used for purposes of communication. But like many contemporary words such as *communication* and *media,* the term is often used to connote both the *process* of communication that uses hardware and the *message* within the cultural context in which a communicative act takes place. Although there may be some disagreement about what actually constitutes IT, it is possible to say that today almost everyone in the world is touched in some way by it. From the largest corporations that use IT for rapid information storage and processing, as well as electronic funds transfer (EFT), to the rural villager who hears a radio message about impending bad weather, IT has become an important system for instantaneous communication.

While the word *technology* almost always describes tools that are applied in systematic or scientific ways, there is generally more disagreement about what the word *information* connotes.

In many western cultures there are two general definitions of *information.* One focuses on the aspect of the *message* in the communicative process and defines information as quantifiable, such as computer data that can be measured and controlled by the number of "bits" that are transferred or stored. In this view, information is considered a commodity that can be bought or sold. The second definition classifies information as *knowledge* and focuses on the *receiver's use* of the material processed by the technology. In this definition, *technology* has significantly less denotative meaning than *information.*

Both of these instrumental definitions focus on only one aspect of the communication transfer. Both also disregard any ties to the cultural context in which a message is stored or transferred, or to the social actions surrounding the application of technology for a specific purpose. Therefore, IT is often viewed as a tool rather than a complex connection and convergence among the hardware, the controllers of the larger infrastructure to support the operation of the IT, the users, and the application of the messages and processes involved in exchanging messages. Feminist scholars have begun to seek connections among these components to better understand the power, impact, and effect of IT within specific contexts.

The cultures that use either of these definitions generally apply the broad term *information technology* to "big media,"—for example, technically complex communication systems such as computers; broadcast, cable, closed circuit, or satellite-distributed television; radio-based technologies; telephony; and large-scale digital technologies; as well as ethnotronic technology (small media), which are small, portable systems that do not require a large, expensive infrastructure for the exchange of messages. Examples of ethnotronic technologies include personal communication services (PCSs) like cellular telephones, portable fax machines, laptop computers, beepers, and small recording devices, such as answering machines.

Many cultures view the process and hardware used for communication by means of "information technology" as more critically synthesized. The French, for example, use the term *telematics* to encompass both the hardware and the process of using information technology for exchanging messages and limit the term *informatics* to strictly computer-based message exchange. In Latin American cultures, the word *informatics* often describes computer science.

IT and Manufacturing Issues

While there may be subtle cultural interpretations of how the term *information technology* is applied, feminists tend to agree that, like other forms of technology, information-related technologies often lead to the oppression of women because the masculine power structures that invent, manufacture, and market these devices support gender hierarchies. The designs often created by men are often used by women, and when people tend to believe that advanced technology is progressive and leads to a better quality of life, they are inclined to support public policies that uncritically perpetuate gendered power relations (Bush, 1983). The research on women and IT has found that although women often are the uses of such technologies, there is little evidence to suggest that they play a major role in the implementation of the designs for IT.

In the latter part of the twentieth century, women in some less economically developed countries have become a significant labor force for multinational electronics manufacturing firms. In particular, Mexico and countries of the Pacific rim have become major electronics manufacturing sites for multinational operations. Jessie Bernard (1987) notes that most of the work concentrated in two industries—textiles (including apparel) and, now, the electronics industry—is supported by female workers. While it is true that IT manufacturing has provided jobs for many unskilled women, this workforce is often exploited, with low wages, few benefits, and exposure to chemicals that are either untested or present in quantities that can have negative effects on health (Ward, 1990; Whitman Hoff, 1994).

Studies on the impact of the growing number of electronics manufacturing operations in these areas are few, though international trade agreements such as the North American Free Trade Agreement (NAFTA) have drawn greater attention to specific effects on women. In particular, NAFTA raises questions about the operation of *maquiladoras* in Mexico, where there are more than 1,300 U.S.-owned factories, employing a significant number of women and children who are paid low wages, who cannot read instructions or warnings printed in English, and who often must live in squatter camps.

Despite the rapid diffusion of IT in the industrialized world, there are surprisingly few studies of the psychological and emotional impact on workers caused by applications of new IT in the modern office. A notable exception is

Zuboff's in-depth analysis of the transformation of some specific tasks and industrial applications of IT (1988).

Between 1960 and 1988, the service sector of the U.S. economy increased by 138 percent, with women workers accounting for three-quarters of the increase (Ries and Stone, 1992: 330–331) and for many of the new jobs created by technical positions related to IT. Despite the increase in women in the labor force, however, the actual proportion of clerical jobs decreased from 31.6 percent in 1975 to 27.8 percent in 1990 (Ries and Stone, 1992: 334). Many market surveys focus on the liberating aspects of IT for women, but it is important to remember that many of the newly created jobs were part-time, nonunion positions without benefits. Alternative work arrangements such as telecommuting, flex-time, and job sharing are sometimes viewed as positive changes that allow women greater flexibility, but these opportunities are often balanced by the reality that clerical work has been reconfigured to piecework, similar to that of the traditional factory assembly line. Evidence indicates that many women who use these alternative work arrangements by bringing computers, fax machines, and other office IT into the home are actually paid less than they would be in full salaried positions. Women working at home may experience additional stress by trying to balance the demands of children, spouse, or older relatives who need care during certain times of the day, while attempting to fit their clerical work into off-hours of the day or night (Schor, 1991). Tensions with and alienation from the organization are also common by-products of these alternative arrangements.

Although there has been some attention to possible negative health effects of working closely with video display terminals (VDTs), such as an increase in miscarriages, no data have yet proved that there are direct adverse health effects caused by working in clerical positions with IT. Contemporary evaluations suggest that reproductive disorders are due more to tasks that require workers to sit in one place for long periods of time than to technology as such.

Newly created jobs have aided some groups of workers, however. Handicapped women and men have used IT more for gainful employment in recent years, with advances in telecommunications devices for the deaf (TDDs), enhanced visual display units, portable transcribers, and speech synthesizers.

Fewer studies have focused on the use of IT by women in the home. Most of the research in this area has fallen to feminists, who write about and evaluate this important aspect of women's history. The collection edited by Cheris Kramarae (1988) was one of the first to include several chapters dedicated to the ways in which women have taken IT and modified it to support their social endeavors. Lana Rakow's chapter on women's use of the telephone (207–228) clearly illustrates how this invention created public jobs for women in the office but also created isolation for women in the home, until they managed to use the technology to overcome geographic boundaries as the population of the United States became further dispersed. In the same collection, Judy Smith and Ellen Balka (42–97) discuss how computer networking has provided an opportunity for women in Canada and the United States to "chat" about developing a feminist assessment of technology.

Questions about assessing technology constitute a key area of concern for feminists seeking to understand the ideological impact of IT. One of the first books to present a history and explanation of technological assessment was Jennifer Daryl Slack's *Communication, Technology, and Society: Conceptions of Causality and the Politics of Technological Intervention* (1984). Other major contributions to the field have included *Women, Work, and Technology,* edited by Barbara Drygulski Wright (1987), and Sue Curry Jansen's article "Gender and the Information Society: A Socially Structured Silence" (1989).

Recent attempts by feminists to conceptualize a uniform methodology to study the impact of IT have further demonstrated how past gender relations within cultures and societies have influenced present practices. Cynthia Cockburn and Ruza Fürst Dilić (1994) edited a volume of research conducted by several women from eastern and western Europe. While the editors discuss the problems inherent in studying contemporary technology due to issues of access, education, and training, they also remind us, in the context of a comparative international study, that the terms *gender, sex,* and *gender relations* are culturally distinct. Despite the difficulty experienced by the researchers, Cockburn and Fürst Dilić suggest that a feminist strategy regarding technology should include "women's right to healthy, sustainable, paid work; [access to] technological design; [development of] supportive domestic technologies;... and reevaluation of the domestic, the private, and the relational [aspects of technology and women's lives]" (19–20).

While the existence of IT appears to be creating a revolution in the way we communicate and in opportunities for employment, it is important to remember that the technology cannot be regarded in isolation. Information technologies are often introduced to environments with a history of practices that are hierarchical and structured by gender differences. As feminists continue to examine the power relations among information technologies, gender relations, and cultural contexts, they may very well continue to find new uses for information technologies and influence their development.

See Also

COMPUTER SCIENCE; COMPUTING: OVERVIEW; COMPUTING: PARTICIPATORY AND FEMINIST DESIGN; CYBERSPACE AND VIRTUAL REALITY; DOMESTIC TECHNOLOGY; INFORMATION REVOLUTION; MEDIA: OVERVIEW; TECHNOLOGY; TELEWORKING; WORK: OCCUPATIONAL EXPERIENCES

References and Further Reading

Bernard, Jessie. 1987. *The female world from a global perspective.* Bloomington: University of Indiana Press.

Bush, Corlann Gee. 1983. Women and the assessment of technology: To think, to be; to unthink, to free. In Joan Rothschild, ed., *Machina ex Dea: Feminist perspectives on technology,* 151–170. New York: Pergamon.

Carter, Barry C. 1999. *Infinite wealth: A new world of collaboration and abundance in the knowledge era.* Boston: Butterworth-Heinemann.

Cockburn, Cynthia, and Ruza Fürst Dilić. 1994. *Bringing technology home: Gender and technology in a changing Europe.* Buckingham, U.K.: Open University Press.

Hudson, Heather E. 1997. *Global connections: International telecommunication infrastructures and policy.* New York: Van Nostrand Reinhold.

Jansen, Sue Curry. 1989. Gender and the information society: A socially structured silence. *Journal of Communication* 39(3): 196–215.

Kramarae, Cheris, ed. 1988. *Technology and women's voices: Keeping in touch.* New York: Routledge and Kegan Paul.

Ries, Paula, and Anne J. Stone. 1992. *The American woman, 1992–1993: A status report.* New York: Norton.

Schor, Juliet B. 1991. *The overworked American.* New York: Basic Books.

Slack, Jennifer Daryl. 1984. *Communication, technology, and society: Conceptions of causality and the politics of technological intervention.* Norwood, N.J.: Ablex.

Ward, Kathryn. 1990. Introduction and overview. In Kathryn Ward, ed., *Women workers and global restructuring,* 1–22. Ithaca, N.Y.: ILR.

Webster, Juliet. 1996. *Shaping women's work: Gender, employment, and information technology.* London and New York: Longman.

Whitman Hoff, J. 1994. Ethics, transnationals, and technology transfer. In Jarice Hanson, ed., *Advances in telematics.* Vol. 2. Norwood, N.J.: Ablex.

Wright, Barbara Drygulski, ed. 1987. *Women, work, and technology.* Ann Arbor: University of Michigan Press.

Zuboff, Shoshana. 1988. *In the age of the smart machine.* New York: Basic Books.

Jarice Hanson

INITIATION RITES

An initiation rite marks a transition to a new social status, whether that new status is adulthood or "entering society" or membership in a special group or association. Arnold Van Gennep (1960) analyzed initiation rites as variations on "rites of passage" through the life cycle, with a similar tripartite process or structure: separation, liminality, and reincorporation. In the first, or preliminary stage, there is a separation or removal from ordinary life. The middle stage, liminality, which often involves tests or ordeals, is characterized by an indeterminate status. ("Liminal" literally means barely perceptible, so it is a useful analogy for indeterminacy.) In the final stage, reincorporation, the new identity is celebrated. Bruce Lincoln (1991) proposed a different tripartite model—enclosure, metamorphosis, and emergence—as a more accurate description of female initiation rites, especially rites surrounding first menstruation and birth.

Studies of Rites

In the Muslim areas of northern Maluku in Indonesia, as in other Malay-influenced areas of southeast Asia, women and their newborns spend 40 days postpartum confined to a birthing room where they experience an elaborate process that resembles initiation rites: it includes "warming" from a small, constantly maintained fire, often built directly under the birthing bed. Catherine Bell (1997: 95–98) describes similar practices in China that involve seclusion and "humoral" concerns about heat and cold; she argues that these rituals surrounding birth "provide some of the most basic models and metaphors for all sorts of ritual processes, as well as religious experience in general." Lincoln used a metaphor, "cocooning," that seems particularly apt in these contexts.

Caroline Bynum (1984) focused on women's experience of initiation in medieval narratives of conversion; this study led her to question the centrality of liminality in models of initiation. An important feature of liminality in male initiation rites, according to Van Gennep and some later theorists, is an experience of identity confusion and gender inversion that includes taking on "feminine" characteristics. While female symbols and femininity are clearly present in men's accounts, Bynum found no evidence of such identity upheaval or gender inversion in these women's accounts of their conversion. Similarly, Bruno Bettelheim (1954) took gender inversion and "symbolic wounds" in male puberty rites as evidence of envy of female sexuality and reproduction, but it is difficult to see how this analysis helps us understand women's experience of initiation.

Quite aside from the issue of the differing experiences and symbols that mark ritual passages to womanhood and manhood, it has often been remarked in the anthropological literature that female initiation rites are cross-culturally less elaborate than male rites, and even that female identity is commonly considered more natural and less problematic than male identity and hence less in need of cultural elaboration (Gilmore, 1990). Some scholars have gone so far as to say that female circumcision and clitoridectomy, where they are practiced, are so unmarked and brutal that they should not be considered initiation rites at all (Lightfoot-Klein, 1989). Others have argued that the violence and anxiety associated even with male circumcision have been underplayed in models of initiation rites, functioning mainly to incorporate new adult members of society (Crapanzano, 1981).

"Reinvention" of Rites

There have been explicit attempts to "reinvent" female initiation rites as part of movements for women's social equality and inclusion. One example is the relatively recent use of the bat mitzvah for girls by many non-Orthodox Jewish congregations. The development of gender-oriented initiatory practices within both women's and men's movements in the United States can also be seen in this context as an explicit response to a felt lack or "loss" of meaningful ritual in ordinary life; the goddess worshipers described by Starhawk (1989) and the drum-beating men described by Robert Bly (1990) are examples. Bell (1997: 259) argues that a romantification of ritual as a basic and necessary aspect of human experience in contemporary "new age" thought is "closely intertwined with the emergence of the very concept of ritual as a universal phenomenon accessible to formal identification and analysis." What seems clear is that although initiation rites tell us a great deal about gender ideology and what it means to be a man or a woman in a particular society, the ways such rites are analyzed—and even the ways they are practiced—are also influenced by changes in gender ideologies.

See Also

DRUMMING; FEMALE CIRCUMCISION AND GENITAL MUTILATION; GODDESS

References and Further Reading

Bell, Catherine. 1997. *Ritual: Perspectives and dimensions.* New York: Oxford University Press.

Bettelheim, Bruno. 1954. *Symbolic wounds: Puberty rites and the envious male.* Glencoe, Ill.: Free Press.

Bly, Robert. 1990. *Iron John: A book about men.* New York: Random House.

Bynum, Caroline Walker. 1984. Women's stories, women's symbols: A critique of Victor Turner's theory of liminality. In Robert L. Moore and Frank E. Reynolds, eds., *Anthropology and the study of religion,* 105–125. Chicago: Center for the Scientific Study of Religion.

Crapanzano, Vincent. 1981. Rite of return: Circumcision in Morocco. *Psychoanalytic Study of Society* 9: 15–36. (Ed. Werner Meunsterburger and L. Bryce Boyer.)

Gilmore, David D. 1990. *Manhood in the making: Cultural concepts of masculinity.* New Haven, Conn.: Yale University Press.

Lightfoot-Klein, Hanny. 1989. *Prisoners of ritual: An odyssey into female genital circumcision in Africa.* Binghampton, N.Y.: Haworth Medical.

Lincoln, Bruce. 1991. *Emerging from the chrysalis: Rituals of women's initiations,* rev. ed. New York: Oxford University Press.

Starhawk [Miriam Simos]. 1989. *The spiral dance: A rebirth of the ancient religion of the great goddess,* 10th anniversary ed. San Francisco: HarperCollins.

Van Gennep, Arnold. 1960. *The rites of passage.* Trans. Monika B. Vizedom and Gabrielle L. Caffee. Chicago: University of Chicago Press.

Karen Frojen Herrera

INSANITY

See MENTAL HEALTH I; MENTAL HEALTH II.

INTERESTS: STRATEGIC AND PRACTICAL

Interests may be defined as the objectives and social outcomes that are held to benefit groups or individuals. In most usages, interests have been understood in primarily economic terms, and social strata were conceived as having different and often conflicting interests. The idea that different social groups had common interests, which could be defended or advanced through legislation and political action, can, however, be found in the works of historians and political theorists of classical antiquity.

Social Theory

In modern social theory the concept of interests has found an application in the analysis of political phenomena such as collective action and social conflict, and in discussions of how far group interests are represented in, and by, states. Theories of interest were developed in opposition to two assumptions. First, in presuming a category of collective interests there is an implicit rejection of a fundamental principle of utilitarian liberalism: competitive individual interests. Second, the idea that struggle and protest served to further certain rational interests and objectives has existed in opposition to the claim that these were the actions of irrational "mobs." That those who rioted, went on strike, protested, demonstrated, or engaged in other forms of collective action were pursuing reasonable, and hence intelligible goals, is an assumption that lies at the heart of theories of interest.

Gender Analysis

The gender analysis of protest movements, such as bread riots, peace movements, and other forms of collective action often associated with women, suggested that there were gender differences in the ways interests were conceived. Women often appeared to submerge their own interests through an identification with the well-being of their family or community. While some analysts argued that women's interests were vested in the family by virtue of their role in social reproduction, others argued that women were motivated by altruism and that interest theory was inappropriate for the analysis of women's politics. In this view, women were governed more by affect than by interest, in contrast to men, who were said to be governed more by interest than affect.

However, general theories of female collective action foundered when confronted with the varied character of women's politics, identities, and motivations. Women have constructed their interests in many different ways and have mobilized to demand rights of various kinds in many different sociocultural contexts. Feminist movements united women around common interests, but such unity has also been fractured by differences of class, ethnicity, religion, and other forms of social diversity. Sex is a necessary but insufficient basis for the construction of female solidarity, and it is not possible to speak of "women's interests" as if these were uniformly shared by women across the class and social spectrum. Moreover, interests cannot be understood as a mere effect of structure on agency, as in Marxist accounts of "objective interests." Rather, although interests are instrumental, they are nonetheless linked to identity formation and are constituted in discourse.

In recognition of this variability and diversity, the present author proposed two sets of heuristic distinctions with regard to women's interests (Molyneux, 1985; 2000). The first involved identifying a category of gender interests as distinct from what were commonly referred to as "women's interests." *Gender interests* referred to interests arising from gender relations; therefore, these interests pertained, in distinct and specific ways, to both men and women. A second distinction identified two ways in which women's gender interests could be derived: *practical* interests, those concerned with the satisfaction of needs arising from women's placement within the sexual division of labor; and *strategic* interests, those involving attempts to transform social relations in order to improve women's position and to secure a more lasting repositioning of women within the gender order and within society at large.

The intrinsically political and potentially transformative nature of strategic interests distinguished them from practical interests. Practical interests are, however, no less "real" than strategic interests, and no static opposition exists between the two categories. Practical interests could be transformed through political action into strategic demands, as when poor women mobilizing around practical gender interests engage in struggles that enhance their ability to satisfy their practical and their strategic interests simultaneously. These distinctions have been adapted to develop guidelines for gender policy and planning and have served as a critique of state programs that failed to address unequal and oppressive gender relations.

See Also

COMMUNITY POLITICS; CONFLICT RESOLUTION: MEDIATION AND NEGOTIATION; INTERNATIONAL RELATIONS; POLITICAL PARTICIPATION; POLITICAL REPRESENTATION; POLITICS AND THE STATE: OVERVIEW; POWER

References and Further Reading

Jonasdottir, A. G. 1988. On the concept of interests, women's interests, and the limitations of interest theory. In K. B. Jones and A. G. Jonasdottir, eds., *The political interests of gender,* 33–65. London: Sage.

Molyneux, M. 2000. Analysing women's movements. In Maxine Molyneux, ed., *Women's movements in international perspective.* London: Macmillan.

———. 1985. Mobilisation without emancipation? Women's interests, state, and revolution in Nicaragua. *Feminist Studies* 11(Summer): 227–254.

Moser, C. 1989. Gender planning in the third world: Meeting practical and strategic needs. *World Development* 17(11): 1799–1825.

Maxine Molyneux

INTERIOR DESIGN AND DECORATION

Ever since humans began constructing shelters, they have constantly refined their designs to serve the activities of daily life, and for much of that time they have also ornamented them to give pleasure and convey social status. These two goals, functional and aesthetic, are reflected in the present distinction between interior design, which addresses the ways a building's interior supports people's activities, and interior decoration, which is concerned more with the choice and placement of finishes, furnishings, and art objects. The two professions overlap, of course: the interior designer makes aesthetic as well as functional recommendations, and the decorator must consider the way a space will be used.

Historical Background

For most of history, interior design was not done by specialists but rather was a collaboration between residents and the craftspeople who worked on the interiors. From the Renaissance to the nineteenth century, architects usually designed the interiors of their own buildings and sometimes even helped to create the furnishings and artworks. It was not until the late nineteenth century that specialists in interior design became prominent. The profession expanded throughout the twentieth century; by 2000, more than 60,000 interior designers and even more decorators were employed in the United States alone.

Interior design was dominated by men earlier in the twentieth century, but women became more prominent beginning in the 1960s. For example, the presidency of the American Society of Interior Designers (ASID) was held only by women in the 1990s, and by 2000, 85 percent of AISD's members were female. Women first entered the field as specialists in residential (home) design, no doubt because of societal constraints against their working with male-dominated commercial clients, architects, and subcontractors and because of their participation in domestic female networks. Most early women interior decorators and designers came from the upper socioeconomic strata, but the field has been democratized in recent years, especially in the commercial sphere.

Women pioneers in the field were known primarily as decorators. The American novelist Edith Wharton (1862–1937) also wrote an influential book, *The Decoration of Houses* (1897). During the first half of the twentieth century, women in England and the United States were responsible for important innovations: Rose Cumming (1887–1968) set styles in the 1920s with bold ideas and bright fabrics; Elsie de Wolfe (1865–1950) let light and space into cluttered, gloomy Victorian rooms; Dorothy Draper (1889–1969) was noted for her hotel interiors and bold architectural details; Frances Elkins (1888–1953) in the United States had an eclectic touch; Syrie Maugham (1879–1955) created a sensation with her all-white rooms; Sister Parish (1910–1994) introduced a "rich country" style characterized by comfort and intimacy; and Ruby Ross Wood (1880–1950) epitomized classical restraint. Women such as Sybil Colefax in Britain and Eleanor McMillen Brown in the United States founded important firms that continued after their death.

Contemporary Figures

Today many top women designers and decorators have headquarters in New York, Los Angeles, or London. A few noted names are Diane Burn, whose painted interiors are unique; Nina Campbell, who is also a designer of fabrics and finishes; Mariette Himes Gomez; Cecil N. Hayes, an African-American whose firm is based in Florida; Anouska Hempel, who is well known for her elegant hotel interiors in England and contintental Europe; and Rose Tarlow, who is a specialist in antiques. Margaret McCurry, one of the world's best-known women architects, formerly worked in interior design.

The Interior Designer's Training and Work

Most interior designers prepare for their profession through programs at colleges and universities. A few specialized professional schools also exist. Training should include not only design principles but also business courses, since many designers will eventually manage their own firms, employ others, and deal constantly with bidding and other financial processes.

Training and qualification programs can take various forms. In the United States, for instance, programs are supported by student chapters of ASID, design firms that offer internships, the Foundation for Interior Design Education Research (FIDER), continuing education, and individual mentors. The National Council for Interior Design Qualification (NCIDQ) administers professional examinations to candidates who have some combination of six years of education and experience in the field; those who qualify are accredited and may append the designation "ASID" to their names. The Interior Designers of Canada conducts similar programs in that country. The International Interior Designers Association is made up of educators and designers who plan educational, commercial, government, health care, hotel, and residential facilities worldwide.

Interior designers are responsible for planning most elements of building interiors, with the exception of load-bearing construction (which is designed by architects) and mechanical and electrical contracting. Designers analyze the client's requirements, activities, and lifestyle and integrate this information with their own knowledge of design. They then formulate concepts that reflect projected use, design principles, and the legal or code requirements for the type of structure being planned. The designer then presents recommendations, often in multimedia format, and after consultation prepares working drawings and specifications for non-load-bearing construction, lighting, materials, finishes, furnishings, fixtures, and equipment. During the construction and installation phase, the interior designer works closely with other professionals and subcontractors; this work includes preparing and administering bids and solving problems as they arise. Designers today assume considerable responsibility for compliance with government regulations on workplace safety and access for people with disabilities.

Interior designers may own and run independent businesses or may work within architectural firms. Work on commercial buildings produces the largest proportion of interior designers' income, but residential work is also important; of about 20,500 members of ASID, for example, 6,500 undertake only commercial projects; 4,500 only residential projects; and 9,500 both. Some interior designers also create furniture, fabrics, and other products, either independently or for large manufacturers.

Interior Decorators

Interior decorators are responsible for selecting and installing surface finishes (walls, floors, and so on), carpets and other fabric elements, furniture, and decorative objects. They may also design these for manufacturers. Decorators work on both commercial and residential projects; in fact, they are employed by a homeowner more often than interior designers are. They are often associated with retailers, such as furniture and flooring stores, where they advise customers; they may also style interior settings for advertising and display. Their work differs from that of interior designers in that they do not usually address construction planning or code compliance.

Interior design and decoration is a professional field that offers remarkable opportunities for women and has been very attractive to women. Women's increasingly dominant presence is certain to benefit not only the profession but also the clients and others who enjoy the results of the designer's work: buildings that function pleasantly, safely, and appropriately for their diverse human occupants.

See Also

AESTHETICS: FEMINIST; ARCHITECTURE; BUILT ENVIRONMENT; WORK, *specific topics*

References and Further Reading

Ching, Francis. 1996. *Architecture: Form, space, and order.* New York: Wiley.

Kirkham, Pat, and Judy Attfield. 1989. *A view from the interior: Feminism, women, and design.* London: Women's Press.

Massey, Anne. 1990. *Interior design of the twentieth century.* London: Thames and Hudson.

Pile, John F. 1988. *Interior design.* Englewood Cliffs, N.J.: Prentice-Hall.

Russell, Beverly. 1992. *Women of design: Contemporary American interiors.* New York: Rizzoli.

Wharton, Edith, and Ogden Codman, Jr. 1997. *The decoration of houses,* reprint ed. New York: Norton. (Originally published 1887.)

Jane McGary

INTERNAL MEDICINE

See MEDICINE: INTERNAL.

INTERNATIONAL ORGANIZATIONS AND AGENCIES

Numerous international agreements and treaties existed prior to the twentieth century, but it has been only since World War I that international organizations and agencies have proliferated. After World War I, a number of largely western state leaders met and agreed to create the League of Nations, an institution aimed at preventing future wars. While the League was unsuccessful in this goal, as evidenced by the outbreak of World War II, a commitment to creating international agencies survived the war and was repeated in the mid-1940s with the creation of a new group of international organizations including the United Nations (UN), the International Monetary Fund (IMF), and the International Bank for Reconstruction and Development (IBRD, also called the World Bank). By the end of World War II, it was considered unlikely that international organizations would actually prevent war, but it was hoped that they could address or manage a variety of issues, including establishing international labor or health standards, managing the international monetary system, promoting population control policies, and so on. In addition to international organizations that have been created by governments (international governmental organizations, or IGOs), there are also numerous international nongovernmental organizations (INGOs or NGOs) created by nongovernmental groups such as the International Red Cross (IRC), the International Planned Parenthood Federation (IPPF), and many others.

Within women's studies, there are a number of ways in which international organizations and agencies have been examined. The first is to document the number of women involved in an organization. In part, the purpose of this research is to discover barriers to women's participation in these agencies. These studies have found that women do not usually reach the upper echelons of power within international organizations, most particularly IGOs, but tend to be concentrated in secretarial or middle-management positions. Cynthia Enloe reports that nearly 90 percent of the secretaries and clerical personnel at the World Bank are women, while less than 3 percent of the bank's senior-level positions are occupied by women. Like wise at the UN, women make up roughly 83 percent of clerical and secretarial positions and only a small fraction of UN undersecretaries or assistant secretary-generals (Enloe, 1989: 121–122). A report by a UN Steering Committee on the Improvement of the Status of Women concluded in the early 1990s that under existing UN personnel policies it would take 50 years to achieve equality in numbers between women and men at the professional level (Kirshenbaum, 1992: 18).

A second way in which women's studies scholars have examined international agencies is to study the policies that they produce and the impact that they have on women. Studies like this reveal that reports and statistics generated by different agencies have often simply ignored women, their activities, their work, and their various contributions to the societies in which they live. Marilyn Waring has documented the ways in which women and women's work are made almost completely invisible within the United Nations System of National Accounts (UNSNA). This invisibility is significant she argues, because national governments and international agencies decide what is important, politically and otherwise, in part on the basis of various measures found within the UNSNA. What this means is that when aid donors use the UNSNA to decide which countries are the most "needy" and which projects are the most important; when governments base their economic policy priorities on UNSNA figures; and when multinational corporations decide where, whether, and how to invest internationally on the basis of what is recorded in the UNSNA, the absence of women and women's work from these figures makes it very convenient to ignore their interests, concerns, and demands (Waring, 1999).

Whether or not international agencies ignore women, it is often the case that their policies profoundly affect women's lives. IMF austerity measures, for example, are imposed on developing countries seeking loans to meet short falls in the balance of payments. When countries agree to these measures, they usually cut food subsidies, limit imports, and take measures to promote exports. Gita Sen and Caren Grown (1987: 34–5) note that IMF austerity measures can also worsen women's loss of control over land, reduce women's incomes, and move women into low-paying jobs within Export Processing Zones.

It is important to note that the impact of international agencies on women will differ dramatically depending on the historical and political context in which the organization is located as well as the race, class, and ethnicity of the women at whom the agencies' policies are aimed. The International Planned Parenthood Federation (IPPF) provides a good illustration, for it has had a variety of effects on women. On the one hand, it is an international organization that has been active in providing birth control and contraceptive services to women throughout the world, and this has benefited many women. On the other hand, the norms by which the IPPF operated throughout much of its history were based on an assumption that global stability would be enhanced if birthrates were reduced in developing countries. This has meant, according to many observers, that the IPPF has often been involved in coercive and dangerous population control programs, usually aimed at poor and rural women. More recently, however, the IPPF has become the focus of New Right and fundamentalist attacks in both North America and many developing countries precisely because it is viewed as empowering women through providing them with access to birth control and abortion services. The orientation of IPPF policies is now shifting to promoting women's and men's reproductive and sexual health in ways defined by those people rather than imposed by an international agency (Whitworth, 1994: chapter 4). Thus a single international organization has meant a variety of things to different women, depending on when and where one studies it.

International agencies can also serve as a vehicle for change for women. Some women have used NGOs, both national and international, as a medium through which to organize in order to lobby governments and international agencies as well as to monitor national and international issues. These nongovernmental organizations include Development Alternatives with Women for a New Era (DAWN), the International Lesbian and Gay Association (ILGA), the Women's International League for Peace and Freedom (WILPF), the African Association of Women for Research and Development (AAWORD), the Greenbelt Movement in Kenya, the Coalition on Trafficking in Women, and many others (Peterson and Runyan, 1999, chapter 5; Stienstra, 1994). International governmental organizations have also addressed women and women's issues. The United Nations declared a Year for Women (1975) and then a Decade for Women (1976–1985), and while women's lives were not necessarily transformed as a result, these declaration did put women's concerns, and women themselves, on the agenda of various international institutions.

This has already had an impact on some policy proposals emerging from international organizations. At the UN Conference on Human Rights in Vienna in 1993, delegates agreed to a series of resolutions that recognized women's human rights as an inalienable, integral, and indivisible part of universal human rights and condemned violence against women in both their public and their private lives. The conference delegates also demanded the eradication of sexual harassment, exploitation, and trafficking in women. Similarly, in 1994 UN Conference on Population and Development in Cario supported in its Programme of Action the importance of empowering women through providing them with access to education, as well as the importance of sharing responsibilities within the home in caring for children and performing household tasks. Delegates also acknowledged the right of all people to decide if, when, and how often they should reproduce.

The Fourth UN Conference on Women in Beijing in 1995 and the parallel NGO Forum were considered an enormous success, attracting some thirty thousand women to the NGO Forum and 189 governments to the formal conference. Though faced with backlash, both within China and beyond, the Platform for Action that emerged from Beijing made a number of important advances, including references to the family "in its various forms," the recognition that human rights of women include their right to decide freely on matters relating to their sexuality and reproductive health, the eradication of violence against girls, an end to female genital mutilation, and an agreement to develop strategies to alleviate poverty (Meyer and Prügl, 1999: 184–189).

These resolutions are significant not only because women's issues are being politicized, but, more importantly, because that politicization is being shaped at least in part by feminist activists who have found spaces within existing international agencies to present and promote their views. There is often a clear link in these cases between NGOs and IGOs, for it is increasingly through NGOs that women are most effectively shaping the policies and strategies of IGOs and are being recognized as important contributors to dialogues and discussions about international issues. In this way, women have found that not merely are they affected by the policies of international organizations and agencies, but they can also, through effective mobilizing, shape and influence those policies.

See Also

DAWN MOVEMENT; DEVELOPMENT: OVERVIEW; ECONOMY: OVERVIEW; NONGOVERNMENTAL ORGANIZATIONS

References and Further Reading

Enloe, Cynthia. 1989. *Bananas, beaches, and bases: Making feminist sense of international politics.* London: Pandora.

Kirshenbaum, Gayle. 1992. Inside the world's largest men's club. *Ms.* 3(2): 16–19.

Meyer, Mark K., and Elisabeth Prügl, eds. 1999. *Gender politics in global governance.* Lanham, Md.: Rowman and Little field.

Peterson, V. Spike, and Anne Sisson Runyan. 1999. *Global gender issues,* 2nd ed. Boulder, Col.: Westview.

Sen, Gita, and Caren Grown. 1987. *Development, crises, and alternative visions: Third World women's perspectives.* New York: Monthly Review.

Stienstra, Deborah. 1994. *Women's movements and international organizations.* London: Macmillan.

Waring, Marilyn. 1999. *Counting for nothing: What men value and what women are worth,* 2nd ed. Toronto: University of Toronto Press.

Whitworth, Sandra. 1994. *Feminism and international relations: Towards a political economy of gender in interstate and non governmental institutions.* London: Macmillan.

Sandra Whitworth

INTERNATIONAL RELATIONS

International relations (IR) is a discipline whose focus of study is world politics, especially relations between states. It is often argued that IR has been constructed around the experiences of (elite western) men, their states, and their wars; and IR has proved one of the disciplines most resistant to feminist scholarship, which has made its mark only since about 1988.

IR Perspectives

IR is a relatively new academic discipline, founded first in the United Kingdom in 1919 in the wake of World War I to study the causes of war with the hope of preventing future wars. Its internationalist and liberal beginnings were discredited by the conflicts of the 1930s, the failure of the League of Nations, and the outbreak of World War II. Since then, IR has been dominated by scholars from the United States and by neorealist perspectives. Predominantly, they see as the key unit of analysis sovereign states, existing in a world of ungoverned anarchy, of power and conflict, where national or state security becomes military security.

There have long been other, though marginal, perspectives in IR. Pluralists see a world of interdependence, of cooperation as well as conflict, and study nonstate actors, including multinational companies and nongovernmental organizations like Greenpeace or the Catholic church. Structuralists see a world of grossly unequal power relations, domination, dependence, and exploitation, where class is a key analytic category. Since the oil crises of the early 1970s, the study of international political economy has been allowed "in," though often in a "states and markets" form that does not affect neorealism's world view. Recently, critical theorists have sought to bring theoretical challenges from other social sciences into the discipline, accusing it of not reflecting on its own knowledge-making politics, and not listening to the many "other voices" in the world. It was caught entirely by surprise by the end of the cold war, the primary framing device for most of its practitioners, and by the subsequent upsurge of nationalist movements and identity conflicts.

Feminist IR

Until very recently—and still, in many places—women were virtually invisible in IR, and feminist scholarship was ignored. The discipline tended to disregard gender, as if diplomacy, war, and trade were men's business, or as if men and women were affected identically by world politics. These assumptions remained unchallenged owing to the small number of women, and the even smaller number of feminists, in the discipline, and to its association with "high politics," especially with defense and foreign policy. Women's relegation to the domestic sphere rather than the public and political sphere meant that the citizen, the statesman, and the soldier became male, and (elite western) men's interests and experiences informed the discipline's theorizing.

There has been considerable writing about, and often by, women with regard to aspects of international relations—for example, war and peace. In recent decades, also, feminist research has told us much about women and development and women and citizenship. These writings were not admitted to a discipline that often defended narrow and exclusive intellectual borders and frequently ignored or dismissed writings from outside the academy. Then a challenge came from the London School of Economics, where Fred Halliday was a prime mover in the first feminist master's IR course. *Millennium* published the first special issues of an IR journal on "Women and IR" (1988), and Rebecca Grant and Kathleen Newland edited the collection *Gender and International Relations* (1991). The shift from "women" to "gender" reflected the structuring effects of gender in IR and drew on vibrant and sophisticated feminist scholarship beyond the discipline.

At the same time, there were feminist moves in the United States, the heartland of IR in both numbers and power. In 1988 the project "The Gendered Construction of the State/Society: Its Implications for IR," with Ann Tickner as director, gathered feminists from inside and outside the discipline. There followed a series of conferences, strategic interventions in the discipline, and the growth of a small but determined feminist IR community. The conferences included the workshop "Women, the State and War" workshop in 1989 and the "Gender and IR" in 1990, with papers published in a collection edited by V. Spike Peterson (1992).

The first specifically directed feminist international politics text came from outside the discipline, from a feminist specializing in comparative government, Cynthia Enloe (1990). She asked: Where are women in international politics? and concluded that women are an intrinsic part of IR, keeping military bases and international tourism and debt repayment strategies going, for example. She maintained that IR was thoroughly gendered, and that it depended on particular constructions of masculinity and femininity. She also included different women's views and stories from different parts of the world.

The first special issue on feminist IR in a North American IR journal (*Alternatives,* 1993) was edited by Christine Sylvester, whose own book on feminist IR theory was published in 1994. Feminist IR textbooks have proliferated (Peterson and Runyan, 1993; Pettman, 1996; Tikner, 1992; Steans, 1998), as have writings that focus explicitly on sexuality, and on the "man" question in IR, exploring different constructions and functions of masculinity in international politics (for example, Zalewski and Parpart, 1998). The main (US-dominated) International Studies Association has an energetic and productive section on feminist theory and gender studies, begun in 1989, with a women's caucus since 1994. The section now runs the Web site Femisa and its list server. *The International Feminist Journal of Politics,* the first feminist IR journal (with IR broadly defined) was launched in 1999.

Despite this remarkable growth and consolidation, there are still few women and even fewer feminist IR academics. Newer "second generation" feminist scholars are making important contributions, often extending the discipline's reach to nonwestern sites (Moon, 1997). Postgraduate students coming from a wide range of academic and other backgrounds form an especially important element of the feminist IR community. Overall, this community is engaged in extensive reconstruction on the basis of women's experiences and gendered explorations of masculinist and universalizing power relations in both the discipline and the world.

Feminist IR has demonstrated that women are present in state politics and foreign policy making, in international organizations and state armed forces, for example, though it argues that they are often in a gendered division of labor that leaves few women in powerful positions and most in feminized or support roles. Women are workers on the global assembly line, international migrant laborers, and activists in nationalist movements. They are often the majority in social movements with international links or an international focus, such as peace and environmental protest groups and nongovernmental development organizations. Increasingly, women's organizations themselves have transnational links or interests.

Feminist IR sees gender relations as power relations, reflecting and reinforcing particular constructions of masculinity and femininity. The discipline, like the international media, was surprised when the invasion of Kuwait and the Gulf War revealed hundreds of thousands of Asian women workers in the Persian Gulf, many of them domestic workers. They were one example of the growing feminization of international labor migration, and they were also seen as an example of gendered politics of foreign debt and "structural adjustment" policies imposed by the IMF and World Bank. They were part of an international traffic in women, where poorer states such as the Philippines and Sri Lanka "export" women's labor in their search for hard currency in the form of remittances, and in turn development policies and restructuring dislocate and impoverish people, leading them to new income-seeking strategies.

The Gulf War was also the first in which the international media focused on women, indeed mothers, as soldiers. Soldiers, like citizens, were long assumed to be male, the protectors, while women (and children) were the protected, those for whom the soldiers fought. This problematic distinction concealed the fact that women have often fought in wars and other armed struggles, and, in representing men as active citizens and women as dependent, compromised women's claims to full citizenship. Since the 1980s, many young women have joined state armed forces, though usually with restrictions on their roles. The furious debates in many states about women and gays in the military, often represented as alternative categories, reveal that particular kinds of heterosexual masculinity are often presumed necessary for soldiering.

The Gulf War also demonstrated the symbolic use of women to mark boundaries of difference and danger in international politics. The international media contrasted the images of U.S. women tank drivers and Saudi Arabian veiled women forbidden to drive cars to suggest a broader contrast between first world and third world, liberated and oppressed peoples and progressive and backward cultures that seemed to be based on a racist and imperialist understanding of the world. It also may have reflected a view of women as national or community possessions, and as physical and cultural reproducers, as "nationalist wombs" (Enloe, 1990: 54). Such constructions make women especially vulnerable to rape during war, to demonstrate their men's "failure" as protectors and to terrorize and humiliate both individuals and communities. However, more recently women's movements in different states and women's international alliances against rape and violence have brought women's rights onto the international agenda.

Women's relations with state, nation, and war suggest that it is difficult for them to be treated as subjects in the practice or study of international relations. It is difficult to "write" women into these relations. The sheer weight of domination and the devastating impact of militarization, war, and ethnic-nationalist and communalist violence, of exploitation and impoverishment, means that making women visible in IR could reinforce images of women as victims. An alternative reading that gives agency to women would also analyze women as active in exclusivist nationalist or fundamentalist movements, including those directed against other women. But there is also much to learn about women's strategies for progressive change.

An expanded and more inclusive IR would need to deal with the vast scope and apparently endless variety of experiences and relations. Feminist IR confronts the usual issues of feminist research and the complex relations between feminist academics and other women, including those they teach or write about. These issues are intensified by the discipline's concentration in the rich, white West. Now, however, there is much writing by third world feminists and by or about women, including rural poor and indigenous women, in settler states and other problematic contexts.

Feminist IR is cross-cultural and transnational. It is crucial, then, to ask not only "Where are the women?" but "Which women?" The huge international processes of colonization, immigration, and nation- and state-making have generated an international power grid in which class, race, nationality, dominant or minority status, religion, and language mesh with gender; thus "difference" implies power relations between women as well as between men and women.

Feminist IR is a huge project, both in terms of the resistance of its "father" or "master" discipline and in terms of the scope of women's different experiences worldwide. At the same time, the relentless globalization and the transnational impact of militarization, for example, need to be contested across, as well as within state boundaries. There is a long tradition of women politicking internationally, especially since the Nairobi conference in 1985. This organizing influenced international women's conferences in Rio, Vienna, Cairo, and Beijing. Such links, along with transnational feminist research, form a working basis for more internationalized feminism, in the academy and in the real world.

See Also

DEVELOPMENT: OVERVIEW; ECONOMY: GLOBAL RESTRUCTURING; GLOBALIZATION; HUMAN RIGHTS; IMMIGRATION; MILITARY; MULTINATIONAL CORPORATIONS; NATION AND NATIONALISM; NONGOVERNMENTAL ORGANIZATIONS (NGOS); PEACE MOVEMENTS, *all regions*

References and Further Reading

Alternatives. 1993. Vol. 18, Special issue: Feminists write IR.

Enloe, Cynthia. 1990. *Bananas, beaches, and bases: Making feminist sense of international politics.* London: Pandora.

Grant, Rebecca, and Kathleen Newland, eds. 1991. *Gender and international relations.* Milton Keynes: Open University Press.

Millennium. 1988. Vol. 17, Special issue on women and international relations.

Moon, Katherine. 1997. *Sex among allies: Military prostitution in US-Korean relations.* New York: Columbia University Press.

Peterson, V. Spike, ed. 1992. *Gendered states: Feminist (re)visions of international relations theory.* Boulder, Col.: Lynne Reinner.

Peterson, V. Spike, and Anne Runyan. 1993. *Global gender issues.* Boulder, Col.: Westview.

Pettman, Jan Jindy. 1996. *Worlding women: A feminist international politics.* London and New York: Routledge.

Steans, Jill. 1998. *Gender and international relations: An introduction.* Cambridge: Polity.

Sylvester, Christine. 1994. *Feminist theory and international relations in a postmodern era.* Cambridge: Cambridge University Press.

Tikner, J. Ann. 1992. *Gender in international relations.* New York: Columbia University Press.

Zalewski, Marysia, and Jane Parpart, eds. 1998. *The "man" question in international relations.* Boulder, Col.: Westview.

Femisa web address: <http://csf.colorado.edu/isa/sections/ftgs/>.

Jan Jindy Pettman

INTERNATIONAL WOMEN'S HEALTH MOVEMENT

See GLOBAL HEALTH MOVEMENT.

INTERNATIONAL WOMEN'S DAY

The origins of International Women's Day (IWD) go back to the late nineteenth and the early twentieth century. On 8 March 1857, women from the garment and textile industry in New York City—many of whom were widowed and poverty-stricken—formed a long cortege and carried picket signs protesting their low wages, their twelve-hour working day, and their increasing workload. They called for improved working conditions, better wages for women, and in general equal rights for women workers. This march was dispersed by the police; some women were arrested, and some were trampled in the confusion.

Fifty-one years later, on 8 March 1908, workers from the same industry went on strike, for similar reasons. On this day, thousands of women marched to protest child labor and to demand safe and reasonable working conditions and the the right to vote. This demonstration drew the attention of Clara Zetkin, a German labor leader, who in turn brought the issues to the attention of the International Conference of Socialist Women.

In 1910, at the second International Conference of Socialist Women in Copenhagen, Zetkin suggested an international women's day to honor the movement for women's rights and to help women achieve universal suffrage. Her motion was passed unanimously by the participants—more than 100 women representing 17 countries, including the first three women elected to the Finnish parliament. This conference did not set an official date for the observance; but in 1911, International Women's Day was observed on 19 March in Austria, Denmark, Germany, and Switzerland, where more than one million women and men attended rallies.

On 25 March 1911, a fire at the Triangle Shirtwaist Factory in New York City took the lives of more than 140 working girls, most of them Italian and Jewish immigrants. This disaster was attributed to substandard working conditions, and the tragedy would be commemorated during subsequent observances of International Women's Day.

In 1913, Russian women observed their first International Women's Day on the last Sunday in February. In 1914, on or around 8 March, women elsewhere in Europe held rallies to protest war or to express solidarity with their sisters. By 1917, two million Russian solders had died in World War I, and Russian women struck for "bread and roses," again chosing the last Sunday in February. That Sunday fell on 23 February according to the Julian calendar then in use in Russia; but according to the Gregorian calendar in use elsewhere, the date was, again, 8 March. Political leaders opposed the timing of this strike, but the women were not deterred. Four days later the tsar was forced to abdicate, and the provisional government granted women the right to vote.

March 8 was officially recognized as International Women's Day by the United Nations during International's Women's Year in 1975. Today, women worldwide celebrate this day to give impetus to their role in working for world peace, although they are divided by national boundaries and by ethnic, linguistic, cultural, economic, and political differences. International Women's Day has taken on a new dimension for women in developed and developing countries alike. It is a day dedicated to reflecting on progress made, calling for further change, and remembering acts of courage and determination by ordinary women who have played an extraordinary role in the history of women's rights. In some countries, the work of the United Nations Development Fund for Women (UNIFEM) is emphasized. This fund provides financial support and technical assistance to innovative programs that promote women's rights and women's economic and political empowerment.

See Also

INTERNATIONAL ORGANIZATIONS AND AGENCIES; NONGOVERNMENTAL ORGANIZATIONS; PEACE MOVEMENTS, *specific regions*; UNION MOVEMENTS; WOMEN'S MOVEMENT, *all entries*

References and Further Reading

Coote, A., and B. Campbell. 1982. *Sweet freedom*. England: Pan.

Stevens, Joyce. 1985. *A history of International Women's Day in words and images*. IWD Press. (Cyber edition, Isis Creation.)

Internet Resources

UNIFEM webpage: http://www.unifem.undp.org.

UNESCO "Women Make the News" Project: <http://www2.unesco.org /webworld/march8/news.shtml>

United Nations Development and Human Rights Section: <http://www.un.org/ecosocdev/geninfo/women/womday07.htm.> (Also at <http://www.un.org/womenwatch>)

Beverley Perel

INTERNET

See CYBERSPACE AND VIRTUAL REALITY; DIGITAL DIVIDE; INFORMATION TECHNOLOGY; NETWORKS: ELECTRONIC.

INTERNET POLITICS AND STATES

Quantitatively and qualitatively, the Internet is changing the context for transnational political activity, with particular significance for women. Three areas stand out. The first and probably the most important area is the new potential for women to establish effective local and global political networks. The second area is the longer-term effect of such political community building: new international processes for raising the profile of women's concerns and for sharing solutions and programs cross-culturally. The third area is the collective thinking these new communities make possible, allowing women to move beyond patriarchal and predominantly state-constructed traditions and visions of politics.

Cyber Meetings and Politics

In the hierarchy of politics, women have historically been least evident in international relations. The international sphere is farthest from the private space of the home, to which women have traditionally been relegated; thus very few women have gained access to international politics. As a result, they have had little influence in this domain and have had limited opportunities to encounter one another internationally, to discover their cross-national political priorities, or to work together on these concerns.

For these and other reasons, networking was a priority in international feminist activism long before the Internet, but the arrival of the Internet brought a major increase in the quantity, the visibility, and the impact of this work, providing a new international space where women can make connections (Youngs, 1999b). The Net has transformed women's political environment and has opened up new paths for challenging male monopolies in global politics. Through this new medium, women have become international explorers and have made their presence known in Web sites that highlight their concerns, their political campaigns, and the ways they can make the most of information and communication technologies (ICTs).

The Beijing Conference and Beyond

The Fourth UN World Conference on Women in Beijing in 1995 and the first Global Knowledge Conference in Toronto in 1997 (GK97, organized by the World Bank and the Canadian government) were part of the dawning of a new Internet age of global feminist politics. Faxing had already become a useful technology for informational and campaign networking; building on this, women's nongovernmental organizations (NGOs) increasingly used ICTs, including electronic mail and conferencing. The Women's Programme of the Association for Progressive Communications (APC) was launched in 1993 as a global initiative for improving women's access to ICTs and addressing gender imbalances in policies and regulations affecting them, as well as issues related to the technology gap between the "North" (the developed nations) and the "South" (the developing nations); this program was the main provider of ICTs for NGOs and UN delegates in the preparatory process for the Beijing conference and at the conference itself (Harcourt, 1999). The focus was on training, support, information exchange, and of course networking.

This aspect of political work related to the Beijing conference was a catalyst for use of ICTs by women and women's organizations globally. A cybercampaign became part of the preparation for GK97 to increase women's presence: the initial list of 600 participants had included only 78 women, but E-mail and institutional lobbying were used to increase the women participants to one-third (Hyer, 1999). Online work also played a major role in the preparations for the Beijing + 5 review in 2000. Moreover, the Net has enabled women's NGOs to expand networks within networks, which link all forms of communications and distribution. This has been particularly important in flows of information in and between "South" and "North." Faxes, photocopiers, telephones, ordinary as well as electronic mail, Web sites, and on-line discussion groups are all used.

Redressing Inequalities

As of the year 2000, concerns centered on the fact that most of the world was not connected to the Net: worldwide, just 2 percent of people were connected; nearly 90 percent of Internet users were concentrated in the industrial countries; and about 80 percent of Web sites were in English. Women's access varied widely, from 38 percent of users in the United States to 16 percent in Russia, 7 percent in China, and only 4 percent in the Arab states (UNDP, 1999). Women and women's NGOs focusing on ICTs undertake all aspects of getting more women on-line, including policy and regulation, software design, access to software, familiarization with and training in technology, Web site development, and ongoing support (Harcourt, 1999).

Net-based debate, work, and political activism by and for women have encountered problems involving women's relationship to this technology and its potential to help them achieve their goals. In this regard, there have been theoretical and philosophical as well as practical developments, since a central theme has been challenging men's greater knowledge about and use of ICTs, and this has entailed a new emphasis on feminist critiques of science and technology and their social applications. Such critiques analyze cyberspace as a "virtual realm" in which women can meet each other away from the "patriarchal gaze" of everyday social settings and can develop new political modes and communities; these critiques also investigate women's potential to harnass and exploit the creative and radical aspects of ICTs. One prominent figure, Donna Haraway, has combined postmodernist thinking about feminism and "technoscience," emphasizing "knowledge projects as freedom projects" and arguing that "the shapes the world takes are conventional and revisable" (1997: 269).

Much new feminist thinking about the Net has involved "politics of place." The growing international networks of women not only make connections that cross various local forms of politics but also create new global communities focused on feminist issues, including violence against women and political, social, and cultural rights and repression. Arguably, such collective voices and campaigns and their presence on the Net represent the most radical and largest-scale challenge to the masculinist political frameworks that tend to omit the personal and the "private" (home, family, relationships, and work associated with social reproduction). Women and women's organizations are using the Net to convey to global audiences that there are many links between the so-called public sphere of institutions and decision making and the private sphere. In this and other ways the Net has become a tool for furthering long-established feminist theoretical and practical campaigns for an integrated approach to politics, which recognizes that social relations of power cross the presumed boundary between public and private and that these dynamics are crucial to global and local change (Youngs, 1999a).

See Also

INFORMATION REVOLUTION; INFORMATION TECHNOLOGY; NETWORKS: ELECTRONIC

References and Further Reading

Haraway, D. J. 1997. *Modest_witness@second_millennium. FemaleMan©_meets_OncoMouse©: Feminism and technoscience.* London: Routledge.

Harcourt, W., ed. 1999. *Women@Internet.* London: Zed.

Hyer, S. 1999. Shifting agendas at GK97: Women and international policy on information and communication technologies. In W. Harcourt, ed., *Women@Internet*, 114–130. London: Zed.

United Nations Development Program (UNDP). 1999. *Human development report.* New York: Oxford University Press.

Youngs, G. 1999a. *International relations in a global age: A conceptual challenge.* Cambridge: Polity.

———. 1999b. Virtual voices: Real lives. In W. Harcourt, ed., *Women@Internet*, 55–68. London: Zed.

Gillian Youngs

INVENTORS

To invent is literally to find. Thus invention in its most basic sense is finding: finding a new or better way (a process, method, or technique) of doing or making something; creating a new or improved material, drug, or medicine; developing a new apparatus or machine; developing a new plant or another organism or chemical compound; or creatively combining or applying earlier inventions.

Inventions, Discoveries, and Patents

Invention differs from discovery. An invention uses or applies a discovery, putting it into practical or useful form. The elasticity of rubber, for instance, was an easy discovery. But the person who applied that discovery to create the elasticized waistband invented something that was a great contribution to human comfort. To take a more complex example, the force of water sprays under pressure and the cleansing power of hot water and soap were known for centuries—but Josephine Cochran, of Shelbyville, Illinois, combined and applied these effects within a closed space to invent the automatic dishwasher.

Cochran obtained several patents (1888–1911), and finally sold his invention to KitchenAid; but many inventors, especially women, never patent their creations. Thus inventions also differ from patents. Every patent involves an invention (by definition of the patent office involved), but not every invention is patented. An idea need be neither patented nor patentable to be a true invention. For example, women who used half of a juiced lemon as a cervical cap, or let their babies smell stale, ammonia-filled diapers to relieve nasal congestion, were also inventing. But they would not have been eligible for patents even if patent offices had existed when they came up with these ideas.

Women As Inventors

To recognize women's inventive contributions, several guidelines are helpful.

Start in prehistory. Women, needing to gather for themselves and a child or two, most likely created two of early humans' first inventions: carriers (for gathered food and infants) and the digging stick (for unearthing roots, bulbs, grubs, and termites). Contrary to the stereotype, women also hunted and had formidable hunting "magic" in menstrual blood. Furthermore, much hunting was probably scavenging or mass drives over cliffs or into ravines, in which everyone participated.

Because women did much of the work of early human groups, they undoubtedly became the first and main technologists, with such fundamental inventions as food processing, storage, and preservation, culminating in the pathbreaking invention of cooking; fiber processing, spinning, and weaving (including combs, distaffs, or spindles and various kinds of looms); dyeing and its applied chemistry; pottery (including early kilns and means of potturning); and horticulture (deliberate cultivation, including early sowing, harvesting, and processing tools such as seed dibbles, hoes, spaces, scratch ploughs, and simple irrigation). Women almost certainly also invented herbal medicine, herbal contraceptives, and various other means of fertility control.

Include anthropology and archaeology. Women's prominent early role in technology is best documented by the division of labor in ancient and surviving nomadic and horticultural groups, especially as noted by recent, mainly female, anthropologists. Also revealing are explanatory and origin myths, taboos, and gender differences in burial goods—even the ancient skeletons of such groups. Recently, for example, an archaeologist found evidence in the spine, feet, and knees of female skeletons that these women had spent long hours kneeling, grinding grain.

When studying modern inventions and technology, examine the received definition of significance in invention. The "establishment" history of technology focuses on weapons and machines, beginning with arrowheads and the wheel—both assumed to be invented by males—and continuing through guns, bombs, steam and internal-combustion engines, rockets, and computers. This male-defined history values "high technology" and "pure" innovation, regardless of social or environmental effects. Women, however, tend to be socialized to ask the purpose of an invention, how it might help people or make lives more comfortable or fulfilling—and conversely to avoid creating harmful or toxic things. Young boys as well as girls need to develop these values.

In an overpopulated, polluted, hungry world, an effective and acceptable long-term male contraceptive, better plastic recycling, or the cheap, nonpolluting fertilizer technology invented by a teenager in the United States, Elisabeth Bryenton, in the 1970s can be far more significant than a more powerful internal-combustion engine or a faster computer. When forests are disappearing faster than they can be replanted, solar cookers become significant, enabling food to be cooked without firewood. The cheap, lightweight solar box cookers recently invented by Barbara Kerr and Sherry Cole of Arizona deserve world renown and distribution.

As higher doses of ultraviolet light penetrate the damaged ozone layer, attacking human immune systems, a crucial invention would be immune-system shields and boosters. Whether some general assault on the immune system underlies the AIDS pandemic remains to be seen. Certainly, a preventive, cure, or more effective treatment for AIDS would win worldwide acclaim today. The Chinese-American researcher Dr. Flossie Wong-Staal is a leader in this area. Among other things, she has created a promising vaccine using a small part of the HIV virus that remains stable through the virus's myriad mutations.

Point out barriers to women's achievements, including the linguistic and symbolic, but avoid focusing on barriers at the expense of achievement and avoid presenting women as victims. Consider using "gather-hunter" (rather than "hunter-gatherer") to describe that mixed form of human economy. Since in all such societies south of the Arctic, women's gathering provides 60 to 80 percent of the food, "woman the provider" joins "man the hunter" as a prehistoric hero.

As a symbolic barrier, consider a common metaphor for invention: building a better mousetrap. Women rarely patent animal traps of any kind and clearly would rather invent items for the care and feeding of animals. An inventive girl, seeing her inclination at odds with the dominant metaphor, may feel it is not acceptable or appropriate for her to invent.

Familiar barriers to women inventors include these. Women have less time, money, and self-confidence than men, and getting a patent takes all three. Girls have more responsibility, less time to daydream, less encouragement to tinker or fix things, and less latitude to explore than boys. They are often given dolls and cooking sets rather than chemistry or erector sets, and a new computer may go to the boy's room rather than to his sister's. Women are still often excluded from technical training and subtly or overtly discouraged from studying advanced mathematics and science. The message is unmistakable: tinkering, technology, and invention are male. Despite progress, these barriers persist.

Emphasize achievement and give effective examples for encouragement and role models. Women have nevertheless contributed far more, and more significantly, to human technology than is generally realized. Four very important modern examples are the DPT (diphtheria, pertussis, tetanus) vaccine, coinvented by Drs. Pearl Kendrick and Grace Eldering; the prototype heart-lung machine, codeveloped by Mary Gibbon and her husband; the cold-precipitation method of isolating factor VIII from human blood, enabling hemophiliacs to live a relatively normal life, invented by Dr. Judith Pool of Stanford University; and radioimmunoassay (RIA), coinvented by Dr. Rosalyn Yalow, a physicist, and her male collaborator, a physician. Dr. Yalow won a Nobel prize for this supersensitive diagnostic test, which could detect a teaspoonful of sugar in a lake 60 miles long, 60 miles wide, and 30 feet deep.

As these four highly significant inventions suggest, women inventors show a strong preference for the vital field of health and medicine. As the world becomes more crowded, disease has more and better chances to attack, and women's propensity for medical invention becomes ever more valuable. Thus women can truly be called the once and future inventors of the world.

See Also

ALTERNATIVE TECHNOLOGY: CASE STUDY—AFRICA; ARCHAEOLOGY; COMPUTING: FEMINIST AND PARTICIPATORY DESIGN; ENGINEERING; PLAGIARISM IN SCIENCE; SCIENCE: FEMINIST CRITIQUES; TECHNOLOGY

References and Further Reading

Barber, Elizabeth. 1994. *Women's work: The first 20,000 years.* New York: Norton.

Baskin, Yvonne. 1991. Intimate enemies. *Discover,* Dec.: 16–17.

Bindocci, Cynthia. 1993. *Women and technology: An annotated bibliography.* New York: Garland.

Dahlberg, Frances, ed. 1981. *Woman the gatherer.* New Haven, Conn: Yale University Press.

Lee, Richard B., and Irven DeVore, eds. 1968. *Man the hunter.* Chicago: Aldine.

Macdonald, Anne. 1992. *Feminine ingenuity.* New York: Ballantine.

Mason, Otis T. 1894. *Woman's share in primitive culture.* New York: Appleton.

Pennisi, Elizabeth. 1993. High-tech gene therapy to target HIV. *Science News* 144: 182.

Stanley, Autumn. 1993. *Mothers and daughters of invention.* Metuchen, N.J.: Scarecrow. Paperback ed., New Brunswick, N.J.: Rutgers University Press, 1995.

Tanner, Nancy, and Adrienne Zihlman. 1976, 1978. Women in evolution, Parts I and II. *Signs* 1(3: Spring): 581–608; 4(1: Autumn): 4–20ff.

Trescott, Martha. 1979. *Dynamos and virgins revisited.* Metuchen, N.J.: Scarecrow.

Autumn Stanley

IN VITRO FERTILIZATION

See FERTILITY AND FERTILITY TREATMENT; REPRODUCTIVE TECHNOLOGIES

ISLAM

Islam (meaning "submission" to the will of God in Arabic) is the name Muslims give to their religion. Islam claims to be a divine revelation communicated to the world through the prophet Muhammad. The doctrine and practice of Islam are based on the word of God as revealed to Muhammad and written in the Qur'an, and the sayings, doings, manners, and customs and the example of Muhammad's life (*sunna*).

Central to Islamic doctrine is the belief that the Qur'an confirmed other revelations. These earlier revelations, however, were incomplete, and because of defects in their transmission, interpretation was distorted by earlier monotheistic communities (mainly Jews and Christians). Thus the Qur'an was believed to correct and complete God's message, to provide guidance for all humankind, and to be the last, unchangeable revelation. Islam, then, is the culmination, rather than a rejection, of Judaism and Christianity.

For Muslims, the Qur'an provides the basis for a complete Islamic ideology—a system of ideas and doctrines regarding duties, ethics, morality, and law—and a reference and guide for a way of life under Allah's (God's) commands and obedient to His will. *Shari'a* (literally, a "way" or "path") is the name given to the whole system of the law of Islam, governing what are familiarly known as both civil and criminal matters, private or personal and also public law. Only a small portion of the Qur'an concerns legal matters; the Qur'an calls itself a *huda,* or guide, not a code of law.

The Development of Islamic Law

The formation and development of *shari'a* law took place over several centuries after the death of Muhammad. The responsibility of interpreting Qur'anic precepts and translating those interpretations into practical decisions devolved on his companions, known as the "four rightly guided caliphs." The period from the death of Muhammed (632 C.E.) to the year 750 C.E. saw the transformation of Islam from a small religious community in Arabia to a vast military empire stretching to the Pyrenees on its western frontier while, on the other, it stood astride the northern approaches to the Indian subcontinent.

The difficulties of interpreting ethical ideas and rendering them into law were compounded by this rapid acquisition of vast foreign territories with diverse cultures and heterogeneous peoples. These societies were more unambiguously patriarchal, more misogynistic, and more restrictive of women than the tribal societies of Mecca and Medina of Muhammad's time. The practices introduced by Muhammad within the first Muslim society were, in their own time and context, progressive; they were instituted in a context of attitudes far more positive toward women than those of the later Abbasid society. (Abbasid rule was ci. 750–1250 C.E.)

As Islamic society was transformed, many local laws were modified on the basis of Qur'anic rules, interpreted by judges and jurists of the time. It was also during this period that religious scholars began to voice their views concerning standards of conduct, expressing Islamic ethics and moral vision. These views later evolved into the early schools of Islamic law (*madhhab*). *Shari'a*—the divine law of the Qur'an—remains dominant in the Muslim world, not only among traditional legal scholars but also among modern politicians and ordinary believers.

Women in Islam

References to women in the Qur'an are found in many kinds of verses, including some that specifically address the wives of Muhammad, some that depict female figures in historical events, and some that merely relate rules of behavior appropriate to female and male Muslims. The Qur'an itself asserts that certain women figures of the sacred past serve as exemplars of sin and righteousness, weakness and strength, vice and virtue (Stowasser, 1994).

In those passages revealed to Muhammad in Medina, the Qur'an introduced substantial reforms affecting the position of women by creating new rules or laws and modifying existing customary practices (Esposito, 1982). For example, "women's right to inherit property was an Islamic decree that Medinans found novel and apparently uncongenial" (Ahmed, 1992). However, by the time of the classical Qur'anic exegetes and historians of the ninth to fourteenth centuries, Islamic tradition and law had formulated a theological-legal paradigm that enshrined cultural assumptions about gender, women, and institutionalized structures governing male-female relations and that mirrored the social reality and practices of the postconquest, acculturated Islamic world (Ahmed, 1992: 82). Once formulated, the paradigm largely prevailed, because of the absence of any large-scale external—or even internal—challenges or pressures to change.

Tenets of Islam Regarding Women

Female actors and subjects in Qur'anic history can be interpreted as religious symbols. For example, verses instituting rules of conduct, dress, and comportment for Muhammad's wives have been interpreted as binding on all Muslim women, since they are based on the *sunna.*

Muslims past and present, from all theological and political persuasions, including conservatives as well as modernists, claim that Islam was the earliest religion to emancipate women, giving them rights unknown in any other society at that time. This classic Muslim view—that women in pre-Islamic Arabian society enjoyed no rights whatsoever and that it was the Qur'an that introduced specific rights for women (such as the right to inherit property, to contract marriage, and to divorce)—pervaded almost all literature on women in Islam until relatively recently. Although serious scholarly work on Middle Eastern women's history has been limited, there is a general consensus that the Qur'an did introduce various positive changes and reforms for women, including outlawing female infanticide, enforcing the payment of the male dower (*mahr*) to the bride herself rather than to her guardian, and securing the right of a woman to inherit property and dispose of it as she pleased.

However, most classical interpretations of the Qur'anic legislative verses rely on the *hadith* as much as on the Qur'anic verses themselves. The *hadith* are a record of what Muhammad actually said and did and also a record of what his community in the first two centuries of Islamic history believed that he said and did.

Not everything that is at present accepted and established as part of Islamic tenets and laws regarding women rests solely on the Qur'an, or on direct interpretations of its text; these tenets include inferences and interpretations drawn from the "Traditions" (*hadith* and *sunna* of the Prophet), as well as the accumulated *tafsir* ("interpretations") of the classical Islamic scholars and exegetes. The Islamic paradigm of the ideal role, status, and duties of Muslim women was thus derived from the *tafsir* of male jurists and scholars, particularly those of the classical age of Islamic civilization.

An overview of its main teachings shows that the Qur'an refers to gender status and relations in both an ethical or universal and a contextual or specific sense. It accords equal status to both sexes in many of its verses on spiritual requirements and on the religious duties and capabilities of men and women. Yet in other, more specific verses it grants a slight edge to men over women, particularly in social and public roles (for example, in women's testimony as witnesses to business contracts) and conjugal and family relations (for example, a wife's slight subordination to her husband); see the Qur'an, 2:282 and 4:34, respectively.

The Qur'an also considers both sexes as having originated from one living essence or being (*nafs,* "living entity") and hence as enjoying equal status from the beginning of creation (Qur'an, 4:1). It therefore imposes on both sexes an equal obligation and duty in observing the basic ritualistic requirements of the faith—belief in the one God, praying, fasting, giving alms to the poor (*zakat*), and making a pilgrimage to Mecca if possible. Equal treatment in terms of punishment in the hereafter is also accorded to both sexes for any laxity in their practice of the faith or any transgression of what is prohibited by the Qur'an.

However, equally central to the Qur'anic precepts on women are those verses that allow polygyny (up to four wives), institute veiling or covering (*hijab*) and seclusion for Muhammad's wives, describe men as having a "degree of superiority over women for whom they are responsible in providing economic sustenance," imply a preference for the testimony of men over women in business contracts, and prescribe the right of female inheritance to the value of half of whatever her male siblings inherit.

Therefore, the message of Islam as instituted by the prophet Muhammad's teachings and practice in his lifetime include two tendencies that are in tension with each other (Ahmed, 1992). The Qur'an strongly advocated ethical egalitarianism as a fundamental part of its broader or universal spiritual and moral message. Yet patriarchal marriage and male dominance were also basic features of family and marriage as established by Muhammad in the first Islamic community of Medina. Examples of androcentric tendencies in early Islam include verses specifying women's rights and position relative to men's in matters of inheritance and marriage; these clearly mandated women's entitlement as less than men's.

This tension is a source of much acrimony, and of many competing interpretations, regarding sexual equality, gender rights, and gender relationships in Islam. Historically, orthodox Muslims view such regulations and practices as having been put into effect by Muhammad and as binding on all Muslims (Ahmed, 1992). Others, specifically the modernists, prefer the ethical and broader moral dimension of the Islamic message. They regard the regulations put into practice by the prophet Muhammad as contextual (*asbab al-nuzul*). As historically contingent expressions of fundamental principles, those forms are not necessarily binding on Muslims at all times in all societies; what matters, the modernists hold, is the principles themselves, whose interpretation and realization must move with the times.

Problems of Interpretation: The Qur'an, Shari'a Law, and Codification of the "Woman Question"

The history of the Qur'anic narrative and the developments of doctrinal teaching and legal interpretations in Islamic exegetic, or explanatory, literature have not always been well understood. Qur'anic precepts consist mainly of broad propositions, rather than specific formulations; as a legislative document, the Qur'an raised many problems without providing any simple or straightforward code of law.

An example of this ambiguity, and of the crucial role played by interpretation, is the Qur'anic reference to polygyny. Polygyny, up to a maximum of four wives, is expressly permitted by the Qur'an, but at the same time husbands are enjoined to treat cowives equally; if a man fears that he will be unable to do this, then he should marry only one wife. The legal basis of marriage and the legal basis of polygyny differ profoundly, depending on whether the ethical injunction to treat wives impartially was judged to be a matter of legislation or left purely to the individual man's conscience.

Another example of a Qur'anic interpretation contested among contemporary Muslims is the rule of veiling and seclusion (*hijab*) for Muslim women. Revelation of the *hijab* (which literally means "curtain") is found in several verses of the Qur'an addressed to the prophet Muhammad's wives in Medina (Qur'an, 33: 28–34). The rule of the *hijab* in those verses is intended as a way of covering Muhammad's wives from the public gaze, ensuring their privacy, and thus maintaining their dignity and status. This requirement was revealed during a period when large numbers of people joined the Islamic community in Medina. An increasing number of Muslims were coming in and out of the place of abode of the Prophet and his wives in order to go to a nearby mosque, which was also a public meeting place for all Muslims. By instituting seclusion, a distance or space for privacy was created between the Prophet's wives and the throngs of Muslims on their doorstep. During that time, this distance was considered appropriate for the wives of a now powerful and successful leader in a newly unambiguously patriarchal society of Medina Muslims. The saying "she took to the *hijab*" also emerged at this time; it meant that a woman had become a wife of the Prophet. It was in this phase of the expanding Medinan Muslim community, too, that verses were revealed to establish some rules of modesty, decorum, and conduct for Muslim men and women (Qur'an, 24: 30–31).

Soon after the revelation of the Qur'anic verse requiring the Prophet's wives to "take the veil," another verse was also revealed, advising the Prophet's wives, his daughters, and all Muslim women to cover their body with a *jilbab* (a long outer garment, like a cloak), whenever they were in public places (Qur'an, 33: 59). The intention of this verse was to ensure the safety of Muslim women and protect them from harassment during a difficult time for Muslims in Medina. The *jilbab* was also a mode of dress congruent with common cultural practices of that time; apparently it indicated that the wearer was a woman of a powerful or upper-class community and under its protection. The mode of dress itself was a form of warning to men who might harass or molest Muslim women.

According to one interpretation, veiling of the face and "donning the *jilbab*" are pre-Islamic practices dating to the Sassanid era, as early as the third century C.E. This custom later spread to many of the pre-Islamic Arab tribes in the Hegaz (peninsula of Arabia). Among the more sedentary tribes it was an indication of the social status of women. However, it was not a common practice among Arab nomadic tribes, slaves, or peasants. It was only after the Prophet's death, and especially during Omar's rule as caliph, that the interpretation of the *hijab* as female seclusion and segregation applying to all Muslim women was gradually accepted as an Islamic ruling. It was also supported by a later *hadith,* attributed to the Prophet, which said that a righteous Muslim woman should not reveal any part of her body except her face and the palms of her hands. This became known as the rule of *'aura* (literally, "that which is exposed or in a state of vulnerability").

Attempts by Modern Muslim Women Regarding Emancipatory and Progressive Interpretations

The gap between the ethical principles of the Qur'an on gender equality and the male-centered interpretations that, over time, were codified into law represents a challenge for modern Muslim women in their pursuit of equality. The endorsement of official androcentric interpretations throughout much of Muslim history has precluded many gender-neutral and other alternative interpretations. The sociocultural bias built into the interpretive process and the exclusively or traditionally male composition of its permitted exponents among *fugaha* and *ulama* (scholars) worked to disqualify and even suppress not only new interpretations but any endeavor to broaden interpretive practices and processes, especially by opening up the contextual and historical bases of interpretive reasoning.

Concerned with the attainment of a Muslim form of modernity, the modernist approach of the twentieth century saw the question of ensuring women's rights as essential to the renovation or reformation of Islamic society. That approach has been somewhat muted by the contemporary rise of various Islamist movements with backward-looking or "restorationist" agendas.

The more progressive attempts at reconstructing a forward-looking Muslim worldview can be divided into four types of approaches. First, there is the approach of some modern Muslims who are regarded as "secularists" by conservatives. Their writings include the few critiques that take a sociological approach, analyzing the social and cultural bases of early and established or classical interpretations. These analyses (see the writings of Nawal el Sadawi, for example) reject any notion of an originally progressive phase in Islam's history and claim that such a notion would be idealized if not mythical. Instead, analyses of this kind seek to show that original Islam was inherently patriarchal. They also argue that a gender hierarchy has operated through class structuring and within the cultural specifics of various Muslim societies.

A second approach, in recent years, is represented by attempts by female (and male) Muslim scholars as well as a number of Muslim women's groups to develop a new critique of the established interpretations within an Islamic framework. An avowedly Muslim orientation or perspective is evident in the writings of this larger group of Muslim scholars. The explanatory writings they have produced rely on a progressive reading of texts such as the Qur'an, the *hadith,* and the life histories of prominent women in early Islam. This approach also relies on the claims that Islam was progressive during its formative period under the guidance of the Prophet. It attempts to establish Islam as compatible with the emancipation of women through a critical review of conventional interpretive methodologies. It also calls for a holistic, contextual reading of the Qur'an that would provide an egalitarian interpretation and a positive legal and institutional view of women. Methodological issues loom large in this kind of progressive reading of the Qur'an (Wadud-Muhsin, 1992).

Not all of these theorists, however, depend only on progressive reinterpretations of the sacred and divine texts. A slightly different tendency—a third approach—is evident in the writings of some Muslim scholars, many of whom identify themselves as Muslim feminists or modernists, criticizing the use of other textual sources besides the Qur'an (for example, the *tafsir* or the *hadith*), and alleging that these sources have undermine the principles of egalitarianism within the Qur'an. They are highly critical of established orthodox interpretations and insist on rigorous analyses to establish reliable historical bases for such views (Engineer, 1992; Hassan, 1985).

A fourth approach applies "historicity" to argue that "cultural encrustations and bias" over time were absorbed and built into many Islamic interpretations, especially legalistic interpretations (Ahimed, 1992). Recognizing the complexity and ambiguity of interpretations of texts and laws, they call for a new *ijtihad* ("individual reasoning"). According to this approach, history holds out new possibilities for the actualization of the Qur'anic ethical and social vision—and for giving evolving sociolegal forms to those possibilities and understandings, forms that were not available to previous generations of Muslims.

Ultimately, all arguments calling for an effective progressive and emancipatory reading of the Qur'an and all its explanatory texts entail the will of Muslims themselves to devise and utilize new methods of sociolegal and religious learning, thereby fashioning an Islamic culture of modernity. This requires a dual recognition: of the moral autonomy and responsibility of the thoughtful Muslim individual; and of a need for *ijtihadic* reasoning to be conducted as a dialogue or as a community matter throughout Muslim *umma* (society).

Women and Islam in the Modern World

The Islamic world encompasses enormous complexity: of social forms and cultural configurations, of modes of consciousness and historical conjunctures. Within the many levels of Islamic society, Muslim women live under very different conditions. Muslim countries such as Pakistan, India, Malaysia, and Indonesia, as well as Tunisia, Morocco, Algeria, Kuwait, and Saudi Arabia, are examples. Accordingly, women's position and the influence they can exert over their own lives also vary considerably, both from one society to another and from one generation to the next (El-Sadaawi, 1980; Mumtaz and Shaheed, 1988; Shaaban, 1988; Smith, 1980; Stowasser, 1987).

In recent times, especially since the Islamic revolution in Iran, there has been a widespread Islamic resurgence among Muslim societies worldwide. In Iran itself, women, through various types of political, feminist, and women's movements, have participated in and contributed much to support the revolution of Imam Khomeini. Yet that revolution ultimately brought to power an Islamic regime that has made strong efforts to retract and obscure the few advances that women in Iran had made in the preceding decades (Tabari and Yenganeh, 1982).

In the context of a worldwide Islamic resurgence, the lives of Muslim women in various societies are fluid and contradictory. What women are and how they should live have become central issues in ideological debates about the nature of Islamic society and history. Controversies over the status of Muslim women are involved in overt political contestation over many other basic issues concerning the future of Islam. As a result, it is not just women's rights and interests that drive these debates about the position of modern Muslim women. Ensuring Muslim women's rights becomes even more hazardous and uncertain as Muslim women and their modernist supporters respond to a variety of state policies, ranging from secular to Islamist, both modernizing and religiously impelled. These contradictory state policies and ideologies provide a challenge for modern Muslim women, especially women who seek to participate on their own terms in efforts toward Islamic renewal or reconstruction and at the same time to achieve more egalitarian treatment.

See Also

FAMILY: RELIGIOUS AND LEGAL SYSTEMS—ISLAMIC TRADITIONS; FEMINISM: MIDDLE EAST; FEMINISM: NORTH AFRICA; HOUSEHOLDS AND FAMILIES: MIDDLE EAST AND NORTH AFRICA; RELIGION: OVERVIEW; SACRED TEXTS

References and Further Reading

Ahmed, Leila. 1992. *Women and gender in Islam: Historical roots of a modern debate.* New Haven, Conn.: Yale University Press.

El Sadaawi, Nawal. 1980. *The hidden face of Eve: Women in the Arab world.* London: Zed.

Engineer, Asghar Ali. 1992. *The rights of women in Islam.* London: Hurst.

Esposito, John L. 1982. *Women in Muslim family law.* Syracuse, N.Y.: Syracuse University Press.

Hassan, Riffat. 1985. Made from Adam's rib: The woman's creation question. *Al-Mushir Theological Journal of the Christian Study Center* (Autumn).

Mumtaz, Khawar, and Farida Shaheed. 1987. *Women of Pakistan: Two steps forward, one step back?* Lahore, Pakistan: Vanguard.

Shaaban, Bouthaina. 1988. *Both right and left handed: Arab women talk about their lives.* London: Women's Press.

Smith, Jane I., ed. 1980. *Women in contemporary Muslim societies.* Lewisberg, Pa.: Bucknell University Press.

Stowasser, Barbara F. 1987. Religious ideology, women, and the family: The Islamic paradigm. In Barbara F. Stowasser, ed., *The Islamic impulse,* 262–296. London: Croom and Helm.

———. 1994. *Women in the Qur'an, traditions, and interpretation.* Oxford: Oxford University Press.

Tabari, A., and N. Yeganeh, eds. 1982. *In the shadow of Islam: The women's movement in Iran.* London: Zed.

Wadud-Muhsin, Amina. 1992. *Qur'an and woman.* Kuala Lumpur: Penerbit Fajar Bakti.

Norani Othman

J

JOBS

See WORK.

JOURNALISM

Journalism is, of course, a topic with many aspects, but this article will focus on the feminist approach. Feminist scholars propose that a critical perspective on journalism requires recognizing that news is a gendered discourse, which both produces and reproduces particular constructions of masculinity, femininity, ethnicity, multiculturalism, sexual orientation, race, and class. For example, Rakow and Kranich (1991:9) have argued that news is a "masculine narrative in which women function not as speaking subjects but as signs." Woman as mother, the lesbian woman, the woman of color, the single woman, and the working woman are examples of how "woman" can function as sign in various social and cultural environments. These are also examples of how the meanings and implications of gender can change, depending on its interplay with factors such as class, race, sexual orientation, ethnicity, and religion. Liesbet Van Zoonen (1994:33), a Dutch scholar, suggests that "gender should thus be conceived, not as a fixed property of individuals, but as an ongoing process by which subjects are constituted, often in paradoxical ways." Sometimes, in opposition to the notion that news is a gendered narrative, other feminists and media scholars suggest that more coverage of women and more women journalists will contribute to a press that is more committed to addressing the actual concerns and needs of women around the world.

In different parts of the world, in different economic, political, and cultural contexts, journalism and the press have adopted certain ideologies: objectivity, a watchdog role, social responsibility, developmental goals, and sometimes the philosophies of political parties, for instance. Whether choosing particular topics, deciding what language to use, interviewing experts as sources, or selecting visuals to accompany written or spoken words, producers of journalism make decisions every day about how to frame a news event. Institutional, structural, and individual ideologies, such as the effects of a news organization's corporate goals and values or the education of journalists and their socialization into the news culture, function to frame, limit, and structure the content of and approach to news stories. Like other social and cultural institutions—such as other media, education, government, and the law—the press reflects mainstream and alternative ideologies and at the same time helps to produce them. Journalism and the press have the power to set the agenda for public discussion of issues and, through particular representations, to instruct us about what is and is not important in the world.

It is because of this agenda-setting function that the press has been an arena where feminists have fought for visibility, increased and more accurate representation, and a political and social voice. Because women have so often been relegated to the private sphere—that is, the family, the home, and the "personal" domain—organizations like the press can be a powerful way for women to enter the public sphere. While the private sphere has historically been viewed as feminine, the public sphere (which includes government, politics, and "high" culture) has been associated with masculinity. These connotations are apparent in all cultures, and particularly in western cultures.

In the context of news coverage, "hard" news is commonly understood to include international topics, economics, science, and politics. "Soft" news, by contrast, consists of more personal human-interest stories that are often also more local (as opposed to national or international); "soft" topics include schooling, education, the family, day care, and the like. The women's liberation movement in the United States coined the phrase "The personal is political," in part to address this divide between so-called public and private issues. However, although the boundaries of this divide may have moved, journalism still tends to categorize certain topics as "women's issues." For example, in a cover story in *TV Guide,* (October 9–15, 1999), Diane Sawyer was quoted as saying, "The definition of hard news is changing, and what was soft news is now hard news—for instance, a story about day care and its effect on women's productivity can be a lead story on the news with Peter Jennings. It's what women in the newsroom and women at home care about more than what's happening in Sri Lanka" (cited in Fairness and Accuracy in Reporting, FAIR, 12 October 1999). According to the article in which this quotation appeared, the influence of women on the news agenda has resulted in "more emphasis on such story topics as child care, education, health and the moral aspect of politics." FAIR noted in its analysis of this article that when the press reports the news as if "women's" concerns are human concerns, then issues like child care, health care, and poverty are considered "hard" news, and women can be understood as equally invested in topics such as economics, international affairs, and technology.

As a social, economic, and cultural institution, journalism has spoken, and often unspoken, values and norms governing the selection of "newsworthy" events. These values and norms are deeply affected by its "business" orientation, which makes news a commodity that is often used to sell advertising (Lupton, 1994). Events considered newsworthy are often dramatic, with an element of crisis (such as airplane crashes and natural disasters), are geographically or culturally close to the audience, concern elite people or elite nations, and are timely (Gitlin, 1980; Lupton, 1994; Tuchman, 1978). As a result of economic pressures, combined with criteria for newsworthiness, news in general tends to be less informative and more entertaining. Also, the press tends to polarize issues as two extremes or opposites: for example, pro-choice versus pro-life or infertility versus overfertility. (The term "binaries" is sometimes used, rather loosely, for such opposed pairs.) The power of the press lies not only in its ability to define a social issue that is worthy of news coverage, but also in how it communicates the ways in which an issue should be understood and what views on an issue are valid or invalid.

Journalistic Representations of Women

Representations in the press contribute to our everyday understanding of identity and experience, including our understanding of ourselves as gendered. Print news and broadcast news have historically underrepresented and misrepresented women. Mohanty, drawing on a global sample, has found that most women and most women's problems are not considered newsworthy; and that when women do appear in the news, they are often represented as sexual or are relegated to the private sphere of the home (Byerly, 1995). According to Tuchman's analysis (1978), the media reflect dominant social values and therefore often show women in traditional, stereotypical roles, or simply do not show them at all.

Interestingly, although women of the third world are at times seen in press coverage, they are rarely heard. Writing about population policy from a postcolonial, feminist perspective, Rashmi Luthra notes, "The term *Third World* conjures up images of poverty, desperation, chaos, and excessive breeding.... *Third World woman* conjures up images of the veil, the harem, the sati, the illiterate, the victim, unable to control her destiny. Historically, the 'Third World' has been represented in the West as the untamed land, the land of darkness, and the woman in this land as mysterious, unaccessible, oppressed" (1995: 197). Valdivia (1995: 15) has argued that the silence of postcolonial women in the media of the United States results partly from an inability on the part of the western press "to envision such women as speaking subjects on public issues." Images of women as silent victims are prevalent in the coverage of women's issues—for example, there are many pictures of women weeping (and usually holding at least one child) after a flood in Africa or during a famine, or after an earthquake in Mexico. Such pictures have connotations of women as emotionally victimized, and these powerful visual mages almost seem to be a substitute for women speaking about their experiences or speaking as experts on an issue.

Experts, authority figures, and other people who appear as sources in the news most often fall into certain categories (Lupton, 1994:25–26): political figures, celebrities, criminals or people accused of crimes, officials, sportspersons, and human-interest figures (including heros and victims of crimes and natural disasters). According to one monitoring group—Women, Men and Media (WMM)—female sources are likely to be ignored by TV correspondents; also, women's participation in the reported news is decreasing: for example, in the United States between January 1994 and January 1995, the number of front-page references to and photographs of women dropped.

To some extent, these problems with the representation of women may be due to a lack of women in journalism. According to a study by FAIR of 185 independent journalists and syndicated columnists listed in the *News Media Yel-*

low Book for Summer 1995 (a journalism directory), only 39 (21 percent) were women. Of these women, almost half gave advice: 19 women columnists focused on topics like nutrition, interior decorating, sex, family psychology, recipes, travel tips, or entertainment reviews (Flanders, 1995). FAIR also found that during the first six months of 1995, men wrote 93 percent of all columns on the op-ed page of the *New York Times.* In 1999, FAIR reported that female journalists were still outnumbered two to one by males. In 1998, female reporters made up only one-third of the correspondent corps and covered only 28 percent of the stories. In terms of news ownership, a survey by Broadcasting and Cable in 1998 found no women heading the top 25 media or television groups, broadcast networks, or major cable programming companies.

Journalism and the Feminist Movement

During the late 1960s and early 1970s, the media became an important target of the women's movement in the United States. Prominent figures in the movement and feminist media scholars publicly critiqued stereotypical images of women in the media and the effects of these images on audience members (Rakow, 1991; Van Zoonen, 1994).

Certainly, the press was taking notice of the women's movement—events like the protest against the Miss America pageant in 1968 were deemed newsworthy, and women burning bras, high heels, and copies of *Playboy* made compelling film footage. However, the coverage of the women's movement tended to focus on these "outrageous" protest's and on individual feminists, such as Kate Millet, who appeared on the cover of *Time* in August 1970 and was described in the accompanying story as a woman who seldom washed her hair (Douglas, 1994:150). Although in general the press endorsed some elements of the women's movement, such as equal pay for equal work, it also frequently misrepresented feminists as man-hating, hairy, aggressive, "radical," bra-burning lesbians. Although the news media of the 1970s did expose millions of women to feminist concerns (such as institutional sexism and racism, harassment, lack of child care, and unequal education), their coverage of these concerns was often ambivalent or dismissive. The depiction of feminism and the women's liberation movement in the press "suggested that women had only two choices of how to be and where to be: compliant, calm, and sexually rewarded in private; or aggressive, strident, and sexually mocked in public" (Douglas, 1994:184). Much of the criticism of "bad" feminists in the media focused on their physical appearance, reinforcing the stereotypical idea that a woman's self-worth is determined by her physical attractiveness and also reinforcing the tendency of media representations to polarize women as "good" or "bad" and to polarize women's behavior as "normal" femininity or inappropriate and unfeminine.

Twenty years later, the media routinely reported the "death" of feminism and a waning of feminist concerns, suggesting that discrimination and sexism no longer existed. The press often featured young women who expressed an aversion to feminism and considered themselves part of a new "postfeminist" generation. In her book *Backlash* (1991), Susan Faludi asserted that the 1980s had seen a powerful counterattack against women's rights—the backlash of the title—that is, an attempt to reverse the progress women had made and the victories they had won. Faludi claimed that the effectiveness of this countermovement was due in part to the way it framed issues of women's rights in its own language. For example, some press reports suggested that conditions such as a "man shortage" and an "infertility epidemic" were the price women had paid for equality or liberation. Press coverage of the United Nations Fourth World Conference on Women (in Beijing in September 1995) tended to focus on only three topics: Hillary Clinton's appearance; "free speech" versus China's "secret police"; and disagreements among the women participants. According to much of the coverage, diversity and difference appeared to result in bickering, indecision, and at one point a "shouting match." For example, an article in *US News and World Report* (11 September 1995) used these words: "Sharp disagreements over women's rights mark a United Nation's conference." Such reporting reduced the complexity of the dialogue among the largest gathering of women in history to "squabbling." Press coverage about issues of women's health, education, and economic well-being and violence against women too often took a backseat to images of stereotypical "petty" or "disagreeable" women.

Global Journalism

Despite their "global reach," contemporary journalism and the contemporary press tend to value western culture above all other cultures. Ella Shohat and Robert Stam describe this as Eurocentrism—a presumed superiority of European-derived cultures and peoples (Europe and the neo-Europeans of America, Australia, and elsewhere). As a result of this tendency, third world and minority cultures are often assumed to be "inferior," if they are visible in the press at all. Eurocentrism "envisions the world from a single privileged point" (Shohat and Stam, 1994:2). Western history, then, is valued and celebrated, while the non-West is represented only in terms of actual or imagined deficiencies. In fact, much of the mainstream press does seem to have a Eurocentric sensibility: voices, coverage, and representations of nonwestern women are affected by the privileged position of western culture. (They are also affected, it is frequently held, by the privileged position of masculinity.)

Nevertheless, there are examples of a progressive, feminist presence in the global press. Carolyn M. Byerly notes that between 1975 and 1985, women began to take an organized approach to changing their relationship to the male-owned global media industries and asks, "How has organized feminist effort, utilizing both mainstream and independent structures, expanded women's voices in world news?" (1995: 106). One answer to this question is the women's feature service project sponsored by the United Nations, and the Women's Feature Service (WFS) based in New Delhi. The original women's feature service project was an effort to increase women's voice in international news. During its five years of operation, the project increased the visibility of issues related to women and to community and national development. It also increased the number of news stories about women by about 1,200—most markedly in Latin America and southeast Asia. WFS is today the longest-lived and largest global news agency controlled by women and has served as a model for other feminist news projects. Among its goals were to determine whether and how the media helped to perpetuate women's "inferior" status and to explore how the media might be used as a vehicle for women's ideas and political power.

Another example of media projects is the Women and Media Monitoring and Advocacy Program, founded in 1997 by the World Association of Christian Communicators (Hermano, 2000). This program advocates specific policies regarding gender and communication, in conjunction with partner groups such as Isis International (Philippines), La Calandria (Peru), Mediaworks (South Africa), Women's Media Watch (Jamaica), WACC-Pacific (Fiji), and the Institute of Women's Studies in the Arab World (Lebanon). In addition, many international and local grassroots women's groups are working toward more visibility in the press and a stronger political voice in global news.

Finally, many feminists and media scholars see the Internet and other computer networks as a location for a new, more available, more open form of journalism. However, plans for privatization and commodification of the Internet may threaten the free access that the information superhighways promise. Some feminists believe that the Internet holds a promise of exchange and debate of information, without regard to gender, race, or ethnicity—that is, without regard to difference. Although it is unclear as yet whether this utopian vision of the Internet as a free, boundless form of communication will be realized, we need to develop more journalistic avenues, both in the mainstream press and in the alternative press, for women's voices, images, presence, and power to be seen, heard, and felt.

See Also

EUROCENTRISM; IMAGES OF WOMEN: OVERVIEW; JOURNALISTS; MEDIA: OVERVIEW; MEDIA: MAINSTREAM; MEDIA AND POLITICS; POSTFEMINISM; PRESS: FEMINIST ALTERNATIVES

References and Further Reading

Beasley, M., and S. Gibbons. 1993. *Taking their place: A documentary history of women and journalism.* Washington, D.C.: American University Press.

Byerly, C.M. 1995. News, consciousness, and social participation: The role of Women's Feature Service in world news. In A. Valdivia, ed., *Feminism multi-culturalism, and the media: Global diversities.* Thousand Oaks, Calif.: Sage.

Douglas, S.J. 1994. *Where the girls are: Growing up female with mass media.* New York: Times.

FAIR's Women's Desk. 1999. Action alert: Women have not "taken over the news." www.fair.org/fair.

Faludi, S. 1991. *Backlash: The undeclared war against American women.* New York: Crown.

Flanders, L. 1995. The pundit spectrum: How many women—and which ones? *Extra!* November/December. New York: Fairness and Accuracy in Reporting.

Gitlin, T. 1980. *The whole world is watching.* Berkeley, Calif.: University of California Press.

Hermano, T. 2000. Programme notes. In *Media & gender monitor.* New York: World Association of Christian Communicators.

Lupton, D. 1994. *Moral threats and dangerous desires: AIDS in the news media.* Bristol, Pa.: Taylor & Francis.

Luthra, Rashmi. 1995. The "abortion clause" in U.S. foreign population policy. In A. Valdivia, ed., *Feminism, multicultural, and the media: Global diversities.* Thousand Oaks, Calif.: Sage.

Mattelart, M. 1986. *Media, women and crisis: Femininity and disorder.* London: Comedia.

Rakow, L., and K. Kranich. 1991. Woman as sign in television news. *Journal of Communication,* 41(1):8–23.

Shohat, E., and R. Stam. 1994. *Unthinking Eurocentrism: Multiculturalism and the media.* London: Routledge.

Tuchman, G. 1978. *Making news: A study in the construction of reality.* New York: Free Press.

Valdivia, A.N. 1995. Feminist media studies in a global setting: Beyond binary contradictions and into multicultural spectrums. In A. Valdivia, ed., *Feminism, multiculturalism, and the media: Global diversities.* Thousand Oaks, Calif.: Sage.

VanZoonen, L. 1994. *Feminist media studies.* London: Sage.

Sara Connell

JOURNALISTS

Scholars and activists cite two major reasons for their interest in monitoring the participation of women in the journalistic workforce, the first having to do with concerns about equal opportunity in employment, and the second having to do with the question of whether women will bring a different perspective to the way news is gathered, framed, and presented to the audience (Gallagher, 1981).

As writers and editors who are directly involved with the gathering and dissemination of news and other information, journalists produce work distributed in a variety of media outlets, including daily newspapers, weekly newspapers, newsmagazines, television stations, radio stations, and news services such as the Associated Press. In all these media, men continue to dominate the higher-paying and most powerful positions.

Women in Journalism

Feminist scholars tend to spend more time studying images of women in the mass media than they do studying women's participation in the media workforce. However, the number of studies of women in the media workforce has increased.

In studying women's participation in the news workforce, it is important to examine the ways that women have created their own media to make their voices heard (Smith, 1993), even if the dissemination of these media is not as widespread or influential as the news messages disseminated by mainstream media. In nearly every part of the world, women have created alternative channels of communication, media monitoring groups, and professional organizations to promote the interests of women (Endres and Lueck, 1996; Gallagher and Quindoza-Santiago, 1994). These groups have challenged the established media not only by seeking more positive media portrayals of women but also by seeking more equitable working conditions for women media workers. Such challenges have come through requests, demands, lawsuits, boycotts, and the individual interventions of women media workers (Lent, 1991).

The United States can serve as a statistical example. When the first major survey of U.S. journalists in mainstream print and broadcast news organizations was undertaken by Johnstone, Slawski, and Bowman in 1971, women made up 20.3 percent of the journalistic workforce. In 1982–1983, when Weaver and Wilhoit conducted their survey again, women made up 33.8 percent of U.S. newsrooms.

Although such increases in the representation of women from the 1970s to the early 1980s made many observers optimistic about women's progress in journalism, women did not make the same inroads into the field during the decade that followed. By 1992, women made up only 34 percent of the journalistic workforce in the United States—an increase of only two-tenths of a percentage point since the previous decade. In the early 1990s, the typical journalist in a mainstream news organization in the United States was still a white, male Protestant, although women made up 45 percent of the journalistic workforce with less than five years of experience and 42 percent of those with five to nine years of experience (Weaver and Wilhoit, 1992: 4–5).

As was true in previous decades, the participation of women in journalism during the 1990s varied tremendously by medium, with women making up 45.9 percent of the staffs of news magazines, 44.1 percent of weekly newspapers staffs, 33.9 percent of daily newspaper staffs, 29 percent of radio newsrooms, 25.9 percent of wire service newsrooms, and 24.8 percent of television newsrooms (Weaver and Wilhoit, 1992).

Meanwhile, the U.S. Bureau of the Census reported that women made up 41.6 percent of the editors and reporters in the experienced labor force as of 1970—with the proportion rising to 49.7 percent by 1992 and 55.7 percent by 1996. These proportions differ from Weaver and Wilhoit's figures, most likely because the Bureau of the Census defined "journalist" more broadly, to encompass writers and editors who work for a variety of publications and organizations that produce written materials, including neighborhood newspapers, small magazines, and other specialized media.

Challenges Faced by Women

Several factors appeared to work against women's making as many inroads into the journalistic workforce in the 1980s as they had made in the previous decade; these factors included a slowdown in the expansion of the journalistic workforce and a decreased commitment on the federal level to affirmative action policies, particularly those applied to the employment of women in broadcast news organizations (Lafky, 1993).

For example, throughout the 1980s, traditional print and media organizations faced decreased profits because of an economic downturn and increased competition for advertising dollars from direct mail, cable television, and other media outlets. Weaver and Wilhoit (1992) estimated that mainstream print and broadcast news organizations employed only 10,000 more full-time journalists in 1992 than they had in 1982—a growth rate of just under 9 percent. In contrast, the mainstream journalistic workforce grew by an estimated 42,572 individuals between 1971 and 1982—a 61 percent increase.

Affirmative action programs first gained momentum in broadcast news organizations after 1971, when the Federal Communications Commission (FCC) added women to an equal opportunity rule that had originally applied only to racial and ethnic minorities. This legislation prohibited discrimination against women and required television and radio stations to file their affirmative action programs with the FCC and outline their efforts to implement equal opportunity employment programs. Under the Reagan administration, however, the FCC's commitment to affirmative action weakened.

Unequal Opportunities

Even when women were hired as journalists, they did not get as many opportunities as men to cover the most newsworthy stories or advance to the highest levels of management (Mills, 1988). Before the second wave of the women's movement in the 1960s, many women journalists were relegated to covering "women's" news. Women's pages, society sections, and broadcast news stories and programs aimed at women's concerns reinforced the notion of separate spheres for men and women. Men were most often in charge of reporting the public-sphere issues and events that dominated the headlines—subjects related to conflict, power, and influence, also known as "hard news." Women most often took responsibility for stories about noncontroversial domestic and social issues and trends in the private sphere, known as "soft news" (Creedon, 1993; Hosley and Yamada, 1987; Marzolf, 1977; Mills, 1988; Sanders and Rock, 1988).

Very few women have held the top jobs in print or broadcast news organizations (Mills, 1988; Sanders and Rock, 1988). Women in the media did celebrate in 1993 when Connie Chung joined Dan Rather as a co-anchor on the *CBS Evening News*, considered by many to be the most prestigious of the network news shows; but the celebration was short-lived—in 1995, Chung left CBS, just as Barbara Walters had lost her co-anchor post at ABC in 1978.

Just a few years earlier, a pioneer newswoman, Marlene Sanders, had noted that it was still being debated whether a woman's voice was authoritative enough to hold the nation's attention in the anchor position on the main news broadcasts (Sanders and Rock, 1988). Certain stereotypes continue to be reinforced by the staffing of anchor positions on television news shows; one joke in the industry is that male-female anchor teams often resemble the second marriages of some men, with a mature, seasoned newsman paired with a younger, pretty TV "wife" (Fung, 1988).

As noted above, women have challenged their underrepresentation in news organizations and in media coverage through requests, demands, lawsuits, and boycotts, and by lobbying for more positive media portrayals and more equitable working conditions (Beasley and Gibbons, 1993). Women undertook a long struggle to be included in previously all-male organizations such as the National Press Club in Washington, D.C. (where women journalists were relegated to the balcony when reporting on national and world leaders who addressed the organization) and the journalistic fraternity Sigma Delta Chi, now called the Society of Professional Journalists (Mills, 1988; Lent, 1991). Before the doors to these prestigious groups opened for them, women formed their own professional organizations, including Theta Sigma Pi (now known as Women in Communications, Inc.) and the now defunct Women's National Press Club.

Like women in other occupational groups, women in journalism, on the whole, make less money than men in the field. When Johnstone, Slawski, and Bowman conducted their study of U.S. journalists in mainstream print and broadcast organizations in 1971, they found that women made an average of 64 cents for each dollar earned by the average man in the field. By 1981, that disparity had lessened considerably, with women earning an average of 71 cents for each dollar earned by men journalists. The earnings gap closed even more by 1992, when the median income of women journalists was $27,669 a year—81 percent of the median income of men journalists, $34,167 (Weaver and Wilhoit, 1992). Still, while women have made inroads in the media workforce—as journalists and in other positions—during the past three decades or so, they remain underrepresented in the highest-ranking positions where policy is determined (Mills, 1988; Weaver and Wilhoit, 1991).

Women as Journalism Students

The past three decades have also seen changes in the percentage of women enrolled in undergraduate journalism programs at colleges and universities in the United States—the pipeline to many jobs in journalism. In the United States, men accounted for 44 percent of the bachelor's degrees in journalism awarded in 1971, but women began to outnumber men in these academic programs starting in 1977, after a 60:40 ratio had favored men for the four previous decades (Peterson, 1979). Since 1988, an average of 6 out of 10 students in undergraduate journalism and mass communication programs have been women. In 1997, 61.3 percent of the undergraduate students, 62.7 percent of the master's degree students, and 54 percent of the Ph.D. students in the field were women (Becker and Kosicki, 1998). In 1996, according to a survey conducted by Dan Riffle, Guido Stempel, and Kandice Salomone of Ohio University, 32.6 percent of the members of the Association for Education for Journalism and Mass Communication were women.

It is important to note, however, that not all journalism students receive their training in university-based journalism and mass communication programs. Some gain their training on the job or through internship programs. In addition, not all journalism majors end up working in newsrooms. Many journalism majors take jobs in related mass communication fields such as public relations and advertising.

See Also

JOURNALISM; MEDIA: OVERVIEW; MEDIA: MAINSTREAM; PRESS: FEMINIST ALTERNATIVES

References and Further Reading

Beasley, Maurine. H., and Sheila J. Gibbons. 1993. *Taking their place: A documentary history of women and journalism.* Washington, D.C.: American University Press.

Becker, Lee. B., and Gerald M. Kosicki. 1993. Annual census of enrollment records fewer undergrads. *Journalism Educator* (Autumn): 76.

Creedon, Pamela. J., ed. 1993. *Women in mass communication,* 2nd ed. Newbury Park, Calif.: Sage.

Endres, Kathleen L., and Therese L. Lueck, eds. 1996. *Women's periodicals in the United States: Social and political issues.* Westport, Conn.: Greenwood.

Fung, Victoria M. 1988. Sexism at the networks: Anchor jobs go to young women and experienced men. *Washington Journalism Review* (October): 20–24.

Gallagher, Margaret. 1981. *Unequal opportunities: The case of women and the media.* New York: United Nations Educational, Scientific, and Cultural Organization (UNESCO).

———, and Lilia Quindoza-Santiago, eds. 1994. *Women empowering communication: A resource book on women and the globalization of media.* New York: International Women's Tribune Center, Isis International, and World Association for Christian Communication.

Hosley, David. H., and Gayle K. Yamada. 1987. *Hard news: Women in broadcast journalism.* New York: Greenwood.

Johnstone, John W. C., Edward J. Slawski, and William W. Rowman. 1976. *The news parade: A sociological portrait of American journalists and their work.* Urbana: University of Illinois Press.

Lafky, Sue A. 1993. The progress of women and people of color in the U.S. journalistic workforce: A long, slow journey. In Pamela. J. Creedon, ed., *Women in mass communication,* 2nd ed., 87–103. Newbury Park, Calif.: Sage.

Lent, John A. 1991. *Women and mass communications: An international annotated bibliography.* New York: Greenwood.

Marzolf, Marion. 1977. *Up from the footnote: A history of women journalists.* New York: Hastings House.

Mills, Kay. 1988. *A place in the news: From the women's pages to the front page.* New York: Dodd, Mead.

Peterson, Paul V. 1979. Enrollment surges again, increases 7 percent to 70,601. *Journalism Educator* 33(4): 3–8.

Sanders, Marlene, and Marcia Rock. 1988. *Waiting for prime time: The women of television news.* Urbana and Chicago: University of Illinois Press.

Smith, Marilyn Crafton. 1993. Feminist media and cultural politics. In Pamela J. Creedon, ed., *Women in mass communication,* 2nd ed., 61–83. Newbury Park, Calif.: Sage.

Van Zoonen, Liesbet. 1994. *Feminist media studies.* London: Sage.

Weaver, David. H., and G. Cleveland Wilhoit. 1991. *The American journalist: A portrait of U.S. news people and their work,* 2nd ed. Bloomington: Indiana University Press.

———. 1992. *The American journalist in the 1990s: A preliminary report of key findings from a 1992 national survey of U.S. journalists.* Arlington, Va.: Freedom Forum.

Sue A. Lafky

JUDAISM

Judaism is one of three monotheistic religions historically rooted in the Hebrew Scriptures, a set of sacred books known to Jews as Tanakh, to Christians as the Old Testament, and to Muslims as the Tawrah (from the first of its three sections, called in Hebrew the Torah). The Scriptures record the early history and religious development of a people known first as Israelites (until the sixth century B.C., when the Babylonians destroyed the First Temple and carried its priests, along with the last king of Judah, into captivity), thereafter as Judeans, and ultimately, in English, as Jews. In their religious writings and documents, however, the Jews continue to designate themselves collectively as Israel, despite the supersessionism of the early church, which (ignoring the persistence of the Jewish people) had appropriated the name Israel for itself. The Israelite religion is the primary historical source of the three western monotheistic religions known as Judaism, Christianity, and Islam. The Israelite religion itself underwent a gradual transformation in the centuries following the Babylonian exile, until, after the destruction of the Second Temple by the Romans in A.D., 70 it emerged in the form now called rabbinic Judaism, which (with minor exceptions) is the basis of all forms of Judaism still practiced in the world today.

The ancient Hebrew Scriptures gave the world a new religious concept, YHWH (pronounced "Yahweh," this name combines the letters of the past, present, and future tenses of the verb "to be," signifying that God was, is, and will be), a God of history who first revealed his will for humankind through the medium of a people called Israel, to whom he appeared at Mount Sinai after the Exodus from Egypt as they journeyed to the Promised Land, and on whom he bestowed a body of religious law called the Torah (literally, "teaching" or "instruction"). The 613 commandments of the Torah encompass sacred and secular law, civil and criminal procedure, law of property, and law of persons.

Prominent in the last category is the personal status of women, which can be gleaned both from the Torah's specific commandments concerning them and from images of women portrayed in the context of patriarchal Israelite culture, with its worship of the original tribal god YHWH. Women's role and status in Judaism, as depicted in legal and homiletical rabbinic literature of the early centuries after Christ (claiming to interpret the Word of God), still rest solidly on these ancient sources—a fact that continues to affect the personal lives of thousands of Jewish women.

In traditional Jewish law (known as Halakhah, literally "the Way"), the theoretical status of women has changed surprisingly little since the editing of the Torah (which modern scholars date to the time of Ezra, around 450 B.C.) Classical sources of halakhic rules that still govern the lives of observant Jewish women include the Hebrew Bible (compiled and edited between 950 and 150 B.C. and finally canonized by the Council of Yavneh around A.D. 90); the Mishnah (a handbook of legal rules compiled in Palestine during the first two centuries after Christ and redacted around 200 C.E.); and the Talmud (a voluminous commentary on the Mishnah compiled in Babylonia between A.D. 200 and 600). There are actually two Talmuds. The earlier but less authoritative is the Talmud of the Land of Israel (also known as the Jerusalem Talmud), compiled in the Hebrew language in Palestine between A.D. 200 and 400. By convention, references to "the Talmud" always mean the later and more authoritative Babylonian Talmud, compiled in the Aramaic language between A.D. 200 and 600 in Babylonia (then part of the Persian Empire but conquered by Islam and renamed Iraq early in the seventh century). These sources were subjected to centuries of interpretation by rabbinic sages, a process that continues. In addition, books of Midrash (biblical exegesis) dating from the talmudic era contain numerous statements, both laudatory and derogatory, regarding the cultural image, social role, and legal status of women. The importance of these statements has not diminished over time; the basic rules in these classical texts continue (for Orthodox and some Conservative Jews) to define women's position in Judaism as one of subordination to men in the private cultural domain and virtual exclusion from the public cultural domain—an arena reserved, as in ancient cultures generally, for men only.

Patriarchal Elements in Judaism

The texts of classical rabbinic Judaism reflect the hierarchical social system called patriarchy. Patriarchies, by definition, subordinate women (along with children, slaves, and foreigners) by assigning them a lower level of personhood, as legally defined by the sum of rights, duties, and powers accruing to a given individual at a particular time.

The Mishnah, the first substantial collection of Jewish law, includes as one of its six divisions a section titled "Women," devoted to defining the status of women in relation to the societal norm, the free adult Israelite male. This article (leaving aside unverifiable claims of divine origin of rabbinic tradition and concomitant beliefs that women's status is ordained by God) analyzes the status of women in Judaism from a social scientific and predominantly anthropological standpoint.

The rabbinic concept of women's place in the cultural life of the people of Israel perpetuated patriarchal norms that had informed Israelite and surrounding cultures for centuries. Talmudic sages distinguished between the status of various *classes* of individual women in the private domain of Judaic culture (determined by their family relationships to men as set forth in the laws of marriage and divorce) and the relationship of women *in general* to the public domain of the culture (with particular regard to communal religious enterprises pursued in the public forums of synagogue, study house, and courthouse, from which women were routinely excluded).

Women in the Private Domain

In the sphere of private law, classical Jewish law divided women into two main groups: those legally dependent on specified men and those who were legally autonomous. This classification turned on a very specific factor, which still controls the matrimonial status of Jewish women—sometimes with unfortunate results: the presence or absence of some man who owned the exclusive right to benefit from the sexual-reproductive function of the woman in question

(Wegner, 1988). Such men fall into three categories: father, husband, or *levir.* The first two require no explanation; the third, a Latin word, denotes the brother-in-law of a woman whose husband died without heirs. The *levir* was bound by biblical law to marry his brother's widow unless he released her by a ritual called *halisah* (Deut. 25:5–10); without such a release, the sister-in-law remained a levirate widow (*yebamah*), tied permanently to her *levir* (even if he never consummated the union) and hence not free to marry any other man. Rabbinic law adopted this biblical rule, with the result that an unreleased levirate widow cannot remarry.

In the biblical and mishnaic taxonomy of women, three categories of female—(minor daughter, wife, and levirate widow)—were under male control, specifically with regard to the disposition or use of their biological function. Conversely, by the dichotomous logic that pervades the Mishnah, their three polar opposites—adult unmarried female, divorcée, and normal widow—were legally autonomous, because no man had the legal right to control their sexual-reproductive function. These three classes form mirror images of their dependent counterparts, especially regarding marriage and divorce. Thus, the marriage of a minor daughter (under 12 1/2 years) was arranged by her father, whereas an adult woman could negotiate her own. A husband could revoke any religious vow made by his wife that might impair their conjugal relations, but no one could countermand the vows of a divorcée because no one "owned" her biological function. Likewise, a husband who divorced his wife—whether for cause or for no stated reason, as permitted in biblical and Mishnaic law—could not restrict her sexual freedom once she was released; just as marriage signified the man's acquisition of an exclusive claim on the woman's biological function, so divorce signified his surrender of that right. Similarly, with levirate widows versus normal widows, the *levir* inherited conjugal rights over his brother's widow, as is still the case (although since the Middle Ages he has been required to release rather than marry her; this modification was necessitated by a ruling, traditionally attributed to the eleventh-century Rabbi Gershom of Mainz, that banned polygyny by Jews in the lands of Christendom). Even today she cannot remarry without such a release. Conversely, a normal widow could remarry at will, because her sexuality would revert to her own control on the death of her husband.

These ancient rabbinic rules, which are still enforced in Orthodox and Conservative Judaism (causing serious problems for thousands of Jewish women unable to obtain release from missing or recalcitrant husbands or *levirs*), reflect and perpetuate a biblical view of women's role and function within the private cultural domain. In the biblical account of origins, God created woman explicitly to be man's "fitting helper" (Gen. 2:18), subordinating her to him as a punishment for tempting him with forbidden fruit (Gen. 3:16). This emphasis on woman's place as childbearer and homemaker, typical of patriarchal societies, appears throughout the Bible (both Old and New Testaments—see Paul's strictures on the conduct of women)—as well as in the literature of diverse cultures of antiquity, including classical Greece; for instance, Plato speaks of the "ploughland of the womb," and Aristotle defines the female as a "defective male" (Plato, *Timaeus;* Aristotle, *De Animalivm Natura;* Wegner, 1991). It is thus a historical error to attribute the subordination of women in western civilization primarily to the influence of Judaism, as was done by some Christian feminists, whose conclusions were later disavowed by their scholarly colleagues (Fiorenza, 1983).

The Dependent Woman: Chattel or Person?

The perception of women as men's subordinates and reproductive vessels obscures the fact that women in the talmudic system were by no means entirely chattels; in fact, they enjoyed many of the rights, duties, and powers that define legal personhood. In private domestic or business transactions, the law treated women unequivocally as persons. The wife participated in a reciprocal nexus of matrimonial entitlements and obligations, performing specified household chores and producing a prescribed amount of economic product (yarn or cloth) in return for maintenance at a standard reflecting her social class. A seemingly unique feature in ancient systems is the Mishnah's specification of conjugal relations as primarily a wife's right and a husband's duty—in contrast to other traditional systems, including Anglo-American common law, which until the late twentieth century construed sexual intercourse as primarily a husband's right and a wife's duty. This anomaly may have resulted from the sages' misconstruing a technical term in Exodus (21:10) to signify conjugal visitation rather than the wife's right to shelter (which, as some medieval commentators proposed, was its more likely meaning).

Another important rule preserved the wife's title to any property she brought to the marriage; under this rule—in contrast to Anglo-American common law until modern times—such property did not automatically accrue to the husband on marriage. A woman also had the power to make contracts of purchase and sale, to appoint agents to conduct her business, to act as her husband's agent to sell his goods, and in some circumstances to sue her husband; for instance, she could petition the court to order him to release her from the marriage if he had infringed on her matrimonial rights.

The common denominator of a wife's rights in Jewish law is that they posed no threat to the husband's claim on his wife's sexuality. This was and is the only context in which Jewish law formally treats a woman as chattel; but the husband's claim on a wife's biological function gave rise to serious halakhic problems that continue to affect Jewish women in matters of marriage and divorce. Not only is the husband's claim exclusive, but it is technically unilateral rather than reciprocal. First, it is formally acquired by a (putative rather than actual) payment of bride price (*mohar,* which is similar to the Arabic *mahr*). In biblical times this went to fathers, who routinely betrothed their minor daughters—with or without consent—delivering them at puberty to the selected husband. Formally, the bilateral contract was between the groom and the bride's father rather than between the spouses themselves (except where a bride fully of age arranged her own marriage or consented thereto). Second, the basically polygynous nature of biblical Israelite marriage law meant that from a strictly legal standpoint the bride had no reciprocal monopoly of the husband's sexual and reproductive function. This inequality remains enshrined in the traditional Jewish marriage ritual, where the groom recites a Hebrew formula declaring that the bride is sexually reserved (*mequddeshet,* literally "set apart") for him alone, while the bride makes no response, remaining silent throughout the ceremony.

The *ketubbah,* a formulaic Aramaic document read aloud during the ceremony, states that the groom has paid the biblical "brideprice of virginity" (except in marriage to a widow or divorcée) and promises to give his bride all rights accorded her by Jewish marriage law. The document also asserts that the bride has formally consented, and it is attested by the signatures of two competent witnesses (usually the officiating rabbis), not those of husband and wife.

The unilateral form of the *ketubbah* is legally significant because it logically dictates the unilateral form of Jewish divorce, in which (as in Islamic law) the husband alone has power to dissolve the marriage bond by relinquishing his exclusive claim on his wife's sexual function. This rule causes serious problems in cases where a husband has disappeared without trace or refuses to give his wife a *get* (writ of Jewish divorce) when so ordered by the rabbinical court. Although the formal power of divorce is vested in the husband alone, the Mishnaic sages had tried to help the wife by endorsing draconian measures (including imprisonment by gentile civil authorities for contempt) to secure compliance; today, Israeli civil law applies the sanction of imprisonment for contempt to husbands who refuse to release their wives following a rabbinical court order. (This does not always have the desired effect; in 1995, one notoriously recalcitrant husband died after spending 32 years in jail for refusing to obey the Israeli rabbinical court's order.)

Jewish courts both in Israel and in the Diaspora likewise continue to apply the archaic law of the *'agunah* (literally, "anchored woman") whose husband has disappeared without trace or gone insane or refuses (often for purposes of extortion) to deliver a *get.* An unreleased levirate widow (whose brother-in-law is still a minor or cannot be found or is uncooperative) is likewise an *'agunah.* Lacking a *get* or *halisah* release, as the case may be, the *'agunah* can never remarry in Jewish law, even after obtaining a civil divorce. This rule, however, is not enforced by Reform Judaism, which has in principle rejected the binding nature of rabbinic Halakhah, whose development it treats as a sociological rather than a theological phenomenon.

The most serious aspect of this continuing problem is the fact that any child born to an *'agunah* by a man other than her husband is considered illegitimate (*mamzer*) with severe legal disabilities; though subject to Jewish law in general, such offspring are disqualified by biblical law (Deut. 23:2) from marrying any Jew except another *mamzer.* This rule, too, remains in force, with disastrous results for thousands of Orthodox and Conservative Jews in Israel and around the world.

In the Diaspora, an *'agunah* can obtain a civil divorce and resort to civil remarriage (though, if the second husband is a Jew, any child of that marriage will be a *mamzer*). In the state of Israel, even this option is not available, because Israel (like Middle Eastern countries generally) lacks provision for civil marriage and divorce. This is the most enduring halakhic problem for Jewish women in the private law of personal status, whose inequity is compounded by a double standard: if a recalcitrant husband succeeds in concealing his delinquency and remarries, the technically polygynous character of Jewish marriage saves his children by the second wife from the stigma of illegitimacy that would attach to future children of the first wife.

The Autonomous Woman: Always a Person

In classical Jewish law an autonomous woman's personal status theoretically exceeded that of a dependent woman, since she controlled every aspect of her private life, whether involving her property or her personal status. Her most significant power was control over her sexual-reproductive function. Thus a widow or divorcée could freely negotiate with any suitor of her choice. Her former husband could not restrict the future sexual relations of his divorced wife; indeed the Mishnah explicitly states that the essence of a writ of divorce is its explicit statement that the divorcée is now "permitted" (that is, sexually available) to other men (M. Git. 9:1–3).

In sum, the effect of the classical rules on a woman's legal status in the private domain was and remains as follows: in the case of a dependent woman, any defiance of the man's exclusive claim on her sexuality (such as remarriage following a civil divorce without first receiving a *get*) justifies overriding her rights of personhood and treating her as, in effect, the husband's chattel. The reason for this is that her reproductive organs, whose function technically belongs to the first husband or *levir,* cannot be detached from the rest of her. But in all other situations, even a dependent woman is perceived as a legal person, with numerous rights, duties, and powers. Autonomous women are treated as legal persons in all circumstances; and all Jewish women, both dependent and autonomous, are viewed as members of the Israelite people, bound by the responsibilities of Jewish personhood and required to observe all rules of Jewish law and custom that pertain to them.

Woman and the Public Domain

In the public cultural domain of Jewish religious practice, the status of women involved different issues—as it still does in the Orthodox, ultra-Orthodox, and Hasidic branches of Judaism. In the public domain Jewish women were neither chattels nor persons; as in most cultures throughout history, they were virtual nonentities. They were simply "not there"—a feature endemic in Middle Eastern countries. The categories of "chattel" or "person," and the subdivisions among women, were irrelevant, because the system decreed (and came to assume) the exclusion of all women from active participation in the public forums of Jewish culture. These public forums included the synagogue (*bet knesset*), where, if present at all, women were seated behind a screen or in a women's gallery and denied participation in the rituals of worship other than silent prayer; the study house (*bet midrash*) and later the Talmudic academy (*yeshivah*), where men could immerse themselves day and night in the study of sacred texts; and the religious courthouse (*bet din*), where men sat in judgment while women in most cases were not competent even to testify. Midrashic exegesis rationalized the exclusion of women by emphasizing their physical, mental, and moral shortcomings (paralleling the classical Greek view of women, as expressed by Plato and Aristotle, among others) and thus justifying the male monopoly of the highest spiritual and intellectual manifestations of a religious culture that, applying a double standard, subjected men and women alike to onerous obligations.

One must bear in mind the virtual lack of literary evidence concerning the intellectual or spiritual lives of Jewish women in antiquity or the Middle Ages. The Talmud mentioned one extraordinary—and possibly fictional—woman, Beruriah (wife of the second-century Rabbi Meir), who "learned three hundred laws from three hundred scholars in a single day" (B. Pesahim 62*b*); but the medieval commentator Rashi later claimed (commentary to B. Avodah Zarah 18*b*) that Beruriah met with unfortunate circumstances when her husband, Rabbi Meir, directed one of his students to try to seduce her after she had derided the Talmudic statement that "women's judgment is unstable" (B. Qidd. 80*b*). However, no one knows how far Mishnaic and Talmudic rules represent historical reality rather than an ideal utopian system. In general, early sages and later rabbis alike discuss women only as peripheral adjuncts in contexts important to men (especially mariage and divorce law) and never speak of women's aspirations, if any, to the life of the mind officially denied them by the rabbinic system.

The sages' antipathy to the presence of women in the public domain was the natural corollary of a cultural imperative that restricted women to the home to keep them in their divinely ordained role of "helpers"—enablers and facilitators of the male cultural enterprise beyond the four walls, especially the study of sacred texts (B. Berakhot 17*a*). But if so, what role was there for autonomous women unattached to men—women who dwelled in their own homes, uncontrolled by fathers or brothers or husbands and thus figuratively, if not literally, on the fringes of the public domain? Rabbinic literature is replete with assumptions that such women must be suspect. The Talmud explicitly notes the three main reasons for women being "out there"—the commonest being prostitution (B. Berakhot 17*a*). The Bible had defined as a harlot even the righteous Rahab, who helped the Israelite spies—why else would she be living in her own house on the outskirts of the city wall? (Josh. 2), and likewise two women living together with their babies, who sought the judgment of Solomon about which was the living child's mother (1 Kings 3:16–28). Again, two women sitting together at a crossroads were assumed to be practicing witchcraft (B. Pesahim 111*a*). Women in the streets might be returning from preparing a corpse for burial—and thus in a state of cultic impurity that, to the Talmudic mind, made it essential to avoid them (B. Berakhot 51*a*). There was, in sum, no "good" reason for a woman to be out in the public domain unchaperoned by men.

Until recent times women's relationship to the public sphere of Jewish religious expression was one of exclusion from the "men's club." On the basis of exegesis of Scripture and on rabbinic innovation where the Bible was silent, women in classical Jewish culture were deemed ineligible for religious leadership roles like rabbi or cantor or religious judge (or even for lay leadership roles in the Jewish community, such as synagogue president); barred from access to Jewish scholarship in Talmudic academies (the functional equivalent of universities in the era before these were founded); and excluded from any active role in the public forums of the rabbinic enterprise. Along with the private-domain problem of the *'agunah* already discussed, women's exclusion from the public cultural domain of synagogue and seminary is the other major focus of contemporary Jewish feminist critiques and has led, in progressive branches of Judaism, to a reassessment, culminating since 1972 in the ordination of women rabbis in the American Reform, Reconstructionist, and Conservative movements and in Reform and Liberal Judaism as practiced in Britain and Europe.

The subordination of women and their exclusion from active roles in the public cultural domain are by no means unique to Judaism; both were endorsed by the church in canonizing the letters of Paul, as also in later centuries by Qur'anic law and *Shari'a* tradition (Wegner, 1982). Subordination of women is a feature of every legal system whose records have survived from antiquity. Despite feminists' success in raising societal consciousness about these issues, legal restrictions on women remain in place in varying degrees in most societies and religions. Hence a balanced appraisal of the status of women in classical Judaism demands comparison with the laws of contemporary surrounding cultures, above all the eastern Mediterranean cultures of the Greco-Roman period—that is, the last few centuries B.C. and the first few centuries after Christ. Seen against that backdrop, Jewish women were, on balance, neither better nor worse off than women in early Christianity or Greco-Roman pagan cultures.

Women and Cultic Pollution

Like most traditional cultures, classical rabbinic Judaism confined women to the private domain in their social role as wives, mothers, and homemakers and their "cottage industry" economic function—often, spinning and weaving in the protective privacy of the home. Women everywhere were barred by law or custom from the highest leadership roles in the public domain of religious worship, which comprised a large part of the world of ideas and virtually defined the creative life of mind and spirit in all cultures of antiquity. But in Judaism women's exclusion from the public domain rested on something more than the conventional notions about "women's place" common to all patriarchies. This fact emerges when we consider women in the context of early rabbinic Judaism, which adopted the worldview of the Israelite priests when Rome's destruction of the Second Temple in 70 A.D. and banishment of Jews from their holy city, Jerusalem, ended the sacrificial cult and rendered the priesthood defunct.

The keynote of the priestly worldview was the concept of holiness: "You shall be holy as I, YHWH your God, am holy" (Lev. 19:2). In rabbinic Judaism holiness meant living one's entire life from morning until night and from birth to death in accordance with rules specially ordained by God for his chosen people. In the public domain those rules included avoidance of women because of their disruptive potential, either through sexual distraction that would deflect men's minds from their religious obligations of study and prayer or (in the case of menstruating women) by imparting a mysterious, invisible, intangible miasma known to anthropologists as cultic pollution. Consequently, women became the focus of certain taboos that led to their exclusion from active participation in such communal religious activities as studying the Torah and worshiping in a synagogue.

The concept of cultic impurity or pollution (associated in many ancient cultures with bodily functions like eating and sexual intercourse) is entirely distinct from modern concepts of cleanliness and dirt, as was demonstrated in Mary Douglas's groundbreaking study of pollution and taboo, *Purity and Danger* (1966, see also Wegner, 1992). Douglas showed how pollution was connected with bodily functions not well understood in primitive societies, especially those related to life and death. In the Hebrew Bible, these pollution-generating processes included the transition from life to death (Lev. 21:2–4); the birth of new life (Lev. 12:1–5); the onset of menstruation, which wastes the life-giving fluid that should ideally nourish a fetus (Lev. 15:19–24); and other uncontrollable genital discharges, both male and female (Lev. 15:2–12, 25–27).

The Holiness Code outlawed inappropriate sexual liaisons (Lev. 18 and 20). Forbidden sexual unions included adultery, homosexuality (see the strictures of Paul on homosexuality, at Rom. 1:26–27), bestiality, and intercourse with a menstruating woman. Biblical rules precluding intercourse with women standing in specified blood or marriage relationships form the basis not only of Jewish marriage law but also of canon law and the incest and marriage rules in the civil and criminal codes of the Christian West.

Jewish Marriage and Divorce

As explained earlier, Jewish marriage involves a man's acquisition of the exclusive right to benefit from a woman's sexual and reproductive capacity. But this transaction is unilateral in form, because in polygynous cultures a wife has no exclusive claim on her husband's biological function. The unilateral character of the Jewish marriage ceremony was preserved even after the triumph of Christianity necessitated a ban on the practice of polygyny by Jews living in the lands of Christendom. This ban, traditionally attributed to the eleventh-century Rabbi Gershom of Mainz, remains in force, though it was never applied to Jews living in the lands of Islam, where the *Shari'a* law of marriage and divorce (virtually identical to Jewish Halakhah) likewise permits polygyny.

Modern Remedies for the Jewish Wife

In secular legal systems laws can be altered in response to social change by the sovereign body that originally created them, whether this be a monarchy, an oligarchy, or a representative assembly, though cultural lag may retard the process. But theocratic systems like Jewish or Islamic law claim that all laws come from God alone—not only in matters pertaining to religious law but also in what is usually perceived as the sphere of secular or civil law. In the case of criminal law, Diaspora Jewry has as a matter of policy submitted to the law of the land ever since the third-century talmudic sage Samuel issued a decree to that effect (*dina de malkhuta dina*), but in all other areas halakhic jurisprudence maintains that since God alone makes Jewish law (albeit mediated by rabbinic jurists), God alone can change it.

The Late Twentieth and Early Twenty-First Centuries

In the late twentieth century Jewish feminist scholars raised the consciousness of the Jewish public to the problems described in this article, and religious leaders in progressive branches of Judaism proposed various solutions, which, however, were mostly devices to preempt or circumvent the law of divorce without disturbing its basic premises. These devices usually take the form of prenuptial contracts to obey any future rabbinical court order to give and receive a *get*, subject to financial penalties for recalcitrant husbands who withhold this after a civil divorce (Riskin, 1989). Such expedients, however, have thus far had minimal effect; they have been generally rejected by Orthodox Jews; all of them fall short of giving a wife the right to divorce her husband (this is conceptually impossible, as explained above); and it is obviously distasteful for couples on the brink of marriage to be forced to contemplate the possibility of a future divorce.

The other set of problems affecting Jewish women relates to the public domain and involves specifically such questions as a woman's capacity to hold a communal religious office such as that of rabbi or cantor. Like the question of Christian women's eligibility for the priesthood in some churches, this question of women holding religious office has been answered affirmatively by the branches of progressive Judaism, beginning with Reform, Judaism in 1972, followed by Reconstruction Judaism in 1973 and Conservative Judaism in 1985; by 1995, the question continued to be rejected by Orthodox and traditional branches of Judaism, just as women's eligibility for priesthood continues to be denied by the Roman Catholic church.

See Also

FAMILY: PROPERTY RELATIONS; FAMILY: RELIGIOUS AND LEGAL SYSTEMS—JUDAIC TRADITIONS; FEMINISM: JEWISH; SACRED TEXTS

References and Further Reading

Douglas, Mary. 1966. *Purity and danger: An analysis of the concepts of pollution and taboo.* London: Routledge and Kegan Paul.

Fiorenza, Elisabeth Schussler. 1983. *In memory of her.* New York: Crossroad.

Riskin, Shlomo. 1989. *Women and Jewish divorce.* Hoboken, N.J.: Ktav.

Wegner, Judith Romney. 1982. The status of women in Jewish and Islamic marriage and divorce law. *American Journal of Legal History,* 26:1–33.

———. [1988] 1992. *Chattel or person? The status of women in the Mishnah.* New York: Oxford University Press.

———. 1992. Leviticus. In Carol A. Newsom and Sharon H. Ring, eds., *The women's Bible commentary.* Louisville, Ky.: Westminster.

———. 1991. Women in Philo: Hebraic or Hellenic? In A.-J. Levine, ed., *Women like this: Women in the Greco-Roman world.* Atlanta, Ga.: Scholars Press.

Judith Romney Wegner

JURISPRUDENCE

See LAW: FEMINIST CRITIQUES.

JUSTICE AND RIGHTS

Social justice, with its emphasis on the idea of equality in all its forms, is an important aspect of feminism, as is the tendency to make political claims in terms of rights. Campaigns led by women have deployed this language of rights and have often sought to use law as a device for social change. In India, for example, efforts to reform laws concerning rape, dowry, and inheritance have involved demands for new legislation and the implementation of existing legal principles, using the discourse of rights in the courtroom. Other such campaigns have developed strategies related to formal declarations of rights, both national and international. However, justice and rights in the legal sphere are not necessarily identical to these concepts beyond the realm of law. Notions of justice, in particular justice for women, are concerned not only with equality and liberty but also with the distribution of resources and opportunities necessary to maintain them. While feminist campaigns involving legal reform may reflect this distributive justice, entry into law implies at least a limited acceptance of formal legal justice, underpinning liberal legalism, which stresses values of reciprocity, neutrality, and abstract rationality. The engagement with law, although open to question, has produced a particular debate concerned with notions of rights and justice in law.

Skepticism Regarding Law and Rights

As Ratna Kapur and Brenda Cossman (1996) argue, there is widespread ambivalence about law, in part because of a gap between women's formal legal rights and their substantive inequality (see also Williams, 1991). Similarly, Silvia Pimentel (1993), discussing challenges facing women in Brazil, mentions equal rights organizations but also mentions doubts about the significance of law in the lives of the majority of women.

Many Anglo-American feminists also have an ambivalent relationship with legal justice. Twentieth-century activists concentrated initially on the extension of civil liberties to women, such as the right to vote, but later were in favor of legislative intervention to enhance opportunities for women in education, health, social security, and employment. In the last two decades of the twentieth century, issues related to reproductive rights were a particular focus. Radical and postmodern theorists have, in different ways, argued that law is not neutral and rights are not abstract. They view law as phallocentric, excluding discourses counter to the masculine worldview; but they nevertheless appreciate that law is a site of struggles.

There are feminsts who argue for changes in the legal order that would proceed from acceptance of a natural and universal sexual difference. For instance, the French writer Luce Irigaray defines a program of civil law for women that includes a series of special rights, such as the right to human dignity, to human identity, and to motherhood as a component of female identity. The language of this code is, however, accompanied by a "speculative" voice, and its details have provoked debate. For example, it is difficult for some women to identify with "the enshrining in law of *virginity* as a component of female identity"(Irigaray, 1994: 60).

Legal Orientalism

International rights are of considerable significance, and the concept of "women's rights as human rights" was prominent in the agenda of the UN Conference held at Beijing in 1995. One instrument, the Convention on the Elimination of All Forms of Discrimination Against Women (CEDAW), which promotes equality as a means to justice, puts women's rights squarely on the international stage. The language of human rights has a power that is denied to women's rights alone. However, it has been argued that western feminists are involved in this rhetoric, with its individualistic assumptions. Their interpretation of women's rights, including their concern with reproductive health, is legitimated, universalized, and projected onto those the West considers "others."

This critique relates to the broader concern that western feminism is implicated in colonial narratives that continue to resonate. In this context, Leila Ahmed (1992: 197–198) comments that the dominant voice of Arab feminism firmly rejects adulation of the West. Instead, it details the "comprehensive rights" provided to women in Islam, while recognizing that these rights are not necessarily manifest in Islamic societies. Ahmed also notes that western feminism often focuses on veiling, and that this focus is an instance of the way in which the struggle for women's rights can become a struggle over the merits and demerits of different cultures.

Rights and the Ethics of Care

Within western feminism itself, the discourse on rights is subject to criticism. This discourse is viewed not only as never fully delivering on its rhetoric, but also as a potential source of oppression. A concentration on rights as autonomy rather than as relationships and community is perceived as alienating and profoundly isolating. In this regard, Carol Gilligan's argument (1982) that women's moral development is silenced by a dominant moral language that takes male life as the norm has been the basis of a debate about an ethics of justice versus an ethics of care.

Gilligan describes a different moral voice, sometimes called "maternal thinking," associated with connection, nurturance, compassion, responsibility, and refraining from hurting others. This "language of the web," she argues, is rarely used by men in their analysis of moral problems and is largely repudiated in the public world. Critics have argued that the notion of women sharing a different voice appears essentialist and reiterates a reactionary idea that women and men occupy separate spheres. Nevertheless, Gilligan's work has many adherents and has inspired many theoretical developments. For instance, the Dutch feminist Selma Sevenhuijsen (1998) suggests a version of democratic citizenship that recognizes vulnerability, together with a new approach both to the "normal subject" and to justice, based on values like reconciliation, reciprocity, and diversity.

Approaches to Justice in Law

In the United States, Susan Moller Okin has argued that contemporary theories of social justice neglect women and ignore gender. She contends that the family perpetuates gender and is a site of injustice to both women and children, but the privacy accorded to it has obscured gender inequalities. For example, divorce laws treat as formal equals those who are highly unequal in terms of their relative economic power. Her solution is to bring justice into the family, protecing the vulnerable.

Okin uses a heuristic device from John Rawls's social theory—imagining rational persons in an "original position" where a "veil of ignorance" conceals any individual characteristics, such as sex and social status. She asks "what social structures and public policies regarding relations between the sexes, and the family in particular," would be agreed upon in this original position (1989:175). Her presumption is a humanist theory of justice, producing public policies and laws that would minimize gender; specific examples would include family leave, state-funded child care, and arrangements to maintain a household's standard of living after divorce.

Drucilla Cornell rejects the "veil of ignorance" in favor of the sanctuary of an "imaginary domain." This too is a heuristic device, a prior moral space where it is possible to focus, in Kantian terms, on what "should be," a space in which women can be evaluated as free persons. For Cornell, this is the "crucial moment in the evolution of a theory of justice" (1998: 14). In this "sanctuary," or place of "dreams," individuals have the right to orient themselves to their own sexual being; thus it provides an opportunity for self-representation and an opportunity to discover what free and equal persons should demand as a matter of justice, before any broader egalitarian theory of distributive justice is addressed. Cornell's theory of justice, unlike Okin's, would not entail legislation or policies aimed at eliminating gender.

Defending Legal Rights

Anticipating that any attempt to universalize the imaginary domain as a legal and moral right will raise the question of imperialism, Cornell suggests that this moral space is not necessarily a western ideal but is necessary for a human rights agenda that addresses sex. However, she avoids appeals to any universal experience of women. Citing Patricia Williams's defense of legal rights, she describes an African-American woman for whom "the brutal legacy of slavery ... is inseparable from how she imaginatively recollects herself," a legacy that "no white woman can know" (Cornell, 1998: 10). Williams herself (1991: 163) observes that African-Americans have never fully believed in rights but "have also believed in them so much and so hard" as to give "them life where there was none before."

Williams's defense shares the more general ambiguity of feminist approaches to rights and justice. However, while rights may be indeterminate and manipulable, the law's individuality, its neutrality, and its failure to deliver the rhetorical good are not in themselves a reason to abandon rights. From Williams's standpoint, the greatest fear is not isolation. For those who have been denied their legal rights, the magic quality of rights may be positive and transforming. Engaging in a commercial transaction, for instance, can be an aspect of gaining a self rather than being an object of property. Elizabeth Schneider, who is a lawyer, teacher, and activist, argues that it is possible to assess the utility of rights only when one sees the political vision that feeds into and emerges out of a claim (1986). Claims of rights can legitimize subordination and affirm the values of subordinated groups. As Kapur and Cossman imply (1996: 336), a part of discovering the "subversive potential of law" is to return, again and again, to these difficult questions about rights and justice.

See Also

ANTIRACIST AND CIVIL RIGHTS MOVEMENTS; COLONIALISM AND POSTCOLONIALISM; ETHICS: FEMINIST; HUMAN RIGHTS; IMPERIALISM; INDIGENOUS WOMEN'S RIGHTS; LAW: FEMINIST CRITIQUES; LIBERALISM; REPRODUCTIVE RIGHTS; UNIVERSALISM

References and Further Reading

Ahmed, Leila. 1992. *Women and gender in Islam*. New Haven, Conn.: Yale University Press.

Cornell, Drucilla. 1998. *At the heart of freedom*. Princeton, N.J.: Princeton University Press

Gilligan, Carol. 1982. *In a different voice*. Cambridge, Mass.: Harvard University Press.

Irigaray, Luce. 1994. *Thinking the difference*. London: Athlone.

Kapur, Ratna, and Brenda Cossman. 1996. *Subversive sites*. Thousand Oaks, Calif.: Sage.

Okin, Susan M. 1989. *Justice, gender, and the family*. New York: Basic Books.

Pimentel, Silvia. 1993. Special challenges confronting Latin American women. In Joanna Kerr, ed., *Ours by right*. London: Zed.

Schneider, Elizabeth M. 1986. The dialectic of rights and politics: Perspectives from the women's movement. *New York University Law Review* 61: 589–652.

Sevenhuijsen, Selma. 1998. *Citizenship and the ethics of care*. London: Routledge.

Williams, Patricia. 1991. *The alchemy of race and rights*. London: Virago.

Hilary Lim

K

KIBBUTZ

The Israeli kibbutz—a communal farm or settlement—was an amalgamation of early twentieth-century socialism and Zionism. Kibbutzim succeeded in establishing communal life and property and in changing traditional patriachical family structure, but they did not succeed in establishing gender equality (Palgi, 1994; Safir, 1983, 1993).

Historical Background

The *kvutza* (the term means "group" or "commune"), a forerunner of the kibbutz, was created for both construction and agricultural work. It was established in both urban and rural areas, but the ideal form became a collective agricultural settlement, which "reclaimed the land" for farming by manual labor. The early *kvutzot* consisted of 10 to 30 men and no more than 1 to 3 women. Because they were so few, women tended to "get stuck" with domestic chores—cooking stews in huge iron pots, laundering with lye in similar pots over open fires, baking bread in ovens constructed from stones. This nonmarketable service work was hard, tiring, and boring and was held in low esteem. Only manual labor was perceived as productive. Men would take turns doing domestic work, but they did so resentfully, and often they accepted women into a *kvutza* only to cook and to do laundry, so as to free themselves for work in the fields.

The first kibbutz was established in 1923–1924. Social and sexual equality were stated goals, but there was no formal planning to establish the conditions necessary for gender equality. According to socialist theory, eliminating exploitative relationships and the traditional patriarchal family would lead to woman's emancipation. What was represented as sexual equality, however, was only a limited movement of women into jobs that were traditionally masculine.

On the kibbutz, production was collectivized. Members of the kibbutz received goods and services according to their needs rather than their individual productivity. Marriage and family were rejected as reactionary and as a threat to group solidarity: the group was to replace the traditional family and to become the "family" for all of its members. When couples formed, they were expected to behave toward one another in the same manner as they behaved toward any other members. In order to prevent "excessive intimacy" that might lead to primary identity as a couple rather than as members of a group, the partners in a couple never worked together and did not receive simultaneous vacations or time off. Since women were outnumbered by at least three to one in the early years of the kibbutz, this was also considered a means of preventing jealousy. Other factors that reinforced antifamilial attitudes were inherent in the original structure of the kibbutz. In addition to being an agricultural settlement, the kibbutz was often a military outpost defending the Zionist enterprise as well as its own members. Following the establishment of the state of Israel in 1948, new kibbutzim were established to guard its borders. Many contemporary kibbutzim began as such outposts.

During the period before statehood, the birth of the first child on a kibbutz set in motion a process that eventually resulted in the extremes found in the modern kibbutzim. A notion prevailed that only the mother or some other woman could properly care for an infant, so no plans were made for communal care of children. The young idealists who were so concerned with establishing a new society unquestioningly accepted traditional values and beliefs about human beings' biological nature and abilities and about the mother-child relationship. Women therefore returned to communal child-rearing functions and service roles. Women might be accepted in masculine jobs when the economy demanded it, but child rearing was automatically considered an exclusively feminine occupation. Bottle-feeding and sterilized milk are relatively recent innovations in Israel (fresh milk was not pasteurized and bottled until 1956), and sanitary facilities and refrigeration were entirely lacking in the early years. Thus for at least the first half year after a baby's birth, the mother was bound to work close to the children's house, for too much time would be wasted traveling back and forth from the fields to nurse. As more children were born, the pace at which women moved from production jobs to lower-status service jobs accelerated. These jobs were lower in status both economically and ideologically, and they tended to be permanent—very few women returned to production. Thus prejudicial beliefs about women's capability were reestablished and reinforced.

Contemporary Kibbutzim

Today, most kibbutz women still work in lower-status service jobs that are analogous to traditional housework. Although there are no salaries, status differences have been found, with production and management rated highest. Of women in service jobs, *metaplot* (child-care workers) and nurses have higher status than women who work in food preparation or clothing care. Because *metaplot* and nurses require long training and specialization, their jobs tend to become permanent assignments. This, in turn, increases the competition for such positions, causing persisting devaluation of unspecialized work and increasing the stress of unspecialized jobs while reducing job satisfaction. For instance, it is relatively easy to plan a menu to the taste of every member of a small family, but preparing meals for, say, 500 people is bound to lead to dissatisfaction and complaints.

Kibbutz women may turn to traditionally female roles, and come to value such roles, as a compensation for their limited and less attractive job choices, or to reduce "cognitive dissonance"—a psychological term referring to inconsistency between an individual's beliefs or opinions and his or her actual behavior. When such a discrepancy develops, it is easier for people to change their attitudes to match their behavior than vice versa (Festinger, 1964; Mednick, 1975; Safir, 1983). For instance, although the kibbutz socializes women to work in agriculture, most prefer to work in education, while in fact most work in service areas. Palgi (1976) found that women who worked in agriculture or industry were not particularly satisfied, felt that they were not making the best use of their skills and abilities, and did not hold positions of responsibility. Thus it was not surprising that research with second-generation kibbutz members revealed that men assigned more importance to work and women assigned more importance to the family (Leviatan, 1983). Women's production jobs are generally unskilled and do not lead to advancement. Service jobs are relatively specific and do not prepare women for leadership roles in the kibbutz structure. This can easily result in lowered aspirations and further channeling of energy into "feminine" pursuits, resulting in a vicious circle.

The contemporary kibbutz is extremely child-centered, and motherhood is a high-status "profession." Children are seen as an important human resource, and as the main way to increase its population. In the early days, collective child rearing and the children's house were the ideal, creating a situation that made it easier for women to have many children while continuing to work and to find time for other activities. Children spent the hours between four o'clock in the afternoon and seven o'clock in the evening with their families and then returned to the children's house to sleep. In the late 1960s, as the economic situation of kibbutzim greatly improved, money was invested in improving and increasing the size of the members' living quarters. This was an impetus for a movement (led by mothers) to bring the children "home" to sleep. The last kibbutz canceled communal sleeping arrangements in 1997.

Evaluating the Kibbutz

The kibbutz has made a number of contributions to social equality within the family. Kibbutz couples share roles to a much greater extent than is typical in Israeli society or western society (Rosner and Palgi, 1989). Wives are not dependent on their husbands economically or for social status. Each adult is a full and independent member of the kibbutz and receives the same economic remuneration, and children are the economic responsibility of the group.

Mothering on the kibbutz is also substantially different from mothering in the cities. The child has both his or her biological mother and a social mother—the *mitapelet*—appointed by the kibbutz and responsible to it for children's socialization. When a child begins school, his or her involvement with the teacher is more intensive as well. This enables the child to have less complicated and warmer relations with both the mother and the father, who can be more nurturing than city parents, since the *mitapelet,* and to a lesser extent the teacher, are responsible for discipline (Keller, 1983). This restructuring of family relations results in much lower domestic violence in the kibbutz than in the city.

However, the economic crisis in Israel at the beginning of the twenty-first century put the kibbutzim under considerable financial strain. Because every member is a worker, a kibbutz can have "hidden unemployment" (Palgi, 1994). Most kibbutzim are trying to reduce service work so that workers can move into and expand kibbutz industry—the current definition of productive labor. Thus, communal services (such as doing laundry and providing daily shared meals) are being restored to the family, as unpaid labor. Economic considerations have taken and still take priority over planning for gender equality, and this has widened the gender gap. The kibbutz was initially successful in removing traditional economic barriers to equality. However, psychological barriers to equality remained, and resulted in a polarization of men and women's work. It seems likely that the current restructuring of kibbutz will result in polarized, traditional family life, wiping out the gains that were part of the communal structure.

See Also

FAMILY: RELIGIOUS AND LEGAL SYSTEMS—JUDAIC TRADITIONS; HOUSEHOLDS AND FAMILIES: MIDDLE EAST AND NORTH AFRICA; HOUSEHOLDS: POLITICAL ECONOMY; JUDAISM; SOCIALISM; WORK, *specific topics*; ZIONISM

References and Further Reading

Festinger, Leon. 1964. *Conflict, decision, and dissonance*. Stanford, Calif.: Standford University Press.

Keller, Suzanne. 1983. The family in the kibbutz: What lessons for us? In Michal Palgi, Joseph Blasi, Menachem Rosner, and Marilyn Safir, eds., *Sexual equality: The Israeli kibbutz tests the theories*. Philadelphia, Pa.: Norwood.

Leviatan, Uri. 1983. Why is work less central for women? Initial explorations with kibbutz samples and future research directions. In Michal Palgi, Joseph Blasi, Menachem Rosner, and Marilyn Safir, eds., *Sexual equality: The Israeli kibbutz tests the theories*. Philadelphia, Pa.: Norwood.

Mednick, Martha T. S. 1975. Social change and sex-role inertia: The case of the kibbutz. In M. T. S. Mednick, S. S. Tangri, and L. W. Hoffman, eds., *Women and achievement*. New York: Wiley.

Palgi, Michal. 1976. Sex differences in the domain of work in the kibbutz. *Kibbutz* 3–4: 114–129. (In Hebrew.)

———. 1994. Women in the changing kibbutz economy. *Economic and Industrial Democracy* 15: 55–74.

Rosner, Menachem, and Michal Palgi. 1989. Sexual equality in the kibbutz: A retreat or a change of significance? *Kibbutz* 3–4: 149–185. (In Hebrew.)

Safir, Marilyn P. 1983. The kibbutz: An experiment in social and sexual equality? A historical perspective. In Michal Palgi, Joseph Blasi, Menachem Rosner, and Marilyn Safir, eds., *Sexual equality: The Israeli kibbutz tests the theories*. Philadelphia, Pa.: Norwood.

———. 1993. Was the kibbutz an experiment in social and sex equality? In Barbara Swirski and Marilyn P. Safir, eds., *Calling the equality bluff: Women in Israel*. New York: Teachers College Press.

Marilyn P. Safir

KINSHIP

The first anthropological concept of kinship referred to systems of social relations defined only by descent and kinship itself. Later this perspective was broadened. Kinship is now regarded as one of the universals of human society, because all cultures recognize not only familial relations but also specific ways of "relating" and creating relationships between people. How relationships are defined informs gender relations and the diverse positions women take within these relations.

Gender relations are embedded within varying and changing kinship relations throughout the world. The complexity of kinship challenges generalizations about the position of women within classes, races, cultures, and nations. Kinship contextualizes gender relations through the immense variation of positions women can hold within the kinship systems into which they are born and marry. These positions are linked to rights and obligations and the ability to maneuver within them.

Kinship studies developed long before women's studies. Here, the history of kinship studies is outlined first, followed by a summary of feminist approaches to kinship studies.

Kinship Studies

For more than a century, kinship studies have been on the scientific agenda, mainly within the discipline of anthropology. The study of kinship started from a perspective of highly stable systems. Soon afterward Morgan (1877) developed a historical and evolutionary perspective. In England, Malinowski and Radcliffe-Brown carried kinship studies further into anthropology. Malinowski (1913) emphasized family as the "initial situation for the development of kinship," on the basis of his fieldwork in the Trobiand Islands. Radcliffe-Brown (1952) argued that kinship systems are composed of both terminology and patterns of social behavior, linked to a larger social structure. His was a functionalist approach, which considered kinship systems as institutions helping to maintain a wider social system. In the 1920s, what became known as the structural-functional approach was developed. Kinship organization was seen as an arrangement that enables people to cooperate with one another in an ordered social life. In this regard, Radcliffe-Brown outlined the relevance of the "unity of the sibling group" and the "unity and solidarity of the lineage" for social life. He emphasized marriage as essential for rearranging social structure.

A different approach was provided by statistical analysis comparing large numbers of societies in terms of their kinship systems. Murdock (1957) carried out a cross-cultural study of 250 societies throughout the world. This approach allowed comparisons between geographically different areas and shed light on social change within kinship relations. Change within kinship relations had been largely neglected by structuralist-functionalists, who saw kinship as an unchanging system and assumed solidarity within the kinship grouping as well as its functional contribution to the consolidation of the wider social structure. Murdock's systems of categorization were criticized, however, for not recognizing the subtle differences of meaning for kin relations that exist within individual kinship systems.

Lévi-Strauss's work (1963) differs fundamentally from the work of the British scholars, in that he questioned the empirical reality of kinship relations. He argued that kinship systems exist largely because of the meaning they are given by their members. Accordingly, they exist in human consciousness and are an arbitrary system of representations of relations, rather than a simple reflection of a real situation. Thus, Lévi-Strauss focused on the meaning natives give to their own models of kinship, rather than meanings created by researchers through external analysis.

Lévi-Strauss drew parallels with linguistics, in which kinship systems, like phonemic systems, were seen as mind-made systems on the level of unconscious thought. Much debate concentrated on the "conscious" or "unconscious" quality of a native's knowledge of his or her own principles of kinship relations.

Lévi-Strauss is also known for his principle of reciprocity based on kinship, which primarily entails the exchange between women and men. Women were implicitly seen as objects of exchange, linking male-based kinship groupings. This assumption, among others, has been criticized by feminist scholars.

Feminist Scholarship and Kinship

The theoretical structures and models of kinship have come under criticism regarding their ethnocentric and androcentric assumptions. Feminist scholars have added the category *gender* to analysis, pointing out that many male scholars of kinship have failed to address the position of women. In 1975, Gayle Rubin studied sexual oppression and patriarchy and their expression within kinship. She proposed a sex-gender system to refer to the domain of oppression, but she also argued against its assumed inevitability. She argued that kinship relations are products of social relations rather than "natural" facts. This perspective later formed part of mainstream kinship studies.

Initially, the feminist debate on kinship centered on analytical dichotomies, such as nature versus culture and domestic versus public life. Women were associated with the less valued nature, and men with the more highly valued, transcendent culture. Women were seen as central in their capacity as mothers, linked firmly to the less important domestic sphere and dissociated from the economic and political activities of the public sphere. This model was later criticized, however, as a legacy of Victorian concepts that "cast the sexes in dichotomous and contrastive terms." Biological motherhood was rejected as an explanation of the universal devaluation of women because it turned women into "victims of a conceptual tradition that discovers 'essence' in the natural characteristics which distinguish" the sexes (Rosaldo, 1980: 401). Focusing on an essence attached to sex implied that the inferior position of women was not only universal but unchangeable.

In the 1980s, a feminist-Marxist debate emerged, involving an opposition between relations of reproduction and production. The unequal value placed on the production of people and the production of things in Euro-American culture was pointed out (Collier and Yanagisako, 1987: 24). Women had often been considered the means of reproduction, and their productive activities had been neglected. This in turn led to the debate about how domestic work was to be defined. The distinction between economic activity and domestic work was seen as problematic because it implicitly presented both as gendered activities, of unequal value.

In Euro-American culture, an assumption prevails that the primary reproductive relationship in all societies is between a man and a woman and is characterized by sexual intercourse and subsequent pregnancy and birth. Questioning the primacy of this relationship leads to a shift from emphasizing biological bonds to emphasizing sociocultural characteristics in which these bonds are embedded; thus marriage, parenthood, and all other kinship relations can be seen as social rather than biological relationships (Schneider, 1984). The pervasive assumptions about kinship have been based on the natural characteristics of women and men and their natural roles in sexual procreation, often embedded in the unformulated assumption of a basic nuclear family.

The premise of sexual difference also hindered the development of a historical perspective of change and the realization that kinship relations are strongly connected to economic and political change in society at large. As kinship studies developed, new questions could be asked about how specific societies create ("fictive") kinship bonds and recognize claims and responsibilities, and how these change over time. Through challenging models and structures as fixed entities, it is possible to analyze how men and women renegotiate, bargain, and create new networks of kin. Attention has also shifted to how gender relations and the socialization of children are interconnected with the social world.

Various folk models of Euro-American origin—such as those identified above—persist and need to be identified and deconstructed; otherwise, anthropologists will continue to find dichotomies that ignore women or makes women inferior. Thus there is a continuous need to review Euro-American theory, not only in terms of kinship and universal womanhood but also in terms of culture and ideology in general.

Women have come to be seen as actors operating within widely differing and changing kinship relations, instead of as mere objects of exchange, or as passive participants in or victims of isolated kinship systems. Marriage, for example, can be seen not as a determinant of social organization but rather as a point at which practice and meaning are renegotiated. Power has become a much debated concept within feminist analysis of kinship, as well as how male dominance has come to exist within most kinship systems.

Examining the changing nature of kin relations, and seeing these relations as negotiated, has also made it possible to analyze a growing matrifocality in kinship relations, as is found in the increasing numbers of women-headed households in Africa, South America, and North America, as well as in several European countries (Molokomme, 1991). Economic forces promoting migratory labor, state-sanctioned individual property and land ownership, and changing agricultural systems of production all influence how individual actors pursue their own ends and undertake responsibilities toward others.

The Future of Feminist Scholarship on Kinship

Feminist scholarship on kinship has been built on prior theory but has also made major changes in order to develop further analyses. One major contribution of feminist scholarship has been to focus on the actors, and especially on the position of women within kinship networks. However, much of feminist scholarship was initially characterized by an emphasis on a domain incorporating the position of women, and it discussed women apart from the context of their relationships. The resulting theories were seldom based on existing kinship theory, which was seen as old-fashioned and unrelated to current realities. Strathern (1992: 55), through her analysis of middle-class English kinship, cites another reason for this neglect. She argues that kinship seems to be implicitly perceived as a reproductive model characterized by "individuals reproducing individuals," rather than as the "reproduction of relationships." An individual is traditionally seen as linear, literally "embodied," coming to life at birth and ending at death; this view tends to disregard the continuity between the dead, living, and unborn. By contrast, many other cultures see the unborn and the dead as part of a collectivity of kin, and the individual as a member of this kin network.

Today, at a time when fundamentalist religious discourses are reinventing the family, masculinity, and femininity, an analysis of kinship and gender must also consider economic, political, and cultural factors. Likewise, much theory on development rests on static notions of the family and the individual and must come to terms with changing family and kinship structures, instead of simply assuming their unchanging continuity as safety nets in a process of economic and political change. The influence of colonial law on family law, which in turn influences current kinship practices and ideologies, also shows how dramatically kinship relations are affected by forces often considered another field of study. Scientific developments in fertility are another example of how insights into other societal areas influence relationships of kinship and gender in different and changing cultural contexts.

Increasingly, kinship is viewed from a historical perspective, taking into account the influence of culture, politics, and economics on kin relations. Feminist kinship studies have contributed to challenging the assumed inevitability of kin relations, showing how women and men shape their lives, and their bonds, responsibilities, and claims to each other, in different cultural contexts.

Future kinship studies will continue to broaden their vision beyond such ethnocentric distinctions as that between the "biological" and the "social," and they can also be expected to take an imaginative view of what falls under the concept of kinship itself. In this context the term "relatedness" has been coined as an analogy to "kinship," in an attempt to regain openness to "indigenous idioms of being related" and to distance theory from earlier definitions

(Carsten, 2000: 4). There is more emphasis on the whole range of possible forms of inclusion and exclusion of persons and on shifting relations of support and neglect (Palriwala and Risseeuw, 1996). Kinship in the 1990s was described as having "risen from its ashes" (Carsten, citing Schneider, 2000: 3).

See Also

FAMILY STRUCTURES; HOUSEHOLDS AND FAMILIES: OVERVIEW; MARRIAGE: OVERVIEW

References and Further Reading

Carsten, J., ed. 2000. *Cultures of relatedness: New approaches to the study of kinship.* Cambridge: Cambridge University Press.

Collier, Jane Fisburne, and Sylvia Junko Yanagisako, eds. 1987. *Gender and kinship: Essays toward a unified analysis.* Stanford, Calif.: Stanford University Press.

Lévi-Strauss, Claude. 1963. *Structural Anthropology.* New York: Basic. (First published in French, 1958. Paris: Plon.)

Malinowski, Bronislaw. [1913] 1963. *The family among the Australian Aborigines: A sociological study.* New York: Schocken.

Molokomme, Athalia. 1991. *Children of the fence: The maintenance of extra-marital children under law and practice in Botswana.* Ph.D. dissertation, Leiden University, Netherlands.

Morgan, Lewis, H. 1964. *Ancient Society.* Cambridge, Mass.: Harvard University Press. (Originally published 1877.)

Murdock, George P. 1957. World ethnographic sample. *American Anthropologist* 59: 664–687.

Palriwala, R., and C. Risseeuw, eds. 1996. *Shifting Circles of support: Contextualizing kinship and gender in south Asia and sub-Saharan Africa.* London: Sage.

Radcliffe-Brown, A. R. 1952. *Structure and function in primitive society: Essays and addresses.* London: Cohen and West; Glencoe, Ill.: Free Press.

Reiter, Rayna R. 1975. Men and women in the south of France: Public and private domains. In Rayna Rapp Reiter, ed., *Toward an anthropology of women,* 252–283. New York: Monthly Review.

Rosaldo, Michelle Zimbalist. 1980. The use and abuse of anthropology: Reflections on feminism and cross-cultural understanding. *Signs: Journal of Women in Culture and Society* 5(3): 389–417.

Rubin, Gayle. 1975. The traffic in women: Notes on the "political economy" of sex. In Rayna Reiter, ed., *Toward an anthropology of women,* 157–210. New York: Monthly Review.

Schneider, David. 1984. *A critique of the study of kinship.* Ann Arbor: University of Michigan.

Strathern, Marilyn. 1992. *After nature: English kinship in the late twentieth century.* Cambridge: Cambridge University Press.

Carla Risseeuw

KNOWLEDGE

One of the principal contributions of women's studies to scholarship is its intimate examination of how we as human beings come to know the world and what counts as knowledge. At the heart of these epistemological questions is the issue of objectivity—as it is currently constructed—which implies that people can and should distance themselves from the object of knowledge in order to see a truth separate from and unaffected by their social and ideological positions. Knowledge is thus referential, about something located in the world outside the knower that can be objectively determined. The judgment of the validity of such knowledge can be tested by universal criteria that are unaffected by the subjective position of the knower. According to this view, such objective judgments are by their nature both unemotional and value-free. In the paradigm case, the knower is the scientist who steps back from his or her object of study in order to understand it. The resultant knowledge is explained, categorized, and organized by abstractions.

Feminists have challenged claims made within this paradigm on two levels. First, they dispute claims of validity and truth made within the paradigm, arguing that much of the research is not objective on its own terms but is gender-biased. Lennon and Whitford (1994:1) argue that one compelling epistemological insight offered by feminists is that claiming knowledge, far from being a neutral practice, is implicated in networks of exclusion and domination. For example, educational and medical studies done primarily on men are generalized to women. The reverse is not the case.

A second objection is to the paradigm itself. From the early second-wave feminists (for example, Simone de Beauvoir and Kate Millet) to modern researchers (for example, Belenky et al., 1986; Kramarae and Spender, 1992; Lennon and Whitford, 1994; Reinharz, 1992; Scheman, 1993), many feminist scholars have argued that the assumed disconnection between knower and known, implicit in "objectivity," is impossible. Human beings cannot completely separate their subjectivity from their knowledge. Further, this specious claim to objectivity is a patriarchal ideological position that devalues the experiences of women as knowers and the content of what women know. If objectivity is the sine qua non of knowledge, then subjective, interpersonal, intuitive experience—that is, these feminists argue, typically female experience—does not count as knowledge. It counts as feeling but not as legitimate and justified knowledge, and as such it is less than the detached, allegedly neutral, objective claims of traditional epistemology. On this view, it is thus masculine to think and feminine to feel. What (mostly) men have thought has become the canon of knowledge. What (mostly) women have felt has not.

The result, it is argued, has been not only that a male view has dominated the production of knowledge but also that the problems addressed have reflected males' experience of the world and ignored females' experience. For instance, economics and political science until recently have both neglected domestic activities as objects of investigation. Thus, the construction of knowledge has had and continues to have political implications. If domestic work has not been worthy of study, it appears less worthy of reform. If there is little shared, recognized knowledge about the major contexts of women's lives, women are disempowered. This is the root of the feminist claim that knowledge is power.

Feminist critiques have led to discussions about how to reconnect the knower to the known, and how to empower female experience. The aim is twofold: first, to value a knowledge-making process that recognizes interdependence and contextual thought (as the process that recognizes independent, dispassionate thought is now valued); second, to represent the products of such a process within academic disciplines as legitimate and justified knowledge.

Despite general agreement among feminist researchers concerning past neglect and current feminist epistemological goals, debate continues on how to represent subjectivity (how to put the knower back into the known) and how to evaluate claims of knowledge in nonpatriarchal ways. On the one hand, a number of feminist scholars have advocated recontextualizing knowledge by using a differently gendered subjectivity and restoring what they see as a predominantly female way of knowing. In other words, if past forms have disconnected the neutral (male) observer from the isolated, independent data, then a new form should connect the (female) participant to the intersubjective, communally determined data. This different emphasis would change the moral dimensions of epistemology as well. If past goals of scholarship implied an ethics of impartial justice and individual rights, future feminist goals would imply an ethics of care and responsibility. This politicizes knowledge in a different way. What we "know" would be judged for its effects on relationships within the world. The basis would be more communal and less individual. For example, a communal understanding of and responsibility for the environment is a basis for ecofeminism and counters a view of the environment as subject to individual control.

On the other hand, some feminists have supported the poststructuralist, postmodern idea of fragmented subjectivity creating many kinds of knowers. Rejecting the idea of a shared, essentially female way of knowing (because of a lack of consensus on exactly what a female way of knowing would be), they instead discuss how different discourses (for example, social and academic) affect our place in the world and lead us to different conclusions. While this addresses the myriad differences in points of view by agreeing to disagree, in its extreme form it encounters a problem of relativism. If knowledge is political and the feminist aim is to empower the disempowered, then how do we accomplish this without some clear standard for evaluating better and worse claims?

Despite the problems with reconstituting epistemology, feminists have begun a number of projects to address diverse canons. Lennon and Whitford (1994) argue that a feminist epistemology is neither an essential female way of knowing nor simply an articulation of diverse female subjectivity. Rather, it is attention to epistemological concerns arising from feminist investigation of women's experience.

See Also

EPISTEMOLOGY; PATRIARCHY: FEMINIST THEORY; SOCIAL SCIENCES: FEMINIST METHODS

References and Further Reading

Belenky, Mary F., Blythe M. Clinchy, Nancy R. Goldberger, and Jill M. Tarule. 1986. *Women's way of knowing: The development of self, voice, and mind.* New York: Basic Books.

Code, Lorraine. 1991. *What can she know? Feminist theory and the construction of knowledge.* Ithaca, N.Y.: Cornell University Press.

Goldberger, Nancy, Jill Tarule, Blythe Clinchy, and Mary Belenky. 1996. *Knowledge, difference, and power: Essays inspired by Women's Ways of Knowing.* New York: Basic Books.

Kemp, Sandra, and Judith Squires, eds. 1997. *Feminisms.* Oxford: Oxford University Press.

Kramarae, Cheris, and Dale Spender, eds. 1992. *The knowledge explosion: Generations of feminist scholarship.* New York: Teachers College Press.

Kramarae, Cheris, and Paula Treichler, eds. 1992. *Amazons, bluestockings and crones: A feminist dictionary.* London: Pandora.

Lennon, Kathleen, and Margaret Whitford, eds. 1994. *Knowing the difference: Feminist perspectives in epistemology.* London: Routledge.

Reinharz, Shulamit. 1992. The principles of feminist research. In Cheris Kramarae and Dale Spender, eds., *The knowledge explosion: Generations of feminist scholarship.* New York: Teachers College Press.

Scheman, Naomi. 1993. *Engenderings: Constructions of knowledge, authority, and privilege.* New York: Routledge.

Ivy Glennon

KNOWLEDGE ECONOMY

See DIGITAL DIVIDE.

KNOWLEDGE: Traditional and Indigenous

See SCIENCE: TRADITIONAL AND INDIGENOUS KNOWLEDGE and TRADITIONAL HEALING.

L

LABOR, DIVISION OF

See DIVISION OF LABOR.

LABOR, DOMESTIC

See DOMESTIC LABOR.

LACTATION

See BREAST; BREAST FEEDING.

LANGUAGE

The relationship between gender and language is complex and has provoked a number of debates within feminist theory, both in linguistics and in literary theory. These debates can be grouped around two main concerns: whether language is encoded in ways that reflect a male perspective, and whether language is spoken differently by women and men.

Language and Male Perspective

Many feminists have been concerned with the analysis of language because they consider language crucial in determining how women and men see themselves and think about themselves as gendered beings. Many feminists believe that the language we speak is a product of social forces; that is, the social system within which we live structures the linguistic choices we have available to us in ways that reflect our society's main concerns. For many theorists, this means that the language you speak imposes limits both on what it is possible to say and, perhaps more important, on what it is possible to think. This can lead you to think about yourself and the world similarly to other people in your language community, even when those ways of thinking are not in your interests. Thus, if we accept the hypothesis that the English language reflects the concerns of those who are in a dominant position in society—for example, in Britain, white middle-class men—then women will tend to consider themselves from the perspective of that dominant position. For instance, to describe a man or woman as an "old woman" is an insult, meaning that he or she is overly fussy; there is no equivalent pejoritive male term. This is not an isolated example, and many feminist linguists contend that this systematic differential encoding of language causes women and men to view themselves from a primarily male perspective. This way of encoding experience in language has been termed *sexism.*

Sexism. Vetterling-Braggin defines a statement as sexist if "it creates, constitutes, promotes, and exploits any irrelevant or impertinent marking of the distinction between the sexes" (1981: 3). Thus, a sexist statement refers to someone's gender when gender is not relevant. In English, one of the main elements of sexism investigated by feminists is the so-called generic pronoun—that is, the use of the pronoun *he* to refer to people in general. For example, consider "When the police officer has taken your statement, *he* will ask you to sign it." Here, it is asserted that *he* is used generically: it refers to both male and female police officers. However, research has found that statements such as this are generally understood to refer specifically to males. Similarly, feminists have argued that generic nouns, such as *police officer, people,* and *neighbor,* despite seeming generic, are often understood to refer specifically to males. For example, in the biblical phrase *thy neighbor's wife,* the generic noun *neighbor* is modified by the term *wife,* indicating that *neighbor* refers only to male neighbors, not female neighbors (see also Cameron, 1985). Feminists in many academic fields have objected to the use of *man* in referring to the human race as a whole, since in English it usually suggests the interests of men. Feminists, successfully, urged publishers and institutions such as universities and trade unions to create guidelines that encourage more inclusive language. For many women, terms such as *chairperson* and *convenor* instead of *chairman* can signal that the environment in which they work acknowledges and values their existence. However, such attempts to reform language so that women will not feel excluded have often met with hostility and have frequently been derided as "political correctness": a form of thought policing and an infringement on freedom of speech.

Semantic derogation of women. Muriel Schultz (1990) has argued that words associated with women generally go through a process of "semantic derogation"—that is, their meaning becomes negative. She analyzes the complex process whereby words such as *witch* and *glamour* that originally have a generic meaning, applying to both women and men, acquire negative connotations when they come to be associated primarily with women. Thus *glamour,* which originally referred to magical power, went through a process of semantic derogation when it began to mean women's power to sexually attract.

This is also the focus of Jane Mills (1989), who has investigated the curious histories of words associated primarily with women. For example, she traces the history of words like *gossip,* which originally meant a sponsor at Christian baptism (kinswoman or kinsman in the Lord: "God-sibb"), and gradually began to refer to seemingly trivial conversation between women. She also traces the history of a great variety of insulting terms for women in English.

Lakoff (1975) observes that when the same words are used to refer to men and women they can acquire different meanings: for example, *tramp,* when used for a male, means only someone who sleeps in the street, whereas when used to refer to a woman it means someone who is sexually promiscuous. Lakoff argues that such sexualizing of words that refer to women is fairly widespread in English. For example, the female equivalents of *courtier, master,* and *host* are, respectively, *courtesan, mistress,* and *hostess*—each of which has or can have a connotation of sexual availability that is not present in the male form. The sexual activity of women is generally negatively encoded in language, so that there is no real male equivalent of the negative *nymphomaniac;* the closest male equivalents are more positively encoded: for example, *stud* or *Casanova* (see S. Mills, 1994).

Women's dictionaries. Many women have found themselves unable to identify words—names—for their own experiences of, for example, menstruation or childbirth. Thus some have developed dictionaries to provide more positive terms for experiences that have been taboo, stigmatized, or put through a primarily male, heterosexual filter. Jane Mills's work (1989) is part of this process; and Kramarae and Treichler's *Feminist Dictionary* (1985) lists contentious words about women, points out some contradictions in their definitions in mainstream dictionaries, and offers new definitions of words for women's experiences.

Mary Daly (1978) takes a more radical approach, suggesting that women should intervene in the actual process of making meaning instead of accepting language as fixed. For instance, women might capitalize words they consider important (*Goddess,* to make it analogous to *God*); might appropriate negative words and give them positive connotations (*hag* and *crone,* referring to strong women); and might break words apart to reveal underlying sexist assumptions (*the/rapist* for *therapist*).

Some women—for example, the science fiction novelist Suzette Hadin-Elgin (1985)—have tried to develop a separate women's language. Hadin-Elgin created a lexicon of words for experiences that are difficult to name within a patriarchal culture. For example, her verb *doroledim* describes the activity of a woman who eats to compensate for a dull life; her noun *radiidin* is a nonholiday, a time ostensibly for rest or celebration that actually generates a great deal of work for women. In such ways, feminist linguists and literary theorists have attempted to challenge language that encodes a male perspective.

Women's Language

There has been considerable debate within feminist linguistics as to whether women speak differently from men and, if so, whether this constitutes a separate language or a "genderlect"—that is, a tendency to use certain elements more or less than men. Similarly, in literary theory, there has been debate about whether women write differently from men. Early feminist linguistic work in this area, such as that by Robin Lakoff (1975) and Dale Spender (1980), tended to assume that women spoke a form of language that reflected powerlessness and deference to men. For example, Lakoff argued that women use forms such as tag questions (*isn't it, don't you?*) at the end of a statement more frequently than men, and that this more tentative form of language conveyed a lack of power. Lakoff also argued that women tend to be more hesitant verbally, weakening the force of their statements.

Lakoff's work, though it has been influential, is rather problematic, in that she draws only on anecdotal evidence and generalizes about the speech of all women from a very restricted survey. Her examples tend to be taken from white middle-class American women in mixed-sex informal speech. Furthermore, although women may experience difficulty in certain domains of speech, they nevertheless communicate clearly and decisively in other domains. For example, women who find public speaking difficult (formal speeches, addressing large groups) may be fluent and confident in more informal settings. Their problems with public speaking may be traced to lack of training, lack of encouragement, and lack of female role models. Similarly, in settings like business meetings, women may tend to carry over the speech patterns they use in informal settings; for instance, they may use cooperative strategies when other participants are using competitive strategies. Thus it may not be appropriate to assume that women always speak in a different way; rather, women may tend to use different patterns in different contexts.

Dale Spender's work has introduced many women to oppression in language and provides an important critique of the way women's language has been evaluated against an assumed male norm and therefore found deficient. Spender also argues that women's informal speech or ("gossip") has been consistently judged to be excessive, and that this judgment implies that women should be silent. However, Spender, like Lakoff, tends to assume that all women speak similarly, and she does not take up the possibility of speaking in different ways in different contexts.

For a more complex view of women's speech, Jennifer Coates and Deborah Cameron's work (1988) is useful. They have collected essays that consider how specific groups of women speak—for example, black British women in the west Midlands, older rural Welsh women, white middle-class British women in an informal single-sex friendship group, and British Gujarati women and their wedding songs. This kind of specificity moves the debate about women's language away from a focus on powerlessness, passivity, and hesitancy to a focus on how particular groups of women find strength in some contexts and difficulty in other contexts. This has led to analyses of the conditions that create difficulties for women as speakers—for example, in a public forum—rather than assuming that such difficulties are due to their sex. This more positive analysis of language suggests that women can develop strategies for change.

Significantly, Coates analyzes how women speak when they are among other women, rather than simply analyzing their speech in relation to an assumed male norm. Hence, she has been able to develop a new, positive way of describing women's language. For example, she describes how white middle-class British women cooperate with one another in informal speech settings and contrasts this style to a competitive male norm in similar settings. The cooperative style is characterized by overlapping speech, which in this context is considered not as an interruption (which would be competitive or aggressive) but as a demonstration of sympathy—one speaker can predict how another will end a statement. Coates finds that some women can behave competitively when necessary, but that when women are among female friends, they generally speak cooperatively, displaying concern and care.

Feminist literary theorists have been interested in the possibility of a women's language for different reasons: for them, feminine, or women's, writing is the way to confront the status quo through language. For theorists such as Julia Kristeva, Hélène Cixous, and Luce Irigaray, the space of the "feminine" is one where the masculine rules of language are subverted and where women can develop new and revolutionary ways of making meaning (Marks and de Courtivron, 1980). However, other feminist theorists, such as Monique Wittig (1992), have been critical of this view of women's writing practice, arguing that it is both essentialist and heterosexist and takes refuge in "nonsense."

Causes of Women's Oppression in Language

Many feminists believe, with regard to language, that women not only are described differently from men but also do not have the same resources as men. Feminists analyze the causes of this oppression variously. Some, like Dale Spender, believe that it is caused by the dominance of males over females, that the patriarchal structure of society is reflected in language. Others, such as Deborah Tannen (1991), believe that differences in language have more to do with the fact that children are socialized in different ways and grow up in gendered subcultures—that is, children are largely brought up in groups divided according to sex. Even in mixed settings, such as coeducational schools, children tend to form single-sex groups for play, friendship, and socializing, and so they develop different ways of speaking and behaving; it is largely because of this initial difference, then, that women grow up speaking differently. Feminists who believe that women speak differently because of such gendered subcultures tend not to be as openly political as feminists who believe that women's language is different because of patriarchy and oppression.

Tannen's work has been especially popular. She argues that because of initial differences in upbringing, women tend to use what she calls "rapport talk"—speech with the primary aim of cementing relationships. Men, on the other hand, tend to use "report talk," with the primary aim of imparting information. As a result of this difference in intention, statements may be understood in different ways by women and men; this in turn can lead to breakdowns in communication.

Tannen's work is suggestive but has the same problems as Lakoff's work: its generalizations are based on descriptions of mainly white middle-class American women, in specific situations—that is, in the context of intimate heterosexual discussions. In this area of research, it is important to clarify which women or men are being discussed.

See Also

LINGUISTICS; LITERARY THEORY AND CRITICISM; SEXISM; WOMEN: TERMS FOR WOMEN

References and Further Reading

Bergvall, Victoria L., Janet M. Bing, and Alice F. Freed, eds. 1996. *Rethinking gender and language research: Theory and practice.* London: Longman.

Cameron, Deborah. 1985. *Feminism and linguistic theory.* London: Macmillan.

———, ed. 1990. *The feminist critique of language: A reader.* London: Routledge.

Coates, Jennifer. 1998. *Women talk.* Oxford, U.K.: Blackwell.

———, ed. 1998. *Language and gender: A reader.* Oxford, U.K.: Blackwell.

———, and Deborah Cameron, eds. 1988. *Women in their speech communities.* Harlow, U.K.: Longman.

Crawford, Mary. 1995. *Talking differences.* London: Sage.

Daly, Mary. 1978. *Gyn/ecology.* London: Women's Press.

Hadin-Elgin, Suzette. 1985. *Native tongue.* London: Women's Press.

Kramarae, Cheris, and Paula Treichler. 1985. *A feminist dictionary.* London: Pandora.

Lakoff, Robin. 1975. *Language and woman's place.* New York: Harper Colophon.

Marks, Elaine, and Isabelle de Courtivron, eds. 1980. *New French feminisms.* Brighton, U.K.: Harvester.

Mills, Jane. 1989. *Womanwords.* Harlow, U.K.: Longman.

Mills, Sara. 1994. *Feminist stylistics.* London: Routledge.

Schultz, Muriel. 1990. The semantic derogation of woman. In Deborah Cameron, ed., *The feminist critique of language: A reader,* 134–147. London: Routledge.

Spender, Dale. 1980. *Man-made language.* London: Routledge.

Tannen, Deborah. 1991. *You just don't understand: Women and men in conversation.* London: Virago; New York: Ballantine.

Vetterling-Braggin, Mary, ed. 1981. *Sexist language: A modern philosophical enquiry.* Lehigh, Pa.: Littlefield Adams.

Wittig, Monique. 1992. *The straight mind and other essays.* Hemel Hempstead, U.K.: Harvester Wheatsheaf.

Sara Mills

LAW AND SEX

"Law" can be many different things. It can be law made by statutes, legislation, or proclamation by sovereign rulers; law made by proclamation of courts (often called "common law"); or law created and enforced by religion, custom, or tradition. The impact of law can be felt directly, when law dictates what can and cannot be done, or indirectly, as when law refuses or fails to provide protection against harmful situations.

Under law, women can be adversely affected in two ways: a law can discriminate "on its face," that is, explicitly; or a law can have a discriminatory impact on women even if it does not specifically treat women differently from men. Of course, a law may not affect women differently at all; and laws may also protect or benefit women.

Laws that explicitly discriminate against women include some that concern reproduction, such as forced sterilization or mandatory family planning. Examples of laws discriminating against women from all walks of life include the "one child" policy in China (which also indirectly encourages female infanticide) and welfare policies designed to penalize low-income women and single women for having children. Other examples are found among laws relating to property and property interests, such as laws preventing married women from owning property and laws concerning dowries. Laws related to dowries, for instance, can encourage a man to kill his wife in order to marry someone else and thus receive another dowry. This has been a serious problem in India, although the Indian government, relatively recently, addressed it by passing a law under which, in certain circumstances, a man will be presumed to have caused his wife's death.

There are also laws that directly discriminate against women by affecting their ability to protect themselves, such as laws that do not recognize marital rape as a crime (as in Uganda) and laws that do not allow women to defend themselves against batterers. Ireland, for instance, long had a constitutional ban on divorce (now repealed), which often prevented women from escaping battering husbands.

Laws that do not discriminate "on their face" but have a discriminatory impact include many laws concerning rape. Traditionally, in prosecutions of rape, the burden of proof has been on the women, and standards of proof have been very hard to meet; moreover, men's experience has counted more than women's experience, so that a man's access to sex has been protected more than a woman's right not to be harmed. Also, rape has not traditionally been considered a war crime—it was not considered an issue at the Nuremberg trials after World War II, for instance. Recognition of rape as a strategy in war, and thus as a war crime, came only when attention was focused on rape as an aspect of "ethnic cleansing" in the former Yugoslavia.

Indirectly discriminatory law also includes many laws and policies regarding immigration; thus a woman may not be granted asylum because her situation does not fall within the tradition categories of persecution, so that her need for asylum cannot be demonstrated. Laws or policies related to child care also tend to be discriminatory, because women traditionally have the greater responsibility for child care. Indirect discrimination results if, for example, such laws do not enforce child support by an absent father, or if they do not realisticially provide for child care when parents work outside the home, making it difficult for a woman to work to support herself and her family.

Discrimination by law is felt not just by individual women or even just by women as a group but by an entire society. For example, women's household work has monetary value, but when (as is often the case) it is not counted in official statistics for production, a nation's gross national product (GNP), or gross domestic product (GDP), will be greatly undervalued.

As noted above, law can also be beneficial to women, though perhaps this does not happen very often. One example from the United States is legislation passed in Florida and Minnesota that allows women who were forced into prostitution to sue those who forced them or held them; a woman who wins such as suit can collect monetary damages. Another example from the United States is also interesting, although this legislation did not succeed: a town in Indiana passed a law prohibiting pornography because of its presumed harm to women. (The law was challenged in the courts as an infringement of freedom of speech and was not upheld.)

See Also

ETHNIC CLEANSING; FAMILY LAW *and* CASE STUDY: INDIA; FAMILY: RELIGIOUS AND LEGAL SYSTEMS, *specific regions;* HUMAN RIGHTS; JUSTICE AND RIGHTS; LAW: FEMINIST CRITIQUES; LEGAL SYSTEMS; PERSONAL AND CUSTOMARY LAWS; RAPE

References and Further Reading

Bartlett, K. 1993. *Gender and law.* Boston: Little, Brown.

Bartlett, Katherine T., and Rosanne Kennedy. 1991. *Feminist legal theory: Readings in law and gender.* Boulder, Col.: Westview.

Chow, Esther N., and Catherine W. Berheide, eds. 1994. *Women, the family, and policy: A global perspective.* SUNY Series in Gender and Society. Albany: State University of New York Press.

Edwards, Susan S. M. 1985. *Gender, sex, and the law.* London and Dover, N. H.: Croom Helm.

Graycar, Regina. 1990. *The hidden gender of law.* Annandale, New South Wales, Australia: Federation.

Levit, Nancy. 1998. *The gender line: Men, women, and the law.* New York: New York University Press.

Tong, Rosemarie. 1984. *Women, sex, and the law.* Totowa, N. J.: Rowman.

Weisberg, D. Kelly, ed. 1982. *Women and the law: The social historical perspective.* Vols. I and II. Rochester, Vt.: Schenkman.

Kirstin Gulling
Jana Kramer

LAW ENFORCEMENT

Women's role in law enforcement has had a distinctive form and history in many countries. In the late twentieth century it altered again, with women seeking employment on equal terms with men in the police forces of numerous nations. Controversies about women's participation in such activities continue.

History

Law and order are chiefly enforced in contemporary societies by civilian police who have powers to arrest citizens, pursue offenders, and detect crime. Patterns of policing are diverse, but two major forms have had great influence. The first modern police in the English-speaking world were the "new" Metropolitan Police of London, set up in 1829, whose organization was widely imitated in the United States and in the countries of the British Commonwealth, through colonial power and influence. In much of Europe a Napoleonic model of high policing predominated with two (or more) agencies operating, one of which was often (and remains) a quasi-military gendarmerie. To none of these bodies were women recruited.

In the mid-nineteenth century, however, members of early feminist groups began campaigns to increase the part played by women in the criminal justice system, especially in law enforcement. Two U.S. organizations, the Women's

Prison Association and the American Female Moral Reform Society, led the way. In 1845 they succeeded in having six matrons appointed to supervise women prisoners in jails in the United States. Their aims were twofold. They wished to protect women from abuse by jailers and fellow prisoners and also to "regulate womanhood"—that is, to ensure that "innocent girls" would not become depraved or be drawn into prostitution by "hardened female criminals." Thus, one of the key issues and debates surrounding women's role in law enforcement was apparent at a very early stage: were female officers to protect women from men or to ensure that women did not harm others?

Throughout the nineteenth and early twentieth centuries there was increasing activity by women, often from the first-wave feminist movement, for a variety of causes related to moral reform. These included the abolition of slavery, attacks on the vice trade (especially childhood prostitution), and campaigns against alcohol abuse. There was a growing conviction that an important way to achieve such aims was for women to become police officers. Groups such as those mentioned above and the Women's Freedom League in Britain were, at this stage, focused on moral welfare rather than on controlling crime. In 1860, for example, Louisa Twining gave evidence to the Royal Commission on Education on the need for "the influence of women of feeling, and education" to staff institutions for girls. Later in the nineteenth century Twining was one of the initiators of the project to introduce women into policing.

In 1905 Lola Baldwin, who was secretary to a protective group for women, was taken on as a "safety worker" in Portland, Oregon, to prevent sexual harassment of women and girls and to protect men from being solicited by prostitutes. She and her staff did not wish to be called police officers, considering themselves to be social service workers. Alice Stebbins Wells, appointed to the Los Angeles Police Department in 1910, was the first official female officer in the United States. She too followed the welfare and reform model in her work, focusing on women and juveniles and emphasizing "protection"—for example, patrolling public places and taking young people into custody or care to prevent them from falling into crime or sin. As well as pioneering this work, which was widely copied across the United States, Wells later toured the country and abroad, proclaiming the value of female officers to all police forces. Several European nations also introduced prison and police matrons into custodial settings at about this time, the first being Germany in 1903.

In Britain the impetus for the introduction of female officers came from participants in the women's suffrage movement. Indeed, some women who had been suffragists, had taken direct action, and had been arrested were leaders of the movement to bring about females into policing. One of these was Mary Allen. Before the outbreak of World War I in June 1914, a delegation of women's groups had approached the home secretary, with the aim of appointing women constables "with powers equal to men." Margaret Damer Dawson and Nina Boyle, who had both been working with war refugees, concluded that female officers should be appointed to offer protection to women and girls in those turbulent and uncertain times. They began to recruit members to the Women Police Volunteers. Although the recruits were unpaid, they did receive some training and were permitted to patrol by the commissioner of police of the metropolis.

The built-in contradiction in the aims of the volunteers soon emerged in a conflict. This concerned the imposition of a curfew on the women of Grantham, Licolnshire, by the general officer commanding the area. The volunteers agreed to help enforce the curfew, which, of course, protected the *male* soldiers. Nina Boyle was outraged, and the movement split, with Damer Dawson taking the majority of members with her into the renamed Women Police Service (WPS). They proved quite successful and popular, even though the historian of women police in Britain suggests that their activities were often intrusive and moralistic. Yet another group, the National Union of Women Workers of Great Britain and Ireland (later the National Council of Women), also launched Voluntary Women Patrols. They, unlike the WPS, wore only armbands, not uniforms, but they also had authority from the Metropolitan Police.

At the end of the war, all the groups were disbanded, but the police strike of 1918 and other political events led to the setting up of peacetime Metropolitan Police Women Patrols in February 1919. Neither Margaret Damer Dawson nor Mary Allen was involved in this project. Both were deemed too radical. Despite numerous reports, petitions, and parliamentary debates (in which Nancy Astor, the first women to take her seat in the House of Commons, played a part), it was not until 1931 that women finally achieved full status as attested police officers in Britain. This did not mean, any more than it did in the United States, that they had achieved equality with their male colleagues. In both countries women worked only on prevention and protection with women and children. In Britain alone, women had their own command structures, could be promoted, and wore uniforms. The British model was exported to Germany during the occupation after World War I. Other European countries, such as the Netherlands and Sweden, also employed small numbers of female officers to work in this significant if limited way.

Latent Years

Between the 1930s, when more than 1,500 women officers were in service in the United States, and the 1950s, when the total was about 2,600, the expansion of women's role in law enforcement was very slow. In Britain, too, recruitment was stagnant, with no growth in numbers in the Metropolitan Police between 1921 and 1939.

Equality and Expansion

However, in the altered political, social, and economic climate of the 1960s and 1970s, change was very rapid and dramatic. First, the numbers of women entering policing doubled in both the United States and Britain by 1960. More significantly, the tasks assigned to female officers and their position in their policing agencies shifted from the restricted "policewomen's" agenda to broader work. In 1968 the Indianapolis police department in the United States sent the first women officers out on patrol. Washington, D.C., followed with a group of women, including several African-Americans, going out to patrol. In Britain police forces were rapidly integrated in the 1970s, with women receiving equal pay and also doing the same work as men.

These changes continued and led to further developments in the 1980s and 1990s. The proportion of female officers has risen in many countries, although in Japan, for instance, it remained at about the same level—2 percent—between 1970 and 1990. By the end of the twentieth century it stood at about 15 percent in Britain and rather less in the United States. Such averages, however, mask considerable local variation: thus the figure for the Detroit police department, in the United States, was 20 percent in 1990, and for the West Midlands, in the United Kingdom, it was 16 percent. Several women have become police chiefs in major U.S. cities—for example, Elizabeth Watson, appointed to head the Houston police department in 1990 and later chief in Austin, Texas; and Elaine S. Hedtke in Tucson, Arizona. In 1994 Beverly Haward became the first African-American woman chief of police when she took over the police department in Atlanta, Georgia. In the same year Martine Monteil took the post of chief of the Brigade de Répression du Banditisme of the Paris police. In the mid-1990s two women, Pauline Clare and Elizabeth Neville, were appointed the first female chief constables in Britain.

At lower levels women have taken on every kind of nontraditional policing task, including arresting violent suspects, piloting police helicopters, and acting as dog handlers. In the United States, women wear the same uniform and carry the same weapons as men. Several women have been killed in the course of their work, in the United States, Britain, and France.

Police agencies have increasingly adopted formal statements and codes of equality. In some countries this has been because of judicial decisions. In the United States, equal rights legislation, as well as laws on employment opportunities in criminal justice and a series of cases brought by women, has ended discriminatory hiring and promotion practices, such as height and athletic requirements. In Britain the Metropolitan Police issued an Equal Opportunities Code in 1989, and other forces followed suit. In 1988 the European Court ordered France to lift quotas on the recruitment of women. International bodies, such as the International Association of Women Police and the European Network for Policewomen, flourish and hold major international conferences.

Evaluation and Research

By many accounts, the role of women in law enforcement is well established and unquestioned. However, there are debates and controversies around a number of issues. One issue on which a considerable body of research exists is women's "fitness" for policing. Because of the danger, disorder, and distress associated with the job, policing has been seen as an unsuitable job for a woman. Moreover, women have been regarded as unsuited to police work because they are presumed to lack brute strength or physical presence.

Extensive research in the United States on women officers' performance on patrol, including comparisons with their male colleagues, has showed these fears to be unjustified. Women did as well as men on most tasks and were better at some. Furthermore, it is clear that the police agenda changed in many societies in the late twentieth century. In particular, gendered offenses became a focus of public concern. Rape, domestic violence, and physical and sexual abuse of children have all been given higher priority. As a result, the skills and talents suitable for modern police work have had to be redefined, brute strength being less vital than interpersonal skill.

Cop Culture and Harassment

Women officers and their role in law enforcement were increasingly prominent in the late twentieth century. They were portrayed in television police series, such as *Cagney and Lacey* (United States, 1980s), a long-running drama about two detectives in the New York City Police Department, and *Prime Suspect,* a miniseries about a chief inspector in the

Criminal Investigation Division in London. These shows, and films such as *Blue Steel,* depicted women as strong, brave, and capable. Nevertheless, they (and news stories) also showed the problems women continued to face *inside* police agencies because of harassment from their male colleagues. One of the most dramatic cases involved Alison Halford, who was assistant chief constable of Merseyside, England, and who brought a suit alleging sexual discrimination against her employers and the Home Office. The ensuing tribunal hearings revealed details of the police culture that were reinforced by other cases brought by more junior officers, as well as findings from a national survey of women officers' experiences of harassment (Anderson et al., 1993). Parallel cases have been publicized in the United States and Australia.

A Role for Women in Law Enforcement

Women all over the world have shown great commitment to working in law enforcement. Often this is because it is a relatively well-paid occupation that has been opened to women only in recent times. There are other issues at stake. Historically, women sought to become law officers for moral, even missionary reasons. They campaigned ceaselessly to achieve their aims. They now participate widely in policing, albeit still usually as a minority. Women increasingly challenge the domination of the apparatus of social control, which in many countries remains almost exclusively in the hands of men. Some commentators question whether women bring distinctive styles or perspectives to their work in law enforcement. What is clear is that many women do seek a role in law enforcement and that their chief obstacle now is resistance, in the form of harassment, from some of their colleagues.

See Also

CRIME AND PUNISHMENT; CRIMINOLOGY; SEXUAL HARASSMENT

References and Further Reading

Anderson, Rhona, Jennifer Brown, and Elizabeth Campbell. 1993. *Aspects of sex discrimination within the police service in England and Wales.* London: Home Office Police Department.

Brown, Jennifer, and Frances Heidensohn. 2000. *Gender and policing.* Basingstoke: Macmillan.

Halford, Alison. 1993. *No way up the greasy pole.* London: Constable.

Heidensohn, Frances. 1992. *Women in control? The role of women in law enforcement.* Oxford: Oxford University Press.

Horne, P. 1980. *Women in law enforcement.* 2nd ed. Springfield, Ill.: Thomas.

Lock, Joan. 1979. *The British policewoman.* London: Hale.

Martin, Susan E. 1990. *On the move: The status of women in policing.* Washington, D. C.: Police Foundation.

Moses, Dorothy Schulz. 1995. *From social worker to crime fighter.* Westport, Conn.: Praeger.

Rafter, Nicole, and Frances Heidensohn, eds. 1995. *International feminist perspectives in criminology.* Milton Keynes, U.K.: Open University Press.

Frances Heidensohn

LAW: Family

See FAMILY LAW.

LAW: Feminist Critiques

In general, law—statute law, common law, and customary law—was developed by men during eras when women were excluded from active participation in this process. Feminism has provided a standpoint from which to critique and change both legal structures and the substance of law. Early feminists examined the openly discriminatory laws that effectively excluded women from participation in public life. Although the status of women improved, feminists in the late twentieth century continued this critique and developed a distinctive field of inquiry: feminist legal theory, or feminist jurisprudence. This field now presents an array of theories about the legal difficulties women continue to encounter and how to change the legal system to remedy these problems. These various approaches both compete with and inform one another and thus increase the understanding of the relationship between women and the law.

Historical Development

Essentially, women's voices were not heard in the processes leading to the formation of customary law; and when more formal legal structures were developed, women were neither judges nor lawyers and thus did not participate in the making of common law. Nor did women sit in legislatures (indeed, they were not even allowed to vote for those who did), so they did not participate directly in the development of statutory law. Because of a dominant ideology of sex inequality, many legal standards were openly discriminatory against women, denying them civil and property rights, excluding them from professions, treating men and women differently upon dissolution of a marriage, and the like. Even where women acquired the right to vote, hold property, enter into contracts, and practice the professions of their choice, the law often remained distinctively "male." In the United States, for example, many laws were sex-specific until well into the mid-twentieth century.

In many other ways as well, legal standards simply did not take the experiences of women into account, because the law had been based on male experiences and male viewpoints. One frequently cited example is the law of justifiable self-defense, which was based on a presumption of a direct confrontation between two roughly equal parties conditioned to use violence defensively. Common law required a defendant pleading self-defense to establish both a realistic fear of imminent physical danger and proportionality between the level of force encountered and the level applied in defense. A battered woman who kills her more powerful abuser with a deadly weapon after a long history of beatings is poorly served by these criteria; the legal requirements developed by and for men do not fit her experience.

The proliferation of feminist critiques of law was a product of the women's movement of the 1960s and 1970s. It began with critiques of outright sex discrimination by feminist activists who undertook campaigns to change the law so that women would be treated similarly to men. As many traditional barriers to women's participation in education, employment, and political life began to fall, these early feminist critiques of law developed and became more nuanced. Academics and practitioners began to focus not only on the unequal treatment of women and men but also on the ways in which women are different from men and may require "different" treatment in order to be genuinely equal. Other academics and lawyers attacked both positions—"equality" and "difference."

By the year 2000, many law schools offered courses in feminist jurisprudence, and feminist legal scholars had produced a substantial literature in many parts of the world (examples include Graycar and Morgan, 1990; Kapur and Cossman, 1996; and Smart, 1989). Yet there is clearly no such thing as a single feminist legal theory. Rather, there are now many contending theories, all critical of legal systems developed by men but differing in their views of how to change the law to include women's perspective and to protect women's interests and welfare. Several influential schools of feminist legal criticism are described below.

Critiques Based on Formal Equality

Formal equality was the predominant legal theory in the early stages of the postwar women's movement; it also dominated the strategy of groups seeking to gain equal rights for women through legislation. Feminist activists challenged exclusionary practices in court on grounds of equality and promoted antidiscrimination laws—that is, laws prohibiting unequal treatment of men and women. Moreover, formal equality theory was embodied in the conventions and declarations issued by the international human rights movement concerning the rights of women.

Formal equality theory, like classical liberal democratic theory, assumes autonomous individuals as actors: each actor seeks to maximize self-interest in the public sphere. However, equality theories (sometimes referred to as "rights theories") do not consider differences among actors in the private sphere, disregarding inequalities in the private sphere that have an important impact on the status of women, such as familial, religious, and customary constraints on women's freedom of action, or women's inability to take advantage of choices in the public sphere. For example, according to equality theories men and women would be treated identically by laws governing divorce, ignoring the fact that a wife may have left the workforce for a long period to care for children and may be ill-equipped to reenter employment on equal terms.

Despite its disregard of the private sphere, formal equality theory was quite successful at gaining initial access for women to many institutions, such as schools and professions, which had previously been closed to them. Critics point out, however, that formal equality theory is best suited to advance the interests of elite women, those who are positioned to compete on equal terms with men in universities and professions. Poorer women, women who lack education, and women whose family obligations prevent them from competing in the world of men could be harmed by legal theories that assume equality where it does not in fact exist. Thus feminists differed about whether the legal changes resulting from a formal equality approach actually benefited women as a group.

In the United States, formal equality theory was well suited to attack the many forms of sex-specific legislation that still existed in the middle of the twentieth century, such as exclusion of women from jury pools, different ages of majority for men and women, different labor standards, and different rules for men and women under family law. In many other parts of the world, equality theory remains a powerful tool in women's struggle against inequalities that are sometimes exempted from guarantees of legal equality. In India, for example, substantial areas of civil law (family and inheritance law) are treated under "personal law" pertaining to an individual's religious community, and many of these communties overtly discriminate against women (Kapur and Cossman, 1996). In such contexts, and in various cases involving sex-discriminatory customary laws in Africa, formal equality theories have provided important weapons for women's rights activists (Stewart, 1996).

Critiques Based on "Difference" or Cultural Feminism

Because the individual actor assumed by formal equality seems, overall, to be male, formal equality theory does not work well in addressing legal issues unique to women, such as issues involving pregnancy. Pregnancy and its disabilities (those based on biology as well as many that may be socially constructed but are nonetheless strongly entrenched) appeared to be "differences" and to require "special" treatment. Hence, legal feminists have debated whether equality or difference is the more beneficial approach to women's rights. While recognition of women's unique needs (such as maternity leave) clearly helps substantial numbers of women, it may also perpetuate stereotypes of women as the weaker sex and an ideology of protection that has kept them out of economic and social life in the past.

The roots of cultural feminism are often traced to an influential book by the psychologist Carol Gilligan, *In a Different Voice* (1982). Gilligan compared male and female moral judgments on a number of issues and concluded that the male perspective tended to rely on notions of individual rights and justice, while the female perspective assigned a greater value to caring and relationships. This insight has led some feminist legal theorists to wonder how including the female voice might transform the law, which in western culture has been influenced by notions of abstract, noncontextual individual rights.

Robin West (1987, 1997) envisages a system in which legal judgments would incorporate empathy, care, and connection among individuals; she has also maintained that women's experiences—their pleasures and pain—are mostly invisible or trivialized in a legal system designed to remedy the types of legal problems that happen to men. For example, assault involving two persons of equal strength is recognized as a compensable harm, but harassment of women that is tantamount to assault has not traditionally been seen as an injury requiring legal redress. West proposes both including women's experiences in the development of law and incorporating into jurisprudence the largely female perspective of caring and connection, arguing that both the "male" rights-oriented approach and the "female" caring approach are necessary to justice.

Critiques Based on Power or Dominance Theory

One very influential feminist legal theorist in the United States, Catharine A. MacKinnon (1989), criticizes both formal equality critiques and cultural feminist critiques of the law. She argues that formal equality approaches take men—the male body, male strength, and men's needs and biographies—as the norm against which females are measured and are found to be different or unequal. With the terms set in this way, a formal equality approach benefits women only to the extent that they are similar to men. For example, women workers are free to compete with men in a workplace structured around an ideal male worker who has a wife at home. If a woman is unable, because of obligations to small children or aged parents, to work long days, she fails to meet the "equal, gender-neutral" standard for employees in that firm. According to MacKinnon, formal equality cannot address this problem: simply treating similarly situated individuals similarly will still result in sex discrimination. MacKinnon is also suspicious of approaches based on women's differences from men, arguing that women's apparent preference for caring and connection may simply reflect qualities and abilities women have learned in order to survive in a world of male dominance.

In MacKinnon's own feminist critque of the law, what is central is the question of power—male supremacy and female subordination. It is through power that differences between the sexes have been assigned their social, economic, and political consequences, by which they are translated into advantages for men and disadvantages for women. MacKinnon's approach, often called dominance theory, has its roots in radical feminism and socialist analysis.

Another important critique of law based on an analysis of power is derived from postmodern or poststructuralist thought. In poststructural theory, power is located not so much in political or juridical institutions as in a more dispersed ability to define and reflect judgments about what is normal. Law in this sense is a form of authoritative discourse. Carol Smart, an English feminist theorist writing from this standpoint, eschews feminist jurisprudence as grand theory, arguing that law is a very limited instrument for effecting change (1989). Whereas MacKinnon has emphasized how her theories might be translated into practice (for example, by litigation and legislation to define sexual harassment as sex discrimination), Smart is skeptical about using law for radical purposes.

Theories based on analysis of power relations are especially useful with regard to violence against women and the legal treatment of "harms"—such as domestic violence, sexual harassment, pornography, and rape—that happen almost exclusively to women. A formal equality approach is inadequate for analyzing these harms because it fails to address the structures of power and dominance that perpetuate them, such as the eroticization of male power over women (MacKinnon, 1989) or familial, religious, and customary hierarchies that the law does not reach (Coomaraswamy, 1994).

Antiessentialism, Critical Race, and Postcolonial Feminism

An important critique of all the feminist legal theories discussed so far is that they "essentialize" woman by ignoring many characteristics other than gender—such as race, class, and sexual orientation—which affect women's interests and perspectives,. "Critical race" feminists suggest that the essential woman assumed by formal equality, cultural feminist, and dominance theories to be the victim of discrimination looks very much like a white, middle-class, heterosexual woman (Harris, 1990). By reducing a woman to her gender, these theories ignore the interests and viewpoints of many women—perhaps the majority of women—and fail to address discrimination against them. Laws concerning sex discrimination, for example, cannot account for discrimination that is motivated by both race and sex and therefore cannot provide adequate remedies. Similarly, feminist theories about rape that take the perspective of white women cannot address African-American women's experience of rape as an instrument of racist domination of black women and black men (Crenshaw, 1989).

Analyses developed by women in the third world bring new depth and complexity to feminist critiques of the law. In India, for example, a woman's identity has traditionally been defined by religion, social class, and family before her subjective identification as a woman (Pathak and Rajan, 1992). Under these circumstances, feminist legal scholars who rely on the universalizing concepts of human rights theory may be seen as alien and as hostile to national identity. In seeking to develop their own legal strategies for effecting change, third world women add an important perspective to feminist analysis of the law.

See Also

FAMILY LAW *and* CASE STUDY: INDIA; LAW AND SEX; LEGAL SYSTEMS; PERSONAL AND CUSTOMARY LAW

References and Further Reading

Coomaraswamy, Radhika. 1994. To bellow like a cow: Women, ethnicity, and the discourse of rights. In Rebecca J. Cook, ed., *Human rights of women: National and international perspectives.* Philadelphia: University of Pennsylvania Press.

Crenshaw, Kimberlé. 1989. Demarginalizing the intersection of race and sex: A black feminist critique of antidiscrimination doctrine, feminist theory, and antiracist politics. *University of Chicago Legal Forum* 139–167.

Gilligan, Carol. 1982. *In a different voice: Psychological theory and women's development.* Cambridge, Mass.: Harvard University Press.

Graycar, Regina, and Jenny Morgan. *The hidden gender of law.* Annandale, New South Wales, Australia: Federation.

Harris, Angela P. 1990. Race and essentialism in feminist legal theory. *Stanford Law Review* 42: 581–616.

Kapur, Ratna, and Brenda Cossman. 1996. *Subversive sites: Feminist engagements with law in India.* New Delhi: Sage.

MacKinnon, Catharine A. 1989. *Toward a feminist theory of the state.* Cambridge, Mass.: Harvard University Press.

Pathak, Zakia, and Rajeswari Sunder Rajan. 1992. Shahbano. In Judith Butler and Joan W. Scott, eds., *Feminists theorize the political.* London: Routledge.

Smart, Carol. 1989. *Feminism and the power of law.* London: Routledge.

Stewart, Ann. 1996. Should women give up on the state? The African experience. In Shirin M. Rai and Geraldine Livesley, eds., *Women and the state: International perspectives.* London: Taylor and Francis.

West, Robin. 1997. *Caring for justice.* New York: New York University Press.

———. 1987. The difference in women's hedonic lives: A phenomenological critique of feminist legal theory. *Wisconsin Women's Law Journal* 3: 81–145.

Cynthia Grant Bowman

LAW: Personal and Customary

See PERSONAL AND CUSTOMARY LAWS.

LEADERSHIP

The visibility of women in positions of leadership increased significantly in the late twentieth century and has continued into the twenty-first, for two main reasons. First, the global women's movement gained momentum from the United Nations Decade of Women, 1975–1985, and from the Beijing World Conference on Women in 1995. Second, scholars of leadership tended more and more to characterize it as relational, contextual, and ethical, rather than as necessarily linked to top organizational positions (Bryson and Crosby, 1992; Bunch, 1987).

The global women's movement and the shift in thinking about leadership were connected. For example, during the UN Decade, women were the chief organizers of international conferences, presided at large public forums, presented visions of how their societies should develop, and negotiated difficult conflicts. In preparation for the international conferences and in their aftermath, women founded new organizations and reinvigorated old ones. Clearly, many women were ably performing what might be called traditional leadership roles.

At the same time, many of these women performed these roles in a consciously groundbreaking manner that combined positional and nonpositional leadership, promoted shared or collective leadership, and celebrated connection and diversity over hierarchy and homogeneity (Basu, 1995). Some women refused to be called leaders at all, because leadership had a traditional association with power, hierarchy, and oppression.

Women's leadership also gained visibility in the late twentieth century because individual women competed successfully with men to win public office, from local to national levels. A few prominent examples were Sirimavo Bandaranaike, prime minister of Sri Lanka; Gro Harlem Bruntland, prime minister of Norway; Margaret Thatcher, the English prime minister; Corazon Aquino, president of the Philippines; and Mary Robinson, president of Ireland. Women were appointed to important positions in United Nations organizations: Mary Robinson became the first UN High Commissioner for Human Rights, Gro Harlem Bruntland was named director general of the World Health Organization, and Sadako Ogata became high commissioner for refugees. More women became judges and chief judges from the local to the international level.

Some women rose to the top of large corporations, although women's leadership in business was perhaps most visible at the grassroots level, whether it was a housewife in the United States starting a successful public relations firm in her living room or a woman in a Bangladeshi village starting a small but profitable vending operation.

Other women broke barriers in sports and outdoor adventure—leading Olympic teams, climbing Himalayan peaks, and conducting polar expeditions. Women leaders also altered women's role in many religious institutions, became high-ranking military officers, and founded an academic field, women's studies.

Altering the Context

Women leaders have taken advantage of political, social, economic, and technological trends that brought new opportunities and challenges at the turn of the twenty-first century; they also helped shape those trends. In political life, women's activism within and outside political parties helped women greatly increase their numbers in elected office. These increases, however, were concentrated at subnational levels; in the year 2000, women still held only 13 percent of the seats in the world's national legislatures. As an outcome of meetings during the UN Decade, women leaders developed and promoted a new international treaty, the Convention on the Elimination of Discrimination against Women, which provided new visibility for women's political, social, economic, and cultural rights and ultimately contributed to a recognition that women's rights should receive attention within any human rights campaign.

The advent of a knowledge-based, consumer-oriented global economy made women more valued as workers and managers but also made them more vulnerable to economic decisions emanating from other parts of the world. Women were still disproportionately concentrated in low-paying jobs and were subject to sexual harassment and other forms of discrimination. Some women responded by becoming union leaders and by organizing campaigns demanding equal pay for equal work. Economists such as Marilyn Waring (1988) led important efforts to have women's paid and unpaid work acknowledged and to have women's vital role in economic development appreciated. Other feminist activists led campaigns to ensure that women could escape domestic violence, benefit from new knowledge and technologies related to family planning, and protect themselves from the AIDS epidemic. Some women also led organizations—such as antiabortion groups—that opposed feminist campaigns.

Visionary Leadership

Women leaders helped create and communicate new shared visions of what girls' and women's lives could be like and new visions of what societies might become. They fought to keep these visions alive under hostile conditions: for example, Aung San Suu Kyi, who won the Nobel Peace Prize in 1991 for leading a democratic reform movement in Myanmar, continued her campaign at great personal sacrifice; the Islamic scholar Konca Kuris of Turkey was tortured and killed for her advocacy of women's rights; many Afghani women risked their lives as to defy the fundamentalist Taliban movement and organized home schools for girls who had been denied public education; and many lesbians around the world were attacked when they led campaigns for lesbian rights.

Team and Organizational Leadership

Much of the U.S.-based research on women's leadership in the last two decades of the twentieth century explored whether women take a different approach from men to building and sustaining teams and organizations. The findings were mixed. Women in "nontraditional" or female-dominated organizations seemed to have a more collaborative, interactive style of leadership than men (Helgeson, 1994; Rosenor, 1990); but in male-dominated organizations women's leadership styles were similar to those of their male colleagues. Other analysts—for example, Felice N. Schwartz (1989), who initiated the debate over the "mommy track"—examined barriers to women's advancement into corporate leadership positions and advocated mentor programs, family-friendly policies, and other initiatives to help businesses attract and retain women managers.

Diversity

At the beginning of the twenty-first century, the diversity of women's leadership was apparent. Women leaders represented a wide range of ideologies and political stances. Women were moving into leadership positions in traditionally male-dominated areas such as electoral politics and corporations, and women were also transforming the definition of leadership as they emphasized networking and collaboration and formed their own organizations. Women and girls were finding more opportunities to train for leadership in programs designed especially for them. Many of these programs were organized by women's nongovernmental organizations (NGOs) as a follow-up to international women's conferences.

See Also

ENTREPRENEURSHIP; ORGANIZATIONAL THEORY; WORK, *specific topics*

References and Further Reading

Adler, Nancy J., and Dafna N. Izraeli. 1994. *Competitive frontiers: Women managers in a global economy.* Cambridge, Mass.: Blackwell.

Basu, Amrita. 1995. *The challenge of local feminisms: Women's movements in global perspective.* Boulder, Col.: Westview.

Bryson, John M., and Barbara C. Crosby. 1992. *Leadership for the common good: Tackling public problems in a shared-power world.* San Francisco: Jossey-Bass.

Bunch, Charlotte. 1987. *Passionate politics.* New York: St. Martin's.

Helgeson, Sally. 1994. *The female advantage: Women's ways of leading.* New York: Doubleday.

Rosenor, Judy B. 1990. Ways women lead. *Harvard Business Review* (November–December): 119–125.

Schwartz, Felice N. 1989. Management women and the new facts of life. *Harvard Business Review* (January–February).

Waring, Marilyn. 1988. *If women counted: A new feminist economics.* San Francisco: Harper.

Web site: Center for Women's Global Leadership <http://www.cwgl.rutgers.edu/index.html>

Barbara C. Crosby

LEADERSHIP, POLITICAL

See POLITICAL LEADERSHIP.

LEGAL SYSTEMS

Legal systems enshrine the cultural values of ruling groups by establishing laws and mechanisms for enforcing those laws. It is often argued that legal systems largely reflect and reinforce patriarchal social relations, confirming the subordination of women through the regulation of their productive and reproductive labor. Yet legal systems are subject to change and operate in complex and contradictory ways. At particular historical moments, women have benefited from legal reforms, although such a gain is often partial and fragile and will have a differential impact on women within a particular society, depending on their racial, ethnic, religious, cultural, sexual, and class position. Guarantees of sex equality are included in state constitutions in many parts of the world, but these provide no more than a framework in the struggle to attain equality in practice. A growing body of international law, including pronouncements on the status of women, provides a focus for challenging oppressive laws at an international level.

The formal sources of law include custom and religion, as well as legislation, judicial decisions, and scholarly writings. Conflicting systems frequently coexist within particular nation-states, for example, when invading powers impose new laws without dismantling indigenous legal systems, when regional and local practices persist alongside developing federal or national systems of law, or when religious leaders give priority to model laws claiming to be derived from holy texts, in preference to secular sources of law. In times of revolution or social upheaval, when legal systems are at their most volatile, rapid changes can occur in the rules governing the position of women. Gender roles may be challenged and the status of women enhanced; alternatively, any gains associated with discredited regimes may be lost and traditional laws confining women to the private sphere reimposed. Where a new regime introduces changes in the status of women that are perceived as too radical by community leaders, women who attempt to claim their new rights may be severely punished and even killed by those leaders.

Two major legal systems emanating from Europe, both underpinned by Christianity and liberalism, have been influential in many parts of the world as a result of colonialism and westernization. First, the Romano-Germanic tradition originated as a system of private law regulating relationships between individuals and developing elaborate systems of legislative codes. It penetrated beyond Europe, influencing legal developments in east Asia, South America, and parts of Africa. Second, the common law is derived from the English system of public law, in which a system of precedent has evolved; that is, cases are decided on the basis of judicial decisions in earlier cases. Its influence extended to North America, Oceania, and parts of south Asia and Africa. Radical transformations occurred in both European systems in the process of transplantation, particularly where they were grafted onto preexisting legal systems by colonial powers. Legal plurism, in which two or more systems of law coexist, became widespread; customary or personal laws regulating the private sphere of marriage and the family were often left intact. Postcolonial governments have inherited the conflicts and inconsistencies that flow from pluralist legal systems which, when coupled with a backlash in many countries against any form of westernization, provide a fertile breeding ground for the reassertion of laws oppressive to women, justified on the basis of cultural tradition and religious edict.

Legal Systems in Western Democracies

With the development of industrialization and a series of bourgeois revolutions in eighteenth-century Europe, in which the rising middle classes successfully challenged the feudal landowners, who had monopolized power, a new set of social and legal relations evolved, grounded in the principles of equality, liberty, contract, and the rule of law. Male heads of households exercised these newly won rights on behalf of women and children. Women's scope for participation in the public sphere was severely curtailed and their activities in the private sphere were regulated by laws on marriage, child custody, and the ownership and inheritance of property, which left power and control firmly in the hands of men. Blackstone's *Commentaries on the Laws of England* are unequivocal: "By marriage the husband and wife are one person in law: that is, the very being or legal existence of woman is suspended during marriage" (Blackstone, 1973–1975: 445).

In order to break free from the shackles of this legal inheritance, women in western democracies have campaigned continuously for full citizenship rights and for legal equality with men in all areas of public and family life (see, for example, the account of these campaigns in Britain and the United States in Sachs and Wilson, 1978). By appealing to the very principal of equality, which gave the legal systems their legitimacy, and by recognizing the importance to nation-states of women's participation in the labor market, women have won important civil, political, and social rights. Yet despite achieving apparent gender neutrality in a great deal of legislation, legal systems in western democracies, it is widely held, continue to underwrite rather than undermine patriarchal structures, and gender stereotypes persist in many areas of law. Formal equality in the public sphere is achieved on the basis of conformity to rules and values designed for the benefit of men, while severe inequalities persist in the private sphere. Much work remains to be done to address the problem of male violence and the ways in which laws define and control women's sexuality and fertility (Smart, 1989; Thornton, 1991).

State Socialist Legal Systems

The most radical overhaul of legal systems takes place in the wake of successful revolutions. Where state socialist societies were created, some of the characteristics of the previous legal system (usually the Romano-Germanic) were preserved, but a new body of legal rules was formulated in order to abolish the private ownership of the means of production and to make the legal system responsive to the will of the people, as expressed through the Communist Party.

In contrast to western democracies, where equality is fought for from below, state socialist governments are committed to a policy of women's liberation through legislation. There is a shift from private forms of patriarchy to public forms: the state provides for women in return for their productive and reproductive labor. The laws confirm the dual role of women as workers and mothers, while men are treated only as workers. Benefits such as paid maternity and housework leave are confined to women, reinforcing the traditional sexual division of labor within households (Einhorn, 1993). The economic and social rights conferred on women by the state are not matched by the civil rights necessary for active participation in political processes. Women's organizations are officially endorsed and controlled by the state and disconnected from grassroots involvement.

In times of economic difficulty, laws benefiting women prove among the most fragile; states waver between proworkerist and pronatalist policies as the need for women in the workforce is balanced against the perceived need for women as mothers. Extreme fluctuations in abortion laws indicate their use as an instrument of population policy rather than of gender equality. Since the collapse of state socialist regimes in the former Soviet Union and eastern Europe, legislative supports for women workers have been dismantled and according to many observers the controls of private patriarchy have been reestablished as religious and nationalist politics gain ascendancy.

In other parts of the world, attempts to impose gender equality as part of a socialist agenda have met with only partial success. In China, changes to women's status were largely restricted to increasing women's participation in economic life and introducing marital rights for women within the legal system. Since the early 1980s, women's reproduction has been strictly controlled through the imposition of policy limiting each family to one child. In Central and South America, the combination of Catholicism and the *machista* culture are said to impede the implementation of equality principles even where socialist revolutions are in progress (Stephens, 1990).

Pluralist Legal Systems

Elements of western and state socialist legal systems have been adopted by or imposed upon countries in many parts of the world, resulting in various forms of legal pluralism.

In postcolonial societies, a multiplicity of customary and religious laws coexist alongside "received" laws from the former colonial states. Local laws governing marriage, postmarital residence, inheritance, and access to property were frequently left intact by the colonial rulers, although they prevent women from becoming economically independent. Western preoccupation with clear and precise rules often produced distortion and ossification in the application of customary law, sometimes accentuating gender inequalities (Armstrong et al., 1993). In some African states, for example, Zimbabwe and Tanzania, laws have been passed to equalize the position of men and women in marriage, but weak enforcement mechanisms and unequal power relations have rendered the laws ineffective. In India, the practice of sati, or suttee, the self-immolation of the widow on the deceased husband's funeral pyre, is increasing, despite its illegality, and the dowry system persists, as does the burning of brides when dowry payments are disputed. The government, caught between fundamentalist forces on the one hand, and pressure from women's and civil rights groups on the other, does little to enforce its own equality laws.

When states actively seek to "modernize" traditional legal systems, the position of many women is rapidly transformed; the extent of their participation in public life becomes a key indicator of social progress. When such regimes fall into disfavor, laws restricting women's activities are reimposed just as swiftly by the incoming regime and carry the same degree of symbolic significance. Such sharp reversals in the position of women have occurred in a number of Islamic states in recent years. In Iran and Pakistan, a selective blend of Islamic law and customary practices has deprived women of many rights previously enjoyed, such as the right to own and inherit property and to contract and terminate marriage freely (Shaheed, 1986).

For as long as the backlash against westernization and secularization is expressed so forcefully and fundamentalist movements are in the ascendancy, governments opposed to such extremist tendencies often seem unwilling or unable to reverse them. In such a climate, it is difficult for women's groups to mount effective forms of resistance, and women who still operate in the public sphere increasingly do so on men's terms. Significantly, this attack on secularism and women's rights is mirrored in a number of western societies, where Christian fundamentalist groups have promoted laws that control women's fertility in the name of religion.

International Law

International law attempts to shape national legal systems by establishing universal principles of conduct, expressed in a series of declarations and conventions. International and internal pressures are used to persuade states to become signatories, and international courts pass judgment on those found guilty of violations. Some transnational laws have a specific geographical range, such as the Treaty of Rome, which established the European Community and included provisions for sex equality, as does the Inter-American Convention on the Prevention, Punishment, and Eradication of Violence against Women. United Nations initiatives potentially have worldwide effects. The UN Convention on the Elimination of All Forms of Discrimination against Women was adopted in 1979 and ratified by more than one hundred states by the beginning of the 1990s. The UN Declaration on the Elimination of Violence against Women was adopted in 1993.

Women's groups are also engaged in campaigns to remove gender bias from international human rights laws to ensure that the seriousness of rape and sexual abuse, especially in situations of war and conflict, is acknowledged, that women seeking refugee status are treated fairly, and that cultural practices such as female genital mutilation, sati, and dowry deaths are internationally condemned.

See Also

CONSTITUTIONS; FUNDAMENTALISM AND PUBLIC POLICY; JUSTICE AND RIGHTS; LAW AND SEX; LAW: FEMINIST CRITIQUES

References and Further Reading

Armstrong, Alice, et al. 1993. Uncovering reality: Excavating women's rights in African family law. *International Journal of Law and the Family* 7: 314–369.

Blackstone, I. W. 1973–1975. *Commentaries on the laws of England.* 12th ed. Oxford: Clarendon. (Originally published 1765.)

Einhorn, Barbara. 1993. *Cinderella goes to market: Citizenship, gender, and women's movements in east central Europe.* London: Verso.

Kandiyoti, Deniz. 1991. *Women, Islam, and the state.* Basingstoke: Macmillan.

McColgan, Aileen. 2000. *Women under the law: The false promise of human rights.* Harlow: Longman.

Mehdi, Rubya. 1990. The offence of rape in the Islamic law of Pakistan. *International Journal of the Sociology of Law* 18: 19–29.

Roach Anleu, Sharon L. 2000. *Law and social change.* London: Sage.

Sachs, Albie, and Joan Hoff Wilson. 1978. *Sexism and the law: A study of male beliefs and judicial bias.* Oxford: Martin Robertson.

Shaheed, Farida. 1986. The cultural articulation of patriarchy: Legal systems, Islam, and women. *South Asia Bulletin* 1: 38–44.

Smart, Carol. 1989. *Feminism and the power of law.* London: Routledge.

Stephens, Beth. 1990. A developing legal system grapples with an ancient problem: Rape in Nicaragua. *Women's Rights Law Reporter* 12(2): 69–88.

Thornton, Margaret. 1991. Feminism and the contradictions of law reform. *International Journal of the Sociology of Law.* 19: 453–474.

Jeanne Gregory

LEISURE

Leisure is usually defined as time free from work or other duties. Feminists and others often comment that in many ways, leisure is a problematic concept for women; some even suggest that "women's leisure" is a contradiction in terms.

One problem is that not everyone has equal access to leisure time. Time free of paid work is typically well defined, but some writers (such as the feminists Deem, 1986; and Henderson and Bialeschki, 1992) have noted that women tend to be disproportionately involved in unpaid work and caregiving, with the result that they often have little or no uncommitted time. A second problem is that the social definition of leisure is sometimes influenced by ideology. In particular, it can be affected by concepts of masculinity and femininity, that is, ideas about appropriate male and female roles, concerns, and behavior; it can also be affected by ideologies of class and race. A third problem, related to the second, is that many women need to choose settings for leisure cautiously and to guard their behavior in these settings. Consequently, the quality of a leisure experience and interactions with companions—and the opportunity for a break, a change, or simply time to themselves—may become more important to women than a specific setting or activity.

Women's Leisure Activities

Historical studies of women's diaries have found some surprising similarities across social classes with regard to leisure. Two examples are the celebrated writer Virginia Woolf and Hannah Cullick, a working-class woman in rural England during the Victorian era, whose leisure was circumscribed by their work and by men's control of their joint and personal incomes (Stanley, 1988). A century later, because of women's primary position as wives, mothers, and caregivers, this was to a considerable extent still true:

> Women's leisure away from home is rarely taken as a right, and even when some women (usually middle-class) do get some "away from home leisure," it often takes the form of family leisure. (Hargreaves, 1994: 187)

Thus for many women, truly free leisure is a precious commodity, often taken in snatched intervals between such tasks as cooking, cleaning, and child care. Women employed full time and married women with children under school age report the least time for personal leisure (Deem, 1986; Green et al., 1990). However, employed women typically feel more entitled to leisure time, and have more varied opportunities for leisure, than women who are dependent on a partner's income. In every social class, earning money tends to make women better able to negotiate time for leisure.

Modern studies in western societies suggest that women's leisure, more than men's, is likely to be based in and around the home. For instance, studies in the United Kingdom (Deem, 1986; Green et al., 1990) found that women's favorite leisure activities were watching television, reading, and crafts done at home. These findings have been replicated in Australian studies (Dempsey, 1990; Wearing and Wearing, 1998) and in North American studies (Bialeschki and Henderson, 1986; Hunter and Whitson, 1991). Although this "domestication" of women's leisure is affected by class and other social and cultural differences, it is evident in very diverse groups of women, and it implies a blurring of work and leisure pursuits.

Women's ability to engage in leisure activities outside the home varies with their domestic circumstances and responsibilities. Young unmarried women, in general, have more potential freedom to "dance the night away" with their friends (McRobbie, 1984), if they have the money to do so, whereas women in partnerships and women with children are of necessity more homebound. In theory, older women whose children are grown up have more freedom for outside pursuits, but in practice they too are often limited by lack of money, lack of friends to go out with, and obligations to care for aging relatives.

In kind, if not in frequency or duration, women's recorded leisure activities in the home are similar to those of men. Outside the home, however, there are sharp gender differences. Because outside activities are subject to a range of constraints, women are less likely than men to go to clubs, restaurants, or cafés, bars, or pubs. These constraints include child care, lack of time, and lack of money. A lack of safe, affordable transportation often keeps women at home, especially after dark, including middle-class women who share a car with a male partner.

The difference between women and men is especially marked in physical recreations: men participate in these far more often than women, and the range of activities is broader for men. In the United Kingdom, according to at least one study (Woodward et al., 1989), the physical activities most popular among women were yoga and keeping fit; these were followed by swimming, badminton, tennis, squash, and running or jogging. Participation in sports increases with higher social class, and with education. In Sheffield, England, for example, middle-class women (as defined by their male partners' occupations) were twice as likely as women from the lowest-income households to enage in physical recreation. It seems likely that women's participation in such activities is related to their own and others' expectations about what pusuits are appropriate and "normal" for women; such expectations are, in turn, strongly influenced by ideologies of family life and domesticity.

Most research on women's leisure has focused on white women in western societies. Much less is known about the effects of ethnicity. One study of male and female shift workers in the United Kingdom (Chambers, 1986) found that for its small, qualitative sample of Asian women, home-based leisure was the norm; their favorite activities included dressmaking and other home crafts. These Asian women engaged in only half as many activities outside the home as white women in the study, mainly visiting and entertaining friends and relatives and taking vacations and day trips. It should be noted, however, that according to Hargreaves (1994), the bulk of research on ethnic women and sports in the United Kingdom has focused on Asians, who are statistically the least likely to engage in sports—probably because of racism; because of problems with westernized sports facilities, which do not accommodate Asian women's cultural or religious needs (for example, these facilities often provide only single-sex enclosed spaces); and because of certain attitudes that may prevail in Asian communities, which tend to give women's sports a low priority, to value homemaking and domestic roles for women, and to fear that women will encounter racist and sexual harassment in the wider society.

Lesbian women are also subject to discriminatory attitudes and practices that can limit their leisure activities. Many lesbian women encounter homophobia and feel alienated when they try to use mainstream leisure and sports facilities. Ironically, stylized, fragmented images of women's bodies are often used to advertise leisure facilities, but lesbian as well as heterosexual women are often warned that they should hide their sexuality in such places. To avoid being marginalized, or having to pass as straight, some lesbians have established their own separate clubs and athletic factilites.

Constraints on the leisure choices of women—whatever their social status, ethnicity, or sexual orientation—and the fact that these choices can be limited by male control, should be a matter of serious concern, because leisure is central to women's well-being, to their enjoyment of life, and even to their empowerment.

The Experience of Leisure

Leisure is not only a choice of activities but also a state of mind. In this regard, too, leisure is affected by social differences and cultural contexts. The mental experience of leisure involves relaxation and pleasure, feelings that can be derived from even the most mundane activities if the conditions are right. As one study participant put it, "Leisure is anything that I can do where I don't have someone to nag at me to do it" (Hunter and Whitson, 1991: 228). But leisure as a mental state can be lacking altogether if the conditions are wrong—for example, in organized activities where women feel that they are being watched and judged, and particularly if they have a sense of being watched and judged as women, not individuals.

A good experience of leisure is often described as a "flow," and crucial elements in this flow are satisfaction, enjoyment, and a strengthened sense of self. For example, daydreaming while gardening can be an occasion for creativity and for the active thinking that helps us make sense of the world, so that we can, as appropriate, preserve or challenge the status quo. This kind of leisure is important to women; and when it involves sharing insights and dreams with other women, it can also provide the support and solidarity essential to self-esteem, and often lacking in work.

One area in which the experience of leisure can vary greatly is family-oriented leisure. As noted above, family leisure is a context in which recreation may not be easily distinguishable from work. On family outings and holidays, women are often primarily responsible for serving others, so that their own experience of leisure is minimal or nonexistent; in addition, there can be a sense of strain or tension because it is difficult to live up to the ideal of family life and family fun fostered by society and the media. Nevertheless, many women do find satisfaction and fulfillment in spending free time with their families and playing with their children. In one study of small towns in Canada, women were invited to talk about experiences that gave them happiness, fulfillment, or pleasure:

> [They] talked about a balance between self and others that is not reducible to specific times or activities. They also talked of times and activities and relationships which clearly were sources of happiness but for which "leisure" did not seem an appropriate name. (Hunter and Whitson, 1991: 223)

"Nights out" are also important in the experience of leisure. A night out with one's partner, away from children and other responsibilities, is often cited as a predominant source of pleasure. Nights out with other women constitute a highlight and are, in fact, often jealously guarded. The importance of women's networks in the experience of leisure is well documented; freed from the scrutiny of their male partners, women can "let their hair down" and indulge in "unladylike" behaviors, such as ribald humor, that can serve as a counterbalance to the gendered aspects of everyday life, and especially to male power:

> We'll put the world to rights, we'll discuss our sexual problems if there are any, have a laugh, talk terrible about our husbands. (Green et al., 1990)

Within such experiences, women's solidarity is reinforced, creating loyalties and bonds that can be called on in times of crisis.

Leisure, Conflict, and Guilt

Leisure, then, is primarily a state of mind. For women, achieving this mental state can be impeded by external constraints and also by conflicting emotions, such as feeling guilty because one needs time away from a partner or children, and anger at being at the service of other people's leisure. But when the "flow" of leisure is achieved, it is a source of personal wholeness and power.

See Also

CRAFTS; FRIENDSHIP; SPORT; TELEVISION

References and Further Reading

Betschild, Myra, and Eileen Green. 1994. Having the time of our lives: Is leisure an appropriate concept for midlife women? In Ian Henry ed., *Leisure in different worlds*. Vol. 1. *Modernity, postmodernity, and lifestyles*. Leisure Studies Association, No. 48. University of Brighton.

Bialeschki, M. Deborah, and Karla Henderson. 1986. Leisure in the common world of women. *Leisure Studies* 5: 299–308.

Chambers, Deborah. 1986. The constraints of work and domestic schedules on women's leisure. *Leisure Studies* 5: 309–325.

Deem, Rosemary. 1986. *All work and no play: The sociology of women's leisure.* Milton Keynes: Open University Press.

Dempsey, Ken. 1990. Women's life and leisure in an Australian rural community. *Leisure Studies* 9: 35–44.

Green, Eileen, Sandra Hebron, and Diana Woodward. 1990. *Women's leisure, what leisure?* London: Macmillan.

Hargreaves, Jennifer. 1994. *Sporting females: Critical issues in the history and sociology of women's sports.* London: Routledge.

Henderson, Karla, and Deborah Bialeschki. 1992. Leisure research and the social structure of feminism. *Society and Leisure* 15: 63–75.

Hunter, Patricia L., and David J. Whitson. 1991. Women, leisure, and familism. *Leisure Studies* 10:219–233.

McRobbie, Angela. 1984. Dance and social fantasy. In Angela McRobbie and Mica Nava, eds., *Gender and generation.* London: Macmillan.

Stanley, Liz. 1988. Historical sources for studying work and leisure in women's lives. In Erica Wimbush and Margaret Talbot, eds., *Relative freedoms: Women and leisure.* Milton Keynes: Open University Press.

Wearing, Betsy, and Stephen Wearing. 1988. All is a day's leisure: Gender and the concept of leisure. *Leisure Studies* 7: 111–123.

Wimbush, Erica, and Margaret Talbot, eds. 1988. *Relative freedoms: Women and leisure.* Milton Keynes: Open University Press.

Woodward, Diana, Eileen Green, and Sandra Hebron. 1989. The Sociology of women's leisure and physical recreation: Constraints and opportunities. *International Review for the Sociology of Sport* 24(2): 121–133.

Eileen Green

LESBIANISM

The terms *lesbianism* and *lesbian* refer to a woman's sexual desire for another woman. Today these terms are usually self-chosen; a woman knows herself and her desires as lesbian and may describe herself to others as lesbian: "A lesbian [is a woman] who says she is" (Clarke, 1983). Lesbianism, in this sense, is a recently constructed concept rather than a biological description.

While some have preferred to define lesbianism in terms of a sexual relationship, this is culturally and historically limiting. A woman who describes herself as a lesbian may or may not choose a woman for her sexual partner. A woman who is a lesbian may find her primary social satisfaction in the company of other lesbians, or she may not. The reverse is also true. Women who are not lesbians can live and have lived together as companions. Women who are not lesbians have sometimes chosen other women for sexual partners (McDaniel, 1995).

Many lesbians insist that lesbian identification means more to them than simply the gender of the person with whom they are being sexual. What "more" consists of, however, has never been defined to everyone's satisfaction. "Women-identified Lesbianism is, then, more than a sexual preference, it is a political choice," wrote Charlotte Bunch in a lesbian newsletter published in the United States in 1973. Others in North American and western European cultures believe that the "more" includes commitment to women's community and culture, as well as sex. Still others feel that the orientation described as lesbian includes psychological, spiritual, and emotional components. For some, *lesbian* includes the political concept of feminism; for others, it does not.

One western lesbian was told by a friend in Benin, West Africa, that the sex they had shared had nothing to do with lesbianism but was rather an offer of comfort and friendship (Foeken, 1989). In China, one synonym for *homosexual* translates as "the foreigner's disease" (Anderson, 1991). In other countries, homosexuality has been described as a sign of "western" decadence. In many countries, however, western and eastern, northern and southern, interconnections of racism, sexism, and homophobia have been the focus of lesbian organizing, transcending local debates about the origins of lesbianism or homosexuality.

The historical debate about who *was* a lesbian has been equally difficult to resolve. Self-definition is not useful for historical periods before a term evolved to describe same-sex activity. Because of the historical invisibility of lesbians, we are ignorant, for the most part, of the ways in which lesbians in previous centuries shaped their lives, coped with their difficulties, or experienced their joys. Two poles of opinion exist about applying the term retroactively—those who insist that lesbianism must include an erotic or sexual component and those who argue that the definition of lesbianism must be broadened to include all women with primary emotional bonds to other women (Vicinus, 1982).

One of the problems exacerbating this discussion is "nature or nurture"—that is, the question whether women can "choose" to be lesbians or are lesbians because of some genetic, biological determination.

Whatever science eventually determines, lesbians live and love in every culture in the world. The International Lesbian Information Service (ILIS) publishes a newsletter and has organized regional and international lesbian conferences. Shelley Anderson, who has served as editor of the ILIS bulletin, has also published a pamphlet describing lesbian political organizing around the world and the conditions under which lesbians are living, country by country.

See Also

BUTCH/FEMME; IDENTITY POLITICS; LESBIAN SEXUALITY; LESBIAN STUDIES; LESBIAN WRITING: OVERVIEW; LESBIANS IN SCIENCE; MOTHERHOOD: LESBIAN; QUEER THEORY; SEXUAL ORIENTATION

References and Further Reading

Anderson, Shelley. 1991. *Out in the world: International lesbian organizing.* Ithaca, N.Y.: Firebrand.

Bunch, Charlotte. 1973. Perseverance furthers: Woman's sense of self. *Furies* (Jan./Feb.).

Clarke, Cheryl. 1983. Lesbianism: An act of resistance. In Cherrie Moraga and Gloria Anzaldúa, eds., *This bridge called my back: Writings by radical women of color,* 128. Latham, N.Y.: Kitchen Table/Women of Color.

Foeken, Ingrid. 1989. In *New Internationalist,* no. 201 (November): Special issue on homosexuality.

McDaniel, Judith. 1995. *The lesbian couples' guide,* 3–8. New York: HarperCollins.

Vicinus, Martha. 1982. Sexuality and power: A review of current work in the history of sexuality. *Feminist Studies* 8(1: Spring): 134–156.

Judith McDaniel

LESBIAN CULTURAL CRITICISM

Like any branch of critical practice and theory, lesbian cultural criticism is a multiform project. It is concerned with both the subjects and the objects of culture, that is, the producers and consumers of culture as well as the products or artifacts themselves. Critical interest initially centered on literary texts and gradually expanded to film, visual and pictorial art, music (in particular popular music), television, advertising, and old and new media generally.

Lesbian cultural criticism has roots in the social movements of the late 1960s. Maintaining its close connections with local politics and social activism throughout its development, it constitutes a specific form of cultural critique: politically informed sociocultural theory and practice. Like other "minority" discourses, including women's, gay, black, and postcolonial studies, lesbian cultural criticism is thus fundamentally an interventionist practice, seeking to focus attention on the role of cultural products in shaping the meanings and values informing social reality. This includes the significance of sexual realities and identities.

While giving relative priority to sexual differences, lesbian cultural criticism has long recognized the multiple forms of differentiation that define identities, both individually and collectively in terms of gender, sexuality, race, class, ethnicity, age, and ability. Even if the issue of race and ethnicity has from time to time been obscured in actual practice, the theoretical insistence on the multiplicity of subjectivity is one of the project's central assumptions.

Another basic assumption is that the various forms of differentiation defining such multiple identities not only acquire meaning within specific sociohistorical contexts but also are learned, constructed, and experienced in an ever-changing cultural realm. Cultural production, in the broadest sense of the word, continually disseminates the highly diverse images, concepts, and beliefs that enable human beings to structure reality and to assign meaning to themselves, to others, and to the world as a whole. In other words, cultural practices provide human beings with the conceptual—or imaginary—scenarios that help them to find their positions in shifting social realities, to situate themselves in the material practices of everyday life. Since not everybody is equally free to assume any position in society, and the positions of power and privilege are unequally divided along the lines of gender, race, class, sexuality, and so on, the gendered and sexually marginalized position of lesbian critics serves as a specific vantage point for considering the interdependent lines of sociocultural stratification, and especially sexual differentiation, as they are realized in cultural practice. The aim of lesbian cultural analysis is to expose and hold up for questioning the inequalities produced by the established structures of differentiation in which both the critical subject herself and her objects of study are necessarily involved.

Situated at the intersections of feminist studies, gay studies, and critical theory, lesbian cultural criticism necessarily operates from already "marginalized" segments of the intellectual domain. With its joint origins in early women's studies and gay (and lesbian) social activism, it is, furthermore, confronted with the sexual bias prevailing in one and the gender bias pervading the other, while simultaneously addressing the sexual and gender biases dominating critical theory, with which it partly overlaps.

The critique of heteropatriarchal power and the fight against inequality through critical intervention in the "sanctified" realm of culture lie at the heart of lesbian cultural criticism. Developments within the larger critical community, as much as changes in society as a whole, have nonetheless resulted in various shifts in thematic emphasis and theoretical focus. Tracing such trends allows for a clearer view of lesbian cultural criticism in contemporary (primarily Euro-American) academe in its interdependent relations with and as distinct from other radical critical projects.

Lesbian critics initially set out to recover a "lost" tradition of lesbian art and writing that, in fact, turned out to be much more expansive and diverse than was first expected. In addition to criticizing the persistently negative portrayal of "the love that dares not speak its name" in mainstream culture, they reconstructed an equally rich stylistic tradition in which the "unspeakable" realities of lesbian experience have historically been voiced, albeit in more or less encoded form. The most abiding and thus perhaps the most distinguishing feature of lesbian criticism, however, is what Sally Munt (1992) has called *dykonstruction,* a term that puts the critical subject herself at the center of the cultural process.

In an overwhelmingly heterocentrist society, lesbian readers have become particularly skilled at reading between the lines of mainstream culture to produce their own "privileged" meanings and interpretations. Hence, as early as the first half of the 1980s—that is to say, even before the influence of poststructuralism made itself felt in the larger critical community—lesbian critics had begun to reflect on the effects of their own sociosexual perspective on the construction of cultural meaning and knowledge. Practicing deconstruction before it became a prevailing mode of critical analysis among Euro-American scholars generally, lesbian critics clearly recognized the operation of cultural differentiation and sociohistorical specificity in determining both the objects and the subjects of cultural analysis.

The idea that the conscious assumption of a "deviant" sociocultural perspective allows for the generation of forms of meanings and knowledge different from those produced by "official" mainstream culture continues to inform lesbian cultural criticism today. While embracing a wide range of disciplinary fields, each with its distinct objects of study and theoretical and methodological tools, lesbian critics tend to take the actual realities of their own sociosexual positioning and experience as the starting point for cultural analysis. Rather than essentializing such experience in order to authenticate their own "alternative" knowledge, however, they actively engage their sociosexual specificity to point up the inevitably politicized nature of all modes of meaning and knowledge, as well as of the subjectivity of the critics producing them, including those situated in the mainstream.

See Also

CULTURAL CRITICISM; CULTURAL STUDIES; CULTURE: WOMEN AS CONSUMERS OF CULTURE; CULTURE: WOMEN AS PRODUCERS OF CULTURE; FILM: LESBIAN; LESBIAN STUDIES; LESBIAN WRITING: OVERVIEW; LITERARY THEORY AND CRITICISM

Reference and Further Reading

Griffin, Gabriele. 1993. *Heavenly love? Lesbian images in twentieth-century women's writing.* Manchester and New York: Manchester University Press.

Hoogland, Renée C. 1997. *Lesbian configurations.* Cambridge: Polity and New York: Columbia University Press.

Innes, Sherrie A. 1997. *The lesbian menace: Ideology, identity, and the representation of lesbian life.* Amherst: University of Massachusetts Press.

Munt, Sally. 1992. *New lesbian criticism: Literary and cultural readings.* New York and London: Harvester Wheatsheaf.

Wolfe, Susan, and Julia Penelope, eds. 1993. *Sexual practice, textual theory: Lesbian cultural criticism.* Cambridge, Mass., and Oxford: Blackwell.

Renée C. Hoogland

LESBIAN DRAMA

Lesbian drama is addressed within the discipline of theater and performance studies, which involves play- or group-specific journal scholarship. This drama is studied in various contexts, including histories of feminist theater and specialist panels at annual conferences sponsored by the North American Assocation for Theater in Higher Education (ATHE) and at the triennial conferences of International Women Playwrights. Useful anthologies include the volume on lesbians in Methuen's series *Plays by Women* and *Amazon All Stars: Thirteen Lesbian Plays,* edited by Rosemary Curb, both of which include works by women of color. There is also much unpublished lesbian drama.

Characters and Plots

Plays in English with lesbian characters increased in number as part of artistic developments within second-wave feminism. There were a few lesbian types in drama earlier than this, usually depicted as internalizing shame; one well-known example is Lillian Hellman's play *The Children's Hour* (1934). In the 1970s the scarcity of plays by women encouraged theater practioners to develop new dramas promoting social change, and this included challenges to stereotypes and misrepresentations of lesbians. Such works were often collaborative and were developed for lesbian audiences. Politically powerful representations of lesbians in mainstream stage productions emerged initially as secondary characters, for example, in Caryl Churchill's *Cloud Nine* in England (1979) and Robyn Archer's *The Pack of Women* in Australia (1983). By the mid-1980s—a decade after the first productions in London by Gay Sweatshop, a company dedicated to gay and lesbian drama—plays with lesbians as central characters were being produced by small professional theaters.

Coming-out stories about the difficulty of being accepted by families and friends predominate in lesbian drama. There are numerous plots in which a heterosexual woman encounters lesbianism and identifies herself as a lesbian—a theme also adopted by some nonlesbian writers. One example is a successful realist play about vacationing lesbian couples, *Last Summer at Bluefish Cove* (United States, 1982), by Jane Chambers, after whom an award has been named. Some dramas reflect long-standing concerns of lesbians. For instance, Michelene Wandor's *AID Thy Neighbour* (England, 1978) is about lesbian motherhood. Alison Lyssa's *Pinball* (Australia, 1981) and Sarah Daniels's *Neaptide* (England, 1986) both present lesbians involved in child custody cases, and also dramatize break-ups of relationships. Biographical dramas about dead and famous lesbians proliferate; one example is Sara Hardy's *Vita! A Fantasy* (1990), about Vita Sackville-West. Another theme is ambiguous sexuality, as in cross-dressing—theatrical cross-dressing is centuries old and now theorized as queer. A relatively early example of this theme is Simone Benmussa's *The Singular Life of Albert Nobbs* (France, 1978), about a historical woman who dressed and lived as a man. By the late 1980s, plays about love and romance were balanced with an increasing number of performances about explicit sexual practices and parodic stagings of butch-femme identities.

Production and Performance

An important source of opportunities for production and touring are venues like Café Wow in New York, Drill Hall in London, and regional women's theater groups such as Canada's Maenad in the 1980s, and, more recently, festivals such as the Gay and Lesbian Mardi Gras in Sydney and It's Queer Up North in Manchester. Writers for these venues are expected to identify themselves as lesbian or bisexual and to write about concerns relevant to their sexual identity. (By contrast, plays with lesbian characters for general audiences are not necessarily written by self-identified lesbians.)

Shows about lesbians remain controversial, as was indicated by the legal battle in the United States to reinstate funding by the National Endowment of the Arts for gay and lesbian artists, and by an attempt on the part of the city councilors at the Edinburgh Festival in 1995 to ban a production of Australia's all-female physical theater group Club Swing—*Appetite* (1993), about food and desire in sexualized aerial acts. Theater practitioners in countries where representing a lesbian remains a political challenge to the law recount threats and vilification.

Performance extends the conceptual meanings of written plays by visually encoding identity. In the 1980s theorists like Sue-Ellen Case and Jill Dolan expanded historical and theoretical knowledge of how innovative theatrical forms capture lesbian sensibility; such theorists argue that innovation is important because realism is by nature politically conservative. In performances by Holly Hughes and Split Britches in the United States, acts of desire between women mimic and parody heterosexual interactions; but they establish a sexualized space, separate from culturally pervasive heterosexuality, by omitting male symbols of desire or treating such symbols ironically. In the 1990s, Linda Hart and Kate Davy contrasted audiences, arguing that a lesbian audience will recognize the "double encoding" of the lesbian subject as an active agent in this kind of seduction, while a general audience will not understand how the use of form suggests an enactment of lesbian sexuality and will therefore interpret the same presentation simply as a satire of heterosexual behavior.

Performances involving lesbian characters have become popular with a range of audiences; this trend and experiments in queer performance promise more complex concerns and representations in future lesbian drama.

See Also

DRAMA; FEMINISM: SECOND-WAVE BRITISH *and* SECOND-WAVE NORTH AMERICAN; QUEER THEORY; THEATER: MODERN AND CONTEMPORARY

References and Further Reading

Case, Sue-Ellen, ed. 1996. *Split britches: Lesbian practice/feminist performance.* London:Routledge.

Curb, Rosemary, ed. 1996. *Amazon all-stars: Thirteen lesbian plays.* New York: Applause.

Dolan, Jill. 1988. *The feminist spectator as critic.* Ann Arbor: University of Michigan Press.

Freeman, Sandra. 1997. *Putting your daughters on the stage: Lesbian theatre from the 1970s to the present.* London: Cassell.

Furtado, Ken, and Nancy Hellner. 1993. *Gay and lesbian American plays: An anotated bibliography.* Lanham, Md.: Scarecrow.

Tait, Peta. 1994. *Converging realities: Feminism in Australian theatre.* Sydney: Currency.

Peta Tait

LESBIAN FEMINISM

See FEMINISM: LESBIAN.

LESBIAN MARRIAGE

See MARRIAGE: LESBIAN.

LESBIAN MOTHERHOOD

See MOTHERHOOD: LESBIAN.

LESBIAN POPULAR MUSIC

Lesbian music can refer to lesbian composers and lyricists, lesbian performers, and lesbian audiences. In all three senses, lesbian popular music has contributed significantly to lesbian and gay cultures.

Beginnings to the 1980s

Historically, music by lesbians has existed as long as lesbianism itself. Sappho of Lesbos (c. 610–580 B.C., or B.C.E.) is said to have created the Mixolydian mode, also called the Lesbian mode; this ancient, jubilant musical scale can still be found in contemporary folk music (Gardner, 1990).

A lesbian, Dame Ethel Smyth (1858–1944), was perhaps Great Britain's foremost woman composer. Smyth was close to Virginia Woolf and was part of several social circles of wealthy lesbians in London and Paris that also included Radclyffe Hall. They called themselves inverts, Uranan women, or Sapphists. Smyth was active in the British suffragist movement, and her "March of the Women" (1911) was a favorite suffragist marching song. She once conducted it, using a toothbrush as a baton, through a window of Holloway Women's Prison, where she was serving a two-month sentence for throwing stones at government officials. Later, in the 1970s, the march would be sung by women's liberationists, consciously acknowledging their debt to the suffragists.

In modern times, music has sustained lesbians in a world that is often indifferent, or hostile and punitive. (Lesbian acts are punishable by law in some African countries, Muslim countries, and Asian countries.) Throughout the western world, Lesbian feminists began to create and circulate music during the women's liberation movement of the late 1960s. Much of their music has been recorded by small independent studios and distributors.

The first lesbian record album, *Lavender Jane Loves Women,* was produced in the United States in 1973 by the singer and songwriter Alix Dobkin and the instrumentalist Kay Gardner (under the label Alix Dobkin Project NY). A second album by Dobkin, *Living with Lesbians,* was produced in 1976 (by 1999 she had created seven albums). Gardner's compositions were released in six albums from 1975 to 1990; they included *Mooncircles* (1975), *Emerging* (1978, by Urana Records), and *A Rainbow Path* (1986, by Ladyslipper Records).

Themes of lesbian music in the 1970s and 1980s were those of feminist and women's music—women's oppression, environmental politics, and peace—as well as lesbian visibility. Lesbian oppression was addressed in 1977 in *A Lesbian Concentrate: A Lesbianthology of Songs and Poems,* produced by Olivia Records in California. The musicians, most of whom had made albums of their own with Olivia, included Teresa Trull, Linda Tillery, Holly Near, and June Millington. Part of the profits went to a National Defense Fund for lesbian mothers. One song in this album, "Prove It on Me Blues," was written by the African-American blues and jazz singer Gertrude "Ma" Rainey (1886–1939), whose music was especially popular with butch and femme lesbians of the 1920s through the 1950s.

Olivia, a nationwide women's recording and distribution company in the United States, was founded in the mid-1970s by lesbians: Ginny Berson and Robin Brooks, with the musicians Cris Williamson and Meg Christian, among others. Olivia and Ladyslipper Records have contributed significantly to the creation and circulation of lesbian music and culture. Another company, Urana Records (Wise Women Enterprises), adopted the name used by some lesbians of the 1890s to 1930s. Alive—five musicians—released an album, also titled *Alive,* on the Urana label in 1979.

In 1975, Cris Williamson's theme of women's spirituality in *The Changer and the Changed* was popular with lesbians. (Williamson and Tret Fure—her musical and personal partner—produced twenty-six albums from 1981 to 2000.) Also in 1975, Isis, a rock band in New York, celebrated women lovers in the song "Bobbi and Maria," from the album *Ain't No Backin' Up Now.*

Strongly political lesbian music flourished from 1975 to 1989, with British, Irish, continental European, Japanese, Australian, and North American lesbian feminist musicians recording original works. *Flying Lesbians* was produced in 1975 by seven singers and instrumentalists in West Berlin, recording in both German and English. The singer and pianist Linda Shear created *A Lesbian Portrait* in 1977. Kathy Fire produced *Songs of Fire: Songs of a Lesbian Anarchist* in 1978. The Canadian singer and songwriter Ferron produced four albums; the second, *Testimony* (Lucy Records, 1980), had strong philosophical and spiritual themes. Beginning in 1979, Ova, two lesbians in London, recorded four albums with a strongly political content including protests against rape and nuclear weapons. Lesbian feminist bands in Sydney, Australia, produced their own albums: Lavender Blues made *Wake Up Sister* in 1978; the band Stray Dags made an album in 1980 (*Stray Dags;* in Australia and New Zealand, "dag" is literally the tailend of a sheep and figuratively an unkempt, uncool person); and the lesbian quartet Kali made an album (*Kali*) in 1987. In the mid-1980s, the Irish lesbian feminist band Major to Minor performed in and around Dublin. In Japan in 1985, the lesbian Yonja Yan released a cassette about her struggles as a woman of Korean descent. Later, an album by Minori Sawada included a song called "Come Out, Lesbian"; and Onna (Women's) Club Band performed translations of Cris Williamson's songs. In 1983, lesbian singers performed at a fund-raising concert for Rape Crisis in Cape Town, South Africa (which is not among the African countries that punish lesbianism). One of the concert's organizers, Mignon Lee-Warden, later emigrated to Australia, where she organized four annual women's music festivals. (At the time of this writing, a fifth festival was planned for February 2001, in Sydney.)

The Contemporary Scene

New styles of the 1990s included punk rock and cyberpunk, and themes included satires of gender stereotypes. Internationally, lesbian musicians have participated in feminist, lesbian-feminist, and queer events, and in women's festivals; one example is the Michigan Womyn's Music Festival, which celebrated its twenty-fifth anniversary in August 2000. Openly lesbian or gay women in the mainstream music industry as of the year 2000 included several singers and songwriters: k. d. lang (Canada); Alix Dobkin, Melissa Etheridge, Julie Cypher, Indigo Girls, Phranc, Cris Williamson, Tret Fure, and Janis Ian (United States); Judy Small (Australia); Topp Twins (New Zealand–Aotearoa); Ova (England); Zrazy and Sinead O'Connor (Ireland); and Minori Sawada and Michuru Sasano (Japan). Sasano was a former vocalist with Tokyo Shonen (Tokyo Boys).

Indigo Girls released nine major albums from 1989 to 1999 and sold 17 million copies. Their lyrics addressed environmental awareness and protested against homophobia—a stance that they backed up with community activism. Janis Ian, who had also been popular earlier, in the 1970s, came out as a lesbian to counter antihomosexual bias. Judy Small, an Australian feminist, performed at international folk and women's music festivals from 1982 on; her seventh original album was *The Rainbow Village: Out and Proud* (1999). Phranc, a Jewish-American lesbian, created original music in styles ranging from folk during the 1980s to punk-popular in her album of 1991, *Positively Phranc.* That album contains a tribute to Billie Tipton, a woman jazz musician in the United States (around the 1930s) who passed as a man for fifty years. Two members of the Irish band Major to Minor became Zrazy in 1992 and performed their own pieces at the Womyn's Music Festivals in Michigan and at Europride Festivals (1994–1995). In 1997, Zrazy's song "Come Out Everybody" was nominated for "best out song" in the Gay and Lesbian American Music Awards.

Festivals have been a significant part of the contemporary scene. From 1989 to 1999, Australian National Lesbian Conference and Cultural Festivals presented lesbian musicians. One example was the National Lesbian Festival in Australia in 1991, at which the Lesbians at the Sydney Opera House Concert drew an audience that may have numbered as many as 4,000 lesbians. The performers included lesbian and feminist musicians such as the Australian singer-songwriters Robyn Archer, Judy Small, Anique Lamerduc, Sue Edmonds, and George (who had recorded *Gutsy Woman* in 1988); and the Topp Twins from New Zealand. This concert also featured Aboriginal musicians such as Betty Little and the gay Koori opera singer Deborah Cheetham. Les Amuse, a group from Adelaide, Australia, that had some writers as members, performed in 1995 at the festival in Alice Springs and also at the Fringe to the Adelaide Arts Festival in 1996. Deborah Cheetham's show *White Baptist Abba Fan* was part of a lesbian and gay festival—called *Feast*—held in Adelaide in 1999.

Some lesbian and queer women musicians worked with multimedia during the 1990s. Scooter, for instance—a nonprofit music collective of queer anarcho-punk musicians—was established in Sydney in 1998. The Butchies, who have performed at the Womyn's Music Festival in Michigan, record for the label Mr. Lady, which describes itself as "dyke-run" and distributes independent women's art and videos as well as music. Mr. Lady's Web site, at the time of this writing, was linked to the site of the United States National Center for Lesbian Rights.

See Also

LESBIANISM; LESBIAN STUDIES; MUSIC: ROCK AND POP; MUSIC: SOUL, JAZZ, RAP, BLUES, AND GOSPEL

References and Further Reading

Cline, Sally. 1997. *Radclyffe Hall: A woman called John.* London: Murray.

Dahl, Linda. 1984. *Stormy weather: The music and lives of a century of jazzwomen.* London: Quartet (Namara Group).

Gardner, Kay. 1990. *Sounding the inner landscape: Music as medicine.* Stonington, Me.: Caduceus.

O'Brien, Karen. 1995. *Hymn to her: Women musicians talk.* London: Virago.

Scooter. 2000. Grrls. *Lesbians on the Loose* 11(2, Issue 122): 17.

Robin Eagle

LESBIAN ROLES: Butch/Femme

See BUTCH/FEMME.

LESBIAN SEXUALITY

Historical Background

Between about 1922 and 1976, lesbians who were studied by researchers in the United States were women hospitalized in psychiatric institutions or in outpatient psychiatric care. These studies, therefore, contributed to a myth that lesbians and lesbian sex were pathological. Before the mid-1960s, lesbians were often considered mentally ill, and stereotyped as looking like men, wanting to be men, hating men, and hating their own lesbianism. Another myth was that lesbians mimicked women and men in their sexual relations. Moreover, the primary way to identify lesbians was to ask who their sexual partners were; and lesbians' sexuality was linked to their status as a presumably pathological minority.

Around 1965, lesbians began to write about their own sexuality. Del Martin and Phyllis Lyon started a lesbian organization, Daughters of Bilitis, which published a newspaper, *The Ladder.* This became an "underground railroad" in print for lesbians worldwide, who began to read about each other's experiences, passions, and sexuality. Lesbians around the world began to write books, poems, and periodicals, spreading the word about lesbians and their sex lives. In the mid-1970s, Pat Califia did research outside the mainstream; she passed out questionnaires to lesbians and published the results in *Sapphistry: The Book of Lesbian Sexuality* (1980). In the 1970 to the 1980s, university courses, traveling lecturers, public forums, talk shows, and magazines exploring more radical forms of lesbian sex added to the growing knowledge about real lesbians. Professional researchers such as Nanette Gartrell, Katherine O'Hanlan, and Esther Rothblum published studies that included lesbians and their sex lives. In 1974, the American Psychiatric Association removed homosexuality from its list of diagnosable psychiatric disorders, describing it instead as simply a variant sexual orientation. Women's (predominantly lesbian) music and cultural festivals around the United States—organized by, among others, Robin Tyler, Lisa Vogel, and Barbara (Boo) Price—provided forums where thousands of lesbians could explore their sexual feelings, thoughts, and politics.

Different strains of writing, thinking, and working with lesbian sex began to emerge, ranging from the purist lesbian feminists, represented by Adrienne Rich and Judy Grahn, to a more radical populist strain that blurred sexual lines, represented by Susie Bright and Arlene Stein, and the new academic world of queer theory, exemplified by Judith Butler, Teresa deLauretis, and Diana Fuss.

By the 1980s, there was enough information to create factions in the lesbian community, which led to what were often referred to as the "lesbian sex wars."—These conflicts involved issues such as being for or against monogamy, sadomasochism, lesbian sex workers, "lesbian night" at gay bathhouses, butch-femme, sex toys, dildos, and even whether anyone should publish information about lesbians and sex. This was an exciting time, however, with lesbian sexual energy in the air.

Lesbians take on the weight of prejudice every time they have sex. They are in a double bind: what brings pleasure is linked to what they are reviled and punished for. A remarkable aspect of lesbian sex is that women are willing to fight for the right to make love to each other. They sense sexiness in the fact that women understand each other's emotions and experience, such as the menstrual cycle and menopause. Genitals, breasts, lips, and other erogenous zones, which are the same for both partners, are a source of comfort and sexual arousal.

Lesbian Sexual Identity

The fact that the etiology of lesbian sex is debatable comes from a belief on the part of mainstream culture that lesbianism is an alternative to a heterosexual norm. (Only homosexual researchers ask where heterosexuality comes from.) Sexual identity is a result of complex variables: background, an internal sense of self, cultural affinities, lifelong erotic experiences, group orientation, current sexual behavior, and inclusion or a sense of belonging.

For any individual, these variables may all align, although commonly this is not the case; rather, one or more variables will usually not fit the profile of a lesbian. Thus it is difficult to give a precise definition of lesbian. It is tempting to define a lesbian simply by whom she is having sex with, or would prefer to have sex with. But although some women who identify as lesbian have ongoing, lifelong, and exclusive sex with women, there are also women who identify as lesbian and do not have sex at all, women who identify as heterosexual but have sex with women, and women who identify as lesbian but have sex with men.

Lesbian Sexual Sensibility

Lesbian sexual sensibility is "woman-based." A primary aspect of lesbian cultural sensibility is the interdependence of sex, love, emotional intimacy, and a close relationship. Whereas casual, uncommitted sex does occur, a high value is placed on sex within the context of a relationship.

There are, however, lesbians who participate in other kinds of sexual associations. These women may have relationships that are polyamorous and include threesomes, open relationships, sex with friends who are not lovers, and deliberate noncommittment in an effort, among other things, to make sex more interesting (Munsen and Stelboum, 1999).

Lesbian Sexual Styles

Lesbian sexual styles span a broad spectrum, and discussion of these styles is controversial within the lesbian community. Regarding many oppressed peoples, there is a notion that if you know one you know all; this is especially true of sexual stereotypes. It is crucial that lesbian sex lives are seen as *individual* lives. That being said, there are some general styles that can be described.

From the 1920 to the 1930s, there emerged the butch-femme sexual style; this has both historical and current significance for lesbian sex. Although it is often said to be a mimicking of men and women, butch-femme is actually a uniquely lesbian sexual style (Nestle, 1992).

There are lesbians who subscribe to the "androgynous imperative"—that "real lesbians" are sexy because of a certain combination of genders. There are those who would say they follow no lesbian cultural style in their sexuality but rather simply follow where their libido and sense of attraction lead them.

There is a myth that lesbians do everything equally in sex; that is not always true. There are differences in who initiates, who is actively making love to whom and for how long, who goes first, and what physical acts are performed.

Problems with Lesbian Sex

Lesbians have never had easy access to information about sex. One persistent problem for lesbians is that as girls they are taught that women are not supposed to be sexual. Compared with men, women often have less varied sexually experiences, fewer partners, and less information about sex. This is also true of lesbian women. Lesbians as a whole have not been able to explore sex openly as teenagers or adults. They have to hide their sexuality to avoid being ostracized, humiliated, and possibly harmed.

Another problem derives from an asset: familiarity. It can be boring knowing and feeling what one's partner knows and feels. Lesbian relationships can lack the diversity needed to make sex exciting. However, there are ways to improve this situation, including sex toys, sexual films, poetry, and how-to books.

Perhaps the most difficult problem is living in a culture in which sexual assault is more likely to be perpetrated against girls and women. Thus in lesbian relationships, there is a greater risk that one of the partners will be a victim of incest, rape, or sexual harassment than there is in heterosexual relationships. This has a considerable impact on sexuality.

Specifics: What Do Lesbians Do?

Lesbians participate in numerous sexual activities, though not all are done by all lesbians and not all are done every time a woman has sex with another woman. Lesbians use the fingers, tongue, hands, legs, breasts, lips, eyes, skin, hair, vagina, anus, clitoris, and other body parts in various combinations to give pleasure to themselves and their partners. They use sex toys such as vibrators, dildos (usually smooth oblong objects made from leather, silicon, vegetables, and other products that can easily be put into the vagina or the anus and moved around), and various objects that can be clipped, wrapped, touched, and rubbed on body parts to increase and diversify stimulation and pleasure. Oral sex (putting one's mouth on the genitals of another person) is widely practiced by lesbians.

To repeat, however, these practices vary among lesbians. Assuming that all lesbians engage in any particular behavior is erroneous. For example, research with 1,500 lesbians revealed that 30 percent did not like or engage in oral sex (Loulan, 1984). It is important for each lesbian to explore what she herself likes and does not like, and to get more information about the ideas of other lesbians.

Lesbians are as varied as anyone else when it comes to sex: some are innovative, some are not, some like to have sex every day, some like to have sex once every three months, some do not like to have sex at all, some are profoundly emotionally affected by sex, some find sex complicated, some find it simple. But lesbian sex is here to stay, and information about it is continually growing.

See Also

BISEXUALITY; BUTCH/FEMME; FEMINISM: LESBIAN; LESBIAN STUDIES; QUEER THEORY; SEXUALITY: OVERVIEW.

References and Further Reading

Bright, Susie, and Jill Posener. 1996. *Nothing but the girl: The blatant lesbian image, a portfolio and exploration of lesbian erotic photography.* London: Freedom.

Butler, Judith. 1990. *Gender trouble: Feminism and the subversion of identity.* New York and London: Routledge.

Califia, Pat. 1980. *Sapphistry: The book of lesbian sexuality.* Tallahassee, Fla.: Naiad.

Clausen, Jan. 1999. *Apples and oranges.* New York: Houghton Mifflin.

deLauretis, Teresa, ed. 1991. Queer theory: Lesbian and gay sexualities. *Differences: A Journal of Feminist Cultural Studies* 3(2).

Fuss, Diana, ed. 1991. *Inside/out: Lesbian theories, gay theories.* New York and London: Routledge.

Gartrell, Nanette, H. K. H. Brodie, and H. Kraemer. 1974. Psychiatrists' attitudes toward female homosexuality. *Journal of Nervous and Mental Disorders* 159(2): 141–144.

Grahn, Judy. 1984. *Another mother tongue: Gay words, gay worlds.* Boston: Beacon.

Hall, Marny. 1998. *The lesbian love companion: How to survive everything from heartthrob to heartache.* San Francisco: HarperCollins.

Loulan, JoAnn. 1987. *Lesbian passion: Loving ourselves and each other.* Duluth: Spinster's Ink.

———. 1984. *Lesbian sex.* Duluth: Spinster's Ink.

Munsen, Marcia, and Judith Stelboum, eds. 1999. *The lesbian polyamory reader: Open relationships, non monogamy, and casual sex.* New York: Haworth.

Nestle, Joan. 1992. *The persistent desire: A femme-butch reader.* Boston: Alyson.

Rich, Adrienne. 1986. Compulsory heterosexuality and lesbian existence. In *Blood, bread, and poetry: Selected prose 1979–1985,* 23–75. New York: Norton.

Stein, Arlene. 1993. *Sisters, sexperts, and queers: Beyond the lesbian nation.* New York: Plume.

Weston, Kath. 1996. *Render me, gender me: Lesbians talk sex, class, color, nation, studmuffins . . .* New York and London: Routledge.

JoAnn Loulan

LESBIAN STUDIES

Lesbian studies refers both to the process of constructing ideas about lesbian identity and history and to formal course offerings in universities, mostly in women's studies programs. Lesbian studies is the production of knowledge from a lesbian perspective. As such, it counters the heterosexist idea that lesbians are deviant, abnormal, or invisible. In lesbian studies, lesbians are the subjects, not the objects, of scholarship and teaching.

Definition of *Lesbian*

Before there can be lesbian studies, there must be some consensus about the definition of *lesbian.* The concept of lesbianism arose along with concepts of homosexuality and heterosexuality in late nineteenth-century Europe and the United States. At that time, sexuality came to be understood as a determining factor in individual identity. With the reawakening of the western women's movement in the 1960s, lesbianism became a large, visible public movement, strongly influenced by feminist ideas.

Lesbianism in contemporary western societies has been defined, variously, in terms of a woman's primary emotional, sexual, or political commitment to women. The definition of *lesbian* has provoked controversy since the emergence of the modern lesbian movement, and, indeed, is part of what lesbian studies is about. The experiences, identities, and communities included under the heading "lesbian" remain a matter of debate today. So too does the historical and cross-cultural dimension of lesbianism. Who is a lesbian and what might be considered part of lesbian studies are not, and perhaps cannot be, strictly defined.

The Study of Lesbians: Deviance and Pathology

It is often argued that since 1869, the beginning of modern sexuality studies, women who prefer their own sex or who express discomfort with the female gender role—in other words, lesbians—have been studied as "objects" in order to reinforce the normality and centrality of heterosexuality. The study of lesbianism (as opposed to lesbian studies) took place primarily within the disciplines of sociology, psychology, and medicine. Lesbians were likely to be defined as "inverts" by biologically oriented scientists, as "perverts" by psychoanalysts, and as "deviants" by functionalist sociologists. Even today, lesbianism may be included in courses on abnormal psychology or sociology of deviance. Against this backdrop it was very difficult for researchers, whether lesbian or heterosexual, to construct unbiased knowledge about lesbians.

The first text that might be considered a precursor to lesbian studies was Jeannette Foster's *Sex-Variant Women in Literature* (1956/1985). Foster's work established the presence of lesbians in literature both as characters and as authors. Her work was expanded and updated periodically by Barbara Grier in *The Lesbian in Literature* (1981). Aside from these literary texts, however, virtually all research and scholarship produced before the 1970s either entirely ignored the existence of lesbians or looked at lesbianism only from a heterosexist perspective. For these reasons, little of this work continues to be used today.

The Origin of Lesbian Studies

Lesbian studies, as it exists in universities today, was a product of social movements in the United States in the late 1960s, specifically women's liberation and gay liberation. Lesbians from both movements (as well as some who had never been involved in any formal organizations) came together to establish an autonomous lesbian identity, politics, and culture. Having little concrete knowledge about lesbians, other than what had been discovered or invented by sexologists, they began the project of research and interpretation. Hence, the establishment of lesbian studies was considered essential to individual and collective identity and survival.

Early work took place primarily outside universities, where lesbian academics were still largely "closeted." Many of the first generation of lesbian scholars had no association with formal academia at all. Most of their work was published in lesbian periodicals like *Conditions* and *Sinister Wisdom* or by small lesbian and feminist presses. For example, J. R. Roberts, a librarian and community activist, compiled *Black Lesbians,* a bibliography published by Naiad Press in 1987. The second issue of *Sinister Wisdom,* in 1976, was devoted entirely to lesbian literature. This journal also published the proceedings of lesbian panels at the meetings of the Modern Language Association, panels that included such influential writers and theorists as Audre Lorde, Adrienne Rich, and Mary Daly. In several cities lesbian libraries or archives were established, the largest and most influential of these being the Lesbian Herstory Archives in Brooklyn, New York. These community-based institutions and scholars paved the way for academic lesbian studies.

Hence, lesbian studies (like women's studies during the same period) was closely linked to grassroots lesbian movements and communities. During the 1970s classes were as likely to be offered at lesbian centers as in universities. This reflects, on the one hand, the strength and activism of lesbian feminism. It also reflects the fact that lesbian studies (again, like women's studies) was largely developed by nonacademics, graduate students, and untenured faculty members. Until these women gained the power to confront and change the entrenched homophobia of the universities, academic lesbian studies would be difficult to establish. As lesbians entered or came out in the universities, the development of lesbian studies accelerated.

During the 1980s there was a shift from community-based lesbian studies to a discipline largely within academia. Lesbian scholarship now appeared in special issues of academic journals such as *Frontiers* (one of the first women's studies journals), *JumpCut* (a radical film journal), and *Radical Teacher.* Lesbian scholars communicated with one another through newsletters like *Matrices* or through the Lesbian Feminist Studies Clearinghouse (both now defunct). Caucuses and divisions flourished in many professional organizations. Lesbian scholarship clearly had made the transition from community to university.

Women's Studies: Silencing and Survival

Lesbian studies was greatly facilitated by the institutionalization of women's studies in colleges and universities in the United States. Throughout the 1970s and 1980s, most courses on lesbianism were likely to be found in women's studies programs. A survey conducted in 1980 found lesbian studies courses in more than a dozen institutions. In 1982 the first anthology of academic lesbian writing, *Lesbian Studies,* included a sampling of course syllabi from nine different campuses, the earliest of which had been offered in 1972. It is not surprising that many lesbians found women's studies a "safe space" in which to come out—that is, to affirm their lesbianism publicly—and to pursue research and teaching on lesbianism. Women's studies, with its base in feminism, valued the diversity of women's lives (in theory if not always in practice). Women's studies primarily involved woman only, especially in its first decade, and thus was congenial to lesbians, who often choose to make a primary commitment to women in all aspects of their lives. Most important, perhaps, women's studies was a new field struggling to change or expand the paradigms and curricula of the traditional universities. Thus, it was the most likely place for new and radical scholarship on women to be taken seriously.

But tension has always existed between women's studies and lesbian studies—as between lesbian and heterosexual feminists in general. Despite the strong presence of lesbians in women's studies, the movement as a whole has been reluctant to acknowledge their role or to place lesbian issues and analyses too close to the center of its work and structures.

There are many reasons for this silencing or marginalizing of lesbians. Since it is common to attempt to stigmatize women's studies (or the women's movement) by labeling all feminists as lesbians, some heterosexual women have been uneasy about associating with open lesbians. In order to attract heterosexual students to classes, or to gain the respect and support of academic colleagues, some women's studies programs have attempted to distance themselves from lesbians. Moreover, since women's studies programs themselves are often under attack or on the defensive, lesbian academics may put the general welfare of the program ahead of a specific lesbian agenda. Finally, both lesbian and heterosexual women may fall victim to homophobia—fear of or discomfort with homosexuality—and avoid bringing lesbianism into the classroom at all.

This tension has been persistant in the relationship of lesbians to the National Women's Studies Association in the United States. Although the most serious conflicts within the organization have been over racism, lesbians (who constitute its largest and most active caucus) have consistently expressed a sense of alienation and marginalization. Since the first national convention in 1979, there has been only one plenary specifically on lesbianism. Nor has lesbianism or sexuality ever been the theme of a conference, although a lesbian institute was held as part of the meetings in 2000. Clearly, there is still room for growth within the discipline of women's studies.

New Lesbian Scholarship

Lesbian studies developed along several fronts, including the creation of courses, the development of concrete knowledge in the disciplines, and the articulation of various theories of lesbian identity and culture. By the late 1980s, a body of contemporary and historical knowledge had been assembled primarily by historians, literary critics, anthropologists, sociologists, and psychologists. Some of this initial research was collected in the first anthology of lesbian scholarship and pedagogy, Margaret Cruikshank's *Lesbian Studies* (1982).

Key articles that shaped early lesbian theory include Carroll Smith-Rosenberg's "The Female World of Love and Ritual" (1975) and Adrienne Rich's "Compulsory Heterosexuality and Lesbian Existence" (1980/1993). Smith-Rosenberg uncovered thousands of letters exchanged among nineteenth-century women portraying a world in which women felt and expressed profound, lasting love for female friends and relatives. For the first time, the homoemotional experiences of women were thoroughly documented. Rich offered two very influential concepts: first, that in a patriarchal society heterosexuality is *compulsory* for women, not freely chosen; and second, that women's same-sex friendships exist on a continuum with lesbian relationships. In this way she replaced the notion of lesbians as a marginalized minority group with that of a lesbian existence potentially present in every woman's life. The construction of lesbianism that emerged from these articles—as deep and primary love between women, whether sexual or not—can also be found in Lillian Faderman's groundbreaking literary history, *Surpassing the Love of Men* (1981). Faderman's thesis was that until the onset of the modern era romantic friendships between women were not only tolerated but idealized in western society. But the identification of lesbianism with emotional rather than sexual bonds has proved highly controversial. Acrimonious debates over the importance of sexuality to definitions of lesbianism persisted throughout the 1980s.

By 1990 academic lesbian scholarship was no longer restricted to "alternative" publications but regularly appeared in mainstream scholarly journals and university presses. For example, historians uncovered evidence of lesbian sexuality or primary emotional commitments in various historical and geographical areas including Renaissance Italy, pre-Bolshevik Russia, and early twentieth-century China. Biographical studies revealed evidence of Rich's "lesbian continuum" in the lives of numerous women, both famous and obscure. Studies of "passing women" explored how working-class women chose to increase their social and economic opportunities by dressing and living as men, often joining their lives with other women. Far from being a curiosity of modern times, lesbianism was found to be a persistent, if differently experienced, phenomenon throughout history and across cultures.

Ethnographic information about lesbians is much rarer than information about male homosexuality, but important anthropological and sociological studies of modern lesbian communities demonstrate how lesbians structure social relationships and individual identities in order to survive in hostile environments. In terms of the individual subject, psychologists have created new models to replace heterosexist ideologies defining lesbians as sick or stunted.

Literary criticism, perhaps, has been most profoundly affected by lesbian scholarship. Lesbian literary studies include investigating the lives of lesbian writers, recovering lost or suppressed texts, reading from a lesbian perspective, analyzing lesbian imagery and characters, establishing traditions and influences, and constructing theories of aesthetics and representation. Currently, lesbian literary scholarship has resulted in books by single authors, edited anthologies, and journal articles too numerous to list here.

This new lesbian scholarship incorporates a variety of theories and methodologies, but it consistently assumes that sexual identity is learned, constructed, or experienced within a particular social structure or historical context, rather than being a biological or universal condition. Lesbian scholarship counters the dominant heterosexual perspective with one that emerges from the experiences of lesbians in various societies and subcultures. Through this scholarship, lesbian studies has been established as a field of inquiry in and of itself, and traditional scholarship has begun to change in response to new knowledge, questions, and theories.

Lesbians of Color and the Reconfiguration of Lesbian Studies

Lesbian studies, like women's studies and the feminist movement, was developed primarily by North American white women who initially resisted the criticism, offered by lesbians of color, that the movement was internally racist. In the 1970s this resistance was reinforced by a tendency to focus only on the similarities among all lesbians and to posit a universal patriarchy that oppressed all women or all lesbians equally. Little attention was paid to the material differences among lesbians or to the possibility that some lesbians might have access to power by virtue of their race or class or that others might feel commitments to men of their cultural groups. It became the task of lesbians of color, joined by antiracist white lesbians, to initiate a new understanding of difference and diversity.

The key texts in redefining lesbian studies include *This Bridge Called My Back* (Moraga and Anzaldúa, 1987), a collection of writings by radical women of color (many of them lesbians); and the works of Audre Lorde, who may be the single most influential figure in lesbian studies. By the 1990s lesbians of color had reshaped lesbian studies in two ways: first, by offering a critique of white racism that changed the way white women undertook scholarship and pedagogy; and, second, by creating texts and curricula that constitute

African-American or Latina lesbian studies, or, more generally, multiethnic lesbian studies.

Lesbian Studies: Present and Future

New theoretical developments in the 1990s further shifted the terms and interests of many lesbian scholars. The feminist construction of lesbianism, which emphasized gender (that lesbians are women) over sexuality (that lesbians are homosexual), increasingly came under attack. Theorists, scholars, and community activists revived interest in the butch-femme role playing that had characterized some mid-century lesbian communities. Explicit sexual imagery and practices became more noticeable in lesbian writing. In short, the new scholarship increasingly emphasized the sexual definition of lesbianism, which had been muted in earlier feminist theorizing.

At the same time, lesbians inside and outside the academy established closer ties with gay men. Many attribute this development to the need for coalitions to combat the increasing threat of right-wing activism and to agitate for increased resources in the fight against the AIDS epidemic. This coalition was reflected in the academy. While lesbian academics worked to place lesbian scholarship in women's studies programs and courses (what is called "mainstreaming"), they had not attempted to establish independent lesbian studies programs. Such structural change has since occurred in the form of gay and lesbian studies programs. Lesbian academics now face choices about where to focus their time and energy: as lesbians within women's studies or as women within gay studies. They must address questions such as these: Do similar paradigms and approaches unite lesbian studies and gay studies? Do lesbians become a mere subset of normative gay male experience?

A new theoretical perspective called "queer theory" is reshaping lesbian studies even more radically. Queer theory rejects entirely the idea of fixed sexual identities, thus questioning the assumption that lesbianism (or any other identity) can be a basis for defining any particular body of knowledge. In place of "lesbian" or "gay," queer theorists posit a fluid, loosely defined notion of queer, which may specify lesbians, gay men, bisexuals, and transgendered individuals. Queer theory has had a profound influence in the universities, particularly on literary theory. Nevertheless, many lesbian scholars question whether queer theory adequately explains differences based on gender and race. They also argue that lesbians' visibility has been too long and hard a fight to be lost in the amorphic notion of queer. This debate—between scholars identifying with lesbian feminism and those adhering to queer theory—no doubt will be among the signal issues in future lesbian studies.

Finally, the most important development of lesbian studies as it moves into the twenty-first century may well be its globalization. Lesbian courses and scholarship already exist in Britain, Canada, Australia, New Zealand, the Netherlands, Scandinavia, and Germany, as well as in the United States; there is increasing interest in such work in Latin America, India, and Japan. As feminist and lesbian movements strengthen in these countries, and women have increased access to higher education, the creation of a truly international lesbian studies is sure to follow.

See Also

ETHNIC STUDIES, *I and II;* FEMINISM: LESBIAN; GENDER STUDIES; HETEROPHOBIA AND HOMOPHOBIA; HETEROSEXISM; LESBIAN CULTURAL CRITICISM; LESBIANISM; LESBIAN WRITING, *all entries;* LESBIANS IN SCIENCE; LIBRARIES; QUEER THEORY; ROMANTIC FRIENDSHIP; WOMEN'S STUDIES: OVERVIEW *and specific entries*

References and Further Reading

Boston Lesbian Psychologies Collective. 1987. *Lesbian psychologies.* Urbana: University of Illinois Press.

Cruikshank, Margaret, ed. 1982. *Lesbian Studies: Present and future.* Old Westbury, N.Y.: Feminist Press.

Duberman, Martin, Martha Vicinus, and George Chauncey, Jr. 1989. *Hidden from history: Reclaiming the gay and lesbian past.* New York: Meridian.

Faderman, Lillian. 1981. *Surpassing the love of men.* New York: Morrow.

Foster, Jeannette. 1985. *Sex-variant women in literature.* Tallahassee, Fla.: Naiad. (Originally published 1956.)

Garber, Linda. 1994. *Tilting the tower: Lesbians teaching queer subjects.* New York: Routledge.

Grier, Barbara. 1981. *The lesbian in literature.* Tallahassee, Fla.: Naiad.

Griffin, Gabriele, and Sonya Andermahr. 1997. *Straight studies modified: Lesbian interventions in the academy.* London: Cassell.

Kennedy, Elizabeth, and Madeline Davis. 1993. *Boots of leather, slippers of gold: The history of a lesbian community.* New York: Routledge.

Lorde, Audre. 1984. *Sister outsider.* Trumansburg, N.Y.: Crossing.

Medhurst, Andy, and Sally R. Munt. 1997. *Lesbian and gay studies: A critical introduction.* London: Cassell.

Moraga, Cherrie, and Gloria Anzaldúa. 1981. *This bridge called my back: Writings by radical women of color.* Latham, N.Y.: Kitchen Table, Women of Color.

Rich, Adrienne. 1993. Compulsory heterosexuality and lesbian existence. In Henry Abelove, Michele Aina Barale, and

David Halperin, eds., *The lesbian and gay studies reader.* New York: Routledge (originally published 1980).

Roberts, J. R. 1981. *Black lesbians.* Tallahassee, Fla.: Naiad.

Smith-Rosenberg, Carroll. 1975. The female world of love and ritual. *Signs* 1 (1): 1–29.

Wilton, Tamsin. 1995. *Lesbian studies: Setting an agenda.* London and New York: Routledge.

Wolfe, Susan, and Julia Penelope. 1993. *Sexual practice textual theory: Lesbian cultural criticism.* Cambridge, Mass.: Blackwell.

Zimmerman, Bonnie, and Toni A. H. McNaron. 1995. *The new lesbian studies: Into the twenty-first century.* New York: Feminist Press.

Bonnie Zimmerman

LESBIAN WRITING: Overview

The word *lesbian* is derived from Lesbos, the name of a Greek island, the home of Sappho (about 600 B.C.E.), who is considered the first woman poet to celebrate her love of women in writing. The meaning of *lesbian* has been a subject of considerable debate, as in the 1970s and 1980s, when definitions ranged from "a woman-identified woman" to "a woman whose sexual focus is other women." Lesbianism has often been taboo in western and many other cultures. The systematic documentation and analysis of lesbian writing in works such as Jeannette Foster's *Sex Variant Women in Literature* (1956), Lillian Faderman's *Surpassing the Love of Men* (1985), and Bonnie Zimmerman's *The Safe Sea of Women* (1992) are a phenomenon of the post-World War II period, related to the civil rights movement and to women's and lesbian liberation.

Background

Because "lesbian writing" was not identified as such until the twentieth century, little is known about lesbian writing predating the late nineteenth century. Scholars have attempted to identify earlier writers and texts, but the marginalization of lesbianism in mainstream culture has meant that such identification often rests on clues suggesting lesbianism (as, perhaps, in the case of Emily Dickinson) rather than on unambiguous proof.

From the late nineteenth century on, changes in women's socioeconomic and political status, debates about their role in society, and the emergence of sexology contributed to a more extensive presentation of lesbians in literature. Lesbian characters, initially described as "inverts"—a term associated with *Studies in the Psychology of Sex: Sexual Inversion* (1897) by Havelock Ellis (who was married to a lesbian, Edith Ellis)—were typically depicted as lonely, tormented, artistically gifted, self-sacrificing middle-class women whose passion for other females remained unfulfilled, owing to the stigma attached to lesbianism. Radclyffe Hall's *The Well of Lonelinesss* (1928), a classic of this kind of lesbian realist fiction, first became famous because it was subjected to a trial for obscenity at Bow Street Magistrates' Court in London the year it was published. Its protagonist, Stephen Gordon, is a woman portrayed as having the soul of a man trapped in a female body; she is driven into exile in France, an exile that symbolizes her alienation from her own society. Similar journeys, fictional—such as H[ilda] D[oolitle]'s *Her* (1927) and Djuna Barnes's *Nightwood* (1936)—and real, were undertaken by many early twentieth-century lesbian writers, who formed circles in Greece and in cities like Paris and Berlin. Writers of this period, described as modernist, were preoccupied with representing the self in language, and this focus enabled lesbian writers such as Gertrude Stein and Renée Vivien to experiment with constructing lesbians in texts.

The Emergence of Lesbian Pulp Fiction

Lesbian pulp fiction began to be published extensively in the 1950s; this genre was later documented in the United States, for example, by Barbara Grier of Naiad Press. Pulp fiction—of which Ann Bannon's "Beebo Brinker" series is typical—continued to portray lesbians as tormented women. These protagonists live in subcultures and are continually threatened by exposure as lesbian in a heterosexual world, by police raids on clubs, and by unstable relationships. They are often presented as butch and femme: the butch characters frequently give themselves a masculine air through their clothing and behavior; the femme characters are frequently described in conventionally feminine terms and are potentially or actually heterosexual. There is a shift away from the earlier focus on middle-class women. Sexual activity between women is described in more detail, but the terminology and rituals are those of heterosexual romantic fiction.

Pulp fiction, like other narratives frequently considered characteristic of lesbian writing, often takes the form of a bildungsroman, or story of education, in this case a story of coming out. The protagonist has to come to terms with her sexual identity; frequently, she leaves her family and place of origin behind in order to find a new place in society—as a rebellious loner, or within a lesbian subculture, or by meeting the woman with whom she will live happily ever after. Classics of this kind of writing included Rita Mae Brown's *Rubyfruit Jungle* (1973) and Audre Lorde's *Zami: A New Spelling of My Name* (1982).

One long-established version of the lesbian bildungsroman is boarding-school fiction, in which the protagonist struggles—often unhappily—with her affection and desire for a classmate, a pupil, a teacher, or a colleague. Examples include Christa Winsloe's *Girls in Uniform* (1933), Antonia White's *Frost in May* (1933), Lillian Hellman's *The Children's Hour* (1934), Rosemary Manning's *The Chinese Garden* (1963), Brigid Brophy's *The Finishing Touch* (1973), and Olivia's *Olivia* (1973). Works in which lesbian relations develop in an all-female setting have led to debates about whether lesbianism is innate or acquired.

Political Activism in Lesbian Writing

Lesbians' political activism in the 1960s and 1970s was another source of debate—in this case, the debates were among lesbians and between lesbians and heterosexual women and had to do with their relative identities and their relation to patriarchy. This controversy is reflected in fictional works such as Gillian Hanscombe's *Between Friends* (1983) and also was a basis for theoretical writings such as Sidney Abbot and Barbara Love's *Sappho Was a Right-On Women* (1972), Jill Johnstone's *Lesbian Nation* (1973), and Ti-Grace Atkinson's *Amazon Oddyssey* (1974).

One of the leading contemporary lesbian feminist poets in the United States, Adrienne Rich, expressed several themes related to political activism: the ideal of a lesbian nation or a unitary lesbian community, the concern of the lesbian liberation and women's liberation movement with oppressive patriarchy, the environmental "green movement," and advances in reproductive technology that suggested the possiblity of fertilization outside the womb. These themes also appeared in lesbian-feminist science fiction. A few forerunners—such as Sarah Scott's *A Description of Millennium Hall* (1762) and Charlotte Perkins Gilman's *Herland* (1915)—depicted all-female utopias. In the 1970s and 1980s, initially in the United States and then in the United Kingdon, lesbian science fiction flourished, issued by newly established lesbian-feminist publishing houses. Examples include Marge Piercy's *Woman on the Edge of Time* (1979), Monique Wittig's *Les Guérrillères* (1979), Katherine V. Forrest's *Daughters of a Coral Dawn* (1984), Joanna Russ's *The Female Man* (1976), and Sally Miller Gearhart's *The Wanderground* (1978).

The questions raised in these texts about women's difference from men and about the role of biology and acculturation, or nature and nurture, in the formation of sexual identity were also debated in theoretical writings by lesbian and heterosexual feminists. The possibility of a specific kind of writing associated with the feminine was discussed by several French writers—lesbian, feminist, or both—such as Hélène Cixous, Luce Irigaray, and Julia Kristeva, who combined an interest in language with critiques of classic psychoanalysis. (According to Freudian psychoanalytic theory, awareness of possessing or lacking a penis is a crucial moment in the individual's psychosexual identity; this concept has often been a focus of feminist and lesbian critiques.)

Cultural Production and Genres

The idea that certain traits are typical in women's cultural production has been much discussed with regard to lesbians' appropriation of some genres traditionally dominated by men. Science fiction is one example; in this genre, male concerns tend to be centered on new technologies and the conquest of new worlds, whereas lesbian feminist science fiction has tended to focus on the need for changes in social structures and relations, and on how women's intuition and nurturance might be manifested in an altered environment. Another example is crime fiction, where questions arise about how the genre is subverted by having a lesbian detective at the center of a plot. The detective novels of Claire McNab, Sarah Dreher, Barbara Wilson, Mary Wings, Val McDermid, and others have established lesbian crime fiction as a favorite form of lesbian entertainment.

Through appropriating such popular genres, lesbian writing has begun to enter mainstream culture. However, the two novels that have perhaps contributed most to this process are both "high culture" works that won literary prizes and were adapted for the screen: Alice Walker's *The Color Purple* (1983, an epistolary novel) and Jeanette Winterson's *Oranges Are Not the Only Fruit* (1985). Each of them presents a female character who is trapped in an oppressive small-town or rural environment but transcends it through a lesbian relationship.

In the 1980s and 1990s, lesbian writers such as Winterson and Sara Schulman experimented increasingly with the novel form, producing texts that reflected the question of lesbian identity. Simore de Beauvoir's dictum that a woman is made, not born, was taken up by theorists such as Monique Wittig, Eve Sedgwick, Judith Butler, and Teresa de Lauretis and resonates in a postmodern culture that sees all ideas about individual identity as constructed and provisional, serving specific ideological and political purposes. In this framework, lesbianism is just one position that anyone can adopt. This is the argument of queer theory, in which the stability implied by the term *identity* is contested, and identity is seen rather as performance.

This notion of identity as performance accords with a whole range of lesbian writing that focuses on the double or multiple lives of its lesbian characters, women who live in a heterosexist society and may have to conceal their lesbianism by enacting a heterosexual, feminine role. It has also been associated with playing with gender—for example, when a lesbian is seen as a man trapped in a female body. Thus it has been important in the reclaiming of lesbian cultural history, in which role playing is a significant aspect of self-definition, and it has helped promote the writings of lesbians such as Joan Nestle, who have participated in changes in lesbian culture and have written autobiographically about these changes.

Lesbian Writing and Performance

The idea of identity as performance is prominent in lesbian writing for the theater. Here, lesbian "context theorists," playwrights, theater groups, and other theater practitioners have become increasingly important. Gay Sweatshop and Split Britches have been at the forefront of this development. However, their work and queer theory itself have been criticized by lesbians who subscribe to the lesbian feminism of the 1970s and 1980s.

According to this critique, "queer" lacks political bite, ignores reality in favor of an idea of "play" and lifestyle politics, leads to an "anything goes" mentality, and marginalizes lesbians by focusing on AIDS, which is more a concern of gay men. This critique has been voiced particularly strongly with regard to lesbian erotica and pornography in writing (and also in photography). Lesbians such as Pat Califa have come under attack because of their representations of sadomasochism, including coercive, painful, humiliating sex between lesbians or between lesbians and heterosexual or gay men; critics such as Sheila Jeffreys argue that such writings replicate heteropatriarcy: its power politics and its subordination and degradation of women in general and lesbians in particular.

Thus although a unitary lesbian nation is an ideal, contemporary lesbian writing reveals very diverse positions and viewpoints. Its proliferation—which is indicated by the lesbian sections in mainstream as well as alternative bookstores—has encouraged debates about differences among lesbians and has increased their cultural visibility.

See Also

BUTCH/FEMME; LESBIANISM; LESBIAN DRAMA; LESBIAN SEXUALITY; LESBIAN WRITING: CONTEMPORARY POETRY *and* CRIME FICTION; LITERARY THEORY AND CRITICISM; QUEER THEORY

References and Further Reading

Butler, Judith. 1994. *Bodies that matter.* London: Routledge.

Faderman, Lillian. 1985. *Surpassing the love of men: Romantic friendship and love between women from the Renaissance to the present day.* London: Women's Press.

Foster, Jeannette H. 1956. *Sex variant women in literature.* New York: Vantage.

Grier, Barbara. 1981. *The lesbian in literature.* Tallahassee, Fla.: Naiad.

Griffin, Gabriele. 1993. *Heavenly love? Lesbian images in twentieth-century women's writing.* Manchester: Manchester University Press.

Hall, Radclyffe. 1928. *The well of loneliness.* London: Cape.

Jay, Karla, and Joanne Glasgow. 1990. *Lesbian texts and contexts: Radical revisions.* New York: New York University Press.

Lorde, Audre. 1982. *Zami: A new spelling of my name.* Watertown, Mass.: Persephone.

Rule, Jane. 1975. *Lesbian images.* Trumansburg, N.Y.: Crossing.

Zimmerman, Bonnie. 1992. *The safe sea of women: Lesbian fiction, 1969–1989.* London: Onlywoman.

Gabriele Griffin

LESBIAN WRITING: Contemporary Poetry

As a rule, poetry embodies thoughts and feelings in its imagery and in its sound patterns, rather than explaining or describing such thoughts and feelings at length. In many lyric poems, these thoughts and feelings concern the relationship of the human to the external—for example, the relationship of the lover to the beloved, the human to the other or to the world, or to God, or to nature, or to the universe. Rather than attempt to define lesbian poetry by means of information about the sexualities or lifestyles of particular poets, or through literalist categorizations of the content of particular poems, it is more useful to place the emphasis on how a lesbian reading of a poem alters traditional assumptions. These assumptions have to do with what constitutes the "human," and what constitutes the "external," as well as how the relationship between the two might be viewed. When the word "lesbian" is used as an adjective, as it is in the term "lesbian poetry," readers and listeners are faced with a difficult choice between either regarding "poetry" as an aspect of lesbian existence or regarding "lesbian" as marking a subspecies of poetry in general. Both viewpoints are valid, but each emphasis leads to different forms of commentary, and within each lie temptations to reduce the complexity and to obscure the understanding of poetic texts.

Visibility and Invisibility

Ways to examine lesbian poetry are many and various, focusing sometimes on sociopolitical phenomena and sometimes on literary-cultural considerations. Within the lesbian and gay rights movements, for example, alliances based on homosexual resistance to heterosexism have resulted in lesbian and gay (male) poetry performances and publications. At the same time, solidarity and identification within feminism between lesbian and heterosexual women in resistance to patriarchy have resulted in feminist poetry performances and publications. With these parameters still pertaining, there have been further alignments and realignments of third world, nonwhite, postcolonial, first nation, working-class, and similarly differentiated groups, both of activists and of scholars, resulting in poetry performances and publications that either include or entirely consist of lesbian work. Much of this poetry is ignored by literary critics; or it is derided as ghettoized, special-interest polemic; or it is simply misread.

In addition, not all languages and cultures recognize as their own the construction of lesbian identity initiated by Western sexologists in the latter part of the nineteenth century—and further challenged, developed, and changed by western feminism during the latter half of the twentieth century. This circumstance, together with the increasing global dominance of English-language use and publishing, means that, at the same time as the reading and the writing of lesbian poetry in English became increasingly visible (c. 1970), the reading and the writing of lesbian poetry in minority western languages, and in all nonwestern languages, became relatively invisible or were declared nonexistent. To uncover and explore texts in these language cultures demands different methods of analysis from those now familiar to students of English, French, and Spanish literature.

Lesbian poetry is hard to find, even with the aid of dedicated scholarship, but, despite dismissal by mainstream critics and scholars, its existence is secure. Its range is prodigious, its production vigorous, its voice authentic, its temper fully human, and its quality equal to anything elsewhere admired. But it is marginalized or excluded from reading lists, publishers' promotions, print and broadcast reviews, awards and prizes, and all of the other literary and marketing showcases used to monitor and manipulate modern readerships.

At the end of the twentieth century, however, many poets were being open about their lesbianism and about linking it to other concerns in their lives. Among them are Audre Lorde (1934–1992) who began writing tight, lyrical poetry about personal relationships as a budding poet in the 1960s and then extended this to an expression of her lesbianism, shaping her sexuality to fit her struggles against personal and social injustice. The later poems of Adrienne Rich (b. 1929) have become openly lesbian and her poetry consistently addresses social and political issues in her distinctive urgent, concerned, incisive voice, while Cherrie Moraga (b. 1952) explores her own multiple identities in her poetry—feminist, Chicana, lesbian—and Judy Grahn (b. 1940) calls herself a gay cultural theorist determined to retrieve gay history both in her poetry and in her other writings.

Poetic Forms and Modes

The combined effects of English-language dominance, late-twentieth-century literary theory, and the development of information technology have resulted in a greater visibility and prominence of twentieth-century Anglo-American writers and readers of lesbian poetry than of similar work in other language cultures. Lists of cited work have tended to include comparatively small numbers of non-English-language writers. As of the end of the 1990s, standard bibliographical searches of major databases and of sites on the World Wide Web, for example, provided accessible references to lesbian poetry by and about more than forty authors. Although the list included some geographical and historical variety, it was dominated by white, western women—in particular, women in the United States.

Given this imbalance, it is reasonable to begin by exploring poetic forms and modes, rather than biographies. The most obviously lesbian poetry can be found in love lyrics, since the love lyric, familiar to all writers and readers, has been the poetic form most commonly used from the late Middle Ages onward. Its use extends throughout the range of crafted diction, from highly wrought literary texts to folk poetry and folk song to greetings cards and popular songs. Lesbian voices have been present in every part of this range. Love—and, more recently, sex—between women has been given shape and expression in love lyrics more often than in any other written form, though the greater part of such texts has never been published. These poems have been regarded by their writers and recipients as private, personal, and particular, and thus devoid of any wider interest or literary status.

In addition to love lyrics, the vast, relatively unexplored body of lesbian poetry encompasses meditations, speculations, insights, affirmations, and examinations concerning every aspect of life, both of the external known world and of the inner landscapes of memory and desire. For isolated writers and readers, poetry has offered comfort, corroboration, and connection; for those who have found social, professional, or activist networks, it has offered clarity, continuity, and celebration.

The body of lesbian poetry established by the end of the twentieth century has both literary and extraliterary resonance. Because women as a group have less disposable income than men, because women's work has had considerably less visibility than men's, and because recognizably lesbian work has been censored or silenced altogether, poetry has always been highly valued by lesbian writers and readers. Writing poetry requires neither expensive equipment nor professional institutions, and, since poems are nearly always shorter than prose works, they have been easier to reproduce and circulate at minimal cost. This has meant that the development of lesbian communities, and of lesbian sensibility, has always been supported by exchanges of poetry with political energies, both celebratory and subversive. This vast body of work is hidden in newsletters, small magazines, and other marginal or short-lived publications stored in specialist archives and in collections of personal papers.

Readers and Lesbian Poetry

More conventional—and, therefore, enduring—modes of publication are obviously easier to locate, so that commentary, which is centered for the most part in the academy, necessarily focuses on work that has found literary, rather than activist, outlets. Even from a literary standpoint, however, lesbian poetry still requires a radical repositioning of its readership if it is to be permitted the full force of its energy and clarity. How lesbian poetry is read, that is, is at least as crucial to its understanding as who wrote it, why it was written, how it has been and will be written, and even what it is, since its proper reading requires a major reassessment of the assumptions brought to the reading of mainstream poetry. These assumptions concern the relationship between the writer and the reader, between the writer and the speaker of the poem, and between the writer or speaker of the poem and the world, the whole of creation, or the "other." Lesbian poetry requires a constant questioning of the notion of the "other" and of the relationship to that other. What is at stake in the reading of lesbian poetry goes beyond relationships between women, though these relationships can have striking results.

Reading poetry involves continually placing the poem in new contexts. For example, Elizabeth Bishop's (1911–1979) refrain to her mentor, in "Invitation to Miss Marianne Moore" (1955), to "please come flying," captures the joyful calling of like to like, regardless of whether either poet might have welcomed or rejected a lesbian identity for herself.

It is the sense of "kinship," rather than the idea of an identity, that is important. What is meant by a sense of kinship is quite simply a strong sense of similarity rather than difference. The "other" is not necessarily different from the "human." A woman addressing another woman inevitably acknowledges the similarity between them. By contrast, in a traditional, heterosexual love poem, the male lover is different from the beloved.

Male-dominated societies generate male-dominated literary traditions. This means that the human is primarily the male human, and the relationship of the human to the external refers—with all the weight of tradition behind it—to "man's" relationship to the external. "Man's" relationship to "God," to the world, to other men, to women, and to the rest of creation has varied in accordance with a particular cultural context and "his" place in it. In no known society, however, has the relationship of the male human being to God and the world been the same as that of a lesbian reader or writer to God and the world. Moreover, it is harder for a woman to idealize or demonize another woman for her own ends, because, despite differences of race and class, for example, the phrase "another woman," with all the weight of tradition behind it, necessarily indicates that they belong to the same category. Simple statements such as "You are like me" and "You are not like me" depend for their precise understanding on who is speaking to whom and in which cultural context, since the relative power, or powerlessness, attributed to the "you"—not just by the speaker, but also by the surrounding mores and conventions—is crucial to understanding what is meant.

This is not to say that lesbian poetry contains no antagonistic figures. Many appear. Men are the obvious example, though a poem like Adrienne Rich's "Phantasia for Elvira Shatayev" (1978), which extends understanding and fellow feeling to the figure of the husband, will often reach out to the male outsider. What matters is how power and kinship are attributed, by whom they are attributed, and to whom they are attributed. What also matters is the value placed on them.

Whatever may be the agenda, the particular politics (Adrienne Rich, for example, feels strongly about the link between poetry and politics), or the individual attitude of a poet declaring herself to be lesbian, these stances have to take place in a context that explores some of the following questions. How does she relate to other women? Does she assume, or not, that her work will be read by other women? Does she speak to a fellow "goddess"—a fellow idealized figure—since she does, after all, inherit the mainstream tradition, however ill or well it serves her? Or does she not address a "goddess"? Is she "human" in that she is separated from the rest of creation? Or is she "human" in that she is not?

Since lesbian role models have not been set up for widespread acclaim, admiration, or imitation by absolutely everyone, it follows that the problems of kinship and of relative power and powerlessness that any lesbian poet faces are being read—when they are read at all—within a mainstream context. This requires a readjustment of all assumptions regarding kinship and the value attached to relative power and powerlessness. A lesbian reading of poetry, in other words, is hard work. Is it, therefore, worthwhile, apart from the novelty it generates and apart from the general principle that any new way of looking at things is worth acquiring?

For many commentators, it is not only worthwhile but absolutely essential at the beginning of the twenty-first century. The central question of the relation of the "I" to the "other" that lesbian poets negotiate and perforce redefine is precisely the question that needs to be renegotiated by everyone, if women, men, God, the world, and the rest of creation—lesbians included—are not to destroy themselves. Lesbian poetry embodies a major and continuing contribution not only to the needs of lesbian writers and readers but also to the civilizing of the wider culture, in that it offers human beings the possibility of seeing themselves as a part of creation, rather than at odds with it.

See Also

LESBIAN WRITING: OVERVIEW; POETRY: OVERVIEW *and* FEMINIST THEORY AND CRITICISM

References and Further Reading

Bulkin, Elly, and Joan Larkin, eds. 1981. *Lesbian poetry: An anthology.* Watertown, Mass.: Persephone.

DeJean, Joan. 1989. *Fictions of Sappho, 1546–1937.* Chicago: University of Chicago Press.

Hanscombe, Gillian, and Suniti Namjoshi. 1991. "Who wrongs you, Sappho?" Developing lesbian sensibility in the writing of lyric poetry. In Jane Aaron and Sylvia Walby, eds., *Out of the margins: Women's studies in the nineties,* 156–167. London: Falmer.

Kennard, Jean E. 1986. Ourself behind ourself: A theory for lesbian readers. In Elizabeth A. Flynn and Patrocinio P. Schweickart, eds., *Gender and reading: Essays on readers, texts, and contexts,* 63–80. Baltimore, Md: Johns Hopkins University Press.

Munt, Sally. 1992. *New lesbian criticism: Literary and cultural readings.* Hemel Hempstead, England: Harvester Wheatsheaf.

Rich, Adrienne. 1979. *On lies, secrets, and silence: Selected prose, 1966–1978.* New York: Norton.

Gillian Hanscombe
Suniti Namjoshi

LESBIAN WRITING: Crime Fiction

The lesbian mystery novel had its origins in lesbian pulp fiction of the 1950s and early 1960s. Its glimpse into an underworld of intrigue and suspense was offered again in the lesbian crime novels that proliferated in British and North American publishing of the 1980s. They allow the reader to step—safely—into a quagmire of sex, violence, and death. Lesbian crime novels are also about discovering and exploring lesbian identities.

M. F. Beal's *Angel Dance* (1977) is generally considered the first lesbian feminist crime novel. Its angry, complex, visionary indictment of heteropatriarchal capitalism reflects the protest culture of the 1970s. The subversive first-person narrator of *Angel Dance,* Kat Guerra, is a Chicana detective who embodies the way class, race, gender, and sexuality combine to maintain the hegemonic order of law; and the state is represented as so powerful and so corrupt that the concept of "justice" can no longer be invoked. This theme is also explored in Barbara Wilson's early classic, *Murder in the Collective* (1984).

The traditional crime novel is a genre in which anxieties about society are expressed and the enemy is named and destroyed. In the lesbian and feminist crime novel, the terms are often inverted, so that the state is identified as the corrupt enemy and the lesbian sleuth, rather than being a feared and hated "other," is the victor. The mystery is solved in two stages: first, by using a process of individuation intrinsic to the thriller, the lesbian protagonist achieves self-determination; second, she becomes integrated into a community. The first phase is often represented as coming out, and the second as finding love (that is, romance) or as discovering the lesbian community in a movement toward politicized integration. A typical example is Katherine Forrest's *Murder at the Nightwood Bar* (1987).

Lesbian mystery fiction has consistently questioned or reexamined the concept of heroism, transgressing the conventions of the genre. Many novels, mostly from the mid-1980s, consciously appropriated the image of the avenging knight, proferring a sexy superdyke striding the city streets in her steel-capped shoes, swinging her double-headed ax, leaving slain patriarchs in her wake. This was one form of transgression; in later forms, the legacy of butch-femme roles in that image became more explicit. As a subcultural stereotype, the butch detective works at two levels of identification: the reader not only may desire the detective but also may want to *be* the detective.

Theorists who have considered the genre of detective fiction have likened it most to satire. Classical Menippean satire (which parodied myth and philosophy and is said to have been invented by Menippus, a Phoenician of the third century B.C.E.) consists of a dialogue between stylized characters who merely mouth ideas: the *ailon,* who is the hero; and an *alazon,* who is usually revealed as a pompous, deluded fool. The dramatic function of the lesbian detective is to expose "alazons" by using her analytical powers, and thus to lead the reader to a changed, enlightened consciousness. In feminist ideology, patriarchy and heterosexism are often synonymous with "alazony," and an investigation of gender relations exposes "false consciousness"—a Marxist term for delusional identification with the wrong interest group. This can be a persuasive structure, artfully seducing a protofeminist reader. The protagonist, the *eiron,* is able to scrutinize and deflate the excesses of masculinity; in these narratives, masculinity usually ends up shooting itself in the foot. Satire of this kind is often used in a popular series by Mary Wing, which starts with *She Came Too Late* (1986).

The crime novel, with its legacy of socialist critiques (Dashiell Hammett, for instance, was a communist), its formal relationship to parody, and its tendency toward antiheroism, has elements that can readily be appropriated by a counterculture. Examples of such appropriation include Sarah Schulman's *After Delores* (1991) and Claire Macquet's *Looking for Ammu* (1992). But the lesbian crime novel had its heyday during an individualistic period of Reaganism (in the United States) and Thatcherism (in Great Britain). Its solutions to social problems and crime often took the form of personal rather than structural justice. In the 1990s, some lesbian crime novels continued the tradition of pulp fiction, while others—such as the verse novel *The Monkey's Mask* (1997) by the Australian writer Dorothy Porter—mutated into formal experimentation.

See Also

BUTCH/FEMME; DETECTIVE FICTION; LESBIAN WRITING: OVERVIEW

References and Further Reading

Munt, Sally R. 1994. *Murder by the book: Feminism and the crime novel.* London and New York: Routledge.

Palmer, Paulina. 1991. The lesbian feminist thriller and detective novel. In Elaine Hobby and Chris White, eds., *What lesbians do in books,* 9–27. London: Women's Press.

Sally R. Munt

LESBIANS: HIV Prevalence and Transmission

The prevalence of HIV (human immunodeficiency virus) among lesbians has been difficult to quantify, compared with its rate of occurrence in other populations, for two main reasons. First, at the time of this writing the survey instruments of organizations monitoring HIV had no category designated "lesbian" or "women who have sex with women." Second, in most cultures women who call themselves lesbian are—as a result of social pressures—generally secretive about their sexual orientation.

Studies that have been done, however, have found that the primary risk factors for HIV among women who have sex with women are sexual contact with a man and the use of injected drugs (Cohen, 1993; Peterson, 1992). In the United States, for example, women who reported having sexual contact *only* with other women represented 0.9 percent of all reported cases of AIDS (acquired immune deficiency syndrome) among adult women. Of that number, 93 percent were users of intravenous (IV) drugs, and the remaining 7 percent had received blood transfusions before March 1985 (Chu, 1992). Current research would seem to indicate that female-to-female HIV transmission through lesbian sex is extremely rare (Raiteri, 1994).

Researchers caution, however, that because women who identify themselves as lesbian may have sex with men as well, these data are relevant only for sexual behavior, not for self-identified sexual orientation (Chu, 1994). Lesbians who engage in behaviors that are known to transmit HIV will, not surprisingly, have a higher prevalence of HIV infection.

Behaviors that transmit HIV include anything that allows infected blood (including menstrual blood) or semen to enter the blood of a previously uninfected person. The highest-risk behaviors include receptive anal intercourse and sharing IV needles. Vaginal heterosexual intercourse poses a slightly lower risk. Female-to-male transmission is considered to have a lower efficiency than male-to-female transmission, because semen carrying HIV is always highly infectious, whereas the viral load of vaginal fluids varies. Although vaginal fluids can carry the virus, they also carry antibodies that may inhibit HIV transmission. In addition, the vagina and cervix are lined with mucous membranes that can absorb the virus. Very young women—preteens and girls in the early teenage years—are at greater risk of HIV infection because at these ages the walls of the vagina, which are lined by the mucous membranes that produce vaginal fluid, are thinner and contain fewer immunity-producing cells than those of women in their mature childbearing years (*New York Times,* 1993). In postmenopausal women, the vaginal walls again begin to thin and vaginal dryness is more common, potentially allowing tearing that would permit infected semen to enter the bloodstream.

Debate in lesbian communities about both the prevalence and the transmission of HIV has focused primarily on the necessity of recognizing that lesbians *do* become infected, in spite of the low probability of woman-to-woman transmission. To say that most lesbians who are HIV-positive probably acquired the virus from shared needles or from sex with an HIV-infected man does *not* imply that these women are not lesbians or that they do not need or deserve support from the lesbian community (McDaniel, 1995).

For women who have sex with women, safe practices to prevent transmission of HIV may include a dental dam as a vaginal barrier, latex gloves or finger cots if there are open cuts or sores on the hands, and a condom on all sex toys.

See Also

AIDS AND HIV; BISEXUALITY; LESBIANISM; SAFER SEX; SEX EDUCATION; SEXUAL ORIENTATION

References and Further Reading

Chu, Susan Y., T. A. Hammett, and I. W. Buehler. 1992. Update: Epidemiology of reported cases of AIDS in women who report sex only with other women. *Journal of AIDS* 6(5):518–519.

Chu, Susan Y., L. Conti, B. Schable, and T. Diaz. 1994. Female-to-female sexual contact and HIV transmission. *Journal of the American Medical Association* 272(6):433.

Cohen, Henry, M. Marmor, H. Woolfe, and D. Ribble. 1993. Risk assessment of HIV transmission among lesbians. *Journal of AIDS* 6(10):1173–1174.

McDaniel, Judith. 1995. *The lesbian couples' guide.* New York: HarperCollins.

New York Times. 1993. UN finds teenage girls at high risk of AIDS (30 July).

Peterson, L. R., L. Doll, C. White, and S. Chu. 1992. No evidence for female-to-female HIV transmission among 960,000 female blood donors. *Journal of AIDS* 5(9): 853–855.

Raiteri, R., R. Fora, and A. Sinicco. 1994. Lesbians safe from AIDS transmission. *Lancet* 344(23 July): 270.

Judith McDaniel
Judith Mazza

LESBIANS IN SCIENCE

Women have long been underrepresented in science. Historically, they were directly discouraged from pursuing scientific careers. In contemporary times, women typically comprise 20 percent or less of the scientific society of their profession. In 1994, a study by the National Science Foundation showed that women and people of color in science and technology comprise only half of their normal proportion of the workforce.

The "glass ceiling" for women becomes a "lavender ceiling" for lesbians, gives society's external and internal homophobia. When these facts are coupled with the invisibility of lesbians and the mutability of sexual orientation in women, lesbians' representation in science is less discernible and less measurable than the representation of women in general. Women in the sciences have often been perceived as asexual, as being married to science and not to a husband and family. Their writings indicate a passionate devotion to science and to their women friends, but for the most part there is little, if any, documentation of the nature of these friendships. It is clear, however, that lesbians face the same career barriers in science and engineering that women in general face, in addition to homophobia.

The forces impeding women's achievement in science are complex, involving not only traditional societal roles and internalized "isms," but also the undeniable biological roles and behaviors expected of women. Women in most cultures are taught to play subordinate roles. Many women must choose between advancing a career and nurturing a family. Many women leave their chosen career because they experience discomfort with the attitudes and opportunities presented to them. They face differences in intellectual and networking styles that can pose a significant but subtle obstacle to acceptance by peers, and to advancement.

Internalized homophobia manifests itself when gender roles are challenged. Women who have chosen to be aggressive in their careers are often labeled as confrontational or uncooperative. If they were men, this aggressiveness would be considered a positive and creative quality. Women who act as aggressors are actually perceived as violating gender-appropriate behaviors, and their sexuality is called into question. In the predominantly male world of science and engineering, many successful women try to separate themselves from feminists who overtly challenge male traditions; they avoid drawing attention to themselves lest they be mistaken for lesbians. Such isolationism deprives younger women of the networking and mentoring they need to achieve parity with their male colleagues.

An underlying cause of internalized homophobia is the overt homophobia that pervades most cultures. Historically, overt acknowledgment of homosexuality could cause a scientist or engineer to lose a security clearance, face a hostile work environment, miss out on promotions or assignments, and possibly even lose a job. In academia, a lesbian scientist could face biased peer review for publication or funding, as well as for tenure. In industry, a company perceived as being run by gays could lose its clientele. Even today, many states in the United States do not have laws that allow for redress in instances of overt discrimination in the workplace based on sexual orientation. In the United States, federal legislation (ENDA) to equalize nondiscrimination in employment regarding sexual orientation throughout the nation has been languishing for several years. With changing times, new institutional and corporate human resource policies, and legislation, most openly discriminatory practices have disappeared. Yet the shadow of past deeds remains, as does the fear of internalized homophobia.

No scientists are immune to these experiences. In 1994, a survey of members of the Gay and Lesbian Medical Association (GLMA) found a clear and disturbing picture of a medical system rife with discrimination against gay, lesbian, and bisexual physicians and their patients. GLMA is actively working to correct this situation.

Communities for socializing hardly existed before the 1990s; but since then, through grassroots networking and activism, lesbians and gay men have banded together to form organizations to combat homophobia. The National Organization of Gay and Lesbian Scientists and Technical Professionals (NOGLSTP) is one such group, dedicated to providing dialogue with professional organizations in order to improve their members' employment and professional environment. An affiliate of the American Association for the Advancement of Science, NOGLSTP has an educational agenda for the gay, scientific, and general communities to eliminate stereotypes and oppose antigay discrimination. Lesbians in Science (LIS), an Internet discussion group, helps provide lesbians with their own "old girls' network" by promoting intercity and intradisciplinary contacts. One of NOGLSTP's many achievements has been to educate U.S. governmental agencies about security clearance processing, which had been a major barrier to lesbian and gay scientists and engineers in the defense industry since the McCarthy era of the early 1950s. Today, for the most part (excluding the military, the FBI and CIA, and the National Security Agency), an executive order bars discrimination on the basis of sexual orientation in federal agencies.

Many universities and educational institutions in the United States, as well as corporations involved in scientific research and technology-intensive industries, have equal employment opportunity policies that do not discriminate on the basis of sexual orientation and offer benefits for employees' domestic partners. Support groups for gays and lesbians abound in technology-based U.S. corporations such as Apple, Lucent Technologies, AT&T, Lotus, Kaiser-Permanente, Xerox, Silicon Graphics, and Genentech. Support groups and employee organizations can also be found at federally funded laboratories and agencies such as the Jet Propulsion Laboratory, the National Institutes of Health, Los Alamos National Laboratory, and the Department of Energy. Human resource departments throughout the United States provide diversity training and make efforts to recruit a diverse workforce. More and more CEOs and human resource managers acknowledge the creative advantage of a diverse workplace and the bottom-line benefits accruing from the productivity and commitment of happy employees. In a work environment where diversity is promoted and appreciated, the lesbian scientist is more likely to find visibly gay and lesbian role models, mentors, and professional networking opportunities. She can be "out" at work—or not, as she feels appropriate—and can direct her energy where it belongs: to the advancement of her career.

Organizing among lesbians and gays in the sciences has occurred mainly in the United States. European countries lack overall organizations, but many scientific meetings and conferences, particularly in Germany, include gatherings of lesbian scientists where they may discuss issues in the scientific community of concern to them. In Asia and Africa, however, such gatherings appear to be nonexistent, unless they are under the umbrella of an international conference that draws scientists from all over the world. Despite these small steps, in most countries outside the United States, science lacks any lesbian viewpoint, and there is no sense of any lesbian community within any of the various branches of the sciences, or indeed within the scientific community as a whole.

In an ideal world of professionals, merit would the only criterion for career advancement, and sexual orientation would not matter. But scientists, like all human beings, bring the subjective experiences of their cultural upbringing to bear on their lives. Nevertheless, sociologists have shown that individuals who know a gay or lesbian person are more likely to have a tolerant attitude toward gays and lesbians in general. Lesbian professionals who have the courage and the resources can and should be open about their sexual orientation. As the pipeline to scientific eminence begins to fill with a more balanced proportion of women, and as society becomes more aware of lesbians, it is only a matter of time until lesbians begin to see their statistical share of contributions to science and technology.

See Also

ANTIDISCRIMINATION; HETEROPHOBIA AND HOMOPHOBIA; SCIENCE: TECHNOLOGICAL AND SCIENTIFIC RESEARCH; SCIENCE: FEMINIST CRITIQUES; SCIENCE: TWENTIETH CENTURY

References and Further Reading

Bell, A., and M. Weinberg. 1978. *Homosexualities: A study of diversity among men and women.* New York: Simon and Schuster.

Diamond, Rochelle A. 1995. Gay scientists improve workplace conditions through visibility and more communication. *Scientist* (6 February): 13.

Duvivier, Elizabeth. 1999. Gaining ground: Gays and lesbians in engineering. *Diversity/Careers* (December–January).

Friskopp, A., and S. Silverstein. 1995. *Straight jobs, gay lives: Gay and lesbian professionals, the Harvard Business School and the American workplace.* New York: Scribner.

Harding, Sandra. 1998. Essays on science and society: Women, science, and society. *Science* 280(8 May): 822.

Isaksson, Eva. 2000. Science. In Bonnie Zimmerman, ed., *Lesbian histories and cultures,* 672–674. New York: Garland.

Jones, Leslie S. 1998. Taking the sciences beyond affirmative action: Cultural impediments to gender and racial/ethnic inclusion. In American Association of University Women Educational Foundation, *Gender and race on the campus and in the school: Beyond affirmative action,* 35–50. Washington, D.C.: American Association of University Women Educational Foundation.

Lawler, Andrew. 1994. Scientific community: Tenured women battle to make it less lonely at the top. *Science* 286(12 November): 1272–1278.

National Science Foundation. 1994. *Women, minorities, and persons with disabilities in science and engineering.* Arlington, Va.: National Science Foundation.

Selby, Cecily. 1998. Choices and successes: Women in science and engineering. *Proceedings of the New York Academy of Sciences Conference* (12 March).

Schatz, B., and K. O'Hanlan. 1994. *Anti-gay discrimination in medicine: Results of a national survey of lesbian, gay, and bisexual physicians.* San Francisco: Gay and Lesbian Medical Association.

Internet Resources

Lesbians in Science, an E-mail discussion list for lesbians in industry, universities, government labs, and other organizations. Send message SUBSCRIBE LIS your name your E-address to: LIS-REQUEST@KENYON.EDU

National Organization of Gay and Lesbian Scientists and Technical Professionals, Inc. (NOGLSTP), P.O. Box 91803, Pasadena, CA 91109. <http://www.noglstp.org>

Queer Resources Directory. <http://www.qrd.org>

Rochelle Diamond
Barbara Belmont

LESBIANS IN THEATER

See LESBIAN DRAMA.

LEVIRATE

See FAMILY: RELIGIOUS AND LEGAL SYSTEMS; JUDAIC TRADITIONS *and* JUDAISM.

LIBERAL FEMINISM

See FEMINISM: LIBERAL.

LIBERALISM

Liberalism is a theory of political rights, corresponding to a rational-individualist theory of human nature, that arose in England in the seventeenth century as a radical alternative to patriarchalism. Patriarchalism had accounted for all social relationships in terms of familial structures in which fathers were unquestionably dominant over wives and children. According to it, everyone in a society was born into a state of subjection to some patriarchal superior, in relationships ordained originally by God; social and political behavior should be governed by principles derivable from those relationships of domination and subordination. The authority of kings was, thereby, linked to the authority of fathers in a system that legitimated both absolute sovereignty in the political arena and patriarchal authority within the family.

Liberalism challenged this view, insisting, principally, on a radical individualism which asserted that everyone was born free and equal, and that political relationships had to be grounded in a recognition of equality. Two major schools of liberal theory and practice have been developed since that time. One, the social contractarian school, expressed in the work of Thomas Hobbes and John Locke—and more recently revived by John Rawls (1971; revised 1999) and Robert Nozick (1974)—insisted that, since all people were born free and equal, the only legitimate political power was grounded in the consent of the governed. A second school, the utilitarian, articulated in the works of Jeremy Bentham and John Stuart Mill, argued that the only legitimate standard for judging social institutions and practices was the principle of utility, "the greatest good of the greatest number." Liberals have debated whether social contractarian or utilitarian perspectives offer the best grounds for structuring a society that truly respects and values individual freedom. Nevertheless, liberalism of either variety is characterized by respect for individuality and individual freedom—with "freedom" understood as protection from social or governmental "interference" with individually chosen ends—coupled with wariness about the exercise of political power.

Despite the seeming absolutism of this valuing of individuality and individual freedom, liberal theory and politics have been far from consistent about according freedom and equality to all. From its beginnings, liberalism struggled with the question of who merited full membership in a citizenry. And, at various places and times, those defined as "dependent" (including people who "depended" on wages for their support, women, slaves, children, and people John Stuart Mill classified in 1859 as "barbarians") were not considered citizens, or accorded rights to freedom and equality, even in paradigmatic liberal societies such as the United States and England (see Ackelsberg, 1994; Shklar, 1991).

Thus, for example, although liberal critics of patriarchalism focused on undermining the connection between patriarchal authority and political authority, with the expressed aim of freeing men to form political communities on a more egalitarian basis, these same liberal theorists were much less attentive to the implications of their arguments either for relations within the family or for relations between the sexes in the liberal polities about which they theorized. Ironically, perhaps, Mary Wollstonecraft (England, 1759–1797), Emilia Pardo Bazan (Spain, 1851–1921), and women in many other countries used liberal arguments about freedom and individual self-development to press for greater equality and rights for women. More recently, Susan Moller Okin (1989) and Zillah Eisenstein (1981) have argued that the liberal critique taken to its logical conclusion would challenge the patriarchal character of family relations as well as the male-dominated structure of broader political institutions and practices.

Most liberal thinkers and writers have failed to make these connections, however. Instead, the "independent" citizen of liberal political theory has been constructed as a male head of household, who could count on the services of his wife (and of servants or slaves as well) in the so-called private realm of the home to provide him with the support that made possible *his* participation in political life. Women's effective exclusion from the social contract and from full and equal participation in most liberal societies has been hidden, and justified, by an unstated (prepolitical) "sexual contract" that subordinated women to men in the private and familial arena (Pateman, 1988). Liberalism failed to recognize the interdependence between public and private arenas in the liberal polity. As a consequence, the theory and practice of liberalism effectively maintains the subordination of women despite its ideological commitment to individuality and individual freedom. Similar arguments could be made with respect to the blindness of liberalism to (or its dependence on) the inequalities manifest in relations between employer and employee, or between colonizer and colonized.

Liberalism, Socialism, and Communitarianism

Although liberalism began as a critique of, and an alternative to, patriarchalism, it has also come to be understood in contrast to other political ideologies, notably socialism and, more recently, communitarianism. Socialist critics have noted that political liberalism arose at roughly the same time as capitalism, and that the two have become almost synonymous. They argue that liberalism's emphasis on individualism and political freedoms blinds it to the workings of power in the (capitalist) economy that effectively belie any meaningful political equality. In this respect, socialists and some feminists offer parallel critiques that focus on related aspects of the assumed distinction between what are termed "public" and "private" arenas: whether in the case of women's subordination in the home, or in the case of the subordination of workers in the economic arena, the claim to individual equality that is at the root of liberal politics, and that liberal institutions supposedly protect, is often false and misleading. The freedom of contract (whether marriage contract or employment contract) on which liberal politics depends only masks relations of dominance and subordination. Similarly, many staunch supporters of liberal political ideology and practices in Europe seemed unaware of the contradictory nature of their simultaneous defense of colonialist practices in Africa and elsewhere (see, for example, Mill, 1859).

In the later years of the twentieth century, communitarians developed yet another set of criticisms of liberalism. Communitarians joined with both socialists and patriarchalists in criticizing the individualism they take to be at the core of liberalism, insisting that fundamental concepts such as liberty, consent, equality, and privacy have no meaning outside of the context of particular communities. In their view, liberalism denies the reality that any social order depends on the common meanings or understandings derived from particular communal traditions. It does not make sense to speak of individuals constituting a community; rather, communities constitute individuals. Although these criticisms are similar to those of many feminists and socialists, who also emphasize the social construction of individuals, communitarian criticism focuses less on gender or class divisions and more on the significance of traditional community values. By contrast, liberals and many feminists have, in turn, criticized communitarians for failing to recognize or acknowledge the relationships of domination and subordination that structure virtually all communities, including (especially) traditional ones.

Evaluating Liberalism

In short, liberalism leaves an ambiguous legacy. On the one hand, it offered a sharp and powerful critique of patriarchal or traditionalist societies, insisting that the protection of individual freedom is the critical value for society. In making this argument, it provided tools and concepts that have been taken up by feminists, and by others struggling against inequality or oppression, to argue for greater freedom and equality for all. On the other hand, all too many liberal theorists (and liberal societies) have ignored the implications of their own analyses with respect to gender relations, failing to recognize the social and political subordination of women as a fundamental challenge to the promises of liberal individualism. Furthermore, to the extent that liberal political institutions have been able to coexist with colonialism, and even with slavery, it is clear that liberal ideology is no guarantee of either freedom or equality. Feminists and others, therefore, continue to debate whether liberalism can be reclaimed to offer a strong ground on which to argue for equality, or whether the ways it has assumed—and thereby made invisible—the subordination of women and other groups in the construction of the liberal citizen make it fundamentally ill-suited to this task.

See Also

FEMINISM: LIBERAL BRITISH AND EUROPEAN *and* LIBERAL NORTH AMERICAN; JUSTICE AND RIGHTS

References and Further Readings

Ackelsberg, Martha. 1994. "Dependency" or "mutuality"? A feminist perspective on dilemmas of welfare policy. *Rethinking Marxism* 7(2): 73–86.

———, and Mary Lyndon Shanky. 1996. Privacy, publicity, and power: A feminist reconsideration of the public-private dichotomy. In Christine DiStefano and Nancy J. Hirschmann, eds., *Revisioning the political: Feminist reconstructions of traditional concepts in western political theory*, 213–233. Boulder, Col.: Westview.

Eisenstein, Zillah. 1981. *The radical future of liberal feminism.* New York: Longman.

Gutmann, Amy. 1985. Communitarian critics of liberalism. *Philosophy and Public Affairs* 14(3: Summer): 308–322.

Mill, John Stuart. 1859. *On liberty.* London: J.W. Parker and Son.

Nozick, Robert. 1974. *Anarchy, state, and utopia.* New York: Basic Books.

Okin, Susan Moller. 1991. *Justice, gender and the family.* New York: Basic Books.

Pateman, Carole. 1988. *The sexual contract.* Stanford, Calif.: Stanford University Press.

Rawls, John. 1971. *A theory of justice.* Cambridge Mass.: Harvard University Press. Revised edition 1999.

Shklar, Judith. 1991. *American citizenship: The quest for inclusion.* Cambridge, Mass: Harvard University Press.

Martha A. Ackelsberg

LIBERATION

Liberation implies freedom from oppression and the power to live differently. Concepts of liberation have been central to feminist theory and numerous women's struggles. There is, though, no general definition that covers all its meanings.

Second-wave feminism drew on concepts of liberation current in black, gay, and left-wing struggles for civil rights in the United States and parts of Europe in the 1960s. This became known as women's liberation. The explicit focus on liberation identified common political interests among all women. But it also raised immediate problems. First, feminism produced incompatible theories of liberation. Second, the idea of common political interests was contested.

Women's Liberation

From the start of second-wave feminism in the United States, there were political divisions over what liberation meant (Firestone, 1970). Liberal feminists had long-standing demands for equal rights with men. Critics found this concept of liberation relatively conservative. Equal rights do not provide freedom from power relations and so may bring limited change.

Ideas of women's liberation are more radical because they claim that men's power over women runs through every area of society and culture. Radical and revolutionary feminists recognized social divisions between women but thought of liberation in terms of all women's shared interests. Women's minds, bodies, sexuality, and labor were seen as dominated by male power.

Since male power is embedded in production systems, women's liberation challenges the structure of local, national, and global economies. Socialist feminists attempted to link the oppression of women to capitalist oppression of workers, the internationalization of capitalism, and theories of the state.

Women's liberation identified all women as oppressed by men and subject to male violence. But heterosexual and lesbian women were seen as standing in different relationships to patriarchy. Socialist feminism identified women as divided by social class and imperialism. Critics of these theories identified racism as dividing women and shaping oppression, and socialist societies as patriarchal.

Feminism has no political center to provide an authoritative definition of common goals and strategies for liberation. In some women's organizations, a list of demands became identified with women's liberation, but these were somewhat varied and also the subject of disputes. In the United Kingdom, for example, these demands included self-defined sexuality; equal pay, education, and job opportunities; contraception and abortion on demand; free 24-hour nurseries under community control; legal and financial independence; an end to discrimination against lesbians; and freedom from male violence and the legal framework and institutions that perpetuated it (Feminist Anthology Collective, 1981).

Such demands for liberation targeted male power. But this power could not be separated in practice from other oppressive relationships, including those that empower and privilege some women at the expense of others (Mies, 1986).

Liberation across Social Divisions

Women's struggles for civil rights and equality with men coexist with more radical struggles against gender oppression. These have their own histories in different parts of the world (Basu, 1995). But women's struggles do not necessarily tackle women's oppression of women. Struggles against male power have often been part of ethnic, nationalist or anticolonial struggles in which divided women share political interests with men (Jayawardena, 1986).

Women can be subordinated by male power but also privileged by race, ethnicity, imperialism, class, party membership, heterosexuality, or physical ability. Subordinated women have voiced their own experiences of oppression from other women (hooks, 1982). This voicing of experience has often been painful and emotional. Women have confronted women's power over others in the range of relationships that both connect and divide them (Afshar and Maynard, 1994; Saadawi, 1980).

bell hooks (1982) points out that change can have different results across the divisions of class and racism. For instance, paid work can offer middle-class housewives some liberation. Women who work as servants for career women, or as cheap immigrant labor, cannot find work liberating in the same way.

The evidence that some women benefit from the oppression of others challenges any universal theory of women's liberation. Strategies for liberation, then, depend on analyzing the everyday realities of different women's lives (Latin American and Caribbean Women's Collective, 1980).

Liberation as Living Differently

The idea of women's liberation, however, does suggest that women have some common political interests. For women to be free, male power must be overthrown, violence ended, and women put in control of their bodies. But this cannot be done without changing all the other forms of power with which gender is connected. Women's liberation, therefore, implies fundamental social change in all areas of public and private life.

Even if liberation on this scale is possible, disagreement remains about what freedom should be like, and what different women might lose. More effort has gone into women's struggles than into designs for liberated societies. Feminists disagree on what women could be liberated to. First, there are different ways of linking local and specific issues to wider changes. Second, visions of liberation vary markedly between cultures. There are many views of how sexuality, reproduction, child rearing, work, and government might be organized. Third, men cannot bear children, so liberation raises questions about whether freed women and men are essentially different. Liberation raises difficult questions about how people can live together in complex societies without oppressing one another.

See Also

EMANCIPATION AND LIBERATION MOVEMENTS; EMPOWERMENT; EQUALITY; ESSENTIALISM; FEMINISM: OVERVIEW; WOMEN'S MOVEMENT, *all entries*

References and Further Reading

Afshar, Haleh, and Mary Maynard. 1994. *The dynamics of "race" and gender: Some feminist interventions.* London: Taylor and Francis.

Basu, Amrita. 1995. *The challenge of local feminisms: Women's movements in global perspectives.* Boulder, Col.: Westview.

Feminist Anthology Collective. 1981. *No turning back: Writings from the women's liberation movement 1975–1980.* London: Women's Press.

Firestone, Shulamith. 1970. *The dialectic of sex: The case for feminist revolution.* New York: Morrow.

hooks, bell. 1982. *Ain't I a woman: Black women and feminism.* London: Pluto.

Jayawardena, Kumari. *Feminism and nationalism in the third world.* London: Zed.

Latin American and Caribbean Women's Collective. 1980. *Slaves of slaves: The challenge of Latin American women.* Trans. Michael Pallis. London: Zed.

Mies, Maria. 1986. *Patriarchy and accumulation on a world scale.* London: Zed.
Ramazanoglu, Caroline. 1989. *Feminism and the contradictions of oppression.* London: Routledge.
Saadawi, Nawal El. 1980. *The hidden face of Eve: Women in the Arab world.* London: Zed.

Caroline Ramazanoglu

LIBERATION MOVEMENTS

Liberation movements are, by definition, actions and endeavors of a body of persons with liberty or release from bondage as their goal. For the purposes of this article, liberation campaigns have been taken to include both revolutionary and nationalist contests for self-determination and struggles for recognition and rights by groups contained within independent communities. Such movements have been especially associated with the nineteenth and twentieth centuries, and they present a number of general difficulties. They are likely to be spearheaded by the middle class, whose members have tended to be their chief beneficiaries. Their leaders may be determined to involve women, in order to increase their support and hence their legitimacy, but liberators who see women in extraordinary roles for specific purposes do not usually free themselves from traditional ideas about women's "proper" long-term roles. Women's movements have frequently benefited from links with other movements—notably abolitionist, peace, temperance, male suffrage, nationalist, and youth campaigns—yet their association with these endeavors may require the subordination of concerns specific to women. It should also be noted that the rights of women—and, subsequently, feminism—have been depicted as bourgeois, western causes, making the highlighting of female objectives problematical in socialist and nonwestern nationalist contests alike (Jayawardena, 1987).

Those liberation struggles that have depended heavily on violence and military confrontations have seldom transformed relation between the sexes. The fabled Amazons of Scythia may have survived in the English language, but the term has denoted a masculine woman, whereas most women in history have preferred to extol the virtues usually associated with their sex. There have been intrepid women warriors, including Boadicea, queen of the Iceni in first-century Britain; the Trung sisters of thirteenth-century Vietnam; Marie Deschamps at the barricades in the 1830 French revolution; and the female guerillas of China's First Revolutionary War (1927–1928). What is more, the techniques of twentieth-century terrorism do not put women at a serious physical disadvantage. However, even during armed conflicts most women have not challenged men's expectation that female militarism should take traditional forms: providing sons and releasing husbands for liberation movements, nursing under dangerous conditions, undertaking masculine jobs on a temporary basis, and taking part in crowd actions to show solidarity with the men of their group or to swell the numbers of protestors. The female form has, of course, been evoked to symbolize reproachful suffering (as in the antislavery crusade), to epitomize the nation (as in the figure of Britannia), and to represent a stern motherland (as in the image of the mother goddess demanding sacrifices from all in the twentieth-century Indian campaign for independence). Nonetheless, in art and literature, the feminine figure has most obviously had an inspirational function. Real women are expected to behave conventionally. Hence, whereas the women who joined all kinds of crowd and community protests have certainly aroused interest, their behavior has been commonly condemned as strident and unseemly: a sign of the world turned upside-down (Krishnamurty, 1989; Rendall, 1985). Women in Britain and the United States were enfranchised at the end of World War I, partly by reminding politicians of the war work they had undertaken, yet that work was generally not violent or military. By contrast, women in France were granted the vote after World War II, partly because of their labors in the wartime Resistance. But in all three countries activists had failed to persuade men in the mass and politicians in particular to embrace the wide-ranging agenda of feminism, as war inevitably brought masculine values and exploits to the fore, and women had helped to popularize the notion that they constituted the selfless sex. When a militaristic government came to power in Japan during the 1930s, agitation for women's emancipation was blocked, and although Japanese society was profoundly transformed by the subsequent military defeat in 1945, traditionalism with regard to women was still entrenched in schools and the family (Lebra, Paulson, and Powers, 1976).

Nationalism and Liberation Movements

Nationalist movements involving political campaigns as well as military confrontations have created comparably mixed opportunities for women. They—like feminist movements—have been crucially shaped by economic change, principally by the modernizing influences of urbanization, industrialization, and capitalism. Economic transformation and the tension generated by colonization have produced constructive resentment in the bourgeois elites that have developed among colonized peoples. The protests of such elites have in turn resulted in the extension of certain rights to bourgeois women in countries revolting against colonialism. Education has been improved, dress reformed, and social etiquette liberalized; marriage and property arrangements have been amended, and economic and recreational opportunities improved. White women who were part of the colonization process sometimes helped to bring about these changes, but their impact was complex. On the one hand, they were inclined to proclaim their cultural superiority and to denounce native practices that they found offensive, notably youthful and arranged marriages, the treatment of widows, polygamy, foot binding, and female seclusion. On the other hand, they might help their indigenous sisters to organize and win welfare and political gains, as happened in India. Yet assistance of this kind did not automatically follow from condemnation of native customs. In Rhodesia, for example, white women accepted restrictions on their own rights, apparently content with the benefits they obtained from exploiting colonial land and labor; for their part, white Rhodesian men helped tribal elders to preserve institutions affecting women that Europeans basically deplored, recognizing that—for their own economic interests—they needed to work with, rather than against, the local authorities (Stichter and Parpart, 1988).

Bourgeois native women resisting colonization were, moreover, hindered as well as assisted by the native men who usually led liberation movements, and whose priorities tended to change after independence had been secured. Where once all had been rallied to a common cause in the face of a common enemy, and previously neglected women might be particularly promising recruits, the desire to protect and confine the female sex might subsequently reassert itself. Because the separate organization of women was not normally thought necessary during liberation drives, their representatives were not well placed to mobilize the mass of women when success was eventually achieved. And as all reformers have found, women discovered that changes in the law were frequently rendered inoperative by a lack of attention to their implementation and by the persistence of conventional attitudes. All these factors were at play in the aftermath of the long twentieth-century campaigns of Chinese, Japanese, and Algerian nationalists (Broyelle, 1977; Gordon, 1968; Young, 1973). In addition, too much often depended on a handful of sympathetic, well-placed male allies, including Gandhi in India and Ben Bella in Algeria. Once Boumedienne had succeeded Ben Bella in 1965, his lesser commitment to women's rights made a noticeable difference in Algerian efforts to achieve female emancipation (Gordon, 1968).

For colonized women drawn to the ideas of nationalism and feminism, it has proved extraordinarily difficult to reconcile their competing claims. In order to break free of foreign control, nationalists have utilized the modernizing forces released by the colonizers but have also been driven to defend their religions and folkways against outsider's criticism. Accordingly, Indian observers have noted that the condition of women is not greatly improved following the replacement of a caste society by a class system, and have suggested that allegations about the inferiority of women are distinctively western. Whereas such allegations undermine women's ability to act on their own behalf, it is maintained, the Indians' recognition of the power of women gives them a secure psychological base for self-assertion (Liddle and Joshi, 1986). In the same vein, attention has been devoted to showing that the Qu'ran, while granting men general superiority over women and certain practical advantages, not least in marital matters, can be interpreted with flexibility in the interest of women. Although this may be so, in countries such as Algeria the opposition of Muslim traditionalists to granting women freedoms that appear to be copied from the West may work against the liberal possibilities of the Qu'ran (Gordon, 1968). In other parts of Africa, there are similar signs of determination to seek progress in the complex context of local attitudes to men, politics, and the family (Bush, 1999: 90, 92, 103; Coquery-Vidrovitch, 1997; Stasiulis and Yuval-Davis, 1995), and there is a similar wariness about a feminist ideology associated with Europe and the United States. As one South African militant put it in the 1980s, "We're in the middle of a liberation struggle, but women's liberation is not necessary at this stage. We are far more concerned about total liberation; and automatically, our own liberation will follow. Most of the factors that make men more dominant arise out of social and political problems—and we plan to resolve those!... But I wouldn't like to dominate any man, as an African woman. So-called equality in America: in fact American women dominate American men, as one big generalisation—I really believe they've gone about things the wrong way" (Lipman, 1984: 130).

The South African situation showed, however, that there is no obvious way forward for women in liberation struggles. Many female campaigners against apartheid were politicized by experiences in their own communities, but other women found it difficult to overcome opposition from their husbands and to give as much time to protest as men, who were less tied to family duties and were employed in less isolating occupations. Women of all races had come together in 1954 in the Federation of South African Women, pledged to strive for "the removal of all laws, regulations, conventions, and customs that discriminate against us as women," and asserting that "we women share with our menfolk the cares and anxieties imposed by poverty and its evils." The Federation reached out to "all progressive men and women" in "the great national liberatory movements." Two years later white liberal women organized themselves in the Black Sash to protest by nonviolent means against the denial of individual rights; they gathered information about government policies and ran advice offices for the black community. Numerous other women's groups subsequently appeared (Barrett et al., 1985: 239, 240; Goodwin, 1984). Yet, understandably, racial and class differences among South African women inclined them toward different tactics and exposed them to unequal economic, community, and political pressures (Bush, 1999: 151–156; Walker, 1982).

Women's relations with nationalist movements have not been easy, even in European countries where feminism has developed without the stigma of being an alien import. Thus, in Poland as in Ireland, in France as in Norway, and in Germany as in Italy, female activists found themselves embroiled in the twists and turns of nation building and political liberalization. But they found, too, that this politicization involved them in quarrels beyond their own cause, particularly between liberals and socialists and between liberal and clerical elements.

Socialist and Liberation Movements

Socialist movements seeking the liberation of the masses have also found themselves at odds with women's aspirations and movements. Although in the utopian socialist experiments of the early nineteenth century, the reformation of all aspects of society had been considered, the Marxian socialism that subsequently developed, focusing on production and class-based revolution, was more problematical. For, whereas bourgeois women reformers initially tended to pursue the individual rights valued in middle-class circles, Marxists laid claim to the loyalties of working-class women and offered collective solutions to exploitation. Social revolution was seen as the way to achieve women's liberation, and undoubtedly women were politicized in socialist campaigns, just as they had been in nationalist contests. But in both kinds of struggle, women were subordinated to men.

Contrary to socialist assertions, female oppression was not simply a feature of capitalism. Bourgeois rights undoubtedly did not transform the structure of society and equally benefit all women; they might, in fact, throw the remaining social inequalities into still starker relief. Bringing women out of family seclusion into production, however, while affording women a new social freedom and esteem, did not commonly result in economic or domestic equality. Hence, in China, it was helpful to women that Mao Tse-Tung acknowledged that they carried "half of heaven on their shoulders," and should be treated accordingly. It was understandable that he believed women would be liberated only "in the course of the socialist transformation of society," and it was encouraging when socialists conceded the inhibiting effect of Confucian ideology, which taught that men were "lords and women their subjects" (Broyelle, 1977: 158, 164, 168). Moreover, the continued upheavals experienced by the Chinese in the twentieth century may have made change appear to be an unavoidable fact of life. In politics and military matters, men have nonetheless continued to dominate, as they do in capitalist regimes, while male babies have continued to be preferred over female. And from at least the 1920s, the economic improvement of the people as a whole has been the dominant objective of Chinese revolutionaries (Young, 1973). In Russian history from the 1860s, feminists have likewise found themselves at odds with male-dominated radical movements whose adherents claimed to offer a broader social liberation: that is, with nihilists, populists, and, finally, Marxists (Edmondson, 1984). Such tension has not by any means been unproductive in Europe, where countries with influential socialist movements—for instance, Italy, Greece, and France—have shown themselves sympathetic to women's demands in the latter part of the twentieth century. But such movements do discourage separate mobilization by feminists and predictably support only those feminist demands that accord with their agendas (Katzenstein and Mueller, 1987).

African-American Movements

For African-American women, aware of their quasi-colonial status in the United States during the nineteenth century, racial organizations frequently seemed to be the best vehicles through which to seek liberation. Black and white campaigners were drawn into the pre-Civil War antislavery movement and, despite pressure on African-Americans from some whites to form separate societies, black abolitionists bestowed crucial authenticity on the movement and many white abolitionists proved capable of transcending contemporary prejudices about race. Unfortunately, the main thrust of the movement had been exhausted by the 1860s, and although black men had been endowed with citizenship rights, including suffrage, some key white women had been alienated from cross-racial endeavors by their failure to persuade abolitionist and Republican allies to accept their case for women as well as African-American men to get the vote. Thereafter, white feminists gave priority to campaigning in the eastern and western states, with black and white southern women being left to form racially separate community groups. From the end of the nineteenth century, black women were taking a keen interest in suffrage, but white suffragists in the National American Women's Suffrage Association, influenced by prejudice and tactical considerations, then came to tolerate separate organization of the races, just as white temperance activists and clubwomen had done. The result was that many black women joined their men in bodies such as the Urban League and the National Association for the Advancement of Colored People, urging that racial and sexual discrimination were intimately linked and that liberation from both should be jointly sought. Relations between black men and women could themselves be difficult, given the strains imposed by white people's attitudes, the large numbers of black women who were forced to be breadwinners, and conventional views on women among black men. The leadership of the black church and mixed-sex protest associations was largely male, and criticism of this state of affairs was difficult for African-American women, torn between gender and racial loyalties. And they, along with white women, were subordinated within the American civil rights movement when it began a new and militant chapter in the 1950s (Crawford, Rouse, and Woods, 1990; Gilmore, 1996; White, 1999).

The feminist upsurge that affected the United States in the two decades that followed was shaped by many factors, one of which was the comparison black and white American women activists made between the sexual and racial caste systems. Working for black liberation, many young women from both races came to think more radically and question their own treatment in the civil rights campaign and the larger society, just as women abolitionists had been politicized and turned to feminism by their experience of working for others. Additional and related developments had profound importance for women. First, student protests in affluent western countries called into question pecuniary values, entrenched inequalities, and elements of cultural conformity within their societies. Second, opposition to war generally, and to specific conflicts such as those in Vietnam and Algeria, provoked a fresh phase of the peace movement, which had always been associated with women. Third, the growth of left-wing groups committed to bold tactics and indifferent to old ideological feuds also helped to create a climate in which debates about women's liberation could flourish (Katzenstein and Mueller, 1987). When the forces of political reaction regrouped, it was discovered, as it always is when women link their movement with others, that female liberation requires a total transformation of society that few nonfeminists can contemplate. Women's political participation has increased since the 1960s, and there is now a discernible female agenda in politics, yet the need for political allies remains. Unhappily, coalitions of the disadvantaged have been urged for decades by minority leaders such as Bayard Rustin and Jesse Jackson without demonstrating that "rainbow" or "alternative" alliances of the young, the old, the poor, the unions, and racial groups can effectively come together outside a few great polyglot cities, or in economic circumstances other than such exceptional ones as helped to create the New Deal of the 1930s.

Conclusion

Nonetheless, by the end of the twentieth century the cause of women's liberation had a distinctive ideology and a wide reach. Association with other liberation movements has given its adherents an appreciation of the dynamics of group oppression. It made them aware of the benefits and difficulties involved in collaborating with other disadvantaged elements in society, and showed them what does and does not work in the light of their historical circumstances and local conditions. Retaining an ongoing involvement with nationalist, working-class, and civil rights campaigns in which women's interests are only one factor among many, feminists have been able to reassess their approach to internationalism and reaffirm their faith in the things that make women different from men. And they have been able to acknowledge that feminism not only can appear in many contexts but also can address a huge range of issues (Basu, 1995).

See Also

ANTIRACIST AND CIVIL RIGHTS MOVEMENTS; COLONIALISM AND POSTCOLONIALISM; DEMOCRATIZATION; EMANCIPATION AND LIBERATION MOVEMENTS

References and Further Reading

Badran, Margot, 1995. *Feminists, Islam, and nation: Gender and the making of modern Egypt.* Princeton, N.J.: Princeton University Press.

Barrett, Jane, Aneene Dawber, Barbara Klugman, Ingrid Olberry, Jennifer Schindler, Jennifer Yawileh, and Joanne Yawileh. 1985. *South African women on the move.* London: CIIR and Australia: Pluto.

Basu, Amrita. 1995. *The challenge of local feminisms: Women's movements in global perspective.* Boulder, Col.: Westview.

Broyelle, Claudie. 1977. *Women's liberation in China.* Hassocks, Sussex: Harvester.

Bush, Barbara. 1999. *Imperialism, race and resistance: Africa and Britain, 1919–1945.* London and New York: Routledge.

Coquery-Vidrovitch, C. 1997. *African women: A modern history.* Boulder, Col.: Westview.

Crawford, Vicki L., Jacqueline Anne Rouse, and Barbara Woods, eds. 1990. *Women in the civil rights movement: Trailblazers and torchbearers, 1941–1965.* Brooklyn, N.Y.: Carlson.

Edmondson, Linda. 1984. *Feminism in Russia, 1900–1917.* Stanford, Calif.: Stanford University Press.

Gilmore, Glenda Elizabeth. 1996. *Gender and Jim Crow: Women and the politics of white supremacy in North Carolina, 1896–1920.* Chapel Hill and London: University of North Carolina Press.

Goodwin, June. 1984. *Cry, Amandla: South African women and the question of power.* New York and London: African Publishing.

Gordon, David C. 1968. *Women of Algeria: An essay on change.* Cambridge, Mass.: Harvard University Press.

Hahner, June E. 1990. *Emancipating the female sex: The struggle for women's rights in Brazil, 1850–1940.* Durham N.C.: Duke University Press.

Jayawardena, Kumari. 1987. *Feminism and nationalism in the third world.* London: Zed.

Katzenstein, Mary Fainsod, and Carol McClurg Mueller, eds. 1987. *The women's liberation movements of the United States and western Europe.* Philadelphia, Pa.: Temple University Press.

Krishnamurty, J., ed. 1989. *Women in colonial India: Essays on survival, work and the state.* Delhi: Oxford University Press.

Lebra, Joyce, Joy Paulson, and Elizabeth Powers, eds. 1976. *Women in changing Japan.* Boulder, Col.: Westview.

Liddle, Joanna, and Rama Joshi. 1986. *Daughters of independence: Gender, caste and class in India.* London: Zed.

Lipman, Beata. 1984. *We make freedom: Women in South Africa.* London: Pandora.

Miles, Angela, 1996. *Integrative feminisms: Building global visions, 1960s–1990s.* New York: Routledge.

Mohanty, Chandra Talpade, Ann Russo, and Lourdes Torres, eds. 1991. *Third world women and the politics of feminism.* Bloomington: Indiana University Press.

Rendall, Jane. 1985. *The origins of modern feminism: Women in Britain, France, and the United States, 1780–1860.* London: Macmillan.

Stasiulis, D., and N. Yuval-Davis, eds. 1995. *Unsettling settler societies: Articulations of gender, race, ethnicity and class.* London: Sage.

Stichter, Sharon B., and Jane Parpart, eds. 1988. *Patriarchy and class: African women in the home and workforce.* Boulder, Col.: Westview.

Walker, C. 1982. *Women and resistance in South Africa.* London: Onyx.

White, Deborah Gray. 1999. *Too heavy a load: Black women in defence of themselves, 1894–1994.* New York and London: Norton.

Young, Marilyn B., ed. 1973. *Women in China: Studies in social change and feminism.* Ann Arbor: University of Michigan Press.

Christine Bolt

LIBRARIES

Libraries are, of course, a large topic; this article will focus on their relation to women's studies. Because women's studies as a field is a recent phenomenon, and because it crosses nearly all disciplinary lines and does not separate scholarly matters from personal experience, traditional libraries are still responding to it in a variety of ways.

Historical Background

From the earliest times all over the world, libraries began as private collections of palaces or courts, individuals, religious centers, or centers of learning. In the modern world, they have come to serve as gatekeepers of knowledge and culture. As Sarah Pritchard (1995) observes, libraries codify knowledge through their decisions about which materials to acquire, which to ignore, and how to make their contents accessible through cataloging and classification. By virtue of such decisions, libraries in effect control access to and impose a structure and a relational value system on all forms of information.

An important aspect of any library is how its collection is organized. Traditionally, libraries in the West organize and provide access to their collections through the use of standardized terminology called "subject headings." The most widely used scheme of subject headings in the world is the Library of Congress Subject Headings (LCSH) and translations or adaptations of it; this system—its name refers to the Library of Congress (LC) in the United States—was developed in the late nineteenth century.

Nonwestern countries where libraries have existed longest, such as India, Egypt, and China, began adopting western models of organization and concepts of librarianship in the nineteenth and twentieth centuries. Libraries in some countries use adaptations of the LCSH scheme to provide subject access to their collections. However, other countries, including India and China, have their own national schemes of subject headings; and many countries, such as Japan, do not commonly use subject headings at all.

Issues of Access

Libraries and women's groups worldwide attempt to provide both scholarly and practical information regarding women and gender issues. However, although many materials that preserve women's history and accomplishments have been held in libraries and archives for many years, they have not necessarily been organized in ways that provide good access to them. One problem is that the LCSH system was based on guidelines intended to meet the needs of a hypothetical reader—evidently assumed to be white, from the United States or western Europe, Christian, heterosexual, and male—whose point of view does not represent the world as a whole (Marshall, 1977).

A crucial issue of access is, therefore, terminology. In most traditional library collections, access to information about, by, and of concern to women is hampered by the use of problematic wording (whether LC or other standard terms). One source of difficulties is "subsuming terminology," such as using the heading "Man" to mean all human beings. A second problem is the misleading use of modifiers, as in the heading "Women as artists," which implies that women are not ordinarily capable of being artists or are not ordinarily qualified to to be artists and thus also implies the stereotype that women's rightful place is in the home as nurturers (Berman, 1993). A third problem is separate and unequal treatment of specific groups of people, which arises when words or constructions connoting inferiority or peculiarity are used. One example is the heading "Woman—Social and moral questions" when there is no parallel heading "Man—Social and moral questions." A fourth problem is the complete omission of terminology of particular interest or concern in women's studies, such as "Gynocide" or "Sex tourism" (Marshall, 1977).

Improving terminology is, therefore, considered essential to improving access. Pioneering work by Joan Marshall and a group of feminist librarians in the United States in the 1970s led to many improvements in Library of Congress terminology, such as changing one heading from the generic "Woman" to "Women." However, despite these improvements and the continuing work of reformers such as Sanford Berman, the LCSH system continues to perpetuate numerous inappropriate headings related to women, and also headings related to people of color, older people, sexual minorities, poor people, and disabled people. There are at least two reasons for this. One reason is cost. Most libraries now use improved terminology for recently published works, but it is expensive to reassign subject headings to older works catalogued before improvements were made. Thus many older works still have the earlier headings, with the result that a substantial portion of library materials by, for, and concerning women are inaccessible. A second reason is that the Library of Congress too frequently does not make full use of improved terminology; that is, it does not assign enough subject headings to books being cataloged. As a result, important content of many books and other materials is invisible.

Problems of sexism in language and in systems of subject terminology are not limited to the English language. Feminist librarians and archivists in several countries are in the process of producing thesauri to reflect the central concerns of those seeking information relevant to women and women's studies. Currently there are women's thesaurus projects in, for example, Austria, Spain, Italy, and South Africa. *The Women's Thesaurus,* a collaborative work involving feminist librarians, scholars, women in the media, and women in nontraditional occupations, was published in the United States in 1987. In Japan, the National Women's Education Center published a *Thesaurus on Women and the Family* at approximately the same time. *Women in Development Thesaurus,* a joint project of the Indonesian Institute of Science and UNICEF, was published in 1991. The International Archives of the Women's Movement (IIAV) in Amsterdam published a thesaurus, *Vrouwenthesaurus,* in 1993, which was translated and adapted in 1998 as the *European Women's Thesaurus.*

Terminology is not the only issue related to access. Another problem is that until as recently as about the mid-1970s, there were very few reference works such as bibliographies, biographical directories, or bibliographical guides. For the most part, therefore, librarians and researchers could find little guidance to information on, for, or by women, which was scattered piecemeal throughout many individual resources generally based on the traditional disciplines. Historically, information about, by, and for lesbians was even more obscured from view. A number of good reference works on lesbian and gay issues were published in the 1990s; but there are still relatively few reference works on lesbians and lesbian studies, and most of them are quite recent (Cruikshank, 1982; Damon, 1967; Maggiore, 1988; Potter, 1986; Roberts, 1981).

Women's Studies in Libraries

Currently, finding information relevant to women's studies entails using several different types of libraries. According to contemporary concepts of librarianship and models of organization, libraries are divided into academic (higher education), school, public, and special libraries or documentation centers. In some countries, such as Japan, the best resources for women's studies are not in university libraries but in special libraries in many women's centers funded by city governments. In other countries, the national government or a supranational organization affiliated with the United Nations (such as UNESCO) funds the best resources for women's studies, again as special libraries or documentation centers, either independent or in women's centers. In the United States, the primary home of women's studies is academia, but this is not the case in most countries, such as Italy. Thus the best resources for women's studies are found in a wide variety of libraries, documentation centers, and archives in different countries.

Europe. In Europe, for the most part—according to a survey by Marieke Kramer (1995) and Jytte Larsen—there are three types of centers of information for the study of women and gender issues. One group, developed as a result of the first wave of twentieth-century feminism in the 1930s, consists of professional, publicly funded, large general collections. These include the International Archives for the Women's Movement (Amsterdam), the Fawcett Library (London), and the Bibliothèque Marguerite Durand (Paris).

A second group consists of centers established as a consequence of the second wave of feminism in the 1970s. These collections tend to specialize by subject and are well-suited for networking, but they are usually not well funded and therefore are maintained by volunteers.

Third, there are centers set up within public bodies and organizations (such as national organizations for equality policy) in the 1980s. These were planned from the start to have professional paid staffs; they are computerized; and they function as national information centers. Some, such as KVINFO (Copenhagen) and ARIADNE (Vienna), originated in national libraries. Others began as affiliates of women's studies units in universities. These centers have a high degree of professionalism and offer extensive coverage of national publications.

Although there are no general information services within the European Union, there are some specialized services, such as the Center for Research on European Women (CREW), which focuses on women and employment. Librarians in European Union countries and in other states (such as Czechoslovakia) are working hard to organize the collection and exchange of information on women and gender issues. For instance, a Women's Library and Information Center was established in Istanbul, Turkey, in 1990.

Asia. In Asia, India has the most women's studies programs and research facilities. Information on women and gender issues is found in special collections in academic libraries and government agencies, in documentation centers within women's studies research centers, and in cells in women's organizations. The Research Center for Women's Studies Documentation Center, at SNDT Women's University in Bombay, is perhaps best known internationally. The largest women's research institute in the world, however, is the Korean Women's Development Institute in Seoul, established by the Korean National Assembly in 1982. Among its divisions is an Information Center that supports the institute's research projects and action-oriented programs.

Middle East. In the Middle East, the Institute for Women's Studies in the Arab World, founded in 1973, is housed at the Lebanese American University (formerly Beirut University College). The university library includes the Women's Documentation Center, which has books and international periodicals.

Latin America. Latin American women's groups, in particular, have used electronic networks and communication systems to meet their information needs. (Women's groups in several members of the Commonwealth of Independent States and in some southeast Asian countries are developing their own information systems patterned on the Latin American systems.) In Latin America, one of the best repositories of information on women is Isis Internacional in Santiago, Chile. Like many women's information centers in other parts of the world, Isis Internacional is a nongovernmental organization (NGO) affiliated with the United Nations; it provides information produced by or for women or about topics of concern to women. Primarily, Isis serves women in Latin America and the Caribbean.

In most Latin American countries, scholarly information for women's studies is best accessed through feminist groups such as the Centro de Investigacion y Capacitacion a la Mujer, in Quito, Ecuador, and CIDHAL (Communication, Exchange, and Human Development in Latin America) Women's Center in Cuernavaca, Mexico. In some countries, such as Brazil, scholarship is relatively recent and resources are scarce; thus the best access to information on women and gender issues in these countries is frequently through private libraries.

Africa. In 1997, the African Gender Institute at the University of Cape Town, South Africa, was host to a pan-African workshop for librarians and documentalists with the aim of exploring ways to share gender-related information and resources throughout Africa. One result is the Gender in Africa Information Network (GAIN), which has established an electronic network that enables libraries of many women's groups—for instance, the African Center for Women in Addis Ababa, Ethiopia, an NGO affiliated with the United Nations; and Women's Research and Documentation Project at the University of Dar Es Salaam in Tanzania—to share resources and improve the flow of information with other entities.

Isis–Women's International Cross-Cultural Exchange (Isis–WICCE) in Kampala, Uganda, is an activist women's resource center. One of its goals is to collect and disseminate information related to women and to facilitate communication and networking between individuals and women's groups from different parts of the world. Its documentation center works with contacts in more than 100 countries.

Issues of Collection Development

Many source materials in women's studies—books, videotapes, CD-ROMs, and other formats—are generated by activist groups and published by feminist enterprises, such as presses, that are small by commercial standards. However, most libraries do not collect materials that are not easily available commercially, and that policy effectively excludes books, journals, and videotapes produced by these small enterprises unless someone in a library makes special efforts to acquire them.

In addition, in most libraries, responsibility for selecting materials to add to the collection is divided up by traditional disciplines—that is, people with particular expertise in a specific discipline usually select materials in that discipline only. Most libraries, however, do not have women's studies specialists per se. Because women's studies involves so many different disciplines, careful coordination among various selectors is required in order to develop a good collection in women's studies. In recent years, increasing numbers of academic libraries are designating one person to have formal responsibility for building the collection in this area (usually along with responsibility for other areas as well).

Women's Studies Librarianship

Women's studies courses began in the United States in the late 1960s and spread from there. Women's studies librarianship also began in the United States, in response to this new scholarship.

The American Library Association has a Women's Studies Section that began meeting in 1979; one of its goals is to promote awareness of women's studies as a multidisciplinary field of research and teaching to which libraries must respond. Several projects initiated by the Women's Studies Section and its members have led to the publication of directories, indexes, bibliographies, and other valuable resources. One project has persuaded producers of standard indexing services and databases to include more periodicals covering women's studies. The Section also maintains core bibliographies in women's studies on-line.

Women members of the International Federation of Library Associations formed a Round Table on Women's Issues in 1992. One aim of this group is to promote awareness of women's issues in libraries; this entails gathering and disseminating information about women in the profession of librarianship and surveying information resources, especially as regards their organization and use.

In 1998, the International Information Center and Archives for the Women's Movement (IIAV) in Amsterdam was host to an international Know-How Conference for librarians and documentalists working with materials relevant to women and gender issues, which attracted approximately 300 information specialists and representatives of government agencies from more than 80 countries. One product of this conference was an on-line guide to collections of women's information in all types of organizations, "Mapping the World of Women's Information"—a continuing service of IIAV that provides keyword and geographic access to collections worldwide.

Prospects

Librarianship is concerned with understanding information and recorded expression: their nature, the ways people seek and use them, and the best structures and processes for organizing, documenting, preserving, and sharing them (Pritchard, 1995). Feminist thinkers examine the nature of knowledge itself and consequently the structures and institutions built around our concepts of what knowledge is. Libraries and librarians must continue to meet the challenges of women's studies as they decide what to make available and preserve (in print, electronic, or other formats). Libraries need to mobilize resources to enable writers, librarians, publishers, academics, teachers, students, policy makers, and women in the community to find information and to use it to create new services and structures (Moseley, 1995).

See Also

INFORMATION TECHNOLOGY; KNOWLEDGE; LESBIAN STUDIES; NETWORKS: ELECTRONIC; NONGOVERNMENTAL ORGANIZATIONS; REFERENCE SOURCES; THIRD WORLD WOMEN: SELECTED RESOURCES; WOMEN'S STUDIES: OVERVIEW *and* RESEARCH CENTERS AND INSTITUTES

References and Further Reading

Berman, Sanford. 1993. *Prejudices and antipathies: A tract on the LC subject heads on people.* Jefferson, N.C.: McFarland.

Cruikshank, Margaret. 1982. *Lesbian studies: Present and future.* Old Westbury, N.Y.: Feminist Press.

Damon, Gene. 1967. *The lesbian in literature: A bibliography.* San Francisco: Daughters of Bilitis.

Kramer, Marieke. 1995. Getting it together: Women's information services in the European Union. In Eva Steiner Moseley, ed., *Women, information, and the future: Collecting and sharing resources worldwide,* 101–102. Fort Atkinson, Wis.: Highsmith.

Maggiore, Dolores. 1988. *Lesbianism: An annotated bibliography and guide to the literature, 1976–1986.* Lanham, Md.: Scarecrow.

Marshall, Joan. 1977. *On equal terms: A thesaurus for nonsexist indexing and cataloging.* New York: Neal-Schuman.

Potter, Clare. 1986. *The lesbian periodicals index.* Tallahassee, Fla: Naiad.

Mosely, Eva Steiner, ed. 1995. *Women, information, and the future: Collecting and sharing resources worldwide.* Fort Atkinson, Wis.: Highsmith.

Pritchard, Sarah. 1995. Women's studies scholarship: Its impact on the information world. In Eva Steiner Moseley, ed., *Women, information, and the future: Collecting and sharing resources worldwide,* 15–16. Fort Atkinson, Wis.: Highsmith.

Roberts, J. R. 1981. *Black lesbians: An annotated bibliography.* Tallahassee, Fla.: Naiad.

Organizations

African Center for Women. United Nations Economic Commission for Africa, Box 3001, Addis Ababa, Ethiopia.

African Gender Institute. Web site: <http://www.uct.ac.za/org/agi>

ARIADNE. Kooperationsstelle fur Frauenspezifische Information und Dokumentation Osterreichissche Nationalbibliothek. Web site: <http://onb.ac.at/ben/ariadfr.htm>

Bibliothèque Marguerite Durand. 79 rue Nationale, 75013 Paris, France. (Telelphone: +33 1 457 08 030. E-mail: bnd75@club-internet.fr)

Centro de Investigacion y Capatacion a La Mujer. Casilla Postal 0901-10201, Guayaquil, Ecuador. (Fax: 593 4 408 087)

Center for Research on European Women (CREW). 21 rue de la Tourelle, Bruxelles B-1040, Belgium. (Telephone: +32 2 230 51 58. Fax: +32 2 230 62 30)

Communication, Exchange, and Human Development in Latin America (CIDHAL). Cuernavaca, Apartado Postal 579, Morelos, Mexico.

Fawcett Library, City of London Polytechnic. Web site: <http://www.lgu.ac.uk/fawcett/main.htm>

Institute for Women's Studies in the Arab World, Lebanese American University. Web site: <http://www.lau.edu.lb>

International Information Center and Archives for the Women's Movement (IIAV). Web site: <http://iiav.nl>

Isis Internacional Santiago. Esmeralda 636 2P, Santiago, Chile. (Telephone: 56 2 633 4582. Fax: 56 2 638 3142. E-mail: isis@reuna.cl)

Isis–Women's International Cross-Cultural Exchange (Isis–WICCE). Box 4934, Kampala, Uganda. (Telephone: 256 41 543-953. Fax: 256 543 954. E-mail: isis@starcom.co.ug)

Korean Women's Development Institute Women's Information Center. Web site: <http://www.kwominet.or.kr>

KVINFO Center for Information on Women's Studies. Web site: <http://www.kvinfo.dk>

National Women's Education Center. 728 Ranzan-cho Oazo Sugaya, Hiki-gun, Saitama-ken 355-02, Japan. (Telephone: 81 0493 62 6711)

Research Center for Women's Studies Documentation Center. SNDT Women's University, Sri Vithaldas Vidyavihar, Juhu Road, Bombay 400054, India.

Women's Library and Information Center. Fener Mahallesi, Fener Vapur Iskelesi Karsisi, Fener-Halic, 34220 Istanbul, Turkey. (Telephone: 90 212 534 9550. Fax: 90 212 523 7408)

Women's Research and Documentation Project, Women's Research and Documentation Center. Box 35185-85-WISH, University of Dar Es Salaam, Dar Es Salaam, Tanzania.

Women's Studies Section, American Library Asssocation. Web site: <http://www.library.wisc.edu/libraries/WomensStudies/core/ coremain.htm>

Beth Stafford

LIFE CYCLE

The term *life cycle* refers to the process by which living organisms are created, develop, mature, die, and are replaced by new organisms in a continuum of energy exchange. This process is basic to all life-forms on Earth, from microorganisms to human beings.

The human life cycle has been viewed in different ways by different cultures. Some eastern philosophies tend to view the continuum of human existence as having no beginning and no end; the life cycle, in this view, allows for an interconnection of life and death, so that life does not cease with death. This cycle of rebirth and renewal has been compared to the four seasons in nature.

By contrast, in western thought—and especially in western psychology—human growth and development are often seen as a linear series of life stages from birth to death. Human development proceeds from infancy through childhood, adolescence, young adulthood, and middle age to old age and senescence. These stages are connected by transition points and rites of passage. According to some theorists (notably Erik Erikson), each physical stage of maturation has its own set of psycholgical tasks that, for healthy development, should be accomplished before the next stage is reached.

Gender is not explicit in either of these general views of the life cycle; rather, the life cycle seems to be gender-neutral. However, some traditional societies have developed concepts of the female life cycle; and toward the end of the twentieth century some scholars and writers examined girls' and women's developmental stages as such—although, as in the work of Carol Gilligan and Gail Sheehy, the focus of such writing was mainly on white, middle-class women in the United States.

In many cultures, the female life cycle has been viewed within the context of reproductive function. The reproductive life span, then, begins with puberty or first menstruation (menarche), which marks the transition from childhood to womanhood and childbearing. It continues through the childbearing years until the perimenopausal or climacteric years, when fertility progressively diminishes and the woman's menstrual cycle becomes irregular. The span ends with the final menstrual period, menopause. In most cultures where food is plentiful, the reproductive life span extends from approximately age 12 to age 50. When a culture sees the female life cycle in this way, its rites of passage have typically been related to these reproductive events. First menstruation, first sexual intercourse (loss of virginity), childbirth, and even menopause have thus been used to define adulthood.

Feminists and others have commented that seeing women's life cycle in terms of reproduction has some troubling implications. For example, it would seem to imply that a women who is, voluntarily or involuntarily, childless is not a real woman or is emotionally dysfunctional—and this was, in fact, a central tenet of nineteenth-century psychoanalytic theory. The terms *hysteria* and *hysterical,* routinely applied to women, were derived from the Greek word for the uterus, and it was widely believed that depression and other disorders in women were due to unresolved conflicts about femininity and the desire for pregnancy.

It can be argued that seeing women's lives as centered on their reproductive function is limiting because women are assumed to have only one biological role, reproduction, and therefore only one social role, child rearing. The reproductive life cycle fails to account for women's multiple and significant roles, in many societies, that are completely separate from reproduction. Some feminists hold that the life cycle, for women, should be reframed to include their role not only in biological reproduction but also in "social reproduction"—such as their contributions to extended families, neighborhoods, and communities, and to national political activism.

See Also

ADOLESCENCE; GIRL CHILD; MENARCHE; MENOPAUSE; MENSTRUATION; PSYCHOLOGY: DEVELOPMENTAL; REPRODUCTION: OVERVIEW

References and Further Reading

Erikson, Erik H. 1980. *Identity and the life cycle.* New York: Norton.

Gilligan, Carol. 1982. *In a different voice: Psychological theory and women's development.* Cambridge, Mass.: Harvard University Press.

Katz, Cindi, and Janice J. Monk. 1993. *Full circles: Geographies of women over the life course.* London and New York: Routledge.

Lichtendorf, Susan S. 1982. *Eve's journey: The physical experience of being female.* New York: Putnam.

Lott, Bernice E. 1987. *Women's lives: Themes and variations in gender learning.* Monterey, Calif.: Brooks/Cole.

Owens, Timothy J., ed. 2000. *Self and identity through the life course in cross-cultural perspective.* Stamford, Calif.: JAI.

Rossi, Alice S., ed. 1985. *Gender and the life course.* New York: Aldine.

Schuster, Clara Shaw. 1992. *The process of human development: A holistic life-span approach.* 3rd ed. New York: Lippincott.

Sheehy, Gail. 1984. *Passages.* New York: Bantam.

———. 1995. *New passages: Mapping your life across time.* New York: Random House.

Nancy Reame

LIFE EXPECTANCY

Life expectancy—a concept that this article can only briefly introduce—is one of several measures used to monitor the health of a population or to evaluate the outcomes of a health program. Put simply, life expectancy is the estimated number of years a child born in any particular year is expected to live (Davis and George, 1993). For most of human history, life expectancy was low; for instance, among workers in Europe as recently as the beginning of the nineteenth century, it was reported to be about 28 years. By the end of the twentieth century, however, life expectancy had increased dramatically.

In most countries throughout the world, people now live longer. In 1998, according to the *World Health Report: Life in the Twenty-First Century—A Vision for All,* average life expectancy has risen to 68 years. By the year 2025, it is predicted to rise to 73 years. These figures are overall averages; life expectancy varies from nation to nation, and in countries such as Angola, Mozambique, Afghanistan, Malawi, and Rwanda, it will probably remain 20 to 30 years lower than the average. Nevertheless, 73 years constitutes a 50 percent improvement over the life expectancy in 1955, which was 48 years (WHO, 1998).

The reasons behind the gradual increase in life expectancy are numerous and complex. They include improvements in the standard of living, such as better food, housing, and sanitation, attributable, at least partly, to global economic and industrial development. Historically, life expectancy has always been linked to wealth and poverty: the poorer one is, the lower one's life expectancy. This is not surprising, since life expectancy is affected by people's living environment: overcrowding, dirt, insufficient or poor-quality food, a lack of safe running water, and poor sewerage and drainage all contribute to early death. Life expectancy is also affected by factors that may seem less obvious, such as literacy, education, and social status—again, the lower each of these measures is, the lower a person's life expectancy will be—and in this regard, too, there have been general improvements worldwide. Medical science is another factor; the risk of infant and maternal mortality and death from infectious diseases has been greatly reduced in many countries.

Today, women live longer than men, although this has not always been the case. In Europe and the United States, women's longer life expectancy first became apparent at the end of the nineteenth century, a point when the life expectancy of both sexes had increased (Hart, 1988). Since then, the gap between men's and women's life expectancies has continued to widen. In the United States, the gap is more than 6 years; in Europe, Latin America, and the Caribbean it is approximately 5 years; in sub-Saharan Africa, it is 3 years; in southeast Asia, 4 years. Only in southern Asia do women and men have equal life expectancy (UNDP, 1995; WHO, 1998). However, life expectancy for women, like overall life expectancy, still differs markedly among regions and societies. In some of the richest countries, the gap between female and male life expectancy is now very wide; in the poorest countries it may be much narrower.

Why women tend to live longer than men is not entirely clear, especially since women in so many parts of the world fare worse than men in terms of access to economic and health resources. Whatever the reasons for women's higher life expectancy, however, it is probable that gender discrimination can and does continue to to prevent many women from realizing this potential.

Although women in general live longer than men, this does not mean that they are necessarily in good health: in many contexts, women's lives are far from healthy. In fact, women's higher life expectancy is itself a cause of a higher rate of morbidity (disease) among women, because their health status deteriorates with advancing years. This anomaly—that women have a greater life expectancy but, often, less healthy lives—has been an impetus for the development of additional, more informative statistical measures to complement life expectancy. Three such measures are quality-adjusted life years (QALYs), disability-adjusted life years (DALYs), and gender-related empowerment (GEM).

See Also

AGING; DEVELOPMENT: OVERVIEW; HEALTH: OVERVIEW; HEALTH CARE, *specific regions;* HEALTH CHALLENGES; POVERTY

References and Further Reading

Davis, A., and J. George. 1993. *States of health and illness in Australia.* Sydney: HarperEducational.

DeBarbieri, T. 1997. Cambios en la situacion de la mujer (Changes in the situation of women). *Demos* 10: 32–33.

Hart, N. 1988. Sex, gender, and survival: Inequalities of life chances between European men and women. In A. J. Fox, ed., *Inequality in health within Europe.* Aldershot: Gower.

Trovato, F., and N. M. Lalu. 1996. Causes of death responsible for the changing sex differential in life expectancy between 1970 and 1990 in thirty industrialized nations. *Canadian Studies in Population* 23(2): 99–126.

United Nations. 1991. *The world's women 1970–1990: Trends and statistics.* New York: UN.

———. 1995. *The world's women 1970–1990: Trends and statistics—Social statistics and indicators.* Series, K. No. 12. New York: UN.

United Nations Development Program 1995. *Human development report 1995.* New York: UNDP.

———. 1999. *Human development report 1999.* New York and Oxford: Oxford University Press.

World Health Organization. 1998. *World health report on life in the twenty-first century: A vision for all.* Geneva: WHO.

Internet Sources

Internet information note: Life expectancy. <http://www.aoa.dhhs.gov/NAIC/Notes/lifeexpectancy.html>

Marchetti, C. 1997. *Longevity and life expectancy.* <http://ideas.uqam.ca/ideas/data/Papers/fthiiasrr97-11.html>

World Health Organization. 1998. *Gender and health: A technical paper.* <http://www.who.int/frh-whd/GandH/GHreport/gendertech.htm#Introduction>

Fiona Stewart

LINGUISTICS

Analysis of the role of language in society and proposals for linguistic change have been important elements of the contemporary feminist movement in many countries. While this work has come from people in a variety of fields, much of it has been done by scholars in linguistics. The founder of the discipline of linguistics is generally considered to be the Swiss linguist Ferdinand de Saussure (1857–1913), whose *Cours de linguistique générale* was published in 1916. Linguistics is frequently defined as "the scientific study of language." In this sense, "scientific" means "objective" and "descriptive," in contrast to previous approaches, which are considered by linguists to be "subjective" and "prescriptive."

Structuralism

Early work in the twentieth century was based on the structuralist model proposed by Saussure. One of the objectives of structural linguistics is to look at "langue," or language, as a system at a given point in time, synchronically, rather than at its development over time, historically or diachronically. Saussure considered the study of "langue" (language shared by community) the central objective of linguistic study, and the study of "parole" (individual examples of speech) as secondary. Saussure's influence on subsequent theories is enormous. Even a contemporary nonstructuralist linguist like Noam Chomsky (b. 1928) uses the terms "competence" and "performance" in a similar way. One result of this approach is to consider that the main branches of linguistics are:

- Phonology: sound systems of language
- Morphology: structure of words
- Lexicology: vocabulary
- Syntax: structure of sentences
- Semantics: formal aspects of meaning

Sociolinguistics

According to Suzanne Romaine (1994: vii), "Modern linguistics has taken for granted that grammars are unrelated to the social lives of their speakers. Thus, linguists have usually treated language as an abstract object that can be accounted for without reference to social concerns of any kind." The field of sociolinguistics has developed with the objective of redressing the balance by studying the relationship between language and society. The development of sociolinguistics could be seen as a reaction against the exclusion of "variation" by "mainstream" linguistics. Its status within linguistics is still a matter of some debate (Cameron, 1990). Even the title of the field is not without its controversies: Should it be called sociolinguistics or the sociology of language? Some book titles testify to the divergence of thought as well as terminology: Ralph Fasold published two complementary titles: *The Sociolinguistics of Society* in 1984 and *The Sociolinguistics of Language* in 1990.

One of the major developments in the field has been the quantitative approach of the linguist William Labov, who studied speech patterns, especially phonological variables, in urban areas of the United States (see, for example, *Sociolinguistic Patterns,* 1972). In the 1970s, Peter Trudgill studied speech patterns in Norwich, England (see, for example, *The Social Differentiation of English in Norwich,* 1974). The findings of such studies were interesting: they revealed that not only did language vary, but it did so in systematic ways. Though their primary objective was to examine differentiation based on social class, such studies also provided data on gender-based distinctions. Trudgill used the term "covert prestige" to explain his finding that men showed a preference for nonstandard speech forms, in contrast to standard speech forms, which have "overt prestige" and were more favored by women, all other factors being equal (see also Lakoff, 1975). Such findings have led to the stereotype that women's speech is more conservative and purist then men's, because women speak more "correctly." (Linguists are reluctant to use words like "correct" because of their connotations of prescriptivism.) The whole idea of women's supposed linguistic conservatism continues to be reappraised by linguists.

In recent years, questions have been raised, especially by feminist linguists such as Deborah Cameron (1985: 50–52), about the ramifications of methodological issues such as data collection. The research by Labov and Trudgill was carried out by middle-class male academics: this may have affected the responses of female interviewees. Another problem arises in the process of assigning married women to social categories based on their husband's occupation: this may also lead to unreliable findings, since it does not allow for other factors that may be relevant, such as level of education. Concern has also been expressed about the unquestioned acceptance of men's speech patterns as the "norm" from which women's speech deviates, though the notion of the "male as norm" is, of course, not peculiar to linguistics. Jennifer Coates (1993: 6) refers to studies confined to male informants, while studies confined to female informants are rare. In the former case, conclusions are often made about language in general, whereas in the latter case this would be extremely unlikely. Such possible biases are particularly problematic in linguistics, which prides itself on its soundly based empirical methods: the claim of linguistic objectivity may be considered spurious in such cases.

Language and Gender

During the past twenty years or so, the field of language and gender has flourished as a subfield of sociolinguistics (Conrick, 1999). "Gender" is the preferred term for most authors, since it refers to a social category, as opposed to "sex," which refers to a biological category. However, in linguistics, it is important to distinguish between this usage and the other usage of the term to mean the grammatical category of "gender." For example, in languages such as French, nouns are either "masculine" or "feminine," and in German, nouns are either "masculine," "feminine," or "neuter."

Robin Lakoff's text *Language and Woman's Place* was published in 1975. It had previously been published in article form in 1973. This event was the beginning of a flurry of interest in the field as sociolinguists began testing the various hypotheses that Lakoff put forward based on her own intuition. There has never been general agreement on the existence of "women's language"—the features that Lakoff suggested were characteristic of women's speech (see Lakoff, 1990: 204, for an updated list)—and her lack of empirical data has been criticized. However, her work provided an impetus to other researchers to investigate both how women speak and how they are spoken about.

Subsequently, work developed along two major lines:

- "Dominance framework," focusing on examining the culture of male dominance and its effects on speech patterns
- "Difference framework," focusing on the differing social experiences of women and men or boys and girls, and consequent acquisition of different speech norms.

Alice Freed (1995: 4–6) gives an overview of these two approaches, as well as the "celebrating difference" model. She concludes: "The 1980s can, therefore, be best characterized as a time when the field of language and gender was polarized into two camps: those who saw the patterns of language variation as a symptom and effect of a male-dominated partiarchal society, and those who saw these linguistic tendencies as a natural outgrowth of a gender-differentiated society" (1995: 6; see also Coates, 1993: chapter 1).

Language and Gender Research in the 1990s

In the 1990s the field widened even further, with the growth of interest in sociolinguistics in general and in women's studies in particular. There has been considerable development of interdisciplinary approaches in related fields such as psychology, sociology, literary criticism, and applied linguistics. The result is that linguistic analysis has become more multidimensional and more complete in its attempts to describe how language portrays women and how women use language in negotiating meaning in society.

However, it is still true to say that most work is done on the English language, especially American English, which represents the most prolific area of research. Much work has also been done on languages such as French, both in mainland France—an early example is Marina Yaguello's *Les mots et les femmes* (1978)—and in French-speaking countries and communities throughout the world. Quebec has taken the lead on an issue that continues to be the focus of much debate in the area of the linguistic representation of women in French—the feminization of professional titles (that is, the creation of new titles for women in professions that were previously male-dominated). Several francophone communities (for example, in Quebec, Belgium, and Switzerland) have issued guidelines on how to feminize titles, while respecting the morphological rules of French (Biron, 1991).

More studies are analyzing women's speech patterns in nonwestern languages. For example, in Coates and Cameron (1989: 158–174), Viv Edwards and Savita Katbamna give an interesting analysis, "The Wedding Songs of British Gujarati Women." (Gujarati is a language of northern India spoken, in this instance, by Indian immigrants in Britain.) Earlier work on nonwestern languages was done mainly on phonology and morphology, and this is reported widely in sociolinguistics textbooks such as Janet Holmes, *An Introduction to Sociolinguistics* (1992: chapter 7), Ronald Wardhaugh, *An Introduction to Sociolinguistics* (1992: chapter 13), and Peter Trudgill, *Sociolinguistics: An Introduction to Language and Society* (1983). There is also an increase in knowledge and awareness of nonwestern perspectives on language and linguistics. Contributions on languages other than English and originating from different ethnic backgrounds are more frequently included in collections and readers (see, for example, Minh-ha and Nkweto Simmonds in Cameron, 1998). Freed summarizes recent directions in research as follows:

> Language and gender studies in the past five years can thus be characterized by three major trends: (1) a move toward multicultural comparison, with an emphasis on examining the interrelation of language in traditional or emerging societies and in minority communities in the West; (2) a realization that in analyzing speech, the specific cultural and situational context of a given communicative act must always be considered; and (3) a growing understanding that the category of gender itself needs to be reevaluated and perhaps redefined. (1995: 8)

Recent Trends

Discourse analysis and conversation analysis. In recent years there has been a significant growth in interest among linguists in the area of discourse analysis. "Discourse" refers to elements of language longer than the sentence. Previously, linguists had concentrated on studying idealized, decontextualized sentences. Discourse analysts, like sociolinguists, would say that you cannot study language without looking at context and at how human beings use language to achieve communicative aims. Conversation is the most common form of discourse studied: it is a "highly structured activity" (Crystal, 1987), where there are rules for openings and closings and so forth. Many features of conversational interaction have been studied extensively by researchers in language and gender—for example, turn-taking and interruptions, topic management, discourse markers, and amount of talk—with a view to establishing whether there are differences in the communicative strategies that women adopt, as opposed to men. Work in this area has been controversial, especially that of Deborah Tannen, whose book *You Just Don't Understand!* (1992) has been influential in popularizing descriptions of the different discourse or communicative styles that she characterizes as a "community" style for women and a "contest" or competitive style for men. Tannen's view (1992, 1993) is that women's style is more associated with the creation of links or rapport. The linguistic consequences of the "community" model would be that women:

- Interrupt less
- Ask more questions
- Use fewer imperatives
- Make more minimal responses (for example, "hmm," "yes")

There is nothing negative in these characteristics either socially or linguistically. They are frequently described as "politeness" strategies (which girls are encouraged to acquire in order to become "ladies"; see Lakoff, 1975, 1990). They could, of course, be seen as crucial for the smooth continuity of social relations in the "celebrating difference" model referred to above. Deborah Cameron, in particular, has been critical of Tannen's work. She suggests that *You Just Don't Understand!* is part of a "you and your relationship genre which is marketed specifically to women.... Preaching gender tolerance to an audience composed overwhelmingly of women means in essence telling women to adjust to male behaviour, to accept a status quo in which their needs for intimacy and connection will continue to go unmet by their male partners" (1994: 194–195). This brings us back to the issue of the "male as norm" and whether women should modify their speech to make it resemble the "male norm"; Cameron (1995) describes such adjustment as "verbal hygiene for women." The result is a classic double bind: if women speak like women, they are unconvincing; if they speak like men, they are strident and aggressive.

On the positive side, research on "turn-taking" and "amount of talk" shows overwhelmingly that, in mixed conversation, men talk more than women and interrupt women more frequently than the other way around; examples of such studies abound in literature. Another subject of interest that comes under the heading "topic selection" is the stereotype that women gossip. One of the *Oxford English Dictionary's* definitions of "gossip" is "a person, mostly a woman, who delights in idle talk." Tannen (1992: 97) suggests that gossip could be redefined as a kind of "rapport-talk" and that its negative connotations come from its associations with the oral rather than the written code. Linguistics has always, since Saussure, asserted the primacy of the oral code, while popular views of language have tended to assign greater prestige to the written code. The question of the acquisition of linguistic gender norms is important. Joan Swann (1992) gives a comprehensive account of linguistic differences in children's behavior (especially in the classroom) based on gender. There is also increasing interest in gender issues in second language acquisition (Freed, 1995). The attribution of gender roles is, of course, highly significant socially. It appears that linguistic gender norms are acquired early.

Linguistic intervention. Some fundamental issues remain problematic for linguists. Romaine (1994: viii) refers to the diversity of approaches and the lack of emphasis, or even agreement, by linguists on a coherent theory of the "socio" element of sociolinguistics. Opinions are divided over the nature of the relationship between language and society, especially in the context of gender. Three possible types of relationship have been discussed:

- Language reflects gender divisions in society.
- Language creates gender divisions in society.
- There is an interplay between language and social structure. (Coates, 1993: vi; Graddol and Swann 1989: 8–11)

The first view suggests that differences in linguistic behavior mirror inequalities in society between women and men. The second position is more radical, suggesting that the language we speak determines how we see the world. This determinist position is what linguists describe as the

Sapir-Whorf (or Whorfian) hypothesis, after the two anthropological linguists who advanced it. A third theoretical possibility is a form of compromise between the first two: that language reflects gender divisions but also helps to create and maintain them.

How one sees the relationship between language and society is crucial for linguists in deciding what role to play in linguistic intervention. If the first position outlined above is adopted, the conclusion would be that since language reflects society, language will not change until society changes and, consequently, any attempts at linguistic change are futile. Cheris Kramarae (1981: 155–156) provides a list of some popularly held assumptions about language and society, some of which fit into this framework; she suggests that they are all the more powerful because they are popular.

The second and third positions form the basis for the kind of intervention that the feminist movement has undertaken over the past few decades (Pauwels, 1998) The idea of prescribed ways of speaking (or not speaking) poses a theoretical problem for linguists, especially feminist linguists, because the rejection of prescriptivism is ingrained at an early stage of linguistic training. However, Cameron (1995: 5) suggests that "the linguist's (often extreme) distaste for prescriptivism is an ideologically non-neutral one dependent on value judgements that are highly resistant to rational examination." In fact, many individuals and organizations have recognized the need not to stand idly by, with the result that many universities and publishing houses have published guides to nonsexist language. These have become a subject of much academic and popular debate. An important indicator of the success of this enterprise is the publication by the Linguistic Society of America (LSA) of the "LSA Guidelines for Non-Sexist Usage," in the LSA bulletin (1992, no. 135: 8–9). This evidence suggests that linguists, as well as the general public, are reappraising strongly held views on the nature of language and linguistic change in the light of feminist contributions to our understanding of language and society.

See Also

COMMUNICATIONS: OVERVIEW; COMMUNICATIONS: CONTENT AND DISCOURSE ANALYSIS; COMMUNICATIONS: SPEECH; CONVERSATION; LANGUAGE; WOMEN: TERMS FOR WOMEN

References and Further Readings

Biron, Monique. 1991. *Au féminin: Guide de feminisation des titres de fonction et de textes.* Québec: Office de la langue francaise.

Cameron, Deborah. 1990. Demythologizing sociolinguistics: Why language does not reflect society. In John E. Joseph and Talbot J. Taylor, eds., *Ideologies of language.* London: Routledge.

———. 1985. *Feminism and linguistic theory.* London: Macmillan.

———. 1998. *The feminist critique of language: A reader.* 2nd ed. London: Routledge.

———. 1995. *Verbal hygiene.* London: Routledge (see especially ch. 5, "The new Pygmalion: Verbal hygiene for women").

Coates, Jennifer. 1993. *Women, men and language: A sociolinguistic account of sex differences in language.* London: Longman.

———, and Deborah Cameron. 1989. *Women in their speech communities.* London: Longman.

Conrick, Maeve. 1999. *Womanspeak.* Dublin: Marino/Mercer.

Crystal, David. 1987. *The Cambridge encyclopedia of language.* Cambridge: Cambridge University Press.

Fasold, Ralph. 1990. *The sociolinguistics of language.* Oxford: Blackwell.

———. 1984. *The sociolinguistics of society.* Oxford: Blackwell.

Freed, Alice. 1995. Language and gender. *Annual Review of Applied Linguistics* 15: 13–22.

Graddol, David, and Joan Swann. 1989. *Gender voices.* Oxford: Blackwell.

Holmes, Janet. 1992. *An introduction to sociolinguistics.* London and New York: Longman.

Kramarae, Cheris. 1981. *Women and men speaking: Frameworks for analysis.* Rowley, Mass.: Newbury House.

Labov, William. 1972. *Sociolinguistic patterns.* Philadelphia: University of Pennsylvania Press.

Lakoff, Robin. 1990. *Language and power: The politics of language.* New York: Basic Books.

———. 1975. *Language and woman's place.* New York: Harper and Row.

Linguistic Society of America. 1992. LSA guidelines for non-sexist usage. *LSA Bulletin* 135: 8–9.

Pauwels, Anne. 1998. *Women changing language.* London and New York: Longman.

Romaine, Suzanne. 1994. *Language in society: An introduction to sociolinguistics.* Oxford: Oxford University Press.

Saussure, Ferdinand de. 1916 *Cours de linguistique générale.* Paris: Payot.

Swann, Joan. 1992. *Girls, boys and language.* Oxford: Blackwell.

Tannen, Deborah. 1992. *You just don't understand: Women and men in conversation.* New York: Ballantine.

Trudgill, Peter. 1974. *The social differentiation of English in Norwich.* Cambridge: Cambridge University Press.

———. 1983. *Sociolinguistics: An introduction to language and society.* Harmondsworth: Penguin.

Wardhaugh, Ronald. 1992. *An introduction to sociolinguistics.* Oxford: Blackwell.
Yaguello, Marina. 1978. *Les mots et les femmes.* Paris: Payot.

Maeve Conrick

LITERACY

In the English language, the word *literacy* has two rather different connotations, which are often confused: the ability to read and write (regardless of the criteria used for measuring this); and being well-read, and therefore knowledgable. This dual meaning suggests that to be literate is to know. The forms of knowledge with which literacy is associated are often closely associated with forms of social power and are historically variable. Therefore, it is rarely appropriate to treat literacy as a portable set of skills, definable in the abstract, on which everyone can agree and to which, in theory, everyone can have equal access. On the contrary, which forms of literacy are institutionally and publicly recognized within particular societies, which forms come to stand for particular kinds of knowledge, and what relative prestige these then attract are highly charged issues. This is especially evident in multilingual societies where only some languages may be represented in their written form within the education system and other state institutions. Definitions of what it means to be literate screen out as well as potentially encompass the range of ways in which people interact with the written word.

Gender and Literacy

Three key questions are how literacy is defined, who exercises it, and for what purposes it is exercised. Many feminist scholars have taken these issues up in relation to gender, identifying and exploring at least four aspects:

1. The role literacy plays in women's lives, especially considering that women often live at the margins of social power (Mace, 1998; Rockhill, 1993).
2. How the forms of literacy most closely associated with women are devalued (Alloway and Gilbert, 1996; Moss, 1989).
3. Gender differences in genre preferences and their ideological consequences (Radway, 1984; White, 1990).
4. The relationship between gender, access to education, and educational achievement (Lee, 1996; Solsken, 1993).

At every level, it is argued, gender and literacy are intimately connected. Feminists' priorities in addressing this relationship vary according to the specific setting. In the context of much of the developing world, where universal education remains a political aspiration rather than a fact, access for girls and women to education and to literacy remains crucial, as does the politics of their entitlement. UNESCO's slogan, "Educate a woman, educate a nation," encapsulates a political hope: that women's entitlement to education must be just as important as men's. Simultaneously, the slogan points to a political reality: that women, disproportionately, are kept out of education by the economic structuring of the domestic sphere and their place within it. The hope cannot be realized unless the reality is corrected.

In the United States and the United Kingdom, there is a superficially similar educational slogan: "Teach the mother, reach the child." However, this slogan is to be read differently (Mace, 1998). It is used by governments to launch family literacy campaigns, aimed at communities where educational achievement is generally low, and some commentators argue that it represents literacy not as a political entitlement but as women's work, tied to the state's functional agenda. Women's aspiration to literacy for themselves, these critics hold, is effectively removed from picture. By implication, women are divided into "good mothers" who already understand their responsibilities and discharge them fully and well, and the irresponsibly ignorant who need to be told what to do.

Governments increasingly emphasize literacy as a social good, a functional necessity in today's global technological economy. They prefer to treat literacy as a potentially finite list of decontextualized skills that can be handed on under almost any conditions. But literacy, in terms of actual individual acts of reading and writing, remains much more than this. Feminists invariably emphasize that it is socially and culturally shaped—as a socially regulated activity, which distributes power unevenly, and as a powerful resource, which can be appropriated for many different purposes. Literacy can be made in women's image, too.

Ironically, in many of the leading western economies, where universal education is well established, official attention has recently turned to boys' comparative underachievement in reading and writing. Perhaps inevitably, attempts to find quick explanations and quick remedies often lead to crude gender stereotyping in which, variously, boys are uniformly represented as lumpen louts, women teachers are accused of unfairly feminizing the reading and writing curriculum, and fathers who do not take the time to serve as role models by reading to their children are viewed as deficient. For feminists, this represents a renewed impetus to understand more fully what links literacy and gender to schooling and to wider social structures. New understanding in this area will create new opportunities for intervention.

See Also

EDUCATION: OVERVIEW; EDUCATION: ACHIEVEMENT; EDUCATION: GENDER EQUITY

References and Further Reading

Alloway, N., and P. Gilbert. 1996. Boys and literacy: Lessons from Australia. *Gender and Education* 8: 3.

Lee, A. 1996. *Gender, literacy, curriculum.* London: Taylor and Francis.

Mace, J. 1998. *Playing with time: Mothers and the meaning of literacy.* London:University College Press.

Moss, G. 1989. *Un/popular fictions.* London: Virago.

Radway, R. 1984. *Reading the romance: Women, patriarchy, and popular literature.* Chapel Hill: North Carolina University Press.

Rockhill, K. 1993. Gender, language, and the politics of literacy. In B. Street, ed., *Cross-cultural approaches to literacy.* Cambridge: Cambridge University Press.

Solsken, J. 1993. *Literacy, gender, and work in families and in school.* Norwood, N. J.: Ablex.

White, J. 1990. On literacy and gender. In R. Carter, ed., *Knowledge about language and the curriculum.* London: Hodder and Stoughton.

Gemma Moss

LITERARY THEORY AND CRITICISM

Feminist literary theory and criticism reflect the diversity of women's experiences in different cultures and at different times in history, as women have developed strategies and techniques for pursuing their political aims through the study of written texts. Feminists believe that literature is an important cultural practice, which not merely reflects but also affects the way women are perceived; they also believe that in reading and writing about literary texts, women can participate in the struggle to change unequal gender relations. Feminists are often accused of bringing politics into literary criticism, but in fact they were among the first critics to argue that there are no neutral texts and no neutral readings. They hold that judgments about the value of different texts—even judgments that seem to be purely aesthetic—are inevitably informed by political beliefs.

Early Criticism and the Literary Canon

The earliest feminist criticism, typified by Kate Millet's *Sexual Politics,* focused on the representation of women in the texts that formed the traditional literary canon. These critics argued that women were often portrayed, consciously or unconsciously, in negative ways, and that such portrayals contributed to broader cultural assumptions about gender differences. The images of maleness and femaleness in literary texts were read as explicitly or implicitly endorsing patriarchal or masculinist assumptions about the structuring of gender relations. In many traditionally acclaimed texts, for example, men are presented as strong, active, and rational and women as weak, passive, and emotional, supporting an underlying belief in the superiority of the male over the female and in the male as the norm and the female as an aberration. As such images purport to represent reality, they contribute to an oppressive or restrictive model of femaleness, with which women are assumed to identify; thus these images perpetuate inequality.

The majority of texts in the traditional canon were written by men. Feminists, therefore, also addressed the neglect of writing by women and endeavored to recover and study previously ignored works produced by women throughout history. Some feminists, for example, challenged current critical judgments whereby a few male novelists in the eighteenth century were celebrated while hundreds of female novelists of that period, who had been both popular and influential in their own time, were ignored. Other feminists turned to previously ignored types of writing, such as journals, letters, and privately circulated texts, through which women found expression in periods when they were denied a public voice. The fact that a text is written by a woman does not necessarily mean that it is feminist, but recovering a diversity of women's writing allowed feminist critics to explore how earlier women participated in debates about gender, sometimes reinforcing and sometimes challenging dominant cultural views.

The approach that emphasizes a positive examination of women's writing is often called "gynocriticism," a term coined by Elaine Showalter; this approach has led, among other things, to the development of courses on women's writing. While this development has been welcomed by most feminists, some have argued that it is not without risks. Women's writing may be ghettoized, leaving the male-dominated canon relatively unchanged, and the formation of an alternative canon of women's writing runs the risk of excluding, through the inevitable process of selection, material that does not fit, such as works from other cultures.

Issues of Difference

Some feminists have also argued that insistence on a distinctively female tradition of writing may imply that men and women are *essentially* different—an implication that is not helpful to the struggle for change. This issue continues to be debated by feminists who disagree about the basis of gender difference. Some feminists believe that there is an essential difference, which is to be celebrated; others argue that subjects, whether male or female, do not have a fixed or essential identity determined by the biological sex designated at birth. Feminists who do not believe in an essential difference argue that the study of writing from various historical periods challenges the idea that gender differences have universal, given meanings. Traditional western accounts generally present gender inequality as a timeless, natural truth; this discourages those who are oppressed from believing that change is possible. By examining changes in how women have been represented, and have represented themselves, at different times, feminists have concluded that what it is to be a woman, or a man, is not fixed but changeable and changing.

Freud and Poststructuralist Theory

Both the position of women and the meaning of "woman" have changed over time. Studies influenced by poststructuralist theories of language and subjectivity have suggested that this instability or fluidity is also evident within a culture and within individuals at any given moment.

One of the most influential twentieth-century accounts of sexual identity is psychoanalysis. Feminist critics have taken various positions on the usefulness of psychoanalytic theory. Initially, they tended to be suspicious of Freud's theory of gender difference, as reinforcing masculinist values through phallocentrism; but later work has stressed the productive possibilities in psychoanalytic examination of people's identification with, and experience of, their position as gendered subjects Feminists' reappraisal and applications of psychoanalytic theory were facilitated by Jacques Lacan's rereading of Freud in the light of structuralist linguistics; and developments in poststructuralist theory have been influential in some branches of feminist literary theory and criticism since the 1960s. While some feminists have remained suspicious of theories that seem to bear traces of the masculinist culture in which they were produced, others have argued that these theories offer useful ways of understanding oppression and resistance.

A key assertion of poststructuralist theory, deriving from psychoanalysis and structuralist linguistics, is that the traditional model of the autonomous individual subject as the source, or author, of meaning is a fiction. The argument that texts and their meanings are products of a culture rather than of an individual challenges the idea that an author's gender is of primary concern to the feminist critic. It encourages ways of reading that pay less attention to the author and more to the text as a site of multiple, complex, and sometimes conflicting meanings. For poststructuralist feminist critics, working on a male author's text in order to examine the contradictions and limits of masculinist ideas is an important contribution to feminist inquiry.

Poststructuralist theories of meaning as contingent and identity as unstable have been strategically applied in many areas of feminist criticism, including analyses of history and literary texts. They have also enabled the development of new feminist theories about relationships between gender, subjectivity, and writing.

Among the best-known exponents of feminist poststructuralist theory are Julia Kristeva, Luce Irigaray, and Hélène Cixous. Although the individual work of such writers is distinct in its claims and implications, all focus on the relationship of woman to language, and on the role of the feminine and desire within language. Irigaray and Cixous see language as a phallocentric symbolic order that subordinates women; they explore ways in which women can subvert or challenge that order through writing. Irigaray writes about "womanspeak," which is bound up with female sexuality and so is available only to women, whereas Cixous argues for *écriture féminine,* which as a feminine discourse rather than a female language is available to both women and men. Both discourses are characterized by openness, nonlinearity, and nonrationality that are seen as subverting normative discourse. The idea that such forms of discourse are connected with the fluidity and plurality of feminine identity has led to suggestions that what is being celebrated is an essentialist view of female difference. In French, *féminine* can mean both "female" and "feminine"; this has led to some confusion for English-speaking readers, as have the poetic, allusive style of Cixous's writing and her refusal to adhere to the conventions of academic writing.

Kristeva's work combines linguistic and psychoanalytic theories to analyze different orders of language, suggesting that the phallocentric symbolic order associated with the father is preceded, and sometimes disrupted by, a "semiotic" order associated with the mother. Although the "semiotic" has many of the characteristics of "womanspeak" and *écriture feminine,* it is seen not as an oppositional form of language but as an intrinsic part of language, operating in a dialectical relationship with the symbolic, as the unconscious operates with the conscious. In Kristeva's work both language and identity are in process, and both are governed by a tension between fixity and fluidity. These theories have been deployed from different feminist positions, essentialist and materialist, in reading literary texts that display the characteristics of subversive forms of language as well as in approaching questions of gender and writing.

In the United Kingdom and the United States, Irigaray and Cixous are called "French feminists," but this is a problematic description. Although their work has been extremely influential, their relationship to feminism and to other feminists has been difficult. Cixous, for example, has rejected the label "feminist," and some have argued that the stress on this body of work has drawn attention away from the diversity of feminist work in France. The label also implies a shared national identity, but although these women have all worked in French academic contexts, Kristeva is from Bulgaria and Cixous was born in Algeria. The fact that they are collectively known as "French feminists" indicates a feature of mainstream academic feminism that has been criticized from a variety of positions—it puts the white, middle-class, heterosexual model of woman in a privileged position, and thus it implicitly excludes or marginalizes the majority of the world's female population.

Issues of Identity

Socialist and Marxist critics have argued that women's class position is a crucial consideration, and that working-class women were often overlooked in traditional studies. Lesbian and bisexual writers have criticized the heterosexist slant of mainstream feminism. Women from diverse cultures, including African-American and Indian writers such as Barbara Smith and Gayatri Chakravorty Spivak, have argued for the importance of issues of racial and cultural difference, criticizing what they consider covert racism in western feminism and developing ways of reading other traditions and cultures. Initial work along these lines included the recovery of neglected material about or by working-class women, lesbians, and women of color, but feminists working in these areas have not merely added these other components of identity to gender. By attending to the diversity of female experience and to the multiple subjective positions women occupy, such studies can explore the complexity of individual and cultural identities and the role played by texts in the construction of these identities.

Issues of identity are a key concern in postmodern writing. Some feminists welcome the postmodern concept that representation is a force in the constitution of reality, and the postmodernists' critique of traditional models of power relations in society. Other feminists, though, fear that feminism may suffer from these challenges to the ontological status "woman." Much debate has surrounded recent developments in queer theory, which explores new ways of understanding the relationship between sex, gender, and sexuality; queer theory is seen by some as subversive of, and by others as complicit with, current cultural and political formations. Feminist literary theory and criticism seem likely to continue to develop in multiple directions as new political, intellectual, and cultural trends emerge.

See Also

ESSENTIALISM; EUROCENTRISM; FEMINISM: OVERVIEW; FEMINISM: CULTURAL; LITEATURE: OVERVIEW; LESBIAN CULTURAL CRITICISM; PHALLOCENTRISM; POETRY: FEMINIST THEORY AND CRITICISM; POSTCOLONIALISM: THEORY AND CRITICISM; POSTMODERNISM: FEMINIST CRITIQUES; POSTMODERNISM: LITERARY THEORY; PSYCHOANALYSIS; QUEER THEORY

References and Further Reading

Belsey, Catherine, and Jane Moore, eds. 1997. *The feminist reader: Essays in gender and the politics of literary criticism.* London: Macmillan.

Butler, Judith. 1999. *Gender trouble: Feminism and the subversion of identity.* 10th anniversary edition. New York: Routledge.

Cameron, Deborah, ed. 1998. *The feminist critique of language: A reader.* London: Routledge.

Greene, Gayle, and Coppélia Kahn, eds. 1985. *Making a difference: Feminist literary criticism.* London: Methuen.

Marks, Elaine, and Isabelle de Courtivron, eds. 1981. *New French feminisms: An anthology.* Brighton: Harvester.

Millett, Kate. 1970. *Sexual politics.* New York: Doubleday.

Moi, Toril. 1985. *Sexual/textual politics: Feminist literary theory.* London: Routledge.

Morris, Pam. 1993. *Literature and feminism.* Oxford: Blackwell.

Showalter, Elaine. 1977. *A literature of their own: British women novelists from Brontë to Lessing.* Princeton, N. J.: Princeton University Press.

Smith, Barbara. 1989. Toward a black feminist criticism. In Elaine Showalter, ed., *Speaking of gender,* 168–185. London: Routledge.

Spivak, Gayatri Chakravorty. 1987. *In other worlds: Essays in cultural politics.* London: Methuen.

Tamsin Spargo

LITERATURE: Overview

"A woman writing thinks back through her mothers," Virginia Woolf wrote in *A Room of One's Own* (1929: 146). Woolf was attempting to explain the scarcity of women writers before the nineteenth century: women, she concluded, had great difficulty in writing because the only literary tradition they could call on was a tradition of men. The woman who took up her pen had too few mothers through whom to think.

Although Woolf may have been right about the importance of literary tradition in encouraging women's creativity, she was wrong to assume that English women had little literary history before Jane Austen in the nineteenth century, and none at all before Aphra Behn in the seventeenth. *A Room of One's Own* has in fact inspired generations of twentieth-century feminist critics to work to uncover the literary mothers of the past, and what these scholars have discovered is the incontrovertible fact that women could and did participate in literary culture throughout human history. In the twenty-first century, women of all cultures have a multitude of mothers who were writers, readers, translators, critics, and editors of literary texts.

Women in Literary Culture

This is not to say that participating in literary culture has always been easy for women. Many societies now and in the past have devalued and constrained women's literary activity, often simply by denying women a basic education. In England in the time of Shakespeare, for example, 90 percent of women were illiterate, compared with 70 percent of men. Such discrepancies between men's and women's ability to read and write existed in most of western Europe until the nineteenth century, and in many developing countries are still evident today (Cressy, 1980; Graham-Brown, 1991).

Even for women who can read and write, there are more subtle ways of restricting literary activity. Many cultures consider writing incompatible with femininity or women's modesty, so that women who write run the risk of being labeled monstrous, masculine, or even whorish. For example, Joan Kelly-Gadol's essay "Did Women Have a Renaissance?" (1987) argues that Italian women of the fifteenth and sixteenth centuries were shackled by a courtier culture, which saw women's primary function as decorative, both physically and intellectually. Thus, as their male counterparts were reviving intellectual inquiry, courtly women of Italy were conjoined to utter nothing that was not pretty or amusing—a constraint that made it extraordinarily difficult to develop the intellectual abilities required of a writer. Mary Wollstonecraft (1759–1797), the pioneering advocate of women's rights in Europe, deplored similar conditions in eighteenth-century England and France: "Women, in particular, all want to be ladies, which is simply to have nothing to do, but listlessly to go they scarcely care where, for they cannot tell what" (1995: 168), and certainly not to become poets, playwrights, or philosophers.

When they are not discouraged altogether, women who do write often find their ambitions limited to certain genres considered suitable for women. Laments in pre-Islamic Arabia, pillow books in medieval Japan, devotional verse in early modern Europe: all these were genres conventionally assigned to women. In more recent times in the West, women's writing became associated with personal, emotional, and familial themes, as opposed to the political, rational, and societal concerns that supposedly prevail in men's writing. Thus in the nineteenth and early twentieth centuries in the West, novels and love poems were viewed as fitting forms for women writers, while epics and political manifestoes were not. Such attitudes not only affected—and in some cases still affect—contemporary women's ability to write but also limited access to earlier women writers, the "literary mothers" Virginia Woolf mentioned. The reason Woolf could not find women writers before Jane Austen was not that no such women had existed, but rather that those who did write had been effaced from a literary history that could not accommodate them in the category of conventional feminine authorship. Dale Spender's study *Mothers of the Novel* (1986) notes that many women novelists who were respected in the eighteenth century had vanished from the canon of English literature by the mid-twentieth century. In companions to literature published as late as the 1960s, many important women writers are ignored where their male counterparts merit mention, often because the women do not conform to traditional notions of "femininity." The militant works of the pre-Islamic poet Al-Khansa (c. 600 C.E.), for example, often go unmentioned in encyclopedias that devote an article to her male contemporary Imru'u'l-Qais, whose poetry is of similar significance in Arab literary history. Where women are not ignored, their work might be marginalized as about "feminine" topics not of interest to the general (male) readership. In the same companions to literature that ignored Al-Khansa, the Greek women poets Corinna and Sapho are described as "limited" to personal (and hence feminine) subject matter for a female audience, although their technique is praised.

And yet, in spite of cultural limitations and historical obscurity, women's literary history is ultimately not a story of victimization. Women from all societies have been active and vocal participants in literary culture, sometimes working within existing cultural frameworks and sometimes working against them. Not all women were always discouraged from writing: convents, courts, communes, radical politics, and literary fashions all enabled and at times even encouraged women's literary production. Around the year 1000 C.E., for example, Japanese ladies-in-waiting and

Byzantine nuns produced influential works of literature in environments that gave them access to education and leisure time and that valued women's literary activity as political, religious, and social currency. Murasaki Shikibu (fl. c. 1000) wrote *The Tale of Genji,* the foremost novel in Japanese literary history, and Anna Comnena (1083–1153) wrote a politically inflammatory history of the Byzantine empire. History is full of examples of radical women, pious women, noblewomen, or simply fortunate women whose circumstances and belief system enabled and encouraged their writing.

Still, the history of women's writing is seldom a narrative of steady progress. The Japanese courtiers writing around the year 1000 have few known successors until the nineteenth century, when Japanese women's writing came into its own again with writers such as Yosano Akiko (1878–1942), who adapted her predecessor's masterpiece, *The Tale of Genji.* Among early modern European writers there are many female "ghosts": women whose manuscripts or printed books are known to have existed but have since disappeared. And in cultures where widespread literacy is a comparatively recent phenomenon, the extent of women's participation in oral literature may never be known. With such gaps in the history, feminist critics may never be able to realize Virginia Woolf's vision of an unbroken heritage of literary mothers, but what such scholars have accomplished is to uncover the literary activity of far more women than Woolf might have imagined.

In addition to this rich early heritage, in the past century and a half women's writing has experienced a true renaissance across cultures, with many more women writing all forms of literature. Women from developing countries, where literacy was once scarce—such as the African writers Ama Ata Aidoo, Flora Nwapu, and Mariama Ba—are producing a written literature of their own; women from cultures with a long tradition of written literature are claiming their place as part of the tradition, among the most respected and widely read poets, novelists, essayists, and dramatists of their times.

Women's Literary Criticism

Women have also taken their place as critics of literature, a phenomenon that has influenced not only how modern readers view women writers but how they view literature itself. Following the work of feminist philosophers like Simone de Beauvoir, feminist critics such as Elaine Showalter, Gayatri Spivak, Sandra Gilbert, Susan Gubar, and Toril Moi, among others, began the project of examining how both male and female writers imagine women in literature, and how that literary imagination might influence a culture's concept of what it is to be a woman. Whether they consider medieval saints' lives or eighteenth-century novels, what such critics contend is that femininity is not a set of innate characteristics, the same in every woman, but in fact is culturally constructed, created in the media and art forms which are the legacy of any culture. This kind of analysis makes it possible to reconsider women writers who may have disappeared from literary history because their writing did not conform with their culture's definition of femininity. It reveals prejudices that led both male and female readers to assume that women's writing was necessarily more personal, more family-oriented, more experiential, and more emotional than men's; and it enables critics to look beyond these constructions of femininity to see women writing against those prejudices and assumptions in order to change them.

Feminist literary criticism has opened up new ways of reading literature by women as well as literature about women; particularly, it can show how such texts challenge traditional constructions of femininity by articulating a woman's experience in a woman's voice. There is, of course, no single way of writing about woman's experience, just as there is no single definition of what it is to be a woman. Modern novelists such as Margaret Atwood, Marguerite Duras, Toni Morrison, and Isabel Allende have expanded the traditional boundaries of literary form in order to rewrite women's experience. These writers disrupt the usual flow of a novel with such techniques as stream of consciousness; mixing in poetry, fairy tales, and other literary genres; and distorting narrative time schemes and the identity of characters. Although such techniques are, of course, also available to men, the ability to disrupt traditional literary forms equips a woman writer with what Virginia Woolf (who was herself such a pioneer) called a "common sentence ready for her use" (1929: 114), the means by which women writers tell of women's experience with narrative techniques defined by women as well as men.

These writers challenge not only how we regard women, but also how we think of literature itself. Women writing in nontraditional forms stretch the boundaries of what is literary; the canon must widen to include *Zami* (1982), the "biomythography" of Audre Lorde, alongside the more linear narratives of Henry James, or even Mary Ann Evans (George Eliot, 1819–1880), one of many women who wrote under a man's name. The challenge comes not only from experimental writers of the twentieth century, but from all women whose literature takes forms that are not considered conventionally literary. Quaker women pamphleteers of England and America in the eighteenth century, African women creators of oral literature, and women of all cultures and times who wrote diaries, journals, and letters that contain gems of literary art—all these have reshaped how critics, readers, and teachers define what is literature.

The Twenty-First Century

At the beginning of the twenty-first century, women have established the long line of literary mothers Woolf dreamed of, and critics and writers are now exploring other forms of identity and tradition that might influence women's writing. Femininity is only one of many culturally constructed identities available to a woman writer: she may also be, for example, white, Jewish, gay, middle-class, an immigrant, educated, or any combination of race, ethnicity, class, religion, sexuality, economics, and many other identities. Within this nexus of identities, what is most important for many modern writers is not to limit the concept of "woman" or "woman writer" to the experience of white middle-class women. Jean Rhys's novel *Wide Sargasso Sea* (1966) makes this point vividly by telling the story of the Creole "madwoman in the attic" who is the dark contrast to the heroine of Charlotte Brontë's *Jane Eyre* (1847). Rhys's novel is a literary demonstration of the way white women's identity can be formed at the expense of marginalized women whose stories are not told. In reading women's writing, therefore, it is important to be sensitive to the stories that might not be told, and to the multitude of identities at work when a woman writes.

See Also

DIARIES AND JOURNALS; DRAMA; FICTION; LESBIAN DRAMA; LESBIAN WRITING, *all entries;* LITERARY THEORY AND CRITICISM; NOVEL; POETRY: OVERVIEW *and* FEMINIST THEORY AND CRITICISM; PUBLISHING: FEMINIST PUBLISHING IN THE THIRD WORLD *and* FEMINIST PUBLISHING IN THE WESTERN WORLD; THEATER, *all entries*

References and and Further Reading

Beauvoir, Simone de. 1989. *The second sex.* Trans. H. M. Parshley. New York: Vintage.

Belsey, Catherine, and Jane Moore, eds. *The feminist reader: Essays in gender and the politics of literary criticism.* London: Macmillan, 1989.

Brontë, Charlotte. 1996. *Jane Eyre.* Ed. Michael Mason. New York: Penguin. (Originally published 1847.)

Cressy, David. 1980. *Literacy and the social order: Reading and writing in Tudor and Stuart England.* Cambridge: Cambridge University Press.

Gilbert, Sandra, and Susan Gubar. 2000. *The madwoman in the attic: The woman writer and the nineteenth-century literary imagination.* 2nd ed. New Haven, Conn.: Yale University Press.

Graham-Brown, Sarah. 1991. *Education in the developing world: Conflict and crisis.* New York: Longman.

Kelly-Gadol, Joan. 1987. Did women have a Renaissance? In Claudia Koonz, Renate Bridenthal, and Susan Stuard, eds., *Becoming visible: Women in European history.* 2nd ed., 175–202. Boston: Houghton Mifflin.

Lorde, Audre. 1982. *Zami: A new spelling of my name.* Freedom, Calif.: Crossing.

Moi, Toril, ed. 1987. *French feminist thought: A reader.* New York: Blackwell.

Rhys, Jean. 1996. *Wide Sargasso Sea.* Ed. Francis Wyndham. New York: Norton. (Originally published 1966.)

Shikibu, Murasaki. 1983. *The Tale of Genji.* Trans. Edward G. Seidenstricker. New York: Random House.

Showalter, Elaine, ed. 1985. *The new feminist criticism: Essays on women, literature, and theory.* New York: Random House.

Spender, Dale. 1986. *Mothers of the novel: 100 good women writers before Jane Austen.* New York: Pandora.

Wollstonecraft, Mary. 1995. *A vindication of the rights of woman with strictures on political and moral subjects.* Ed. Ashley Tauchert. London: Everyman. (Originally published 1792.)

Woolf, Virginia. 1929. *A room of one's own.* London: Hogarth.

Erica Longfellow

LITERATURE: Arabic

Before World War II, Arabic literature was primarily the province of males. This is not surprising, given the fact that until the mid-twentieth century Arab men were much more likely than Arab women to be literate. However, women authors played a minor role in earlier Arabic literature and have played an increasingly important role in the postwar period.

Earlier Writers

The most important genre in which premodern Arab women wrote (and one which was theirs almost exclusively) was the *marthiyah,* a short, fatalistic, dirge-like poem about a male relative who has fallen heroically in battle. *Marathi* (plural) first became popular during the pre-Islamic period. The most famous *marthiyah* author was al-Khansa (d. c. 630 C.E.), who wrote so movingly about the death of her father and two brothers that her work served as an inspiration to other women writing in this genre.

Not until the nineteenth century, it seems, did another Arab woman make a name for herself as a writer. Aisha al-

Taimuriyya (1840–1902) was born and raised in Cairo, Egypt, although her parents were ethnic Kurds. In addition to writing poetry in Arabic, Persian, and Turkish, she composed several prose pieces that addressed social issues. A contemporary of al-Taimuriyya's was Zainab Fawwaz (1846–1914), a Lebanese who also lived for long periods of time in Syria and Egypt. She wrote poems as well as newspaper articles, fiction, and a play. Many of her works advocate the emancipation of the Arab woman. Despite its modern subject matter, much of her writing is in the style of *magama,* a premodern literary form that employs a sophisticated vocabulary and many rhetorical flourishes.

During the first half of the twentieth century, at least five Arab women became known for their writing. May Ziyada was a Palestinian who moved to Cairo with her family at a young age. She published a volume of poems in French under the name Isis Copia and wrote a number of essays on social topics. Al-Anisa Dananir, Salma Jayusi, and Fadwa Tuqan, three Jordanian women, wrote poetry that is more personal, dealing with the sorrow and pain of loneliness. Like al-Taimuriyya and Fawwaz, Bint al-Shati wrote about social issues, such as the inequality of land distribution in her native Egypt and the plight of women in the Arab-Islamic world. Unlike them, she wrote mostly in prose. Her short novel *Sayyid al-Isba: The Story of a Fallen Woman* (1944) may be the first work in this genre by an Arab woman, and it inspired many other Arab women to write novels after World War II.

Writers of the Postwar Period

This discussion of postwar literary work by Arab women is organized in four parts, following the various stages of feminist consciousness and social orientation. The first section deals with North African writers from the mid-1940s to the mid-1950s, and with issues of biculturality and the search for identity. The second section covers the mid-1950s to the mid-1960s, exploring the relationship among romanticism, traditionalism, and rebellion. The third section, covering the mid-1960s to the mid-1970s, considers the trend toward a more universalized, socially conscious political commitment. The fourth section assesses feminist writings from the mid-1970s to the present.

1. Biculturality and the search for identity can be represented by three Algerians who wrote in French. Marguerite Taos-Amrouche's *Jacinthe noire* (*Black Hyacinth,* 1945), Djamila Debeche's *Leila, jeune fille algerienne* (*Leila: A Young Algerian Girl,* 1947) and *Aziza* (1955), and Assia Djebar's *La Soif* (*Thirst,* 1957) were at least partly a result of the French colonial influence in North Africa. This forced contact with western culture created strong bicultural stress in North African society, presenting alternative life patterns and diluting the strength of local tradition.

2. Djebar's *La Soif* is, perhaps, transitional between the first two stages because its heroine, Nadia, frantically rebels against tradition but, in the end, numbly accepts the existing order. The Lebanese author Layla Ba'labakki further developed the theme of romanticism and rebellion against tradition in *Ana Ahya* (*I Live,* 1958; translated into French as *Je vis,* 1961). This novel describes the life of Lina Fayyad, a young woman who wants to rise above the hypocrisy of her environment, which she does by rebelling violently and self-destructively. Ba'labakki's portrayal of Lina is edged with a criticism of die-hard traditionalism as well as of superficial modernity.

The Syrian author Kulit Suhayl al-Khuri deals extensively with the position of women in Arab society. She wrote poetry in French and prose in Arabic. Her first two novels, *Ayyam Ma'ah* (*Days with Him,* 1959) and *Laylah Wahidah* (*A Single Night,* 1961), explore the theme of women rebelling against the restricted roles traditionally ascribed to them in Islamic culture.

3. Assia Djebar's *Les enfants du nouveau monde* (*Children of the New World,* 1962) was one of the first novels to acknowledge that inner problems can be embedded in larger political issues. This theme was further developed by the Moroccan author Khanata Bannuna in *Al-Nar Wal-Ikhtiyar* (*Fire and Choice,* 1969) and by the Palestinian author Sahar Khalifeh in *Al-Subar* (*Wild Thorns,* 1976). All three novels advocate a redirection of all members of the community, female as well as male, toward the accomplishment of communal goals.

4. Since about 1975, Arab women writers have reflected a greater awareness of and commitment to the political, social, and sexual issues facing Arab women today and seek to find new ways to help them escape their entrapment. Within this shared concern, however, they take multifaceted approaches to the problems and show considerable stylistic differences.

Nawal Al-Saadawi uses her experiences as a doctor and psychiatrist in Egypt to express the internal and external conflicts brought about in women's lives through repression. Her style is direct and realistic. Her best-known works that have been translated into English are *The Hidden Face of Eve* (1981), *Woman at Point Zero* (1983), *Two Women in One* (1985), *God Dies by the Nile* (1985), *Memoirs from the Women's Prison* (1986), *She Has No Place in Paradise* (1987), and *Searching* (1991). Her most controversial work, *Women and Sex,* is a frank and scientific discussion of the customs and taboos surrounding Arab women and their sexuality. When the book was first published in Egypt, it caused such a furor that she was dismissed from her job and was forced to take refuge in Lebanon. *Women and Sex* was subsequently republished (in Arabic only) and widely read by women throughout the Arab world.

The Lebanese author Hanan Al-Shaykh worked as a journalist for the Lebanese daily newspaper *An-Nahar* before devoting her full attention to writing novels. She approaches women's problems through an extreme sensitivity that helps her grasp more acutely and fully the magnitude of women's oppression from within. Her style is poetic, sensual, and highly suggestive. Her best-known works translated into English are *The Story of Zahra* (1986) and *Women of Sand and Myrrh* (1989).

Etel Adnan was born in Beirut to a Syrian Muslim father and a Greek Christian mother. She studied philosophy at the Sorbonne in Paris and at Harvard University in the United States before becoming a poet, novelist, and essayist. She writes with poignancy, political commitment, and urgency in conveying her ideas about justice and freedom. Her best-known collections of poems in English are *Moonshots* (1966), *Pablo Neruda Is a Banana Tree* (1971), *Five Senses for One Death* (1982), and *From A to Z* (1982). Her one novel, *Sitt Marie Rose* (1977), is about a young woman who stands courageously alone for what she believes and is not afraid to tell men what is wrong with their values, even when she knows they may kill her for defying them. Her collections of essays include *Of Cities and Women (Letters to Fawwaz)* (1993) and *Paris, When It's Naked* (1993).

Ghada Al-Samman, a writer of short stories and essays, was born in Syria but relocated as an adult to Beirut, Lebanon. She worked as a civil servant, journalist, and university lecturer before finally founding her own publishing house so that she could disseminate her own works and avoid censorship. Her early stories use fantastic and occult plots to portray women striving for self-realization. A good example is *La Bahra Fi Bairut* (*There Is No Sea at Beirut,* 1963). In the works of her middle period, she revolted against traditional Islamic attitudes toward love and social hypocrisy. Her later works describe women revolting against being treated as sexual objects by despotic husbands or as slaves by authoritarian parents. Her highly symbolic style is sometimes poetic and suggestive, sometimes surrealistic and irrational. Her nonfiction work includes *Ar-Ragheef Yanbud Kal Qalb* (*The Loaf Beats Like a Heart,* 1975), a treatise on the Arab struggle against Zionism and imperialism; and *Al-A'mal Ghair Al-Kamilat* (*Unfinished Works,* 1979), descriptions of her travels to various European capitals, including London, Berlin, and Rome.

Venus Khoury-Ghata was born in Lebanon but lives in Paris. She writes poetry, novels, and essays in French. She employs sarcasm, irony, surrealism, unexpected images, parody, and a sensuality that can seem close to pornography, as well as tenderness, poetry, despair, anguish, and admonitions. The Lebanese tragedy is the central topic in several of her novels. One of her best works is *La Maitresse du notable* (1992).

The short stories of Daisy Al-Ameer and the novels of Emily Nasrallah are frank and acutely perceptive of the issues now facing Arab society in general and Arab women in particular. Their style is usually realistic and thought-provoking.

Andree Chedid was born in Cairo to Lebanese parents but has spent most of her life in Paris. She writes poetry, novels, short stories, plays, and essays in French with love, vision, an understanding of life's universal complexities, and a commitment to nonviolent peace activism. Her favorite topic is the peacemaking role played by women in the Middle East, where East meets West, races mix, religions clash, languages blend, and history is at a frightening turning point, all the while revolting against the traditional roles that society tries to impose in their personal lives. Her best-known works in English translations are *The Multiple Child* (1995) and *The Return to Beirut* (1989).

Assia Djebar has developed a nearly perfect style that shows great maturity. *Loin de Medine* (*Far from Medina,* 1991) is a collection of tales, narratives, visions, scenes, and recollections inspired by her reading of some Muslim historians who lived during the first centuries of Islam. Her goal is to give a voice and a presence to the many women who have been forgotten by the traditional recorders and transmitters of the Islamic tradition.

The blunter and more open treatment of the oppressive aspects of Arab societies in late twentieth-century women's literature is not simply a more daring exercise of literary freedom, although we must never lose sight of the courage these authors have shown. Rather, the increasing clarity and frankness with which the social context is presented suggest that it is no longer merely a backdrop for the action of the story. In these works Arab society itself comes forth as a character, complete with principles of choice and action and with both trivial and tragic flaws.

See Also

EDUCATION: MIDDLE EAST AND NORTH AFRICA; FEMINISM: MIDDLE EAST *and* NORTH AFRICA; FICTION; LITERATURE: OVERVIEW; POETRY: OVERVIEW

References and Further Reading

Accad, Evelyne. 1990. *Sexuality and war: Literary masks of the Middle East.* New York: New York University Press.

———. 1978. *Veil of shame: The role of women in the contemporary fiction of North Africa and the Arab world.* Sherbrooke, Canada: Naaman.

Chaitanya, Krishna. 1983. *A history of Arabic literature.* New Delhi: Manohar.

Cooke, Miriam. 1988. *War's other voices: Women writers on the Lebanese civil war.* Cambridge: Cambridge University Press.

Haywood, John A. 1972. *Modern Arabic literature, 1800–1970.* New York: St. Martin's.

Makar, Ragai. 1998. *Modern Arabic literature: A bibliography.* Lanham, Md.: Scarecrow.

Malti-Douglas, Fedwa. 1991. *Woman's body, woman's world: Gender and discourse in Arabo-Islamic writing.* Princeton, N.J.: Princeton University Press.

Evelyne Accad

LITERATURE: Australia, New Zealand, and Pacific Islands

Often rooted in ancient oral traditions, the printed literature of Australia, New Zealand, and the Pacific Islands in the nineteenth and twentieth centuries has been written primarily in the English language and has been influenced by English and European literary styles and culture. The English language and its literature in turn have been enriched by the introduction of colorful phrases and stylistic innovations from these cultures, often by women writers who have achieved both national and international recognition.

Australia

The orally transmitted narratives and songs of the Aborigines were mostly unknown to non-Aborigines until the last half of the twentieth century, when researchers began to collect, transcribe, and translate them. More recently, some Aborigines have begun to write in English, and others in what is called Aboriginal English, an adaptation of English to Aborigine-style narration. For example, the poet Oodgeroo Noonuccal (Kath Walker) wrote her collection of poems *We Are Going* (1964) in Aboriginal English; and Sally Morgan's *My Place* (1987), an autobiographical work that contributes to social and cultural history, is also written in Aboriginal English.

During the nineteenth and twentieth centuries, many Australian women writers, like women in the other arts, studied and lived for extended periods in Europe and North America. Their writings often reflect their home country, with Australian and Aboriginal settings, characters, and themes. One of the first to achieve fame was Henrietta Richardson (1870–1946), who wrote under the pen name Henry Handel Richardson and spent most of her life in Germany and England. Her work has both European and Australian themes and is rich in psychological character study. Her trilogy *The Fortunes of Richard Mahony* (1930) was widely thought to be the best work of Australian fiction published up to that time. Richardson's other novels include *Maurice Guest* (1908) and *The Young Cosima* (1939), a fictional retelling of the love triangle of Cosima Liszt, Richard Wagner, and Hans von Bülow.

Miles Franklin (1879–1954) was the author of *My Brilliant Career* (1901), a novel that became an internationally known film in 1980. Her own real-life career and her writings were controversial in her homeland because of her forthright feminism and her uncompromising rejection of women's traditional roles. She lived in the United States and England from 1906 to 1927 and then returned to Australia. *My Career Goes Bung,* a sequel to *My Brilliant Career,* was initially considered so recklessly daring that it was not published until 1946. After her death, the prestigious Miles Franklin Award for Australian fiction was founded, supported by the estate she left for that purpose.

Katharine Susannah Prichard (1893–1969), who wrote novels, short stories, plays, and verse, was much affected by workers' hunger marches in London—where she was working as a freelance writer—in 1909. Her writing from that time on reflected Marxist influences. She returned to Australia in 1916 and joined the Communist Party of Australia in 1920. Her novel *The Pioneers* (1915) was made into a film in 1926. Two other novels, *Working Bullocks* (1926) and *Coonardoo* (1929), are often considered her best fiction. *Coonardoo,* a story of interracial marriage, was controversial in its time.

Christina Stead (1902–1983) is considered a feminist, but she herself firmly rejected that description. She lived in Paris, London, and the United States from the 1940s until 1974, when she returned to Australia. Her best-known and most critically admired novel is *The Man Who Loved Children* (1940), although it achieved wide recognition only with the publication of a revised edition in 1965. This novel depicts relations between the sexes as a relentless war, in which marriage is the battleground, children are cannon fodder, and the attempt to win both love and independence is doomed.

Elizabeth Jolley was born in England in 1923 and moved to Australia in 1959. A novelist and short-story writer with a dry, humorous style, she is noted for writing openly about lesbian relationships and for contrasting what she regards as the staleness of Europe with the raw vitality she finds in Australia. She won international recognition with her third and fourth novels, *Mr. Scobie's Riddle* (1983) and *Miss Peabody's Inheritance* (1983). *Palomino* was written in the 1950s but was considered so daring that it was not published until 1980.

Thea Astley (b. 1925), a teacher and novelist, has lived her entire life in Australia. She thoroughly examines the effects of colonialism on current relations between Aborigines and whites, often writing in a wryly humorous, satirical style. The effects of white domination—racism, rage, violence, infection, destruction, and displacement—are depicted throughout her work, from an early novel, *A Kindness Cup* (1974), to *The Multiple Effects of Rainshadow* (1999). Astley's work is considered difficult; it has earned critical recognition and has been influential but has not achieved wide popularity. Her other novels include *Beachmasters* (1985) and *It's Raining in Mango* (1987).

Shirley Hazzard, who was born in Australia (in 1931) and lives in New York, is known for her refined prose. Her work shows an Australian influence in its search for meaning and destiny, while its literary qualities, emotional complexity, and psychological insight reflect strong influences from English literature. Her *People in Glass Houses* (1967) is a series of character sketches satirizing the world of the United Nations. A prize-winning work, *The Transit of Venus* (1980), brought her fame on an international level.

A number of other Australian women writers emerged in the twentieth century, including Judith Wright, a poet with an international reputation whose work speaks with a modern intonation; Eleanor Dark, author of historical novels, such as *The Timeless Land* (1941); Joan Lindsey, whose novel *Picnic at Hanging Rock* was made into a film of the same name (1975); Colleen McCullough, whose novel *The Thorn Birds* (1977) was translated into many languages and became an international best-seller; and Patricia Wrightson, who used Aboriginal figures and motifs in her novels for children in the 1960s and 1970s.

New Zealand

New Zealand, like Australia, has a rich tradition of oral literature and mythology. Though Maori myths and legends are well known today, the oral tradition had little influence on written literature until about the 1970s. Writing in New Zealand during the nineteenth century and the early twentieth century consisted mainly of English-language journals, letters, and factual descriptions of immigrant life. Among the first published works was *Station Life in New Zealand* (1870), by Mary Anne Barker (1831–1911), an Englishwoman who lived on a sheep farm in New Zealand for three years. Blanche Edith Baughan's *Reuben and Other Poems* (1903) was one of the first purely literary works to be published; it was followed by other books of poetry, including Mary Ursula Bethell's *From a Garden in the Antipodes* (1929) and *Collected Poems* (1950).

Jane Mander (1877–1949) was noted for her realistic novels about New Zealand and for writing openly about sexual themes. While studying in New York, she became involved in the women's suffrage movement and began writing about independent young women who pursue unconventional lives in New Zealand. Her novels include *The Story of a New Zealand River* (1920) and *The Passionate Puritan* (1921).

Katherine Mansfield (1888–1923) was the first New Zealand writer to capture the attention of an international literary audience. Though she was influenced by Anton Chekhov, she developed her own distinctive, poetic style in her stories of internal psychological conflicts. Mansfield contributed signficantly to the development and refinement of the short story as a form of English literature. Her work has also had a tremendous influence on the direction and development of literature in her native land. She lived in London from age 19 until her death at age 35 and published several collections of short stories, including *In a German Pension* (1911), which revealed an early sense of disillusion; *Bliss* (1920), containing stories evocative of her homeland; and *The Garden Party* (1922), considered her finest work.

Ngaio Marsh (1899–1982) is one of the most popular New Zealand authors. A Shakespearean actress, she lived for a while in England, where she wrote her first novel, *A Man Lay Dead* (1934). Returning to New Zealand, she produced Shakespearean repertory theater there from 1938 to 1964. Marsh, a celebrated writer of mysteries, helped the detective genre gain literary respectability; two of her best-known detective novels are *Final Curtain* (1947) and *Death of a Fool* (1956). She was made a Dame of the Order of the British Empire in 1948.

Sylvia Ashton-Warner (1908–1984) was a dedicated teacher as well as a writer of fiction, nonfiction, and poetry. As an educator, she was also committed to improving communication between Maori and Europeans, and most of her writing, both fiction and nonfiction, reflects this commitment. Her best-selling novel *Spinster* (1958) was made into a British film, *Two Loves* (1961), and brought her international attention; some of her other novels, including *Incense to Idols* (1960) and *Greenstone* (1966), were also best-sellers. Her nonfiction, including her autobiography, *I Passed This Way* (1979), has in general received less attention.

Janet Frane (b. 1924), in contrast to Ashton-Warner, wrote an award-winning autobiography that attracted a great deal of attention itself and also drew attention to her novels, her other fiction, and her poetry. The autobiography, a three-volume work—*To the Is-Land* (1982), *An Angel at My Table* (1984), and *The Envoy from Mirror City* (1985)—was made into an internationally distributed movie, *An Angel at My Table,* in 1990 by the New Zealand director Jane Campion. Frame's frank revelations about her early life, when she was hospitalized because of a mistaken diagnosis of schizophrenia, have aroused much interest, as have her literary experiments and her inventive use of language. Her novels include *Owls Do Cry* (1957) and *The Carpathians* (1989).

Patricia Grace (b. 1937) writes narratives of Maori life in which she sometimes blames European settlers for the ills suffered by indigeneous people. Her novels include *Mutuwhenua: The Moon Sleeps* (1978) and *Potiki* (1986).

Keri Hulme (b. 1947), a novelist, poet, and short-story writer, is of mixed English, Scottish, and Maori ancestry. She identifies closely with her Maori heritage and purposely introduces Maori-style mysticism and lyrical qualities into her writing. Her best-known work is *The Bone People* (1983), which won New Zealand's Pegasus Prize in 1984 and the United Kingdom's prestigious Booker Prize in 1985.

Pacific Islands

Perhaps because of variable rates of literacy—since literacy is a requisite for the development of written literature—little or no literature has been published in many of the Pacific Islands. In many islands, English is an official language, but it tends to be reserved for government uses; in their everyday life, citizens of, for example, Papua New Guinea, Fiji, and the Easter Islands often use their native languages. Written literature in English is beginning to appear in areas served by the University of Papua New Guinea (established in 1965) and the University of the South Pacific (1968). Literary journals in the 1970s and later—including *Mana,* a publication of the South Pacific Creative Arts Society; and *Kovare,* a journal of New Guinea writing—have been published mainly in the English language, but interest in writings in local languages is emerging.

An exception is Hawaii, a locale long romanticized in western fiction. The setting of an idealized island paradise is being countered by the more realistic views of Hawaiian authors, who are both natives and immigrants. This new literary wave is based on an oral tradition known as "talk story." It deals with issues of gender and sexuality, along with knotty problems of race and class connected, in many instances, with the sensitive issue of how to define the "authentically" Hawaiian. Writers of fiction include Lois-Ann Yamanaka (*Blu's Hanging,* 1997) and Nora Okja Keller (*Comfort Woman,* 1997); many Hawaiian writers are women and are members of Bamboo Ridge, a publishing group founded in 1978.

See Also

LITERATURE: OVERVIEW; POSTCOLONIALISM: THEORY AND CRITICISM

References and Further Reading

Anderson, Don, ed. 1996. *Contemporary classics, 1965–1995: The best Australian short fiction.* New York: Vintage.

Dann, Jack, and Janeen Webb, eds. 1998. *Dreaming down under.* New York: HarperCollins.

Dhawan, R. K., and David Kerr, eds. 1992. *Australian literature today.* Chicago, Ill.: Advent.

Dutton, Geoffrey, ed. 1976. *The literature of Australia.* New York: Penguin.

Hagedorn, Jessica. 1997. Review of *Blu's Hanging* by Lois-Ann Yamanaka. *Harper's Bazaar* (1 April): 64. (On-line: Encarta Electric Library <http://encarta.nsn.com>)

Kramer, Leonie, ed. 1981. *The Oxford history of Australian literature.* Oxford: Oxford University Press.

Sturm, Terry, ed. *The Oxford history of New Zealand literature.* Oxford: Oxford University Press.

Themes in Australian literature. 1999. In *Encyclopedia of Australia.* Webster/Infrosentials Group (<http://www.insentials.com>).

Williams, Mark, ed. *Postcolonial literatures in English: Southeast Asia, New Zealand, and the Pacific, 1970–1992.* New York: Hall.

———, and Michele Leggott, eds. 1995. *Opening the book: New essays on New Zealand writing.* Auckland: Paul; Auckland University.

Georgia Kornbluth

LITERATURE: Central and South America

The late 1960s witnessed an explosion of international interest in Latin American literature. A whole series of novelists—Garcia Marquez, Fuentes, Cortazar, and Vargas Llosa—became household names around the world, along with Borges and Paz. Significantly, though, this list does not include women; only since the 1980s has the contribution of women writers in Latin America has become better known beyond their own region.

The absence of women from the list of "new wave" writers of the 1960s and 1970s may be explained in a number of ways, not least of which is a lack of translations of a great deal of work. The process of canonization, whether on economic or on aesthetic grounds, tends to ensure that translation takes place, but this has not been the case with Latin American women writers. Isabel Allende (Chile) has acquired a considerable reputation, due to the popularity of *The House of the Spirits* (1985); and translations of Clarice Lispector (Brazil) led Hélène Cixous to single her out for special attention. Otherwise, most of the magnificently varied women's writing in Latin America is known only to a small minority around the world.

This is ironic when we reflect that not only was the first Latin American writer to be awarded the Nobel Prize for literature a woman—the Chilean poet Gabriela Mistral (1889–1957)—but the first writer of any significance to emerge from the New World in the seventeenth century was also a woman, the controversial Sor Juana de la Cruz (Mexico, 1651–1695), whose powerful anticonformist voice was finally suppressed by the ecclesiastical authorities, so that she ended her days in silence. Sor Juana may be seen as emblematic of the situation of many women writers in the colonies; she was a woman of great intelligence who fought for the right to be educated and wrote expressive erotic metaphysical poetry in defiance of the authorities, against whom she defended herself until the last. Significantly, Octavio Paz, who had earlier defined the Mexican woman as a passive, secretive "other" to the macho male, became fascinated by his countrywoman, Sor Juana, who was forced into passivity and secrecy by a repressive authoritarian system.

Early Latin American writing by women is predominantly in the form of letters and diaries, and these modes have continued to be utilized a great deal in contemporary fiction. Novelists such as Laura Esquivel, Elena Poniatowska, and Margo Glantz (Mexico); Luisa Valenzuela (Argentina); and Marvel Moreno (Colombia) follow the precedent established by an earlier generation of writers such as Rosario Castellanos (Mexico) and Silvina Ocampo (Argentina), subverting conventional narrative structures through the inclusion and adaptation of all kinds of texts, such as diaries, letters, recipes, tape-recorded conversations, and autobiography. The boundary between fact and fiction is often deliberately blurred, and in a novel such as Valenzuela's *The Lizard's Tail,* which deals with the terror in Argentina in the 1970s, the writer herself enters the narrative as a character. Esquivel's *Like Water for Chocolate* is constructed around a series of recipes, while Poniatowska's *Querido Diego, te abraza Quiela* consists of 12 invented letters supposedly written by the Russian painter Angelina Beloff to her unfaithful lover, Diego Rivera.

The impact of surrealism has been powerfully felt by many Latin American women writers. Clarice Lispector, Silvina Ocampo, Maria Luisa Bombal, and Alejandra Pizarnik all acknowledge a debt to surrealism, and it is interesting that a movement that was so male-dominated in Europe should have become so women-centered in Latin America; this is perhaps because it could be fused with other traditions, such as the fantastic. It is important also to remember that in the early Spanish colonies, the novel was forbidden by the Inquisition; the first published novel did not appear until 1816, in Mexico. Moreover, at different times repressive dictatorships imposed ruthless censorship on writers. At such times, surrealism, antirealism, or magical realism have offered ways of communicating that avoid overly literal messages, which government censors would be able to recognize and suppress.

The violent history of much of Latin America is reflected in women's writing. From the Guatamalan Rigoberta Menchu, winner of the Nobel Peace Prize in 1993, to the Argentinian playwright Griselda Gambara and her fellow countrywoman, the novelist Marta Traba, to the Chilean Marjorie Agosin, writing about exile and torture, women writers have exposed the suffering of their people under corrupt governments and violent dictatorships. It could be argued that Latin American women's writing has frequently been an act of defiance, or an act of testimony, bearing witness to atrocities and injustice, in the same way that the Mothers of the Plaza de Mayo, in the 1980s, became a symbol of the refusal to forget the countless numbers of the "disappeared" in Argentina, their children arrested in the night by the secret police and never seen again. The need to bear witness against abuse of power and to resist violence by speaking out against its many forms is a powerful theme in much Latin American writing, especially women's writing.

Perhaps the best-known visual images of Latin American women, created by a woman, are the self-portraits of the Mexican artist Frida Kahlo. These images are often violent and brutal, simultaneously self-mocking and tragic. Images of great violence are likewise often to be found in women's writing. Many writers from Argentina and Mexico, in particular, hold a mirror up to a violent history in their novels, plays, or stories. Alejandra Pizarnik, in her famous short story "The Bloody Countess," chooses as a subject a woman who is said to have obtained her pleasure through the torture and murder of hundreds of young girls. Pizarnik uses this narrative to examine the meaning of freedom in the world, and the relationship between a concept of freedom and responsibility, starting from Sartre's proposition that absolute freedom is the ultimate horror. In their explorations of violence, many Latin American women writers describe the physicality of horror, in much the same way as Frida

Kahlo explored her own sensuality and the pain that afflicted her body throughout her life.

Marjorie Agosin's anthology of Latin American women poets (1994) is entitled, fittingly, *These Are Not Sweet Girls,* a deliberate reference to an ironic poem by Anabel Torres (Colombia), "These Are the Sweet girls." Sweetness is definitely not a characteristic of Latin American women poets. Sor Juana, who wrote so passionately and with such rage in the seventeenth century, was followed by countless others, struggling to express themselves through powerful imagery and innovative uses of Spanish or Portuguese. Apart from the great Gabriela Mistral, the early twentieth century saw writers such as Delmira Agustini (Uraguay, 1886–1914) and Alfonsina Storni (Argentina, 1892–1938), whose intensely personal, highly erotic poetry has had an impact on many Latin American writers. They can be said to have established a tradition of women's erotic poetry that many later writers were able to develop.

Any attempt to categorize or even list leading Latin American women poets is doomed to failure, simply because there are so many poets, with such varied styles, all of whom write so well. A brief survey might include Julia de Burgos (1914–1953) from Puerto Rico, Nancy Morejon from Cuba, Violeta Parra (1904–1967) from Chile (best known for her songwriting), Alejandra Pizarnik (1936–1972) from Argentina, Claribel Alegria and Gioconda Belli from Nicaragua, Marjorie Agosin and Paz Molina from Chile, Adelia Prado from Brazil, Clementina Suarez (1902–1991) from Honduras, Ana Istaru from Costa Rica, and Montserrat Ordonez from Colombia. Many of these women have won major awards for their poetry, but few are well known in the English-speaking world. Novelists have enjoyed rather more success internationally, but there are only a limited number of writers whose work has been successfully marketed.

In contrast to the relative neglect of Latin American literature until recently, Latin American writers, both men and women, have always been interested in the works of other writers, and many have actively sought to bring in new writing from around the world. One of the most influential critics and publishers of the twentieth century was a woman, Victoria Ocampo (Argentina, 1890–1979), sister of the novelist Silvina, who founded the extremely influential literary journal *Sur.* Ocampo introduced all kinds of writers into Latin America, and as a literary patron she had incalculable influence. In the 1930s, she met Virginia Woolf; she published *A Room of One's Own* in *Sur* in 1935–1936, followed closely by *Orlando* and *To the Lighthouse.* Victoria Ocampo pursued a deliberate policy of trying to widen the range of Latin American writers by introducing new ideas and techniques, not only from Europe but also from Asia.

The pioneering work of Victoria Ocampo is only one aspect of the cosmopolitanism of Latin American writing. Other factors have also contributed: many Latin American writers have spent time in exile (for example, Julia de Burgos, and Luisa Valenzuela), escaping from repressive dictatorships. Many studied abroad, in France or the United States in particular (for example, Alejandra Pizarnik and Claribel Alegria). Many have worked for their countries as diplomats or cultural attachés (for example, Rosario Castellanos and Margo Glantz). What is striking about so much Latin American writing (by both men and women) is a fusion of diverse elements, a willingness to experiment with different styles and voices, and the way in which writers convey a sense of being Latin American—often of belonging to one specific part of Latin America—combined with a sense of cultural displacement, of eternal exile. Exile, whether physical or psychological, is a powerful theme. Women as diverse as Clarice Lispector, who creates female characters who are exiles in their own communities and even in their own families, or Gabriela Mistral, whose poetry returns again and again to explorations of exile, exemplify the persistence of this theme in both poetry and prose. Many writers use their own families as material, writing about mothers and grandmothers, who were often immigrants or exiles fleeing persecution or wars in Europe.

The richness of Latin American women's writing reflects the multifaceted nature of Latin American societies, where diverse languages and traditions combine. This writing deserves to be much better known. Nevertheless, the fact that some women's work has found its way into English is due as well to the skill of translators, many of whom are also women. As interest in Latin American women's writing continues to grow, the number of texts translated is also increasing.

See Also

IMAGES OF WOMEN: CENTRAL AND SOUTH AMERICA; LITERATURE: OVERVIEW; POETRY: OVERVIEW

References and Further Reading

Chanady, Amaryll Beatrice, ed. 1994. *Latin American identity and constructions of difference.* Minneapolis: University of Minnesota Press.

Condé, Lisa P., and Stephen M. Hart, eds. 1991. *Feminist readings on Spanish and Latin American literature.* Lewiston, N.Y.: Mellen.

Sommer, Doris, ed. *The places of history: Regionalism revisited in Latin America.* Durham, N.C.: Duke University Press.

Virgillo, Carmelo, and Naomi Lindstrom, eds. 1985. *Woman as myth and metaphor in Latin American literature.* Columbia: University of Missouri Press.

Susan Bassnett

LITERATURE: Children's

See CHILDREN'S LITERATURE.

LITERATURE: China

Women writers and women as figures in men's literary imagination are the two main aspects of feminist study of literature in China, the world's longest written tradition. Representations of women and the feminine by men have had important consequences for Chinese women writers, who are best known for their work in the dominant genres of their times: poetry in the traditional period and fiction in the modern period.

This article will discuss, first, traditional literature, and then modern literature. All Chinese names are transliterated in pinyin, the standard romanization now used in China and in scholarship on China. However, much scholarship on the traditional period and many library catalogues use the Wade-Giles system, which spells many sounds quite differently (such as Lady Ho, Chuo Wen-chün, Pan Chao, Ts'ai Yen, Tz'u Yeh, Hsüeh T'ao, Li Ch'ing-chao, and Chu Shu-chen).

Traditional Literature

Canonical literature of the traditional period is written in classical Chinese, a terse language quite different from speech. Only an elite minority could afford the years of study it took to acquire literacy in classical Chinese, memorize the canon, and master the prestigious art of writing poetry—requirements for the highly competitive exams for government office, from which women were excluded. Some women were educated, yet during most of the traditional period, because of the Confucian injunction that women's words should not pass beyond the women's quarters, it was common for elite women or their families to burn their work; thus most of these women's writing has been lost. Many of the women whose works survive, albeit sometimes anonymously, were courtesans or nuns.

In textual records before the seventeenth century, women's lives are generally obscured, although for various reasons certain women writers are sporadically highlighted (Change and Saussy, 1999). These include Lady He (c. 300 B.C.E.), Zhuo Wenjun (second century B.C.E.), Ban Zhao (first century C.E.), Cai Yan (c. 200), Zi Ye (third to fourth century), Xue Tao (768–831), Yu Xuanji (c. 843–868), Li Qingzhao (1084?—1151), Zhu Shuzhen (early twelfth century), Guan Daosheng (1262–1319), and Huang E (1498–1569). Names of women also appear among the ranks of professional storytellers in twelfth- and thirteenth-century texts, and many anonymous ballads and love songs can be attributed to women. China's earliest collection of poetry, the *Shijing* (*Poetry Classic,* c. seventh century B.C.E.), includes many pieces in a woman's voice; but these folk songs were heavily edited, and it is impossible to say with certainty which of them, if any, were actually written by women. Creating verse was a standard part of the courtesan's repertoire, and anonymous female entertainers of the fifth and sixth centuries are credited with having originated a verse genre called *ci* ("song lyric"), which then gained respectability in the hands of famous male poets (Wagner, 1984).

In the late sixteenth century, women of the ruling class in an area in southeastern China known as Jiangnan begin to emerge in the record in greater numbers as poets, editors, and critics, and much more of their work has been preserved (Chang and Saussy, 1999). By this time, the poetic tradition was well established, with over a thousand years' worth of images of women and a feminine voice that articulated men's preoccupations. For instance, the image of a woman pining for her absent male lover was an analogy for a government official longing to be recognized by his ruler; and male poets used the voice of an abandoned woman as a code in which they could speak of their own frustrated political ambitions. Around the time that women, in greater numbers and more visibly, were fashioning such literary resources into expressive instruments of their own (Robertson, 1992), and men were extolling women's emotional authenticity and debating the proper scope of women's education and writing, vernacular fiction was filled with representations of temptresses and shrews. A few scholars argue that such representations were realistic and attribute them to something like feminist consciousness; but most scholars agree that these characters—who are portrayed (usually grotesquely) as ravenous for money, sex, and power—represent forces of chaos in a world out of balance (McMahon, 1995).

Late in the traditional period, women were also known as writers of various regional genres involving narrative performance, like the *tanci* of the Jiangnan area or the "wooden fish" songs of the Canton delta region; but little of this work is available in translation. Women in one part of Hunan wrote letters, autobiographies, and narratives in a script called *nüshu* ("women's script"), which men did not read or write (Silber, 1994).

Modern Literature

Prose of the late nineteenth century and the early twentieth century continued to use images of women to represent powerlessness. Now, however, the trope of the oppressed woman in traditional Chinese society represented national weakness—a moribund China threatened by imperialist powers. The reforms that ended the imperial examination system in 1905, the promulgation of colloquial Chinese as the standard written language that began about a decade later, and calls for women's rights—greater access to education, and the abolition of foot binding, arranged marriage, polygamy, and female infanticide—were all part of a broad project of national salvation. Poetry, which had been the predominant genre, was replaced by realistic fiction, serving as an instrument of social and political change. In the twentieth century, women emerged as writers of novels and short stories.

In the early twentieth century, young intellectuals, both men and women, addressed the "woman question" and the concept of the "new woman" in stories and essays published in scores of new periodicals. Most of the young women who were writing at this time did not continue to write beyond the 1920s; perhaps for this reason, their place in literary history has been obscured until recently (Dooling and Torgeson, 1998). The women whose enduring reputation has already been established are the radical writer Qiu Jin (1875–1907), who became a martyr of feminism and nationalism when she was executed for treason; Bing Xin (b. 1900), who began as a poet and then wrote fiction and autobiography; Ling Shuhua (1900–1990), whose stories address the position of women in traditional culture and changing gender relations; the novelist and essayist Xiao Hong (1911–1942); the fiction writer Zhang Ailing (Eileen Chang, 1921–95); and Ding Ling (1904–1986), a preeminent woman writer of twentieth-century China, whose career reflects the political as well as the literary trends of her time.

Ding Ling became a literary sensation with the publication in 1927 of *Miss Sophie's Diary*, an exploration of female subjectivity and sexuality, and she would be plagued throughout the rest of her career by readers' insistence on interpreting this first-person narrative as autobiographical. Her writing in the 1930s and 1940s addressed the plight of the proletariat, while continuing to focus on women's issues, and she became a powerful literary figure in the communists' base area. Her essay "Thoughts on March Eighth," which discussed the inequality of women in that region, made her a target of political criticism. She went on to write stories and novels in the style of socialist realism that was the communist literary standard, but she came under attack again in the 1950s and spent more than 20 years in exile, in labor camps, and in jail. In 1979 she was rehabilitated and alienated other writers by supporting political orthodoxy; but the year before her death, she founded a literary magazine that published controversial writers and was shut down.

With the end of the cultural revolution in the late 1970s, a period of greater literary freedom began. Despite sporadic campaigns and crackdowns, that period has continued to the present day. After several decades during which women's issues had been buried by official proclamations of equality and women's personal concerns had been subordinated to the state's political agenda, women again became central to literature, restoring personal subjectivity and gender issues, especially in the 1980s. In 1956, Zong Pu (b. 1928) was severely criticized for writing about love in her story "Red Beans"; in 1979, by contrast, the story "Love Must Not Be Forgotten" by Zhang Jie (b. 1937), although controversial, was acclaimed for questioning the sacrifice of personal fulfillment to politics. Zhang Jie's novella *The Ark* (1981) explored many facets of sexism through the lives of three main women characters.

In the 1980s, a younger generation of writers introduced narrative innovations to Chinese fiction in their attempts to write about contemporary life from a woman's perspective. Zhang Xinxin (b. 1953) took up the problem of femininity in the story "How Did I Miss You?" (1980) and depicted the struggle of a woman trying to reconcile marriage and a career in the novella *On the Same Horizon* (1981). Wang Anyi (b. 1954) is best known for the trilogy *Love on a Barren Mountain* (1986), *Love in a Small Town* (1986), and *Brocade Valley* (1987), and for the novella *Bao Town* (1985), which involves a "search for roots" and explores women's issues and the essence of Chinese culture. Can Xue (b. 1953) wrote surreal avant-garde works, best represented in translation by *Dialogues in Paradise* (1988). Li Ang (b. 1952), from Taiwan, created a sensation with her novella *The Butcher's Wife* (1983), in which an abused wife kills her husband. Shu Ting (b. 1952) is China's best-known contemporary woman poet.

Since the late 1980s, several of the best women writers in Chinese have emigrated and continued their careers abroad. Liu Suola (b. 1955) wrote *Chaos and All That* (first published in Hong Kong in 1991), in which the jaded, irrepressible protagonist recounts absurd episodes of her childhood during the cultural revolution in China from the perspective of her present absurd life in London. Yan Geling (b. 1958), originally from Shanghai and now living in San

Francisco, explores life as a Chinese woman in the West in impressive fiction that is beginning to be widely known in translation.

See Also

FEMINISM: CHINA; LITERATURE: OVERVIEW; IMAGES OF WOMEN: ASIA; MEDIA: CHINESE CASE STUDY; WOMEN'S STUDIES: EAST ASIA

References and Further Reading

Barlow, Tani E., ed. 1993. *Gender politics in modern China: Writing and feminism.* Durham, N.C.: Duke University Press.

Chang, Kang-i Sun, and Haun Saussy, eds. 1999. *Women writers of traditional China: An anthology of poetry and criticism.* Stanford, Calif.: Stanford University Press.

Denton, Kirk, and Jeremy Sieg. *Modern Chinese literature and cultural resource center* (MCLC). Web site: <http://deall.ohiostate.edu.denton.2/biblio.htm>

Dooling, Amy D., and Kristina M. Torgeson, eds. 1998. *Writing women in modern China: An anthology of women's literature from the early twentieth century.* New York: Columbia University Press.

Ko, Dorothy. 1994. *Teachers of the inner chambers: Women and culture in seventeenth-sentury china.* Stanford, Calif.: Stanford University Press.

Mann, Susan. 1997. *Precious records: Women in China's long eighteenth century.* Stanford, Calif.: Stanford University Press.

McDougall, Bonnie S., and Kam Louie, eds. 1997. *The literature of China in the twentieth century.* New York: Columbia University Press.

McMahon, Keith. 1995. *Misers, shrews, and polygamists: Sexuality and male-female relations in eighteenth-century China.* Durham, N.C.: DukeUniversity Press.

Roberston, Maureen. 1992. Voicing the feminine: Constructions of the gendered subject in lyric poetry by women of medieval and late imperial China. *Late Imperial China* 13(1): 63–110.

Silber, Cathy. 1994. From daughter to daughter-in-law in the women's script of southern Hunan. In Christina Gilmartin et al., eds., *Engendering China: Women, culture, and the state,* 47–68. Cambridge, Mass.: Harvard University Press.

Wagner, Marsha L. 1984. *The lotus boat: The origins of Chinese tz'u poetry in T'ang popular culture.* New York: Columbia University Press.

Widmer, Ellen, and Kang-i Sun Chang, eds. 1997. *Writing women in late imperial China.* Stanford, Calif.: Stanford University Press.

Cathy Silber

LITERATURE: Drama

See DRAMA.

LITERATURE: Eastern Europe

After World War II, the introduction of communist regimes in eastern European countries—including Albania, Bulgaria, former Czechoslovakia (the Czech Republic and Slovakia), Hungary, Poland, Romania, and the former Yugoslav federation (Bosnia–Herzegovina, Croatia, Macedonia, Montenegro, Serbia, and Slovenia)—fostered a perception of homogeneity for a region that in reality encompasses countries with different traditions and cultures. While women writers were marginalized in literary histories published before the fall of communism in 1989, the 1990s marked a period of rapid growth in the study of women's literature in most of the countries concerned. This should soon be reflected in a greater availability of reference books.

Writing Before the Nineteenth Century

Before the nineteenth century, there were comparatively few women writers in eastern Europe. One of the earliest was Jefimija (1349–1405), the first Serbian woman poet. Married to a Serbian feudal ruler, Jefimija became a nun after his death. Her deeply religious poetry belongs to the Byzantine tradition. Among her preserved writings is an elegy over the death of her child, written on the back of an icon miniature. Her best known work is "Pohvala Knezu Lazaru" ("A Eulogy to Prince Lazar," 1402), embroidered in gold on the prince's shroud by the poet herself.

Many of the early women writers in eastern Europe were members of the aristocracy and are known for autobiographical writings, often with religious themes. The Czech noblewoman Zuzana Černínová z Harasova (1601–1654) is remembered for her letters about the hardships of the Thirty Years' War. Countess Kata Bethlen (1700–1759), a Hungarian aristocrat from Transylvania, wrote a powerful memoir, *A Short Description of the Life of Countess Kata Bethlen Written by Herself,* in her early 1930s. This book, published in 1762, conveys the suffering and self-torture of a devout Protestant woman who was, at the age of 17, forced to marry her Roman Catholic half-brother. One of Bethlen's contemporaries was a prolific Polish poet Elżbieta Drużbacka (1695–1765), whose *Zbiór rytmów duchownych, panegirycznych, moralnych i światowych* (*A Collection of Rhythms, Spiritual, Panegyrical, Moral and Worldly*), was published in 1752. Her compatriot, Konstancja Benisławska (1747–1806), wrote baroque-inspired religious hymns gathered in *Pieśni sobie śpiewane* (*Songs Sung to Oneself*, 1776).

Nineteenth-Century Literature

In the nineteenth century, patriotic movements in many eastern European countries awoke a new interest in folklore and oral literary tradition. In eastern Europe, as in many other parts of the world that had been under foreign domination, folklore offered some of the best expressions of native languages. Collections of eastern European fairy tales, legends, and epic and lyric poetry contain the works of many otherwise forgotten women. In Serbia, for example, shorter lyric poems were originally gathered as "women's poems" These included a variety of subgenres, from rhythmic verse which accompanied particular types of work (for example, harvesting and weaving) to lullabies, riddles, or charms. Although collected as "men's poetry," longer epic poems were also frequently recorded as dictated by women. A number of blind Serbian women are known to have earned their living as professional performers of epic poetry. The best known of them, Slepa Živana (Živana the Blind), died in 1828. Similar traditions existed in other eastern European countries.

The romantic movement, which is, in eastern Europe, inseparable from the struggle for national liberation, had a number of prominent female proponents. In Poland, Narcyza Żmichowska (1819–1876)—an emancipated woman, a private teacher, and, for two years, a political prisoner who "presided over a group of intellectual women who banded together for mutual support" (Wilson, 1991)—wrote poetry and a novel in lyrical verse called *Poganka* (*The Heathen Woman,* 1846). The Serbian poet Milica Stojadinović-Srpkinja (1830–1878) wrote patriotic verse. She was known as the "muse of the 1848 generation" and her exceptional beauty was usually praised more than her poetry. Elements of late romanticism can be found in patriotic poetry written by Luiza Pesjak Crobath (1828–1898), a Slovene poet who tried her hand at fiction, plays, and children's poetry.

In the second half of the nineteenth century, a number of eastern European women achieved recognition as novelists. Among the most notable is Božena Němcová (1820–1862), the first eminent woman novelist in the Czech language. *Babička* (*Grandmother,* 1855), reputedly her best novel, describes Czech village life. Němcová's contemporary, the novelist Karolína Světla (1830–1899), was an influential proponent of Czech romantic realism. In Poland, Eliza Orzeszkowa (1841–1910) was one of the first women to earn her living as a professional writer. She was a prolific novelist who drew her inspiration from provincial Polish life, adopting a didactic, populist tone. The position of women was one of the dominant themes examined in her novels. She spent most of her life in the provincial town of Grodno, where she had been kept under surveillance by the tsarist Russian police for her political activities. Her contemporary and friend, the poet Maria Konopnicka (1842–1910), married early to a much older landowner, "bore him six children and then rebelled, throwing aside all the standards of the manor, moving to Warsaw, and embarking upon a career of her own" (Miłosz, 1983). A campaigner for women's rights, violently anticlerical, radical in denouncing the predicament of the oppressed as well as tsarist censorship, Konopnicka faced many obstacles in her writing career. She wrote poetry, short stories, and novellas in verse, often about the plight of the exploited classes.

Like Konopnicka, many eastern European women writers of the period explicitly questioned the position of women through their work. The Croatian Dragojla Jarnević (1812–1875) highlights in her diaries "the conflict between intellectual activity and household chores, which plagued her despite her resolve not to marry" (Hawkesworth, 1991). The Serbian actress and poet Draga Dejanović (1843–1870) titled one of her articles with a question, "Are Women Capable of Being Equal with Men?" (1870). The Slovene novelist and playwright Zofka Kveder (1878–1926), best known for her novel *Njeno življenje* (*Her Life,* 1914), demanded social rights for women in her articles and edited an influential protofeminist magazine. The novelist Marija Jurić-Zagorka (1873–1957) was among the first Croatian women to express feminist ideas in her journalism. Her adventure novels achieved great popularity but were attacked as pulp literature. The Polish actress, playwright, and novelist Gabriela Zapolska (1857–1921), a "woman in revolt, surrounded by scandalous gossip" (Miłosz, 1983), wrote naturalist plays aimed at exposing the hypocrisy of the bourgeoisie, frequently with a female heroine.

The Twentieth Century

One of the best Hungarian novelists, Margit Kaffka (1880–1918), was among the first women writers to explore the position of an educated career woman in *Mária évei* (*The Years of Maria,* 1913). Her other novels explore the restrictions facing women who do not espouse their traditional role in society. Among the women novelists who influenced modern eastern European prose in this century, one of the earlier examples is Czech novelist Růžena Svobodová (1868–1920). Her often sentimental prose reflects "much of the emancipationist ardour of the age" (Hawkesworth, 1991). Svobodová inspired a generation of Czech women novelists, most notably Božena Benešová (1873–1936), whose novel *Don Pedro, Don Pablo, and Véra Lukašová* (1936) represents "a gently ironic depiction of an 11-year-old girl's achievement of emotional maturity through an encounter with a child molester" (Pynsent, 1993). The Romanian novelist Hortensia Papadat-Bengescu (1876–1955) was a sharp observer of suburban life and the *nouveaux riches.* The Slovak writer Elena Maróthy-Soltesová (1855–1939), who moved from ideal to social realism in her novels, was a pioneer of the Slovak women's movement and reputedly the first female literary critic in Slovakia. Maria Dąbrowska (1889–1965) wrote one of the most influential Polish novels, *Noce i dnie* (*Nights and Days,* 1932–1934). Many consider this *roman fleuve* in four volumes to be among the best examples of Polish prose available. The Serbian writer Isidora Sekulić (1877–1958) enjoys a similar reputation for the elegant style of her essays, stories, and travel writing.

At the turn of the twentieth century, many women writers also became involved in magazine publishing. Among them, the Czech writer Eliška Krásnohorská (1847–1926) was the founder–editor of the influential women's magazine *Ženske listy,* while Marica Bartol Nadlišek (1867–1940) founded and edited the first Slovene women's magazine, *Slovenka* (*The Slovene Woman*). Some of the leading national writers of the era contributed to its literary pages. In Hungary, the novelist Cécile Tormay (1876–1937) was the editor of the leading conservative literary magazine, *Napkelet* (*The East*), the forum of the Christian–National revival. Historical novels written by Irén Gulacsy (1894–1945) and Mária Szabó (1888–1982) belong to the traditions of this revival.

In poetry, the Hungarian Minka Czóbel (1855–1947) wrote symbolist, decadent verse during the 1890s, and, like her counterpart Emily Dickinson in the United States, "lived in isolation in the depths of countryside" (Czigány, 1984). The Polish poet Maria Komornicka (1876–1949) embraced the philosophy of Friedrich Nietzsche. Her poems, often in free verse, vehemently defend total freedom for the individual. Many influential women poets continued to achieve prominence in the first half of the century. Elisaveta Bagryana (1893–1991) was the leading Bulgarian poet of her era. She was an independent-minded, emancipated woman, and many of her lively, direct poems create a strong image of a woman "whose desire for freedom is elemental" (Pynsent, 1993). The Slovene poet Lily Novy (1885–1958) wrote expressionist poetry, often with erotic or existential themes. Desanka Maksimović (1898–1993), the leading Serbian woman poet of the twentieth century, succeeded in linking personal, lyric expression with wider national themes.

It was in poetry, rather than prose, that eastern European women continued to enjoy greater prominence after World War II. In Croatia, Vesna Parun (b. 1922) rejected social realism and was attacked by the communist establishment for her collection *Zore i vihori* (*Dawns and Whirlwinds,* 1947). The leading contemporary Bulgarian poet, Blaga Dimitrova (b. 1922), who in 1992 became the country's vice president, published establishment-approved poetry in the 1950s but subsequently drifted away and was considered a dissident. Her novel *Litse* (*Face,* 1991) was originally banned. The leading Polish poet Wisława Szymborska (a Nobel Prize-winner, b. 1923) and the leading Romanian poet Nina Cassian (b. 1924) are both translated and widely known abroad. The Romanian poet Ana Blandiana (b. 1942), the Polish poet Ewa Lipska (b. 1945), the Slovene Svetlana Makarovič (b. 1939), the Czech Sylva Fischerová (b. 1963), and the Albanian Natasha Lako (b. 1948) were among the leading poets in eastern Europe at the end of the twentieth century.

Among writers of fiction, Elena Kadare (b. 1943) is reputed to be the first Albanian woman to publish a novel. More recently, her compatriot Diana Çuli (b. 1951) published short stories and a novel to great critical acclaim. The Czech novelist Zdena Salivarová (b. 1933) wrote two highly regarded novels in exile and worked as the head of the leading Czech publishing house in exile, 68 Publishers, in Toronto, Canada. She published, among other things, the novel *Pera a perutě* (1989, available in English as *Truck Stop Rainbows*), by Iva Pekárková (b. 1963), a delinquent teenager who became a New York taxi driver and later a novelist.

The Twenty-First Century

Two of the leading eastern European women novelists at the beginning of the twenty-first century are the Croatian writers Dubravka Ugrešić (b. 1949) and Slavenka Drakulić (b. 1949), both widely translated. Ugrešić's irreverent and funny novels preserve some of the best tradition of eastern European bittersweet satire. Exiled in the West since the early 1990s, she has brilliantly examined the desintegration of Yugoslavia in essay collections and memoirs including *The Museum of Unconditional Surrender* (1996) and *The Culture of Lies: Antipolitical Essays* (1998). Drakulić's novels—*Hologrami straha* (*The Holograms of Fear,* 1987), which explores her experience of kidney dialysis; and *Mramorna Koža* (*Marble Skin,* 1989), a haunting story of a mother–daughter relationship—could perhaps be more readily compared to the writings of the French novelist Marguerite Duras. Very different in style are Drakulić's accounts of women in eastern Europe, gathered in *How We Survived Communism and Even Laughed* (1992), and her experiences of the Yugoslav war described in *Balkan Express* (1993) and *Café Europa: Life After Communism* (1997). She remains one of the leading figures of eastern European feminism today. While women's writing in the former Yugoslavia continues to be profoundly influenced by the experience of war and displacement, in other eastern European countries women writers face the more typical challenges of the postcommunist era, including the survival of indigenous publishing in an increasingly commercialized book market flooded by western best-sellers.

See Also

FEMINISM: EASTERN EUROPEAN; LITERARY THEORY AND CRITICISM; LITERATURE: OVERVIEW; WOMEN'S STUDIES: CENTRAL AND EASTERN EUROPE

References and Further Readings

Chester, Pamela, and Sibelan Forrester, eds. 1996. *Engendering Slavic literatures.* Bloomington: Indiana University Press.

Czigány, Lóránt. 1984. *The Oxford history of Hungarian literature from the earliest times to the present.* Oxford: Oxford University Press.

Elsie, Robert. 1986. *Dictionary of Albanian literature.* New York, Westport, Conn., London: Greenwood.

Hawkesworth, Celia. 1991. Feminist writing in Eastern Europe: The problem solved? In Helena Forsås-Scott, ed., *Textual liberation: European feminist writing in the twentieth century,* 100–129. London and New York: Routledge.

———. 2000. *Voices in the shadows: Women and verbal art in Serbia and Bosnia.* Budapest: Central European University Press.

Labon, Joanna. 1992. Eastern Europe. In Claire Buck, ed., *Bloomsbury guide to women's literature,* 106–109. London: Bloomsbury.

Miłosz, Czesław. 1983. *The history of Polish literature* (2nd ed.), Berkeley, Los Angeles, and London: University of California Press.

Pynsent, Robert B. (ed). 1993. *The everyman companion to east European literature.* London: J.M. Dent.

Wilson, Catharina M. (ed). 1991. *An encyclopedia of continental women writers.* 2 vols. New York and London: Garland.

Vesna Goldsworthy

LITERATURE: Erotic

See EROTICA.

LITERATURE: Fairy Tales

See FAIRY TALES.

LITERATURE: Fiction

See FICTION.

LITERATURE: Japan

In the history of Japanese literature, women's writing has occupied a somewhat contradictory position. On the one hand, the works of *joryūsakka,* or the female school, have been relegated to a secondary literary rank; but on the other hand, women's works have been central to the formation of the literary canon—indeed, from the inception of written language in Japan to the first literary forms that emerged thereafter, women's voices have sounded a keynote. Recognition of women's contributions to literature in Japan has been to a great extent been determined by the sociopolitical environment of each historical period, and changes in women's status have been directly related to their access to authorship.

Ancient Period

During the ancient period women had high social and spiritual status, playing significant roles as political leaders and shamanesses—Shinto priestesses who served as mediums for gods and spirits. Hieda no Are, who was most likely a shamaness, was charged with the task of memorizing the history and legends of Japan's creation and of the female deity Amaterasu Ōmikami to be included in the first written chronicle of Japan, the *Kojiki* (*Record of Ancient Matters,* 712 C.E.; translated 1969). In the eighth century, the *Man'yōshu* (c. 759; translated 1940), an anthology of poetry primarily made up of the 31-syllable *waka* (in modern times referred to as *tanka*), included the work of more than 130 women poets. Evidence suggests that a matrilineal system existed during this period.

Heian Period (794–1185)

From the sixth century on, the matrilineal family gave way to patriarchal structures as Buddhism and Confucianism gained currency. Most women's status was lower as a result, but upper-class women in the imperial courts wrote literature that forms the foundation of Japan's literary heritage.

Women began to produce literature after the invention of the native Japanese written language in the form of *kana,* or phonetic syllabaries, in the ninth century. Men continued to use Chinese characters for official writings, considering *kana* to be less sophisticated and mainly the language of poetry and women. Many noblewomen, however, were well-educated and learned *kana* so as to become accomplished writers of poetry and prose for the Fujiwara imperial court, where they were consorts and governesses. The first poetry collection authorized by the imperial court, the *Kokinshū* (905, translated 1984), includes *waka* poems by well-known women poets, among them Izumi Shikibu's poems of passionate love and Ono no Komachi's poems describing cruel love and jealousy.

The crowning achievement in prose was Murasaki Shikibu's *Genji Monogatari* (*The Tale of Genji,* c. 1000, translated 1976), a Heian court romance that tells of Prince Hikaru Genji and the distinctive gallery of women who cross his path. Often cited as the world's first novel, this long fictional narrative embodies *mono no aware,* a heightened sense of life's transient beauty. Sei Shonagon's *Makura no Sōshi* (*The Pillow Book of Sei Shonagon,* c. 1000, translated 1967) is an intriguing collection of vignettes and essays spiced with witty observations of court life. The prolific diary literature of the time included *The Diary of Murasaki Shikibu* (translated 1987); *Kagerō Nikki* (*The Gossamer Years,* 954–994, translated) by the mother of Fujiwara no Michitsuna; *The Diary of Izumi Shikibu* (c. 1010; translated 1969); and a diary by the daughter of Sugawara no Takasue, the *Sarashina Nikki* (*As I Crossed a Bridge of Dreams,* c. 1059, translated 1971). Each work chronicles the innermost feelings of its author and traces her life as a woman.

Medieval (1200–1600) and Edo (1600–1868) Periods

The medieval period was characterized by war and instability; for women's writing, it marked the beginning of the dark ages. Anything that women may have written during this period was deemed neither important nor worth preserving. As feudalistic, Confucian ethics became more repressive and highly codified, any attempt by women to express themselves was virtually forbidden. These conditions persisted even when stability and peace returned during the Edo period, the more than 250-year military reign (shogunate) of the Tokugawa family. However, some neglected writings by women from this period—diaries, *waka,* and *haiku* (17-syllable verse)—have recently been unearthed, offering feminist scholars promising directions for future research.

Meiji Period (1868–1912)

Immediately after the collapse of the Tokugawa shogunate, the Meiji period began, with restoration of the imperial government and renewed contact with the West. A wave of democratization and modernization swept the country during the Meiji era, and new opportunities began to open up for women to express themselves, particularly through literature. During this time, the novel became the dominant form, partially because of the *genbun itchi* literary movement, which stressed the unification of written and spoken Japanese.

The first women writers to appear on the literary scene after centuries of virtual silence were Miyake Kaho, Kimura Akebono, and Higuchi Ichiyō. Miyake's *Yabu no Uguisu* (*Nightingale in a Thicket,* 1888) is a lively story of a westernized debutante attending dances and coming out in the social world. Writing in a different mode, Kimura Akebono described impoverishment and overwork among female textile workers in *Fujo no Kagami* (*A Mirror for Womanhood,* 1889, translated 1988). Higuchi wrote about Japanese women still burdened with the weight of traditional Confucian morals. One of her representative works is "Takekurabe" ("Growing Up," 1895, translated 1957), a sad romance of a young girl compelled to become a geisha (an entertainer and consort for male patrons) just as her sexuality is awakening. Higuchi was significant for looking back to the tradition of her Heian literary ancestors, and also for incorporating romantic ideals of love and individualism seen in the new literature coming from the West. The writers of the Taishō period were to inherit these new developments in Japanese literature.

Taishō (1912–1926) and Early Shōwa Periods

The first feminist movement in Japan was born with *Seitō* (*Bluestocking*), a journal dedicated to women's writing under the editorship of Hiratsuka Raichō. This movement came into being with Japan's rapid industrialization and urbanization, as a middle class emerged and educational opportunities for women improved. The original contributors to *Seitō* included two feminist writers, Yosano Akiko and Tamura Toshiko. Many critics find Yosano's *tanka* poetry, particularly the distilled verses of passionate love in *Midaregami* (*Tangled Hair,* 1901, translated 1971), to be among the best of its genre. Tamura's short fiction, as in "Miira no Kuchibeni" ("The Painted Lips of a Mummy," 1913), deals with the fierce conflicts facing the "new woman" caught in traditional heterosexual arrangements.

Seitō had come into being as an extension of the first wave of a worldwide feminist movement, but it eventually collapsed because of financial difficulties and its own elitism, making room for a proletarian movement in Japanese women's literature. Miyamoto Yuriko and her writings can perhaps be seen as a bridge between these two movements. Her autobiographical *Nobuko* (1925; excerpts were translated in 1987), depicts an independent woman breaking out of a stifling marriage and is a classic work of feminist fiction. She later turned to proletarianism with such works as "Chibusa" ("The Breast," 1935). Other important proletarian works that emphasized the need to improve labor and social conditions, such as Sata Ineko's "Kyarameru Kōjō kara" ("From a Caramel Factory," 1928) and Hirabayashi Taiko's "Seryōshitsu nite" ("In the Charity Ward," 1922), explicitly linked social conscience to the aims of artistic expression. Other significant women of this period were Hayashi Fumiko, who wrote *Hōrōki* (*Vagabond's Song,* 1928; excerpts were translated in 1987); Nogami Yaeko, who wrote *Machiko* (1928–1930); and Okamoto Kanoko, who wrote "*Rōgishō*" ("The Tale of an Old Geisha," 1937, translated 1985). The beginning of the Shōwa period saw the imprisonment and harassment of many writers by an increasingly militaristic government as the free-spirited quality of the early Taishō period faded away in an oppressive, censorious climate.

Post-World War II Period (1946–Present)

After Japan's defeat in World War II, women gained many rights under the occupation forces. The country quickly moved from devastation to a period of unparalleled economic growth. Some women writers who had first written before the war began to publish again, such as Uno Chiyo, with *Ohan* (1957, translated 1961); and Enchi Fumiko, with *Onnazaka* (*The Waiting Years,* 1957, translated 1971). In the latter, a wife's outward "feminine" submission to Confucian family values is undercut by an inner spirit of rebellion.

Other women who lived through wartime hardships began to write only after the war's end. Their writings were often characterized by a general disillusionment in the wake of war and an undercurrent of revolt against the circumscribed roles of women under the prewar dictum "*ryōsai kenbo*"—"good wife, wise mother." Moving toward the internal realm of fantasy and away from real-life descriptions of the plight of women, fiction writers such as Ōba Minako with "Sanbiki no Kani" ("Three Crabs," 1968, translated 1978), Takahashi Takako with *Ronrī Ūman* (*Lonely Woman,* 1977), Saegusa Kazuko with *Hibikiko Bishō* (*Hibikiko's Smile,* 1988), and Tomioka Taeko with "Shokubutsusai" ("Feast of Vegetation," 1973), explore isolation, violence, and distorted sexuality. For example, Kōno Taeko's skillfully wrought fictional world centers on obsessive themes of sadomasochism and repressed fantasies of violence against children and against motherhood itself in such stories as "Yōjigari" ("Toddler-Hunting," 1961, translated 1991). Tsushima Yūko, however, turns away from these writers' more pessimistic preoccupations to treat the family in a more affirmative, though not uncritical, manner in *Chōji* (*Child of Fortune,* 1978, translated 1983).

Some writers attack social injustice and deal actively with contemporary problems. Their works include Ariyoshi Sawako's *Fukugō Osen* (*Compound Pollution,* 1974) and Ishimure Michiko's *Kugai Jōdo: Waga Minamatabyō* (*Paradise in the Sea of Sorrow,* 1968, translated 1990), both of which deal with the issue of chemical pollution in Japan. Another socially conscious writer, Hayashi Kyōko, relates the experience of the atomic bombing in *Matsuri no Ba* (*Ritual of Death,* 1975, translated 1978).

Japanese women writers often use themes, narrative techniques, and images that reflect the influence of world literature. Kurahashi Yumiko's "Parutai" ("Partei," 1960, translated 1982) reveals a strong influence of existentialism in her veiled treatment of student protests and the Communist Party of the 1960s. Kanai Mieko's fiction, woven of long, sensual sentences in complex narrative structures, tends toward a lyrical self-reflectiveness reminiscent of Borges and Kafka ("Puratonteki Ren'ai," 1979; translated as "Platonic Love" in 1985). The contemporary poetry of Shiraishi Kazuko, collected in *Seinaru Inja no Kisetsu* (*Seasons of Sacred Lust,* 1970, translated 1975), reveals a marked debt to jazz culture. Kōra Rumiko's poetry, as seen in *Kamen no Koe* (*Voices of the Mask,* 1987), is inspired by Asian and African cultures.

Recently, some writers have struck a chord in contemporary readers by refiguring gender roles and appropriating images from popular culture—comics, film, and the youth scene. In Yoshimoto Banana's best-selling *Kitchen* (1988; translated 1993), for example, the "mother" is really a man who has had a sex change operation. Yamada Eimi's fiction (*Bedtime Eyes,* 1985) often deals with liberated sexuality and interracial relationships. Ogawa Yōko's *Ninshin Karenda* (*Pregnancy Calendar,* 1991) depicts repressed violence and ambivalence toward family and motherhood in a manner reminiscent of earlier postwar writers. In addition to the science fiction of Ōhara Mariko and the treatment of lesbian sexuality in the works of Matsuura Rieko, the innovative writings of Masuda Mizuko, Nakazawa Kei, Matsumoto Yūko, and Ogino Anna continue to present diverse fictional worlds.

While it remains to be seen how the next generation of writers will deal with the new set of social problems and difficult choices confronting Japanese women today, it seems certain that they will not only continue to trace a tradition begun centuries ago with the voices of Heian women but will also create new and increasingly imaginative expressions of social life and individual experience.

See Also

BIOGRAPHY; ÉCRITURE FÉMININE; FICTION; LITERATURE: OVERVIEW; POETRY: OVERVIEW; PUBLISHING; TRAVEL WRITING; UTOPIAN WRITING

References and Further Reading

Gessel, Van C., and Tomone Matsumoto, eds. 1985. *The Shōwa anthology: Modern Japanese short stories, 1929–1984*. Tokyo: Kodansha International.

Hibbett, Howard, ed. 1977. *Contemporary Japanese literature: An anthology of fiction, film, and other writing since 1945*. New York: Knopf.

Kobayashi, Fukuko. 1999. Killing motherhood as institution and reclaiming motherhood as experience: Japanese women writers, 1970s–1990s. In Shirley Geok-Lin Lim, Larry E. Smith, and Wimal Dissanayake, eds., *Transnational Asia Pacific: Gender, culture, and the public sphere,* 134–144. Urbana and Chicago: University of Illinois Press.

Mizuta, Noriko, and Kyoko Iriye Selden, eds. 1982. *Stories by contemporary Japanese women writers.* New York: Sharpe.

Manola, Claire Zebrowski. 1992. *Japanese women writers in English translation: An annotated bibliography.* New York and London: Garland.

Mulhern, Chieko, ed. 1994. *Japanese women writers: A biocritical sourcebook.* Westport, Conn.: Greenwood.

Rexroth, Kenneth, and Ikuko Atsumi, eds. 1977. *The burning heart: Women poets of Japan.* New York: Seabury.

Schalow, Paul Gordon, and Janet A. Walker, eds. 1996. *The woman's hand: Gender and theory in Japanese women's writing.* Stanford, Calif.: Stanford University Press.

Sekine, Eiji, ed. Love and sexuality in Japanese literature. *PMAJLS* 5 (Summer).

Tanaka, Yukiko, ed. 1987. *To live and to write: Selections by Japanese women writers, 1913–1938.* Seattle, Wash.: Seal.

———. 1991. *Unmapped territories: New women's fiction from Japan.* Seattle, Wash.: Women in Translation.

———, and Elizabeth Hanson, eds. 1982. *This kind of woman: Ten stories by Japanese women writers, 1960–1976.* Stanford, Calif.: Stanford University Press.

Fukuko Kobayashi
Mary A. Knighton

LITERATURE: Lesbian

See LESBIAN WRITING.

LITERATURE: North America

Women's writing in North America—the United States and Canada—dates back to colonial times, but it has flowered particularly in periods that also had strong feminist movements. In common with men's writing, literature by women includes letters, novels, political tracts, poetry, drama, short stories, and autobiography, but women have often adapted these literary forms to their own uses. In that sense, North American women's writing was and remains distinctive.

Beginnings: The Needle and the Pen

The first black and white American poets were women: Anne Bradstreet, a Puritan refugee from England who arrived in Massachusetts in 1630; and Phillis Wheatley, an African who was bought as a slave in 1761 by a master in Boston. Because it was virtually unheard of at that time for a woman to aspire to be a writer, Bradstreet's poems, collected in *The Tenth Muse Lately Sprung Up in America,* were published, without her knowledge, by her brother-in-law in London in 1650. Wheatley's *Poems on Various Subjects Religious and Moral* (1773) were also published in London, prefaced by various testimonials to establish their authenticity and the author's status as a prodigy. Both women wrote in a classical form, and in a tone of humble subservience to the presumably superior judgment of (white) men. Bradstreet concerned herself with her love for her children and husband, as well as homages to the queen of England; Wheatley wrote more public poems dedicated to political figures such as George Washington. Humility and feminine decorum were, however, a mask that occasionally slipped. In "The Prologue," Bradstreet defiantly wrote, "I am obnoxious to each carping tongue/Who says my hand a needle better fits"; these lines made her a foremother of many women writers in centuries to come who would also protest against their limiting domestic role (Gilbert and Gubar, 1996: 84). Wheatley's famous poem "On Being Brought from Africa to America" voices a daring warning against racial prejudice: "Remember, Christians, Negroes black as Cain/May be refined and join the Angelic train" (Gilbert and Gubar, 1996: 247).

Other genres of the colonial period practiced by women, but considered less threatening to the male domain, were letters and captivity narratives. *A Narrative of the Captivity and Restoration of Mrs. Mary Rowlandson* (1682) recounts the author's spiritual crisis when she was captured, with her three children, by a group of Wampanoag in New England. It reads like an adventure story, but it is also an episode in which a Christian woman is forced to test her beliefs and—somewhat—to revise her prejudices: she notes, for example, that the Wampanoag do not seem to know sexual violence. Rowlandson's story, like much early writing by Canadian women, offers readers a glimpse of women's lives on the frontier. Frances Brooke's novel *The History of Emily*

Montague (1769) draws a parallel between the colonization of Quebec and the position of women under the domination of British men. Anna Brownell Jameson published *Winter Studies and Summer Rambles,* a three-volume diary about life in Canada, in 1838. The sisters Susanna Moodie and Catharine Parr Traill expressed their diametrically opposed views of what it was like, for an English gentlewoman, to make a life in the colonies in *Roughing It in the Bush* (1852) and *The Backwoods of Canada* (1836). Moodie rejected life on the frontier, whereas Traill's letters preached that women created problems for themselves by not being subservient enough to their husbands (Fraser, 1991). Like Traill's, Abigail Adams's letters to her husband, John (who became the second president of the United States), give a vivid impression of the plight of a politician's wife at the time of the American Revolution. Adams is by turns submissive, as when she writes about domestic life, and adamant—as when she writers that the legislators for the new republic should "remember the ladies" lest women stage a rebellion of their own (Gilbert and Gubar, 1996: 231).

First Flowering: Abolitionists and Feminists

Writings protesting against domesticity and slavery proliferated during the nineteenth century, when campaigns for women's suffrage and the abolition of slavery gained momentum. These two issues were intertwined in the powerful speeches of Sojourner Truth, an illiterate slave whose words were recorded by her white friends. "Ain't I a Woman?" is a famous speech in which she analyzed the double standard by which "women" (meaning white women) were considered too delicate to take part in politics whereas black women like herself, a field slave who had borne thirteen children and had seen them sold, were not considered women at all. Elizabeth Cady Stanton was also a well-known figure on the lecturing circuit. It was Stanton who drafted a Declaration of Sentiments (modeled on the United States' Declaration of Independence) for the women's rights convention in Seneca Falls in 1848. Her autobiography *Eighty Years and More* (1898) documents her struggle for (white) women's suffrage.

Apart from speeches, nineteenth-century activist literature also included a considerable number of slave narratives, of which *The Narrative of the Life of Frederick Douglass, an American Slave* (1845) is probably best known. *Incidents in the Life of a Slave Girl* (1861) by Harriet Jacobs was written from a deliberately female perspective under the pseudonym Linda Brent. Jacobs mixed conventions of the slave narrative and the sentimental novel in order to touch the hearts of America's white mothers. Like Mary Rowlandson, she emphasizes her concern for her children and the protection of her virtue, realizing full well that in society's view, a slave woman's virtue is far less precious than the virtue of a middle-class white woman.

Jacobs and Truth are important voices from the nineteenth century, because the overwhelming majority of women writers of that era were white and middle-class. Of these, the writer with the widest popular reputation is Harriet Beecher Stowe, whose antislavery novel *Uncle Tom's Cabin; or, Life Among the Lowly* (1852) was highly effective and caused a storm of controversy, though today it is considered rather patronizing and sentimental. Stowe belonged to a generation that Nathaniel Hawthorne called "a darn mob of scribbling women," because they could earn their living by writing. Another member of this generation was Fanny Fern, whose novel *Ruth Hall* (1855) openly advocated financial independence for women. In this regard, Fern went further than the Transcendentalist philosopher Margaret Fuller, who in *Woman in the Nineteenth Century* (1845) had called for women's spiritual and intellectual independence from men. Fuller's feminism was infused with Transcendentalist ideas.

Nineteenth-century women's writing, then, reflected and was motivated by political causes—feminism and abolitionism—but it should also be said that these women's writing, and their public speaking, took place in a generally hostile climate. A "cult of true womanhood," as it has often been described, was in full swing at this time, and women's writing was deemed appropriate only if it concerned motherhood, the family, and domestic duties. The sentimental tradition therefore informs white and black women's writing, such as Frances Ellen Watkins Harper's *Iola Leroy, or Shadows Uplifted* (1892), an antislavery novel with a fair share of coincidences and tearful reunions.

Second Flowering: Modernism and Misogyny

Like her contemporary Walt Whitman, the poet Emily Dickinson was very much an original, and a forerunner of the modernist movement. Although her reclusive lifestyle and spiritual subject matter belong to the late nineteenth century, the formal innovations of her poetry link her with Marianne Moore, H. D. (Hilda Doolittle), Mina Loy, and other women poets in the circle of Ezra Pound and T. S. Eliot. Modernism, in part characterized by Eliot's doctrine of impersonality, was on the whole hostile to women and to the feminine. Yet these women poets, as well as the lesbian writer Gertrude Stein, brought to their art a dedication and a professionalism that echoed Dickinson and could not be ignored by the male establishment.

In addition to the white modernists (many of whom emigrated to Europe), there was also a surge of creativity among black women in the 1920s. This was the time of the Harlem renaissance, an African-American cultural movement that included such writers as Jessie Redmon Fauset, Nella Larsen, and Zora Neale Hurston. Larsen was a pioneer who (unlike her foremothers Harriet Jacobs and Frances Ellen Watkins Harper) explored black women's sexuality in her novellas *Quicksand* (1928) and *Passing* (1929). Hurston—an anthropologist as well as a writer—was revolutionary in her poetic use of the black vernacular, especially in her novel *Their Eyes Were Watching God* (1937).

In the early twentieth century, autobiographies by women from other nondominant groups began to appear. Mary Antin's *The Promised Land* documented her experience as a young Jewish woman emigrating from Russia to the United States. Zitkala-Sa (whose nontribal name was Gertrude Bonnin) published *The School Days of an Indian Girl* in *Atlantic Monthly* magazine in 1900, and Sui Sin Far (Edith Maud Eton) wrote *Leaves from the Mental Portfolio of an Eurasian* in 1909. By contrast, in Canada, where autobiographical writing had been most prominent to begin with, the novel now gained ground. Jeannette Duncan and Nellie McClung both wrote fiction that addressed the struggle for women's suffrage, Duncan in *The Imperialist* (1904) and McClung in *Purple Springs* (1924). Martha Ostenso's *Wild Geese* of 1925 returned to one of the most frequent themes in Canadian women's literature, the domination of men over women and nature; it echoed Frances Brooke's work and pointed forward to a work of 1972, Margaret Atwood's *Surfacing* (Fraser, 1991).

Between the 1930s and the 1960s, although the vote had been won, the social and intellectual climate for women's writing in North America was still not very favorable. Now, there was little feminist activity to inspire or complement women's literature, and writers who did have careers in fiction, poetry, drama, or journalism were often not writing specifically as women. This is not to say that they did not address female themes, or that their work cannot be read, with hindsight, as subversive in some ways. Mary McCarthy's *The Group* (1963) for example, is quite similar to Sylvia Plath's better known-novel *The Bell Jar* (1962), because both present a critical examination of women's dilemma—torn between education and ambition and the expectation of marriage and motherhood. In this respect they were like the earlier feminist writer Charlotte Perkins Gilman, who had protested against the stifling of women's talents by a patriarchal society in her story "The Yellow Wallpaper" (1892) and a utopian novel, *Herland* (1915). Women's sexual desires had also been explored by Kate Chopin in her classic novel of the southern United States, *The Awakening* (1899).

Several women writers gained honors and won literary prizes in midcentury. African-Americans such as the poet Gwendolyn Brooks and the playwright Lorraine Hansberry were very successful during the 1950s, as was the poet Elizabeth Bishop (who was a friend of another celebrated poet, Marianne Moore). Bishop articulated the attitude of many women writers of the period when she wrote in a letter that, although gender does matter in the making of art, it should play no role in how art is received: "art is art," and there is nothing to be gained from having separate categories for women's and men's writing (Gilbert and Gubar, 1996: 1667).

Third Flowering: Literature and Liberation

Since the advent of the women's liberation movement in the late 1960s, women have been writing in ever greater numbers and in every conceivable genre. Feminist criticism has developed as well, rediscovering earlier women's writing and reading it in new, feminist ways. For the first time in American theatrical history, there was a critical mass of women dramatists. Before the 1970s women had been prominent as actresses, but rarely as directors or playwrights. Susan Glaspell's *Alison's House* (1930), a dramatization of the life of Emily Dickinson, and Lillian Hellman's *The Children's Hour* (1934), controversial because it addressed lesbianism, had been among the few exceptions to the rule that theater was dominated by men. Today, that rule no longer holds. In 1977 *Uncommon Women and Others,* Wendy Wasserstein's play about college-educated women in a world hostile to their aspirations, was produced to critical acclaim, and in 1983 Marsha Norman won the Pulitzer Prize for *'night Mother.* In some ways *'night Mother* can be seen as a counter to the oedipal plays of Arthur Miller: it examines the mother-daughter relationship and ends with the daughter's suicide. Such a resolution is deliberately avoided in the African-American playwright Ntozake Shange's celebration of young black women's lives, *For Colored Girls Who Have Considered Suicide/When the Rainbow Is Enuf* (1976).

Black, white, Asian-American, Native American, and Chicana women have transformed the modern novel, which had, according to many critics, become increasingly stale and self-conscious in men's hands during the 1960s. Maxine Hong Kingston's *The Woman Warrior* (1977), for example, became one of the most-taught texts in universities in the United States; and in 1993 Toni Morrison was the first African-American to win the Nobel Prize for literature. Morrison's novels, such as *Sula* (1973) and *Beloved* (1987), address black feminist themes, as does the work of Alice Walker, who won a Pulitzer Prize for *The Color Purple* in 1983. The Chinese-American Amy Tan, the Native Americans Leslie Marmon Silko and Louise Erdrich, and Chicana writers like Sandra Cisneros and Gloria Anzaldúa have written fiction challenging not just gender stereotypes but also cultural and racial prejudice, in highly imaginative ways. By comparison, the important fiction of the women's movement itself—such as Marilyn French's *The Women's Room* (1978) and Marge Piercy's *Braided Lives* (1982)—now seems rather less radical in that it reveals the limitations of white feminism in the 1960s and 1970s.

Canadian women's writing is also strong in the area of fiction. Besides Margaret Atwood, who is still preeminent, there is Alice Munro, who shares with Atwood a distinctive blend of realism and gothic fantasy (Howells, 1987). There are also Margaret Laurence, Joan Barfoot, Marian Engel, and the Quebecois writers Anne Hébert, Nicole Brossard, and Marie-Claire Blais. Blaise's *Les Nuits de l'Underground/Nights in the Underground,* set in Montreal, is about lesbian women's lives, like much of Jane Rule's fiction. In the United States, too, the women's movement has brought lesbian writing out of the closet: Audre Lorde (who wrote *Zami: A New Spelling of My Name,*), Rita Mae Brown, and Sarah Schulman have all contributed to lesbian literature and history. Women's poetry has flourished in the works of African-Americans like Rita Dove (who served as poet laureate of the United States) and Lucille Clifton and the Hawaiian Cathy Song, and in the extensive oeuvre of Denise Levertov and—particularly—Adrienne Rich. Rich is a lesbian poet and essayist whose writing has in many ways charted the development of second-wave feminism, as in her collection *Diving into the Wreck* (1974), her meditation on motherhood *Of Woman Born* (1976), and her essays "Compulsory Heterosexuality and Lesbian Existence" and "When We Dead Awaken: Writing as Re-Vision" (1971). "When We Dead Awaken" begins by lamenting that the study of literature was dominated by, in Virginia Woolf's words, a "procession of the sons of educated men" (Gilbert and Gubar, 1996: 1981). Today, by contrast, the study and the production of literature are shared by a procession of educated and creative mothers and daughters, whose words are being read and heard the world over.

See Also

CULTURAL STUDIES; FEMINISM: FIRST-WAVE NORTH AMERICAN *and* SECOND-WAVE NORTH AMERICAN; LESBIAN DRAMA; LESBIAN WRITING, *all entries;* LITERARY THEORY AND CRITICISM; LITERATURE: OVERVIEW; LITERATURE: NORTH AMERICA—NOTE ON AFRICAN-AMERICAN, LATINA, AND NATIVE AMERICAN POETS; POETRY: OVERVIEW *and* FEMINIST THEORY AND CRITICISM; THEATER: *selected topics*

References and Further Reading

Carby, Hazel V. 1987. *Reconstructing womanhood: The emergence of the Afro-American woman novelist.* New York: Oxford University Press.

Fraser, Wayne. 1991. *The dominion of women: The personal and the political in Canadian women's literature.* New York: Greenwood.

Gilbert, Sandra M., and Susan Gubar. 1989. *No man's land: The place of the woman writer in the twentieth century.* 2 vols. New Haven, Conn.: Yale University Press.

———, eds., 1996. *The Norton anthology of literature by women: The traditions in English.* 2nd ed. New York: Norton.

Howells, Coral Ann. 1987. *Private and fictional worlds: Canadian women novelists of the 1970s and 1980s.* New York: Methuen.

Lauret, Maria. 1994. *Liberating literature: Feminist fiction in America.* New York: Routledge.

Moers, Ellen. 1977. *Literary women: The great writers.* New York: Doubleday.

Pryse, Marjorie, and Hortense Spillers, eds. 1985. *Conjuring: Black women, fiction, and literary tradition.* Bloomington: Indiana University Press.

Scheier, Libby, Sarah Sheard, and Eleanor Wachtel, eds. 1990. *Language in her eye: Writing and gender. Views by Canadian women writing in English.* Toronto: Coach House.

Wagner-Martin, Linda, and Cathy Davidson, eds. 1995. *The Oxford book of women's writing in the United States.* New York: Oxford University Press.

Zamora, Lois Parkinson, ed. 1998. *Contemporary American women writers: Gender, class, ethnicity.* New York: Longman.

Maria Lauret

LITERATURE: North America—Note on African-American, Latina, and Native American Poets

On January 20, 1993, Maya Angelou, who is African-American, addressed the audience at the inauguration of President Clinton, reading one of her own poems, "On the Pulse of Morning." We might see this occasion as signifying a greater recognition of women poets of color, who have often been marginalized in North American literature in three senses: as women, as members of minorities, and as poets—since in modern times poetry has tended to be far less popular than novels, stories, and drama.

These notes on African-American, Latina and Chicana, and Native American poets include some resources that can serve as an introduction to voices who are important, distinctive, individualistic, and rewarding but, for some readers, perhaps unfamiliar. In multiethnic countries such as the United States and Canada, people of color, minorities, may make up nations within a nation, and their poets might not always be counted within the mainstream. For example, Arna Bontemps says of African-American poetry:

> [It] sometimes seems hard to pin down.... From spirituals and gospels songs to blues, jazz and bebop, it is likely to be marked by certain special riff, an extra glide, a kick where none is expected, and a beat for which there is no notation. It follows the literary traditions of the language it uses, but it does not hold them sacred. As a result, there has been a tendency for critics to put it in a category by itself, outside the main body of American poetry. (1974: xv)

African-Americans

Harper and Walton's anthology of African-American poetry (2000) covers two centuries of poets and their works. Among the earliest women is Lucy Terry Prince (1724–1821), a semiliterate slave girl who wrote "Bar Fight." An important figure from this time is Phillis Wheatley (c. 1754–1784), who was born in Senegal, West Africa, and brought to Boston in 1761. Her *Poems on Various Subjects, Religious and Moral* was printed posthumously in 1793, making her the first African-American to publish a volume of literature

The poet and activist Francis Harper was born free in Baltimore in 1825. She worked with the Maine Anti-Slavery Society, the Woman's Christian Temperance movement, the American Equal Rights Association, the National Council of Women, and the National Association of Colored Women and was also involved in the Underground Railroad (which was not an actual railway but a cooperative system that spirited fugitive slaves to northern states or Canada). Harper's *Poems on Miscellaneous Subjects* was published in 1854, with a preface by the abolitionist William Lloyd Garrison.

Ward's anthology of African-American poets (1997), which is organized in periods spanning 250 years, begins with oral poetry by slaves, including spirituals—gospel hymns—such as "Were You There?" and "Do Lord." A second period, from 1746 to 1865, described as "voices before freedom," includes Prince, Wheatley, and Ann Plato (born around 1820). A third period, from 1865 to 1910, includes the work of Henrietta Cordelia Ray (1852?—1916).

For the twentieth century especially, Ward's chronology indicates when a poet arrived on the literary scene. Many of the women included—such as Margaret Walker and some of her contemporaries—continued to write well into a later period, and indeed some are still productive.

Ward designates 1910 to 1960 as the early twentieth century. This period includes Anna Spencer, Georgia Douglas Johnson, May Miller, Clarissa Scott Delany, Gwendolyn Bennett, Margaret Walker, Margaret Esse Danner, Gwendolyn Brooks, and Naomi Long Madgett. Of these, Brooks (born in 1917) is particularly well known; she was the first African-American to win the Pulitzer Prize (in 1950, for her book *Annie Allen*), and in 1968 she was named the poet laureate of Illinois.

Ward characterizes the period beginning in the 1960s as "voices from a new age." One of these voices is Maya Angelou (born in 1928); others are Elma Stuckey, Mari Evans, Sarah Webster Fabio, Audre Lorde, Sonia Sanchez, Lucelle Clifton, Jane Cortez, June Jordan, Julia Field, Nikki Giovanni, and Alice Walker. During the 1980s and 1990s, African-American poets have included Colleen McElroy, Sybil Kein, Angela Jackson, Harryette Mullen, and Rita Dove, who was a poet laureate of the United States. Another contemporary poet, Sapphire, published several books, including *Black Wings and Blind Angels.*

Though we cannot look individually at all these poets, we can focus on a few. Margaret Walker, for instance, was born in 1915 in Birmingham, Alabama, and died in 1998. Her first collection of poems, *For My People,* which celebrates the African-American experience, won the Yale University Younger Poets Award. Walker also wrote a novel, *Jubilee,* published in 1966; a biography of the American author Richard Wright, *Daemonic Genius,* published in 1988; and two other volumes of verse. The lesbian feminist and poet Audre Lorde (1934–1992) writes compellingly, often in a sad or melanholy tone. Lorde tends to be succinct, but although she is frequently a writer of few words, those words have bite and convey a message. Sonia Sanchez (born in 1934) published a collection of poems and vignettes, *Shake Loose My Skin,* in 1999. A selection of Nikki Giovanni's poetry was published in 1996, with an introduction by Virgina Fowler. Fowler referred to Giovanni and other black poets as "daughters of the diaspora"—a description that can include Latinas and Native Americans as well.

Latinas and Chicanas

The Chicana poet Gloria Anzaldúa (born in 1942) has written a great deal of poetry drawing on her experiences as a Mexican-American, including *Chiautlyotl, Woman Alone* (1986); *The Cannibal's Canción;* and *La Curandera.* The anthology *!Florincanto Si! A Collection of Latina Poetry,* edited by Bryce Milligan, Mary Guerrero Milligan, and Angela De Hoyos (1988), includes Anzaldúa as well as many other Latina and Chicana poets: Majorie Agosin, Norma E. Cantú, Sandra Cisneros, Rosario Ferré, Rita Magdaleno, Anabella Paiz, Beatriz Rivera, Evangelina Vigil-Pinon, Alma Luz Villanueva, and Bernice Zamora.

Espada's anthology *El Coro: A Chorus of Latino and Latina Poetry* (1997) includes Sandra Cesneros, Sandra María Esteves, Diana Garcia, Magdalena Gomez, and Elizabeth Perez, among others. Another anthology, Gonzalez's *Touching the Fire: Fifteen Poets of Today's Latino Renaissance* (1998), presents works by Mexican-Americans, Puerto Ricans, and Cuban-Americans; the poets represented include Silvia Curbelos and Sandra M. Castillo.

Native Americans

Janet Witalec's important anthology *Native North American Literary Companion,* published in 1995 and 1998, covers other genres as well as poetry. Paula Gunn Allen (born in 1939) is one of the writers and poets featured in this collection. According to Allen, "The purpose of traditional American Indian literature is never simply pure self-expression. The private soul at any public wall is a concept alien to American Indian thought." Rather, "The tribes seek—through song, ceremony, beyond, sacred stories (myths), and tales—to embody, articulate, and share . . . to actualize, in language, those truths that give humanity its greatest significance and dignity." She describes her own poetry as having "a haunted sense to it and it has a sorrow and grievingness" (15).

Witalec's collection also includes Jeannette Armstrong, the first Native novelist in Canada, who born in 1948 on the Okanagan Reserve in British Columbia. Beth Brant is of Mohawk ancestry; her first published volume was *Mohawk Trail.* Elizabeth Cook-Lynn, whose grandparents were also writers, was born on a Sioux reservation. Witalec notes of Cook-Lynn, "In her work she implements a variety of perspectives and forms such as verse, narrative, oral history and story" (109). Louise Erdrich, who is of Chippewa and German-American descent, published her first two books—*Jacklight: A Volume of Poetry* and *Love Medicine: A Novel*—when she was just 13 years old. Joy Harjo—who was born in 1959 in Tulsa, Oklahoma, and is of Muskogee and Creek heritage—has published two poetry collections: *Secrets from the Center of the World* and *In Mad Love and War.* Witalec also presents, among others, Linda Hogan, Lee Maracle, Wendy Rose, Leslie Marmon Silko, Luci Tapahonso, and Anna Lee Walters, who have all made significant contributions as poets.

See Also

LITERATURE: NORTH AMERICA; POETRY: OVERVIEW; POETRY: FEMINIST THEORY AND CRITICISM

References and Further Reading

Angelou, M. 1994. *The complete collected poems of Maya Angelou.* New York: Random House. ("On the Pulse of the Morning" appears in this volume.)

Bontemps, A. 1974. *American Negro poetry.* New York: Hill and Wang.

Clifton, L. 1980. *Good woman: Poems and a memoir 1969–1980.* New York: BOA Editions.

Dove, R. 1993. *Rita Dove: Selected poems.* New York: Vintage.

Espada, M. 1997. *El coro: A chorus of Latino and Latina poetry.* Boston: University of Massachusetts Press.

Giovanni, N. 1996. *The selected poems of Nikki Giovanni.* New York: Morrow.

González, R. 1998. *Touching the fire: Fifteen poets of today's Latino renaissance.* New York: Anchor.

Harper, M, and A. Walton. 2000. *The Vintage book of African-American poetry: 200 years of vision, struggle, power, beauty, and triumph from fifty outstanding poets.* New York: Vintage.

Sanchez, S. 1999. *Shake loose my skin.* Boston: Beacon.

Simonson, R., and S. Walker. 1988. *The Graywolf annual five: Multicultural literacy.* Saint Paul, Minn.: Graywolf.

Milligan, B., M. Milligan, and A. De Hoyos. 1998. *!Floricanto si! A collection of Latina poetry.* New York: Penguin.

Sapphire. 1999. *Black wings and blind angels: Poems by Sapphire.* New York: Knopf.

Ward, J. 1997. *Trouble the water: 250 Years of African-American poetry.* New Yor'k: Penquin.

Wheatley, P. (1969). *Poems of Phillis Wheatley: A native African and a slave.* Boston, Mass.: Applewood.

Witalec, J. 1998. *Native North American literary companion.* New York: Visible Ink.

Barbara K. Curry

LITERATURE: Novel

See NOVEL.

LITERATURE: Persian

Although the history of Iranian literature goes back 1,000 years, it is only in the modern age—the period since the early nineteenth century—that women have gained recognition as contributors. The traditional patriarchal society and Islamic laws interpreted by and from the viewpoint of men ensured that women were kept secluded within the walls of their homes, their bodies veiled and hidden, their voices muted. Access to literacy was limited to a minority of women in the court and the upper class. If women were attempting to express themselves through literature in premodern Iran, neither they nor their works reached farther than their homes, where their involvement was confined to the oral tradition of plays and poetry, recited and performed at female gatherings.

Nineteenth Century and Earlier

It is true that the names of several exceptional women poets have survived, such as Rabe'e Ghazdari (tenth century), Mahasti Ghanjavi (twelfth century), Jahan Malak Khatun (fourteenth century), and Khadijeh Soltan Daghestani (seventeenth century). However, these women are remembered, in general, not so much for their poetry as for transgressing boundaries safeguarded by men, who accused them of engaging in forbidden love affairs. The most famous of the traditional women poets in Iran is perhaps Zarrin-Taj Bareghani (1817–1852), known as Tahereh Qorratol-Eyn, who was executed for her belief in the Bahai religion. She violated tradition by leaving her home and her designated role as wife and mother to become a religious scholar, unveiling, entering the male world, giving sermons in public, and expressing her religious devotion through her poetry (Milani, 1992).

The increase in cultural and political interactions between Iran and Europe in the early nineteeth century initiated a gradual transformation of traditional society and began the discourse of modernity. It is at this time that intellectuals first raised questions regarding traditional conventions and the role of women, opening debates between modernist intellectuals, who advocated a liberated woman like the western model, and upholders of the long-standing Islamic restrictions. Women's writing about their position in society emerged in the midst of these debates. In 1894, in response to a misogynous text written by a man (*Ta'dib al-Neswan,* "Disciplining Women"), Bibi Khanum Astarabadi wrote *Ma'ayeb al-Rejal* ("Vices of Men"). Drawing from classical poetry and religious texts, Astarabadi scrutinized men's behavior in her own society. In the early 1900s, a Qajar princess, Taj-ol Saltaneh, wrote *Khaterat,* a memoir in which she criticizes men for perpetuating the situation of women in Iran (Najmabadi, 1993).

Early Twentieth Century

The period of constitutional revolution (1906–1909) was a turning point: schools for women were established, women's journals were published, and women participated in protests against the absolute power of the ruler and the involvement of foreign countries (Britain and Russia). Thus, the social movement was an opening for women to enter the literary scene.

The first published woman poet, Parvin E'tesami (1907–1941), was born during this new era of modernity in Iran. Her father, a man of letters and one of the intellectuals who advocated women's liberation, may have provided a channel for her at a time when only men's work was printed. In her collection of poems, *Divan* (1935), E'tesami delineates for the public the mundane details of women's secluded domestic lives.

The Pahlavi Regime

The Pahlavi regime (1925–1979) was a time of rapid societal change as the nation aspired to modernity and westernization, and women were seen as the embodiment of the new Iran. One of the most significant decrees of this period was a law mandating unveiling, issued by Reza Shah Pahlavi in 1936. Ostensibly, this law facilitated women's entry into the public domain, although critics have seen it as another way of controlling a woman's body. The rapid changes occurring at this time resulted in a complex duality for women: on the surface they were unveiled, modern, and western, but they were still firmly rooted in the traditional patriarchal restraints (Najmabadi, 1991).

E'tesami's poetry broke through the wall of silence that had surrounded women's "interior" in the sense of their domestic lives; later in this era women began to speak of their "interior" in the sense of the body and the soul. Forugh Farrokhzad (1935–1967), the most celebrated woman poet of Iran, reflects on her awareness of herself as a woman and an individual in three collections of poems, *Asir* ("Captive," 1955), *Divar* ("Wall," 1956), and *Tavalodi Digar* ("A Rebirth," 1964). Her oeuvre represents a transgression of taboos against writing about a woman's body, sexuality, or ideas. Other women poets of this period include Simin Behbahani, (b. 1927), Zan-Dokht Shirazi (1911–1952), Jaleh Esfahani (b. 1921), Parvin Dowladabadi (b. 1922), and Tahereh Saffarzadeh (b. 1936). Saffarzadeh represented a new trend: although she did share her contemporaries' concerns about women's position, she voluntarily took up the veil as a protest against western influence and cultural imperialism, and she framed her expression within the tenets of Islam (Milani, 1992).

Initially, it was as poets that women carved out a space for themselves in literature. Despite the fact that storytelling was traditionally a woman's domain and women had for generations recounted tales to their children, it was not until 1947 that a woman, Simin Daneshvar, published a collection of stories, *Atash-e Khamush* ("Extinguished Fire"). Daneshvar's later published writing includes *Shahri Chon Behesht* ("A City Like Paradise," 1961); a celebrated novel, *Sauvashun* (1969); and three works published after the Islamic revolution of 1979, *Be Ki Salam Konam?* ("Whom Should I Salute?"), *Jazireh-ye Sargardani* ("Island of the Lost"), and *Az Parandeha-ye Mohajer Bepors* ("Ask the Migrant Birds"). Through the genre of the story, Daneshvar depicts the lives of ordinary women and their distinctly female problems. Her powerful women characters are active agents in their society (Milani, 1992).

Women who followed Daneshvar, writing prose during the Pahlavi era and the era of the Islamic revolution, include Mahshid Amirshahi, with *Kucheh-ye Bonbast* ("The Blind Alley," 1966), *Sare-Bibi Khanom* ("Bibi Khanom's Starling," 1968), *Ba'd Az Ruz-e Akhar* ("After the Last Day,"1969), and an autobiography that she began after the revolution: *Dar Hazar* ("At Home") and *Dar Safarr* ("Away from Home"). Another writer of this time is Shahrnoosh Parsipour, author of *Sag va Zemestan-e Boland* ("The Dog and a Long Winter," 1970) and *Avizeha-ye Bolur* ("Crystal Earrings," 1977), and two works published after the revolution: *Tuba Va Ma'na-ye Shab* ("Tuba and the Meaning of Night") and *Zanan Bedune Mardan* ("Women Without Men"). A third author, Goli Taraghi, wrote *Khab-e Zemestani* ("Winter Sleep," 1973) and *Bozorg-Banu-ye Ruh-e Man* ("The Grand Lady of My Soul," 1979).

The Islamic Revolution

The revolution of 1979 had an immense impact on the position of women. During the Pahlavi era, as noted above, women had been expected to embody modern western ideals. With the Islamization of society—a direct reaction against the contradictions of the Pahlavi era—women and the female body were still a focal symbol, but they now symbolized the ideal Islamic woman. Obligatory veiling and similar measures were setbacks in women's lives and women's position in society. However, many women continued to write and publish despite these new problems. In fact, the number of women writers increased dramatically after the revolution. Vulnerable and veiled, women spoke powerfully through their writing and used writing as a way to search for the roots of their difficulties. Women were active in several literary genres, but short stories and novels provided the best outlet for their discoveries. Drawing on their own experiences—the psychological dimensions of their existence and their externally controlled bodies—women have been writing the stories of their lives in various innovative narrative styles.

Although some of these women were established writers before the revolutionary era, many others began their literary careers after the revolution. Contemporary women writers include Moniru Ravanipour, with such works as *Ahle-Gharg* ("People of Gharg"), *Sangha-ye Sheytani* ("Satanic Stones"), *Dele Fulad* ("The Iron Heart"), and *Koli Kenar-e Atash* ("The Gypsy by the Fire"); Ghazaleh Alizadeh, with *Do Manzareh* ("Two Views"), *Khanehe Edrisiha* ("Edrisi's House"), and *Chahar Rah* ("Crossroad"); and Mihan Bahrami, who has published individual stories and a collection, *Heyvan* ("Animal").

The 1990s and Today

A younger generation of promising women writers, published in the 1990s, includes Shiva Arastui, Farkhondeh Hajizadeh, Zoya Pirzad, Banafsheh and Khatereh Hejazi, Farkhondeh Aghai, Fereshteh Sari, Farideh Golbu, and Mansureh Sharifzadeh (Vatanabadi and Khorrami, 2000). Women writers have been supported by a significant increase in the number of women readers, and by the emergence of publishing houses such as Nashr-e Roshangaran that predominantly issue works by women.

Contemporary Iranian women are now successful not only in literature but in all creative fields, including cinema, theater, and the fine arts. Their road has not been smooth, and they have been constrained by a patriarchal society in general and by specific institutions and laws, such as those requiring veiling, then unveiling, and then reveiling. But women's voices, once muted and secret, are a distinct and powerful force in the public domain of Iran.

See Also

HOUSEHOLDS AND FAMILIES: MIDDLE EAST AND NORTH AFRICA; FEMINISM: MIDDLE EAST; FEMINISM: NORTH AFRICA; ISLAM; LITERATURE: OVERVIEW; POETRY: OVERVIEW; VEILING

References and Further Reading

Afshar, Haleh, 1998. *Islam and feminisms: An Iranian case study.* New York: St. Martin's.

Bayat, Mangol. 1978. Women and revolution in Iran, 1905–1911. In Lois Beck and Nikki Keddie, eds., *Women in the Muslim world,* 295–308. Cambridge, Mass.: Harvard University Press.

Lewis, Franklin, and Farzin Yazdanfar, eds. 1996. *In a voice of their own.* Costa Mesa, Calif.: Mazda.

Milani, Farzaneh. 1992. *Veils and words: The emerging voices of Iranian women writers.* Syracuse, N.Y.: Syracuse University Press.

Moghadam, Valentine. 1993. *Modernizing women: Gender and social change in the Middle East.* Boulder, Col.: Lynne Rienner.

Moghissi, Haideh. 1994. *Populism and feminism in Iran: Women's struggle in a male-defined revolutionary movement.* New York: St. Martin's.

Najmabadi, Afsaneh. 1991. Hazards of modernity and morality: Women, state, and ideology in contemporary Iran. In Deniz Kandiyoti, ed., *Women, Islam, and state,* 48–76. Philadelphia, Pa.: Temple University Press.

———. 1993. Veiled discourse, unveiled bodies. *Feminist Studies* 19(3: Fall): 487–518.

Nashat, Guity, ed. 1983. *Women and revolution in Iran.* Boulder, Col.: Westview.

Rahimieh, Nasrin. 1992. Beneath the veil: The revolution in Iranian women's writing. In Anthony Purdy, ed., *Literature and the body,* 95–115. Amesterdam and Atlanta, Ga.: Rodopi.

Sullivan, Soraya Paknazar, trans. 1991. *Stories by Iranian women since the revolution.* Austin: Center for Middle East Studies, University of Texas at Austin.

Vatanabadi, Shouleh, and Mehdi Khorrami, eds. 2000. *A feast in the mirror: Stories by contemporary Iranian women.* Boulder, Col.: Lynne Rienner.

Shouleh Vatanabadi

LITERATURE: Poety

See LESBIAN CONTEMPORARY POETRY; POETRY: OVERVIEW; and POETRY: FEMINIST THEORY AND CRITICISM.

LITERATURE: Romantic Fiction

See ROMANTIC FICTION.

LITERATURE: Russia

Since the collapse of the Soviet Union in 1991, Russia's women writers are no longer writing within a cultural and political context bound by the ideological rigor of the preceding 75 years. Their writing—whether it involves experimentation with new forms and narrative techniques or a new consciousness of gender and women's roles—mirrors the enormous changes that are taking place in post-Soviet society as a whole. Their writing is produced against the backdrop of an economy that is now largely market-driven, and of a nation in the throes of rethinking its relationship to its own past and to the West.

History

During the Soviet era, the arts functioned as an arm of the Communist Party. In 1932, an artistic credo known as socialist realism set forth how the arts, including literature, were to serve the state. The early architects of cultural policy wanted literature to point the way to a "radiant future" by providing heroes and optimistic endings, clearly demarcating the forces of good and evil, and avoiding psychological conflict. Private life and its attendant emotions were seen as holdovers of western decadence, detracting from the new socialist order. Soviet men and women were exhorted to merge private life with public life, and personal desires with the larger goals of building the new state. Socialist realism was the official doctrine until the Gorbachev era, although it was relaxed somewhat during World War II and the "thaw"—the liberalization that followed the death of Stalin in 1953. For the most part, Soviet writers produced the presecriptive literature the Party demanded, or they rejected the official literary establishment entirely by publishing through nonofficial channels, or—in the great majority of cases—they worked within the official literary establishment but tried to extract small concessions from the Party that would enable them to write more critically and truthfully.

Soviet rule had a number of consequences for women's writing, one of which has been a reluctance to speak about issues of gender. While many authors, such as Vera Panova and I. Grekova, wrote about women's lives, the family, and domestic issues, most stopped short of identifying themselves as "women writers." For example, Natalia Baranskaia's novella *A Week Like Any Other Week (Nedelia kak nedelia,* 1969), which chronicles a week in the life of a woman who is attempting to work and raise her family in Soviet society—was heralded in the West as a feminist tract, but Baranskaia herself denied any feminist leanings. The term "woman writer" (*pisatel'nitsa*) had extremely pejorative connotations, including a suggestion of lightweight, sentimental prerevolutionary romance. Thus women tried to put as much distance as possible between themselves and what was perceived as "women's literature."

Another effect of Soviet rule was the development of certain ideologically correct stereotypes, to which both women and men were meant to conform. The mold for a woman was a strong, desexualized socialist worker marching cheerfully beside her husband but retaining the qualities of the nurturing, semisanctified mother—a figure from

Russia's religious and folkloric past. The image of the nurturing mother was periodically invoked by Soviet leaders (especially Stalin) for propaganda and to mobilize national sentiment during war, famines, and purges.

Prose Writers

By the 1970s, Russia's women writers, like many Soviet writers in general, were beginning to move away from imposed artistic credos. In particular, Liudmila Petrushevskaia, who remains a major voice, published works that in several ways ran counter to the expectations of Party ideologues. First, she included characters who did not officially "exist" in the Soviet Union—the "lost people"—and chronicled their lonely, uprooted lives; her female protagonists are alienated or disengaged even from their own narratives. Second, she engaged in dialogue with the male masters of classical nineteenth-century Russian literature. In her novella *Our Crowd (Svoi krug),* for instance, she rewrote the story of Dostoyevsky's underground man, turning him into a female narrator. Third (like many younger writers of the 1990s), she reworked many traditional Russian myths that had helped shaped women's image. For instance, in her novel *The Time: Night (Vremia noch',* 1992) she turned the venerated image of the mother into a manipulative, vampire-like figure whose "love" suffocates everything and everyone in its path.

Gorbachev's policy of *glasnost*—candor—first enunciated for writers in 1986, opened the door for freer expression of ideas. This development coincided with the beginning of the literary careers of writers such as Tatiana Tolstaia, Valeriia Narbikova, Marina Palei, Nina Sadur, and Liudmila Ulitskaia. Tolstaia's career, however, suggests that even under glasnost there was still resistance in certain circles to writing that departed radically from socialist norms. Tolstaia's first vignettes and monologues were not well received by publishers and critics, who could not understand why she created fictional types who were of little consequence for Soviet society. Her protagonists—dreamers, misfits, old women remembering long-lost love, mamma's boys—are indeed a throwback to prerevolutionary days, as is her highly figurative prose style: Soviet prose was expected to be linguistically accessible to all.

Nevertheless, many writers whose careers coincided with glasnost experimented with new themes and narrative tropes in the late 1980s. The fiction of Narbikova, Palei, Petrushevskaia, Nina Gorlanova, Larisa Vaneeva, Svetlana Vasilenko, Iulia Voznesenskaia, and Tolstaia herself (among others) has taken up images of the body and has searched for new heroines. The sudden appearance of bodily functions in women's writing is a sharp contrast to the sanitized Soviet ideology, and the body often functions as a trope. Tolstaia, for example, describes pre-Soviet bodies that symbolize social and psychological displacement; and critics have suggested that in Petrushevskaia's prose, bodily functions and acts become metonyms for the collapse of a larger moral order. In Marina Palei's story "Kabiria from the Obvodnyi Canal" ("Kabiria s Obvodnogo kanala," 1991), the body becomes a site for the tenacity of life in the face of poverty and disease; *joie de vivre* transcends ideology as Palei's protagonist, Monka, dying of cancer, still ponders what color dress and lipstick she should wear. Palei creates a new type of post-Soviet heroine, whose unabashed delight in her body and in amorous adventures defies the sexual repression of Soviet socialist romances.

Many Russian women writers in the post-Soviet era are seeking new prototypes and new heroines. In some cases—as in Liudmila Ulitskaia's novel *Sonechka* (1992)—an author experiments with incorporating the traditional mother figure into post-Soviet reality, attempting to integrate the qualities of this figure into daily life and to ennoble and enable women rather than put them on a pedestal.

Some female prototypes in post-Soviet women's fiction are a result of the appearance of pulp fiction. As readers—looking for a respite from the economic and political problems of a country in transtion—have been increasingly drawn to popular light fiction, new protagonists have emerged. One example is "Anastasiia Kamenskaia," the woman protagonist of a series of 21 police detective novels written since 1992 by Aleksandra Marinina, a former lieutenant-colonel in the police. "Kamenskaia" is thoroughly undomesticated and has few of the qualities of traditional Russian or Soviet heroines. Rather, her outstanding traits are logic and intelligence—sitting at her computer, she lets her male assistants do the legwork; then she solves the case through cold, hard reasoning. Polina Dashkova has also written successful mass-market detective fiction.

Poetry

In general, the post-Soviet era has been a good time for Russian women poets. New publishing houses have provided new channels; moreover, increased contact with western feminists and the discovery and publication of some lost works by eighteenth- and nineteenth-century women poets have contributed to an atmosphere conducive to poetry and have given women broader experiences that find expression in poetry. However, like women prose writers, Russia's contemporary writers of poetry are noticeably reluctant to be called "women poets" (*poetessy*); according to Stephanie Sandler (2001), none of these women "makes genuine and complete sense outside the context of... male contemporaries and precursors."

Among the voices of the 1990s are Bella Akhmadulina, Tatiana Bek, Inna Lisnianskaia, Iunna Morits, Olesia Nikolaeva, Ol'ga Sedakova, Tat'iana Shcherbina, and Elena Shvarts. Again like the prose writers, these women are engaged in the often complicated process of reworking the Russian past and their own identity as Russian poets in post-Soviet society. Many of them find contemporary post-Soviet reality and the persistent questions about the direction of post-Soviet society problematic and disturbing. Some, such as Ol'ga Sedakova, have chosen to distance themselves from the present and re-create the poetry of the past. Sedakova is fairly typical of Russian women poets whose traditional response to ideology and to the various "isms" of the twentieth century has been to write apolitical verse. Others, though, have taken the opportunity to shed some of the ideological baggage of the Soviet era. Traditionally, Russian poets have held a special place in the national consciousness, becoming—as Anna Akhmatova did during World War II—spokeswomen for an entire nation. Poets such as Shcherbina now welcome the chance to free themselves from the historical image of women as bearers and articulators of their country's suffering.

See Also

DETECTIVE FICTION; FEMINISM: COMMONWEALTH OF INDEPENDENT STATES; HOUSEHOLDS AND FAMILIES: COMMONWEALTH OF INDEPENDENT STATES; LITERATURE: OVERVIEW; LITERATURE: EASTERN EUROPE; LITERATURE: UKRAINE; POETRY: OVERVIEW; WOMEN'S STUDIES: COMMONWEALTH OF INDEPENDENT STATES

References and Further Reading

Barker, Adele, and Jehanne Gheith, eds. 2001. *A history of women's writing in Russia.* Cambridge: Cambridge University Press.

Gessen, Masha, ed. and trans. 1995. *Half a revolution: Contemporary fiction by Russian women.* Pittsburgh, Pa.: Cleis.

Goscilo, Helena. 1996. *Dehexing sex: Russian womanhood during and after glasnost.* Ann Arbor: University of Michigan Press.

———, ed. 1993. *Fruits of her plume: Essays on contemporary Russian women's culture.* Armonk, N.Y.: Sharpe.

———. 1995. *Lives in transit: A collection of recent Russian women's writing.* Dana Point, Calif.: Ardis.

Kelly, Catriona. 1994. *A history of Russian women's writing 1820–1992.* Oxford: Oxford University Press.

Nepomnyashchy, Catharine Theimer. 1999. Markets, mirrors, and mayhem: Aleksandra Marinina and the rise of the new Russian detektive. In Adele Barker, ed., *Consuming Russia: Popular culture, sex, and society since Gorbachev,* 161–191. Durham, N.C.: Duke University Press.

Sandler, Stephanie. 2001. Women's poetry since the sixties. In Adele Barker and Jehanne Gheith, eds., *A history of women's writing in Russia.* Cambridge: Cambridge University Press.

———, ed. 1999. *Rereading Russian poetry.* New Haven, Conn.: Yale University Press.

Women's view. 1992. In *Glas: New Russian writing,* Vol. 3. Moscow: Russlit; and Somerville, Mass.: Zephyr.

Adele Barker

LITERATURE: Science Fiction

See SCIENCE FICTION.

LITERATURE: South Asia

The history of women's writing in the Indian subcontinent, as elsewhere in the world, is only recently coming to light. Even a casual glance at women's writing in the south Asian region today reveals a wealth of forms and genres, an intricate interweaving of the political and the personal, a range of subjects and ideas, and often the heavy hand of official and unofficial censorship. The conditions under which women wrote in earlier times may not necessarily have been very different from what they are today, but clearly the environment in which such writing is produced and received has changed considerably. Today, south Asia, and particularly India, offers a vigorous publishing scene in which women's writing occupies a place of considerable importance. Women writers have made a name for themselves, both in their own countries and internationally. Every major publisher in India, Pakistan, Bangladesh, Sri Lanka, Nepal, Bhutan, or the Maldives has books on and by women as a major part of its list. However, even the somewhat patchy history of women's writing that is available to us at present shows that these gains have not come easily: women have often had to battle against tremendous odds to make their voices heard.

Early Writings

The earliest known anthology of women's literature, dating back to the sixth century B.C.E., is the *Therigatha,* a collection of songs composed and sung by Buddhist nuns. The 522 surviving verses were written down much later, in 80 B.C.E., but the original poets are known to have been contemporaries of Buddha. Another important collection of writing by women is the work of the Sangam poets (100 B.C.E. to 250 C.E.), who wrote in Tamil. Of the 2,381 surviving poems of this period, 154 are by women; in addition, about 102 are anonymous, and some of these could also have been by women. In general, the songs in the *Therigatha* focus on a quest for nirvana, or release; the Sangam women poets turn their attention to plants, animals, nature, and everyday relationships of love and caring. It should be noted that our knowledge of these early periods is sketchy.

Beginning in the eighth century C.E., an important tradition of women's writing, known as *bhakti,* spread through Karnataka, Maharashtra, Gujarat, and Rajasthan; at a later stage, its sweep also took in Kashimr and Punjab, as well as some parts of Bengal and Assam. The best-known exponent of *bhakti* is Mirabai (c. 1498–1565), who came from a royal family in Rajasthan; but many others—such as Janabai, Gangasati, Akkamahadevi, and Lal Ded—had walked this path before her and would do so after her. Literally, *bhakti* means devotion; this movement drew in a vast number of the poor and marginalized because it did away with the trappings of institutionalized religion, allowing people to relate directly to their god. A large number of *bhakti* poets were women who rejected the bonds of home, family, and institutionalized religion, preferring to seek god—often in the guise of a lover—directly; they also rejected the stranglehold of Sanskrit, considered the language of high literature.

It is believed that during what has come to be known as the Mughal period, women, particularly those from royal families, were well versed in literature and that many wrote their own compositons. A woman who stands out among these is Gul Badan Begum (1523–1603), the daughter of the Mughal king Babur; she wrote the *Humayun Nama,* a much acclaimed history of the reign of her brother Humayun. Apart from women at court, there were others, the *tawaifs,* or courtesans, who sang and danced and were generally regarded as women of great independence and learning. *Tawaifs* composed and often sang their own verses. Two of the best-known women from this time are Umrao Jan and Mahlaga Bai. A woman who created a controversy that lasted into the early twentieth century was the Telugu courtesan Muddupalini, whose erotic epic, *Radhika Santwanam* ("Appeasing Radhika"), was republished by another woman, Bangalore Nagarathnamma, in 1910 and was subsequently banned by the colonial authorities for its supposed pornographic content.

The Modern Period

By the time of Muddupalini, the British had already arrived on the shores of the subcontinent; over time, relations that began as trade and commerce were transformed into power and rulership. In the years to come, upper-class and upper-caste women would be privileged while the voices of "other" women would be marginalized; and Indian languages were also marginalized because the British closed many indigenous schools and brought in English education. Nonetheless, women continued to write, often facing opposition not only from the colonial powers but also from their own men. These women wrote autobiographies (two of the best known are *Amar Jiban,* 1868, by Rashsundari Debi; and *Amar Katha,* 1912, by Binodini Dasi, an actress), novels (for example *Suguna, Kamala,* c. 1887–1888, by Kruppa Sathianandan, who lived from 1862 to 1894), political tracts, and so on.

During the social reform movement of the nineteenth century, and, later, during the nationalist movement of the early twentieth century, women writers continued to address and resist some dominant discourses. Many issues of the reform movement—including women's education, remarriage by widows, and religious reform—were reflected in the writings of women such as Tarabai Shinde (c. 1850–1910) and Pandita Ramabai (1858–1922).

An important development for writers in the 1920s and 1930s was the founding of the Progressive Writers Association, whose membership included some women—for example, Ismat Chugtai. From the 1950s on, a traumatic event shaped much writing by women such as Chugtai, Quratulain Hyder, Jyotirmoyee Debi, and Krishna Sobti: this was the partition of India in 1947, which tore apart the fabric of social life in north and east India. In later years, social movements of all kinds—including peasant rebellions, protests against rising prices, land reform, and, later, a widespread and growing women's movement—were the context for much women's writing.

In the aftermath of the partitioning of India, what had until then been a shared history became divided. The subcontinent, which is much of the region we now call south Asia, became India and Pakistan; in the 1970s, a third country, Bangladesh, would be created there. Ceylon (Sri Lanka), Nepal, Bhutan,and the Maldives are also part of this geographical region. Women's writing in the different countries now followed somewhat separate courses, with the freedom to write being more or less circumscribed according to the laws of each place. In some ways, women's writing was most viable in India, which was large and relatively prosperous and had been formed, politically, as a democracy.

Women always continued to write, and they produced a wide range of material; but only in the early 1980s did a market open up for their work. When this market did emerge, it was partly as a result of the growing strength and extent of the women's movement, which provided a hospitable environment for women's writing. In the late 1970s and early 1980s, women's studies institutes were set up in different parts of the subcontinent, and these generated a considerable amount of academic writing. Another factor that help to create a space for women's writing was the publication, and recognition, of a number of important books by women in the West as well as in India; one example is Arundhati Roy's *The God of Small Things* (1998).

Today, virtually every major publisher in south Asia offers books by and about women, and these often form the most successful part of the list. Consequently, writers have a greater choice of publishers; and publishers, in turn, now seek out women writers. One legacy of colonialism has been that writing in English received much more attention than writing in indigenous languages, but this too is beginning to change, with considerable attention being paid to translations. It would not be wrong to say that in the future women's writing in south Asia promises to go from strength to strength.

See Also

FEMINISM: SOUTH ASIA; LITERATURE: OVERVIEW; POETRY: OVERVIEW; PUBLISHING: FEMINIST PUBLISHING IN THE THIRD WORLD; WOMEN'S STUDIES: SOUTH ASIA

References and Further Reading

Azam, Ikram. 1989. *Literary Pakistan.* Rawalpindi: Nairang-e-Khayal; and Islamabad: Margalla Voices.

Azim, Firdous, and Niaz Zaman, eds. 1994. *Infinite variety: Women in society and literature.* Dhaka, Bangladesh: University Press.

Bose, Mandakranta, ed. 2000. *Faces of the feminine in ancient, medieval, and modern India.* New York: Oxford University Press.

Bahri, Deepika, and Mary Vasudeva, eds. 1996. *Between the lines: South Asians and poscoloniality.* Philadelphia, Pa.: Temple University Press.

Johnson, Gordon. 1996. *Cultural atlas of India: India, Pakistan, Nepal, Bhutan, Bangladesh, and Sri Lanka.* New York: Facts on File.

Natarajan, Nalini, and Emmanuel S. Nelson, eds. 1996. *Handbook of twentieth-century literatures of India.* Westport, Conn.: Greenwood.

Verma, K. D. 2000. *The Indian imagination: Critical essays on Indian writing in English.* New York: St. Martin's.

Urvashi Butalia

LITERATURE: Southeast Asia

Geographically, southeast Asia comprises ten countries: Vietnam, Cambodia, Myanmar (Burma), Laos, Thailand, Malaysia, Indonesia, Singapore, Brunei, and the Philippines. Through trade, immigration, and conquest, major civilizations and their religions have marked the region—the Chinese and Indians, Hinduism, Buddhism, Confucianism, and Islam, followed most recently by the Europeans and Christianity. Until the period after World War II, Vietnam, Laos, and Cambodia were still under French rule; Burma, Malaysia, Singapore, and Brunei were under the British; Indonesia was under the Dutch; and the Philippines, after 300 years of Spanish rule, were under the United States.

Generalizations about women's literature in this region must therefore consider the context: complex diversity including literary production in the western colonial languages—Spanish, Dutch, French, and English—and in national languages such as Vietnamese, Lao, Khmer (in Cambodia), Thai, Burmese, Malay (in Malaysia, Indonesia, and Brunei), and Tagalog (in the Philippines), as well as immigrant languages such as Chinese and Tamil. Singapore uses four official languages, mainly English and Chinese, but its national language is Malay. Women's writing is also diverse in complex ways. For example, there is little at all from Brunei; women's writing in the formerly francophone countries—Laos, Cambodia, and Vietnam—was influenced since the 1960s by prolonged armed conflict; and in Burma, women writers were affected by ideological imperatives and isolation.

Effects of Colonialism

One common factor—western colonialism—is crucial to the beginnings of literary production by women in southeast Asia, and to their emancipation. Even uncolonized Thailand embarked on modernization and westernization in the nineteenth century. Colonial rule and westernization brought in their wake western education and modern liberal ideas about universal education and equality, which were given practical force by Christian mission girls' schools. Until the twentieth century, educated or even literate women were rare in this region and so, therefore, was writing by women; but the prestige of a western education for both sexes among the influential classes would gradually change this. In 1912, about a decade after the Philippines were occupied by the United States, the University of the Philippines produced its first woman graduate. The University of Rangoon was established in 1920, and Thailand passed a Compulsory Education Act in 1921.

Initially, women from the aristocratic and wealthy classes, having obtained an education abroad or locally, were able to produce literature in a western language or the national language. The earliest Filipina poet and dramatist, Leona Florentino (1849–1884), was from a wealthy family and had learned Spanish through religious instruction. Two early women writers in Thailand were half-sisters from the nobility: M. L. Bupha Kunjara (1905–1963), generally regarded as a pioneer of modern Thai literature; and M. L. Boonlua (1911–1982). The well-known early Burmese writer Khin Khin Lay (b. 1913) was the granddaughter of a minister at court. These members of the native elite and a growing middle class of native western-educated intellectuals—literate in the European imperial languages, and with literary tastes influenced by their education—soon began using western literary forms such as the sonnet, the short story, and the novel.

Influence of Nationalism

The emergence of women's writing coincided, too, with the creation of a modern literary tradition in every southeast Asian country in the context of nationalist struggles for independence from colonial rule. The nationalism that instituted national languages also inspired the beginnings of national literature as a form of resistance to western influence through the expression and fostering of a national cultural identity. Such literature, written by both men and women, therefore addresses contemporary national sociopolitical and cultural issues, especially the effects of westernization, modernization, and individualism on traditional values and institutions, and hence, for the women writers, on the situation or role of women in modern society.

Significantly, it was a young Dutch-educated Indonesian woman of noble birth, Raden Adjeng Kartini (1879–1904), who, confined by aristocratic tradition, wrote a series of letters to Dutch friends in Holland calling for the emancipation of women and describing the kinds of opportunities women could be given to fulfill their potential as individuals. Kartini's letters, published as *Door Duisternis tot Licht* (*Through Darkness to Light*), are considered an important literary work, and Kartini is considered a national heroine.

The growth of urban centers under colonial rule established the conditions for modern print technology, the mass media, and sophisticated distribution networks. As literacy spread, prose fiction, including some written by women, published or serialized in serious journals or, later, in mass-circulation popular magazines, began to displace imported literature, existing oral traditions, and the traditional prestige of poetry, usually produced by men.

Literary Magazines

In Thailand, the influential literary journal *Thai Kasem* first published in serial form the novel *Sattru Khong Chao Long* (*Her Enemy,* 1929) by Dok Mai Sod (M. L. Bubpha Kunjara). Another magazine, *Narinat,* published her first major work, *Khwam Phit Khrang Raek* (*The First Mistake,* 1930). Both novels have achieved the status of classics for their combination of traditional Buddhist didacticism and the responses of their characters to contemporary sociocultural change and conflict. Politicized journals edited by women for a female readership also emerged, including *Satri Thai* (*Thai Women*) in the 1920s, the feminist periodical *Lep* (*Fingernails*) in 1973, and another, *Satri Thai,* in 1976, by the National Council of Women of Thailand. Mass-circulation magazines continue to publish fiction, mainly serialized romances, written by women.

Filipinas were the first women in this region to obtain suffrage—in 1937, after a long struggle during which, in the 1930s, magazine publishing rapidly grew in both English and Tagalog. These magazines featured the work of early nationalist or feminist women writers in Tagalog, such as the prolific Magdalena Jalandoni (1891–1978). Some women writers even took the names of the well-known magazines with which their fiction and writing were associated, such as Liwayway Arceo, whose name came from a famous Tagalog magazine of the 1940s, *Liwayway.*

This was the case, too, in Burma, where the first serious literary journal, *Myanma alin Metgazin* (*The Light of Burma Magazine*), usually regarded as the midwife of modern Burmese literature, appeared in 1912. The most prominent prewar magazine was *Dagon Metgazine,* founded in 1920. Several women writers, including Dagon Khin Khin Lay, attached its name to their own. Dagon Khin Khin Lay herself later published *Yuwadi Gya-ne* (*Women's Journal*) in 1946; it encouraged writing for and by women. Gya-ne-gyaw Ma Ma Lay, the pen name of the influential Burmese national writer Ma Tin Hlaing (1917–1982), derived from the journal *Gya-ne-gyaw* (*The Thunderer Journal*), which she founded with her husband. She wrote her first short story for it in 1941 and later wrote many others, which were collected by popular demand under the title *Shu Manyi* (*Ceaseless Delight*) in 1948. Believing in the equality of women, she edited a magazine for women, *Kalaungshin,* for the League of Women Writers in the 1950s, and she was among the most frequent contributors of short fiction to one of Burma's leading journals, *Shumawa,* in the 1950s.

It has been said that modern Indonesian literature is "magazine literature" (*sastra majalah*) because many early literary works, especially prose fiction, appeared in magazines before being collected for publication or published as books. Here, as elsewhere in the region, women's magazines provided an avenue for expression and a source of income, and by the 1970s many had established a large readership, among them *Kartini, Femina, Gadis, Ajah-Bunda, Sarinah, Pariwi,* and *Mode.*

For Malayan women writers, too, it has been noted that the initial breakthrough of women's involvement in literary writing was a women's magazine, *Bulan Melayu* (*The Malay Moon*), published in 1930 by the Malay Women Teachers' Association, founded by Hajjah Zainon Sulaiman (Ibu Zain). It is important less for its publication of women's literary efforts than for its campaign for the preconditions of such writing—women's literacy and education. Ibu Zain's own two daughters distinguished themselves as writers in both Malay and English, particularly Adibah Amin (b. 1936), an award-winning journalist, translator, novelist, and radio dramatist.

Fiction and Poetry in Southeast Asia

The earliest novels by Malay women appeared in the 1940s, and women are now among the ranks of established novelists. Notable examples include Salmi Manja (b. 1939), who is also a poet; Fatima Busu (b. 1948); and the journalist Khadijah Hashim (b. 1945). Their works, while socially realistic, are written within an Islamic culture and tend toward conservatism and didacticism. The women poets, all also born about the 1940s, are generally more radical, experimental, and frank, meshing personal and public themes. Outstanding examples are Zurinah Hassan, Siti Zainon Ismail, Zahrah Nawawi, and Salmah Mohsin.

In Singapore, unlike Burma, Thailand, or the Philippines, women's writing in English, appearing later, is less sociopolitically oriented and more personal. Furthermore, in Singapore—unlike Indonesia or the Philippines—there is less of a market for popular romance. The first book by a woman author in English was, in fact, an autobiography, *Sold for Silver,* by a nurse, Janet Lim, published in 1959. Writers of poetry and fiction tend to be university graduates and to write in English. Beginning in the 1960s and 1970s, the best-known poets and writers included Lee Tzu Pheng (b. 1946), Christine Su-chen Lim (b. 1949), and Catherine Lim (b. 1942). Lim's short fiction falls somewhere between serious literature and entertainment. She is among the most popular and prolific writers, and her readers readily identify with her characters, who are often caught between tradition and modern ways. She portrays this conflict vividly in her best-selling collections *Little Ironies: Stories of Singapore* (1978) and *Or Else the Lightning God* (1980).

The division between serious literature and entertainment has always been controversial. In Thailand, for instance, educated people once considered fiction—*nangsu an len* ("books for pleasure") potentially corrupting, but since the 1950s fiction has been used by both women and men writers to explore social and political themes reflecting contemporary concerns. In Thailand, Indonesia, and the Philippines, short stories popularized by women's magazines and some novels by women writers are still regarded as light fiction or merely "ladies' writing," while the so-called literary novel, addressing social and political issues, is associated more with men writers. In fact, popular women's novels, such as those by the Indonesian writers Nh. Dini and Marga T, are not necessarily escapist and can address serious concerns, especially regarding social, familial, and sexual relationships.

Women's writings from southeast Asia remain relatively unknown or inaccessible outside the region, and sometimes even within the region, unless they have been written in or translated into English. Apart from writers in English from Malaysia and Singapore, critically acclaimed Filipinas who have published in English include Edith Tiempo (fiction and poetry), Kerima Polotan (fiction), Gilda Cordero Fernando (fiction), and Linda Ty-Casper (fiction and historical fiction). Among the best-known Thai works in English translation is the award-winning *Letters from Thailand* (*Chotmai Chak Muang Thai,* 1969), by one of Thailand's outstanding women novelists, Botan (Supa Sirisingh). It explores the conflict between Chinese immigrants and their children, who feel more Thai than their parents. The first Burmese novel to be translated into English and published outside Burma is the award-winning *Not Out of Hate* (*Monywei Mahu,* 1955) by Ma Ma Lay. It is set in the war years, and its main theme is self-deceiving love, but its underlying concern is the threat of western ways to Burmese tradition and culture, exemplified by the break-up of a traditional family by the western-educated Burmese protagonist.

See Also

FEMINISM: SOUTHEAST ASIA; LITERARY THEORY AND CRITICISM; LITERATURE: OVERVIEW

References and Further Reading

Allot, Anna. 1991. Introduction to Ma Ma Lay, *Not out of hate.* Athens: Ohio University Center for International Studies.

Kintanar, Tahir, Koh and Heraty. 1994. *Emergent voices: Southeast Asian women novelists.* Diliman, Quezon City: University of the Philippines Press.

Koh, Tai Ann. 1995. History/his story as her story: Chinese women's biographical writing from Indonesia, Malaysia, and Singapore. In Leo Suryadinata, ed., *Southeast Asian Chinese: The sociocultural dimension.* Singapore: Times Academic.

———. 1992. Southeast Asia. In Claire Buck, ed., *Bloomsbury guide to women's literature.* London: Bloomsbury.

Mattani Mojdana Rutnin. 1988. *Modern Thai literature: The process of modernization and the transformation of values.* Bangkok: Thammasat University Press.

Nguyen Tran Huan. 1981. The literature of Vietnam, 1954–1973. In Tham Seong Chee, ed., *Essays in literature and society in southeast Asia.* Singapore: Singapore University Press.

Polotan, Kerima. 1975. The woman as writer. *Focus Philippines* 25 (November).

Rosnah bte Baharuddin. 1989. Women writers in Malaysian literature. *Sari: Journal of Malay language, literature, and culture* (July).

Supa Sirisingh. 1990. Women and books in Thailand. *Asian/Pacific Book Development Quarterly* 21 (3).

Tai Ann Koh

LITERATURE: Southern Africa

The history of women writing in southern Africa is multinational and intricately layered. Most critical attention has focused on texts written in English, but there is a very strong tradition of writing in local, indigenous languages as well as a long history of writing by white Afrikaaner women and European women. Throughout this region, the development of literature has been influenced by tension related to formal education, migration, and patriarchy, albeit uniquely in each country. This article is divided into categories that should help clarify connections between black women's literary work, black feminist discourse, and the publishing and internationalization of southern African women's writing.

Black Women Writing in English

Critical work on black women writers from southern Africa was perhaps first identified in print in Amelia House's bibliography *Black South African Writers: A Preliminary Checklist* (1980), which includes writers of poetry, short stories, and novels. Although it is, as the title states, preliminary, it remains the most extensive bibliography to date; it opened the world's eyes to the literary contributions of black women in this region. However, there is still very little women's work in historical anthologies for southern Africa; this gives the impression that women in this region began writing only in the late 1980s—when in fact several researchers have uncovered works by women dating back through the nineteenth century.

There is also an imbalance in published theoretical work, not only between women and men but also between black women and white women (criticism of the latter discrepancy emerged in the late 1980s). The major publishing outlet for black women writers has been magazines—particularly *Agenda* and *Staffwriter.* It should be noted that although *Staffwriter,* for example, did consistently publish work by select black women writers such as Miriam Thali, the only black woman on its editorial board was Gcina Mhlope, who was also the only black woman editorial member of virtually all of the literary magazines publishing creative work by black people in the 1970s and the 1980s, including *Drum, Contrast, Quarry, Bloody Horse, New Coin,* and *New Contrast.* Literature in southern Africa has been extremely male-dominated. Women, especially black women, have historically been ignored or overlooked in literary anthologies and criticism. Texts that have attempted to correct this underrepresentation of black women include *Lip: From Southern African Women* (1983), *Vukani Makhosikazi: South African Women Speak* (1985), *Sometimes When It Rains: Writings by South African Women* (1987), *Women in South Africa: From the Heart* (1988), and *One Never Knows: An Anthology of Black South African Women Writers in Exile* (1989).

Black working-class women are oppressed on many levels, and this fact has implications for the position of black women writers. Urban migration, forced labor, domestic service, unequal access to education, westernization, and other factors have had drastic effects on the development of black women's literature. It is important to understand that although Nadine Gordimer and Doris Lessing are considered southern African writers on the basis of their subject matter, their lives as writers are not representative of other southern African women. Black women writers are still not as celebrated as white women writers; nor do black women or girls who want to write receive the same ecouragement and critical help as whites.

In addition to these imbalances, yet another imbalance exists between the nation of South Africa and the rest of southern Africa, which is far less industrialized and has an even stronger tendency to marginalize women's writing. In considering the writing emerging from this region, one is immediately struck by the relative abundance of writers from South Africa and the extremely limited number of notable writers from other countries. South African literature is actually a vast enough category to warrant treatment on its own.

Contemporary Literature

Most published writing by black women in southern Africa can be categorized as "life writing," narrowly defined as autobiography. Contemporary work in this genre is historically connected to the pastoral autobiographies of the nineteenth century. During the later stages of the antiapartheid movement in South Africa, many autobiographies were written by politically active black women; these contrast strikingly with the masculinist constructions of the liberation movement that dominated the world market. Black South African women writers of autobiography include llen Kuzwayo (*Call Me Woman*), Winnie Mandela (*Part of My Soul Went with Him*), Caesarina Makhoere (*No Child's Play*), Emma Mashinini (*Strikes Have Followed Me All of My Life*) and Mamphele Ramphele (*A Life*). The autobiographies of Christine Sybia, Poppie Nongena, Phyllis Ntalatala, and Noni Jabavu are also noteworthy. Recent autobiographical collections such as *Basali! Stories by and About Women in Lesotho* (1995) and *Coming on Strong: Writing by Namibian Women* (1996) have expanded the literary history of southern Africa by bringing to a wider audience the work of writers in countries where women's literature has not received much attention.

In fiction, on the other hand, writing by black women is a relatively recent development. The 1960s are often called the "silent decade" because so many southern African writers were in exile, and although literary production did begin again after that time, creative writers such as Gcina Mhlope have remarked that black women still lacked both time and space for writing. Most black women are preoccupied with the work—within or outside the home—that must be done for day-to-day survival, with persistent financial pressures, and with problems of finding adequate housing and education for themselves and their children; they simply do not have enough time to produce, say, an entire novel, or, often, even to read one. Because of the politics of time and location, then, there has been virtually no reading or writing culture among black women; until very recently it would have been futile to ask rural or urban black women about the work of black women writers.

Today, a significant number of literacy programs and writing circles have been established, making creative writing more accessible for women throughout the region. Autobiographical narratives (understood as a broad range of "life story" writings) remain a primary literary mode—understandably, since there is a social impetus toward autobiography, and since this genre can be so cathartic. Poetry and the short story are also important forms. Several writing projects sponsored by universities, nongovernmental organizations, and government programs have contributed to women's writing. For example, Zimbabwe Women Writers facilitates the publication of women's writing and has among its members rural as well as urban women, ranging in age from schoolgirls to grandmothers.

The Novel

Bessie Head is perhaps the best-known woman writer from southern Africa. She was born in South Africa, but her writing career took shape after her self-exile to Serowe, Botswana, and she is often considered a Botswanan writer because of her deep insights into its culture. Head addresses issues of race, class, culture, gender, and sanity, which are at the core of sociocultural conflicts in southern Africa.

Prominent South African women novelists include (among many others) Lauretta Ngcobo (*Cross of Gold,* 1981; *And They Didn't Die,* 1990); Miriam Thali (*Muriel at Metropolitan,* 1975, titled *Between Two Worlds* when it was published in London; *Amandla,* 1980; and *Mihloti,* 1984); and Joyce Sikane (*A Window on Soweto,* 1972).

In Zimbabwe, several young women have published novels that are gaining much critical attention. Tsitsi Dangarembga's *Nervous Conditions* (1988) is often cited as the first black Zimbabwean novel written by a woman in English and is widely taught at international universities, specifically for its critical analysis of colonization. J. Nozipo Maraire's novel *Zenzele,* published in 1996, takes up many contemporary issues.

Zabela: My Wasted Life (1996), by Binto Sitoe, is one of the very few novels in circulation by Mozambican women.

Unfortunately, little information is available about indigenous-language novels by women in countries such as Angola, Botswana, Malawi, Mauritius, Swaziland, and Zambia.

Literature on Feminism

Amina Mama, one of the foremost radical scholars of women's studies in Africa, notes in *Women's Studies and Studies of Women in Africa During the 1990s* that "regional and national diversities notwithstanding, there is [little] discussion and less clarity on the politics of women's studies in the region. The only point of consent is that most of us would prefer there to be more African women scholars involved in the theoretical and empirical production of women's studies.... There is not even much consensus on using the term 'women's studies,' which is often jettisoned in favor of 'gender' to gain acceptability among the men and allow them to feel, and be, included. 'Feminism,' as a term and a concept, is now marginally less contentious then it was a few years ago. Although there are not yet many 'centers for feminist studies' in Africa, there is an increasing acceptance of the goal of 'gender equality' if not 'women's liberation.'"

This passage indicates some of the major problems at the root of feminist literature in southern Africa. The lack of centers for feminist studies is tied to state politics, but it is also related to divisions with the black women's movement that continue to separate women ideologically and practically. Many spaces designated "feminist" were closed soon after being established; Zimbabwe is a prime example.

In South Africa, there is much more feminist literature, which receives much more, and more varied, critical consideration. This may be partly attributable to the fact that South Africa is thought of as part of the first world; but contemporary writing in South Africa has also clearly been influenced by internal state politics: the new, equitable, nation-state is allowing the voices of every representative group to be heard.

See Also

APARTHEIT, SEGREGATION, AND GHETTOIZATION; AUTOBIOGRAPHY; FEMINISM: SOUTH AFRICA; LITERATURE: OVERVIEW; LITERATURE: SUB-SAHARAN AFRICA; NOVEL; POLITICS AND THE STATE: SOUTHERN AFRICA

References and Further Reading

Barnett, Ursula. 1983. *A vision of order: A study of black south African literature in English (1914–1980).* London: Sinclair Brown.

Barrett, Jane, et al. 1985. *Vukani makhosikazi: South African women speak.* London: Catholic Institute for International Relations.

Brown, Susan, et al., eds. 1983. *Lip: From South African women.* Johannesburg: Ravan.

Boyce-Davis, Carole. 1990. Private selves, public spaces: Autobiography and the African woman writer. *Neoheloicon: Acta Comparitonis Litterarum Universarum* 17(2): 1983–1210.

———. 1986–1987. Finding some space: Black South African women writers. *A Current Bibliography of African Affairs* 19(1).

Chapman, Michael. 1996. *Southern African literatures.* London: Longman.

Clayton, Cherry, and Craig Mackenzie, eds. 1989. *Between the lines: Interviews with Bessie Head, Sheila Roberts, Ellen Kuzwayo, and Miriam Thali.* Grahanstown: National English Literary Museum.

Gaidzanwa, Rudo. 1985. *Images of women in Zimbabwean literature.* Harare: Zed.

Head, Bessie. 1979. Social and political pressures that shape literature in southern Africa. *World Literature Written in English* 18 (1 April).

House, Amelia. 1980. *Black South African women writers in English: A preliminary checklist.* Evanston, Ill.: Northwestern University Program on Women.

Jabavu, Noni. 1982. *Drawn in color.* London: Murray.

Joubert, Elsa, ed. 1980. *The long journey of Poppie Nongena: One woman's struggle against apartheid.* New York: Holt.

Kendall, K. Limakatso. 1995. *Basali! Stories by and about women in Lesotho.* Pietermaritzburg: University of Natal Press.

Kitson, Norma, ed. 1994. *Zimbabwe women writers: Anthology No. 1.* Harare: Zimbabwe Women Writers.

Kuzwayo, Ellen. 1985. *Call me woman.* San Francisco, Calif.: Spinster Ink.

Makhoere, Caesarina. 1988. *No child's play: In prison under apartheid.* London: Women's Press.

Mama, Amina. 1996. *Women's studies and studies of women in Africa during the 1990s.* Dakar: Codesria.

Mandela, Winnie. 1984. *Part of my soul went with him.* New York and London: Norton.

Maraire, J. Nozipo. 1996. *Zenzele: A letter for my daughter.* Johannesburg: Donker.

Mashinini, Emma. 1989. *Strikes have followed me all my life: A South African autobiograpy.* London: Women's Press.

Meena, Ruth. 1992. *Gender in southern Africa.* Harare: SAPES.

Mhlope, Gcina. 1981. The toilet. In Ian Gordon, ed., *Looking for a rain god.* London: Macmillan Education.

Ndebele, Nhabulo S. 1994. *South African literature and culture: Rediscovery of the ordinary.* New York: Manchester University Press.

Ntantala, Phyllis. 1992. *A life's mosaic.* Cape Town: David Phillip.

Orford, Margie, and Nepeti Nicanor, eds. 1996. *Coming on strong.* Windhoek: New Namibia.

Ramphele, Mamphela. 1995. *A life.* Cape Town: David Phillip.

Shava, Pinel Viriri. 1989. *A people's voice: Black South African women writing in the twentieth century.* London: Zed.

Van Neikerk, Annemarie, ed. 1990. *Raising the blinds: A century of South African women's stories.* Pretoria: Donker.

Keshia Abraham

LITERATURE: Sub-Saharan Africa

The African proverb "When an old person dies, a library has burned" is beautiful but ironic from a woman's viewpoint. It suggests the traditional African respect for knowledge—the accumulated lore of centuries, passed down through the generations orally and in performance arts, in poetic and narrative forms, including myths, legends, and folktales that convey cultural values, and proverbs and epigrams that are considered revealed wisdom and are used in resolving disputes. This traditional respect for knowledge has been extended to the printed word, encouraging the growth of a vigorous publishing industry throughout sub-Saharan

Africa. But the great value given to tradition also tends to discourage the publication of women's writings, just as it tends to discourage some other changes that would allow women to live contrary to patriarchal rules—indigenous or colonial. Nevertheless, many women writers are participating in today's prolific publishing. Works are being printed in African languages, English, French, and Portuguese.

Literature in African Languages

Much modern literature in African languages had its beginning in colonial educational systems, and its forms and styles are based on European models—although an exception is found in Ethiopia, where Amharic has been a written literary language since the fourteenth century. Writers in sub-Saharan languages who wish to preserve or revive ancient African traditions often use them primarily as subject matter, seeking substantive rather than stylistic continuity—a characteristic they share with writers, both female and male, who work in European languages.

Written literature in African languages is frequently unavailable to both African and non-African readers and sometimes even to scholars, since any individual scholar may know, at most, one or two of these languages. Too little African-language literature is available in translation, and translations of works by women are even fewer.

A great part of written literature in sub-Saharan Africa, whether it is based on traditional lore or deals with present-day or European subject matter, has been published in English, French, or Portuguese.

Literature in English

British holdings in sub-Saharan Africa included Uganda, Kenya, Ghana, Sierra Leone, Nigeria, Zambia, Zimbabwe, and Botswana. English-speaking poets and fiction writers were generally part of an intellectual class that considered the *négritude* of the French colonies (discussed below) excessive and undesirable.

Literature in English—which acccounts for the largest quantity of published works in sub-Saharan Africa—began to emerge as a major strain in the 1950s, arising out of a smattering of publications going back to the late eighteenth century. The first well-known woman writer to publish fictional works set in sub-Saharan Africa was Doris Lessing (b. 1919). Lessing is known primarily as a British novelist and short-story writer, but she was raised in southern Rhodesia (now Zimbabwe) and continued to live there as a young adult, moving to England only in 1949. At least two of her early works have African themes and settings: her first novel, *The Grass Is Singing* (1950), and her collection of short fiction *African Stories* (1951).

In 1966 Grace Ogot (b. 1930) of Kenya become the first woman to publish a novel in English on the African continent—*The Promised Land.* Originally a nurse by profession, Ogot went on to a diverse career, working as a television scriptwriter and an announcer for the British Broadcasting Corporation and the Voice of America, and as a columnist for the *East African Standard.* She has become one of the few well-known women fiction writers of Kenya. Ogot has often used her nursing experience as source material, focusing on the conflict between traditional African and western medicine. Some of her stories highlight other conflicts between ancient traditional culture and the new ways of life introduced by colonialism and modernization. She has contributed stories to European and African journals, and her works have been published in several collections, such as *The Island of Tears* (1980).

Two other women novelists from Kenya have also achieved recognition for novels set in Africa—Rebekah Njau, for *Ripples in the Pool* (1975), which tells a story of a woman's marital problems; and Lydia Nguya, for *The First Seed* (1975), which describes the conflict between urban and rural cultures and values.

Buchi Emecheta (b. 1944) of Nigeria went to London with her husband in 1962 and began publishing novels in 1972 with *In the Ditch.* In *The Joys of Motherhood* (1979), one of her best-known works, she highlights the protagonist's relationship with her *chi,* or spirit being, as a way of showing the conflict between traditional and modern ways. Many of Emecheta's novels, such as *The Bride Price* (1976), *The Slave Girl* (1977), and *Nowhere to Play* (1980), deal with a woman's quest for identity and dignity. She writes about the Biafran civil war (1966–1969) in *Destination Biafra* (1982).

Ama Ata Aidoo (b. 1942) of Ghana has taken up some difficult subjects—for instance, intercultural marriage in the play *The Dilemma of a Ghost* (1965) and the moral barrenness of slave trading in *Anowa* (1980). In *The Dilemma of a Ghost* a Ghanian student returns from abroad, bringing his African-American wife with him into a traditionally repressive environment. Aidoo returned to this theme in her semi-autobiographical first novel *Our Sister Killjoy; or, Reflections from a Black-Eyed Squint. Anowa* is built on an elaborate and intriguing metaphor that exemplifies African uses of dreams and spirit messages. The slave trader's wife is portrayed as barren, and therefore worthless; at the end, she tells for the first time a prophetic dream she had as a child, revealing that it is the slave trader himself who is sterile. Aidoo has also written other novels, poetry, and a collection of children's stories.

Efua Sutherland (b. 1924), also of Ghana, studied at Cambridge and at the School of Oriental and African Studies at the University of London. On her return to Ghana, she established the Drama Studio in Accra (now the Writers' Workshop in the Institute of African Studies, University of Ghana, Legon) and helped establish the literary magazine *Okyeame,* also in Accra. Her play *The Marriage of Anansewa: A Storytelling Drama* (1975) draws on traditional lore and is often said to be her most valuable work. Besides several other plays, she wrote works for children, pictorial essays, and short stories. Her *Voice in the Forest* (1983) is a collection of folklore and fairy tales.

The novelist and short story writer Bessie Head (1937–1986) was a child of an interracial liaison—a circumstance that had profound effects on her life. She was born and grew up in South Africa but moved to Botswana in 1964; thus she may be discussed as a South African or a Botswanan writer. She wrote revealingly about personal issues as well as racial and social problems, including taboos against interracial sex. Head published three novels during her lifetime—*When Rain Clouds Gather* (1968), *Maru* (1971), and *A Question of Power* (1973); a fourth, *The Cardinals* (1993), was published posthumously. She also wrote stories and many autobiographical letters, some of which have been collected in *A Gesture of Belonging: Letters from Bessie Head, 1965–1979* (1991).

Flora Nwapa (1931–1993) was born in Nigeria and educated there and at the University of Edinburgh. When she returned to Nigeria, she worked as a teacher and an administrator. After the Biafran civil war ended, she formed her own publishing company, Tana Press/Flora Nwapa, issuing African books. Her first novel, *Efuru* (1966), is based on an old folktale in which a barren, newly widowed woman, in despair over her childlessness, follows her husband to the land of the dead. In other novels, such as *Women Are Different* (1986), Nwapa writes about social problems faced by women in Nigerian culture. She also published a volume of poetry, *Cassava Song and Rice Song* (1986).

Poets of sub-Saharan and southern Africa include Tsitsi Dangarembga, whose first collection was *Nervous Conditions* (1988–1989). Dangarembga is a descendant of the Shona people of Zimbabwe who seeks to reclaim her ancestral values and culture through myth and story-telling. The novelist Buchi Ememcheta is also a poet; her poetic works include *The Family* (1989). Another poet writing in English is Micere Githae Mugo of Kenya; her anthology *My Mother's Poem and Other Songs* was published in 1994.

Literature in French

From the 1930s to the 1960s, fiction and poetry in French-speaking sub-Saharan Africa (including what is now Mauritania, Mali, Niger, Chad, Côte d'Ivoire, Senegal, and Madagascar) were imbued with the ideals of *négritude,* a belief that everything African was better than its European counterpart. After colonialism ended, the literary mood shifted to focus as well on political, social, and economic reform.

Fiction in French by women writers from sub-Saharan Africa began to be published in the 1970s and 1980s. The Senegalese writer Mariama Bâ won the first Noma Award for publishing in Africa, for *Une si longue lettre* in 1980 (published in English translation as *So Long a Letter* in 1980). Aminata Sow Fall, also of Senegal, wrote *La grève des bàtta* (1979), which received much critical acclaim for its skillfully handled irony; it was published in English translation as *The Beggars' Strike* in 1980.

Literature in Portuguese

Portugal's sub-Saharan African empire (comprising Angola, Cape Verde, Guinea Bissau, São Tomé, Príncipe Island, and Mozambique) was smaller than the empires of Great Britain and France. Comparatively little literature of this area has been written in Portuguese, and still less is available in English translation. Poetry was the first lusophone (Portuguese) literary form to flourish in sub-Saharan Africa, starting in the 1930s. After Portuguese colonialism ended in 1975, Portuguese-speaking African poets begin to take a special pleasure in language.

Noémia de Sousa was the first woman poet from sub-Saharan Africa to publish her work. Her best-known poem is "Sangre Negro" ("Black Blood," 1976). Other sub-Saharan women poets who write in Portuguese are Paula Travares of Angola, author of *Rotos de Passagem* ("Rites of Passage," 1985); and Ana de Santana, also of Angola, who wrote *Sabores, odores & sanho* ("Flavors, Scents, and Reveries," 1985).

See Also

LITERTURE: OVERVIEW; LITERATURE: ARABIC; LITERATURE: SOUTHERN AFRICA

References and Further Reading

Anyinefa, Koffi. 1995. Litteratures en langues africaines (Literatures in African languages; book review). *Research in African Literatures* 26 (1 March): 164.

Bruner, Charlotte H. 1997. Postcolonial subjects: Francophone women writers (book reviews). *World Literature Today* 71 (1 January): 235.

Desai, Gaurav. 1998. Reviews of Julie Newman, "The ballistic bard," and Vera Mihailovich, ed., *"'Return' in postcolonial writing." Research in African Literatures* 29 (22 March): 211.

Finnegan, Ruth. 1976. *Oral literature in Africa.* Oxford: Oxford University Press. (Originally published 1970.)

Gérard, Albert S. 1981. *African-language literatures: An introduction to the literary history of sub-Saharan Africa.* Colorado Springs, Col.: Passeggiata.

Gover, Daniel. 1996. Bessie Head: Thunder behind her ears (book review). *Research in African Literatures* 27 (1 September): 138.

Jack, Belinda. 1996. *Francophone literatures: An introductory survey.* Oxford: Oxford University Press.

Jahn, Janheinz, and Claus Peter Dressler. 1973. *Bibliography of creative African writing.* Millwood, N.Y.: Kraus-Thomson.

Jones, Eldred Durosimi, Eustace Palmer, and Marjorie Jones, eds. 1987. *Women in African literature today: A review.* Lawrenceville, N. J.: Africa World.

Lewis, Desiree. 1996. "The cardinals" and Bessie Head's allegories of self. *World Literature Today: South African Literature in Transition* 70 (1 January): 73.

Mihailovich-Dickman, Vera, ed. 1994. *"Return" in postcolonial writing: A cultural labyrinth.* Amsterdam: Rodopi.

Mulala, Beatrice. 1999. Francophone literatures. *Research in African Literatures* 30 (15 October).

Newman, Judie. 1995. *The ballistic bard: Postcolonial fictions.* London: Arnold.

Phillips, Maggi. 1994. Engaging dreams: Alternative perspectives on Flora Nwapa, Buchi Emecheta, Ama Ata Aidoo, Bessie Head, and Tsitsi Dangarembga's writing. (Cluster on South African writing.) *Research in African Literatures* 25 (2 December): 89.

Review of National Literatures. 1971. 2(2: Fall) Special issue devoted to black African literatures.

Taiwo, Oladele. 1985. *Female novelists of modern Africa.* New York: St. Martin's.

Web Sites

Clarke's Books (South Africa): <http://www.clarkesbooks.co.za>

Encarta Electric Library (sources accessed on-line): <http://www.elibrary.com>

Georgia Kornbluth

LITERATURE: Ukraine

Over the centuries, foreign rulers of Ukraine, wary of the role of culture in a Ukrainian national revival, have made numerous attempts to "flatten out" or "equalize" Ukrainian language and literature, applying policies such as "Russification," "Germanization," "Polonization," and "Romanianization." As a result, Ukrainian cultural, social, and political life in the modern era has been motivated to a considerable extent by nationalism as well as socialism, and this has had implications for women's literature. In the late nineteenth century, for example—a time when Ukrainian writing was populist in mood, realistic in style, and concerned with oppressed individuals and national conditions—there was no feminist literature as such. Just as socialist women in general were willing to defer their own needs until the emancipation of the workers, the broad base of Ukrainian women tended to defer their aspirations for the sake of the national cause. Thus feminist issues such as equal rights were actually goals for the entire community; exclusively women's issues were secondary (Bohachevsky-Chomiak, 1988: xix; Zhurzhenko, n.d.: 2).

Russian and Austro-Hungarian Occupation

Literature, especially poetry, was the first public arena open to Ukrainian women, and numerous women, particularly in Russian-occupied Ukraine, entered it. For example, poets active in the women's movement and public organizations included Hanna Barvinok (Oleksandra Bilozerska-Kulish, 1828–1911), the "poet of women's fate" (Bohachevsky-Chomiak, 1988: 10); Dniprova Chaika (Liudmyla Berezyna Vasylevska, 1861–1927), an early practitioner of symbolism; Hrytsko Hryhorenko (Oleksandra Sadovshchyk Kosach, 1867–1924); Liubov Ianovska (1861–1941); and Uliana Kravchenko (Julia Schneider, 1861–1947).

In prose, Marko Vovchok (Maria Vilinska Markovych Zhuchenko, 1834–1907) was the first influential modern writer. Her work, critically acclaimed in the late 1850s and 1860s, shaped the development of the Ukrainian short story. Vovchok wrote realistic stories, often narrated by a peasant woman, about women's difficult lot under serfdom (*Narodni opovidannia, Folk Stories,* 1857); she also wrote about provincial women's lives (*Institutka, After Finishing School,* 1860; and *Zhiva dusha, A Living Soul,* 1868). Her novella *Marusia* (1871) was widely popular in Ukraine and western Europe. Despite Vovchok's critical success, women writers who moved beyond populist writing were often labeled "elitist" by critics—one example is Olena Pchilka (Olha Drahomaniv Kosach, 1849–1930), a cultural and women's activist whose characters resembled Jane Austen's.

By the end of the nineteenth century, two modernists—Lesia Ukrainka (who was Pchilka's daughter) and Olha Kobylianska—were at the forefront of Ukrainian literature. Both stressed aesthetics ("art for art's sake") rather than social commentary.

Ukrainka (Larysa Kosach, 1871–1913) is considered Ukraine's foremost woman poet; in childhood, she was stricken with tuberculosis of the bone, but her poetry is life-affirming and calls for an obstinate struggle. Her first collections—*Na krylakh pisen, On Wings of Song* (1893); and *Nevilnychi pisni, The Songs of Slaves* (1895)—prompted one critic to praise her courage and her poetic boldness and to say that she was "more of a man" than anyone else in Ukraine (Luckyj, 1992: 15). Her lyric poems "Contra Spem Spero," "Always a Wreath of Thorns," and "Word, Why Are You Not Like Tempered Steel?" are highly regarded.

Ukrainka was also a dramatist. Her dramatic poems include "Oderzhyma" ("A Possessed Woman"), "Na ruinakh" ("On the Ruins") and "U pushchi" ("In the Wilderness"); her plays include *Boiarynia* (*The Boyar's Wife,* 1910), *Lisova pisnia,* (*A Forest Song,* 1911), and *Kaminny hospodar* (*The Stone Host,* 1912). *Boiarynia* remained unpublished in Ukraine until 1989 because of its anti-Russian sentiment; it portrays a seventeenth-century Ukrainian woman who marries a Russian and is faced with a Tatar-influenced subordination of women that is foreign to Ukrainian society. However, Ukrainka rejected feminism as irrelevant to the "liberation of the masses" (Bohachevsky-Chomiak, 1988: 41). Because Ukrainka often took her subject matter from world literature and history, critics accused her of being contemptuous of ordinary people.

Olha Kobylianska (1863–1942), a prominent prose writer, had a strong influence on women's consciousness. Many of her works are feminist; she believed that women's liberation involved individual effort, but she often emphasized the support of other women. Kobylianska was from southwest Ukraine (Bukovyna), which was under the Austro-Hungarian Empire. The empire had a policy of Germanicization, but Kobylianska was pursuaded to write in Ukrainian rather than German by Natalya Kobrynska (1851–1920), who was a leader of the Ukrainian feminist movement and an author of symbolist stories.

Although many of Kobylianski's short stories are considered fine examples of Ukrainian modernism, she is best known for her novels. In fact, she wrote the first Ukrainian feminist novel, *Tsarivna, The Princess* (1896), about a woman in search of autonomy, individualism, and self-esteem. Because the protagonist's obstacles are a result of her gender, few male critics or readers understood that this novel was concerned with individual emancipation, not just women's liberation (Bohachevsky-Chomiak, 1988: 109). Two powerful novels by Kobylianski have a village setting: *Zemlia, The Earth* (1902); and *V nediliu rano zillia kopala, On Sunday Morning She Dug for Herbs* (1909). In these works, the female protagonists are uneducated and close to nature, but Kobylianska saw neither nature nor romance as "ennobling," "since neither promoted individual autonomy" (Bohachevsky-Chomiak, 1988: 110).

The Soviet Period

During the Soviet period, at least 500 Ukrainian writers were killed in the Stalinist purges of the late 1930s (Luckyj, 1992: 53). Soviet ideology saw women as combination of traditional traits (mother, nurturer) and socialist virtues (worker, member of the labor collective). "Socialist realist" literature extolled such women, ignoring the gender inequality implied by this double burden. In the Soviet period, there was little notable literature by Ukrainian women. However, with Stalin's death (1953), the Soviet Union experienced a series of cultural and political "thaws" (although these alternated with "freezes") that allowed the publication of many works dealing with previously banned themes and characters.

The poet Lina Kostenko (b. 1930) began writing her profoundly searching, experiential, introspective lyric poetry during a "thaw." She was the most talented of the *shestydesiatnyky,* "poets of the sixties" (that is, the 1960s), a loose group that, after three decades of programmatic socialist realism, became important for a new awareness of the function of poetry. These writers also became a symbol of their generation, which could not forgive the previous generation's complicity with Stalinism.

Kostenko's first collections were *Prominnia zemli, Earthly Rays* (1957); *Vitryla, Sails* (1958); and *Mandrivki sertsia, Wanderings of the Heart* (1963). Then, during a "freeze," she was accused of "nihilistic moods" and of being interested in "formalist currents" (Naydan, in Kostenko, 1990: 144) and had great difficulty publishing her poetry; from 1967 to 1977, she published nothing in Ukraine. However, in 1979 Kostenko published *Marusia Churai,* an eponymous historical novel in verse about a semilegendary seventeeth-century Ukrainian folksinger-songwriter. Eight years later this work was formally acknowledged and was awarded Ukraine's highest literary honor, the Shevchenko Prize. Kostenko continued publishing in the 1980s; *Vybrane* (*Selected Works,* 1989) contained many poems written during her decade of silence, along with new poetry and some previously published works.

Like Lesia Ukrainka, Kostenko fuses many literary sources—Ukrainian, western, and Russian literature; the Bible; classical Greek and Roman literature—with her own experience. Her style is controlled yet natural, with little if any linguistic or metrical experimentation; and she has helped poets to reclaim "the lyrical 'I'" (Naydan, in Kostenko, 1990: 149).

Glasnost and Independence

After *glasnost* (1985–1991, the period of "openness" at the end of the Soviet era), Ukraine's declaration of independence in December 1991, and the collapse of the Soviet Union soon afterward, there was a new, freer climate that stimulated a flood of ideas. Ironically, however, creative writing has suffered. Many writers become preoccupied with politics and had less desire—or less time—to write. There were also practical factors, such as the realities of free-market publishing, a severe paper shortage, and spiraling inflation.

However, a new group of poets did emerge: the *visimdesyatniki,* "poets of the eighties," notable for a multiplicity of styles, techniques, and themes. This group included Natalya Bilotserkivets (b. 1954) and Oksana Zabushko (b. 1960), who is also a literary scholar; Zabushko's *Dyrygenty ostannoi svichky, Holders of the Last Candle* (1990), is considered to be among the best recent poetry collections. The "poets of the eighties" preferred personal writing, though common themes include the nuclear disaster at Chernobyl (as a symbol on many levels), ecology, the fate of future generations, and a concern for Ukrainian culture, often epitomized by the Ukrainian language. Another significant figure is Solomiia Pavlychko (1958–1999), a literary scholar and translator who was among the first to study feminism in Ukrainian scholarship and culture. Since Ukrainian independence, Zabushko, Pavlychko, and the poet Oksana Paxl'ovs'ka have been especially successful at establishing contacts with western scholars.

Ukrainian women writers have always tried to be active members of their community, emphasizing not so much the rights of women or the benefits of women's independence but rather "the importance of women and the need to expand opportunities for them" (Bohachevsky-Chomiak, 1988: xxii). This type of feminine identity, reflected in women's writing, is likely to continue well into the future.

See Also

FEMINISM: COMMONWEALTH OF INDEPENDENT STATES *and* EASTERN EUROPE; LITERATURE: OVERVIEW; LITERATURE: EASTERN EUROPE; LITERATURE: RUSSIA

References and Further Reading

Bohachevsky-Chomiak, Martha. 1988. *Feminists despite themselves: Women in Ukrainian community life, 1884–1939.* Edmonton, Alberta: Canadian Institute of Ukrainian Studies.

Cyzevsky, Dmytro. 1997. *A history of Ukrainian literature.* 2nd ed. New York: Ukrainian Academic.

Cummins, Walter, ed. 1993. *Shifting borders: East European poetries of the eighties,* 363–400. London: Associated University Presses.

Kostenko, Lina. 1990. *Selected poetry: Wanderings of the heart.* Trans. Michael Naydan. New York: Garland.

Luckyj, George S. N. 1992. *Ukrainian literature in the twentieth century: A reader's guide.* Toronto: University of Toronto Press.

Morris, Sonia, ed. 1998–2000. *Women's voices in Ukrainian literature,* Vols. I–VI. Trans. Roma Franko. Saskatoon: Language Lanterns.

Onyshkevych, Larissa. 1993. Ukrainian literature in the 1980s. In Walter Cummins, ed., *Shifting borders: East European poetries of the eighties,* 363–368. London: Associated University Presses.

Ukrainka, Lesia. 1985. *Forest song: A faery drama in three acts.* Kiev: Dnipro.

———. *Hope: Selected poetry.* 1981. Trans. Gladys Evans. Kiev: Dnipro.

Vovchok, Marko. 1983. *After finishing school.* Trans. O. Kovalenko. Kiev: Dnipro.

Zhurzhenko, Tatiana. (n. d.) Nation-building, citizenship, and women's political identities in postsocialist Ukraine. Online: <http://www.unl.ac.uk/ukrainecentre/WP/10.html>

Teresa Polowy

LITERATURE: Western Europe

The common literary heritage of western Europe originated in ancient Greece and Rome. Spread through Christianity, models of poetry, drama, and prose came into contact with and influenced the local languages and cultures of Europe. Feminists tend to analyze the gender-related aspects of this process, and of the literature that resulted.

Background

Standard literary histories—even today—list only a tiny minority of female authors, and the masterpieces of European literatures are associated with the names of men: Aeschylus, Dante, Cervantes, Shakespeare, Goethe, Molière. Only four European women writers have won the Nobel Prize, and one of these prizes was shared. In literature by men, feminists argue, women rarely occur as autonomous subjects; they more often figure in restricted roles, frequently as stereotypical representations or embodiments of archetypal themes: as the classical "eternal feminine" formulated by Goethe; as silent objects of the erotic impulses of the romantics; as the prostitutes, hysterics, and adulterers of the realists; or as the demons, vampires, and androids of the fin de siècle.

Despite their near-invisibility as active participants in culture and literature, there is a long tradition of writing by women. However, their work has often been trivialized and marginalized, and only a small proportion has survived for later generations. This "erasure" is, arguably, a result of excluding most women's writing from the canon—the body of works considered to be representative of great art and a repository of accepted cultural beliefs. In a culture, the canon is said to be formed by selecting those texts considered worth preserving and, even more important, by excluding other works on aesthetic, formal, and sometimes ideological grounds. In the twentieth century, this selection process worked in favor of "universal" aesthetic values such as complexity, ambiguity, tension, and irony and worked against depictions of social and cultural contexts; the effect was to exclude most works by women and ethnic minorities. The primarily male, western canon was increasingly criticized by feminist and postcolonial scholars. Feminist work from the 1970s concentrated on recovering women's cultural history and establishing a genealogy of women writers by rediscovering and reprinting earlier authors. There has also been a focus on reevaluating woman-centered themes, genres, and ideas.

These approaches have produced evidence of a rich body of work. Women have always been writing, and although the history of this writing is discontinuous and sporadic, continuities in gender-specific themes and strategies can be seen across Europe from the beginning. Women, like men, have been poets, dramatists, novelists, satirists, and biographers, but the themes and formal features of their work are different from those of male authors, and their writing rarely fits in with dominant literary periods or definitions of high culture. Working on the margins and against prevailing standards, women have needed subversive, challenging, unconventional strategies, and through these they have often provided new impulses for mainstream culture.

These features characterize women's work across the different western European traditions, but there are also substantive differences. Although it is certainly true everywhere that education, wealth, leisure, and an enlightened attitude are factors in women's opportunities and in their access to cultural and intellectual life, contradictions appear nevertheless between different cultures. For example, in Spain and Italy the romantic period was one of stagnation and cultural silence for women authors, but in Germany romanticism proved to be one of the most productive times for influential figures such as Rahel Varnhagen (1771–1833) and Dorothea Schlegel (1763–1839). Similarly, although education is one of the most important indicators of women's participation in culture, eighteenth-century Italy was far advanced in appointing some female professors (Laura Bassi, 1711–1778; and Maria Dalle Donne, 1777–1842) whereas other countries at the same time did not even allow women to attend university lectures. However, Italy has the least representation of women writers, and many women writers in Italy have antifeminist or self-censoring tendencies (Russel, 1997), whereas in France, the *salonnières* asserted a feminine culture based on democratic values and respect for women's intellectual powers as an alternative to the dominant culture of the court of Versailles.

Early Writings

Throughout the ages, various arguments have been used to exclude women from creative work. The idea that women lack the ability to produce texts of outstanding value, for instance, is linked partly to an association of men with divine creativity and language (New Testament, John 1:1) and also partly to the teachings of the church fathers, who laid down accepted roles for men and women. Women were not allowed to teach orally or in writing, and this proscription was only partially qualified for nuns, who were considered to have renounced their womanhood. Thus the earliest recorded writing by European women is from religious women, often nuns, who wrote in Latin but also in the vernacular. Examples are the German abbesses Hrotsvith von Gandersheim (c. 935–after 973) and Hildegard von Bingen (?1098–1179); Birgitta av Vadstena (1303–1373) in Sweden; and Margery Kempe (c. 1373–after 1439) and Julian of Norwich (c. 1342–after 1416) in England. The most widely known of the Spanish mystics is Saint Teresa de Jesús (also called Teresa of Avila, 1515–1582), whose works are world classics.

Didactic or visionary, prose or poetry, this early devotional literature from across Europe introduces many features and themes that were to remain important characteristics of women's writing. Concern with the personal and identity, placing the writer and her body in the text (Kempe); rootedness in the everyday, in the joys and sorrows of this world rather than the eternal (Birgitta); the use of domestic imagery (Julian); affinity with the human body and the feminine (Hrotsvith); and themes of mothering and nurturing (Teresa)—these are aspects that shape the work of such women and differentiate them from their male contemporaries.

Nondevotional writing in the vernacular is extant in the twelfth-century *lais* of Marie de France, who is considered one of the finest medieval prose writers. Her personal voice is clear in her passionate short narratives, which focus on and identify with the fate of frustrated young women. She was a champion of her sex, and her sympathetic woman-centered perspective makes her a precursor of Christine de Pisan (1364/5–?1434), whose most famous book—*La Cité des Dames* (1405; *The Book of the Cities of the Ladies,* 1521)—provided an influential analysis and critique of women's roles and asserted their capacity for learning. This initiated the *querelle des femmes* ("woman question"), a sustained debate about whether women are by nature intellectually, physically, or morally inferior to men. (The notion that women were inferior in these ways was enshrined by Aristotle and St Paul.) Conducted mainly in French, such argumentative and rhetorical literary exchanges continued until the seventeenth century, with many famous writers taking sides. (Rabelais and Montaigne, for example, took the negative side; Ariosto and Marguerite de Navarre, 1492–1549, took the positive side). The themes of the debate—education, sexuality, marriage and the family, women's right to work—were taken up and articulated in private and public writing in Germany (where the "woman question" is the *Frauenfrage*) from the eighteenth century, and in England in the nineteenth century; and they continue to be relevant today.

The Renaissance through the Enlightenment

With the Renaissance (fourteenth to seventeenth centuries), the Reformation (sixteenth century), and the Enlightenment (eighteenth century), education became a central interest and was increasingly extended to women. But despite humanist reforms, the belief that only aristocratic women should be educated persisted, and women from other classes received only a rudimentary education or none at all. Thus the majority of writers continued to be aristocrats or middle-class. Interestingly, although the church fathers' teaching was instrumental in excluding women from creative work, nevertheless the church had long been associated with literacy and with offering a life outside the family.

In the seventeenth century, the first professional writers—for example Sophia Elisabeth Brenner (1659–1730) in Sweden—emerged across Europe. In England, the poet and dramatist (and spy) Aphra Behn (1640–1689) wrote eighteen plays; the best-known today are *The Rover* (1679) and *The Lucky Chance* (1686), which deals with the plight of young women married off to rich old men, a theme familiar from the work of Marie de France. In France, the phenomenally successful Mme de Villedieu (1640–1683) broke established conventions in her wide-ranging work by fusing history and fiction. In Germany in the eighteenth century, Sophie de la Roche (1730–1807) became the first woman there to support herself by her writing.

The spread of female teaching orders (most famously the Ursulines) at the beginning of the seventeenth century contributed to making women's education a social reality. Although this extended opportunities to a greater body of women than ever before, women's literacy still lagged behind men's: for instance, in France the literacy rate for men at the end of the eighteenth century were 47 percent but the rate for women was only 27 percent (Sartori, 1999). (Education would remain the province of the upper and middle classes until legislation in the nineteenth and twentieth century provided general elementary schooling.) This increasing interest in and access to education is reflected to some extent in an increase in publications by women, from 1 percent of texts in the seventeenth century to 20 percent in the nineteenth century (Wilson, 1991). However, the scope for intellectual and creative activity remained restricted, and a demand for equal educational opportunities continued to be a theme of women's fiction.

The increasing importance of the salons—regular public gatherings in the homes of prominent aristocratic women—in seventeenth- and eighteenth-century France provided an alternative intellectual and cultural arena where women could engage in intellectual debates as equals and circulate their work. Among the most influential hostesses were Madeleine de Scudéry (1607–1701), Mme de Lambert (1647–1733), Mme d'Epinay (1726–1783), and Mlle de Lespinasse (1732–1776). In Italy, prestigious salons were led by Maria Pizzelli Cuccovilla (1735–1807) and Maria Vittoria Serbelloni (d. 1790), and the tradition was continued in Germany by Rahel Varnhagen, Henriette Herz (1764–1847), and Dorothea Schlegel. The *salonnières* are often said to have been the true founders of Enlightenment, pioneers of new cultural and democratic forms of social organization. Many of them were also famous authors who introduced formal innovations. Madeleine de Scudéry's historical novels (for example, *Le Grand Cyrus,* 1649–1653; and *Clélie,* 1654–1660) blurred the distinction between fiction and official (male) history. Using dialogue rather than action, these novels achieve psychological depth and offer social critiques, as does Mme de Lafayette's acknowledged canonical masterpiece, *La Princesse de Clèves* (1678).

Constrained by their marginalization and by the conventions of the dominant literary discourse, women often "invented" new genres to explore female experience. The first sentimental novel in France was written by Hélisenne de Crenne (1510?–1560?); Georgette de Montenay (1540?–1607) created the first book of Christian emblems;

and the Dames des Roches, a mother and daughter, produced the first collection of private letters (1587), which included poetry, prose dialogues, first translations from the Latin, and even a tragicomedy. In Germany, Varnhagen and Bettina von Arnim (1785–1859) are credited with the creation of a new aesthetics in epistolary literature, the exchange and publication of consciously literary letters. The novel was introduced to Spain by the work of Cecilia Böhl de Faber (1796–1877), and Rosalía de Castro (1837–1885) has been posthumously rediscovered as a precursor of *modernismo.*

Nineteenth Century

Innovation was often necessitated by subversion, and although more women than ever before were writing and publishing by the eighteenth and nineteenth century, increasing moral and ideological restrictions were placed on them. When public and private life were separated, women were relegated to the private sphere, and this is reflected in the personal nature of women's genres such as travel literature and autobiography. The domestic ideal of the nineteenth century—the "angel by the hearth"—also required strategies to overcome the taboo against public expression. While medieval writers often inserted themselves into their texts, women authors now increasingly attributed their work to men (Colette, 1873–1954, is an instance) or used male pseudonyms. Famous examples are George Sand (France, 1804–1876), Charlotte and Emily Brontë (England, 1816–1855 and 1818–1848), and George Eliot (England, 1819–1880). Some research indicates that at least 50 percent of women writers in Germany used a pseudonym in the eighteenth and nineteenth centuries (Eigler and Kord, 1997: 33).

With the beginning of feminist movements in the late nineteenth century, demands for women's civil rights and legal and intellectual autonomy were expressed increasingly assertively. Writers as far apart as Colette and Louise Aston (1818–1871) combined the political with the personal, challenging bourgeois standards of morality with calls for social and sexual equality, and depicting clashes between the sexes and classes. Questions of sexuality, and of lesbian identity, began to be addressed early in the century by writers such as Renée Vivien (1877–1909) and Radclyffe Hall (1880–1943).

Twentieth Century

The two world wars, fascism, and the domestic ideology of the 1950s brought setbacks to women's opportunities; but with the second wave of feminism, beginning in the 1960s, there was an unprecedented representation of women in public life and cultural production. Initial demands for equality and the validation of women's everyday experiences produced documentary literature such as Erika Runge's *Frauen: Versuche zur Emanzipation* ("Women: Attempts at Emancipation," 1968) and Maxie Wander's *Guten Morgen, du Schöne: Protokolle nach Tonband* ("Good Morning, Beautiful: Transcripts from Tapes," 1973).

Increasingly, sexual difference and the relationship between language and the body became the focus of much feminist work. Hélène Cixous's essay "Le Rire de la Méduse" ("The Laugh of the Medusa," 1976) challenged traditional representations of women by examining language, identity, and the body—as did novels such as Verena Stefan's *Häutungen* ("Shedding," 1975) and Marie Cardinal's *Les Mots pour le dire* ("The Words to Say It," 1975). Luce Irigaray's *Spéculum de l'autre femme* ("Speculum of the Other Woman," 1974) provided a critique of patriarchal western philosophic traditions from Plato to Hegel. Revisionist mythmaking has been a strategy for writers such as Irmtraud Morgner (1933–1990), Christa Wolf (b. 1929), Nathalie Sarraute (b. 1902), Esther Tusquets (b. 1936), Carmen Martín Gaite (b. 1925), and Angela Carter (1940–1992), who have reworked the structures and themes of myths, fairy tales, and legends.

More recently, women's work has taken new directions, introducing sexual, thematic, and aesthetic diversity and including issues of minority, old age, and ethnicity. An increasing awareness of Eurocentrism and of the differences between women has meant that, for example, the voices of Turkish women in Germany, black and Asian women in England, and Algerian and Moroccan women in France have become more prominent.

See Also

FEMINISM, *specific topics;* LITERATURE: OVERVIEW; LESBIAN WRITING: OVERVIEW; THEATER, *specific topics;* WOMEN'S STUDIES: WESTERN EUROPE

References and Further Reading

Buck, Claire. ed. 1992. *Bloomsbury guide to women's literature.* London: Bloomsbury.

Eigler, Friederike, and Susanne Kord, eds. 1997. *The feminist encyclopedia of German literature.* Westport, Conn., and London: Greenwood.

Gilbert, Sandra, and Susan Gubar. 1988–1994. *No man's land: The place of the woman writer in the twentieth century.* 3 vols. New Haven, Conn.: Yale University Press.

Gould Levine, Linda, Ellen Engelson Marson, and Gloria Feiman Waldman, eds. 1993. *Spanish women writers: A bio-bibliographical sourcebook.* Westport, Conn., and London: Greenwood.

Larrington, Carolyne. 1995. *Women and writing in medieval Europe: A sourcebook.* London: Routledge.

Russell, Rinaldina, ed. 1997. *The feminist encyclopedia of Italian literature.* Westport, Conn., and London: Greenwood.

Sage, Lorna, ed. 1999. *The Cambridge Guide to women's writing in English.* Cambridge: Cambridge University Press.

Sartori, Eva Martin, ed. 1999. *The feminist encyclopedia of French literature.* Westport, Conn., and London: Greenwood.

Weedon, Chris, ed. 1997. *Postwar women's writing in German: Feminist critical approaches.* Oxford: Berghahn.

Wilson, Katharina M., ed. 1991. *An encyclopedia of continental women writers.* Chicago and London: St. James.

Women in context. 1993–1998. Ed. Janet Garton et al. Atlantic Highlands, N.J.: Athlone. (See volumes on women's writing in specific European countries.)

Karen Seago

LONGEVITY

See AGING; LIFE EXPECTANCY.

LONG-TERM CARE SERVICES

Long-term care is the help people need to cope, and sometimes to survive, when protracted physical or mental disabilities impair their capacity to perform the activities of everyday life, such as eating, using the toilet, bathing, dressing, getting in and out of bed, and moving about (Rivlin and Weiner, 1988: 3). Though associated with the elderly, long-term care services are needed by people of all ages. In fact, most people over age 65 are physically active and able to care for themselves. The prevalence of disability, however, rises steeply with advancing age. In the United States, only 14 percent of people aged 65 to 74 are disabled, but that proportion rises to 58 percent for people aged 85 and over (Rivlin and Weiner, 1988: 5). Senile dementia of the Alzheimer type affects 25 to 50 percent of those over 85 and requires special long-term care (Doress-Worters and Siegal, 1994: 7). The fastest-growing age group in the population is the very elderly, the group most likely to need long-term care.

Long-Term Care, Women, and Families

Long-term care is overwhelmingly a women's issue (Adams, Nawrocki, and Coleman, 1999). Because the majority of unpaid and paid caregivers are women, the responsibility for providing long-term care services for people of all ages falls disproportionately on them. Also, because women live longer than men, more of the very elderly who need long-term care services are women. Old women, as a group, are poorer than old men, so they are more likely to be unable to pay for themselves and to be dependent on public programs for long-term care services. In the United States, over 15 percent of older women are poor, compared with less than 8 percent of older men. Thirty-eight percent of older black women and 25 percent of older Hispanic women are poor (Doress-Worters and Siegal, 1994: 187). Indeed, very elderly women who are alone are the main users of long-term care yet are among the poorest people everywhere (Rivlin and Weiner, 1988: 45).

Throughout the world, care of the elderly is primarily a family responsibility. For instance, although the United States is considered a culture that favors the young and discriminates against the old, family-provided help remains the backbone of in-home care for the elderly there. Roughly 90 percent of the older persons in the community who have a chronic disability depend on family or friends in order to remain at home (Rivlin and Weiner, 1988: 179). Other countries are likely to face challenging problems in the future. The Scandinavian countries, for example, have developed excellent programs, but the cost of these programs is rising, so relatives may need to become more involved in care. China will face problems as its one-child-only policy reduces the number of caregivers for the elderly, and young Japanese are becoming more reluctant to bring their elders into their homes.

Aspects of Community Care

Most old people want to remain independent and to live in their own homes as long as possible. Home-equity conversion may allow homeowners to draw on the value of their homes to raise money to pay for home-care services. Living arrangements for persons needing a supportive environment include cohousing, developed first in Denmark to combine individual and family privacy with community (McCaman and Durrett, 1994); congregate housing with private rooms and shared common space; shared living in houses or apartments; accessory apartments built within or adjoining larger homes; senior housing, which is often subsidized and open also to younger disabled persons; retirement communities; supported group living such as rest homes and board-and-care homes; and assisted living with some nonmedical assistance.

Long-term care services are available for people living in the community. These include professional case managers who will come into the client's home, home-care and community service workers such as homemakers and people who do chores, personal care attendants, mental health and counseling services, and friendly visitors. Other services that help people stay in their homes include meals on wheels, transportation, protective arrangements to safeguard elderly people against abuse, congregate meals, emergency alert systems, and telephone reassurance. Structured programs outside the home include senior centers and adult day care. Help for overburdened caregivers includes support groups and respite-care services.

In-home health care services include home visits by physicians, skilled nursing care, therapy (by physical, occupational, health, speech, and other therapists), visits from social workers and home health aides, and provision of medical supplies. Day health centers provide more medical supervision than adult day care programs.

Another model is the life-care or continuing-care community, which offers a range of accommodations from independent through assisted to nursing home residences, all on the same premises. However, people with low or even moderate incomes cannot afford to live in these communities without subsidies.

Care in Nursing Homes

In the United States, nursing homes serve less than a quarter of the disabled elderly but cost four times as much as home care services (Rivlin and Weiner, 1988: 7). Because the high cost of nursing home care exceeds the financial resources of most of the elderly, well over half of the residents depend on Medicaid—the programs that pay for medical care for the indigent. To control costs, admission to nursing homes is mostly limited to the severely disabled. Although private long-term care insurance (with both in-home and nursing home coverage) is now available, few elderly people can afford it. Thus, the United States has depended on a welfare model rather than a public or private insurance model to pay for nursing home care. New models, such as increased support for family caregivers, private insurance incentives, and individual medical accounts, are being considered.

Nursing homes include profit-making, nonprofit, and public facilities. Vigilance, compliance with state and federal regulations, family and community involvement, a staff that is adequate in terms of both training and numbers, maintenance of residents' rights and autonomy, and freedom from abuse and unnecessary restraints help to ensure residents' dignity, their quality of life, and their own control over their lives.

Funding

The terminology describing types of services and residences varies throughout the world, as do the sources of funds to pay for these services and the actual availability of specific arrangements. In the United States, the federally funded Medicare program pays primarily for acute-care services, with only limited benefits for skilled nursing care. Federal funding for elderly home care services comes from Medicare, Medicaid, the social services block grant, the Veterans Administration, and the Older Americans Act. States also contribute to Medicaid and may supplement home-care services and other local programs and facilities. Nursing home care is paid for by residents, by some private insurance, and by Medicaid.

In the United States, several models, such as the experimental social–health maintenance organizations (S/HMOs) have tried to combine social and medical services for a given population group. Because a sharp distinction is made between medical and nonmedical long-term care services and because each program is unique, it is difficult to coordinate a comprehensive set of home-care services. Other developed countries have universal coverage for medical services, have usually not used a medical model for home-care services, and have more successfully integrated the continuum of services.

AIDS and Long-Term Care

The rapidly increasing number of people stricken with and dying of HIV/AIDS is an acute and devastating public health crisis spreading rapidly through many countries. In most of the world, the disease is transmitted primarily through heterosexual sex and is transmitted to women more easily than to men. Large numbers of children are being orphaned, requiring long-term care in countries that have no adequate programs to care for them. In the United States, public health education and advances in treatment have slowed both the transmission of the virus and the conversion of HIV to full-blown AIDS, and have allowed people with AIDS to survive longer. Under these circumstances, people with AIDS will need long-term medical and supportive care. Because of the lack of education for older people, HIV/AIDS is increasing among the elderly, especially women, in the United States.

The aging of the post-World War II baby boom generation, combined with rapidly falling mortality rates for the aged, will lead to a sharp increase in the demand for long-term care. Meeting and financing this increased demand will be one of the great challenges of the twenty-first century.

See Also

AGING; AIDS AND HIV; DISABILITY AND FEMINISM; DISABILITY: HEALTH AND SEXUALITY; DISABILITY: QUALITY OF

LIFE; ELDERLY CARE: WESTERN WORLD; ELDERLY CARE: CASE STUDY—CHINA; ELDERLY CARE: CASE STUDY—INDIA; HEALTH: OVERVIEW; NURSING HOMES

References and Further Reading

Adams, Stephanie, Heather Nawrocki, and Barbara Coleman. 1999. *Women and long-term care.* Washington, D.C.: Public Policy Institute, American Association of Retired Persons, November, Pub. ID: FS77. (AARP's Public Policy Institute, 601 E Street, N.W., Washington, DC 20049, publishes extensively on long-term care issues.)

Doress-Worters, Paula B., and Diana Laskin Siegal, in cooperation with the Boston Women's Health Book Collective. 1994. *The new ourselves, growing older: Women aging with knowledge and power.* New York: Simon and Schuster.

McCaman, Kathryn, and Charles Durrett. 1994. *Cohousing: A contemporary approach to housing ourselves,* Rev. ed. Berkeley, Calif.: Ten Speed.

Rivlin, Alice M., and Joshua M. Weiner. 1988. *Caring for the disabled elderly: Who will pay?* Washington, D.C.: Brookings Institution.

Diana Laskin Siegal

M

MADNESS

See MENTAL HEALTH I and MENTAL HEALTH II.

MAGAZINES

For two centuries or more, women's magazines have brought their predominantly female audiences issues that concern them. They cover a vast range of topics of interest to women from many socioeconomic classes, races, ethnicities, ages, and geographical regions: fashion and feminism, cooking and sports, romance and finance. No matter what a woman's interests are, she can probably find a magazine that addresses them.

This popular and inexpensive medium has attracted millions of readers around the world. In Japan, the magazines *With* and *Mrs.* are popular with adult women, while *Puchisebun, Olive, Seventeen,* and *MC Sisters* appeal to younger ones. In Germany, *Bravo Girl!* attracts a teenage audience, and *Jackie* is popular with young women in Great Britain.

Some of the most successful women's magazines today focus on fashion. The fashion magazine has a long history. An American, Sarah Josepha Buell Hale, started editing the *Ladies' Magazine* in 1828. Renamed *Godey's Lady's Book* in 1837, it became one of the most successful fashion magazines of the nineteenth century. *Godey's* was also the first women's magazine to last longer than five years. Hale's magazine succeeded because she was an astute analyzer of middle-class tastes. Another successful early fashion magazine, *Frank Leslie's Lady's Journal,* began in 1871 and was edited by Miriam Folline Leslie, one of the most important women journalists of her era. Hale and Leslie were two early pioneers in the field of women's fashion magazines who recognized how popular and lucrative they could be. Hundreds of publishers have since followed in these women's footsteps, producing fashion magazines such as *Vogue* and *Vanity Fair*—which emphasize elite styles—and the more middle-class *Redbook, Essence, Mademoiselle, Glamour, Elle,* and *Cosmopolitan. Seventeen, Sassy, Teen,* and *YM* are popular fashion magazines targeted at younger women.

Fiction, especially that directed to a female audience, has also been a staple in women's magazines. The popular *Peterson's Ladies' Magazine,* which began publication in 1842, based its success mainly on the fiction it featured. Gloria Steinem found the magazine a useful medium for spreading feminist and political messages when she founded *Ms.* Growing interest among women in physical well-being, sports, and fitness has motivated the creation in recent decades of women's magazines like *SELF.* There are also more specialized women's health, fitness, and sports magazines—for example, *American Cheerleader.*

Despite their popularity, women's magazines that focus on politics (*Ms.*) or physical fitness (*SELF*) have not attracted the large readership of some women's magazines that concentrate on home and lifestyle. Such magazines as *Good Housekeeping, Family Circle, Ladies' Home Journal,* and *Woman's Day* are fixtures in magazine racks across the United States—perennial best-sellers, read by generations of American women. Their editorial focus on middle-class tastes in fashion, food, crafts, and home decor has attracted an audience of millions. This success has stimulated many new ventures—for example, Martha Stewart's upscale *Living*—but none has achieved the success of its early predecessors.

Despite their great popularity, magazines aimed at women and girls are not always viewed positively by the mainstream press. Often, women's magazines are depicted as mindless entertainment without redeeming social value. Nonetheless, these magazines play an important role, as Naomi Wolf writes in *The Beauty Myth: How Images of Beauty Are Used against Women* (1992) because they "are the only products of popular culture that (unlike romances) change with women's reality, are mostly written by women for women about women's issues, and take women's concerns seriously." Around the world, the part played by magazines in spreading women's ideas and issues has been crucial, because many other media have traditionally disregarded or ghettoized those concerns. Women's magazines have given their readers a voice they might otherwise lack.

See Also

FASHION; IMAGES OF WOMEN: OVERVIEW; JOURNALISM; JOURNALISTS; POPULAR CULTURE; PUBLISHING; ZINES

References and Further Reading

Duffy, Margaret, and J. Michael Gotcher. 1996. Crucial advice on how to get the guy: The rhetorical vision of power and seduction in the teen magazine *YM. Journal of Communication Inquiry* 20: 32–48.

Duke, Lisa L., and Peggy J. Kreshel. 1998. Negotiating femininity: Girls in early adolescence read teen magazines. *Journal of Communication Inquiry* 22: 48–71.

Durham, Meenakshi G. 1998. Dilemmas of desire: Representations of adolescent sexuality in two teen magazines. *Youth and Society* 29: 369–389.

Evans, Ellis D., Judith Rutberg, Carmela Sather, and Charlie Turner. 1991. Content analysis of contemporary teen magazines for adolescent females. *Youth and Society* 23: 99–120.

Frazer, Elizabeth. 1987. Teenage girls reading *Jackie. Media, Culture and Society* 9: 407–425.

Hermann, Mareike. 1998. "Feeling better" with *BRAVO:* German girls and their popular youth magazine. In Sherrie A. Inness, ed., *Millennium girls: Today's girls around the world,* 213–242. Lanham, Md.: Rowman and Littlefield.

McCracken, Ellen. 1993. *Decoding women's magazines: From Mademoiselle to Ms.* New York: St. Martin's.

McRobbie, Angela. 1991. *Feminism and youth culture: From Jackie to Just Seventeen.* Boston: Unwin Hyman.

Peirce, Kate. 1990. A feminist theoretical perspective on the socialization of teenage girls through *Seventeen* magazine." *Sex Roles* 23: 491–500.

———. 1993. Socialization of teenage girls through teen-magazine fiction: The making of a new woman or an old lady? *Sex Roles* 29: 59–68.

Schrum, Kelly. "Teena means business": Teenage girls' culture and *Seventeen* magazine, 1944–1950. In Sherrie A. Inness, ed., *Delinquents and debutantes: Twentieth-century American girls' cultures,* 134–163. New York: New York University Press.

Wolf, Naomi. 1992. *The beauty myth.* New York: Doubleday.

Julie Hucke
Sherrie A. Inness

MAKEUP

See COSMETICS.

MANAGEMENT

In the twentieth century, the number of women in the paid labor force increased worldwide, and most of this growth occurred after 1980. This increase in women's workforce participation has been especially evident in industrialized countries. In the United States, the leading nation in the employment of women in management, women constitute 44 percent of the managerial workforce (Powell, 1999). Despite great progress, however, the picture is not entirely positive.

Representation of women in management has not yet reached 50 percent in any country (Harris, 1995). Women are almost entirely absent from the highest levels of management in organizations worldwide (Powell, 1999). Even in the United States, women constitute less than 5 percent of top-level managers (Ragins, Townsend, and Mattis, 1998). In the past, the absence of women at the highest levels of management was attributed to the fact that women had not been in the workforce long enough to achieve such success. This explanation is no longer relevant, particularly in the United States, where women began entering management in appreciable numbers in the early 1970s. Almost 30 years later, women still have not reached the highest levels of management in significant numbers.

Models of Women's Roles in Management

Several explanations have been proposed for the absence of women in upper-level management positions (Fagenson, 1993; Gutek, 1993). The first is called the "person-centered" or "gender-centered" model. According to this explanation, women lack the skills or characteristics necessary to attain high-level organizational positions. This model suggests that when women are able to develop the skills and characteristics they need to be top managers, they will secure high-level jobs. Evidence to support this model is lacking, however. Reviews of the literature on women in management report few differences between men and women with regard to their managerial skills and business education (Adler and Izraeli, 1994; Fagenson, 1993). In fact, some research suggests that women possess better skills than men, especially for supporting and empowering others (Fagenson, 1993). Interestingly, these skills have been identified as critical to managerial success, particularly in international contexts (Harris, 1995). The application of this model does not offer much hope for the rapid advancement of women in high-level managerial positions, if women's skills and educational achievements in the business field are already equivalent or superior to those of men.

A second explanation for the scarcity of women in executive positions is the "situation-centered" approach (Fagenson, 1993; Gutek, 1993). According to this model, sex discrimination results in women's being placed in organizational positions that confer little or no power and offer few opportunities for advancement. These limitations exert the greatest impact at higher organizational levels as a result of the "pyramid" shape typical of organizations. The end result is that very few women ever rise to hold positions in the executive suite. The situation-centered model suggests that vigorous enforcement of equal opportunity laws will result in greater progress for women in management. Although such laws exist in many countries, enforcement varies across countries and over time within countries (Gutek, 1993). Even when a reasonable amount of enforcement has occurred, as in the United States and Australia, the situation for women in management has not greatly improved (Harris, 1995).

A third approach, the "gender-organization-system" model, integrates the person-centered and the situation-centered models (Fagenson, 1993). This perspective suggests that men and women in organizations behave differently as a result both of their gender and of the situations they face within organizations. This model further suggests that individual, organizational, and systemic factors external to the organization interact to hinder the progress of women in management. Enhancing women's progress, according to this approach, would require taking into account these complex sets of interactions. Changes in the legal system, the economic system, societal beliefs and values, organizational structures and processes, and individuals are all important in facilitating the movement of women into top levels of management. Thus, the gender-organization-system model suggests that a multipronged approach to advancing women in management is likely to be the most successful strategy. Research so far has provided support for this theory (Fagenson, 1993; Powell, 1999).

Education

A primary requirement for advancement into management is an appropriate level of education. At present, the representation of women in U.S. business schools, including MBA programs, is approaching 50 percent. Women outside the United States are also pursuing educational opportunities in greater numbers. These trends indicate that women are entering the business world with the same educational preparation as men and, therefore, should hope to advance as far and as fast as men do. However, it is unlikely that education alone will be sufficient to break the barriers to women's progress into executive management. There is, in fact, an inverse relationship between educational credentials and position level: the higher the position sought, the less reliance individuals place on "objective" credentials such as education when deciding who will be promoted (Antal and Gnath, 1994). Although increased education might bring more women into management positions, it is probably not enough in and of itself to help them advance to the highest organizational levels.

Equal Opportunity Laws

Equal employment legislation is another factor that has helped women to enter and advance in the management hierarchy. The United States, Australia, and Great Britain have been the most vigorous with respect to passing and enforcing equal employment legislation. Most European Union countries have passed such legislation, but the strength and enforcement of the laws vary (Harris, 1995). The equal employment legislation that exists in Japan, for instance, is only rarely enforced (Adler, 1993). Women in Japan are frequently employed as casual labor, to be hired and fired at will.

Equal employment legislation has been instrumental in bringing women into the business world and into management, but it is unlikely to eliminate all the impediments they face. Legislation has the effect of forcing employers to select and promote employees on the basis of job-related criteria, but reliance on such objective criteria, diminishes as the level of the position within an organizational hierarchy rises, as noted above.

Work and Family Balance

Managerial work makes very high demands on employees' time, and these time demands often conflict with the pressures posed by family life. In the past, when most managers were men with wives who stayed at home and took care of the household and child-rearing tasks, these time demands could be met. As more women have entered the ranks of management, companies have started to look at making accommodations for dual-career couples with children. However, accommodations such as child care assistance, flexible work schedules, and telecommuting have only infrequently been offered by employers. Thus, little has been done to reduce the unequal burden women carry with respect to household management (Morrison et al., 1992).

In European countries, maternity leave and child care policies are more liberal than in the United States. In many Asian countries, however, married women and women with children are still expected to remain at home (Adler and Izraeli, 1994).

Organizational Culture

The culture of an organization can also limit women's ability to rise in the organizational hierarchy. Organizational culture is heavily influenced by senior company executives. A recent survey of chief executive officers of *Fortune* 1000 companies found that most of them believed that women had not been in management positions for a sufficient period of time to progress into the highest levels of management, and that women lack the general management experience necessary to do so. In contrast, the highest-ranking female executives in the same companies found stereotyping by male executives, exclusion from work-related networks, and a hostile organizational climate to be the major obstacles to women's advancement (Ragins et al., 1998).

In Japan, women are kept out of important decision-making positions, and anti-nepotism rules are used to force a woman married to a fellow employee to resign. In Malaysia and Singapore, women's presumed lack of geographic mobility is cited by male managers as a reason why few women have been promoted into managerial positions. In Germany, advertisements for executive positions routinely use the masculine pronoun (Adler, 1993).

Women may also face sexual harassment on the job. Anti-harassment laws in the United States have not been effective in eliminating this problem. Sexual harassment is widespread in Japan and is common in many European Union countries. When it is ignored or even tolerated by top-level managers, as is often the case, the climate for women in management can be quite hostile (Fagenson, 1993; Powell, 1999).

Male chief executive officers tend to view the organization as a "level playing field" where every individual has an equal opportunity to succeed. The obstacles identified by women are not apparent to them. One promising strategy for improving the situation is to have women work directly with top-level managers in order to make their superiors aware of the obstacles female employees face. In a second approach, women can cultivate mentors among high-level managers. This strategy has proved successful in facilitating women's advancement to higher levels of management (Fagenson, 1993; Ragins et al., 1998).

A feminist approach to women's advancement in organizations suggests a very different third strategy. It suggests that the male model of management—which advocates domination and hierarchy as the best systems for running organizations, and devalues child-rearing activities as detrimental to organizational efficiency—should be discarded. A woman-centered view of organizations should be adopted in its place (Fagenson, 1993). A more woman-friendly approach to the design of organizations would promote equality and participation; it would also allow women to have and care for children without making substantial economic sacrifices. This proposal calls for a total restructuring of the workplace, based on appreciating and valuing what women bring to it (Harris, 1995).

Women have made much progress in the field of management during the past few decades. Their movement into the management profession has been both supported and facilitated by changes in social, legal, and business environments in many countries. As competitive pressures increase in the global economy, businesses will need to make the most of the human resources available to them, and women represent resources that companies have not yet fully utilized. The companies that are best able to capitalize on this resource will be the most likely to succeed.

See Also

ENTREPRENEURSHIP; EQUAL OPPORTUNITIES; LEADERSHIP; ORGANIZATIONAL THEORY; WORK: EQUAL PAY AND CONDITIONS; WORK: OCCUPATIONAL EXPERIENCES

References and Further Reading

Adler, N. J. 1993. An international perspective on the barriers to the advancement of women managers. *Applied Psychology: An International Perspective* 42: 289–300.

———, and Izraeli, D. N., eds. 1994. *Competitive frontiers: Women managers in a global economy.* Cambridge, Mass.: Blackwell.

Antal, A. B., and Gnath, C. K. 1994. Women in management in Germany: East, West, and reunited. In N. J. Adler and D. N. Izraeli, eds., *Competitive frontiers: Women managers in a global economy.* Cambridge, Mass.: Blackwell.

Fagenson, E. A. ed. 1993. *Women in management: Trends, issues, and challenges in managerial diversity.* Newbury Park, Calif.: Sage.

Gutek, B. A. 1993. Changing the status of women in management. *Applied Psychology: An International Review* 42, 301–311.

Morrison, A. M., White, R. P., and Van Velsor, E. 1992. *Breaking the glass ceiling.* Reading, Mass.: Addison-Wesley.

Powell, G. N. 1999. *Handbook of gender and work.* Newbury Park, Calif.: Sage.

Ragins, B. R., Townsend, B., and Mattis, M. 1998. Gender gap in the executive suite: CEOs and female executives report on breaking the glass ceiling. *Academy of Management Executive* 12: 28–42.

Ellen A. F. Eland

MARKETING

See ADVERTISING and ADVERTISING INDUSTRY.

MARRIAGE: Overview

Marriage is a culturally approved relationship that legitimizes a sexual and economic union, usually between a man and a woman. All national states have definitions of what constitutes a legal marriage and under what circumstances it can be lawfully dissolved; indeed, there may be as many definitions of marriage as there are cultures and legislatures. Marriage is one of the most important events in a person's life. In many cultures a person may marry only once, or at least that may be the ideal, particularly for women. Marriage always carries an implication of permanency, even in cultures where divorce is not unusual. In many cultures, girls are trained from an early age to be good wives and mothers, and those who never marry are generally considered unlucky outsiders, unless they join a convent or another institution for celibates.

Defining the Union

Most societies and religions have rituals marking the onset of the union. Marriage certificates, wedding banquets, and other ceremonies show that an alliance has taken place and that the two people involved have certain duties, rights, and obligations to each other, their families, and the children engendered or adopted by them.

Societies may distinguish between legal marriages—those recognized by civil or religious authorities—and common-law or consensual unions. Consensual unions can be an alternative when divorce is not permitted or when a new marriage would mean losing an inheritance or a widow's pension. In many places, consensual unions are forbidden, and any children produced are considered illegitimate and may not have the same rights as those of legal unions.

Marriages can be dissolved by death, divorce, invalidation, separation, or abandonment. However, not all societies permit dissolution of a marriage. Divorce is still prohibited in many countries, and where it is possible, it may be seen as morally wrong. In some cases, not even death ends the surviving partner's obligations.

Selection of Marriage Partners

All societies have rules and restrictions determining whom one can marry, when one can marry, where a married couple should reside, the number of spouses one may take, and to whom the children produced belong. The incest taboo, a restriction known to all human societies, bans sexual relations and marriage with certain culturally defined kin members. Some societies—such as the Inca, ancient Egyptians, and Hawaiians—have permitted royal marriages between brothers and sisters. Other societies entirely forbid marriage between cousins, while still others permit marriage only between cousins of a certain degree. There are also rules of endogamy, which oblige people to marry only within their own or some other specified group, and rules of exogamy, which state that people must marry outside their kin group or another close community. The societal rules pertaining to marriage may be different from those regulating permitted sexual relations, and they may also vary in their interpretation of economic and moral alliances, rights, and obligations.

Arranged marriages have been the norm in many cultures; a "go-between," or marriage broker may be given charge of finding a suitable match. In arranged marriages, neither the man nor the woman may have much choice; often they have not even seen each other before the ceremony. On the other hand, there are societies in which the idea of mutual love and consent is an important precursor to marriage; societies that have long elaborate courtship rituals; and societies in which it is acceptable for couples to live together before formal marriage. Most societies have restrictions in regard to the minimum age at which one should or may marry. Children are still betrothed very early in some areas of the world (for instance, India), even though this may be illegal. Recent Chinese law, in an attempt to regulate the birthrate of the population, authorized women to marry only after age 26; in contrast, a traditional Chinese practice existed in which baby girls were adopted by their future parents-in-law as a way of minimizing conflict between marital expectations and family obligations. Sometimes, when a boy died, his child fiancée would be widowed without ever having been married.

In societies where marriage partners are selected more freely, people of marriageable age have to find their own suitable mates, who are likely to belong to the same ethnic group, socioeconomic class, race, and religion. Courtship practices in these cases include dating, going to singles bars, and participating in a trial marriage, a period in which couples have an opportunity to get to know each other better and to see if they are compatible and willing to enter into long-term legal marriage. Industrial societies may also have marriage brokers and sophisticated matchmaking systems in which each interested party pays a fee for a list of available persons who fit designated expectations and requirements. Love marriages stress the emotional attachment and solidarity of the couple over the obligations that each person has to his or her own birth family.

Same-sex marriages have been reported in the ethnographic record from Africa to native North America. The Cheyenne Indians allowed married men to take male transvestites as second wives. Female husbands have been reported among the Bantu and other African groups. In the late twentieth century, industrialized countries such as the United States began debating whether to legalize same-sex unions. In some states, the "domestic partner" can be a beneficiary of his or her partner's insurance and can obtain financial indemnization, child custody, and visitation and other rights nearly equal to those of a legal spouse.

Marriages that involve only two people are known as "monogamous." The custom of marrying more than one person, or polygamy, can involve unrelated men or women or a group of brothers and sisters. When societies allow a man to have more than one wife, the practice is known as "polygyny"; this is found in many Muslim groups. The custom of polyandry permits a woman to have several husbands simultaneously. The practice of consecutive monogamous marriage—that is, divorcing a marriage partner and then marrying someone else—is considered by some to be a form of "serial" polygamy.

Residence and Familial Affiliation after Marriage

Once couples get married, they have to find a place of residence. In many societies, the chosen place is an independent dwelling away from parents and relatives, termed neolocal residence. Other types of residence include matrilocal, in which couples live with or near the wife's parents; patrilocal, in which they settle with or near the husband's parents; avunculocal, in which both partners leave their original places of residence and move in with or near the husband's mother's brother; and bilocal, in which couples live with or near either the wife's parents or the husband's parents.

The question of familial affiliation of the children produced in a marital relationship and of custody in case of parental death or divorce is not simple. Although some industrialized states have laws giving equal privileges to both mothers and fathers, other societies follow a pattern—known as "rules of descent"—of connecting particular individuals with sets of kin. In patrilineal descent, the children belong to the line of the father, and affiliation is transmitted through sons to their children. The mother's last name—which was her father's—is lost. In matrilineal descent, an individual is affiliated only through the female line, and children belong to the mother and her kin group. There are societies that affiliate some children with the father and others with the mother, a situation known as "ambilineal" descent.

Marriage and the Social Order

Marriage systems are related to kinship and gender systems and are tied in to economic and political structures. An analysis of any marriage system naturally includes the ideological, sexual, and economic aspects of the relationship. In many societies, this can be translated into the ways in which women are exchanged or used to cement political alliances. Sometimes the number of wives a man has reflects on his status, wealth, and occupation. In some societies, women are seen only as wives and mothers at the service of men. Gender relations are socially constructed in relation to kinship and marriage systems and are a function of wider socioeconomic and political systems.

In kin-based and nonstratified societies in which the division of labor is determined primarily by sex and age, marriage is a controlling factor in the distribution of rights, privileges, and obligations. Marriage, as the basis of kinship, thus often perpetuates social inequality in these societies and does little to alleviate the chronic disputes that occur between men over rights to women (Collier, 1988).

Theories explaining marriage restrictions were long the domain of male scholars who saw marriage as a relation of reciprocity in which men exchange women—in other words, as the "union of a man and a woman who is either someone's daughter or sister, by the union of daughter or sister of that man or another man with the first man in question" (Lévi-Strauss, 1959). New approaches to the study of marriage have demonstrated that women are not passive objects of rules governing the rights that men allegedly have to transfer women from group to group. However, a feminist critique of the institution of marriage has suggested that women are often the pawns in marital transactions by men. Females are used as "bait" in the acquisition of male prestige, power, and property. Many traditional practices that are detrimental to women—foot-binding, female circumcision, the enforcing of virginity, and the seclusion of women in purdah—increase the desirability of a daughter as a future wife or the prestige of her parents and husband.

Some scholars have argued that marriage and kinship systems are at the root of male aggression and dominance (Rubin, 1975). In many places, marriage still involves a relationship in which husbands and fathers are the rulers, while women are considered legal minors and are confined to the domestic sphere. Male and female relations outside the home often tend to reproduce this patriarchal structure. In the workplace in industrialized societies, women usually are subordinate to men, and they may receive a lower salary, in part because it is assumed that working is a discretionary activity for women, whereas men work in order to provide for dependents. Family reform movements are calling for a change in the distribution of power within the marital relationship (Harding, 1981) as well as in the public sphere. There is also an international movement to improve the situation of women and to change women's and men's roles in both private and public domains. At the same time, choices like celibacy as an alternative to marriage or the election of childlessness are increasingly accepted.

Feminist researchers have challenged many of the assumptions of the social science literature, including the family as a biological given, the mythologizing of women's experiences, the glorification of motherhood, and the emphasis on domestic harmony (Thorne, 1982). They have also contested the ideological notion of the nuclear family and the concept of "family values," in particular the ways in which these are defined and distorted in order to fit political agendas.

See Also

COURTSHIP; DOWRY AND BRIDEPRICE; DIVORCE; FAMILY: RELIGIOUS AND LEGAL SYSTEMS, *regional entries;* KINSHIP; MARRIAGE: INTERRACIAL AND INTERRELIGIOUS; MARRIAGE: LESBIAN; MARRIAGE: REGIONAL TRADITIONS AND PRACTICES; MARRIAGE: REMARRIAGE; POLYGYNY AND POLYANDRY; WIDOWHOOD; WIFE

References and Further Reading

Bohannan, Paul, and J. Middleton, eds. 1968. *Marriage, family, and residence.* Garden City, N.Y.: Natural History.

Collier, Jane Fishburne. 1988. *Marriage and inequality in classless societies.* Stanford: Stanford University Press.

Fox, Robin. 1967. *Kinship and marriage.* Cambridge; Cambridge University Press.

Gough, K. 1959. The Nayars and the definition of marriage. *Journal of the Royal Anthropological Institute* 89: 23–34.

Harding, Susan. 1981. Family reform movements: Recent feminism and its opposition. *Feminist Studies* 7(1): 57–75.

Lévi-Strauss, Claude. 1959. *The elemental structures of kinship,* 116. Boston: Beacon.

Rubin, Gayle. 1975. The traffic in women: Notes on the "political" economy of sex. In Rayna Rapp Reyter, ed., *Toward an anthropology of women,* 157–210. New York: Monthly Review.

Thorne, Barrie. 1982. Feminist rethinking of the family: An overview. In Barrie Thorne with Marilyn Yalom, eds. *Rethinking the family: Some feminist questions,* 1–24. New York: Longman.

Patricia Tovar

MARRIAGE: Interracial and Interreligious

Many societies have prohibitions or preferences regarding intermarriage that serve to link groups and establish alliances. In many parts of the world, including Europe and South Asia, aristocratic women were long given away in marriage to seal military and trade alliances and to unify territories. Exogamy is the practice by which a particular societal grouping favors marriage outside its own kin group, village, or language group. Endogamy, in contrast, requires people within a society to marry within a specified group, which may be defined in terms of region, community, ethnicity, religion, caste, or social class. Arab societies, for example, have a preference for marriage between parallel cousins—that is, between children of same-sex siblings, especially one's father's brother.

Sometimes the offspring of interethnic marriages are the first victims when conflict arises, as in the case of the former Yugoslavia. In India, marriage between people of different castes or different religions can lead to ostracism of the couple or interfamilial strife in the village, even though such harassment is illegal.

Although the prohibition of marriages between blacks and whites common in many U.S. southern states was declared unconstitutional in 1967, the number of married interracial couples remains low. In the United States, the most frequent type of interracial marriage is between black upper- or middle-class males and lower-class white females (Zack, 1993). This in part reflects the taboos of slavery, where white women were not allowed to have sex with black males, while white men had sexual relations with black women but did not marry them. In this instance, intermarriage is related to an increase in one's status.

Theories of racial purity and superiority—as well as the interrelation among class status, women's subordination, and racism—have played a large role in marriage prohibitions throughout history (Martinez-Alier, 1989). Racism permits the perpetuation of economic privilege and rank, thus reproducing and reinforcing inequality. Governments may restrict citizenship privileges or invoke immigration policies that manipulate perceptions of "melting pots" and "color blindness," and they may encourage or discourage intermarriage according to the needs and ethnic makeup of the ruling class. A marriage does not always guarantee that the spouse and the children will have full citizenship rights. Before 1974, Portuguese women could lose their citizenship if they married foreigners. In Israel, matrimonial law is determined by Jewish religious regulations that prohibit mixed marriages (Mayer, 1987).

Data are controversial about whether interracial and intercultural marriages have higher rates of conflict, either within the family or in the society at large. Clearly, the couple has to compromise in terms of the languages spoken at home, the religions practiced, the values and traditions acceptable in the household, and the obligations to kin. Because they can also raise issues of racism and class, conflicts may be tolerated less or dealt with in a different manner than in a nonmixed marriage. Conversely, a decision to marry outside one's group may also make a family more open to compromise and cooperation.

See Also

FAMILY: RELIGIOUS AND LEGAL SYSTEMS: *regional entries;* MARRIAGE: OVERVIEW; RACISM AND XENOPHOBIA

References and Further Reading

Martinez-Alier, Verena. 1989. *Marriage, class, and color in nineteenth-century Cuba.* Ann Arbor: University of Michigan Press.

Mayer, Egon. 1987. *Love and tradition: Marriage between Jews and Christians.* New York: Schocken.

Zack, Naomi. 1993. *Race and mixed race.* Philadelphia, Pa.: Temple University Press.

Patricia Tovar

MARRIAGE: Lesbian

Though many lesbians and academics explicitly use the term *lesbian marriage* to express their activism in favor of legal recognition of lesbian partnerships, in no nation (as of this writing) do lesbian unions yet enjoy the same legal rights and status as heterosexual marriages. The struggle for recognition of lesbian marriage has shifted from early feminist critiques of marriage as a patriarchal and inhibiting institution to a recognition of the legal and political benefits of marriage. Legal benefits at issue include securing health insurance coverage for lesbian and gay partners, ensuring inheritance and residential continuity for partners of the deceased, counteracting discrimination in the workplace, and preserving child custody rights. A useful resource for tracking progress on these issues and their regional solutions in the United States is the legal handbook by Curry (1994 and future editions). It is notable that cities have taken the lead in this regard; changes in city ordinances have then prompted changes at the state level in New York, California, Minnesota, and Oregon. These city and regional laws recognizing gay and lesbian partnerships have faced opposition from reactionary state and national level countermovements against gay and lesbian rights.

Issues of responsibility have been as important as rights in winning legal recognition for lesbian unions. The issue of responsibility to former partners has come to the fore with several widely publicized cases in which dissolving partners were found liable for alimony-type payments to former partners.

Stereotypes of lesbian unions as inherently more supportive than heterosexual unions have been challenged in a study of partner abuse in the former (Renzetti, 1992). Other issues that have emerged in the recent literature recognizing lesbian and gay family forms are their long history, and the relationship of lesbian and gay couples to their "families of origin" (Weston, 1991).

Social and political movements in support of recognizing gay and lesbian partnerships have been prominent mainly in western societies, and the view from Asia and Africa on the legal status of lesbian partnership has been little studied. Topics needing investigation include the degree of societal institutionalization of lesbian partnerships, the gender status of lesbians, and the cross-cultural recognition of lesbian commitment ceremonies. The existence of female "husbands" in some African herding societies is often cited as evidence of social institutionalization of lesbian partnerships in those societies, but the social recognition of intimacy and sexuality within these "marriages" is still not well understood.

See Also

HOUSEHOLDS: FEMALE-HEADED AND FEMALE-SUPPORTED; LESBIANISM; MOTHERHOOD: LESBIAN

Reference and Further Reading

Curry, Hayden. 1994. *A legal guide for lesbian and gay couples.* 8th ed. Berkeley, Calif.: Nolo.

Johnson, Susan E. 1990. *Staying power: Longterm lesbian couples.* Tallahassee, Fl.: Naiad.

Renzetti, Claire M. 1992. *Violent betrayal: Partner abuse in lesbian relationships.* Newbury Park, Calif.: Sage.

Sherman, Suzanne, ed. 1992. *Lesbian and gay marriage: Private commitments, public ceremonies.* Philadelphia: Temple University Press.

Weston, Kath. 1991. *Families we choose: Lesbians, gays, kinship.* New York: Columbia University Press.

Karen Frojen Herrera

MARRIAGE: Regional Traditions and Practices

Most societies have rituals and ceremonies to mark engagement, the closing of a marital contract, and the onset of living together in a marriage. Marriage practices are historically and economically rooted and often include property exchanges that seal a union and determine the role women will have, both as wives and as daughters. These economic transactions have profound implications for the social structure. Dowry and bride-price or bride wealth are the most common transactions (Goody, 1973); other marriage arrangements include gift exchange, token payment, and sister exchange.

Bride wealth is a gift in goods, livestock, or cash given by the groom or his family to the bride's family. In case of divorce, her family usually has to return the bride wealth. Bride wealth is considered a compensation given to the bride's parents for their granting the groom the right to her children and her labor. It does not mean buying a woman as a slave or a servant. Indeed, it may increase the prestige of women. Bride wealth is practiced in a wide range of societies: nonstratified groups such as the Gusii of Kenya, certain groups in New Guinea and the Philippines, the Hopi and Navajo of North America, the Guajiro of south America, and many non-Brahman groups in traditional south India, to name a few. Grooms may spend years accumulating bride wealth until they can afford to get married. This means that elderly men often control large households of women.

Other societies practice brother–sister exchange, in which a groom can exchange one of his female relatives for a bride. Some groups of hunter-gatherers and hunter-horticulturalists have the bride-service model, in which the groom has to work for his bride's family either before or after the marriage. Some men may exchange their sisters or other female relatives for brides as an alternative to bride service.

Dowry is property in the form of land, cash, or goods that is given by the bride's family to the prospective husband or his family. The trousseau—clothing, linens, and sometimes furniture—that women assemble (beginning in childhood) is also part of the dowry. The bigger the dowry, the higher the woman's desirability and therefore also her chances of increasing the social standing of her family. In highly stratified societies like those in north India, families start saving for dowries right after girls are born. The practice of dowry seems to correlate with low status for women and to intensify the chances that women will be unfairly treated. The abortion of female fetuses, female infanticide (to forestall the need to provide dowries), and killing of brides (to seize their dowries) are some consequences of this practice. On the other hand, a dowry may be the only insurance that a woman has if she becomes a widow (Kaplan, 1985). Dower is similar to dowry, except that the money is given to the woman herself at the time of marriage, though she may subsequently give it to her husband for family needs. Dower tends to give women more autonomy, although it may be manipulated by husbands. It is also less common than dowry.Egypt is one example of a society in which dower is used.

Elopement and bride theft are other ways to enter a marital relationship, and these are reported in different areas of the world, such as Polynesia (Ortner, 1981). Another alternative is mail-order brides. Mail-order wives from poor countries are selected by men from affluent countries, sometimes because they are thought to be more submissive. There have, however, been a variety of other circumstances in which marriages have come about by this means. For a while in the nineteenth century, no Chinese women were allowed to migrate to the United States, creating a situation of extreme scarcity of Chinese wives. Chinese men later solved this scarcity by ordering brides through the mail.

See Also

COURTSHIP; DOWRY AND BRIDEPRICE; INFANTICIDE; SUTTEE (SATI); WEDDINGS

References and Further Reading

Goody, Jack. 1973. Bridewealth and dowry in Africa and Eurasia. In Jack Goody and Stanley Jeyaraja Tambiah, eds., *Bridewealth and dowry*, 1–57. Cambridge: Cambridge University Press.

Kaplan, Marion. 1985. *The marriage bargain: Women and dowries in European history.* Binghamton, N.Y.: Harrington Park.

Ortner, Sherry. 1981. Gender and sexuality in hierarchical societies: The case of Polynesia and some comparative implications. In Sherry Ortner and Harriet Whitehead, eds., *Sexual Meanings*, 359–409. Cambridge: Cambridge University Press.

Patricia Tovar

MARRIAGE: Remarriage

The degree to which a society restricts or permits women's remarriage is closely related to customs of divorce and widowhood. In many societies, marriage is allowed only once, even if the spouse dies. Some religions have strict prohibitions regarding remarriage, as is case among higher Hindu castes.

Many Roman Catholic countries do not recognize divorce to dissolve church marriages, and an ideology of "eternal love" is enforced. Other countries grant civil divorces, but the church may consider the remarriage of divorcees adultery; only when a marriage is annulled can the partners remarry. When divorce is stigmatized, people have less chance of remarrying because they are inhibited by ideas of wrongdoing, fault, and guilt, and perhaps also by the notion of holiness attached to the first marriage.

Remarriage of widows is prohibited or discouraged in many parts of the world. In India, for example, one indication of high caste has traditionally been an interdiction against remarriage. In China, arches were built to honor widows who never remarried but remained filial daughters-in-law. Although the remarriage of widows is not forbidden in the Christian Bible, it is seen as undesirable; Saint Paul suggested (in I Corinthians) that people, including widows, stay unmarried unless they were unable to control their passion. In general, the Catholic church regards second nuptials less highly than first marriages. In many parts of preindustrial Europe second weddings, especially of mismatched couples, were ridiculed in a ritual called *charivari:* villagers expressed their disapproval of the union by making loud noises and singing rowdy songs to the newlyweds (Goody, 1976).

Remarriage has religious, economic, and demographic implications. It affects inheritance, family structure and size, and the socialization of children. Historical studies in Europe have found that remarriage of widowed people occurrs more frequently in the lower classes (Sogner and Dupaquier, 1981). Men remarry more than women, and young people more than old. The marriageability of a divorced or widowed person has to be compared with that of never-married people of the same age. Widows may be more independent than married women, and they may not want to relinquish that freedom through a second marriage unless they are forced to do so by strong economic or social pressures.

When widowed or divorced people remarry, step-relationships are often formed. Customs of property disposal usually permit widowers to remarry and keep full rights to the property and children of the first marriage. Some countries, however, require that people who are remarrying keep their property separate in order to preserve the inheritance rights of existing children. In most societies, divorced women are entitled to alimony and their children to child support from the father. Deciding to remarry sometimes involves weighing the risk of losing alimony or a widow's pension.

In many polygynous societies, a widow is expected to marry her husband's younger brother, a practice known as the *levirate.* This was customary in the Jewish and Islamic worlds, in some African patrilineal societies, and among Native Americans. This relationship does not necessarily impry a sexual obligation, but the *levir* (Latin, "brother-in-law") may have the duty to provide the dead man with an heir; at the same time, the survival of the widow and orphans is ensured by the patrilineal group.

See Also

ADULTERY; DIVORCE; JUDAISM; MARRIAGE: OVERVIEW; STEPFAMILIES; WIDOWHOOD

References and Further Reading

Goody, Jack. 1976. Inheritance, property and women. In J. Goody, J. Thirsk, and E. P. Thompson, eds., *Family and inheritance: Rural society in western Europe 1200–1800.* Cambridge: Cambridge University Press.

Sogner, S., and J. Dupaquier. 1981. Introduction. In J. Dupaquier, E. Helin, P. Laslett, M. Livi-Bacci, and S. Sogner, *Marriage and remarriage in populations of the past.* London: Academic Press.

Patricia Tovar

MARTYRS

Martyrdom—the willingness to sacrifice one's life in the name of one's faith—has been a common theme in religious history. Various religions, including early (c. 200–400 C.E.) and medieval (ca. 1200–1400 C.E.) Christianity and Neo-Confucianism (ca. 960–1279 C.E.), have taught that martyrdom enables believers to achieve spiritual perfection and a position among the blessed. An emphasis on sexual renunciation and asceticism in both Christianity and Neo-Confucianism, combined with the association of women with carnality, led both traditions to encourage women to a general martyrdom of resignation in the face of suffering. Images of female martyrs in the "martyr literature" of both traditions reflect an obsession with ensuring women's virginity or chastity.

The emergence of Neo-Confucianism included a revised moral code for women that reflected a view of them as the dangerous hosts of sensual desires that must be controlled so as not to block men's progress toward sagehood. The most influential Neo-Confucian texts contain numerous models of exemplary women martyrs who are willing to mutilate themselves, submit to cruel debasement, or commit suicide rather than lose their chastity before marriage or violate the chastity of widowhood by entering into a second marriage. These texts helped create a chastity cult for women that became a new religious and social orthodoxy (Kelleher, 1987). Although most women in China have come to reject this Neo-Confucian ideal of female martyrdom as clearly oppressive to women, feminist scholars have a more ambivalent view of the Christian martyr literature.

Women are often the heroes in Christian martyr tales written by both men and women. Because the martyr represents the ultimate image of Christ, the repeated theme of women's power to be sanctified through martyrdom shows women's equality with men in the ability to achieve this ideal state. Some feminist interpretations see an important early vision of female heroism in these tales of women willing to endure brutal torture, persecution, and death rather than lose their virginity or violate vows of chastity through rape or marriage to pagan men. As Rosemary Radford Ruether (1987) states, "This literature held up to women the vision of a new equality in Christ and a heroism available through rejection of family and state authority and the adoption of celibacy" (217).

Other feminist readers of the martyr literature, however, are more critical of them as grisly fantasies of torture and butchery that reinforce patriarchal abhorrence of women's sexuality. Further, according to critics such as Barbara Walker (1983), "The real martyrs of the early Christian era were not made by the pagans so much as by their fellow Christians [who] massacred thousands of 'heretics' " including pagan women who refused to renounce their own Goddess religion (600–602 C.E.). From this perspective, the politico-religious persecution of the heretics and witches is the more important focus of any study of "women martyrs."

Finally, it may be that an ideal of individual martyrdom is inconsistent with the character of women's religions and feminist theology because it individualizes women's problems and solutions rather than focusing on the structural oppression that is ultimately responsible for much of women's suffering. In contrast to the promise of otherworldly beatitude inherent in martyrdom, feminist theology tends to focus on women's lives in this world.

See Also

CHRISTIANITY: FEMINIST CHRISTOLOGY; CONFUCIANISM; HERESY; THEOLOGIES: FEMINIST; SAINTS

References and Further Reading

Kelleher, Theresa. 1987. Confucianism. In Arvind Sharma, ed., *Women in world religions,* 135–159. Albany: State University of New York Press.

Lerner, Gerda. 1993. *The creation of feminist consciousness, from the Middle Ages to 1870.* New York: Oxford University Press.

Ruether, Rosemary Radford. 1987. Christianity. In Arvind Sharma, ed., *Women in world religions,* 207–233. Albany: State University of New York Press.

Walker, Barbara. 1983. Martyrs. In *The woman's encyclopedia of myths and secrets,* 600–602. San Francisco: Harper and Row.

Cathy Peppers
Ivone Gebara

MARXISM

Marxism is one of several socialist economic and social theories that developed in response to the oppression that emerged with the growth of western industrial capitalism. The Marxist materialist conception of history proposes ways in which humans can act on their environment, in a politically conscious movement, to create more equal situations in which human potential can be developed. Karl Marx and Friedrich Engels, the founding theorists of Marxism in the middle to late nineteenth century, stated that liberal ideas of justice, individual rights, and human nature were by no means universal or immutable but were rather the product of a particular historical period, and they could therefore be changed. Marx was deeply concerned with exploring inequalities in societies because he believed that democracy cannot exist alongside inequality and special interests. In Marxism, a faith in human consciousness is set alongside concentration on the organization of society and a conception of man's mastery of nature as a driving force of history. The theory of human progress in Marxism views history primarily in terms of the development of efforts to dominate production processes.

Marxism and Society

Broadly speaking, Marx outlines six stages in the development of societies: primitive communism, slavery, feudalism, capitalism, socialism, and communism. These stages develop different forces of production (means of production and labor power) and varying relations of production (class relations or the organization of production). For Marx, the period of slavery ended not because society became enlightened about its immorality, but because it was no longer profitable or successful as a relation of production. Nineteenth-century capitalism was seen as a form of human society important for accelerating man's mastery, while at the same time its economic system contained the seeds of its destruction in favor of the creation of a socialist society, from which a classless communist society would develop in turn. Because production is carried out within social organization, historical analysis of the relation between the forces and relations of production reveals the changes in social systems. Marx's belief that history is progressive is supported by human domination over nature. In capitalist societies, this development of forces takes place within an increasingly oppressive social organization, and the relations of production move beyond human control. Capitalist societies are defined by the division into classes, which are determined by their relation to the means of production. In capitalism, the bourgeoisie and ruling class own the means of production, while the propertyless workers are forced into the laboring class, owning only their own labor power under conditions that they do not determine.

Socialism requires a particular stage of development of capitalism as its precursor. Class conflict—the economic exploitation of workers by the bourgeoisie—is the dynamic of change. The coming to consciousness by the mass of workers of the injustice of their exploitation and their realization of their power to effect change can result in a revolutionary situation in which the capitalist order is overturned and a socialist society organized. Marx did not specify whether this revolution would be spontaneous or organized, violent or peaceful. A classless communist society would develop out of the stage of socialist organization. These ideas were popularized in works such as *The Communist Manifesto* (1848). Although the ideas of thinkers such as Marx and Engels had far-reaching implications within societies at the time of their distribution, the influence of their works came to fullness with the Russian Revolution of 1917.

Marxism and Women

Marx and Engels do not place women in the center of their analyses; indeed, they have little to say directly about women's subordination and oppression as something particular, apart from the general oppression of workers. The tools of Marxist theorizing, however, were to have beneficial effects within early feminist liberation thinking. For instance, the socialization of domestic work—envisaged by Engels in *The Origin of the Family, Private Property and the State* (1884) as a stage toward equalizing relations between men and women in society—had a profound impact on feminist debates. Engels outlines the appalling conditions under which women had to labor and the changed nature of public and private aspects of familial oppression. This formulation of women's participation in social production and the question of relations between individual and society became a central theme in much socialist feminist analysis. Engels's critiques of household work's becoming privatized under capitalism, and of women's position as "slaves of the workers," alienated from one another, are powerful; however, he views the family solely in the context of the social division of labor and assesses women's oppression mainly with reference to different forms of ownership. Ideas of women's personal oppression are absent.

Feminist thinkers have criticized Marx and Engels for their lack of a systematic study of the specific oppression of women or of the gendered nature of power relations. Engels does not attempt to explore implications of the changes to occur under socialism. His critique of existing gender relations is based on the dominance of economic power rather than on that of male power, and it is more cautious than the writing on free love by the utopian socialists who were his contemporaries. Engels does not recognize male and female sexuality equally but instead assumes that men have greater needs and women wish to submit; that heterosexuality is natural; and that economic factors outweigh other motivations. In the classless society Engels foresees, male domination over women would cease, yet the bases of this domination are inadequately theorized, so his assumed "inevitable" harmony between men and women is at best naive in ignoring the benefits men gain from their dominance.

Women and Work in Marxism

It was in the area of women and work that Marxism had its most powerful impact on later generations of socialists and feminists. The two essential preconditions for women's emancipation—women's participation in the workforce and the socialization of domestic work—could not happen under capitalism; they would have to take place in a system in which industry was socialized or communally owned, and within a society in which the nuclear family model was not underpinning private property and profits. Liberation was to be gained by workers' efforts to control the external world of work. It was assumed that with this control and the achievement of a socialist revolution, the contradictions of women's oppression would be overcome, and the expression of fully human development would be realized.

Even though Marxist political writings provide limited theoretical guidance on the problems of women's oppression and women's liberation, the work of Marx and Engels and their "scientific" brand of socialism had a significant impact on nineteenth- and twentieth-century feminism in at least five major ways:

- Marx is the philosopher of the oppressed, and women are oppressed.
- Marx is also the preeminent theorist of revolution, and liberal and socialist thinkers recognized the liberation of women as a revolutionary proposition centered on challenging the "sacred" social institution of the family.
- Placing family and sexual relationships in a historical context, along with other forms of social organization, meant that they could be challenged and changed.
- The impact of economic factors on the condition of women, as the result of a particular historical stage of development, made Marx's critique of political economy particularly appropriate to women.
- Marxism is about *praxis,* and so it was important for later feminists in outlining the importance of "changing the world" on the basis of practical experience—the impact of theory, practice, and reflection. New methods of analysis were offered for feminist thinking (see Corrin, 1999).

Nevertheless, the basic Marxist categories—such as value of labor—remain ungendered and do not explain why women are oppressed differently from men. Because the proletarian struggle would allow automatic emancipation for all people, little attention was paid to sexual relations, which were deemed to be determined largely by economic relations. On these and other crucial issues of organization, anarchist thinkers such as Emma Goldman broke with the Marxists. Goldman argued that the exploitation of women took on an extra dimension in terms of male–female relations; she was passionate in her defense of women's right to "be women," whatever that entailed, and she voiced her disdain for the state as a vehicle for women's liberation. It was in part the disputes on these issues between the Marxists and anarchists that helped to dissolve the First International, a conference held in 1864. The impact of the thought of Marx and Engels on the Russian revolutionaries was to have consequences for women's "liberation" under socialism and to generate debates regarding socialist feminism internationally.

Impact of Marxism on Women's Studies

In extending earlier Marxist discussions, Marxist, materialist, and socialist feminism engendered vigorous debates about the roots of women's oppression under capitalism and showed that women's oppression had a material foundation. Within the materialist strand, a division is generally made between economic materialists, such as Christine Delphy and those—for example, Adrienne Rich—who view sexuality as the prime basis of oppression. Although Marxist methods proved useful for feminists analyzing the ongoing causes of women's oppression, a break with orthodox Marxism soon became apparent in debates concerning the linking of capitalist and patriarchal systems of oppression. In one break, radical feminists claim that at some level all previous theorizing on patriarchy was itself patriarchal. Another major feminist contribution has been the broadening of conceptions of "work" to include domestic labor, which enabled feminists to argue that the invisibility of domestic work underpins the capitalist division of labor.

In the 1970s, Marxist feminists found themselves confronting two major problems. They recognized that women's subordination predated capitalism, and that Marxist theory had no developed means for exploring gender divisions. Although Marxism had analyzed the "woman question" in relation to economy, it had not addressed the "feminist question," which centers on women's relation to men. Women's oppression is functional for capitalism: women provide a cheap and flexible source of labor power, and their domestic labor services reproduce and sustain more workers. Marxist considerations of "the family" as subject to changing status in historical development meant that the form of the family could be questioned and opened up possibilities for radical changes in viewing sexual relations. What was new about the Marxist feminist analysis was the linking of capitalist and patriarchal systems of oppression. It was apparent that the particular form of family actively promoted within capitalist societies (men as fathers, heads of household, and breadwinners, and women as mothers, caregiver for children, and subordinate to men) was well suited to supporting both capitalism and patriarchy. Even though relatively few family structures in the late twentieth century conformed to it, the ideology of this family form as normal and desirable, along with ideas about the "family wage," were powerful in reinforcing women's oppression. Marxist thinkers here point to the ruling ideas as those of the ruling class, and to the power of ideology in dominating people's everyday lives. This ideology of "man the breadwinner and woman the domestic" continues to have repercussions for women's lives across many countries today.

Mitchell (1974) extends Simone de Beauvoir's analysis of women's oppression from family ideology (perceiving themselves as wives and mothers) by separating the *economic* mode of capitalism from the *ideological* mode of patriarchy. Mitchell believes that the latter functions through the unconscious; her use of psychoanalysis is important for later feminist debates, especially those regarding women's agency, consciousness, and cultural politics. Each of the four structures identified by Mitchell—production, reproduction, sexuality, and the socialization of children—needs to be examined in order to see how it maintains women's oppression and to identify potential areas of change. Mitchell argues that, rather than entering the workforce in poorly paid jobs, women have to enter on the same terms as men, which means changing the other structures of oppression. Her argument that a cultural and ideological revolution was required together with a politicoeconomic one has been taken up by radical feminists in various contexts.

Sokoloff (1980) proposes that the idea of the family wage as a point of intersection between capitalism and patriarchy enabled men to be paid a wage deemed sufficient to reproduce their labor power through support of their wives' household and child rearing work. This fixed women into an identity with a "natural" role in the family. The idea of the family wage, however, was certainly not realistic for most working people. Applying Marxist methods to consider the ways in which patriarchy operates through the domestic mode of production, Christine Delphy writes, "All contemporary 'developed' societies, including 'socialist' ones, depend on the unpaid labour of women for domestic services and child-rearing" (1984: 60). In noting patriarchal exploitation as the "common, specific and main" oppression of women, Delphy raised important points for feminist debates. Patriarchy was seen by radical feminists as the key form of women's exploitation, and theoretical priority was given to patriarchal systems of male domination. A "dialogue" emerged, in which Marxist methods and concepts provided a starting point for many radical feminists, while many Marxist feminists used the concept of patriarchy. In recognizing that patriarchal systems of control are not inevitable and can be changed, Adrienne Rich acknowledges, "We tear open the relationship at the core of all power-relations, a tangle of lust, violence, possession, fear, conscious longing, unconscious hostility, sentiment, rationalization: the sexual understructure of social and political forms . . ." (1981: 56). This critique shows the powerful impact of theorizing about the personal as political, and the revolutionary ways in which human relations and women's oppression can be considered. Once we recognize how patriarchal relations engage with other forms of social relations, we can accomplish holistic analyses of race, class, and gender as interlocking systems of power. Avtar Brah writes, "Patriarchal relations are a specific form of gender relation in which women inhabit a subordinated position. In theory, at least, it should be possible to envisage a social context in which gender relations are not associated with inequality" (1996: 109). Patriarchal relations can then be assessed in terms of how they combine with other forms of social relation in particular contexts.

Women, Marxism, and the State

Definitions of the state focus on the set of structures that mediate power relations in society; the state also represents a higher consensus, shown in its authoritative provision of law and its monopoly of coercive power. Liberal feminists view the state as the main engine of change, because it is the arena in which rights can be formalized in laws. Marxist, socialist, and radical feminists explicitly reject this liberal conception of politics and view the state as representing the economic forces of capitalism. Marxist and socialist feminists also have argued that the state and the ideologically defined family operate in tandem to support capitalism (McIntosh, 1978). The state promotes women's oppression through regulation of education, representation of sexuality, and the underlying gender assumptions of the legal, judicial, and penal systems (Barrett, 1980).

Those radical feminists who reject the state outright as a patriarchal institution share shades of nineteenth-century anarchist thinking. Radical feminists' beliefs in working collectively within communities to regenerate or revolutionize society from within—a characteristic of utopian socialist thinking—were taken up in many feminist campaigns from the 1970s on. For radicals, state power is male power, and feminism is the "final critique" of Marxism (MacKinnon in Mies, 1986).

Marxist methods of analyzing women's struggles through *praxis* (uniting theory and practice in action) in a dialectical frame of historical materialism are highlighted by feminist thinking. Within this frame, issues of public versus private, paid versus unpaid, and valued versus undervalued work are important. That humans make our own history (but not as we choose) is a basic tenet of historical materialism. As societies in Europe, China, and Africa, and political parties in India developed toward communist organization after World War II, "work" in all its contested forms became a major focus in feminist debates.

Theories of freeing women from domestic work and child care and substituting alternative family forms have been considered by political theorists from Plato to Marx, with suggestions for anonymous parenting, female collectives, and socialized child care. These models, however, deny the experience of motherhood outlined by Rich. Women's labor in families has different aspects, depending on which women are being considered. Black women in the United States historically worked as caregivers in white homes, and as a group, "Women of color are the lowest paid wage-earners in America. We are the primary targets of abortion and sterilization abuse, here and abroad" (Lorde, 1984: 20). For radical black thinkers, the international dimension is integral to black politics in the context of women's work and the impact on women's lives of global shifts in capital.

Addressing the question of the relationship between capitalist patriarchy and the exploitation and subordination of colonies, Maria Mies writes that it is important for "every woman in her everyday life, and the feminist movement in its political goals and existence" (1986: 2). Reducing the incentives for multinational companies to further colonize countries in Asia, Africa, and Latin America through the unjust international division of labor, Mies argues, could become a focus for feminist-led consumer liberation movements in underdeveloped countries. In tandem, such movements could cause the "bourgeois model of the housewife" to lose its ideological status as a symbol of progress. Taking Marxist thinking on *praxis* (theory and practice united in action) forward into the internationalist dimension of political thinking is of primary significance.

In outlining how the global division of labor operates, Swasti Mitter (1986) explains that the older division of labor, an artifact of colonialism, was one in which European "mother" countries provided manufactured goods, while the "children," the colonies, provided raw materials. The emerging order was legitimized in classical economic literature as one of reciprocal benefit. The scope of the division of labor declined with the independence of former colonial teritories from 1947 on, as many countries developed their own industrial bases with production policies of import-substitution. When these policies failed for various reasons, models of export-oriented industrialization were supported by richer "first world" countries that provided capital, while the undifferentiated category "third world" provided cheap labor. The development of computer and satellite technology permitted global supervision and separation of production. "The centralization of market and technology, together with the decentralization of production, have turned out to be the major features of the new international division of labour" (Mitter, 1986: 8). Feminists analyze the specific oppression of women in respect to the international division of labor.

Women's marginal role in the mainstream labor population makes them particularly attractive as employees in "flexible" arrangements, where the key desire is to be able to hire and fire workers rapidly. A polarized labor market is now emerging in which women constitute the majority of the casual workers with little job security or benefits, while a small core elite of multiskilled male workers enjoys benefits and job security with the support of trade unions. Key issues for feminists are working women's ability to control their working conditions and the democratization of power over state economic policies. The ways in which women in developing countries have been resisting oppressive working conditions are a major focus of women's studies in the 2000s, and this raises questions of oppression and domination that are central to Marxist theory.

Conclusion

It was in the area of women and work that Marxist theory had its most powerful impact on later feminist thinkers. Marxist and socialist feminists soon had to make some breaks with "malestream" Marxist thinking because the bases of male domination over women were inadequately theorized in the writings of Marx and Engels. By the 1970s, the recognition through Marxist and feminist methods of analysis that women's oppression is particular in its underpinning of capitalism, coupled with the developing dialogues between feminist liberation theorists and activists, moved feminists to wider areas of consideration. What distinguished feminist politics in the 1970s and beyond was the emphasis given to aspects of explanation of the *specific* oppression of women. Class relations within an international perspective are still at the center of much feminist thinking. Moving forward from Marxist thinking, many feminists continue to believe that economic and cultural revolutions are still required to overcome liberal capitalism and challenge international divisions of labor. Exploding the myth of the family as the basic "natural" unit of society exposed the negative impact of such conservative ideology in supporting particular family forms. The positions of Marxist, radical, and socialist feminisms in the 1970s were not mutually exclusive, and some feminists campaigned across several levels of struggle in a variety of coalitions. By 1990, with the demise of the Soviet-type societies in Central and Eastern Europe, questions were raised internationally concerning the rhetoric and reality of women's liberation with regard to Marxism, communism, and socialism. These have since been debated from various standpoints.

See Also

ANACHISM; CLASS AND FEMINISM; COMMUNISM; FEMINISM: ANARCHIST; FEMINISM: MARXIST; FEMINISM: SOCIALIST; SOCIALISM FEMINIST PERSPECTIVES

References and Further Reading

Barrett, Michele. 1980. *Women's oppression today: Problems in Marxist-feminist analysis.* London: Verso.

Brah, Avtar. 1996. *Cartographies of diaspora: Contesting identities.* London, Routledge.

Corrin, Chris. 1999. *Feminist perspectives on politics.* London: Longman.

Delphy, Christine. 1984. *Close to home: Materialist analysis of women's oppression.* London: Hutchinson.

Engels, F. (1884–1968). Origins of the family, private property and the state. In *Marx and Engels: Selected Work's* 461–566. London: Lawrence and Wishart.

Lorde, Audre. 1984/96. Sister outsider. In Alice Walker, ed., *The Audre Lorde Compendium: Essays, Speeches and Journals.* London: Pandora.

Marx and Engels: Selected Works in One Volume. 1968. London: Lawrence and Wishart.

MacKinnon, Catherine. 1982. Feminism, Marxism, method, and the state. In N. O. Keohane et al., eds., *Feminist theory: A critique of ideology.* Cambridge, Mass.: Harvard University Press.

McIntosh, Mary. 1978. The state and the oppression of women. In Annette Kuhn and Ann Marie Wolper, eds, *Feminism and materialism.* London: Routledge.

Mies, Maria. 1986. *Patriachy and accumulation on a world scale: Women and the international division of labor.* London: Zed.

Mitchell, Juliet. 1974. *Psychoanalysis and feminism.* Harmondsworth: Penguin.

Mitter, Swasti. 1986. *Common fate, common bond: Women in the global economy.* London: Pluto.

Rich, Adrienne. 1981. *Compulsory heterosexuality and lesbian existence.* London: Onlywomen Press.

Sokoloff, Natalie. 1980. *Between money and love: The dialectics of women's home and market work.* New York: Praeger.

Vogel, Lisa. 1983. *Marxism and the oppression of women: Towards a unitary theory.* London: Pluto.

Chris Corrin

MARXIST FEMINISM

See FEMINISM: MARXIST.

MASCULINITY

Masculinity is an arbitrary quality associated with men's appearance or behavior as the social and cultural construction of maleness. Its scope varies historically, cross-culturally, and among social classes and ethnic groups. However, it is usually valued over femininity: masculinity creates males as dominant and females as dependent; masculinity enables men to act out their power by subordinating and controlling women.

Masculinity is seen as positive and as the norm. Men are constructed as rational, logical, truth-seeking, strong, powerful, and "naturally" authoritative. "Real men" are seen as being able to gratify their sexual needs. The sexual control of women—power over women—is central to masculinity and masculine identity. However, masculinity is also cast as an orientation to the outside world: man as the protector of women and children, man as the provider and as head of the household.

Masculinity is valued over femininity in patriarchal societies; men fear failure, weakness, and loss of control, which may be perceived as "feminine" qualities. In the late twentieth century, some male writers (Hearn, 1987) have examined the unproductive aspects of masculinity—for example, not being able to express emotions. However, despite growing recognition that the social construction of masculinity may prevent men from expressing certain emotions, it is important not to lose sight of the rewards it brings its possesors in a patriarchal society.

See Also

FEMININITY; GENDER; MEN'S STUDIES; OTHER; PATRIARCHY: FEMINIST THEORY

References and Further Reading

Hearn, Jeff. 1987. *The gender of oppression: Men, masculinity and the critique of Marxism.* Brighton, U.K.: Harverter Wheatsheaf.

Pamela Abbott

MASCULINITY, FEMALE

See BUTCH/FEMME; GENDER; and TRANSGENDER.

MASTURBATION

Masturbation—sexual self-stimulation—is a practice that is probably universal, or nearly so, and can take various forms. Phallic batons from the Ice Age were probably used in rituals. Touching one's own genitals for sexual gratification has been known since the beginning of recorded history. Small clay sculptures of masturbating figures have been found, dating as far back as the Neolithic period. In ancient Egypt, the most popular creation myth was based on masturbation by a deity and was commemorated in a daily ritual that took place in the Karnak temples, built over 4,000 years ago: at dawn every morning, the priests and priestesses would reenact this original masturbation at the shrine of Amon. Greek pottery from the fourth and fifth centuries B.C. shows both women and men masturbating, along with graphic depictions of the use of dildos.

In ancient Ireland, the Gaelic word for masturbation was "self-love," but with the arrival of Christianity it was changed virtually overnight to "self-abuse," religion having turned this basic sexual act into a sin. The biblical story of Onan was originally interpreted as referring to masturbation (in fact, masturbation has sometimes been called onanism), although later scholars reinterpreted Onan's act as coitus interruptus. To this day, many clerics and religious doctrines continue to consider "self-pollution" a sin. Masturbation is a major sin in Orthodox Judaism, for example; Mormons, too, consider it a sin—a bad habit that separates a person from God and defeats the proper use of human procreative power.

In the late eighteenth century, doctors began to hold that masturbation was an illness, for which science alone had the cure. Masturbation was cited as causing every imaginable sickness and as ultimately leading to insanity. Elaborate and cruel restraining devices, pills, injections, electrical shocks, surgical removal of the clitoris, circumcision, and other means were employed to stop children and adults from masturbating. Still, this "awful vice" continued.

Then, by the late nineteenth century, doctors, as an accepted medical practice, began performing genital massage to induce orgasm in "hysterical" women. Hysteria was seen as chronic in women—the result of sexual deprivation. Because masturbation was forbidden, and marital sex presumably consisted solely of a penis penetrating a vagina, which does not always produce orgasm in women, medical authorities were able to justify this clinical practice. In response to the demand from physicians, the first electric vibrator was invented as a medical instrument. These machines reduced from one hour to ten minutes the time it took the physician to give a woman an orgasm, and this made their practices even more lucrative.

Eventually women were able to buy electric vibrators for home use, even before vacuum cleaners or electric irons were available. Vibrators were offered in Sears, Roebuck catalogs and advertised in respectable women's magazines. But when vibrators began appearing in pornographic films in the 1920s, they were made unavailable to the general public. From then on, electric vibrators were sold primarily as massage machines, ostensibly to soothe sore muscles or to prevent male baldnesss by stimulating the scalp.

In 1970, the author of this article—Betty Dodson, an artist in New York—became the first recognized feminist to publicly reintroduce electric vibrators to women solely for producing orgasms. Dodson made drawings illustrating women masturbating with vibrators, wrote articles about their most effective use, and gave workshops to teach women how to harness their energy for sexual pleasure. In 1974, she wrote, and published herself, the first feminist book devoted entirely to self-pleasuring, entitled *Liberating Masturbation: A Meditation on Selflove.* In 1975 another feminist in New York, Dell Williams, opened Eve's Garden, the first sex store for women.

Throughout the 1970s and thereafter, sex stores owned by women cropped up across the United States and in Europe. At the turn of the twenty-first century, such shops continue to be safe havens where women can buy sex toys, books, and videos that offer the information they need to think of the clitoris, not the vagina, as a woman's primary sex organ.

In 1972, the American Medical Association declared that masturbation is a normal sexual activity. Sex education about masturbation has taken longer to be accepted: there have been religious and political efforts to limit sex education in public schools to procreation, and as late as 1995 the U.S. surgeon general, Joycelyn Elders, was fired for suggesting that masturbation "might be taught."

Acceptance of masturbation continues to grow. It has freed many adults from suffering unnecessary sexual guilt. More marriages are sexually happier because the partners include self-loving, shared or enjoyed separately. Perhaps most important, children of parents who understand the natural role of masturbation are no longer punished for touching their own genitals.

Masturbation is our first natural sexual activity. It is a way to discover our erotic feelings, a way to learn to like our genitals, and a way to build sexual self-esteem. Self-sexuality is a natural part of human sexuality throughout the life span.

See Also

EROTICA; LESBIAN SEXUALITY; PORNOGRAPHY IN ART AND LITERATURE; SAFER SEX; SEX: BELIEFS AND CUSTOMS; SEX EDUCATION; SEX AND CULTURE; SEXOLOGY AND SEX RESEARCH; SEXUALITY: OVERVIEW; TABOO

References and Further Reading

Dodson, Betty. 1974. *Liberating masturbation.* Published and distributed by the author.

———. 1996. *Sex for one: The joy of selfloving.* New York: Three Rivers/Crown.

———. n.d. <www.bettydodson.com> (Web site).

Hyde, Janet Shibley, and John D. DeLamater. 1997. *Understanding human sexuality.* 6th ed. New York: McGraw-Hill.

Marcus, Irwin M., and John J. Francis. 1975. *Masturbation: From infancy to senescence.* New York: International Universities Press.

Betty Dodson

MATERNAL HEALTH AND MORBIDITY

Maternal health and morbidity refers to the health of women during pregnancy, childbirth, and the puerperium (the time from childbirth until the uterus returns to its normal size) and includes long-term morbidity or disability resulting from these events. Maternal health and morbidity can be described but is difficult to measure. A useful proxy indicator is *maternal mortality,* which describes women's risk of dying as a result of pregnancy or childbirth and is usually measured as a rate: the ratio of number of maternal deaths to the number of women at risk. The maternal mortality rate includes events taking place before childbirth (for example, abortion or ectopic pregnancy), events taking place during pregnancy (for example, hemorrhage), and events taking place afterward (for example, infection or sepsis).

Statistics

Most of the world's women bear their children in very unsafe conditions, and they suffer as a result. The extent of maternal morbidity and mortality has always been underestimated, because two-thirds of the world's women live in countries with either nonexistent or inadequate death registration systems, and most pregnancies and deliveries take place outside the health system. The World Health Organization (WHO) has estimated that some 500,000 women die from pregnancy-related causes each year, 99 percent of them in developing countries. The lifetime risk of dying from pregnancy-related causes is 100 times higher for a woman in Africa, for example, than for a woman in the United States—a far greater discrepancy than for any other health indicator, such as infant mortality. Maternal mortality is highest in southern Asia (650 per 100,000 births) and Africa (640) and lowest in Europe (generally under 10). Maternal deaths, however, are only the tip of the iceberg; for every maternal death, countless other women suffer damage to their health during pregnancy, childbirth, and the postpartum period.

Causes

The causes of maternal morbidity and mortality are many-layered. The most common direct medical causes are hemorrhage, unsafe abortion, sepsis, and eclampsia (convulsions). The indirect or contributing causes include AIDS, malaria, viral hepatitis, and anemia. Anemia, which is widespread, lowers women's resistance to infection, increases fatigue, and increases the dangers of puerperal hemorrhage. About two-thirds of pregnant women in the developing world are anemic, compared with about 14 percent in developed countries. Very young women (under the age of 18) and women over the age of 38 are more likely to encounter complications, as are women with a large number of previous pregnancies. Genital mutilation puts women at risk of obstructed labor and hemorrhage.

Underlying these more direct causes of maternal morbidity and mortality are logistical causes, which include unavailability, high cost, or poor quality of general health care, coupled with lack of access to a hospital for complicated deliveries or in emergencies. The root cause, however, is low social status of women in the community. For instance, in societies with a marked preference for boys, girls are perceived as a burden; they are undernourished as children, are married at a very early age, and then begin childbearing while still children themselves. In Ethiopia, where development of a fistula (an opening between the vagina and the bladder or rectum resulting from prolonged obstructed labor) is common, nearly all the women being treated for this condition are under the age of 14. Fertility tends to be high in such cultures because large families are often the only way for women to achieve social status in the community.

Interventions

A few of the complications of pregnancy and childbirth (for example, anemia) can be prevented, and those that cannot be prevented usually can be treated. Trained traditional birth attendants can provide prenatal care and carry out clean, uncomplicated deliveries, a solution that has been tried in several developing countries; but in emergencies access to skilled obstetric care (including blood transfusion, cesarean section, and treatment of complications of eclampsia and abortion) is crucial. Unlike many other health conditions, obstetric emergencies cannot usually be treated at home or at the primary level.

Obstetric services are not available to the majority of women in the world. These services are expensive to provide and in most countries are given low priority, reflecting the low value given to women's health. Maternal and child health (MCH) services have traditionally emphasized the child, with women seen only as the vehicle for childbearing and child care. It was not until the mid-1980s that the first calls were made to "put the M back into MCH." The Safe Motherhood movement, launched at an international conference in Nairobi in 1987 and supported by women's groups in many developing countries, has done much to sensitize policy makers. But implementation is slow and has no doubt been hampered by increasing poverty in many countries.

The problems encountered by women in wealthier countries are in many ways the obverse. In an effort to ensure complete safety (and to protect themselves from charges of malpractice), doctors have been carrying out an ever larger number of surgical interventions, cesarean sections, routine episiotomies, and so on. This trend has spread to countries such as Brazil, where pregnant women who are hospitalized are routinely given a cesarean section. Western women who have become dissatisfied with the medicalization of pregnancy and childbirth are calling for a return to more natural, women-centered care, including home births and fewer interventions.

This polarization of problems has meant that women's health advocates working at the international level must be very sensitive to the priorities and needs specific to each situation. It would be irresponsible and even dangerous to adopt or transfer the demands of western health activists to women in countries with a poor health care infrastructure. A woman having her eighth child in an Indian village, told that hospital deliveries are dangerous, is likely to die if she hemorrhages at home, whereas her counterpart in the United States can be rushed to a hospital for a blood transfusion.

The emphasis placed on women's right to control their fertility, including the right to a safe abortion, should not be allowed to obscure the fact that the vast majority of women in the world want to bear children. Bearing a child without risking their own health is one of women's basic human rights. Women have children not only for themselves but for their family, community, and society as a whole. Society, in turn, has a duty to ensure women's health and safety.

See Also

ABORTION; CHILDBIRTH; FEMALE CIRCUMCISION AND GENITAL MUTILATION; FERTILITY AND FERTILITY TREATMENT; FETUS; HEALTH CARE: OVERVIEW; MIDWIVES; OBSTETRICS; PREGNANCY AND BIRTH; REPRODUCTION: OVERVIEW; REPRODUCTIVE HEALTH

References and Further Reading

Abou Zahr, Carla, and Erica Royston. 1991. *Maternal mortality: A global factbook.* Geneva: World Health Organization.

Berer, Marge, and T. K. Sundavi Ravindran. 1999. *Safe motherhood initiatives: Critical issues.* Oxford: Blackwell Science.

Maine, Deborah. 1997. Prevention of Maternal Mortality Network. *International Journal of Gynecology and Obstetrics.*

Royston, Erica, and Sue Armstrong. 1989. *Preventing maternal deaths.* Geneva: World Health Organization. (Also in French and Spanish.)

Web Sites

<www.cdc.gov/nccdphp/drh/mh.htm> (maternal health)
<www.rho.org> (reproductive health)
<www.safemotherhood.org> (safe motherhood)

Erica Royston

MATERNITY LEAVE

Maternity leave is time a woman is entitled to take away from a paid job to give birth and care for her baby. The term usually implies that the woman's job will be protected while she is absent, and that she can return to the same employer and position after a specified period. Guaranteed maternity leave is essential if women are to be equal participants in the labor force; otherwise, they risk losing all their acquired rights in a job each time they have a child, while most men continue in their jobs without such interruptions. (A more recent development is paternity leave, which usually covers a shorter period than maternity leave.)

Although in many countries maternity leave is required by law, not every country has such legislation. There is a great deal of variation in protection from country to country, and even within countries. Union contracts often account for the differences. When unions negotiate collective agreements, maternity leave is usually included, and these agreements may provide rights in addition to those covered by government legislation.

The differences in maternity leave provisions are related primarily to eligibility, benefits, and enforcement. In some cases, only women who have worked for an employer for a specified period of time are eligible; in other cases, all employed women are eligible, whatever their employment record. Although some women are allowed only six weeks away from the job—and these six weeks must be taken at specified periods before and after delivery—others can extend their leave up to two years and choose when the leave begins or ends.

Women may or may not receive some or all of their usual pay and benefits while on leave. Some women have the right to return to their former positions, while others simply have the right to a job. There are also differences in how easy it is for employers to evade the law.

See Also

CHILD CARE; EQUAL OPPORTUNITIES

References and Further Reading

Brannen, Julia. 1991. *Managing mothers: Dual-earner households after maternity leave.* London and Boston: Unwin Hyman.

Kamerman, Sheila B. 1983. *Maternity policies and working women.* New York: Columbia University Press.

Pat Armstrong

MATHEMATICS

It is a prominent myth of western culture that women cannot do mathematics. Since the middle of the nineteenth century, evidence to the contrary has been accumulating; at the beginning of the twenty-first century, that evidence is overwhelming.

Before 1850

Five women are generally identified as the only female contributors to mathematics before the middle of the nineteenth century: Hypatia (370?–415 C.E., Alexandria), Gabrielle-Émilie Le Tonnelier de Breteuil, Marquise du Châtelet (1706–1749, France), Maria Gaetana Agnesi (1718–1799, Italy), Sophie Germain (1776–1831, France), and Mary Fairfax Greig Somerville (1780–1872, England). Of these, only Germain made original contributions to mathematics; each of the others made some significant contribution to the transmission of mathematical ideas.

Besides the historical visibility of these five women, there is evidence that other women enjoyed doing mathematics. Bhāskara's *Siddhā nta-siromani,* a twelfth-century Indian text on astronomy, contains arithmetic and algebra problems in verse, a number of which are worded as questions posed to a girl or to a woman. The *Ladies' Diary,* a popular English magazine of the eighteenth century, consisted mainly of mathematical problems and puzzles.

Late Nineteenth Century

Starting in the second half of the nineteenth century, more women were trained in mathematics beyond arithmetic, and some of them became mathematicians. Among the earliest were two women who left Russia in the 1860s in pursuit of higher education: Sofia Vasilevna Kovalevskaia (1850–1891), the most celebrated of the pre-twentieth-century women mathematicians, and Elizaveta Fedorovna Litvinova (1845–1919?), the first woman to be awarded a PhD in mathematics based on a regular course of study (1878, Bern). Kovalevskaia, who became professor of mathematics at the University of Stockholm, received a PhD from Göttingen in 1874, after having studied privately in Berlin because the universities controlled by the Prussian government were not open to women.

In 1882, Christine Ladd-Franklin (1847–1930, United States) earned a PhD in mathematics at Johns Hopkins University but was denied the degree because of her gender. In 1885, Charlotte Angas Scott (1858–1931, England) received a DSc from the University of London for work done while a lecturer at Girton College, Cambridge. Scott became particularly influential in the training of American women mathematicians as the head of the mathematics department of Bryn Mawr College in Pennsylvania, the only independent women's college in the United States ever to grant doctorates in mathematics.

Toward the end of the nineteenth century, many exclusively male American and European universities that were centers of mathematical research began to allow women to attend graduate courses and receive graduate degrees. In fact, mathematics and physics were used as the testing ground to establish the fitness of women to pursue advanced degrees in German universities because, it was argued, the criteria for correctness in those disciplines are more objectively defined than in other subjects.

Until about 1890, it was unusual for a woman to publish an article in a mathematical journal or attend a mathematical meeting. Starting in the 1890s, women—with and without doctorates—became more visible in the mathematical community through these activities.

Early Twentieth Century

The four decades before World War II saw a dramatic rise in the number of women educated as mathematicians. In the United States, for example, eight women were awarded the PhD in mathematics during the 1890s, but there were 114 during the 1930s. Although many women succeeded in being trained as mathematicians, finding appropriate employment was more difficult, especially for those who married.

As the number of women mathematicians increased, so did their visibility in the mathematical community, and they began to be recognized for their accomplishments. The women mathematician who received the most recognition was Amelie Emmy Noether (1882–1935, Germany). Universally recognized within the discipline as one of the outstanding mathematicians of the twentieth century, Noether is also well known among physicists, although mathematicians and physicists tend to be familiar with different aspects of her work. In 1932, she became the first woman invited to give a plenary address at an International Congress of Mathematicians (ICM). Although she taught at Göttingen for many years, first without compensation and then for a small salary, she never held a professorship in Germany. In 1933, she was dismissed from her lectureship by the Nazi government and came to the United States as a guest professor at Bryn Mawr.

Since World War II

In the years since World War II, the participation of women in mathematics has become so extensive that women mathematicians are no longer seen as anomalous by virtue of their gender, at least within the mathematical community. However, the proportion of women among mathematicians varies widely on a geographic basis; it is, in general, higher in eastern and southern Europe than in northern Europe. At American universities during the 1990s, more than 2,500 women earned PhD's in mathematics.

Women mathematicians still do not occupy prestigious positions or receive prestigious speaking invitations in proportion to their numbers, but they are receiving increasing recognition for their mathematical contributions. On the international level, this recognition is coming slowly. The second woman (after Noether) to give a plenary address at the quadrennial ICM was Karen Uhlenbeck (b. 1942, United States) in 1990; she was followed in 1994 by the Belgian-born Ingrid Daubechies (b. 1954, United States) and the Russian-born Marina Ratner (United States). At the end of the twentieth century, no woman had been awarded the Fields Medal, generally considered the mathematical equivalent of a Nobel Prize but restricted by tradition to mathematicians under the age of 40.

Since the early 1970s, the improved position of women in mathematics has been due in part to the formation, in 1971, of the Association for Women in Mathematics (AWM). In addition to the United States-based AWM, other, younger organizations also work toward the broader inclusion of women in mathematics—for example, European Women in Mathematics (EWM).

See Also

EDUCATION: MATHEMATICS; PHYSICAL SCIENCES; SCIENCE: OVERVIEW

References and Further Reading

Association for Women in Mathematics (AWM) Newsletter. 1971–. College Park: University of Maryland; Association for Women in Mathematics.

Grinstein, Louise S., and Paul J. Campbell, eds. 1987. *Women of mathematics: A bibliographic sourcebook.* New York: Greenwood.

Lewis, Albert C. 2000. Women in mathematics. In Albert C. Lewis, ed., *The history of mathematics from antiquity to the present: A selective bibliography.* Providence, R.I.: American Mathematical Society.

Judy Green

MATHEMATICS EDUCATION

See EDUCATION: MATHEMATICS.

MATRIARCHY

Matriarchy is a complex subject which is difficult to define and often evokes strong reactions. The word *matriarchy* is used in several senses. It has often been used to denote a social-cultural organization in which women are the recognized leaders in the community. In other instances, it refers to a social organization in which the political status of a person depends on matrilineal descent, or to a cultural system in which the mother is the head of the family, or in which inheritance of family property is through the maternal line. It has also been used to define the social pattern of societies in which the deity is a goddess.

So far, there is no evidence of a complete matriarchy—a society in which women had the final say on every aspect of communal life. At the same time, there is no known society in which women had absolutely nothing to say about any aspect of communal or personal life. Evidence from African societies, though strongly suggesting that there are no purely matriarchal societies, nevertheless shows many traits of matriarchal practices in the sense that, even in what appears to be all-male rule, one finds tendencies of mother-centeredness. With this understanding, what follows is an attempt to map a range of matriarchal possibilities.

In order to understand the problems of using terms such as *matriarch*, *matriarchy*, and *matriarchal*, it is important to look at the areas of power, the means of such power, and the mechanisms used to enforce decisions. A closer examination of female leadership often reveals that the relative position of women, in terms of freedom and control, depends largely on the size and nature of the group being discussed. It seems that women have always had the greatest possibility of governing at the level of the family, whether nuclear or extended. Women also appear to have more responsibility in relation to matters affecting other women, both in modern industrialized society and in peasant societies. Only rarely have women governed entire nations. In addressing the sphere of women's power, scholars point to the education of children, arrangements for marriages, types of work, the ownership of property or things, social status, and the spiritual welfare of the community.

Most writing on matriarchy is the work of anthropologists. Some theorize that matriarchal societies were earlier stages of societal development, or as primitive. The community of the Iroquois Indians has been singled out as one in which women had great influence. Iroquois women could take the role of *sachems* (chiefs) and, as such, constituted an important part of the governing segment of the society. Even here, however, the physical strength of men, their dominance in fighting, and their tendency to compete led to attitudes involving superiority and control. Among the Kuna Indians of Panama, women are described as being physically as strong as men, or even stronger. As a result, Kuna women control drunkenness and fighting at fiestas: if the men become too drunk and begin to fight, the women simply move in and separate them.

One important source of power for women in nonindustrialized societies is food production and business entrepreneurship. The areas where women are the food producers are also the areas in which women have the most say. When the pattern changes either to industry or to cash-crop farming, a shift of power also takes place. Similarly, in areas where women have a prominent position in business entrepreneurship, as do the so-called market women of west Africa, they have freedom of movement and more self-determination. These factors often bring out aspects of female leadership or female power that may be referred to as matriarchal.

In Africa, matriarchal features are evident among communities such as the Ibo of Nigeria, the Ashanti/Akan of Ghana (west Africa), the Kwaya of Tanzania (east Africa), and the Chewa of Malawi (southern Africa). Sjöö and Mor (1976) report that many indigenous communities in Asia, the Pacific, and North and South America are "matriarchal." What these groups have in common are strong female roles in food production and strong community adhesiveness. In many of these societies, the role of women is more important than that of women in typical western societies, but this does not mean that they are truly matriarchal, except in a very limited way.

The word *matriarch* is used to refer to a woman who has a prominent leadership role in her community or is publicly respected especially for her long and consistent impact on society or the family. In Chinese and African societies, the oldest woman in the family—often a grandmother or the great-grandmother—is a matriarch because she commands a great deal of authority. She has to be consulted on all family decisions, and she has the veto power. The rest of the family respects her and gives her a place of honor in the home. Each family has its own matriarch, and her power is recognized in her own immediate and extended family setting to a greater extent than in the society as a whole, even though generally these matriarchs are respected by the entire communities. Age plays a very important role, because *matriarch* is not a title but a status. Younger women do not qualify to be called matriarchs even if they provide leadership in the family. Age in these societies is a positive and powerful sign of experience and wisdom.

In some polygamous societies, the oldest wife is a matriarch. She is expected to provide leadership to junior wives and has a special supervisory role over family matters. There is also considerable authority invested in her by society. She can stop the male members of the family from taking an action pertaining to family property or family members. She is immune from being beaten or ordered around by her husband, and in many cases she is the only wife allowed to sit in the council of men when important decisions regarding family matters are being made. If she is not present in person, she is the first to be told about the decisions made, and she is the one who tells the other wives. She is also expected to be responsible and fair in her judgments and actions. This is what makes polygamy work and what makes communally structured societies appear to be matriarchal.

Some matriarchs gain this status by relationship to men considered to be patriarchs, such as presidents, chiefs, or bishops. In the Anglican churches in Africa, the wives of bishops act as patrons of churchwomen's organizations, such as the Mothers' Union, and are treated as matriarchs.

In the Bible, matriarchs are the wives of patriarchs, the key figures in the patriarchal history of Israel. In these narratives, Sarah seems to be the only one whom traditional biblical scholarship recognized as a matriarch. This may be due to the emphasis in the biblical text and subsequent tradition that Sarah, and not Hagar, bore the son promised by God, and thus became the mother of the people who inherit the promise given to Abraham. Jeansonne (1990) and Bellis (1994) include particularly good references to the biblical matriarchs.

Present-day biblical scholarship, such as that exemplified in the *Oxford Companion to the Bible* (Metzger and Coogan, 1993), recognizes the bias in the traditional interpretation of biblical stories, and in particular, the patriarchal history of Israel as told in the book of Genesis. In order to reclaim the inclusivity of history, rather than referring to patriarchs, the dictionary adopts the term *ancestors of Israel.* With the use of such an inclusive term, it becomes possible to name all the other women in the Genesis history who would warrant the recognition as matriarchs: Sarah, Hagar, Rebecca, Leah, Rachel, Bilha, and Zilpa. All these women were related to the patriarchs of Israel, and they, too, contributed to the history of Israel.

Matriarchs are also women who have been prominent and powerful and made great achievements in their own right. In Africa, women who have founded indigenous African churches are often considered matriarchs. Women such as Indira Gandhi and Golda Meir may eventually be seen by history as matriarchs for the prominent roles they played in world politics at a time when they had few female counterparts. Thus, the use of the term can be determined by context or group.

When linked to property inheritance, matriarchy is sometimes confused with matrilineage. Matrilineal descent exists in a societal structure in which inheritance and family descent pass through the female line. Men or children may have access to property only as a result of their relationship to the woman who is the legal owner. This means that the children are recruited into and given inheritance through the lineages of their mothers, hence *mater-linear.* In this system, it is the brother of the mother, the maternal uncle, and the birth mother who give the children their identity and inheritance. Marriage does not confer rights of inheritance or descent on the spouse. Identity and inheritance are therefore passed on to the children through a brother–sister relationship and not through a husband–wife relationship. Males in this system are the source of lineage, identity, and inheritance not for their direct progeny but rather for those of their female siblings.

Matrilineal descent does not always translate into matriarchy, but it paves the way for matriarchal possibilities. Logically, it seems that matrilineal practices have the potential to influence the status of women in society. The subleties of economic superiority deriving from ownership of land, a house, or other properties give these women a head start and greater bargaining power than their sisters who have no right to ownership of family property except through their male associates.

The Ashanti/Akan people of Ghana, for example, are definitely matrilineal, but one would not necessarily describe them as matriarchal. The *ohemaa* (queen mother) occupies a prominent role in the governance of community matters, but the public image of the ruler is the *ohene* (king). The queen mother presides over the team of kingmakers. Akan women are very powerful and control most family decisions. Local folklore has it they would have been even more powerful were they not prone to menstruation and pregnancy.

Nsugbe (1974) describes the Ohaffia Ibo leadership as having two headships of matrilineage, one generally male and the other always female. The male attends to secular duties such as the settling of disputes among the patrilineage, protection of the rights and properties of the clan, and the appointment of those who apportion matrilineal lands. In the absence of the male heads, the females act. But the main responsibility of the female heads is to attend to the sacred duties of society. The female head presides over the patrilineage for ritual events such as sacrifice to the sacred pots, each of which represents an ancestor. A male cannot be ritual head; the status is obtained matrilineally and by lineage seniority.

Among the indigenous Yoruba (Nigeria), although most political rulers are males, the women do have representation at the highest level, the king's council, through their leader, the *iyalode* (Bolanle Awe, 1977). Unless one were to argue that African patriarchies like the Yoruba make provision for women's voices, it would be unthinkable to describe the Yoruba as matriarchal.

For the past three decades, the study of matriarchy by female scholars has taken on a new dimension by shifting its setting from the social-cultural realm into the religious. With the focus on worship of the female deity, the Goddess became the anchor of this search. Although the rewriting of women's religious history may be one of the results, the main aim of these studies has been to establish whether the worship of a female deity had any effect on the status of women in cultures where one was worshiped.

Ancient Goddess-worshiping societies are sometimes referred to as "matriarchal." Two views of these societies compete for recognition. One assumes that because these societies worshipped the Goddess, women must have had a high status. If this theory were true, it would support women who have argued that a society's deity and symbols of worship, if cast in a particular gender, influence the way society shapes its views about gender and power. Hence, the male core symbols of Judeo-Christianity—evident in the male deity, God the Father, male meditating persons, and male-dominated language of the Scriptures repeated in prayers and worship rituals—impart a higher regard for men in these societies, at the expense of women. A potential conclusion of this argument is that matriarchy is good for women and bad for men, just as patriarchy is good for men and bad for women. Another issue for women is that in almost all instances in which there are female deities, there are complementary male deities. The female deities are usually assigned fertility roles, and therefore there is almost always a relationship between male deities and female deities. Women are presently challenging the interpretations that have tended to regard female deities merely as symbols of sexual relations.

The converse view says that in early matriarchal societies, women held high status; therefore, the Goddess was worshipped. This theory underscores the argument that whoever has the dominant power in society determines not only the secular but also the religious agenda. In Greek society, where there was much emphasis on female deities, there were certain religious rites in which only women engaged. Then women were indeed in complete control and made all decisions, which excluded men. Some of these rites were not necessarily symbolic of women's high status. The feminist investment in this view is meant to lay a foundation for the advocacy of shared leadership. Women have over time argued that many world religions are a result of the dominance of patriarchy, and the low status of women in society is a result of its religious practice as translated into sexism. The men rule and name the world and all that is in it, and they have also determined how religion is to be organized in this world; even the male God is a result of men is determining who should be worshiped. This state of affairs is not good for the whole society, and it can change only if one group does not become hegemonic.

Some women scholars of matriarchy have been interested in the search for models of female leadership. This search has taken the form of archaeological documentation and revisiting the interpretation of the religion of the Goddess (Sjöö and Mor, 1976; Stone, 1976). By exploring how the Goddess was worshiped, they have attempted to reconstruct what may have been the role of women in such a society. They have also posited theories that attempt to explain how and why change came about. They have speculated on the kind of leadership that matriarchy could have produced as a way of debating whether males and females differ in how they conduct the affairs of society. For example, is matriarchy any more just and peaceful than patriarchy? Some scholars offer evidence that suggests that ancient matriarchal societies had more balanced and egalitarian communities. In order to avoid being snared in the trap of pitting matriarchy against patriarchy, they suggest that the study of matriarchy should use other terms, such as *matrifocal* or *matristic* societies, which help retrieve such special features of matriarchy as its communitarian orientation.

For feminists, patriarchy does not mean only the rule of the father—or the rule of males—but carries connotations of an unjust hierarchical and dualistic ordering of life that discriminates against women. Though some have argued that matriarchy should not be seen as the opposite of patriarchy, the popular mind will always see the two in opposition. The latter says that ancient matriarchal social systems and religions were organized on different premises from patriarchy. Matriarchy, on this view, indicates an entirely different orientation of consciousness around which entirely different patterns of personal, social, cultural, and spiritual relationships could and did occur. According to this understanding, some women conclude that the central characteristics of matriarchy are the gathering and binding of peoples, the care of the weak and vulnerable, and the conservation of what promotes the community.

The recent interest of woman scholars in the study of matriarchy focuses on the connections among power, control, property ownership, and the status of women. A further factor needing consideration is the source of power. This cannot be explained simply as a result of tradition in a society. The evidence points to the strength of individual personalities and their reputation for having been successful in previous social crises. Women who are thought to control supernatural powers also inevitably have a certain corresponding power within society.

See Also

FAMILY: RELIGIOUS AND LEGAL SYSTEMS, *all entries;* GODDESS; GRANDMOTHER; MATRILINEAL SYSTEMS; MOTHER; PATRIARCHY: DEVELOPMENT; PATRIARCHY: FEMINIST THEORY

References and Further Reading

Bellis, Alice Ogden. 1994. *Helpmates, harlots, and heroes: Women's stories in the Hebrew Bible.* Louisville, Ky.: Westminster John Knox.

Bolanle Awe. 1977. The Iyalode in the traditional Yoruba political system. In Alice Schlegel, ed., *Sexual gratification: A cross-cultural view.* New York: Columbia University Press.

Busia, K. A. 1958. *The position of the chief in the modern political system of Ashanti: A study of the influence of contemporary social changes on Ashanti political institution.* Oxford: International Africa Institute.

Eisler, Riane. 1987. *The chalice and the blade.* San Francisco: Harper.

Heine, Susanne. 1989. *Matriarchs, goddesses, and the image of God: A critique of feminist theology.* Minneapolis, Minn.: Augsburg.

Jeansonne, Sharon Pace. 1990. *The women of Genesis: From Sarah to Potiphar's wife.* Minneapolis, Minn.: Fortress.

Metzger, Bruce M., and Michael D. Coogan, eds. 1993. *The Oxford companion to the Bible.* New York: Oxford University Press.

Nsugbe, Philip O. 1974. *Ohaffia: A matrilineal Ibo people.* Oxford: Clarendon.

Sjöö, Monica, and Barbara Mor, eds. 1976. *The great cosmic Mother: Rediscovering the religion of the earth.* San Francisco: HarperSanFrancisco.

Stone, Merlin. 1976. *When God was a woman.* New York: Dial.

Musimbi R. A. Kanyoro

MATRILINEAL SYSTEMS

Matrilineal systems trace descent through the mother. This means that children bear their mother's name and become members of her kin group. It is the mother, not the father, who formally and functionally determines the child's position in the social structure. The father, by comparison, has a structurally weak position, and it is the mother's brother who—together with the mother, and often with her other matrikin—represents adult authority in the child's life. Accordingly, the cross-sex-sibling relationship (that between brother and sister) has a more structurally significant function in matrilineal systems that does the spousal bond, which tends to be of diminished importance. This stands in stark contrast to western culture, which emphasizes the heterosexual spousal link as the most important social bond between women and men. By means of the matrilineal principle, people can build corporate kin groups that unite members in their social, economic, and political interests, organizing them into lineages and clans, though the significant social unit might be a smaller group, such as the household.

Studies of Matriliny

There have been major disagreements in the social sciences about the meaning of matrilineal descent and what it entails. In their quest for answers, scholars have focused mainly on the search for the origins of matrilineal descent and on the distribution of authority between the sexes in such systems. One of the many difficulties plaguing the research of matrilineal systems is that of definition—as reflected in the rather common confusion with "matriarchy," a term implying a state of women's power or even female rule. The concept of matriarchy was introduced into the scholarly debate by the nineteenth-century Swiss evolutionist Johann Jakob Bachofen, who postulated a universal matriarchal stage for early human history on the basis of data from the matrilineal Lycians and other ancient cultures. Only later, according to Bachofen, did men and male principles assert themselves. His views found much opposition in his lifetime and have been rejected by the majority of twentieth-century scholars as well. Matriarchy as a system of absolute female rule has so far not been found in human history—though, by the same logic, the universality of patriarchy has not been proved either.

Mainstream scholarship under the premise of universal male dominance claims instead that men have always been in control of women and children. Furthermore, according to this axiom, male authority is concentrated and expressed in the roles of father and husband—that is, in the sexual male persona. Matrilineal systems, however, challenge this assumption because the father and husband in such societies play marginal roles compared with those of brother and maternal uncle. Western observers were puzzled by this and assumed that a man's relationship with his wife's matrilineal relatives, especially her brothers, had to be tension-ridden because both sides would wish to have control over the woman and her children. In 1950, the British anthropologist Audrey I. Richards coined the term "matrilineal puzzle" to describe this alleged conflict between husbands and brothers. It was quickly accepted into anthropological scholarship; it fit the western assumption of universal male dominance and its implication that this dominance be "naturally" vested in the figures of husband and father. The matrilineal puzzle postulated that matrilineal systems were structurally weak. The goal became to understand male dominance under these special circumstances. Many scholars focused on males and especially on the mother's brother, whose role seemed to resemble that of the western father and thus came closest to the western ideal of the controlling authoritarian male.

The problem leaves out the cornerstone of matrilineal systems: the women, and especially women in the role of mother. There have been few systematic in-depth studies of mothers and motherhood in matrilineal systems. By ignoring women, many scholars lost sight of the crucial fact that the significant cross-sexual dyad in matriliny is represented by the woman and her brother or mother's brothers, rather than the wife and her husband. This is a critical factor because it means that nonsexual relationships take center stage and determine the structural impact of heterosexual bonds.

Following western androcentric thinking, much of the literature on women in matrilineal systems focused on the role of wife, while the mother's ties to other matrikin, male and female, have been referred to as only a link between generations. It follows that the significance of women's structural centrality, as well as the mother's personhood and agency, has been seriously downplayed in all but a few writings (see Mencher, 1962, 1963, for examples). Western stereotypical perceptions have created barriers to understanding motherhood in matrilineal systems, as well as matrilineal ideology.

The available data reveal that matrilineal reality frequently reflects a view of gender dynamics different from the one suggested by the paradigm of universal male dominance. At the same time, as we review the matrilineal world, we must understand that matrilineal systems embrace a wide range of variation with respect to female and male authority and control. The archaeological record thus far does not permit us fully to explain these differences or to clarify the origins of matrilineal systems, and the ongoing westernization of the world makes it difficult to determine precisely how internal factors, external factors, or both affect gender dynamics in these cultures. It should, however, be pointed out that matrilineal systems were found as late as the early twentieth century in a wide range of societies—from groups that were part of very hierarchical state societies, such as the Nayar of Kerala, to simple horticultural ones, such as the Seneca. The details of how the systems functioned also varied.

Basic Elements of Matrilineal Systems

In spite of the variations among matrilineal peoples, certain basic principles in the social, economic, and religious or ideological spheres stand out. The marital bond is structurally weak, and divorce is accordingly easy, with few major consequences for women and children. Various forms of conjugal residence support this weak marital scenario. The husband might move into his wife's place years after the wedding. After coresidence is established, he might spend considerable time elsewhere with his sisters or his mother. In some societies, women and men never set up a common household as a conjugal unit but instead remain in their natal matrilineal homes, keeping only visiting spousal relationships. These relationships might be temporary or of a more lasting nature. Furthest removed from the western ideal in this respect are probably the Mosuo of southwestern China, who, though familiar with the institution of marriage, prefer visiting relationships that can easily be entered and terminated by either partner. Forceful attempts by the Communist Party of China to assert the value of monogamy and paternal legitimization led to reluctant marital unions that were, however, abandoned by the Mosuo as soon as the cultural policies of the Communist government eased up in this respect. A preference for visiting relationships was also found among the south Malabar Nayars of southwestern India until the mid-nineteenth century. In Kerala, the impact of British colonialism and the introduction of capitalist land relations led to a gradual breakup of Nayar households. The Nayars had formal rituals that have been compared to weddings, but the marital bond was structurally weak and as late as the 1970s spouses did not often set up common households.

Among the Akan people of west Africa, colonization and its aftermath have led to an uneasy coexistence of different marital concepts, which include a variation of residence patterns somewhat similar to those already mentioned. Western observers are frequently uncomfortable with the implications, such as the nonexistent or weak roles of wife and husband, and the freedom this implies for women, sexually and otherwise.

Status of Women in Matrilineal Kinship

Such arrangements enable women to hold high positions in the domestic sphere. Among the pre-nineteenth-century Iroquois of North America and the Minangkabau of Indonesia, for example, we can clearly speak of female leadership in the household. The challenge to western observers lies here in the significance that matrilineal systems assign to the domestic sphere, as compared with the prestige associated with the public sphere in the West. Matrilineal systems, furthermore, elevate the significance of the domestic sphere by emphasizing the interplay between the two arenas.

Women in matrilineal systems usually fare better economically than their counterparts in other groups. They own and control property, including animals, as among the pastoralist Navaho (North America) and Guajiro (South America). Spousal property is normally separate, implying that husband and wife do not represent the important economic unit they are expected to form in the West. Among contemporary Asante (west Africa), for example, husband–wife partnerships are rare. An Asante woman's identity depends not only on her ability to achieve motherhood, but also on her economic independence. A woman who depends solely on her husband for sustenance is considered "foolish"by the Asante, a grave insult. The Iroquois represent another example of women's powerful control of resources. Iroquois women controlled all food obtained through their own horticultural and gathering activities, as well as all game hunted by men. This applied to all occasions of food consumption—daily meals and food eaten on ritual occasions. Women were also in charge of food provisions for soldiers and thus were able to prevent wars by withholding food or, conversely, to encourage warfare, Clearly, women's management and manipulation of food resources affected life in the household and beyond.

In matrilineal systems, women usually enjoy a high degree of control over their sexuality and their procreative powers, although there is wide variation. For example, among the Guajiro, brides must be virgins, which is in stark contrast to the premarital sexual freedom found in most matrilineal systems. But Guajiro women are in full control of their reproductive potential. At the time of menarche, the young Guajira is instructed in the preparation and application of contraceptive medicines. Such knowledge is exclusively held and controlled by women; men do not interfere. In the past, men were required to make a payment to the wife's matrikin after she gave birth, in compensation for the inconvenience caused by the pregnancy, the pain suffered, and the blood lost during delivery. The Mosuo are at the other end of the spectrum. They place no sexual restrictions on women or men, and illegitimacy is not an issue. Traditionally, among the Nayars a girl's first marital alliance was arranged by her mother's brother and mother's mother, but then she was free to divorce and to take more than one husband, even simultaneously. By the end of the twentieth century, women in Nayar culture rarely divorced and were much more downtrodden.

Gender Dynamics

Members of matrilineal systems attach high value to women's role as links between generations, and they develop what Alice Schlegel (1972) has called "a cognitive orientation towards women," which is reflected in their religions as well as their gender ideologies. The Iroquois pantheon, for example, includes powerful goddesses who represent the life-giving and life-sustaining activities of women. Female deities among the Mosuo represent intelligence, prosperity, and fertility. However, it is important to note that it is not goddess-worship per se that is characteristic of matrilineal systems: female deities are also worshiped in patrilineal and other male-dominant societies without signaling high female status. In matrilineal systems, it is the specific perception of a divine female principle that expresses the expectations and confidence that matrilineal people have toward the female members of society.

Attitudes toward violence provide additional insight into gender dynamics in matrilineal systems. In spite of different styles and methods for dealing with aggressive tendencies, matrilineal societies in general do not idealize or glorify aggression (or, at least, not within the group) and, furthermore, they do not approve of expressing it in the form of violence against women. Data on rape give further insight into this manner of thinking. Although systematic studies on this topic do not exist—another serious gap in our knowledge—there are data to confirm that rape is rare or even nonexistent among matrilineal groups such as the Guajiro, Iroquois, Mwera (east Africa), Minangkabau, and Mosuo. It was rare among the Nayar, and when it did occur, it represented power relations between different or lower-ranking Nayars or lower castes.

Modern Systems of Matriliny

The difficulty of defining and identifying matrilineal systems makes it hard to assess the number of people who live according to this principle today. The *Atlas of World Cultures* (Murdock, 1981), using a sample of 563 so-called preindustrial societies for which extensive ethnographic records exist, identifies 15 percent of those as matrilineal. Today these groups constitute ethnic minorities and subgroups in their respective nation-states; the 3.8 million Minangkabau of Indonesia probably represent the largest contemporary matrilineal system. Differing views exist regarding the future of these cultures in modern society. Kathleen Gough (Schneider and Gough, 1961) voices the mainstream view that westernization leads to disintegration of matriliny and replaces it with the nuclear family. Mary Douglas (1969), on the other hand, sees the flexibility of matrilineal systems, as expressed in membership recruitment and weakly ascribed authority patterns, as an adaptive strategy that can be successful in an expanding market economy. A great deal depends on the particular circumstances of westernization, its depth of penetration, its relationship to global capitalism, and the surrounding culture.

The reason for the survival of a matrilineal system is not easy to determine. In the case of the Mosuo, it seems to be their refusal to adopt external practices, while among the Minangkabau, the tolerated coexistence of *adat* (the matrilineal philosophy) and Islam (with its male-oriented view) has made survival of matriliny possible. Modern scholarship, including feminist scholarship, has shown very little interest in these groups. The reason for this must be sought in the West's own preoccupation with everything masculine, and, following from this, an inability to acknowledge women-centeredness and its implications. It remains to be seen if people still situated in matrilineal systems will be able to affect mainstream national cultures more deeply. The struggle of the Mosuo to be acknowledged as an ethnic subgroup by the Chinese government serves as an example of the challenges these societies face. But it would seem that matrilineal systems—with their acknowledgement of women's resourcefulness and authoritarian abilities—have the potential to be useful models for a changing modern world in which the number of female-headed households increases annually worldwide.

See Also

FAMILY: POWER RELATIONS AND POWER STRUCTURES; FAMILY STRUCTURES; HOUSEHOLDS: FEMALE-HEADED AND FEMALE-SUPPORTED; HOUSEHOLDS AND FAMILIES: OVERVIEW; KINSHIP; PATRIARCHY: DEVELOPMENT; PATRIARCHY: FEMINIST THEORY

References and Further Reading

Bachofen, Johann Jakob. 1861. *Das Mutterrecht.* Stuttgart: Krais and Hoffmann.

Clark, Gracia. 1994. *Onions are my husband: Survival accumulation by west African market women.* Chicago: Chicago University Press.

Douglas, Mary 1969. Is matriliny doomed in Africa? In Mary Douglas and Phyllis M. Kaberry, eds. *Man in Africa,* 121–135. London: Tavistock.

Mencher, Joan. 1962. Changing familiar roles among South Malabar Nayars. *Southwestern Journal of Anthropology* 18: 230–245.

———. 1963. Growing up in South Malabar. *Human Organization* 22: 54–65.

———. 1965. The Nayars of South Malabar. In M. N. Nimkoff, ed., *Comparative family systems,* 163–191. New York: Houghton Mifflin.

Murdock, George Peter. 1981. *Atlas of world cultures.* Pittsburgh, Pa.: University of Pittsburgh Press.

Richards, Audrey I. 1950. Some types of family structure amongst the Central Bantu. In A. R. Radcliffe-Brown and Daryll Forde, eds., *African systems of kinship and marriage,* 207–251. London: Oxford University Press.

Sanday, Peggy Reeves. 1990. Androcentric and matrifocal gender representations in Minangkabau ideology. In Peggy Reeves Sanday and Ruth Gallagher Goodenough, eds., *Beyond the second sex: New directions in the anthropology of gender,* 139–168. Philadelphia: University of Pennsylvania Press.

Schlegel, Alice. 1972. *Male dominance and female autonomy: Domestic authority in matrilineal societies.* Washington, D.C.: Human Relations, A. F. Press.

Schneider, David M., and Kathleen Gough. 1961. *Matrilineal kinship.* Berkeley, Calif.: University of California Press.

Shi, Chuan-Kang. 1993. *The Yongninp Moso: Sexual union, household organization, gender, and ethnicity in a matrilineal duolocal society.* PhD diss., Stanford University.

Stivens, Maila. 1996. *Matriliny and modernity: Sexual politics and social change in rural Malaysia.* Sydney: Allen and Unwin.

Stone, Linda. 1997. Through the Mother. In *Kinship and gender,* 109–153. Boulder, Col.: Westview.

Volger, Gisela, ed. 1997. *Sie Eruund: Frauenmacht und Männerherrschaft im Kulturverpleich.* Vol. 1. Cologne: Rautenstrauch-Joest Museum.

Watson-Franke, Maria-Barbara. 1987. Women and property in Guajiro society. In Gudrun Dahl, ed., *Ethnos,* special issue, Women in pastoral production 1–2: 229–245.

Weng, Naiqun. 1993. *The motherhouse: The symbolism and practice of gender among the Naze in southwest China.* PhD diss., University of Rochester.

Maria-Barbara Watson-Franke

MEDIA: Overview

Feminist scholars focus on issues related to the mass media because of the popularity of these forms of culture. Drawing on a vast variety of theoretical strains, feminist work on media studies begins with the assumption that the mass media are implicated in ideological and material processes that support, exacerbate, and re-create sexism in patriarchal cultures. When studying the media, we can divide the field into four major areas: production, content, audiences, and effects (McQuail, 1987). Many topics of study overlap these four areas, and dividing the field into categories is difficult because of the theoretical and methodological complexity and the interdisciplinary nature of contemporary feminist media studies. In addition, most contemporary scholars at least acknowledge, if not attempt to engage in, research projects that span more than one of the four major areas. A variety of scholars using a broad range of methodologies and philosophical positions raise topics of lively and impassioned debate. Finally, scholarship still pays varying degrees of attention to issues of diversity, such as race, class, and sexual orientation. Today there is at least acknowledgment of these issues, which was not the case in the early days of the modern women's movement. Some scholars bracket these issues in sections of books or particular chapters (for example, Lont, 1995; van Zoonen, 1994), whereas others make issues of diversity the organizing focus of an entire reader (for example, Dines and Humez, 1994; González et al., 1994). Nevertheless, for the purposes of clarity, we will consider feminist media studies within McQuail's four-part division of the field, including issues of diversity throughout.

Production

Scholars in the area of production examine the setting within which the mass media are produced. Within this area of study, there are three levels of analysis: institutional, organizational, and individual. The institutional level of analysis examines "the spirit of one or more normative press theories and... the more general and enduring rules of the game for handling questions of function or purpose in society, the differentiation between media, the scope of media activity vis-à-vis other institutions... and the degrees of freedom appropriate for media activity in what they make public" (McQuail, 1987: 137). Within feminist studies, there is a relative scarcity of work in this area; much of the existing work focuses on issues of journalism and the press. In terms of institutional norms and values that guide the production of media, multiculturalism and gender sensitivity are not highly valued. Even critical scholars' overviews of the field (Herman and Chomsky, 1988) ignore sexism and racism as forces influencing the production of media messages. Thus, though values such as freedom of expression are touted, feminist scholars find that gender issues and a focus on women are neglected. The large volume of work on women and pornography, for example, suggests that freedom of expression is operationalized as a positive freedom not for women but rather for the pornographers. Similar findings apply to advertising: advertisers have freedom of speech, but women do not have the power to counter images of beauty that have been shown to have negative effects on women in general, girls in particular, and society at large. Here, however, there are national differences. For example, within the United States, advertisers have been successful in arguing that commercial speech falls within freedom of expression guidelines, whereas in many other countries, commercial speech is subject to regulations that may include restrictions on gender portrayals, as was the case in Sandinista Nicaragua. Even in those particular cases, however, legal measures are not necessarily followed in practice.

The organizational level of analysis examines the practices and conventions at the actual site of production. For example, the use of sources within mainstream journalism almost always favors white, middle-class, western or westernized, heterosexual male subjects. The same can be said of the gaze of Hollywood film: the point of view of most films is male. News organizations prefer to schedule events during the workday mostly within male, middle-class, and dominant institutions, while alternative organizations such as the women's movement usually conduct business and events after hours. Routines that have been established to ensure the repeated, consistent, and timely production of media artifacts contain elements of gender, race, and class bias. For example, newspapers can cover late-night sports or theater events, but not women's-movement or civil rights meetings. Thus, embedded in the very practices of media organizations are gender, race, and class assumptions that favor one group and disadvantage others. Organizations with nonhierarchical (horizontal) structures find that news organizations are unable to cope with their lack of spokespeople or leaders. Within broadcasting, other visual and supposedly technical matters contain racial biases that have the potential to influence the coverage of women of color. For example, until quite recently students in broadcast classes were not trained in the use of the color contrast adjustment when taping people of color. Even seemingly neutral practices may in fact contain gender, race, and class components.

The individual level of analysis examines the single mass communicator. At a very basic level, women own and control minimal interest in media industries and production. They tend to be clustered in entry- to middle-level media industry positions, with some exceptions (for example, Oprah Winfrey in the United States). There has been improvement since the women's movement began monitoring media employment in the 1960s, though the gains in the United States have been made mostly by white, middle-class women. Specific occupations such as advertising and journalism have experienced such an influx of female workers that they are sometimes referred to as "pink-collar jobs" because of the gender makeup of the workforce, as well as the resulting decline in status and real wages that accompanies such a workforce shift. Many studies show that there is a gender wage gap within most occupations in media industries, as in other fields throughout the economy. Women have had to sue the *New York Times,* for example, to achieve pay equity, promotion, and access to job postings. Legal measures are necessary but not sufficient to guarantee parity at work. Broadcasting in the United States is a special case, since the public interest standard allows women and minorities a window of opportunity during license renewal time. By filing a brief with the Federal Communications Commission (FCC), women and other oppressed groups have sometimes won greater workforce participation in broadcasting industries and symbolic awareness of sexist issues. However, these gains have often been transitory and problematic, as the "two-fer" practice suggests—that is, broadcasters can satisfy two quotas by hiring one woman of color. Another finding at the individual level of analysis is that simply adding women to media industries does not change sexist practices. It is important to remember that women enter the workforce in organizations that have preexisting practices and conventions and that, in turn, answer to larger institutions with preexisting norms and values. This is why, when we study production, we have to consider all three levels of analysis. We find that women as individuals are placed in double-, triple-, or multiple-bind situations in the workplace. That is, they have to follow rules that compromise their gender, race, class, sexual orientation, and other vectors of oppression.

Content

Content is the second major area of media studies, and the one on which most feminist scholarship has focused. Whereas production studies focus on material issues, content analysis focuses on symbolic issues. Scholars begin from the assumption that symbolic reality affects material reality. Thus, analysis of content is conducted because content is said to influence, in direct and indirect ways, both individual behavior and public policy. Studies have been conducted both from a social science, quantitative framework and from a humanistic, qualitative framework, involving systematic counting and measurement in the former and interpretation in the latter. Feminists have analyzed film, newspapers, women's magazines, *fotonovelas,* romance novels, comic books, popular music, television, advertisements, pornography, and just about any other type of media content. The overall finding, dating back to the early 1960s and global in scope, has been one of "symbolic annihilation." This is a two-step finding: first, women and minorities are underrepresented in media content; second, when they are represented, women and minorities are trivialized, victimized, or ridiculed. This applies particularly to women of color in white-dominant culture regions and to third world women in a global context.

Early work on images that measured presence and frequency has been largely replaced by work on representations. Though much criticized, early work on images inspired a whole generation of media scholars and activists to challenge sexism within the media. Work on representations accounts for multiple levels of mediation and meaning, acknowledging that mass media do not directly reflect culture, and that counting can serve as an initial indicator of complex layers of meaning that often rely on omissions or intertextuality. For example, what may first appear as exceptions to the finding of symbolic annihilation are in fact more complex processes of signification. So, while symbolic annihilation applies to international, national, and local news, in both pornography and advertising women are overrepresented, though still trivialized, victimized, or ridiculed. Women's appearance in these media is mostly circumscribed within an overall framework that objectifies them. By contrast, melodramatic genres in print, television, and film often focus on women and, somewhat less often, on gender issues. The latter genres themselves are gendered feminine and, not surprisingly, are very popular among the female audience.

The popularity of these feminine forms among women is attributed to social rather than biological reasons and forms the bulk of the next area: audience studies. Thus, from within content analysis, there is an abundance of studies of romance novels, soap operas, *telenovelas,* and women's movies. Following the two major methodologies, quantitative and qualitative, studies find that melodramatic genres focus on women's talk and the domestic sphere. Quantitatively, the narrative structure of melodramatic genres differs from the more action-oriented, technology-intensive, single-plotted, episodical resolution, and capital-intensive male-gendered narratives. Women's melodrama is multiplotted, focuses on talk in domestic or low-technology settings, and has less or no closure, as is the case in televised or radio soap opera. Feminist scholars suggest that news as a genre is so male-gendered that women can appear only as signs within news stories (Rakow and Kranich, 1991). In general, content analysis supports feminist critiques of patriarchal mainstream culture, though the manifestations of sexism are varied and demonstrate a great ability to co-opt strategies and themes of the women's movement.

Audiences

A third area of media studies is audience analysis. Beyond the attempt to find out who is watching or reading what from a marketer's perspective, media scholars are interested in understanding individuals' and groups' media choices: Why do certain people or groups expose themselves to particular types of media products? What gives them pleasure, anger, or other emotions? In recent work, much attention has focused on how groups and individuals, usually from a subculture or oppressed group, can derive pleasure from media content that on a manifest level appears to annihilate them symbolically. Thus, feminist film scholars attempt to understand why it is that, even though Hollywood film symbolically annihilates women, women still account for half of the moviegoing public (Pribram, 1988). Building on theoretical perspectives ranging from psychoanalysis to cultural studies, feminist film theorists have explored some of the possible audience positions offered to or taken by women in response to dominant male-gendered content. For example, Christine Gledhill (1988) has suggested that *Coma* (1977) offers the possibility of a feminist negotiated reading. Similarly, Jacqueline Bobo (1988) finds that African-American women derived pleasure by engaging in an oppositional reading of *The Color Purple* (1985). Certain recent popular movies, such as *The Silence of the Lambs* (1991) and *Thelma and Louise* (1991), and more recently *Election* (1999), and *Dick* (1999), continue to underscore the possibility of gendered readings of popular culture; men and women come out of the movie with different interpretations about who the protagonist was and what the plot was, as well as whether the movie was pleasurable or not. Similar work has been done regarding soap operas by Mary Ellen Brown (1990) and romance novels by Janice Radway (1984). These authors celebrate the active audience—women whose resistant practices enable them to get pleasure and gain possible empowerment as a result of interpreting media texts in other than their intended manner. Other scholars caution that celebrating the active audience takes attention and effort away from the fact that much of the mass media is formulaic and produced by and for males within a patriarchal setting. Or, as van Zoonen suggests, "It becomes increasingly difficult to find moral justifications for criticizing their [women's genres'] contribution to the hegemonic construction of gendered identities" (1994: 35). Feminist audience research in media studies is a nascent area of work. Much remains to be done, especially in regard to oppressed groups such as women of color, working-class women, lesbian women, and globally diverse women.

Effects

Given the predominance, among academics in the United States, of positivist approaches in general and structural functionalism in particular, it is not surprising that much of the work in media studies has been conducted within the framework of effects. The effort has historically been to show or disprove claims that the media cause or contribute to particular individual or social outcomes. This research focus has not necessarily predominated in other countries and regions. For example, in Europe—including Britain—as well as throughout Latin America, most of the feminist work in media studies has been conducted within literary or semiotic frameworks of analysis. However, in the United States and in many other countries where the export of U.S. academic models has been somewhat successful, there are some significant areas of study that apply social scientific methodologies. Indeed, early research on women in the media was criticized for methodologically equating gender and race studies with studies on the effects of violence on particular audiences. Given the pervasiveness and basic identity issues related to race and gender, it was inadequate to conceive of these issues as merely ones of effect. Moreover, as Tuchman (1979) noted, the mimesis theory (that audiences reenact what they see) had been largely disproved throughout the social sciences. Thus, it was problematic to posit that merely increasing the portrayal of women and minorities in the mass media by itself would generate a chain of actions that would end sexism. Indeed, as subsequent research has shown, an increasing volume of images does not necessarily mean an improvement in portrayal. This is why the previously mentioned work on representation is so important. Nor does an increased amount of images end sexism. As Susan Faludi argues in her best-selling book *Backlash* (1991), increased images are largely used to attack the women's movement and to undermine any gains that it may have achieved.

Still, there are some important contemporary research projects that attempt to link media to effects. In particular, studies about pornography have attempted to establish a causal link between explicit and violent sexual material and violence against women. However, pornography cannot easily be fitted into just effects. Results have been generally inconclusive: some studies show a link, but others do not. Similarly, many studies suggest that current ideals of beauty that border on anorexic thinness affect both girls and women in a negative manner, causing many to have a distorted body image and to engage in dangerous and unhealthy diets that can, in the extreme, cause death. Though a real concern and health issue, this is a problem only in a society where food is overabundant; for most of the world's women, overeating and expanding body weight are not problems. Another area of studies is sex-roles research. Here scholars have found that media images contribute to young people's notions about appropriate gender roles. For all three of these highlighted effects, the key word is *contribute*—that is, the media contribute to but are not the sole causal agent of a particular action or attitude. There is much disagreement about whether the contribution is large, small, or insignificant. Social scientific methodologies nearly preclude proof, especially in terms of individual behavioral research: so many variables could account for a particular action. A similar problem of methodology pervades at larger levels of analysis—that is, it is nearly impossible to say that the media were important or even the most significant contributors to a particular social outcome or issue. Nevertheless, research suggests that the media contribute to sexism in general, and in particular to a climate that makes violence against women and children acceptable or "normal," as well as to body image and to sex roles. The language and theoretical concept of "normalization" has proved immensely fruitful in poststructuralist feminist scholarship, which draws heavily but not solely on Michel Foucault's work and has been applied to issues of gender and the body (Balsamo, 1997; Bordo, 1997). Thus, the "sex roles" approach continues and also has been picked up by critical qualitative scholars.

See Also

COMMUNICATIONS: OVERVIEW; CULTURE: OVERVIEW; IMAGES OF WOMEN: OVERVIEW; MEDIA: ALTERNATIVE; MEDIA: GRASSROOTS; MEDIA: MAINSTREAM; MEDIA AND POLITICS

References and Further Reading

Balsamo, Anne. 1997. *Technologies of the gendered body: Reading cyborg women.* Durham, N.C.: Duke University Press.

Bobo, Jacqueline. 1988. *The color purple:* Black women as cultural readers. In E. D. Pribram, ed., *Female spectators.* London: Verso.

Bordo, Susan. 1997. *Twilight zones: The hidden life of cultural images from Plato to O.J.* Berkeley: University of California Press.

Brown, Mary Ellen, ed. 1990. *Television and women's culture.* Newbury Park, Calif.: Sage.

Dines, Gail, and Jean M. Humez, eds. 1994. *Gender, race, and class in media: A text reader.* Newbury Park, Calif.: Sage.

Faludi, Susan. 1991. *Backlash: The undeclared war against American women.* New York: Crown.

Gledhill, Christine. 1988. Pleasurable negotiations. In E. D. Pribram, ed., *Female spectators.* London: Verso.

González, Alberto, Marsha Houston, and Victoria Chen, eds. 1994. *Our voices: Essays in culture, ethnicity, and communication.* Los Angeles: Roxbury.

Herman, Edward, and Noam Chomsky. 1988. *Manufacturing consent: The political economy of mass media.* New York: Pantheon.

Lont, Cynthia M., ed. 1995. *Women and media: Content/careers/criticism.* New York: Wadsworth.

McQuail, Denis. 1987. *Mass communication theory: An introduction.* Newbury Park, Calif.: Sage.

Pribram, E. Deidre, ed. 1988. *Female spectators.* London: Verso.

Radway, Janice. 1984. *Reading the romance: Women, patriarchy and popular literature.* Chapel Hill: University of North Carolina Press.

Rakow, Lana F., and Kimberly Kranich. 1991. Woman as a sign in television news. *Journal of Communication* 41 (1): 8–23.

Tuchman, Gaye. 1979. Women's depiction by the mass media. *Signs: Journal of women, culture, and society* 4 (3): 528–542.

Zoonen, Liesbet van. 1991. Feminist perspectives on the media. In James Curran and Michael Gurevitch, eds., *Mass media and society.* London: Edward Arnold.

———. 1994. *Feminist media studies.* Newbury Park, Calif.: Sage.

Angharad N. Valdivia

MEDIA: Alternative

Since the mid-eighteenth century, women have used their own media to dramatize their specific interests and to define identities for women that give their lives meaning and significance. In experimenting with alternative content as well as alternative structures and processes for production and distribution, women have derived intellectual and emotional satisfaction from producing and supporting their own media. "Massified" media organizations have been hostile to women's attempts to articulate alternative ways of being and models of womanhood. Mainstream, commercial mass media typically ignore or trivialize the women's movement; at best, they co-opt its philosophy. Nonetheless, in and through their own alternative media—whether or not they label these as "feminist"—women empower themselves.

These transformative and oppositional possibilities are particularly well served by print media—magazines, newspapers, pamphlets, and newsletters, as well as books from feminist publishing houses. Print is a relatively cheap medium. It does not require large bureaucratic structures or centralized distribution systems, although these may serve it. Women-controlled national and international wire services and news bureaus in Europe, North and South America, and Asia help to spread news of feminist activities and achievements. One of these, the Women's International Network News, was founded in 1975 as a worldwide, open, participatory communication system by, for, and about women of all backgrounds, beliefs, nationalities, and age groups. Over the past few decades, feminist collectives have occasionally produced radio programs, and feminist radio stations have operated in Central and South America and Europe. On the whole, however, radio and television have proved far less useful than print to women's alternative purposes—in part because channel space, a limited resource, has been monopolized by institutions with strong access to capital and technology. Some feminist collectives have produced shows for the public access channels on cable systems, although it is not clear what type or size of audiences they reach. Women have successfully used film, although feminist filmmaking groups like Studio D of the National Film Board of Canada are rare. The monetary costs and the social and technical skills perceived as necessary have kept computer technologies out of reach for many women, but electronic bulletin boards and list serves may eventually prove ideal for worldwide feminist communication.

Suffrage and Feminist Periodicals

If nothing else, alternative media let like-minded women know that they are not alone. As Jo Freeman, founder of the *Voice of the Women's Liberation Movement,* explains, "Its purpose was to reach any potential sympathizer in order to let her know that there were others who thought as she did and that she was not isolated or crazy" (1975: 110). Periodicals were particularly important to geographically isolated nineteenth-century women seeking alternatives to dominant conceptions of "true womanhood." Once paper and postage costs dropped, literacy spread, and printing technology became easier, women found print highly accommodating. In 1746, the *Female Spectator* was first published in Dublin; another magazine for women began publication in London in 1759 as *The Lady's Magazine, or Polite Companion for the Fair Sex.* New York saw its first newspaper for women in 1834; its editor, Ann Oddbody, declared, "There is a paper *Man* published, why shall not a paper *Woman* be also seen daily in the City of Gotham" (quoted in Ross, 1976: 14). Originally founded as a temperance organ, *The Lily's* advocacy of women's suffrage made it one of the first "feminist" publications in the United States. "It is WOMAN that speaks through *The Lily,*" Amelia Bloomer promised in her debut editorial in January 1849.

Most of the eighty or so suffrage periodicals published in the United States were short-lived and had limited distribution (primarily in the East, but also in the Midwest and Far West). Several, however, enjoyed fame and national circulation, such as *The Woman's Journal* (1870–1931), which suffrage leader Lucy Stone published in Boston with the help of her family. The "Votes for Women" movement in England spawned several newspapers. Some periodicals served more specific populations, such as *The Farmer's Wife,* (1891–1894) and *The Woman's Exponent* (1872–1914) for Mormon women. Nonsuffrage periodicals included Charlotte Perkins Gilman's *Forerunner* (1909–1916) and Margaret Sanger's *The Woman Rebel* (1914) and *Birth Control Review* (1917–1940).

The second wave of the women's movement, too, could hardly have emerged or survived without alternative media. Just as nineteenth-century reform-minded women objected to their second-class status in the abolition and temperance movements, the sexism of their "radical" male colleagues in the 1960s prompted feminists to establish their own media. According to one estimate, between 1968 and 1988, around 1,500 women's liberation newspapers, magazines, and journals were published, however briefly, in the United States. Periodicals emerged in Senegal, Ghana, Uruguay, Japan, Holland, South Africa, and the Soviet Union. *Spare Rib* and *Outwrite,* both British periodicals, were particularly long-lived; *Emma,* still published in Germany, has achieved the largest circulation among feminist periodicals. Many feminist and lesbian periodicals speak to "hyphenated identities" and address particular interests such as health, separatist politics, philosophy, or the arts. Still others express the particular concerns of African-American, Latina, Asian, and Indian women.

Feminist publishing houses are relatively recent but highly ambitious and successful. They generate women's work and also shape and encourage it. For example, the Kitchen Table–Women of Color Press publishes works by third world women, particularly lesbians; it was self-consciously designed as a revolutionary tool for shaping ideology and promoting change. Some emerging computer indexes and on-line bibliographic databases that include alternative resources hold out the promise of even greater access to feminist literature. Feminist bookstores, like live performances by feminist artists, offer not only literal spaces in which women can come together but also opportunities for exhibiting and distributing alternative materials—books, periodicals, recordings, comics, posters, and other works.

Feminist Structures and Processes

One defining feature of women's alternative media has been a commitment to "authentic" communication and to social and political transformation, regardless of commercial possibilities. The Onlywoman Press, a publishing and printing collective, for example, asserts that "We are quite committed to making what we do an act of participation within the Women's Movement instead of turning out products like hot dogs" (Cadman et al., 1981: 35). Even when these alternative media are not committed to losing money, their lack of profit motivation nearly ensures that they will not earn large profits. Very few have managed to negotiate a middle ground that allows for economic solvency without compromising their politics. Even relying on passionate volunteer labor, as most of them do, many of them must resort to personal donations and institutional subsidies. If they run advertising, women's alternative media usually choose to limit what kinds they will accept; even so, the relatively narrow and often anticonsumerist vision articulated by these media and the small size of their audience tend to alienate potential advertisers. The economic problems of many women's alternative media are compounded by their concerns regarding access. Since women in general, or the specific kinds of women they hope to reach, are the least able to afford high subscription rates, several feminist publications have designed innovative ways to be affordable to poor women.

Women's alternative media typically try to demystify technology and involve women in production; often, every worker learns every part of the process. *The Woman's Advocate,* begun in Philadelphia in 1855, took its subtitle literally: "Devoted to the elevation of the Female Industrial Classes, and produced exclusively by the joint stock, capital, energies, and industry of females" (27 January 1855: 2). Likewise, Olivia, the oldest and largest women's record label, emphasizes its interest in training women in technical fields. Sometimes this commitment among women's alternative media has entailed accommodating the human needs and family responsibilities of women workers even when this has required altering production schedules or skipping issues. Some women's record labels, film companies, and publishing houses have operated with a high level of technical proficiency and sophistication. Others—whether because of indifference to achieving a slick commercial appearance or because they cannot afford fancy production values—have often produced work that "looks" quite different from mainstream media.

Despite their dependence on volunteers, most feminist media limit men's participation, sometimes with fairly specific rules about this. Some of the best-known papers of the women's suffrage movement, however, enjoyed significant help from men. For example, *Revolution* (1868–1870), published by Susan B. Anthony, was coedited by Elizabeth Cady Stanton and a male abolitionist, Parker Pillsbury, and it had several regular male contributors. Commitment to sisterhood among some feminist performers has sometimes entailed trying to exclude men from the audience, too. Nonetheless, most alternative mass media seem open to the possibilities of winning male converts.

Nineteenth-century suffrage journals usually had fairly conventional management structures. (Often, however, one or two women performed all tasks.) Many second-wave feminist media organizations, in contrast, have tried to design collectivist or fluid protocols that bypass or eliminate masculinist hierarchies of power, authority, and status. In many instances, after varying degrees of political debate, the practical demands of efficient, on-schedule production have dictated a return to a more clearly delineated distribution of responsibilities and duties. The founder of the *Pittsburgh Feminist Network News,* explaining the failure of subscribers to take advantage of her experiment, concluded, "Perhaps as more and more women learn to speak for themselves, and find they have a voice in some feminist periodical, the time will come again to try to build a communications medium, based on trust, a common worldview and equally shared power" (Downie, 1989: 201). Nevertheless, several women's recording labels, publishing houses, and especially periodicals have been more or less successfully run with leaderless groups and anti-elitist decision making. The mission statement of the periodical *off our backs* in 1970, emphasized the personal and political consequences of promoting "non-exploitative ways of relating to one another based on trust and concern rather than political expediency" (Ferro et al., 1993: 117).

Experiments with Electronic Media

The highly bureaucratized structure of broadcasting corporations demands huge audiences, given the potential for earning enormous profits by "selling" audiences to advertisers. Especially in the United States, therefore, broadcasting has not served as an outlet for alternative interests. The economics of cable television might make alternative programming feasible on that medium, especially on public access channels; however, cable companies too have consistently sought the widest possible audiences and therefore resist oppositional messages. Furthermore, the feminist collectives that are creating cable programming have tended to focus their attention increasingly on technique and technology so that the shows look good. Therefore, for those seeking new mechanisms for social change, even cable's public access feature has been disappointing.

With respect to the "information superhighway," computer literacy, the cost of hardware and software, and sheer access remain problematic at the global level, although they will become less so over time. Computer technology was not invented and developed with women's specific needs in mind, but access is expanding beyond the academics and professionals who initially were the only women able to afford online services. Furthermore, the opportunities for using the Internet to spew out antifeminist propaganda, including some viciously directed at individuals, should not be underestimated. Nonetheless, computer networks may be—now and in the foreseeable future—the most efficient and convenient means of collaborative communication for both groups and individuals dissatisfied with dominant ideology. At least theoretically, feminist bulletin boards and chat lines can reach urban and rural women across the world, enabling them to interact, exchange ideas and information, support one another, and sustain a sense of community on a global scale.

Some scholars in cultural studies have offered plausible feminist readings of television shows (talk shows, soap operas, or situation comedies), feature films, and romance novels. These media may reduce the isolation of homebound women and even provide opportunities for a bit of consciousness-raising. As market-driven media that treat audience members as consumers, however, they are not radicalizing or liberating in the way or to the extent that women-controlled and women-oriented periodicals have been, nor can they be. Conversely, women's alternative media suggest a model for oppositional media and critique the structures and content of dominant media. More important, they dramatize women's attempts to redefine themselves and remake their world.

See Also

MEDIA: OVERVIEW; MEDIA: GRASSROOTS; MEDIA: MAINSTREAM; MEDIA AND POLITICS; PUBLISHING: FEMINIST PUBLISHING IN THE THIRD WORD; PUBLISHING: FEMINIST PUBLISHING IN THE WESTERN WORLD

References and Further Reading

Armstrong, David. 1981. *A trumpet to arms: Alternative media in America.* Los Angeles: Tarcher.

Bate, Barbara, and Anita Taylor, eds. 1988. *Women communicating: Studies of women's talk.* Norwood, N.J.: Ablex.

Burt, Elizabeth V., ed. 2000. *Women's press organizations, 1881–1999,* Westport, Conn.: Greenwood.

Cadman, Eileen, Gail Chester, and Agnes Pivot. 1981. *Rolling our own: Women as printers, publishers and distributors.* London: Minority.

Doughan, David, and Denise Sanchez. 1987. *Feminist periodicals 1855–1984: An annotated critical bibliography of British, Irish, Commonwealth and international titles.* New York: New York University Press.

Downie, Susanna. 1989. A community-based medium: The story of the *Pittsburgh Feminist Network News.* In Ramona R. Rush and Donna Allen, eds., *Communications at the crossroads: The gender gap connection.* Norwood, N.J.: Ablex.

Endres, Kathleen L., and Therese L. Lueck, eds. 1996. *Women's periodicals in the United States: Consumer magazines.* Westport, Conn.: Greenwood.

———. 1996. *Women's periodicals in the United States: Social and political issues.* Westport, Conn.: Greenwood.

Farrell, Amy F. 1998. *Yours in sisterhood.* Chapel Hill: University of North Carolina Press.

Ferro, Nancy, Coletta Reid Holcomb, and Marilyn Saltzman-Webb. 1993. Statement of purpose from *off our backs,* March 1970. In Maurine Beasley and Sheila Silver, eds., *Women in media: A documentary source book,* 193–95. Washington, D.C.: American University Press.

Freeman, Jo. 1975. *The politics of women's liberation.* New York: Longman.

Kessler, Lauren. 1984. *The dissident press: Alternative journalism in American history.* Beverly Hills, Calif.: Sage.

Kimball, Gayle, ed. 1981. *Women's culture.* Metuchen, N.J.: Scarecrow.

Kramarae, Cheris, ed. 1988. *Technology and women's voices: Keeping in touch.* New York: Routledge and Kegan Paul.

Mather, Anne. 1975. A history of feminist periodicals: Part II. *Journalism History 1:* 108–111.

Rakow, Lana, ed. 1992. *Women making meaning: New feminist directions in communication.* New York: Routledge.

Riaño, Pilar, ed. 1994. *Women in grassroots communication.* Thousand Oaks, Calif.: Sage.

Ross, Ishbel. 1974. *Ladies of the press.* Reprint, New York: Arno. (Originally published 1936.)

Rush, Ramona R., and Donna Allen, eds. 1989. *Communications at the crossroads: The gender gap connection.* Norwood, N.J.: Ablex.

Linda Steiner

MEDIA: Chinese Case Study

By 1999, China had 1,900 newspapers; 7,900 magazines; 260 television stations; and 560 cable television stations. The television networks reached 83 percent and the radio stations reached 77 percent of the national population, which was then 1.2 billion. Internet communication was expanding rapidly: in 1995, about 50,000 Chinese had access to the Internet; by the beginning of 2000, that figure had increased to about 8 million.

Although there are no privately owned publishers or broadcasters in China, media can be owned by various institutions. There are newspapers and magazines run by Communist Party committees at the central, provincial, or municipal level; publications operated by what are known as "people's organizations," such as China Women's News, run by the All China Women's Federation; and publications run by administrative departments and large enterprises. As alternatives to these often serious-looking publications, a variety of tabloids have sprung up for entertainment and commercial purposes.

It has been estimated that there are 78 newspapers and magazines especially aimed at women readers in China. Of the top 10 magazines with a circulation of more than one million each, three are women's magazines. Also, some newspapers run a regular page dedicated to women.

Women in Media Organizations

Women can be found in virtually every news organization throughout the country today. Statistics are incomplete, but probably about 200,000 people have professional jobs in journalism, as reporters, editors, translators, announcers, or program anchors. There are three grades of titles for professional journalists in China: junior (editor or reporter), middle, and associate or full senior. About 87,000 journalists have midlevel or upper-level professional titles, and about 28,000 (32 percent) of these are women.

China's constitution specifies that men and women are equal in every sphere of life, and this provision was reinforced in 1992 by the Law on the Protection of Rights and Interests of Women. The enforcement of the law leaves something to be desired, and there is no quota system for hiring women in media organizations, but professionally qualified women do have equal opportunity with men in entering journalism. In fact, some news organizations have hired more women than men in recent years, although many others continue to prefer males.

Women journalists are encouraged to cover politics, economics, and law. A problem arises, however, because some young women journalists focus only on culture and the arts. Measures have been taken to broaden their horizons; in 1996, for example, Capital Women Journalists Association, a Beijing-based nongovernmental organization (NGO) of women in media, ran a series of lectures by leading government officials and senior journalists on "National Affairs and News Reporting," mainly for the benefit of women journalists.

According to a nationwide survey on women journalists conducted in 1995 by Professor Chen Chongshan of the Media and Communication Institute of the Chinese Academy of Social Sciences and Chen Xiuxia of the All China Journalists Association, women accounted for 8 to 9 percent of the people on executive and editorial boards of news organizations. Of leaders at the level of news departments, about 18 percent were women. Thus women were still underrepresented among media decision makers. The survey also found that women journalists seemed insufficiently assertive: 72 percent of them agreed that "If the work suits me, it is not necessary to compete with men for higher positions."

Women's Role in Media

Most women journalists in China regard themselves as equals of their male colleagues, and their main concern is performing their professional duties. Since the UN's Fourth World Conference on Women in Beijing in September 1995, however, more women journalists have become conscious of the importance of gender equality and have used their position to promote gender awareness. They have also taken advantage of the Development Program for Chinese Women (1995–2000), announced by the Chinese government before the Beijing conference. Its guidelines include enhancing awareness of women's role in civilization and social progress; advocating equal personal dignity, rights, and status for women; promoting role models of women who have high self-esteem and are self-confident, independent; and enterprising; preventing movies, television programs, books, newspapers, and magazines from using language that is derogatory or insulting to women; eliminating social discrimination and prejudice against women; and increasing all people's understanding of women's legal rights and interests.

One action women journalists have taken is to publicize and implement the basic state policy of gender equality, as announced by President Jiang Zemin at the Beijing Conference. In particular, they have addressed gender inequality in power-sharing and decision making at all levels. *China Women's News,* which has been in the vanguard, has interviewed a number of provincial leaders to ascertain their understanding of the basic policy and the actual measures being taken to implement it; this newspaper has also published a series of investigative reports on women and power-sharing. On March 8, 1997, in recognition of International Women's Day, China's leading newspaper, the *People's Daily*, had a front-page editorial calling on the whole nation to implement the basic policy of gender equality.

In 2000, China did not yet have a national organization of women in media, but it did have several regional associations of women journalists. The largest, Capital Women Journalists Association, established in 1986, had 8,000 members, working in more than 100 news organizations based in Beijing. This association established a Women and Media Watch Network, which has been conducting surveys and monitoring media coverage of gender-related issues. On 5 March 1997, it set up a Media Monitoring Hotline, soliciting criticism and comments from the general public on images of women in the media. In the first year, 1997, one of these surveys found that a third of television commercials relegated women to obedient, domestic roles, and few commercials presented women as decisive leaders or as working in creative, high-tech environments. The findings were fed back to advertising agencies and sponsors, who agreed to receive training on gender awareness.

Capital Women Journalists has also undertaken activities to alert the media to neglected groups of women, such as women in poverty-stricken areas. For example, after one of five fact-finding trips to mountainous counties in northwestern, southwestern, and central China, dozens of impoverished but dauntless mothers made their way to the leading Chinese newspapers, and the public has become more concerned about them. Women in media have also become more concerned with domestic violence. Wang Li, deputy editor-in-chief of *Women's Friend*, a monthly magazine based in Harbin (in China's northernmost province, Heilongjiang), describes this as the least visible type of violence against women and says that journalists should be "obliged to make it known to all that such violence is against the law."

With a circulation of nearly 300,000, *Women's Friend*, run by the Provincial Women's Federation of Heilongjiang, is the most active of the 78 publications devoted to women in the campaign against domestic violence. From 1993 to 2000, each issue had at least one report on typical cases of domestic violence. Rather than dramatizing or sensationalizing violence, it emphasizes educating its readers, using the cases it reports as a means of spreading legal literacy. "We mean to enhance public awareness that women's rights should be respected as human rights," Wang Li says. This publication also encourages women to stand on their own and fight for their dignity, using the law as a weapon and safeguarding their legal status at home, instead of enduring humiliation for the sake of "face."

Thus women in the media have played an active role in implementing China's basic state policy of achieving gender equality, and they have made an impact on society. But so far their concerns, their research, and their views have been largely confined to female media—the concept of gender consciousness is not yet shared by the majority of their male colleagues. The Women and Media Watch Network is dominated by women, and in the long run this may not be conducive to raising general public consciousness of gender equality or to establishing a partnership of equality between men and women.

See Also

JOURNALISM; JOURNALISTS; MEDIA: OVERVIEW; VIOLENCE: EAST ASIA (CHINA) *I and II.*

References and Further Reading

Chang, Won Ho. 1989. *Mass media in China: The history and the future.* Ames: Iowa State University Press.

Jernow, Allison Liu. 1993. *"Don't force us to lie": The struggle of Chinese journalists in the reform era.* New York: Committee to Protect Journalists.

Lee, Chin-Chuan. 1994. *China's media, media's China.* Boulder, Col.: Westview.

Xiong Lei

MEDIA: Grassroots

The use of communication media by women at the grassroots level is a worldwide initiative that reaches women of all socioeconomic and educational levels and many different cultural backgrounds. Grassroots media are those owned and operated by nonprofessionals and produced and distributed in noncommercial formats, including the use of video, radio, print, or theater by social action groups, local communities, or other grassroots organizations. This article reviews the use of media by women at the grassroots level as a means to foster participation in their communities, as alternative representations of women and other disempowered groups (ethnic minorities, gays and lesbians, the poor), and as tools for social and political action (for better living conditions, for the defense of women's rights). Although these grassroots movements support demands for access and equity of representation of women in mainstream media, their media production practices are intended to recognize and give a place to the voices of those who traditionally have not been represented and heard in the mainstream commercial media.

Women's use of traditional or folk media in regions such as Africa, Asia, or Latin America dates to precolonial times. This legacy emphasizes women's crucial role as storytellers, keepers of oral traditions, and practitioners of informal communication. It also highlights the fact that the knowledge, skills, and abilities that women bring to media production have their foundation in such informal networks. During the 1960s and 1970s, women's interventions in grassroots media proliferated. During these decades, movements such as the Theatre for Development movement in Africa and Asia and the Popular Radio movement in Latin America were initiated. In the 1980s and 1990s, video production reached a large number of women's grassroots organizations as the use of other audiovisual and print media expanded. Examples are publishing houses such as Kali for Women in India, Kitchen Table Books in the United States, and Sechata Publishers in Africa; alternative film movements and centers such as Cine Mujer in Colombia or Invisible Colors in Canada; journals such as *Speak* in South Africa and *Asmita* in Nepal; and communicative networks such as Rede Muhler in Brazil or the European Network of Women in the Audiovisual Arts (Pandora). The conference "Women Empowering Communication" (Bangkok, 1994) evidenced the magnitude of grassroots media production. More than 400 women from 80 different countries shared their communication strategies and their work in media production as they met to strengthen their global network. The conference testified to the growing movement and networks of independent video and filmmakers, community and feminist radio, and women's journals, and to the variety of media interventions by women in the performing arts (theater, dance) and in writing.

Characteristics and Examples

Control over decision making, planning, access to resources, production, and distribution is a crucial element in media production at the grassroots level. Areas of control vary according to the context and focus of the individual project. In Zimbabwe, leadership in the villages and community development are being supported through a community publishing project in which books are collectively produced by more than a thousand people. The community is involved at every stage, deciding on the theme and the content, writing, drawing, and providing feedback on the book's drafts. Once the book is printed, it is translated into all five Zimbabwean languages, and workshops discuss its possible uses.

In Canada, immigrant women have used video to discuss their experiences and initiate processes of dialogue and education. Once a group is identified and committed to follow a production process, its members become involved in every step of the process, from the critical analysis of mass media to investigation, group building, script development, shooting, editing, and distribution. The emphasis of the production process is on allowing individuals to investigate their own lives and then describe and represent them through the video. During this process, women have realized that they not only have the right to express themselves but also have abilities and resourcefulness that are artistic, social, and political (Kawaja, 1994).

Empower, a nongovernmental organization in Bangkok, offers sex workers programs of English-language classes, continuing education, and health and AIDS education. Health education programs use drama and humor inspired by the dramatic and performing tradition of Thai cultures. Performances are presented by the sex workers themselves, with the philosophy that drama encourages people to take their roles and respect the roles of others. Using humor and drama to educate people about health and AIDS is seen as providing a safe communication space for the sex workers, while enhancing equality and respect among the sex workers, customers, and business owners. This example demonstrates that in order for grassroots media to foster participation and to become effective vehicles of communication, the individual's social and cultural concerns and background need to be incorporated and recognized.

In Tanzania, popular dance and theater have been used in development programs for women. In theater-training workshops, villagers identify the community's needs and perceptions of its problems and decide on the dramatic content. Through the theater workshop and acting—along with dance, which is a traditional female means of communication—women have rediscovered their dramatic potential to represent specific problems and the situation in which these problems emerge (Mlama, 1989).

Club Mencia is a women's radio program in the southern region of the Dominican Republic. Women from the area participate in the program, which is structured as a listeners' club. Women join the club by sending in their names, addresses, and other information. Audience participation is the most important element of the program, and it relies on such formats as on-air discussion and letters. The producers invented a pirate station called "Radio Macho" ("the radio station for men who wear the pants") to introduce the problem of *machismo* with a combination of humor and critical reflection. Radio Macho's interruptions of the women's program are discussed on the air. Listeners' perception of messages that have been disseminated by others "like them" is crucial to their awareness and to the continuity of the process of communication.

Technology

According to the conventional description, communication technologies are inaccessible and complex, requiring professional expertise and male-gendered technological abilities. Women's participatory communication experiences question this idea by promoting the direct use and manipulation of the technology. This process assists participants to look critically at technology instead of passively accepting it or taking it for granted. The experience of the Self-Employed Women's Association (SEWA) in Ahmadabad, India, illustrates this. The association assists its members (20,000 home-based workers, vendors, and providers of labor and services) with skill training, social services, and advocacy of their rights. The organization formed a cooperative, "Video SEWA," to support its organizational activities. The participants, all women, receive training and produce videos on themes of their concerns, such as child labor and the struggle for better working conditions. They travel from village to village producing the videos, involving the community and finally showing the videos.

In Bolivia, the Gregoria Apaza Center for the Advancement of Women trains native urban Aymara women in radio, video, and television. The center supported the creation of a network of Aymara women television journalists who document and report the living conditions and initiatives of their urban native communities. These women have acquired leadership in their communities because the message received from a woman "of the people" has been more fully accepted.

Contributions to a Global Debate

Since the 1990s, after more than a decade of advocating for the democratization of communications and recognizing small changes in the structure of the communication industries, women have demanded new strategies and ways of rethinking the movement toward democratization. Grassroots media interventions may suggest some of these alternative ways and strategies. They reveal some of the contributions women are making as media and communications producers, and the ways they are making possible the presence of women's voices in the larger societal context.

The global debate about the democratization of communications has acknowledged that women's access to mainstream media is crucial, but it has ignored the widespread social movements of women who are building new communication alternatives and propositions for change at the grassroots level. The omission is significant: these grassroots efforts not only demonstrate the advances made by women's movements in opening democratic spaces for people's communication but also address concerns about unbalanced information flows, concentration of resources, and negative portrayals of women and other groups—concerns shared by the developing world.

Engrained in grassroots media production is the belief that there must be an infrastructure of direct participation for democracy to work. Grassroots media have that potential, not just by putting media in the "hands of the people," but also by exercising the right to acquire and produce information and by opening spaces for people's cultural expressions.

The participatory style of grassroots media allows a range of individual explorations and group explorations of issues of identity and representation (as poor, as women, as colonized, or as disempowered). The absence of women's voices from the mainstream media is a central concern of women's grassroots media, which their advocates define as spaces for grassroots communication and for building new representations.

Although individuals involved in grassroots media might have diverse social goals, experiences, and knowledge of media operations (called "media literacy"), they find themselves becoming part of a collective experience that develops and reinforces individual and group identity and confidence. The function of grassroots media goes beyond being instruments of "information" to becoming means of inquiry into problems of identity and representation, social and political concern (demands, problems, and policies), or social consciousness.

Myths of Women's Silence

Women's silence has been a dominant metaphor used to refer to women's marginal position in public communication and in the communication industries. Grassroots media projects question the validity of this metaphor for explaining women's communicative and social situation. Women, as communicators within their communities, have actively and informally shaped their self-definition by their complicity with, acceptance of, or rejection of dominant definitions of themselves (Riaño, 1994).

The manipulation and control of the media technology and the media language and genres that are fostered by grassroots media are fundamental in breaking the fear of speaking and in challenging the myth of women's silence. That myth assumes that women do not already have a voice, and that the goal of media interventions is "to give" women a voice. Women have challenged that notion by arguing that the issue is not the lack of women's voices, but rather the absence of women's words in the public space. Participatory processes of media production establish a presence of women at this level.

Skills Development

Participation in broadcasting, visualizing, or dramatizing is a way of discovering and developing participants' creative skills. Women's communication skills and knowledge can be discovered and furthered by participatory media production. Furthermore, this kind of participation sharpens their perception of specific issues (such as their understanding of the causes of specific problems) and their problem-solving skills. Dialogue and collective production reinforce individual perceptions and analytical skills and enhance the development of a collective message. Through the process of collectively producing a video or a radio program, individuals enhance their dramatic and visual skills. When this production is made to promote a social or community goal, dramatic and visual skills become tools that assist individuals and groups in expressing their needs, interests, and perceptions of reality. This process is characterized as a cyclical one of analysis and reflection that involves a third and necessary element: action.

See Also

MEDIA: OVERVIEW; MEDIA: ALTERNATIVES; MEDIA: MAINSTREAM; MEDIA AND POLITICS

References and Further Reading

Callagher, Margaret, and Quindoze-Santiago, Lilia, eds. 1994. *Women empowering communications.* London: WACC.

Kawaja, Jennifer. 1994. Process video: Self-reference and social change. In Pilov Riaño, ed., *Women in grassroots communications,* 131–148. Thousand Oaks, Calif.: Sage.

Media Development Journal. Vols. 38 (1991) and 61 (1994).

Mlama, Penina. 1989. Culture, women and the media. In S. K. Kwame Boafo, ed., *Communication and culture: African perspectives,* 11–18. African Region: WACC.

Riaño, Pilar, ed. 1994. *Women in grassroots communications.* Thousand Oaks, Calif.: Sage.

Stuart, S. 1989. Access to media: Placing media in the hands of the people. *Media Development* 36(4): 8–11.

Pilar Riaño

MEDIA: Mainstream

Since the 1960s, when what is generally referred to as the second wave of feminism in the United States began, feminists—especially in nations where U.S. media products are widely available—have had a special interest in the ways mass media advertising, movies, television, popular fiction, magazines, and music have represented girls and women, and the ways in which women and girls have been affected by these images. It is not coincidental that the rise of second-wave feminism ran parallel with the enormous expansion of mass media—especially home television—in the post–World War II industrialized world. In deploying a profuse and constant barrage of generally stereotypical and demeaning images of women and femininity, the media themselves played a part in arousing the consciousness and anger of young women, particularly of the white, educated classes, at the ways in which society contrives to keep females in subordinate and relatively powerless positions. Women have been portrayed as wholly sexualized objects or wholly desexualized, nunlike "spinsters"; as "good girls" endlessly serving the needs of men and children, at home and in the workforce, or "bad girls" defying the behavioral norms set by patriarchal institutions, especially the nuclear family; as brainless, ditzy "dumb blondes" or "unnaturally," brainy (and thus asexual) nerds. The mass media representations have been almost exclusively one-dimensional, stereotypical, and marked by qualities predetermined by male values and needs. It is thus understandable that feminist activists, writers, and scholars have, from the start, put great energy into critiquing and working to change gender stereotypes in media and to empower women to resist them.

Early Activist Campaigns against Media

It was perhaps Betty Friedan, in her influential book *The Feminine Mystique* (1963), who first called attention to the sexism of media gender stereotypes. Her work was instrumental in raising consciousness about media sexism and inspiring women to organize against these and other sexist social norms. By the late 1960s, many national and grass-roots campaigns around sexist media images were active and visible. In the early stages of the second wave in the United States, the campaign to change media stereotypes took a predominantly activist form. Flora Davis (1991) chronicles in detail the various campaigns undertaken by feminist activists both within and outside the media in the late 1960s, during the period when the mass women's movement in the United States was just reaching its height. In 1968, members of New

York Radical Women demonstrated against the Miss America pageant, a symbol of the sexual objectification of women through media images. In the early 1970s, major sit-ins by female employees took place at *Newsweek* and the *Ladies' Home Journal,* two popular magazines, demanding that media institutions respond to feminist demands.

In the next few years, feminist groups across the country mobilized demonstrations against a variety of sexist media forms—pornographic magazines, particularly offensive movies, rock music album covers, and billboards. These actions garnered some media attention and were responsible for certain changes in media personnel and content. They were also responsible for increased interest in feminist critiques of sexist representational practices, and several feminist books—most notably Kate Millett's *Sexual Politics* (1970) and Germaine Greer's *The Female Eunuch* (1970)—became best-sellers. But by and large, the mainstream media remained highly sexist, and what progress was made was largely in the interest of white middle-class women and tended to ignore the often very different, and more severe, prejudices against women of color and poor women.

Feminist Media Theory and Criticism

Campaigns against media stereotypes continue to be waged, and mainstream critiques of sexist media continue to be published in magazines and books—for example, Susan Faludi's *Backlash* (1991) and Naomi Wolf's *The Beauty Myth* (1991). Perhaps the most attention and insight into mainstream media's gendered representational practices since the early 1970s, however, has been within the academy, where the influx of students and professors affected by the work of second-wave activists and writers has led to the widespread esablishment of women's studies programs, as well as particular courses in many departments, in which critiques of all kinds of representational forms, including media genres, are studied.

Media studies itself, as an academic field, developed rather late. Early women's studies courses tended to stress literary criticism more than media criticism per se, because literature was an already established academic field and was highly respected. Popular culture only slowly came into its own as an area of academic study and teaching. Nonetheless, the influence of feminism, with its targeting of media images as key agents of socialization and, by extension, oppression of women and minorities, led to increasing academic interest in media studies. As more former activists and young people influenced by feminist ideas and feminist targeting of the media entered the academy and began writing and teaching, the academic field grew.

The dominant focus of early feminist scholarship, one that is still a major focus for feminist writers inside and outside the academy, was the critique of negative stereotypes. Feminists show great and warranted concern about the powerful role of mass media in educating and socializing people, especially young children, to imitate and passively accept the polarized sex roles engendered by sexist and, consumerist society. And since U.S. mass media are today globally ubiquitous and almost as powerful in their impact in other countries as in the United States, concern about these negative images has spread to women everywhere on the globe. Not only do U.S. media images objectify and demean white, middle-class women; the racist and class-biased thrust of American media images doubly and trebly oppress women of color and poor women, within the United States and elsewhere.

The works of Tuchman et al. (1978) on the treatment of women in television, newspapers, and magazines; of Katherine Fishburne (1982) on the history of women's portrayal in media and popular culture; of John Berger (1975) on the traditions of gender representation that carry through from the age of oil painting to the age of advertising; and of Erving Goffman (1979) on the symbols and rituals surrounding gender representation in advertising have become classics in an enormous body of work in this tradition of feminist media critique of negative images.

In more recent years, this tradition has expanded to include studies of women of color and working-class women. bell hooks's (1990) work points out how white feminists have failed to address the many ways in which women of color do not fit classic feminist truisms, and Patricia Turner (1994) has analyzed how images from black popular culture have had an enormous, if often unsung, influence on the larger white culture. Many other writers, most prominently Cherríe Moraga and Gloria Anzaldúa in the anthology *This Bridge Called My Back* (1981), have protested the particular, often invisible, ways in which women of color in many ethnic groups have been victims of media sexism different from that directed at white, middle-class women. Lillian Robinson (1978) has analyzed the similarly demeaning ways in which working-class women have been made invisible, and often doubly oppressed, through media representational norms.

Media History and Women's History

As the study of gender and mass media has developed, much has been learned about the complex ways in which the media themselves are implicated in the history of women's struggles to free themselves from sexist constraints. Feminist historical studies of early mass media by Stuart Ewen (1976) and Lynn Spigel (1992) reveal how the advertising, magazine, and television industries sought to "sell" women on new consumer goods and lifestyles as a way of "liberating" them from current forms of oppression, only to trap them in new modes of life that were equally constraining. Indeed, the history of commercial mass media of all kinds reveals a clever strategy by which media executives have attempted to channel women into new roles, jobs, and lifestyle habits that were primarily meant to stimulate the growth of the consumer society. When society needed women in the workplace, media pushed the image of the career woman. When consumption of household appliances and prepared foods was needed, women were seen as "domestic engineers" or sophisticated "modern" wives and mothers serving their families the "latest" food products.

As time has gone by, however, and the women's movement itself has become increasingly influential in public debate and consciousness, media industries have been forced to take account of women audiences' increasing awareness of and resistance to negative stereotypes and industry ploys to exploit and manipulate them. Women are the major consumers of many forms of popular culture, especially television, magazines, pulp fiction, and advertised products; and, influenced by the urging of the women's movement that they be educated for careers, increasing numbers are becoming media producers, writers, and directors themselves. These two trends have led to a contradictory media situation in which forces of backlash against feminist gains war with the ever more active push by women for more progressive images.

Julie D'Acci's study (1994) of the production of the television series *Cagney and Lacey,* about two female police officers, reveals the intricate, contradictory process by which media producers have incorporated feminist ideas and values into media texts while still maintaining most of the basic sexist norms of the industry. Elayne Rapping's study (1992) of female-oriented television movies reveals similar contradictions, which nonetheless show that the industry has indeed been affected and changed by feminism. Lisa Lewis's study (1992) of MTV, the music video channel that now reaches a global audience with satellite channels in Europe, Australia, China, and Latin America, demonstrates that female artists, producers, and even teenage fans have had an enormous effect on the once institutionally sexist and racist network, whose initial target audience was young, white, suburban males. Lewis shows how the demands of women consumers and the strong will of women performers forced MTV to air more strong women artists with feminist messages. Tricia Rose (1991) has done similar work on the rise of black women rap musicians with strong feminist messages and attitudes. Even Naomi Wolf's scathing study of increasing sexism in magazines as a kind of "backlash" against feminism also reveals a grudging move toward inclusion of more feminist-influenced editorial content. Wolf argues that it is this very feminist-informed editorial content that has moved advertisers to up the ante, so to speak, in their push to sexualize and objectify women's images, creating a kind of double bind in which women who "want it all"—career, family, sexual pleasure—must struggle to reach a perfection of appearance that is far more rigorous than the beauty norms of earlier times.

Women as Readers and Consumers

As studies of the industry continue to reveal contradiction, so do studies of texts themselves. Feminist scholars have been looking more closely at the very texts that have generally been considered most sexist—soap operas, romance novels, sitcoms—and finding them less one-dimensionally oppressive than they might seem on the surface. Tania Modleski's *Loving with a Vengeance* (1982) analyzes some of these forms and finds more value in their representation of women's lives than has generally been granted. She and many other recent scholars argue that women's forms have been unfairly devalued precisely because they *are* women's forms and speak to women's concerns and values, which the male critical establishment discounts or ignores.

Studies of women readers and viewers of mass culture have furthered insight into the way texts created by sexist institutions may nonetheless reveal contradictions internally, and the ways women themselves receive the texts. Ien Ang (1982), John Fiske (1987), and Janice Radway (1983) have done studies of audience's "reading practices" that reveal that women may often "read against the grain," finding ways to interpret texts to suit their own values and resisting the oppressive dominant messages of texts in order to focus on minor subtextual meanings that are more progressive. That texts do not hold a single, one-dimensional, unambiguous meaning is a position increasingly taken by media scholars. Similarly, readers themselves are increasingly being seen as having power to subvert and reformulate the meaning of even the most oppressively sexist texts. Thus, women who read romances, says Radway, find in them moments of liberation from the very different worlds they inhabit within their own sexist marriages. Bobo and Seiter (1991) have done similar work on black women audiences and reached a similar conclusion. Far less work has been done on women in other cultures, however.

As refreshing as all this inquiry is, it does not take away from the fact that mass media, today as in the 1950s, are a commercial industry in a society in which sexism and patriarchal values and traditions still reign supreme. For this reason, the representation of women and girls in movies, TV, music, magazines, and advertising remains predominately sexist, manipulative, and exploitive of women, especially women of color, poor women, and sexually unconventional women. Lesbians are still largely invisible in media, and women who are sexually unconventional in lifestyle—for example, prostitutes or single mothers—are still demonized. The work of women scholars, activists, and media professionals is far from done, and indeed is more urgent than ever as the range and power of the media continue to spread over the globe and to fill greater and greater portions of our days and nights.

See Also

CULTURAL STUDIES; FEMINISM: SECOND-WAVE NORTH AMERICAN; IMAGES OF WOMEN: OVERVIEW; MEDIA: ALTERNATIVE; MEDIA: OVERVIEW; REPRESENTATION

References and Further Reading

Ang, Ien. 1982. *Watching "Dallas": Soap opera and the melodramatic imagination.* New York: Methuen.

Berger, John. 1975. *Ways of seeing.* New York: Penguin.

Bobo, Jacqueline, and Ellen Seiter. (1991). Black feminism and media criticism: *The Women of Brewster Place. Screen* 32: 286–302.

D'Acci, Julie. 1994. *Defining women: Television and the case of "Cagney and Lacey."* Chapel Hill: University of North Carolina Press.

Davis, Flora. 1991. *Moving the mountain: The women's movement in America since 1960.* New York: Simon and Schuster.

Ewen, Stuart. 1976. *Captains of consciousness: Advertising and social roots of consumer culture.* New York: McGraw-Hill.

Faludi, Susan, 1991. *Backlash: The undeclared war against American women.* New York: Crown.

Fishburne, Katherine. 1982. *Women in popular culture: A reference guide.* Westport, Conn.: Greenwood.

Fiske, John. 1987. *Television culture.* New York: Methuen.

Friedan, Betty. 1963. *The feminine mystique.* New York: Norton.

Goffman, Erving. 1979. *Gender advertisement.* Cambridge, Mass.: Harvard University Press.

Greer, Germaine. 1970. *The female eunuch.* New York: Bantam.

hooks, bell. 1990. *Yearning: Race, class, gender, and popular culture.* Boston: South End.

Lewis, Lisa. 1992. *Voicing the difference: Gender politics and MTV.* Philadelphia: Temple University Press.

Millett, Kate. 1970. *Sexual politics.* New York: Doubleday.

Modleski, Tania. 1982. *Loving with a vengeance: Mass-produced fantasies for women.* New York: Methuen.

Moraga, Cherri, and Gloria Anzaldúa. 1981. *This bridge called my back: Writings of radical women of color.* Watertown: Persephone. Press.

Radway, Janice. 1983. *Reading the romance: Women, patriarchy, and popular culture.* Chapel Hill: University of North Carolina Press.

Rapping, Elayne. 1992. *The movie of the week: Private stories/public events.* Minneapolis: University of Minnesota Press.

Robinson, Lillian. 1978. *Sex, class, and culture.* New York: Methuen.

Rose, Tricia. 1991. Never trust a big butt and a smile. *Camera Obscuna* 23: 109–132.

Spigel, Lynn. 1992. *Make room for TV: Television and the family ideal in postwar America.* Chicago: University of Chicago Press.

Tuchman, Gaye, Arlene Daniels, and James Benet. 1978. *Hearth and home: Images of women in the mass media.* Oxford: Oxford University Press.

Turner, Patricia. 1994. *Ceramic uncles and celluloid mammies: Black images and their influence on culture.* Berkeley: University of California Press.

Wolf, Naomi, 1991. *The beauty myth.* New York: Doubleday.

Elayne Rapping

MEDIA AND POLITICS

The complex connection between women, politics, and the media involves numerous issues and topics such as images of women, citizenship, political participation and representation, feminism, journalism, mainstream mass media, and alternative media. Here, the starting point will be mainstream mass media and research on women and politics oriented toward media studies. Within this framework, feminist scholars consider how women are portrayed in the media as participants in the public sphere, and how the media define and represent feminist issues or other political issues particularly relevant for women. Feminist analysis includes production processes (asking, for example, whether journalists' own gender influences their choices with regard to representing women in politics) and gendered media genres: for instance, factual journalism, including reporting on politics, is often considered a masculine genre; entertainment and drama are seen as feminine genres. A supposed "lightening" of journalism has interested political scientists, since this trend may be linked to broader changes in political culture and may enhance women's status and visibility in media organizations and in the content of journalism. However, much less is known about women and men as audiences or about the effects of the media on political participation.

Representations of Women in Public Life

Women are increasingly gaining access to politics and public life, but the media still tend to give a more traditional picture. Quantitative monitoring of women's representation in the media seems to produce similar figures both over time and across national or regional boundaries.

For example, the Norwegian public broadcasting company (NPK) studied men's and women's participation in its radio and television programs at five-year intervals beginning in 1973 and found that, with only slight fluctuations, the proportion of women remained about 30 percent. A study comparing prime-time programming in six northern European countries found about the same proportion of women in all six—32 percent (Who Speaks, 1997–2000). Men were the majority in all categories of roles and were especially prominent as politicians (72 percent) and experts (80 percent).

News reporting is a primary focus of research on women's representation in the media, since this genre is perceived as the media's most "official" source of information about social reality, as the main mediator of political matters to the public, and as a masculine genre (Tuchman et al., 1978). The Global Media Monitoring Project (GMMP) examined a news day in 71 countries—over 15,000 news items from the press, radio, and television—and found no large differences in the portrayal of women in various parts of the world (MediaWatch, 1995). Of all interviewees, 17 percent were women; among interviewees above age 35 in "higher-influence" occupations—such as politicians, government spokespersons, and professionals—there were 10 times as many men as women. In stories covering political issues, only 7 percent of the interviewees were women. Such research indicates that women, including women politicians, are not as newsworthy as men (Kivikuru et al., 1999; Norris, 1997).

Media content remains traditional not only numerically but also in more subtle ways. The media seem to reinforce traditional assumptions about gender relations and appropriate female behavior, and when women step outside their accustomed roles, news coverage often suggests a reluctance to accept this. For instance, coverage of women politicians tends to focus more on personal character, looks, family, and private life, and on the competing demands of private and public life. Women in politics are conscious that the images and language used to portray them differ from those used to portray men (Sreberny-Mohammadi and Ross, 1996; van Zoonen, 1998).

Representation of Women's Issues and Feminist Politics

Some research has addressed media coverage of feminist politics and women's political issues—although definitions of these areas vary. The GMMP found that, on average, only 11 percent of news stories covered changing roles of women, violence against women, harassment of women, portrayal of women in the media, women's wages, women's working conditions, women's health, birth control, or women with disabilities. Frequently, to be considered newsworthy, women-specific issues have needed a "soft" or sensational element, such as violence or some other kind of tragedy (Carter et al., 1998; Joseph and Sharma, 1994). The Foreign News Flow Project, an international effort involving some 50 countries, found that coverage of the Fourth United Nations Conference on Women in 1995 concentrated on polarization of various political views, had more of a human-interest orientation, and used a more entertaining style than "conventional" foreign news items (Aslama and Kivikuru, 1999). Studies on coverage of the women's movement and feminism, mostly conducted in the United States, suggest that the media focus on preferred individuals and organizations as representatives of the movement. Thus, they narrow the definition and scope of the movement and its everyday relevance to other women, men, and groups (Norris, 1997).

Women, Politics, and Journalists

Despite an increase in women in the media, as journalists and other professionals who influence content, women remained a minority at the decision-making level during the 1990s; and a journalist's own gender did not necessarily change content or approach (Leonard, 1998). The GMMP found that even though women were 44 percent of the journalists reporting on politics and government, their stories hardly ever included women as interviewees. The increasing use of entertainment style in factual journalism, sometimes described as "feminization of news," may give women more opportunities as media professionals and thus more influence over content; however, this tendency is most clearly seen in "infotainment" programming and is more subtle in conventional news.

Audiences and Effects

Feminist media scholars have not given extensive attention to women as audiences of political material in the mass media. Standard quantitative audience measurements, mostly conducted by broadcasting organizations, provide the only systematic data; these measures and other research show that in the western world there is a fairly predictable pattern: women tend to prefer more entertaining genres while men prefer more informative genres, such as news and current affairs. Surprisingly little research is conducted on why these gender differences exist or on how female audiences—in terms of ethnicity, age, education, and geographical location—relate to political communication in the media. Certain results suggest, however, that many women do not associate news with their everyday life but simply accept existing criteria of newsworthiness. Studies of audiences during political campaigns find that gendered social reality affects how women identify and reflect upon political issues, and that voters' perception of a political message depends considerably on the gender of the politician.

Changes in Political Culture; Changes in Journalism

The popularization of politics and the market-driven orientation of journalism toward entertainment and human-interest stories are interconnected trends. Gender differences in both public and private life are reflected in "hard" (factual, masculine) and "soft" (entertaining, feminine) news topics—a division criticized by feminist political scientists and media scholars. Neverthless, more entertaining news covereage can create a "popular public sphere," addressing issues and speaking to audiences which might be relegated to the margins of conventional journalism, and providing an alternative forum for political education and discussion. Also, by focusing on private and personal aspects of life, these "soft" genres include female audiences and women's politics and portray women more often, thereby at least opening up the possibility of alternative gender representations.

On the other hand, popular journalism, especially in political news and reporting, has provoked rethinking of the media as a potential link between civic society and the state. It has been argued that politicians have become yet another group of celebrities, subjects of gossip as much as serious reporting; that citizens are regarded as media consumers and are offered entertainment instead of political information; that emotionality has become more important than analysis or criticism; and that political issues are distorted by personalization. Some scholars describe this as a "crisis of communication for citizenship" (Blumler and Gurevitch, 1995). In certain ways, softer journalism is a response to feminists' criticism of traditional news journalism, but it does not necessarily make women's issues more political; rather, it still tends to reinforce gender stereotypes, as in the representations of female politicians.

Finally, it has also been argued that the media have abandoned the role of watchdog or objective observer and have become an active participant in political processes, with the result that anyone who wants to participate in politics must use publicity efficiently.

Guidelines for Change

The media are important for politics and thus for women and politics, and various suggestions have been made for addressing these concerns and thereby improving the status of women in society. Initiatives and proposals include a news service covering women, particularly in developing countries (Byerly, 1995); recommendations for governments and media organizations by the United Nations Platform for Action of 1995 (Section J: Media); and consciousness-raising for journalists and women political candidates, such as the Screening Gender Project. The GMMP has recommended four strategies to achieve gender equality in the world's media:

1. Transforming the coverage of traditional politics, government, and business to include women's perspectives.
2. Increasing access to power and decision-making. Although women do participate in the media, their participation in politics, business, and the economy is much lower.
3. Discussing the merits of regulation, such as affirmative action.
4. Conducting ongoing analysis in order to develop an empirical, scientific basis for increasing the participation of women in the mass media.

See Also

EDUCATION: POLITICAL; IMAGES OF WOMEN: OVERVIEW; JOURNALISM; JOURNALISTS; MEDIA: OVERVIEW; POLITICAL REPRESENTATION

References and Further Reading

Aslama, Minna, and Ullamaija Kivikuru. 1999. The Beijing controversies: Finnish news coverage of the Fourth World Conference on Women, Beijing 1995. *Nordicom Review* 20(2): 101–109.

Blumer, Jay, and Michael Gurevitch. 1995. *The crisis of public communication.* New York: Routledge.

Byerly, Carolyn M. 1995. News, consciousness, and social participation: The role of Women's Feature Service in world news. In Angharad N. Valdivia, ed., *Feminism, multicul-*

turalism, and the media: Global diversities. London and Thousand Oaks, Calif.: Sage.

Carter, Cynthia, Gill Branston, and Stuart Allan, eds. 1998. *News, gender, and power.* London and New York: Routledge.

Joseph, Ammu, and Kalpana Sharma. 1994. *Whose news? The media and women's issues.* London and Thousand Oaks, Calif.: Sage.

Kivikuru, Ullamaija, et al. 1999. *Images of women in the media: Report on existing research in the European Union, employment and social affairs, equality between women and men.* Luxembourg: European Commission Directorate-General for Employment, Industrial Relations, and Social Affairs Unit V/D.5, Office for Official Publications of the European Communities.

Leonard, Pauline. 1998. Women behaving badly? Restructuring gender and identity in British broadcasting organizations. *Harvard International Journal of Press/Politics* 3(1): 26–47.

MediaWatch. 1995. *Global Media Monitoring Project: Women's participation in the news.* Toronto: MediaWatch.

Norris, Pippa, ed. 1997. *Women, media, and politics.* New York and Oxford: Oxford University Press.

Screening gender—Promoting good practice in gender portrayal in television. (Project of five European broadcasting companies.) Web site: <www.yle.fi/gender>.

Sreberny, Annabelle, and Liesbet van Zoonen, eds. 1999. *Women's politics and communication.* New York: Hampton.

Sreberny-Mohammadi, Annabelle, and Karen Ross. 1996. Women MPs and the media: Representing the body politic. In Joni Lovenduski and Pippa Norris, eds., *Women in politics.* Oxford: Oxford University Press.

Tuchman, Gaye, Arlene Kaplan, and James Benet. 1978. *Hearth and home: Images of women in the mass media.* New York: Oxford University Press.

van Zoonen, Liesbet. 1994. *Feminist media studies.* London and Thousand Oaks, Calif.: Sage.

———. 1998. "Finally, I have my mother back": Politicians and their families in popular culture. *Harvard International Journal of Press/Politics* 3(1): 48–64.

———. 1991. A tyranny of intimacy? Women, femininity, and television news. In Peter Dahlgren and Colin Sparks, eds., *Communication and citizenship.* London: Sage.

Who Speaks (1997/2000). *Who speaks in television? A comparative study of female participation in television programs.* Helsinki: Screening Gender Project, Finnish Broadcasting Company. See also: Birgit Eie and Herö Hege. 1994. *Who speaks in NRK? A report on the participation of women and men in radio and television programs in 1994.* Oslo: Norwegian Broadcasting Company (NRK), Equality Council.

Minna Aslama

MEDIA AND VIOLENCE

See VIOLENCE: MEDIA.

MEDICAL CONTROL OF WOMEN

Medical control of women refers to biomedical practices and discourses through which explicit or implicit power is exerted over women's bodies, behaviors, and identities essentially on the basis of their sex and gender. It includes government implementation of health technologies, especially in the service of population planning programs, that have legitimized and outfitted medical regulation of female sexuality and reproductive capacities. Medical treatment need not be coercive, of course: individuals can and do participate in medicine's conceptual framework; internalize its theories of disease, health, and the body; and more or less willingly assimilate to its disciplinary regimes (Foucault, 1975). Further, receptivity to therapies is heterogeneous and can incorporate modes of resistance as well as provide avenues for empowerment and enhanced physical and mental well-being. However, it is frequently held that too much medicine does represent "control of women."

Medicine's jurisdiction over women has effectively been established through its ideological authority to define the very nature of women's biology, including its tendency to characterize female anatomy as a natural determinant of women's lesser sociopolitical opportunities. Although actual practices vary widely by cultural and historical context, medical subordination of women has ranged from the instrumental management of normal physiological events (like childbirth, menstruation, and menopause) to invasive technologies that augment or inhibit fertility.

Western Medicine and Medical Control

Western medicine, which is traceable to the ancient world, has for centuries assigned an inferior status to the female body, based on its periodicity and on presumed innate deficiencies relative to a male standard. A brief glance at the history of various "women's diseases" illustrates the influential role that the medical profession has played in circumscribing women's lives within conservative expectations about domesticity, dependency, and motherhood.

For example, European physicians from the Middle Ages through the Renaissance frequently made a diagnosis of hysteria for a disparate assortment of symptoms (including melancholy, anemia, anxiety, and insomnia) believed to result from a wayward uterus that wandered listlessly through the body. Well into the seventeenth century, hysteria was attributed to dissatisfied maternal longings; accordingly, the most widely prescribed cure for hysteria was sexual intercourse, within a heterosexual union sanctioned by law. Physicians of the day advocated early marriage, frequent pregnancies, and penetrative therapies—anal enemas, vaginal douches, and venal punctures (bloodletting)—that were recognized as analogous to the sex act (Dixon, 1995); such ideas reflected and reinforced the doctrine that uterine woes could best be satisfied by male seed, or, alternatively, by phallic surrogates.

In the Victorian era, a new variant of hysteria and related disorders like neurasthenia became virtually epidemic among affluent women in Europe and the United States (Ehrenreich and English, 1979). Symptons included fainting and fits of temper (which were supposed to be brought on by masturbation, among other proclaimed vices). Again, heterosexual intercourse was presumed to be curative; prescribed therapies also included applying leeches to the labia or the vagina, primitive hysterectomies, and even castration of the clitoris—and, above all, the injunction to restrict activities to feminine, that is, domestic, purposes.

At the turn of the twentieth century, psychoanalysis redefined hysteria as an unconscious affliction triggered by frustrated libidinal fantasies—and thereby tacitly disavowed much sexual violence against women. Madness, however, was still typically linked to the (female) body.

Since the inception of psychiatry, women have statistically predominated in most categories of mental, or emotional, deviance (Ussher, 1991). During the middle of the twentieth century, the majority of victims of lobotomies were women; and women far more often than men have been prescribed tranquilizers and antidepressant drugs. Hysteria was based on the notion that female sexuality is fraught with neuroses, and the legacy of that notion has included modern infirmities such as frigidity, nerves, and hypochondria. In fact, the codification of premenstrual syndrome (PMS, a malady with more than 150 variable traits) as a disorder of raging hormones can be read as a conceptual extension of the wandering womb. Thus female psychology and physiology regularly devolve into biologically determined pathology. Some contemporary medical textbooks depict even "normal" menstruation in terms of atrophy, degeneration, and lost production, that is, as a departure from the implied optimal condition: conception and implantation (Martin, 1987). Menopause, too, has largely been presented as a deficiency disease in need of antidotes, despite the fact that for many women, particularly in nonwestern cultures, the climacteric is regarded not as an illness but rather as a new stage of opportunity. Moreover, menopause treatments like hormone replacement therapy have been prescribed well in advance of adequate information concerning their long-term risks.

Modern Obstetrics and Fertility

The image of women as weak victims of their biology has proved not only tenacious but also conveniently (and lucratively) exploitable, nowhere more so, it is often held, than in the technological co-option of childbirth by modern obstetrics (Arditti et al., 1984; Corea and Klein, 1985). According to this view, which is widespread, the medicalization of childbirth virtually eliminated female practitioners from the healing profession until relatively recently, first by delegitimizing traditional midwifery (a process that may date from the medieval witch-hunts) and then by excluding women from higher education at the same time that a university education became increasingly mandatory.

Although in exceptional cases parturition may have benefited from the forceps and hooks wielded by medical practitioners, by and large medicalized childbirth, over the course of two centuries, has had a number of negative effects on the health of women as a group. These practices date from at least the eighteenth century, when fatalities from puerpural sepsis, or "childbed fever," increased among women attended by hospital physicians (who unwittingly spread infection from patient to patient and from cadavers to patients), and have prevailed through decades of aggressive gynecology and surgical interventions. The general disempowerment of women in labor, by which a woman participated less and less in the the delivery of her own child, is often said to have reached an extreme in the mid- to late twentieth century in developed nations and among the elite of the developing world, with routine episiotomies, induced labor, amniotomics (puncture of the amniotic sac) and forced extractions, high rates of cesarean section, heavy anesthesia, poorly tested pharmaceuticals (for example, the carcinogenic drug diethylstilbestrol, DES, for threatened miscarriages), and prenatal diagnostic screening. In particular, prenatal screening (for example, amniocentesis, fetal ultrasound, and electronic and genetic monitoring) has become increasingly imperative.

From the outset, modern obstetrics has been instrumental in the professionalization of medicine, in part simply because childbirth is so common, but also because an emergent partnership between urban universities and charity hospitals made working-class women available as clinical material for training physicians. The resultant trend toward discriminatory experimentation, particularly on poor and disenfranchised women, continues today, especially in developing countries. On the one hand, research into reproductive biology focuses almost exclusively on women; on the other hand, research on women's more general health concerns has been neglected. This disparity has often been rationalized on the basis of the risk of pregnancy and the difficulties of "controlling for" female hormonal cycles under the experimental protocols. Such gender bias has been pervasive in medical research and has been coupled with class and ethnic stratification of reproductive health care (Ginsburg and Rapp, 1995). With respect to contraceptive development, women's bodies often have become, in effect, laboratories for testing new methods, in the absence of conclusive data about side effects or potential carcinogenicity (for example, the risk of morbidity associated with the Dalkon shield, an intrauterine device; and the increased risk of cancer associated with prolonged hormone therapy).

Infertility is widely seen as another area of medical control of women, who are the major recipients of infertility management (even in cases when the cause is traceable to a male partner's low sperm count). Women carry the primary burden of physical discomfort and emotional stress from infertility treatments such as in vitro fertilization and artificial insemination, despite their relatively low success rates (Oakley, 1993). Furthermore, while research gravitates toward prestigious high-tech interventions, basic investigation into the causes and prevention of female infertility—including the influential role played by sexually transmitted diseases—is notably lacking.

With regard to sexually transmitted diseases (STDs), such omissions and paradoxes also have a long history. For example, in Europe from the fifteenth to the twentieth century, women were deemed more likely to contract and spread syphilis and gonorrhea, because the female body was at once more delicate and more contagious. Nonetheless, treatment generally prioritized men (Spongberg, 1997). As late as the 1970s, the technique most commonly used to diagnose gonorrhea was highly effective for men but unreliable for identifying infected women (Corea and Klein, 1985).

Morality and Coercion

Such inequities in health care agendas and medical applications illustrate the power of medical authority to moralize. One example is contraceptive development during the first half of the twentieth century: in the United States, the medical establishment was morally opposed to birth control and abortion services until pressure from women's lobbies and the threat of lost profits prompted a pragmatic adoption of contraceptive methods and research already under way. In one of medical history's darker episodes, sympathy on the part of some physicians for the contemporaneous eugenics movement also played a role in this ideological shift, which, at its most extreme, culminated in the forced sterilization of minority, handicapped, and impoverished women in many western nations. Coercive birth control measures are part of the population planning programs of many developing nations today.

Conclusion

Essentially, then, the concept of medical control means that the medical regime portrays women's bodies as constitutionally delicate—and thus in need of protection by the male medical profession. Along with this portrayal, women's bodies are also depicted as simultaneously problematic and polluting—and thus in need of policing by patriarchal institutions. In overt and subtle ways, biomedicine has worked in concert with the political, economic, and technological sectors to perpetuate ideological and practical means for controlling female sexuality and motherhood.

See Also

CHILDBIRTH; CONTRACEPTION; ETHICS: MEDICAL; EUGENICS; EXPERIMENTS ON WOMEN; FERTILITY AND FERTILITY TREATMENT; GENITAL MUTILATION; GYNECOLOGY; HEALTH CHALLENGES TO WOMEN; MADNESS AND HYSTERIA; MENTAL HEALTH, *I and II*; OBSTETRICS; REPRODUCTIVE HEALTH; REPRODUCTIVE RIGHTS

References and Further Reading

Arditti, Rita, Renate Duelli Klein, and Shelley Minden, eds. 1984. *Test tube women: What future for motherhood?* London: Pandora.

Corea, Gena. 1977. *The hidden malpractice: How American medicine mistreats women.* New York: Harper and Row.

———, and Renate Duelli Klein, eds. 1985. *Man-made women: How new reproductive technologies affect women.* London: Hutchinson.

Dixon, Laurinda S. 1995. *Perilous chastity: Women and illness in pre-Enlightenment art and medicine.* Ithaca, N.Y.: Cornell University Press.

Ehrenreich, Barbara, and Deirdre English. 1979. *For her own good: 150 years of the experts' advice to women.* London: Pluto.

Foucault, Michel. 1975. *The birth of the clinic: An archaeology of medical perception.* Trans. A. M. Sheridan Smith. New York: Vintage.

Ginsburg, Faye D., and Rayna Rapp, eds. 1995. *Conceiving the new world order: The global politics of reproduction.* Berkeley: University of California Press.

Martin, Emily. 1987. *The woman in the body: A cultural analysis of reproduction.* Boston: Beacon.

Oakley, Ann. 1993. *Essays on women, medicine, and health.* Edinburgh: Edinburgh University Press.

Spongberg, Mary. 1997. *Feminising venereal disease. The body of the prostitute in nineteenth-century discourse.* New York: New York University Press.

Ussher, Jane M. 1991. *Women's madness: Misogyny or mental illness?* New York: Harvester Wheatsheaf.

Kyra Marie Landzelius

MEDICAL ETHICS

See ETHICS, MEDICAL.

MEDICINE: Internal I

Internal medicine is the medical specialty that provides health care, excluding surgery, to adults. The "internal" in its name suggests that it is concerned not merely with outward appearances of illness but rather with the deep and invisible causes of disease. The internist, as the specialist in internal medicine is called, develops competence in diagnosing and treating the diseases of the human body's major organ systems—the heart and blood vessels, the lungs, the digestive system, the kidneys, the blood, the joints and muscles, and the circulating hormones—as well as diseases that transcend any one organ system, such as infections and cancer. Although many internists choose to undergo additional training to become subspecialists in cardiology, pulmonary medicine, gastroenterology, nephrology, hematology, rheumatology, endocrinology, infectious disease, or oncology, the the majority practice general internal medicine; that is, they are professionally equipped to care for patients with a wide range of ailments, including coronary artery disease, asthma, peptic ulcer disease, anemia, diabetes, and arthritis.

Internal medicine—or simply "medicine," as it is known within the medical center—provides the intellectual and clinical backbone of the hospital or medical school. Unlike surgery, gynecology, or neurology, medicine attempts to understand the basic mechanisms of disease, no matter what treatment is indicated or what bodily function is affected. The internist acts as a consultant for surgeons, obstetricians, psychiatrists, and family physicians in diagnosing and treating adults with particularly complex diseases. From its early discoveries of antibiotics, insulin, thyroid hormone, and steroids to its recent dazzling progress in the treatment of heart disease, AIDS, diabetes, and many cancers, internal medicine has provided the most sustained basic and clinical research into the causes and treatments of human diseases.

Internal medicine is a creation of the American medical system and does not exist formally in other countries. Although what in the United States is called internal medicine is practiced everywhere, the specialty is usually referred to elsewhere as "general practice."

The principles that have guided internal medicine since its inception include the rigorous application of scientific knowledge to clinical care, commitment to the whole patient in his or her illness, collegiality with all other health professionals, and social responsibility as a curator of medical expertise. The field of general internal medicine, in particular, has taken responsibility for research, teaching, and exemplary practice in such aspects of medical care as communication skills, effective doctor–patient relationships, preventive medicine, patient education, and end-of-life care. More urgently with every decade, internists envision their duties to include recognition of each patient's singular emotional and personal experiences of illness, advocacy for justice, and commitment to the highest standards of professionalism and ethics.

History of Internal Medicine

Arising in the United States in the late nineteenth century, the specialty of internal medicine was created for those physicians whose clinical actions were based on the emerging sciences of pathology, bacteriology, biochemistry, and physiology. At a time when commercial U.S. medical schools awarded diplomas after less than two years of haphazard lectures and apprenticeships to local general practitioners, internal medicine endorsed for its trainees in the United States the rigorous, university-based, four-year scientific education obtained by physicians in England, Germany, and France.

At its inauguration in 1888, U.S. internal medicine was the vision of white, upper-class, European-schooled male physicians. Several elite doctors of Boston, Philadelphia, Baltimore, and New York were driven to distinguish their practice from the slipshod practice of graduates of commercial medical schools. The emerging field of internal medicine, in the persons of such early leaders as Sir William Osler and Francis Delafield, allied itself unequivocally with the European university model. In 1910, with the support of the Carnegie Foundation, the educator Abraham Flexner evaluated the medical schools of the United States and recommended closure of the majority of the so-called irregular schools—the non–university-based and nonelite schools, including many that had been founded specifically to train women doctors. When these schools were closed, women and members of minority groups who wanted to become doctors had no place to go. The educational quality of the irregular schools was indeed inferior to the university training, but their closure incurred social debts still outstanding a century later (see Morantz-Sanchez, 1985).

Women in Early Internal Medicine

Late nineteenth-century medicine in general had a distinct and troubling relationship with women. Women were accepted grudgingly, if at all, into the university medical schools—Victorian sensibilities were shocked by the thought of coeducational discussions of intimate bodily functions and were unused to the idea of professional women in any field. Women intent on becoming doctors found that they had to go to Europe to obtain decent training.

If there were few women doctors, there was no dearth of women patients, at least among the moneyed classes. The sick poor of either gender had difficulty obtaining care. Care for the sick rich, however, was overflowing. Mainstream medical theory of the time dictated that a woman was inherently weak and sickly—her menstruation, pregnancies, breast-feeding, and powerful emotions subjected her to storms of nervous delicacy, fainting spells, and invalidism. The doctor was the constant companion of such enfeebled women, ready at a sneeze to prescribe lengthy rest cures and bleedings. Both physical and intellectual activity were banned as dangerous to the uterus. And so, for decades, women were prevented from writing, working, and becoming professionals by internists, neurologists, and gynecologists armed with their theories of the hormonal inferiority of women (Ehrenreich, 1973).

Such women physician pioneers as the neurologist Mary Putnam Jacobi and the public health reformer Elizabeth Blackwell challenged this misogynist ideology. Modeling an intellectual and physical stamina to match their male colleagues, these turn-of-the-century women physicians and their women colleagues contributed enormously to the health of all women by puncturing theories about women's inherent inferiority and by proving themselves to be at least equal to their male counterparts.

Women and Healing

Do women and men internists practice medicine differently? At the risk of seeming essentialist—that is, ascribing characteristics to women just by virtue of their being women—many commentators note that women's experiences of childbirth and motherhood equip them with the practical habits of nurturing and compassion required of the physician. Some psychologists and philosophers have tried to delineate the differences between women's and men's modes of relating to other people, their development of moral standards, and their ways of knowing (Gilligan, 1982; Belensky et al., 1986). These observations are particularly salient for internists and the other primary care physicians who devote themselves to long-term, comprehensive, and loyal care of their patients. Indeed, differences between women doctors and men doctors are evident whenever sought: women doctors spend more time with their patients, seem more attentive to the life contexts of their patients' illnesses, and demonstrate such qualities as empathy and attunement more predictably than do men (Bowman and Allen, 1990; More, 1994). If some negative aspects of medicine have been termed "paternalistic"—its arrogance, its power-hoarding, and its dominance in decision making—other healing aspects might be characterized as maternalistic: medicine's unconditional regard for the other, its altruism, and its nurturing impulses (More, 1999).

Internal Medicine's Attention to Women's Health Concerns

Despite its gendered past, internal medicine has become highly attuned to the needs of women patients. Since the 1980s, women have been actively sought as participants in research projects so that medicine can learn the different physiological and pharmacological workings of the female body, rather than generalizing to women what has been learned about men. Contrary to the false beliefs of the nineteenth century, women are now understood to have longer survival rates than men and to be protected from a host of ailments that cut short men's lives. For example, the female hormone estrogen exerts healthful effects on the circulation, lipid levels, and the heart, preventing heart attacks at an early age. Women's longer life span can be explained by the survival edge donated by their female physiology.

Teaching and practice in internal medicine have increasingly emphasized women's health issues, as demonstrated by the rise of internal medicine practices devoted to the care of women. The research agenda of internal medicine has embraced such issues as the treatment of osteoporosis, breast cancer, ovarian cancer, and symptoms of menopause, as well as social issues affecting women, such as domestic violence and sexual abuse. There is growing recognition that women experience diseases differently from men, and this is motivating efforts to train internists to diagnose common diseases accurately as they present in women as well as in men.

The care of women patients has perhaps helped internal medicine to become attuned to the lived experience of illness. The emerging interests within internal medicine in narrative medicine, humanistic medicine, and relation-centered care emphasize the singularity of each experience of illness (Charon, 2000). As primary caregivers of family members and as patients, women can teach doctors about the journeys undertaken as health fails, about the search for meaning inaugurated by suffering and loss, and about the humility and courage required of the effective doctor in accompanying patients through their illnesses.

Internal Medicine's Commitment to Women Physicians

Internal medicine is the specialty that claims the highest number of women physicians in the United States; almost 20 percent of the women physicians in that country are internists. At the turn of the twenty-first century, women students make up more than 40 percent of the incoming classes of United States medical schools, yet women are still underrepresented among the profession's leaders. Women chairs of internal medicine departments are few, as are women chiefs of the subspecialty divisions of internal medicine departments. Women internists take longer than their male counterparts to achieve promotion and tenure, and they have lower salaries than men in comparable positions. Although vigorous efforts are being made by departments of medicine and deans of medical schools to redress these inequalities, they are decreasing only slowly. However, the increase in numbers of women entering internal medicine has changed the field by motivating institutions to grant leaves for childbearing and time for child rearing, and to extend the timing of tenure decisions for both men and women. Finally, the influx of women internists must be responsible, in part, for internal medicine's increased attentiveness to such dimensions of medicine as relationships with patients, humanism and professionalism, and respectful care of dying patients.

See Also

HORMONE REPLACEMENT THERAPY; MEDICINE: INTERNAL II

References and Further Reading

Belenky, Mary Field, Blythe McVicker Clinchy, Nancy Rule Goldberger, and Jill Mattuck Tarule. 1986. *Women's ways of knowing: The development of self, voice, and mind.* New York: Basic Books.

Bowman, Marjorie A., and Deborah I. Allen. 1990. *Stress and women physicians.* 2nd ed. New York: Springer-Verlag.

Charon, Rita. 2000. Medicine, the novel, and the passage of time. *Annals of Internal Medicine* 132: 63–68.

Ehrenreich, Barbara, and Deirdre English. 1973. *Complaints and disorders: The sexual politics of sickness.* Old Westbury: Feminist Press.

Friedman, Emily, ed. 1994. *An unfinished revolution: Women and health care in America.* New York: United Hospital Fund.

Gilligan, Carol. 1982. *In a different voice: Psychological theory and women's development.* Cambridge, Mass.: Harvard University Press.

Maulitz, Russell. 1986. *Grand rounds: One hundred years of internal medicine.* Philadelphia: University of Pennsylvania Press.

Morantz-Sanchez, Regina. 1985. *Sympathy and science: Women physicians in American medicine.* New York: Oxford University Press.

More, Ellen. 1999. *Restoring the balance: Women physicians and the profession of medicine, 1950–1995.* Cambridge Mass.: Harvard University Press.

———, and Maureen A. Milligan, eds. 1994. *The empathic practitioner: Empathy, gender, and medicine.* New Brunswick, N.Y.: Rutgers University Press.

Starr, Paul. 1982. *The social transformation of American medicine.* New York: Basic Books.

Stevens, Rosemary. 1986. Issues for American internal medicine through the last century. *Annals of Internal Medicine* 105: 592–602.

Rita Charon

MEDICINE: Internal II

The feminist movement of the last third of the twentieth century raised issues regarding health care and health care systems which challenged prevailing notions of gender neutrality in medicine, including internal medicine—the medical specialty, practiced by internists, that provides health care other than surgery to adults.

In the United States, where internal medicine as a concept originated (though it is actually practiced everywhere under names such as family medicine), the roles of women as both patients and providers changed dramatically in the years between 1970 and 2000. More women became physicians, and more women patients challenged their health care providers, demanding respect for concerns and conditions that had previously been thought trivial because they happened only to women. In the fields of internal medicine and family medicine, physicians learned that their treatment of adult women could not be based solely on a model of health and disease in adult men. Women's health was no longer just reproductive health, and therefore no longer just the province of the gynecologist. Instead, the traditional biomedical areas of adult health—oriented according to systems such as heart, lungs, gastrointestinal, endocrine, and musculoskeletal, among others—were reexamined for gender-specific aspects. This reexamination was done in the context of the social factors relating to women's status which had an impact on women's health: power differentials at work and at home, emotional health, and the attitude of the medical system toward women. The result has given us new diseases and conditions, new treatments, and new areas for research. In internal medicine, the feminist movement has brought about a new look at old diseases, a new focus by treatment and research on previously ignored problems, and a new definition of medical problems that are either a result of gender equity in the society or a result of gender discrimination. The examples to be discussed are but some of many in these categories.

Cardiovascular Disease

Cardiovascular disease is the best example of an old disease looked at anew. Hypertension, heart attacks, and strokes are the leading cause of death for women in the United States. Being female, particularly because of the presence of estrogen, has been presumed for many years to be a protective factor against heart disease, since the incidence of heart disease in premenopausal women is less than in men. However, studies in the last ten years have shown that women are more likely than men to die from a second heart attack, are more likely to wait before going to an emergency room, and are less likely to receive appropriate diagnostic evaluation if they do not have the typical male pattern of cardiac pain. In the United States, these differences in treatment and outcome are compounded by racial and class differences.

The presumption that estrogen has a protective effect led to widespread prescribing of estrogen replacement therapy as a preventive measure to decrease heart disease in women. However, two large-scale studies published in the year 2000 have questioned this benefit, and the optimal postmenopausal use of estrogens for preventing heart disease is a controversial topic. One of these studies was a preliminary report from the Women's Health Initiative (WHI), a 15-year research program conducted in the United States by the National Institutes of Health. WHI focuses on the major causes of death, disability, and frailty in postmenopausal women; its overall goal is to reduce coronary heart disease, breast and colorectal cancer, and osteoporotic fractures in these women.

Osteoporosis

The Women's Health Inititiave and the creation of the Office of Research in Women's Health exemplify a second impact of the women's health movement—increased research on health problems that primarily affect women. These problems include the diseases women die from (such as lung and breast cancer, cardiovascular disease, and AIDS), the diseases women suffer from but do not die from (complications of pregnancy, arthritis, hypertension, depression), and the diseases which disproportionately affect women (thyroid disease, bladder disorders, migraine headaches, and systemic lupus).

Osteoporosis, a thinning of the structure of the bones, is one such condition. It can occur in men or women, and at any age, but it is primarily a problem of women over age 70. It affects Caucasian (white) American women and women in northern Europe disproportionately, compared with African-American women or women in many other countries around the world. Osteoporosis is a problem because it leads to fractures, particularly hip fractures, which are a major cause of disability and death for older women. While new diagnostic methods have been developed to detect osteoporosis and new drugs, including hormone treatments and biphosphonates, have also been developed, the role of a simpler treatment approach consisting of exercise, supplemental calcium, and supplemental vitamin D remains controversial. Research in the next decade should help elucidate factors that determine why osteoporosis affects women around the world so differently, and what the best diagnostic and treatment approach will be.

Effects of Gender Equity

Gender equity in employment, social status, and education has been a goal of the United Nations and its member countries, but becoming more like men may not necessarily have a positive health benefit for women. The growing rate of lung cancer among women is a result of the social acceptability of women smokers. In the United States, lung cancer is the most common cause of death from cancer in women. Increased awareness of the dangers of nicotine, smoking cessation programs, and limitations on smoking in public spaces may begin to decrease this risk in the United States. However, American tobacco companies have increased advertising and exports of cigarettes around the world, enlarging this health risk for men and women. Internationally, the employment of women in factory jobs which may involve poor environmental conditions, repetitive motions on machines, and inhalation of toxic substances used in manufacturing will expose women to new health risks.

Effects of Domestic Violence

Although gender equity contributes to some health problems, gender inequity—domestic, social, and economic oppression of women—has created many more health problems. Domestic violence is the most common cause of nonfatal injury to women in the United States. Recognition of the large numbers of women who have been victims of rape and incest in childhood has also led to a greater understanding of the health consequences of these occurrences in adult life. In particular, childhood sexual abuse has been shown to be a risk factor for irritable bowel syndrome, severe obesity, chronic pelvic pain, substance abuse, and syndromes of chronic undiagnosed body pain over many years.

AIDS

AIDS, initially thought to be a man's disease, has become a women's problem worldwide, as a result of factors such as rape, both within and outside of marriage; men's refusal to use condoms; and the large number of women in developing countries forced to earn a living by their bodies. Research into AIDS in women has been limited because physicians failed to recognize the problem or its special manifestations, including increased cervical cancer and transmission of AIDS to newborns. Currently, increased research into women and AIDS offers promising treatments. However, because of cost, they are not available in many third world countries, where they are most needed.

Geriatric Issues

Finally, many diseases treated by internists become women's diseases late in life, because women's life expectancy is greater than men's. In the United States, women constitute 60 percent of the population over age 65, and 71 percent over age 85. By 2030, according to current estimates, one in five women will be 65 years of age or older. Men are more likely to die younger from acute cardiovascular-cerebrovascular disease and cancer; elderly women live for long periods of time functionally impaired by multiple chronic illnesses. Also, women are disproportionately represented among elderly people whose income is below the poverty line.

The common geriatric issues—urinary incontinence; memory loss and dementia; degenerative arthritis of the hips, knees, and hands; diminished sight and hearing; and depression and loss—are primarily women's concerns. Men receive more of their end-of-life treatment either in acute-care hospitals or from their spouses at home. Women's chronic conditions are cared for at home, by themselves, until they are no longer able. In the United Sates, 75 percent of long-term residents of nursing homes are female. Current areas of research in the care of older women include alternatives to nursing home care, prevention and treatment of chronic disabilities, and adjustment of preventive care and treatment regimens developed for younger populations to meet the realistic life expectancies of older populations.

Access to Information

As the concept of women's health has expanded to include women's comprehensive physical and emotional well-being beyond their reproductive organs, a challenge for both patients and health care professionals is to stay well informed. Medical information on the Internet has the potential to keep practitioners around the world up to date, and to empower patients. As an unregulated resource, however, the Internet also has the potential to offer biased and unsubstantiated information and advice. Users of women's health care sites will want to evaluate the sites carefully in terms of funding and sponsorship, advertising, and sources of information. Government and nonprofit sites, in the United States and elsewhere, provide a point of departure.

Women's health issues are no longer just childbirth, contraception, and reproductive cancers. As physicians, patients, and researchers look at women's health through the lens of gender, it becomes clear that women's health is not just how we become ill and die, but how we live.

See Also

AGING; AIDS AND HIV; HEALTH CHALLENGES; HORMONE REPLACEMENT THERAPY; HYPERTENSION: CASE STUDY—CLASS, RACE, AND GENDER; MEDICINE: INTERNAL I

References and Further Reading

Blumental, S. J. 2000. Critical women's health issues in the twenty-first century. *MsJAMA* 283: 667–668.

Candib, Lucy M. 1995. *Medicine and the family: A feminist perspective.* New York: Basic Books.

Carlson, K. J., and S. A. Eisenstat. 1995. *Primary care of women.* St. Louis, Mo., Mosby.

Dan, A. J. 1993. Integrating biomedical and feminist perspectives on women's health. *Women's Health Issues* 3(2): 101–103.

Eastell, R. 1999. Treatment of postmenopausal osteoporosis. *New England Journal of Medicine* 338(11): 376.

Grisso, J. A., et al. 1999. Violent injuries among women in an urban area. *New England Journal of Medicine* 341(25): 1899–1905.

Hulley, S. B., D. Grady, et al. 1998. Randomized trial of estrogen plus progestin for secondary prevention of coronary heart disease in postmenopausal women, Heart and Estrogen/Progestin Replacement Study (HERS) Research Group. *Journal of the American Medical Association* 280: 605–613.

Julian, D. G., and N. K. Wenger. 1997. *Women and heart disease.* London, Martin Dunitz.

Rich-Edwards, J. W., et al. 1999. Primary prevention of coronary heart disease in women. *New England Journal of Medicine* 332(26): 1758.

Internet Sources

<www.womenshealthnetwork.org>

Site of the National Women's Health Network, a consumer advocacy organization based in Washington, D.C . The organization runs an Information Clearinghouse on women's health.

<www.4women.gov>

Site of the United States federal government, Office of Women's Health. Provides up-to-date information and links to many other government sites oriented both to professionals and to laypersons interested in women's health.

<www.bwhbc.org>

Site of the Boston Women's Health Book Collective, publishers of *Our Bodies, Our Selves,* the landmark work of the early women's health movement. The site has excellent health information and provides an annotated listing of other women's health sites, including those in Spanish or French.

Gene Bishop

MEDICINE: Traditional and Complementary

See HOLISTIC HEALTH I; HOLISTIC HEALTH II; TRADITIONAL HEALING.

MEN'S STUDIES

Men's studies as a field of study is a recent development in higher education, mainly in North America and Europe. Its institutionalization, infrequent at the end of the 1990s, had its origins in the "men's movement" (particularly in the United States) and in the context of diverse group of "men against sexism" in various western countries.

In general terms, men's studies has been defined as "the study of masculinities and male experiences as specific and varying social-historical-cultural formations" (Brod, 1987: 40). The need for such an interdisciplinary subject area has been premised on the idea that traditional scholarship, though seemingly about men, precludes the study of masculinity as a specific male experience. Men's studies, like women's studies, is opposed to "patriarchal ideology's masquerade as knowledge"; it raises new questions while simultaneously revealing the inadequacy of established frameworks of knowledge to answer old ones (Brod, 1987).

Men's studies has not been without its critics and controversies among both its practitioners and feminists. Feminists have voiced diverse opinions on the relevance and relationship of men's studies to women's studies and feminist theory.

History and Influences

In the United States and Europe, early writings from men's groups of the 1960s and 1970s and later, more academic writings led to the institutionalization of men's studies. There are now international journals, conferences, and textbooks that are concerned with masculinity and masculinities. (See Hearn and Morgan, 1990, and Morgan, 1992, for historical detail on the origins of men's studies.)

Research by men on masculinity has covered many areas: sexuality, health, violence, culture, male friendships, men's roles as fathers and workers, and so on. Central issues have been the definition and discussion of the "crisis in masculinity" and male identity (Morgan, 1992). Academics in men's studies have also been concerned with the impact of this study of masculinity on the disciplines (Kimmel, 1990).

To varying degrees, those involved in men's studies have recognized the influence and vital importance of feminist ideas. Though some have only paid lip service to the debt men's studies owes to feminism, others have acknowledged it fully: "Feminism provided the context, the overall set of assumptions within which the current studies of men and masculinities are being conducted" (Morgan, 1992: 6). Other practitioners of men's studies have argued that feminism has ignored the specific experiences of men, or that it is not politically correct for men to study women. Some base their segregation of their field on recognition of the distinctiveness of male power and the specificity of male experience. It is clear that some men have reflected on their own motivations for such an engagement.

Inclusiveness

Men's studies has recognized that it "owes much to those voices proclaiming the legitimacy of experience and the need for recognition of the inherent dignity of other marginalized groups (gays, lesbians and people of color)" (Doyle, 1994). Thus, it is claimed that the early works in men's studies, in which masculinity was constructed by generalizing from white, heterosexual, and middle-class experiences, have been superseded by acknowledgment of the diversity of male experiences: classism, homophobia, and "racism" should not inform and limit the analyses of masculinity. Not all scholars agree, however, that men's studies' practitioners have fully, theoretically embraced diversity and difference.

Writing in 1988, Kobena Mercer and Isaac Julien argue that men against sexism and male theorists in the British context had not recognized the "racial" differences of masculine identities. The 1990s saw more recognition of this, but still no comprehensive engagement. A later theorist, writing on the issue of gay studies and masculinity, concludes: "In addition, men's studies of masculinity added some insights into masculinity and male experience though frequently excluded full consideration of sexual orientation and heterosexuality as a component of masculine identity" (Edwards, 1994: 1).

Central Ideas

The notion of hegemonic masculinity has recently been central. It has been defined as investigating how particular groups of men inhabit positions of power and wealth, as well as how they both legitimate and reproduce the social relationships that generate their dominance (Carrigan et al., 1985).

Another central idea has been the notion that there are multiple masculinities—black, white, working-class, and middle-class, for instance. Thus, theorists of men's studies now increasingly use "masculinities" instead of "masculinity" (see Connell, 1995, for a critical discussion of this concept).

As in any field of study, there are different approaches and viewpoints among those involved. These include the "mythopoetic vision" of Robert Bly and Sam Keen in the United States, the profeminist approach, the men's rights perspective the spiritual quest, and the views of gay men and men of color such as black men (see the *Journal of Men's Studies,* 1994, for discussion of these groups).

Debates within men's studies have focused on such issues as the relationship of men's studies to feminism and the methodologies to be used. A central controversy has concerned the actual naming of the field. The relationship to feminism can be either male-identified, female-identified, or antifeminist (see Renzetti and Curran, 1989). Some men involved have accepted and encouraged the defining of the area as "men's studies." This view is typified by Michael Kimmel, who has asserted: "Men's studies doesn't seek to supplant women's studies. It seeks to buttress, to augment women's studies, to complete the radically redrawn portrait of gender that women's studies has begun" (1988: 20).

Such practitioners see the naming of the area, like its purpose and relationship to women's studies, as unproblematic. Men's studies is merely adding to the knowledge of gender relations that feminist theory began. To call this new field "men's" studies seems obvious, given both its subject matter and the fact that its practioners and students are assumed to be male. Others, such as Jeff Hearn and David Morgan (1990) in Britain, have been critical of the presumed complementary relationship of men's studies to women's studies. Hearn has suggested "critique of men" as an alternative title that would recognize the tension and problems related to definitions and naming. Others still have favored "critical studies of men and masculinity" (or "masculinities") and some prefer to theorize about masculinity outside men's studies.

Men have also considered the methodologies they have employed in this "critical study of men." For instance, there have been various criticisms of the sex-role paradigm used within men's studies. The sex-role concept, originally developed by Talcott Parsons, sees masculinity as a fixed and easily defined set of behavioral norms into which all men fit, but it has been criticized by feminists and by practitioners of men's studies (see Brod, 1987; Kimmel, 1990).

In addition to scrutinizing functionalist concepts like sex roles, exponents of men's studies have criticized biological determinism, which has underpinned some thinking on male behavior and identity. The general theoretical consensus, as in feminism, is that social constructionist theories are better suited to explaining men's behavior in contemporary, historical, and cross-cultural contexts.

Responses from Women

Feminists have fairly recently turned their theoretical attention to men's studies and its objects, though it should be noted that feminists have always been studying masculinity. Among various criticisms made by feminists, the central ones—similar to those that have concerned some male theorists—have addressed the politics of naming "men's studies"; the relationship of men's studies to feminism, women's studies, and gender studies; and the methodologies and perspectives employed by advocates of men's studies. Even feminists who have welcomed these male initiatives, such as Lynne Segal (1990), have been cautious in their optimism. Some women fear that both theoretical attention and institutional position and rewards will move from women's studies, which has still only limited institutional recognition and security, to the newer area of men's studies. Men are in more senior positions within the university system and higher education generally and are better positioned to argue the case for men's studies in both financial and academic terms.

The defining of a new area of study called men's studies as such has been seen, on one hand, to reflect shifts within the academy to extend the scope of theoretical inquiry to both female and male experience. On the other hand, some feminists argue that the existence of men's studies and gender studies can lead to a narrower political and theoretical agenda in terms of analyses of women's experience. For instance, many men and some women welcome the shift to using the category of "gender" instead of the categories of "woman" and "man." Harry Brod (1987) links this shift to the study of men, which he sees as a fundamental part of this trend. But concentrating on "gender" rather than on "woman," for instance, has been seen to lead to the stance, adopted by some male theorists, in which "issues of gender and masculinity are now central to social theory, while in the early eighties Marxism and feminism were" (Seidler, 1992: 20; see Richardson and Robinson, 1994, for a full discussion of these trends).

Other feminist criticisms have centered on men's motives for creating a new field of study. Caanan and Griffin (1990) contend that men's studies could be seen as a source of research opportunities publishing contracts, and more jobs for the "already well-paid boys" in a climate of competition for funds and positions. A general concern has been the fear that men's studies and the establishment of a new "male canon" represent another attempt to reassert traditional male academic hegemony—to reinvent the old "men's studies" as defined by Dale Spender (1981). In that approach, knowledge about "mankind" was presented as objective and representative of both sexes.

Although the male scholars newly engaged in men's studies claim to share a goal with feminist scholars, some feminists, like Hanmer (1990), observe that some of them only pay lip service to feminism. Taking this viewpoint further, the feminists Andrea Cornwall and Nancy Lindisfarne (1994) assert that some practitioners of men's studies emphasize the personal at the expense of the political, and that the works of certain feminist scholars are utilized while others are ignored. For example, the work of Nancy Chodorow, which has been criticized within anthropology as reductionist and Eurocentric, is said to be overused. "Men's studies theory" has also been linked to social and developmental psychology; these are perspectives that feminists have questioned. Male theorists are also said to caricature certain groups within feminism, such as radical feminists (Robinson, 1996).

Some male theorists have reflected critically on these and other issues raised by feminists. Furthermore, even though many women have been critical, many have also supported theoretical and personal efforts by men to analyze male experiences and power.

Future Directions

The future of men's studies, like that of women's studies, is uncertain, not least because of economic constraints. There have been initial stages of self-definition and some reflection on theoretical omissions, such as the experiences of black, gay, and working-class men, and varied responses to feminism and feminist scholarship. It remains to be seen if men's studies will become further institutionalized, though the publishing and the marketing of writings on masculinity and men's studies continue to expand rapidly. It will also be interesting to observe whether men's studies will develop and flourish outside the United States and the West. The field's links to the men's movement in its diverse forms will also develop as the nature and character of the movement change.

In relation to feminism and women's studies, some feminists assert that it is still unclear whether men's studies will be part of the problem of women's oppression or part of the solution to it. The relationship among feminism, women's studies, men's studies, and the critical study of men and masculinities needs to be continually reconceptualized to ascertain whether earlier feminist critiques have been addressed.

See Also

BIOLOGICAL DETERMINISM; EDUCATION: HIGHER EDUCATION; GENDER; GENDER STUDIES; MASCULINITY; WOMEN'S STUDIES: OVERVIEW

References and Further Reading

Brod, Harry. 1987. *The making of masculinities: The new men's studies.* Boston: Allen and Unwin.

———, and Michael Kaufman, eds. 1994. *Theorizing masculinities.* London: Sage.

Caanan, Joyce E., and Christine Griffin. 1990. The new men's studies: Part of the problem or part of the solution? In Jeff Hearn and David Morgan, eds., *Men, masculinities, and social theory.* London: Unwin Hyman.

Carrigan, Tim, Bob Connell, and John Lee. 1985. Towards a new sociology of masculinity. *Theory and Society* 14(5).

Connell, R. W. 1995. *Masculinities*. Cambridge: Polity.

Cornwall, Andrea, and Nancy Lindisfarne. 1994. *Dislocating masculinity: Comparative ethnographies*. London: Routledge.

Digby, Tom. 1998. *Men doing feminism*. New York: Routledge.

Doyle, James A. 1994. Editorial. *Journal of Men's Studies* 3(2).

Edwards, Tim. 1994. *Erotics and politics: Gay male sexuality, masculinity, and feminism*. London: Routledge.

Hanmer, Jalna. 1990. Men, power, and the exploitation of women. In Jeff Hearn and David Morgan, eds., *Men, masculinities, and social theory*. London: Unwin Hyman.

Hearn, Jeff, and David Morgan, eds. 1990. *Men, masculinities, and social theory*. London: Unwin Hyman.

Kimmel, Michael. 1990. After fifteen years: The impact of the sociology of masculinity on the masculinity of sociology. In Jeff Hearn and David Morgan, eds., *Men, masculinities, and social theory*. London: Unwin Hyman.

———. 1988. The gender blender. *Guardian* 29 (September): 20.

Mercer, Kobena, and Isaac Julien. 1988. Race, sexual politics, and black masculinity. In Rowena Chapman and Jonathan Rutherford, eds., *Male order: Unwrapping masculinity*. London: Lawrence and Wishart.

Morgan, David H. J. 1992. *Discovering men*. London: Routledge.

Renzetti, Claire M., and Daniel J. Curran. 1989. *Women, men and society*. Boston: Allyn and Bacon.

Richardson, Diane, and Victoria Robinson. 1994. Theorizing women's studies, gender studies, and masculinity: The politics of naming. *European Journal of Women's Studies* 1(1): 11–27.

Robinson, Victoria. 1996. Heterosexuality and masculinity: Theorizing male power or the male wounded psyche. In Diane Richardson, ed., *Telling it straight: Theorizing heterosexuality*. London: Open University Press.

———, and Diane Richardson. 1994. Publishing feminism: Redefining the women's studies discourse. *Journal of Gender Studies* 3(1): 87–94.

Schacht, Steven P., and Doris W. Ewing, eds. 1998. *Feminism and men: Reconstructing gender relations*. New York: New York University Press.

Segal, Lynne. 1990. *Slow motion: Changing masculinities, changing men*. London: Virago.

Seidler, Victor. 1992. Sobs for the boys. *Guardian* (30 June): 20.

Spender, Dale. 1981. *Men's studies modified: The impact of feminism on the academic disciplines*. Oxford: Pergamon.

Victoria Robinson

MENARCHE

Menarche is a conspicuous and meaningful event in every woman's life. Unlike the more gradual changes that occur during puberty, the onset of menstruation is dramatic and memorable. In one study of recollections of menarche, almost all of the 137 women, ranging in age from 18 to 45, remembered their first menstruation; most could describe in detail where they were when it happened, what they were doing, and whom they told.

Pubertal Development

Menarche is preceded by characteristic body changes that occur sometime between the ages of 9 and 16. Breast development usually, but not always, occurs first. There is an increase in body hair, a growth spurt, and a weight gain prior to menarche, along with a change in body proportions as the hips become fuller. Sweat glands become more active, and a body odor develops that is thought to be related to an increase in the secretion of sex hormones from the adrenal glands. The skin becomes oilier, sometimes giving rise to skin problems. While these external changes are going on, there are concomitant changes occurring within the body: the uterus and vagina are growing.

The average age at menarche ranges from between 12.8 and 13.2 years of age, with extremes at 9 and 17 years. The age of menarche in the United States and much of western Europe has declined greatly in the past 100 years. The decline, sometimes referred to as the "secular trend," is presumed to be related to better nutrition and health. Famine amenorrhea was reported in both world wars, and young women who are undernourished because of excessive dieting or anorexia nervosa often do not have menstrual periods. The fall in age at menarche that has occurred between 1830 and 1960 coincides with increased availability of protein in the diet of developed countries. In some countries, particularly those in which nutrition has remained inadequate, age of menarche is comparatively high: in Bangladesh it is just under 16, and among certain New Guinea tribes it is about 18.

Significant hormonal changes occur at puberty, although they are incompletely understood. The female sex hormones, adrenal hormones, and hormones originating in the brain and pituitary gland are of major importance. It is the interrelationship of these hormones that later controls the female reproductive cycle. Endocrinologists now believe, however, that the hormonal changes associated with sexual maturation are genetically programmed at the time of conception. By the third trimester of pregnancy, the negative feedback system that will regulate hormonal secretions is established in the fetus. During infancy, the hypothalamic gonadotropin regulating mechanism—the signal system regulating menstruation, which works as an intricate feedback loop in which the brain responds to different levels of sex hormones in the blood—is "set" at a low level. It remains there until around the time of puberty, when there is an increase in the secretion of follicle stimulating hormone (FSH) and luteinizing hormone (LH) and a decrease in hypothalamic sensitivity.

The main female sex hormone secreted by the ovaries is estradiol, which is present in relatively small amounts in the blood until about age 8 or 9, when it begins to rise. This increase in blood levels of estradiol causes growth of the breasts, uterus, vagina, and parts of the pelvis. Menstruation, as well as earlier pubertal development, is thought to begin with a signal to the hypothalamus from the central nervous system.

Genetic factors play a role in determining rate of growth, pubertal development, and age at menarche. Studies of identical twin sisters growing up together indicate that they reach menarche about two months apart, with the first-born twin—for some unknown reason—more likely to menstruate first. Mother–daughter and sister–sister correlations have also been reported to be significant. Swedish researchers who studied a large sample of mothers and daughters found other menstrual similarities: significant correlations between mothers' and daughters' length of cycle, duration of menstrual flow, and symptoms of dysmenorrhea and premenstrual tension. Lest it be thought that only mothers influence their daughters' menstrual cycles, however, researchers believe that mother and father exert an equal influence on rate of growth and maturation. Thus, a late-maturing girl is as likely to have a late-maturing father as a late-maturing mother.

Women who experience high energy outputs, such as ballet dancers and athletes who train intensively, have a later age of menarche and a high incidence of amenorrhea. This is particularly true when intensive training begins at an early premenarcheal age. It is not known whether the delay in menarche seen among young athletes is due to an altered lean–fat ratio or to the direct effects of exercise on hormonal secretion and metabolism. Intensive sports activity and thinness have a synergistic effect in delaying the onset of menstruation.

Climatic and Seasonal Effects

Climate has only a very minor effect on age at menarche. Contrary to earlier beliefs, people who live in tropical countries are somewhat more likely to have a *late* menarche. This is thought to be related to nutrition rather than to climate, because children in the higher socioeconomic groups in these countries experience menarche at about the same time as children living in temperate zones.

Season of the year does have an effect on pubertal development. Height increases twice as fast in the spring: peak growth is seen between March and July in the Northern Hemisphere. The greatest gains in weight occur in the autumn. Girls are most likely to have their first menstruation in the late fall or early winter; they are least likely to experience menarche in the spring.

Some illnesses can delay menarche, probably because of their effects on nutrition. This is most likely to be true in cases of ulcerative colitis, regional enteritis, cystic fibrosis, congenital heart disease, uremia, and diabetes mellitus. Conversely, conditions that can advance the age of menarche include hypothyroidism, central nervous system tumors, encephalitis, head trauma, and some virilizing disorders. Inactive, retarded, or bedridden children also reach menarche at an earlier age than their more active counterparts. Blind children have a younger age at menarche, which may be related in part to their relative inactivity.

Psychological Effects of Menarche on the Early Adolescent Girl

Much of the early writing about the psychology of menarche presented it as a traumatic experience: the early adolescent is ashamed of her growing breasts and pubic hair and horrified by menarche. There is no mention of the excitement and anticipation experienced by preadolescent girls who are waiting expectantly to "get it."

Menarche can have an organizing effect for the adolescent girl by helping her to clarify her perception of her own genitals, particularly in confirming the existence of the vagina and correcting the confusion she may have had about the female genitalia. Indeed, menarche may serve as a reference point around which girls can organize their pubertal experiences—a landmark for feminine identification. Certainly, awareness of sexual differentiation between males and females sharpens greatly at this time.

Reactions to Menarche

In several studies, menarche has been found to be an anxiety-producing or negative event. Mixed feelings, such as being "excited but scared" or "happy and embarrassed," are common. Changes in the way girls see themselves, however, are among the most dramatic reactions to menarche. During puberty, body changes occur gradually, but girls expect to act differently after menarche, and they also perceive themselves quite differently. In a clever study of 12-year-old girls, Elissa Koff asked them to draw male and female human figures on two occasions, approximately six months apart. The findings were striking: postmenarcheal girls produced drawings that were significantly more sexually differentiated than those of their premenarcheal peers. Most notable was the difference between the drawings done by the girls whose menarcheal status changed during the course of the study. Their drawings at the second testing were of females with breasts and curves, very different from the childlike drawings done at the first, premenarcheal testing session.

These studies clearly demonstrate that girls experience menarche as a turning point in their development, and that they apparently reorganize their body image in the direction of greater sexual maturity. Postmenarcheal girls are more aware of the differences in secondary sex characteristics of males and females in general, and of themselves as women, than are premenarcheal girls of the same age; however, they are also more self-conscious, embarrassed, and secretive about their bodies.

The Importance of Timing

The age at which a girl experiences menarche seems to affect her reaction to it, in that early-maturing girl have a harder time. There is some support, however, for the idea that the time around menarche is turbulent for most girls, regardless of when it occurs. Mental health surveys among young people in the United States, New Zealand, Canada, and Puerto Rico highlighted certain risks: for girls, the likelihood of severe depression doubles in the year after the onset of menstruation, and it reaches a peak rate of 7 percent in girls around the ages of 13 and 14.

Girls who are out of synchrony in the timing of menarche, especially those who experience menarche at 11 years of age or younger, seem to have more difficulty with it. Unlike boys, who are eager for their growth spurt and physical signs of maturity, girls prefer to mature at the same time as other girls. This may result from the age difference between the sexes in the onset of puberty—boys normally start later than girls—or perhaps it is another example of the pressure early adolescents feel to conform. Girls' attitudes about early development may also be related to the changes in their lives that occur when they develop breasts and curves. There is some evidence that girls who are already pubertal at age 11 or younger are more likely to be dating and, somewhat paradoxically, these girls also have lower self-esteem, lower school achievement, and more behavioral problems than otherwise comparable boys and nonpubertal girls.

Impact on Relationships: Parents, Peers, and Sex

In addition to adjusting to their own changing bodies and developing closer relationships to their peers, adolescents have to establish greater independence from their parents. In view of the changing perceptions that girls have of themselves at menarche, it is reasonable to expect that menarche also affects their relationships with family members. Sixth- and seventh-grade girls who had begun to menstruate were significantly more likely to be left alone when parents were not home, to baby-sit, and to care more about independence from their parents. Similarly, postmenarcheal girls were more likely to wear makeup or a bra, to shave their legs, and to date. They also slept less on school nights, moving from nine or more hours a night toward the more usual adult eight-hour sleep cycle. Thus, it seems that girls who look older (that is, have attained menarche) are also treated differently by their parents—they are allowed to act older. The postmenarcheal girls also were more uncomfortable in discussing emotionally charged topics such as love, sex, drugs, and alcohol with their parents, and they reported having more conflict with parents than did premenarcheal girls. Menarche thus seems to mark the end of one phase of a girl's life and the beginning of another.

Beliefs about Menarche

Although beliefs and behaviors associated with menstruation vary across cultures, myths, misconceptions, and taboos are universal. A study by the World Health Organization of patterns and perceptions of menstruation among women in 10 countries found wide differences in attitudes; for example, the proportion of women who viewed menstruation as an illness ranged from 3 percent in Pakistan to 67 percent in Egypt. Seventy-two percent of women in Korea and the Philippines, 45 percent in Yugoslavia, and only 2 percent in Indonesia held the belief that bathing should be avoided during menstruation, and a majority of women in all countries studied said that sexual intercourse was to be avoided when they were menstruating.

Belief about menstruation are acquired at an early age, and adolescent girls who report being adequately prepared have a more positive initial experience with menstruation. Girls want to know about menstrual physiology and menstrual hygiene—the facts that are usually included in menstrual education materials. They also want information about menstruation as a personal event. They need to know about the normality of menstruation; it must be distinguished from disease, injury, and uncleanliness. And they need an opportunity to talk about their reactions to body changes, looking older, growing up, and parental and peer expectations. Because girls' attitudes and ways of thinking change during early adolescence, menstrual education needs to be an ongoing process. It should begin before menstruation occurs and continue throughout adolescence.

See Also

ADOLESCENCE; CURSE; GIRL CHILD; HEALTH EDUCATION; INITIATION RITES; MENSTRUATION

References and Further Readings

Delaney, J., M. J. Jespton, E. Toth. 1990. *The curse: A cultural history of menstruation.* Chicago: University of Illinois Press.

Gardner-Loulan, JoAnn, Bonnie Lopez, and Marcia Quackenbush. 1991. *Period.* Volcano, Calif.: Volcano.

Gillooly, Jessica B. 1998. *Before she gets her period.* Glendale, Calif.: Perspective.

Goleman, D. 1989. Pioneering studies find surprising high rate of mental ills in young. *New York Times* (10 January).

———. 1991. Theory links early puberty to childhood stress. *New York Times* (30 July): C1, 6.

Golub, Sharon. 1983. *Menarche.* Lexington, Mass.: Lexington.

———. 1992. *Periods: From menarche to menopause.* Newbury Park, Calif.: Sage.

Snowden, R., and B. Christian, eds. 1983. *Patterns and perceptions of menstruation.* New York: St. Martin's.

Sharon Golub

MENOPAUSE

Orthodox medical doctors see menopause as ovarian failure. Women stop producing estradiol and after menopause are "estrogen-deficient." According to this viewpoint, deficiency leads to osteoporosis and heart disease, so women need hormone *replacement.* Menopausal women are portrayed as patients or even as victims, and are told that they are incapable of being healthy without help because their bodies are undependable.

However, many women worldwide—western and eastern, northern and southern—experience a different reality. They know that menopause promotes health, not just for individual women but for society as a whole. They see menopausal distress as normal and menopause as a time for intense personal introspection and growth. They do not use (and indeed most do not have access to) "replacement" hormones, yet many lead vigorous, active lives into their nineties.

This woman-centered cross-cultural perspective on menopause is neither superstition nor mindless custom, but a result of careful observations by wise women over many generations. They believe that natural menopause is a gift to us from our foremothers, women who were deeply intuitive and in tune with women's emotional, spiritual, and physical needs (Northrup, 1998).

When Does Menopause Take Place?

All women are born making estrogen. At puberty, a very active estrogen, estradiol, begins to be produced for about 24 hours during each menstrual cycle. From puberty until the mid-twenties, estradiol levels increase with each cycle. Thereafter, estradiol decreases each month until, usually by the mid-forties, ovulation is no longer triggered. Eventually (the mean age is 50) women stop making estradiol, although they continue to make estrogen. Science calls the last drop of menstrual blood menopause and the years of change preceding this perimenopause (*peri-* means "around"). Most women, however, call this entire span of time—from the first signs of approaching menopause to several years after the last menstruation—their menopausal years. Postmenopause refers to all the years of a woman's life after her last menstrual period.

Menopause and Hormones

Many well-educated women believe, mistakenly, that their ovaries stop making estrogen when their menstrual periods stop, and that all postmenopausal women are therefore "estrogen-deficient." Using the word "replacement"—as in estrogen *replacement* therapy (ERT) or hormone *replacement* therapy (HRT)—reinforces this erroneous belief. Of the many kinds of estrogen made by women, only estradiol ceases to be made after menopause. The ovaries do not "die" or "fail." Ovarian cells that produced estrogen and progesterone during the fertile years are gradually replaced during the menopausal years by stromal cells that produce androgens (Greer, 1991). Furthermore, fat cells and adrenal glands produce estrogens (estrone and estriol) from cholesterol during and after menopause.

Menopause is a time not of decreases in hormones but of exceptionally *high* levels of hormones. Estradiol does decline and eventually cease, but levels of luteinizing hormone (LH) and follicle-stimulating hormone (FSH) increase by 30 to 50 percent. Menopausal symptoms are generally a result of dealing with this vastly *increased* hormone load (Love, 1997). Estrogen replacement therapy reduces these symptoms by stopping that process, but the symptoms will resume if ERT is no longer taken, and ERT is not the only way to eliminate them. Mineral-rich herbs, for instance, provide raw materials for hormone production, help women compensate for minerals lost in sweaty hot flashes, and protect the heart and the bones against mineral loss while easing symptoms. A diet high in protein and fat helps by providing the amino acids and lipids required for hormone production.

Hormone replacement therapy has been an ongoing controversy, since estrogen supplements have been linked to an increased risk of cancer (*JAMA*, 2000), stroke, and heart attacks. In the United States, for example, only 15 percent of menopausal American women were choosing HRT as of the year 2000—although this was enough to make estrogen the most widely prescribed drug in the nation.

Menopause Is Healthy

Menopause promotes health and extends life; it is not a state of deficiency caused by "living too long." Menopause and the cessation of childbearing are positive events in most women's lives—not an end but a beginning. Menopause may be a prime factor in women's greater longevity. Throughout history—and probably in prehistory as well—postmenopausal women have been invaluable to the community, serving as judges, visionaries, teachers, healers, and wise women. Many women in many cultures have menopausal symptoms, but, like women in childbirth, they know that they will be rewarded at the end of their travail with increased status in the family and greater freedom in society.

Kristen Hawkes of the University of Utah posits that postmenopausal women have been the most industrious members of hunter-gatherer societies, gathering more food than men or than women of other ages; and that they have been important to the survival of their grandchildren—as important as the childen's own mothers. Hawkes believes that prehistoric postmenopausal women were instrumental in freeing our ancestors to explore new habitats, and ultimately to spread across the entire planet. She calls this the "grandmother hypothesis."

Menopause Is Not a Modern Artifact

One hundred years ago the average life expectancy for an American woman was only 50 years; before that, and in some other cultures, it was even shorter. However, this does not mean that widespread survival to menopause is a new phenomenon created by modern advances in health. Life expectancy is an average, which is lowered significantly by infant, childhood, and maternal mortality; even in the past, most women who survived childhood and childbirth lived to be postmenopausal.

Healthy postmenopausal women are the rule, not the exception, and for millennia women have managed postmenopause without the help of technology. Archaeologists have found thousands of large-breasted, large-bellied figurines from the Paleolithic era, such as the "goddess of Willendorf," which is 30,000 years old. These are said to be pregnant fertility goddesses, but if we look carefully we see that the pendulous breasts, downward-folding belly, and small vulva appear to be those of a postmenopausal woman, not the protruding belly, breasts, and vulva of a pregnant women.

Perspectives on Menopause

Women in different cultures have varying explanations of and approaches to menopause. Following are just a few of the many examples that could be cited.

Menopause as "puberty": The physical and emotional symptoms of menopause and puberty are similar: months or even years of erratic menses with surges and drops of hormones that aggravate breast tenderness, menstrual pain, acne, and emotional sensitivity. Body hair changes. Fat fills in breasts, hips, buttocks, and thighs; curves appear where there were once angles. Depression, self-loathing, suicidal thoughts, a distorted body image, and anxiety can afflict even the most stable mind when the body image differs from what a culture deems beautiful. Our deepest beliefs about ourselves may come into question.

Thus both puberty and menopause require changes in self-perceptions; and both also allow other, heretofore unknown, aspects of the self to emerge. Menopausal women—like girls experiencing puberty—may find their relationship with their family strange, strained, and different (Roth, 1999).

Menopause as an awakening of kundalini: There are also many similarities between menopausal symptoms and an awakening of "kundalini"—a hot, fast, powerful energy that is said to be the root of all spiritual experiences and to exist within the earth, all life, and every person. The term itself is Sanskrit; but many different cultures, including Sumerian, Chinese, Irish, Aztec, and Greek as well as Indian, acknowledge something like kundalini. When kundalini awakens, it uncoils and rises, affecting every part of the body, especially the endocrine, cardiovascular, and nervous systems. Awakened kundalini sends powerful surges of superheated energy up the spine, like a hot flash.

Kundalini does not suddenly happen at menopause. Before puberty, it is outside the body. As puberty commences, an energy "gate," an imaginary opening in the "root chakra" (located at the base of the spine or in the uterus), opens and kundalini flows into the uterus and pelvic tissues, where it builds up until menstruation. As it accumulates, it intensifies emotions and sensations; this intensification is then released with the menses.

At menopause, one "valve" of the gate closes. The open valve allows kundalini to enter; at the same time, the closed one prevents it from leaving. Kundalini now builds up in the pelvic tissues until it pushes up, through the spine, and out of the top of the head: the crown. The energetic function of menopause is to awaken kundalini and confer "enlightenment."

As kundalini rises, it opens other energy gates, awakening new abilities that may cause the menopausal woman (or her family and friends) to think she is crazy. She might observe that men fear her when she reaches this stage (Walker, 1985). Actually, she has never been more sane and has never seen her life more clearly. If the energy centers triggered by kundalini are resistant to being activated, symptoms such as menstrual pain, bloating, indigestion, heart palpitations, thyroid malfunctions, headaches, and memory loss may occur.

After several years most women naturally establish an even flow of kundalini, but training in hatha yoga, pranayama, or tai chi helps many women handle both the postmenopausal increase in energy and the erratic flows of the menopausal years.

Menopause as a "strong liver": A theory in traditional Chinese herbal medicine is that menopausal symptoms arise because too much energy enters the liver and not enough leaves (Wolfs, 1990). Favorite liver-strengthening herbs include dandelion (*Taraxacum officinale*), yellow dock (*Rumex crispus*), milk thistle seeds (*Psylibum mariannum*), and burdock root (*Arctium lappa*). A tincture of milk thistle seeds is used to ease hot flashes, improve mood, and relieve menopausal skin problems such as acne and itchiness. Burdock root is also used to cool hot flashes, and to nourish the heart and bones.

Menopause as adrenal stress: During and after menopause, estrogen is supplied by the adrenal glands, which must therefore work harder. If a women's adrenal glands are already producing a high level of stress hormones, the extra demand represented by estrogen may create extrasensitive, hyperalert behavior not unlike an adrenal crisis. Adrenal stress contributes to menopausal symptoms such as panic attacks, emotional swings, night sweats, and extreme fatigue or its opposite, sleeplessness. According to herbalists, the stinging nettle (*Urtica dioica*) builds, restores, and tones the adrenals.

Menopause and the Bones

One reason that menopausal women take hormones is to prevent or mitigate osteoporosis—thinning of the bones. It is true that HRT, ERT, and some nonhormonal drugs increase bone mass; but these drugs need to be taken for decades and may pose substantial risks. Moreover, preventing osteoporosis does not necessarily lead to better health or longer life, and increased bone mass may not itself be healthy. Postmenopausal women with the highest bone mass are two and a half to four times more likely to be diagnosed with breast cancer than those with the lowest bone mass. Therefore, changes in lifestyle may be more efficacious than drugs: such changes not only protect the bones but can benefit health without creating risks.

Flexibility may be more significant than bone mass. Flexible bones, whether thick or thin, are resistant to breakage; brittle bones, even if thick, tend to break. Regular exercise and a good supply of dietary minerals keep bones flexible. Exercise increases the utilization of calcium, improves balance (and so prevents falls), and increases muscular flexibility—which, in women, is associated with bone flexibility. Diet is also important. A diet based on plant foods, including leafy vegetables, is typical in rural China, which has the lowest known rate of fractures among middle-age and older women, and also significantly low rates of many diseases (including osteoporosis). Minerals are crucial: because so many hormones are produced during the menopausal years, the diet should be rich in minerals; otherwise, the deficit may be drawn out of the bones.

Menopause and the Heart

Hormone replacement therapy has been urged as a means of preventing heart disease postmenopausally, but many doubts have been raised about this approach (Trickey, 1998). Limiting, or eliminating, saturated fats and foods rich in cholesterol is also said to prevent heart disease; however, major studies and population-based data from other countries seem to invalidate this theory. Greek women, who have the lowest incidence of heart disease in the world, have a diet containing 40 to 60 percent fat. Thus a diet rich in healthful fats, such as organic butter and olive oil, may provide optimum health postmenopausally.

Heart disease correlates more strongly with mineral deficiencies than with fat consumption. Coronary heart disease is lowest where drinking water is naturally rich in minerals. Herbs rich in potassium (nettle, red clover, sage) help maintain proper blood pressure; herbs rich in calcium (peppermint, chickweed, thyme) protect the heart and help it maintain a steady rhythm; and herbs rich in magnesium and potassium (dulse, nettles, yellow dock, burdock) help keep blood pressure low.

Menopause and Breast Cancer

Breast cancer is a major health concern of postmenopausal women, and this is one aspect of the debate over HRT: supplemental estrogen increases the risk of breast cancer, and not everyone agrees that this risk is outweighed by estrogen's protection against osteoporosis. Evidently, too, a low-fat diet does not prevent breast cancer, although research findings are somewhat inconsistent. A study of more than 60,000 Swedish women aged 40 to 76 found that their risk of breast cancer fell as consumption of monounsaturated fat from dairy products and meat rose, but their risk rose as consumption of polyunsaturated fat from vegetable oil rose. Greek women, on the other hand, were found to have a lower risk when they consumed more olive oil.

Menopause, in brief, is a social as well as a physical phenomenon. In many cultures women are changing the meaning of menopause as they consider their own emotional, spiritual, and physical needs.

See Also

AGING; BIOLOGY; BODY; GRANDMOTHER; GYN/ECOLOGY; HEALTH: OVERVIEW; PHYSIOLOGY

References and Further Reading

Bergner, Paul. 1997. *The healing power of minerals and trace elements.* Rocklin, Calif.: Prima.

Costlow, Judy, Maria Christina Lopez, and Mara Taub. 1991. *Menopause: A self-care manual.* New Mexico: Santa Fe Health Education Progect.

Crawford, Amanda McQuade. 1996. *The herbal menopause book.* Freedom, Calif.: Crossing.

A friend indeed, for women in the prime of life. P.O. Box 260, Pembrina, North Dakota 58271.

Greer, Germaine. 1991. *The change: Women, aging, and the menopause.* Canada and New York: Knopf .

Journal of the American Medical Association (JAMA). 2000. (January.)

Kenton, Leslie. 1995. *Passage to power: The natural menopause revolution.* London: Ebury.

Love, Susan. 1997. *Dr. Susan Love's hormone book.* New York: Random House.

Nissim, Rina. 1995. *La menopause: Réflexions et alternatives aux hormones de remplacement.* Paris: Éditions Mamamelis.

Northrup, Christiane. 1998. *Women's bodies, women's wisdom.* New York: Bantam, 1998.

Reitz, Rosetta. 1979. *Menopause: A positive approach.* New York: Penguin.

Roth, Dick. 1999. *No, it's not hot in here: A husband's guide to menopause.* Georgetown, Mass.: Ant Hill.

Taylor, Dena, and Amber Sumrall, eds. 1991. *Women of the fourteenth moon: Writing on menopause.* Freedom, Calif.: Crossing.

Trickey, Ruth. 1998. *Women, hormones, and the menstrual cycle: Herbal and medical solutions from adolescence to menopause.* London: Allen and Unwin.

Walker, Barbara. 1985. *The crone: Woman of age, wisdom, and power.* New York: Harper and Row.

Weed, Susun S. 2000. *Menopausal years, the wise woman way.* Woodstock, N.Y.: Ash Tree.

Wolfs, Honora Lee. 1990. *Second spring: Healthy menopause through traditional Chinese medicine.* Boulder, Col.: Blue Poppy.

Susun S. Weed

MENSTRUATION

Menstruation is the natural process of shedding the cyclic buildup of uterine tissue, blood vessels, and the unfertilized egg when a pregnancy has not occurred. In human females, and in females of other higher primate species, menstruation marks the end of one reproductive cycle and the beginning of the next. The term *menstruation* is derived from the Latin *mensis,* "month," and that is the approximate length of the *menstrual cycle*: in well-nourished women menstrual "periods" occur on average every 28 days, though the normal range across groups of women is from 21 to 35 days. The length and regularity of each individual woman's cycle are determined by family history, age, general health, diet, body weight, emotional stress, environmental factors, and the use of drugs, medications, and hormonal contraceptives. Cycles that are more or less regular are considered "normal."

The Menstrual Cycle

Menstruation is controlled by two hormones: estrogen and progesterone, naturally occurring steroids produced by the ovaries. Beginning at puberty (which takes place at about age 12 in healthy girls), estrogen and progesterone are released in a fluctuating rhythm; their source in the ovary is specialized balls of cells called follicles that carry a single egg and the genetic material for producing a new human being. During each cycle, only one follicle will fully mature and release its egg—a process known as *ovulation.* During the ovulation phase, the follicle produces just estrogen, which stimulates the uterus to develop a thick lining—and an increased blood supply—for nourishing a potential pregnancy.

After ovulation, the transformed follicle, now called a corpus luteum, produces both estrogen and large amounts of progesterone for approximately 12 to 14 days. If the egg is fertilized (by sperm), the hormones produced by the corpus luteum will help to maintain the pregnancy. But if there is no pregnancy, hormone production by the corpus luteum gradually decreases to the preexisting low levels. In response, the tiny blood vessels in the uterus close and, without further nourishment, the uterine lining sheds off. At the same time, the uterine muscle also loses its supply of steroid hormones; this causes chemical reactions that in turn cause muscle contractions—which, if strong enough, result in menstrual cramps. Mild to moderate cramps lasting only 1 or 2 days at the beginning of the period are common in healthy women and are considered a sign of fertility.

The sloughed-off tissue and blood cells form what is called the menstrual flow or period, which lasts on average 4 days. For any single period, the total volume of flow is usually only 2 to 3 ounces or about 4 to 6 tablespoons. Menstrual flow, like the length of the cycle, varies from woman to woman and for the same woman over time: the duration and amount of the flow depend on a variety of factors.

Perspectives on Menstruation

Menstruation as a normal physiologic event has been overshadowed by its impact on human cultures worldwide. Throughout history, it has been seen as a powerful, mystical, and even dangerous event from which men and children need to be protected. In the literature, art, politics, and social practices of many cultures, the menstruating woman has been sometimes revered, sometimes vilified, and sometimes isolated (Delaney, Lupton, and Toth, 1988). Taboos, myths, and misunderstandings associated with menstruation have served as a rationale for avoiding or forbidding sexual intercourse, sports, manual work, bathing, and other activities during the menstrual period, and for excluding women from political leadership and managerial positions. Many such ideas persists in both developed and developing societies. For example, the term *menstrual politics* was coined relatively recently to refer to sociopolitical constraints on women's lives deriving from the fact that women menstruate. Gloria Steinem (1995) was one of the first feminist writers to argue that social context can influence and distort the salience of menstruation as a sociocultural event.

Historically, menstruation has been subjected to concealment, as something private, secret, or even shameful or unclean. Consequently, most cultures have developed rituals, procedures, and devices to hide the menstrual flow. In the developed world, the manuufacture and sale of menstrual hygeine products became a commercial enterprise—which came under scrutiny in 1980, when a link was found between a type of tampon and a potentially fatal disorder, toxic shock syndrome. Since then, there have been some improvements in product labeling; but advocates of women's health continue to be concerned about the safety of devices such as tampons.

Some researchers have argued that the concept of repetitive menstrual cycles as the norm for female reproductive functioning is new and artificial—an idea unique to contemporary societies where fertility rates are low, health standards are high, and abortion and contraceptives are available. In these cultures, a woman will have, on average, 400 menstrual cycles during her reproductive years. This is about 10 times higher than the number in countries where women are impoverished and have no access to contraception, and thus experience successive pregnancies, long intervals of breast feeding, and episodes of amenorrhea (absence of menstrual periods) resulting from starvation or malnutrition. Women in western societies have higher rates of endometriosis, premenstrual syndrome (PMS), and cancers of the breast, ovaries, and uterus; researchers are examining whether this is related to their longer exposure to steroid hormones.

On the other hand, Margie Profet (1993) has argued that mensturation functions to protect the uterus and oviducts from colonization by pathogens—the bacteria from the male and female genitalia that tend to cling to sperm tails; that is, menstruation serves to flush away these bacteria. This theory has been marginalized by mainstream science, on the assumption that menstruation is not needed for such cleansing: for example, the nose manages to cleanse itself with mucus. However, it can be held that not all bodily systems necessarily use the same cleaning mechanisms, and Profet's argument has received considerable attention from feminists.

How the cyclic fluctuations in estrogen and progesterone that produce the menstrual cycle are characterized has guided the development of contraceptive agents and the medical management of some reproductive processes, including the normal transition to menopause, the final menstrual period. In biomedical research and literature, this medicalization of women's biological and menstrual functioning has tended to predominate, with little attention to the interaction of psychologic, sociocultural, and health factors. But in North America, at least, feminist researchers are now increasingly interested in defining and describing psychosocial and cultural influences on the range and diversity of the menstrual cycle, and on health and illness related to it (Dan, 1994).

See Also

ESTROGEN; HORMONES; MENARCHE; MENOPAUSE; PREMENSTRUAL SYNDROME (PMS); REPRODUCTIVE PHYSIOLOGY

References and Further Reading

Boston Women's Health Book Collective. 1998. Anatomy and physiology of sexuality and reproduction. In *Our bodies, ourselves for the new century.* New York: Simon and Schuster.

Dan, Alice. 1994. *Reframing women's health: Multidisciplinary research and practice.* Thousand Oaks, Calif.: Sage.

Delaney, Janice, Mary Jane Lupton, and Emily Toth. 1983. *The curse: A cultural history of menstruation.* Chicago: University of Illinois Press.

Profet, Margie. 1993. Menstruation as a defense against pathogens transported by sperm. *Quarterly Review of Biology* 68(3): 335–371.

Steinem, Gloria. 1995. If men could menstruate. In *Outrageous acts and everyday rebellions.* New York: Holt.

Nancy King Reame
(with Board Members of the Society for Menstrual Cycle Research)

MENTAL HEALTH I

The concept of mental health encapsulates both psychological well-being and psychological problems. Since statistics were first recorded in the early nineteenth century, women have outnumbered men in the population treated for mental-health problems (Showalter, 1987). Today, according to data from both community surveys and hospital statistics, women are two to four times as likely as men to be identified as having neurotic disorders (which include anxiety, eating disorders, neurotic depression, and phobias) and depressive disorders. Women are significantly more likely than men to be admitted for inpatient psychiatric care; four to twelve times as likely as men to be referred to a psychiatrist, clinical psychologist, or therapist; and twice as likely to be prescribed psychotropic medication or given electroshock therapy (ECT) (Ussher, 1991). A major question facing both mental-health professionals and feminist critics is whether these statistics reflect a real difference in the incidence of mental health problems in men and women, or whether women are merely more likely than men to be labeled mentally ill (Stoppard, 1999). Both arguments are outlined in this article.

Misogyny and Labeling

Feminist critics have argued that, across cultures and throughout history, definitions of mental health take "male as norm," and moreover that women are labeled mentally ill when they present any challenge to patriarchy (Ussher, 1991). Historically, women defined as "mentally ill" have often been those who reject the traditional feminine role, refusing to be passive, inactive, and sexually controlled. The many women convicted as witches, whom psychiatric historians have latterly claimed to be "undiagnosed madwomen," were often women who desired independence, sexual freedom, and the ability to treat other women and help them through childbirth (Ehrenreich and English, 1978). In the nineteenth century, women who demanded education, the freedom to divorce, and a right to a mind or a "room of their own" were frequently categorized as neurasthenic or hysterical, and their protests were thus dismissed and controlled (Showalter, 1987).

Today, both women who reject the feminine role and, paradoxically, women who are archetypally feminine may be at risk of psychiatric diagnosis. A number of research studies have demonstrated that mental health professionals classify similar traits as characteristic of both femininity and mental disorders; these include "more submissive, less independent, less adventurous, more easily influenced, less aggressive, less competitive, more excitable in minor crises, having their feelings more easily hurt, more conceited about their appearance, [and] less objective" (Broverman et al., 1970; Ussher, 2000). At the same time, there is evidence that "unfeminine" behaviors such as violence, anger, and aggression are seen as signs of pathology in women, but not in men. This led Phyllis Chesler to write: "What we consider 'madness,' whether it appears in women or in men, is either the acting out of the devalued female role model or the total or partial rejection of one's sex-role stereotype" (Chesler, 1993). It is a double bind in which women cannot win.

Sexuality and reproduction are linked with discourses associated with women's madness and badness, with the female body seen as both a site of dysfunction and a focus for intervention. As far back as Plato and Hippocrates, philosophers and physicians attributed female ailments to the womb, which was reputed to travel about the body, leaving madness in its wake. Spinsters and "barren women" were seen to be particularly at risk, so sex with a man and motherhood were oft-advocated cures (Showalter, 1987). In the witch trials of the Middle Ages, madness, sexuality, and menstruation were again linked; central to the persecution of women as witches was the fear and disgust associated with their "boiling menstrual blood" and their supposed sexual proclivities, including sex with the Devil, the stealing of men's penises, and group orgies. Female sexuality outside patriarchal control has been viewed as a threat to be curbed (Ussher, 1991; Ussher, 1997): the nineteenth-century woman who demonstrated sexual desire or autonomy was frequently pathologized, as lesbian women have been throughout history and across cultures.

The argument that madness and mental health problems are merely artifacts of misogyny carries the risk that we might appear to dismiss the reality of women's distress. By contrast, the vulnerability model accepts the reality of women's mental health problems and adopts either a biomedical model or a psychosocial model to explain them.

The Vulnerability Model: Biomedical Explanations

Traditional biomedical explanations attribute women's mental-health problems to imbalances in female hormones and to reproduction (Nicolson, 1998). Premenstrual syndrome (PMS), postnatal depression (PND), and the menopause have all been pathologized in this way. However, the notion of a simple causal relationship between hormones and reproductive syndromes has been severely criticized on the ground that there is no clear evidence for a simple biological substrate underlying PMS, PND, and menopausal complaints. Many of the psychological symptoms attributed to reproduction have been explained within a psychosocial model, which posits that psychological and social factors are at the root of mental-health problems. For example, premenstrual symptoms have been found to be associated with stress, or with the differential attribution of negative moods to menstruation and positive moods to life events, as a result of the negative expectations associated with menstruation. Equally, there is no agreement in the medical literature about the hormonal or biochemical causes of PMS, and no one medical treatment for it has been found to be consistently more effective than a placebo (Ussher, 1989). The attribution of female distress and dysfunction to reproduction may be a continuation of the centuries-old practice of pathologizing female sexuality and attributing madness to the womb.

Psychosocial Explanations

A number of psychological and social factors clearly contribute to women's mental-health problems. Economic factors, such as poverty and economic powerlessness, are known to be major risk factors for a range of physical and psychological problems. The World Health Organization's statistics, collected over successive decades, provide evidence of women's relative poverty across cultures: women earn significantly less than men even when equally qualified and are far more likely to lack independent income. The resulting powerlessness and economic dependence are factors associated with mental-health problems. For this reason, older women and women from ethnic minority groups are at higher risk. Powerlessness also has been posited as an explanation for the finding that women in traditional marital relationships—those who do not work outside the home and are responsible for the full burden of domestic work and child care—are at higher risk of mental-health problems than are single women, women in more egalitarian relationships, or women in paid employment. The traditional female caring role can in itself increase vulnerability: caring for young children, for elderly relatives, or for a dependent spouse is a major risk factor for depression (Ussher, 1991).

Sexual violence and childhood sexual abuse have also been posited as important in the etiology of women's mental health problems. Survivors of abuse report significantly higher rates of problems than are found in nonabused populations. A history of sexual abuse and violence is found in between 40 and 70 percent of many clinical populations, including those diagnosed with eating disorders, depression, anxiety, gynecological complaints, and sexual problems (Browne and Finklehor, 1986). Many women, internalizing the shame and guilt associated with sexual violence and abuse, blame themselves and often become depressed as a result. In countries where such statistics are collected, it is estimated that 70 percent of women have experienced sexual harassment; that between one-tenth and one-quarter of all women have experienced rape; and that between 10 percent and 30 percent of girls have been sexually abused as children. Rape and child sexual abuse may represent merely the extreme end of a continuum of objectification and sexism that faces all women and puts all women's mental health at risk (Chesler, 1993).

Conclusion

Women may be at higher risk than men for diagnosis and treatment for mental health problems. As a result of feminist critiques, however, many women have began to challenge descriptions of normality imposed on them. Many women reject the very concept of "mental illness"; they see "madness" as a reflection of society's underlying misogyny. The challenge for feminism is to reconcile radical critiques of mental-health theory and practice with the reality of distress experienced by many women. The move toward feminist therapy, nonblaming theories, and woman-centered mental-health research is one positive consequence of this debate (Brodsky and Hare-Mustin, 1980; Sherr and Lawrence, 2000; Fee, 2000).

See Also

ABUSE; DEPRESSION; EATING DISORDERS; MENTAL HEALTH II; MISOGYNY; PREMENSTRUAL SYNDROME (PMS); PSYCHIATRY; PSYCHOLOGY: OVERVIEW; STRESS

References and Further Reading

Brodsky, A., and R. Hare-Mustin, eds. 1980. *Women and psychotherapy.* New York: Guilford.

Broverman, K., et. al. 1970. Sex role stereotyping and clinical judgment of mental health. *Journal of Consulting and Clinical Psychology* 34(1): 1–7.

Browne, A., and D. Finklehor. 1986. Impact of child sexual abuse: A review of the research. *Psychological Bulletin* 99(1): 66–77.

Chesler, P. 1993. *Women and madness.* New York: Doubleday. (First published 1972.)

Ehrenreich, B., and D. English. 1978. *For her own good: 150 years of experts' advice to women.* New York: Doubleday.

Fee, D. 2000. *Pathology and the postmodern: Mental illness as discourse and experience.* London: Sage.

Nicolson, P. 1998. *Post-natal depression: Psychology, science and motherhood.* London: Routledge.

Sherr, L. and J. St. Lawrence, ed. 2000. *Women, health and the mind.* London: Wiley.

Showalter, E. 1987. *The female malady.* London: Virago.

Stoppard, J. 1997. *Fantasies of feminity: Reframing the boundaries of sex.* London: Penguin.

———. 1999. *Understanding depression: Feminist social constructionist approaches.* London: Routledge.

Ussher, J. M. 1997. *Fantasies of femininity: Reframing the boundaries of sex.* London: Penguin.

———. 1989. *The psychology of the female body.* London and New York: Routledge.

———. 2000. Women and mental illness. In L. Sherr and J. St. Lawrence, eds., *Women, health and the mind.* 77–90. London: Wiley.

———. 1991. *Women's madness: Misogyny or mental illness?* Hemel Hempstead: Harvester Wheatsheaf.

Jane M. Ussher

MENTAL HEALTH II

Historical Background

Much of the knowledge of psychology that we take for granted today was not even whispered about fifty years ago. During the 1950s and 1960s, for instance, clinicians were still being taught that women suffer from penis envy, are morally inferior to men, and are innately masochistic, dependent, passive, heterosexual, and monogamous. Women were told that mothers—not fathers, genetic predisposition, accidents, or poverty—caused neurosis and psychosis in their children. Neither women nor men were told that oppression is traumatizing—especially when those who suffer are blamed for their own misery and diagnosed as pathological. Medical students and clinical psychologists were not taught how to administer tests for mental health—only for mental illness.

Madness and posttraumatic stress symptomatology certainly exist, but throughout history in Europe and North America, many sane women who were victims of violence, who were viewed as too independent, or who were resented and feared as healers and mystics were condemned as witches and, from the sixteenth century on, psychiatrically imprisoned. In the nineteenth and twentieth centuries, a man had the legal right to lock his perfectly sane wife or daughter away in a mental asylum, and some did. Authoritarian, violent, drunken, or insane husbands could punish their wives for resisting them, or discard them in order to marry other women. The woman patient was seldom treated with kindness or medical expertise, whether she was entirely sane, was experiencing postpartum or other depression, heard voices, or was "hysterically" paralyzed; whether she was well-educated and well-to-do, or an illiterate member of the working poor; whether she had led a relatively privileged life or had been repeatedly beaten, raped, or abused in other ways; whether she accepted or could no longer cope with her narrow social role; whether she had been idle for too long, or had worked too hard for too long and was fatigued beyond measure. If she fought back, she was seen as in need of psychiatric treatment. As recently as the early 1990s, Lieutenant Darlene Simmons, a U.S. Navy lawyer, was ordered to take a psychiatric exam after she accused her commander of sexual harassment.

Bias of Clinicians

In the 1970s and 1980s, pioneer feminist clinicians were derided, fired, and forced out of graduate programs because they refused to diagnose other women within the prevailing model. When psychiatrists and clinical psychologists refused to medicate their female patients or treat lesbianism as an illness, or when they were seen as too "sympathetic" to their female patients, their professional credentials were challenged. In 1983, presumably in the postfeminist era, the psychotherapist Miriam Greenspan, author of *A New Approach to Women and Therapy,* was told by her supervisors that "excessive anger in a woman was a sign of a character disorder, that an inordinate preoccupation with spiritual matters is a symptom of schizophrenia, that too much empathy is a serious lapse in professionalism, [and] that too much compassion is an impediment to one's expertise as a psychotherapist." In 1996, the social worker and scholar Nzinga Shaka Zula wrote, "Therapists are often the soft police of the dominant culture." Often, female clinicians are much harder on women patients than are male clinicians. They may feel they must do so in order to distance themselves from a despised group.

Furthermore, when western medicine does not understand or cannot cure an illness, it often first denies that the illness is real by saying it is "merely" a psychiatric disorder. Increasingly, women with disabling medical illnesses are being psychiatrically diagnosed and sedated rather than tested or treated for a nonpsychiatric illness. Asthma and arthritis were once viewed as psychosomatic; today lupus, multiple sclerosis, Lyme disease, chemical and food allergies, Gulf War syndrome, chronic fatigue immune dysfunction syndrome, and certain neurological and endocrinological diseases may be dismissed and denigrated as primarily psychiatric in nature. Patients—usually women—are told that they are probably imagining their pain, that their illness is "all in their heads." Many psychiatric inpatients are still not believed when they complain of physical pain. Nonpsychiatric medical care is often withheld until a psychiatric patient collapses.

According to the psychotherapist Marcia Hill (1996), "Class and classism are in the position that gender and sexism were thirty years ago: denied, surrounded with myth, silenced." If every woman is, indeed, one man away from welfare or homelessness, to what class do women themselves belong? According to the psychotherapist Bonnie Chalifoux (1996), "working-class women live on a fault-line, as Lillian Rubin has described it. They are only one crisis away from falling into poverty, and they walk the line without a safety net." A poor woman can't afford to be neurotic; she has to keep going, no matter what. When the workload, stress, heartbreak, and tragedies mount up, and she succumbs—as most human beings would under similar circumstances—many psychiatrists may think that there is nothing to do but diagnose and medicate her. The state can't afford to shelter and treat her, she can't afford private therapy, and no family member will take care of her for very long.

The stereotype expressed in the saying "The more a woman is oppressed the stronger she is" is neither fair nor true. In fact, in 1972, *Women and Madness* wrote: "The problems of being both black and female in a racist and sexist society are staggering, the permutations of violence, self-destructiveness, and paranoia endless. Racism in psychiatric diagnosis and treatment is usually further confused by class and sex biases." Although such bias is increasingly challenged, double (and triple) diagnostic and treatment standards still exist. Native American, African-American, Hispanic, and Asian-American women have good reason to mistrust the mental health care system. They know they are often seen as inferior, even at their psychological and moral best, and as commendably self-sufficient when they are about to expire of grief. Furthermore, if a woman is poor or is not a native speaker of English, her chances of getting the psychological help she may need are minimal. Continuing, unexamined anti-Semitism also exists. Evelyn Torton Beck (1994) notes that "in the swiftly growing body of multi-cultural psychology, Jews are often omitted (or) misrepresented, oppressed by the myths and stereotypes of the dominant Christian culture." Jewish women—like African-American women—have often been viewed as tough, angry, strong, even pushy, when they have stood up for themselves.

Culture

Society changes slowly. Thus, most women have grown up in families in which boys were preferred, fathers were absent, and God was conceived of as male, not female. The cumulative effect of being forced to lead circumscribed lives as second- or third-class citizens, both psychologically and economically, is toxic. The psychic toll is measured in anxiety, depression, phobias, suicide attempts, eating disorders, and such stress-related illnesses as addiction, alcoholism, high blood pressure, and heart disease. It is therefore not surprising that many women—whether or not they are educated and have careers—behave as if they have been colonized physically as well as psychologically; they blame themselves (or other women) when they are captured (she really wanted it, she freely chose it) and defend their colonizers' right to possess them (God or nature has ordained it). Most women are still trained to put their own needs second, and the needs of any man—including a violent man—first.

Institutions

In the past thirty years we have learned a great deal about the genetic and chemical bases of mental illness. Those suffering from manic depression, depression, or schizophrenia often respond to the right drug at the right dosage level; all drugs have negative side effects; we should not prescribe the same drug for everyone, especially without continually monitoring the side effects; and verbal or other supportive therapies are often impossible without such medication. Despite the progress in biological psychiatry, however, both women and men are still wrongfully or overly medicated or denied proper medication by harried psychiatrists and psychopharmacologists. Psychiatric inpatients are often overly tranquilized for the convenience of overworked staff, who do not always treat the drugs' side effects with compassion or expertise.

Women who have been repeatedly raped in childhood—often by adult men in their own families—are traumatized; as such, they are often diagnosed with borderline personality disorder. If they are institutionalized, they are rarely treated as the torture victims they are. On the contrary, in state custody, women are more likely to be raped again, and each time it is more traumatic. Instead of being trained to understand this, most institutional staffs do not believe the rape victims, nor do they think of rape as a lifelong trauma.

The Feminist Alternative

Feminist psychologists and psychiatrists understand that both female and male psychology has been shaped not only by biology and anatomy but also by patriarchal culture and its devaluation of women. As a caste, women have not controlled the means of production or of reproduction; in addition, girls and women have routinely been shamed sexually and persecuted in other ways by men—but also by other women. Feminist psychological practice tries to understand what a struggle for freedom might entail, psychologically, when the colonized group is female.

The most important feminist work has "disappeared" from (or never made its way into) the graduate and medical school canon. This is astounding, because contemporary mental-health professionals did not learn about incest, rape, sexual harassment, wife-beating, or child abuse from graduate or medical school textbooks, but rather from feminist consciousness-raising and research, and from grassroots activism. Activists learned from the victims themselves, who had been empowered to speak not by psychoanalysis but by feminist liberation.

We now understand that women and men are not "crazy" or "defective" when, in response to trauma, they develop posttraumatic symptoms including insomnia, flashbacks, phobias, panic attacks, anxiety, depression, dissociation, a numbed toughness, amnesia, shame, guilt, self-loathing, self-mutilation, and social withdrawal. Victims of trauma may attempt to mask these symptoms with alcohol, drugs, overeating, or extreme forms of dieting. We understand more about what trauma is, and what it does. Chronic, hidden family and other domestic violence is actually more traumatic than sudden violence at the hands of a stranger, or of an enemy during war. After even a single act of abuse, physical violence is only infrequently needed to keep a victim in a constant state of terror, dependent on her captor and tormentor.

We understand, too, that rape is not about love or even lust, but about humiliating another human being through forced or coerced sex and sexual shame. The intended effect of rape is always the same: to utterly break the spirit of the rape victim, to drive her out of her body and quite often out of her mind, to render her incapable of resistance. The effects of terror on men at war and in enemy captivity are equivalent to the trauma suffered by women at home in violent "domestic captivity."

Rape has been systematically used by men of every class and race to destroy women within their family or community and, during war, wives, mothers, and daughters of the enemy. This terrorist tactic, coupled with childhood sexual abuse and shaming, works. Most women do not resist, escape, or kill their rapists in self-defense. When women do try to resist, they are often killed by their rapists, jailed, or executed. For example, in 1995 Sarah Balabagan, a Filipina maid, was condemned to death for having killed her employer-rapist in Abu Dhabi. Rape has also become a weapon of war. The women who were systematically gang-raped in northern Africa, Central and South America, and Rwanda and Bosnia have received neither justice nor adequate treatment. A psychiatrist in Zagreb, Vera Folnegovic-Smalc, noted the following rape trauma symptomatology: "anxiety, inner agitation, apathy, loss of self-confidence, an aversion to sexuality. Rape is one of the gravest abuses, with consequences that can last a lifetime."

The Feminist Therapist

A feminist therapist tries to believe what women say. Given the history of psychiatry and psychoanalysis, this alone is a radical act. A feminist therapist believes that a woman needs to be told that she's not crazy; that it's normal to feel sad or angry about being overworked, underpaid, and underloved; and that it's healthy to harbor fantasies of running away when the needs of others (aging parents, needy husbands, demanding children) threaten to overwhelm her.

A feminist therapist believes that women need to hear that men "don't love enough" before they're told that women "love too much"; that fathers are as responsible as mothers for their children's problems; that no one but herself—not even well-meaning feminist saviors—can rescue a woman; that self-love is the basis for love of others; that it's hard to break free of patriarchy; that the struggle to do so is both miraculous and lifelong; and that very few of us know how to support women in flight from—or at war with—internalized self-hatred and violence.

A feminist therapist tries to listen to women respectfully, rather than in a superior or contemptuous way. She or he does not minimize the extent to which a woman has been wounded, but nevertheless remains resolutely optimistic. No woman, however wounded, is beyond the reach of human community and compassion.

A feminist therapist does not label a woman mentally ill because she expresses strong emotions or is at odds with her "feminine" or maternal role. Feminists do not view women as mentally ill when they engage in sexual, reproductive, economic, or intellectual activities outside of marriage. They do not pathologize women who have full-time careers, are lesbians, refuse to marry, commit adultery, want a divorce, choose to be celibate, have an abortion, use birth control, choose to have a child out of wedlock, choose to breast-feed against expert advice, or expect men to be responsible for a full 50 percent (and when necessary, 100 percent) of child care and housework. Women have lost custody of their children for these very reasons and have been pronounced unfit parents by courtroom psychiatrists or social workers.

A feminist therapist believes that a woman's control of her body is as important as sexual pleasure, and that women must be able to defend themselves against violent or unwanted invasions such as rape, battery, unwanted pregnancy, or unwanted sterilization. As the feminist clinician Janet Surrey says, "The work of feminist healers is to integrate our minds and our bodies, ourselves and others, human community and the life of the planet. I question our profession's fear of feminism. I refuse to do psychology without a feminist liberation theology."

As much as the therapist for an imprisoned human rights activist requires a political and human rights movement behind her, the prisoner also requires freedom. The same is true for every women being held against her will in a marriage or a brothel, or trapped in a family system in which starvation or poor nutrition, genital cutting, little education, no religious power, early and repeated pregnancies, and other psychological disfigurements remain the norm, not the exception. As the psychiatrist Judith Herman wrote in *Trauma and Recovery* (1992), "The systematic study of psychological trauma depends on the support of a political movement. In the absence of strong political movements for human rights, the active process of bearing witness inevitably gives way to the active process of forgetting."

Herman models a new vision of therapy and of human relationships in which a therapist is called on to "bear witness to a crime" and to "affirm a position of solidarity with the victim." Herman's ideal therapist cannot be morally neutral but must make a collaborative commitment and enter into an "existential engagement" with the traumatized. Such a therapist must listen, solemnly and without haste, to the factual and emotional details of atrocities, without flight or denial, without blaming the victim or identifying with the aggressor, and without "using her power over the patient to gratify her personal needs." Although the love and understanding of relatives, friends, and political movements are necessary, they are not substitutes for the hard psychological work that victims must also undertake with the assistance of trained professionals; in fact, even enlightened professionals like Herman cannot undertake this work without a strong support system of their own.

Bearing witness is important; being supported instead of punished for doing so, especially by other women, is also important. Putting one's suffering to use through educating and supporting other victims is important; so are drafting, passing, and enforcing laws. Testifying as an expert witness is crucial. It is also critical that we support women who have fought back against their rapists and batterers and who have been jailed for daring to save their own lives. They are political prisoners and should be honored as such—not seen as pathological masochists who "chose" to stay until they "chose" to kill.

Historical accounts of asylums strongly suggest that most women in asylums were not insane; that help was not to be found in state-run institutions; and that what we call "madness" can be caused or exacerbated by injustice and cruelty within the family and society. Freedom, radical legal reform, political struggle, and kindness are crucial to psychological and moral mental health.

See Also

ABUSE; BATTERY; DOMESTIC VIOLENCE; EMPOWERMENT; MENTAL HEALTH I; PSYCHIATRY; PSYCHOLOGY: OVERVIEW; PSYCHOLOGY: PSYCHOPATHOLOGY AND PSYCHOTHERAPY; RAPE

References and Further Reading

Beck, Evelyn Torton. 1995. Judaism, feminism, and psychology: Making the links visible. In Kayla Weiner and Arianna Moon, eds., *Jewish women speak out: Expanding the boundaries of psychology.* Seattle: Canopy.

Caplan Paula. 2000. *Don't blame mother.* New York: Routledge.

Chalifoux, Bonnie. 1996. Speaking up: White, working-class women in therapy. *Women and Therapy* 18.

Chesler, Phyllis. 1998. *Letters to a young feminist.* New York: Four Walls Eight Windows.

———. 1986. *Mothers on trial: The battle for children and custody.* New York: McGraw-Hill.

———. (1979) 1998. *With child: A diary of motherhood.* Reprint, New York: Four Walls Eight Windows.

———. *Women and madness.* (1972) 1997. 25th Anniversary edition, New York: Four Walls, Eight Windows.

———, Esther D. Rothblum, and Ellen Cole, eds. 1996. *Feminist foremothers in women's studies, psychology, and mental health.* Binghamton, N.Y.: Haworth.

Dusky, Lorraine. 1996. *Still unequal: The shameful truth about women and justice in America.* New York: Crown.

Folnegovic-Smalc, Vera. 1994. Psychiatric aspects of the rapes in the war against the Republics of Croatia and Bosnia-Herzegovina. In Alexandra Stiglmayer, ed., *Mass rape: The war against women in Bosnia-Herzegovina.* Lincoln: University of Nebraska Press.

Geller, Jeffery L., and Maxine Harris. 1994. *Women of the asylum.* New York: Doubleday.

Greenspan, Miriam. 1983. *A new approach to women and therapy.* New York: McGraw-Hill.

Hill, Marcia. 1996. We can't afford it: Confusions and silences on the topic of class. *Women and Therapy* 18.

Herman, Judith Lewis. 1992. *Trauma and recovery.* New York: Basic.

Shaka Zulu, Nzinga. 1996. Sex, race, and the stained-glass window. *Women and Therapy* 19.

Surrey, Janet. 1989. Personal interview.

Wood, Mary Elene. 1994. *The writing on the wall: Women's autobiography and the asylum.* Chicago: University of Illinois Press.

Phyllis Chesler

MIDWIVES

From the earliest times, women worldwide have helped other women in childbirth. The English word *midwife* derives from Middle English and means "with woman"—the one who stays with the childbearing woman. The Danish word is *jordmor* ("earth mother"); in France, a midwife is called *sage-femme* ("wise woman"). The midwife knows how to prepare mothers for childbirth, calm them in labor, and turn a malpositioned baby. Her knowledge includes how to shorten a labor, free a breech baby, and unwrap an entangled cord. Where no doctor or technology is available, she applies the time-honored, empirically derived skills that help mothers and babies through childbirth.

Modern times have changed midwifery by medicalizing childbirth, particularly in the industrialized nations but in much of the rest of the world as well. Where midwifery has remained strong, it serves as a bulwark against the loss of basic skills that often accompanies the use of high technology. At the time of this writing, according to data gathered by the World Health Organization (WHO), midwives were the only attendants in the birth room in 70 percent of births in the countries losing the fewest babies at birth. The Netherlands, one of the top five, has most successfully resisted the advance in the use of technology in childbirth; there, 40 percent of births still occur in the parents' home, attended by midwives.

At the other extreme, the United States and Canada allowed midwifery to virtually disappear by the mid-twentieth century. By 1970, only a few hundred traditional midwives (called "grannies" or "grand midwives" in the southeastern United States and *parteras* in the Southwest) remained to serve the rural poor. A decade later, the grand midwives' work was made illegal, despite shortages of maternity-care providers in their rural states. Midwifery in the United States and Canada is now enjoying a resurgence, however, because of public and legislative reactions to rising costs of maternity care and high rates of cesarean section. Access to a midwife is still not possible for most women, though, because the number of midwives is small.

If the midwife lives in an industrialized nation, she works in a hospital surrounded by technology, in a birth center, or, more rarely, in the homes of the mothers she serves. She may also provide prenatal care and help with contraception, breast feeding, care of newborns, sex education, primary health care, identification and referral of high-risk patients, and "well woman" gynecological care.

In areas in developing countries where traditional midwives represent the norm and childbirth practices are more rooted in ancient cultural ways, birth usually takes place in the home. Traditional midwifery training is passed from generation to generation through oral tradition and apprenticeship, and it usually is not regulated by law. The philosophy underlying traditional midwifery does not view childbirth as an illness needing treatment; it both celebrates and works with the natural process. In 1972, WHO began to call traditional midwives "traditional birth attendants" (TBAs), to distinguish them from their more formally trained counterparts in Europe and other industrialized regions. To reduce infant and maternal mortality in poor nations, WHO has proposed that traditional midwives be taught to work alongside—not within—the organized formal health system. Critics of the technological excesses of western obstetrics, many of them midwives, believe that this profession has as much to learn from traditional midwives (about the importance of upright positions and continuous emotional support in labor, for instance) as it has to teach them about preventing neonatal tetanus and other complications.

See Also

CHILDBIRTH; GYNECOLOGY; MATERNAL HEALTH AND MORBIDITY; NURSING; OBSTETRICS; PREGNANCY AND BIRTH

References and Further Reading

Oakley, Ann, and Susanne Houd. 1990. *Helpers in childbirth: Midwifery today.* New York: Hemisphere.

Wagner, Marsden. 1994. *Pursuing the birth machine.* Ace Graphics.

Ina May Gaskin

MIGRATION

Who Is a "Migrant"?

Today, fewer people are on the move than during the uncontrolled migrations preceding World War I. Nevertheless, in recent times wars, ethnic cleansing, and the process of economic globalization have engendered massive movements within countries and across international boundaries.

Identifying who is a "migrant" is problematic. In contrast to *refugees* and women *trafficked* for marriage, domestic service, or prostitution, demographers define *migrants* as those who choose to move. Economic exigencies may, however, blur such distinctions. Nowadays, whole towns and villages in the third world consist of children, increasingly older women, and old men. Can we say with any certainty which of the absent left freely?

How many people move? Almost a decade after the census rounds of 1990, precise statistics were still not available, nor have demographers found a reliable method to count the undocumented.

Women Migrants

Women who choose to migrate are not a discrete category. They are young, middle-aged, and older; their economic and social statuses vary; their education and work experiences differ. Women may migrate alone or with family members; they may go a short distance to a town or city in their own countries, or to another country. They may be prosperous professionals, or poor, uneducated, and unskilled. National origin and ethnic and racial identities are other important variables that differentiate female migrants.

When younger women migrate, they often go alone and are isolated in the new place. They leave their natal families behind because there is insufficient food, space, or access to education at home—and their earnings help sustain their families. Or they go because professional opportunities are better in the receiving country, but they still may be isolated. Thus, Daisy, a young diplomat in New York, spends most of her weekends alone; she is too junior to socialize with her coworkers and has little in common with the large working-class colony from her country.

It is often asserted that women migrate alone because they have a better chance than men of finding work in the cities. Yet except for certain professional fields, most of the jobs open to women may be little better than slavery: operators in factories where women assemble garments or electronics for a pittance; household (domestic) workers who labor long hours with few rights or protections; workers in agriculture and agricultural processing enterprises; or sex workers. Even some professionals find that they cannot practice until they retrain and are accredited in the new country. Teachers and nurses may work for years as domestic servants or in factories.

Women with children often must seek work in a new place because their male partners desert them. These women make hard decisions: whether to leave their children behind in the care of relatives or to take them along. In Jamaica, Margaret, a 102-year-old, nearly blind woman was caring for two toddlers; her granddaughter left them with her one day, saying she was "going to foreign."

Many migrant women send money to support their children in the home place; others lose contact. Iris returned to Colombia after six years as a household worker in New York. She told her husband, an unemployed alcoholic, that he should stay behind. Undocumented, she was never able to visit her family, but her remittances financed a modest new house and educated her two sons.

Are these women "migrants," or are they "economic refugees"? Their migration often is de facto involuntary: move or starve. In the early days of research, demographers used an odd phrase to describe why people migrate: the pull of "bright city lights." Today, it seems clear that few women leave home to seek adventure. In the Spanish phrase, desperate women say, "*No me queda otra*": "I don't have any alternative." Thus, Mani from Cambodia and Hoanh from Vietnam work night shifts in auto parts assembly and turkey processing near Iowa City. They work seven nights a week and never know ahead of time whether their shift will last eight or twelve hours. Then, at 9:00 A.M., they struggle to stay awake in English classes. "Bright lights" were not what drove them to migrate.

Studying Women Migrants

Until recently, women were not considered serious subjects for migration research. When Youssef et al. (1979) published their pioneer work on migration and third world women, they found only two publications that quantified sex differences in migration. Since then, there have been a dozen UN conferences or publications dealing with the issue.

Sassen (1988) was able to document that "new" immigration countries—the Philippines, Korea, Jamaica, Dominican Republic, China, and several smaller ones—had mostly female migrants, while "traditional" migrants from countries such as Italy, Portugal, and Greece were mostly male.

Even when women began to migrate in large numbers, they were rarely noticed. Until the mid-1970s, social demographers, sociologists, and anthropologists focused on migration and urbanization in terms of race, class, and ethnicity (ignoring gender); women-in-development scholars discovered the richness of studying women cross-culturally, but most of them ignored women's cross-cultural migratory movements.

Indeed, most scholars assumed that women had no independent role in migration. If wives and daughters migrated, they "accompanied" their husbands and fathers. If women stayed behind, they simply waited for their men to return. Now we not only know that more women than men are swelling many migrant streams, but we also are learning about those who stay behind.

Female researchers dominate the new field of migration studies on women. From the mid-1970s onward, their studies began appearing in every world region. Illustrative studies are Chant (1992) and Sweetman (1998).

Literature on Women Migrants: Focuses

Literature on women in migration until recently focused on two main themes, each with several subthemes. *Destination country studies* dominated the earlier literature. This research explores how women and girls adapt to their new homelands, particularly how their relationships to their male partners, fathers, and brothers may change in countries that offer them new freedoms to study and to work outside the home.

Destination research also includes an important subtheme: free-zone export manufacturing industries in the Caribbean, southeast Asia, and the Middle East OPEC countries that draw women migrants from the rural areas of their own countries and the surrounding region. Sassen was the pioneer in this area, pointing to two processes that she would later name "circuits": labor going from the periphery (poor countries) to work in the core (industrialized) countries, and capital going from the core to the periphery to finance production plants, particularly to third world export-processing zones that still mainly employ young women (Nash and Fernández-Kelly, 1983; Ward, 1990). Government aid agencies tout a variation on this approach: aid instead of migration.

Curiously, few scholars have studied the far greater numbers of women who migrate to cities to work in the informal sector as street vendors, domestic workers, and sex workers. Workers in export processing appear to have a certain cachet for researchers; sellers and servants do not (but see Chaney and Garcia Castro, 1989).

Another subset in destination studies is an older (and continuing), voluminous popular literature on undocumented migrants, which is often racist and hostile. In prosperous times, migration may be viewed in destination countries as culturally and economically enriching, and doors are open to reasonable numbers of legal migrants as well as to those seeking asylum from mortal danger. Historically, however, hard times bring a vicious backlash against migrants, even in countries that actively recruit migrant labor—in particular, where the migrant population is large (for example, about one-quarter of the population of New York City is foreign-born). Migrants typically are blamed for economic downturns and for taking the jobs of citizens. Campaigns to deny social services have a special impact on women, who are the largest users of publicly financed health, education, and welfare systems.

Another group of studies focuses on the *sending countries.* In the early years of migration research, scholars were interested almost exclusively in finding out whether migration was positive or negative for receiving countries (and, sometimes, for the migrants); there was little research on the impact of migration on the countries of origin. Studies on the importance of remittances to both household and national economies came first; then studies centered on the household, exploring how women in both sending and receiving societies balance their productive and reproductive roles, and how changing family relations affect their lives and attitudes.

Many women are left behind by male out-migration, with a consequent increase in the incidence of female-headed households. Studies show that mothers, wives, and daughters do not sit passively awaiting remittance checks. They often are overwhelmed by the many new tasks they must assume to replace the labor of absent husbands, fathers, and brothers. Boserup (1970/1989) was the first to note how African male migration (forced or voluntary) to the mines and plantations affects women who take over the farming operations and provision of food—indeed, often carrying food to their male relatives in town. If the men stay away for a long time, women often pool their resources, forming new domestic units with other women, including their grandmothers, mothers, and sisters.

Scholars have long noted that migration has ceased to be a once-in-a-lifetime venture; many migrants go back and forth repeatedly from host to home country. These observations have evolved into important new research linking migratory processes in the sending and receiving countries as "transnational communities." This focus gives a new twist to the sociological category of "social field," the idea that research must include both ends of the continuum if the complexity of migration is to be understood.

Whether in Europe, the United States, or Canada, many migrants maintain strong ties to their natal countries through a constant circulation not only of people and cash, but also of newspapers and magazines, music and indigenous celebrations, literature and the arts, and invitations to home-country sports stars, beauty queens, and politicians. Colombian teenagers in Queens, New York, dance to the latest music from Bogotá or Medellín. Presidential candidates from several Caribbean and Latin American countries regularly travel to campaign among their nationals abroad, who can vote in their respective embassies. (Examples of this new research include Glick Shiller et al., 1992; Pessar, 1997; Sutton and Chaney, 1987.)

A fourth important focus in migration research is the *level of analysis.* Researchers working from the standpoint of international capital accumulation or other world systems, for example, may define migrant women garment workers in Ciudad Juarez or Turkish women in Germany as exploited. Case studies of women workers themselves, however, may reveal that these women consider themselves fortunate to be working at all.

There is, however, an overriding concern with the notion of "capital in place of migration." Offshore industries financed from abroad may lessen the flow of the poor into the richer nations, but capital migrates to poor countries without the safeguards to health, safety, and environment that workers have gained in the industrialized West.

Contributions to Theory

Has migration research on women enriched feminist theory? The earlier literature is primarily descriptive. Now, important theoretical work is being done by scholars linking the household to the international system; on the new international division of labor; on race, class, and ethnicity; and on transnational communities.

See Also

DEMOGRAPHY; IMMIGRATION; POPULATION: OVERVIEW; REFUGEES

References and Further Reading

Boserup, Ester. 1970. *Women's role in economic development.* London: Allen and Unwin (rev. ed. 1989, London: Earthscan).

Chaney, Elsa M., and Mary Garcia Castro, eds. 1989. *Muchachas no more: Household workers in Latin America and the Caribbean.* Philadelphia: Temple University Press.

Chant, Sylvia. 1992. *Gender and migration in developing countries.* London: Belhaven.

Glick Schiller, Nina, Linda Basch, and Cristina Blanc-Szanton. 1992. *Toward a transnational perspective on migration: Race, class, ethnicity, and nationalism reconsidered.* New York: New York Academy of Sciences.

Nash, June, and Maria Patricia Fernández-Kelly eds. 1983. *Women, men, and the international division of labor.* Albany: State University of New York Press.

Pessar, Patricia, ed. 1997. *Caribbean circuits: New directions in the study of Caribbean migration.* New York: Center for Migration Studies.

Sassen, Saskia [Sassen-Koob]. 1988. *The mobility of capital and labor: A study in international investment and labor flow.* Cambridge: Cambridge University Press.

Sutton, Constance R., and Elsa M. Chaney, eds. 1987. *Caribbean life in New York City: Sociocultural dimensions.* New York: Center for Migration Studies.

Sweetman, Caroline, ed. 1998. *Gender and migration.* Atlantic Highlands, N.J.: Oxfam.

Ward, Kathryn, ed. 1990. *Women workers and global restructuring.* Ithaca, N.Y.: ILR Press.

Youssef, Nadia H., Mayra Buvenic, and Ayse Kudat. 1979. *Women in migration: A third world focus.* Washington, D.C.:

Office of Women in Development, Agency for International Development.

Elsa M. Chaney

MILITANT FEMINISM

See FEMINISM: MILITANT.

MILITARIZATION

See ARMAMENT AND MILITARIZATION.

MILITARY

The military is a politically charged institution. Most government officials and many ordinary citizens believe that their country is not authentic, sovereign, safe, or developed unless its government has a military force at its disposal. Precisely because so many people believe that a military force is at the heart of political independence and maturity, who serves in the military has become a salient public question, raising issues of racism, class inequality, sexual ideology, and sexism.

In some countries—for instance, Algeria, Australia, Canada, the United States, Israel, Austria, Nicaragua, and Zimbabwe—whether and how women should serve in the military are policy questions that have set off wide-ranging public debates. There have been arguments among friends and family members, as well as court cases, legislative lobbying, public opinion polls, and television features on the issue. The question that provokes such national controversy does not seem to be simply whether women should don uniforms (or be allowed to stay in uniforms they are already wearing), but whether women's being allowed to serve as soldiers undermines the desired character of society. Consequently, the controversy touches something deep in the culture: anxieties about preserving a social order based on masculine privilege or aspirations for revolutionary ideals.

In many other countries, women's role in the military has not been discussed. For instance, in present-day Ghana, the Netherlands, Chile, China, Egypt, France, and Japan, it scarcely seems to be an issue at all. Women may have been, or are, in those countries' armed forces, but the absence of broad public debate about women's serving in the military suggests that most people in power and most ordinary women and men, including feminists, just do not deem it very important.

In both these sets of countries, the questions of whether, how, and when women serve in the military have political ramifications—for the way masculine privilege is sustained, the way women participate in public life, and the way governments manipulate ideas about gender to maintain their own authority and to conduct relations with other states. The end of the cold war had not changed this fact.

It is tempting to imagine that the percentage of women in any country's military rises and falls because of women's own actions, but that is not usually the way the gendered politics of military personnel work. Far more typically, those (predominantly men) who make the policies to ensure that the government has the desired number of soldiers (a term that, for convenience, can represent people in any branch of the armed forces) identify certain sorts of men as the optimal material—men who are young; men who are heterosexual; men whose race and ethnicity seem to the military's commanders to foster political loyalty; men who can speak (though perhaps not write) the language that dominates government affairs. But sometimes a government runs short of these "ideal" men, especially if the military undergoes technological modernization that requires more educated soldiers to operate complex weaponry, or if the government expands the military's role so that it has more missions internally and abroad. Militaries rarely stand still. They are subject to pressures from their own generals, from local civilian elites, and from foreign arms sellers and allies to adopt new technologies, take on new responsibilities, and confront new perceived threats. With each change, military personnel planners rethink what numbers they require, and in what ideal mix. This is a crucial political moment in the evolution of any government's relationship to women.

At the moment that these military planners start to run out of the male soldiers they deem trustworthy, they begin to consider recruiting young men from ethnic and racial groups that they do not trust, and women, first from the dominant community and later from other communities. In all armed forces, gender, race, class, and ethnicity are woven together in a government's "manpower" calculations. Officials conventionally accept women as soldiers if they can be deployed in the least masculine-gendered positions, such as medicine, communications, and clerical duties. Only rarely are they placed in frontline combat posts. Thus, in the 1990s, the majority of women in the U.S., German, and British armed forces were nurses and administrative workers. The patriarchal white regime of pre-1994 South Africa demonstrated the larger military pattern of racialized gender strategizing. It began deliberately recruiting white women into its armed forces in the 1980s, even though this violated its own Calvinist presumptions about white femininity, because pro-apartheid white officials believed that they were facing a growing threat of black resistance and did not have enough young white men to fill the ranks. By 1989, at the height of South Africa's militarization, women had become 14 percent of the government's active-duty defense force. Most were white women. Similarly, the British, American, Canadian, and Soviet governments' overwhelmingly male military elite recruited women volunteers during World War II, especially after it became clear that this would be a prolonged war causing extraordinary numbers of deaths and casualties. When the war was won, all but a very small remnant of these women soldiers were demobilized.

The sexual politics of armed forces have to be monitored constantly, not just when war seems imminent or during wartime. There are times in many countries when a shift in economic resources, a change in demographic trends, or a realignment of international cooperation allows citizens to debate whether they should have a standing army at all. A sovereign state without a military is not unthinkable. In 1948, Costa Ricans made precisely that decision; so did the new civilian regime of Haiti in the mid-1990s. Post-Soviet Russians in the 1990s heatedly discussed what the relationship of their military should be to democratic institutions, to citizenship, to non-Russian minority peoples, to young men's coming of age, and to patriotic motherhood. Nothing has been taken for granted. It was in the 1990s that Russian military commanders began recruiting thousands of women. They still had a male conscription law, but from 1989 to 2000 so many young Russian men refused to answer their conscription call-ups that the Russian officials began to rely more on women volunteers. They were following a well-worn path. British, Australian, Canadian, and U.S. defense strategists likewise began recruiting women in large numbers in the 1970s, when male conscription ceased. The timing was confusing. Coming in the 1970s, this looked as though it might have been a government response to the rise of the second wave of feminism.

Ten years later, many feminists—especially in the United States, Australia, and Canada (much less so in Britain)—took up women's equal access to military careers and benefits as their own issue. They developed political campaigns to press for more women in all military roles, at the time of the government's initial switch from male conscription to an all-volunteer force in the 1970s. Most women did not see the military as an essential arena for political activism. In fact, because so many American feminists had been opposed to the United States' waging war in Vietnam, there was considerable puzzlement when the leadership of the National Organization for Women (NOW) participated in a Supreme Court case designed to compel the government to require not only young men but also young women to register with the draft board on their eighteenth birthday. In the late 1970s, NOW's leaders saw a women's "draft" as a matter of equal opportunity to full citizenship. Some of NOW's critics inside the women's movement, by contrast, saw the registration law as a matter of militarism. By "militarism" these peace activist feminists meant a viewpoint that sees a world composed of friends and enemies where many problems must be resolved by force, and that imagines a government to be "mature" only if it possesses a major instrument of coercion. In that view, discipline and regimentation are valued traits in citizens, and patriarchal forms of masculinity are raised to the status of the best defense of the country's sovereignty.

A principal debate among feminists in many countries at the beginning of the twenty-first century remains this: Does it make more political sense to think of women gaining entrance into armed forces as an issue of equal rights or of militarism? A group of Italian feminists held a meeting in 1992 to try to answer this. Most of them had not paid much attention to women in the military; until 1999, the Italian military did not have any women in uniform—it stood out in the 1990s as the lone member of NATO prohibiting women from joining the active-duty armed forces. Moreover, many Italian feminists looked back with profound misgivings on their country's period of fascism during the 1930s and 1940s, and on their government's recent support for wars such as that waged against Iraq in 1991. To most Italian feminists, antifascist and peace activism appeared far more urgent and meaningful than working to get more women inside the state's military. Yet, with the end of the cold war, Italian policy makers were gingerly considering an end to all-male conscription. They would not follow Costa Rica and dissolve the military altogether; they wanted Italy to remain a member of NATO, and they were watching the unstable situations next door in the Balkans. But if male conscription ended, the military would need to enlist volunteers with enough education to handle the increasingly sophisticated weaponry. In this likely new postconscription setting, even Italy's conservative politicians would follow their NATO allies Portugal, Spain, and Turkey by bringing into the military a small number of women. Some Italian feminists came to this meeting in 1992 convinced that Italian women as a whole should work through the puzzles surrounding women as soldiers before the masculinized political elite made decisions for them, perhaps even in the name of "women's liberation."

In the decade since the collapse of the Soviet Union and the end of the cold war, many governments have refashioned their military personnel policies. Some governments, such as Canada, Ireland, Fiji, and Finland, have deliberately oriented their armed forces toward United Nations peacekeeping operations, while others have ended male conscription (for example, Belgium, the Netherlands, France). Some regimes have tried to end civil wars by incorporating rebel soldiers into a new state military (El Salvador, Angola, South Africa), while still others have reduced total personnel but have compensated by spending a great deal on the latest weaponry. There are also new governments that have been building new military institutions from scratch: Lithuania, Estonia, Armenia, Slovakia, Azerbaijan, Slovenia, Croatia, Bosnia. In every one of these countries, even those with only a handful of women in uniform, all women have a stake in what choices these officials make.

Policy elites refashioning their military personnel strategies look around for precedents while they decide. Perhaps they will think the Israelis made the right choice. When the Israeli state's military was formed out of guerrilla units in the late 1940s, women were kept in uniform but restricted to noncombat roles, so that combat became a "manly" occupation in Israeli culture. Or perhaps officials will feel more comfortable with the choices made by the largely male leaderships of revolutionary regimes. When the regular units of the Vietnamese military were scaled back in the mid-1980s, it was left a mainly male force; so were the Zimbabwean and Nicaraguan state armed forces when their civil wars ended. In contrast, Mozambique's military, even in 1992, more than a decade after independence, was still 20 percent women, and the new Eritrean military, having won independence from Ethiopia in the early 1990s, refrained from the usual practice of demobilizing almost all the women guerrilla fighters in the process of transforming itself from an insurgent force into a state institution. Precedents can be powerful, but military precedents are gendered and are chosen very selectively.

If male conscription is ended but the government still demands a sizable military, personnel planners may be tempted to attract at least some women as volunteers to fill particular roles, especially if they can manage this without surrendering the image of soldiering as a manly occupation. They may decide to repress those women who may see enlisting as a way to move away from home, live with other women, and gain some of the public respect, technical training, and alleged adventure that traditionally have been accorded male soldiers. Both the Slovak and the Dutch military attachés posted in Washington in the early 1990s expressed interest in the American model of incorporating women into an all-volunteer military, as a way of making up for the dearth of men (particularly educated men) that would follow the end of all-male conscription. But this raises the question whether the U.S. experience should serve as anyone else's model. The Dutch military in 1992 had a mere 1.7 percent women. If it adopted the "U.S. model" as it actually has worked, would this mean that Dutch women, like their U.S. counterparts, would pay for their training and media coverage with lesbian witch-hunts and sexual harassment? By the year 2000, women of color, especially African-American women, were almost half of all the enlisted women in the U.S. Army. What did this trend imply for Dutch women of color?

If a new military is being created or a military is being thoroughly reformed at the end of a civil war, the inclusion or exclusion of women could be taken as a significant sign of women's status as revolutionary heroes, patriots, or citizens precisely at a moment in the country's history when such a status is weighted with public significance. This does not have to be so. If "citizen," "patriot," or "revolutionary hero" were instead popularly imagined as being entirely separate from soldiering, and if soldiers did not get any special material privileges like technical training or veterans' benefits, then women's-rights advocates could disregard women's access to military jobs without risking very much. However, if a soldier, especially a combat soldier, is popularly deemed conventionally heterosexual, especially patriotic, suited for elective office, mature, deserving of public respect, or (if a senior military officer) influential in government decision making or eligible for a corporate executive job later in life—that is, *if any society is militarized*—then women' rights advocates face a serious dilemma. On the one hand, they can argue that women should eschew militarism and thus not seek places in the military, though this strategy risks leaving women out of an arena that accords men many privileges. On the other hand, they can work hard to ensure that women in large numbers get into the reformed military and get assigned to combat and promoted to senior officers' positions; but this campaign risks relegitimizing the military at the very time when its influence in society could be rolled back.

In conclusion, women's role in any country's military has political significance, even when their number is small, because the military often has great influence and because the masculinization of soldiering has been tied closely to citizenship. In every country, women's relationship to soldiering is subject to change—not often through feminist campaigning, but usually through male officials' strategizing. When women activists do take up women's role in their country's military as an important issue, they cannot define it narrowly. Precisely because the military can insinuate itself so deeply into family dynamics, industrial structure, the human psyche, the electoral system, class and racial interactions, historical memories, and popular culture, when women question the gendered fiber of any armed forces, they find themselves engaged in analyzing the very definition of personhood and of the nation.

See Also

DISARMAMENT; WAR

References and Further Reading

Cock, Jacklyn. 1993. *Women and war in South Africa.* Cleveland, Ohio: Pilgrim.

Enloe, Cynthia. 2000. *Maneuvers: The international politics of militarizing women's lives.* Berkeley, Calif.: University of California Press.

Maisels, Amanda, and Patricia M. Gormley. 1994. *Women in the military: Where they stand.* Washington, D.C.: Women's Research and Education Institute.

Office of the Inspector General, Department of Defense. 1993. *The Tailhook report.* New York: St. Martin's.

Randall, Margaret. 1994. *Sandino's daughters revisited: Feminism in Nicaragua.* New Brunswick, N.J.: Rutgers University Press.

Cynthia Enloe

MISOGYNY

Misogyny, the systematic cultural and ideological hatred of women, has both overt and covert manifestations across the globe. As an ideology that rationalizes men's hatred and hostility toward all things female, misogyny is manifest in a variety of laws, legends, and prohibitions relating to women, "from the early patriarchal myths, through medieval witch-massacres and genocide of female infants, to modern day rape laws, mother-in-law jokes, and sadistic pornography" (Rich, 1976–113).

Misogyny at its most overt is expressed in forms of violence against women such as rape, sexual abuse, and sex tourism. In Europe—from the middle of the fifteenth century to the end of the eighteenth century—the most famous historical example of misogyny is the great witch-hunt. The misogynistic link between sex and violence is seen in its most horrendous expression in times of war. Two contemporary examples are the rape of Muslim women by the Serbian army in Bosnia and Croatia and the prostitution on a massive scale of Filipina women at U.S. bases in the Philippines. In addition to blatant forms of violence, misogyny informs the systematic discrimination against women in social institutions such as law, government, religion, education, prison systems, police forces, and the military. Misogyny is reflected, too, in the silencing of women's voices and the erasure or distortion of women's presence in history. Hatred of women also pervades human speech, in the "harmless" humor permitted on the subject of women, their sexuality, their dress, and their behavior, and in the crude and violent songs about women and their sexual organs that emanate especially from military environments.

Psychological Roots of Misogyny

Feminist psychologists and anthropologists suggest that the roots of misogyny lie in men's fear and envy of women's association with the fundamental mysteries of life and death. Some feminists use the concept of "womb envy" to explain men's psychological and cultural revolt against women's organic connection to the creation of life and to the return to the "womb of earth" in death, drawing on Melanie Klein's definition of envy as "the angry feeling that another person possesses and enjoys something desirable—the envious impulse being to take it away or spoil it" (quoted in E. Keller, 1992: 51). They invoke the ancient, continuing envy, awe, and dread of the male for the female capacity to create life, which has repeatedly taken the form of hatred for all aspects of female procreativity, creativity, and labor. Men's misogynistic fantasies of female—especially maternal—power can be seen in the myriad representations in many cultures of women's power as hostile, destructive, controlling, or malign. The various manifestations of misogyny thus reveal themselves as a male tendency to project fears and anxieties onto women as evil, inferior beings whose threat to the patriarchal order must be neutralized; behavior that threatens patriarchal institutions, such as illegitimacy, abortion, and lesbianism, is labeled "deviant" or "criminal."

Feminists have also argued that women's internalization of misogyny—the self-hatred of women who believe patriarchy's message about their innate inadequacy, inferiority, even monstrosity—is both a cause of women's depression, dependency on approval, eating disorders, and other crippling behaviors, and a means by which women collude in their own oppression. Misogyny, therefore, can be seen as rationalizing and perpetuating fears of women's power, which in turn works to conceal from men and women the illusory nature of a supposedly inherent male superiority.

Origins of Misogyny

Misogyny is commonly held to date from the rise of patriarchy (c. 2000 B.C.); there is some evidence that earlier matricentric or matrilineal societies held women in greater respect. The rise of patriarchy, with its inherent misogyny, is associated with the idea that military conquests disturbed agrarian and more peaceful societies. This origin of misogyny in the overthrow of earlier goddess-worshipping societies appears cross-culturally in ancient myths that reflect a fear and envy of women's power and authority, rationalizing men's taking over of women's responsibility for agriculture, pottery, ownership of land, and household management. Some scholars relate the warrior-hero myths of many cultures with the destruction, devaluation, or degradation of the body of the woman, mother, or goddess figure (C. Keller, 1986; Warner, 1994); one of the most famous examples is the earth mother goddess Tiamat, who was slain by the young warrior god Marduk in the Babylonian *Enuma Elish* (Sproul, 1979). Ancient misogynistic attitudes are also reflected in the myths of many cultures that symbolically replace maternal procreativity with a male takeover of procreative power. Fear and hatred of the maternal are identified in Hesiod's Olympian eogony, which supplants earlier chthonic goddesses (Harrison, 1991); in the ancient and widespread myths of men stealing the procreative bullroarer from women (E. Keller, 1992: 45–48); and in the creation of male sacrificial religious rituals (Jay, 1985). In addition to this ancient resentment of women's power to create new life, many cross-cultural mythic images also reflect a fear of woman as sexual temptress and consumer of male sexual energy, as exemplified by the fanged blood goddess Kali and widespread myths about the vagina dentata or the vaginal serpent (Weigle, 1982: 118–128).

These myths suggest that misogyny can be a consequence of rejection and fear of embodiment and connection with the Earth's cycles of life, death, and regeneration. What men reject and fear is projected onto women, who then become icons of despised carnality from whose powers men must protect themselves by keeping women subjugated. This subjugation is accomplished by creating images of the idealized mother, cut off from all sexuality, who is all-nurturing and self-sacrificing for the son (as with the Virgin Mary), as well as by instituting societal control over women's bodies, their reproductive processes, and their sexual activity. Although there is some debate about the validity of a direct correlation between prepatriarchal goddess worship and higher status for real women (see Ruether, 1992), certain precolonial cultures—such as the pre-fifteenth-century Philippines and Latin America—did evidence greater respect between women and men before they were replaced by colonialist regimes. Capitalist conquerors (*conquistadores*) in Latin America, the Philippines, and parts of Africa, with their contempt for indigenous populations and their determination to plunder the wealth and resources of the conquered country, introduced new forms of devaluing women—a legacy of feudal Europe combined with racism and ecocidal or earth-destroying tendencies.

The mythic conquering warrior-hero, victorious over the slain body of the mother, has also been psychoanalytically understood to represent the struggle of the son to attain liberation from the mother and to transcend and rupture the connections that link him with the affective life. This psychology underpins and legitimates cultures that glorify "freedom," individualism, and separation from intimacy and the limitations of attachment (Baker Miller, 1976; Chodorow, 1978). Drawing a linguistic connection among *monstrum, mater, mother, and matter,* Jung saw a psychic fear and hatred of the "terrible mother" represented mythically in images of dragons, witches, and devouring animals (Neumann, 1963). Thus, a fundamental misogyny undepins the male ego-liberation struggle and the superman hero as a model of the human subject.

Misogyny in Modern World Religions

Modern world religions also must bear their share of responsibility for both actively and passively promoting misogynistic thought and practices. At best, the patriarchal mind-set that governs their structures and thought patterns has been blind to the situation and suffering of women and has considered them the possessions of their husbands, essential only for the procreation and rearing of children, and thereby for the continuing of the race. As Jahweh, God of the Hebrew Bible, says, through the prophet Malachi: "Has not the one God sustained us for the spirit of life? And what does he desire? Godly offspring." A dramatic illustration of the misogynistic practice of linking sex, violence against women, and war is the biblical story of Judges 19. A concubine is gang-raped all night by a mob in the town of Gibeah. In fury because his possession has been violated, her master chops her body into twelve pieces and distributes them to the twelve tribes of Israel. A massacre of the tribe of Benjamin follows, and more slaughter is needed to provide 600 kidnapped virgins for the Benjamites, in order that the tribe should not die out. Until recently, this story has never been proclaimed as an example of violence against women that manifests the most extreme form of misogyny.

The focus on the continuation of the race has led to the toleration of practices that, if not blatantly misogynistic, contribute to the consistent undervaluing of women's persons and bodies. Various practices reflect the ways that women are valued solely for their usefulness within marriage. Women have been punished—frequently with death—for independent action or any transgression against the marital bond, and the position of women outside marriage has been surrounded with controls and prohibitions at best, and cruelty and brutality at worst. Thus, the position of the widow in some Indian and African cultures is fraught with restrictions. In parts of India where the practice of *suttee (sati),* self-immolation on the funeral pyre of the dead husband, is now forbidden by law, the widow is virtually under house arrest, restricted in diet and clothing, considered to bring bad luck, and frequently blamed for her husband's death. The alternative to abiding by these restrictions is beggary or prostitution. Some religions condone cruel practices designed to control and prevent sexual activity in young girls. In some Muslim countries, especially in Africa, female circumcision and genital mutilation are practiced. The increase in female infanticide and abortion of female fetuses in India—made easier by technologies such as ultrasound—points to the fact that misogynistic practices are to be found not only in so-called primitive stages of society's development but also in modernized cultures.

One way in which misogyny persists in churches, synagogues, and temples is through lack of interest in, or rationalizing of, the suffering that women undergo specifically as women, as seen in all aspects of the feminization of poverty (Cooper-White, 1995). From the perspective of many religions, if suffering and sacrifice point the way to holiness, then women are natural bearers of suffering who need to atone for the inherent sin of being women (Grey, 1989). Only recently has this perception begun to be addressed by such organizations as the United Nations and the World Council of Churches.

A number of other specific theological factors facilitate misogynistic attitudes toward woman. Myths of creation that hold women responsible and guilty for sin and evil, such as the Judeo-Christian Eve or the Greek Pandora, reflect sharp dualisms—good-evil, earth-sky, body-spirit, emotion-rationality, human-nonhuman—fundamental to many religions. Such Manichaean systems rationalize the association of women with the negative pole of the dualisms—with embodiment, emotion, sexuality, earthiness—all that *Homo spiritualis* must shun. In the ascetic spirituality of certain Christian Fathers, women, in order to be holy, must become like men (Grey, 1993). The predominance of the male god, always superior to the female if an image of female deity is present at all, is an ever-present reminder that women cannot imagine the divine on their own terms.

Psychological, cultural, and spiritual sources of misogynistic attitudes also indicate directions for correcting them. Feminists' identification of misogyny as a source of crippling effects in women's lives has been the first step toward creating psychological, spiritual, and social solutions. Other signs of progress in eradicating misogyny can be seen in the increased acceptance of women in government and many professions, the creation of equal opportunities in many working situations, the improved prosecution of rape and harassment, and the redefinition of pornography as a civil rights issue. Future progress will depend on a persistent, careful analysis of particular form of misogyny and a willingness to call on all the resources—philosophical, legal, psychological, and theological—that enable equal partnership, mutuality in relationships, and a healing of the thousands of years of injustice and cruelty that this disordered pattern of relating has produced.

See Also

ARCHETYPE; CREATION STORIES; CURSE; INFANTICIDE; MATRIARCHY; PATRIARCHY; RAPE; THEOLOGIES: FEMINIST; VIOLENCE AND PEACE: OVERVIEW; WAR; WITCHES: ASIA; WITCHES: WESTERN WORLD

References and Further Reading

Baker Miller, Jean. 1976. *Toward a new psychology of women.* Boston: Beacon.

Chodorow, Nancy. 1978. *The reproduction of mothering: Psychoanalysis and the sociology of gender.* Berkeley: University of California Press.

Cooper-White, Pamela. 1995. *The Cry of Tamar: Violence against women and the church's response.* Minneapolis, Minn.: Augsburg Fortress.

French, Marilyn. 1992. *The war against women.* London: Hamish Hamilton.

Grey, Mary. 1989. *Redeeming the dream.* London: SPCK.

———. 1993. *The wisdom of fools?* London: SPCK.

Harrison, Jane Ellen. 1991. *Prolegomena to the study of Greek religion.* Princeton: Princeton University Press. (First published 1903.)

Jay, Nancy. 1985. Sacrifice as remedy for having been born of woman. In Clarissa Atkinson et al., eds., *Immaculate and powerful,* 283–301. Boston: Beacon.

Keller, Catherine. 1986. *From a broken web: Separation, sexism, and self.* Boston: Beacon.

Keller, Evelyn Fox. 1992. *Secrets of life, secrets of death: Essays on language, science, and gender.* New York: Routledge.

Kennedy, Helena. 1992. *Eve was framed: Women and British justice.* London: Chatto and Windus.

Neumann, Eric. 1963. *The Great Mother: An analysis of the archetype.* Kingsport, Ky.: Pantheon.

Noddings, Nel. 1989. *Women and evil.* Berkeley: University of California Press.

Rich, Adrienne. 1976. *Of women born: Motherhood as experience and institution.* New York: Norton.

Ruether, Rosemary Radford. 1992. *Gaia and God.* San Francisco: Harper.
Smith, Joan. 1989. *Misogynies.* London: Faber and Faber.
Sproul, Barbara. 1979. *Primal myths: Creating the world.* San Francisco: Harper and Row.
Warner, Marina. 1994. *Managing monsters: Six myths of our time.* London: Vintage.
Weigle, Marta. 1982. *Spiders and spinsters: Women and mythology.* Albuquerque: University of New Mexico Press.

Mary Grey

MISTRESS

The term "*mistress*" refers to a female extramarital partner of a married man whose relationship to the man has a certain degree of longevity and intimacy and at least part-time residential cohabitation (Orth, 1972). The role of mistress is essentially adulterous and may be subject to legal or social sanctions.

Sanctions against adultery are more socially marked for women than for men. In English, a correlate of this is a more developed vocabulary for female extramarital partners than for males. The term *mistress* lacks a readily available masculine equivalent, and *kept woman* is much more common than *kept man.* These differences imply that, although both male and female extramarital partners experience social stigma, the role of a female as extramarital partner is more socially expected, if not accepted, than that of a male. It is important to note that the term *mistress* was once reserved for a woman in a position of authority as head of a business or household. Though its usage in this sense is on the wane, the multiple meanings of the term reflect the ambiguous power relations among the mistress, her lover, his legal family of marriage, and society at large.

The degree of cultural elaboration and political and economic institutionalization of the role of mistress has varied considerably across cultures. Mistresses were common among wealthier men in most recent Asian and Middle Eastern societies, as well as in Spain, Portugal, and their former colonies, and in France. The harem in Middle Eastern societies is stereotyped in the West as an extreme institutionalization of the role of mistress. The difference, however, is that although an Egyptian consort or cowife generally does not have the same rights and status as a principal wife, the role of consort carries no sanction and little social stigma. Malek Alloula's study (1986) of nineteenth-century French picture postcards depicting "Moorish women" of Algeria suggests that the western eroticization of the "colonial harem" generated a confused association between the illicit role of the western mistress and the legal role of cowives and consorts in other societies.

The Egyptian cowife or consort shares with the western mistress a figurative (and to some extent literal) hiddenness from society. Though the academic literature on mistresses is rather small, the importance of mistresses in the popular imagination is obvious from their frequent appearance in fiction and folktales, and from the recent spate of popular psychology and self-help literature on dealing with experiences of adultery and the mistress role (an example of the latter is Richardson, 1985).

See Also

ADULTERY; IMAGES OF WOMEN: MIDDLE EAST; MARRIAGE: REGIONAL TRADITIONS AND PRACTICES; SINGLE PEOPLE; WIDOWHOOD; WIFE

References and Further Reading

Alloula, Malek. 1986. *The colonial harem.* Trans. Myrna Godzich and Wlad Godzich. Minneapolis: University of Minnesota Press.
Orth, Penelope. 1972. *An enviable position: The American mistress from slightly kept to practically married.* New York: McKay.
Richardson, Laurel. 1985. *The new other woman: Contemporary single women in affairs with married men.* New York: Free Press.

Karen Frojen Herrera

MODERNISM

The term *modernism* is associated with various European and North American forms of artistic production that are characterized by self-consciousness in style and content and that originated in a more or less narrowly defined historical period (roughly from the end of the nineteenth century to the middle of the twentieth).

Modernist Writers

Modernist writers such as Gertrude Stein, H. D. (Hilda Doolittle), Dorothy Richardson, Katherine Mansfield, and Virginia Woolf broke from nineteenth-century traditions that regarded the individual as knowable and unitary. These writers were much influenced by the newly emerging ideas of psychoanalysis, specifically the notion of a conscious and an unconscious mind. The self was seen as fragmented; some aspects of the psyche were not immediately accessible and not within the conscious control of the individual. Modernist writers explored ways of representing this fragmented self in artistic production.

Modernist writers rejected the idea that language reflects reality. Instead, they saw language as constructing reality. They began to experiment with style and narrative in order to bring to the surface the "inner" reality that they regarded as governing consciousness. The most striking technique they brought to this task was the "stream-of-consciousness" style of writing. These attempts to represent the workings of the mind on the printed page encoded thought fragments, incomplete musings, and associative, simultaneous, and discontinuous thoughts in written language. To do this, modernists experimented with innovative sentence construction and punctuation. Gertrude Stein, for example, omitted most punctuation in her work, whereas Virginia Woolf used punctuation in an elaborate way in complex, embedded sentences that are intended to present the complex workings of the mind. Katherine Mansfield, by contrast, frequently used short, incomplete sentences.

The modernist writers also experimented with narrative structures. Instead of constructing stories that had a beginning (introduction), a middle (crisis), and an end (resolution), they offered narratives which showed the daily repetition of certain experiences and in which problems tended not to be resolved. They experimented with representations of time and space; moments or short periods of time may be extended over many pages, or long periods condensed into a single sentence.

Such experimentation was in part a result of a perception that the conventions of written language are arbitrary and changeable. This understanding went together with a more generalized view that all conventions are temporary agreements between people, and therefore subject to change. The result was a sustained questioning of rules and regulations that constructed as "natural," "objectively true," *and* "universal" certain notions which were now increasingly viewed as provisional, socially constructed, and specific to particular situations. This questioning was facilitated by the gradual disintegration of the colonial empires and by the two world wars, events that prompted a reappraisal of women's and men's roles in society, including their sexual identity. Women writers of the first half of the twentieth century such as Radclyffe Hall, Djuna Barnes, Natalie Barney, and Renée Vivien portrayed lesbians in their work. Others, such as Olive Schreiner, pleaded for androgyny—the conjoining of female and male attributes in one individual—as a way of enabling women to move beyond traditional heterosexual femininity.

Modernism as a Concept

Women who wanted to live outside conventional feminine roles broke away from their background by moving from North America and Britain to continental Europe, usually to Paris. This uprooting resulted in a sense of alienation and detachment heightened by life in the city—a sense of being aimless and adrift. This was the basis of the figure of the *flâneuse,* a wandering urban character who spent her time watching people and sitting in cafés.

Within the modernist period, many artistic movements and schools existed, each of which reflected some but not all of the characteristics mentioned here. The very concept of monolithic modernism has therefore been questioned. Ray Chow (1992), for example, suggests that modernism is exclusionary, elitist, middle-class, white, and western in orientation. But the high modernism of Virginia Woolf and Gestrude Stein may be juxtaposed with the work of Katherine Ransfield and Jean Rhys, which suggests a rather different world from the one critiqued by Chow—a world that still needs to be fully explored in modernist studies.

See Also

POSTMODERNISM: LITERARY THEORY

References and Further Reading

Ankum, Katharina von, ed. 1997. *Women in the metropolis: Gender and modernity in Weimar culture.* Berkeley: University of California Press.

Benstock, Shari. 1987. *Women of the Left Bank: Paris, 1900–1940,* London: Virago.

Berg, Christian, Frank Durieux, and Geert Lernout, eds. 1995. *Le tournant du siècle: Le modernisme et modernité dans la littérature et les arts* (The turn of the century: Modernism and modernity in literature and the arts). Berlin: de Gruyter.

Chow, Ray. 1992. Postmodern automatons. In Judith Butler and Joan W. Scott, eds., *Feminists theorize the political.* London: Routledge.

Felski, R. 1995. *The gender of modernity.* Cambridge, Mass.: Harvard University Press.

Gilbert, Sandra M., and Susan Gubar. 1988. *No man's land: The place of the woman writer in the twentieth century.* New Haven, Conn.: Yale University Press.

Griffin, Gabriele, ed. 1994. *Difference in view: Women and modernism.* London: Taylor and Francis.

Miller, Jane Eldridge. 1997. *Rebel women: Feminism, modernism, and the Edwardian novel.* Chicago: University of Chicago Press.

Rado, Lisa, ed. 1997. *Modernism, gender, and culture: A cultural studies approach.* New York: Garland.

Scott, B. 1995. *Refiguring modernism.* Vol. 1, *The women of 1928;* Vol. 2, *Postmodern feminist readings of Woolf, West, and Barnes.* Bloomington: Indiana University Press.

Scott, Bonnie Kime, ed. 1990. *The gender of modernism.* Bloomington: Indiana University Press.

Waugh, Patricia. 1989. *Feminine fictions: Revisiting the postmodern.* London: Routledge.

Gabriele Griffin

MODERNIZATION

The concept of modernization is related to a theory of development that explains changes in economic, political, and social systems as societies move from "traditional" to "modern." It is often associated with westernization because industrialization had its origins in Europe; however, modernization is no longer thought of as a process of Europeanization because modernity takes a variety of forms. The theory can, however, be attributed to several western scholars.

Parsons (1971) developed the idea of *pattern variables,* a term which describes the shift from traditional to modern societies as a movement from sacred, diffuse values to secular, more specific values, and from ascriptive characteristics to those based on achievement; for example, leaders are chosen on the basis of universal characteristics that are measurable (such as performance on examinations) rather than through inheritance. Rostow (1960) described five stages of growth, moving from traditional to high mass consumption, with an underlying assumption that each society evolves on a unilinear path toward increasing use of technology based on the values of rational, impersonal decision making, where capital-intensive rather than labor-intensive methods are applied with increasing specialization and greater economies of scale. This is accompanied by an expansion of scientific knowledge based on empirical methods, which leads to progress.

Modernization theory is criticized for failing to explain why many third world countries do not follow a unilinear path. Writers such as Frank (1969) explain this in terms of "underdevelopment" and blame capitalism for creating dependency—that is, countries in the Southern Hemisphere depend on those in the Northern Hemisphere and therefore experience stagnation rather than economic growth. Modernization theory underlies most development programs, especially those initiated from the 1960s to the 1980s, and it is criticized by feminists because it marginalizes women or simply adds them into male-centered economic programs, often neglecting crucial social factors. Ester Boserup (1989) was the first to point out the differential impact of modernization and technology on the work of men and women; she noted that men benefited more than women from these programs.

See Also

DEVELOPMENT: OVERVIEW; ECONOMY: OVERVIEW; ECONOMY: GLOBAL RESTRUCTURING; GLOBALIZATION

References and Further Reading

Boserup, Ester. 1989. *Woman's role in economic development.* London: Earthscan. (Originally published 1970.)

Frank, A. G. 1969. *Capitalism and underdevelopment in Latin America.* New York: Monthly Review.

Parsons, Talcott. 1971. *The system of modern societies.* Englewood Cliffs, N.J.: Prentice Hall.

Rostow, W. W. 1960. *The stages of economic growth: A non-communist manifesto.* Cambridge: Cambridge University Press.

Jan Currie

MONEY

Women undertake two-thirds of the world's work and own 70 percent of the world's small businesses, yet they own only one-tenth of the world's money and less than one-hundredth of the world's property (United Nations Statistics, 1997). Research by the International Fund for Agricultural Development (IFAD) shows that in developing countries, women are responsible for most food production. On the African continent, it is estimated that women produce 70 percent of the food. Yet in these developing countries, nearly 570 million rural women—60 percent of the rural population—live below the poverty line (International Labour Organisation, 2000).

These statistics reflect the fact that there is no direct connection in money economies between money and the labor that produces goods and services. In these economies, money can be owned, accumulated, and used to exercise power and influence quite independently of the production and sale of goods and services. Whether money exists as cowrie shells and salt or as coins, notes, checks, credit cards, and e-money, it shares certain universal characteristics. Money carries with it power, influence, independence, and mobility. And worldwide, women have always had less access to money and less use of it than have men. In most cultures, the church, the state, social mores, and women's own biology have all played roles in separating women from money. The result is that of the planet's three billion women, 70 percent are poor—that is, they lack adequate money to access basic health and education for themselves and their children.

The Christian religion, for example, has played a major role in keeping women from acquiring money and the benefits it can bring. Matilda Joslyn Gage claimed that the churches' attitudes and behavior toward women in 1893, when she wrote, was "the most stupendous system of organised robbery known" (1980: 238). Although her concerns were broader than the churches' control of money, she made the clear connection between Christian values espoused and enforced by the church through canon law between the tenth and sixteenth centuries and its robbery "of the fruits of woman's industry, the exercise of her judgement, her own conscience and her own will." In particular, she pointed out that by the end of the sixteenth century in England, laws of succession introduced by the church "constantly sacrificed the interests of wives and daughters to those of husbands and sons" (1980: 60)

By the eighteenth century, control by church and state of women's lives meant that, under English common law, women lost all legal rights and identity when they married. Legally, they could neither hold nor manage money in their own right, and any money that a woman might have earned from her own labor was automatically regarded by the law as belonging to her husband. Changes to the law in the nineteenth century gradually removed these formal barriers to women's owning money, but the attitudinal aftermath remained and, even at the turn of the twenty-first century, it is still generally true that women apply for and receive less money in the form of bank loans and advanced credit. This is in spite of the fact that, under special development programs in the developing world, 97 percent of loans to women are repaid in full and on time (United Nations statistics, 1997).

For the quarter of the world's population that is Muslim, the Qur'an has for centuries officially granted women the right to keep their own earnings, inherit property, and manage it as they wished. But the reality is that for many Islamic women today, the principles espoused in the Qur'an have been overtaken by strict rules of Islamic law, which have confined women to the private sphere and denied them equal education and equal opportunities to earn money in the paid workforce (Muftuler-Bac, 1999: 306). Arab countries have the lowest official rates of women in the workforce, with 8 percent of women employed in Algeria and 10 percent in Egypt, Saudi Arabia, Oman, and Jordan.

Social mores also have played a role in separating women from money and from the power and independence that money can bring. Women's restricted access to education and their subsequent higher levels of illiteracy in almost every country (United Nations statistics, 1997) have limited their access to money by consistently preventing them from participating in higher-paying spheres of work. In both developing and developed countries, it is still regular practice for males to be given greater access than females to education and to the money that better job and career prospects can bring. In the paid workforce, women almost always earn less than their male counterparts, even when their work can be assessed to be of equal value. For example, in the manufacturing industry, women in Singapore earn 72 percent of men's wages. In Hong Kong, women earn 63 percent of men's wages, and in the Republic of Korea—again in the manufacturing sector—women earn only 57 percent of men's wages (United Nations statistics, 1997).

In agricultural societies, feminist research reveals similar inequalities. In a study of women in agriculture in Nigeria (Adekanye, 1984), 89 percent of the women investigated indicated that monthly incomes in agriculture were generally higher for men, and 77 percent felt that government programs addressing credit sources, cooperative development, and supply of fertilizer were mainly aimed at men. It is not uncommon for women to manage farming activities until an excess is produced that can be exchanged for money; at this point, the status of agricultural work rises, and men tend to take over the cash crops and the money.

Although there is no direct connection between women's biology and their ability to earn and manage money, childbearing inevitably limits women's mobility and their ability to travel to sell their labor to the highest bidder. In 120 nations, women's activism has resulted in legal requirements for women to be offered paid maternity leave. Canada has the best provisions, allowing paid maternity leave for 17 weeks, but even in relatively poor countries, such as Madagascar and Mauritania, women are guaranteed 14 weeks' paid maternity leave. In Australia, paid maternity leave is mandatory for employees in the public sector, and 30 percent of workplace agreements in the private sector also include paid maternity leave.

In developed countries, recent studies indicate that even today, there are forces operating to limit women's access to and knowledge about money (White and

Spender, 1994). For reasons of patriarchy, pride, or power, men tend to keep information about money from their partners, ostensibly because women should not have to worry their "pretty little heads" about such unpleasant matters. Women should be wary of this seemingly protective attitude in the men to whom they are connected financially. Many women who have allowed men to control the purse strings have been left—through divorce or death of a partner—with no money or no understanding of their financial situation.

The Internet has created a new way for women to access information about money, although in most countries men use Internet resources more often than women do. Even so, Web sites relating to women and money have proliferated in response to women's increasing interest in money, investment, and finances. Most are commercial sites that provide advice and information about money management and investment, as well as profiles and stories about successful women. Women's overt and increased interest in money is undoubtedly connected to the current and changing status of women. In Australia, for example, it is estimated that within the foreseeable future, 40 percent of women will never marry, 43 percent of women will divorce, and 80 percent of women will spend at least a decade of their lives on their own (Australian Bureau of Statistics, 2000). Their concern with money is born of necessity.

The United Nations Web site, <www.un.org>, is a mine of statistical information about the status of women throughout the world. One of the main conclusions to be drawn from the UN information is that women still have a long way to go in terms of achieving equal access to money as well as to the benefits it can bring to their lives and those of their families.

See Also

ECONOMIC STATUS: COMPARATIVE ANALYSIS; ECONOMY: OVERVIEW; ECONOMY: HISTORY OF WOMEN'S PARTICIPATION; ECONOMY: INFORMAL; POVERTY; WORK: EQUAL PAY AND CONDITIONS; WORK: OCCUPATIONAL SEGREGATION

References and Further Reading

Adekanye, Tomilayo O. 1984. Women in agriculture in Nigeria: Problems and policies for development. *WSIF* 7(6): 429–430.

Australian Bureau of Statistics. 2000. <http://www.abs.gov.au>

Bennett, David, and McColl, Gina. 1999. Filthy lucre. *Sydney Morning Herald Magazine* (October 23).

Gage, Matilda Joslyn. 1980. *Woman, church and state.* London: Persephone.

Muftuler-Bac, Meltern. 1999. Turkish women's predicament. *WSIF* 22(3).

Statistics Division of United Nations Secretariat. 1997. *The world's women 1995: Trends and statistics.* <http://www.un.org>

White, Shelby, and Spender, Lynne. 1994. *What every woman should know about her partner's money.* Hodder and Stoughton.

Lynne Spender

MORALITY

See ETHICS *and* RELIGION: OVERVIEW.

MORMONS

The Mormons—the Church of Jesus Christ of Latter Day Saints (LDS)—originated in the visionary experiences of Joseph Smith (1805–1844), a farmer's son who grew to young manhood in upstate New York's "Burned-Over District" during a period of religious ferment referred to by historians as the "second great awakening." The church Smith founded in 1830, like several other communitarian movements of the period, claimed to be less a new religious phenomenon than a restoration of the spirit of original Christianity. Like those other sectarian movements, the Mormons generated considerable hostility wherever they sought to settle. However, unlike the other movements, most of which failed to survive for more than a generation, Mormonism represents a genuine American success story. It is a story with complex implications for women.

Mormonism developed in the context of westward expansion. Smith and his followers were driven successively from New York to Ohio to Missouri to Illinois (where Smith was assassinated by a mob in 1844), and finally to present-day Utah, where under the leadership of Brigham Young (1801–1977) they established the independent theocratic state of Deseret. From the outset, when Joseph's wife Emma helped him to transcribe what would become the *Book of Mormon* (to which the LDS Church accords religious authority equal to that of the Bible), women had active roles in the church-ruled state. Smith created a Female Relief Society in 1842, giving women an institutional identity and a mission to educate and provide comfort to the poor; Smith's successor, Young, continued to encourage women's education, and their socially and economically productive activity. Mormon women were given the vote in 1870, and they generally supported the nineteenth-century women's suffrage movement. From 1872 to 1914 they published their own newspaper, *Women's Exponent.* Though they could not be priests or elders, women were allowed—indeed, encouraged—to heal and to prophesy in Mormon temples, and to share in various aspects of the church's internal life. As in the broader society of the time, however, their role was clearly subordinate to men's, and defined primarily in terms of their duties as wives and mothers. Theology provided the justification.

The God revealed in the *Book of Mormon* is both Father and Mother. The purpose of human existence is to rise, through worship, to an afterlife in a spiritualized material realm called the celestial kingdom, where men and women will live "as Gods." The primary vehicle for this rising to godhood is marriage—more specifically, in what to many outsiders is Mormonism's best-known doctrine, plural marriage, the goal of which is to bring as many preexistent souls into the world and the church as possible, duplicating the creative activity of the Father-Mother God and populating the celestial kingdom.

The doctrine of "celestial marriage" evolved over time. Smith saw it as appropriate only for a select group of elders, himself among them; his wife Emma, however, rejected this teaching of her husband's as "straight from hell." Emma was not alone in her disapproval, but the idea began to catch on in Mormon circles, in part through an appeal to Old Testament patriarchal precedent. The men of Nauvoo, Illinois, shut down the Female Relief Society, apparently suspecting it to be a hotbed of antipolygamy sentiment. In Deseret under Young, plural marriage became a key tenet of Mormonism, and Mormon women eventually came to argue its benefits: it ensured that there were enough good husbands to go around, it restrained men's sexual passion within the bounds of holy matrimony, and it provided a context for raising healthy children communally. Politics, however, conflicted with theology. The LDS church revised its policy on plural marriage in 1890, to pave the way for Utah's admission to statehood in 1896. Despite the church's change of policy, there are nevertheless some Mormons who to this day have refused to abandon the practice.

Ironically, the LDS church was in some ways more congenial to feminism in the nineteenth century than in the twentieth. Over time, Mormon women retreated into ever more traditional roles. The church explicitly opposed, and was a major force in defeating, the Equal Rights Amendment (ERA); and in 1980 it excommunicated a fifth-generation Mormon, Sonia Johnson, because of her vocal support of the ERA. Efforts to introduce feminist theology into the church—or even to revive the now deemphasized idea of the Mother God—have been resisted by the LDS hierarchy. However, through endeavors such as *Exponent II,* a Mormon feminist journal, efforts to challenge the traditional male-dominant hierarchy of the Church continue.

See Also

CHRISTIANITY: STATUS OF WOMEN IN THE CHURCH; POLYGYNY AND POLYANDRY; RELIGION: OVERVIEW

References and Further Reading

Beecher, Maureen Ursenbach, and Lavina Fielding Anderson, eds. 1987. *Sisters in spirit: Mormon women in historical and cultural perspective.* Urbana: University of Illinois.

Brodie, Fawn. 1945, 1971. *No man knows my history: The life of Joseph Smith, the Mormon prophet.* New York: Knopf.

Cannon, Janath, Jill M. Derr, and Maureen U. Beecher, eds. 1992. *Women of Covenant.* Salt Lake City, Utah: Deseret.

Johnson, Sonia. 1981. *From housewife to heretic.* New York: Doubleday.

Ludlow, Daniel H., ed. 1992. *Encyclopedia of Mormonism.* 4 vols. New York: Macmillan.

Mary Zeiss Stange

MOTHER

The term *mother* usually denotes a female who has undergone the biological process of parturition (giving truth to offspring) although the word often has connotations that are more social than biological. *Mothering* refers more to maternal obligation to nurture, raise, and socialize children than to the birth process itself. In many societies, a woman's status undergoes a profound transformation with the birth of a child, and the mother–child dyad assumes central importance, often until the child is weaned. The socialization of girls in many societies prepares them for motherhood, and coming-of-age and marriage ceremonies ritually announce a girl's readiness to bear children. The absence of or misinformation about effective birth control practices in many rural communities and the cultural or economic preference for having many children mean that many women spend much of their productive lives bearing, caring for, and rearing children.

In traditional Hindu society in India, for instance, it is only as a mother that a woman attains significant status in the household, and the onset of pregnancy signals a shift in status from that of virtual servant to that of future mother.

A mother of sons, particularly a firstborn son, is revered, and the birth of a daughter at least proves that a woman is not barren (Kitzinger, 1978). In other societies, the generative power of motherhood is applied to all women; among the Bamenda of central Africa, for example, funerary rituals for women last for four days, while a man is mourned for only three. Because women are producers of children, they are rendered almost godlike and worthy of extreme respect. Pre-Hispanic Aztec religion deified women who died in childbirth just as it did warriors who died in battle.

Mothers have appeared in symbol, myth, religion, and cosmology since earliest times. Venus figurines, female carvings with prominent secondary sexual characteristics that emphasize fertility, were common in the Gravettian period in central Europe 25,000–18,000 years ago, and stone figurines, often with accentuated hips and breasts and bellies swollen by pregnancy, were widespread throughout the world during the Neolithic period. Inspired by Morgan's work on the Iroquois and by Bachofen's *Das Mutterrecht,* Engels theorized in the nineteenth century that the earliest type of kinship structure was matriarchal, characterized by female rule and religious expression. This concept has been impossible to prove empirically, however, and has since been rejected by many anthropologists and other social scientists.

In *The Reproduction of Mothering* (1978), Nancy Chodorow argues that the process of mothering itself, with women raising both female and male children, differentiates gendered personality structures. According to Chodorow, mothers unconsciously respond to each child's gender in different ways, and male and female personalities are shaped accordingly. However, there is great cultural variation in the ways in which women mother. In many hunting-gathering societies, such as the Efe of central Africa, mothers habitually care for others' children, even breastfeeding them, while the children's mothers are out foraging (Peacock, 1991). Mingling children is common throughout much of the Caribbean, China, and western Africa, and especially in polygynous societies, where cowives share household duties. Although a mother retains ultimate control over her child, the child is socialized by all adults in the group. Other societies allow for social maternity, or the adoption of children by non-kin. Among the Baule people of the Ivory Coast, adoption reflects the desire on the part of a woman to care for a dependent on whom her husband has no corresponding claims. Among the Baule, as elsewhere, degrees of fosterage precede permanent adoption. In these cases, the child is generally less well treated, is more like a servant than a natural child, and is eventually returned to its natal kin group (Etienne, 1993).

See Also

CHILD DEVELOPMENT; CHILDCARE; GRANDMOTHER; MOTHER EARTH; MOTHERHOOD

Reference and Further Reading

Chodorow, Nancy. 1978. *The reproduction of mothering: Psychoanalysis and the sociology of gender.* Berkeley: University of California Press.

Etienne, Mona. 1993. The case for social maternity: Adoption of children by urban Baule women. In Caroline B. Brettell and Carolyn F. Sargent, eds., *Gender in cross-cultural perspective,* Englewood Cliffs, N.J.: Prentice-Hall.

Kitzinger, Sheila. 1978. *Women as mothers: How they see themselves in different cultures.* New York: Vintage.

Peacock, Nadine. 1991. Rethinking the sexual division of labor: Reproduction and women's work among the Efe. In Micaela di Leonardo, ed., *Gender at the crossroads of knowledge: Feminist anthropology in the postmodern era.* Berkeley: University of California Press.

Maria Ramona Hart

MOTHER EARTH

The idea that the Earth is a mother, whence all life comes and to which it returns in a continuous cycle of birth, death, and rebirth, dates to early Paleolithic cultures. In the small cave of La Ferrassie, Dordogne, six Neanderthal people were interred some 100,000 years ago. They were buried in a fetal position, their bodies marked with red ocher, the pigmented earth that may have been a symbol of the color of life-giving blood. The east–west arrangement of the tomb, pointing to the rising sun and typical of burial sites up to the Middle Ages, further reflects a cyclical understanding of life: all creatures are born and die in order to be born again.

In analogy with the cyclical processes they observed in women's bodies, many early peoples saw the earth as the great womb, out of which all life emerged and to which, eventually, it returned. Ritual life was probably closely connected to this worldview. Caves were considered the entrance to the sacred womb of mother Earth, as is evidenced by female sexual symbols, particularly the vulva, often painted near the entrance of Paleolithic caves.

In a period of human development when the relationship between sexual intercourse and procreation was little understood, evolving religious concepts had to do with the female principle as it related to life and fecundity, but also to death and to the mysterious process of transformation into new life, as observed in nature. Countless small artifacts, the so-called Venus statues, emphasize the female procreative organs; they were produced over a period of more than 10,000 years (approximately between 25,000–15,000 B.C.E.) and have been found near cultic sites in locations that range from northern Spain to Siberia (König, 1986).

Elinor Gadon (1990) rightly argues that "Venus" is a misnomer because it associates these artifacts with the patriarchal goddess of sexual love, whereas the statues "represent the fecundity of the earth in all its abundance, bounty and creativity." These "earth mothers" were manifestations of mother Earth, before the concept of *goddess* emerged in Mediterranean, Asian, and Native American high cultures.

The earth aspect of the great goddess was still central in what are believed to have been matrifocal high cultures (such as Catal Hüyük in Turkey), ensuring the cycle of life and fertility. Silbury Hill near Avebury, England, is now considered a cultic site of the Earth goddess. Built in female shape, it was intricately laid out to incorporate the cycle of the seasons and the movements of moon and stars into the body of the goddess.

The patriarchal reimaging of earlier cultural and religious concepts, though still acknowledging mother Earth as the primordial force out of which all life has come, put her lowest in the slowly emerging divine hierarchies of patriarchy. The Olympian creation myth tells of a chthonic Goddess, mother Earth (Gaia), who emerged out of chaos, created heaven (Ouranos) seas, and mountains, but in the ensuing battle lost against her own offspring. Though Zeus became the supreme symbol of patriarchal power, however, the Olympian gods swore their binding oaths by mother Earth (Walker, 1983).

The memory of Earth as mother from whom all life issues and where it eventually returns lived on in most religious traditions. Many creation myths understand human beings as "earthlings." Adamah—made of earth—is the name of the first human, created by God in the Hebrew creation story. The universally known ritual of giving birth squatting on the ground, still practiced in rural areas in some parts of Africa and Asia, evoked the presence of Earth as mother and child, allowing every woman to reenact the drama of the great mother Goddess (Eliade, 1978; Moltmann et al., 1999).

Perhaps the idea of all creatures returning into Earth's womb has been even more tenacious in the cultural memories of peoples all over the globe. Some Native American religions included a central doctrine of reincarnation in a new body from mother Earth's womb.

The symbolism of Jesus' burial in a cave (the womb) and his resurrection after three days must also be seen in this context. The Christian tradition quietly acknowledged the popular religious undercurrent that understood the Earth as a protecting, embracing, motherly resting place. The original meaning of the word *heir* meant "to protect, to envelop" and was the name of the old Nordic goddess of death, Her, one of the aspects of the Earth mother.

The word *earth* stems from a Sanskrit root, *artha,* signifying material wealth and bounty. However, a popular feminist etymology that connects the "material" (Latin *material,* the bodily) to *mater terra* (mother Earth) cannot be proved, through the relationship to mater/mother is perhaps more tenable (Deshowste 1963).

Feminist theologians, such as Rosemary Radford Ruether (1992), have consistently critiqued the dualisms of Christian Hellenistic tradition, which put mind over matter and thus helped to legitimize the exploitation of nature by western civilizations "Mother Earth" has become an important metaphor in the search for a new integrative paradigm, which puts sustainability, justice for the living Earth, and healing at its center. It inspires both ecofeminist political struggles and performance artists who combine art and ritual in a new way, evoking the great cosmic forces of mother Earth (Gadon, 1990: 365ff).

See Also

CREATION STORIES; DEATH; EARTH; ECOFEMINISM; GAIA HYPOTHESIS; GODDESS; NATURE; WOMANSPIRIT

References and Further Reading

Drosdowski, Gunther, Wolfgang Mütter et al., eds. 1963. *Der Duden.* Vol. 7: *Etymologie.* Mannheim, Wien, Zürich: Verlag Duden.

Eliade, Mircea. 1978. *Earth, water and fertility: A history of religious ideas.* Chicago: University of Chicago Press.

Gadon, Elinor W. 1990. *The once and future Goddess.* London: Aquarian. (Originally published 1989.)

König, Marie. 1986. *Die Frau im Kult der Eiszeit.* In *Frau und Macht: Fünf millionen Jahre Urgeschichte der Frau.* Hamburg: Fischer.

Moltmann, Elisabeth, Maria Schwelien, and Barbara Stamer. 1994. *Erde, Quelle, Baum, Lebenssymbole in Märchen, Bibel und Kunst.* Stuttgart: Kreuzverlag.

Riencourt, Amaury de. 1983. Sex and power in history. In Barbara G. Walker, ed., *The women's encyclopedia of myths and secrets.* San Francisco: Harper and Row.

Ruether, Rosemary Radford. 1992. *Gaia and God: An ecofeminist theology of Earth healing.* New York: HarperCollins.

Walker, Barbara G., ed. 1983. *The women's encyclopedia of myths and secrets.* San Francisco: Harper and Row.

Reinhild Traitler–Espiritu

MOTHERHOOD

Motherhood can be conceptualized on several different levels (Adams, 1995; Bernard, 1974; Rotherman, 1989). It is (1) a biological universal, in that it is the female of the species that gives birth; the reproductive aspects of motherhood (conception, gestation, birth, lactation) are fairly constant. Motherhood is also (2) a cultural institution, a set of practices for dealing with the care and rearing of children. These are subject to geographic and historic variety in traditions, customs, attitudes, beliefs, rules, laws, and norms. Motherhood is also (3) an identity, based on experience. It gives women a sense of who they are and what their place is in society. Part of this identity arises out of motherhood as (4) an activity or a project. It is mother work, reproductive or caring. The latter aspect also entails motherhood as (5) an emotional and psychological relationship or a bond between a mother and a child. Like other institutions, motherhood is (6) an ideology containing powerful symbolic components, expressed in culture, including religion, art, and literature. On the basis of these ideological connotations, motherhood also has (7) a political dimension: reproduction is subject to political manipulation in policies that encourage or discourage high birthrates. It involves intense debate on family policy (maternity and parental leave and day care), abortion, birth control, and reproductive technologies.

Ideals

Modern western motherhood is shaped by the privatization of family and household. Sole or primary responsibility for child care rests on the mother in an isolated household. This is rooted in the nineteenth century and the history of the industrial revolution, during which productive activities were gradually removed from the household as men and unmarried and childless women engaged in wage work. Reproductive work, or child care, became the exlusive domain of biological mothers, most of whom were married. The ideology of exclusive motherhood united women of all strata. However, whereas the wealthy had nannies and wet nurses and even today have access to paid child care help in their homes, most women of the less privileged classes are unable to employ private household help.

In a privatized setting, there is a focus on the special bond between mother and child. Motherhood is women's primary occupation, requiring her to render round-the-clock tender, loving care. The mother becomes a symbol of privatized homes and altruistic, self-sacrificing love. Having children becomes idealized as something that is highly satisfying. Motherhood is supposed to be the fulfillment of womanhood, based on a presumed natural tendency to want and care for children.

This idealization also appears in the way religion, literature, and art have traditionally treated motherhood. Many cultures and religions of the world revere the mother as a symbol of fertility and sacrifice. This is exemplified by the Virgin Mary in Christianity and by the mother-goddess Kali in Hinduism. Religion also plays a large part in family size. For example, Catholic women have more children than non-Catholic women as a result of the birth control policies of the Roman Catholic church.

Practically every young woman anticipates children and motherhood in response to institutional pressures on girls and women. The phrase *maternal instinct* captures both the psychological need of women to have children and the social definition of women as nurturing and caring. Women are socialized into motherhood very early, and motherhood is glorified in the mass media and other social institutions. Women are made to feel deviant if they choose not to have children or do not love motherhood. Similarly, infertility tends to be perceived as a personal flaw. Jessie Bernard (1974) argues that in fact, women have traditionally had very little choice about motherhood. It was only in the latter part of the twentieth century that nonmotherhood became an acceptable option for women, and that women were able to acknowledge that motherhood was not the most fulfilling task in their lives.

The Work of Motherhood and Women's Status

Motherhood involves a range of activities required to ensure the emotional and physical health of infants and small children, and added housework caused by the addition of children. When caring for babies is exclusively the mother's responsibility, any help that she may be given, even by the father, is seen as a gift, not an obligation (Bernard, 1974).

The work of a mother in this kind of setting can be highly stressful and can bring little satisfaction because it is characterized by low levels of control and high levels of demand. The work is monotonous, fragmented, and isolated. Women with young children often experience postpartum depression, which, aside from metabolic changes following childbirth, is related to the fundamental change in women's lives after the birth of a child. In modern societies, a new mother may receive little help from her husband, relatives, or the larger community. Thus, Adrienne Rich (1976) describes the experience of motherhood as "anger and tenderness," capturing the contradictory aspects of the experience. On the one hand, women are told, and many believe, that they should find motherhood fulfilling. On the other hand, they struggle with the demands it puts on their time, energies, and identity.

Nor is exclusive, privatized mothering necessarily beneficial for children. There are ongoing debates about children's need for wider social contact with other adults and peers once they are past infancy. However, Barbara Katz Rothman (1989) cautions against overly zealous claims about the ill effects of exclusive mothering and the danger of blaming women's child-rearing practices for the perpetuation of male domination. It is not clear whether women rear children because they have low status, or whether they have low status because they rear children. The idea that one must break up women's monopoly of early child care gives mothering a negative connotation. Rothman suggests that it is more fruitful to encourage nurturant behavior in all—men and women alike—rather than to blame women for their nurturant behavior.

Forms of Motherhood

There is a wide range of child-rearing arrangements around the world. In nonindustrial societies, motherhood is an enterprise for the whole extended family unit, including grandparents, uncles, aunts, and older siblings (Bernard, 1974). For example, Uche Isiugo-Abanihe (1984) points out that 33 percent of Ghanaian mothers and 24 percent of Nigerian mothers reported a child living away from home, usually with relatives, in order to strengthen kinship ties and to reduce economic burdens on families with several children. Less emphasis is put on the biological mother as an exclusive provider of child care.

Single motherhood is prevalent phenomenon not only in the industrialized nations of the West but also in the less developed countries in Africa and South America. For example, about half of rural households and about 40 percent of urban households in Botswana are headed by unmarried, widowed, divorced, or deserted women (van Driel, 1994). These mothers and their families are usually poor, as a result of rapid changes in the economic and social organization of society. There is a lack of male support for women who migrate and hold jobs, and women who stay behind in villages depend on subsistence agriculture and small-scale domestic production.

Traditionally, extended families in much of the colonialized areas of the world provided economic stability, security, and emotional support. Colonization introduced new economic patterns as well as new norms, customs, values, and laws, including changes in the structure of families and the role of the mother. In Jamaica, for example, the common matricentric and matrifocal household type is rooted partially in polygamous west African traditions that assign women the sole responsibility for child care. It is also a product of colonialism, and especially of slavery, which removed the maintenance of families from slave fathers. Furthermore, European men who had intercourse with female slaves often would not acknowledge their offspring. In contemporary Jamaica, the lack of men's participation in children's upbringing is also associated with the low status of women, as well as with internal migration of both women and men in search of work (Brody, 1981).

Changing Motherhood

One important problem for twentieth-century wage economies is the reconciling of motherhood with wage work. This is reflected in the negative relationship between fertility and women's labor force participation. As women entered the wage labor force en masse in the second half of the twentieth century, fertility rates plummeted in the industrialized West. This reflects rising levels of education among women. The more educated women are, the fewer children they tend to want, and the less conservative they are in planning their families. Women who must or prefer to engage in wage labor often suffer conflict and guilt over balancing motherhood and jobs.

With these changes, motherhood has become increasingly politicized in the public arena. The women's movement has drawn attention to policies designed to help women cope with their dual roles of mother and wage worker, including maternity leaves and day-care provision. In addition, technology has invaded the biological aspects of motherhood through the medicalization of motherhood and childbirth, abortion, and innovations in birth control, as well as reproductive technology such as in vitro fertilization and surrogate motherhood, all of which are subject to intense public debate.

See Also

ADOPTION; CHILD CARE; FERTILITY AND FERTILITY TREATMENT; INFERTILITY; MOTHER; MOTHERHOOD: LESBIAN;

PARENTHOOD; PREGNANCY AND BIRTH; REPRODUCTIVE TECHNOLOGIES

References and Further Reading

Adams, Alice. 1995. Maternal bonds: Recent literature on mothering. *Signs* 20: 414–427.

Bernard, Jessie. 1974. *The future of motherhood.* New York: Dial.

Brody, Eugene B. 1981. *Sex, contraception, and motherhood in Jamaica.* Cambridge, Mass.: Harvard University Press.

Hare-Mustin, Rachel T., and Sharon E. Hare. 1986. Family change and the concept of motherhood in China. *Journal of Family Issues* 7: 67–82.

Isiugo-Abanihe, Uche C. 1984. Child fostering and high fertility interrelationships in west Africa. *Studies in Third World Societies* 29: 73–100.

Rich, Adrienne. 1976. *Of women born: Motherhood as experience and institution.* New York: Norton.

Ross, Ellen. 1995. New thoughts on the oldest vocation: Mothers and motherhood in recent feminist scholarship. *Signs* 20: 397–413.

Rothman, Barbara Katz. 1989. *Recreating motherhood: Ideology and technology in a patriarchal society.* New York: Norton.

Thurer, Shari L. 1994. *The myths of motherhood: How culture reinvents the good mother.* Boston and New York: Houghton Mifflin.

van Driel, Francien T. M. 1994. *Poor and powerful: Female-headed households and unmarried motherhood in Botswana.* Saarbrucken: Nijmegen Studies in Development and Cultural Change.

Vappu Tyyska

MOTHERHOOD: Health Issues

See MATERNAL HEALTH AND MORBIDITY.

MOTHERHOOD: Lesbian

In the United States in the late twentieth century, a social movement emerged around the recognition of the role of lesbian and gay parents in "reinventing the family" (Benkov, 1994). Motherhood became an explicit and celebrated choice within lesbian marriages (Martin, 1993). Important academic work and political activism in the lesbian and gay community centered on the issue of lesbians' rights to child custody. Useful legal resources for lesbian mothers include a casebook (Achtenberg, 1992) and a litigation manual (Achtenberg, 1990). The movement has also seen the publication of books for children that address their experiences in gay and lesbian families, like Leslea Newman's *Heather Has Two Mommies* and Michael Willhoite's *Daddy's Roommate,* both published by Alyson Wonderland in Boston.

Ellen Lewin views the struggle for recognition of the "rightful place for lesbian mothers in the feminist reexamination of the family" as allied with the larger issue of the needs of female-headed households in general. In her view, "Research needs to be more sociological and structural than psychological, shifting concern from how the mother's sexuality or the absence of a father would affect the children's development to the ways in which the daily lives of lesbian and heterosexual female-headed families would tend to coincide" (1993: 3–4).

Issues that have emerged with the recognition of gay and lesbian families as alternative and "normal" families include the political and ideological nature of conventional definitions of family, the former invisibility of lesbian and gay families in family research and in the public consciousness, the relationship of lesbian and gay families to wider lesbian and gay culture and community, intergenerational issues of the relationship of lesbian and gay families to their "families of origin," and social myths and concerns about role confusion and gender identity among children in lesbian and gay families (Laird, 1993).

See Also

HOUSEHOLDS: FEMALE-HEADED AND FEMALE-SUPPORTED; LESBIANISM; MARRIAGE: LESBIAN; MOTHER; MOTHERHOOD; PARENTHOOD

References and Further Reading

Achtenberg, Roberta. 1990. *Lesbian mother litigation manual.* 2nd ed. San Francisco, Calif.: National Center for Lesbian Rights.

———. 1992. *Lesbians and child custody: A casebook.* New York: Garland.

Benkov, Laura. 1994. *Reinventing the family: The emerging story of lesbian and gay parents.* New York: Crown.

Laird, Joan. 1993. Lesbian and gay families. In Froma Walsh, ed., *Normal family processes,* 2nd ed., 282–328. New York: Guilford.

Lewin, Ellen. 1993. *Lesbian mothers: Accounts of gender in American culture.* Ithaca, N.Y.: Cornell University Press.

Martin, April. 1993. *The lesbian and gay parenting handbook: Creating and raising our families.* New York: Harper Perennial.

Karen Frojen Herrera

MULTICULTURALISM

Is Multiculturalism Bad for Women? That is the title of a relatively recent collection of essays (Cohen et al., 1999), and its succinct formulation is eliciting many responses. There are many versions of multiculturalism throughout the world, formed by different histories. There have always been migrations and diasporas, but after two world wars and many other armed conflicts during the twentieth century, the mixing of peoples within political borders increasingly renders traditional national models obsolete.

Definitions and Categories

The concept of multiculturalism was developed by nations and other aspirants to geopolitical cohesiveness as a strategy to represent themselves as homogeneous, despite their inclusion of people from varied ethnic, cultural, and linguistic groups. For cultural analysts, the politics of representation is at the heart of multiculturalism; for sociologists, a major concern is the specifics of legislation and public policy and their often arbitrary implementation—a sphere in which women are strongly affected. Multiculturalism may also be invoked as a way of signaling a community's divergence from the notional monoculturalism often wrongly identified with "the West" or "Europe."

Multiculturalism is a concept associated with minorities, and this implies a relationship with a majority; however, how these two categories are defined and applied in relation to each other is controversial. Defining multiculturalism is further complicated by differences between developed capitalist societies and the third world or developing world—for example, between the European community and "settler societies." In general, the minorities are organized by such categories as race, ethnicity, and indigeneity, and their presence is causally linked to migration, colonization, and other forms of subjugation. All these ways of identifying groups are problematic.

It is more accurate to refer to processes of *racialization* involved in representing minorities than to assume the existence of clear-cut "races." *Ethnicity* was originally used as a defining term in order to avoid using *race,* with its implications of now discredited "scientific" racism; *ethnicity* was also easier to attach to the European migrations that surrounded the world wars. In North America, phrases such as *visible minorities* (in Canada) and *people of color* (in the United States) were introduced to categorize non-European immigrants in the mass diasporas; these also encompassed Native Americans and the descendants of African slaves. Hence, multiculturalism is often perceived as a covert way to indicate racialized differences.

The need to deconstruct the "natural" facade of racialization is clear when we recall that such groups as Ukrainians in Canada and Greeks and Italians in Australia were once designated "black" (Gunew, 1994). The picture is also complicated by the presence of oppressed indigenous groups: in Australia, some Aborigines refuse to be included in multicultural discourses on the ground that these refer only to cultures of migration; in New Zealand, *biculturalism* is the preferred official term, because the notion of multiculturalism is seen as diverting attention from the Maori sovereignty movement. In Canada, the indigenous groups—called the First Nations—are occasionally included in multicultural discourses and practices, but they are also consistently trapped between the two "founding nations," French and English. This has produced continuing debates on *cultural appropriation,* the act of adopting another culture's emblematic characteristics (Crosby, 1994).

State and Critical Multiculturalism

We can distinguish between *state multiculturalism,* which addresses the management of diversity, and *critical multiculturalism,* which is used by minorities as a lever to gain participation in the public sphere on the strength of their differences. Minorities use various strategies to overcome the assimilationist presumptions of most state multiculturalism. Essential to both concepts, however, is the notion of "community," a sphere in which women are particularly affected.

State multiculturalism is a successor of assimilation—the "melting pot" ideal in which immigrant minorities adopt patterns from the majority—and of integration, in which separate communities move toward common values. It is often held to represent a kind of liberal pluralism that assumes a hidden norm from which minority groups diverge, and to disregard prevailing power differentials (Goldberg, 1994; Yuval-Davis, 1997). State multiculturalism operates most clearly in the theories and practices of education, sociology, law, and immigration, but it tends to be contradictory in both assumptions and applications. In education, it is often manifest in the celebration of cultural differences as apolitical ethnic accessories displayed in multicultural festivals of costumes, foods, and music. This liberal framework may be racked by dilemmas, as it was in

France in the 1990s, when Muslim schoolgirls were barred from wearing headscarves in the classroom. This precipitated a debate in which the traditional left aligned with the far right because both identified Islam with religious bigotry that was supposedly at odds with the secular, rationalist values of the French republic (Silverman, 1992).

In sociology and immigration studies, the "migrant problem" and "minority problem" are common themes. There is considerable emphasis of compatible differences and the minority's need to obey the host country's laws and conform to its mores. Despite professed tolerance, the minority is often represented as primitive or uncivilized, importing its social pathologies—for example, criminal gangs, arranged marriage, or clitoridectomy.

Women and Multiculturalism

In all these approaches, the "community" is taken as the locus of cultural difference, and within it, women are rarely accorded agency. In the exceptional cases where they are, as in the women's movement, other internal differences such as class loyalties tend to be suppressed (Ali, 1997). Communities of a diaspora are often characterized by outsiders as static and ahistorical (Yuval-Davis, 1997); even internally, compensatory nostalgia may lead to rather rigid constructions of perceived traditions, particularly those associated with the struggle to maintain religious beliefs. In such situations, women are often designated the bearers of tradition but are not granted agency in their interpretation, or as community leaders (Cohen et al., 1999).

A telling example of how women can be caught between the forces of the majority nation and their immigrant tradition is provided by the case of Shahbano, a 73-year-old divorced Muslim woman who was awarded spousal maintenance by the High Court of India after a ten-year legal battle. This led to accusations by India's Muslim minority that their constitutional right to judge family matters under Islamic law (*Shari'a*) was being undermined by the Hindu majority. Shahbano herself eventually rejected the court's decision in what was interpreted as an act of Muslim solidarity. As Pathak and Rajan (1992) point out, apparent respect for minority rights can trap women between the private and public spheres. It remains to be seen how the European Community will legislate to deal with minority communities within separate nations and with differences among its member nations.

Future Directions

Multiculturalism implies a focus on culture—understood as intellectual and artistic production—and this can can occlude or minimize historical events and political movements. Hazel Carby (1992) notes that academic emphasis on black women's texts can function as a substitute for actual social relations or the continuing work of desegregation and antiracism.

There is also a danger that, within multicultural initiatives, minorities may internalize "identity politics"—the expectation that all members of an identified group share not only history and language but also beliefs and goals. This can lead to competition among groups and the construction of a hierarchy of legitimation based on degrees of oppression, and eventually to a backlash and to accusations of "political correctness" and "thought police" from the watching majority.

The future of critical multiculturalism depends on awareness of the inherent "hybridity" and diverse affiliations of all the subjects that may be mobilized by specific projects and events. Provisional coalitions can be built around "mutual and reciprocal relativization" (Shohat and Stam, 1994). The meaning and symbolic force of multiculturalism, as well as its mechanisms of implementation, are produced within specific contexts. Multiculturalism is a two-edged sword: it can be invoked to counter exclusionary, hegemonic practices, but its appeal to nostalgic histories can reinstate a conservative status quo that is rarely beneficial to women.

See Also

COMMUNITY POLITICS; ETHNICITY; IMMIGRATION; SETTLER SOCIETIES; MULTICULTURALISM: ARTS, LITERATURE, AND POPULAR CULTURE

References and Further Reading

Ali, Yasmin. 1992. Muslim women and the politics of ethnicity and culture in northern England. In Gita Saghal and Nira Yuval-Davis, eds., *Refusing holy orders: Women and fundamentalism in Britain,* 101–123. London: Virago.

Carby, Hazel. 1992. The multicultural wars. In Gina Dent, ed., *Black popular culture,* 187–199. Seattle, Wash.: Bay.

Cohen, Joshua, Matthew Howard, and Martha Nussbaum, eds. 1999. *Is multiculturalism bad for women? Susan Mollor Okin with respondents.* Princeton, N.J.: Princeton University Press.

Crosby, Marcia. 1994. Construction of the imaginary Indian. In Wendy Waring, ed., *By, for, and about: Feminist cultural politics,* 85–113. Toronto: Women's Press.

Goldberg, David Theo. 1994. Introduction: Multicultural conditions. In D. T. Goldberg, ed., *Multiculturalism: A critical reader,* 1–41. Oxford: Blackwell.

Gunew, Sneja. 1994. *Framing marginality: Multicultural literary studies.* Melbourne: Melbourne University Press.

Pathak, Zakia, and Rajeswari Sunder Rajan. 1992. Shahbano. In Judith Butler and Joan W. Scott, eds., *Feminists theorize the political,* 257–290. New York: Routledge.

Shohat, Ella, and Robert Stam. 1994. *Unthinking Eurocentrism: Multiculturalism and the media.* London: Routledge.

Silverman, Max. 1992. *Deconstructing the nation: Immigration, racism and citizenship in modern France.* London: Routledge.

Yuval-Davis, Nira. 1997. *Gender and nation.* London: Sage.

Sneja Gunew

MULTICULTURALISM: Arts, Literature, and Popular Culture

As multiculturalism becomes a social reality in most countries of the world, differentiating multicultural arts from the general category of the arts becomes increasingly difficult. Multicultural arts are usually defined as those associated with artists and communities not of the dominant culture; they also can be examples of collaboration between dominant and minority cultures. Many multicultural artists and practitioners struggle with tokenistic representation, restricted funding, and overdetermination of content and style in audiences' expectations.

On the one hand, multicultural arts are expected to exemplify the exotic for the dominant culture and thus to reflect the host society's toleration and appreciation for "other" cultures. On the other hand, multicultural arts can be vibrant, challenging, and hungry interventions in the shaping of national identities and representations. It is often within texts of multicultural arts that the sharpest critiques of nationalism and society occur. This probably explains why, within studies of national arts, there is a marked resistance to multicultural forms, authors, and practitioners. National cohesion is encouraged by the ease with which dominant cultures can sideline or co-opt multicultures, but it is also threatened by the gathering momentum of these "other" representations and perspectives as communities and individuals develop their artistic confidence. For women artists and practitioners in particular, community values can dictate the types of participation available to them if they wish to gain or maintain the support and encouragement of their own communities.

Defining Multiculturalism

When we use the term *multiculturalism* with regard to the arts, an important demarcation is whether we are discussing official multiculturalism (such as the forms found in Canada and Australia) or descriptive multiculturalism (the mixing of cultures found in any country). In many nations, especially those in which multiculturalism is officially promoted, multicultural arts have been viewed as inferior and compromised. They often are not considered challenging, excellent, or particularly creative—they are thought to be merely reflective of the cultures from which the artists or styles come. The desire for the "other's" viewpoint often does not extend beyond a few best-selling novels, one different face reading the news, and someone with an accent in an advertisement. The tokenistic melding of these elements is most often referred to as *cosmopolitanism,* the practice of experiencing the world in bite-sized (and, increasingly, byte-sized) pieces.

Multiculturalism is in many ways a more powerful and loaded term than *cosmopolitanism* because it refers to difference within a nation not as an individual choice but as a political and cultural reality. Multiculturalism, however, can also be perceived as compromising artistic integrity by dictating the boundaries of available representation and thus signaling the burden of "authenticity" or "ethnicity" that artists from non-mainstream cultures must negotiate. These suspicions and undervaluations continue even though some of these communities have had continuous representation in the population over many generations. Considering this extended presence, it is not surprising that multicultural work not only represents immigrant tales but also includes productions that extend the boundaries of what any arts can be.

Criticism of Multicultural Arts

The minority status of ethnic communities often means that the majority believes that their literary and other creative works are of interest and benefit only to their source communities. Criticism of multicultural arts in most national contexts has taken place largely in historical and sociological scholarship. With preconceived ideas of what certain ethnic groups are "really like," critics viewed their literature as documentary evidence of their opinions and ways of living. Many critics read multicultural texts only as examples of personal narratives, incapable of irony, devoid of style, and inadmissible to national literary canons. Women artists have even more limited horizons; the narrow history of women's arts always tends to shunt their work into "life-writing." Many establishment narratives in the arts for various communities (out of necessity) seek to legitimize the presence of the artist's community or family. Many editors have attempted to extend narrow reading practices by bringing together works they believe are good literary examples (battling the stereotype that multicultural writing is bad writing). Other anthologies are designed to display the fascinating diversity of a nation's writers.

The knowledge that ethnicity, as a category, can be manipulated confuses identity ascription. It also can devalue multicultural arts because of the view that the area cannot be trusted to offer a form of cultural truth. In contrast, this knowing manipulation can also leave space for alternative responses and challenges for identity and community politics. What is needed in discussions of the multicultural arts is constant questioning of the terms *ethnic* and *community.* Especially crucial is the question of who is representing whom, given the nature of gender relations in many ethnic communities and the overwhelming predominance of male representatives for multicultural communities in most nations. Furthermore, strained relationships often exist between artists and their own ethnic or cultural communities. The nature of artistic endeavor means that boundaries are necessarily pushed and overstepped, sometimes resulting in censure or rejection by ethnic cultural communities.

See Also

IDENTITY POLITICS; MULTICULTURALISM

References and Further Reading

Bennett, David. 1998. *Multicultural states: Rethinking difference and identity.* London and New York: Routledge.

Castles, Stephen, Mary Kalantzis, Bill Cope, and Michael Morrissey. 1992. *Mistaken identity: Multiculturalism and the demise of nationalism in Australia.* Sydney: Pluto.

Clark, Gordon L., Dean Forbes, and Roderick Francis. 1993. *Multiculturalism, difference and postmodernism.* Melbourne: Longman Cheshire.

Goldberg, David Theo, ed. 1994. *Multiculturalism: A reader.* Cambridge, Mass.: Blackwell.

Gordon, Avery F., and Christopher Newfield, eds. 1996. *Mapping multiculturalism.* Minneapolis: University of Minnesota Press.

Gunew, Sneja, and Kateryna Longley. 1997. *Striking chords: Multicultural literary interpretations.* Sydney: Allen and Unwin.

Gunew, Sneja, and Fazal Rizvi. 1994. Introduction. *Culture, difference, and the arts,* xi–xvi. St. Leonards: Allen and Unwin.

Hage, Ghassan. 1998. *White nation: Fantasies of white supremacy in a multicultural society.* Sydney: Pluto.

Hutcheon, Linda, and Marian Richmond, eds. 1990. *Other solitudes: Canadian multicultural fictions.* Toronto: Ontario University Press.

Pizanias, Caterina. 1994. *Making the grade: Multiculturalism and the arts in Canada.* Calgary: Egg.

Shohat, Ella, and Robert Stam. 1994. *Unthinking Eurocentrism: Multiculturalism and the media.* London and New York: Routledge.

Tseen-ling Khoo

MULTINATIONAL CORPORATIONS

A multinational corporation (MNC) or transnational corporation (TNC) is a formal business organization that operates in more than one country. Such an enterprise owns assets, undertakes investments, and produces goods and services around the globe. Multinationals have their origin in the charter companies that spearheaded European conquest and global capitalist expansion beginning in the sixteenth century. They have emerged among the world's most powerful institutions in the current era of globalization. This article provides an overview of the expanding control of multinationals, their impact on women's lives, and the urgent need for a global citizens' movement to regulate their activities.

The imperative of competitive growth driven by the twin forces of capital accumulation and technological expansion has allowed multinationals to penetrate practically every realm of life. They now account for at least two-thirds of world trade. Just one hundred multinationals control one-fifth of all foreign-owned assets in the world. In every sector, from natural resources and food to finance and the media, markets are controlled increasingly by a handful of firms whose net worth is greater than the gross national product (GNP) of many countries in the world. According to Lazlich (1997), three to six giant corporations control more than 80 percent of the global markets in forest products, wheat, copper, iron ore, tin, and bauxite. Five companies control 75 percent of the global vegetable seed market. Ten companies control about 60 percent of the global animal health industry. Ten large banks control 77 percent of global investment capital markets. Four western news agencies control about 90 percent of information provided to newspapers around the world, while four western television and broadcasting networks—Reuters, Worldwide Television, Cable News Network (CNN), and the British Broadcasting Corporation (BBC)—control practically all foreign news distributed to television stations worldwide.

Through billion-dollar mergers and acquisitions (such as the $80-billion merger of the oil companies Exxon and

Mobil in 1998), International Monetary Fund (IMF) and World Bank policies for privatization and deregulation, and new instruments such as the World Trade Organization (WTO), and the Multilateral Agreement on Investment (MAI), multinationals are augmenting their power over nation-states, local economies, and communities at an unprecedented rate. Although "new multinationals" have emerged in recent decades in southeast Asian nations such as Taiwan and Korea, multinational power continues to be concentrated in industrialized countries in the Northern Hemisphere (the "North"). In 1995, 193 of the 200 largest corporations in the world had headquarters in the United States, Japan, and Europe. This reality underlies the problem of widening global inequality. In 1995, the 80 percent or so of the world population that lived in the poor countries of the Southern Hemisphere (the "South") received 15 percent of global income, whereas the 20 percent that lived in the rich "North" received 85 percent of it. Multinational power is also concentrated largely in the hands of men. This exacerbates the feminization of poverty: 70 percent of the world's poor are women.

Alternative Perspectives

Multinationals are widely regarded as a rational and progressive force. They are credited with the economic dynamism and material advancement of the modern world and frequently are viewed as defenders of global democracy and freedom. Many liberal feminists subscribe to this view. They recognize that the benefits of global economic development have accrued mostly to men, and so they call for a fuller integration of women into the global economy as the solution to their subordination. While middle-class women struggle for professional careers and executive positions in corporations, liberal feminism (as represented, for example, by the Women in Development School) advocates the expansion of income-generating work for poor women at the lower levels of the global economic pyramid. The Platform of Action of the 1995 Beijing Women's Conference also seeks gender justice, women's economic empowerment within the MNC paradigm of market and technological growth, and an end to violence against women.

More radical perspectives, however, see multinationals as largely an irrational and destructive force that is responsible for many of the social and ecological problems in the world. The convergence of the perspectives of socialists, ecofeminists, and women of color has produced a powerful critique showing that the MNCs' unbridled growth and relentless pursuit of profit have victimized, not empowered, the majority of the world's women.

Victimization of Women

Women grow more than half the food produced in the countries in the "South." Yet, with the industrialization of agriculture and corporate control over biodiversity, the amount of land and resources available to female subsistence producers is rapidly declining. Large-scale single-crop agriculture and use of sterile genetically engineered cultivars by agribusiness corporations threaten the environment's capacity for renewal and small farmers' ability to continue farming. The large-scale dumping of pesticides and toxic wastes by multinationals poses severe threats to the environment and human health and reproduction. Big dams, structural adjustment, and other policies sponsored by the World Bank also exacerbate gender, race, and class inequalities and threaten the survival of communities.

Global economic restructuring since the 1970s has involved a shifting of multinational production facilities from the "North" to the "South." The reasons for this shift include lax environmental standards and the availability of cheap nonunionized labor—especially "docile" young female labor—in the "South." Faced by high unemployment, many young women clamor for jobs in the electronics and textile factories in the free trade zones operated by multinationals, yet this "feminization of manufacturing" has not provided better working conditions or improved standards of living. On the contrary, many women suffer from health problems and sexual and other forms of harassment. Upon dismissal, lacking transferable skills and labor rights, many women find themselves destitute.

Likewise, population control programs exported from the "North" have not necessarily eradicated poverty or improved the social position of women in the "South." Contraceptives like Norplant and Depo-Provera produced by multinational pharmaceutical companies have helped bring down fertility and population growth rates. However, the use of such experimental, provider-controlled methods in regions that lack basic health care facilities frequently contributes to coercion and abuse.

With nothing but their bodies and bodily services to sell, many young men and women enter the expanding service sector of the global economy known as the "skin trade," which includes billion-dollar multinational enterprises such as pornography and prostitution. Ultimately, corporate power is maintained partly through the media and militarism. Media images presenting women as sex objects disempower women, robbing them of alternative self-enhancing images.

The victimization of women is perhaps most evident in situations of war. Seventy-five percent of the refugees of armed conflicts in the 1990s were women and children. The weapons for these wars, which are being fought mostly in the countries of the "South," are supplied by defense companies based mostly in the "North." Indeed, defense is the largest sector of the global economy. The prosperity and power of the industrialized "North," and the United States in particular, rest ultimately on the competitive advantage of their defense companies.

Toward Empowerment

A wide spectrum of local and international efforts has arisen to challenge the hegemony of the multinationals. There are campaigns to halt the production of nuclear weaponry and genetically engineered food, to ban pornography and child labor, and to eliminate the World Bank and the World Trade Organization. Many of these efforts are led by women: farmers and environmental activists in India struggle to stop the spread of new seed varieties and dam projects; young workers in the free trade zones in southeast Asia demand labor rights; indigenous women in the United States organize against uranium mining and toxic-waste dumping; and victims of corporate disasters sue for reparations.

What is urgently needed is the consolidation of these separate struggles into a worldwide nonviolent movement to impose ethical, social, and ecological criteria on multinational policymaking and action. Through such measures as consumer boycotts, socially and environmentally responsible investing, campaigns to reform electoral finance, and resistance against war taxes, citizens in the "North" can play a leading role in the effort to regulate the multinationals. Most women and men in the "South" do not enjoy the freedom, resources, or leisure needed for this kind of activism. In this era of corporate empires, the democratization of multinationals needs to be the central organizing strategy of progressive social change movements. It is doubtful that either environmental sustainability or human rights—including women's rights—can be achieved without a fundamental transformation of the multinationals. This calls for a vision of a new global society where cooperation and survival are valued before corporate competition and profit maximization.

See Also

CAPITALISM; DEVELOPMENT: OVERVIEW; ECONOMY: OVERVIEW; ECONOMY: GLOBAL RESTRUCTURING

References and Further Reading

Bandarage, Asoka. 1984. Women in development: Liberalism, Marxism, and Marxist-feminism. *Development and Change* 15: 495–515.

———. 1997. *Women, population, and global crisis: A political-economic analysis.* London: Zed.

Economic Justice News. Declaration: Addressing the global economic crisis. 1999. *Economic Justice News* 2(1): 12.

Lazlich, Robert S. 1997. *World market share reporter.* Detroit: Gale Research.

Rafi Communiqué. 1999. The gene giants. <http://www.rafi.ca> (posted 3 March).

Verité Monitor. 1999. Verbal, physical, and sexual abuse in the factory. *Verité Monitor* 3 (Fall): 6–7.

Asoka Bandarage

MUSIC: Anglo-American Folk

The tradition that the folk singer Peggy Seeger has called a "water table of cultural expression" (O'Brien, 1995: 176) was originally the music of working rural communities, encompassing sea chanteys, protest songs, and love ballads, among other forms, and handed down from generation to generation. Folk music is a tradition in which women figure strongly, partly because this music, in general, is not commodified or dependent on male patronage. Folk music also offers greater independence to women performers because in its basic form it is acoustic and portable, and therefore economically viable. This article will focus on modern Anglo-American folk performers.

Much folk music reflects women's lives and expresses feminist ideas. Seeger has noted, "There are ballads that talk about ownership of women by fathers, sons, and families, plus women's social positions and rights. There were revenge songs in code showing women to be smarter than men or dressed as men proving themselves just as good in certain situations" (O'Brien, 1995: 176). Seeger—who is the sister of the U.S. folk artists Mike and Pete Seeger and was married to the late Scottish folk singer Ewan MacColl—was one of the first women to become prominent in the folk "revival" of the 1950s and 1960s. She was born in New York but settled in England in the mid-1950s, and over the next forty years she released more than thirty solo albums, specializing in feminist ballads. The varied topics included the Asian women who led a strike against the Grunwick photo-processing plant in the United Kingdom in 1976–1978 and the women peace campers in "Carry Greenham Home."

A leading figure in the postwar folk revival in the United States was Jean Ritchie, a traditional folk singer from Kentucky who accompanied herself on the dulcimer. Her parents collected songs and were visited by the British folklorist Cecil Sharp. Ritchie was recorded by the Texan archivists John and Alan Lomax, and in 1946 she recorded for their Library of Congress Archive. She also performed with the Weavers, Woody Guthrie, and Oscar Brand. Delving into the songs of the Appalachian mountains, where she grew up, Ritchie (like Peggy Seeger) did much to keep folk traditions alive; she was also on the original board of directors of the Newport Folk Festival.

By the 1960s, audiences seemed hungry for authentic, "unplugged" music, and folk reached a wider popular public. Female artists during these years concentrated on musical innovation. The French-Canadian sisters Kate and Anna McCarrigle fused folk rhythms with Cajun music from Louisiana; Joni Mitchell, another Canadian, combined folk-inspired songwriting with jazz. Other women artists—notably, in the United States, Joan Baez and the black gospel-based singer and guitarist Odetta—used folk more as a form of political protest. Folk music of the 1960s took on a radical tinge after it was taken up by the U.S. Communist Party as the music of roots and revolt. Joan Baez, in particular, found in folk a voice of emotional integrity that spoke to a younger generation protesting against the Vietnam War and the right-wing legacy of the 1950s, when Senator Joseph McCarthy had led a notorious crusade against domestic communism. Baez was a prominent activist and was often described as the "yin" (feminine) to Bob Dylan's "yang" (masculine). Her popularity and her musical production declined in the 1970s, when commercial folk music was being eclipsed by punk, disco, and loud guitar rock; but around 1985 she made women's acoustic songwriting important again.

Suzanne Vega, another figure of note, was a veteran of the folk scene in Greenwich Village in New York City; as a child, she had sung at Pete Seeger's knee. Vega had the ability to combine the pared-down narrative approach of folk with the pop sound of the late 1980s, and her two successful record albums *Suzanne Vega* and *Solitude Standing* began a wave of folk-inspired performance by other artists. Michelle Shocked's *Texas Campfire Tapes* (1987), which became a worldwide success, was produced with a pocket-side audiocassette recorder. Tracy Chapman, a former street musician from Cambridge, Massachusetts, who wore dreadlocks, sang songs of love and protest that sold in the millions around 1988.

In the late 1980s, new audiences for folk music began to rediscover earlier artists such as Baez and Judy Collins in the United States and Anne Briggs, Maddy Prior (who had been a vocalist with Steeleye Span), June Tabor, and Frankie Armstrong in Great Britain. Country music, a genre with roots in folk music, also enjoyed a revival. Established country performers such as Dolly Parton and "new traditionalists" such as Nanci Griffith and Mary Chapin Carpenter had a more urban style of storytelling.

In the 1990s, world music opened up new possiblities for folk and new defininitions of folk—much as it did for rock. Women like Mari Boine, a Sami (Lapp); Emma Junaro, from Bolivia; and Talitha Mackenzie, from the Scottish highlands, combined music from indigenous communities with western pop.

See Also

LESBIAN POPULAR MUSIC; MUSIC: SOUL, JAZZ, RAP, BLUES, AND GOSPEL; MUSIC: COMPOSERS; MUSICIANS

References

Armstrong, Frankie. 1992. As far as the eye can sing. London: Women's Press.

Baez, Joan. 1988. *And a voice to sing with.* London: Century Hutchinson.

Gavin, James. 1992. For baby, the circle comes back around. *International Herald Tribune* (2 December).

Mellers, Wilfrid. 1986. *Angels of the night: Popular female singers of our time.* New York and Oxford: Blackwell.

O'Brien, Lucy. 1995. *She bop: The definitive history of women in rock, pop, and soul.* New York and London: Penguin.

Ritchie, Jean. 1997. *Celebration of life.* New York: Music Sales.

Romalis, Shelly. 1998. *Pistol-packin' mama: Aunt Molly Jackson and the politics of folk song.* Music in American Life Series. Champaign: University of Illinois Press.

Stanton, Phil, ed. 1999. *Irish folk music: The Rough Guide.* London: Rough Guide.

Lucy O'Brien.

MUSIC: Composers

Women in Music Before the Nineteenth Century

The earliest acclaimed women composers of music in the western classical tradition were also poets: the Greek Sappho (seventh century B.C.) is probably the first, followed by Hildegard of Bingen, abbess of Rupertsberg (1098–1179). Some music by women also is found among that of the troubadours and trouvères of the twelfth and thirteenth centuries. In the sixteenth century, women composers were principally performers. In Italy, Francesca Caccini (1587–after 1638), the first woman known to have composed opera (*La liberazione de Ruggiero dall'isola d'Alcina,* Florence, 1625), produced one of the largest and most varied collections of early monody; extant music by Barbara Strozzi (1619–after 1664) includes ariettas, arias, and cantatas for solo voice. In France, the career of Elisabeth-Claude Jacquet de la Guerre (1665–1729), a child prodigy as a harpsichordist and composer, was encouraged by Louis XIV, who permitted her to dedicate her publications to him. In the next century, the Italian composer, violinist, and singer Maddelena Lombardini Sirmen (1745–1818) performed throughout Europe; her violin music was praised by many, including Leopold Mozart. In France in 1792, Julie Candeille (1767–1834) took the title role in her *Catherine, ou la belle fermière* at the *Théâtre Français,* singing and playing in 154 performances. In England, women composers included the singer Harriet Abrams (c. 1758–c. 1822) and the virtuoso keyboard players Mary Jane Guest (c. 1765–after 1814). Jane Savage (fl. 1780–1790) and Maria F. Parke (1772 or 1773–1822), as well as members of two illustrious families: Maria Barthélemon (c. 1749–1799) and her daughter Cecilia (1769 or 1770–after 1840); Katerina (1769–1833) and Sophia Dussek (1775–1847); and Sophia Dussek's daughter, Olivia Buckley (c. 1795–after 1845).

Nineteenth-Century Composers

The two best-known women composers of the nineteenth century, Fanny Mendelssohn (1805–1847) and Clara Wieck Schumann (1819–1896), also came from established musical families. Mendelssohn's output comprises about 500 compositions. Her only known public appearance was in 1838, at a charity benefit where she played a piano concerto by her brother Felix, although she often performed in the salon. Schumann, however, was a concert pianist. She bore her husband Robert eight children and resumed her career after his death in 1856. Almost all her works were published. Other nineteenth-century women composers include the singer Pauline Viardot (1821–1910), Viardot's eldest daughter Louise (1841–1918), and Louise Farrenc (1804–1875). Later in the century, Cécile Chaminade (1857–1944) wrote approximately 400 compositions, nearly all of which were published in her lifetime; in 1913, she was awarded the Legion d'Honneur. In the same year, Lili Boulanger (1893–1918) became the first woman to win the Prix de Rome at the Paris Conservatoire—with her cantata, *Faust et Hélène.* She died in 1918, leaving her opera, *La Princess Maleine,* unfinished.

Maude Valerie White (1855–1937) and Liza Lehmann (1862–1918), although among Britain's foremost composers of song at the turn of the twentieth century, remain in the shadow of Dame Ethel Smyth (1858–1944). The second of Smyth's six operas, *Der Wald,* was performed in Berlin in 1902, in Covent Garden three months later, and at the Metropolitan Opera House, New York, in 1903. Her third, *The Wreckers,* is generally considered her masterpiece. Smyth also wrote 10 books, mostly autobiographical. Opera composers of this time in Russia include Ella Adayevskaya (1846–1926) and Valentina Serova (1846–1924), wife of the composer Alexander Serov.

In the United States, Mary Ann Pownall (1751–1796), an English actress, published songs in New York in 1794. In 1864, a *Select Catalogue of Mrs. E. A. Parkhurst's Compositions,* mostly popular songs and parlor piano pieces, was issued by a New York publisher, Horace Waters. Constance Runcie (1836–1911), raised in New Harmony, Indiana, was probably the first American woman to compose in large forms; she paved the way for Margaret Ruthven Lang (1867–1962), Amy Marcy Beach (1867–1944), and Emma Roberto Steiner (1850–1928), all of whose works were played at the World's Columbian Exhibition in Chicago. The first two enjoyed careers that included performances by major orchestras—in particular Beach, whose *Gaelic Symphony* was performed by the Boston Symphony Orchestra in 1896. Steiner is said to have conducted more than 6,000 performances of operas and operettas and several concerts of her own works. Mary Carr Moore (1887–1957) completed her opera *Narcissa* in 1911, conducting it in Seattle (1912), in San Francisco (1925), and—many years later—in Los Angeles (1945).

Women in Music in the Twentieth Century

In the twentieth century, women have contributed to every important musical movement and style. Abstract modernism was espoused by Ruth Crawford (1901–1953), whose *String Quartet* (1931) is a shining example of the style, and by Rebecca Clarke (1886–1979), whose *Viola Sonata* has likewise entered the canon. Elisabeth Lutyens (1906–1983) in England and Barbara Pentland (b. 1912) in Canada were noted serialists. Other women—including Germaine Tailleferre (1892–1983), the only female member of *Les Six;* the Americans Louise Talma (b. 1906) and Miriam Gideon (b. 1906); the Polish composer Grazyna Bacewicz (1909–1969); and the British composer Elisabeth Maconchy (b. 1907)—eschewed rigorous precompositional systems and turned instead to neoclassicism. The style of many of these women cannot be rigidly defined. The Russian Galina Ustvolskaya (b. 1919), for instance, although influenced by neoclassicism, has—like her younger compatriot, Sofia Gubaidulina (b. 1931)—developed a distinctive voice, quite outside the mainstream. And, as the language of abstract modernism has changed, so has that of the composers who espoused it, such as the Americans Ellen Taaffe Zwilich (b. 1939) and Joan Tower (b. 1938).

Women also have helped to broaden the horizons of twentieth-century music. Like the nineteenth-century Queen of Hawaii, Lili'uokalani (1838–1917), many women of other cultures have been educated in the western musical tradition; some, such as Kimi Sato (b. Japan, 1949, the first non-French recipient of the Prix de Rome), have adopted a western language; others—such as Younghi Pagh-Paan (b. 1945), a Korean living in Germany—have actively striven to fuse contrasting styles. Some have inherited two cultures simultaneously, like Gillian Whitehead (b. 1941), who is part Maori, and the African-American Florence Price (1887–1953). At the same time, western-born women composers have looked beyond their own culture. Lily Strickland (1887–1958) turned to African-American, Indian classical, and—like Catherine Urner (1891–1942)—Native American music; the South African Priaulx Rainier (1903–1986) was influenced by the language and music of the Zulus; the Australian Peggy Glanville-Hicks (1912–1990) drew on Hindu sources for her first opera, *The Transposed Heads* (1953). Many western composers have found Balinese and Javanese music a rich trove. The logical goal of such a merging process is "musical eclecticism." The Australian Florence Ewart (1864–1949), writing before World War II, drew on sources including Verdi, Bizet, and Puccini, Greek classical references, American Indian melodies, Corsican folk songs, and an Indian *rektah.* Later eclectics include the Russian song composer Alexandra Pakhmutova (b. 1929), the American Sheila Silver (b. 1946), and the Canadian Alexina Louie (b. 1949). Judith Weir (b. 1954), although writing in a noneclectic musical style, has used texts ranging from an early Icelandic saga to Chinese Yuan dramas, as well as several from her own Scottish tradition.

Women composers have made a significant contribution to the development of the medium in the twentieth century. They have helped not only to extend the range of existing instruments, particularly the human voice (Joan La Barbara, b. 1947, and Cathy Berberian, 1925–1983), but also have added others, including folk instruments (for example, the *bayan* in Gubaidulina's *Seven Last Words,* 1982) and newly invented ones (Lucia Dlugoszewski's "timbre piano," Laurie Anderson's tape-bow violin, and Annea Lockwood's "glass concert"). Women also have helped to develop electronic music; for instance, Bebe Barron in the United States was a coauthor of the music for the film *Forbidden Planet* in 1956, and Daphne Oram was a cofounder of the BBC Radiophonic Workshop in Britain in 1958.

Although women composers have contributed to every aspect of the composition of western art music, until recently historians and critics viewed them as marginal figures. Now that the number of women composers, teachers, and role models is burgeoning, the need to define and acknowledge the female composer's contribution—not only by critics, but also by women composers themselves—has become urgent.

References and Further Reading

Ammer, Christine. 1980. *Unsung: A history of women in American music.* Westport, Conn.: Greenwood.

Bowers, Jane, and Judith Tick, eds. 1986. *Women making music: The western art tradition, 1150–1950.* Urbana: University of Illinois Press.

Citron, Marcia. 1993. *Gender and the musical canon.* Cambridge: Cambridge University Press.

Cohen, Aaron L. 1987. *International encyclopedia of women composers.* 2nd ed. New York: Books and Music.

Lefanu, Nicola. 1987. Master musicians: An impregnable taboo? *Contact* 31: 4–8.

Lepage, Jane Weiner, ed. 1980. *Women composers, conductors and musicians of the twentieth century: Selected biographies.* New Jersey: Scarecrow.

McClary, Susan. 1990. *Feminine endings.* Minneapolis: Minnesota University Press.

Pendle, Karin, ed. 1990. *Women and music: A history.* Bloomington: Indiana University Press.

Sadie, Julie Anne, and Rhian Samuel, eds. 1994. *The new Grove dictionary of women composers.* London: Macmillan.

Zaimont, J. L., C. Overhauser, and J. Gottlieb, eds. 1984–1991. *The musical women: An international perspective.* Westport, Conn.: Greenwood.

Rhian Samuel

MUSIC: Drumming

See DRUMMING.

MUSIC: East Asia

Religious philosophy has been a powerful force shaping gender relations in east Asian society. In China, Korea, and Japan in particular, Confucianism has influenced the strict gender division that persists today. As a result of Confucian ideals, women are often relegated to the home and act as primary caregivers in the family, while men are responsible for providing for the family through work in the public sphere. Thus men continue to enjoy more opportunities in business, government, and, of course, professional music. Although these expectations have changed over time and continue to change today, throughout much of east Asia women still do not have opportunities to perform certain music professionally, and thus their contributions to music in general have often been ignored. There is a lack of information on women and music in east Asia, but we can gain a sense of their role by examining traditional, folk, and popular genres.

Traditional Music

East Asian traditional music includes many theatrical genres, most notably *kabuki* in Japan and Peking (Beijing) opera in China. In these genres, historically, women were either legally banned or socially discouraged from performing onstage, even if they had been significantly involved in the initial development of a theatrical form. As a result, in *kabuki* and Peking opera males often perform both male and female roles. Despite the legal and social pressure not to perform onstage, women found ways to participate through the many concert genres that developed from the major theatrical forms. For example, Coaldrake (1997: 14) discusses women who performed in *gidayū,* a type of musical narrative associated with Japanese *bunraku*—puppet theater. According to Coaldrake, although women were banned from public stage performance from 1629 to 1877, they were very successful as professional *gidayū* performers in a concert setting, but such performances were less celebrated than the original theatrical genre.

Another reason for the difficulty women have faced in performing traditional arts relates to music education. In Japan, for example, traditional arts historically have been passed from generation to generation through the *iemoto* system, by which musical expertise and professional titles were transmitted primarily from male to male within families. Women contributed greatly to the development of the arts, but often a talented woman could not take her father's professional name. Linda Fujie gives an example of one such woman, O-Yo (1840–1901; the instrument mentioned in this passage, the *shamisen,* is a three-stringed lute):

> The daughter of the head master of *kiyomoto* (a style of *shamisen* music used in *kabuki*), O-Yo was an excellent musician. As a woman, she was not allowed to take over her father's position after his death; instead she married a man who then inherited his title. But O-Yo took up most of his duties. O-Yo was not allowed to play the *shamisen* on the *kabuki* stage, since only males appeared there. She was, nevertheless, an active performer at private parties in teahouses and restaurants. . . . O-Yo herself was an important transmitter of the *kiyomoto* tradition of her father, teaching it to many people from all parts of Japan. (1992: 335)

Women like O-Yo were active participants in teaching such art forms to men who could perform professionally, thus preserving the tradition.

Women were also actively involved as courtesans in the performance of traditional music in east Asia. In Korea, for example, *kisaeng,* female court entertainers, learned court instrumental music, songs, and dancing. The *kisaeng* had low status, and their family background was insignificant, but their contribution to Korean music and dance was important: "It was through *kisaeng* that the songs and dances of the court music (called *yoak,* 'female music') were carried beyond the palace and transmitted to the general public" (Lee, 1980: 201). In Japan, too, traditional music was historically performed by courtesans and *geisha,* who continue to be well-trained in dance, singing, and often the *shamisen,* which they use to accompany such song forms as *kouta* (Fujie, 1992: 337). According to Nora Yeh, both elite men and women courtesans historically performed *nanyin,* a type of Chinese vocal music (1990: 157–172). *Nanyin* song texts often deal with "love between men and women, tragic separations and the unfortunate fate of women" (158). Although both men and women have performed *nanyin,* Yeh argues that "beyond entertainment and self-expression, the *nanyin* tradition has served to edify women. Equally useful was singing as a veiled way of entreating men not to mistreat women and to be conscientious or sympathetic toward their needs" (158). Yeh emphasizes the creative freedom available through singing in an often oppressive social situation. *Nanyin* performance continues today, and young women may participate until they are married, when they are expected to devote all their attentions to family duties.

Folk Music

Women performers have also been important in folk genres. In Korea, for example, many women serve as shamans, and much music is associated with shamanistic rituals, though the role of women in this music is unclear. The Korean vocal genre *p'ansori*—in which a single person tells a dramatic story, sometimes lasting from four to eight hours—was originally performed only by men; but the scholar Sin Chae-hyo (1817–1884) began training female performers, and there are still women *p'ansori* singers today (Lee, 1980: 207). Women have also been actively involved in Japanese folk song, *minyo,* and their particular vocal style has helped to define the unique sound of Okinawan folk music.

Popular Music:

Throughout east Asia, women have been well represented in popular music, although it is often difficult to determine which women have been artistically autonomous and which have been creations of the male-dominated music industry. Several female artists have contributed to developing a distinct sound in Korean popular music (Fisher and Kawakami, 1994: 471). Lee Sun-hee, a prominent popular musician, "has brought issues of real importance into her songs. Typically these often refer back to the period of Japanese occupation, as in her 1992 album, featuring songs recounting the misery of women forced into camps as prostitutes under the occupation—currently a significant political issue between Korea and Japan." Lee Mi-ja, who has remained popular since the 1960s, performs *ponchak* rock, "a Korean combination of sentimental song and danceable beat," and "is so highly regarded as the archetypal voice of the Korean spirit that when the influential *Korea Daily* published a special feature on New Year's Day 1985, entitled 'The Hundred People Who Have Shaped the Republic of Korea,' she was the sole representative of the entertainment world."

Scholarship on Chinese popular music focuses primarily on the expressive possibilities of rock and its potential as voice of resistance. Few women are mentioned in this research, but one Taiwanese singer, Teresa Teng (Deng Lijun), introduced Taiwanese pop songs to mainland China from the late 1970s through the 1980s (Mimic, 1995: 78).

In Japan, women have had considerable commercial success in many areas of mainstream popular music, such as *enka,* a type of sentimental popular song (Clewley, 1994: 459–467). *Takarazuka,* an interesting popular theatrical genre that developed in the early twentieth century, is all-female vaudeville, in which women perform both male and female roles onstage; they often carry their stage personas into everyday life. *Takarazuka* continues to have ardent fans in contemporary Tokyo (Robertson, 1998). Japanese female underground rock groups, such as Super Junky Monkey (now disbanded), have received much attention from the media and academics and represent a growing area of female performance (McClure, 1998; Milioto, 1998).

In Summary

Despite the rapid changes in east Asian society, many traditional genres remain predominantly male, and women must continue to find alternatives. Women seem to have been most successful in playing instruments considered appropriate for female performance by prevailing social systems, or in traditional and popular vocal genres. Nora Yeh (1990: 161) suggests that singing, especially, has given women freedom to express themselves despite societal oppression; although she is referring to *nanyin,* it can also be argued that traditional, folk, and popular music have been a creative outlet for female performers in east Asia. Thus the scarcity of publications on women and music in east Asia reflects not a complete absence of female performers in vocal and instrumental genres but the historical position of women in the private sphere rather than the public sphere. Much work remains to be done on women and music in east Asia.

See Also

MUSIC: COMPOSERS; MUSIC EDUCATION; THEATER: WOMEN IN THEATER

References and Further Reading

Clewley, John. 1994. Enka, Okinawa, and the masters of Clone: The Japanese are coming! In Simon Broughton, Mark Ellingham, David Muddyman, Richard Trillo, and Kim Burton, eds., *The Rough Guide: World music,* 459–467. London: Rough Guides.

Coaldrake, A. Kimi. 1997. *Women's gidayū and the Japanese theatre tradition.* London and New York: Routledge.

Fisher, Paul, and Hideo Kawakami. 1994. Eastern barbarians: The ancient sounds of Korea. In Simon Broughton, Mark Ellingham, David Muddyman, Richard Trillo, and Kim Burton, eds., *The Rough Guide: World music,* 468–472. London: Rough Guides.

Fujie, Linda. 1992. East Asia/Japan. In Jeff Todd Titon, ed., *Worlds of music: An introduction to the music of the world's peoples,* 318–375. New York: Schirmer.

Lee, Byong Won, et al. 1980. Korea. In Stanley Sadie, ed., *The new Grove dictionary of music and musicians,* Vol. 10, 192–208. London: Macmillan.

McClure, Steve. 1998. Where the girls are. In *Nippon pop,* 77-78. Vermont: Tuttle.

Milioto, Jennifer MJ. 1998. Women in Japanese popular music: Setting the subcultural scene. In Mitsui Toru, ed., *Popular music: Intercultural interpretations,* 485–498. Japan: Kanazawa University.

Mimic, Peter. 1995. A bit of this and that: Notes on pop/rock genres in the eighties in China. *CHIME Journal* 76–95.

Robertson, Jennifer. 1998. *Takarazuka: Sexual politics and popular culture in modern Japan.* Berkeley: University of California Press.

Yeh, Nora. 1990. Wisdom of ignorance: Women performers in the classical Chinese music traditions. In Marcia Herndon and Susanne Ziegler, eds., *Music, gender, and culture,* 157–172. Wilhelmshaven: Noetzel.

Jennifer MJ Milioto

MUSIC: Education

Women and girls are successful in music education but form a small minority in many professional realms of music. How and why this reversal takes place is one area of research in gender and music education studies. The gendered musical practices and values of girls, boys, and teachers; the gendered content of the music curriculum; and the gendered nature of pedagogy, assessment, and evaluation are being studied from psychological, sociological, and philosophical perspectives.

Women and Girls in Music Education

In many countries with formal education systems, the curriculum is based on western classical music. This applies not only to the West but also to places as far apart as Brazil, Ghana, Hong Kong, and Singapore. The majority of classroom teachers and specialist instrumental teachers are women. This situation can be traced back to the eighteenth century, when domestic music-making was seen as a feminine accomplishment (Ehrlich, 1985). Playing the piano and singing, in particular, were believed to enhance the marriage prospects of young women. For women who did not marry, teaching music was one of the few respectable alternatives. In higher education, however, women lecturers are few; they are most prominent in areas that have traditionally been female strongholds, such as singing, piano playing, and teacher training.

The precedence of classical music as a feminine accomplishment persists in many countries where girls rather than boys are still encouraged to learn an instrument in the home. Consequently, at school, girls form the majority of school choirs, bands, and orchestras and take optional music courses and activities in much greater numbers than boys. Research conducted in England (Green, 1997) and Canada (Hanley, 1998) suggests that teachers in those countries perceive girls as considerably more interested and involved than boys in school musical activities. However, boys dominate in at least two areas: popular music and music technology (Colley et al., 1993; Green, 1997).

Scholarship

Early work in the 1970s focused on differences between girls' and choices of boys' instruments, and this is still an active research area (see O'Neill, 1997). In general, girls tend to choose instruments that are associated with classical music, are high-pitched, or have a history of being played by females; therefore, the piano, violin, and flute feature strongly. In contrast, boys choose instruments that are associated with popular music and that are loud, low, or conventionally associated with masculinity, such as drums, trombone, or electric guitar. By the late 1980s, work on gendered instrument choice had been joined by appeals for the inclusion of women musicians and music by women in the curriculum, to counteract an earlier exclusive focus on male musicians and their works. These developments were closely followed by philosophical and sociological perspectives (Lamb, 1991, 1994).

In the sole twentieth-century monograph on music education and gender, Green (1997) argues that, despite appearances, schools reproduce women's and men's historical musical practices. This occurs because, although girls and boys have an equal opportunity to take up any instruments and to become involved in any musical style, they tend to choose particular activities and styles that symbolically affirm femininity or masculinity in the world outside the school. Their involvement in these areas within school then acts to confirm the apparent truth of this symbolic affirmation. Thus, choirs, violins, and classical music in schools are not merely the sphere of girls; they also symbolize "femininity." Rock bands and electric guitars are not merely more attractive to boys but also symbolize "masculinity."

The area of composition is particularly interesting. Although music teachers interviewed by researchers overwhelmingly agree that girls are more musically active and motivated than boys, they perceive boys as possessing more "natural" talent than girls, especially in composition. They even tend to regard boys' compositional mistakes as examples of brilliance or spontaneity, and girls' successful products as the mere results of hard work. Such perceptions are paralleled in the conversations and self-images of pupils themselves. A similar situation exists in many other school subjects; mathematics is both analogous and highly pertinent to discussions of music.

Pupils use music to hide or to express something about their gender as well as their sexuality. Thus, girls and boys can symbolically cross over gender divides through music, just as they can use music to affirm gender. Musical activities are not simply something to do or not do; they also harbor deep personal significance. In general, girls and boys fulfill preexisting gendered musical archetypes locked into conventional definitions of femininity and masculinity. Although boys are less numerous in music, those who persist are, by definition and necessity, outstanding. It is they who will eventually take up conventionally male roles in music. Meanwhile, the more numerous girl musicians will be drawn toward teaching, and relatively few will enter the professional world of performance and composition.

Future Directions

Women's studies in relation to music education is still in its infancy, but research and networks devoted to gender and music education in Australia, Brazil, Canada, Germany, Great Britain, Japan, Spain, and many other countries provide possibilities for the future. Potential research topics include gendered differences in music education in different social classes, age groups, ethnic groups, nationalities, religious groups, subcultural groups, and other categories; the development of further strategies in relation to curriculum content, pedagogy, assessment, and evaluation; and international comparative perspectives.

See Also

FEMININITY; MASCULINITY; MUSIC: COMPOSERS; MUSIC: OVERVIEW; MUSICIANS

References and Further Reading

Colley, Ann, Chris Comber, and David J. Hargreaves. 1993. Girls, boys and technology in music education. *British Journal of Music Education* 10(2): 123–134.

Ehrlich, Cyril. 1985. *The music profession in Britain since the eighteenth century.* Oxford: Clarendon.

Green, Lucy. 1997. *Music, gender, education.* Cambridge: Cambridge University Press.

Hanley, Betty. 1998. Gender in secondary music education in British Columbia. *British Journal of Music Education* 15(1): 51–70.

Lamb, Roberta. 1994. Feminism as critique in philosophy of music education. *Philosophy of Music Education Review* 2(2): 59–74.

———. 1991. Including women composers in school music curricula. In Judith Zaimont, Jane Gottlieb, Joanne Polk, and Michael Rogan, eds., *The musical woman: An international perspective,* vol. 3, 682–713. Westport, Conn.: Greenwood.

O'Neill, Susan. 1997. Gender and music. In David J. Hargreaves and Adrian C. North, eds., *The social psychology of music.* Oxford: Oxford University Press.

Lucy Green

MUSIC: Latin America

Latin America, comprising Mexico, Central America, South America, and the Caribbean countries, is generally Spanish-speaking, with the exception of Brazil, where Portuguese is spoken. Common to the entire region is the confluence of three principal cultural groups whose prolonged contact and interaction have been responsible for the development of various styles of music: the indigenous, the African, and the European. The intermixing of these cultures has resulted in large populations of mestizos, or mixed race groups. Important cultural influences have formed and shaped music in Latin America, as have religious practices of indigenous peoples and descendants of Africans. This mix of European, indigenous, and African cultures has created different musical styles in each country, linked to specific historical, social, and cultural experiences.

Gender Ideologies and Music

Factors related to race, gender, and class are a basis of power relations in Latin America. Recent studies suggest that gender is a dynamic social and cultural construct, which tends to be continually negotiated across social boundaries. Gender-based social structures are often described as falling into two categories: (1) structures based on complementarity, that is, two separate but equal spheres, which interact in the creation of culture; and (2) structures based on intrinsic inequality, in which one gender is dominated by the other. In Latin American musical culture, complementarity exists side by side with extreme inequality: many indigenous and African cultural groups are characterized by complementarity, while the European legacy has tended to foster unequal gender relations.

Musical practice varies: in some spheres, there is complete gender separation; in other spheres there are mixed groups in which men and women perform separate, distinct gender-based forms; in a third, more recent sphere, musical roles are relatively equal. Often, all three spheres appear within the same cultural community. To these distinct musical spheres must be added another classification, traditional versus popular music; these categories, too, determine roles available to women in musical practice. Although it is difficult to generalize about an area as large and varied as Latin America, women tend to be singers and dancers while men are instrumentalists. This can be seen in indigenous contexts such as the Quechua- and Aymara-speaking Indians of Peru and Bolivia, in mestizo-based folk music, and in popular musical styles such as salsa and other dance-related genres. Certain instruments have specifically male conotations and are forbidden to women; these include *batá* drums in Afro-Cuban religious practice and flutes in some indigenous communities.

Women in Indigenous Religious Contexts

Indigenous cultures, as noted above, tend to be characterized by complementarity in gender relations. One striking example is the Mapuche, the main ethnic minority in Chile and parts of Argentina. In most indigenous Latin American cultures, shamans are male; but among the Mapuche the shamans are women (Robertson, 1989). These female shamans are the leading performers in spiritual and healing rituals. They are responsible for performing a type of song, known as *tayil,* that is believed to maintain cultural lineages and to be a vehicle of communication between the present and the past. In the Mapuche shamanic traditions, female healers known as *machi* play sacred instruments: the *kultrun* (a small kettledrum); the *wada* (a gourd rattle), and the *kaskawilla* (a bell rattle). During the past four generations, Mapuche women have come to be considered increasingly important as healers and as a link to the supernatural—this is a result of forced migrations of some Mapuche groups, who have perpetuated these traditions in an effort to preserve community and maintain the social order.

African-Derived Music Practices

In Cuba and Brazil, African-derived musical and religious practices have included powerful priestesses. In Cuba, the Yoruba tradition created Santería, a practice combining African deities and Christian saints. Santería temples are headed by a religious godfathers (*babalochas*) or godmothers (*iyalochas*). Both male and female priests lead the rhythmic patterns that invoke the gods (*orishas*). These rhythms are played on drums, the most important being the two-headed *batá* drums, played by men only. Two groups of Yoruba instruments are or can be played by women: the *shekere,* large gourds covered with beaded nets; and a smaller gourd rattle, the *marúga,* which is shaken by the chief singer.

In Brazil, Candomblé—a fusion of African and Christian religious beliefs that can be seen as a form of cultural resistance during centuries of confrontation between these two groups—also has a tradition of priestesses (Béhague, 1977). These women, the *ialorixa* or *mae de santo,* are the ultimate authority regarding music and dance in religious rituals, with full responsibility for liturgy, from leading the proper sequence of songs to directing the cycle of initiation rites. Their power derives from their knowledge of ritual, in which music and dance are integral. The ceremonies frequently use an overlapping type of singing in which solo vocal lines are sung by a male drummer while choral responses are sung by a group of women.

Women in Secular and Social Music

Music is important in agricultural and religious festivals, life-cycle ceremonies, and community festivals in both indigenous and mestizo Latin America. In these contexts, women generally sing and men play instruments. For example, as noted above, women are the preferred singers among the Aymara- and Quechua-speaking peoples of the Andes. Historically, women often played drums to accompany singing and men's instruments, but women as drummers were restricted to a few specific rituals. There is a preference for high-pitched sounds, so young women often sing at the top of their range, using falsetto as well as nasal head and throat techniques that create a dense, overlapping vocal sound. A song is considered incomplete without women's voices (Stobart, 1998).

In highland Bolivia and Peru, music is an aspect of courtship. Certain instruments, such as a small stringed instrument called a *charango,* are specifically associated with young unmarried people, and are played by men to court young women. Young women and men meet, sing, and dance at fiestas. However, musical activity by married women is sometimes frowned on, owing to its association with courtship—although married men of all ages are expected to play in the bands that perform at highland festivals.

The division between women as singers and men as instrumentalists is found in many settings throughout Latin Americas. Among the Yekuana Indians of Venezuela, for instance, women sing—in a high, falsetto register—at large communal garden-song festivals, while men play bark trumpets. In coastal Peru, two traditional Afro-Peruvian genres, *festejo* and *landó,* involve singing and dancing by women while men play guitars, the *cajón* (a box drum), and other percussion instruments. Popular music ensembles typically feature male instrumentalists and sometimes, though not always, women singers.

Folklore Revivals: Traditional Music in Urban Contexts

Women have played a prominent role in the revival of folklore in Latin America, as both researchers and performers, particularly in Chile and Argentina. Reviving folklore and presenting folk genres to urban audiences often reflected a search for cultural and national identity. Violeta Parra, who is considered the "mother" of *nueva canción*—the politically and socially conscious "new song" that emerged in Latin America in the 1960s—began traveling throughout Chile collecting folk songs. These became the inspiration for her own songs, which are composed but are all based on folk models. Margot Loyola, another Chilean researcher and performer, was also active in collecting folk music at this time, and in the formation of several Chilean folk ensembles. Mercedes Sosa, an internationally known exponent of "new song," began her career in the folklore festivals in Argentina in the late 1950s. Important female interpreters of *nueva trova,* the Cuban version of "new song," include Sara Gonzalez and Miriam Ramos. These women have been involved in a musical movement that has encouraged cultural, national, and pan-Latin American solidarity as a counterbalance to the cultural hegemony of Europe and North America.

Popular Music Genres

Many popular genres in Latin American have become internationally known as commercial music. Here too the general pattern of men as instrumentalists and women as singers has prevailed, but there have been a few exceptions; in Cuban music of the 1940s, for example, the all-female Orquesta Anacona broke new ground (Pacini Hernández, 1998).

Female singers of popular Mexican *boleros*—such as Toña la Negra, from Veracruz—specialized in interpreting works written by male composers such as Augustín Lara. *Musica romántica,* the romantic pop ballad whose roots can be traced to *bolero,* has had the largest presence of Latina singers in popular music. Afro-Cuban music has also featured female singers, such as Celia Cruz and La Lupe, two well-known Cuban-born artists who made their careers in salsa in New York. Since the 1970s, all-female groups have emerged; examples include the *megengue* band Las Chicas del Can from the Dominican Republic and the *vallenato* band Las Musas from Colombia (Aparicio, 1998). Recent all-female ensembles include the Cuban group Las Perlas del Son and several *mariachi* bands. This trend will no doubt continue as women achieve more equality with men in wider social and political spheres.

See Also

DRUMMING; MUSIC: COMPOSERS; MUSICIANS; TRADITIONAL HEALING: CENTRAL AND SOUTH AMERICA AND THE CARIBBEAN

References and Further Reading

Aparicio, Frances R. 1998. *Listening to salsa: Gender, Latin popular music, and Puerto Rican cultures.* Hanover, N. H.: Wesleyan University Press.

Béhague, Gerard. 1977. Some liturgical functions of Afro-Brazilian religious music in Salvador, Bahia. *World of Music* 19(3/4): 4–23.

Pacini Hernández, Deborah. 1998. Popular music of the Spanish-speaking regions. In Olsen Dale and Daniel Sheehy, eds., *Garland Encyclopedia of World Music,* Vol. 2: *South America, Mexico, Central Amercia, and the Caribbean.* New York: Garland.

Robertson, Carol. 1989. Power and gender in the musical experiences of women. In Ellen Koskoff, ed., *Women and music in cross-cultural perspective.* Urbana: University of Illinois Press.

Savigliano, Marta E. 1995. *Tango and the political economy of passion.* Boulder, Col., and San Francisco: Westview.

Stobart, Henry. 1998. Bolivia. In Olsen Dale and Daniel Sheehy, eds., *Garland Encyclopedia of World Music,* Vol. 2: *South America, Mexico, Central Amercia and the Caribbean.* New York: Garland.

Washabaugh, William, ed. 1998. *The passion of music and dance: Body, gender, and sexuality.* Oxford and New York: Berg.

Loren Chuse

MUSIC: Lesbian

See LESBIAN POPULAR MUSIC.

MUSIC: North Africa and Islamic Middle East

The Islamic Middle East includes Iran, Iraq, Syria, Lebanon, Jordan, Saudi Arabia, Yemen, and usually Turkey. Sometimes Egypt is included; at other times, it is considered part of north Africa, which also includes Libya, Tunisia, Algeria, and Morocco. These countries share a pan-Islamic Arab tradition, although they also exhibit a great deal of social, cultural, and musical diversity.

Impact of Islam

Beginning in 622 C.E., Islamic Arabs extended their influence across the Arabian Peninsula and beyond, spreading as far as the Persian Gulf, western Iran, northern Africa, and the Iberian Peninsula. The people they conquered gradually absorbed some elements of Islamic culture, including musical traditions and attitudes about the appropriate roles of men and women—attitudes that they superimposed to varying degrees on their own deep-seated cultural values.

Although Muhammad, the founder of Islam, was not opposed to music, he warned Muslims to avoid the kinds of music that could lead to frivolous or lewd behavior. Orthodox Islamic worship does not include ceremonial music. The melodic call to prayer and the practice of intoning the Qur'an, the Muslim scripture, are not considered music by orthodox Muslims, who are ambivalent about music. Arabic classical music is somewhat acceptable to them, however, because of its associated music theory and scholarship.

Despite orthodox ambivalence, music is a vital part of Islamic societies. The Islamic mystics called Sufis use music, dance, and chanted verse in their worship services, and folk music is so highly valued that specialists rather than amateurs generally perform it.

One notable characteristic of orthodox Islam is its social separation of men and women. Men have tended to occupy the public sphere, and women the private sphere. These attitudes vary greatly from society to society, however. In some Arab countries, men are restricted from seeing the faces of women or being in physical contact with women who are not family members; in others, men and women socialize in public. Such variations greatly affect women's roles in music—for example, they determine whether men and women dance together and whether women sing in public. In general, there is a negative attitude toward women's performing in public.

Types of Music

The golden age of Arabic music occurred in eighth-century Baghdad. Classical Arabic music later diverged into eastern Arab and Maghreb (western Arab) traditions. The eastern tradition emphasizes virtuosity; performers express their individuality in improvisation based on Arabic classical musical structures. Western Arab music continues the court music tradition of suites based on prescribed melodies with different rhythmic patterns, and it places less emphasis on improvisation. Middle Eastern and north African music includes folk, military, classical, and popular genres, each with its characteristic instruments and styles.

Common Characteristics

Pan-Islamic music has a distinctive monophonic sound. In principle, there is only one melody and one constant, often complex, rhythmic pattern. Although a vocalist and one or more instrumentalists work with the same basic melody, they often do not sound quite alike, either because each is improvising or because the voices or instruments are performing the same melody at different pitch levels. Vocal and instrumental ensembles generally perform in unison. In folk music, call-and-response and solo singing are both common.

Another feature of Arabic music is that it is made up of combinations and repetitions of melodic patterns or modes, called *makam* in Turkey and *dastgah* in Iran. The mode is a set of rules for composing melody. The *makam* designates the scale of the music (which can include as many as 22 divisions of the octave); it also determines which kinds of ornamentation and melodic movements among notes are permitted. It contributes strongly to the emotions evoked in the listeners.

The predominant style of singing and playing is highly decorated: notes are "bent" and embellished with trills and glissandos. The characteristic singing style of the region is "tense-sounding and has a harsh, throaty, nasal tone, with a certain flatness. . . . Men sing high in their range, and women usually low" (Nettl, 1992: 59).

Instruments used in folk music include single-headed frame drums, goblet-shaped drums played with the hands and fingers, tambourines, metal finger cymbals, conical reed aerophones, end-blown flutes, and an assortment of stringed instruments, including plucked or bowed lutes, several kinds of fiddles, and struck or hammered zithers. Depending on the community, women may play some of these instruments. Other typical accompaniments include hand-clapping and female yodeling.

Arabic classical music uses the zither, the hammered dulcimer, the bowed lute, the western violin (played on the knee, not the shoulder, in north Africa), and the goblet-shaped drum. Usually the classical instrumentalists are male, although women play some of these instruments.

Women Music-Makers

Professional women singers and dancers are a significant part of pan-Islamic culture, a necessity at weddings and other celebrations. Their singing and dancing are often accompanied by drums, tambourines, double-reed aerophones, or hand-clapping.

In some communities, for example, Saudi Arabia, women's privacy is strictly guarded, and they are usually restricted from performing with men or in mixed company. Among the Tuareg of north Africa, however, men and women perform together in public. Tuareg women traditionally are the instrumentalists, and they play a one-stringed fiddle, drums, and tambourines. Tuareg men are known for their highly ornamented love songs, which they sing to the accompaniment of a one-stringed fiddle, usually played by a woman. The popular Lebanese singer Fayrouz (b. 1934) performs in public before mixed audiences.

Egypt—land of the pyramids, female pharaohs, and Cleopatra—has complex and ambivalent attitudes toward female performers. In late eighteenth-century Cairo, highly regarded female performers called *cawalim* ("learned women") were trained in singing, musical composition, instrumental performance, and writing poetry. They were a necessity at any important celebration, but they performed only for women in the harem, screened off from but overlooking the male reception space. They could be heard but not seen by men, an arrangement that preserved their respectability. A second category of female entertainers, mainly dancers, was the *ghawazi,* who often performed at saint's day celebrations. The *ghawazi* were generally not considered decent women because they danced for men in public with unveiled faces (Van Nieuwkerk, 1998: 22). A third category, "common *cawalim,*" consisted of lower-class singers and dancers who performed for the poor.

As a result of changing politics and western influences, female performers gradually lost status. Today, some dancers are considered more respectable than others, but all are regarded with ambivalence, and most are regarded as "fallen women" who shamefully exhibit their bodies in public. They are perceived as having traded their virtue (either literally or figuratively) for money. Nonetheless, dancing has continued to be a vital part of many celebrations, and talented belly dancers are able to earn a good income at deluxe cabarets.

The Banat Mazin in Upper Egypt are a highly sought-after group of *ghawazi* who belong to an extended Gypsy family. Because it is considered inappropriate for local Egyptian women to dance in public, people hire Gypsy professionals—cultural outsiders—to perform. The Banat Mazin move their hips loosely from side to side and keep time with finger cymbals; small metal disks or coins sewn to their dresses symbolize wealth and add to the musical accompaniment. They are accompanied by a traditional folk ensemble that includes a kind of fiddle, a goblet-shaped drum, and a large frame drum, played by male family members.

The Egyptian *zar* ritual is performed to appease and dispel a spirit thought to be causing illness or misfortune. It involves music, dance, and trance. Often the leader of the ritual is female. The ceremonial personnel include male dancers performing a twirling dance, male musicians playing on reed flutes and drums, female drummers and singers, and the subject who is possessed by the spirit. Different rhythms are associated with different spirits, so a number of rhythms are played until the offending spirit is identified.

Umm Kulthum (1908–1975) is considered the "the diva of Arab music." Born in Egypt, she became a superstar in the Arab world. The best composers and poets competed to provide her with songs, weekly radio programs broadcast her performances throughout the region, and she was thought of as the "voice of the nation." Some of her concerts resembled political demonstrations. Umm Kulthum possessed a commanding presence, a golden throat, and the ability to express deeply felt emotions through song. Always self-consciously appealing to local values, portraying herself as a *bint al-balad* ("daughter of the country"), she was able escape the moral stigma associated with women in the performing arts.

See Also

HOUSEHOLDS AND FAMILIES: MIDDLE EAST AND NORTH AFRICA; ISLAM; MUSIC: EDUCATION; MUSICIANS

References and Further Reading

Danielson, Virginia. 1997. *The voice of Egypt: Umm Kulthum, Arabic song, and Egyptian society in the twentieth century.* Chicago, Ill.: University of Chicago Press.

Malm, William P. 1996. *Music cultures of the Pacific, the Near East, and Asia.* 3rd ed. Upper Saddle River, N.J.: Prentice-Hall.

Nettl, Bruno. 1992. Music of the Middle East. In Bruno Nettl, Charles Capwell, Philip V. Bohlman, Isabel K. F. Wong, and Thomas Turino. *Excursions in world music.* Englewood Cliffs, N.J.: Prentice Hall.

Van Nieuwkerk, Karin. 1995. *A "trade like any other": Female singers and dancers in Egypt.* Austin: University of Texas Press.

———. 1998. Changing images and shifting identities: Female performers in Egypt. In Sherifa Zuhur, ed., *Images of enchantment: Visual and performing arts of the Middle East.* 21–35. Cairo: American University in Cairo Press.

Elyn Aviva

MUSIC: Opera

The word *opera* (the plural of Latin *opus,* "work") was first used in 1639 to denote a dramatic production combining speech, singing, gesture, dance, and instrumental accompaniment in a scenic stage setting. The first opera in the modern sense was written in 1598, although masques and other dramatic forms including song had existed for centuries in Europe. An opera usually includes separate compositions in several forms: arias, choruses, and recitatives. In most cases, the music is written by the composer, and the text by another artist known as a librettist.

Women Composers of Opera

Most operas were commissioned by male patrons, and so women composers were rarely engaged. The Italian composer and singer Francesca Caccini (1587—after 1637) is the first woman known to have written music for operas, but only one of these operas has survived—*La liberazione di Ruggiero dall'isola d'Alcina* (1625). The French composer and harpsichordist Elisabeth-Claude Jacquet de la Guerre (1665–1729) wrote one opera, *Cephale et Procris* (1694), which was successfully revived in 1989.

During the eighteenth and nineteenth centuries, some aristocratic women—for example, Wilhelmina, Markgrafin of Bayreuth (1709–1758); and Princess Amalie of Saxony (1794–1870)—wrote operas for performance at their courts. The rise of bourgeois society strengthened the association of political and artistic activities with males and relegated women to less public genres, such as song and chamber music. There were exceptions, however: the semipublic career of Maria Teresa Agnesis (1720–1795) as a theatrical composer enabled her to have her operas staged; and the blind Austrian pianist and composer Maria Theresia von Paradis (1759–1824) wrote at least five operas, though only one (*Der Schulkandidat,* 1792) has survived.

In the late nineteenth century and throughout the twentieth, women wrote an abundance of ballets, children's musicals, lyrical scenes, and other theatrical music. Some who composed operas were Augusta Holmes (1847–1903), Louise Bertin (1805–1877), and Germaine Tailleferre (1892–1983) in France; Erzsébet Szönyi (b. 1924) in Hungary; and Mary Carr Moore (1873–1957) in the United States. The English composer Ethel Smyth (1858–1944) wrote six operas, of which *The Wreckers* is the best known; the first three premiered in Germany. Elisabeth Lutyens (1906–1983) wrote ballad operas, lyric dramas, dramatic scenes, and three full-length operas. Successful contemporary figures include Betsy Jolas (b. 1926), composer of *Schliemann* (1990); Nicola LeFanu (b. 1947), composer of *Blood Wedding* (1992); and Meredith Monk (b. 1943), composer of *Atlas* (1991). Some women who have received commissions from major opera companies are Thea Musgrave (b. 1928), who wrote *Mary, Queen of Scots* for the King's Theatre in Edinburgh; Judith Weir (b. 1954), who wrote *Blond Eckbert* for the London Coliseum in 1994; and Adriana Hoelszky (b. 1953), who wrote *Die Wände* for the Theater an der Wien in 1995. Pauline Oliveros (b. 1932) in 1991 began an international project titled *Njinga, the Queen King,* which is intended to run for 10 years and to integrate various cultures, races, and genders.

Feminist Debate on Models of Femininity in Opera

In western art music, the highest voices have always been most valued. In the eighteenth century, castrati (male singers castrated before their voices deepened) and prima donnas (female sopranos) were adulated and very well paid, though the women were regarded as sexually licentious. The profound pleasure that the female voice evokes gives women a unique position and thus challenges male authority.

Feminist scholars have studied both the ideological milieu in which operas are written and produced and the music itself. Historical research has disclosed how the operatic genre collaborated with textual and sociocultural practices to afect gender roles. One often-cited example is Mozart's *Die Zauberflöte* (*The Magic Flute,* 1791); Mozart divided this opera into the male world of Sarastro, associated with day and rationalism, and the dark world of the queen, associated with emotionalism. Pamina is one of a long line of suffering heroines who live and die for their male partners. This fundamental opposition between male and female is mirrored in the music: the queen sings in the old-fashioned *opera seria* style, whereas Sarastro is accompanied by chorale-like chords in the manner of church music and thus represents a more "natural" order.

In nineteenth-century operas, women are depicted either as models of chastity or as exotic *femmes fatales;* the pure heroines are doomed to tragic death or domestication, and the seductively powerful women to destruction. This dichotomy was not wholly an invention of the Enlightenment or the romantic era; it can be discerned in a number of operas by George Frideric Handel (1685–1759), such as *Agrippina, Teseo, Amadigi,* and *Orlando,* in which we find similarly opposed pairs of female protagonists.

Throughout the history of opera, allegories of male control over females have been prominent themes. In Claudio Monteverdi's *Arianna,* the "Lamento" "served as a floating cautionary to all women tempted to choose their own partners" (Cusick, 1994: 36).

Two threads—one textual and the other contextual—are prominent in today's feminist scholarship in this field. The philosopher Cathérine Clément concentrates on the narrative plots and finds that women are portrayed as victims, suffering most of the grief and conflict. Lawrence Kramer, a professor of English and comparative literature, devotes much attention to misogynistic imagery in his analysis of Richard Strauss's *Salome* and points out that the "chromatic" world of Salome is set against the "diatonic normality" of the prophet Jochanaan. Other writers, such as the musicologist Carolyn Abbate, attack the traditional assumption that the authorial voice in opera is solely that of the male composer. They identify multiple voices within the work of art and stress the composer's dependence on women, a characteristic unique to opera: "As a voice she [the female singer] slips into the 'male/active/subject' position" (Abbate, 1993). Both approaches can be said to demonstrate the ambivalence within a patriarchal system that simultaneously denigrates and idealizes women.

It is interesting to investigate whether women composers treat their female characters and their plots differently.

Caccini's *La liberazione* allegorically explores women's relationship to power in a patriarchal world (Cusick, 1993). Ethel Smyth used opera as a means to reveal and reshape her struggle with what she called "the eternal sex problem between men and women." Her heroines personify and dramatize sexual ambiguity and the image of women drawn close in a natural world of powerful, protective maternal myth and female symbolism (Wood, 1987). In *Bremer Freiheit,* Hoelszky constructs a female victim of male violence who transforms her position into one of power over men by poisoning her friends and relatives.

The relationship between music and language in opera has yet to be fully plumbed. Abbate claims that straightforward analogies between music and language are unacceptable (1991: 18); Kramer, in contrast, maintains that "the supposition that music represents a nonlinguistic immediacy creates the mutually reinforcing necessities of positivist and formalist musicology" (1992: 9). Profound analyses of musical structure and its contexts have only begun to be made.

See Also

MUSIC: COMPOSERS; MUSIC: WESTERN CLASSICAL

References and Further Reading

Abbate, Carolyn. 1993. Opera; or, the envoicing of women. In Ruth A. Solie, ed., *Musicology and difference: Gender and sexuality in music scholarship,* 225–258. Berkeley: University of California Press.

———. 1991. *Unsung voices: Opera and musical narrative in the nineteenth century.* Princeton, N.J.: Princeton University Press.

Boneau, Denise Lynn. 1989. *Louise Bertin and opera in Paris in the 1820s and 1830s.* Chicago: University of Chicago Press.

Clément, Cathérine. 1991. *Opera, or the undoing of women.* Minneapolis: University of Minnesota Press.

Cusick, Suzanne. 1993. Of women, music, and power: A model from Seicento Florence. In Ruth A. Solie, ed., *Musicology and difference: Gender and sexuality in music scholarship,* 281–304. Berkeley: University of California Press.

Ford, Charles. 1991. *Così? Sexual politics in Mozart's operas.* Manchester and New York: Manchester University Press.

Freedman, Deborah. 1985. *Thea Musgrave's opera "Mary, Queen of Scots."* Thesis, Johns Hopkins University.

Kramer, Lawrence. 1990. Culture and musical hermeneutics: The Salome complex. *Cambridge Opera Journal* 3: 269–294.

———. 1992. The musicology of the future. *Repercussions* 1(1): 5–18.

Rieger, Eva. 1995. Zustand oder Wesensart? Wahnsinnsfrauen in Opern. In Sibylle Duda and Luise Pusch, eds., *Wahnsinnsfrauen,* Vol. 2, 366–389. Frankfurt: Insel.

Solie, Ruth A., ed. 1993. *Musicology and difference: Gender and sexuality in music scholarship.* Berkeley: University of California Press.

Wood, Elizabeth. 1987. Gender and genre in Ethel Smyth's operas. In Judith Lang Zaimont, ed., *The musical woman: An international perspective,* 493–507. Westport, Conn.: Greenwood.

Eva Rieger

MUSIC: Rock and Pop

Since rock 'n' roll launched the modern pop industry in the mid-1950s, women writers and performers of rock and pop music have had to struggle against sexism and segregation to establish a place for themselves. In 1953, for instance, the full-throated Big Mama Thornton reached number one with the song "Hound Dog" on the U.S. rhythm and blues charts (a euphemism for "race" record, or black, charts), only to be eclipsed by Elvis Presley, whose cover version of the same song topped the mainstream pop charts three years later.

In the tradition of black blueswomen such as Ma Rainey and Bessie Smith, who paved the way for latter-day soul and pop, Thornton set a new standard of performance in rock 'n' roll that was copied but rarely credited. The segregated nature of music marketing meant that Thornton had considerably less access to mainstream pop audiences than did white 1950s stars such as Peggy Lee, who in the first 18 years of her career had more than 40 hits, including the classic "Fever" in 1958.

Pop music of the 1950s was marked by a transition from the big band era of jazz swing to rock 'n' roll, and it was an era when female performers had limited options. Either—like Thornton and Chess Records' star Etta James—they sang gritty, emotive rhythm and blues, or they aimed for the pop charts, where women were required to sing anodyne standards and dress in sequined glamorous outfits. Singers such as Great Britain's Alma Cogan became as famous for their dresses as for their songs, and most women had to struggle to avoid trivial material.

By the early 1960s, women were beginning to break through with a fresh identity. Male beat groups like the Beatles and the Dave Clark Five owed much of their phenomenal success to the inspiration of the "girl group" sound. In the late 1950s, four teenage girls from New York known as the Chantels combined doo-wop street harmonies with echoes of Gregorian chant in the national pop hit "Maybe," and the Shirelles hit the U.S. number one spot in 1960 with "Will You Still Love Me Tomorrow?" With their success, small independent record labels such as Red Bird, Dimension, and Scepter tapped into a new huge new teen pop audience.

"The reason [this music]...spoke to us so powerfully, was that it gave voice to all of the warring selves inside us... to forge something resembling a coherent identity," writes Susan J. Douglas (1994: 77). The downside of girl groups' commercial success was that women, enthusiastic and new to the industry, were often exploited by producers or record companies.

Most notorious was the pop Svengali, Phil Spector, architect of the "wall of sound," a layered harmonic overload exemplified by songs like the Crystals' "Then He Kissed Me" and The Ronettes' "Be My Baby." Between 1961 and 1965 he had 17 records in the top forty—but he achieved this by operating his Philles label like a factory production line. The Crystals, for instance, were cheated out of royalties when Spector hired the session singer Darlene Love to record songs like "He's a Rebel" and "He's Sure the Boy I Love" for a flat studio fee. The group then had to tour and perform number one hits they had not recorded.

Berry Gordy's Tamla Motown, too, was run like a car-production line in Detroit. Girls were plucked from the public housing projects to work with talented young songwriters such as Smokey Robinson and the team of Holland–Dozier–Holland. As an upwardly mobile, black-owned independent company, however, Motown was as enabling as it was exploitive. "Until Motown, in Detroit, there were three big careers for a black girl. Babies, factories, or daywork. Period," said Mary Wells, who became Motown's first female star with her international number one song hit "My Guy" (quoted in Hirshey, 1984).

Ruthless in his search for a black female singer on a par with white mainstream stars like Debbie Reynolds and Doris Day, Gordy passed over Motown women like Martha Reeves—one of the label's most talented performers, whose dark soul voice led the Vandellas to the top of the charts with such hits as "Nowhere to Run" and "Dancing in the Street"—in favor of Diana Ross. From their first number one single, "Where Did Our Love Go?" (1964), to "Automatically Sunshine" (1972), the Supremes had 30 hit singles. One of the first black acts to play New York's Copacabana night club, they were soul divas who sold massively to the white mainstream.

When beat rock and the girl group sound faded in the late 1960s, "progressive" rock, heavily influenced by the West Coast hippie scene and a revival of the blues, increased in popularity. In this exclusively male scene, it took a young, headstrong woman with Bessie Smith blues riffs in her head and a fierce anti–prom queen attitude to make an impact on her own terms. The Texan-born singer Janis Joplin became the first of the serious rock chicks. From Big Brother and the Holding Company to her last band, Full Tilt Boogie, Joplin rewrote the protocol for women in rock—in terms not just of sound (her unfettered, aching snarl made classics out of such songs as "Piece of My Heart" and "Cry Baby"), but also of image. In tune with the hippie "revolution," Joplin proved that women could be successful performers without being traditionally pretty or sweet.

Apart from Joplin, Jefferson Airplane's Grace Slick and Mo Tucker, drummer with the Velvet Underground, women found it hard to make inroads into rock. Instead, they began to colonize an area less dominated by the standard male rock band. Artists such as Joni Mitchell, Carole King, and Joan Baez carved out a place for female singer-songwriters in the late 1960s and early 1970s, and this genre by the late 1980s had become the main route for women into the business. Artists like Suzanne Vega, Tracy Chapman, and Jane Siberry wrote their own million-selling commentaries on life and relationships.

In the late 1970s, women launched an assault on music via punk, with female acts like the Raincoats, X Ray Spex, Siouxsie (Sioux of Siouxsie and the Banshees), and the Slits deliberately playing against the grain of guitar rock and experimenting with androgynous imagery. Though punk spawned a few high-profile acts, it wasn't until the early 1990s that women made an impact on rock in greater numbers and at a grassroots level. The fame of "hard-core" girl bands like Babes in Toyland, Bikini Kill, and Courtney Love's Hole was fueled by the "riot grrrls," an underground movement originating in Olympia, Washington, and Washington, D.C., in 1991 that spread via fanzines and female bands throughout the United States and then to Great Britain. Chaotic and not necessarily coherent, the movement was nonetheless still empowering for women, both as fans and as performers. This, combined with the success of mixed-gender college rock groups like Throwing Muses and the Breeders, gave exposure to women who were assured and forceful in their negotiation of rock.

The rebel spirit of rock means that, to some extent, women can get away with not looking conventionally attractive; but in pop music, where chart hits and immediate profit are more pressing, women continually have to deal with questions of sexuality and image. After MTV was launched in 1981, this issue became more acute. Pop video regularly reduces women to the role of sexy chicks flanking male stars. To some extent, Madonna overturned these conventions by placing herself center-stage and projecting an overtly sexual image that mixed female fantasy and parody. As she played with images of soft porn, however—from the "peepshow" video "Open Your Heart" in 1986 to the explicit coffee table snaps in her book *Sex* in 1992—her message was often contradictory. Madonna may have preached control, but she created an illusion of sexual availability that many female pop artists felt compelled to emulate. The demand for short-term profit throughout the 1980s saw an industry sticking to salable images; its most dependable agent was MTV, and its corporate artist was Madonna.

Madonna was a more successful role model as a businesswoman, achieving the kind of financial control that women had long fought for within the industry. In 1991, she formed a joint company with Time Warner and received a $60 million advance for the multimedia production *Maverick.* A rival to male artists like Michael Jackson and Bruce Springsteen, Madonna generated sales for Time Warner of over $1.2 billion in the first decade of her career.

By the late 1980s, black women, too, were achieving greater financial success in the pop mainstream. Artists such as Janet Jackson, Tina Turner, and Whitney Houston reached superstar status. The legacy of chart segregation meant that black female artists were frequently pushed toward disco and soul music. Although both genres have produced major stars (Aretha Franklin, Donna Summer), one important struggle for black women has been in their "crossover" from dance music to white-dominated pop and rock.

Women's contributions enriched pop's vocabulary further when, in the 1990s, they made an impact on the charts through the emerging genres of rap, reggae, and world music. The success in the West of African artists like Mali's Oumou Sangare, South Africa's Yvonne Chaka Chaka, and Benin's Angelique Kidjo created new possibilities for female performers worldwide. By the mid-1990s, women were injecting the most creative ideas into a rock and pop world where the male guitar solo and 4/4 drumbeat had become a cliché; and in terms of integration and experimentation, women were leading the way.

See Also

IMAGES OF WOMEN: OVERVIEW; MUSIC: ANGLO-AMERICAN FOLK; MUSIC: SOUL, JAZZ, RAP, BLUES, AND GOSPEL

References and Further Reading

Andersen, Christopher. 1991. *Madonna unauthorized.* New York: Simon and Schuster.

Bayton, Mavis. 1998. *Frock rock: Women performing popular music.* Oxford and New York: Oxford University Press.

Betrock, Alan. 1982. *Girl groups: The story of a sound.* New York: Delilah.

Douglas, Susan J. 1994. *Where the girls are: Growing up female with the mass media.* New York: Times Books.

Garr Gillian G. 1993. *She's a Rebel: The history of women in rock and roll.* London: Stanford.

Garratt, Sheryl, and Sue Steward. 1984. *Signed sealed and delivered: True life stories of women in pop.* London: Pluto.

Grieg, Charlotte. 1989. *Will you still love me tomorrow? Girl groups from the 50s on.* London: Virago.

Hirshey, Gerri. 1985. *Nowhere to run: The story of soul music.* London: Pan.

Joplin, Laura. 1992. *Love, Janis.* New York: Villard.

Juno, Andrea, and V. Vale, eds. 1991. *Angry women.* San Francisco: Re/Search.

Leonard, Hal, ed. 1999. *Lilith Fair: A celebration of women in music.* New York: Hal Leonard.

O'Brien, Lucy. 1995. *She bop: The definitive history of women in rock, pop and soul.* New York and London: Penguin.

O'Dair, Barbara. 1997. *Rolling Stone book of women in rock.* New York: Random House.

Post, Laura. 1997. *Backstage pass: Interviews with women in music.* New York: New Victoria.

Turner, Tina, with Kurt Loder. 1987. *I, Tina.* New York: Avon.

Lucy O'Brien

MUSIC: Soul, Jazz, Rap, Blues, and Gospel

Blues

Blues—a twelve-bar rhythic structure, and also a style of performance—is a basis of many genres from rock 'n' roll to reggae, and it is a very strong element in soul, jazz, rap, and gospel, genres that are predominantly African-American. Blues originated in African tribal chants; it was transported with the slave trade to the Caribbean and the southern United States, where it intermingled with white church and folk music. Blues was central to women's experience, accompanying cleaning, tending the garden, cooking, and soothing children. By the early 1900s, traveling tent shows featured blues singers; one of the first women to popularize blues in this way was Georgia-born Gertrude Malissa Rainey, known as Ma Rainey. With her bulging eyes, gold teeth, and direct, folksy style, Rainey epitomized the country blueswoman as mother and preacher.

One of Ma Rainey's protegés, Bessie Smith, became a vaudeville star in the 1920s and took blues singing to a new level of professionalism; she, Ida Cox, and Ethel Waters were major figures in the emerging "race" records market, music by black artists for black consumers. Smith's first recording, the world-weary yet vulnerable "T'Ain't Nobody's Business If I Do" (1923), became an early anthem of women's independence. As the rural blues of the 1920s developed into the urban Chicago and electric blues of the 1930s and 1940s, a few female instrumentalists came to the fore, such as the pianist and composer Lovie Austin and the guitarist Memphis Minnie, who was also a singer. Minnie, a dedicated documenter of domestic life, sang about crime and prostitution as well as baking biscuits and feeding roosters; between 1930 and 1960 she made more than 200 recordings for several labels, including Columbia and Bluebird, and she influenced artists as diverse as Muddy Waters, Big Mama Thornton, and Chuck Berry. After 1935, the blues faded as dance bands became popular; but from the late 1970s on, much painstaking work was done to keep the history of blueswomen alive by people like the singer Bonnie Raitt, with her Blues Foundation, and the New York archivist and label owner Rosetta Reitz.

Jazz

Women singers brought the blues into jazz and pioneered a new style of vocal performance as jazz and big band vocalists. Billie Holiday, for instance, was the bridge between the vaudeville "mamas" and the era of jazz swing. With her languid, idiosyncratic style, she reworked banal pop standards into classics. Ella Fitzgerald combined show tunes of the 1940s and 1950s with improvisatory scat singing. Artists like Sarah Vaughan, Anita O'Day, and Peggy Lee introduced jazz to the mainstream cabaret audience.

Although women were often overlooked when it came to hiring "sidemen"—band instrumentalists—there were many top female jazz instrumentalists, such as the bandleader and trumpet player Valaida Snow, the composer and pianist Lil Hardin Armstrong (who often collaborated with her famous husband, Louis Armstrong), and the bandleader Anna Mae Winburn, who led the all-female International Sweethearts of Rhythm. Because access to the male bands of the day was restricted, many women players formed their own groups. These women's groups were often dismissed as gimmicks or novelty acts, and sometimes women gave in to pressure and emphasized their physical allure over their musicianship—one group, for instance, was billed as "The Band with a Bosom." Many achieved long-term success, however: for example, the pianist Sarah McLawler formed her own all-woman bebop combo, the Synconettes, in Chicago; and Ivy Benson, an important figure in the 1930s and 1940s, led a band that was a major route for women instrumentalists into jazz and studio work in Britain. By the mid-1950s, artists such as Dinah Washington and Nina Simone were combining the emerging rock 'n' roll and rhythm and blues (R&B) with jazz to create a sophisticated crossover style. This tradition has been continued up to the present day by jazz vocalists like Cassandra Wilson and Dianne Reeves.

Gospel

Many vocalists were influenced by gospel music, a genre that developed alongside blues and jazz. Black American Pentecostal churches added instrumentation and tempo changes to spirituals or "hillbilly hymns," creating a new devotional music that by the 1920s was being performed by touring gospel groups. These church congregations consisted largely of women and children, so women's contribution to gospel has been huge.

The Chicago-based gospel artist Sister Rosetta Tharpe was the first to try to dissolve the line between sacred and secular, rephrasing the music for a jazz audience at the Cotton Club in New York in the 1930s. Although church elders were outraged, Tharpe expanded the concept of "the church," maintaining that the Lord was ready to listen wherever he was addressed. She developed a flamboyant style, and her recordings, including such hits as "Rock Me" and "Trouble in Mind," appeared in the R&B charts throughout the 1940s.

Another major gospel singer of the 1940s and 1950s, Mahalia Jackson, campaigned against the "cheapening" of pop gospel in nightclubs and resisted the attempts of bandleaders like Louis Armstrong to turn her into a jazz singer. Jackson's voice—a majestic, soaring contralto—conveyed simple dignity and rich spirituality. In 1946 she recorded "Move On Up a Little Higher," which sold more than two million copies. She sang at the inauguration of President Kennedy in 1961 and performed before 200,000 civil rights demonstrators at the Lincoln Memorial in 1963. When she died, in 1972, thousands of mourners came to her funeral, including the young Aretha Franklin, who sang "Gracious Lord, Take My Hand."

Soul

Aretha Franklin combined Tharpe's commercial sensibility with Jackson's gospel purity to create one of the most powerful voices of the "soul generation" of the 1960s. The girl group pop sound grew up overnight in 1967, when Franklin's first single, "I Ain't Never Loved a Man (The Way I Love You)" became number one in the R&B charts. The daughter of a Baptist minister, Franklin brought a sense of pride and a mature vision to soul classics such as "Respect" and "Say a Little Prayer." She is a dominant figure in a genre that encompasses many different styles, from the blues-tinged R&B of divas of the 1940s like LaVern Baker, Ruth Brown, and Etta James to the southern sound of Irma Thomas and Ann Peebles and the international pop of the Supremes, Dionne Warwick, and the Three Degrees. The Three Degrees exemplified the heavily orchestrated Philadelphia sound; their hits included "Year of Decision" and "When Will I See You Again?" and one of their members, Sheila Ferguson, remarked, "We were as soulful as white people could handle at the time—glitzy, feminine and smooth" (O'Brien, 1995).

By the 1970s, women had a crucial role in disco soul music, but (much as girl groups of the 1960s were exploited for a mass-produced sound) many disco stars found themselves regarded as vocal clothes-horses and stereotyped as "foxy black chicks." Only a few artists—such as the girl group Sister Sledge and Donna Summer, whose risqué, hypnotic "Love to Love You Baby" was one of the first 12-inch vinyl disco hits—managed to sustain long-term careers and win respect on their own terms.

During the 1980s, more women crossed over successfully from soul to mainstream pop, with singers like Whitney Houston, Sade, and Anita Baker leading the way. By the end of the 1990s, black women were accepted as innovators, producers, and songwriters; artists such as Lauryn Hill, Erykah Badu, and Macy Gray redefined soul as postmodernists, working jazz and blues history into their sound.

Rap

Women also had to fight for a corner in rap, a genre that combines sung-spoken lyrics with electronically assembled music. Rap, an important sector of the music industry, is part of the hip-hop culture, which also includes breakdancing and graffiti. With its emphasis on marketable male stereotypes—black cowboy, pimp, hustler, gang leader, black nationalist hero—and its assumption that women performers were not likely to be big sellers, rap did not leave much room for women except as cheerleaders or decoration. Despite this male skepticism, women have proved themselves in rap, evolving their own cast of characters from fly girl to earth mother to black "sista."

Female rap can be traced back to the soul singers of the 1970s, such as Millie Jackson, who matched male bravado with comic tales of her own sexual exploits. In 1979, the first female rap group—the Sequence—emerged from the club scene in the Bronx (in New York City), though they were considered a novelty. Female rap came of age shortly thereafter, in the early 1980s, when Roxanne Shante recorded "Roxanne's Revenge," an answer to the sexist rap of UTFO's "Roxanne Roxanne." The trio Salt-N-Pepa followed; their album *Hot, Cool, and Vicious* (1986) brought rap into the pop mainstream.

By the early 1990s, women were making inroads into all areas of rap. Queen Latifah projected a sense of pride and dignity as part of a "back to Africa" movement, which had a major impact on hip-hop. She also became a Hollywood actress, with a role in Spike Lee's film *Jungle Fever,* and starred in a popular television sitcom, *Living Single.* MC Lyte, from Brooklyn, New York, used street poetry in her rhymes; her "I Cram 2 Understand U" (late 1980s) became a hip-hop classic. Sister Souljah adopted militant black nationalist rhetoric. Yo Yo performed hard-core rap evoking the mores of street gangs in Los Angeles, but she reached out to women with her campaign organization, the Intelligent Black Women's Coalition.

Women also reflected the more negative aspects of rap in the 1990s. Groups like BWP (Bytches with Problems) and HWA (Hoes—meaning whores—with Attitude) appropriated the misogynist image of "skeezers," gold-digging, money-fixated women. In the middle 1990s, female rappers were sidelined during a very public episode of hip-hop wars (which resulted in the death of two male rap stars, Tupac Shakur and Biggy Smalls). However, in 1997, a new female voice emerged: Missy Elliot issued the satirical, joyful *Supa Dupa Fly,* which was hailed as a stylistic masterpiece in the world of rap, R&B, and rock. Like female blues, jazz, and soul artists before her, Elliot showed how a genre could be transformed.

See Also

LESBIAN POPULAR MUSIC; MUSIC: ROCK AND POP; MUSICIANS

References and Further Reading

Barkley Brown, Elsa, Darlene Clark Hine and Rosalyn Terborg-Penn, eds. 1994. *Black women in America: An historical encyclopedia.* Indianapolis: Indiana University Press.

Clarence Boyer, Horace, and Lloyd Yearwood. 2000. *The golden age of gospel.* Music in American Life Series. Chicago: University of Illinois Press.

Clarke, Donald. 1994. *Wishing on the moon: The life and times of Billie Holiday.* London: Penguin.

Dahl, Linda. 1989. *Stormy weather: The music and lives of a century of jazzwomen.* New York: Limelight Editions.

Feinstein, Elaine. 1986. *Bessie Smith: Empress of the blues.* New York: Viking Penguin.

Finn, Julio. 1998. *The bluesman: The musical heritage of black men and women in the Americas.* New York: Interlink.

Garon, Paul, and Beth Garon. 1992. *Woman with guitar: Memphis Minnie's blues.* New York: Da Capo.

George, Nelson. 1994. *Buppies, B-boys, baps, and bohos: Notes on post-soul black culture.* New York: HarperCollins.

Hirshey, Gerri. 1994. *Nowhere to run: The story of soul music.* New York: Da Capo.

Nathan, David, and Luther Vandross. 1999. *The soulful divas.* New York: Watson-Guptill.

O'Brien, Lucy. 1995. *She bop: The definitive history of women in rock, pop, and soul.* New York and London: Penguin.

Rose, Tricia, and Andrew Ross, eds. 1994. *Microphone fiends: Youth music and youth culture.* New York and London: Routledge.

Simone, Nina, with Stephen Cleary. 1992. *I put a spell on you: The autobiography.* New York: Pantheon.

Werner, Craig. 1999. *A change is gonna come: Music, race, and the soul of America.* New York: Plume.

Lucy O'Brien

MUSIC: South Asia

The assertion that the public sphere of south Asian societies is male, and the private sphere female, can be misleading when it is applied to musical performance. Although is true that numerous genres are performed by women only within the domestic realm, there is a long history of female performance in the public spaces of fields, courts, temples, and concert halls. The division between caste and class, or professional and nonprofessional, may be as profound as that between male and female environments.

Professional Specialists

The earliest references to female performers are found in the *Ṛg-veda* (c. 1500–1000 B.C.E.), although not in ritual contexts. Later texts such as the *Rāmāyaṇa, Mahābhārata,* and *Nāṭyaśāstra* (c. 200–300 C.E.) provide further evidence of these secular female dancers (*gaṇikā*) and musicians. The early Tamil *caṅkam* poets (100 B.C.E.–300 C.E.) mention female "bards" (*viṟali,* who are said to sing, dance, and play a lute, and *pāṭiṇi*) and dancers (*āṭumakaḷ*) of the court, possibly the forerunners of *devadāsī* temple dancers (Kersenboom-Story, 1987: 11–16). It is likely that there was little distinction between these highly skilled court and temple performers (Marglin, 1985: 8–11).

The advent of Muslim rule in south Asia (1206) brought a greater distinction between professional female musicians (who came to be known variously as *tawā'if, kalāvant, naikin,* and, by the colonial British, "nautch girls") patronized by the aristocracy and Muslim and Rajput courts, and the ritual dancers and musicians of Hindu temples. In central and northern India, where Muslim influence was strongest, temple dance had died out by around 1300 (Post, 1992: 99); in southern and eastern India, it continued until the mid-twentieth century. Although the *devadāsī* and *tawā'if* or *kalāvant* performed different music, in different contexts, Post notes four similarities between them: their roles were hereditary female occupations; they received instruction, usually from a male teacher, in music and dance from an early age; patronage was supplied through the court, the temple, or a wealthy individual; and they would be asked to perform privately for groups of men (1992: 99). These musicians received far more education than other women of the time, and they were allowed fuller expression of their sexuality, but the boundaries and rules of their world were still delineated by men.

The women who performed at the courts and in the temples had sexual relations with men outside marriage. Although the *devadāsī* were "married" to the deity and were held to be *nityasumaṅgalī* ("ever-auspicious women") because they could never be widowed, they would also take as sexual partners the temple priests and the king who served as patron to the temple. The *kalāvant* or *tawā'if* would form exclusive sexual relationships with their patrons. This, in addition to their highly skilled performance of music and dance, distinguishes them from prostitutes (*peśavālī*), who also sing and dance (now, usually to *filmī gīt,* "film songs") but who lack the education and training of the *kalāvant.* These overt expressions of female sexuality outraged European colonial observers and Indians who had taken on the social mores of Victorian England, and by the early-twentieth century an "anti-nautch" campaign sought to ban temple dance, culminating in the Madras Devadasi (Prevention of Dedication) Act of 1947.

The *tawā'if,* often identified by the addition of the honorific *bai* to their names, are most closely associated with the vocal genre *ṭhumrī,* whose Hindi texts are romantic and mildly erotic, often alluding to the god Kṛṣṇa as an absent lover. They also excelled in the performance of the Urdu poetic form *ghazal.* These genres were and remain overwhelmingly the preserve of women musicians (Neuman, 1980: 207). In addition to these so-called light classical forms, the *tawā'if* were noted performers of *khayāl,* a genre associated with the male *gharānā* (lineages) of court musicians.

With the decline of the patronage of the courts and landowners during the period leading up to India's independence, and with increasing state repression, the milieu in which the *tawā'if* had flourished disappeared. This change, combined with greater mobility for women and access to instruction from famous male musicians, enabled a number of female singers to make the transition from performing for intimate gatherings of aristocratic patrons (known as *mujra*) to the public space of the concert hall. Notable among these were Gauhar Jan from Calcutta, Keserbai Kerkar from Goa, Siddeshwari Devi from Varanasi, and Begum Akhtar from Faizabad.

The rise of the sound film industry in the 1930s also provided an outlet for female vocalists. *Filmī gīt* ("film song"), popularized by singers such as Noorjehan (who moved to Pakistan after independence), drew on precisely those styles that had been the province of the *tawā'if.* Since the early 1940s, Lata Mangeshkar has been the most influential of all performers in this field. Her distinctive voice has been featured in thousands of songs, and, along with singers such as her sister, Asha Bhosle, and Geeta Dutt, she has dominated the genre.

A different process occurred in southern India. The movement to ban temple dance coincided with a nationalist desire to see a "pure" form of the dance (*bharata-nāṭyam*) introduced to the concert stage. The main driving force behind this was the *Brāhman* dancer Rukmini Devi. This "*Brāhmanization*"—and, therefore, greater respectability—of female professional performance started in 1910 with the singer Sarasvati Bai, the first non-*devadāsī* to perform Karnatak music professionally. Numerous schools were established where girls could study music and dance, and these fast became essential social accomplishments; according to Neuman, "Women form the vast majority of students in music colleges in both North and South India" (1980: 21). In most cases, the completion of a successful *arangēṟṟam* (public debut) does not lead to a professional career on the stage, but it serves as a social marker of the achievement of a high standard. The most famous south Indian female singer, M. S. Subbalakshmi, is noted in particular for her performances of *bhajan* (devotional songs); other prominent singers include D. K. Pattamal and the sisters C. Saroja and C. Lalitha of Bombay.

The playing of instruments, particularly professionally and in public, is traditionally the preserve of men in both the north and the south. A notable acception is the south Indian *vīṇā,* which has a long tradition of female performers; the most famous are M. S. Subbalakshmi's mother, Vina Shanmukhavadivu, and Vina Dhanammal. There are also a number of prominent female violinists, including A. Kanyakumari and Viji Krishnan Natarajan. While the playing of chordophones (stringed instruments) by women seems to cause little controversy in contemporary India, this is certainly not true for professional performers on membranophones (drums). The only professional female *tablā* (hand drum) player in south Asia, Anuradha Pal, has experienced considerable hostility from some male musicians, particularly when she is playing as an accompanist. It is also unusual for women to play aerophones (wind instruments); notable exceptions are the south Indian Sikkil sisters, who are both flutists. These continuing proscriptions may be due in part to the belief that animal skins and saliva are polluting. They are strengthened by a myth propagated by some male musicians that, although women may have great insights into *rāga* (in terms of pitch, melody, and *gamaka,* "ornamentation"), they have a lesser grasp of *tāla* (rhythm and time-keeping).

Nonspecialist and Collective Traditions

In addition to the music of female professionals, there are many local nonspecialist genres performed by women across south Asia. Many of them are associated with life-cycle rituals, and often the texts form a means of challenging dominant ideologies and the place of women in society.

At any Hindu rite, music is seen as auspicious (*maṅgal*). This is particularly true of weddings and funerals, where it is most often provided in north Indian villages by womens' singing (Henry, 1988: 25). Henry divides the songs sung by women at Bhojpuri weddings into three types: those that accompany specific stages of the ritual; those sung in the evenings before the wedding (*sagun*); and abusive songs (*gālī*) performed only when men from outside the family are present (1988: 28–29). Many wedding songs express either the sense of loss of both the bride and her family, or the tyranny she will suffer as a member of a new household. *Gālī,* in contrast, hurl abuse at the men of opposite family, serving to dissipate the tension surrounding the wedding—proprietary feelings over the bride, the extent of her dowry, and the lavishness or meagerness of the celebrations—by enacting the conflicts in song (Henry, 1988: 58–61).

The *oppāri* laments and *ayiṟa pāṭṭu* ("crying songs") of Tamil Nadu fulfill functions similar to the wedding songs of north India, although in differing contexts. *Ayiṟa pāṭṭu,* or vocalized complaints, are spontaneously sung by women of the low *Paṟaiyar* caste, who cry as they perform. Egnor notes that the performance is in "semiprivacy" in order that the song's message, which tends to concentrate on the position of women within marriage, becomes publicly known (1986: 303). *Oppāri* are improvised mourning songs performed on the death of a male relative. The texts concentrate on the inauspiciousness of becoming a widow and how, on the death of a husband, the wife will be divested of his property.

Whereas the genres above articulate concerns that transcend caste, the *Rāmāyaṇa* songs of Andhra Pradesh contrast performance spaces and caste positions. *Brāhman* women sing passages from the epic at private gatherings or while doing domestic work. Although the songs are sung primarily as an act of devotion, the women replace the ideal family of the epic with a family closer to their everyday experience (Narayana Rao, 1991: 128–130). In contrast, low-caste *Māla* and *Mādiga* women sing *Rāmāyaṇa* songs in the fields, a public space. The passages they perform avoid gender issues and concentrate on the subversion of the caste system.

Hindu women in north and south India also take part in group devotional singing of *bhajan* to various deities, both in the private space of the home and in the public space of the temple. The *bhajan* groups may include both men and women, spatially segregated; they are usually accompanied by *ḍholak* (barrel drum), harmonium, and *tāl* (cymbals), played by the singers, including the women. In this context, the ideological strictures against women's playing instruments in public spaces lose their force.

See Also

DANCE: SOUTH ASIA; HINDUISM; HOUSEHOLDS AND FAMILIES: SOUTH ASIA; MUSIC: NORTH AFRICA AND ISLAMIC MIDDLE EAST; MUSICIANS

References and Further Readings

Egnor, Margaret T. 1986. Internal iconicity in Paraiyar "crying songs." In Stuart H. Blackburn and A.K. Ramanujan, eds. *Another harmony: New essays on the folklore of India.* Delhi: Oxford University Press. 295–344.

Henry, Edward O. 1988. *Chant the names of God: Music and culture in Bhojpuri-speaking India.* San Diego, Calif.: San Diego State University Press.

Kersenboom-Story, Saskia C. 1987. *Nityasumaṅgalī: Devadasi tradition in south India.* Delhi: Motilal Banarsidass.

Kippen, James. 1988. *The tabla of Lucknow: A cultural analysis of a musical tradition.* Cambridge: Cambridge University Press.

L'Armand, Kathleen, and Adrian L'Armand. 1978. Music in Madras: The urbanization of a cultural tradition. In Bruno Nettl, ed. *Eight urban musical cultures,* 115–145. Urbana: University of Illinois Press.

Marglin, Frédérique Apffel. 1985. *Wives of the god-king: The rituals of the devadasis of Puri.* Delhi: Oxford University Press.

Neuman, Daniel M. 1980. *The life of music in north India: The organization of a musical tradition.* Detroit, Mich.: Wayne State University Press.

Post, Jennifer. 1992. Professional women in Indian music: The death of the courtesan tradition. In Ellen Koskoff, ed., *Women and music in cross-cultural perspective,* 97–109. New York: Greenwood.

———. 2000. Women and music. In Alison Arnold, ed. *The Garland encyclopedia of world music. Vol. 5, South Asia: The Indian subcontinent,* 407–417. New York: Taylor and Francis.

Raghunathji, K. 1884. Bombay dancing girls. *The Indian antiquary* 13: 165–178.

Ramaswamy, Vijaya. 1994. Women and the "domestic" in Tamil folk songs. *Man in India* 74(1): 21–37.

Rao, Velcheru Narayana. 1991. A *Ramayana* of their own: Women's oral tradition in Telugu. In Paula Richman, ed., *Many Rāmāyaṇas: The diversity of a narrative tradition in South Asia,* 114–136. Berkeley: University of California Press.

Trawick, Margaret. 1991. Wandering lost: A landless laborer's sense of place and self. In Arjun Appadurai, Frank J. Korom, and Margaret A. Mills, eds., *Gender, genre and power in south Asian expressive traditions,* 224–266. Philadelphia: University of Pennsylvania Press.

Maria Lord

MUSIC: Sub-Saharan and Southern Africa

Africa, the second largest continent on Earth, contains more than 50 countries and more than 700 distinct ethnolinguistic groups. Because north African languages and cultures have been heavily influenced by the Arab world of the Middle East, it is usual to discuss north African music separately from that of sub-Saharan Africa—a term that will be used here to refer to the southernmost region as well.

Ethnic and Musical Diversity

The most important characteristic of indigenous sub-Saharan African music is its diversity. The music of Africa, like its languages, is "ethnic-bound" rather than "nation-bound," and traditionally each ethnic group has practiced its own musical varieties, which have changed over time. Factors accounting for the diversity of musical traditions include ecology, migration, socioeconomic systems, and colonization. Sub-Saharan Africa includes savanna and grassland, tropical forests, river basins, and highlands. Sedentary agriculturists, nomadic pastoralists, hunters and gatherers, and urban dwellers populate these different environments, forming a variety of societies that range from kingdoms with hereditary aristocracies to decentralized, egalitarian, kinship-based groups.

It is inaccurate to think of African music as a single entity because of this diversity, which influences "differences in conceptions about music, the role and status of musicians, and the types of repertory, instruments, and dances performed." (Turino, 1992: 172). Nonetheless, some generalizations can be made.

Shared Musical Features

Most of African music is communal and functional; it is performed in a particular context, and not outside that context. Hunting songs, for example, are sung only in preparation for or during a hunt, and songs for girls' puberty rites are sung only during those ceremonies.

In Africa, there is often no real distinction between music and dance; some ethnolinguistic groups use one word to denote both. Many articles of dress (such as bracelets, anklets, and belts) have a musical function: the dancers often use them to mark the beat. The line between audience and performer is blurred, and often everyone present participates.

An African musical composition is not an abstract object but rather an event, something that occurs in a particular context at a particular moment. In this regard it contrasts with western compositions, which typically exist in written notated form and can be played in a variety of settings—for example, a recorded church composition may be played as background music in a secular setting.

Complex polyrhythmic patterns, interlocking singing, and variation characterize indigenous African music. Multipart patterns occur in singing and in instrumental music, with the particular nature of the tonal material varying from region to region. Widespread techniques include call-and-response, hocket (each performer in turn sounds a different note or part of the melody), and overlapping one phrase with the next. The result is musical continuity based on complementary contributions made by individuals.

Traditional Performing Groups

In traditional African societies, music is usually a collective social event in which members of a community gather together for work, a religious ceremony, or recreation. Participation may be voluntary or obligatory, imposed because of one's age, sex, status, or occupation. Several types of groups perform music: autonomous, spontaneous groups, formed for specific occasions; organized musical societies, either separated by gender or mixed; organized associations, such as warrior or hunting groups, whose members perform distinctive ritual music during their ceremonies; and groups of musical specialists attached to the traditional establishment—for example, to a royal court. Sometimes music is performed by only a particular section of the community. For example, certain songs are performed only by women in such female-focused rituals as girls' puberty rites or ceremonies celebrating the birth of twins. According to a noted Ghanaian ethnomusicologist, J. H. Kwabena Nketia (1974: 38), "Among some societies in eastern, central, and southern Africa, rites for healing the sick or for correcting certain disorders are performed by women who sing special songs and accompany themselves with rattles and drums. Mention should also be made of the special musical role that women play at funerals."

Musical Instruments

Although people often associate African music with drumming, African musicians play a wide variety of instruments, often ritualistically made from local plant and animal products. The importance of a particular instrument varies from one society to the next, and each ethnic group places different restrictions on who may play a specific instrument. Certain musical instruments are associated with both sexes; others are played only by men or only by women. Among the Xhosa, for instance, women play the mouthbow but men do not. In some societies, women are forbidden to play any kind of drum—because of taboos surrounding the drums, it is believed that a woman who plays them will become infertile. In other societies, however, women play several kinds of drums.

African musical instruments range from the simple bull-roarer (a board attached by a rope to a stick and whirled through the air) to multistringed instruments. Instruments can be divided into four main groups: (1) Stringed instruments include zithers, lutes, harps, fiddles, lyres, and musical bows. (2) Wind instruments include flutes, reed pipes, and trumpets. (3) Instruments in which a membrane vibrates include an assortment of drums, some of which are sacred objects used in religious rituals. (4) Instruments whose bodies vibrate when they are rattled, hit, struck, rubbed, or scraped include shakers and rattles, used to produce rhythm, and xylophones and thumb pianos, which are tuned and played melodically.

One famous African instrument is the "talking drum." This is a drum constructed so as to produce specific pitches as well as rhythms that imitate speech. It is used among west and central African groups whose languages rely on pitch (tone) to carry lexical meaning. Although principally used to send messages, the talking drum is also played along with animal-horn trumpets to declaim praise of important people.

Musical instruments are used in many settings. Some instruments are traditionally used only in religious rituals. Others are played for recreation or to accompany dance. Still others are used in work settings, such as cattle grazing. Some instruments are used only to accompany song; for example, Zulu solo songs were often accompanied on a gourd bow.

Two African Ethnic Groups and Their Music

African music is inextricably linked to the ethnolinguistic community in which it is performed. A brief description of the Pygmies of central equatorial Africa and the Manding of west Africa will serve to indicate the range of musical and cultural diversity.

The Pygmies still maintain a semiautonomous hunting-and-gathering existence. BaMbuti net-hunters are nomadic bands of nuclear families who move from place to place in the forest in search of game. Much of their way of life is communal and egalitarian, based on consensus. There is very little ownership of goods or private property. Survival depends on communal activity and cooperation, but men and women may have different roles, depending on the task to be accomplished.

These traits are evident in the musical culture of the Pygmies. They own few instruments, for example. The instruments they have include whistles and flutes, used to accompany singing or in informal musical duets; and rhythm sticks, rattles, several kinds of trumpets, and a musical bow. Although individuals sing cradle and hunting songs, communal singing for collective ceremonies is most important. Singing is nonspecialized: everyone participates, with leadership shifting from individual to individual, although an individual with expertise may begin or lead a song. Music performance may be gender-specific. In the *molimo* ceremony, during which the spirit of the forest is invoked, male singers take the primary role; during the *elima* puberty ceremony, however, women are the primary singers. Pygmy musical style and practice have developed from, and reflect, social and economic egalitarianism (Turino, 1992: 174).

The Manding trace their ancestry to the powerful thirteenth-century Mali empire. Contemporary Manding societies have maintained an elaborate social hierarchy, as well as hereditary occupational guilds. One of these guilds is that of the *jalis,* whose role combines functions of the musician, journalist, historian, go-between, and praise singer. Over the centuries, the *jalis* have been politically powerful, capable of encouraging heroic action in battle and embarrassing government officials through ridicule.

Not all *jalis* are men. Women are also trained to compose verses and to recite the complex genealogies, epic narratives, and songs of praise that make up a jali's performance. Male *jalis* play the xylophone, harp lute, or five-stringed plucked lute to accompany their singing; women *jalis* beat on a cylindrical piece of iron. The vocal function is primary for female *jalis,* whereas men concentrate on the instrumental function.

The relationship between a *jali* and his or her patron is very important but is not based on deference. The *jalis* interpret events of the present and the past, negotiate delicate economic and political matters, and patch up quarrels and feuds. In recent years, a number of female *jalis* have become popular recording stars. Some of them have moved to Europe and the United States, and their fame has accompanied them.

In brief, certain similarities are found in African music, such as its communal and functional nature, its complex polyrhythmic patterns, and the interconnection between music and dance. However, this music is also very diverse, as is women's participation in it.

See Also

ANCIENT INDIGENOUS CULTURES: WOMEN'S ROLES; DRUMMING; MUSIC: NORTH AFRICA AND ISLAMIC MIDDLE EAST; TRADITIONAL HEALING: AFRICA, *I and II;* TABOO

References and Further Reading

Koetting, James T. 1992. Africa/Ghana. In Jeff Todd Titon, ed., *Worlds of music,* 67–105. New York: Schirmer.

Kwadena Nketia, J. H. 1994. *The music of Africa.* New York: Norton.

Stone, Ruth M., ed. 1998. *The Garland encyclopedia of world music.* Vol. 1, *Africa.* New York and London: Garland.

Turino, Thomas. 1992. The music of sub-Saharan Africa. In Bruno Nettl et al., eds., *Excursions in world music,* 165–192. Englewood Cliffs, N. J.: Prentice-Hall.

Elyn Aviva

MUSIC: Western Classical

"Women and music" is a phrase often equated with feminist approaches to music. Feminist musicology has addressed the repertoire of inscribed—that is, written—music and the construction of music history as a manifestation of patriarchal structure and has explored this concept in various ways.

History and Historiography of Women in Music

Women have worked creatively in every era of western classical music, sometimes winning recognition, and even fame, in their own time: Hildegard of Bingen and Elisabeth Claude Jaquet de la Guerre are two examples. But until the last two decades of the twentieth century, their activity was often obscured by the constructs of music history and the musical canon. The persistent question "Why have there been no great women composers?" suggests that "greatness" is a gendered construction, and is constructed as male; this question also reveals a certain ignorance of the range of women's creativity in music. Much work by women in the classical music tradition remains hidden from view, but historical excavation is increasing.

Because music requires performance to bring it to life, it demands more intensive and authoritative negotiation with the public sphere than perhaps any other art form. Thus music is a form of creativity more comparable to playwriting than to arts such as literature or painting. Gendered ideology has traditionally impeded women who tried to enter the public sphere and has led societies to ignore, marginalize, or label as inappropriate women's public activities. To a great extent, this is still true today. Awareness of this bias results in a confrontation with "meritocracy"—the assumption that worthwhile artists or their creations will always, eventually get the attention they deserve. To feminists, meritocracy is a myth that ignores market forces and the intricate social networks controlling access to public performance.

Virginia Woolf once suggested that "for most of history, Anonymous was a woman." This is perhaps especially true of music. In the Middle Ages, anonymity was the norm; it was only later in history that the practice of affixing the artist's name to a work became widespread, possibly because names are useful in organizing, and in marketing. Hildegard, then, was not only an exceptional woman and an exceptional composer but also exceptional in that we know her name: she was one of the first composers of either sex to have a body of music survive under her authorship. Anonymity remained the norm in the fourteenth and fifteenth centuries, although the conventional history of music of that time tends to focus on the few named figures. Considering that the study of women's communities such as beguinages, convents, and abbeys has barely begun, the assumption that women did not compose in this era is ill-informed. Extensive information exists about women performers, and noblewomen were highly trained in music; this suggests that women may have composed a great deal, because performers often are also composers. It is entirely possible that works by women were sometimes attributed to men—we know, for instance, that by the sixteenth century music publishers attached the name of the famous composer Josquin des Prez to many pieces by others, simply to enhance the prestige of these works.

Women singers were not banned from early opera (as is sometimes erroneously stated), but female opera singers did face the same social stigma as actresses—an inappropriate inference about sexual availability was drawn whenever a woman made any public display. Two women composers of the early seventeenth century highlight the contrast between this stigma and its alternative. Barbara Strozzi, a courtesan who was the illegitimate daughter of her patron, Giulio Strozzi, had ready access to the audience of his all-male academy and was able to publish several volumes of her music. A recently identified painting shows her playing the viola da gamba, though she is depicted in a courtesan's pose, with one breast exposed. In contrast, Francesca Caccini published little, and she was portrayed as a background figure in humble attire, placed modestly behind her domineering father, her creativity subordinated to his showmanship. Painstaking research by Cusick (1993) has revealed the extent of Francesca's creative accomplishments.

The "great man" approach to history has influenced much writing about music, and the designation of standard "great works" is so ingrained that any assertion of women's contributions to music or women's distinct perspective on the musical experience is likely to elicit a defensive response. Furthermore, despite the current increase in compositions by women and scholarly interest in gender issues, major orchestras still program very few works by women, and presentations at scholarly meetings seldom focus on women composers. Most scholars have made no efforts to topple works by men from their dominant position in the repertoire; even those scholars who examine gender ideology in canonic music such as opera tend to concentrate on social and economic power and control in an abstract aesthetic sense (examples include Clément, 1998; Curtis, 2000; and McClary, 1992). Still, it is significant that issues such as sexism, which have long been apparent to many audience members, are beginning to be addressed.

In the 1990s, feminist scholarship and what is sometimes called the "new musicology" gained attention (McClary, 1991), but valuable work that focused on women (rather than on critical theory) had already been going on for some years. Judith Tick (2000) and Julie Anne Sadie (1995) note a long history of scholarship, particularly by women, about women composers. However, some of this material is not entirely satisfactory. In the 1970s, for instance, research on women in music was undertaken in response to feminst activism and consciousness-raising, but some of this enthusiastic compensatory work was inaccurate and lacked documentation. More recently, *The Norton/Grove Dictionary of Women Composers* (1995) covers 875 women, yet in many cases it remains difficult to find out how to obtain their music; and in the current edition of the Grove dictionary of music, the volume *Women* is strikingly brief; in fact, not one article on a woman composer comes even close in length to the article on the metronome in *The New Grove Dictionary of Musical Instruments.* Smith (1997) and Solie (1997) offer provocative interpretations of Grove's agenda, arguing that the editors systematically avoided feminist scholarship. More thorough information on sources is provided by Barbara Garvey Jackson (1994), but only for a specific period.

Feminist and Critical Methodologies

The dichotomy between scholarly interest in women's musical creativity and more abstract feminist theorizing has concerned many scholars. Some prominent musicologists have aligned with elite academic theorists and distanced themselves from those doing the practical recovery work of gathering empirical information and materials about women. For instance, Susan McClary (1991) has reinterpreted numerous canonical works and investigated current figures (both "serious" composers and popular musicians) but has not addressed historical female composers or musicians (Higgins, 1993).

Perhaps the most compelling scholarship has been informed by a range of feminist and critical methodologies but has also recognized that basic, positivistic work on women remains to be done (Solie, 1993). Information as such is a crucial first step in understanding women's impact on music, but further steps, including methodological considerations and contextualizing, are needed.

Gender, Categories of Music, and Musical Language

Is music gendered? This question can be approached from many angles. One approach involves developing repertories and practices to solidify, celebrate, and empower women's political and cultural identity. For example, the repertories of Cris Williamson and Holly Near (who founded Olivia Records), were based on a folk revival and in turn served as a historical underpinning for the overtly political music of Ani deFranco in the 1990s. (DeFranco, like Near, maintains economic control over her creative work through her own record company, Righteous Babes).

Another approach is to examine gender in the musical language of the western classical tradition. For instance, characters in canonical works often reflect the gender ideology of a male composer and his time (Solie, 1992; McClary, 1992). Such studies consider works with texts (including songs and operas) in which musical language complements or reinforces characterization through lyrics.

Music without a text can also be examined. Music is often said to be a "universal language," transcending any limiting aspects of identity, such as gender. Some scholars have challenged this concept, which informs most discussions of canonic "great works," arguing that it actually assumes a specifically male perspective as normative. Studies of gender roles manifested in music have sought to dispel the idea of music as universal and have described it instead as a conveyor of gender ideology. Practitioners of formal musical analysis (that is, analysis of music apart from any social or cultural functions) have tended to feel most threatened by this approach, possibly because formal dissection seems justifiable only if a work is presumed to be important.

One way to consider gender in music is to compare musical organization with literary and narrative procedures. This approach is stimulating, often has metaphorical value, and can sometimes be used in conjunction with contextual considerations. However, it has been overused and occasionally applied arbitrarily. For example, A. B. Marx described sonata form as having a "masculine" first theme and a "feminine" second theme, clearly intending this as just one possible strategy for understanding the form, and most other theorists who have used such terms had similar intentions; but McClary (1991) and Citron (1993) take Marx's description as a principle for explication of all works in sonata form. In her own study of sonata form (Curtis, 1997), the present author has argued for careful consideration of historical specifics as a way of understanding gender in this genre, rather than seeing thematic content as anthropomorphic. Historically grounded considerations of gender in musical form include Kallberg's study (1996) of noctournes by Chopin, Clara Wieck Schumann, and Fanny Mendelssohn Hensel; and Block's study (1998) of Amy Beach's piano concerto—these scholars both take the composer's milieu into account.

McClary's liveliness, energy, and polemical style have made hers a refreshing voice in academic conversations, although her heightened rhetoric has sometimes elicited criticism not only of her own arguments but of broader feminist scholarship, including some that seems more solidly grounded. McClary has been especially compelling in offering her subjective interpretations of women characters as presented by men, and of the perspectives taken by some current women composers and performers.

Ruth Solie (who was elected president of the American Musicological Society in 1997) has contributed methodologically sophisticated assessments of women performers and scholars. She considers the relevance of a range of feminist theory to music, evaluates various directions of music scholarship, and offers reasoned responses to attacks on feminist perspectives.

Practical Implications of Musical Scholarship

The scholarly focus on cultural contexts and ethnographic studies of women as performers and patrons and of music in communities have led to a broader and more reasoned understanding of music's functions; but this theoretical emphasis can also lead to neglect of basic biographical recovery work. Arguably, we need to offer "great women" as a counterpart of "great men"; arguably, too, we should not allow theories of music's social functions to distract us from the practical need of performing ensembles to present innovative, cohesive programs. Audiences and established traditional ensembles want concerts and recitals to be inclusive, fresh, and varied. Feminist musicology is likely to be most broadly influential when it is keeps listeners and practitioners in mind; scholarship should be carried out with an awareness of actual musical life—the world of audiences, listeners, performers.

During its early stages, much recovery work on women was done by scholarly amateurs, and their work is still consulted, although—as noted above, it may include some inaccuracies. Even biographical studies of individual women, such as Amy Beach and Ruth Crawford Seeger, have had to contend with inaccurate and stereotypical images or—as with Clara Schumann—myths built up by the woman herself and perpetuated by her family and authorized biographers. More recent biographers of Beach, Seeger, and Clara Schumann (Block, 1998; Reich, 1985; Tick, 1997) have produced more balanced and judicious studies, combining feminist methodologies and traditional scholarship. Such scholars have been influential in "changing the subject" (as Solie, 1993, puts it), and they exemplify the importance of studying women in music history.

See Also

HISTORY; MUSIC: COMPOSERS; MUSIC: OPERA; MUSICIANS

References and Further Reading

Ammer, Christine. 1980. *Unsung: A history of women in American music.* Westport, Conn.: Greenwood (2nd ed., Amadeus, 2001).

Barr, Cyrilla. 1998. *Elizabeth Sprague Coolidge: American patron of music.* New York: Schirmer.

Block, Adrienne F. 1998. *Amy Beach: Passionate Victorian.* New York: Oxford University Press.

Citron, Marcia J. 1993. *Gender and the musical canon.* Cambridge: Cambridge University Press.

Clément, Catherine. 1988. *Opera, or, the undoing of women.* Trans. Betsy Wing. Minneapolis: University of Minnesota Press.

Cook, Susan C., and Judy S. Tsou. 1994. *Cecilia reclaimed: Feminist perspectives on gender and music.* Urbana: University of Illinois Press.

Curtis, Liane. 1997. Rebecca Clarke and sonata form: Questions of gender and genre. *Musical Quarterly* 81: 393–429.

———. 2000. The sexual politics of teaching Mozart's Don Fiovanni. *NWSA Journal* 12: 119–142.

Cusick, Suzanne G. 1993. "Thinking from Women's Lives": Francesco Caccini after 1627. In Kimber Marshall, ed., *Rediscovering the muses: Women's musical traditions.* Boston: Northeastern University Press.

Gillett, Paula. 2000. *Musical women in England, 1870–1914: Encroaching on all man's privileges.* New York: St. Martin's.

Higgins, Paula. 1993. Women in music, feminist criticism, and guerrilla musicology: Reflections on recent polemics. *19th Century Music* 17(Fall): 174–192.

Jackson, Barbara Garvey. 1994. *"Say, can you deny me": A guide to surviving music by women from the sixteenth through the eighteenth centuries.* Fayetteville: University of Arkansas Press.

Kallberg, Jeffrey. 1996. "The harmony of the tea table: Gender and ideology in the piano nocturne. In *Chopin at the boundaries: Sex, history, and musical genre.* Cambridge, Mass.: Harvard University Press.

Locke, Ralph P., and Cyrilla Varr, eds. 1997. *Cultivating music in America: Women patrons and activists since 1860.* Berkeley: University of California Press.

McClary, Susan. 1991. *Feminine endings: music, gender, and sexuality.* Minneapolis: University of Minnesota Press.

———. 1992. *Georges Bizet, Carmen.* Cambridge: Cambridge University Press.

Pendle, Karin. 1991. *Women and music: A history.* Bloomington: University of Indiana Press. (2nd ed. 2000).

Reich, Nancy. 1985. *Clara Schumann: The artist and the woman.* Ithaca, N.Y.: Cornell University Press.

Sadie, Julie Ann, and Rhian Samuel, eds. 1995. *The Norton/Grove dictionary of women composers.* New York: Norton. (Also publilshed as *The New Grove Dictionary of Women Composers.* London: Macmillan, 1994.)

Smith, Catherine Parsons. 1997. "A distinguishing virility": Feminism and modernism in American art music. In Susan C. Cook and Judy S. Tsou, eds., *Cecilia reclaimed: Feminist perspectives on gender and music,* 90–106. Urbana: University of Illinois Press.

———. 1997. Review of the *Norton/Grove dictionary of women composers. Women and music: A Journal of Gender and Culture* 1:79–84.

Solie, Ruth A. Changing the subject. *Current Musicology* 53: 55–66.

———. 1997. Defining feminism: Conundrums, contexts, communities. *Women and Music: A Journal of Gender and Culture* 1: 2–11.

———. 1992. Whose life? The gendered self in Schumann's Frauenliebe songs. In Steven Paul Scher, ed., *Music and Text: Critical Inquiries,* 219–240. Cambridge: Cambridge University Press.

———, ed. 1993. *Musicology and difference: Gender and sexuality in music scholarship.* Berkeley: University of California Press.

Tick, Judith. 1997. *Ruth Crawford Seeger: A composer's search for American music.* New York: Oxford University Press.

———. 2000. Women and Music. *The new Grove dictionary of music and musicians,* 2nd ed. London: Macmillan.

Zaimont, Judith Lang, et al., eds. 1984–1991. *The musical woman: An international perspective.* 3 vols. Westport, Conn.: Greenwood.

Liane Curtis

MUSICIANS

Study of Women as Musicians

There is almost no culture in the world that does not have significant genres of music created by women, and some of these are exclusively for women. Western society is the notable exception, yet it is here that most writing about women as musicians has been done. The two main approaches are musicological (the history and analysis of western music) and ethnomusicological (the anthropological study of music in culture). Some larger reference works and musicological texts attempt to span both approaches, and these books are usually the major source of technical information about music (Sadie and Tyrell, 1999). Women as musicians are also discussed in many other disciplines, such as history, women's studies, and theory of culture. Where the research is focused elsewhere, however, one often must read between the lines.

Gender Bias in Musicology and Ethnomusicology

In ethnomusicology it is fairly common practice to study genres distinct to women and men because music is studied in respect to activities often specific to male and female roles in society. In musicology, however, the assumption is still that music is "normally" written by men. One does not talk of Gustav Mahler's and Ludwig van Beethoven's music as "men's music," for example, nor are they generally discussed in critical writing in terms of their gender. This assumption reinforced, if not fostered, the neglect of women as musicians in musicological study, especially in work done before 1970. This neglect is reflected in the absence of women composers from many standard music dictionaries. To offset this omission, numerous bibliographies and studies of women as musicians have been published in the past twenty years. An attempt to address gender imbalance in musicological reference works has begun, and in both musicology and ethnomusicology, women are increasingly being represented in their own words (Vander, 1988). Gender bias in musicology has also become a focus of study (McClary, 1991; Solie, 1993).

Perspective of the Writer

The way women musicians have been discussed in writing is often determined by the culture and gender of the writer. The fact that Navajo women choose male dance partners in the Enemyway Ceremony is seen by one writer as a reflection of the power women have in that society (McAllester, 1992). Another, more influenced by women's studies, sees Cherokee women's music as structured sound promoting the notions of gender balance and harmony characteristic of Cherokee society (Herndon, 1990).

Role of Women and Its Relationship to Music

In many cultures, including western culture, women's roles as caretakers, educators, upholders of tradition, and monitors of important rites of passage determine their role as musicians. In a number of societies, professional lamenters at funerals or weddings are women; in the Japanese tea ceremony, the koto is usually played by a woman; lullabies are the prerogative of women worldwide; teaching pieces in the western classical repertoire are often composed by women; and women in south India are celebrated gurus of Karnatak music. Distinct genres of music are often associated with rites surrounding menstruation, circumcision, marriage, childbearing, menopause, death, healing, and the cycle of daily work. Such music can assert women's identity and status, even within societies oppressive to women. Without a Zulu bride's performance of song and dance at her wedding, for example, the marriage is not considered sanctified. Swazi women can sing publicly of the abuse inflicted by their husbands, even though they are unable to protest to them in private. Thonga women steadfastly maintain a different language from men's, which empowers their music as well as other aspects of their life (Hansen, 1991).

Women's Music and Abuse

Abuse is the theme of many blues lyrics. Bessie Smith (1894–1937) and Billie Holiday (1915–1959) are popular not only as singers but also as icons of female suffering. It has been argued that the tragic demise of operatic heroines like Tosca, Madama Butterfly, Carmen, Brünnhilde, and Violetta elicited some of men's most richly sensual music, and that the male audience and male managers of singers and opera houses demanded the dramatization of women threatened, ill-treated, abandoned, put to death, or committing suicide (Clément, 1989). And, of course, the heroines sing their most glorious music just before they die. Opera prima donnas, or divas, as they became known, were usually more celebrated than their male counterparts. Their manipulation by men itself became the subject of artistic treatment, as in Offenbach's opera *Les contes d'Hoffmann* and George du Maurier's novel *Trilby.*

Composer and Performer

The western distinction between composer and performer that underpins these examples is a notable subtext in musicology. It has had a far greater negative impact on women musicians than on men, although it has affected both. Marriage frequently underscores the distinction. Clara Wieck (1819–1896) was brought up to consider herself a pianist-composer. After marrying Robert Schumann, she wrote that women were inherently weaker than men at composition and she spoke disparagingly of her Piano Trio in G Minor, Op. 17, as "woman's work" (Neuls-Bates, 1986). The American musician Amy Beach (1867–1944) became a full-time composer in response to her husband's discouragement of her concert career as a pianist (Cohen, 1987). Much of the early feminist literature on women as composers was concerned primarily with bringing into prominence women whom disparagement and neglect had made disappear altogether (Stern, 1978). More recent studies are concerned with why and how women's compositions survive at all (Garvey Jackson, 1994).

Acceptability of Women as Performers

One issue frequently brought out in musicological writing is the greater acceptance of women as performers than as composers. Performers in western society rose to prominence in early nineteenth-century opera, particularly through the development of Italian bel canto singing and the demise of the male castrato. Distinguished women singers include Jenny Lind (Sweden, 1820–1887), Anna Bahr-Mildenburg (Germany, 1872–1947), and Maria Callas (United States, 1923–1977). Women as string or keyboard players have in certain periods been undervalued, viewed simply as a fulfillment of men's domestic needs (Leppert, 1987). In other periods and cultures, they have been exalted and even deified; examples are the Hindu goddess Sarasvati and the Christian saint Cecilia.

Women as Instrumentalists

Women drummers are rare in the classical music of India, Pakistan, Africa, and western Europe, and percussion instruments carrying high status are generally not played by women (gongs or metallophones in Indonesia and *timbila* xylophones in Mozambique). Hand cymbals, bells, shakers, and leg rattles, however, are often associated with women musicians and dancers. In contemporary avant-garde music of the West, women percussionists have recently made a significant impact (for example Robyn Schulkowsky and Eveleyn Glennie); but in jazz, rock, and pop music, it is normal to find women as singers, but rare to see them playing instruments. Women in western classical music seem to favor strings, small wind instruments, harp, or keyboard (piano, organ, harpsichord). From the beginning of the orchestra in the late seventeenth century, women were often excluded. During the nineteenth century, such exclusion developed into normal practice and in some cases policy. A considerable number of all-women symphony orchestras were organized from the end of the nineteenth century, particularly in the United States, to counter this prejudice against employing women as orchestral musicians. Although the number of women in the major orchestras of the world is now higher than ever before, it is still low.

Prominent Women Composers

The links among the women's movement, political struggles, and musical emancipation remain severely underresearched despite the example of the composer and suffragist Ethel Smyth (1858–1944). Smyth not only challenged the British political establishment; she also challenged the prevailing notion that women's work was intimate and insipid by writing large-scale, bold compositions such as her opera *The Wreckers* (1939). Other prominent and influential women composers from different countries, periods, and traditions are Hildegard of Bingen (Germany, 1098–1179), Francesca Caccini (Florence, 1587–1640), O-Yo (Japan, 1840–1901), Nadia Boulanger (France, 1887–1979), Constance Magogo (South Africa, c. 1900–1984), and Nicola Lefanu (Britain, b. 1947). There are many good bibliographies, dictionaries, and encyclopedias of women composers and performers in which thousands of other examples can be found.

Critiques of Women Musicians

Women fill most of the supportive roles in music (librarianship, teaching, volunteer work), while men fill the senior institutional positions (Kosloff, 1984). The odds against women's orchestral works being played by a major symphony orchestra or conducted by a woman are high. Even when such obstacles are overcome, most of the senior full-time newspaper reviewers whose opinions make or break a composer's career are male. An interesting case involving prejudiced criticism is that of the Benedictine monk Marian Stecher. His fugues were derided in 1825 because they were thought to be a woman's work (his name was misspelled in print as Mariane Stecher) but praised by a twentieth-century author who did not think a woman could write such good fugues (Garvey Jackson, 1994). Gender-free or gender-aware criticism is certainly more common in ethnomusicology than in musicology. In this regard, the International Council for Traditional Music's Study Group on Music and Gender plays an important role, not only linking women as musicians interculturally but also helping to forge connections between different academic ways of approaching the study of women as musicians.

See Also

MUSIC, *specific entries*

References and Further Reading

Clément, Cathérine. 1989. *Opera, or the undoing of women.* Trans. Betsy Wing. London: Virago.

Cohen, Aaron. 1987. *International encyclopedia of women composers.* 2nd ed. New York: Books and Music.

Garvey Jackson, Barbara. 1994. *"Say can you deny me": A guide to surviving music by women composers from the sixteenth through the eighteenth centuries.* Fayetteville: University of Arkansas Press.

Hansen, Deirdre. 1991s. My research among the Tembe-Thonga of the Kosi Bay Area. In Carol Muller, ed., *Papers presented at the Tenth Symposium on Ethnomusicology,* 40–48. Grahamstown: International Library of African Music.

Herndon, Marcia. 1990. Biology and culture: Music, gender, power and ambiguity. In Marcia Herndon and Susanne Ziegler, eds., *Music, gender, and culture,* 11–26. Wilhelmshaven: Florian Noetzel Verlag.

Kosloff, Doris Lang. 1984. The woman opera conductor: A personal perspective. In Judith Lang Zaimont, ed., *Musical women: An international perspective,* 235–243. Westport, Conn.: Greenwood.

Leppert, Richard. 1987. Music, domestic life and cultural chauvinism: Images of British subjects at home in India. In Richard Leppert and Susan McClary, eds., *Music and society: The politics of composition, performance and reception,* 63–104. Cambridge: Cambridge University Press.

McAllester, David. 1992. North America/Native America. In Jeff Todd Titon, gen. ed., *Worlds of music: An introduction to the music of the world's peoples.* 2nd ed., 16–66. New York: Schirmer.

McClary, Susan. 1991. *Feminine endings: Music, gender, and sexuality.* Minneapolis and London: University of Minnesota Press.

Neuls-Bates, Carol, ed. 1986. *Women in music: An anthology of source readings from the Middle Ages to the present.* New York: Harper and Row.

Sadie, Stanley, and John Tyrell, eds. 1999. *New Grove dictionary of music and musicians.* 2nd ed. London: Macmillan.

Solie, Ruth A. 1993. *Musicology and difference: Gender and sexuality in music scholarship.* Berpeley: University of California Press.

Stern, Susan. 1978. *Women composers: A handbook.* London: Scarecrow.

Vander, Judith. 1988. *Songprints: The musical experiences of five Shoshone women.* Urbana and Chicago: University of Illinois Press.

Christine Lucia

MUSLIMS

See FAMILY: RELIGIOUS AND LEGAL SYSTEMS—ISLAMIC TRADITIONS AND ISLAM.

MYSTICISM

The word *mysticism* is derived from Greek *mystikos,* "initiated person," which can be traced to a root meaning "to shut one's eyes." It denotes a range of beliefs and practices associated with experiences of a reality other than what can be perceived by the ordinary human senses or understood through reason. Although such experiences are empty of the data of ordinary consciousness, they are accompanied by deep emotion—often, joy and peace. The *mystic*—a practitioner of mysticism—seeks to realize ultimate reality through an arduous psychological process that may be equated with a passage through death to a new life. Thus, the mystical experience is not an end in itself but a gateway into a more desirable way of living in the world. Zen Buddhism calls this final stage a "return to the marketplace"; as the sixteenth-century Christian saint Teresa of Avila expressed it from a woman's viewpoint, "The spiritual marriage is good for this: giving birth to works, always works" (1957: 172).

Ethical integrity stands at the beginning and the end of the mystical way. Wise guidance is generally considered to be important for the seeker. Many different schools believe that the signs that distinguish true from false mysticism are the former's humility, selflessness, love, and compassion.

The terms *mysticism* and *mystical* are widely and loosely employed in modern western societies, especially in the "new age" movements. Evelyn Underhill attempts to clarify the resulting confusion:

> [One might] end with a vague idea that every kind of supersensual theory and practice is somehow "mystical." ... Mysticism in its pure form means ... union with the Absolute, and nothing else, and the mystic is the person who attains to this union ... brushing aside the visible universe, even in its supernormal manifestations—It is not philosophy, it has nothing in common with occult knowledge—It is the art of establishing a conscious relation with the Absolute. (1967: 71, 72, 81)

History and Forms of Mysticism

Cultures in many parts of the world have myths of a former time when human beings lived naturally in unity with ultimate reality. In 350 B.C.E., Dshuang Dai of China spoke of the "true human being" in reference to people of archaic consciousness who lived in total unity—nothing outside them, no ego, no time, no space.

Mystics view human history as an evolution and differentiation of consciousness. In this process, the primordial unity is lost as some part emerges from the whole and humans are tempted to become caught up in this separate part. At the same time, they begin to feel a longing to recover their lost unity, as well as to reintegrate the parts of the consciousness that emerged in the past and became lost. This mystical longing is perceived in different forms at different stages in the evolution of consciousness, which may be designated *magical, mythical, mental,* and *integral.*

The magical consciousness evidently arose when human beings were aware of the world "outside" them, though the "I" was almost unrecognized. Paleolithic people lived by hunting and gathering. Women were closely linked with the powers of life and may thus have developed great receptivity and creativity. People began to use magic rituals for protection and domination. Male and female shamans may have begun to seek ecstasy and trance states not only to dominate natural forces but also to ascend to heaven and thus restore unity between heaven and earth.

Human consciousness developed through many millennia, as humans became increasingly aware of the individual "I." This was a time when myths were woven. These ancient narratives, full of archetypal symbolism, present various versions of the human soul's nature and its difficult path back to unity. In the Neolithic era, some peoples settled in villages and cultivated crops, a task that probably was the special realm of women. Many later mythologies still center on an Earth Goddess or Great Mother: Cybele in Anatolia, Isis in ancient Egypt, Demeter in Greece, or Ceres in Rome. (The mysticism of the Eleusinian mysteries of classical Greece centered on Demeter.) Most of the world's polytheistic religions include numerous goddesses who are archetypes of womanhood—for example, Artemis, Pallas Athene, Hera, and Aphrodite in ancient Greece.

During the last millennium B.C.E., people in certain cultures developed ways to approach reality conceptually and formulated principles of order and domination, first through philosophy, later through the sciences, and finally through technology. Greek philosophy shaped the western mentality and through European colonization permeated much of the world. This mental mode of consciousness is often seen as closely linked to patriarchy.

Mysticism seems to have become most highly developed when world religions moved beyond the bounds of single cultures. The Vedas and Upanishads, sacred writings of Hinduism, were produced during the first millennium B.C.E.; Shakyamuni Buddha lived in the sixth century B.C.E.; Lao Tzu formulated Taoism in the sixth century B.C.E.; and at the same period, the Hebrew prophets were setting down their scriptures. Christian mysticism followed within three centuries of the death of Jesus, and Sufism was present in Islam after about the same length of time.

The mysticism of mental conscousness seeks to recover unity by going beyond thinking and knowing. Zen, a Buddhist mystic school, is called "a special transmission beyond teaching, no leaning on words and letters." A body of Christian mystical writings from the fourteenth century are titled *The Cloud of Unknowing.* The very strength of conceptual thinking, it is held, can also be its weakness, just as eating enough brings health but eating too much causes sickness. Reason can make good maps, but depending entirely on them can cause one to lose touch with the reality that they do not portray.

Modern-day mystics attribute many problems to loss of unity, from mental illnesses to ecological catastrophes. They seek fulfillment of their mystical longing in traditions from around the world: yoga from India, Zen's "awakening to the realization of empty oneness," or nearly forgotten disciplines of Christian mysticism. Many seekers combine these traditions and find new depths in the resonances among them.

As the mystic exposes the long-buried layers of consciousness, "the archetype [of the priestess] becomes active" (Dunn Mascetti, 1996: 208). Feminist spiritual movements such as goddess worship, Wicca, and ecofeminist or Gaia cults focus on the unity of all living things and the interconnection of human and cosmic life. Joanna Macy writes, "I believe that we are summoned now to awaken from a spell. The spell we must shake off is a case of mistaken identity, a millennia-long amnesia as to who we really are. . . . We are called to rediscover our true nature, coextensive with all life on this planet" (1989: 201).

Because the true mystic wants to give, rather than to get, by becoming forgetful of the "I," magic power is no longer sought as a form of domination but instead is a manifestation of "not-I," or oneness. Myths, rites, and doctrines are no longer expressions of dominance and hegemony but symbolic manifestations of oneness. Awakening must be forgotten—not rationalized—if one is to become a truly natural human being.

Mysticism is expressed in many different ways, but the most common are in terms of vision, knowledge, union, and love. The Jewish, Christian, and Islamic traditions use personal language, while Buddhist tradition prefers impersonal, abstract language. Some mystics withdraw from the world, like Hinayana Buddhists or Christian hermits; others, like Mahayana Buddhists or Sufis, return to the marketplace. In yoga and Zen, great importance is given to the body, mainly to posture and breathing, whereas western spirituality has paid these matters much less attention. Mysticism is central to some orthodox religions while others have marginalized it. Even the scope of mystical realization can be seen to vary: gnostics limit it to only some people, but Zen holds that everyone is essentially Buddha and capable of realizing it.

Mysticism and Women's Spirituality

Patriarchal religions have often cast doubt on whether women are perfect human beings with a capacity to become enlightened, but true mystics around the world have looked beyond gender distinctions. St. Paul wrote that in the Christian church, "There are no distinctions between Jew and Greek, slave and free, male and female, but all of you are one in Christ Jesus" (Galatians 4:28). In the thirteenth-century *Shobogenzo Raihai Tokuzai,* Dôgen Zenji wrote, "Emptiness is emptiness . . . that is the same in a woman [as in a man]." His contemporary, the Sufi poet and mystic Attar, said, "In the Unity, what remains of 'I' or 'thou'? So how can 'man' or 'woman' continue to be?" (Gürsoy-Maskali, 1979: 239).

Some mystics have contended that women are especially open to mystical experience. Teresa of Avila observed, "There are many more [women] than men, who receive these gifts from the Lord. . . . They improve much more on this way than men" (1957: 244). Some twentieth-century psychological theorists have claimed that women have a natural tendency toward knowing by unification because they start identifying with their mothers when they discover their female identity, whereas men realize their male identity through separation from their mothers.

Many cultures have viewed women as especially sensitive to the unconscious levels of life and gifted as intermediaries between the human and supernatural worlds. Greek oracles and Roman sybils were women who were believed to deliver messages from beyond the human world. In some Siberian and Native American cultures, male shamans assumed female dress and gender roles.

Mysticism is often related to extraordinary phenomena such as visions and "out-of-body" experiences, but these are not the core of the mystical experience. Where it is expressed in symbolic terms, however, women's experience tends to differ from that of men. Reported visions that stem from the experience of being female include the images of Sophia Maria (Wisdom Mary) experienced by Hildegard von Bingen, Julian of Norwich's perception of God as Mother, and many of the tropes used by Teresa of Avila.

Western patriarchal culture emphasizes experimental and rational knowledge and has tended to marginalize mysticism as dangerous or useless, or even to criminalize it as heresy. Mystics have been persecuted because of their inner freedom and their resistance to manipulation by the powerful. Christian contemplatives like Teresa of Avila were often suspected of heretical practices by Roman Catholic authorities, and some women mystics were even executed as witches—for example, Joan of Arc in the fifteenth century. Until recent times, women particularly have suffered through their exclusion from an orthodox spirituality that stressed thinking and activism. The myticism that plays an important part in many women's belief has often been as marginal as the women themselves.

Mystic Cults and Women

From ancient times, mystic cults (systems of religious practice) have centered on mystical death that leads to new life and to unity with heaven, the divine or ultimate reality. This symbolism is a part of many rituals that celebrate life-cycle passages, including birth, menarche, marriage, and death. All of these can be initiatory moments for women. The symbolism of life through death is still present in the initiation into some women's Christian communities, where entrants "die to the world" in order to be reborn into eternal life.

In the mythical stage, women's communities developed secret rituals that became a basis for women's mystic cults—for example, the Maenads in Greek Dionysian mysteries, or the witches' covens in medieval Europe. Some present-day feminists in the United States and elsewhere are reconstructing such cults: "Women [are] trying to create covens in which worship of the Goddess, special reverence for nature, and new ways of bonding might flourish" (Carmody, 1989: 222).

The woman approaching mysticism must always ask: What is happening in this mystical experience, or in this cult? Is it true realization of ultimate reality, or has it been deformed by anger, greed, or folly? Is it stalled at the level of the magical, mythical, or mental, or has it progressed to the final level of integration? Participation in true mysticism is often seen as a path to safeguarding all life on earth. "What are the ways for the future?" asks the Kiowa Apache mystic Chasing Bear (1992: 4, 5), founder of the Sisters of the Sacred Circle. She answers: "To get in balance with the earth ... to sit very quietly within yourself."

See Also

HERESY; MARTYRS; MOTHER EARTH; MYTH; NUNS; SAINTS; SPIRITUALITY: OVERVIEW; WITCHES: ASIA; WITCHES: WESTERN WORLD; WOMANSPIRIT

References and Further Readings

Adams, Carol J., ed. 1992. *Ecofeminism and the sacred.* New York: Orbis.

Carmody, Denise Lardner. 1989. *Women and world religions.* 2nd ed. Englewood Cliffs, N. J.: Prentice-Hall.

Chasing Bear, OowahNay. 1992. Spirituality: A threat to genocide. In *Common ground.* Philadelphia: Wider Quaker Fellowship.

Dunn Mascetti, Manuela. 1990. *The song of Eve.* London: Labyrinth.

Giles, Mary E., 1982. *The feminist mystic.* New York: Crossroads.

Gürsoy-Maskali, Emine. 1979. Women mystics in Islam. In Bo Utas, ed., *Women in Islamic societies: Social attitude and historical perspectives,* 238-243. London: Curzon.

Halkes, Catharine J. M. 1991. Ecology and feminism. In *New creation: Christian feminism and the renewal of the earth.* Louisville, Ky.: Westminster/John Knox.

Harding, M. Esther. 1976. *Women's mysteries, ancient and modern.* New York: Harper Colophon.

Kienzle, B., and P. Walker, eds. 1997. *Women prophets and preachers.* Berkeley: University of California Press.

King, Karen L. 1997. *Women and goddess traditions.* Philadelphia: Fortress.

Macy, Joanna. 1989. Awakening of the ecological self. In Judith Plant, ed., *Healing the wounds.* Philadelphia: New Society.

Teresa of Avila. 1957. *Su vida* and *Las moradas.* Madrid: Espasa Calpe. (Originally published 1565, 1577; trans. as "The book of her life" and "Interior castle" in her *Collected works,* 2nd ed. Washington, D.C.: ICS Publications.)

Tooker, Elisabeth, ed. 1979. *Native North American spirituality of the eastern woodlands.* Mahwah, N. J.: Paulist.

Underhill, Evelyn. 1967. *Mysticism.* London: Methuen.

Warledo, Jackie. 1992. A tenderness for their people. In *Common ground.* Philadelphia: Wider Quaker Fellowship.

Ana María Schlüter Rodés

MYTH

The contemporary interest in women and mythology arises from several distinct sources. Some early feminists tended to ignore religion, but now there is a new appreciation of the role played by systems of representation in the formation of consciousness. Images and symbols can affect not only the mind but also the body and its drives, and the development of an enabling female subjectivity.

Some feminists, in reaction to the pervasiveness of traditional and new forms of patriarchal mythology, are attempting to develop a woman-based spirituality. Others are concerned that, despite the advent of "scientific" consciousness, layers of irrationality continue to govern the social world, often underpinned by new forms of patriarchal representation whose power needs to be confronted.

Two main questions can be said to arise in any approach to myth: How do we read, evaluate, or relate to existing mythological systems, ancient or contemporary? How do we construct female symbolic systems and myths that are genuinely emancipatory?

Evaluating Existing Myths

In evaluating existing myths, one difficulty is that there is no universal definition of what constitutes a myth. Moreover, mythological studies often reflect the fashions and gender-related prejudices of the last two hundred years of intellectual history.

One theory sees mythic consciousness as a protoscientific attempt to explain social, theological, or biological phenomena, by people who had not yet developed technology or deductive logic. Today it is frequently argued that this theory is based on a fairly imperialist or ethnocentric notion of what constitutes "truth," and on an assumption that advanced scientific consciousness will eventually supersede mythic consciousness. Rather, it is held, the evidence suggests that the demise of a religious worldview—corresponding with a rise of new, largely militaristic, myths and rituals—may signal, not secular enlightenment, but shifts in the boundaries of patriarchal consciousness.

Another, related theory is that myth has its origin in primitive ritual, and that ritual is a precursor of conceptual thought. This theory too has been questioned; the empirical evidence against it includes the rituals of the ostensibly atheistic Soviet Union and of other western cultures. Another objection to this theory has to do with its implications, given the almost unilateral exclusion of women from officiating at rituals in patriarchal culture: the theory seems to imply that if women cannot officiate at public rituals, they cannot develop the capacity to think.

Archetypal and structuralist theories of myth are also problematic, especially from a feminist perspective. Archetypal theories often "freeze" socially specific male and female characteristics, viewing them as enduring features of "masculinity" and "femininity," and ignoring the social contexts in which such traits develop. Structuralist theories sometimes ignore the fact that myth is malleable, multivalent, and subject to the reversals and unresolved paradoxes of life. Like archetypal theorists, structuralists sometimes freeze what are essentially imaginative and creative categories of thought into predetermined logical structures, ignoring such issues as power, economics, and ethnicity.

Theories of the origins of myths often contain unexamined suppositions favoring powerful interest groups; the weakness of such theories is, precisely, their failure to take account of, or to challenge, the subordinate position of women. For instance, these theories often reinforce and perpetuate dichotomies such as culture versus nature and sacred versus profane; they seldom ask why mythology so often places women at the impure or "natural" end of the human spectrum, values the particular over the collective, or depicts women as disruptive forces threatening the order of the universe—or why folklore, magic, and some rituals have nevertheless remained within the province of women. It is often argued that until the advent of feminist scholarship, theories about the origins of myths took for granted what needed to be explained.

A feminist analysis or concept of myth, however, has not yet been definitively formulated; in fact, establishing such a definition might be more like creating a new myth than analyzing an existing one. Feminists often say that they need an approach to the politics of myth, and that many factors—materialist, genealogical, and psychodynamic—will affect their strategies of questioning and interpretation. These factors will also need to be taken into account in contemporary efforts to revive or construct mythological systems—a problematic area because myths are essentially collective rather than individual creations.

Theorists now tend to see myths and rituals as both reflecting and affecting social reality. Myth and ritual can be part of the strategy of a dominant culture—as, for example, when its members reserve to themselves the right of interpretation, so that myth and ritual become dogma rather than playful or imaginative realms of discouse. Thus, like many other features of patriarchy, rituals and myths that are reappropriated, reimagined, or simply invented carry a power that is useful for subverting and transforming existing cultures or envisioning new ones.

With regard to examining or constructing myths, certain generalizations are frequently offered:

1. The written versions of myths are almost always androcentric. The reasoning behind this generalization is that the development of writing presupposes some degree of elitism and cultural petrifaction, and elites are typically male.
2. Although women often appear in these myths, they usually appear only if they serve a patriarchal order; this generalization would follow from the first. Generalizations 1 and 2 imply that feminist interpretation will involve the art of reading between the lines, to identify

subtexts and to understand what is being written by the winners about the losers.

3. Analysts should be concerned as much with the effects of texts as with their origins. The reasoning behind this generalization is that if a myth (such as the story of Adam and Eve) has contributed to the oppression of women, no amount of revisionist thinking (such as arguing that oppression was not the author's intention) can compensate for it. (The story of Adam and Eve, for example, was the impetus for centuries of patriarchal propaganda buttressed by various subsidiary myths.)
4. Every version of a myth has its own integrity and must be interpreted in, but not reduced to, its particular social context. This generalization is based on the observation that a myth, being multivalent, has many lives: the cast of characters may change, and the plot or the moral may be reversed.

The Essence of Myths

Myths often address questions of enduring human concern: Where did we come from? What is the correct relationship between the sexes? What is the relationship between ecology and justice? Is there an afterlife? How can we explain human suffering? The fact that mythology addresses such concerns is one reason why it is so compelling. In addition, myths often serve as "charter texts" of identity for individuals, ethnic groups, religions, and nations. Myths of origin, for instance, are likely to be concerned not only with a past golden age but with a golden future.

One way to distinguish myths from folktales, fairy tales, sagas, and legends is that a myth claims to be about an enduring supernatural reality. In the light of history, however, such a claim can often be seen as partisan, worldly, and serving particular interests, especially the interests of those who hold power. Even though the human concerns might be similar, then, a critical examination of how a culture addresses and resolves them mythologically can tell us a great deal about that culture.

Neither the glorification nor the denigration of women in mythology is necessarily a reliable guide to what women were actually doing when a myth was created. Likewise, there is no necessary or causal relationship between the gender of a deity in a culture's mythology and the subordination or liberation of its women. Thus the mere existence or absence of female goddesses tells us little. The image of the Virgin Mary, for example, is ambivalent across cultures and over time: sometimes it empowers women, but at other times it is used against women's efforts for liberation. The origins of a myth, therefore, might bear no relationship to its subsequent use. Due attention must be paid to historical mutations, such as the degeneration of myth into literary patriarchal propaganda.

In interpreting or constructing mythologies, the following questions might be useful. First, how does the image of women in a specific myth compare with the actual condition of women (not just elite women but all women) in a particular society? For instance, while feminist myth-making and rituals often attempt to break down the dichotomy between sacred and profane, they do not necessarily challenge other oppressive realities, such as economic and ethnic inequality. Some new myths might serve the interests of upper-class women but have negative effects on other classes or other ethnic groups.

A second question follows from the first: What factors related to power are operating? This question implies a group of additional points: Who are the "keepers" of the myths, the interpreters, the recorders? Might the transition from an oral to a written (often elitist) mythology affect the form of the myths themselves? Is the underlying concern of a myth (such as an ancestral myth) relations among the living rather than the dead? Who benefits from the recitation of a myth?

Third, what psychodynamic factors are at stake and at what level is a myth speaking? For instance, a myth may address a concern that is psychological, historical, theological, or philosophical, and so on. Such concerns may be universal, but some theorists, especially those influenced by psychoanalysis, suggest that men resolve these concerns at women's expense, by making a woman (like Eve or Pandora) the repository or cause of evil, death, or shame.

In the interpretation or construction of myth, the mere presence of women, even if women are idealized, may be less imporant than female agency. Therefore, a fourth question—perhaps, for feminists, the ultimate question—is this: Does a myth use female agency to support a patriarchal power structure or to perpetuate women's position within such a structure, or does it put female agency at the service of all women?

See Also

ARCHETYPE; CREATION STORIES; FAIRY TALES; GODDESS; MATRIARCHY; RELIGION: OVERVIEW; REPRESENTATION; SACRED TEXTS; WOMANSPIRIT

References and Further Reading

Barthes, Roland. 1972. *Mythologies.* Trans. Annette Lavers. London: Palladio. (Originally published in 1957.)

Condren, Mary. 1989. *The serpent and the goddess: Women, religion, and power in Celtic Ireland.* San Francisco: HarperCollins.

Doniger, Wendy. 1998. *The implied spider: Politics and theology in myth.* New York: Columbia University Press.

Erickson, Victoria Lee. 1993. *Where silence speaks: Feminism, social theory, and religion.* Minneapolis, Minn.: Fortress.

Gimbutas, Marija. 1991. *The civilization of the goddess: The world of old Europe.* Ed. Joan Marler. San Francisco: HarperCollins.

Harrison, Jane. 1962. *Prolegomena to the study of ancient Greek religion.* London: Merlin.

Larrington, Carolyne, ed. 1992. *The feminist companion to mythology.* London: HarperCollins; Pandora.

Patton, Laurie, and Wendy Doniger, eds. 1996. *Myth and method.* London and Charlottsville: University Press of Virginia.

Walker, Barbara. 1985. *The woman's encyclopedia of myths and secrets.* New York: Harper and Row.

Warner, Marina. 1994. *Managing monsters: Six myths for our time.* London: Vintage.

Weigle, Martha. 1991. *Creation and procreation: Feminist reflections on mythologies of cosmogony and parturition.* Philadelphia: University of Pennsylvania Press.

Mary Condren

N

NAMING

> My name is the symbol of my identity and must not be lost (Lucy Stone, cited in Miller and Swift, 1991).

Women's interest in naming themselves and their experiences is central to feminist theories of identity, knowledge, and language. Its most obvious manifestation is the continuing debate in the United States about women who do not change their surnames on marriage. The first-wave women's rights advocate Lucy Stone made the issue prominent when she retained her name in her marriage in 1855 to Henry Blackwell. Nineteenth- and early twentieth-century women who followed suit were often ridiculed as "Lucy Stoners."

Dale Spender (1980) argues that the practice of taking a husband's surname reinforces the idea that women's family names do not count. The custom (now largely outdated) of referring to women in the workplace by their first names and to men by their surname and title implies more power for men. In recent years, women have also begun choosing new surnames for themselves, but the practice is not widespread, and the taking of the husband's name remained the norm in the 1990s.

Surname debate, however, is only the most obvious manifestation of this issue. What women call themselves, their feelings, thoughts, relationships, and experiences defines them and their possibilities in the world. Betty Friedan (1963), in describing educated, middle-class women's discontent in the United States in the late 1950s and early 1960s, observed that the women were frustrated partly because they could not define what was wrong. They had the "problem that has no name." Naomi Scheman's (1993) discussion of anger expands on the idea that to name an experience is to feel less frustrated and disempowered. She argues that women are often reluctant to invoke the name *anger* because they cannot see this name as justifiable or themselves in a position to judge. This refusal to name leaves them wondering why they feel so "guilty" and why they so "irrationally" blow up at family members when they have no "reason" to. Scheman claims that naming anger would provide coherence and legitimacy to the emotion and authority to the women. To discover what women are feeling means to name it (22).

Writers often recognize the power of naming in individual and social contexts. For instance, Suzy McKee Charnas (1978) and Johanna Bolton (1988) both place a naming ceremony as definitive of communities in their feminist science fiction novels. Donald Barthelme (1976) describes the perfect woman in his story, "The end of the mechanical age" as Maude, who named the tools.

Just as naming has creative power, false names have destructive power. In the 1970s, Adrienne Rich argued that the names of *love, motherhood,* and *natural law* were false because they were not defined by the people to whom they were applied. Others held the naming power. The same is true about *work.* When caring for home and family is unpaid, it does not count and cannot claim the name *work* implied in "Does your mother work?"

Thus, part of the feminist project is to claim the power to name and to redefine names applied to women. An early second-wave document illustrates the point. Called "The BITCH Manifesto" (Joreen, 1969), it defines a "bitch" as a woman with personality, strength, and a sense of identity independent of what others think of her. A bitch is a woman who has harnessed her anger with political consciousness and directed it at its source—a sexist social system.

See Also

FEMINISM: OVERVIEW; KNOWLEDGE; LANGUAGE; WOMEN: TERMS FOR WOMEN

References and Further Reading

Barthelme, Donald. 1976. *Amateurs.* New York: Farrar, Strauss and Giroux.

Bolton, Johanna. 1988. *The alien within.* New York: Del Rey.

Charnas, Suzy McKee. 1978. *Motherlines.* New York: Berkley.

Flexner, Eleanor. 1968. *Century of struggle: The women's rights movement in the United States.* Rev. ed. Cambridge: Belknap Press of Harvard University Press.

Friedan, Betty. 1963. *The feminine mystique.* New York: Dell.

Granfors, M. n.d. Account of the Lucy Stone league. *her-self* 3(3):17; cited in Cheris Kramarae and P. Treichler, eds., *Amazons, bluestockings and crones: A feminist dictionary.* London: Pandora, 1992.

Joreen. 1969. The BITCH manifesto. In Betty Roszak and Theodore Roszak, eds., *Masculine/feminine: Readings in sexual mythology and the liberation of women.* New York: Harper Colophon.

Kramarae, Cheris, and Paula Treichler, eds. 1992. *Amazons, bluestockings and crones: A feminist dictionary.* London: Pandora.

Miller, Casey, and Kate Swift. 1991. *Words and women: New language in new times.* Garden City, NY: Doubleday.

Rich, Adrienne. 1977. Foreword. In Sara Ruddick and P. Daniels, eds., *Working it out.* New York: Pantheon.

Scheman, Naomi. 1993. *Engenderings: Constructions of knowledge, authority, and privilege.* New York: Routledge.

Spender, Dale. 1980. *Man-made language.* New York: Pandora.

Ivy Glennon

NATION AND NATIONALISM

The notion of "the nation" must be analyzed and related to nationalist ideologies and movements on one hand, and to the institutions of the state on the other. Nations are situated in specific historical moments and are constructed by shifting nationalist discourses promoted by different groups competing for hegemony. Their gendered character can be understood only within such a context. The concept of the nation-state assumes a complete overlap between the boundaries of a nation and the boundaries of those who live in it, but this is a fiction almost everywhere. There are people living in all societies and states who are not considered to be (and often do not consider themselves to be) members of the hegemonic nation; there are members of national collectivities who live in other countries; and there are nations that never had a state (like the Palestinians) or that are divided across several states (like the Kurds). Nevertheless, this fiction is at the basis of the nationalist ideal.

The fiction of "the nation" naturalizes the hegemony of one collectivity and its access to the ideological apparatuses of both state and civil society. This naturalization casts minorities as deviants from the "normal" and excludes them from important power resources. It can also lead to "ethnic cleansing." Deconstructing it is crucial to tackling racism and understanding the state itself.

If nations are not to be identified with nation-states, one questions if there are any objective characteristics according to which nations can be recognized. This question is not purely theoretical, given the wide consensus, affirmed by the United Nations, regarding "the right of nations to self-determination." Some define "nations" as communities that have their own history, language, territory, economic life, and culture. Greenfeld (1992), on the other hand, argues that the only underlying principle common to all nations is the fact that their members feel that their nation is superior. Anthony Smith (1986) argued for the ethnic origin of nations. Otto Bauer's equally important notion of "common destiny" is oriented toward the future, rather than just the past; it can explain the subjective sense of commitment to collectivities and nations—such as settler societies or post-colonial states—in which there is no shared myth of common origin. It can also explain the dynamic nature of any national collectivity and the perpetual process of boundary reconstruction that takes place within them via immigration, naturalization, conversion, and similar social and political processes. "The United States of the World," which Greenfeld sees as a possible nation, would have to gain this sense of shared destiny before it could evolve into a national collectivity, since collectivities are organized around boundaries that divide the world into "us" and "them."

National projects are usually complex and multidimensional, and different dimensions are emphasized in particular historical moments or by particular segments within the national collectivity. For this reason, one cannot simply (and historically) divide nations and nationalist projects into types. Instead, this article differentiates four major dimensions of nationalist projects that tend to relate in somewhat different ways to gender relations. The *genealogical dimension,* constructed around the specific origin of a people (or their race), involves the myth of common origin or shared blood (that is, genes), which tends to construct the most exclusionary and homogenous visions of the nation. In the *cultural dimension,* the symbolic heritage provided by some combination of language, religion, and other customs and traditions is constructed as the essence of the nation; although this construction allows for assimilation, it tends to have little tolerance of "non-organic" diversity. Constructions of the Other—the stranger, the enemy—are crucial in that respect. Citizenship in the state is a third dimension that determines the boundaries of a nation. Although, in principle, anyone can be "naturalized" and become a citizen, in reality the pathways to becoming a citizen of a particular state—even a settler society without a formal myth of common origin—are usually ethnocentric and often racialized as well as gendered. Finally, the notion of the "homeland" and the territorial/spatial location of "the nation" often embodies the emotional attachment to the nation; indeed, claims to land and contestations of borders are the most common triggers for wars.

Gender Relations and the Reproduction of the "Biological Stock" of the Nation

Theorists of nationalism have tended to look to intellectuals (Smith, 1986) and state bureaucrats as to the reproducers of the nation. However, because one usually must be born into a national collectivity in order to join it, the centrality of women as bearers of the collective (Yuval-Davis, 1980) is immediately apparent.

The inclusion of a new baby in a national collectivity is far from a purely biological issue. Depending on religious and customary laws, the membership of a child might depend exclusively on the father's membership (as in Islam), or on the mother's membership (as in Judaism), or the child may be eligible for dual or voluntary membership. The legitimacy of the child of a legal or customary marriage is often crucial, and a variety of control mechanisms exist, in varying degrees of rigidity, to ensure that women raise their children within the "proper" social circumstances.

Depending on the hegemonic discourses that construct nationalist projects at specific historical moments, women may be encouraged to have children, or discouraged from it, perhaps forcibly; especially since the development of the appropriate prenatal tests, they maybe compelled to have children of a particular sex. One or more of three major discourses tend to dominate nationalist policies of population control. In the people as power discourse, the future of the nation depends on its continuous growth, and immigration does not seem to constitute the solution for such continuous growth. The need for people—primarily for men—can result from various nationalist purposes, both civil and military. Men might be needed as workers to support an aging population; as settlers, to make the new society socially and economically viable; as soldiers; to replace those lost in national disasters; or as part of a "demographic race" with an enemy population. In all such cases, women are called on to produce as many babies as possible.

Often, however, the nationalist project is about national quality rather than just quantity. Although welfare states developed largely in order to improve the quality of life of the people, especially the poor and working class, sometimes states have followed the eugenicist discourse, in which the "quality" of the people is equated with selective breeding. This involves giving a variety of economic and social incentives to women of an admired racial, ethnic or class background to bear more children, while those who are from the wrong origin or have disabilities are prevented from having children by a variety of means, often involving coercion.

The third is the Malthusian discourse, which is driven by fear of population explosion and the consequent inability to provide enough resources to feed all the people. Its present focus on the rate of population growth in the Third World combines a racist fear of being swamped by the non-Western Others with a conscience-soothing explanation for the persistence of poverty and low standard of life in postcolonial Third World countries. Most important, however, Malthusian discourse is a cornerstone of population policies in many Third World countries, a major strategy for solving economic and social problems. The fear that economic and political destabilization will result if the balance between supply and demand for labor power is threatened by uncontrolled growth of the population. Women are often pressured to be sterilized or to use long-term contraceptives.

Cultural Reproduction and Gender Relations

Women are not only the biological reproducers of the nation: often they are its cultural reproducers as well. Because of the central importance of social reproduction to culture, gender relations are often seen as constituting the essence of a culture—as a way of life to be passed from generation to generation. The construction of "home" is of particular importance here, including relations among adults and between adults and children in the family, ways of cooking and eating, domestic labor, play, and bedtime stories. Out of these, a whole worldview, ethical and aesthetic, can become naturalized and reproduced. One can hold on to the problematic notion of reproduction, however, only if processes of growth, decline, and transformation are included in it. Cultures operate within both social and spatial contexts which cannot be understood separately from the time dimension. Different social and geographical factors affect the ways cultures are articulated and used, both inside and outside collectivities.

Rather than being seen as a fixed and homogenous body of tradition and custom, culture should be described as a rich resource, usually full of internal contradictions, which is used selectively by various social agents in projects within specific power relations and political discourses, both in and outside the collectivity. Defining culture in this way preempts debates on the notion of "authenticity." Authenticity assumes fixed, essential, and unitary constructs of cultures, identities, and groupings. Authenticity can become a political and economic resource in itself in particular ethnic projects. It can also give rise to what Kubena Mercer (1990) calls "the burden of representation," and Amrita Chhachhi (1991), in a somewhat different context, calls "forced identities."

Women are often required to carry this burden of representation, because they are constructed as the symbolic bearers of the collectivity's identity and honor, both personally and collectively. The burden of representing the collectivity's identity and future destiny has also brought about the construction of women as the bearers of the collectivity's honor. Women, in their "proper" behavior, their "proper" clothing, embody the line that signifies the collectivity's boundaries. Women in many societies are tortured or murdered by their relatives because of adultery, flight from home, or other cultural breaches of conduct that are perceived as bringing dishonor and shame on their male relatives and community. Another version of retaliation against women who betrayed the collective honor was the mass shaving of the heads of women who were accused of befriending the occupying Nazi armies following World War II. Women are often raped in war as a way of shaming and dishonoring the enemy community as a whole.

Women usually have an ambivalent position within the collectivity. On one hand they may symbolize the collectivity unity, honor and raison d'être of specific national and ethnic projects. On the other hand, they are often excluded from the collective "we" of the body politic and retain an object rather than a subject position. In this sense, the construction of womanhood has a property of Otherness. Strict cultural codes of what it is to be a "proper woman" are often developed to keep women in this inferior power position.

Women and Citizenship

T. H. Marshal, the most famous theoretician of citizenship in the welfare state, defined citizenship as "full membership in the community" with the rights and obligations such membership entails. The notion of citizenship began in the Greek polis, where women—like slaves, resident foreigners, and all other members of the community who were not men with property—were excluded from "the right to rule and be ruled," as citizenship was defined then. After the French Revolution, citizenship became attached to the nation-state. Women were excluded from citizenship then as part of the "sexual contract" which defined the fraternal relationship between the citizens and the state, in which they agreed to be ruled by the state in exchange for the right to rule in their households. Even when women were first awarded citizenship rights, they would lose them when they married or, later on, if they married a foreigner. In most European countries, women did not achieve the right to transfer their citizenship to their children until the 1980s. Even when sex equality legislation was passed and women got their political rights, their civil and social rights often lagged behind. Constructions of culture and tradition are often used to block attempts to equalize women's citizenship's rights. In recent decades, a number of women's organizations have been fighting to improve women's citizenship rights by appealing to international human rights as another layer of global citizenship.

Gender Relations and "The Homeland"

The object-like characteristic of women in the collectivity finds its strongest expression in the construction of women—especially, mothers—as the embodiments of the homeland. In peasant societies, the dependence of the people on the fertility of Mother Earth has undoubtedly contributed to this close association among collective territory, collective identity, and womanhood. Women are associated in the collective imagination with children and therefore with the collective future as well as the familial future. A figure of a woman, often a mother, in many cultures symbolizes the spirit of the collectivity: Mother Russia, Mother Ireland, or Mother India. The symbol of the French Revolution was "La Patrie," a figure of a woman giving birth to a baby; in Cyprus, a crying woman refugee on roadside posters was the embodiment of the pain and anger of the Greek Cypriot collectivity after the Turkish invasion. Women represent the homeland as well as the home. In diasporic communities, it is in the homeland that young men search for "proper brides."

Women, or, rather, "womenandchildren" (to use Cynthia Enloe's 1990 expression) are constructed as organically attached to the homeland. Enoch Powell defined the nation as "two males plus defending women and children in a specific territory." Mothers are trusted to teach their children the proper love of their country: "Every true republican has drunk in love of country, that is to say love of law and liberty, along with his mother's milk. This love is his whole existence," claimed Rousseau.

Nationalist Movements and Women's Liberation

The service of women in the military, as well as other changes in traditional sexual divisions of labor, has occupied central space in discourses of national liberation movements and is part of the complex relationship that has grown between feminist and nationalist movements, especially in the postcolonial world.

In the West, national independence and women's suffrage generally came at two different historical moments. Although women took an active part in the French Revolution, they were excluded and marginalized in the consequent political community. Marianne was the Republic's symbol, but the "woman question" as such was not part of its political agenda. In the twentieth century, however, women's roles and women's emancipation were at the heart of the cultural-political agenda. Chatterjee (1986) observes that cultural decolonization has anticipated and paved the way for political decolonization—the major rupture that has marked the twentieth century. This process involved a growing sense of empowerment, a development of a national trajectory of freedom and independence. A central theme in this process of cultural decolonization was the redefinition and reconstruction of sexuality and gender relations, as in Franz Fanon's famous call (1986 [1952]) for the black man to "reclaim his manhood." As Ashis Nandy (1983) argues, the colonial man was constructed as effeminate in the colonial discourse, and the way to emancipation and empowerment was seen as the negation of this assertion. In many cultural systems, potency and masculinity seem to be synonymous. Such a perspective not only legitimized the extremely "macho" style of many anticolonialist and black power movements but also reinforced the subordinate position of women in these national collectivities.

Nevertheless, the emancipation of women has come to signify wider political and social attitudes toward social change and modernity in a variety of revolutionary and decolonization projects, such as Turkey, India, Yemen, and China (Kandiyoti, 1991). As Chatterjee (1986) points out, because the position of women has been so central to the colonial gaze in defining indigenous cultures, many symbolic declarations of cultural change have involved women's status. This has been one of the important ways in which ethnic and national projects signified—inwardly and outwardly—their move toward modernization. However, these changes did not lack ambivalence; at the same time, they signified modernization and national independence.

One focal point of debate has been the extent to which modernization should be equated with Westernization. For many national leaders of the colonial world, nationalism and socialism were measures of modernity which they had to adopt in order to defeat the European colonial enemy. This is why Chatterjee (1986), for instance, has seen nationalism in the postcolonial world as a derivative discourse. However, this does not mean that the two should be equated. Anzaldua's collective model of empowered hybridization is a much better way of describing the process. Many indigenous cultural and religious traditions were appropriated, at least symbolically, as a resource to establish national emblems and symbolic "border guards" (Armstrong, 1982) of identity.

Because the hegemony of the modern nation-state in the postcolonial world has been very limited and confined mostly to urban centers and the upper classes, the use of cultural and religious traditions as symbolic border guards has enabled the continued coexistence of the modern center with the premodern sections of society. It also enabled the rise of a new generation of leadership who could turn to such customs and traditions and develop ethnic and national projects of a very different kind. In such projects, what had formerly symbolized progress and modernity was now constructed as European cultural imperialism. As an alternative, a fundamentalist construction of the true cultural essence of the collectivity has come to be imposed. These constructions, however, are often no more similar to the ways people used to live historically in these societies than the previous national liberation ones, nor have they abandoned modernity and its tools, such as the modern media and high-tech weaponry.

Once again, women occupy an important role in these projects. Rather than being symbols of change, women are cast as the carriers of tradition. The symbolic act of unveiling, which took center stage in certain emancipatory projects, is now being superseded by campaigns of forced veiling, as in postrevolutionary Iran. Even practices like *sati* (widows' suicide) in India can become foci of fundamentalist movements that see in these traditions the safeguard of the national cultural essence, in a reversal of the colonial employment of focus on these practices to construct Otherness (Mani, 1989; Chhachhi, 1991).

Conclusion

Women affect and are affected by national and ethnic processes in a variety of ways, and it is impossible to understand constructions of nations, nationalist projects, and national conflicts without analyzing their gendered aspects. However, it is important to emphasize that not all women fulfill the same roles in nationalist projects. Ethnicity, class, stage in the life cycle, sexuality, ability, and other factors influence which women fulfill which roles for the nation. Nevertheless, it is "woman" and "womenandchildren" as symbolic constructs that symbolize the nation as a whole.

See Also

DEMOCRACY; ETHNICITY; POLITICAL PARTICIPATION; POLITICAL REPRESENTATION; POLITICS AND THE STATE: OVERVIEW

References and Further Reading

Armstrong, John. 1982. *Nations before nationalism.* Chapel Hill, N.C.: University of Carolina Press.

Chatterjee, Partha. 1986. *Nationalist thought and the colonial world: A derivative discourse.* London: Zed.

Chhachhi, Amrita. 1991. Forced identities: The state, communalism, fundamentalism and women in India. In D. Kandiyot, ed., *Women, Islam and the state,* 144–175. London: Macmillan.

Enloe, Cynthia. 1990. Women and children: Making feminist sense of the Persian Gulf crisis. *Village Voice,* 25 September.

Fanon, Franz. 1986. *Black skin, white masks.* London: Pluto.

Greenfield, Liah. 1992. *Nationalism: Five roads to modernity.* Cambridge, Mass.: Harvard University Press.

Kandiyoti, Deniz, ed. 1991. Identity and its discontents: Women and the nation. *Millennium* 20(3): 429–424.

———, ed. 1991. *Women, Islam and the state.* London: Macmillan.

Mani, Lata. 1989. Contentious traditions: The debate on Sati in colonial India. In K. Sangari and S. Vaid, eds., *Recasting women: Essays in colonial history.* New Delhi: Kali for Women.

Mercer, Kubina. 1990. Welcome to the jungle: Identity and diversity in postmodern politics. In J. Rutherford, ed., *Identity, community, culture, difference.* London: Lawrence and Wishart.

Nandy, Ashis. 1983. *The intimate enemy: Loss and recovery of self under colonialism.* Oxford: Oxford University Press.

Smith, Anthony. 1986. *The Ethnic Origin of Nations.* Oxford: Basil Blackwell.

Yuval-Davis Nira. 1980. The bearers of the collective: Women and religious legislation in Israel. *Feminist Review* 4: 15–27.

———. 1993. Gender and nation. *Ethnic and Racial Studies* 16(4): 621–632.

Nira Yuval-Davis

NATURAL RESOURCES

Victoria Chitepo, Zimbabwe's Minister for Natural Resources and Tourism, has suggested that "women are taking action against the destruction of natural resources on which their lives depend" (quoted in Dankelman and Davidson, 1988: ix). These actions take many forms. For example, in India the Chipko movement involved women entering the Reni Forest to save 2,500 trees from removal by contractors. The women joined hands and told the contractors that they would need to cut off their heads before they could fell the trees. The contractors withdrew from the forest. Another example is the Green Belt movement, led by the National Council of Women of Kenya, which successfully combined the planting of trees with the development of leadership among women. The Green Belt movement became known throughout the world for the way it addressed natural resource issues and considered the development of women as natural resource managers.

Clearly, women throughout the world are influenced directly and indirectly by natural-resource and natural-resource-management issues. Women are often the first members of a community to identify environmental problems such as natural-resources depletion and degradation because they notice the effects on the health of their children and family, or they feel an impact on their ability to provide food, shelter, and clothing. Ecofeminists such as Karen Warren (1998: 264) also point out the more general connections between the domination of women and the domination of nature, a perspective embraced by others whom Val Plumwood (in Braidotti et al., 1994: 161–68) calls "cultural" ecofeminists, who see women and nature as both being the victims of patriarchy. Ecofeminists generally consider the oppression of women's ways of knowing and connecting with nature as standing in the way of the achievement of sustainability. This article explores the meaning of the term "natural resource" and the need for natural-resource management to achieve sustainability. It also outlines the issues, dilemmas, controversies, and contributions of women in reconfiguring natural-resource regimes toward sustainability.

Definitions

A *resource* is typically defined as something of value to humans; those aspects or parts of the environment that fulfill the needs of people are considered *natural resources* (Omara-Ojungu, 1992: 1). Natural resources typically are classified into two groups: renewable and nonrenewable. Renewable natural resources, such as forests and animals, can be regenerated or restocked over time. By contrast, coal and oil are nonrenewable resources; they are available in limited amounts and cannot be regenerated or restocked. Colette Dehlot (in Rodda, 1991: 72) suggests that water, land, and soil should be considered nonrenewable resources: Humans can influence the *quality,* but they cannot increase the amount, of these finite resources. The quality of both renewable and nonrenewable resources can be improved by natural-resource management, and this approach is a key strategy for sustainable development across the globe.

The most enduring and popular definition of *sustainability* is "development which meets the needs of the present generation without compromising the ability of future generations to satisfy their needs" (World Commission on Environment and Development, 1987: 8). As governments grapple with natural-resource issues and their effects on the environment, it is sustainability that they are seeking. This call for sustainable use of natural resources at the international level has led most countries of the world to establish legislation and regulation of the use of natural resources (Braidotti et al., 1994: 123). Four main approaches have been identified for the negotiation and reconstruction of resource regimes: (1) the management and restoration of ecosystems; (2) local environment or development projects; (3) environmental education; and (4) the development of and participation in networks and alliances (Lipschutz and Mayer, 1996: 57).

Management and Restoration of Ecosystems

The Indian Chipko movement of 1974 and the Green Belt movement in Kenya are two examples of the role women have played in the management and restoration of ecosystems. One method increasingly used by governments to address issues of sustainability of resources is the development of protected areas as a means of conservation. Beti Astolfi, the senior advisor to the United Nations Development Fund for Women (UNIFEM), in 1995 suggested a range of issues that need to be considered if women are to be partners in the management of these protected areas. Even though planners and managers have been urged to include women and issues related to women in their planning, many lack the skills to consider gender issues within their work. The consideration of gender issues in resource management requires the careful reconsideration of policy within governments, agencies, and nongovernmental organizations (Astolfi, 1995).

More success is evident when women—such as Sithembisco Nyoni, the founding director of the Organisation of Rural Associations for Progress (ORAP)—take the lead in the management and restoration of ecosystems. ORAP is a nongovernmental organization that works at the village level to encourage women and children (often the only ones left in the village, as everyone else has left to seek work in the city) to understand their local environment and its ecosystems. Women in these villages explore the return to planting many crops together (instead of using Western monoculture practices) and using compost to enrich the soil. This allows the women in these communities to restore the quality of their soil and once again feed their villages (Williamson-Fien, 1993: 65).

Local Environment or Development Projects

Many nations still believe that the natural-resource base within their country would not be depleted so quickly if the number of people it supported were not so large. For this reason, some development projects focus on family planning. But Jodi Jacobson (1994) suggests that use of natural resources is not an issue that can be dealt with by reducing the population. A more relevant issue is that 22 percent of the world's people consume 70 percent of the world's energy and 60 percent of its food (Jacobson, 1994: 9). At the international level, there is increasing pressure to consider processes that will help reduce the consumption levels of this 22 percent of the world's population.

Environmental and development projects need to consider the following range of issues when working with women:

1. It is important that participation by women occurs throughout the problem-solving process, beginning with the identification of the problem and moving on to the identification of solutions, choice of actions, and choice of ways to evaluate whether the actions have achieved their goal. This process is most useful when dealing with natural-resource issues because it takes advantage of the vast knowledge of these women and gives them the power to make decisions and to direct and monitor their actions (Rodda, 1991: 150).
2. The potential for women to influence or make decisions in relation to natural resources sometimes depends on circumstances that are essentially out of their control. For example, as landownership changes from customary to private property rights, women's access to land, water, and trees is altered. In many cases, men own many natural resources. Without ownership, women feel powerless to make changes or take actions that will improve the quality or quantity of a resource.
3. Women develop and maintain complex networks within their communities. These networks and ways of passing on or protecting traditional knowledge within communities and cultures need to be considered carefully in the preparation and implementation of development and environmental projects within communities.

Environmental Education

The work of Maria Mies and Vandana Shiva (1993) has been integral to the acknowledgment of the role of women as natural-resource managers. Particularly in countries of the South, the connection and knowledge women have with their surrounding environment is gaining increasing prominence as part of the solution to environmental problems. But women, in both the North and the South, do not always have access to education programs.

The limitations on the way women access agricultural extension programs were demonstrated in a study of women farmers in Kapokina village Uganda. This research suggested that poor participation of women in extension programs was the result of four major factors: (1) the poor status of women; (2) traditional gender divisions of labor; (3) women's lack of control or access to resources; and (4) timing and inadequacy of the programs offered. The study acknowledged that the participation of women could have been facilitated, in some cases, by the provision of food supplies to ensure health and nutrition and by providing access to basic services such as water and electricity. In most cases, consideration of child-care arrangements would have helped allow for participation, and there also needed to be attention to the issues of ownership that inhibit or empower women to enact the suggested techniques and processes suggested by the extension program (Okurut, 1997).

Two Canadian women, Darlene Clover and Shirely Follen from the Transformative Learning Centre in Toronto, began working to develop adult educational programs that help women to value their knowledge. They created workshops designed to fulfill the learning needs of women, with a focus on giving women a voice through activities that use small groups work, poetry, and art. Clover etal. (1998: 107) recounts the story of a group of women concerned with fishery and coastal environmental issues. The Atlantic Women's Fishnet of Canada has developed a theater presentation for men and women in their local community to convey the environmental implications of corporate dragnet fishing. This education program aimed to provide knowledge and awareness to their local community to protect their fishery resources. In addition, the community group newsletter provides a forum for women to address their role in government research and planning. The process of networking and discussing ideas has been very powerful for women as a strategy for self-education and empowerment.

International and National Networks and Alliances

Women are operating at the national and transnational level to develop networks and alliances that promote sustainable natural resource use and management. The Women's International Network (WIN) has a newsletter that provides a forum for many of the issues outlined above.

At the national level, in Australia, the Rural Women's Network seeks to encourage rural women to share ideas, take an active role in public life, and develop skills for handling change. Some women in the network have conducted programs to introduce other women to issues of wildlife corridors, while others have developed training programs (such as one called "Paddock to Plate") that educate women about farm processes generally (Campbell and Siepen, 1994: 129). A newsletter was established as one of the main methods for women within the Australian network to communicate, but rural women have also been able to share their ideas through conferences such as the Women and Agriculture Conference held at Melbourne University in 1994 and, more recently, on the Internet.

Women have an important link with natural resources and an important role to play in striving to achieve sustainability. They need to be both participants and leaders in reconfiguring the use of resources through ecosystem management and restoration, environment and development projects, environmental education, and the development of networks and alliances. The challenge is to engage as many women as possible in research and practice in the area of natural-resource management, to ensure that gender issues are addressed and the move toward sustainability is achieved.

See Also

ALTERNATIVE ENERGY; DEVELOPMENT: OVERVIEW; EARTH; ECOFEMINISM; ENERGY; ENVIRONMENT: *all regions*

References and Further Reading

Astolfi, Beti. 1995. How to involve women in protected area issues. In Jeffrey McNeely, ed., *Expanding partnerships in conservation.* Washington: Island Press.

Braidotti, Rosi, Eva Charkiewicz, Sabine Hausler, and Saskia Wieringa. 1994. *Women, the environment, and sustainable development: Towards a theoretical synthesis.* London: Zed.

Campbell, Andrew, and Greg Seipen. 1994. *Landcare: Communities shaping the land and the future.* St. Leonards, NSW: Allen and Unwin.

Clover, Darlene, Shirley Follen, and Budd Hall. 1998. *The nature of transformation: Environmental, adult, and popular education.* Toronto: University of Toronto Press.

Dankelman, Irene, and Joan Davidson. 1988. *Women and environment in the Third World: Alliance for the future.* London: Earthscan.

Jacobson, Jodi. 1994. Population mythology. *Amicus Journal* 16 (1):9–10.

Lipschutz, Ronnie, and Judith Mayer. 1996. *Global civil society and global environmental governance: The politics of nature from place to planet.* Albany, N.Y.: State University of New York.

Mies, Maria, and Vandana Shiva. 1993. *Ecofeminism.* London: Zed Books.

Okurut, H. E. 1997. Constraints to participation of women in agricultural extension programmes in Kapokina village, Uganda. In Akim Okuni and Juliet Tembe, eds., *Capacity building in educational research in East Africa: Empirical insights into qualitative research methodology.* Bonn: German Foundation for International Development Education, Science and Documentation Centre.

Omara-Ojungu, Peter. 1992. *Resource management in developing countries.* Harlow, UK: Longman Scientific and Technical.

Rodda, Annabel. 1991. *Women and the environment.* London: Zed Books.

Warren, Karen. 1998. Ecofeminism introduction. In M. Zimmerman, J. Callicott, G. Sessions, K. Warren, and J. Clark, eds., *Environmental philosophy: From animal rights to radical ecology.* 2nd ed. Upper Saddle River, N. J.: Prentice-Hall.

Williamson-Fien, Jane. 1993. *Women's voices.* Brisbane: Global Learning Centre.

World Commission on Environment and Development. 1987. *Our common future.* Oxford, UK: Oxford University Press.

Debbie Heck

NATURE

Definitions

The concept of nature is a cultural construct, and, therefore, its meaning changes as cultures change over time. The word comes from Latin *natura,* which means "birth" and "essence." It refers to the vital strength, impulse, or substance of a thing; Chaucer and later English writers used *nature* to mean "semen" or "menses." *Nature* also signifies the constitution or course of things: the inherent disposition or character of a person, animal, or place.

When applied to the world or the universe, *nature* refers to the creative and regulative physical power that operates in the material world. Thus, seventeenth-century writers spoke of nature's laws, and subsequent scientific inquiry has attempted to uncover them. The most comprehensive meaning is that nature is the immediate cause of all phenomena.

Through centuries of Western history, the meanings of nature have shifted, reflecting the dominant worldview of the time. This is paradoxical because *nature* is often used to say that a particular thing or living process is immutable. Phrases such as "man in a state of nature" or "it is a woman's nature to be . . ." are generalizations that seek to state the inherent and immutable quality of one gender. Men's or women's "nature" is stated as an essential principle, or a law of the world. One can thus see how statements about nature have been used as cultural instruments of social control.

In Christian thought, nature was the innocence of Adam and Eve before the fall. The term speaks of the need to be redeemed from the consequences of female action, and the Christian church has a long history of using sin and redemption ideology as an instrument of social control. Matthew Fox (1991) calls this "religious terrorism." The many medieval women who were condemned as witches were often midwives, herbalists, and healers, close to nature. Most of what they knew about the natural world died with them. In the process of destroying those women and their wisdom, centralized religion became more masculinized, as did the whole culture. Today, some feminists celebrate the lives of those women and reclaim their wisdom wherever possible. Women sometimes use the Old English term *wicca* to reclaim the original meaning of *witch,* in an attempt to resacralize nature, along with the body, mind, and sexuality (Adler, 1986).

From the time of Chaucer, nature was usually personified as a female being, often in terms of respect like "Dame Nature" or "Lady Nature." Since the seventeenth century, however, nature has become increasingly depersonalized so that only the material, nonhuman world is designated as *nature.*

Before the Enlightenment, there was some ambiguity about where the inherent and essential principles of the world resided. At the level of official institutions, however, these principles were synonymous with the power of God. Raymond Williams (1980) describes how, with the beginning of empirical science and capitalism, nature had to be separated from God. Nature was objectified so that natural processes could be described on their own terms. Objects and processes could be examined without any prior assumption of a divine plan. One could experiment to see how things worked, and then control them. Exploitation of natural resources was a predictable consequence of this separation.

Since the nineteenth century, the Darwinian paradigm has powerfully shaped Western culture. Nature has often been evoked as an essential principle, in statements such as "man in a state of nature is in a ruthless struggle for existence," or "it is the nature of our genes to be selfish." Such statements are attempts to state an immutable law of science that can then be extended to demonstrate the "logic" of much political theory about human society and the living world.

The technological culture of the twentieth century has held out the promise that we can control nature, or even escape from it. Yet on another level, we know we are dependent on nature for our ultimate survival. Trying to escape from something we are dependent on breeds a love–hate relationship with it. At perhaps an unconscious level, this love–hate relationship with nature has permeated industrial society, causing people to want to possess and—intentionally or not—destroy. The desire to possess and the desire to destroy amplify each other in a feedback relationship. We build military arsenals to ensure access to the raw materials we want, but this threatens existence itself. To sustain our technological capacity to destroy, we require increasing amounts of raw materials. The cycle continues exponentially, and feminist writers have made a great effort to think and feel their way out of it (see Macy, 1991).

Today there is a wide spectrum of meanings of nature. This diversity is seen at the level of whole cultures and single individuals. When people think about nature in terms of work, business, or politics, they tend to think of it as the inanimate source of raw materials that can be exploited for economic gain. But those same people, in private moments, may think of nature as the countryside, the place to escape to from the city.

The heterogeneity or fragmentation of thought about nature is one of the legacies of post-Cartesian dualistic thinking, which separated materialist science and technology from spiritual and ethical considerations. René Descartes argued that the human organism was made up of palpable body and intangible mind. By splitting us in two, Descartes could remain within Christian orthodoxy, preserving the soul as the domain of theology and establishing the body as the legitimate domain of science.

Feminist Views of Nature

Simone de Beauvoir accepted the Cartesian dualism of mind and body, and she used the material facts of women's menstruation, pregnancy, and childbearing to argue that women have little control over their cycles and body processes. They live lives of biological necessity, as animals do, and repetitively produce human lives in a process that mirrors their own biological cycles. Men, in contrast, are not tied to natural cycles and are therefore above biological necessity. However, de Beauvoir's thought was also characterized by a rejection of determinism, and she thus believed that women could overcome their second-class status through individual effort.

One of the first books of feminist critique in the social sciences, edited by Michelle Rosaldo and Louise Lamphere (1974), was influenced by de Beauvoir. Most contributors to that volume believed that universal female subordination existed, and they explained it by women's being closer to nature than to culture. Claude Lévi-Strauss and other structuralists designated the binary opposites of nature and culture as master categories. The raw and the cooked, or female and male, were metaphoric transformations of nature and culture. Lévi-Strauss (1978), influenced by linguistic theory, was convinced that binary categories were homologous with nature itself and that they arose from the structure of the human brain. After grounding this dichotomy in immutable nature, structuralists generalized far beyond European social thought, selecting confirming myths and rituals to "prove" that all humanity valued culture over nature—and, by implication, male over female.

However, the empirical studies in *Nature, Culture, and Gender* (MacCormack and Strathern, 1980) describe how, in some societies, "nature's wild" was the domain of maleness, not femaleness. Indeed, some societies do not even have a concept of nature that might be opposed to, and ranked below, culture. The link between nature and women is not an immutable "given." Gender and its attributes are not pure biology, and in a crosscultural comparative framework, the meanings given to *male* and *female* are as arbitrary as the meanings attributed to *nature* and *culture*.

In *The Death of Nature* (1981), Carolyn Merchant warns women in the ecofeminist movement against projecting female attributes onto nature. To personify the earth as a woman would be to invite its being treated as the same kind of second-class object of male activity that women have been. In *The Rebirth of Nature* (1990), Rupert Sheldrake, a radical biologist, skillfully demolishes the idea of nature as the World Machine. In reanimating the world, he inexorably feminizes it. His images of the feminine, drawn from deep levels of culture and the psyche, are powerful. He arrives intellectually at the same place many contemporary feminist poets and artists reach experientially.

There is no single women's view of nature, as shown by Lorraine Anderson's 1991 collection of women's prose and poetry about nature. But many women do seem to relate to nature in a caring rather than controlling way. They tend to seek harmony rather than mastery. Where de Beauvoir saw women's attunement to natural rhythms as weakness, these women writers find that such attunement enhances their identity and adds sensory, aesthetic, and spiritual qualities to their lives, especially during life-crisis periods. Closeness to nature helps them transform their lives and experience positive growth out of a life's transitions, such as menopause.

The natural world, seen as a single living organism of which we are a small part, is imagery rich with interconnectedness. It is experienced as a healing, holistic alternative to the fragmentation and frenzy of industrial society. For other writers, the negative metaphor of rape and environmental degradation speaks powerfully to their experience.

Nature and Ecofeminism

Two views exist of how to relate to the world within the current ecofeminist movement. One view is that biological determinism is still salient in Western culture, and the status of women will not improve until the connection between women and nature is severed. Women who share this view tend to be activists and have put much energy into political resistance movements among women throughout the world. Saving trees or clean water often broadens out into resistance to domestic violence and other gender injustices (see Richters, 1994).

Other ecofeminists wish to stay close to nature. They seek to change Western culture, often by drawing on its roots in Goddess myths, rituals, and symbols (Adler, 1986). Some see a more universal synthesis of ancient Western tradition, traditions of indigenous peoples, and, often, Buddhist thought (Macy, 1991).

Virtually all ecofeminists, in common with those in the creation spirituality movement (Fox, 1991), tend to emphasize that the earth, its forests, rivers, and creatures have intrinsic value; in other words, they are sacred. Human life is dependent on the earth, and therefore our fates are intertwined. Changes in nature change us. We now have many metaphors and images of our shared distress. For example, cutting the forest in Thailand displaces people and thus intensifies migration, prostitution, and AIDS; put more simply, the cut forest is AIDS. The need for all people, women and men, to balance the masculine and feminine in themselves seems to be an integral part of regaining harmony with nature.

See Also

ECOFEMINISM; FEMINISM: EXISTENTIAL; NATURAL RESOURCES; NATURE; WICCA

References and Further Reading

Adler, Margot. 1986. *Drawing down the moon.* 2nd ed. Boston: Beacon.

Anderson, Lorraine, ed. 1991. *Sisters of the Earth: Women's prose and poetry about nature.* New York: Vintage.

Beauvior, Simone de. [1949] 1972. *The second sex.* New York: Knopf.

Fox, Matthew. 1991. *Creation spirituality.* San Francisco: Harper.

Lévi-Strauss, Claude. 1978. *Myth and meaning.* London: Routledge and Kegan Paul.

MacCormack, Carol, and Marilyn Strathern, eds. 1980. *Nature, culture, and gender.* Cambridge: Cambridge University Press.

Macy, Joanna. 1991. *World as lover, world as self.* Berkeley, Calif.: Parallax.

Merchant, Carolyn. 1981. *The death of nature: Women, ecology, and the scientific revolution.* San Francisco: Harper and Row.

Richters, Annemiek. 1994. *Women, culture, and violence.* Leiden University: Women and Autonomy Centre (VENA).

Rosaldo, Michelle, and Louise Lamphere, eds. 1974. *Women, culture, and society.* Stanford, Calif.: Stanford University Press.

Sheldrake, Rupert. 1990. *The rebirth of nature.* London: Century.

Williams, Raymond. 1980. *Problems in materialism and culture.* London: Verso.

Carol MacCormack

NATURE-NURTURE DEBATE

> Men have not only excluded the Women from partaking of the Sciences and Employ by long prescription, but also pretend that this Exclusion is founded in their natural Inability. ("By a Lady," 1763)

Western culture has taught that genius is a male monopoly belonging to the white races. Charles Darwin, an advocate of this point of view, argued in respect to women: "If two lists were made of the most eminent men and women in poetry, painting, sculpture, music—comprising composition and performance, history, science, and philosophy, with half-a-dozen names under each subject, the two lists would not bear comparison" [1871] 1981, vol. 2: 327). Darwin saw intellectual prowess as the chief characteristic distinguishing men from women. Except for what he called the "law of equal transmission of characters," man would have become as superior in mental endowment to woman "as the peacock is in ornamental plumage to the peahen" (Darwin [1871] 1981, vol. 2: 328–29).

In fact, women have not been as prominent in cultural achievement as men have been. How do we explain this phenomenon? There are two poles in this debate: *nurture,* which holds that perceived sexual differences are the product of history and therefore of socialization; and *nature,* which holds that something in the physical, psychological, and intellectual nature of women prohibits them from producing great works of art and science. The distinction is significant: if gender roles or personality traits are rooted in the body, traceable ultimately to congenital or genetic factors, it is easier to argue that the predominant sexual divisions of labor and power are natural, and that efforts to transform social relations between men and women are misconceived or foolhardy. If, by contrast, gender roles are rooted in culture, then they can be changed.

The nature/nurture debate arose alongside Western-style democracy and liberal commitment to ideologies of freedom, individualism, and merit. Before the rise of liberal democracies, European social standing had been determined largely by birth. Paternity determined one's standing in a rigidly hierarchical system of "estates." The Enlightenment posed a challenge to existing orthodoxies of inequality with its rallying cry: "All men [often interpreted to include women] are by nature equal." Philosophers and politicians attempting to build a just society sought to ground the laws of men in what they considered a higher authority—the laws of nature (Fauré, 1991). Natural law (as distinct from positive law of nations) was held to be immutable, either given by God or inherent in the material universe. It is this appeal to nature—as prior to and transcending society—that grounds the nature side of the debate.

Three other factors buttress the nature side. First is the authority given to science as a privileged source of knowledge about nature. As claims to equality increasingly came to be considered matters not of ethics but of science, scientists became the preferred mediators between the laws of nature and legislatures. Second, gender became grounded in biology as modern science privileged the physical over the intellectual and cultural. The body—seemingly stable, ahistorical, and sexed—became the epistemic foundation for prescriptive claims about social divisions of labor, power, and privilege. Third, the belief that science is neutral in respect to value and gender sealed an already self-referential system. Scientists' self-proclaimed neutrality was often premised on the absence of dissenting points of view. Those who might have criticized new scientific views were barred from the outset, and the findings of science (crafted in their absence) were used to justify their continued exclusion. These elements taken together—the authority given to nature and to science as the knower of nature, the grounding of gender in biology, and the belief that science is value-neutral—created a self-reinforcing system that rendered invisible (at least to some) the injustices women have suffered (Schiebinger, 1989).

History of the Debate

The attempt to keep woman in her place by showing that women are inferior to men in body and mind is an ancient one, dating back at least to Classical Greece. Aristotle argued that women are colder and weaker than men, and that women lack sufficient heat to cook the blood and thus purify the soul (Cadden, 1993; Tuana, 1993). This strain of argument was put on a "scientific" foundation in the seventeenth and eighteenth centuries with the rise of modern science (though the view of woman as a lesser being remained remarkably the same) (Laqueur, 1990; Schiebinger, 1989). In the eighteenth and nineteenth centuries, craniometrists accounted for alleged sexual differences in intellectual achievement by measuring skulls. Anatomists assumed that the larger male skull was loaded with a heavier and higher-powered brain (Fee, 1979; Gould, 1980). In the mid-nineteenth century, Social Darwinists invoked evolutionary biology to "prove" that woman was a man whose evolution—both physical and mental—had been arrested in a primitive stage (Russett, 1989). In the late nineteenth century, Edward Clark, a Harvard doctor, argued that women should not be admitted to universities because their intellectual development could proceed only at great cost to their reproductive development: if women exercised their brains, this doctor held, their ovaries would shrivel.

This line of reasoning did not end in the twentieth century. In the 1920s and 1930s, arguments for women's different (and inferior) nature were based on hormonal research (Oudshoorn, 1994; Angier, 1999). Today we are still inundated with the argument that biology is destiny. Evolutionary psychologists, for example, try to persuade us that women do poorly in mathematics because their brains are not as highly specialized as men's. Sociobiologists, such as Harvard's E. O. Wilson, teach that genes dictate social inequalities; even in "the most free and egalitarian of future societies . . . men are likely to continue to play a disproportionate role in political life, business, and science." These studies are not profoundly different from those of Aristotle or Edward Clark. They seek to provide scientific justification for enduring divisions in power and privilege between the sexes (Fausto-Sterling, 1992).

Today, in the heat of the Women's Health Initiative, grave concerns have been raised about inadequate knowledge of the female body (Ruzek et al., 1997). There is, however, a certain irony in this. Scientists have tended to slight research on women's health while all too often jumping to reductionistic, biologistic explanations of human inequality. Western science has wrought a double-edged sword of sexual science—the simultaneous exaggeration of sexual differences to the detriment of women and neglect of research potentially beneficial to women.

Gender, Race, and Sexuality

Protagonists on the nurture side of the debate argue that subtle and not-so-subtle forms of discrimination are built into social and scientific institutions. They emphasize that differences between men's and women's achievement result from inequalities in opportunities—including differences in expectations, education, income levels, and verbal and nonverbal behaviors. The fact, for example, that women were excluded from universities for more than seven hundred years (from their inception in the twelfth century until the late nineteenth century) goes a long way toward answering Darwin's challenge that women have lagged behind men in producing great art and science. Not only were women barred from the production of knowledge, but certain problematics and values historically associated with women also were excluded from knowledge (Schiebinger, 1993).

A vast nurturist literature documents how, from moments after birth, boys and girls, and men and women, are treated differently, and how this molds behavior. Boy and girl babies are handled differently, given different toys to play with, and taught to behave differently. This continues as boys and girls enter school. Even when sitting in the same classrooms, boys and girls often receive very different educations. In Western societies, men and women of the same class and ethnic background tend to inhabit separate cultures, which many nurturists trace to foundational gender divisions in emotional, intellectual, and physical labor.

The same nature/nurture duality concerning gender has structured debates surrounding race and sexual orientation. Racists since at least the eighteenth century have argued that innate differences in intelligence determine wealth, poverty, and social status. Because they see intelligence as inborn instead of environmental, they argue that social programs aimed at ameliorating poverty and discrimination (such as Head Start programs and affirmative action) waste precious resources. Nativist-backed eugenics programs have not been confined to Nazi Germany. In 1966 in the United States, William Shockley advocated the sterilization of people with low IQs (intelligence quotients) and supported a sperm bank for geniuses. In the nineteenth century, this kind of reasoning served as a rationale for slavery; in the twentieth, it served as an apology for poverty and racial inequalities (Rose et al., 1984). The notion that human nature is all in the genes also fuels the scientific search for a "gay gene"—said to adhere to the matrilineally inherited X chromosome (it has yet to be found). The Western proclivity to privilege the male as the measure of all things has fueled the search for a distinctively *male* "gay gene."

Beyond Nature and Nurture

One of the fallacies of sexual science has been the belief that nature—bodies and brains—is less mutable than culture. Nativists see the body as a static bedrock of organic life, a firm foundation on which to build natural relations between the sexes. Men's and women's bodies do, however, respond to culture. Critical biologists have emphasized the dialectic of biology and culture. Although biology may condition behavior, it also is constantly being molded and changed by diet, occupation, quality of healthcare, income levels, stress, and exercise, among other things. Women, for example, have grown taller and heavier in proportion to men as nutrition has improved. Women's records in sports have been improving more rapidly than men's as women are encouraged to participate more in physical culture. Nature is plastic: it can and does respond to culture (Hubbard, 1990).

Sexual science has also suffered from assuming rigid distinctions between the sexes and thus failing to recognize that there is often as much variation *within* groups as *across* groups. Any individual woman may be physically and mentally as distinct from any other woman as from any one man—even in relation to primary sexual characteristics. It is important to keep in mind that, in Western culture, sexually ambiguous babies (estimated at 4 percent of births) are "fixed" (Kessler, 1998).

But the fault does not rest with the nativists alone. Nurturists all too often try to explain away difference. For them, sexual science is simply "bad science," overheated with simplistic and exaggerated notions of sexual difference. Fighting science with science, nativists often tend to deemphasize—almost to the point of denying—sexual differences. Much in nurturist arguments (since the eighteenth century) has assumed *sameness* as the only ground for equality. This all too often requires that women be like men—culturally or even biologically (as when working women are not expected to need time off to have children). A simple call for equality ignores the complexities of gender in modern life. Why should women have to assimilate to the dominant culture in order to succeed? Why cannot people be genuinely different in their skills and outlooks and still be equal? Rather than attempting to trace behavior to a single root cause—nurture or nature—we need to understand what is at stake in the debate.

See Also

ANATOMY; BIOLOGICAL DETERMINISM; BIOLOGY; BODY; DIFFERENCE I AND II; ESSENTIALISM; EVOLUTION; LESBIANS IN SCIENCE; PSYCHOLOGY: NEUROSCIENCE AND BRAIN RESEARCH; RACISM AND XENOPHOBIA; SCIENCE: FEMINIST PHILOSOPHY; SEXISM; SEXUAL DIFFERENCE

Reference and Further Reading

Angier, Natalie. 1999. *Woman: An intimate geography.* Boston: Houghton Mifflin.

By a Lady. 1763. *Female rights vindicated: or the equality of the sexes morally and physically proved.* London.

Cadden, Joan. 1993. *Meanings of sex difference in the Middle Ages: Medicine, science, and culture.* Cambridge, UK: Cambridge University Press.

Darwin, Charles. [1871] 1981. *The descent of man, and selection in relation to sex.* Princeton, N.J.: Princeton University Press.

Fauré, Christine. 1991. *Democracy without women: Feminism and the rise of liberal individualism in France.* Trans. Claudia Gorbman and John Berks. Bloomington: Indiana University Press.

Fausto-Sterling, Anne. 1992. *Myths of gender: Biological theories about men and women.* New York: Basic Books.

Fee, Elizabeth. 1979. Nineteenth-century craniology: The study of the female skull. *Bulletin of the History of Medicine* 53: 415–433.

Gould, Stephen Jay. 1980. *The panda's thumb.* New York: Norton.

Hubbard, Ruth. 1990. *The politics of women's biology.* New Brunswick, N.J.: Rutgers University Press.

Kessler, Suzanne. 1998. *Lessons from the intersexed.* New Brunswick, N.J.: Rutgers University Press.

Laqueur, Thomas. 1990. *Making sex: Body and gender from the Greeks to Freud.* Cambridge, Mass.: Harvard University Press.

Oudshoorn, Nelly. 1994. *Beyond the natural body: An archeology of sex hormones.* London: Routledge.

Rose, Steven, Leon Kamin, and Richard Lewontin. 1984. *Not in our genes: Biology, ideology, and human nature.* New York: Pantheon.

Russett, Cynthia. 1989. *Sexual science: The Victorian construction of womanhood.* Cambridge, Mass.: Harvard University Press.

Ruzek, Sheryl, Virginia Olesen, and Adele Clarke, eds. 1997. *Women's health: Complexities and differences.* Columbus: Ohio State University Press.

Schiebinger, Londa. 1989. *The mind has no sex? Women in the origins of modern science.* Cambridge, Mass.: Harvard University Press.

———. 1993. *Nature's body: Gender in the making of modern science.* Boston: Beacon.

Tuana, Nancy. 1993. *The less noble sex: Scientific, religious, and philosophical conceptions of woman's nature.* Bloomington: Indiana University Press.

Londa Schiebinger

NATURE: Philosophy and Spirituality

The dominant Western view of nature bears a patriarchal stamp and is imbued with the dichotomy or duality between man and woman, person and nature, spirit and matter. Nature is perceived as inert—as dead matter—and has been repeatedly symbolized as female in its passive aspects.

The subjugation of nature and of women is intimately associated in the ecofeminist perspective. In the ecofeminist approach, nature and women are creative, not inert. People are part of nature, not external to it. And every aspect of nature is an expression of divine creativity.

In patriarchal religions, the creator is treated as external to creation. Patriarchal science pushes this alienation further, and turns creation into dead, inert matter.

Modern science is projected as a universal, value-free system of knowledge that has displaced all other belief and knowledge systems by the logic of its method to arrive at objective claims about nature. The dominant stream of modern science, the reductionist or mechanical paradigm, is a particular response of a particular group of people. It is a specific project of Western man that came into being during the fifteenth to seventeenth centuries as the "scientific revolution." In the latter decades of the twentieth century, feminist scholarship began to recognize that the dominant science system had emerged as a liberating force not for humanity as a whole (though it legitimized itself in terms of universal betterment of the species), but as a masculine and patriarchal project that necessarily entailed the subjugation of both nature and women. Harding (1986) has called it a "Western, bourgeois, masculine project," and, according to Keller,

> Science has been produced by a particular sub-set of the human race, that is, almost entirely by white, middle class males. For the founding fathers of modern science, the reliance on the language of gender was explicit; they sought a philosophy that deserved to be called 'masculine', that could be distinguished from its ineffective predecessors by its 'virile' powers, its capacity to bind Nature to man's service and make her his slave. (1985)

Francis Bacon (1561–1626) was the father of modern science, the originator of the concept of the modern research institute and industrial science, and the inspiration behind Britain's Royal Society. His contribution to modern science and its organization is critical. From the point of view of nature, women, and marginal groups, however, Bacon's program was not all-inclusive. It was a special program benefiting the middle-class, European, male entrepreneur through the conjunction of human knowledge and power in science.

Bacon's experimental method, which was central to this masculine project, created false dichotomies between male and female, mind and matter, objective and subjective, and rational and emotional; it established a conjunction of masculine and scientific forces dominating nature, women, and the non-West. His was not a neutral, objective, scientific method—it was a masculine mode of aggression against nature and domination over women. The severe testing of hypotheses through controlled manipulations of nature, and the necessity of such manipulations if experiments are to be repeatable, are formulated in clearly sexist metaphors. Both nature and inquiry appear conceptualized in ways modeled on rape and torture—on man's most violent and misogynistic relationships with women—and this modeling is advanced as a reason to value science. According to Bacon, "The nature of things betrays itself more readily under the vexations of art than in its natural freedom" (Anderson, 1960). The discipline of scientific knowledge and the mechanical inventions it leads to do not "merely exert a gentle guidance over nature's course; they have the power to conquer and subdue her, to shake her to her foundations" (Spedding, 1963).

In *Tempores Partus Masculus,* or *The Masculine Birth of Time,* translated by Benjamin Farrington in 1951, Bacon promised to create "a blessed race of heroes and supermen" who would dominate both nature and society (Keller, 1985). The title is interpreted by Farrington as suggesting a shift from the older science, represented as female—passive and weak—to a new masculine science of the scientific revolution, which Bacon saw himself as heralding. In *The New Atlantis,* Bacon's utopian community of Bensalem was administered from Solomon's House, a scientific research institute, from which male scientists ruled over and made decisions for society and decided which secrets should be revealed and which should remain the private property of the institute.

Science-dominated society has evolved much in the pattern of Bacon's Bensalem, with nature transformed and mutilated in modern Solomon's Houses—corporate laboratories and the university programs they sponsor. With the new biotechnologies, Bacon's vision of controlling reproduction for the sake of production is being realized, while the green revolution and the bio-revolution have realized what in *The New Atlantis* was only a utopia.

"We make by act trees and flowers to come earlier or later than their seasons, and to come up and bear more speedily than by their natural course they do. We make them by act greater, much more than their nature, and their fruit greater and sweeter and of differing taste, smell, colour and figure from their nature" (Merchant, 1980). For Bacon, nature was no longer Mother Nature, but a female nature, conquered by an aggressive masculine mind. As Carolyn Merchant points out, this transformation of nature from a living, nurturing mother to inert, dead, and manipulable matter was eminently suited to the exploitation imperative of growing capitalism. The nurturing earth image acted as a cultural constraint on the exploitation of nature. "One does not readily slay a mother, dig her entrails or mutilate her body." But the mastery and domination images created by the Baconian program and the scientific revolution removed all restraint and functioned as cultural sanctions for the denudation of nature.

> The removal of animistic, organic assumptions about the cosmos constituted the death of nature—the most far reaching effect of the scientific revolution. Because nature was now viewed as a system of dead, inert particles moved by external, rather than inherent forces, the mechanical framework itself could legitimate the manipulation of nature. Moreover, as a conceptual framework, the mechanical order had associated with it a framework of values based on power, fully compatible with the directions taken by commercial capitalism. (Merchant, 1980)

The Royal Society, inspired by Bacon's philosophy, was clearly seen by its organizers as a masculine project. In 1664, Henry Oldenberg, secretary of the Royal Society, announced that the intention of the society was to "raise a *masculine philosophy*... whereby the Mind of Man may be ennobled with the knowledge of solid Truths" (Easlea, 1981). And for Glanvill, the masculine aim of science was to know "the ways of captivating Nature, and making her subserve our purposes, thereby achieving the Empire of Man Over Nature" (Easlea, 1981). Glanvill advocated chemistry as one of the most useful arts for "by the violence of its artful fires it is made to confess those latent parts, which upon less provocation it would not disclose" (Merchant, 1980). The "demothering" of nature through modern science and the marriage of knowledge with power was simultaneously a source of subjugating women as well as non-European peoples. Robert Boyle, the famous scientist who was also the governor of the New England Company, saw the rise of mechanical philosophy as an instrument of power not just over nature, but also over the original inhabitants of America. He explicitly declared his intention of ridding the New England Indians of their ridiculous notions about the workings of nature. He attacked their perception of nature "as a kind of goddess," and argued that "the veneration, wherewith men are imbued for what they call nature, has been a discouraging impediment to the empire of man over the inferior creatures of God" (Easlea, 1981).

Today, with new ecological awareness, ecologists the world over turn to the beliefs of Native Americans and other indigenous peoples as a special source for learning how to live in harmony with nature. There are many today from the ecology and women's movements who see irrationality in Boyle's impulse for the empire of white man over nature and other peoples, and who see rationality in the words of Chief Smohalla when he cried out: "You ask me to plough the ground: shall I take a knife and tear my mother's bosom? You ask me to cut grass and make hay and sell it and be rich like white men; but how dare I cut off my mother's hair?" (Easlea, 1981)

In the ecofeminist perspective, creation is an expression of the divine. Nature is thus part of the spiritual domain, and has its own integrity and sanctity.

The ecofeminist perspective transcends the patriarchal divide between spirit and matter and gives spiritual meaning and status to the material world. It also transcends the dichotomy and alienation between people and nature. In ecofeminism, nature is characterized by five sets of principles: (1) creativity, activity, productivity; (2) diversity in form and aspect; (3) connectedness and interrelationship of all beings, including humans; (4) continuity between the human and natural; and (5) the sanctity of life.

The ecofeminist perspective identifies the desacralization of nature and its reduction into raw material for commercial and industrial exploitation as a significant aspect of the environmental crisis. The patriarchal worldview that underlies the exploitation of nature treats it as inert and passive, uniform and mechanistic, separable and fragmented within itself, separate from man, and inferior to man, to be dominated and exploited by him.

Ecofeminist spirituality recognizes the sacred in the earth. It is not just a theoretical stand. It is the philosophy that has guided ecological activism worldwide. In every site, conflict is not just a conflict of interests but worldviews and concepts of nature.

See Also

ECOFEMINISM; NATURE; SCIENCE: FEMINIST CRITIQUES; SPIRITUALITY: OVERVIEW

References and Further Reading

Bacon, Francis. 1960. *The new Organon and related writings.* Anderson. Indianapolis: Bobbs Merrill.

Easlea, Brian. 1981. *Science and sexual oppression: Patriarchy's confrontation with woman and nature.* London: Weidenfeld and Nicholson.

Harding, Susan. 1986. *The science question in feminism.* Ithaca: Cornell University Press.

Keller, Evelyn F. 1985. *Reflections on gender and science.* New Haven: Yale University Press.

Merchant, Carolyn. 1980. *The death of nature: Women, ecology, and the scientific revolution.* New York: Harper and Row.

Spedding, J. et al., eds. 1963. *The works of Francis Bacon.* Stuttgart: F.F. Verlag.

Vandana Shiva

NAZISM

SEE FASCISM AND NAZISM.

NEPOTISM

Organizations such as universities have often discouraged and sometimes prohibited the employment of close relatives, particularly where a supervisory relationship is involved. This is referred to as the "nepotism rule." It is intended to ensure the integrity of the merit principle and of supervisory relationships, but it has typically disadvantaged women, who are usually junior in academic terms to their partners.

Other organizations have tried to protect confidential information by preventing the employment of those with a close relative working for a rival firm. This has been particularly so where intellectual property is at stake, as in the computer and pharmaceutical industries. This concern has again led to discrimination on the grounds of identity of spouse and has again disadvantaged women.

A common fear is that women will betray their employer's secrets through "pillow talk." The assumption is that women are subordinate to their husbands rather than independent professionals. Women are perceived as less able to maintain boundaries between their personal lives and their careers than men are, and more subject to the influence of their partners.

There have been conflicting decisions under antidiscrimination law concerning whether or not discrimination on the grounds of identity of spouse is covered by the prohibition of discrimination on the grounds of marital status.

See Also

ANTIDISCRIMINATION

References and Further Reading

BNA Books, ed. 1988. *Corporate Affairs: Nepotism, Office Romance, and Sexual Harassment.* Washington, D.C.: BNA Books.

CCH Australia LTD. 1984. *Australian and New Zealand equal opportunity law and practice.* North Ryde, New South Wales: CCH Australia.

Marian Sawer

NETWORKING

Perhaps the ultimate outcome of networking is to *feel* connected by *being* connected. Most humans are social animals and form groups for a variety of reasons: efficiency, survival, and enjoyment. The so-called good old boys' network has been in effect for most of humans' literate history because men have controlled most of the public communications and information technology. Men have also controlled the private networks of communication and information under the economic construction of the "individual" entity within the business and corporate world, which allows co-optation of the masses through a structural "father" image.

Such economically, legally, and socially sanctioned networking among men as corporations has kept adult women and female children wards of the state and the property of all males. In at least the Western model, this condition is likely to persist as long as women and children are restricted to and isolated in the domestic sphere by males—husbands, fathers, sons, priests, teachers, judges, or bankers.

Historical Networking

Some think that women have had a preliterate history that has mostly been lost, excised, distorted, and remythologized to alter a Goddess or Gaia society and culture (Gimbutas, 1989) into one headed by an abstract malelike God who, through anointed emissaries, has shifted an egalitarian, sharing life to one in which wealth and power accrue to a few. Women's networking has been constrained by the limitations imposed by the powerful, which usually can be described in sociostructural terms as patriarchal, hierarchical, and capitalistic. The result for women was restriction to domestic, private spaces, silent voices, and isolation, depression, frustration, and, too often, intentional abuse.

Women historically have used collective production gatherings—sewing bees, childcare, and food processing—to come together in interpersonal networks. Social collectives created through religious and educational study and teaching also brought women together in meaningful groups.

Because such informal networks were permitted in domestic and private spheres, they have been important to women. Some of them have become institutionalized at various levels of politics: nongovernmental organizational activities like violence hotlines and centers, or local sociocultural spaces like the poor urban neighborhood (Riaño, 1994: 39). Riaño points to the works of Alfaro (1994), "who examines how women have transformed their motherhood (individual level) into a social maternity (the public). The neighborhood constitutes a symbolic and material space in which their social motherhood is exercised by supporting informal networks of exchange and collective strategies of survival" (39).

Alternative and Emerging Networking

Alternative networks and media are also routes of communication for those outside the mainstream (or "malestream") of traditional media. Riaño (1994) points to the importance of such group communication processes in reclaiming cultural and ethnic concerns, "to facilitate the recovery of indigenous knowledge and historical memory" (35). She describes the work of Mata (1994), who "explores how the discourses created through grassroots communication are not about the Other but about a We. In conclusion, the recognition of the otherness (of gender, race, and class) is achieved in grassroots communication through the dynamic building of group bonds; through identifying a common project, a sense of belonging (ours); and through the recognition of the participants as a collective subject (we)" (35).

When discussing the regional and international levels, women writers usually note how the establishment of 1975 as International Women's Year and the declaration of the United Nations Decade for Women (1976–1985) strengthened the momentum of women's movements through the growth of women's networks and media. The Beijing Women's Conference in 1995 generated many more strands in women's worldwide webs.

Women's emerging communications channels and networks have been so resilient in their resistance to being silenced that women scholars have come to regard them as more than merely alternative media and as deserving increased research and financial commitment. After Martha Allen's impressive 1988 work, "The development of communication networks among women 1963–1983," Annabelle Sreberny-Mohammadi issued a 1996 update, "Women communicating globally: Mediating international feminism," a compendium of women's communication channels and networks. Sreberny-Mohammadi examines women's publications, press services, broadcasting, film video, networks, indigenous culture and performance, and archives, and databases. She notes that Isis International in 1990 published a directory, *Third World Women's Publications,* which at the time listed more than three hundred publications, and that some of the newer publications come from nations of the South. She describes women's press services that feed both nontraditional and traditional media, and notable examples of broadcasting channels by and for women (Sreberny-Mohammadi, 1996: 234).

Various technologies, although largely created and controlled by men in their own images and for their own uses, often have been taken up by women for intellectual stimulation, education, occupation, and liberation. The printing press, for example, affected women through the bookstore, the library, and the school, where they were employed as clerks, librarians, and nurturing elementary teachers (Kramarae, 1988). The typewriter likewise has affected them, but gendered role stereotypes often dictated its use by women; (Corporations long restricted them to secretarial pools where they could do little for the advancement of their sex, except in group bargaining for higher wages). The telephone, an electronic connection for women, also has been described both as an instrument of oppression and a community-building technology for women (Rakow, 1988).

Empowerment Through Networking

Networking among women has brought individual empowerment through sharing information and knowledge in direct and mediated messages and channels, and through their discovering commonality of social treatment and status. Most important, networking for and by women has allowed them to work toward social equality with men. Women and persons of color have deconstructed the social reality erected by men for a materialistic reward system (that is, positions of hierarchical power with economic, educational, and social levels of comfort and dominance beyond individual and even group needs).

Women have had to figure out, time and again, that although each one of us is unique, our experiences have common theads which allow us to share our ordinary, unusual, and unique experiences. When networking works as it should, both efficiently *and* equitably, then it is analogous to the tides coming in and going out according to the rhythms of nature. In human terms, networking ripples out across collective unity levels, from the family to the United Nations, and flows back again, collecting and distributing information and knowledge as it travels.

Networking is what it sounds like: working the net, the web. We are all websters and spinsters, according to the feminist theologian Mary Daly, and thus we are all networkers and are usually networking. (Rush and Grubb-Swetnam, 1996). Daly defines the network as "the Gyn-Ecological context: tapestry of connections woven and re-woven by Spinsters and Websters; the Net which breaks the fall of Journeyers experiencing the Earth Phenomenon (beyond patriarchy and phallocentric attacks and into surviving, spinning, and weaving cosmic connections) and springing us into New Space (space created on the boundaries of patriarchal institutions where women create real alternatives and presence)" (1987: 149).

As the twenty-first century envelops us, computer networks seem to be primarily the realm of academics and white-collar workers who have the time, skills, and resources to own and use them. Women are increasingly using electronic networks as a way of identifying interest and political groups, but their entry has lagged, because science and technology are sanctioned as the invention and activity domain of men. According to estimates, only 15 to 30 percent of Internet users are women. As Kramarae notes, "Thus, gender-differentiated technology deepens women's economic and social dependence" (1998: x). She cites Berch, who "states that despite the appearance of new opportunities for women, the new technology represents 'more than anything else the reconstruction of domination: new technology bears the sexist/classist [and to which could be added, racist and ageist] import of its designers'" (Berch, 1984: 42; Kramarae, 1988: 12). As this author has noted elsewhere, "Communication revolutions may come and go, but the actors remain the same" (Rush et al., 1982; Rush, 1989b: 9).

Humans have entered the twenty-first century with a far greater potential for "being through connection" than at any time in previous literate history because of powerful advances in communications and information technology. Yet the social construction of reality of a relatively few elites—usually male, usually white, heterosexual, highly educated, wealthy in monetary terms, and of higher class status—has made more disparate the ways in which people relate to one another, as individuals and as groups.

This paradoxical situation is known by many names and is a centerpiece for the worldwide elite agenda for discussion and action. It appears that as regional entities become fewer in number and more concentrated in monolithic market economies, financial networking is the economic veneer of the planet. Under this cover, however, there are many fragmented networks of social movements that are also connecting—they include First Nations, peace, environment, women, people of color, the disabled, the homeless, migrants, and refugees, to name a few.

People within these social movements transcend and connect across class, race, gender, and age barriers largely through the efforts of educational elites and technocrats whose expertise is directed toward praxis and social action research. These social movements tend to network through local, state, national, regional, and international conferences, either electronic or traditional. Important to networking across social movements are crossover members and cooperating groups. There are many examples, but four will be offered here: Women's Studies groups, alternative media, nongovernmental organizations (NGOs), and computer network groups.

Women's Studies in US universities may fall within a longer-established academic discipline, such as sociology, but it links colleagues across disciplines in courses, research, services, and conferences. The impact of Women's Studies on campuses was considerable in the past three decades and is predicted to increase, largely because of powerful networking capabilities.

Electronic telecommunication networks are plentiful, and the benefits of their increase seem unpredictable. An example of "numerous alternative media outlets which are trying to make an 'end-run' around the information monopolies using a worldwide metanetwork of highly decentralized technologies—computer networks, fax machines, amateur radio, packet data satellites, VCRs, video cameras, and the like" is the Association for Progressive Communications (APC) (Frederick, 1993: 125). "APC carries a number of important alternative news sources serving nongovernmental organizations. These include InterPress Service (the Third World's largest news agency), Environmental News Service (Vancouver), the United Nations Information Centre news service, Agencia Latinoamericana de Información (Ecuador) and Alternet (Washington, DC)," Frederick writes (125). The APC network, as chronicled by Frederick (1993: 97), was the world's first computer communications system dedicated solely to peace, human rights, and environmental preservation.

In all of this, even with the best intentions, most (an estimated 75–90 percent) of the world's inhabitants are not touched by this technology, networking, and communication of information. If being connected is *being,* then those persons do not exist.

Other network combinations are emerging to provide such crucial bridging. For example, environmentalists and feminists are attempting a remarkably inclusive and diverse merging: in which Mother Nature—Gaia—is taken as the ultimate network, in which all living and nonliving matter participate. Two groups now immersed in this planetary philosophy and ethical debate are known as deep ecologists and ecofeminists (Rush and Grubb-Swetnam, 1996). Their ongoing discussion is well worth surfing the nets of communication and information technology to join.

See Also

CYBERSPACE AND VIRTUAL REALITY; GAIA HYPOTHESIS; GLOBALIZATION; MEDIA: ALTERNATIVE; MEDIA: GRASSROOTS; INFORMATION TECHNOLOGY; NETWORKS; NONGOVERNMENTAL, ELECTRONIC ORGANIZATIONS (NGOS); PUBLISHING; SOCIAL MOVEMENTS; WOMEN'S CENTERS

References and Further Reading

Alfaro, Rose Maria. 1994. Women as social agents of communication: Social maternity and leadership. In Pilar Riaño, ed., *Women in grassroots communication: Furthering social change,* 260–278. Thousand Oaks, Calif.: Sage.

Allen, Martha. 1988. *The development of communication networks among women, 1963–1983.* Unpublished doctoral dissertation, Howard University, Washington, D.C.

Berch, B. 1984. For women the chips are down. *Processed World II* (Summer): 42–46.

Bryant, Bunyon. 1995. *Environmental justice: Issues, policies, and solutions.* Washington, DC: Island Press.

Daly, Mary, in cahoots with Jane Caputi. 1987. *Websters' first new intergalactic weckedary of the English language.* Boston: Beacon.

Frederick, Howard H. 1993. *Global communications and international relations.* Belmont, Calif.: Wadsworth.

Gimbutas, Marija. 1989. *The language of the goddess.* San Francisco: Harper and Row.

Kramarae, Cheris, ed. 1988. *Technology and women's voices keeping in touch.* New York: Routledge and Kegan Paul.

Mata, Marita. 1994. Being woman in popular radio. In Pilar Riaño, ed., *Women in grassroots communication: Furthering social change,* 192–211. Thousand Oaks, Calif.: Sage.

Rakow, Lana F. 1988. Women and the telephone: The gendering of a communications technology. In Cheris Kramarae, ed., *Technology and women's voices keeping in touch,* 207–228. New York: Routledge and Kegan Paul.

Riaño, Pilar. 1994. Gender in communication: Women's contributions. In Pilar Riaño, ed., *Women in grassroots communication: Furthering social change,* 30–44. Thousand Oaks, Calif.: Sage.

Rush, Ramona R. 1989a. Global eco-communications: Assessing the communication and information environment. Paper presented to the International Communication Association, May, San Francisco.

———. 1989b. Communications at the crossroads: The gender gap connection. In Ramona R. Rush and Donna Allen, eds., *Communications at the crossroads: The gender gap connection.* Norwood, N.J.: Ablex.

———. 1992. Global eco-communications: Grounding and re/finding the concepts. Paper presented to the International Association for Mass Communication Research, August, Brazil.

———. 1996a. 10 tenets of deeper communication: Transforming communications theory and research. In Donna Allen, Ramona R. Rush, and Susan J. Kaufman, eds., *Women transforming communications: Global Intersections.* Thousand Oaks, Calif.: Sage.

———. 1996b. Introduction: Websters and spinsters. In Donna Allen, Ramona R. Rush, and Susan J. Kaufman, eds., *Women transforming communications: Global intersections.* Thousand Oaks, Calif.: Sage.

———, and Autumn Grubb-Swetnam. 1996. Feminist approaches. In Michael B. Salwen and Don W. Stacks, eds. *An Integrated Approach to Communication Theory and Research.* Mahwah, N.J.: Lawrence Erlbaum Associates.

———, Elizabeth Buck, and Chris Ogan. 1982. Women and the communications revolution: Can we get there from here? Chasqui (Quito, Ecuador: Centro Internacional de Estudios Superiores de la Comunication para America Latin [Ciespal]).

Sreberny-Mohammadi, Annabelle. 1996. Women communicating globally: Mediating international feminism. In Donna Allen, Ramona R. Rush, and Susan J. Kaufman, eds., *Women transforming communications: Global intersections.* Thousand Oaks, Calif.: Sage.

Ramona Rush

NETWORKS, ELECTRONIC

Growing access to venues for electronic communication has led to the emergence of a number of on-line resources for women. World Wide Web sites and various discussion groups and their archives provide repositories for documents, papers, and resource guides, while groups and lists provide an opportunity to share ideas, request information, and engage in dialogues of interest and importance to women.

There are sites on the Web for every conceivable interest, and many are specifically tailored to the needs and interests of women. Myriad women's health sites, for instance, address topics from contraceptives and sexuality to food and fitness. One such site, <www.obgyn.net>, includes directories of doctors and their specialties as well as expanded medical directories. Such sites often host discussions on every aspect of women's health, and access to professional medical articles. Increasingly, electronic networks provide access and information to women about "alternative" or complementary forms of medicine and health practices.

Web sites devoted to women's scholarship also abound. The Feminist Collections, found on the Women's Studies section of the University of Wisconsin Website (<http://www.library.wisc.edu/libraries/Women'sStudies/>) is an excellent example. The site features extensive bibliographies, key books in Women's Studies, and recent "Computer Talk" columns. In recent years, growth in the presence and diversity of women on-line has resulted in a vast array of sites representing the various interests, concerns, and backgrounds of women around the world. There are sites for affirmative action and diversity (<http://humanitas.ucsb.edu/aa.html>), Afghan women (<http://women3rdworld.miningco.com/msub30.htm>), and African women's rights (<http://www.africapolicy.org/action/women.htm>). A South African feminist journal has expanded to create its own site (<http://www.oneworld.org/agenda/>). The Library of Congress's American Memory Project has many sections dedicated to women (<http://lcweb2.loc.gov/amhome.html>). Asian and Pacific women have a space on the Web (<http://www.sequel.net/~isis/links.html>), and the Beijing Declaration and Platform for Action is found on the Web (<http://www.undp.org/fwcw/plat.htm>). Other sites are devoted to topics as diverse as black women in the United Kingdom (<http://www.vvv.com/~careers/>), Chicana feminists (<http://chicanas.com/>), women and religion (<http://aquinas.gtu.edu/Centers/cwr/>), and gay and lesbian studies (<http://www.inform.umd.edu/EdRes/Topic/Diversity/Specific/Sexual_Orientation/Syllabi/>).

New sites and links are added daily, and many disappear just as quickly. The sheer number of sites demonstrates the fluidity and diversity of the Web and the wide range of information available. Topics on the feminist movement and of general interest about women are readily accessible. The Internet has made communication among women easier and dispersal of vital information simpler. Information concerning women around the world and contact among women in every continent can be accessed with a click of the mouse.

On-line discussion groups and electronic mailing lists provide opportunities to share ideas, request information, and engage in dialogues on issues of interest to women. Many groups provide forums around common interests, often occupational; such lists help professional women develop a common way of communicating by providing otherwise inaccessible contacts and mentoring. Other groups provide forums for discussion of women's studies, feminist theory, and the like. Not all women's lists, however, have a feminist orientation.

Electronic forums help individual women and women's centers in rural areas overcome isolation, and they assist women in long-distance education and job training (Balka in Shade, 1994). The collected material stored in various World Wide Web sites allow for the distribution of documents and other resources on women's studies, gender issues, and feminist research, and provide pointers to conferences, nonelectronic materials, and other electronic resources.

Despite the proliferation of these resources, feminist analyses of computing raise serious questions with regard to women's participation in electronic communities. Although their participation has increased in recent years, women are still underrepresented both on the Internet and on commercial networks and the gap between the experiences of men and women with electronic technology is still significant. Women comprise a tiny proportion of creators and/or moderators of Web sites or other electronic sources. Webmasters are largely male, as are software developers, engineers, animators, and technicians. Individual women and women's centers have less money to purchase computers and network services, and women are less likely to have jobs with Internet access. Gender is often overlooked in mainstream accounts of the usage patterns and practices of technology and in the development of information technology infrastructures (particularly with respect to poor women and women in developing nations).

On-line, women are subject to many of the same forms of communicative dominance found in face-to-face interactions: Men contribute disproportionately to discussions (more frequent and longer posts), and they receive more direct responses from other discussion members. Women report dissatisfaction in these interactions and sometimes consider leaving the forum altogether (Ebben, 1994). Such experiences become catalysts for creating women-only lists (e.g., systers), lesbian-only lists (sappho), or commercial networks such as The Women's WIRE and e-village.

Female characters in MUDs, Internet text-based virtual reality systems, are subject both to special "chivalrous" treatment and harassment. In the context of these electronic games, women's characters are faced with sexually explicit statements and "virtual rape" (Reid, 1994), in which a male character symbolically enacts a rape scene with a female character against that character's will. In addition, women playing male characters are tracked down and "killed" symbolically. While "romance via the Internet" gets press in popular articles and Internet guides, electronic anecdotes warn of women robbed, assaulted, raped, or murdered by men they met electronically.

Some issues may be generational. Women who are acquainted with electronic technologies from a young age may become very effective "weavers of webs" on-line, integrating electronic conversation spaces into their everyday social world (Kaplan in Shade, 1994).

See Also

CYBERSPACE AND VIRTUAL REALITY; INFORMATION TECHNOLOGY; LIBRARIES; NETWORKING; REFERENCE SOURCES; THIRD WORLD WOMEN: SELECTED RESOURCES

References and Further Reading

Ebben, Maureen. 1994. *Women on the net. An exploratory study of gender dynamics on the soc.women computer network.* Department of Speech Communication, University of Illinois at Champaign-Urbana.

Herring, Susan C. 1996. Posting in a different voice: Gender and ethics in computer-mediated communication. In Charles Ess, ed., *Philosophical approaches to computer-mediated communication.* Albany: SUNY Press.

Kolko, Beth, Lisa Nakamura, and Gil Rodman. 2000. *Race in cyberspace.* New York: Routledge.

Markham, Annette. 1998. *Life online: Researching real experience in virtual space.* Walnut Creek, Calif.: Alta Mira.

Reid, Elizabeth. 1994. *Cultural formations in text-based virtual realities.* Master's thesis, Cultural Studies Program, Department of English, University of Melbourne (full text available via anonymous ftp on parcftp.xerox.com as file/pubfMOO/paper/CulturalFoundations.txt).

Selfe, Cynthia L. and Paul Meyer. 1991. Testing claims for on-line conferences. *Written Communication,* 8(2): 163–192.

Shade, Leslie Regan, ed. 1994. *Special issue: Gender issues in computer networking,* The Arachnet Electronic Journal on Virtual Culture, GOPHER to gopher.cic.net 70, Electronic Serials/Alphabetic ListfE/Electronic Journal on Virtual Culture! *or* send GET EJVCV2N3 CONTENTS to listserv@kentvm.kent.edu.

Taylor, H. Jeanie, Cheris Kramarae, and Maureen Ebben, eds. 1993. *Women, information technology, and scholarship.* Urbana, Ill.: Center for Advanced Study.

Wakeford, Nina. 2000a. Gender and the landscapes of computing in an Internet café. In *The Gendered cyborg: A reader.* Ed. Gill Kirkup, Linda Janes, Kath Woodward, and Fiona Hovender. New York: Routledge.

———. 2000b. *Networks of desire: Gender, sexuality, and computing culture.* New York: Routledge.

Webster, Juliet. 1996. *Shaping women's work: Gender employment and information technology.* New York: Longman.

Wincapaw, Annette. 2000. Lesbian and bisexual women's electronic mailing lists as sexualized spaces. *Journal of Lesbian Studies* (forthcoming).

Pointers to Electronic Resources

Gopher for women's studies information and other resources: gopher.umbc.edu, #6 Academic Department Information, #9 Women's Studies (WMST).

Hudson, Judith, and Kathleen A. Turek. 1992. *Electronic access to research on women: A short guide.* Institute for Research on Women, University at Albany, SUNY; call 518-442-4801 for ordering information.

USENET newsgroup soc.feminism; moderators maintain a resource directory of further readings, addresses, and subscription information for electronic groups and lists, available via anonymous ftp to rtfm.mit.edu under/pub/usenet/news. Answers/feminismlresources.

Women's International Electronic University: <http://www.wvu.edu/~womensu>.

Women's International Net magazine: winmagazine@oaknet-pub.com.

Women's resources on the internet: <http://sunsite.unc.edu/cheryb/women/wresources.html>

The Women's Wire (Worldwide Information Resource & Exchange), commercial network: 1-800-210-9999 or info@wwire.net.

Women's writing and resources: <http://www.mit.edu: 800 l/people/womenlindex.html>

Karen Ruhleder
Maureen Ebben

NEWSPAPERS

See JOURNALISM; MEDIA: OVERVIEW; PRESS: FEMINIST ALTERNATIVES.

NONGOVERNMENTAL ORGANIZATIONS (NGOs)

Nongovernmental organizations are the building blocks of civil society. They provide the infrastructure through which citizen's voices can be heard and their energy harnessed to support social and political structures—both for stability and for change. Women always have found ways to make connections with other women to "get the job done," whether the job is making quilts or changing the government. In the latter half of the twentieth century, they became increasingly sophisticated in organizing themselves to affect the world around them, took a more assertive role in public life, and learned the skills necessary to provide services more effectively and to make an impact on public policy. They have become a highly visible and essential component of the NGO world.

What Is an NGO?

By definition, nongovernmental organizations (NGOs) operate *external* to government. Their role is to provide services, discussion forums, and communication channels that are neither provided nor controlled by government. Some NGOs may receive funding from their own or other governments, and most are regulated in some way by registration requirements or tax laws. Many have close connections to one or more government ministries or political parties, which are necessary for obtaining information and planning effective program strategies. One of the key challenges in the NGO world is balancing the relationship to government with the mandate to serve citizens, sometimes in opposition to government positions.

The relative strength—indeed, the very existence—of nongovernmental organizations within any country is directly related to the history and nature of the country's culture and form of government. Certain countries, such as China, have throughout history been so culturally and politically inhospitable to structures and views outside their official ones that NGOs as defined in this article simply cannot exist there; citizen organizations are seen as inherently subversive, professional organizations are allowed but tightly controlled, and the only political organizations are arms of the ruling party. The only recognized women's political organization is the All China Women's Federation, an arm of the Communist Party. Other authoritarian governments allow NGOs to exist but monitor them closely and will not tolerate the possibility of their becoming a threat to established power. In such settings, even nonpolitical NGOs, not identified with political opposition or human rights causes, can be in danger of harassment of members or deregistration if their positions are seen as inherently critical of the government. Even in more open societies, NGOs that are critical of government may experience limited access to information channels, harassment by political opponents, and inadequate funding. And in countries in transition from authoritarianism to democracy, particularly those that never had a tradition of civil-society involvement, NGOs continue to struggle with basic issues such as recruitment, internal organizing and agenda-setting, and government recognition of citizens as credible participants in social and political development.

In other words, making civil society work can be extremely stressful, if not downright dangerous. Yet in every part of the world, under every type of government and in every social setting, citizens continue to find each other, to organize, to carry on discussions, and to carry out action plans designed to make their society better—and to make it their own.

Types of NGOs

Nongovernmental organizations have a variety of missions and organizational structures. They can be constituted as a nonprofit corporation, a resource and communications program, a membership organization, a network, or some combination of these. The single common element, from the smallest local self-help group to the largest international organization, is a commitment to work together to accomplish a mission that cannot be accomplished by individuals working alone.

Throughout the world, *grassroots self-help groups* provide members with resources (such as loans or basic goods) and exchange or pool services (such as childcare or marketing of products) to help them improve their lives. One of the best-known examples of such efforts is the Grameen Bank in Bangladesh, which was not established exclusively for women but which has a high proportion of female participants; countless women's credit cooperatives all over the world have been established on the Grameen model.

Service-oriented NGOs provide women with counseling, legal aid, training and literacy programs, employment placement, family planning services, and the like. A critical service area is violence—provision of counseling, shelters, and advocacy assistance in courts and social agencies. Service-oriented NGOs tend to be staffed by professionals, either paid or volunteer, with a less educated clientele. One of their key challenges is respectful treatment of the clients, particularly where numerical performance goals are involved.

Some service-oriented NGOs are funded at least in part by governments, on the premise that they provide a service that governments should provide but cannot perform as well, or for which NGOs are seen as more trustworthy (such as shelters or legal aid) and thus more effective in outreach to potential clients. In some cases, well-organized NGOs that have built solid programs and credibility with donors, such as the Bangladesh Rural Action Committee, have supplanted government as a primary provider of certain services. Although this benefits citizens, it is problematic in that it relieves governments of full responsibility for citizens' welfare.

Professional organizations, such as the Federation of Women Lawyers (FIDA), give professional women a space for sharing the frustrations and the learning experiences of operating in what still is, in most places, a "man's world." They frequently provide continuing professional education and referral services for their members and services for citizens. Some professional organizations engage in policy study and advocacy as well.

Unions can be a potent force as nongovernmental organizations. They frequently have been at the forefront on issues of workers' rights. Those that take political positions can have significant impact because they speak for a large number of people. One of the key players in opposition to apartheid and in the establishment of the new South Africa, for example, has been the Congress of South African Trade Unions (COSATU). Historically, however, unions have not taken on issues of sex discrimination in the workplace and sometimes have been highly discriminatory themselves. Women have been almost invisible in union governance and policy-making, except in unions that have predominantly female membership.

Policy-oriented NGOs focus primarily on monitoring government performance and developing and lobbying for alternative policy approaches to accomplish certain purposes. Human rights organizations, including those focusing on the human rights of women, and activist groups concerned about specific issues such as the environment or consumer rights, fall into this category. These groups frequently are "ahead of the culture" in defining and pursuing issues that affect people's lives.

NGOs in Action

NGOs operate on local, national, regional, and international levels. The measure of their effectiveness is not their visibility on a particular level, but their impact on the lives of their members and target clientele. A 15-member local self-help group can be more effective in its context than an international NGO with a multimillion-dollar budget. The key to success is choosing the battle and pursuing the project with consistency. Some examples:

- A small women's legal aid and information center in Botswana (with four staff members) succeeded in massively increasing child maintenance awards by bringing multiple lawsuits in the local courts—until the judges had to take notice of the issue. Unwed mothers now can bring suit for child maintenance and claim an appropriate percentage of the father's income, instead of settling for the few dollars per month prescribed by statute.
- A coalition of local and national women's groups succeeded in making a local version of the Convention on the Elim-

ination of All Forms of Discrimination against Women (CEDAW Convention), the international women's human rights treaty, a centerpiece of municipal policy in São Paulo State, Brazil. In 1988, the municipalities of the state adopted the "Paulista Convention" as a policy blueprint. In the United States in 1998, the efforts of a coalition of local groups resulted in the adoption of the CEDAW Convention—which has not been ratified by the United States—as a policy blueprint for the city of San Francisco.

- For many decades, well-established international women's organizations, representing thousands of educated women in hundreds of chapters around the world (primarily, but not exclusively, in the industrialized nations), were privileged to be represented at the United Nations and had direct access to meetings of bodies such as the Commission on the Status of Women. During those same decades, despite the presence of these groups, the Commission on the Status of Women worked in relative obscurity and produced policy statements, resolutions, and even treaties that had little direct effect on governments, while the United Nations human rights bodies totally ignored women. But in the last 15 years of the twentieth century, powered by the voices of groups—many from the global South—representing grassroots women, new professional organizations, and women who became involved in human rights organizations, the international women's NGO community demanded, and received, a new quality of attention to the human rights of women. As a result of NGO organization and lobbying on national and international levels, the International Decade for Women (1975–1985) produced a women's human rights treaty, the Convention on the Elimination of All Forms of Discrimination against Women (1979). As of January 2000, that treaty had been ratified by 165 countries.
- With women's human rights defined by treaty, the international NGO community—consisting of groups from the grassroots to the international—succeeded in bringing human rights to the center of the discussion at the Fourth World Conference on Women in Beijing, 1995. Governments could not ignore women who taught themselves how to identify issues, state them clearly to their national governments, and lobby delegates from other countries in regional and international forums.

Conclusion

NGOs have been the mechanism by which women have made themselves visible in the late twentieth century as potential equal partners in social, political, and economic development. In the new millennium, that potential promises to become reality. The development of civil society rests on the contributions of NGOs, and women's NGOs promise to be at the forefront of that development.

See Also

DAWN MOVEMENT; GLOBAL HEALTH MOVEMENT; GOVERNMENT

References and Further Reading

Hudock, Ann C. 1998. *NGOs and civil society: Democracy by proxy?* New York: Blackwell.

Marsha A. Freeman

NONPROFIT ORGANIZATIONS

See CHARITY; NONGOVERNMENTAL ORGANIZATIONS.

NONVIOLENCE

Defining Nonviolence

Nonviolence is more than the absence of violence; it is the creation of something new to replace violence—a different way of relating to others. Nonviolence means respecting all human life, refusing to kill or do violence to a person either physically or psychologically. Advocates of nonviolence act on the basic assumption that there is value in all life and therefore do not commit or tolerate violations of others. Nonviolence implies not seeking revenge or retaliation for injustices done to oneself or others. Its goal is change: a transformation of the self and others, while seeking truth and justice for all.

Nonviolence has a long and distinguished history, though that history is rarely included in histories of wars and violence. Two figures associated with nonviolence in recent times are Mohandas K. Gandhi (1869–1948) in India and Martin Luther King, Jr. (1929–1968) in the United States: Gandhi led a nonviolent stuggle to make India independent of British rule; King, the leader of a nonviolent movement for African-Americans' civil rights, was greatly influenced by him. A common criticism of nonviolence is that it is an easy way out, an approach for people who are not oppressed; but both Gandhi and King belonged to oppressed groups. Feminists may disagree with some of Gandhi's ideas, especially his attitude toward women, but there is much to be learned from his life and work.

Adhering to nonviolence does not guarantee that there will be no violence—Gandhi and King, for example, were both assassinated—but it does tend to reduce violence, because it can psychologically disarm aggressors and because it prevents violence from escalating. Barbara Deming, an American advocate of nonviolence, has observed (1971):

> We can put more pressure on the antagonist for whom we show human concern. It is precisely solicitude for his person in combination with the stubborn interference with his actions that can give us a very special degree of control.... We put upon him two pressures—the pressure of our defiance of him and the pressure of our respect for his life—and it happens that in combination these two pressures are uniquely effective.... In nonviolent struggle, the violence used against one may mount for a while,... but the escalation is no longer automatic; with the refusal of one side to retaliate, the mainspring of the automation has been snapped and one can count on reaching a point where deescalation begins. One can count, that is, in the long run, on receiving far fewer casualties.

Nonviolence confers power, but not as power is commonly defined. In most societies, power usually is thought of as power over others—that is, the power to control and dominate. But nonviolence implies the power to *be*. Nonviolence, then, means acting on the belief that one has the power to resist through noncompliance, exercising the power to be who one chooses to be. Advocates of nonviolence refuse to be victims, to violate their own conscience, to be passive, or to ignore injustice.

A common misconception about nonviolence is that it does not allow anger. Rather, nonviolence acknowledges anger but channels it into creative rather than destructive energy; thus, for instance, anger is said to be part of the process of defining injustice. Advocates of nonviolence distinguish betwen "just" or "good" anger, which is a response to someone else's control, and anger that is not good, which comes from loss of control over another. Nonviolence is held to confer attitudes and tools that can allow people to free themselves from being controlled.

Comparing Feminism and Nonviolence

Feminism may be defined as women's recognition of and opposition to male domination and oppression, rejection of traditional concepts of masculinity and femininity, valuing of themselves and their ideas, and taking control of their own lives and choices. With such a definition, it is possible to see common and complementary elements in feminism and nonviolence. Both feminism and nonviolence identify and resist systems that dominate and oppress by misusing power; both encourage their adherents to refuse to be victims; both consider the personal and the political; both demand action; and both are processes in which people explore and experiment with their view of themselves and others and their relationship to others.

Feminism and nonviolence both analyze social and political oppression and power relationships. According to feminist analyses, men dominate women; and values such as competition, aggression, domination, and superior strength are inherent in patriarchal societies and institutions, leading to rape, battering, racism, war, ecological destruction, and even the threat of nuclear annihilation. Such systems have little concern for human needs; their priorities tend to be conflict and weaponry.

Nonviolent analysis recognizes that means determine ends—outcomes depend on what people do, not what they hope for. Thus peace, justice, and equality cannot be achieved by using oppression or violence or by imposing a hierarchy. In a conflict, the "other" must be respected; and respect for others is possible only with self-respect. Those who respect themselves refuse to be victims; those who respect others refuse to be oppressors.

The process people use in relating to one another and making collaborative decisions is an important part of both feminist and nonviolent ideology and strategy. Because of this shared concern for process in personal and political relationships, feminists and advocates of nonviolence have influenced each other. Each movement has observed how members of the other get things done, work together, and respect each other. One example is decision making by consensus—that is, by taking all the participants' input and ideas into account and then coming to an agreement as a group. Consensual decision making promotes responsibility, cooperation, and respect for others, which are all elements of both the feminist and the nonviolent vision of a just society.

However, it can also be illuminating to observe differences between feminism and nonviolence. One such difference has to do with leaders: in general, there has been more inclination toward leaders, especially as developers of strategy, in the nonviolent movement. Examples of charismatic leaders include Gandhi, King, and Cesar Chavez (b. 1927), the labor organizer who led a nonviolent farmworkers' protest in the United States. By contrast, feminists often say that they do not need leaders. Many women, of course, have contributed to the feminist movement as activists, organizers, writers, creative artists, and inspirational models, but the movement does not describe itself as a group of leaders and followers; feminists hold that the nature of their movement makes them all participants.

Nonviolent Feminism

Nonviolent feminism as a specific approach requires specific strategies and tactics; in this regard, feminists can often follow or adapt steps that have been used in other nonviolent struggles. A nonviolent campaign has certain typical components: training participants so that they can be more fully involved, identifying allies and supporters, agreeing on nonviolent discipline, negotiating, issuing ultimatums, deciding how to exert pressure (for instance, by a strike or an economic boycott), demonstrating, using civil disobedience, and setting up alternative institutions and constructive programs. This last element—alternative institutions—has been a strong strategy in the feminist movement. Examples are rape crisis centers and shelters for battered women, which offer options to women in need, providing support, safety, and understanding in societies where violence against women is common.

Another aspect of feminist nonviolence is antimilitarism. One example is the Women's Peace Camp at Greenham Common in England, which began in September 1981 and lasted for more than ten years. The Peace Camp was a constant presence outside the gates of Greenham Common Air Force Base, a site for cruise missiles carrying nuclear warheads; these women encircled the nine-mile perimeter of the base, repeatedly blocked the entrances, made their way onto the base, and danced on missile silos and runways. During the 1980s, dozens of other women's peace camps and other actions against the proliferation of weapons were inspired by Greenham Common.

Nonviolent feminism is always growing and changing, and its adherents do not think in terms of a hierarchical list of concerns. They regard their work as decentralized, so that each individual can contribute to vision, strategy, and action. Finally, they see all the issues they choose to confront—sexism, racism, and militarism—as connected. In each struggle, as individuals become aware of their power through feminist nonviolence, more possibilities are created for social and political change.

See Also

FEMINISM: OVERVIEW; PACIFICISM AND PEACE ACTIVISM; PEACEKEEPING; PEACE MOVEMENTS, *specific regions;* VIOLENCE AND PEACE: OVERVIEW

References and Further Reading

Blackwood, Caroline. 1984. *On the perimeter.* London: Heinemann.

Brock-Utne, Birgit. 1985. *Educating for peace: A feminist perspective.* New York: Pergamon, Athene Series.

Cook, Alice, and Gwyn Kirk. 1983. *Greenham women everywhere: Dreams, ideas, and actions from the women's peace movement.* London: Pluto.

Deming, Barbara. 1971. *Revolution and equilibrium.* New York: Grossman.

Harford, Barbara, and Sarah Hopkins. 1984. *Greenham Common: Women at the wire.* London: Women's Press.

Harris, Adrienne, and Ynestra King. 1989. *Rocking the ship of state: Toward a feminist peace politics.* Boulder, Col.: Westview.

Oldfield, Sybil. 1989. *Women against the iron fist: Alternatives to militarism, 1900 to 1989.* New York: Blackwell.

Reardon, Betty. 1993. *Women and peace: Feminist visions of global security.* Albany: State University of New York Press.

Joanne Sheehan

NORPLANT

Norplant, a long-acting all-progestin contraceptive, was developed by the Population Council in the United States, assembled by Leiras Pharmaceuticals in Norway, and distributed in the United States by Wyeth-Ayerst (which also owns its constituent hormone, levonorgestrel). Norplant is a system of six matchstick-sized Silastic capsules, which are implanted in the fleshy underside of a woman's arm. They contain levonorgestrel, a synthetic progestin, which slowly leaks out of the capsules and enters the bloodstream. About half the time, the progestin suppresses ovulation; if ovulation does occur, the thickened cervical mucus prevents sperm from migrating through the cervical canal to the uterus. Moreover, levonorgestrel suppresses the endometrium, so that a pregnancy cannot easily be supported. Norplant is highly effective in preventing pregnancy, though useless in preventing sexually transmitted diseases (STDs). The pregnancy rate with Norplant is approximately one per 100 users per year in women weighing under 154 pounds, and two per 100 for heavier women.

Risks

Norplant is safer than the oral contraceptive known as "the Pill" because it seems not to increase the risk of life-threatening conditions such as deep-vein blood clots and strokes. However, Norplant is associated with other problems—there are significant risks as well as many discomforts. The rate of ectopic pregnancies occurring in women on Norplant is disturbingly high: 18 percent. The U.S. Food and Drug Administration (FDA) has cautioned users that "any Norplant patient who presents with pain in the lower abdomen must be evaluated to rule out ectopic pregnancy." Because the individual cannot remove it on her own, Norplant presents abundant opportunities for coercion and social control. For example, a common side effect is irregular bleeding, or "menstrual chaos"; but in developing countries such as Indonesia, family planners have refused to remove Norplant when such bleeding occurs. In the United States, some judges, penal authorities, and state legislators have tried to mandate Norplant for women convicted of child abuse, as well as for poor women receiving financial aid.

At least one Norplant user in six has experienced difficulties at the time of removal. Product information brochures assure the user that "capsules are removed under local anesthesia through the same incision in which they were placed. The removal procedure usually takes 15 to 20 minutes." This seems misleading. Thousands of women in the United States have sought damages for "severe pain and scarring" they suffered when practitioners attempted the removal: large, impenetrable masses of scar tissue, called "fibrous envelopes," had formed around the capsules; or the capsules had been incorrectly implanted and proved difficult to find; or the capsules broke; or the capsules became dislodged from their original location and moved to areas deeper in the body; or the practitioners lacked training and expertise.

Although levonorgestrel provides protection against pregnancy for five years, it can also be associated with uncontrollable menstrual chaos. Some women on Norplant may bleed for two to three weeks, then spot for days, then bleed again for another two to three weeks. Other women may go several months without a period, then bleed or spot irregularly. For some women—a minority—menstrual chaos resolves after the early months of use, but for up to two-thirds it continues. To control menstrual chaos, some doctors prescribe estrogen, which increases both the cost of contraception and the level of risk, while leaving the crucial question of protection against STDs still unaddressed.

Laboratory research on Norplant began in 1966, and the first clinical experience with progestin-only Silastic capsules was reported in Santiago, Chile, in 1968. Some ten different progestin compounds were tried before levonorgestrel was settled on. Yet follow-up has been so incomplete that little, if any, information has been published about Norplant's long-term effects on the women themselves, much less on any children they may have conceived or breast-fed while using it. Norplant is widely offered to nursing mothers even though the hormone makes its way into breast milk and thus can be ingested by the baby.

Research by independent evaluators suggests that Norplant is often pressed on women in a manner that is neither safe nor respectful of their rights. At the very least, providers should be thoroughly trained and certified in both insertion and removal; coverage of the cost of removal should be guaranteed at the time of insertion; and the risk of menstrual chaos should not be minimized because, depending on a woman's culture and religion, even mild to moderate menstrual chaos may require that she refrain from cooking and agricultural work, religious ceremonies, or sex relations.

Feminists and Norplant

During the twenty-four years that Norplant was in development, an assertive movement of second-wave feminism, focused on health and reproductive issues, emerged in the United States and spread around the world. The early birth control pills and intrauterine devices (IUDs) had been linked to many severe adverse reactions; it was in this context that feminist researchers, including those at the Women's Health Action Foundation in Amsterdam, Netherlands, collected and published data on Norplant. These feminist investigators reported that the population controllers who were trying Norplant out often neglected to follow up; that although menstrual chaos was a hardship for many women, family planners were instructed not to remove the rods "just" for irregular bleeding; and that difficulties with removal might be occurring more often in dark-skinned than in light-skinned women, perhaps because dark skin has a greater tendency to form keloid tissue.

These matters were brought to the attention of the U.S. FDA before approval of Norplant in 1990. At that time, feminists demanded that the drawbacks be thoroughly explained to users beforehand, and that recipients of Norplant be provided with consent forms to think over and sign. To block these regulations, Norplant's developers and distributors mounted a public-relations campaign, which seemed to be aimed largely at discrediting the activists, who were presented as "antitechnology." The targets of this campaign included the present author and the Boston Women's Health Book Collective, which had written *Our Bodies, Ourselves,* (for example, see Hilts, 1990).

In the year 2000, a decade after Norplant's approval by the FDA, several authoritative scientific papers commented that Norplant had "not fulfilled its promise." In an article entitled "Why Are U.S. Women Not Using Long-Acting Contraceptives?" *Family Planning Perspectives* reported that in 1993 only 1.2 percent of women of childbearing age were using Norplant, a figure that had shrunk to 0.9 percent by 1995. More than half of the women surveyed said that "using the implant would be bad for them."

In the United Kingdom, Norplant—which had been introduced in 1993—was withdrawn from sale altogether in

1999. *The Lancet* observed, "Norplant's image in the newspapers was suddenly transformed from that of a wonderful new contraceptive into a 'controversial implant' that became a 'nightmare' for women who used it. Norplant's media downfall was apparently triggered when women and solicitors started to tell the media about individual experiences of problems with Norplant—some of which involved well-known side effects."

Even many of the feminists who first raised and publicized concerns about Norplant would have preferred to see this contraceptive succeed, since part of their agenda has been to offer women with as contraceptive options as possible. Some still believe that if Norplant had been introduced more realistically and more cautiously, with full disclosure of its risks and better protection of users' rights, comfort, and dignity, it might have found a suitable niche—and fewer women in the United States and the United Kingdom would have felt betrayed. As of the early 1990s, however, too many population controllers and pharmaceutical manufacturers still seemed unaware that women everywhere, in growing numbers, would insist on their health rights.

See Also

CONTRACEPTION; CONTRACEPTIVES: DEVELOPMENT; ESTROGEN; ETHICS: MEDICAL; FAMILY PLANNING; MEDICAL CONTROL OF WOMEN; MENSTRUATION; PHARMACEUTICALS; THE PILL; POPULATION CONTROL

References and Further Reading

Asetoyer, Charon. 1994. *The impact of Norplant in the Native American community.* Available from Charon Asetoyer, Lake Andes, S.D. Telephone: 605-487-7964.

The case of Norplant as an example of media coverage over the life of a new health technology. 2000. *Lancet* 355(6 May): 1633–1636.

Hilts, Philip J. 1990. Birth-control backlash. *New York Times Magazine,* 16 December: 41, 55, 70, 72–74.

Long-acting contraception: Moral choices, policy dilemmas. 1995. Available from Hastings Center, Briarcliff Manor, N.Y.

Norplant: Under her skin. n.d. Available from Women's Health Action Foundation, Amsterdam, Netherlands. Also available from Boston Women's Health Book Collective, Somerville, Mass.

Orrick, Phyllis. 1997. *Skin deep: Seldom-told tales of Norplant.* Video. (Produced by Deb Elllis and Alexandra Halkin, 145 Lakewood Parkway, Burlington, Vt. 05401.)

Seaman, Barbara. 1995. Norplant: The contraception you're stuck with. In Barbara Seaman, *The doctors' case against the Pill* (25th anniversary updated ed.). Alameda, Calif.: Hunter House.

Why are U.S. women not using long-acting contraceptives? 2000. *Family Planning Perspectives* 32(4: July-August): 176–183.

Barbara Seaman

NOVEL

Women's ability to write novels has depended in large part on women's ability to write; this explains why much of early novel-writing, across cultures, has come from women of means and of noble birth. To become writers, women needed access to education and literacy—and the aids of pen, paper, lighting, and leisure time.

Historical Background

Lady Murasaki Shikibu, a Japanese aristocrat in the early eleventh century, had access to these resources. She is thought to have written one of the earliest novels, a 54-volume story entitled *Tales of Genji,* about an aristocratic hero and his love of a number of noblewomen. In the Western world, however, novel-writing did not come until much later, after the invention of the printing press.

Women needed more than printing presses to become published writers. They were often frustrated by social and political barriers. A women who gave voice, who could be heard by other women and men, could also be penalized for her audacity. At times and in places where women had no rights—where they were the property or chattels of men—the very act of writing could be seen as one of defiance, an assertion of independence, and women writers who gave offense could find themselves treated as mad or bad.

Historically, there appear to have been fewer women writers than men, and this is understandable given women's relative absence of property and position. Because women have only rarely controlled publishing houses, they have generally required the approval of men to achieve published status. There were a few exceptions, including a woman's press in England during the suffrage era in the early years of the twentieth century, and the Hogarth Press, controlled by Virginia Woolf (1882–1941) and her husband. Toward the end of the twentieth century, the explosion of women's presses associated with the second wave of the women's movement ensured that women were published in appreciable numbers.

Even those women who did break the boundaries and who were able to become published writers were less likely than men to be included among the acknowledged "greats" or to have their works preserved and passed on to future generations. Once a piece of writing was known to have been done by a woman, it was generally rated lower than writing by men (see Russ, 1983; Spender, 1989). To avoid such negative professional responses (and to avoid negative personal attacks), many women did not use their own names. So frequently did women write as "Anonymous" that its use was taken as a sign of female authorship; other women (including Jane Austen) used such terms as "By a Lady." The use of pseudonyms, particularly those that did not reveal the gender of the writer, was also popular; examples are A. M. Barnard (Louisa May Alcott), Currer Bell (Charlotte Brontë) and George Eliot (Mary Ann Evans). In *The Pen Names of Women Writers* (1985), Alice Kahler Marshall lists 4,000 different pen names used by 2,650 women writers.

This invisibility of women writers also contributed to their misrepresentation and their disappearance from the literary tradition. Although much credit is given to a few male authors for the invention of the English novel, certain records suggest that the novel was initially "the women's form" and that more women then men were involved in its conception (Spender, 1986). In fact, so successful were the women in the earliest days of the novel, and so clearly was the novel seen as their genre, that some men even resorted to female pseudonyms to impress a prospective publisher.

Rise of the Novel in Europe

Apart from the eleventh-century Japanese examples, the birth of the novel is associated primarily with the Western tradition following the invention of the printing press. Madeleine de Scudéry (1607–1701), one of the earliest and most prolific of the French novelists, has been called "the mother of the historical novel" in that country. The Spanish writer María de Zayas y Sotomayor, who also wrote during the seventeenth century, was known for her "romances," *Exemplary Love Stories* (*Novelas amorosas y exemplares*) and *Disillusionment in Love* (*Desengaños amorosos*). In England, Fanny Burney is sometimes referred to as "the mother of the novel," although Aphra Behn (1640–1689), more often acclaimed as a playwright, also wrote novels. *Love Letters between a Nobleman and his Sister* and *Oroonoko or The Royal Slave* (c. 1680) are among the best known.

Clear links can be established between letter-writing and the early novel: even when all other forms of writing were seen as inappropriate for women, it was usually permissible for them to write letters. In this role, they could communicate with other women and could amuse, entertain, and reflect on the complexity of human relationships. Fanny Burney (1752–1850), one of the first women to earn her living by the pen, turned such letter-writing into an art form when she wrote the best-selling *Evelina* (1788).

Until relatively recently, women were systematically denied experience outside their own private sphere. Until the advent of the bicycle (and the demise of the chaperone, in some circles), women's mobility was extremely limited to the "here and now," and their exclusion from formal education and professional occupation further restricted women's opportunities to enter the public world. These restrictions on women's experience helped account for the novel's popularity. Readers could "encounter" a range of characters and incidents outside their daily reality and could explore the problems of relationships (including romantic ones) and their solutions.

Although their focus was primarily on the private or domestic sphere, women also wrote public, political, and protest novels. *The Beth Book* (1897) by "Sarah Grand" (Frances Elizabeth Clarke, later McFall) tackled the terrible consequences of the sexual double standard and venereal disease; Rosa Praed (1851–1935) covered the political debates in Australia's new Queensland parliament (1880) and raised the issue of women's "duty" in relation to domestic violence in *The Bond of Wedlock* (1886). In *Say No to Death* (1951), Dymphna Cusack (1902–1981), another Australian novelist, confronted the public with its denial of tuberculosis and the suffering that it caused; her evocation of terminal illness changed social attitudes toward those who were ill and toward their treatment. Throughout women's novels runs a constant criticism of exploitation and oppression, as reflected in the number of antislavery novels produced by women in different cultures.

With the eighteenth- and nineteenth-century novel's emphasis on distinguishing between right and wrong (often in relation to the qualities of the hero) and its questioning of women's place in society, the novel extended women's understanding of human nature and the relationship between the sexes. To some extent, novels gave women their education. Insights into the human condition—why individuals do what they do, whether they could do it differently, what constitutes "happiness"—are still of interest to women today. This is one reason that women constitute the majority of the novel-reading public.

In the English tradition, Eliza Haywood (1690–1756) was among the first (in *Miss Betsy Thoughtless,* 1751) to introduce a contemporary young woman as heroine. Charlotte Smith (1748–1806) created as heroines some middle-aged women who were unsatisfactorily married (*The Old Manor House,* 1793), but this approach to plot and character was not to be widely adopted. With the exception of the irony of Jane Austen (1775–1817), as seen in her novel *Emma* (1816), the recognized plot of the nineteenth century was more often one in which the heroine—usually, a motherless daughter—made the right choice, got married, and lived happily ever after, as if women's existence ceased at marriage.

This version of reality was challenged dramatically by the women's movement of the 1970s. Margaret Drabble (b. 1939) was among those whose novels *started* with marriage and went on to explore the ways in which the institution constrained women and led to unhappiness (*A Summer Bird Cage,* 1963; *The Millstone,* 1965).

In the English tradition, alone, there are far too many great novelists to list the contributions of each to the novel. But there is ample evidence that women have written novels—and read novels—with some sense of subversion. As recently as the late nineteenth century, some in the medical profession believed that because women who read novels knew more about the world and about emotion, and because they exercised some independence (after all, they read on their own) and were often "opinionated," it was evident that novels were not good for their health; an American, Dr. Kellog, went so far as to claim that novel-reading was the greatest cause of uterine disease among young women. So novel-reading was often banned; in the United States, it was not uncommon for women's dresses to contain "novel pockets" in which the offending material could be quickly hidden.

NonWestern Traditions

At much the same time that the novel began to evolve within the English tradition, "story"-writing began to make its appearance in China. During the Qing Dynasty (1644–1911), both the short story and narrative verse became established forms. Yet in China, unlike some other countries, no great women's novel tradition developed during the twentieth century.

From the 19th century on, many influential women novelists emerged in many societies. In Sweden, for example, Selma Lagerlof (1858–1940) won the Nobel Prize for literature in 1909. Sigrid Undset (1882–1949), a Norwegian, wrote *Kristin Lavransdatter* (1920–1922), which also enjoyed international acclaim. In 1839, the Cuban writer Gertrudis Gomez de Allvallaneda wrote an antislavery novel, *Sab,* which was widely read in Spain and Spanish America; the first Indo-Anglian novel is thought to be *Rajmohan's Wife,* written in 1864 by a Bengali, Bankim Chandra Chatterjee.

In Africa, the majority of women novelists, until recently, have come primarily from the English-speaking tradition. Grace Ogot, author of *The Promised Land* (1966), is one of the first black women writers from East Africa, and her work marks the beginning of a new and vital period. Olive Schreiner, Doris Lessing, and Nadine Gordimer have all made valuable contributions to the novel, and the potential of South African black women novelists found expression once they gained access to the printing press. Examples are Lauretta Ngcobos, who wrote *Cross of Gold* (1981), and Farida Karodia, who wrote *Daughter of the Twilight* (1986). In West Africa, there has been much activity since the 1960s, with Flora Nwapa's *Efuru* (1966) symbolizing the independent woman. Buchi Emecheta has also enjoyed international success with *The Slave Girl, Bride Price,* and *Joys of Motherhood* (1979).

North American Women Novelists

North America has been the home of many internationally acclaimed women novelists with whom much of the form of the contemporary women's novel originated. Harriet Beecher Stowe's *Uncle Tom's Cabin* (1852) is still widely known, and Kate Chopin's *The Awakening* (1899) is a classic account of women's consciousness and liberation. For further reference to the earlier novels, see Baym (1993). Charlotte Perkins Gilman's *Herland* (1915) stands as one of the best examples of utopian fiction, and the writing of Willa Cather and Ellen Glasgow represents an alternative tradition that provides a critique of love and romance. Edith Wharton's distinctive New York novels offer another view of women's role, while Sylvia Plath's *The Bell Jar* (1963) is an exposé of a young woman's mental life.

More recently, women's horizons have been expanded by the work of such feminist novelists as Marge Piercy (see especially *Woman on the Edge of Time,* 1976, in which a woman is incarcerated in a mental hospital, and *She,* an exploration of women and cyberspace) and Alice Walker (b. 1944) whose Pulitzer Prize–winning novel *The Color Purple* (1982) caused controversy with its depiction of the oppression of black women by black men. The Canadian novelist Margaret Atwood (b. 1939) has been a powerful force, from the publication of *The Edible Woman* (1969) through the chilling dystopian saga *The Handmaid's Tale* (1985), which depicts a society in which women are defined entirely by their reproductive role.

Australian women writers have challenged their country's myth of "mateship" and have provided a very different, and often satirical, view of the land and its culture and customs. Miles Franklin helped to forge such a tradition with her novel *My Brilliant Career* (1901), sometimes seen as the first genuine Australian novel; *Coonardoo* (1929) by Katharine Susannah Prichard deals with the shocking relationship between an Aboriginal woman and a white property owner. Sally Morgan's *My Place* (1987) remains one of the most moving accounts of Aboriginal history and the consequences for family life.

In New Zealand, Janet Frame enjoys the status of the most famous woman writer. Although Keri Hulme's *the bone people* has achieved international fame, Hulme is but one of the many Maori women novelists to have been published in the last decades of the twentieth century.

The Future of the Novel

In the early years of the twenty-first century, most countries can boast of women novelists who reflect on human experience and explore human relationships with particular reference to women's place. Indeed, many are using the novel to critique and change women's status. But many of the feminist publishing houses founded in the 1970s, which were responsible for getting so many women novelists into print, have since faded, with predictable consequences. The book itself is being displaced as the primary information medium, and the novel may also be at risk. But the women's novel—a direct product of the printing press and a force in the creation of the woman reader—has played a crucial role in the shaping of women's perceptions and the changing of women's place, over the centuries, and so it may continue.

See Also

LITERATURE: OVERVIEW; LITERATURE, *all entries*

References and Further Reading

Baym, Nina. 1993. *Woman's fiction: A guide to novels by and about women in America, 1820–1870.* 2nd ed. Chicago: University of Illinois Press.

Marshall, Alice Kahler. 1985. *The pen names of women writers.* Harrisburg, Pa.: Alice Marshall Women's History Collection, Pennsylvania State University.

Russ, Joanna. 1983. *How to suppress women's writing.* London: Women's Press.

Spencer, Dale. 1986. *Mothers of the novel: 100 good women writers before Jane Austen.* London: Pandora.

———. 1989. *The writing or the sex? Or why you don't have to read women's writing to know it's no good.* New York and Oxford: Athene Series, Pergamon.

Dale Spender

NUCLEAR WEAPONS

With the dropping of the first atomic bombs on Hiroshima and Nagasaki, Japan, in August 1945, the peace movement, including women's organizations, felt a renewed sense of urgency. Organizations such as the Women's International League for Peace and Freedom (WILPF) recognized the dangers of the new nuclear age. Dorothy Detzer, the executive secretary of the WILPF, said that the "atomic bomb fell not only on Hiroshima and Nagasaki but, in a psychological sense, on all of us" (Alonso, 1993: 162).

Since that time, women, as individuals and in groups, have protested the proliferation of nuclear weapons. One such organization is Women's Action for New Directions (WAND). Originally Women's Action for Nuclear Disarmament, WAND was founded by Dr. Helen Caldicott (b. 1939) to end the threat of nuclear annihilation. Its three main goals are (1) the promotion of alternatives to violence as the solution to conflict; (2) the cleanup of the environmental effects of nuclear weapons production, as well as toxic waste at military facilities, and prevention of further contamination; and (3) the elimination of the testing, production, sale, and use of weapons of mass destruction (WAND, 2000 Web site).

Numerous protests have been organized over the years. Among the more significant actions was the Greenham Common Women's Peace Camp, begun in 1981 in reaction to the placement of NATO cruise missiles at that British airbase. From individual women such as Manami Suzuki, an antinuclear campaigner and conservationist (Cambridge Women's Peace Collective, 1984: 255), to grassroots organizations such as Sisters Opposed to Nuclear Genocide and the WISE women's project of World Information Service on Energy, to anonymous demonstrations such as the placing of thousands of paper cranes every year in the Hiroshima Peace Park, women still seek an end to nuclear weapons.

Miyako Shinohara, whose mother was pregnant with her when the Hiroshima bomb fell, believes that women "must take the firmest possible stand in the name of peace and the protection of their children" (Women's Division of Soka Gakkai, 1986: 142).

See Also

PACIFISM AND PEACE ACTIVISM; PEACE MOVEMENTS: ASIA; PEACE MOVEMENTS: EUROPE; PEACE EDUCATION

References and Further Reading

Alonso, Harriet Hyman. 1993. *Peace as a women's issue: A history of the U.S. movement for world peace and women's rights.* Syracuse, N.Y.: Syracuse University Press.

Cambridge Women's Peace Collective, comp. 1984. *My country is the whole world: An anthology of women's work on peace and war.* London: Pandora.
Women's Action for New Directions (WAND). 2000. Web site: <http://www.wand.org.>
Women's Division of Soka Gakkai, comp. 1986. *Women against war.* Tokyo and New York: Kodansha International.

Laura Daly

NUNS

Religious women, particularly in the traditions of Catholicism and Buddhism, have chosen to pursue vocations as nuns for both spiritual and social reasons. As an institutionally sanctioned role for women within otherwise patriarchal religions, life as a nun has allowed women to express spiritual visions of divinity or the mysteries of life that come from their experiences as women. Living in all-female communities organized according to vows of celibacy, poverty, and obedience, nuns may lead religious lives that are more "contemplative" or more "active," depending on whether more emphasis is placed on living separate from the world in monasteries or convents, or on ministering to the sick or poor, or on teaching.

In Western culture until the seventeenth century, and especially during the Middle Ages, restricted access to education meant that women were, in essence, "forced to choose between the life of a woman or the life of the mind" (Lerner, 1993: 30). Because only those women who were members of a ruling family or those who could afford the dowry to enter a convent had access to education, many women chose a cloistered life as an escape from forced marriages and as one of the only means available to continue their intellectual pursuits. Significant contributors to Western intellectual and theological thought such as Hildegard of Bingen (1098–1179) and Sor Juana Ines de la Cruz of Mexico (1651–1695) exemplify the tradition of women who joined convents as a way to free themselves from traditional gender roles. Living as part of a female community of nuns provided such women freedom from domestic and reproductive responsibilities, and the opportunity to achieve some authority as thinkers, speakers, and writers.

For Buddhist women in China, Japan, and Southeast Asia, nuns' orders have been important institutions that have historically allowed women the opportunity to live respectable, active lives outside traditional family structures. Buddhist nuns, or *bikkhunis,* have drawn on the Buddha's original relatively positive views of women's spiritual potential to use the monastic life as a means for fulfilling their spiritual, intellectual, and educational goals.

The relative freedom women have historically found in the monastic or cloistered life has been, however, an attenuated one within patriarchal institutions in which the highest positions of power are held only by men. In the Catholic tradition, even though nuns had more authority than most laywomen to express themselves, the struggles of various convents against the restrictive church hierarchy also led to persecution and charges of heresy. Buddhist nuns have had to struggle against later monastic interpretations of the Buddha's teachings that have kept nuns subservient to monks and limited the scope of their authority as teachers. In more recent times, in both Buddhism and Catholicism, the inferior status of nuns relative to monks or priests has led to important debates about allowing women to achieve full ordination within religious hierarchies.

See Also

BUDDHISM; CELIBACY; CHRISTIANITY: STATUS OF WOMEN IN THE CHURCH; HERESY; MARTYRS; SAINTS

References and Further Readings

Bancroft, Anne. 1987. Women in Buddhism. In Ursula King, ed., *Women in the world's religions, past and present,* 81–104. New York: Paragon.
Lerner, Gerda. 1993. *The creation of feminist consciousness, from the Middle Ages to 1870.* New York: Oxford University Press.

Cathy Peppers
Ivone Gebara

NURSING

Definitions of nursing since the late nineteenth century have focused on caring for persons so that they can achieve the highest level of health possible. A succinct definition of nursing was published by the American Nurses Association (ANA) in 1980 and again in 1995: "Nursing is the diagnosis and treatment of human responses to actual and potential health problems" (ANA, 1995).

Nursing is accountable to provide professional services that optimize health. Optimum health is viewed as body, mind, and spirit in balance. The professional services provided by nurses include:

1. Delegated—services which enhance the health of a person and require a physician's order;
2. Interdependent—services which enhance health by assessing, monitoring, detecting, and preventing complications associated with certain health situations or treatment plans; and
3. Independent—services which enhance health by assessing, monitoring, detecting, diagnosing, and treating the human responses. (CPM Resource Center, 1995)

Nurses function in a variety of roles and settings and constitute the largest health professional group in the United States. They provide direct services in hospitals, nursing homes, and community health settings such as factories, nursing clinics, doctors' offices, schools, homeless shelters, and public health agencies. Nurses also function in leadership roles and as educators and researchers in academic settings. Wherever nurses work, in whatever role, they are advocates for persons dealing with health concerns and with the health care system.

Nursing as Women's Work

Although an increasing number of men are entering the nursing profession, nursing continues to be viewed as women's work. Historically, the first nurses were mothers who cared for family members during illness and death.

Throughout the history of health care, technology and quantifiable outcomes have been more valued than caring. Caring, the essence of nursing, is a subjective experience for both the caregiver and the recipient of care. Because caring is difficult to measure, it cannot easily be categorized in order to charge for units of service. Even so, an increasing number of clients and health professionals are valuing caring, and medical centers are focusing much more on customer satisfaction.

The historically subservient nature of nurses' roles and practices within the patriarchies of the hospital and the medical profession is also important. This subservient status has been challenged in numerous ways over time. In the last half of the nineteenth century, Florence Nightingale challenged the old ways of providing medical care by conducting scientific studies and refusing to serve with physicians who would not permit her to provide nursing services as she wished. For example, after Nightingale and her nurses provided nursing care to wounded soldiers during the Crimean War, the death rate was lowered from 50 percent to 2.2 percent.

Throughout the twentieth century there were both advances and declines in the status and roles of the nursing profession. At the turn of the twenty-first century, more health care professionals are working as partners to provide the best possible treatment and care for patients. Many nurses, doctors, and other health professionals view one another as colleagues, all with their own valuable expertise.

There are many levels of nursing education and several points of "entry into practice," a situation that can be problematic for the profession. To become a registered nurse in most states, a person can graduate from a two-year associate degree program, a three-year diploma (hospital) program, or a four-year baccalaureate program. All three groups take the same examination for licensure as a Registered Nurse. Licensure as a practical nurse can occur after a twelve- to eighteen-month program of study in a technical school. Various ancillary titles, such as certified nursing assistant, compound the confusion.

Finally, nursing services as woman's work are not valued in the US health care reimbursement system. Lack of unity, and therefore lack of power, has kept most nurses dependent on institutional structures for financial security. Changes are taking place, however, and advanced practice nurses (e.g., nurse practitioners) can be reimbursed by third-party payers in some states for services provided.

Nursing and Feminist Movements

Lack of unity among nurses also is reflected in nursing's involvement in women's issues in the political and social arenas. Nurses who have been activists in the women's movement often were stimulated to action by concerns for women's health issues.

During the first wave of feminism, nurse-activists were those who were working in the community, visiting the homes of poor, often immigrant women in urban areas who were ill or dying because of botched abortions, malnutrition, or lack of medical care. The nurses Margaret Sanger, Lavinia Dock, Lillian Wald, and Adelaide Nutting were outspoken activists who marched in suffrage parades, provided birth control information, and spoke out in public about women's health needs. However, the majority of nurses were not involved in political and social action.

During the second wave of feminism, nurses were involved, but the number was not significantly different from those involved during the first wave. Chinn and Wheeler (1985: 74) state that nurses experience oppression as women and can benefit from the feminist "world view that values women and that confronts systematic injustices based on gender."

A number of nurses identify themselves as feminists, but many do not. Some who do not define themselves as feminists nevertheless work for women's rights, reproductive choice, freedom, and equality. Other nurses have accepted the values of the health care arena's patriarchy, values that contribute to the oppression of women as a group and of nursing as a profession.

Nursing: Now and in the Future

The essence of nursing is caring for persons who are dealing with health and illness issues. Inclusivity and advocacy are important foci of nursing practice that do not fit well into health care hierarchies. Thus, nursing continues to struggle with lack of status and power within a system that is hesitant to recognize their value and professionalism.

Nurses provide educational and referral services to assist individuals, families, groups, and communities in improving their health by making health-promoting choices. Nurses work as partners with patients or clients to improve their health status.

With its client-centered focus, nursing's active participation in health care reform is essential. The need to contain cost while providing appropriate health care access for all persons is a continuing challenge of nurses and other health care professionals.

See Also

CAREGIVERS; ELDERLY CARE, *all entries;* HEALING; HEALTH: OVERVIEW; HEALTH CARE; HEALTH CAREERS; NURSING HOMES; WORK: EQUAL PAY AND CONDITIONS

References and Further Reading

American Nurses Association. 1995. *Nursing's social policy statement.* Washington, D.C.: Author.

Chinn, P. L., and C. E. Wheeler. 1985. Feminism and nursing. *Nursing Outlook,* 33(2): 74–77.

CPM Resource Center. 1995. *Core beliefs.* Grand Rapids, Mich.: Author.

Encyclopedia Britannica. 1993. Nursing, Vol. 23: 814–817.

Lynaugh, J. E., and C. M. Fagin. 1988. Nursing comes of age. *Image: Journal of Nursing Scholarship,* 20(4): 184–190.

Reverby, S. M. 1987. *Ordered to care: The dilemma of American nursing, 1850–1945.* Cambridge: Cambridge University Press.

Miriam E. Martin

NURSING HOMES

Women are the world's caregivers and the world's nurses. Women care for children, for the elderly, and for those who require chronic or long-term care because they are frail, ill, or disabled. Most often, caregiving takes place at home as an unpaid activity. Friends and family may provide respite care, visiting nurses and home health care aides may provide routine medical care, and hospitals may provide overnight or short-term care during medical emergencies. When home-based care and hospital care are inappropriate or unavailable, people who require long-term medical care turn to nursing homes. Institutions that provide this intermediate level of care between homes and hospitals include adult day care centers, assisted-living residences, skilled nursing facilities, and hospices.

Nursing homes are considered skilled nursing facilities. Most people admitted to nursing homes stay for one to six months, but about 25 percent of nursing home residents stay for three years or longer, often exhausting their life savings within six months of admission and requiring government subsidy thereafter (American Health Care Association, 1998). Assisted-living facilities provide their residents with custodial care—beds, meals, and housekeeping—and also offer social involvement, recreational opportunities, and help with such activities of daily living as bathing, dressing, walking, shopping, and managing medications. The goals are to promote independence, to maintain or improve physical and mental functioning, to reduce pain, and to reduce hospitalizations. Nursing homes provide not only custodial care but also complex medical care and rehabilitation services for injuries, strokes, illnesses, and disabilities. Nursing home residents include people of all ages with physical disabilities, developmental disabilities, mental retardation, and chronic diseases such as AIDS, emphysema, diabetes, and Alzheimer's disease. Many nursing home residents are frail, and common medical problems include nutritional deficiencies, vision and hearing problems, gait disorders, pressure sores, incontinence, infections, depression, delirium, and dementia (Ouslander et al., 1991). Because women live longer than men in most areas of the world and have different health care needs (Golub and Freedman, 1985; Guralnick et al., 1995; Kaiser et al., 1998; Kosberg and Kaye, 1997), the majority of nursing home residents are women. Women make up 75 percent of the nursing home population age 65 and older, and 80 percent of the population age 85 and older, and those percentages are projected to remain stable through the year 2030 (US National Center for Health Statistics, 1996).

Regulatory agencies usually require licensed and accredited nursing homes to have at least one skilled medical professional on site supervising residents at all times. Most often, this is a registered nurse or a licensed practical nurse, although a part-time physician or medical director is likely to be on call. The geriatric nurse practitioner is an emerging clinical subspecialty in the United States. Daily, hands-on care for nursing home residents usually is provided by certified nursing assistants. As with unpaid nursing care at home, most paid caregivers in skilled nursing facilities are women.

Too many health care needs and not enough money to pay for them result in most of the problems common to the nursing home industry, particularly in the for-profit sector. Fiscal irregularities are common, working conditions and salaries for caregivers are low, and quality of life is poor for most residents. Problems range from inadequacies in food sanitation, housekeeping, and accident prevention to overuse of physical restraints and overmedication of residents who wander and patients with dementia. In the United States, the Nursing Home Reform Law passed as part of the 1987 Omnibus Budget Reconciliation Act (OBRA) attempted to remedy some of those problems. OBRA 1987 specified that nursing home residents had a right to dignity, self-determination, and communication with people outside the nursing home; it set minimum standards for quality of care and for staffing; it placed limits on the use of physical restraints for custodial purposes; and it restricted the use of psychoactive medications to specific medical conditions and symptoms.

An emerging trend for nursing home residents is the use of health care proxies and "advance directives" advising caregivers not to resuscitate patients or not to hospitalize them. These "planned deaths" present caregivers with many of the same ethical challenges as assisted suicide and euthanasia. Sexism and ageism are likely to play a role in interpreting and implementing advance directives because most nursing home policy makers are men, and most nursing home residents are elderly and disabled women.

See Also

AGEISM; AGING; DEATH; DISABILITY, *all entries;* ELDERLY CARE: WESTERN WORLD; EUTHANASIA; HEALTH CARE, *all entries;* LONG-TERM CARE SERVICES; SUICIDE

References and Further Reading

American Health Care Association. 1998. *Profile: Nursing facility resident.* <http://www.ahca.org>

Golub, Sharon, and Rita Jackaway Freedman, eds. 1985. *Health needs of women as they age.* Binghamton, N.Y.: Haworth.

Guralnick, Jack M., Linda P. Fried, Eleanor M. Simonsick, Judith D. Kasper, and Mary E. Lafferty, eds. 1995. *The women's health and aging study: Health and social characteristics of older women with disability.* Bethesda, Md.: US National Institute on Aging. <http://www.nih.gov/nia>

Kaiser, Fran E., F. Nourhashemi, M. C. Bertiere, and Y. Ouchi, eds. 1998. *Women, aging and health: Nutritional intervention and women after menopause.* New York: Springer.

Kosberg, Jordan I., and Lenard W. Kaye, eds. 1997. *Elderly men: Special problems and professional challenges.* New York: Springer.

Ouslander, Joseph G., Dan Osterweil, and John Morley. 1991. *Medical care in the nursing home.* New York: McGraw-Hill.

United Nations Statistics Division. 1999. *Health.* <http://www.un.org>

US National Center for Health Statistics, Centers for Disease Control and Prevention. 1996. *Aging into the 21st century.* <http://www.aoa.dhhs.gov>

Faye Zucker

NURTURE

See NATURE-NURTURE DEBATE.

NUTRITION I

Good nutrition is critically important to every known form of life. The biochemical and energetic nutrients that we digest, absorb, and metabolize from foodstuffs are the foundation of all cellular activity in the body, including growth, repair, reproduction, maintenance, and resistance to disease. Much of nutrition is, of course, common to males and females, but women do have some specific nutritional concerns.

The Spirit of Food

Human nutrition begins in the womb and with milk from mother's breast; and finding, growing, preparing, and storing food seem always to have been preeminently women's work and women's genius. In earth-centered cultures, the harvesting, gathering, and consumption of food are considered sacred or sacramental. This aspect of nutrition is invisible, unmeasurable, and often undiscussed, but it is of utmost importance to the health of the individual and the ecology.

Healthy and Unhealthy Diets

When food choices are limited, women eat whatever is available. As long as adequate carbohydrates, protein, fats, vitamins, and minerals are consumed and clean water is available, health is easily maintained (Price, 1954). However, restricted diets—such as those of vegans, vegetarians, and the poor—generally fail to provide adequately for women; milk products, eggs, or meats need to be added to optimize health. When the food supply is abundant and foods are highly refined, as is the case in most western countries, food choices may adversely affect health. This is due in part to a degradation of the foodstuffs themselves and in part to an innate (and healthy) craving for sweets, salt, and fat, which are scarce in nature but commercially abundant, leading to overconsumption.

Protein

After water, protein is the most plentiful substance in our bodies. Without protein the body could not create enzymes, antibodies, breast milk, skin, hair, nails, or muscle; the brain, the heart, and the other organs could not develop; and women could not menstruate. Amino acids are the building blocks of protein; we require twenty-two different amino acids, of which eight are considered essential nutrients. For protein synthesis to take place, all the amino acids must be present simultaneously in the body, and in the correct proportions. If even one essential amino acid is low or missing, even temporarily, protein production slows or stops altogether (Dunne, 1990).

Animal foods contain all the essential amino acids. No single foods of vegetable origin contain them all, although certain combinations do, such as corn plus beans. Adult women can be healthy on a low-protein diet, but children and pregnant, lactating, and menopausal women require high levels of protein.

Fats

Fat, the most concentrated source of energy in the diet, is found in all animal products; in vegetable seeds, beans, and nuts; and in certain fruits, such as olives and avocados. Fat is vital to women's health; but unfortunately, many women in affluent nations avoid it. American women are an example; a study reported in 1999 found that 26 percent of them were deficient in vitamin E because of a low-fat diet.

Linoleic, linolenic, and arachidonic fats are the essential fatty acids, but all fats, especially cholesterol, are vital for the formation of sex hormones (particularly after menopause), adrenal hormones, vitamin D (which is needed to strengthen the bones), and bile. A low-cholesterol diet can dry women's skin and vaginal tissues and impede the functioning of the brain and nervous system.

The belief that saturated fats elevate blood cholesterol, causing blocked blood vessels, strokes, and heart attacks, has prevailed since the mid-1960s. However, many researchers now consider this theory simplistic and without adequate scientific justification. In the Framingham Heart Study (conducted in the United States), the greater the subjects' intake of total fat, saturated fat, and monounsaturated fat, the *lower* their risk of stroke. In this study, too, although high levels of blood cholesterol were a risk factor for heart diseease, the dietary intake of fat and cholesterol was *inversely* correlated with blood cholesterol. Swedish studies have found that saturated fats promote breast health, while vegetable oils (such as canola, safflower, corn, cottonseed, and sunflower oils) promote breast cancer.

Animal fats are relatively stable. Vegetable oils, by contrast, become rancid within days after pressing; and rancid fats promote cancer and heart disease. Hydrogenation and partial hydrogenation slow rancidity but create trans-fatty acids that leave deposits on the blood vessels. Even unhydrogenated vegetable oils are unhealthy: they flood the body with omega-6 fatty acids—the primary fat component of arterial plaque—and they contribute large amounts of free radicals that damage the arteries and initiate plaque deposits.

Vitamins

Vitamins are small organic compounds made by all living tissues. They are found in whole fresh foods but are absorbed best from dried, fermented, or cooked foods. Some vitamins are fat-soluble (vitamins A, E, and D); some are water-soluble (vitamins B and C). All vitamins are groups of related enzymes that function together. Eighteen hundred carotenes and carotinoids contribute to the liver's production of vitamin A; two dozen tocopherols function together as vitamin E; and only when ascorbic acid is joined by bioflavonoids and carotenes does it function as vitamin C.

A healthy diet supplies adequate vitamins so long as refined foods are rarely eaten. "Enriched" flour, for example, is really impoverished, as it does not contain the entire complement of B vitamins and minerals found in the whole grain.

When vitamins are synthesized in the laboratory, their complexity is reduced to one active ingredient. In situations of impoverishment and famine, supplements have health benefits. They do not replace healthful food, however, and long-term use of vitamin supplements poses health risks, including an increased risk of heart disease and cancer (from supplemental beta carotene), more aggressive cancers (from supplemental alpha tocopherol), and faster-growing cancers (from supplemental ascorbic acid).

Minerals

Minerals are inorganic compounds found in all plant tissues; in all animal tissues, such as bones, hair, teeth, fingernails and toenails; and, of course, in rocks. Minerals are critical for the optimum functioning of the nervous, immune, and hormonal systems and all muscles, including the heart. We need a fairly large amount of some minerals, such as potassium, magnesium, manganese, and calcium; but we have only a minuscule need for trace minerals, such as selenium, iodine, molybdenum, boron, silicon, and germanium (Ziegler and Filer, 1996).

Minerals may be difficult to get, even in a healthy diet. Overuse of chemical fertilizers reduces the mineral content of plant products. During the period 1963–1992, according to U.S. Department of Agriculture, the amount of calcium in fruits and vegetables declined an average of 30 percent. In white rice, calcium declined 62.5 percent, iron 32 to 45 percent, and magnesium 20 to 85 percent (Bergner, 1997). Not only are commercially grown grains low in minerals, but refining then removes what little minerals they do have.

Seaweeds and herbs are dependable sources of minerals when eaten, brewed in water, or infused into vinegar, rather than taken in capsules or tinctures. Many herbs, such as dandelion leaves, peppermint, red clover blossoms, stinging nettle, and oatstraw, are exceptional sources of minerals (Bergner, 1997; U.S.D.A., 1986). For instance, 100 grams of dried nettle contains 3,000 milligrams of calcium.

Phytochemicals

Individual nutrients can be created in the laboratory, but they are unlikely to have the life-giving, spirit-enhancing properties of real food. Hundreds of chemicals occur naturally in foodstuffs, many of which may avert cancer, promote cardiovascular health, improve sexual functioning, enhance energy, and contribute to longevity. Among these chemicals, the class of compounds known as phytoestrogens are especially important for women.

When phytoestrogens are plentiful in the diet, the incidence of breast cancer is significantly lower. Phytoestrogens probably also help prevent osteoporosis, high blood pressure, congestive heart disease, and senility. A phytoestrogen-rich diet also protects against the harmful effects of estrogen-mimicking chemicals in the environment and in food. Whole grains, beans, vegetables, and fruits are high in phytoestrogens.

Sources of Vitamins and Minerals

Boron: Organic greens, nettles, dandelion, yellow dock.

Calcium: Yogurt, leafy greens, seaweed, dried beans, nettles, mint, sage, yellow dock, red clover, oatstraw, plantain leaf, dandelion.

Carotenes: Dandelion leaves, violet leaves, nettles, kale, dark leafy greens, carrots, winter squash, sweet potatoes, tomatoes, papaya, apricot, watermelon.

Chromium: Mushrooms, nuts, liver, beets, whole wheat, oatstraw, nettles, red clover, seaweed, echinacea.

Copper: Seafood, leafy greens, bittersweet chocolate, whole grains, dried beans, nuts, skullcap, sage, horsetail, chickweed.

Folic acid (one of the B vitamins): Nettles, kale, leafy greens, whole grains.

Iodine: Seaweed, seafood, mushrooms, beets, parsley, celery.

Iron: Molasses, leafy greens, liver, bittersweet chocolate, mushrooms, whole grains, potatoes, seaweed, burdock, milk thistle seed, dandelion, yellow dock, echinacea, plantain, nettles, licorice, mint.

Laetrile (vitamin B-17 or amygdalin): Fruit pits, almonds, millet, grasses, roots.

Magnesium: Seaweed, leafy greens, yogurt, whole grains, nuts, oatstraw, licorice, nettles, burdock, sage, red clover, yellow dock, dandelion, parsley, potato skins.

Manganese: Seaweed, leafy greens, milk thistle seed, yellow dock, ginseng, nettle, dandelion.

Potassium: Fruits, vegetables, sage, seaweed, mint, red clover, nettle, plantain leaf or seeds.

Selenium: Seaweed, organic garlic, mushrooms, liver, seafood, milk thistle seeds, yellow dock.

Sulfur: Eggs, yogurt, garlic, cabbage family, nettles, plantain.

Vitamin A: Produced from carotenes by the liver.

Vitamin B complex: Whole grains, greens, dried beans, seafood, red clover, parsley.

Vitamin B-6: Potato skins, broccoli, dried beans, lentils, meat, fish.

Vitamin C: All fresh fruits and vegetables, pine needles, dandelion greens, red clover, parsley, plantain leaf, paprika.

Vitamin D: Sunlight, butter, egg yolks, fatty fish, liver.

Vitamin E: Olive oil, butter, cold-pressed food oils, freshly ground whole grains, nettles, seaweed, dandelion, nuts, greens, sunflower seeds.

Vitamin K: Nettles, alfalfa, kelp, green tea.

Zinc: Pumpkin seeds, sage, echinacea, nettle, seaweed, milk thistle.

See Also

COOKING; FOOD AND CULTURE; FOOD, HUNGER, AND FAMINE; HOLISTIC HEALTH, *I and II;* NUTRITION II; NUTRITION AND HOME ECONOMICS; TRADITIONAL HEALING: HERBALISTS

References and Further Reading

Bergner, Paul. 1997. *The healing power of minerals and trace elements.* Rocklin, Calif.: Prima.

Dunne, Lavon. 1990. *Nutrition almanac.* 3rd ed. New York: McGraw Hill.

Johnson, Cait. 1997. *Cooking like a goddess.* Fort Collins, Col.: Healing Arts.

Lewallen, Eleanor, and John Lewallen. 1996. *Sea vegetable gourmet cookbook.* Mendocino, Calif.: Sea Veg.

Margen, Sheldon, and Editors of University of California at Berkeley Wellness Letter. 1992. *The wellness encyclopedia of food and nutrition.* New York: Rebus.

Mollison, Bill. 1993. *Permaculture book of ferment and human nutrition.* Califon, N. J.: Tagari.

Price, Weston. 1945. *Nutrition and physical degeneration.* New Canaan, Conn.: Keats.

Sokolov, Raymond. 1991. *Why we eat what we eat: How the encounter between the new world and the old changed the way everyone on the planet eats.* New York: Summit (Simon and Schuster).

U. S. Department of Agriculture (U.S.D.A). 1986. *Nutritional value of foods in Common Units.* Agriculture Handbook No. 456. Mineola, N.Y.: Dover. (Originally published in 1975.)

Weatherford, Jack. 1988. *Indian givers: How the Indians of the Americas transformed the world.* New York: Fawcett Columbine.

Weed, Susun. 1989. *Healing wise.* Woodstock, N.Y.: Ash Tree.

Ziegler, Ekhard, and L. J. Filer. 1996. *Present knowledge in nutrition.* 7th ed. Tacoma, Wash.: International Life Science.

Susun S. Weed

NUTRITION II

Women have a particular interest in nutrition for many reasons. Their nutritional needs—far more than men's—vary throughout life, owing to pregnancy, lactation, menstruation, and menopause. Also, women traditionally plan the family's meals, shop for food, and cook; and a "good wife and mother" is expected to provide well-balanced, nutritious meals. In addition, there is increasing interest in natural health and healing, and in a healthy diet as a way of preventing, minimizing, or possibly even curing disease.

Folic acid, a nutrient that can actually prevent disease, provides a case study in public health priorities. In the mid-1980s, students of nutrition were taught that for a woman who had borne a baby with spina bifida (a potentially debilitating spinal cleft), supplemental folic acid could dramatically reduce the risk of having a second baby with that birth defect. However, adding folic acid to foods for the general public was not considered a good idea, because it could mask the effects of vitamin B-12 deficiency, which in the later stages are quite severe and irreversible—although the treatable signs and symptoms of vitamin B-12 deficiency usually appear long before the irreversible neurological damage. (The reason for not simply adding vitamin B-12 as well as folic acid was probably that people with vitamin B-12 deficiency often develop it by being unable to absorb it from their food in the first place.) This public health decision seems logical, until we note that the discovery that supplemental folic acid also reduces the incidence of heart disease, a malady mainly of men (until women reach the age of menopause, at which time the rates are more similar), roughly coincided with the consensus that folic acid supplementation of common foods was not so bad after all. In fairness, it should be said that heart disease affects many more people than spina bifida, and that we cannot be sure why this shift in opinion occurred. Still, this does seem to suggest something about public health priorities—that it may be acceptable for people with undiagnosed vitamin B-12 deficiency to suffer the consequences for the sake of (mostly) men with heart disease but not for the sake of babies (numbering 1 in every 1,000 to 2,000) born with spina bifida.

This is not to imply that there is an across-the-board disregard for women's special nutritional needs. In fact, the well-intended promotion of supplemental iron, which can indeed benefit menstruating and pregnant women, may be detrimental to men and postmenopausal women because elevated iron levels increase the risk of heart disease. This is not parallel to the issue of folic acid, since the increased risk of heart disease was discovered relatively recently and did not require years of debate, and the nutrition community, including supplement manufacturers, responded promptly (special iron-free supplements are now widely available). Another example of women-oriented public-health information has to do with calcium: the scientific community has long promoted an adequate intake of calcium in the premenopausal years to stave off osteoporosis later on. (Note, however, that protein increases the excretion of calcium from the body, so women whose intake of protein is low—yet still adequate—need not have such a high intake of calcium.)

Overall health is obviously affected by nutrition, and the specific benefits of good nutrition are too numerous to list here. It is useful, however, to list some nutrients that are important to women even more than to men. (This partial listing does not address the many aspects of health, such as fertility and a decreased risk of cancer and cardiovascular disease, that are affected by nutrition in general.)

Vitamins

A good vitamin and mineral supplement is a sensible start for any woman trying to maximize her health, although the flavonoids, essential fatty acids, trace elements, and other constituents of good food cannot all be found in a single capsule.

Vitamin A: Because potentially serious birth defects may result from high levels of vitamin A, women who may become pregnant, whether intentionally or not, should avoid vitamin A supplements and instead take beta-carotene, which is converted to vitamin A in the body. Beta carotene is safer than vitamin A because as the level of vitamin A increases, absorption of beta carotene decreases, as does the rate of its conversion to vitamin A.

Cervical dysplasia may be associated with low levels of vitamin A. Also, vitamin A and, especially, beta carotene are important to the immune system. A women whose immune system is weaker than it should be is more susceptible to catching the illnesses of the people around her and is also likelier to have repeated vaginal yeast infections, which have been linked to a low intake of beta carotene.

B vitamins: Most health-care practitioners who prescribe nutritional therapies recommend that if the B vitamins are taken long-term, they should be administered all together as the B complex rather than singly.

People who are subject to migraine—most of whom are women—may benefit from a three-month trial of 400 milligrams of riboflavin (vitamin B-2) per day.

Women with recurrent menstrual cramps may benefit from taking niacin (vitamin B-3) for the seven to ten days preceding menstruation. Niacin is more effective taken with vitamin C and rutin. An incipient migraine headache may be avoided by taking niacin. Niacin can cause flushing because of its effect on the blood vessels and is better taken with meals. Timed-release niacin should be used only under the supervision of a health-care practitioner because it can, in rare cases, damage the liver.

Women taking birth control pills are often low in pyridoxine—vitamin B-6. (They are also often low in other nutrients, including folic acid.) These women should take a good supplement and consume a well-balanced diet. The mood changes and depression sometimes experienced by women taking oral contraceptives may be due to low serum levels of vitamin B-6. Vitamin B-6 can also reduce the severity of morning sickness. This nutrient is also well known for relieving premenstrual syndrome (PMS). Less well known is the fact that a deficiency of vitamin B-6 (and of folic acid and vitamin B-12) can increase the risk of heart disease.

Vitamin B-6 is one of the water-soluble vitamins, which tend to have a much lower toxicity than fat-soluble vitamins. Still, people vary considerably in their reaction to suppelmental vitamin B-6. It is a good idea to start at a level as low as 50 milligrams a day and if the dosage is increased, to spread doses throughout the day so that no more than 50 milligrams is taken at any one time.

A lower-protein diet can reduce the body's excretion of calcium—an important consideration for women who are concerned about osteoporosis. A vegetarian diet is lower in protein; however, supplemental vitamin B-12 is needed by vegetarians whose diet contains no animal products at all.

Vitamin C: The risk of breast and cervical cancer (and many other cancers) increases in women whose intake of vitamin C is low; in pregnant women, the risk of preeclampsia and premature rupture of membranes also increases. Vitamin C plays a well-known role in maintaining a strong immune system.

Vitamin D: Exposure of the skin to sunlight is required to convert a precursor into active vitamin D. The incidence of breast cancer (and colon cancer) is highest in areas where people are exposed to the least sunlight. Vitamin D is also required for absorption of calcium and is therefore important in preventing osteoporosis. However, vitamin D can be quite toxic, so supplementation above the recommended daily intake should be avoided by the general population unless there is a deficiency.

Vitamin E: This vitamin can be used (for at least the ten days before menstruation) to reduce the discomfort of fibrocystic breasts (premenstrual pain and tenderness) and menstrual cramps; it can also reduce the hot flashes and vaginal discomfort of menopause. Vitamin E is the least toxic of the fat-soluble vitamins and is safe at the recommended level, 600 to 800 international units (IU), although women with high blood pressure and those on blood-thinning medications should check with their physician before taking this supplement.

Vitamin K: Most infants born in health-care settings are given an injection of vitamin K after birth to prevent the bleeding (due to inadequate blood clotting) that is possible in people with a deficiency. It is also used to treat osteoporosis and morning sickness.

Pantothenic Acid

Supplemental pantothenic acid may reduce symptoms in people with rheumatoid arthritis, a disease that affects two to three times more women than men.

Folic Acid

As noted above, supplemental folic acid early in pregnancy reduces the risk of neural tube defects in babies. It also reduces the risk of cervical dysplasia and plays a role in preventing osteoporosis.

Calcium

Calcium is available in many forms and is taken by many women to reduce the risk of osteoporosis. This is a good beginning to a prevention regimen, but other factors are also important. For example, many people, especially older people, have inadequate levels of stomach acid. The least expensive calcium supplement, the antacid calcium carbonate, reduces these levels even more and thereby dramatically reduces absorption of calcium. Calcium citrate, another popular form of calcium, is absorbed better by these patients and possibly even by people with normal levels of stomach acid. A vegetarian diet, which is lower in both protein and phosphorus, also reduces the risk of osteoporosis by decreasing the rate at which calcium is excreted from the body.

Calcium may also reduce the risk of hypertension and preeclampsia in pregnant women, and it may be helpful in treating postnatal and postmenopausal depression.

Phosphorus

Most people, especially those who eat large quantities of meat, poultry, fish, and eggs, consume more phosphorus than they need, thereby increasing their risk of osteoporosis, because phosphorus competes with calcium for absorption. Many food additives, including the phosphoric acid in many sodas, contain phosphorus. Unless there is an actual deficiency, phosphorus should not be part of a multivitamin supplement.

Magnesium

Supplemental magnesium (especially when combined with vitamin B-6) may be helpful for women with PMS and menstrual cramps. It may also relieve the symptoms of fibromyalgia (insomnia and painful muscles, tendons, and ligaments), which occurs mostly in women. Magnesium may alleviate chronic fatigue syndrome and migraine, both of which are seen more often in women, and decrease the risk of osteoporosis and preeclampsia. People with kidney disease or severe heart disease should check with their doctor before taking supplemental magnesium. Even in healthy people, large doses may cause diarrhea.

Zinc

Adequate zinc is essential to a healthy pregnancy; it reduces the risk of preeclampsia and improves the health of the baby. Zinc is also important to the immune system; but high doses can have a detrimental effect both on the immune system and on the metabolism of copper, another essential nutrient. Zinc deficiency may be associated with an increased risk of cervical dysplasia. Some researchers believe that zinc deficiency, which leads to abnormalities in taste, may be linked to some forms of anorexia nervosa.

Boron

Boron has not received much attention, but it is important in preventing osteoporosis and possibly menopausal symptoms, probably through its action on estrogen metabolism. It may also relieve the symptoms of various kinds of arthritis, including rheumatoid arthritis.

Iodine

Adequate iodine is essential during pregnancy to avoid cretinism in the baby—a syndrome that may include decreased mental ability, retarded growth, and hypothyroidism, among other problems. Iodine deficiency may also increase the risk of miscarriage and infant mortality. Iodine affects estrogen metabolism and may therefore be helpful in treating fibrocystic breast syndrome and PMS. However, self-treatment with iodine should be strictly avoided because high levels of iodine affect the thyroid gland.

Iron

Menstruating women are at increased risk of iron-deficiency anemia because of their monthly loss of blood; it is counterintuitive but true that heavy bleeding during menstruation can be due to iron deficiency (although there are many possible causes), as well as vice versa. Pregnancy creates a huge need for extra iron that very few women can meet through diet alone. The elderly are also likely to be iron-deficient.

A proper diagnosis of iron deficiency is important because, like men, most women who are no longer menstruating should take iron-free vitamin supplements to reduce the risk of heart disease. Parents of young children might be unaware that a child can be seriously or even fatally poisoned by an overdose of iron-containing vitamins, so it is important to keep them out of reach.

Selenium

Some researchers believe that during pregnancy and lactation, women should consider supplementing their diets with 200 micrograms (not milligrams—an important distinction because of the possibility of toxicity) of selenium to reduce the risk of sudden infant death syndrome, SIDS. Vitamin E and selenium work together, so supplemental vitamin E should also be considered; and low levels of vitamin C and of biotin may also be related to SIDS. Selenium is important in preventing many other diseases that are not exclusive to women; it is an antioxidant and thus may reduce the risk of cancer and cardiovascular disease.

It should be emphasized that this list is not complete in terms of either medical conditions or nutrients. Also, there is much more to good health than swallowing pills, and usually more to curing disease or relieving a symptom than supplementing a single nutrient. People taking medication should check with their physicians to make sure there are no known interactions (for example, between vitamin K and anticoagulant medication or between folic acid and certain anticancer drugs). A healthy diet, adequate sleep and rest, exercise, fresh air, sunshine, plenty of water, and emotional well-being are all more important than any individual nutrient listed here.

See Also

COOKING; FOOD AND CULTURE; HOLISTIC HEALTH, *I and II*; NUTRITION I; NUTRITION AND HOME ECONOMICS

References and Further Reading

Beers, Mark H., and Robert Berkow, eds. 1999. *The Merck manual of diagnosis and therapy.* Whitehouse Station, N.J.: Merck Research Laboratories.

Garrison, Robert, Jr., and Elizabeth Somer. 1995. *The nutrition desk reference.* New Canaan, Conn.: Keats.

Marz, Russell. 1997. *Medical nutrition from Marz.* 2nd ed. Portland, Ore.: Omni-Press.

Murray, Michael. 1996. *Encyclopedia of nutritional supplements.* Rocklin, Calif.: Prima.

Pizzorno, Joseph E., and Michael T. Murray, eds. 1999. *Textbook of natural medicine.* London: Churchill Livingstone.

Brinlee Kramer

NUTRITION AND HOME ECONOMICS

During the twentieth century, home economics arose as a service-oriented academic discipline and research field addressing the sciences of maintaining a household. These include such diverse subjects as nutrition, sanitation, consumption, textiles, management, and technology as they affect the home. In its early years, home economics became institutionalized in the United States and Europe by offering careers to women who were discouraged or barred from entering male-dominated sciences such as chemistry. The field continues to employ primarily women, though there have been recent efforts to bring in more men.

The early-twentieth-century professionalization of home economics rested on two countervailing efforts: the denigration of traditional housework practices, and the rigid adherence to traditional gender ideologies that glorified housework as women's most appropriate occupation. This ideological underpinning has clashed with feminist thought and practices in various historical and social contexts. The formal attachment of U.S. home economics to agricultural colleges shaped the channels through which its findings have reached women both domestically and internationally. On an international scale, home economics has been viewed by some observers as a tool for empowering the world's poorest women; others see it as a strand of postcolonialism aimed at displacing indigenous work practices with Western alternatives in order to satisfy Western strategic and economic interests. This criticism applies particularly to cases in which Western nutritional standards and practices have been introduced to non-Western cultures without adequate sensitivity to the existing socioeconomic and cultural context. Home economics has attempted to correct this deficiency by bringing cross-cultural issues into the college classroom. An examination of the history of home economics as it developed in the West and expanded internationally highlights its awkward relationship with the interests of various categories of women throughout the world.

History of Home Economics as a Profession

Many writers trace the historical roots of home economics to advice books, cookbooks, women's magazines, and household manuals published in the nineteenth century. Catharine Beecher wrote the first comprehensive manual on housework in 1841 under the title *A Treatise on Domestic Economy,* and in the decades after its publication a number of social forces increased the demand for information of this nature. Industrialization and urbanization in the United States and Europe meant that many women who had grown up on farms were now living in towns and cities, with new infrastructures and technologies to manage. Many women accepted unpaid housework as their ideal role but felt uncertain about how to incorporate new technologies and knowledge into their homes. By the turn of the twentieth century, material feminists—who condemned men's exploitation of women's unpaid domestic labor—proposed remuneration for this work, along with a transformation of the material culture of homes and communities. They argued that the formation of day care centers, community dining clubs, and public kitchens would lessen the spatial isolation that impeded women from gaining equality with men (Hayden, 1981). Despite their profound differences, both the household advice writers and the material feminists urged women to distrust tradition and personal taste and to adopt scientifically tested methods of housework.

The same ideologies of gender segregation that kept many women in the home full-time also impeded the entrance of educated women into male-dominated sciences. These women found a new field of inquiry in the realm of domestic work. A handful of these skilled scientists—including chemists Ellen Swallow Richards and Isabel Bevier, sanitation scientist Marion Talbot, and nutritionist Mary Davies Swartz Rose—met for a series of conferences on "domestic science" beginning in 1899 in Lake Placid, New York; their meetings led to the 1908 formation of the American Home Economics Association (AHEA). Two of the AHEA's original officers were men; otherwise, this was almost exclusively a women's organization from the start. The AHEA reaffirmed the need for full-time female labor in the home, and it sought to train college women for their inevitable roles as mothers and housekeepers. As AHEA members cooperated to establish home economics departments in colleges across the United States, they created a curriculum attractive to many young women of the day. However, feminists and other women with nondomestic ambitions struggled against the underlying assumption that it was women's natural role to do housework. Many saw the new, sex-segregated field as a conservative force that delayed true coeducation in colleges. From a broader historical perspective, it is clear that both home economists and their feminist critics concerned themselves with the lives of white, middle-class women and gave scant attention to women of color and new immigrants, who lacked educational opportunity and who often performed a double shift of housework each day, one for pay and one for their own families.

In the United States, the Smith-Lever Act of 1914 united home economics departments with the colleges of agriculture of land grant and state universities and established home economics rural extension work as part of the U.S. Department of Agriculture. The Smith-Hughes Act of 1917 mandated vocational training for future teachers of home economics and for extension workers, although the funding necessary to enact this mandate took more than a decade to arrive. Poverty in the southern states and a deepening shortage of skilled domestic servants during the first decades of the century motivated the training of women of color to work as home economics teachers in segregated schools. A 1923 study on the subject concluded that several factors, including a lack of well-trained teachers, had retarded the transfer of domestic skills to this segment of the population, and it recommended that teacher-training institutions for African Americans adopt a curriculum that included courses in chemistry, advanced food study, textiles and clothing, dietetics, home management, bacteriology, and household physics (*A study of home-economics education in teacher-training institutions for Negroes*). The expense of setting up practice kitchens added to the wide variance in the quality of home economics education received by different segments of the population.

As home economics was producing its second generation of practitioners, it drew important allies from the growing population of women working in related fields. Many women with expertise in subjects such as management and architecture could stabilize their scientific careers only by focusing their attention on the home, an area where their gender helped rather than hindered them. Some joined the technocratic bandwagon of the Progressive Era by insisting that technical answers for the social inequities of domestic life could be found through science. A case in point was the housewife Christine Frederick, who, in 1913, proposed that industrial scientific management could be applied to the home to lighten women's loads. This involved establishing time and fatigue standards for various tasks against which women's existing housework habits could be measured. In 1927, Lillian Gilbreth, a pioneer of industrial motion study and mother of eleven, became a household engineer by spelling out how women could minimize their motions and maximize their psychological health by scientifically planning their housework. In the 1930s and 1940s, she implanted these ideas into home economics departments through a new specialty area called "work simplification."

The politically charged question of why women should want to change their housework habits fueled debates in the United States and Europe. In early-twentieth-century Britain, working-class mothers with little formal education were blamed for the high infant mortality rate and the falling birth rate. Rather than expanding social services and thereby ameliorating poverty, government leaders borrowed the rhetorics of nationalism and eugenics, urging women to improve their homemaking skills for the sake of the nation and the race. In the United States, the business philosophy of "Fordism" held that only a stable, healthy, and comfortable home life could produce the dependable, productive workers needed for industrial expansion. It was thus the housewife's moral duty to acquire the necessary domestic skills. The growth of the human sciences after 1920 added "family psychologist" and "intelligent consumer" to the duties of the "homemaker," a title that emphasized women's expanding domestic role. In turn, home economics expanded its scope into child development and family relations.

Manufacturers and service-sector companies have made use of home economics chiefly in their research and marketing work. Eager to show women the benefits of purchasing their product or service, companies have employed home economists to reach women consumers through a combination of scientific authority and gender-based empathy. National governments have also used home economists as spokespersons; for example, Lillian Gilbreth was hired to spread knowledge about good nutrition and wise spending practices to women across the United States during the Great Depression. The growth of home economics as a profession has been publicly associated with the spread of consumerism because of the way in which the available consumer products have shaped research topics such as clothing design and food preparation.

International Home Economics and Nutrition

Food selection and preparation have always received substantial attention in home economics. In the 1960s, research on food and nutrition accounted for nearly half of the projects completed in U.S. university home economics programs. Larger universities sometimes have a separate department of nutrition that brings together research expertise in physiology, chemistry, biology, pathology, microbiology, medicine, agriculture, animal husbandry, public health, food production, and technology. The origins of inquiry into nutrition go back to the identification of proteins, fats, and carbohydrates in the early 1800s, the establishment of the need for specific minerals in the late 1800s, and the identification of human vitamin requirements in the 1920s and 1930s. The first recommended dietary allowances were formulated in the United States in 1943; other countries soon developed their own lists, which the World Health Organization attempted to coordinate in 1950 (*Present knowledge in nutrition,* 1976).

Whereas research on nutrition has often been propelled by the need to find the cheapest healthy diet for poor populations, food production and processing have been heavily influenced by consumer demand, especially in the United States. Classes in food preparation from the 1940s to the 1980s emphasized the importance of four food groups: grains, fruits and vegetables, dairy, and meat. With the environmentalism of the 1980s and 1990s, agricultural and nutritional experts provided environmental, economic, and nutritional reasons for reducing the energy-intensive production and consumption of beef and other meats and increasing human consumption of grains. The American Dietetic Association (ADA) now monitors food safety and establishes the dietary guidance messages that appear next to the food pyramid on food packaging. Members of the ADA are progressively becoming more sensitive to the interactions between nutrition, age, medical conditions, cultural influences, income, race, sex and ethnicity.

Research on nutrition has been especially important for home economists intent on reducing global malnutrition by finding the common ground between culturally specific food habits and basic dietary requirements. The International Federation for Home Economics (IFHE) works to bring the skills of home economists to bear on such issues of international development. This federation, which originated in 1908 as a link among emerging European home economics programs, has since incorporated members from all over the world (Firebaugh, 1985). Since 1915, when the AHEA forged its ties with the IFHE, a small but dedicated cohort of U.S. home economists have participated in teacher exchange programs and international conferences.

For professionals interested in international research, the IFHE, international agricultural research centers, and aid organizations offer a structure. However, several factors have prevented home economists from making great strides on the global level. First, the discipline has always been organized by concepts emerging from Western and industrial societies. For example, the "household" that is often the focus of home economics research has turned out to be a very Western ideal, not a natural or universal phenomenon. The image of the "homemaker" does not fit well into many horticultural societies in Africa and South America, where women are involved in agricultural production and may even own and control the seeds that are planted and the food that is harvested. Second, home economists have seldom acquired the expertise in agriculture and economics that would allow them to aid such women. Third, because of the gender composition of the field, many practitioners cite their commitments to their families as a reason for not undertaking the prolonged foreign fieldwork necessary for effective international work.

To counter criticism from cultural anthropologists and others with insight into indigenous cultures, the home economics profession has begun to broaden its training. Since 1976, when an "International Section" was formed within the AHEA, the need for greater sociocultural understanding has been recognized among members. Some have suggested including cultural anthropology and foreign language courses as requirements for the college major (Firebaugh, 1985). However, international work is still rare and is not viewed as a priority by the larger profession. The work of establishing the discipline across the world and forging ahead with culturally specific research has fallen to international students who complete advanced home economics degrees in the United States, Canada, or Europe. In Pakistan, where most home economists hold such a degree, U.S. textbooks are used in courses at the elementary, secondary, and college levels. There is still little rural extension work in Pakistan, and so rural and illiterate women have yet to be reached (Saeed and McClelland, 1991). It appears that in most countries, home economics programs at the college level continue to cater to the needs of the middle and upper classes without doing much for the women who face the most intense poverty and malnutrition.

Prospects for the Future

Home economics as a profession has lost some of the momentum it enjoyed in earlier decades when there were fewer career opportunities for women. Between 1972 and 1991, there was a decline of 14 percent in enrollment in U.S. home economics undergraduate programs (Moe et al., 1991). Many feminists, women of non-Western descent, and women of color remain critical of the ethnocentrism and traditional gender-role assumptions built into the discipline. The future of home economics will rest in part on its response to these criticisms.

See Also

AGRICULTURE; COOKING; DOMESTIC LABOR; DOMESTIC TECHNOLOGY; FOOD, HUNGER, AND FAMINE; HOUSEHOLDS: POLITICAL ECONOMY; HOUSEWORK; SCIENCE: TRADITIONAL AND INDIGENOUS KNOWLEDGE; WIFE

References and Further Reading

Beecher, Catharine. 1841. *A treatise on domestic economy.* Boston: Marsh, Capen, Lyon, and Webb.

Cowan, Ruth Schwartz. 1983. *More work for Mother.* New York: Basic Books.

Firebaugh, Francille M. 1985. Women in development and home economics. *Journal of Home Economics,* Winter: 41–45.

Hayden, Dolores. 1981. *The grand domestic revolution.* Cambridge, Mass.: MIT Press.

Matthews, Glenna. 1987. *"Just a housewife": The rise and fall of domesticity.* New York: Oxford University Press.

McIntosh, Elaine N. 1995. *American food habits in historical perspective.* Westport, Conn.: Praeger.

Moe, Cindy, Ann Mullis, David Dosser, and Ron Mullis. 1991. Descriptions of home economists from three perspectives. *Home Economics Research Journal* 20(1: Sept): 6–15.

Palmer, Phyllis. 1989. *Domesticity and dirt.* Philadelphia: Temple University Press.

Present knowledge in nutrition. 1976. New York: Nutrition Foundation.

Saeed, Fouzia and Jerry McClelland. 1991. Home economics curricular in Pakistan: Time for reform? *Journal of Home Economics,* Winter: 33–37.

Sobal, Jeffrey and Donna Maurer, eds. 1999. *Interpreting weight: The social management of fatness and thinness.* New York: Aldine de Gruyter.

Stage, Sarah, and Virginia Vincent, eds. 1997. *Rethinking home economics: Women and the history of a profession.* Ithaca, N.Y.: Cornell University Press.

Strasser, Susan. 1982. *Never done: A history of American housework.* New York: Pantheon.

A study of home-economics education in teacher-training institutions for Negroes. 1932. Home Economics Series no. 7, Bulletin no. 79. New York: Negro Universities Press.

Laurel Graham

O

OBESITY

See EATING DISORDERS *and* FOOD AND CULTURE.

OBSTETRICS

In modern medicine, obstetrics includes the care of women before conception, during pregnancy, and immediately postpartum—that is, after childbirth. Because medicine has long been a microcosm for a culture at large, the evaluation and care of pregnant women provide a key to societal values and attitudes. As an illustration, this article will focus on the United States, where, today, issues in bedrooms and legislative chambers are reflected in examination rooms and insurers' boardrooms.

Nineteenth-Century Obstetrics

Although women have always been healers, pharmacists, abortionists, midwives, and herbalists, much of modern western obstetrics derives from the nineteenth century, when male physicians rather than traditional female folk healers became dominant. Medical textbooks mention many "fathers" of obstetrics and gynecology, but no "mothers." These men shared the attitudes toward women that were prevalent at the time. In 1845, Dr. Meigs, one of the earliest fathers of obstetrics, described women as "feeble and sensitive at birth, and destined by nature to give us existence and to preserve us afterwards by means of... tender and watchful care. Woman, the most faithful companion of man, may be regarded as the very complement of the benefits bestowed upon us by the Divine Being. Whereas before puberty she existed but for herself alone, when all her charms are in full bloom, she now belongs to the entire species which she is destined to perpetuate by bearing almost all the burden of reproduction." Lecturing a class about vaginal examinations, Dr. Meigs remarked apologetically, "I am bound to say that it will be your painful, even your distressing duty, to condescend to the task of making exploration." Presumably the pain and distress arose because the doctor was invading his patients' purity, or because he himself might experience temptation.

In the 1800s, medical training was haphazard—two months to two years, with no clinical facilities and virtually no scientific understanding—and care was characterized by bleeding, leeches, large doses of laxatives, and opium. Athough lay practitioners, who used methods such as herbs, diet, and emotional support, were often safer and more effective than physicians, 13 American states outlawed "irregular" doctors in 1830. This led to popular protests. "Ladies Physiological Societies," early self-help groups, were organized; they emphasized prevention, bathing, loose-fitting clothes, temperance, whole-grain cereals, and birth control and opposed the elitism of regular doctors—"doctorcraft," which they considered one of four great evils, the others being kingcraft, priestcraft, and lawyercraft. By the 1840s, in response to this popular health movement, almost all licensing laws had been repealed. Nonetheless, the regular doctors, backed by class and power, continued to set the standards for medical practice, many of which remain today.

For example, physicians controlled the use of drugs. This dates back to 1846, when Dr. Channing, another father of obstetrics and gynecology, administered ether for the first time during childbirth. (However, since the Bible states, "In sorrow thou shalt bring forth children," this pain relief was seen as immoral, and Channing was accused of blasphemy.) Also, it was assumed that the physician had technical expertise which must be actively used. Discussing a birth in which forceps had been used unnecessarily, Channing said that the physician "must do something. He cannot remain a spectator merely, where there are too many witnesses and where interest in what is going on is too deep to allow inaction." Thus obstetrical forceps, long protected as a trade secret, established the superiority of doctors over midwives.

The physician was admired for his self-restraint and omniscience. In the 1820s—a time of intense modesty—pregnancy and childbirth, with their obvious connection to sexual relations, were considered embarrassing and were described in euphemisms: "expecting," "in a delicate condition," "confinement," "lying-in." Discussion of women's bodies and disorders became associated with a sense of shame and secrecy which to some degree still exists today.

Physicians learned their craft on poor women but practiced their profession on upper-class women. Only poor women fully exposed their body, and this exposure often resulted in a public outcry—out of concern not for poor patients but for the doctor's reputation and its effect on respectable women. As late as the 1970s, medical schools taught pelvic examination using prostitutes. The speculum (the instrument inserted during a pelvic examination) was denounced by the American Medical Association in 1851 as embarrassing to women, and it too was seen as jeopardizing the physician's reputation; not until the 1970s were women able to appropriate the speculum and use it with a mirror and flashlight to perform vaginal self-examination. In the nineteenth century, an essentially prescientfic era of medicine, reputable physicians believed that reproductive difficulties reflected women's own defects—social, cultural, religious, moral, physical, or behavioral. Moreover, the medical community infantalized women. An obstetrical text of 1848 described women as having "a head almost too small for intellect but just big enough for love" and menopause as "the change of life that unhinges the female nervous system and deprives women of their personal charms."

The Early Twentieth Century

In 1900, only 5 percent of women in the United States gave birth in hospitals. By 1939, this had changed dramatically: 50 percent of American women had hospital deliveries. The physician's convenience was an important factor; doctors needed access to technology such as X-rays and anesthesia and also trained their students in hospitals.

Hospitalization brought some new difficulties, espcially infection associated with birth—puerperal fever. It took time to realize that this danger, among others, was related to hospital practices such as not washing the hands; doctors went from patient to patient, and even from cadavers to patients, without washing. To combat puerperal fever, birth became standardized, or ritualized. Wards were aired and disinfected regularly. Nurses bathed and changed their uniforms. Patients' clothes were removed; patients were bathed and given special gowns; their pubic hair was shaved; and enemas and douches were routinely administered during labor. Birth became defined as dangerous, and consequently women were defined as defective and in need of the physician's expertise.

By 1920, physicians believed that normal deliveries were rare and that intervention was justified in virtually all births. In 1920, Dr. DeLee, another famous figure, recommended routine use of forceps and episiotomy (surgical enlargement of the vulva). Women in labor were sedated with ether, and ergot was used to maintain contractions. During delivery, the woman lay flat on her back with her legs in stirrups, because this position gave the doctor the easiest access to the perineum—the pelvic outlet. After delivery, the perineum was repaired. The rationale for these procedures was to prevent "permanent invalidism due to prolapsed uterus and fistulas and to decrease pelvic relaxation," to restore "virginal conditions," and to "prevent brain damage and a life of crime." DeLee compared unaided birth to a mother's falling on a pitchfork and a baby's head being caught in a doorjamb; he described labor as "a decidedly pathological practice," noting, "So frequent are these bad effects, that I have often wondered whether Nature did not deliberately intend women to be used up in the process of reproduction, in a manner analogous to that of the salmon which dies after spawning." By the 1930s, DeLee's advice was widely, if not universally, followed, although in fact there were no data on its efficacy.

By contrast, however, Dr. Williams—another famous obstetrician—documented the terrible state of education and the lack of clinical training. Williams urged educational reforms, obstetrics as a speciality for abnormal births, and the establishment of maternity hospitals.

In Europe, midwives were being educated and upgraded; but by 1900 they had been outlawed in the United States. At this time, medical schools were closed to almost all women, so nursing became the only professional option for women in the United States. This decline of the midwife had to do with cultural attitudes about women's proper place and with midwives' lack of organization, leadership, and power; but whatever the cause, American midwives were left to care for immigrants, the poor, and African-Americans and became stereotyped as immigrants themselves, ignorant and incompetent. A study conducted in 1912 found that physicians were actually less competent than midwives and more likely to intervene with risky surgery; but this report had no effect on physicians' power.

By 1930, the American Board of Obstetrics and Gynecology was established to set standards of obstetrical care. Investigations had found that the two main causes of infant mortality were inadequate prenatal care and excessive or improper interventions by physicians. This was very troubling to the profession and led to further investigations and the beginning of regulations. As maternity hospitals were established, there was also a growing concern about maternal mortality. In the United States after World War I, maternity—which should be a normal life event—was found to be a leading killer of women ages 15 to 45, second only to tuberculosis. Women saw hospitals as clean, safe, and technologically up to date, and the postpartum hospital stay of two to three weeks as preferable to home care by relatives and friends. However, there were no rules about who could do what regarding obstetric care, and maternal and infant health was not improving. Infant deaths from birth injury rose by 50 percent from 1915 to 1929.

At this time, feminism affected obstetric standards. Women campaigned for painless labor: "twilight sleep," a combination of narcotics, sleep medication, and amnesiacs. In fact, twilight sleep became a war cry of feminists and suffragists—joined by wealthy society women—and in 1914, the New England Twilight Sleep Association forced hospitals to provide it. By the 1930s, twilight sleep was used in all hospitals. In addition to its intended effect, relief of pain, it streamlined hospital care, and it made women more passive and manageable.

The Later Twentieth Century

By the end of World War II in 1945, maternal and infant mortality rates were decreasing in the United States; and by 1955 the risk of dying or contracting a serious disease in childbirth had been largely eliminated by antiseptic measures (such as handwashing), antibiotics, and blood transfusions. On the other hand, the hospital had become a difficult and frightening place to have a baby. Maternity wards developed complex, impersonal rules and routines; and women were divided by social class—private rooms versus charity wards—and thus also by race.

By the 1970s, maternity wards seemed to some observers to have lost any human element whatsoever. For many women, childbirth was a time of alienation, loneliness, and powerlessness, of forced immobility and muffled screams. Normal deliveries included stimulation of labor; twilight sleep; leather straps on the beds; open labor wards, from which women were rushed down a hallway to a separate delivery room as the baby's head was crowning; the lithotomy position—the position used in bladder surgery—for delivery; forceps; and separation of mother and baby postpartum. Every labor was seen as a disaster waiting to happen; the emphasis was on efficiency and routine.

With the new wave of feminism, many women questioned the necessity for, and the safety of, such interventions and began to focus on their own need for self-fulfillment and control. Grantly Dick-Reed's book *Childbirth Without Fear* became popular, as did *Thank You, Dr. Lamaze,* which described a method of natural childbirth orginated by the French obstetrician Fernand Lamaze (1890–1957). Dick-Read and Lamaze thought of birth as a normal, benevolent, joyful experience. Ideas such as these—along with taking control of health issues in general—became tenets of the women's liberation movement. In the 1970s, as feminists began to investigate many aspects and assumptions of medicine, as cultural attitudes changed, and as the birthrate dropped, obstetrics became more open to women's demands. Another turning point was the publication of *Our Bodies, Ourselves,* by the Boston Women's Health Book Collective; this was the first book that shared information about women's bodies and health, and the first popular book to link sexism, racism, and health care.

From about 1970 to the end of the twentieth century, dramatic changes in society were reflected in obstetrical training, in an increase in female residents and practicing obstetrican-gynecologists, and in clashes between women's sensibilities and sexist textbooks, medical assumptions, research, and obstetrical practices. For example, in 1975, only 5 percent of applicants for obstetrical residencies were women; by 2000 the proportion was 33 percent. In these three decades, obstetrical practices improved significantly. Labor and delivery suites became more "family-friendly"; epidural anesthesia became safer and more effective. There were also enormous improvements in the care of premature babies and of women in childbirth with HIV.

However, some "high-tech" procedures and practices still devalue the normality and strength of the woman's body in labor and keep the physician in control of the birth process. (An example is fetal monitoring during labor and delivery; although this is a standard of care, there are actually no long-term data indicating improved outcome.) Moreover, with the predominance of managed health care in the United States, the insurer also assumed a position of power, a development that could further distance women from birth as a mysterious, sexual, distinctly female event, central to the creation of a family.

See Also

CHILDBIRTH; PREGNANCY AND BIRTH; SURGERY, *I and II*

References and Further Reading

Benson, Ralph. 1971. *Handbook of obstetrics and gynecology.* Los Altos, Calif.: Lange Medical.

Boston Women's Health Book Collective. 1992. *The new our bodies, ourselves: A book by and for women.* New York: Touchstone. (See also *Our bodies, ourselves for the new century.* 1999. New York: Simon and Schuster.)

Dick-Read, Grantly. 1970. *Childbirth without fear.* New York: Harper Perennial.

Ehrenreich, Barbara, and Deidre English. 1973. *Complaints and disorders: The sexual politics of sickness.* Old Wesbury, N.Y.: Feminist Press.

———. 1973. *Witches, midwives, and nurses: A history of women healers.* Old Westbury, N.Y.: Feminist Press.

Ehrenreich, John. 1978. *The cultural crisis of modern medicine.* New York and London: Monthly Review.

Mitford, Jessica. 1992. *The American way of birth.* New York: Dutton.

Rothman, Barbara Katz. 1982. *Giving birth: Alternatives in childbirth.* New York: Penguin.

Wertz, Richard, and Dorothy Wertz. 1979. *Lying-in: A history of childbirth in America.* New York: Schocken.

Woolhandler, Steffie, and David Himmelstein. 1998. *For our patients, not for profits: A call to action.* Cambridge, Mass.: Center for National Health Program Studies at Harvard Medical School/Cambridge Hospital.

Alice Rothchild

OCCUPATIONAL EXPERIENCES

See WORK: OCCUPATIONAL EXPERIENCES.

OCCUPATIONAL HEALTH AND SAFETY

In the last two decades of the twentieth century, in all industrialized nations, there was a dramatic increase in the number of women, particularly women with small children, working outside the home. Despite this, the role of women as workers and the hazards they may face on the job are still not fully appreciated or well understood. In 1997, one author in a leading medical journal, describing depression in women, wrote: "What about work? Work outside the home is beneficial to women's mental health except when it creates difficulties with housework and childcare" (Meagher and Murray, 1997). In this statement, we see encapsulated a major dilemma facing women, particularly those trying to balance work lives and family obligations: the role of work is not seen as central to a woman's life, as it is to a man's.

Women at Work

Women's lives at work and at home are strongly interconnected. The most obvious connection is the juggling act that most women must perform in order to meet their responsibilities. In industrialized nations, employed women, on average, work about 80 hours per week, compared to about 50 hours per week for their spouses. In developing nations, it is difficult even to analyze women's "juggling acts," because much of the paid work that they do is in the "informal" sector of household-based industries, and the unpaid work of food growing, gathering, and preparation and their other household duties, though uncounted, provides much of the labor by which their society survives.

The paid jobs that women hold tend to be a reflection of their caregiving and household roles. Around the world, women work as nurses and nurses' aides (health caregiving role), as lower-grade schoolteachers (childcare role), as secretaries and clerks (reflecting the seldom recognized role of women as administrators in the home and voluntary organizations). Women who work in industrial jobs are concentrated in the textile trades (traditional sewing) or in assembling small machines or other light objects (reflecting the endless fix-it, make-it work in the home). Women are waitresses—at home and on the job. In retail trades, women are the cashiers and the clerks who sell domestic products, clothing, foods and so on—very few women are involved in the sale of durable industrial items or even heavy-duty home products. Women work in cleaning—commercial dry cleaning and laundries, as well as cleaning in offices and private homes. Traditional women's jobs, which some experts call "female job ghettoes," account for about 80 percent of all the jobs that women do.

Throughout most of the twentieth century, traditional women's work was widely viewed as "safe," although adequate studies demonstrating such safety have never been carried out. Many male jobs were considered too strenuous or too dangerous for women, but the often similar dangers in traditional female ghetto jobs have been ignored. These gender-based notions of comparative risk often have been used as arguments for keeping women out of better-paying jobs in factories and transport, and they have led to legislation, often called "protective," prohibiting the employment of women in a large number of industries and jobs. But "protections" that barred women from equal employment opportunities were never applied to jobs or conditions in traditional women's work. A woman may have been barred from working in a lead-battery production plant, but she was never prohibited from working in a lead-battery production plant, but she was never prohibited from working in the pottery industry, where the levels of lead contamination might well have been higher. Women were banned from night work, with its higher pay scales and better hours for combining with childcare—unless they were nurses and were needed at night. Equal opportunity legislation has been changing these restrictions, and more and more women are entering into nontraditional jobs, but such notions and practices still persist. Indeed, the International Labor Organization still maintains discriminatory language in several of its employment conventions and recommendations governing the employment of women.

Women's role in childbearing has been a major focus of differential occupational health and safety regulations and practices. "Fetal protection policies," whereby all fertile women are banned from certain jobs and workplaces with potential exposure to toxins while men are permitted to work in these environments, were widely practiced throughout the world. These policies galvanized opposition in the feminist and labor communities, particularly in the United States, where it eventually led to the landmark, unanimous U.S. Supreme Court decision in *UAW v. Johnson Controls* (1991), in which the Court declared fetal protection policies to be invalid. In its opinion, the Court stated that fetal protection policies failed to protect the reproductive health of males, who could also be affected by such hazards. The policies also were found to contradict laws prohibiting employment discrimination on the basis of pregnancy.

Are separate standards and separate considerations ever warranted for women? Is there really a separate field of "women's occupational health?" It is difficult to answer this question completely, because there are almost no data on whether women develop *different* occupational diseases or suffer different *injuries* than men do, as Messing and other commentators have discussed. Some reasons for this difficulty are:

- Men and women have greatly different employment patterns, so accurate gender-based extrapolations are challenging.
- The full health and safety implications of the multiple-role issue are not understood.
- There has not been much research devoted to comparative gender rate studies.
- Research into the health and safety hazards of female-dominated industries is still sparse.

Occupational Hazards

The absence of definitive data on where women work, the hazards they face, and the extent to which they may develop disease or disability reflects the discrimination against women workers that exists at the turn of the twenty-first century. The hazards cover the full gamut of exposure to chemical and physical agents, infectious agents, ergonomic injury, and traumatic injury. In addition, it should not be forgotten that the vast majority of women laborers bear the burden of multiple roles and are thus perhaps exposed to the hazards of more than one sector. The following paragraphs describe some of these hazards in detail.

Occupational stress: In general, women are paid less than men, even for similar work, and their occupations offer less room for advancement. Many women are not in decision-making positions. Less money, less opportunity, and less power on the job all contribute to occupational stress, a major hazard for women workers. Long-term stress can contribute to cardiovascular diseases. Stressed people also find it difficult to take proper care of themselves. They exercise less frequently and may smoke cigarettes and drink too many alcoholic beverages as a way of relieving stress. No one has yet done a definitive study on the relationship among work, stress, and health. It is known that unless a woman is satisfied with each of her multiple roles, her well-being will be adversely affected.

Back injuries and *repetitive strain injuries* (RSIs) are a major cause of occupational disease in women workers. Lifting and carrying, particularly carrying awkward loads like bundles of laundry or lifting patients unassisted, can lead to serious and often permanent back injury. Many women work in jobs where they are required to repeat the same small motions during the course of the work day. Computer users may suffer from injury to the wrist (carpal tunnel syndrome) resulting from long hours of data entry. Women who assemble small machines or who work in the meat and poultry industries, where they have to make thousands of reaches and cuts each day, also may develop carpal tunnel syndrome. In the United States, nearly 80 percent of all RSI-related problems were found among women workers, and labor experts expect this trend to grow as industry becomes more automated and service oriented (U.S. Bureau of Labor Statistics, 1994).

Ergonomic hazards need not be exotic. Sitting or standing all day can also be hazardous. Sitting in an ill-proportioned chair—a chair that doesn't "fit"—can cause backache, fatigue, headaches, and eyestrain, particularly if combined with using a computer on the job. Standing or sitting for long periods causes static load. Experts often ignore the biomechanical strain associated with static loads and concentrate on activities involving a lot of movement, lifting, and carrying. But careful study has shown that a woman continuously sitting and laundering hundreds of pounds of linens can actually be "working" harder than a man who lifts heavier weights a few times an hour. It is important to note, however, that some women workers do lift and carry heavy weights, such as patients or meal trays. In many developing nations, it is the women who perform the physical labor of lifting and carrying in agriculture, home maintenance, and the construction industries.

Work with computers can be especially taxing and may pose ergonomic risks, particularly if the computer screen is not adjusted properly or there is glare on the screen from improper lighting. Use of eyeglasses that have not been prescribed to take into account the particular distances and needs of computer viewing may lead to headaches, eyestrain, and general stress.

Women who stand on the job also may be wearing uncomfortable shoes. Both fashion and a lack of well-designed shoes for women workers contribute to occupational injuries to working women's feet. In some occupations, women may actually be required to wear shoes with high heels, even though their jobs involve standing and walking, because such shoes are thought to "look" better. A cocktail waitress in high heels will be a waitress with back and foot problems if she continues to wear such shoes on the job.

Infectious diseases. Women workers with jobs that bring them into contact with the sick, with children, and with the public are, in general, at increased risk of exposure to dangerous microorganisms. Unfortunately, there is no accurate count of how many workers develop infectious diseases on the job. Although most countries require hospitals to keep track of infections that develop among patients while in hospital—nosocomial infections—the registries contain data on only patient illnesses, not illnesses developed by the staff. A recent review of infections in health-care workers produced the following list of occupational infectious diseases in health-care work: hepatitis (B, C, D non A-E), tuberculosis, varicella (chicken pox), measles, mumps, rubella (German measles), HIV/AIDS, Epstein-Barr virus (EBV), and cytomegalovirus (CMV).

Other female-dominated occupations with infection risks include childcare, social work, and schoolteaching, particularly in the lower grades. Women workers in the meat and poultry industry and those who work with animals also may be at significant risk for occupational infections. Molds and spores can be sources of infection and of serious allergies. People who work in jobs as varied as mushroom growing, handling old books and papers, and textile manufacturing can be exposed to highly toxic molds and spores. Indoor air quality also may be compromised by microorganisms in addition to low levels of chemical contaminants. Diseases such as Legionnaires' disease and a host of allergy-type responses can be caused by contaminated indoor air. Many buildings have inadequate ventilation systems, so polluted air is recirculated. Many office machines, furnishings, and supplies emit gases containing low levels of toxic chemicals.

Chemical hazards are found in many working women's environments. Some of the exposures may not be obvious. Textile workers can be exposed to formaldehyde in permanent press finishes. Workers who administer drugs with hypodermic syringes will be exposed to a backspray of drug with every injection. Nurses administering drugs to cancer patients have been found, in studies, to have the toxic drugs in their own bodies. Some health-care workers have developed allergies or skin problems from exposure to antibiotics. Syringes designed to avoid the problem have been developed, but many institutions will not expend the additional funds to buy them.

Many women work in research and clinical laboratories where they may be exposed to chemical hazards. Women who handle animals may have all the same chemical and infection hazards that health-care workers have—and also be at risk for being bitten or attacked by their "patients." Because latex gloves that were dusted with talc for ease of use have caused serious, sometimes fatal, allergic responses in both workers and patients, talc-free gloves are now widely available.

The overall burden of occupational cancer and other diseases related to toxic exposure in women workers is not known. Some examples include health-care workers who—again—are in one of the most important occupations with potential exposure to carcinogens (X-rays, ethylene oxide, dichloromethane, and ethyl acrylate, for example). Other hazards include cadmium oxide and lead in the glazes used in ceramics, pottery, and bricks (refractories), all female-intensive occupations. Artists and craftsworkers also could be at risk from these exposures. Dry cleaning, laundries, electrical appliances, and electronics industries are noteworthy for their potential exposure to chlorinated solvents such as chloroform, 1,2-dichloroethane, and tetrachloroethylene. Many of these small establishments have employees who are not necessarily provided with adequate ventilation or protective equipment, and whose illnesses and injuries are unlikely to be reported. Environmental tobacco smoke can be an occupational health hazard for women employed in hotel and food service establishments.

Reproductive health: Some pregnant women can be exposed to hazards that may affect a pregnancy, leading to spontaneous abortion or even to defective births, but the list of causative agents is comparatively small, and most effects are not yet defined. Several studies have found an association between certain occupational requirements—awkward working postures, extensive standing, and increased physical loads—and preterm deliveries. Male fertility also may be affected by chemical and physical exposures. The actual burden of birth defects attributable to either male or female workplace exposure is not known.

Some chemicals, such as aromatic solvents, may affect a woman's menstrual cycle. Exposure to alkylating agents, lead, mercury, DDT, lindane, toxaphene, PCBs, PBBs, and cadmium has been associated with altered menses. These agents also have led to ovarian atrophy, as has azathioprine. Exposure to the herbicide 2,4-D has lead to infertility in women.

Future Trends

As more women enter the paid workforce and remain in the active workforce for ever-increasing periods of time, more women will be exposed to occupational hazards. Because employed women's home and caregiving responsibilities are not likely to diminish, it is essential that society establish greater social supports and services in order to help working women cope with so much work and stress. More research is needed into the hazards of female-dominated jobs, including the ways that the work is organized. The economic value and social prestige of traditional women's employment also should be reconsidered, because women continue to be paid far less than men for their labor. In order to accomplish many of these goals, better surveillance of health and its relationship to workplace conditions is urgently required.

See Also

HEALTH CHALLENGES; HEALTH: OVERVIEW; WORK: EQUAL PAY AND CONDITIONS; WORK: OCCUPATIONAL EXPERIENCES; WORK: OCCUPATIONAL SEGREGATION; WORK: PATTERNS

References and Further Reading

Goldman, M., and M. Hatch. 2000. *Women and health.* New York: Academic.

International Union, UAW v. Johnson Controls, Inc. 111 Supreme Court, 1196, 1991.

Messing, K. 1998. *One-eyed science.* Philadelphia: Temple University Press.

Stellman, J. M., ed. 1998. *Encyclopaedia of occupational health and safety.* 4th ed. Geneva: ILO.

———. 1999. Women workers: The social construction of a special working population and the hazards they face on the job. *State of the Art Reviews* 14(3):559–581.

United Nations. 1995. *The world's women 1995: Trends and statistics, social statistics and indicators.* Series K, No. 12. New York: United Nations.

Wikander, Ulla, Alice Kessler–Harris, and Jane Lewis, eds. 1995. *Protecting women: Labor legislation in Europe, the United States and Australia, 1880–1920.* Urbana: University of Illinois Press.

Jeanne Mager Stellman

OCCUPATIONAL SEGREGATION

See WORK: OCCUPATIONAL SEGREGATION.

OESTROGEN

See ESTROGEN.

OLD AGE

See AGING.

ONCOLOGY

See CANCER.

ONLINE EDUCATION

See EDUCATION: ONLINE.

ONLINE RESOURCES

See REFERENCE SOURCES *and* THIRD WORLD WOMEN: SELECTED RESOURCES.

ORAL CONTRACEPTIVES

See THE PILL.

ORAL TRADITION

The term *oral tradition* refers broadly to the whole body of a population's knowledge that is passed by word of mouth from one generation to another. In some cultures, oral tradition is the primary medium of transmission; in the postmodern West, it is just one of several communicative media and interacts simultaneously with print and electronic channels. Students of oral tradition have stressed the verbal arts—aesthetic practices largely learned and transmitted orally. They also study particular genres of vernacular expressivity, kinds of verbal art, and forms of oral tradition—from the conversational to the performative. Women and gender-linked materials are central to the study of oral tradition.

Feminist scholars in particular have begun to explore and examine women's verbal art. They have tried to determine, for instance, if it is different from men's—in style, topic, genre, context, or function. Numerous studies suggest some tentative conclusions: that in general, men and women use the same genres, but they may select thematic topics of gendered interest; that women often "perform" their materials most successfully in private, intimate settings, often among female peers; and that women's style may be more connective and less competitive than that of men. The relationship of women and men to oral tradition is clearly linked to the larger cultural context, and specifically to gender roles and expectations; as culture has changed and continues to change, so access to oral traditions is altered.

Perhaps the quintessential oral form is conversation, and so scholars in sociolinguistics look for repeated patterns of tradition within ordinary discourse. Various genres such as sayings, proverbs, jokes, and other narrative forms are often embedded in talk. Conversation itself may be rule governed; there may be unstated rules of politeness for instance, that determine interactions. Studies of women's consciousness-raising groups suggest that in effective conversation, everyone should have a turn at speaking, collaborative building of topics from similar experiences is common, and competitive breaking into another's discourse is frowned on. There also are unarticulated rules for gossiping, which, as a conversational form, is very much about comparative identity: an individual comments on the behavior, dress, or attitudes of an absent other to someone familiar with the missing individual in such a way as to affirm her own perspectives. Analysts have suggested that women tend to talk with a rising intonation, that they use many descriptive words and phrases, and that they take particular care to connect their conversational contributions with those previously offered.

Various narrative forms are often routinely shared in conversational settings, particularly the personal experience story—an account of something that happened to the speaker that has been told frequently enough to have been shaped by traditional patterns. These autobiographical moments often recount periods or episodes of heightened identity, such as a lesbian coming-out story, or an account of an interaction with an authority figure. Personal experience narratives are presentations of self. Legends—often-told stories with a believable core—also figure prominently in conversations. Some forms, such as "urban legends" may recount stories of the discovery of inappropriate matter in fast food; others, more age-linked, may describe adolescent fears of haunted places and escaped convicts, and are favorite slumber-party fare.

Special attention has been paid to performance of verbal arts—to tellers of tales and singers of songs. The formal study of oral tradition originated in the eighteenth and nineteenth centuries with the interest of European scholars in narrative forms they found preserved in the vernacular language. Early folklorists often collected oral traditions with the aim of demonstrating "national character." *Märchen,* or Germanic fairy tales, are fictional accounts that feature stories set in unnamed kingdoms in far-away places and times, usually with royalty as characters, magical occurrences, and a successful denouement that typically involves a main character's rise from obscurity. Although folk tales are told by both men and women, some studies suggest that the very selection of stories to be learned and retold reflects individual concerns. Thus, one Hungarian woman expanded a seemingly insignificant aspect of a narrative to underline the fact that "women's work is never done."

The earliest studies focused on the national character of tales in the vernacular language, but subsequent study has affirmed the existence of similar tales in many parts of the world and has led to the development of tale type indices that aid the recognition and cataloguing of similar materials. Other studies have focused on form rather than content, and on interpretation of narrative meaning. More recently, scholars have shown an interest in studying the entire repertories of gifted performers, connecting tales, songs, and other verbal forms to their individual and collective contexts. Other scholars are focusing on particular performance situations—the nuances of interactions between performer and audience, and how best to transfer the oral performance to the printed page. There is a lively contemporary interest in reviving storytelling in the postmodern West, where folk oral transmission of *Märchen* and other complex tales has all but ceased.

Still other scholars are studying women singers of traditional songs—lyric folksongs, lullabies, and particularly ballads, or stories told in song. Some debate surrounds the movement of certain "commonplaces" or formulae from one ballad example to the next. What, for instance, might account for the similarity of structure—especially the pairing of characters, stanzas, and actions in twos and threes?

The repertory of a late-eighteenth-century Scottish woman, Mrs. Brown of Falkland, has been used to support the idea that the classic ballads were orally formulated, re-created in each performance using formulae and familiar structuring devices. This theory (first published by Albert Lord in 1960) would account for variations that occur from performance to performance.

Oral tradition is a communicative resource available to all people in all times and places. As such, it has been nurtured by all those who privilege face-to-face communication. Among women, oral traditions remain conversational and performative options, richly patterned ways of connecting with others—family, friends, neighbors—in twice-told tale and song, with old sayings and stories, with proverbs, and in predictable and recognizable styles.

See Also

AUTOBIOGRAPHY; COMMUNICATIONS: SPEECH; FAIRY TALES

References and Further Reading

Abrahams, Roger. 1970. *A singer and her songs: Almeda Riddle's book of ballads.* Baton Rouge: Louisiana State University Press.

Degh, Linda. 1969. *Folktales and society: Story-telling in a Hungarian peasant community.* Bloomington: Indiana University Press.

Farrer, Claire, ed. 1975. *Women and folklore.* Austin: University of Texas Press.

Jordan, Rosan A., and Susan J. Kalcik, eds. 1985. *Women's folklore, women's culture.* Philadelphia: University of Pennsylvania Press.

Pentikainen, Juha. 1978. *Oral repertoire and world view: An anthropological study of Marina Takalo's life history.* Helsinki: Suomalaihen Tiedeakatemia.

Radner, Joan Newlon, ed. 1993. *Feminist messages: Coding in women's folk culture.* Urbana: University of Illinois Press.

Spacks, Patricia Meyer. 1986. *Gossip.* Chicago: University of Chicago Press.

Mary Ellen Brown

ORGANIZATIONAL THEORY

Organizational theory is the analysis of the theoretical assumptions that underlie how and why people organize. In traditional or modernist organizational analysis, organizational participants are sexually neutral; the organization is understood as a fixed and presumably hierarchical structure; power is inseparable from either the position or the person; reason is an arbiter, and efficiency a goal; and managers and their skills are the preeminent vehicles of organizing.

Feminist organizational theorists have different categories of analysis and different questions. What they want to find out does not preclude analyzing how to get work done better, but their approach introduces questions rendered irrelevant by the traditional or modernist approach to organizational theory, which is primarily a technocratic theory of *management.* Very broadly, feminist theorists have focused on how power and the sexually specific subject intersect, how unequal relations are constructed between and among those who organize, and how the processes of organizing are linked to female emancipation. In ways that traditional organizational theory cannot, feminists have questioned both the means and the ends of organizing, asking: For what purpose? And: Who benefits?

Initial feminist analyses of organizations focused on moving women into organizations, primarily into management. They either emphasized women's essential sameness to men—and, therefore, the irrationality and inefficiency of excluding women from positions of power—or they emphasized women's essential difference from men and, hence, their ability to reform organizations through their innate nurturing or caring qualities. In the popular press and in most standard organizational texts, where women are mentioned at all, these views continue to hold sway.

Later feminist theorists changed their focus. In order to consider the broader question of the relationship between the means and the ends of organizing, they turned to the analysis of organizational structure and, in particular, to an analysis of hierarchical structures. Rather than presuming their efficiency and rationality, feminists focused on the creation and re-creation of relations of domination and subordination within hierarchy, and the inconsistency of those processes with feminist goals of emancipation. This focus is most clearly seen in Ferguson (1984), Brown (1992), and Young (1993). Kathy Ferguson, drawing on the work of Michel Foucault, emphasizes that bureaucratic discourse is inseparable from hierarchical relations of domination and subordination, and she links bureaucracy to the inevitable marginalization and exclusion of women. In *Women Organising,* Helen Brown maintains that all the skills of organizing—including those most often associated with management, such as leading and political strategizing—can be learned and shared by all the participants as they organize, and that this form of organizing is indispensable if larger political goals are to be achieved. Kate Young concurs in her work on women in development and the transformative role of politically adept nongovernmental organizations. Working in an area that deserves a closer look by feminist organizational theorists, Young links successful advocacy to nonhierarchical forms of organizing; she points out that those development organizations that are nonhierarchical are the most effective in contributing to women's development.

In the 1990s, the struggle to accommodate the insights of postmodernist philosophers like Foucault, Jacques Derrida, and Luce Irigaray to the political project of feminist organizational analysis has moved feminist theorists to a notion of organizing as discursive strategies—the speech or talk that positions participants as it organizes—or, following Irigaray, as discursive strategies operating within a sexually indifferent symbolic order of myth, stories, ceremonies, and language that has no place for sexual difference as other than lesser or "erased." In this form of analysis, organizational theory itself becomes a ritual of male projections masquerading as a tale with a neutral subject. An important work by Calas and Smircich (1991) exemplifies this approach. Using Derrida, they deconstruct the definition of *leader* to show how it is predicated on a notion of maleness that continually rewrites femaleness as lesser. In doing so, they call into question both the prevailing theories of organizations and the organizing strategies through which women are to attain emancipation. If women are constantly reconstructed as lesser in our present, sexually indifferent symbolic order of myth, religion, language, stories, and ceremonies—through which our organizing strategies are given expression—what are women to do?

Some feminist organizational theorists use the work of Luce Irigaray and her theorizing of juxtaposed sexual differences to evade this relentless repression or erasure of women in organizations. Irigaray emphasizes that in our present, sexually indifferent symbolic structure, women are either erased in the guise of sameness to men or are consigned to the place of the different as lesser. By theorizing sexual difference as contiguous, however, Irigaray creates a place for subject-to-subject positions that provide for new forms of social organization not based on relations of domination. These contiguous relations form the basis for *entrustment,* a transformational organizing strategy through which the woman who wants is linked to the woman who knows in order to accomplish what neither can separately. This is an organizational move in which women's collective advancement is predicated neither on the erasure of women as the same as men, nor on their repression as lesser; it opens up organizing strategies that allow women to shape organizations in a way that suits them.

See Also

DIFFERENCE I; DIFFERENCE II; ESSENTIALISM; LEADERSHIP; MANAGEMENT; POLITICAL LEADERSHIP

References and Further Reading

Brown, Helen. 1992. *Women organizing.* London: Routledge.

Calas, Marta, and Linda Smircich. 1991. Voicing seduction to silence leadership. *Organization Studies* 12(4): 567–601.

Ferguson, Kathy. 1984. *The feminist case against bureaucracy.* Philadelphia: Temple University Press.

Irigaray, L. 1991. Women-amongst themselves: Creating a woman to woman sociality. In Margaret Whitford, ed., *The Irigaray reader,* 190–197. Oxford: Basil Blackwell.

Johansson, Ulla. 1998. The transformation of gendered work: Diabolical stereotype and paradoxical reality. *Gender, Work and Organization* 5(1):43–58.

Kanter, Rosabeth M. 1977. *Men and women of the corporation.* New York: Basic Books.

Lewis, Debra, with Jan Barnsley. 1992. *Strategies for change: From women's experience to a plan for action.* Vancouver: Women's Research Centre.

The Milan Women's Bookstore Collective, eds. 1990. *Sexual difference: A theory of social-symbolic practice.* Bloomington: Indiana University Press.

Oseen, Collette. 1997. Luce Irigaray, sexual difference and theorizing leaders and leadership. *Gender, Work and Organization* 4(3):170–184.

Young, Kate. 1993. *Planning development with women.* New York: St. Martin's.

Collette Oseen

OTHER

The French philosopher Simone de Beauvoir (1908–1986) is credited with publishing the first extensive analysis of the way in which women are defined as the "other"—the ways in which women are invisible in culture and in which female experience is ignored. De Beauvoir argued that man was the subject, the norm, and that women were *defined* as the "other." Men are defined positively, and women negatively. Woman is not just different from man, but the antithesis of man. To be like a man is to be not like a woman—woman is "that-by-which-men-define-themselves-as-not-being" (Haste, 1993: 6).

Women are defined from a male perspective. Men are seen as cultured, as rational, as the possessors of scientific knowledge. Women are seen as "natural" and as the object of scientific knowledge rather than its producers. They are seen as controlled by their bodies and their hormones. Scientific knowledge, of which men are the possessors, is concerned with controlling nature, and by derivation "natural" woman is controlled by "cultured" man. De Beauvoir thought that by accepting themselves as defined by men—as other to men—women allowed themselves to be dominated by men.

Feminists have challenged man-made "scientific" definitions of women and men's dominance as definers of reality. While some feminists have argued for androgyny, others have stressed the need for discourses that offer self-definitions for women that value their unique characteristics as much as those of men—or more.

See Also

FEMINISM: EXISTENTIAL; GENDER; REPRESENTATION

References and Further Reading

Beauvoir, Simone de. 1972 (1949). *The second sex.* Harmondsworth, U.K.: Penguin.

Haste, Helen. 1993. *The sexual metaphor.* Hemel Hempstead, U.K.: Harvester Wheatsheaf.

Holland, Janet, Caroline Ramazanoglu, Sue Sharpe, and Rachel Thomson. 1998. *The male in the head: Young people, heterosexuality and power.* London: Tufnell.

Pamela Abbott

P

PACIFISM AND PEACE ACTIVISM

Opposition to war or violence is not the sole domain of women. Also, just as, over the millennia, there have been women who have opposed conflicts, there have been others who have promoted wars. Yet, traditionally, women have been viewed as the more peace-loving gender because of their roles in child rearing and in maintaining the tranquillity and stability of the home.

The need for pacifism and peace activism can be summed up in this one figure: Between 1496 B.C. and A.D. 1941, there were 3,357 documented wars—about one per year (Meltzer, 1985: 10). Since 1941, there have been one world war, several major conflicts (Korea, Vietnam, Iraq-Iran, Afghanistan), numerous civil wars (Central America, former colonial holdings in Africa and Asia, Chechnya), assorted regional crises (India–Pakistan, Middle East, Northern Ireland), and the occasional genocide (Cambodia, Rwanda, Bosnia).

Early History

The role of women throughout history, at least as recorded in history books, has not been one of authority, so their impact on the waging of wars until fairly recently was minimal. Still, there are examples of women pacifists and activists.

One of the earliest recorded examples is Hatshepsut (c. 1540–1481 B.C.), who ruled Egypt with her husband and half brother, Thotmes II, and continued to rule after his death. Her 20-year reign was noted as a peaceful and prosperous period, a time of increased trade with other countries, in contrast to that of preceding pharaohs, who had expanded the empire through the power of the Egyptian armies.

Greek amphora record scenes of women in two roles: arming warriors and greeting returning warriors, dead or alive. In scenes of departure, women, assumed to be mothers, bestow arms on the males. One krater (c. 450 B.C.) shows a young warrior receiving his helmet and shield from a woman, who passes them over an altar (Pantel, 1992: 175). The mythological source of this scene is Thetis bestowing arms on her son Achilles. In scenes of return, women, assumed to be wives, are shown in mourning, bestowing gifts on the dead. In the quintessentially male domain of warfare, women were the lone welcoming committee of slain heroes. In either case, women, as wives or mothers, are keepers of the *oikos* (household), of peace, as men go off to war.

An early example of nonviolent protest led by women occurred in 195 B.C., when women took to the streets of Rome to object to a law that barred women from wearing purple and gold in public and riding in horse-drawn carriages in town, both signs of state (thus male) authority. The law was repealed (Brill, 1997: 20–21).

Despite the Beatitudes' praise of peacemakers, the rise of Christianity eventually led to the spread of war through the Crusades. Women participated in church-sponsored Truce of God campaigns, which called for a limit to the days on which fighting could take place and a prohibition against the involvement of or attacks on women, nuns, clergy, peasants, and shepherds, among others (Elshtain, 1987: 99).

The Middle Ages in Europe saw the establishment of home as a symbol of stability. Following Aristotelian texts, as well as the teachings of St. Augustine, the focus of women's peace activism was the home, not the state. The Franciscan Gilbert of Tournai (d. 1284) used St. Jerome's pleas and the biblical model of Judith to remind women that their duty was to provide a quiet area in the home for prayer, thus transforming domestic space into religious space and women into keepers of the peaceful home fires (Klapisch-Zyber, 1992: 127).

In Japan, women were attracted to the *samurai* (warrior-aristocrats) concept of *bushido* ("the way of the warrior"). Like their counterparts who had been recorded for posterity on Grecian urns, the wives of *samurai* watched and prepared themselves for the worst when their husbands left home to serve the *daimyo* (feudal lord). An eighth-century poem by one *samurai* wife, Yosami, tells of her sorrow at the news of her husband's death following battle:

> Day after day I've longed for my husband,
> thinking each day he would return.
> Now they tell me that he lies buried
> in the Canyon of Stone River. (Knapp, 1992: 20)

In North America, Iroquois tradition speaks of Jigonsasee (Great Peace Woman), who was directed by the prophet Deganawidah to preserve the "Good Tidings of Peace and Power, so that the human race may live in peace in the future" (Rappaport, 1990: 40). She accomplished this by refusing to feed the tribe's warriors until they agreed to live in peace. Later generations of Iroquois women took on the role of peace brokers between warring tribes.

In colonial America, "peace" churches—the Society of Friends (Quakers), Brethren, Mennonites, Rogerenes, and Schwekenfelders—all of whom opposed war as a matter of Christian principle, were among the first to oppose conflict between European settlers and Native Americans. Women were especially active in the Society of Friends, urging nonviolence and later supporting conscientious objectors during the revolution.

The late eighteenth century witnessed women-led protests in various parts of the world for peace and freedom: bread riots in France, challenges to colonial rule in South Africa and Spanish-controlled Central America, and antislavery demonstrations in Europe, among others.

Peace and Other Issues

In the nineteenth century in the United States, peace activism on the part of women was associated with the abolitionist movement. Organizations such as the American Peace Society and the New England Non-Resistance Society linked the abolition of slavery and pacifism. Two prominent figures were Angelina (1805–1879) and Sarah (1792–1873) Grimké, the only southern white women to become leading abolitionists. The sisters became the first female agents of the American Anti-Slavery Society; their lectures drew large audiences of both men and women. They were especially influential at the 1837 Anti-Slavery Convention of American Women, introducing resolutions against racial prejudice. Their pamphlets included *Appeal to the Women of the Nominally Free States* and *Epistle to the Clergy of the Southern States* (both 1836). In 1838, Angelina Grimké became the first American woman to address a legislative body, the Massachusetts legislature, when she presented tens of thousands of antislavery petitions that had been collected by women.

Another figure was Lucretia Mott (1793–1880), a Quaker who helped found the Philadelphia Female Anti-Slavery Society in 1833 and served as its president. She became prominent in the national organization after it admitted women. In 1840, Mott was denied a seat at the World Anti-Slavery Convention because of her gender. As a result, she lectured outside the hall where the meeting was being held, calling for female equality (Clinton, 1991: 753–754). Mott went on to help organize the meeting in Seneca Falls, New York, in 1848 that launched the women's rights movement in the United States.

Also taking an active role in the elimination of slavery, Harriet Tubman (1815?–1913) is best known as a "conductor" on the Underground Railroad, which brought escaping slaves from the South to the North and freedom. Tubman also helped in the planning of John Brown's raid on Harpers Ferry, Virginia (now West Virginia), in 1858 and served as a nurse, scout, and spy for Union forces during the American Civil War. In 1896, she appeared at the organizing meeting of the National Association of Colored Women, encouraging her listeners to continue their struggle for respect and equality.

The actions of these abolitionists and others set the groundwork for the emerging women's rights movement. Abolition, peace activism, and equality for women were part of a chain that led to women's suffrage, in the United States and elsewhere. It was a natural link. The abolitionist movement had encouraged women to become activists, from participating in organizations promoting antislavery to boycotting products from slaveholding states and countries to actively aiding the war cause. Women's rights as citizens were the next focus. Among the early abolitionists-turned-women's rights activists in the United States were Elizabeth Cady Stanton (1815–1902) and Susan B. Anthony (1820–1906). Julia Ward Howe (1819–1910), an abolitionist and women's rights advocate, turned her energies to uniting women worldwide in a peace movement. In reaction to the Franco-Prussian War of 1870–1871, she wrote an antiwar article, "Appeal to Womanhood throughout the World," that called on women "to unite across national borders to prevent the waste of human life which they alone bear and know the cost" (Swerdlow, 1993: 27). Ironically, Ward is best remembered for her poem "The Battle Hymn of the Republic," which was set to the music of "John Brown's Body" and became a rousing patriotic tune.

"Lay Down Your Arms!"

In Europe in the late nineteenth century, women, and men, reacted to the seemingly endless conflicts that resulted from empire building. The writer Bertha von Suttner (1843–1914), an Austrian aristocrat, was one of the most outspoken advocates for peace in Europe and the world. Derided as a "shrew of peace" and a "hysterical bluestocking" (Fraisse and Perrot, 1993: 511), she organized hundreds of pacifist meetings and tried to persuade politicians of the logic of peacemaking. Her masterpiece—the antiwar novel *Lay Down Your Arms!*—tells of the horrors of the recent Prussian campaigns and ends with its heroine whispering to an unhearing world: "Lay down your arms!" (Lengyel, 1975: 77). Suttner inspired her friend, the Swedish inventor and advocate of world peace Alfred Nobel, to create his Peace Prize. She was the first woman to receive it (in 1905)—indeed, the first woman to receive any Nobel Prize. (See the table for other women who have won the Nobel Peace Prize.)

The first international gathering of pacifist women was held in The Hague, Netherlands, in 1899. The conference was the result of efforts by the International Council of Women, a global women's suffrage organization. Speakers proclaimed that the "woman question" and the "peace question" were inseparable: "Both are in essence a struggle for the power of law and against the law of power" (Fraisse and Perrot, 1993: 504).

By 1914, feminism was an international movement that combined two causes: winning women the right to vote and proclaiming peace. With the declaration of war in Europe that year, however, the emphasis switched to organizing for peace. The Woman's Peace Party was founded in January 1915 at a women's peace rally organized by Jane Addams (1860–1935), the social reformer and founder of Hull House. During the war, Addams spoke out against the violence and was vilified for her efforts. After the armistice, she helped found the Women's International League for Peace and Freedom, serving as its president from 1919 until her death in 1935. In 1931, she was awarded the Nobel Peace Prize.

Other organizations that rallied against World War I included the International Congress for the Future Peace, organized by, among other feminists, Jane Addams of the United States and Dr. Aletta Jacobs of the Netherlands; the International Women's Committee for the Permanent Peace, which in 1919 became the Women's International League for Peace and Freedom (WILPF; the league is the oldest extant women's peace organization); and the National Civil Liberties Bureau, organized by Crystal Eastman (1881–1928), a lawyer and journalist who helped establish the bureau to protect conscientious objectors and "to maintain something over here that will be worth coming back to when the weary war is over" (Cook, 1991: 307). Although Eastman was never fully credited as the founder of the organization, which became the American Civil Liberties Union, she was the attorney in charge.

Following the war, and the successful campaign for the right to vote (achieved, for example, before the end of World War I in Australia, Finland, New Zealand, Norway, Denmark, the Netherlands, and the Soviet Union; in 1918 in Sweden, Great Britain, Germany, and Austria; and in 1920 in the United States and Canada), organized efforts by women's groups to maintain peace continued. The Red Scare of the 1920s in the United States created some casualties among organizers, who were linked with socialists and suspected of plotting the overthrow of the government. Among the casualties was Emily Greene Balch (1867–1961), a leader of the WILPF, who was dismissed from her teaching position at Wellesley College because of her antiwar activities. Balch was awarded the Nobel Peace Prize in 1946.

Groups active in the United States in the period before World War II included the Women's Peace Union, which sought a constitutional amendment to make war illegal, and the National Committee on the Cause and Cure of War, an umbrella organization of women's organizations that supported the Kellogg-Briand Pact outlawing war. Individuals included Dorothy Day (1897–1980), a peace activist and founder of the Catholic Worker movement. But war came

Winners of the Nobel Peace Prize

- 1905. Baroness Bertha von Suttner. Austrian honored for her writing and work opposing war.
- 1931. Jane Addams. International president, Women's International League for Peace and Freedom.
- 1946. Emily Greene Balch. Honored for her pacifism and work for peace through a variety of organizations.
- 1976. Betty Williams and Mairead Corrigan. Founders of the Northern Ireland peace movement to bring together Protestants and Catholics to work for peace.
- 1979. Mother Teresa. Honored for her "work in bringing help to suffering humanity" and her respect for individual human dignity.
- 1982. Alva Myrdal. Honored with Alfonso García Robles for their work with the United Nations on disarmament.
- 1991. Aung San Suu Kyi. Burmese activist honored for nonviolent work for human rights in Myanmar.
- 1992. Rigoberta Menchú Tum. Honored for her work for "ethno-cultural reconciliation based on respect for the rights of indigenous peoples."
- 1997. Jody Williams. Honored for her work with the International Campaign to Ban Landmines.

Source: <http://womenshistory.miningco.com/education/womenshistory/msobnobel.htm>

despite the efforts of such groups and individuals. Although many groups in the United States and other countries maintained their pacifist position during World War II, others supported the war effort. In 1943, for example, the National Committee on the Cause and Cure of War became the Women's Action Committee for Victory and Lasting Peace. (After the war, the words *Victory and* were dropped.) The committee, including the former suffragist Carrie Chapman Catt (1859–1947), supported the idea of the United Nations and accepted the fact that U.S. "boys" would have "to be prepared to fight to uphold the rule of law... before war spreads all over the world" (Alonso, 1993: 152).

The use of atomic bombs in 1945 brought new urgency on the part of peace groups. In the aftermath of the war, the focus became opposition to the arms race and the growing tensions leading to the cold war. Organizations included the Women's International Democratic Federation and the Congress of American Women. Their efforts were viewed with suspicion, given the growing anticommunist sentiment. In 1950, for example, the Department of Justice ordered the board of the Congress of American Women to register as "foreign agents." The group voted to disband but reemerged as American Women for Peace, only to succumb by 1953 (Alonso, 1993: 190).

Recent History

Growing unrest, fear of the nuclear arms buildup, and a greater resolve led to increased activity on the part of groups. Among the first actions was Women Strike for Peace, organized in 1961, in Washington, D.C., by concerned mothers led by Dagmar Wilson. The group held demonstrations, organized marches, and arranged petition drives against the nuclear arms race. On November 1, 1961, the group led a one-day strike of some 50,000 women across the United States. To avoid "pro-Red" charges, the group members distanced themselves from other pacifist groups like the WILPF.

This was just the start. With the Vietnam War, the numerous civil wars in Africa and Asia in the former colonial holdings, tension in the Middle East, the push for civil rights by African-Americans, and growing unrest on the part of youth throughout the world, the peace movement gained momentum. Actions were not just on the part of organized groups, however. In Vietnam, Nhat Chi Mai, a Buddhist nun, immolated herself in protest against the war. She left the following letter to explain her action:

> I offer my body as a torch
> to dissipate the dark
> to waken love among men
> to give peace to Vietnam

It was signed "The one who burns herself for peace" (Cambridge Women's Peace Collective, 1984: 178).

The women's peace movement in the 1960s and 1970s took on various issues: war resistance (for example, Women Strike for Peace, War Resisters League, Another Mother for Peace, and other groups held mass rallies), civil rights (in the United States, Coretta Scott King [b. 1927] and others sought to work through groups such as the Southern Christian Leadership Conference), tensions in Northern Ireland (peace movement led by Betty Williams and Mairead Corrigan, who were awarded the Nobel Peace Prize for their efforts), atomic bomb testing (for example, Helen Caldicott [b. 1939], an Australian pediatrician, organized opposition to French atomic bomb testing in the South Pacific in 1971; she went on to head Physicians for Social Responsibility), and nuclear energy (demonstrations led by women against nuclear power stations, including Torness in Britain), to name only a few.

The 1980s witnessed growing resistance to the nuclear arms race. Activities included the Women's Pentagon Action in 1980 and 1981; a 1982 joint tour of Britain by Soviet and American women sponsored by Mothers for Peace; and the Ribbon Project in 1985, which featured such creative and dramatic protests as a 10-mile "ribbon" around the Pentagon.

One of the most striking types of protests during this period was the peace camp. Of particular importance was the Greenham Common Women's Peace Camp near London. The camp was established to protest the NATO decision to place cruise missiles at the Greenham Common airbase for the U.S. Air Force. More than 30,000 women participated in the camp over the next decade and a half. The last of the protesters left on 1 January 2000, with the site being set aside as a peace memorial.

Peace efforts have continued, both through groups and by individuals. In the Middle East, for example, Hanan Ashrawi, a principal spokesperson for the Palestinian cause, was instrumental in bringing the Palestine Liberation Organization to the negotiating table. The organization Four Mothers protested the Israeli presence in Lebanon. Yona Rochlin, a homemaker-turned-activist, has helped to organize descendants of former Jewish residents of Hebron to counteract the hard-line stance of Jewish settlers there and develop peaceful coexistence between the Jewish and Muslim populations.

In Guatemala, Rigoberta Menchú Tum (b. 1959) voiced the plight of refugees and victims of the military crackdown there. In 1992, she was awarded the Nobel Peace Prize. Her efforts today focus on the struggle for Indian peasants' rights not only in Guatemala but throughout the Western Hemisphere.

One focus of the current women's peace movement has been the use of antipersonnel landmines in numerous areas of conflict throughout the world. In 1997, the International Campaign to Ban Landmines (ICBL), represented by its coordinator, Jody Williams (b. 1950), was awarded the Nobel Peace Prize. The ICBL was an important force behind the convention to ban landmines signed in Ottawa in December 1997 by more than 120 countries.

In Africa, women's organizations, including the Rwanda Women's Network, have been active in helping to resolve conflicts and deal with the aftermath of regional and civil wars, especially AIDS and refugee displacement. In Sudan, women have held meetings on how to be part of the peace process. In Uganda, women are beginning to assert authority over some of the youngest soldiers, often children, and are fighting the abduction of young people by guerrilla bands. In Somalia, one woman, Starlin Arush, set up a demobilization program, in which young guerrilla soldiers exchanged guns for food, shelter, and education (Crossette, 2000: 4).

From protests against the use of child soldiers in Sudan to street rallies against policy decisions by the World Trade Organization, World Bank, and International Monetary Fund, peace activism continues, and women are often at the forefront.

See Also

FEMINISM: NINETEENTH CENTURY; FEMINISM: SECOND-WAVE BRITISH; FEMINISM: SECOND-WAVE EUROPEAN; FEMINISM: SECOND-WAVE NORTH AMERICAN; INTERNATIONAL ORGANIZATIONS AND AGENCIES; MILITARY; NONGOVERNMENTAL ORGANIZATIONS (NGOS); NUCLEAR WEAPONS; PEACE MOVEMENTS; WAR

References and Further Reading

Alonso, Harriet Hyman. 1993. *Peace as a women's issue: A history of the U.S. movement for world peace and women's rights.* Syracuse, N.Y.: Syracuse University Press.

Blight, David W. 1991. Truth, Sojourner. In Eric Foner and John A. Garraty, eds., *The reader's companion to American history,* 1087–1088. Boston: Houghton Mifflin.

Brill, Marlene Targ. 1997. *Women for peace.* New York: Franklin Watts.

Cambridge Women's Peace Collective, comp. 1984. *My country is the whole world: An anthology of women's work on peace and war.* London: Pandora.

Clinton, Catherine. 1991. Mott, Lucretia. In Eric Foner and John A. Garraty, eds., *The reader's companion to American history,* 753–754. Boston: Houghton Mifflin.

Cook, Blanche Wiesen. 1991. Eastman, Crystal. In Eric Foner and John A. Garraty, eds., *The reader's companion to American history,* 307. Boston: Houghton Mifflin.

Crossette, Barbara. 2000. Women seek louder voices as world peacemakers. *New York Times* (28 May): 4.

Elshtain, Jean Bethke. 1987. *Women and war.* New York: Basic Books.

Fraisse, Geneviève, and Michelle Perrot, eds. 1993. *A history of women.* Vol. 4, *Emerging feminism from revolution to world war.* Cambridge, Mass.: Harvard University Press.

Klapisch-Zyber, Christiane, ed. 1992. *A history of women.* Vol. 2, *Silences of the Middle Ages.* Cambridge, Mass.: Harvard University Press.

Knapp, Bettina L. 1992. *Images of Japanese women: A westerner's view.* Troy, N.Y.: Whitston.

Lengyel, Emil. 1975. *And all her paths were peace: The life of Bertha von Suttner.* Nashville and New York: Thomas Nelson.

Meltzer, Milton. 1985. *Ain't gonna study war no more.* New York: Harper and Row.

Pantel, Pauline Schmitt, ed. 1992. *A history of women.* Vol. 1, *From ancient goddesses to Christian saints.* Cambridge, Mass.: Harvard University Press.

Rappaport, Doreen. 1990. *American women: Their lives in their words.* New York: Crowell.

Swerdlow, Amy. 1993. *Women strike for peace.* Chicago: University of Chicago Press.

Laura Daly

PAINTING

See FINE ARTS: PAINTING.

PARENTHOOD

Parenthood refers to an adult's relationship to a child as either biological procreator or legal guardian. The term *parenting* refers to the act of looking after a child's daily needs and his or her socialization in accordance with cultural norms and expectations. Parenting and parenthood are divided differently between the sexes. The mother usually has primary responsibility over the daily care and nurturing of children, whereas the father is customarily considered the head of the household, with responsibility for any children in economic and legal terms.

According to Janice Drakich (1988), the legal right of fathers to children weakened in western countries with the privatization of the family and the emphasis on the male as wage earner. The mother–child bond became the focal relationship within the household as the family came to be seen as a source of emotional security. When divorced, mothers were increasingly awarded custody of their children. However, many mother-headed households faced poverty, due to women's lower wages, defaulted child support payments by the fathers, and the lack of social support.

Among twentieth-century trends in western countries, there is a shift away from parenthood toward couplehood as the central feature of family life, due to increased longevity and a lowered fertility rate (the latter is the result of postponed marriages, rising divorce rates, better birth control, and abortion, as well as changes in the roles of women and men). There is also an increasing stress on the commonalities between motherhood and fatherhood, related to rising maternal labor force participation and increased involvement in child care by fathers among the younger generations. These still rare highly involved fathers are usually satisfied with the experience, and children seem to benefit in terms of emotional and social adjustment (Stebbins, 1988).

The European emphasis on couplehood and marriage contrasts with the African stress on parenthood as the central relationship in families. In large parts of Africa, parenthood and especially grandparenthood are fulfillments of individual, kinship, religious, and political obligations. A child is born not only to its parents but also to a lineage, clan, and community that share parenting responsibilities. Polygyny is prevalent in west Africa, and there are strict rules about the legitimacy of children. In some areas of Africa, marriages are often not recognized until a child is produced (Fortes, 1978).

Social support for parenting varies around the world. In the West, women's increased labor force participation has led to calls for more government and community support for dual-earner families with children, through maternity leaves, parental leaves, and day care policies. A study by the present author, Vappu Tyyska (1995), of child care policies in Canada and Finland shows that the degree of development of these provisions depends, among other things, on the degree to which women have been able to secure positions in official politics. Thus in Finland, where women are well represented in the parliament, family policy is among the most comprehensive in the world and includes generous maternity and parental leaves, as well as universal day care and a system of mothers' wages.

See Also

CHILD CARE; HOUSEHOLDS AND FAMILIES: OVERVIEW; MOTHERHOOD

References and Further Reading

Drakich, Janice. 1988. In whose best interest? The politics of joint custody. In Bonnie Fox, ed., *Family bonds and gender divisions: Readings in the sociology of the family.* Toronto: Canadian Scholars' Press.

Fortes, Meyer. 1978. Parenthood, marriage and fertility in west Africa. *Journal of Development Studies* 14(4): 121–149.

Stebbins, Robert A. 1988. Men, husbands and fathers: Beyond patriarchal relations. In Nancy Mandell and Ann Duffy, eds. *Reconstructing the Canadian family: Feminist perspectives.* Toronto and Vancouver: Butterworth.

Tyyska, Vappu. 1995. *The politics of caring and the welfare state: The impact of the women's movement on child care policy in Canada and Finland, 1960–1990.* Helsinki: Federation of Finnish Scientific Societies.

Vappu Tyyska

PART-TIME AND CASUAL WORK

Part-time and casual are forms of *contingent work:* work that is less than permanent or less than full-time, or both. Contingent workers include homeworkers, seasonal and migrant workers, and temporary nonaward workers, whose jobs fall outside the criteria for workplace agreements and state and federal government award systems. Contingent workers earn less, have less job security, and have poorer award conditions than full-time workers. In the 1980s, almost half of all jobs created in industrialized economies were part-time and temporary, most in the service sector. Women, and particularly married women, hold the majority of these positions. Across 14 industrialized nations, Joni Seager and Ann Olson (1997: 19) document a range between 10 and 49 percent of women workers working part-time. Women as a proportion of all part-time workers varied from 65 percent in the United States to 90 percent of all part-time workers in Belgium and Germany. Sylvia Walby (1986: 207) argues that part-time work represents a "new form of the compromise between patriarchal and capitalist interests.... [W]omen's labor was made available to capital, but on terms which did not threaten to disrupt the patriarchal status quo in the household, since a married woman working part-time could still perform the full range of domestic tasks."

See Also

WORK: PATTERNS

References and Further Reading

Seager, Joni. 1997. *The state of women in the world atlas.* New rev., 2nd ed. London: Penguin.

Walby, Sylvia. 1986. *Patriarchy at work: Patriarchal and capitalist relations in employment.* Cambridge, U.K.: Polity.

Beverly Thiele

PATRIARCHY: Development

Patriarchy is best understood as an institution of power and authority that is interwoven with other dimensions of social and cultural life. Cross-culturally, the institution of patriarchy is frequently embedded in the framework of kinship, in which individual members are not simply categorized as "men" or "women," but as "fathers," "mothers," "sons," "daughters," "father's brothers," "mother's sisters," "paternal parallel cousins," "maternal cross-cousins," and so on. Gender intersects with a complex web of social relations and obligations; as a result, each individual embodies multiple roles that tend to be diacritical, relational, and situational. Literally "the rule of father," *patriarchy* refers to "elder male authority in a gerontocracy [that] provides reciprocal benefits to the subordinate females and youths in . . . societ[ies] where it prevails" (Nash, 1988: 15). Membership in the descent group defines each individual's primary rights and responsibilities as well as self-identity. Although patriarchy has emerged as the predominant form of social organization, historically the institution of patriarchy has been most prevalent in pastoral societies and early states in the Middle East and Asia, where women were subjugated to elder males within domestic or kin-based modes of production. In the case of early states, the social relations in the household were often appropriated by the state as a foundation of social order and social control.

Accordingly, patriarchy is not universal. Anthropological studies indicate that variation in gender status is closely related to rules of descent and postmarital residence (Stone, 1997), and ethnohistorical evidence shows that European colonization played a central role in spreading patriarchy in its modern form (Etienne and Leacock, 1980). Prior to European expansion and colonization, some societies were—and in a few cases, continue to be—matrilineal and uxorilocal (that is, a man leaves his natal family to join his wife at marriage), where women formed the center of the social fabric and were essential to the administration of political and legal authorities. Through uxorilocality, female kin were able to create solidarity clusters by living nearby to one another. Likewise, land and other valuable resources in matrilineal societies were allocated to individuals through their maternal affiliations. Yet it is important to note that matriliny is not synonymous with matriarchy, in the sense that females in a matrilineal society never assume the same degree of control over males as their male counterparts in a patrilineal society have often done to their female kin. Some feminist authors have argued that it is often the brothers of female kin, rather than the female kin themselves, who hold positions of power as well as make daily decisions in matrilineal societies. Although this is indeed true of the Trobriand Islanders of Papua New Guinea, one needs to keep in mind that males in a matrilineal society obtain authority through ties with their mothers, sisters, or wives (Weiner, 1976). This is very different from patrilineal societies (often with a virilocal postmarital residence pattern), where males form the core of the society, and around whom major social, political, and economic institutions revolve. By the same token, given the fact that women are the ones who bear children, the need to clearly and unambiguously ascertain the identity of the father causes perpetual anxiety among patrilineal societies, leading to great concern and control over women's bodies and sexuality, whereas in matrilineal societies fatherhood is much less an issue, as one's affiliation with a descent group derives from one's own mother, whose identity is more directly demonstrable. Ethnohistorical research also shows that gender roles and relations in many nonwestern small-scale societies were egalitarian, symmetrical, and complementary, where all adults participated fully in producing or manufacturing and in distributing and consuming food and other necessities.

Patriarchy and the World Economic Systems: A Historical Perspective

Frederick Engels (1972) attributed women's subjugation to the institution of private property, as human societies progressed into an industrial age in which surplus accumulation was made possible and preferable. Through the separation of the family from larger kin groups such as the clan and the institution of monogamy, Engels argued, the male became the dominant figure in the family, now a self-governing economic unit, and he was able to pass his individual property to his sons. Although Engels's formulation might have come close to the experience of western societies, historical and cross-cultural evidence has made it clear that his portrait of the preindustrial communal society—in which men, women, adults, and children worked together in family-centered enterprises and all participated in community life equally—is inaccurate; neither was his vision of women's liberation as a result of a fuller proletarianization of men and women in a later stage of the industrial revolution credible. Nevertheless, the link he made between patriarchy and capitalism became the entry point for the later understanding of gender and global capitalist expansion.

The distinction between forms of male dominance that rest on patriarchy and those whose male hegemony is imposed by other means played an essential role in clarifying the specific historical circumstances in which gender became a decisive factor in the world economic systems (Nash, 1988). In a society in which patriarchy preceded the penetration of European capital, capitalist institutions have often built on, and in turn strengthened, the preexisting patriarchal relations. One example was the lace makers in Narsapur, India (Mies, 1985). Although the rural lace industry was incorporated into the world market, the traditional production organization based on individual households continued to prevail. Women remained the primary workforce—often unpaid or underpaid—under the supervision of male household heads. Yet the persistence of patriarchy not only secured the control of men over their female family members' labor, thus ensuring a smooth operation of production, but also granted them the disposition of surpluses and profits by marketing women's household-produced commodities as well as the rights to redistributing resources. This further reinforced their authority in the family.

Similar situations are observed in rapidly industrializing east Asian countries. In Taiwan, where small-scale family-centered factories constitute an important part of the industrial sector, industrial-entrepreneurial families rely on female family members and children to provide a flexible workforce essential to compete in the ever-changing global economy. Family loyalty or filial piety is often called on to ensure their cooperation. Young Taiwanese women's roles in the family also made them an ideal source of cheap labor in Taiwan's early export industrialization. The patriarchal authority they faced in the family was often modeled by management of multinational firms to form discipline codes on the shop floor (Kung, 1994).

These processes differ from the promotion of male domination in developing nations, in which gender hierarchy was originally absent but was fostered by the introduction of capitalist enterprises. As a result of European expansion, gender symmetry and female autonomy among indigenous populations were frequently destroyed or weakened, and male dominance was imposed at the expense of women. The assault was twofold. First, European colonial processes had a general tendency to commodify local economies and to enforce the institutions of nuclear family and private property in land. These often favored men's access to money, means of production, and technical innovations in areas where women had traditionally acted as farmers and horticulturalists. Subsequently, women's control over and access to land, credit, and other resources were reduced, while at the same time they were excluded from newly created wage work. The transformation of the Iroquois society under European expansion and American colonization illustrates many of these changes. Prior to European contact, women in the matrilineal Iroquois society enjoyed a strategic position in social life. They were the major food producers and controlled the distribution of their crops on which Iroquois male hunters relied for their provision. Iroquois women also made decisions about which of their male kin would sit on the village council representing their lineages. The fur trade with Europeans temporarily enhanced Iroquois women's status. Yet the eventual introduction of a sedentary lifestyle, and the cultural ideology of—and legal provisions that supported—man-the-farmer and woman-the-homemaker by missionaries and the American government shattered the foundation of Iroquois social structure. This cost women their autonomy and social roles of significance.

Second, in societies where women were the preferred industrial labor force, they also were subjected to patriarchal ideologies that characterized them primarily as homemakers whose wages were only complementary to the family. Such ideological devaluation of women's labor provided a rationale for lower wages and introduced a wage gap between men and women. Yet a restructuring of local economies that reshapes job opportunities for both men and women often accompanies global industrialization. Many of these societies also had a high unemployment rate for men, because of changes in the local wage labor market, which obliged women to take paid work in order to support their families. This is evident in the early stages of the *maquiladoras* (Mexican assembly plants) along the U.S.–Mexican border (Fernandez-Kelly, 1983) and in the recent industrialization in the Caribbean (Safa, 1995), where the penetration of capitalist production accorded with a reorganization of the economies, notably the decline of jobs in traditional men's domains in the agricultural sector and a rapid increase in jobs in light industries that go to women. Women in these societies were thereby subjected to the double burden of being homemaker and wage worker, despite getting low pay.

From Private to Public Domain: Patriarchy and Global Industrialization

Under the worldwide incorporation of women into the wage labor force, women's subordination should no longer be defined solely by men's domination at home. With the development of industrial capitalism and modern nation-states, the primary focus of patriarchy has shifted from the private to the public sphere (Safa, 1995). That is, despite the fact that women's contribution to the family economy may have helped to redefine their roles at home and changed the gender dynamics in the household, the cultural ideology of the male breadwinner has been absorbed in the workplace and by the state. Women's productive labor remains undervalued in the workplace, making them dependent on the state's labor protection policy and social programs, whereas their reproductive roles are emphasized in the state policy of many countries.

This is exemplified in the shift of the Dominican economy from one based on agrarian industries to one based on manufacturing and exporting light consumer goods (Safa, 1995). In the new economy, women are the favored workers in export processing zones, whereas men have lost their traditional jobs on sugar plantations. Women's earning ability in the industrial sector may have won them recognition as well as granted them a greater voice in their families, but their wage-earning power has not fundamentally challenged the perception of gender roles (that is, men as the breadwinners) in the workplace. On the contrary, women are the preferred labor force precisely because of their designated role as secondary wage earners. Export-oriented industrialization has thus reinforced their subordination through poorly paid, dead-end jobs, while at the same time resulting in a decline of the total family income that impoverished the average families. Hence, women's participation in paid work cannot simply be taken as a sign of liberation but is a result of local economic restructuring within the global context, which brought both positive and negative effects to women's and men's lives. To focus on the change in women's status at home, and especially on the conjugal bond, thus misses the crucial and defining features of the new international division of labor.

See Also

ANCIENT INDIGENOUS CULTURES: WOMEN'S ROLES; ANCIENT NATION-STATES: WOMEN'S ROLES; ANTHROPOLOGY; COLONIALISM AND POSTCOLONIALISM; DIVISION OF LABOR; GLOBALIZATION; INDUSTRIALIZATION; MATRILINEAL SYSTEMS; PATRIARCHY: FEMINIST THEORY

References and Further Reading

Engels, Frederick. 1972. *The origin of the family, private property and the state.* New York: International.

Etienne, Mona, and Eleanor Leacock, eds. 1980. *Women and colonization: Anthropological perspectives.* New York: Praeger.

Fernandez-Kelly, M. Patricia. 1983. *For we are sold, I and my people: Women and industry in Mexico's frontier.* Albany: State University of New York Press.

Kung, Lydia. 1994. *Factory women in Taiwan.* New York: Columbia University Press.

Mies, Maria. 1985. *Lace makers of Narsapur: Indian housewives in the world market.* London: Zed.

Nash, June. 1988. Cultural parameters of sexism and racism in the international division of labor. In Joan Smith, Jane Collins, Terence K. Hopkins, and Akbar Muhammad, eds., *Racism, sexism, and the world system,* 11–38. New York: Greenwood.

Safa, Helen I. 1995. *The myth of the male breadwinner: Women and industrialization in the Caribbean.* Boulder, Col.: Westview.

Stone, Linda. 1997. *Kinship and gender: An introduction.* Boulder, Col.: Westview.

Weiner, Annette B. 1976. *Women of value, men of renown: New perspectives in Trobriand exchange.* Austin: University of Texas Press.

Anru Lee

PATRIARCHY: Feminist Theory

Patriarchy is a cardinal concept of the radical second-wave feminists, who define it as "a system of social structures, and practices in which men dominate, oppress and exploit women" (Walby, 1990: 214). This use of the concept of patriarchy has enabled the development of some of the most significant feminist ideas and programs worldwide; at the same time, the concept has been criticized, modified, and in many cases abandoned.

The Context for the Term *Patriarchy*

The feminist concept of patriarchy as a widespread social system of gender dominance evolved in the context of the emerging North American and European women's liberation movements and the intellectual and political climate of the late 1960s to 1970s, which emphasized large-scale social systems and structures—capitalism, colonialism, and racism. In particular, Marxism, with its compelling explanation of inequality and a charter for social change, provided one of the most influential models for progressive thinking. Feminists borrowed these frameworks and described male–female relations as colonial or class relations, but also concluded that women's subordination could not be explained by, or with the terms of, those other systems of inequality. The rubric of patriarchy presented one particularly influential effort toward developing a general theory of sex–gender oppression.

In her groundbreaking book *Sexual Politics,* Kate Millet (1970) introduced the feminist use of the term *patriarchy.* The term *patriarch* derives from the Old Testament paternal ruler of a family, tribe, or church, and patriarchy is a formal sociological or anthropological category for societies organized into kinship groups and governed or dominated by the elder male. Commentators of all stripes agree that these archaic societies and early civilizations were patriarchal; some refer to these social forms as "classical" or "historical" patriarchy.

The innovation of radical feminists was to reinterpret patriarchy as a distinct and intractable social system parallel to—yet preceding—class and race stratification. In this view, both the "feudal character of the patriarchal family" and "the familial character of feudalism" (Millet, 1970: 33) endure. Therefore, most, if not all, of the societies we know of—including socialist and revolutionary societies—remain patriarchal. It is important to understand the feminists' use of patriarchy as a strategic and political redefinition—"a struggle concept," as Maria Mies explains, "because the movement needed a term by which the totality of oppressive and exploitative relations which affect women could be expressed as well as their systemic character" (1986: 37).

Patriarchy Redefined

Succinctly, in the radical feminist understanding, patriarchy is a "sexual system of power in which the male possesses superior power and economic privilege" (Eisenstein, 1979:17). In a more elaborate definition provided by Marilyn French, patriarchy is "the manifestation and institutionalization of male dominance over women and children in the family and the extension of male dominance over women in society in general. It implies that men hold power in all the important institutions of society and women are deprived of access to such power. It does *not* imply that women are either totally powerless or totally deprived of rights, influences, and resources" (French, 1985: 239; see also Lerner, 1986: 238–239). In this view, the United Nations, the highlands of New Guinea, France, and Cuba can all be seen as patriarchal social forms.

The political view captured by the term *patriarchy* is different from those conveyed by the phrase "male chauvinism," a now outmoded term that emerged around the same time, or the widespread term *sexism.* Compared with sexism, the feminist concept of patriarchy is more radical, in the sense of challenging the very definitions and standards of equality. Whereas "male chauvinism" and "sexism" imply that the problem of women's inequality has to do with individual men, and that the path to change lies in reform, education, and incremental steps, the theory of patriarchy implies that the problem is society itself and calls for revolution of, or escape from, the patriarchal status quo.

Fundamental to this feminist theorizing is the understanding of patriarchy as institution or system, a powerful mode of organizing society, culture, and individuals. The rubric of patriarchy opened up an intellectual and imaginative space, and provided a vocabulary and model for understanding male dominance and female subordination as systemic, political, and self-reproducing. This view understands politics as "a set of stratagems designed to maintain a system," and therefore patriarchy as "an institution perpetuated by... techniques of control" (Millet, 1970: 23, note 1). The feminist projects since the second wave—whether they use the term *patriarchy* or not—have elaborated on this premise by showing how many mundane, seemingly private and personal experiences operated as the stratagems and tactics that underwrote and reproduced a social system of gender inequality. In this systemic view, such disparate phenomena as wedding rituals, civil law, occupational structures, housework, conversational styles, and psychiatry are seen in a new light as the creations and mechanisms of a patriarchal order.

Variations of Patriarchy

Even working with a similar model, feminist theorists and activists bring different understandings and emphases to the analysis of patriarchal institutions and the strategies for its transformation. If patriarchy is a system structured by sex or gender, was domination based on the role of father, husband, or boss, or simply on maleness? In turn, were women subordinated by virtue of their role as wives, mothers, and sex objects, or else more subjectively, through ideology and psychology?

Materialist feminists or socialist feminists, coming from Marxist and leftist movements, attempted to ground the understanding of male dominance in terms of economic exploitation and control, particularly in the family and labor markets: "The patriarchal system is preserved, via marriage and the family, through the sexual division of labor and society" (Eisenstein, 1979: 17). Although socialist feminists have debated the complex interconnections between capitalism and patriarchy, many considered them to form a collaborative system of capitalist patriarchy (Eisenstein, 1979). The political organizing in line with these theories accordingly works to change laws, policies, and practices that allow the exploitation of women's unpaid household labor and underpaid wage work (Delphy, 1984; Eisenstein, 1979; Mies, 1986). In more recent years, the British sociologist Syvia Walby (1990) proposed understanding patriarchy as a complex combination of six separate arenas: household work, paid work, sexuality, cultural institutions, the state, and male violence.

Perhaps the most popularized expression of the radical feminist theory of patriarchy has been in the interconnected realms of reproduction, sexuality, and violence. The feminist analysis of rape radically reconceptualized men's sexual assault on women as a political use of violence that regulated and punished women and maintained patriarchal power. Similarly, the concepts of wife battering and sexual harassment emerged as political issues because feminists identified them as patriarchal tactics that effectively kept women subordinate in the home and uncomfortable in the public sphere. The translation of these feminist discoveries into gender-neutral policies about "spousal abuse" or inappropriate displays of sexuality at work have, however, erased these radical origins. Relatedly, a very influential if polarizing interpretation of patriarchy, associated with the legal theories of Catharine A. MacKinnon, locates sexuality as the key tactical arena within patriarchal arrangements. Taking a completely different perspective on patriarchal sexuality, the term *heteropatriarchy* emphasizes the specifically heterosexual character of gender and sexual oppression, similar to the ideas of compulsory heterosexuality and heteronormativity. Perhaps paradoxically, but to great effect, the political struggle against these realms of patriarchy has often relied on the state to intervene in domestic realms.

The radical feminist theories of patriarchy often are viewed as theories of ideology, analyzing the ways that male domination is fostered and perpetuated by culture, religion, and science, as well as socialization and psychic development. Many of the large-scale discussions of patriarchy have emphasized the role of male-dominated religions (Daly, 1978; Lerner, 1986), "male principles" (French, 1985), and "patriarchal attitudes" (Figes, 1971), and characterized the patriarchal worldview as one founded on dichotomies (or binaries), hierarchies, and power. The view of patriarchy as most deeply cultural, psychic, and mental—or even spiritual—has motivated the search for alternatives to patriarchal religions and mind-sets, for example, in revitalized goddess worship or witchcraft or the feminist reinterpretations of orthodox religious traditions (Daly, 1978). In fact, feminist theology is one domain where the concept of patriarchy continues to hold much relevance. The view of patriarchy as a total system has led to the search for alternatives. If male-dominated societies position women as objects and not subjects, one clear political strategy lies in escaping this society, and building new relationships, pathways, and cultures with other women; indeed, such a vision informed numerous experiments in separatism and women's culture mainly in the United States, Europe, and Australia. One well-known example is Greenham Common, where throughout the 1980s thousands of women camped and protested around the perimeter of a U.S. military base in England. Other examples from the United States include rural and urban women's collectives, "womyn's music" and a nationwide circuit of music festivals, and, on a more modest scale, events such as art performances, social gatherings, and college classes that create a temporary space dedicated to women only.

One Patriarchy or Many?

Many feminists who employ an idea of patriarchy insist that it represents not one monolith but different forms, seeing significant differences from the classic patriarchal families of antiquity to Chinese extended families to the contemporary western nuclear family ideal (French, 1985; Walby, 1990). In the field of women in development, many feminists worldwide have applied the concepts of patriarchy and patriarchal institutions in evaluating how women's positions have changed with "modernizing" states and the spread of capitalism (Agarwal, 1988; Moghadam, 1996). Feminists in Asia and Latin America also have analyzed their societies as patriarchal, pointing to Confucianism, machismo, and feudalism, for example. In India, feminists have chronicled the enduring legacies of patriarchal feudal relations of property, kinship, and ideology, such as primogeniture and preference for sons. This use of patriarchy in the global "South" generally refers to specific social and cultural forms of male domination rooted in kinship, production, and ideology; today, the patriarchal nature of this local level is seen as inextricable from economic and gender oppression by colonialist, nationalist, and capitalist regimes. Such usage differs from the more diffuse western feminist understanding of society itself.

Others have interpreted patriarchy as one worldwide system (Lerner, 1986; Millet, 1970). For these feminists, male dominance over women represents the original social hierarchy, a template from which other forms of exploitation evolved. Slavery, racism, capitalism, and the exploitation of nature can all be seen, in this view, as predicated on an initial domination of women by men. Such analyses naturally raise the question of when and how patriarchy began, and have prompted research and speculation on what Engels described as "the world historical defeat of the female sex." Scholars used history, mythology, classics, and anthropology to propose the overthrow of matriarchal societies or religions and installation of male-dominated civilizations in Mesopotamia (French, 1985; Lerner, 1986). A vision of patriarchy as global and universal also informed the efforts of first-world feminists to work with women internationally, especially in the South, and to establish "global sisterhood" in a struggle against a presumably similar—if not single—form of oppression by gender.

Limits and Differences

The idea of patriarchy as a single social form across place and time (which often is mistaken as the only feminist understanding of patriarchy) has been subject to much criticism for being totalizing, essentialist, and inaccurate. One of the criticisms of the political theory of patriarchy, especially the notion of one unitary patriarchy, is that it implies a biological basis for a social arrangements (Barrett, 1980; Rowbotham, 1981). Some discussions certainly suggest that patriarchy is based, in the final instance, on biology (Eisenstein, 1979; French, 1985). Most agree, however, that "patriarchy's biological foundations appear to be so very insecure" (Millet, 1970: 31) and stress the social, ideological, and psychic bases of patriarchy more than literal physical sex. It is worth noting that the concept of patriarchy was developed before the powerful feminist formulation of gender; hence, many of these feminists did not deconstruct biological sex in the way that later theorists did. In considering the spirit if not the letter of the discourses about patriarchy, it is clear that these rely on a conceptualization of "sex" that is close to that of gender, meaning a constructed social status and "power division" (Millet, 1970).

Many feminists, particularly academic feminists, reject the radical feminist notion of patriarchy as systematic male dominance and the belief in one patriarchy that is transhistorical and cross-cultural (Barrett, 1980; Rowbotham, 1981; "What Comes after Patriarchy," 1998). Marxist feminists, for example, insisted that much of what counted as the subordination of women was created by capitalism, colonialism, and world systems. For example, the isolated nature of women's domestic work, the separation of the private realm from public life, and the glorification of women as frail dependents—all of these were a product of the shift from agriculture to industrial economies. Anthropologists and historians have criticized the ways that radical feminists take specific practices and relationships out of their particular cultural and historical contexts.

From the point of view of political change, the theories of an all-encompassing patriarchy raise troubling questions about the possibilities and mechanisms of change. The view that all societies are patriarchal, critics suggest, locks women into the position of victims and precludes any sense of how they can resist or change their circumstances, as they do. What is clear is that one obvious strategy for change explicitly or implicitly suggested by analyses of patriarchy—that is, separatism—was unpalatable to most feminists. Moreover, these critiques also meld with a broader problem within second-wave, "1970s," or "Euro" feminism: the problem of addressing seriously the differences among women. By basing the analysis of patriarchal dominance on the powerful but largely western, white, and bourgeois form of the nuclear family, feminist theorists do not account for the ways that the public–private divide and forms of family life vary, especially in terms of race, ethnicity, nationality, and class. Furthermore, the image of a "global sisterhood" struggling against a "global patriarchy" obscures the real power that women of racial, economic, or national privilege hold over other women and men.

After Patriarchy?

By the mid-1980s, the use of the concept of patriarchy waned in academic and many political arenas, perhaps not coincidentally at the same time that "gender" was becoming a more accepted rubric in academic, public policy, and activist worlds. Indeed, it is possible to see a transfer of the intellectual power and political energy associated with analyses of patriarchy to the newer politics of gender. Whereas the widespread use of patriarchy in feminist analysis has declined, the insights that the space of patriarchy allowed continue as key understandings of feminism: the idea that certain seemingly private and individual interactions, events, and emotions—rape, sexual harassment, psychiatric diagnoses, and self-sacrifice—are in fact stratagems of a larger system predicated on male–female difference and inequality. Patriarchy helped feminists think systematically about sex and gender, in ways that borrowed from, but also necessarily separated from, the Marxist analysis of capitalism.

The feminist term *patriarchy,* and the idea of specific patriarchal beliefs and practices, still serves as an important politicized term in theology and radical politics and colloquially in feminist circles. The more technical, specific usage of a kin-based patriarchal social system continues to be used to describe particular historical moments or lingering ideologies across the globe. The terms *patriarchy* and, especially, *patriarchal* are used as a generic category for all kinds of male domination. In a number of cases, *patriarchal* is used as a modifier to suggest just about any form of ranking or oppression, so that highly structured and hierarchical forms of teaching, thinking, theology, or decision making can all be said to be patriarchal, whether or not they suppress women in particular. In this usage, the analysis has shifted away from the systemic social structures to the behavioral and individual.

See Also

DIVISION OF LABOR; FEMINISM: OVERVIEW; FEMINISM: MARXIST; FEMINISM: RADICAL; FEMINISM: SECOND-WAVE BRITISH; FEMINISM: SECOND-WAVE NORTH AMERICAN; FEMINISM: SOCIALIST; HETEROSEXUALITY; PATRIARCHY: DEVELOPMENT; RAPE

References and Further Reading

Agarwal, Bina, ed. 1988. *Structures of patriarchy: State, community and household in modernising Asia.* New Delhi: Kali for Women; London: Zed.

Barrett, Michelle. 1980. *Women's oppression today: Problems in Marxist feminist analysis.* London: NLB.

Daly, Mary. 1978. *Gyn/ecology: The metaethics of radical feminism.* London: Women's Press (2nd ed. 1990).

Delphy, Christine. 1984. *Close to home: A materialist analysis of women's oppression.* Trans. and ed. Diana Leonard. Amherst: University of Massachusetts Press.

Eisenstein, Zillah R., ed. 1979. *Capitalist patriarchy and the case for socialist feminism.* New York: Monthly Review.

Figes, Eva. 1971. *Patriarchal attitudes.* Greenwich, Conn.: Fawcett.

French, Marilyn. 1985. *Beyond power: On women, men, and morals.* New York: Summit.

Lerner, Gerda. 1986. *The creation of patriarchy.* New York: Oxford University Press.

MacKinnon, Catharine A. 1989. *Toward a feminist theory of the state.* Cambridge, Mass.: Harvard University Press.

Mies, Maria. 1986. *Patriarchy and accumulation on a world scale: Women in the international division of labour.* London: Zed.

Millett, Kate. 1970. *Sexual politics.* Garden City, N.Y.: Doubleday.

Moghadam, Valentine M., ed. 1996. *Patriarchy and economic development: Women's positions at the end of the twentieth century.* Oxford: Clarendon; New York: Oxford University Press.

Rowbotham, Sheila. 1981. The trouble with "patriarchy." In Feminist Anthology Collective, ed., *No turning Back,* 301–369. London: Women's Press.

Walby, Sylvia. 1990. *Theorizing patriarchy.* Oxford: Blackwell.

What comes after patriarchy? Comparative reflections on gender and power in a "post-patriarchal" age. 1998. Forum. *Radical History Review* 71 (Spring): 53–195.

Ara Wilson

PEACE AND PEACE ACTIVISM

See CONFILICT RESOLUTION: MEDIATION AND NEGOTIATION; PACIFISM AND PEACE ACTIVISM; PEACE MOVEMENTS; *and* VIOLENCE AND PEACE: OVERVIEW.

PEACE EDUCATION

Peace Education as a Field of Study

The concept and practice of *peace education* exists within the larger field of *peace studies.* The *International Peace Research Association (IPRA)* was established in 1966, and the *Peace Education Commission (PEC)* commands a certain status as the largest commission within IPRA. Members of the PEC are largely well-established educators, ranging from those with standard teaching positions to political scientists interested in the dissemination of findings from peace research. There exists a certain tension within the PEC between those who see peace education as the act (and ethic) of teaching *for* peace (generally educators) and those who view peace education as a means of teaching *about* peace (generally political scientists). Another area of contention is the conflict between regarding peace education as a gender-neutral issue and regarding it as an issue requiring an awareness of gender.

Feminist Peace Education

One example of feminist peace education occurs within the exploration of children's socialization: A peace educator working from a feminist position analyzes the way that boys and girls are raised, with an awareness of gendered differences, in an attempt to deconstruct such sex-role stereotypes and concepts as femininity and masculinity (Brock-Utne, 1989: 153). Feminist peace education attempts to render visible the long-ignored works and writings by women for peace, thus creating new models and examples for both men and women from the ways in which women work for peace.

In the novel *Three Guineas,* Virginia Woolf (1938) raised many questions that are still being asked by feminist peace educators today. She questioned the ability of women to assist men in the achievement of peace when women are themselves so oppressed; when what little education they *do* get is not enough to examine peace issues with a view to enlisting the cooperation of men. Woolf viewed regular education in school as an education for war, encouraging competition and creating a compartmentalized knowledge, divorcing the issue of social and human concerns from technical issues and concepts. In school the achievements of women are being ignored and masculine values cherished.

Even after the publication of *Three Guineas,* the field of peace education continued to be considered gender-neutral. It was not until feminist scholars combined peace education with their awareness of sexism (particularly within the field of gender-role socialization) that certain gender-specific questions began to be asked within the fields of peace research and peace education (Brock-Utne, 1985, 1989; Reardon, 1985, 1988). Such questions included: Do we educate boys for war and girls for peace? Are girls more socialized in empathy than boys are? What are the consequences of having those (males) who are socialized both less in empathy and more in aggressive behavior rule the world? What will the application of feminist theories to the fields of disarmament and human rights and development mean for the movement of peace studies (Brock-Utne, 1985, 1989, 1997)? What is the relationship between militarism and sexism (Easlea, 1983; Reardon, 1985)? Between globalization, peace education, and gender (Brock-Utne, 2000)?

The Invisibility of Women's Works on Peace

Women have written some of the most penetrating works on global questions concerning peace in the broadest definition of the word. These works, however, have largely been ignored, and one of the precepts of feminist peace education is that of rendering these works both valid and visible.

An evaluation of the content of eight books in peace education written in Swedish and currently in use in Swedish schools from preschool through high school showed that a feminist perspective is still lacking (Brock-Utne, 1992). One high school text consists of an anthology of writings on peace from 23 authors. Among those, only two are women, and one of these wrote her article with a man as coauthor. Thus less than 6 percent of the articles in a book that defines peace as "justice" are written by women.

The present author's *Educating for Peace: A Feminist Perspective* (Brock-Utne, 1985) gives many illustrations of the attempts to silence women working for peace. One mechanism (being used, for example, in the textbook anthology) is the way in which women's contributions are "forgotten" after their deaths—that is, not recorded in history books. Yet another silencing tool is ridicule. The famous pacifist novel *Die Waffen Nieder* (*Lay Down Your Arms!* 1889), by the Austrian peace heroine Bertha von Suttner, was a work that escaped being silenced by the oppressive establishment of the author's time. Von Suttner, however, has been excluded from many history books relating to peace activism. This is particularly ironic (in the example of the Swedish textbook anthology), given that this discrimination occurs in a country where such well-known women as Frederika Bremer, Ellen Key, and, more recently, Alva Myrdal, Inga Thorsson, and Maj-Britt Theorin have been leading figures in the struggle for global disarmament.

One of the earliest critics of the way humans are destroying Earth was the Swedish author Elin Wagner (1941). Later followed Rachel Carson with *Silent Spring* (1964), Carolyn Merchant with *The Death of Nature* (1980), and Rosalie Bertell with *No Immediate Danger* (1985). Katarina Tomasevski's work (and wide perspective) on human rights (1989) is especially valuable. By stressing economic rights as much as the more commonly mentioned civil rights, she also takes the fate of impoverished people of the world, particularly women, as the main concern of her work. The structural violence committed in the so-called third world is dealt with brilliantly by Susan George in her books. Helen Caldicott examines the arms race and collective direct violence intelligently and thoroughly in her book *Missile Envy* (1986). There are, however, strong psychological mechanisms at work against these women and their writings. The strongest among them are the constant attempts to silence women and make their works invisible. As mentioned, the Swedish books in peace education provide a good example because they exclude so many important works written by women.

Peace Education within Women's Peace Groups

In the 1980s and mid-1990s there were many local peace groups of the Nordic Women for Peace in Norway, Sweden, and Finland. The discussions initiated in these groups were impressive, and they are here viewed as the best application one can find of the pedagogic principles that peace educators, as well as feminist educators and adult educators, want to adhere to. The atmosphere was one of sharing information and learning from each other.

An analysis of the way women work for peace in this world brought out the following three main characteristics:

- Women working for peace make use of a varied set of nonviolent techniques, acts, and strategies.
- Women take as their point of departure the concern for, and ultimate value of life, especially the life of children, but also the life of all human beings and of nature.
- Women's work for peace is transpolitical, often transnational, aimed at reaching women and sometimes also men and state leaders in the opposite camp (Brock-Utne, 1985: 35–70).

Often women working for peace try to envision a new world, a new "pragmatopia" where power is divided evenly between women and men, where everyone has satisfied the basic necessities of life, and where conflicts are solved nonviolently.

Are Boys Educated for War and Girls for Peace?

There is enormous pressure on mothers who would like to give their sons an education that is aligned with feminist ideas: an education through which the sons are taught to cooperate, care, show tender emotions, and share household chores rather than compete and be tough (see Arcana, 1983; Brock-Utne, 1991; Forcey, 1987). In a study of 20 feminist mothers of sons and 20 traditional mothers of sons, it was found that most of the mothers, regardless of the category in which they had been placed, wanted to give their sons a different education from the one most boys get in our societies. Neither of the groups felt that they had succeeded in raising their sons the way they had wanted.

The only clear difference that could be detected between the two groups of mothers was the way they had explained their lack of success. The traditional mothers blamed genetics: "Boys will be boys." The feminist mothers put the blame instead on environmental factors, including themselves, their lack of time, absent fathers, the influence of sports coaches, and the influence of the fathers of the friends of their son, of television, and of video games.

Peace Education—Taking Gender into Account

Peace educators with a gender perspective try to counteract the way socializing agents influence children—most often boys—to be tough, insensitive, violent, competitive, and oppressive. They also try to counteract the way children—most often girls—are taught to be submissive, inconspicuous, and silent. Peace educators with a gender perspective see that neither the typical way boys are brought up nor the typical way girls are brought up provides a good example of peace education. Good peace education teaches both boys and girls to stand up for their rights and for those of oppressed groups, to speak up against injustice, to be self-reliant and strong yet to cooperate and show compassion and empathy. Good peace education leads to an awareness of injustices and of the need to work for a more equal distribution of the resources of the world.

See Also

GENDER; GENDER CONSTRUCTIONS IN THE FAMILY; NONVIOLENCE; PEACE MOVEMENTS; VIOLENCE AND PEACE: OVERVIEW

References and Further Reading

Arcana, Judith. 1983. *Every mother's son: The role of mothers in the making of men.* London: Women's Press.

Bertell, Rosalie. 1985. *No immediate danger? Prognosis for a radioactive earth.* London: Women's Press.

Brock-Utne, Birgit. 1985. *Educating for peace: A feminist perspective.* New York: Pergamon.

———. 1992. Evaluering av undervisningmateriell til bruk i fredsundervisningen (Evaluation of teaching material to be used in peace education). In *Sartryck och smatryck.* Malmo, Sweden: Institutionen for pedagogkik och specialmetodik.

———. 1989. *Feminist perspectives on peace and peace education.* New York: Pergamon.

———. 1997. Linking the micro and macro in peace and development studies. In Jennifer Turpin and Lester R. Kurtz, eds., *The web of violence.* Champaign: University of Illinois Press.

———. 2000. Peace education in an era of globalization. *Peace Review* 12(1): 131–138.

———. 1991. The raising of a peaceful boy. *Peace Education Miniprints,* no. 8 (January).

Caldicott, Helen. 1986. *Missile envy: The arms race and nuclear war.* Toronto, London, New York: Bantam.

Carson, Rachel. 1964. *Silent spring.* London: Penguin.

Easlea, Brian. 1983. *Fathering the unthinkable: Masculinity, scientists, and the nuclear arms race.* London: Pluto.

Forcey, Linda Rennie. 1987. *Mothers of sons: Towards an understanding of responsibility.* New York: Praeger.

Merchant, Carolyn. 1980. *The death of nature.* San Francisco: Harper and Row.

Reardon, Betty. 1988. *Comprehensive peace education: Educating for global responsibility.* New York: Teachers' College Press.

———. 1985. *Militarism and sexism.* New York: Teachers' College Press.

Suttner, Bertha von. 1889. *Die Waffen Nieder.* (Lay down your arms!) Dresden: Pierson.

Tomasevski, Katarina. 1989. *Development aid and human rights.* London: Pinter.

Wägner, Elin. 1941. *Vackerlocka* (Alarm clock). Stockholm: Delfin.

Woolf, Virginia. 1938. *Three guineas.* London: Hogarth.

Birgit Brock-Utne

PEACEKEEPING

Peacekeeping missions are normally conducted by the United Nations (UN), although the UN Charter itself makes no actual mention of peacekeeping. Peacekeeping was employed for the first time in 1956 during the "Suez crisis"; throughout its history, peacekeeping has been viewed as a welcome alternative to the traditional use of military force. In part, this is because there is a requirement that peacekeeping forces are brought into a situation only with the consent of the parties involved, and that they will fire only in self-defense. One of the early architects of peacekeeping, Canada's Lester B. Pearson, won the Nobel Peace Prize in 1957 for his involvement in the creation of that first mission; the UN's Blue Berets and Blue Helmets won in 1988.

That faith in peacekeeping increased with the collapse of cold war tensions, as peacekeeping missions, and peace operations generally, moved center stage within the UN's repertoire of diplomatic and military instruments. Where previously there had been just a handful of peacekeeping missions, in the so-called new world order those missions proliferated, and became more far-reaching in their scope and mandate. Early- or first-generation missions were involved simply in establishing an interposition force between belligerent groups, whereas the newer second-generation missions involve a whole host of tasks, including military and police functions, the monitoring of human rights, the conduct of elections, the delivery of humanitarian aid, the repatriation of refugees, and the creation and conduct of state administrative structures.

The hope that peacekeeping might serve as an important alternative to the traditional use of military force is one shared by some feminists. As Cynthia Enloe has observed: "The form of military force that is inspiring perhaps the greatest hope is the United Nations peacekeeping force. It inspires optimism because it seems to perform military duties without being militaristic" (Enloe, 1993: 33). Enloe cautions, however, that "[to] date we in fact know amazingly little about what happens to a male soldier's sense of masculine license when he dons the blue helmet or armband of the United Nations peacekeeper" (1993: 33).

One of the reasons that women's studies researchers and activists know so little about what actually happens on peacekeeping missions is that much of the information concerning a mission remains secret. When reports are made by official sources, they seldom raise the kinds of concerns about which feminists remain curious. The UN peacekeeping mission to Cambodia provides a good illustration of this. The United Nations Transitional Authority in Cambodia (UNTAC) was an 18-month mission to Cambodia in the early 1990s and was considered something of a success story for the UN. One observer called it an "international triumph," and then-UN Secretary General Boutros Boutros-Ghali wrote that UNTAC "set a new standard for peacekeeping operations" and that the "international community can take satisfaction from the peacekeeping operation it mounted and supported in Cambodia" (Boutros-Ghali, 1995: 3, 55). The success included the repatriation of 370,000 Khmer refugees and the conduct of a relatively free and fair election in which some four million people, or 85 percent of Cambodia's registered voters, participated. The UNTAC effort also achieved some important successes for women; most notably, the efforts of the United Nations Development Fund for Women (UNIFEM) to incorporate women's issues into the general election and to get women out to vote. UNIFEM is credited with encouraging the emergence of a growing indigenous women's movement as well as a number of indigenous women's nongovernmental organizations, or NGOs (Whitworth, 1998: 177).

But there were other issues that emerged during UNTAC and that seldom appear in the accounts of the mission given by the UN and mainstream observers. Chief among these was the enormous social dislocation that resulted from the deployment of 23,000 foreign personnel—some 16,000 of whom were soldiers—into a relatively fragile, conflict-weary society. That social dislocation included skyrocketing inflation, with the price of basic foods such as rice quadrupling and that of fish increasing by 80 percent; the cost of housing increasing four times; and the value of the local currency, the riel, being devalued by some 70 percent (Curtis, 1994: 60–64).

The social dislocation also included an eruption in prostitution to service UNTAC personnel, with the Cambodian Women's Development Association estimating that the number of prostitutes in Cambodia grew from about six thousand in 1992 to more than twenty-five thousand at the height of the mission. With the sharp increase in prostitution also came a dramatic increase in HIV and AIDS in Cambodia. Although HIV/AIDS most likely did not originate with the UN, the increase in the use of prostitutes certainly contributed to its spread. UNTAC's chief medical officer predicted at the time that as many as six times more UN personnel would eventually die of AIDS contracted in Cambodia than had died as a result of hostile action (Arnvig, 1994: 152, 165; Kien, 1995: 132; Kirshenbaum, 1994; Whitworth, 1998: 179).

Along with an increase in prostitution came the phenomenon of "fake marriages": UNTAC personnel pretended to marry local women, only to abandon them at the end of the mission. Cambodian citizens also reported an increase in physical and sexual assaults against women and children, as well as general problems of drunkenness and drunk driving on the part of UN personnel, which too often resulted in injuries to Cambodian citizens, and even fatalities. Although some mainstream observers described the UN peacekeepers in Cambodia as being "well received" by the local population, in fact an open letter was delivered to the UN secretary-general's special representative in Cambodia, Yasushi Akashi, complaining about the behavior of UNTAC personnel. In the letter, 165 Cambodian and expatriate women and men accused UNTAC personnel of sexual harassment and assault, drunkenness, violence against women and against prostitutes, and responsibility for the rise of prostitution and HIV/AIDS within Cambodia. Akashi responded by saying that it was natural for hot-blooded young soldiers who had endured the rigors of the field to want to have a few beers and to chase "young beautiful beings of the opposite sex." The UN also issued memos requesting that UNTAC personnel not park their distinctively white UN vehicles outside brothels and not frequent brothels while in uniform (Arnvig, 1994: 163–172 and appendix; Kirshenbaum, 1994; Ledgerwood, 1994: 7; Whitworth, 1998: 179–181).

Far from "setting a new standard" for peacekeeping operations, as Boutros-Ghali had claimed, soldiers deployed on this mission—and the attitudes of their military and political leaders—were operating on the same assumptions about women as soldiers deployed on more properly "militaristic" missions have operated on throughout history. "Bringing peace to Cambodia," in other words, was accomplished in part through the deployment of soldiers who assumed that their prerogatives as militarized men included access to prostitutes as well as a freedom to pursue, harass, and assault local women. As Kien Serey Phal wrote, "The peacekeeping operation may have contributed to or compounded problems of declining human security for women" in Cambodia (1995: 131).

Arguably, one of the main reasons these kinds of incidents have occurred is that, whereas the *idea* associated with peacekeeping is far different from the traditional use of militarized force, its *practice* remains unaltered. Yeshua Moser-Puangsuwan notes, for example, that many of the soldiers deployed to Cambodia were members of elite combat units, and received only additional training in counterinsurgency warfare or refresher courses in combat and commando training in preparation for their assignment to UNTAC (1995: 106–107). Few had received any specific training concerning Cambodia, in terms of language, history, social conditions, or customs.

Feminists have tried to suggest alternatives to this way of approaching peacekeeping, which might address these various problems. Judith Hicks Stiehm suggests that increasing the number of women deployed on peacekeeping missions will improve the impact of mediation efforts by peacekeepers, because women are viewed as more empathic by local peoples and tend to ensure that human rights and gender issues protocols are observed (1999: 41–57; United Nations Division for the Advancement of Women, 1995: 1–10). Others disagree and suggest that it is not the presence or absence of women that is the problem, but overreliance on the military. Barbara Ehrenreich, for example, argues that "peacekeeping is the right thing to do, it's just that the military is the wrong thing to do it with," and suggests that people trained in language skills, mediation skills, construction skills, first aid, and primary medicine, as well as people with multicultural training in anthropology, psychology, history, and philosophy, need to be deployed on these missions (1997: 5–6). Often, the nonmilitaristic skills of soldiers deployed on peacekeeping missions contributed most to local people's sense of security: in Phnom Penh, citizens reported that Canadian peacekeepers were exceptional—exceptional because they helped to build a park for children. In other countries, peacekeepers are well remembered for helping to reopen local schools and hospitals, contributions that do not require military training. Whether in the end more women are deployed on peacekeeping missions as soldiers, or whether peacekeeping begins to incorporate both women and men with a wide variety of skills and backgrounds beyond soldiering, feminists have been active in making sure critical questions get asked about this increasingly common UN activity.

See Also

INTERNATIONAL ORGANIZATIONS AND AGENCIES; MILITARY; NONGOVERNMENTAL ORGANIZATIONS (NGOS)

References and Further Reading

Arnvig, Eva. 1994. Women, children and returnees. In Peter Utting, ed., *Between hope and insecurity: The social consequences of the Cambodian peace process.* Geneva: United Nations Research for Social Development.

Boutros-Ghali, Boutros. 1995. Introduction. In Boutros Boutros-Ghali, ed., *The United Nations blue book series. Vol. 2: The United Nations and Cambodia, 1991–1995.* New York: United Nations.

Curtis, Grant. 1994. Transition to what? Cambodia, UNTAC and the peace process. In Peter Utting, ed., *Between hope and insecurity: The social consequences of the Cambodian peace process.* Geneva: United Nations Research for Social Development.

Ehrenreich, Barbara. 1997. Peacekeeping. *Z Magazine* (January): 5–6.

Enloe, Cynthia. 1993. *The morning after: Sexual politics at the end of the cold war.* Berkeley: University of California Press.

Fetherston, A. Betts. 1995. UN peacekeepers and cultures of violence. *Cultural Survival Quarterly* 19(1): 19–23.

Kien, Serey Phal. 1995. The lessons of the UNTAC experience and the ongoing responsibilities of the international community for peacebuilding and development in Cambodia. *Pacifica Review* 7(2): 129–133.

Kirshenbaum, Gayle. 1994. Who's watching the peacekeepers? *Ms.* (May/June): 10.

Ledgerwood, Judy L. 1994. UN peacekeeping missions: The lessons from Cambodia. *Analysis from the East-West Center No. 11* (March).

Moser-Peangsuwan, Yeshua. 1995. U.N. peacekeeping in Cambodia: Whose needs were met? *Pacifica Review* 7(2): 103–127.

Stiehm, Judith Hicks. 1999. United Nations peacekeeping: Men's and women's work. In Mary K. Meyer and Elisabeth Prügl, eds., *Gender politics and global governance*, 41–57. Lanham, Md.: Rowman and Littlefield.

United Nations Division for the Advancement of Women. 1995. The role of women in United Nations peacekeeping. In *Women 2000*. New York: United Nations Division for the Advancement of Women.

Whitworth, Sandra. 1998. Gender, race and the politics of peacekeeping. In Edward Moxon-Browne, ed., *A future for peacekeeping?* Basingstoke: Macmillan.

Sandra Whitworth

PEACE MOVEMENTS: Asia

Just as there has been a broad campaign across Asian nations for women's rights and to improve their security and status, there has been a parallel and complementary peace movement in the region. Women have been at the forefront of efforts to end state and ethnic conflicts and to cease military repression within nations. In order to facilitate this effort, several regional women's networks have emerged in the 1980s and 1990s, which promote advocacy for women's human rights and which organize advocacy programs for peace.

Challenges

For women's groups in Asia, several themes have emerged that cross national borders and are common to peace advocates. The first theme is the growing militarization of the region. Asia has displaced the Middle East as the number one region in the world for arms sales and weapons transfers. There also has been a proliferation of ever more sophisticated military technology, including ballistic missile technology. The second theme is the presence of the U.S. military and the impact of U.S. security policy throughout the region. Security relationships between the United States and individual nations have had positive impacts; however, U.S. support for totalitarian regimes and the negative impact of U.S. military bases has brought into question the overall costs and benefits of such deployment. The third theme, and central concern, remains the ongoing interstate and intrastate conflicts in the region and the potential for the expansion of such conflicts.

Women's peace groups have asserted that the failure of the United States to reorient its security policy in the post–cold war era has led to the continuation of policies that support repressive regimes and that have fostered the militarization of the region. The result at a micro level has been numerous examples of individual violence perpetuated by U.S. military personnel against women, including incidents in South Korea in 1992 and in Okinawa in 1995 and 1997. There are 37,000 U.S. troops permanently stationed in South Korea, and these forces have committed over 1,000 crimes (AFSC, 1999). Protests against the U.S. military presence in the Philippines resulted in base closings, and growing opposition in Japan to U.S. bases has resulted in renegotiations over the size and long-term future of these institutions. In South Korea, groups such as the National Campaign for the Eradication of Crime by U.S. Troops in Korea have regularly protested the U.S. presence. For some 270 consecutive Fridays, activists and students held a weekly protest outside the U.S. embassy in Seoul to highlight the crimes of the U.S. military. After this regular protest was initiated, crimes by U.S. servicemen in Korea were dramatically reduced as the military implemented tougher penalties and increased educational programs.

Another consequence of the substantial U.S. military complex is the large number of Amerasian children in the region. Although the 1982 Immigration and Naturalization Act facilitated the emigration of Amerasian children who were born between 1950 and 1982 from Vietnam, Cambodia, Laos, Thailand, and Korea, there continues to be a growing population of Amerasian children who are the offspring of U.S. servicemen. These children often are not acknowledged by their U.S. parents and face enormous discrimination and abuse in their native countries. Asian women's groups are working to reintroduce legislation in the United States to make it easier for Amerasian offspring of U.S. servicemen to emigrate to the United States. These groups also are endeavoring to develop support groups within Asian nations for Amerasian children and to pass laws in these nations to end discrimination against this population.

Women's peace movement activists in Asia also have confronted the enormous environmental costs of militarism. They have been among the few groups to directly point out the links between military bases and increased environmental stresses. Various groups have endeavored to collect data on the impact of military facilities, but varying regulations in different countries have made coordinated responses to the problem difficult. Myrla Baldonado, the leader of the People's Task Force for Bases Clean-Up in the Philippines, and her group have been especially active in exposing the environmental costs of the U.S. presence. Many groups have now joined with environmental organizations in coalition-building efforts to secure more thorough and comprehensive environmental and public safety laws.

Responses

In response to these myriad concerns, women in the region have endeavored to both utilize existing and proven means to influence national policy and to develop new and alternative methods to exert influence. One method is to promote women's empowerment. The various women's movements recognize that women who are empowered will be able to change their situations of violence as well as their low legal and social position in society. These groups seek to define an agenda for change and effect the social mobilization of millions of women in the region.

Because many governments in the region are controlled by elites within society, the type of direct government lobbying common in western nations has not been a common tool of the peace movement. Groups do not have the resources to compete with the military-industrial complex of many of these nations, and governmental leaders often are unresponsive to pressure from activists. Instead, many of the women's peace groups have made a tactical decision to rely on mass protest and techniques to highlight specific concerns and issues. In this way, they hope to first gain the support of the people, which can then be used to pressure government.

These groups also endeavor to focus world attention on the issues of violence, conflict, and the militarization of Asia. Groups such as the Asia Pacific Women for Law and Development, consisting of women lawyers and activists, and the Asian Women's Human Rights Council (AWHRC) promote the study and rethinking of human rights from a feminist perspective and from the eyes of women of the "South." In particular, the AWHRC has been active in exposing violence and exploitation directed against women, including the trafficking in Asian women, oppression of minority women, and organized prostitution around U.S. military bases in the Philippines, South Korea, and Okinawa. Efforts to institute legal protections for women also have been promoted by international organizations, including the International Commission of Jurists and the Women's International League for Peace and Freedom.

The peace movement in Asia has worked to expand women's empowerment for a variety of reasons. One of the main goals of the movement is to increase women's participation in politics so that women's priorities are reflected in national politics. Proponents of this line of reasoning believe that by reshaping national interests, women's groups can slow or stop the militarization of the region by diverting funds away from the acquisition of new weapons or from military spending in general and, instead, direct them toward causes and programs that have a greater societal influence. Hence, reduced military spending would have two main positive effects: first, it would lessen the growing arms races in the region and reduce hostility between nations, and therefore reduce the likelihood of armed conflict; second, it would allow national governments to devote greater resources to social problems such as poverty, health care, and education.

In response to the large U.S. military presence in the region, Asian women's peace groups have worked to reconfigure the Status of Forces Agreements (SOFA) and the Visiting Forces Agreements (VFA) between the United States and various nations in the region including Japan, South Korea, and the Philippines. One result of these agreements has been the realization that similar agreements between the United States and European nations such as Germany and the United Kingdom provide much greater protections for local citizens and easier procedures for redress against U.S. military personnel. The East Asia–U.S. Women's Network Against U.S. Militarism established a working group in 1998 to rewrite the existing Japanese and Korean agreements so that citizens of these nations would receive the same guarantees and protections as their counterparts in Europe. The working group also helped coordinate campaigns in Japan and the Philippines to oppose the new VFA for the Philippines and bilateral agreements between the United States and Japan, which extended the U.S. military presence in those nations.

One unique feature of the women's peace movement in Asia has been the effort to expose the violence directed toward women during World War II. The Asia Tribunal on Women's Human Rights in Tokyo released a declaration on 12 March 1994 that condemned the horrendous crimes of organized and systematic rape, torture, detention, forced displacement, and abduction. The declaration described Japan's "Operation Comfort Women" as a war crime, and condemned all overt acts of military sexual slavery. The document expressed deep concern over the unprecedented proportions of trafficking in women, including the *devadasi* (temple prostitution) system in India, the sex workers in Japan, and profiteering in the sex industry, which perpetuates the massive export of female labor for entertainment and prostitution.

In 1991, Kim Hak Sung, a Korean woman, filed a lawsuit against the Japanese government in Tokyo District Court. She was one of an estimated 250,000 women from Korea, the Philippines, and Malaysia, and both native and Dutch women from Indonesia, who were forcibly drafted by the Japanese military to be sex slaves as part of the comfort women system. This system is an extreme example of violence against women during wartime. Comfort women were repeatedly raped, up to 50 to 60 times per day in some cases, and were held prisoner from periods that ranged from three weeks to eight years. For some 50 years, the Japanese government endeavored to hide its involvement in the comfort women system and refused to acknowledge the extent of the system.

The original lawsuit has since been joined by dozens of women. The lawsuit aims not to only secure financial compensation but also to seek recognition by the world community that sex is a war crime. By doing so, it seeks the restoration of the honor and dignity of the victims of this crime. Many Asian women's groups and international human rights groups have actively supported the effort as a means to highlight the potential violence of conflict toward civilians, and toward women in particular.

The Asia Tribunal on Women's Human Rights has been effective in challenging mainstream definitions and perceptions of women and violence against women. The tribunal produced a plan of action that included data collection, education, lobbying, support and assistance for victims, information, and services for communities to discourage the need of women to migrate for work. On the issue of comfort women, the tribunal's specific recommendations included full investigations and data gathering, trial and punishment of criminals, guaranteed compensation for survivors, public education, and strengthening of international women's solidarity.

The tribunal reveals the connections between violence against women and the patriarchal socioeconomic arrangements that dominate them. By creating new spaces for women to speak, the tribunal makes public various forms of violence against women during military conflicts. This violence includes rape, sex trafficking, and military sexual slavery. However, it has heretofore been relegated to the domain of personal experience and, therefore, has not been accepted as an issue in domestic and international politics. By privatizing these crimes, the violence becomes invisible. One of the aims of the peace movement is to pierce this wall of invisibility and to make the public aware of the links between military conflict and violence directed toward women.

Regional organizations and networks help Asian women to sustain their vital links to each other, across national borders and cultures, in order to formulate common agendas in the struggle for their rights. For instance, the AWHRC has been active in building groups and holding national conferences of women's groups in Indonesia, Cambodia, Pakistan, India, Thailand, and the Philippines. It also has directed efforts in Nepal, Vietnam, Mongolia, South Korea, and Bangladesh. The importance of women in peace movements in Asia was underscored by the historic Fourth World Conference of Women in Beijing, China, in 1995.

One worldwide movement that has influenced the various women's peace movements in Asia was the "Women in Black." This initiative began in Israel, with women standing silently in protest over the violence in the Palestinian occupied territories. Both Israeli and Palestinian women participated in an effort to highlight the problems for women, children, and families that resulted from the ongoing armed struggle in the region. The movement later surfaced in Argentina, when grief-stricken women in the Plaza de Mayo in Buenos Aires displayed photographs of their disappeared and dead sons. Before long, the movement spread to Asia and other parts of the world. Soon the movement spread to the Philippines, where women protested with banners, lanterns, and posters in an effort to remember in silence the innocent victims of violence and war.

Another regional project of Asian women was the "Woven Rug in Magic." Women's organizations throughout Asia wove rugs to symbolize the struggles of their society. The rugs were sewn together in a moving ceremony held on Beijing in September 1995. In many indigenous cultures in Asia and throughout the world, weaving has been associated with women as their expression of life and struggle, especially within societies that seek to oppress and silence them. The AWHRC sponsored another project to raise political awareness in Asia. This initiative was the World Public Hearing on Crimes Against Women. As in past tribunals, the World Public Hearing aimed to create an outcry and focus international attention on the violence that Asian women suffer in their private and public lives.

The women's peace movement in Asia has had its greatest impact in those nations where there are democratic governments and where there is a relatively open society and the ability to protest and undertake mass action. Thus, it is strongest in Japan, the Philippines, and, to a lesser extent, South Korea. In Japan, however, the peace movement has declined from its height in the 1970s, and internal dissension prevented the movement from being a force in opposing military operations such as the Gulf War. The peace movement has faced immense difficulties in China and Vietnam because of government efforts to control or censor women's groups.

Asian women's groups hope to build on the success of governmental accomplishments such as the creation of a zone in the Pacific free of nuclear weapons, to erode the militarism of the region; they want to create a similar zone in northeast Asia to include Japan and Korea. They also want to continue the momentum gained in the effort to end the use of landmines. Throughout Asia, women are raising their voices across distances of the vast continent, and seeing with new eyes. They are voices of hope and struggle. They are the eyes of those who believe that there are other ways of knowing the world, different from the existing condition of domination based on objectification and subjugation. Women are advocating a new perspective founded on a paradigm of diversity and justice, and, by so doing, are transforming a world that has known suffering for so long.

See Also

INTERNATIONAL ORGANIZATIONS AND AGENCIES; MILITARY; NONGOVERNMENTAL ORGANIZATIONS (NGOS); PEACE EDUCATION; VIOLENCE: EAST ASIA (CHINA); VIOLENCE: SOUTH ASIA; WAR

References and Further Reading

American Friends Service Committee. 1999. *Linking arms: Asia-Europe cooperation on alternative security strategies.* The Hague: American Friends Service Committee.

Asian Women Human Rights Council. 1994. *In the court of women II: Asia tribunal on women's rights in Tokyo.* Tokyo: Asian Women Human Rights Council.

Kumar, Corinne, Kalpana Chkravarthy, Donna Fernandes, Celine Saguaa, Gowramma, R. L. Kumar, Madhu Bhushan, and Bhogari. 1995. *Speaking tree women speak.* Bangalore: Asian Women Human Rights Council.

———, R. L. Kumar, Madhu Bhushan, and A. L. Georgekutty. 1995. *Sacred mountains everywhere: Essays on the violence of universalism.* Bangalore: Asian Human Rights Council.

Morrison, Charles E., ed. 1999. *Asia Pacific security outlook, 1999.* New York: APAP.

Sancho, Nelia, Indai Lourdes Sajor, Lynie Olimpo, and Adriano Cervo Jr. 1994. *Update on the Filipina victims of sexual enslavement by Japanese armed forces during World War II.* Quezon City: LILA-PHILIPINA.

Waylen, Georgina. 1995. *Gender in third world politics.* New York: United Nations Development Fund for Women.

Nelia Sancho

PEACE MOVEMENTS: Australia, New Zealand, and the Pacific Islands

Peace movements in Australia, New Zealand, and the Pacific Islands have arisen in response to particular issues that have emerged and that have been shaped by common features of the geography and history of the region. This area includes the vast continent of Australia and thousands of smaller islands in Polynesia, Melanesia, Micronesia, New Zealand, and Papua New Guinea. Throughout the region, women have been influential in the peace movement. Although this region has many widespread features, it is marked by its extreme contrasts. The Austronesian language family is the largest in the world in terms of the number of languages within the group (more than 800), but in terms of the number of speakers, it is relatively small. In addition, the differing legacies of the various individual territories' colonial and cold war legacies have had significant impact on the peace movement. Most important, the distinctions in culture and tradition have greatly affected the role women have played within the peace movement in the region. The women's peace movement, however, has been able to educate the peoples of the region that it is often women and children who bear the greatest burdens during times of armed conflict, and often end up caring for the victims of violence. Women's groups also have alerted the public to the dangers of militarism and the lost social revenues spent on weapons systems and how these losses detract from government's ablility to address social and economic problems. In line with the Beijing platform of 1995 for action and the Vienna declaration of 1993 on the indivisibility of human rights and women's rights, women's peace advocates have brought to the public's attention how lingering colonialism and human rights abuses dramatically affect people in general, and women in particular.

Culture and History of Precolonial Societies

A recurrent metaphor in the region involves the canoe. The canoe evokes the idea of passages, of traveling in group formation, of contact with other cultures, of moving with the prevailing tides and conditions. The canoe as metaphor is taken quite literally by a number of cultures. For example, the Tanna of Vanuatu define social position through seating in an imaginary canoe, with the aristocrats seated in the prow and women seated behind men. Creation stories in the region see the land and sea as the source of life, the geographic formations as signs of the sacred beings of the past, and people as the keepers or custodians of the land. In this context, although there was warlike behavior, it tended to be localized, and there were a variety of indigenous strategies to prevent conflict or to reconcile disputants (Behrendt, 1992). The overriding societal control is adherence to sacred law and a cosmology that does not see land as a possession. Disputes between warring clans may be heard by a council of elders and can be resolved by restitution, perhaps in the form of gifts to relatives. Gift ceremonies bind not only the disputants but their whole community to the agreed settlement. The dynamics of the social group is such that the threat of ostracism is a powerful deterrent to committing violent acts.

These factors have significantly influenced both the peace movements in the region and the role of women in these movements. The strong attachment to land and sea and the respect for nature have prompted mass movements to oppose the devastation caused by nuclear testing and the environmental damage caused by military bases and military exercises in the region. The traditional patriarchal nature of many of these cultures was reinforced during the colonial period. The introduction of iron tools would cut the time needed for men to complete work but did little to ease the workload of women. On many islands, men gained leisure time and expanded their ambitions toward material accumulation, whereas women held on to the traditional values of the society. As time went by and the armed resistance to colonial rule was overcome island by island, there were differing outcomes from the colonial struggles. The aboriginal people of Tasmania suffered wholesale genocide, whereas the people of Guam eventually adopted the goals and aspirations of their colonial power and became U.S. citizens, and the Maori peoples of New Zealand signed the Treaty of Waitangi, which gave them some legal rights and served as the basis for reconciliation. Through all of this, women emerged as the keepers of culture. In this capacity, they would serve as the foundation for the later peace movements, despite the patriarchal nature of their cultures.

Other important influences from the colonial period that would affect the peace movement include the transportation of Indian and other workers to islands, creating ethnic and class divides where there had been none. In addition, the introduction of written languages transformed the oral traditions of the region. The adoption of colonial languages and the emergence of class created hierarchies within the indigenous societies. These hierarchies tended to deemphasize the role and place of women, as they seldom received education or economic opportunities for advancement. This created enormous hurdles within the cultures of the region that women would have to overcome in their efforts to oppose militarism and develop grassroots peace movements.

Emergence and Development of the Peace Movement

The idea of a peace movement implies a loose coalition of organizations and individuals who are motivated to protest about war and work toward the prevention of war and the end of militarism. The first voices of the peace movement were those raised to protest the treatment of indigenous peoples. Often led by European female missionaries or the wives of male missionaries, these women protested the brutal means used to subdue the native peoples of the region and the subsequent oppression used to destroy their culture and integrate them into the imposed colonial society.

One of the first organized mass peace movements in the region developed in Australia in response to the use of Australian troops by the British during the Second Boer War (1899–1902). Women were in the forefront of this movement, and opposition to the war became tied into the broader women's movement, including the struggle for suffrage. It also was this first antiwar movement in the region that brought together religious pacifists, socialists, and academics with the working class and trade unions. These groups would subsequently form the core of later peace movements. In this historical context, it can be noted that the women's peace movement was drawn largely from the ranks of English-speaking white colonial settlers.

Although World War I was largely supported by the Australian populace, it gave rise to the formation of the Sisterhood of International Peace. Believing that "war begins in the minds of men," its members felt that children should be educated in the ideals of peace. In 1920, the Sisterhood became the Australian section of the Women's International League for Peace and Freedom (WILPF). The strength of the WILPF was demonstrated by its ability to collect 118,000 signatures on a petition to send to the world Disarmament Conference in Geneva in 1932. WILPF continues to be a strong force in the Australian peace movement.

The impact of World War II, in terms of the damage done to particular areas and the deployment of millions of troops and their impact on islands and culture, helped spark the peace movement among indigenous peoples in the region. Following the war, many military bases were retained, even as the general trend in the region was toward decolonization. Added to these military stresses came the aftermath of World War II and the onset of nuclear testing.

Women's peace movements in the region began to agitate for the establishment of a nuclear-free zone to end the atomic testing undertaken by the United States, Great

Britain, and France. These groups also sought an end to the docking of nuclear-powered and -armed ships, the mining and transport of uranium, and the disposal of radioactive waste. Finally, women's peace groups also urged the abandonment of U.S. military bases, whose functions supported the nuclear web. This included bases that relayed signals to nuclear submarines. These efforts often ran counter to many vested interests on the various islands, which endeavored to maintain and even expand the military facilities as a means to bolster local economies.

Meanwhile, the women's peace movement in Australia and New Zealand gained renewed prominence as a result of its opposition to the conflict in Vietnam in the 1960s. Women's groups helped lead the protest movement that prevented New Zealand from escalating its involvement in the early 1960s. Australian troops were sent there in 1962, however, and in 1966 conscripts began being deployed in the conflict. Following the Tet Offensive in 1968, the peace movement gathered momentum, and women's groups helped link opposition to conscription with opposition to the war in general. They also were able to mobilize mothers who opposed the deployment of their sons to Vietnam. This effort was organized by Jean Maclean through an organization called Save Our Sons. The result of this movement was that in 1972, the newly elected Labour governments of Australia and New Zealand quickly fulfilled campaign pledges to withdraw their troops from Vietnam.

Opposition to armed conflict would reemerge in the 1990s with the advent of the Gulf War. From its established base, the women's peace movement was able to mobilize protests against the Gulf War with a rapidity that far exceeded that of the Vietnam effort. Significantly, women were brought into the ranks of the antiwar effort against the Gulf War with few personal incentives—compared with the concern for "our sons" that existed in the Vietnam conflict because of conscription. Women's groups in the South Pacific region continue to protest the ongoing economic sanctions against Iraq and New Zealand's participation in the naval blockade of that nation.

In the wake of the Vietnam conflict, the women's peace movements in Australia and New Zealand took somewhat different courses. The movement in Australia continued to work to oppose broad issues of militarism, including nuclear testing and the deployment of troops in the region, but the New Zealand movement really became identified with and concentrated on the nuclear-free zone. In Australia, feminists in the women's peace movement have been torn by the issue of military service. Women are 10 percent of Australia's military, and many feminists feel compelled to support the rights of women to serve in the armed forces as a form of gender equality. Yet such service also runs counter to the basis of the peace movement.

Elsewhere in the Pacific, the women's peace movement has faced other dilemmas. For example, the deployment of Australian and New Zealand troops as UN peacekeepers to East Timor presented a dilemma, because the women's peace movement opposes armed conflict but supports the self-determination movement of the East Timorese for independence from Indonesia. This support is especially broad among women's groups in areas that remain under colonial rule, such as French Polynesia. One compromise has been support for Peace Brigades International, which provided unarmed protective escorts to human rights activists and has sent 40 such escorts to East Timor.

The major issue for many women's peace groups remains the nuclear-free zone. Advocates in New Zealand led this effort, which culminated in the establishment of one such zone in the South Pacific. New Zealand's stance even led to the demise of Australia, New Zealand, and the United States's military alliance, in effect since World War II, when, in 1985, the government would not allow a U.S. naval vessel to visit New Zealand because the United States would not confirm or deny whether it carried nuclear weapons. Since then, New Zealand women have joined others around the world in advocating the establishment of a Southern Hemisphere Nuclear Free Zone, and the extension of the existing nuclear-free zone in the South Pacific to other areas, including Latin America, the Indian Ocean, and Africa.

The nuclear issue reemerged in a dramatic fashion in the 1990s, when the French government announced its intention to resume nuclear testing in Muraroa in the region. This led to mass protests by people in French Polynesia and condemnation by nations around the world, including the nation-states of the South Pacific. Nevertheless, the French doggedly persisted in their efforts. They even initiated covert operations to disrupt protests by the environmental group Greenpeace, which resulted in the sinking of the Greenpeace ship *Rainbow Warrior* in New Zealand. The resumption of nuclear testing galvanized the women's peace movement in the island nations of the region. Indigenous women were particularly concerned over the long-term potential health consequences of the tests and the environmental damage done.

Women's groups continue to protest the deployment of troops on bases in the region because of the environmental impact of such facilities. In addition, women's peace advocates form the basis in many nations in the region for the opposition to the arms trade and weapons sales. In New Zealand and Australia, these groups have led opposition to weapons sales to Indonesia, and the purchase of weapons systems from the United States, including the purchase of advanced and expensive aircraft such as the F-16 fighter.

Feminists note that the overall peace movement is better at promising women a place in some utopian future than that addressing inequalities evident in its own practices. People of color are underrepresented in the peace movement. Ideological and adversarial approaches alienate some potential recruits. The result has been that a number of former women's peace activists who were involved in groups such as People for Nuclear Disarmament now work instead for nongovernmental organizations such as the International Women's Development Agency and other groups that promote development, gender equality, and the eradication of poverty. The history of the peace movement in the region suggests, however, that quiescent periods—when activists get on with their lives and work toward other gender issues in society—should not be confused with going out of business. Women continue to work quietly for peace. As consumers, they form groups and resist the sale of war toys and violence in popular culture. Maori women have been in the forefront of efforts to lessen violence on television and in other forms of entertainment media. On Tahiti and other islands, women have worked to promote conflict resolution instruction in the classroom and peace education. In many schools, methods that once were the province of the women's peace movement, including conflict resolution and mediation, are included in the curriculum, and mediation has become a standard technique taught in law schools in the region. When events such as the Gulf War and renewal of French nuclear testing have occurred, however, the women's peace movement has demonstrated its power through large-scale mobilization and mass demonstrations.

See Also

COLONIALISM AND POSTCOLONIALISM; ENVIRONMENT: AUSTRALIA AND NEW ZEALAND; ENVIRONMENT: PACIFIC ISLANDS; MILITARY; NONGOVERNMENTAL ORGANIZATIONS (NGOS); NUCLEAR WEAPONS; PACIFISM AND PEACE ACTIVISM; POLITICS AND THE STATE: AUSTRALIA, NEW ZEALAND, AND THE PACIFIC ISLANDS; VIOLENCE: AUSTRALIA, NEW ZEALAND, AND THE PACIFIC ISLANDS; WAR

References and Further Reading

Alves, Dora. 1985. *Anti-nuclear attitudes in New Zealand and Australia.* Washington, D.C.: National Defense University.

Behrendt, Larissa. 1992. *Aboriginal dispute resolution.* Sydney: Federation.

Burgman, Verity. 1993. *Power and protest: Movements for change in Australian society.* Sydney: Allen and Unwin.

Locke, Elsie. 1992. *Peace people: A history of peace activities in New Zealand.* Auckland: Hazard.

Reardon, Betty. 1993. *Women and peace: Feminist visions of global security.* New York: State University of New York.

Robillard, Albert B. 1992. *Social change in the Pacific Islands.* London: Kegan Paul.

Saunders, Malcolm, and Ralph Summy. 1986. *The Australian peace movement: A short history.* Sydney: Australian National University Peace Research Center.

Diane Bretherton

PEACE MOVEMENTS: Central and South America

In Latin America, many women are hungry, exploited, and poorly educated, and peace for them is not only the absence of killing, torture, and "disappearances," but also a roof over their heads and a meal on the table. In this article the term *peace movements* will refer to any attempt by women to create the just conditions that make peace possible. These efforts include managing soup kitchens, teaching literacy, demonstrating against repression, documenting human rights violations, instigating dialogues between hostile factions, and developing democratic party platforms.

Historical Trends

When in 1975 women from all over the world went to Mexico City to share their views on the Women's Decade, those from the industrialized countries talked about women's rights and peace, whereas women from the so-called third world stressed survival issues: a new economic order and respect for human rights. At the end of the decade, both sides had learned from each other. At the conference in Nairobi in 1985, human rights and peace were discussed as interrelated issues, and the western term *feminization of poverty* fit exactly the experience of women from the southern part of the globe.

In the late nineteenth and early twentieth centuries, a first wave of feminism had affected most of the Latin American countries. It was often connected with national liberation movements, and women frequently became active participants in war. Many of them contributed to peace, however, by working for equal rights of all racial and ethnic groups. It was not until the 1970s and 1980s that a second wave of feminism came to South America. In Peru, Brazil,

Argentina, Chile, Uruguay, and Mexico, for example, women had played an important role in various social movements of the mid-twentieth century, and many of them had later come in contact with feminism while in exile. On this ground the women's movement could gain a foothold.

The military dictatorships that had come to power in Chile (1973), Uruguay (1973), and Argentina (1976) promoted the traditional ideals of motherhood and family, but their brutal repression tactics gave women an incentive to mobilize. By resisting dictatorships in imaginative ways, women decisively influenced their societies. When unions, political parties, and public gatherings were not permitted and thousands of activists were "disappeared" or murdered, women, with the help of human rights groups, organized demonstrations against military procedures and established a network of self-help centers, transferring their domestic skills to larger societal tasks. When the military dictatorships broke down in Argentina (1983), Uruguay (1985), and Chile (1990), the women's movements in these countries were pushed aside. With the pressure toward democracy, political parties played an important role, and women had to learn how to influence them or identify with them—if the men allowed them in.

Since the mid-1990s, many Latin American countries have been hotly debating the issue of amnesty laws. Many women are incensed that the murders, tortures, and disappearances of their men are being swept under the rug by these laws in the name of national reconciliation. (Innumerable women are, of course, also among the victims, and innumerable men have joined those who are protesting the amnesties, but men had been the foremost targets of the dictatorships and women the foremost protesters.) Among other countries, Chile, Argentina, Uruguay, Panama, and Peru have passed amnesty laws.

Argentina

In Argentina, the human rights organizations were the first to challenge the dictatorship. Among them, the Mothers of the Plaza de Mayo were the most radical and most effective. The group was founded in 1977 (at the height of repression) by 14 mothers of disappeared persons. By the end of that year there were 300 women. In 1986 the organization had 4,000 to 6,000 members and existed in 26 cities. The women were on average 50 years old, middle-class, and inexperienced in politics. They protested on the Plaza de Mayo, with forced interruptions, every Thursday from 3:30 to 4:00 P.M., wearing white scarves around their heads. They sent notices to the media with the names of the *desaparecidos,* the disappeared ones. They hung posters with these names all over the city. In October 1977 they collected 24,000 signatures from people demanding an investigation and the release of the disappeared without charges. They turned in a huge number of legal claims, initiated hunger strikes, gathered for silent demonstrations, and kept close contact with foreign correspondents. In the late 1970s, some of the women traveled to other countries to spread their message.

The *madres* emphasized their role as mothers and thereby gained a certain protection beyond parties or ideologies. They have sometimes been described as apolitical. The military, however, definitely saw them as a danger. They branded them as terrorists and, after 1977, arrested, threatened, and beat some of them. Thirteen mothers died as victims of the system. It is estimated that about 30,000 people disappeared in Argentina, among them 400 children who were illegally adopted. With the help of a blood bank and genetic tests, women are now trying to identify children and to return them to their families. In 1983, the military junta of Argentina published a report admitting its responsibility for the disappearances as "justified measures against terrorism." However, some horrifying revelations about the fate of many disappeared persons hardly left room for justification. How to pacify the country without a blanket amnesty created a problem even among the mothers. Some considered the group's tactics too strident and wanted more cooperation with the elected government, whereas a large part of the original group considered any cooperation a shallow compromise because the government had not made a serious effort to prosecute guilty military leaders. In the 1990s, mothers and grandmothers of the disappeared continued to fight for a peace with justice and against a cover-up in the name of reconciliation. They opened the Osvaldo Bayer Literary Café in downtown Buenos Aires to support their cause. In March 2000 they even launched a public university.

Peru

From 1980 to 1992, Peru suffered from the guerrilla war unleashed by the Maoist movement Sendero Luminoso, or Shining Path. The country lost over 27,000 people, and the material destruction amounted to billions of dollars. During this time, many Peruvian women became active guerrillas. Sendero gave them leadership roles, taught them how to lead assassination squads, and promised them a glorious revolution that would end poverty and injustice. Many more women, however, worked for peace in visible and invisible ways, creating alternative social strategies.

Because the ruthless tactics of Sendero Luminoso were answered with brutal measures by the government, countless families were caught in the middle. Women were the majority of thousands of refugees, suffering rape, torture, hunger, unemployment, and disappearance. Some peacemakers courageously tried to stand between the warring parties. Outstanding among them was María Elena Moyano, a black feminist and the acting mayor of Villa El Salvador, a huge settlement on the outskirts of Lima. She publicly protested the violence of Sendero, but also refused the support of the military, because she knew that the army was guilty of brutalities as well. On 15 February 1992 Moyano was assassinated by Sendero as she left a fund-raising barbecue to benefit local children. A woman disguised as a mountain peasant carried the 10 pounds of dynamite that would blow María Elena's body to pieces in front of her two young sons. Twenty thousand people gathered for her funeral, from the poorest settlers to the heads of church and state, chanting, "María Elena Moyano, for life and peace" (Herzog, 1993).

The Peruvian women's movement has been one of the strongest in Latin America. Its work has been effectively supported by many nongovernmental organizations, represented, for example, by the powerful women's centers Flora Tristan and Manuela Ramos in Lima. During the last years of the guerrilla war, their work suffered from being threatened by Sendero as well as by right-wing extremists. After President Alberto Fujimori was able to incarcerate a large part of the leadership of Sendero in 1992, these threats diminished, but the centers lost much of their foreign support, partly because European foundations now had to support suffering people in eastern Europe.

Only 15 percent of the Peruvian population were living above the poverty line in 1993, and the following years have shown increasing poverty and unemployment. To ensure the survival of their families, women depended even more on the community kitchens they had established earlier because common meals were less expensive than private cooking. A very successful program provided every needy child with a daily glass of milk. Women also became active in health care, craft cooperatives, legal counseling centers, and street vending. Women who had never been publicly active now learned to organize or to be involved in politics. One woman, Elvira Torres Arias, rose from community kitchen organizer to candidate for Congress in 1995.

The Peruvian women's movement remains active at the beginning of the twenty-first century, exploring new directions in terms of self-help groups and human rights organizations. Many are fighting against a reintroduction of the death penalty and against any attempt by the government to influence women's votes by undemocratic measures.

Guatemala

What Guatemala, especially its indigenous population, has suffered during nearly four decades the 36 of civil war can be imagined by reading *I, Rigoberta Menchú: An Indian Woman in Guatemala.* In what may be a partly fictional or composite account, Menchú describes how her brother, father, and mother were killed by the army. In an attempt to root out communist infiltration from Cuba and Nicaragua, atrocities were used to frighten and subdue the peasants. Violence from all sides eventually caused about 200,000 refugees to flee to Mexico. In 1994, many of them returned because the country appeared more stable again. Some of what Menchú recounts was questioned by the anthropologist David Stoll in 1998, but this cannot undo the enormous importance of her books and her person in calling attention to the plight of indigenous Guatemalans. Since receiving the Nobel Prize in 1992, Menchú has spent much time in Guatemala to press for nonviolence and democratic elections, efforts described in her book *Crossing Borders.* She also supported the research into human rights abuses before and after the murder of Bishop Juan Gerardi in 1998.

The National Association of Guatemalan Widows (CONAVIGUA) was founded in 1988. When the women used a radio station to publicize their meetings, the military searched their office, seriously threatened several workers, and organized civil patrols in order to stage demonstrations against the widows. At the beginning of the twenty-first century, CONAVIGUA works for better nutrition, health care, housing, and child care and raises women's awareness of exploitation and rape. It also tries to prevent violence by promoting the right to refuse military service. CONAVIGUA has documented many human rights violations in the conscription procedures and has created a public awareness of military abuses. Other groups, such as Grupo de Ayuda Mutua (GAM), concentrate on work for the disappeared, and Mama Matin, created in Mexico in 1990, works for issues such as literacy, women's health, and children's vaccinations. Indigenous women of Guatemala celebrated their hope for peace when on 21 July 1999 their representatives officially entered the Guatemalan government.

Conclusion

In most Latin American countries, the intimate connection between public and private violence, between patriarchal domestic habits and "official" military abuses, has not been sufficiently recognized. Chilean women, however, emphasized this connection from the beginning of the resistance, and they continually try to influence politics in this regard, especially in view of the former dictator Augusto Pinochet's possible prosecution since 1998. Another cultural factor insufficiently analyzed pertains to concepts of education: manhood is still widely identified with domination, and womanhood with submissiveness and domestic nurturing (Garcia, 1983).

Women's peace movements in Latin America are nevertheless strong and unique in their diversity. In Panama, a section of the peace organization Servicio Paz y Justicia (SERPAJ) published a booklet on new women's models of development. In Ecuador and Costa Rica, women have used alternative radio stations to reach a wide spectrum of the population. In El Salvador, the "Platform of Salvadoran Women" (1993) represented a radically feminist attempt to make concrete proposals for a just peace. The document contains 300 demands and suggestions, concerning issues such as women's ownership of land and labor laws that protect women workers from exploitation in the free trade zones. In Brazil, a branch of SERPAJ teaches literacy to keep illiterate people from being manipulated by those in power. The famous *arpilleras* (colorful fabric pictures) of Chile and Peru have often been subversive means of depicting violence and injustice. In Colombia, nearly 86,000 "community mothers" take care of displaced children, each keeping 15 of them in her house, so that the parents can go to work. Gloria Cuartas, a former mayor in northwestern Colombia, earned the United Nations Educational, Scientific, and Cultural Organization's (UNESCO) Peace Mayor Award in 1996 because of her courageous way of communicating with hostile factions without being dependent on either side. Cuartas next headed UNESCO's Cities for Peace program, based in Caracas, Venezuela.

In most Latin American countries, women created their own network of nongovernmental organizations that served specific cultural needs. Although these structures carried the danger of dependence on foreign money, they also facilitated an unprecedented interaction of diverse women from within each country and from the international community and directed attention to the poorest parts of the population. As Nelsa Curbelo of SERPAJ-Ecuador has stated, "Cultural violence is lodged within our own personal and collective unconscious.... The culture of peace has to be invented.... The change will come from the world of the poor. New life is created there, because flowers grow out of rubbish, not diamonds" (Bensing, 1992).

See Also

FEMINISM: CENTRAL AND SOUTH AMERICA; HUMAN RIGHTS; POLITICS AND THE STATE: CENTRAL AND SOUTH AMERICA; TERRORISM; VIOLENCE: CENTRAL AND SOUTH AMERICA

References and Further Reading

Arditti, Rita. 1999. *Searching for life: The grandmothers of the Plaza de Mayo and the disappeared children of Argentina.* Berkeley: University of California Press.

Barrios de Chungara, Domitila, with Moemi Viezzer. 1978. *Let me speak! Testimony of Domitila, a woman of the Bolivian mines.* New York: Monthly Review.

Bensing, Elisabeth, Gaby Franger, and Agatha Haun, eds. 1992. *Living reconciliation—making peace: Women's strategies against oppression, war, and armament.* Nuremberg: Germany: Frauen in der Einen Welt.

García, Celina. 1983. Latin American traditions and perspectives. *International Review of Education* 29(3): 369–389.

Herzog, Kristin. 1993. *Finding their voice: Peruvian women's testimonies of war.* Valley Forge, Pa.: Trinity.

Jelin, Elizabeth, ed. 1990. *Women and social change in Latin America.* London: Zed.

Menchú, Rigoberta. 1998. *Crossing borders: An autobiography.* Trans. and ed. Ann Wright. London: Verso.

Mujeres ALAI. Spanish-language Web site on women's movements in Latin America. <http://www.alainet.org/mujeres>.

Scheper-Hughes, Nancy. 1992. *Death without weeping: The violence of everyday life in Brazil.* Berkeley: University of California Press.

Tabak, Fanny. 1984. Women and authoritarian regimes. In Judith H. Stiehm, ed., *Women's views of the political world of men,* 99–119. Dobbs Ferry, N.Y.: Transnational.

Latinamerica Press/*/Noticias Aliadas.* Weekly publication, Lima, Peru. Also on the World Wide Web. <http://www.cnr.org.pe/na-lp>.

Kristin Herzog

PEACE MOVEMENTS: Europe

Early History

Writing in A.D. 98, the Roman historian Tacitus spoke admiringly of German women, who accompanied their husbands into battle and, on marriage, received from their grooms a shield and spear or sword: "The wife... is thus warned by the very rites with which her marriage begins that... her fate will be the same as [her husband's] in peace and in battle, her risks the same" (quoted in Gies and Gies, 1978: 15).

Despite this record of early European women's participation in battles, women other than members of royalty generally had limited involvement in the public sphere, and therefore little say on when or if wars should be fought.

The Crusades (1095–1272), the series of military expeditions undertaken by western European Christians to reclaim the Holy Land from the Muslims, were an early catalyst for opposition to war. Although their role outside the home—and, thus, their influence—was still generally limited, women joined with men to protest the violence. Church leaders reacted to these calls for peace by instituting Truce of God campaigns. Women joined in these campaigns to limit the days on which fighting could take place.

Individual women conducted peaceful protests, including dancing and washing clothes on Sundays and holy days, which were forbidden. Other women became "unmannerly" in churches (Brill, 1997: 22).

Christine de Pisan (b. 1364–?), a poet at the court of Charles VI of France, expressed her disgust at war and noted that women

> Murder no one, nor wound, nor harm,...
> They do not cheat men of their lands,
> Nor make false contracts, nor destroy
> Kingdoms, duchies, empires ...
> Nor wage war and kill and plunder....
> (*Epistle to the God of Love,* quoted in Gies and Gies, 1978: 15)

Women turned to religious communities as an alternative to marriage and in an effort to maintain peaceful lives. One such group was the Beguines, a twelfth-century movement that began in what is now Belgium. The Beguines, without the approval of church officials, divided their time between prayer and work, and preached peace and good deeds. Essentially urban, the movement spread to France and Germany in the thirteenth century. Because they were not an order and were independent of male monasticism, they were viewed with suspicion; some Beguine leaders were tortured for preaching peace in public. In 1318, the archbishop of Cologne ordered Beguine associations dissolved and integrated into orders approved by the pope, and in subsequent years members were absorbed into established convents (Gies and Gies, 1978: 92). Some Beguine communities reemerged in the seventeenth century. At the beginning of the twenty-first century, there are still a few communities in Belgium and the Netherlands.

Still, throughout much of European history, women were forbidden by church and state officials to participate in public issues, such as war. Occasionally there were organized protests. In 1649, for example, hundreds of women petitioned the English Parliament for the release of four parliamentary radicals, but they were contemptuously rebuked: "That the matter they petitioned about was of a higher concern than they understood... and therefore desired them to go home, and look after their own business" (Miles, 1988: 145).

With the development of religious sects such as the Society of Friends (Quakers) in England, the Mennonites in Germany and the Netherlands, and the Moravian Church in eastern Europe, women gained opportunities to express their pacifism. The Society of Friends, in particular, believed in nonviolence and welcomed women's participation. The influence of the Quakers was long-lasting: many later women leaders of peace and women's rights movements, both in Europe and in the United States, were members of the sect.

"A Woman's Dream"

It wasn't until the nineteenth century that pacifism and organized peace movements gained momentum. Local peace groups and anticonscription clubs organized by men sprang up. Women's auxiliaries to these men's groups soon developed. Among these women's groups were the Olive Branch Circles, which were popular in England during the first half of the nineteenth century. There were also mass antislavery demonstrations in various cities in Europe, along with challenges to British and Spanish colonialism as it existed in Africa and Central America. European women joined in these protests and supported the free produce movement, which involved agreeing not to purchase products made by slave labor.

As in the United States, the abolitionist movement in Europe was linked directly to peace activism. But European organizations were directed and controlled by men, to the exclusion of women. At the 1840 World Anti-Slavery Convention in London, for example, women were denied full participation. One of the protesters to this policy was the U.S. delegate Lucretia Mott (1793–1880), who would later help organize the women's rights movement in the United States.

In the 1860s, other movements were beginning to take shape in Europe, from free churches to workers' rights to antimilitarism to democratic to women's suffrage. Alliances were being formed among the members of the various groups, and women in particular, as early feminists, were making contact with democratic-republican internationalism and pacifism groups (Fraisse and Perrot, 1993: 504). Women's concerns crossed borders; hence, women's groups, whether focused on peace or women's suffrage, developed international links and were not just limited to Europe.

One of the first organized women's peace demonstrations was on Mothers' Peace Day on 6 June 1873 , which took place in Manchester (England), London, Rome, Geneva, and Constantinople, along with a handful of U.S. cities. Women in these cities gathered to protest militarism and the military training of young boys. The peace rallies were originally the idea of the U.S. suffragist and author Julia Ward Howe (1819–1910). These "Women's Peace Festivals" became annual events for the next three decades. As part of the rhetoric, many participants pressed for women's right to vote. The link between the peace and women's suffrage movements became apparent.

The first international women's peace conference was held in The Hague in 1899. The conference was organized by Margarethe Selenka, a German, with the support of Bertha von Suttner, an Austrian aristocrat. The Hague peace conference grew from the work of the International Council of Women (ICW), which had been founded in Washington, D.C., in 1888 as an international suffrage organization and boasted some 15 million members in 25 affiliated national councils (Thébaud, 1994: 58). The meeting of 1899 drew representatives from the Netherlands, Denmark, Great Britain, the United States, Canada, Ireland, Wales, Germany, Sweden, New Zealand, and Tasmania. The ICW embraced efforts for both suffrage and peace, becoming a worldwide voice for women's issues. Out of it grew the International Woman Suffrage Alliance, founded in 1902 and later known as the International Alliance of Women (Alonso, 1993: 54). The organization later focused its efforts on international women's suffrage within the context of world peace. In the 1 May 1914 issue of the *International Woman's Suffrage News,* peace was referred to as "a woman's dream . . . a vision of justice and peaceful evolution" (Alonso, 1993: 54).

One of the leaders of the peace movement at this time was, as noted above, Baroness Bertha von Suttner (1843–1914). A passionate advocate of world peace, she wrote of the horrors of war in short stories, articles, and novels. Her most famous work—*Lay Down Your Arms!*—gained worldwide attention for its antiwar theme.

Suttner first became involved with the peace movement in 1885, when, on her return to Europe from the Caucasus after an extended period there with her husband, Baron Arthur von Suttner, she experienced the heightened militarism on the continent. She contacted the International Arbitration and Peace Association, headquartered in London, and vowed to "make war on war" (Lengyel, 1975: 63). Her response was the two-volume novel *Lay Down Your Arms!* (subtitled *A Human Destiny*), first published in 1889. The novel gained critical acclaim and was translated into all of the major languages. On reading it, the Russian novelist Leo Tolstoy commented: "What [Harriet Beecher Stowe's] *Uncle Tom's Cabin* did against slavery in America, your magnificent book should do for peace" (Lengyel, 1975: 80).

After the success of her book, Suttner founded the Austrian Peace Society in 1891 and was the cofounder of the Peace Society Central Office in Bern, Switzerland. She also founded the periodical *Lay Down Your Arms!* (which later became *Peace Watchtower*). In it, she reported on the activities of peace movements throughout the world. Suttner later inspired her friend Alfred Nobel, the Swedish inventor and peace advocate, to establish the Nobel Peace Prize. Suttner was the first woman to receive the award (1905).

New peace societies sprang up throughout Europe. These societies worked closely with the Interparliamentary Union, consisting of members of legislatures of key countries. There were major peace marches sponsored by feminist organizations in 1899 and 1907. Despite the efforts of these organizations and individuals like Bertha von Suttner, however, war broke out in 1914. One of the first organized reactions to World War I was the International Congress of Women, which met in The Hague in April 1915. Organized by Aletta Jacobs, a physician and president of the Dutch suffrage organization, and Chrystal Macmillan, a Scottish lawyer and secretary of the International Woman Suffrage Alliance, the meeting was a response to the cancellation of the European suffragists' annual meeting planned for Berlin. Because of the war, travel was restricted, so the meeting was transferred to the neutral Netherlands, and world peace became the prime issue.

The meeting attracted 1,136 delegates from 12 countries, despite efforts by some governments to prevent their attendance. For example, 180 British women were refused passports, and the closing of the North Sea prevented even those with passports from attending. Because of the war, no Russian or French women attended (Alonso, 1993: 66–69). A concluding document stated that "one of the strongest forces for the prevention of war will be the combined influence of the women of all countries. . . . But as women can only make their influence effective if they have equal political rights with men, this Congress declares that it is the duty of the women of all countries to work with all their force for their political enfranchisement" (quoted in Alonzo, 1993: 68).

Among the resolutions passed were the decision to plan a meeting to be held at the same time and place as the end-of-war treaty meeting, so that the women could pressure the major powers to include women's equality in the peace talks, and the creation of two delegations to visit national leaders to urge mediation. One of the speakers supporting the latter resolution was Rosika Schwimmer (1877–1948), who said: "If brains have brought us to what we are in now, I think it is time to allow our hearts to speak. When our sons are killed by the millions, let us, mothers, only try to do good by going to the kings and emperors, without other danger than a refusal" (quoted in Steinson, 1977: 62). Schwimmer, a Jewish Hungarian feminist, was the international press secretary of the International Woman Suffrage Alliance. As a result of her speech, two delegations were formed after the meeting adjourned. The first, composed of Jane Addams of the U.S. delegation, Aletta Jacobs, and Rosa Genoni of Italy, met with leaders of England, Germany, Hungary, Italy, France, Belgium, the Netherlands, and Switzerland. The second delegation, which included Schwimmer, the U.S. feminist Emily Greene Balch, Chrystal Macmillan, and Cor Raymondt-Hirsch of the Netherlands, visited Norway, Sweden, Denmark, Russia, and the Netherlands. The two groups paid a total of 35 visits urging the leaders to seek mediation or a full truce.

With the ending of the war in November 1918, the organizers of the Hague conference began coordinating another ICW meeting, as they had planned. Unfortunately, they could not meet in Versailles, where the peace negotiations were being held, because German women could not travel there, so they met in Zurich instead. The ICW conference, held 12–17 May 1919, attracted delegates from Great Britain, France, the United States, Germany, the Central Powers, and neutral nations. The delegates agreed that the blockade of Germany should be lifted and supported in principle the League of Nations, which they felt should address such issues as child labor, racism, and arms reduction. Additionally, the ICW urged that a "Women's Charter" be included in the final peace treaty, covering topics such as universal suffrage, property and civil rights after marriage, equal pay for equal work, and "economic provision for the service of motherhood" (quoted in Alonso, 1993: 82). Delegates also agreed to continue their efforts as the Women's International League for Peace and Freedom (WILPF), headquartered in Geneva. The U.S. delegates Jane Addams and Emily Greene Balch were nominated as president and secretary-treasurer, respectively. The WILPF is the oldest extant women's peace organization.

Both during and after the war women joined socialist groups. In March 1915, 70 women from eight European countries attended an international conference of socialist women in Bern. The chief organizer, Clara Zetkin, had first attempted to mobilize the left wing of the German Social-Democratic Party and was later imprisoned. Luise Zietz, who took Zetkin's place, was forbidden to speak in public (for having discussed wartime shortages in Germany too frankly) and was later expelled from the party. In France, Louise Saumoneau founded the Socialist Women's Action Committee for Peace and Against Chauvinism. Women also organized unions. In Britain, for example, the National Federation of Women Workers was formed, but the union agreed that women workers should be dismissed when the soldiers returned: the price of admission to British trade unionism. In France, strikes were carried out by women munitions workers, if not for peace, then at least for the return of the troops (Thébaud, 1994: 61–62). Union and socialist activities throughout Europe continued through the 1930s, creating tension in women's organizations between moderate and more radical elements.

The growing tide of fascism in Germany and Spain brought even more urgency to peace efforts. Many women joined relief organizations for the Spanish Civil War, for example. In Germany, a handful of women swam against the tide of enthusiasm for Hitler, including a schoolgirl, Hiltgunt Zassenhaus, who thrust her arm through a pane of glass rather than give the Nazi salute (Miles, 1988: 227). European branches of the WILPF were harassed and its members arrested. Nazis raided the Munich WILPF office, destroying files and arresting workers. The Swiss government accused WILPF's international secretary Camille Drevet of spreading lies and ordered her expelled from the country. After a storm of protest, Swiss authorities dropped the charges (Brill, 1997: 85).

With the outbreak of war, a split in the European women's peace movement developed, with hardcore pacifists urging strict nonviolence and moderates supporting the war effort, often joining local chapters of the Resistance. Members of the Polish WILPF snatched Jewish children from trains headed for death camps. Women in other occupied countries hid children and adults who were wanted by the Nazis. Members of the Danish WILPF were able to bring 300 Jewish children out of Vienna, then helped them escape to Sweden (Brill, 1997: 87–88). Many women peace workers themselves died in German concentration camps.

Recent History

The use of atomic bombs energized the peace movement. In November 1945, women from the French Resistance hosted a meeting of more than 800 women from 41 countries. From this meeting emerged the Women's International Democratic Federation, representing 81 million women worldwide (Brill, 1997: 95). The WILPF took the lead in organizing women's responses to the new threat. Members from 15 countries met in Luxembourg in August 1946 and voiced their support of the United Nations and of disarmament. Later, many members of the WILPF opposed the North Atlantic Treaty Organization (NATO), seeing any such military union as threatening to world peace.

In her writing, the British essayist and novelist Vera Brittain (1896–1970) addressed the horrors of war. Beginning with the memoirs *Testament of Youth* (1933) and continuing with *Testament of Friendship* (1940) and *Testament of Experience* (1957), she wrote eloquently of the disillusionment of war and of the chances of peace, with the first volume speaking of the "lost generation." She remained active in the peace movement, in such organizations as the Peace Pledge Union and the Campaign for Nuclear Disarmament, and urged nonviolent direct action. Her writing inspired many women peace activists in Europe (Berry and Bostridge, 1995).

The 1950s and 1960s saw organized demonstrations against the arms race, colonialism, racism, the Korean War, French and later U.S. involvement in Vietnam, restrictions on freedom in eastern Europe, and nuclear testing, among other concerns. An early demonstration was the Women's International Strike for Peace, with protests in Geneva in March 1962 (the international organization was an offshoot of the U.S. Women Strike for Peace). In an echo of the women's peace conference in Zurich in 1919, Strike for Peace held an alternative conference in May 1965 in the Netherlands at the same time as NATO's general meeting in The Hague (Alonso, 1993: 209). The chief issue for women's peace organizations such as the WILPF through the mid-1970s, however, was the Vietnam War. There were numerous public demonstrations throughout Europe, including on International Women's Day, 8 March 1971.

Another focus was the strife in Northern Ireland. The movement against the violence was led by Betty Williams and Mairead Corrigan, who organized marches in which Protestants and Catholics demonstrated together for peace. In the citation for the Nobel Peace Prize, which they were awarded in 1976, Williams and Corrigan were praised for having "shown us what ordinary people can do to promote peace" (Nobel Prizes Web site, 2000).

In the late 1970s and 1980s attention on the part of women's peace organizations shifted to nuclear arms proliferation and nuclear power. In 1975–1977 women participated in the occupation of the Wyhl nuclear power plant in southwestern Germany, as well as at protests at plants in Brokdorf and Grohnde, Germany (1976 and 1977, respectively), and Malville, France (1978). Women in Gorleben, Germany, organized a picnic in the woods about to be felled for construction work on one nuclear power plant. The trees were cut down with demonstrators still in them. On 15–16 September 1979, more than 1,000 women met in Cologne, Germany, for a Women's Congress Against Nuclear Power and Militarism. The meeting ended with a "die-in," with participants lying down in the street in simulation of a nuclear accident (Gyorgy, 1980:8). The Nordic Peace March of March 1982, organized by Women for Peace from Scandinavia, was a three-week-long journey by foot, boat, and train, from Stockholm to Minsk. It was the first time the slogans "No to Nuclear Weapons in Europe, East and West" and "Yes to Disarmament and Peace" were carried by Europeans in Russia (Cambridge Women's Peace Collective, 1984: 268–269).

A common form of protest was the peace camp. The most imitated was the Greenham Common Women's Peace Camp, which began in August 1981 as a march from Cardiff, Wales, to the Greenham Common Royal Air Force base near London. The women were protesting the decision of NATO to site U.S. cruise missiles there. On arrival, the women set up the peace camp outside the main gate of the base. The camp became known as Yellow Gate when other satellite camps sprang up around the nine-mile perimeter fence of the base. Each camp chose a color of the rainbow to distinguish it. The missiles arrived in November 1983, and the round-the-clock encampment continued, with demonstrators being routinely arrested. In 1991, the last of the cruise missiles were removed, and the U.S. Air Force left the base in September 1992. The last of the satellite camps closed in January 1994. Today, there is a movement to turn the site into a peace park. Plans include a circle of stones inspired by Stonehenge (Greenham Common Women's Peace Camp Web site, 2000).

Other issues since then have included environmentalism, human rights abuses, use of antipersonnel landmines, forced involvement of child soldiers in local conflicts, and problems arising from the global economy.

See Also

ACTIVISM; ENVIRONMENT: WESTERN EUROPE; INTERNATIONAL ORGANIZATIONS AND AGENCIES; MILITARY; NUCLEAR WEAPONS; PACIFISM AND PEACE ACTIVISM; PEACE MOVEMENTS: NORTH AMERICA; WAR

References and Further Reading

Alonso, Harriet Hyman. 1993. *Peace as a women's issue: A history of the U.S. movement for world peace and women's rights.* Syracuse, N.Y.: Syracuse University Press.

Berry, Paul, and Mark Bostridge. 1995. *Vera Brittain: A life.* London: Chatto and Windus.

Brill, Marlene Targ. 1997. *Women for peace.* New York: Franklin Watts.

Cambridge Women's Peace Collective, comp. 1984. *My country is the whole world: An anthology of women's work on peace and war.* London: Pandora.

Fraisse, Geneviève, and Michelle Perrot, eds. 1993. *A history of women.* Vol. 4, *Emerging feminism from revolution to world war.* Cambridge, Mass.: Harvard University Press.

Gies, Frances, and Joseph Gies. 1978. *Women in the Middle Ages.* New York: Crowell.

Greenham Common Women's Peace Camp Web site. <www.web13.co.uk/greenham/stonecircle/html>.

Gyorgy, Anna. 1980. Europeans oppose nukes. *Clamshell Alliance News* 4 (Feb./Mar.): 8. Reprinted in Elliott Shore, Patricia Case, and Laura Daly, eds. 1982. *Alternative Papers.* Philadelphia: Temple University Press.

Lengyel, Emil. 1975. *And all her paths were peace: The life of Bertha von Suttner.* New York: Thomas Nelson.

Miles, Rosalind. 1988. *The women's history of the world.* Topsfield, Mass.: Salem House.

Nobel Prizes Web site. <www.nobel.se>

Steinson, Barbara Jean. 1977. Female activism in World War I. Ph.D. diss., University of Michigan.

Thébaud, Françoise. 1994. The Great War and the triumph of sexual division. In Françoise Thébaud, ed., *A history of women.* Vol. 5, *Toward a cultural identity in the twentieth century,* 21–75. Cambridge, Mass.: Harvard University Press.

Laura Daly

PEACE MOVEMENTS: Israel

This article describes the development of women's peace groups in Israel, presenting the main groups and their activities between 1988 and 1995. Women's peace groups are defined as groups consisting only of women and opposing the Israeli occupation of the West Bank and the Gaza Strip.

Historical Background

The conflict between Israel and Palestine has been an ongoing struggle in the Middle East lasting almost a century, and especially since 1948, when Israel was established. In the 1967 war, Israel occupied the West Bank and Gaza Strip and since then has ruled forcefully over 1.5 million Palestinians. Women in Israel, both Jewish and Palestinian (Muslim and Christian), have worked for peace in various organizations for many years. Some women's organizations, such as Tandi (Movement of Democratic Women), have been active since 1948. However, political and historical circumstances in Israel have prevented the growth of mass peace movements. Demonstrating against the politics of the government on issues of war and peace has been a relatively new experience for Israelis in general and for women in particular. Reluctance to challenge government policies can be traced to the widespread perception of Jews that Israel has been under a state of siege since its inception. This mentality produced a consensual Jewish society in which any opposition has been difficult to sustain. In addition, the strong influence of orthodox Jewish sectors and the nature of the state as a Jewish state have caused public opposition by women to be regarded as unusual (Swirski and Safir, 1991). At the same time, the Palestinians who remained in Israel after 1948 were subject to military rule until 1966 and thus were prevented from political activities.

The first popular peace movement of Jewish men and women was Peace Now, established in 1977. The Israeli invasion of Lebanon in 1982 prompted the first two women's peace groups. These were small but vocal and used single-gender demonstrations as a political tool. Parents Against Silence centered on the idea of women as mothers and focused on the demand to return their sons from the war. Women Against the Invasion of Lebanon was more direct in its opposition to the Israeli occupation of Palestinian territories and emphasized the role of women as an independent political entity for the first time. Both groups were part of the growing peace movement, which until then had been dominated by men. The inception of both groups was influenced by women's traditional role as mothers on the one hand and the growing frustration of women with their place in the male preserve on the other hand. When Israel withdrew (partially) from Lebanon, these groups ceased their activities (Gillath, 1991).

The Growth of Women's Peace Groups

The second wave of women's peace organization began early in 1988 with the start of the Palestinian uprising, the Intifada, in the occupied territories. The women's peace movement succeeded in mobilizing women who had not previously been active politically and bringing them together with activists of other left-wing, peace, and feminist groups. Single-gender organizations gave women a place to formulate opinions and work their way into the political sphere. This has presented a challenge to the traditional place of women in Israeli society that might have long-term consequences.

The first initiatives were a street slide show in Tel Aviv and the peace quilt. The slide show was organized by members of the feminist magazine *Noga.* The slides, taken by journalists and not shown to the public, exposed the consequences of Israeli military actions in the occupied territories (Young, 1992). The intention was to reveal the connection between the oppression of women and of the Palestinian people.

For the peace quilt, women from all over Israel decorated squares of material expressing the desire for peace and an end to the occupation. Four thousand pieces were sewn together to form the quilt. This project culminated in June 1988, when about 400 Israeli Jewish and Palestinian women, carrying the quilt, marched around the Israeli Parliament protesting the occupation.

Women in Black

At the same time, starting in January 1988, a small group of women in Jerusalem organized a protest vigil against the occupation. The women, dressed in black, stood in silence for one hour each Friday in a major city square. Each carried a sign saying "End the Occupation." The vigils soon spread over the country and become a national protest, with 33 vigils held at the same time every week.

Participation in the vigil was open to any woman, regardless of political, social, or personal background, who wished to join and who agreed to the group's slogans. By creating women-only vigils, the demonstrations of Women in Black became a place not only to voice opposition to the occupation but also to protest women's oppression. Women in Black has been the most visible, long-standing public protest in Israel. The group had no name, but within a short time the black clothing formed its identity. The association of black with mourning and death (in both Jewish and Palestinian traditions) was acknowledged by the women and the public alike as an expression of outrage. The color was also instrumental in creating a distinctive demonstration that could not be ignored. These vigils formed a decentralized network of primarily local, autonomous groups. With no formal or hierarchical structure, decisions were made by consensus, and local resources were used in recruiting, negotiating with the police, changing slogans, and organizing beyond the weekly vigils. The message was a broad one, based on criticism of the Israeli occupation. The public reaction was a mixture of sexual and verbal abuse, and anger against the women and their politics.

This blatant visibility, together with its underlying sexual politics, so strongly reacted to by the public, gave Women in Black the power to make an impact on society in general and on left-wing activities in particular. Women in Black participated as a group in other national demonstrations and left-wing activities where their point of view could no longer be ignored. In time, the model of these vigils was adopted by women in other countries, first in support of the Israeli vigils and later against war and local conflicts.

Various Women's Peace Groups

January 1988 saw the start of another group, Shani—Israeli Women Against the Occupation. This group of leftist, feminist, Jewish women in Jerusalem began with the aim of providing a framework for political education and protest. This was done through house meetings, study groups, and discussions with Palestinian women from the occupied territories. Shani produced fact sheets and initiated protest campaigns on some of the key issues concerned with the occupation (for example, the closure of all schools in the West Bank by military order for most of 1988–1989). Shani reached hundreds of Jewish women and was a strong factor in the growth of Women in Black in Jerusalem. It provided Jewish women with an opportunity to meet Palestinian women and to discuss controversial topics with them while searching for a joint political solution.

In December 1988, at the end of the first year of the Intifada, a conference, "A Call for Peace: Feminist Perspectives on the Occupation," was held and resulted in the formation of the first nationwide coalition of Israeli women (both Jews and Palestinians) and organizations active in the struggle for peace: Women and Peace. This coalition comprised women from two groups that long preceded the Intifada, Tandi, and the Israeli section of the Women's International League for Peace and Freedom (WILPF), as well as new groups such as Women in Black, Shani, and, for a short time, Women for Women Political Prisoners, a group dedicated to the defense and support of women prisoners. The aim of Women and Peace was to work for an end to the occupation in solidarity with Palestinian women from the occupied territories and to foster the connection between women and peace in public consciousness.

One of the coalition's main activities was the organization of an annual conference. In 1989, at the end of the conference "Women Go for Peace," 6,000 Israeli and Palestinian women and women from Europe and the United States marched from West Jerusalem to East Jerusalem. The marchers called on the Israeli government to recognize and negotiate with the Palestine Liberation Organization (PLO) and to agree to an international peace conference and to the establishment of a Palestinian state alongside Israel.

Working together in a coalition enabled Israeli Jewish and Palestinian women to broaden and deepen their political agenda. The political platform of Women and Peace called for negotiations with the PLO and a solution based on two states, as well as for immediate Israeli withdrawal from the occupied territories. Some of the women in the coalition urged soldiers to refuse to serve in the occupied territories. The coalition was only one of the many groups in Israel to organize a demonstration against the Gulf War. It also openly advocated sanctions as a means of pressuring the Israeli government to change its policy of occupation.

Another women's initiative was the Israeli Women's Peace Net (Reshet), formed in 1989 after an Israeli Palestinian women's conference in Brussels. The Peace Net began by holding house meetings and discussions between Israeli women and Palestinian women from the occupied territories. They were successful in reaching Israeli women holding positions of strength in the establishment groups and in centrist and leftist political parties (Chazan, 1991).

During the third year of the Intifada, women from the Peace Net, together with Women and Peace and Palestinian women from the occupied territories, formulated a peace treaty between Israelis and Palestinians based on feminist principles (Espanioly and Sachs, 1991). The Coalition of Women and Peace and the Peace Net formed a joint delegation to a Geneva Women's Peace Conference in May 1991 and cooperated on other occasions in demonstrations and solidarity visits to Palestinian women and women's organizations in the occupied territories.

On the basis of an ongoing dialogue between Israeli and Palestinian women's peace groups, the Israeli Women's Peace Net and Palestinian women's organizations established the Jerusalem Link in 1994. The Link is the coordinating body of two independent women's centers, one Palestinian and one Israeli, located in East and West Jerusalem, respectively. The Link was designed to serve the interests of the women of each community. Its focus is on women's issues, the advancement of peace, and the relationship between these two areas.

The signing of the Declaration of Principles between Israel and the PLO created a new reality for the women's peace groups in Israel. Only a few vigils of Women in Black still stand; other women's peace groups and the coalition of Women and Peace are looking for new strategies for action. This new area presents challenges to women who are concerned about the implications of peace treaties signed by men who were previously involved in warfare and about how to deal with the continuous atmosphere of hatred and oppression that affects women on both sides.

See Also

FEMINISM: JEWISH; FEMINISM: MIDDLE EAST; PEACE MOVEMENTS: MIDDLE EAST AND THE ARAB WORLD; POLITICS AND THE STATE: MIDDLE EAST AND NORTH AFRICA; VIOLENCE AND PEACE: OVERVIEW; VIOLENCE: MIDDLE EAST AND THE ARAB WORLD (LEBANON)

References and Further Reading

Chazan, Naomi. 1991. Israeli women and peace activism. In Barbara Swirski and Marilyn Safir, eds., *Calling the equality bluff: Women in Israel.* New York: Pergamon.

Cohen, Ruth. 1993. Women in Black step down. *Challenge* 22: 11–13.

Deutsch, Yvonne. 1992. Israeli women: From protest to a culture of peace. In Deena Hurwitz, ed., *Walking the red line.* Philadelphia: New Society.

Espanioly, Nabila, and Dalia Sachs. 1991. Peace process: Israeli and Palestinian women. *Bridges* 2(2: Fall): 112–119.

Gillath, Nurit. 1991. Women against war: "Parents Against Silence." In Barbara Swirski and Marilyn Safir, eds., *Calling the equality bluff: Women in Israel.* New York: Pergamon.

Montell, Jessie. 1991. Israeli identities: The military, the family and feminism. *Bridges* (Fall): 99–111.

Ostrowitz, Rachel. 1990. Dangerous women: The Israeli women's peace movement. In Rita Falbel, Irena Klepfisz, and Donna Nevel, eds., *Jewish women's call for peace.* Ithaca, N.Y.: Firebrand.

Rosenwasser, Penny. 1992. *Voices from a "promised land."* Willimantic, Conn.: Curbsrone.

Swirski, Barbara, and Marilyn Safir, eds. 1991. *Calling the equality bluff: Women in Israel.* New York: Pergamon.

Women in Black. 1992–1993. National newsletter, nos. 1–6. Jerusalem.

Young, Elise. 1992. *Keepers of the history: Women and the Israeli-Palestinian conflict.* New York: Teachers College.

Debbie Lerman

PEACE MOVEMENTS: Middle East and the Arab World

The Middle East and north Africa have been no more warlike than many other regions of the globe over the course of history, but recent events and reports in the western media have led many to believe that this region and its predominant religious tradition, Islam, are irrevocably committed to warfare both against outsiders and among their own nations. There is also a widespread perception that women in these regions are confined to domestic settings and profoundly disempowered. Neither of these stereotypes is entirely accurate. The activities of indigenous women's and peace movements in Arab countries, though often conducted in the face of official disapproval and even brutal repression, have contributed to a slowly growing hope of achieving a just and secure society.

Almost all Middle Eastern countries have women's councils and federations that address such issues as education, women's legal rights, and economic improvement. Women's attitudes toward peace vary from country to country and from one historical period to the next. Much depends on the level of state control of feminist movements, as well as on the maturity and experience of the leadership. But there are undeniable dimensions to the question of women and peace in the Middle East, related to the extreme suffering of women and their courage in confronting the ravages of war and national liberation struggles.

Peace movements in the Arab world and its neighboring countries are often confined to state elites, some of whom engage in a limited number of peace activities. This behavior is both surprising and explainable. The Middle East is largely in the midst of national liberation movements, rather than being the arena of world conflicts and struggle. With the exception of the Gulf War, most conflicts have been the result of postcolonial adjustments and the desire to safeguard vulnerable borders and demarcation lines. Naturally, the potential of these wars to arouse feelings of intense patriotism and nationalism precludes the development of a peace constituency. In only one of these wars, the Lebanese civil war of 1974–1989, was there a discernible and vocal female peace movement. Pitting brother against brother and, by extension, sister against sister, the Lebanese conflict could not stir up feelings of patriotism while the country was torn asunder by internal forces and actors. By contrast, the long Palestinian–Israeli conflict (1919 to the present) has all the makings of an intense national liberation confrontation. Here, it is often held, patriotism and nationalism emerged as the mobilization tools of nationalist elites, leaving little room for peace sentiments and gestures. This conflict, however, experienced female peace activities and serious, though intermittent, efforts to bridge the gap between enemies.

Lebanon: Making Peace in Civil War

While Beirut, the capital of Lebanon, was torn apart by 17 years of factional war, women wove links between the sectors of the city when men did not dare to do so, traveling despite the danger of snipers and communicating with one another. They provided for their families despite scarcity of food, electricity, and fuel. Many started small enterprises to help their families, and these often persisted after the war ended, especially when women entrepreneurs found themselves widowed.

Nongovernmental organizations (NGOs) proliferated to provide humanitarian assistance and messages of peace. Some of these were led by women who raised their voices to condemn violence. In 1984, Iman Khalifeh, a young kindergarten teacher who had worked with families on both sides of the divided city, coined the slogan "No to war. No to the tenth year of war! Yes to peace," which drew 70,000 signatures on petitions circulated on both sides of Beirut. In 1986, the late Laure Moghaizel, an eminent lawyer and cofounder (with her husband) of the Lebanese Association for Human Rights, joined Afifa al-Sayed, Leila Harb, Morma Melhem, and Amal Dibo (one of the present authors) to form a movement for nonviolence in Lebanon. These NGOs collaborated in organizing marches, sit-ins, and other demonstrations against war, violence, and human rights violations. The Lebanese Women Council resisted the divisions that racked the country; its members from all regions continued to attend meetings and to take positions in favor of peace and unity.

A three-day march for peace and human rights was sponsored in October 1987 by the Lebanese Association for the Rights of the Handicapped and the nonviolence movement. In July 1988, a sit-in in front of the temporary parliament called for peace, unity, independence, and human rights; for this occasion, Dibo wrote a "hymn for nonviolence" that was later adopted nationwide. The movement also sponsored blood drives in association with the Red Cross–Red Crescent, children's peace poster contests, and several conferences. Although most of these activities were initiated by women, who participated intensively, many men also contributed significantly.

Women also had leading roles in international organizations active in Lebanon, including Frances Moore of Save the Children Federation, Sanàa Osseiran of IPRA-Paris, and Nahla Haidar of the United Nations (UN) in Geneva. By bringing both relief assistance and conflict resolution strategies these women linked war-isolated Lebanon to the international community and kept channels of communication open through humanitarian appeals and exchanges. The offices of the UN agencies in Lebanon, though headed by men, were often maintained by women such as Lina Sultani at the United Nations High Commission for Refugees (UNHCR), Amal Dibo and Anna Mansour at the United Nations Children's Fund (UNICEF), and Jacqueline Abdel-Massih at the World Health Organization. The Lebanese High Relief Committee was headed by the only woman in high government office, Ne'mat Kan'an. Nadia Tawtal, a Christian, constantly kept open a social center for mothers and children in Burj el-Barajneh, the most deprived area in the Muslim sector of Beirut. These women served the whole population as if it were their family.

Women wrote many articles, essays, studies, short stories, and novels during the war years, as a means not only of denouncing war but also of liberating women from the passive silence of the victim. Perhaps the greatest literary novel to express the sentiments of these women during the

Lebanese Civil War was Etel Adnan's *Sitt Marie Rose.* Adnan, an unusual product of Lebanon's ethnic and religious mélange, had a Syrian Muslim father and a Christian Greek mother. The plot of her novel, the torture and killing of a Christian Lebanese schoolteacher by a Christian gang as punishment for her love affair with a Palestinian doctor, is also a meditation on the relationship between masculinity and violence. The protagonist is presented as strong and defiant, which challenges preconceptions equating femininity with weakness or dependency. The plot is deepened by its description of the killing, deliberately staged before a class of deaf-mute children, symbolizing the silence of the Arab regimes in the face of Lebanon's agony and disintegration. Such writers gave to the voiceless a voice that was not to be silenced, even after the war ended. Women maintained the trust and networks they had built during the conflict and turned to healing society's wounds. Women opened at least 10 art galleries with an agenda of helping Lebanon recover its sanity and its historical leadership in the cultural life of the eastern Mediterranean.

In civil society and industry, women also became prominent. Mona Hraoui and the deputies Nayla Mouawad and Bahia Hariri asserted their responsibility in rebuilding postwar government functions. Increasing numbers of women workers joined trade unions. In nearly every town, women were candidates for municipal elections, though few were elected.

Limits of Women's Peace Movements in the Middle East

Although many women in Lebanon, Israel, and Palestine have succeeded in crossing the ideological and physical barriers imposed by war, mass women's peace movements are generally not a common phenomenon in the region. To appreciate the inherent limitations on women's roles as peacemakers, one must examine the level of female political participation in Middle East governments and movements. First of all, women are still banished from the realm of international relations and are rarely consulted in matters of state. National liberation movements often diverge from this pattern in order to mobilize the energies of the largest number of followers. Women have regarded these movements as an opportunity to empower themselves and to prove their capacity for political decision making. Women's organizations and public committees, particularly in the Palestinian case, carve a niche for themselves in the space separating the leadership from the masses. This civil society, which has great potential for democratizing the future of Palestine, also represents a golden opportunity to build female institutions of a lasting quality. However, the Palestinian case is also instructive in a different manner. Opportunities for the consolidation of women's gains and rights always come with strings attached; women are expected to postpone their quest for equal civil rights in order to maintain the unity of the struggle. Thus they plunge into the throes of the political and national resistance battle with no guarantees for a future of equality and full participatory rights. Women's loyalty to the national cause became the only passport to emancipation. Under these conditions, women themselves sought to offer the supreme national and patriotic sacrifice in order to prove their worthiness as citizens in the community of the future. The route to female political legitimacy was through the battlefields of national liberation.

Nationalism also limited involvement in peace movements of Egyptian feminists who had mostly experienced semiofficial state feminism beginning with the years of Gamal Abdel Nasser. However, Egyptians still marvel at the quixotic adventure of Sanaa Hassan, a highborn Egyptian determined to build her own bridges to the Israelis in the 1970s. She came to Israel from a European port of entry and mingled with various symbols of Israeli society. When she returned to Egypt, however, her testimony about her experiences lacked legitimacy as well as substance largely because it was an individual effort. Although there were generally few calls for peace with Israel by Egyptian feminists, Nawal Saadawi and her group, the Arab Women's Solidarity Association, have joined other groups in expressing opposition to their countries' foreign policies by joining the movement against economic sanctions in Iraq. In so doing, they express a pan-Arab solidarity while also publicizing the suffering of women and children under the sanctions.

The case of Syria and Iraq, but especially Iraq, illustrates the difficulty of exercising autonomous control when the ruling party dominates and incorporates all institutions of society. Under these conditions, women's progress and their political expression are delimited by the ideological needs of the state. Since the late 1970s, no women's group has organized to pursue its own social agenda independent of the state; instead, Iraqi women have focused their energies and loyalties on the General Federation of Iraqi Women, which is considered a cadre of the ruling Baath Party. The state permitted minor changes in Islamic Personal Status Law only in order to avoid any clashes with Islamist groups. The intense suffering and great losses of women during the Gulf War and the UN-imposed economic sanctions did not give rise to any feminist peace expressions.

Conclusion

Sharing in the making of society, nations, and the world is the secret of peace; justice and mercy are the only guarantors of its maintenance. These are human qualities, regardless of gender. Dissociating women's and men's roles led to women's becoming peacemakers, while men became warriors. But women and men together are called to make peace and sustain it. The role of women as promoters of peace is most often recognized in wartime, and they have been denied full partnership in the building of society in peacetime. The greatest challenge for men and women is to balance the aggression and care within each of them, and to choose in freedom to weave peace in society and among nations, based on equality, dignity, and justice.

See Also

NATION AND NATIONALISM; PEACE MOVEMENTS: ISRAEL; VIOLENCE AND PEACE: OVERVIEW; VIOLENCE: MIDDLE EAST AND THE ARAB WORLD (LEBANON); WAR

References and Further Reading

Accad, Evelyne. 1990. *Sexuality and war: Literary masks of the Middle East.* New York: New York University Press.

Aghacy, Samira. 1997. *Modern Lebanese feminine literature.* Beirut: Institute for Women's Studies in the Arab World.

Cook, Meriam. 1987. *Women write war: The centering of the Beirut decentrists.* Oxford: Center for Lebanese Studies.

Cutting, Pauline. 1988. *Children of the siege.* London: Pan.

Einstein, Hester. 1984. *Contemporary feminist thought.* London: Unwin.

Ghoussoub, Mai. 1998. *Leaving Beirut: Women and the wars within.* London: Saqi.

Makdissi, Jean Said. 1990. *Beirut fragments: A war memoir.* New York: Persea.

Sabagh, Sura, ed. 1996. *Arab women between defiance and restraints.* New York: Olive Branch Press.

Amal Dibo
Talhami Ghada

PEACE MOVEMENTS: North America

The women's peace movement in North America had its origins in the outbreak of war in Europe in 1914. World War I galvanized women in both the United States and Canada to organize in opposition to the war and in support of a negotiated settlement between the belligerent nations. Since then, women on both sides of the border have worked in a variety of organizations that address issues of international relations, peace, and justice and work to define the role of women in these areas.

In the United States, the first organized response by women to the European war was the Peace March in New York City on 29 August 1914. This rally, organized by suffragists and social reformers, brought together some 1,500 women dressed in mourning in an early protest against the war. The Peace March signaled the need for a permanent political structure to bring a feminist point of view to the international dispute. The year 1915 marked the creation of two significant peace organizations. In the United States, the Women's Peace Party (WPP) was established, with the social reformer Jane Addams as the chair. The WPP demanded that the United States remain neutral and sought to bring the belligerent nations to the peace table. Within months, Addams had joined Rosika Schwimmer of Hungary, Emmeline Pethick-Lawrence of Great Britain, and U.S. suffragist Carrie Chapman Catt in creating an international feminist peace organization. Meeting in The Hague, the women established the Women's International League for Peace and Freedom (WILPF), with the primary objective of bringing about a negotiated settlement of the war. The WILPF was to become the most enduring women's peace organization of the twentieth century.

Canadian women were similarly dismayed by the outbreak of the war, but as citizens of the United Kingdom they were already committed to sending sons and husbands off to the European battlefront. Their antiwar sentiment was directed at reversing the conscription policy and promoting a peace settlement between Britain and Germany. Canadian women such as the journalist Nellie McClung, agricultural activist Francis Beyon, and suffragist Laura Hughes headed the peace movement and worked tirelessly for a settlement of the war. Many Canadian women joined the WILPF, thereby linking themselves with the growing movement of feminist pacifists.

It was a bold move for a woman to criticize her government during the course of World War I, and many were widely rebuked for their efforts to work for peace. These activist women represented a wide social and political spectrum. Most had been involved in the social reform movements of the period, and many considered themselves socialists or socialist-practicing Christians. Others, particularly in the United States, were reformers committed to the politics of the center, as represented in the United States by the Republican or Democratic Party. Regardless of their backgrounds, they generally agreed that war was an evil that could be controlled and eliminated. They acknowledged that the principal causes of war were increased military buildups, the economic profiteering that came from increased military spending, the spread of nationalism, and the failure of men to respond to international crises in a civilized fashion. Above all, they believed that women could change the context in which international events were constructed. They argued that if the nurturing elements of womanhood were brought to the development of public policy, this gentle influence would lead to the total elimination of the brutality and destructiveness of war.

At the end of World War I, the WILPF held a second meeting at The Hague to parallel the Paris Peace Conference of 1919. Their purpose was to impress upon the men meeting at Versailles the need for a nonpunitive peace accord that would guarantee a just and lasting peace. Although a lasting peace was an ephemeral goal, the women's peace movement began to have an impact on structures of international relations.

During the 1920s, feminist pacifism expanded and played a key role in the worldwide effort for disarmament. In the United States, many women continued to work for the WILPF or joined other fledgling peace organizations. Carrie Chapman Catt orchestrated a conference for women to study the causes of war and its cures. The conference ultimately became an umbrella organization, known as the Committee on the Causes and Cures for War, which linked numerous women's clubs together to lobby for U.S. participation in the League of Nations and the World Court, for a decrease in military budgets, and for aid to women and children suffering the economic cataclysm of postwar Europe. The United States did not join either international body during this period. However, Catt, Addams, and others were successful in engineering Senate investigations into military profiteering during the war, the signing of the Kellogg-Briand Pact that called for the elimination of war, and a decrease in naval spending through the provisions of the Washington Naval Conference. In 1931, Jane Addams received the Nobel Peace Prize for her efforts to outlaw war.

When the Great Depression of the 1930s gave rise to the fascist governments in Europe, the pacifists were alarmed but began to splinter in their approach to the new threat of world war. Many American women, believing that the United States must stay out of any conflict abroad, pushed for neutrality and an isolationist foreign policy. Others, such as Eleanor Roosevelt, who was then the first lady, believed that the threat to democracy was too great to allow the United States to remain neutral and that ultimately the defense of democracy outweighed the demands of the feminist peace movement. Throughout the decade, the WILPF and others, in both the United States and Canada, continued to argue that war was not inevitable but could be prevented through education and by letting the maternal nature of women guide world affairs.

When war officially came to Canada in 1939 and to the United States in 1941, very few women could maintain their opposition to war in light of the threat to Anglo-American democracy. Once war was declared, the WILPF issued statements about supporting the war effort and proposals to seek a negotiated settlement. Ironically, women in both countries recognized that civilian and military war work would help expand their economic rights. The peace movement had to mediate among conflicting demands—the need for national defense, the war's economic benefits to women, and the long-term goals of feminist pacifism. It did so in working for wartime civil liberties, tolerance among the peoples of all nations regardless of governmental disputes, and a postwar world that would be built upon the principles of freedom and peace.

The Allies' victory in 1945 aroused hopes for international peace through the creation of the United Nations but also gave rise to immense new problems created by the use of atomic weapons on Japan. The breakdown of relations between the United States and the Soviet Union also meant new problems for feminist pacifists. The WILPF continued through World War II, but the tensions of the cold war in the postwar years nearly brought about its demise. Its president, the longtime activist Emily Greene Balch, won the Nobel Peace Prize in 1946, but at the same time her organization and the entire women's peace movement were in disarray. Growing suspicion that communists had infiltrated the women's peace movement and that women's activism reflected national disloyalty caused a marked decline in interest and membership.

The postwar "red scare" had an impact on the peace movement, and the widespread movement to the suburbs in the 1950s led to a further decline in numbers. The WILPF shifted its agenda to attract new and younger members and to insulate itself from further criticism as a haven for communist sympathizers. WILPF activists targeted young suburban mothers, with the message that support of peace and freedom was the patriotic duty of every intelligent woman. Furthermore, they suggested that such women would support the efforts of the United Nations and various nongovernmental organizations (NGOs) to limit testing and development of nuclear weapons.

Canadian women were similarly embattled by the paranoia created by the "red scare," when anticommunist fears dominated Dominion policy, but a few brave women publicly objected to the U.S. military's use of Canadian territory for nuclear defense. Most Canadians, like most Americans during this period, found it difficult to agree with women who wanted to eliminate the nuclear arms race. Furthermore, many of the Canadian peace activists were avowed socialists, a political strain that did not attract many so-called traditional homemakers to the peace movement. Soon, however, the fear of fallout from nuclear testing and the threat of a nuclear holocaust would transcend political orientation in both countries.

By 1957, international scientists had begun to call for the end of nuclear testing as evidence mounted that the fallout from nuclear tests had serious consequences for public health. For women, the revelation that atmospheric testing endangered lives brought the nuclear arms race directly into their homes. Awareness of environmental contamination and fear of nuclear war prompted a renewed interest in the peace movement. Like the previous generation of peace activists, these new activists, many of them mothers with no political experience, believed that they had a particular interest in shaping international policy to conform to the well-being of all individuals. Their goal, more formidable than outlawing war, was to bring an end to the nuclear arms race and its threat of global destruction.

Each new cold war crisis, from Sputnik to the U-2 spy plane incident and the Berlin Wall, intensified East–West tensions and sent men and women scurrying to fallout shelters for air raid drills. Lotta Dempsey, a journalist with the Toronto *Star,* viewed the cold war as the failure of men to provide global security. Early in 1960, she suggested in her column that women might be better suited to conduct world affairs. Legions of Canadian women responded and organized the Voice of Women (VOW), or La Voix des Femmes, to make a collective reply to cold war politics and the threat of nuclear war. Their mission was a single demand for a world free of nuclear weapons in which it would be safe to raise a family. The organization, requiring only a small membership fee, grew rapidly, and the women established chapters across Canada, with the largest in Montreal. They lobbied the government in Ottawa to make Canada a nonnuclear nation and sought research information on strontium-contaminated milk and other by-products of atmospheric atomic testing.

Women in the United States raised the same issues. Dagmar Wilson, an illustrator of children's books who was the American wife of a British attaché, initiated the idea that women should "strike for peace." On a day set aside in November 1961, women across the United States went "on strike" from their daily household routines to demonstrate the fallacy of the idea of national security through nuclear armaments. As in Canada, the response was overwhelming. Like VOW, Women Strike for Peace was an organization made up of middle-class wives and mothers, generally nonideological and sharing one clear objective—to save the human race by ending the arms race.

On both sides of the border, women lobbied their governments, wrote articles, created peace programs for classrooms, developed strategies for arms reductions, and planned for the end of the cold war. Whereas U.S. women were often condemned as communist sympathizers and many were called to testify before Congress, Canadian women courageously traveled to Moscow to meet with Soviet women who held the same concerns for the welfare of their own families. Despite many obstacles, these seemingly quiet traditional homemakers began to have an effect on East–West tensions. The year 1963 saw their first tangible success in the signing of the Nuclear Test Ban Treaty, which eliminated aboveground atomic weapons tests.

In the late 1960s and early 1970s, the war in Vietnam sparked massive demonstrations and global antiwar sentiment. Feminist pacifist organizations struggled to find a constructive role to bring about the end of the war and assist the victims of war in southeast Asia. The WILPF and Women Strike for Peace organized peaceful demonstrations against the war, lobbied the president and Congress, and established draft counseling centers. A group of mothers, envisioning a world in which children would be free of the threat of war, created an organization called Another Mother for Peace. Their most memorable contribution to the peace movement was a poster designed by Lorraine Schneider that showed a bouquet of flowers with the caption "War is not healthy for children or other living things."

Canadian women had more freedom to give aid to the Vietnamese people. VOW began a campaign to knit dark-colored sweaters and blankets for North Vietnamese children; the dark color served to camouflage the children from U.S. bombing raids. VOW also brought women from both South and North Vietnam to Canada, where they met with peace activists from the United States. The Vietnam War stimulated much interest in the women's peace movement, but by the war's end in 1975 some women believed their work was complete. Many others remained peace activists but transferred their efforts to include women's rights, environmental protection, domestic violence, and children's peace education.

The 1980s saw a renewed military buildup in both the United States and the Soviet Union. Ronald Reagan's characterization of the Soviet Union as an evil empire, coupled with covert U.S. military operations in Latin America, once again forced women's organizations to confront the power structures that promoted militarism. The WILPF in both Canada and the United States renewed its call for a feminist dialogue in the structuring of foreign policy. In the United States, a unique group emerged that involved the wives of congressmen and other governmental officials. Betty Bumpers, wife of a U.S. senator, forged a bipartisan coalition whose goal was to promote a better understanding between U.S. and Soviet women. This group, known as Peace Links, was structured much like the pre–World War II Committee on the Causes and Cures for War. It attracted both feminist pacifists and women who were active in many other organizations. Unlike other groups, Peace Links had the ability to bring women from all walks of life, in both the Soviet Union and the United States, close to the centers of power. Peace Links coordinated a series of international conferences at which women could meet with high-level governmental officials, as well as women's exchanges between the United States and the Soviet Union and a pen pal program that endured the political upheaval in the former Soviet Union.

The last decades of the twentieth century witnessed numerous violent upheavals throughout the world. Peace activists have come to recognize that their efforts can no longer be a mere response to individual crises but, rather, must be a long-term, persistent effort to ensure social justice, human rights, and democracy. To meet these ongoing worldwide demands, women's peace organizations have established many programs to aid victims and refugees of conflict, famine, and terrorism. The WILPF, Voice of Women, Peace Links, and others have continued to work to create a culture of peace in areas of conflict, to eliminate racism and sexism, to end all forms of violence—especially violence directed at women—and to demand worldwide disarmament.

In May 1999, women from around the world gathered in The Hague to celebrate the hundredth anniversary of the first peace conference called by Czar Nicholas II. The backdrop to this celebration was NATO's bombing of Yugoslavia, and so the women once again found themselves called to condemn militarism and violence in the Balkans, just as they had in the early years of a century of unprecedented warfare. The women's nongovernmental peace agencies formulated an appeal for peace that reflects the expansion of institutionalized violence. Focusing on twentieth-century resurgence of genocide, the Coalition to End Genocide catalogued the millions of dead from World War I through the crisis in Kosovo in 1999. Noting that global response is always too little, too late, they called upon the United Nations and its member states to end genocide by reforming UN policy making and improving early warning mechanisms. In the early years of the twenty-first century, women peace activists continue to confront the same issues as their foremothers while acknowledging that world peace is a far more comprehensive quest than was once imagined—a quest that requires constant vigilance.

See Also

ARMAMENT AND MILITARIZATION; DISARMAMENT; FEMINISM: FIRST-WAVE NORTH AMERICAN; PACIFISM AND PEACE ACTIVISM; VIOLENCE AND PEACE: OVERVIEW

References and Further Reading

Adams, Judith Porter. 1991. *Peacework: Oral histories of women peace activists.* Boston: Twayne.

Addams, Jane. 1907. *New ideals of peace.* New York: Macmillan.

Alonso, Harriet Hyman. 1993. *Peace as a woman's issue: A history of the U.S. movement for world peace and women's rights.* Syracuse, N.Y.: Syracuse University Press.

Chatfield, Charles. 1971. *For peace and justice: Pacifism in America, 1914–1941.* Knoxville: University of Tennessee Press.

Cortwright, David. 1993. *Peace works: The citizen's role in ending the cold war.* Boulder, Col.: Westview.

DeBenedetti, Charles. 1980. *The peace reform in American history.* Bloomington: Indiana University Press.

Foster, Catherine. 1989. *Women for all seasons: The story of the Women's International League for Peace and Freedom.* Athens: University of Georgia Press.

MacPherson, Kay. 1994. *When in doubt do both: The times of my life.* Toronto: University of Toronto Press.

Peace, Roger C., III. 1991. *A just and lasting peace: Theoretical, historical and practical perspectives.* London: Croom Helm.

Solo, Pam. 1988. *From protest to policy.* Cambridge: Ballinger.

Swerdlow, Amy. 1993. *Women strike for peace: Traditional motherhood and radical politics in the 1960s.* Chicago: University of Chicago Press.

Williamson, Janice, and Deborah Gorham, eds. 1989. *Up and doing,* Toronto: Women's Press.

<www.igc.org>—PeaceNet

<www.PeaceLinksUSA.org>—Peace Links

<www.ploughshares.ca>—Canadian Voice of Women for Peace

<www.wilpf.org>—Women's International League for Peace and Freedom

Paula C. Barnes

PEDAGOGY: Feminist I

Feminist pedagogies occur at the interface of feminisms and emancipatory education theories. They developed initially out of a western, historical concern about women's exclusion from and experience of discrimination within masculinist educational institutions. The pedagogical focus was on access, particularly to disciplines in which women had been traditionally underrepresented (for example, the sciences), equity, and the recovery of subjugated knowledge.

Shifts in feminist thinking about sexual difference in the 1980s informed the ways feminist educators addressed inequities. These new conceptualizations about how sexed bodies influenced gendered possibilities moved beyond biological or constructionist understandings about difference. Psychoanalytic feminisms challanged the mind-body split. They saw the body and desire as central to the understanding and production of lived experience. This enabled feminist educators to locate the differences and specificities of gendered, raced, and classed bodies as productive sites for theory and practice.

Feminist pedagogies have always been part of a more general cross-cultural, historical tradition in education that saw social justice as a central concern. By the 1970s, "critical pedagogies" had emerged as a movement within educational sociology. Prior to this, educators concerned with the underachievement of particular students had tried to address inequity by incorporating students' subjectivity and background knowledge into the curricula. Structural reproduction theorists criticized this approach for failing to recognize the structural and ideological constraints that determine lived experience and the production of meaning . They suggested that oppressive class and gender relations were reproduced through education, thereby preventing students' agency or positive transformation at the intersubjective level of the classroom.

Critical pedagogies emerged from these positions that simultaneously acknowledged the structural constraints on subjectivity and reinscribed the agency and consciousness of the student. Key influences were the Frankfurt School of Critical Theory, Gramscian concepts of hegemony, and Freirean *conscientizacao* (*conscientization*). The project of critical pedagogies was to enable students to articulate their experiences in order to analyze how meanings and identities are constructed within, across, and against ideological and structural constraints. These critical tools enable students' to act in ways that challenge individual and collective oppression, thus effecting social transformation—the goal of critical pedagogies.

The emphasis on subjective experience, empowerment, the student's voice, and dialogue within critical pedagogies correlates with feminist concerns about subjectivity. Feminist educators critiqued critical pedagogues' continued dependence on masculinist assumptions about the centrality of the rational subject and the positioning of the teacher as the key to students' agency. These critiques acknowledged a debt to critical pedagogies while insisting that they have not sufficiently interrogated the power relations of the classroom. Key theorists include Ellsworth, Gore, Lather, Luke, and Walkerdine (in Luke and Gore, 1992).

What poststructural feminists brought to critical pedagogies was a threefold awareness that (1) teachers must recognize that they are always already involved in a disciplinary and discursive relationship with students, (2) power and agency in the classroom are always shifting and contingent because subjectivity is multiple and contradictory, and (3) the insistence on a coherent pedagogical narrative erases the contradictions within and between subject positions that prevent effective learning and lead to violence in the classroom.

Poststructural feminist educators insist on risks being taken, trust being negotiated, and fears and desires being acknowledged. In this way, poststructural feminist pedagogies use the omissions of critical pedagogies as starting points from which to teach through difference. Some poststructural feminist pedagogies also engage with queer, indigenous, and cross-cultural pedagogies (see De Castell and Bryson, 1997).

See Also

DIFFERENCE, I AND II; DISCRIMINATION; EDUCATION: GENDER EQUITY; EMPOWERMENT; EPISTEMOLOGY; KNOWLEDGE; PEDAGOGY; FEMINIST II

References and Further Reading

Cohee, Gail, et al., eds. 1998. *The feminist teacher anthology: Pedagogies and classroom strategies.* New York: Teachers College Press.

De Castell, Suzanne, and Mary Bryson, eds. 1997. *Radical in(ter)ventions: Identity, politics, and difference/s in educational praxis.* Albany: State University of New York Press.

Hernandez, Adriana. 1997. *Pedagogy, democracy, and feminism: Rethinking the public sphere.* Albany: State University of New York Press.

hooks, bell. 1994. *Teaching to transgress.* New York: Routledge.

Hughes, Kate Pritchard. 1994. *How do you know? An overview of writings on feminist pedagogy and epistemology.* Melbourne: Victoria University of Technology Monograph Series.

Jackson, Sue. 1997. Crossing borders and changing pedagogies: From Giroux and Freire to feminist theories of education. *Gender and Education* 9(4): 457–467.

Luke, Carmen, ed. 1996. *Feminisms and pedagogies of everyday life.* Albany: State University of New York Press.

Luke, Carmen, and Jennifer Gore. 1992. *Feminisms and critical pedagogy.* New York: Routledge.

Maher, Frances, and Mary Kay Tetreault. 1997. Learning in the dark: How assumptions of whiteness shape classroom knowledge. *Harvard Educational Review, 67*(2: Summer): 321–349.

Mayberry, Maralee, and Ellen Rose, eds. 1999. *Innovative feminist pedagogies in action: Meeting the challenge.* New York: Routledge.

McIntosh, Peggy. 1992. White privilege and male privilege: A personal account of coming to see correspondences through work in women's studies. In Margaret Andersen and Patricia Hill Collins, eds., *Race, class and gender, an anthology,* 70–81. Belmont, Calif.: Wadsworth.

Ropers-Huilman, Becky. 1998. *Feminist teaching in theory and practice: Situating power and knowledge in poststructural classrooms.* New York: Teachers College Press.

Galina Laurie
Jen Skattebol

PEDAGOGY: Feminist II

> If you want to take a class with women, with people of color, . . . come to Women Studies and start learning about things that they told you you didn't need to know. . . . Learning about me, instead of learning about them, learning about her instead of learning about him, it's a connection that makes education education. (Jilchristina Vest, cited in Maher and Tetreault, 1994: 56)

The term *pedagogy* commonly refers to teaching practices: the approaches teachers use to convey their subject matter to students. "Feminist pedagogies" are designed to make the voices of students, particularly women and other marginalized groups, the center of the educational process; such pedagogies seek to create an education for personal and community awakening and growth as well as social equality and justice.

Although originally focused primarily on methodologies, as distinct from subject-matter content, the term *feminist pedagogy* increasingly embraces the whole process of classroom knowledge construction. Feminist pedagogies, originally conceived primarily in terms of women's perspectives, increasingly reflect students' and teachers' multiple positions in settings of increasing educational diversity—identities given by class, race, culture, age, and other dimensions, as well as gender.

Thus work in feminist pedagogy has embraced what Carmen Luke (Luke and Gore, 1992), in Australia, calls a "foundation of difference," and what Maher and Tetreault (1994) call "pedagogies of positionality." In these new approaches, the exploration of participants' social locations, both consciously understood and unconsciously felt, both relative to each other and as they reflect wider societal networks, becomes central to the educational process. Knowledge for liberation and social change comes from exploring these relationships.

The principles behind the development of feminist pedagogy in the past 20 years reflect many strands of educational thought. These include the work of John Dewey and his followers in the 1920s and later, who believed in the classroom as a student-centered learning community whose values could help lead to a more egalitarian social order, and more recently the work of Paulo Freire, whose "liberation" model of pedagogy stems from his literacy work with Brazilian peasants and is rooted in Marxism and Latin American liberation theologies.

Freire assumed that the oppressed, and their teacher allies, would all speak in the same voice. His theories ignored contradictory identities that make most people simultaneously members of both oppressed and oppressor groups; in particular, he ignored exploited working-class men's subjugation of women (Weiler, 1991). Feminist teachers, although sharing Dewey's and Freire's commitment to students' empowerment, thus also differ from these schools in that they claim a particular commitment to women students, a concern with gender as a category of analysis for their teaching practices, and a notion that women and men (and by extension other diverse groups) might have divergent needs and interests in the classroom.

The assertion that education needs to be attentive to the particularities of women students is an example of the broader challenge posed by women's studies and feminist theory to what is described as the universalism and false objectivity of male-dominated western thought. Both feminist and postmodern scholars assert that knowledge is always constructed in a social context; the fact that the "norm," according to many scholars, is always male, white, and privileged and that other perspectives are ignored represents the dominance of a repressive minority over political, educational, and cultural institutions. As women's studies has transformed the academic disciplines to include the experiences of women, people of color, and other previously unheard groups, so the classroom has increasingly become an arena for the intersection of these new perspectives, rather than the imposition of one. (For the impact of the scholarship about women, African-Americans, and other marginalized groups on the curricula in American universities, see hooks, 1994; Tetreault, 1985.)

Feminist pedagogies are also rooted in the women's liberation movement of the 1960s. Along with initiating women's studies programs in colleges and universities worldwide, the women's movement engendered the consciousness-raising groups in which women began to explore and articulate their own perspectives and feelings publicly for the first time. In resistance to the more intellectual and abstract focus of the New Left in general, and its refusal to theorize about women or organize women, but sharing its commitment to fundamental political change, these small, informal groups of women delved into their subjective experiences and their personal histories to articulate theories that could lead to common social action to improve women's lives. Typically, these groups were leaderless, localized, collective, and unstructured, assuming and relying on a commonality of female concerns. They bequeathed to formal educational settings, and to feminist pedagogy, an attentiveness to students' personal experience and feeling as a source of knowledge. They also fostered a view of the teacher as a facilitator and equal participant rather than a distant authority (Weiler, 1991).

Another inspiration for feminist pedagogies has been the ongoing research on female students at all levels, from kindergarten through college, which finds that they are consistently disadvantaged by the practices and atmosphere of traditional, male-dominated, hierarchically organized classrooms. At every educational level and in every country that has been studied, female students are found to speak less than males and to receive less attention and mentoring from teachers. Although females tend to do well in school, it is males who excel, particularly in the higher grades and in math and science (Hall and Sandler, 1982). Besides identifying many other instances of sexism in education, researchers have suggested that traditional pedagogical approaches favor males; girls and women benefit from a classroom atmosphere that is collaborative rather than competitive, and that is concerned with "connected" and relational, rather than strictly analytical and rational, approaches to learning (Belenky et al., 1986).

In weaving together these complex legacies and lessons, feminist teachers by the mid-1980s had evolved a variety of specific teaching methods. These included collaborative learning groups and projects and evoking students' personal reactions and experiences through journals, shared classroom decision making, and student-led discussions. Feminist pedagogies have enriched programs and classes for adult and returning students as well (Maher and Tetreault, 1994: 77–82). Several collections of essays documented feminist teachers' accomplishments and struggles with the creation of a genuinely democratic and specifically feminist pedagogy. See Bunch and Pollack (1983), Culley and Portuges (1985), and Schniedwind and Maher (1987). More recent works include Luke (1996), Ropers-Huilman (1998), Cohee et al. (1998), and Mayberry and Rose (1999). The journals *Feminist Teacher* and *Radical Teacher* are also devoted to these issues in the classroom.

However, just as in the evolution of feminist theory itself, upheavals in the past decade have transformed the early models of feminist teaching. Women of color and lesbians, particularly the former, pointed out in the late 1970s that many white, middle-class, heterosexual feminists had created women's studies scholarship in their own image, ignoring many women, just as male theory had ignored all women. For example, the emphasis in the classroom on sharing individual "personal experiences" sometimes silenced the women, often women of color, who were in the minority in most settings. Searches during discussions for *commonalities* in the experiences of all women thwarted the evolution of knowledge from a variety of different perspectives, leaving its construction to the dominant group—white, heterosexual women—and ignoring the input of women of color and others.

Despite the adoption in feminist theory of situated knowledge and multiple partial perspectives, white students even today resist seeing themselves as socially positioned and privileged by their whiteness. Frequently they like to speak simply as individuals (or globalized "just people"), while treating women of color as anomalies. As one said, "I just don't like saying that white women are this and African American women are that. Why can't we all be women?" (Maher and Tetreault, 1994: 174). As bell hooks put it:

> Black students sometimes get the feeling that feminism is a private white cult. [Their] efforts to link all discussions of gender with race may be contested by white students, who see this as moving away from feminist concerns. And so suddenly the feminist classroom is no longer the safe haven many women students imagined. Instead it presents conflict, tension, hostility. (1990: 29)

The challenge mounted by lesbians and students and faculty members of color to these preceived false commonalities of experience and theory has been been expanded to include the assumption underlying early ideas of feminist pedagogy—that feminist teachers could relinquish their authority in the name, again, of sisterhood. As academics, they have had to confront the hierarchical nature of the academy, the need to establish themselves within their academic fields, the expectation of both female and male students that teachers be experts, and the responsibilities of evaluating students. Unable to relinquish it altogether, feminist pedagogues are challenged to come up with new grounds for their authority, in the context of creating democratic and feminist classrooms within undemocratic and androcentric educational institutions (Culley and Portuges, 1985; Maher and Tetreault, 1994; Weiler, 1991).

Faced with such challenges, which split the presumed unities of teacher and student, women of color and white women, and lesbian and heterosexual women, as well as assumed dichotomies between males and females, feminist teachers have begun to explicate these "conflicts, tensions, and hostilities" in their classrooms. How can heterogeneous student groups face and work through such divisions, which place people in the same room on various sides of multiple divides between oppressor and oppressed?

Differences of power, authority, learning styles, cultural and class backgrounds, and other variables that students and teachers bring to the classroom are no longer avoided by feminist teachers, but, in fact, form the theoretical foundations for current feminist "pedagogies of positionality." The goal is not to replicate social power relationships but to challenge and change them. For example, much work has recently been done on the concept of whiteness and other positions of privilege; pedagogies of positionality encourage excavation of relations of privilege in the classroom (McIntosh, 1994; Maher and Tetreault, 1997). If white students come to see that whiteness is a position, just as gender is, then race and gender can be seen as relational and interactive. Each side constructs the other in constantly shifting dynamics that feminist teachers can work both to reveal and to transform.

In a study by Maher (the present author) and Tetreault, the themes of "master," "voice," "authority," and "positionality" address these issues. For example, whereas in early formulations of feminist pedagogies, "voice" meant simply the awakening of students' own responses, today it is understood as a complex fashioning of identity-in-context through which people focus on different aspects of their own and one another's positions to shape their personal narratives as well as the subject-matter mastery they achieve. After struggling alongside women of color through novels about and by African-American women, one white woman said, "I thought we all thought alike, but it seems a lot of Black people think differently than I do. I mean they were always working for equality, but there's so much racism that, with things they see every day, they look at things a different way" (176). An African-American male in the same class said that he had learned a lot about the "ways we perpetuate our sexism": "It's good for me to step back and look at [oppression] in another way because usually I'm always seeing it from a racist standpoint.... I am a male, so in some ways I feel the oppressor category, and it is a strange feeling.... I've never developed a lot of the views [the instructor] says men have" (177). Similarly, classroom authority is not fixed, but rather a set of relations that can be acknowledged as grounded in teachers' and students' evolving (and various) connections to one another and the material. The resulting knowledge is not hierarchically ordered but rather always contextualized—and evolving. As one African-American scholar put it:

> The different ways we are engaged in feminist discourse do not elevate Black women scholars, in relation to other women of color or European-American women, to the heights of some [new] exemplary level of knowing. Instead [we] attempt to situate Black womanists/feminists, to account for radically new interpretations of feminism and the ways we teach it. (Chinosole, personal communication, 1994)

The acknowledgment of these dynamics changes neither the teaching practices per se engaged in by feminist teachers nor the difficulties they encounter. Experimentation with collaborative classroom arrangements, positioning students as authorities, and pushing them to articulate their experiences in relation to one another go on, and feminist teachers are always "in process."

Yet to see everyone as positioned is not to make every position equally valid, but rather to explore the complex (and always shifting) relations of privilege that are masked by any one ideology of oppression, even that of "all women." Furthermore, to shift "feminist pedagogy" toward "pedagogies of positionality" does not mean forsaking commitments to social justice for actual women and others beyond the classroom and beyond local borders. As Carmen Luke, from Australia, says:

> Deferrals to the local and to specificity do not mean that anything goes, that we do not take a position in classroom encounters. That position can only be emancipatory if our attention to [local] politics is tied to engagement with the politics of global structures and their justifying narratives of oppression. (Luke and Gore, 1992: 48–49)

The future of feminist pedagogy, of pedagogies of difference and of positionality, lies, like other educational issues, in societal changes beyond the classroom and beyond educational institutions. Students' and teachers' visions of empowerment and community need sustenance from developments outside, just as the women's movement and the civil rights movement have provided the continuing inspiration for many feminist teachers in the United States. The current decline in emancipatory projects worldwide makes feminist and antiracist educational projects difficult. Yet although classrooms reflect the power dynamics of the larger society, they also offer arenas to observe and challenge them. Furthermore, the increasing diversity of educated populations throughout the world makes for far richer and more complex classroom environments. It is in this fertile soil that we hope feminist pedagogies will continue to both struggle and flourish, and that the term *pedagogy* will retain its emancipatory possibilities.

See Also

CONSCIOUSNESS-RAISING; EDUCATION: ANTIRACIST; EDUCATION: GENDER EQUITY; EDUCATION: HIGHER EDUCATION; EDUCATION: NONSEXIST; KNOWLEDGE; PEDAGOGY: FEMINIST I; RACE; WOMEN'S STUDIES: OVERVIEW

References and Further Readings

Belenky, Mary, Blythe Clinchy, Nancy Goldberger, and Jill Tarule. 1986. *Women's ways of knowing: The development of self, body and mind.* New York: Basic Books.

Bunch, Charlotte, and Sandra Pollack. 1983. *Learning our way: Essays in feminist education.* Trumansburg, N.Y.: Crossing.

Cohee, Gail, Elizabeth Daumer, and Theresa D. Kemp, eds. 1998. *The feminist teacher anthology: Pedagogies and classroom strategies.* New York: Teachers College Press.

Culley, Margo, and Catherine Portuges, eds. 1985. *Gendered subjects: The dynamics of feminist teaching.* London: Routledge and Kegan Paul.

Hall, Roberta, and Bernice Sandler. 1982. *The classroom climate: A chilly one for women.* Project on the Status and Education of Women. Washington, D.C.: Association of American Colleges.

hooks, bell. 1990. From skepticism to feminism. *Women's Review of Books* 7(5): 29.

———. 1989. *Talking back: Thinking feminist, thinking black.* Boston: South End.

———. 1994. *Teaching to transgress.* New York: Routledge.

Luke, Carmen, ed. 1996. *Feminisms and pedagogies of everyday life.* Albany: State University of New York Press.

Luke, Carmen, and Jennifer Gore, eds. 1992. Feminist politics in radical pedagogy. In *Feminisms and critical pedagogy.* New York: Routledge.

Maher, Frances A., and Mary Kay Thompson Tetreault. 1994. *The feminist classroom.* New York: Basic Books.

———. 1997. Learning in the dark: How assumptions of whiteness shape classroom knowledge. *Harvard Educational Review* 67 (2: Summer): 321–349.

Mayberry, Maralee, and Ellen Rose, eds. 1999. *Innovative feminist pedagogies in action: Meeting the challenge.* New York: Routledge.

McIntosh, Peggy. 1994. White privilege and male privilege: A personal account of coming to see correspondences through work in women's studies. In Margaret Andersen and Patricia Hill Collins, eds., *Race, class and gender. An anthology,* 70–81. Belmont, Calif.: Wadsworth.

Ropers-Huilman, Becky. 1998. *Feminist teaching in theory and practice: Situating power and knowledge in poststructural classrooms.* New York: Teachers College Press.

Schniedwind, Nancy, and Frances Maher, eds. 1987. Feminist pedagogy (special issue). *Women's Studies Quarterly* 15(3–4). Reissued with addition in 1993: 21(3–4).

Tetreault, Mary Kay. 1985. Feminist phase theory: An experience-derived evaluation model. *Journal of Higher Education,* 56(4: July/Aug.): 363–384.

Weiler, Kathleen. 1991. Freire and a feminist pedagogy of difference. *Harvard Educational Review* 61(4: Nov.): 449–474.

Frances A. Maher

PERFORMANCE ART

Performance Art is a fairly new artistic style, created by the neo-avant-garde (largely North American and European artists) in the 1970s. This style combines various forms of expression of all classical genres in their ephemeral states, freely experimenting with forms of spontaneous direct communication, without being constricted by conventional definitions of the fine arts.

From its beginnings, performance art distinguishes itself by an intermedial mix in which traditional pictorial means, movements, theatrical staging, music, photography, electronic media, film, and video are used to create a critical interpretation of materialism and social inequality.

The roots of performance art go back to the early 1900s, when the European avant-garde began critiquing bourgeois aesthetics, challenging traditional conceptions of art by attempting to establish or reestablish it as a sensible function in the coherence of everyday life. Futurists, dadaists, and surrealists questioned the social order with cabaret-like appearances, which inspired reactions as diverse as laughter, protests, and sometimes even action. These appearances, however, demonstrated the available possibilities and strategies for change within the art establishment. The immediate confrontation between all varieties of performance art (such as happenings, actionism, and fluxus) and the audience was not only required but unavoidable.

In the early 1970s, performance art became the name for the actions of pictorial artists in California. By labeling a specific presentation technique, the performer—as subjective first-person narrator—illustrated personal experiences and sensations: interpretations of reality in the form of a living picture. Structurally, performance art is more related to the archaic act of ritual than to the conventional dramatic arts. The "actors" represent *themselves* without exception; the space and time of the actions are real.

Thematically, performance art focused essentially on the proportion of the social allocation of obligatory cultural stereotypes in order to analyze their influencing mechanisms beyond the existing establishment. In the 1970s, this aspect interested female artists, who, under the influence of the feminist movement, engaged themselves for the equality of the sexes, rendering their double roles as women and as artists the central accusation in this new genre. This aspect of performance art—like no other art form—was created and maintained by women, even though they have been only modestly represented and recognized.

This new medium guaranteed the greatest possible freedom and an immediacy of artistic expression; it also shows no formal or thematic restrictions of the conventional points of a male-dominated cultural management. Performance art allows the female artist to glance into the mirror of art, which reflects a complex self-image for the first time, a process and social (and critical) view that aims at the private and intimate life and also at the general life with psychoanalytic accuracy. The artistic search of the new self-portrait of the woman should occupy these positions, which until now (arguably) were held by the established clichés, stereotypes, and misogynistic images of the dominant patriarchal order.

Valie Export (b. 1940, Austria) analyzed the biological and social components of sex-specific role attitudes and female body language in direct contact with the street audience. In *Tapp und Tastkino* (1968), Export hid her breasts in a cupboard behind a black curtain into which people passing by (after having paid) could put their hand.

Ulrike Rosenbach (b. 1943, Germany) physically confronts medieval paintings of women with her own body, pointing out the difference between the wishful thinking of men and female physical reality. In her video *Madonna im Rosenhag* (1975), she fires arrows at the idealized picture of the Mother of God; the pierced face then fades into her own portrait.

Iole de Freitas (b. 1945, Brazil) used a mirror as an instrument and symbol in *Glass Pieces Life Slices* (1975), to search for the position of herself. In mirrors spread in a circular shape on the floor, she examines the sectional reflections of her body with a camera and documents—in a photographic installation—a fragmentary perception of her own womanliness; of a utopian, not estranged self.

Gina Pane (1939–1990, France) injured herself in the course of her performances, thereby damaging the untouchable picture of the woman. In *Psyche* (1977), she cut both of her eyelids and let the blood drip onto her (reflected) image, in order to demonstrate the discrepancy between the image of female wholeness and the effect of a repressive reality (confirmed by a daily glance into the mirror).

Colette (b. 1953, Tunisia) reacted with irony to male appropriations of female self-understanding. She styled herself as a spoiled woman who existed passively, locked into a frilled luxurious world of silk and satin from which there was no escape. In *The Wake of Madame Recamier* (1975), Colette sleeps, a doll-like creature, in a narrow grotto and reclaims a total unconnectedness to a repressive reality.

Orlan (b. 1947, France), pushed the finishing strategies that women (willingly) undergo in order to meet male ideals. In *La reincarnation de Sainte Orlan* (1990), Orlan creates a synthetic image of woman out of pictures of Europe, Venus, Psyche, Diana, and the Gioconda on her computer, and gradually matches her own appearance to this image after several plastic surgeries. Each operation is a performance, documented on video.

Joan Jonas (b. 1936, United States) also used video as an electronic mirror, enabling the dimensions of space and time to be manipulated. In *Double Lunar Dogs* (1980), Jonas directs the most important passages of the cave parable in the form of a science-fiction story, using this medium to comment on the exemplary effort to escape the narrow bourgeois mentality that prevents the development of any independent female identity.

Laurie Anderson (b. 1936, United States) used her own experiences to theorize about American political understanding. This is demonstrated in *United States—Part II* (1980), as she analyzed the loss of identity in the western civilization. This is decried as the effect of modern communication technologies, whose functions are no doubt understandable for the user, but which also increasingly confront the individual with a semiotic world, the complex meaning of which can no longer be reliably deciphered.

Siglinde Kallnbach (b. 1956, Germany) reactivated in *Nach (N)omen or Der Sensenmann kann mich mal(en)* (1990) shamanistic rites and techniques to recall the forgotten magical power of women. Kallnbach entered into a trance and painted bloody images onto a wall, before she tore her clothes and attacked the audience, who were then sprinkled repeatedly with color-soaked material.

See Also

AESTHETICS: FEMINIST; GAZE; THEATER: OVERVIEW; THEATER: MODERN AND CONTEMPORARY; THEATER: WOMEN IN THEATER

References and Further Reading

Goldberg, Roselee, and Laurie Anderson. 1998. *Performance: Live art since 1960.* New York: Abrams.

Jones, Amelia. 1998. *Body art/performing the subject.* Minneapolis: University of Minnesota Press.

Juno, Andrea, and V. Vale, eds. 1992. *Angry women.* New York: Juno.

O'Dell, Kathy. 1998. *Contract with the skin: Masochism, performance art, and the 1970s.* Minneapolis: University of Minnesota Press.

Pontriand, Chantal. 1981. *Performance: Text(e)s and documents.* Montreal: Parachute.

Roth, Moira, ed. 1983. *The amazing decade: Women and performance art in America 1970–1980.* Los Angeles: Astro Arts.

Edith Almhofer

PERFORMANCE TEXTS

Performance texts are theatrical shows, spectacles, or events. Images and visual effects are especially meaningful, and therefore, ideally, performance texts are viewed as they are performed. A performed script outlines the conceptual spaces for bodies in a performance text. A performance text might include written material and words for players to speak, other media (artwork, slides, video, computer-generated images), and might juxtapose live and recorded bodies. In its most abstract version, a performance text presents fragmented sequences suggesting impressions of fleeting interiors and irrational imaginings seemingly at random. Less abstract performance texts include monologues and come closer to, but differ from, the stylized format of plays with their psychologically coherent characters and thematic messages. A heightened sensory and cerebral engagement is central to, rather than incidental to, experiencing a performance text. Ideas and images are open-ended and collide across conceptual terrain that often refers to without reproducing other theatrical texts and cultural representations.

Women have been important figures in the artistic movement creating performance texts that has bridged performance art and experimental group theater since the 1960s. Their work innovatively explores space, performer–spectator relationships, and intellectual discourses. Creators of performance texts usually direct or perform their own work (or both). Female performers train within and against the larger, male-dominated field in eastern and western theatrical traditions, for example, in movement, dance, butoh (a post–World War II Japanese movement style), and physical theater. Directors' textual production can be analyzed with gender theories about self and embodied identity. Even if the artists do not identify as feminist, their processes align with feminist theater that blurs the traditional roles of performer, writer, and director. Some performance texts overtly contest racial and gender orthodoxies.

Since the 1980s the Magdalena Project (based in Wales) has developed collaborative works with international artists including those from eastern Europe and South America. Most performance writers are also directors, many with theater backgrounds, such as Japan's Kishida Rio, the United States' Omaha Magic Theater, the United Kingdom's, Rose English, and Australia's Jenny Kemp, Clare Grant, ex-Sydney Front, and Virginia Baxter, cofounder of Open City. Although performance texts are generally produced by groups of artists, since the 1960s individuals such as Rachel Rosenthal, Carolee Schneemann, and Meredith Monk have expanded the genre in the United States, where monologues predominate. These include the extraordinary solo shows of Anna Deavere Smith, who performs over 30 identities across race and gender in each show, and sexually explicit shows by visual artists such as Karen Finley, and the ex-porno film star Annie Sprinkle.

Performance texts can range from the spoken works of the British novelist Deborah Levy writing on cultural dislocation, to France's visual artist Orlan restaging her plastic surgery in art gallery installations, to the United Kingdom's Bobby Baker's satirical cooking demonstrations as high art, to queer parodic body shows. They can be grouped with postmodernism in theater, as well as intercultural performance projects, as for example, by Australian and Japanese performers, or with both, as in the shows by the United States' Spiderwoman.

Documentation requires visual and written records and often includes theoretical analysis and sometimes performance artifacts. Articles in journals such as *Women and Performance, Performance as Research, Text and Performance*

Quarterly, and Australia's *Real Time* critique performance texts. Organizations such as Performance Studies International sponsor conferences. Performance-specific venues seem connected to a noticeable increase in women's performance texts since the early 1980s, for example, in Manhattan's P.S. 122 and at Sydney's The Performance Space.

Peggy Phelan is perhaps the leading performance theorist. She writes across artistic modes on the (gender and race) politics of visibility and the philosophical implications of performing presence and absence. Feminist theorists such as Jill Dolan, Elin Diamond, and Elinor Fuchs outline the main debates since the 1980s with the rejection of conventional realist forms (including Brechtian) and the preference for the radicalism of innovative performance texts. Feminist performance theory and its pedagogy might investigate the imagistic representation in the visual text, its surface coding, and implied subjectivities, and might utilize philosophical ideas of the body (for example, the philosopher Judith Butler's embodied performative social self and Elizabeth Grosz's sexed bodies). Performance makers are often familiar with these discourses, and spectators' and readers' responses should recognize ongoing influences and exchanges between performance texts and the ways that these texts often preempt theoretical approaches.

See Also

DRAMA; LESBIAN DRAMA; PHILOSOPHY; RACE

References and Further Reading

Fuchs, Elinor. 1996. *The death of character.* Bloomington: Indiana University Press.

Phelan, Peggy. 1993. *Unmarked.* London: Routledge.

———. 1997. *Mourning sex.* London: Routledge.

Schneider, Rebecca. 1997. *The explicit body in performance.* London: Routledge.

Tait, Peta, ed. 2001. *Body show/s: Australian viewings of (live) performance.* Amsterdam: Rodopi.

Peta Tait

PERIODICALS

See MAGAZINES.

PERSONAL AND CUSTOMARY LAWS

Legal systems in postcolonial societies are a product of complex histories. The variety of regulatory regimes that affect women's lives include *customary laws,* based on the customs and practices of the indigenous people; *personal laws,* based on religion; and *state laws.* Feminist legal discussions have concentrated on the contribution of customary and personal laws to women's inequality within their societies, but feminist legal scholars, particularly those from the "North," have placed too little emphasis on understanding the plurality of laws—specifically, the relationship of customary or personal laws to state law (Manji, 1999). However, a new scholarship is emerging from the "South" that starts by tackling the issues women face in family and property-related matters.

Personal or customary laws once covered all aspects of life, but colonial interventions and the development of the modern state formally restricted their domain to "private" matters, including family relations (such as marriage, divorce, maintenance, and custody of children), and property relations (for example, inheritance). Personal laws based on religion cover family and related matters in many countries: in India, for example, there are Hindu, Muslim, and Christian personal laws. Islamic personal laws are practiced in many countries in north Africa, the Middle East, south Asia, and southeast Asia. Customary laws prevail in much of sub-Saharan Africa.

There is a debate within feminism on the contribution of customary and personal laws to women's position in their societies. In the dominant view, these laws are reflections of women's subordinate position: thus within many customary systems in Africa, marriage is based on a payment by the man to the woman's family, not on the consent of the woman; children are the property of their fathers; and women cannot own or inherit land. Similarly, personal laws based on religion are seen as contributing to women's subordination; for example, Islamic law permits a man to have more than one wife and to divorce with little formality.

Customary practices are viewed as a reflection of gender relations that are rooted in the past and in need of reform through the creation of equal rights for women. One strategy has been to campaign for the recognition of women's rights as human rights. The Convention on the Elimination of All Forms of Discrimination against Women, ratified in 1981, urges states to eliminate discriminatory practices based on custom and tradition and to ensure that personal laws are not discriminatory. Some campaigners have struggled to incorporate clauses within their country's constitution to outlaw discriminatory practices and promote equality.

Some feminists, often from societies where personal and customary laws exist in a complex relationship to state law, argue that this approach fails to acknowledge the complexity of the issues but constructs women merely as victims of oppressive systems. They argue that feminists from the North tend to impose their own analysis (Stewart, 1996).

Centralism versus Pluralism

To discuss the significance of customary or personal laws, it is necessary to consider briefly the nature of law. Can nonstate regulatory regimes be law? Legal analysts debate this issue in terms of a dichotomy: centralism versus pluralism. Proponents of centralism insist that the term *law* be confined to rules created by the state that are uniform and exclusive in their application (Dengu-Zvogbu et al., 1994: 13–14). Legal centralists distinguish between law and morality but ignore the impact of the law on society and the ways in which people regulate their lives to comply with or avoid the law (Dengu-Zvogbu et al., 1994: 15).

Legal pluralism, by contrast, suggests that two or more legal systems can coexist within the same social system (Merry, 1988: 870). Interest in legal pluralism developed from the study of what is known as *juristic* (Griffiths, 1986) or *classical* (Merry, 1988) legal pluralism—that is, the dual legal systems created when European countries established colonies and superimposed their legal systems (known as general or received laws) on preexisting systems. In this situation, the sovereign entity commands different bodies of law for different population groups, varying by ethnicity, religion, nationality, or geography. These parallel legal regimes are all dependent on the state legal system (Merry, 1988: 871).

On family and related matters, the colonial regimes imposed legal segregation between the indigenous peoples and themselves. The received law of the colonizers, covering law and order, commercial, property, and criminal matters, remains the dominant legal normative order today (Bentzon et al., 1998: 32).

Newly independent states sought to deracialize and "modernize" their inherited legal systems, often by creating a new constitution embodying liberal democratic concepts of the rule of law and individual rights and, in sub-Saharan Africa, by transforming the laws of the colonizers into general laws applicable to all citizens. The segregation persists but is now based on whether a person is deemed to follow customary ways or live by "modern" standards. Citizens in postcolonial societies inhabit a complex legal world in which who you are and how you live determine which type of law applies to you (Merry, 1988: 871).

Family and property relations are good examples of the multiple regulatory regimes that women in many countries must negotiate. For example, historically, land in eastern and southern Africa was held communally by a clan or kinship group, with its disposition organized within and through this kinship network by elders. In this system, based on status, women generally were not recognized as actors. For example, land was inherited not by a widow but by a male relative of the deceased.

These customary laws not only constructed the property relations within the clan but also were used to challenge the colonial state's objective of exploiting the land through private ownership and sale. Historical research has shown how the clans organized their resistance to these developments. The colonial state had to rely on the chief's authority to regulate relations within rural areas and ultimately had to accept the validity of the chiefs' customary definitions of land use and allocation (Chanock, 1991). Through the struggle to retain control over the land within the clan, the chiefs and the colonial state constructed an understanding of what was customary land tenure. By defending their custodianship over land and preventing it from being turned into private property, the kin groups resisted state authority over them. At the same time, however, they constructed customary laws that maximized gender hierarchies.

This history has influenced the way in which the interaction between gender relations and customary practices is understood in the postcolonial era. Some see customary practices as the basis for resisting exploitation, whereas others see them as impediments to progress, including progress for women.

Current Research Projects

The Women and Law in Southern Africa (WLSA) organization and a regional Women's Law program in southern Africa set out to break through this constructed dichotomy by adopting a legal pluralistic grounded approach (Bentzon et al., 1998). They have concentrated on family-related matters such as maintenance and inheritance in a number of southern African countries (see, for example, Dengu-Zvogbo et al., 1994). Both projects have worked in collaboration with Scandinavian women's law researchers and have been influenced by this approach (see Dahl, 1987). Their research and action concentrate on women's position within customary law as it is actually practiced, which is often very different from how it is understood formally. This approach has led to an understanding of women's legal issues that takes full account of the plurality of normative orders outside state law that affect women's lives (Bentzon et al., 1998).

Research on widows' rights to inheritance in Uganda reveals the importance of understanding the impact of customary law and practices on the construction of rural women's existence. Mwaka (1999) shows how rural widows struggle to ensure their access to property by making use of a range of agencies, in particular the newly constituted local courts, to protect their position within the customary and state systems. The analysis that emerges does not confine women to the status of victims, unable to access state laws, but sees them as actors negotiating and manipulating within and between the various normative orders.

A feminist legal analysis emerging in India since the late 1990s (Kapur and Cossman, 1996; Mehra, 1998) has tended to concentrate on women's engagement with the formal legal system in areas such as violence against women, rather than on the personal laws that regulate family matters such as divorce, maintenance, and the transmission of property in each of the main communities—Hindu, Muslim, and Christian.

Impact of Colonialism

Those tackling personal law issues such as women's access to property must take into account the impact of colonialism on gender relations. Historians do not agree on the extent to which colonial law was able to break up village solidarity and impose new forms of organization on peasant economies. Some imbue colonial law with great power; others question its effectiveness. Washbrook (1987: 162) contends that the colonialists were not able to use the law to impose the necessary conditions for market capitalism. Instead, the laws were used to support traditional social institutions and rights rather than to move toward a society based on individualism and competition.

As in Africa, this situation limited the capacity for exploitation by the colonizers, who feared both a possible revolt of the dispossessed and resistance to change from the powerful village-level groups that the state needed to maintain rural order. Thus the colonial state accommodated the dominant local groups by leaving "private" property laws within their domain and, in so doing, constructed a set of property relations based on the local groups' interpretation of Hindu law and social practice, which reflected the power of male elders to the detriment of women.

Impact of Religious Law and Custom

Research on access to land by women peasant farmers in Orissa illustrates the importance of understanding the interaction between the various normative orders within their historical contexts. Patel (2000) considers the way in which women who live and work with their husbands on small subsistence farms in rural Orissa perceive their entitlement to property. As Hindus, these women can make claims to a share of the property under the Hindu Succession Act of 1956, enacted by the newly independent Indian State. In addition, Article 15 of the Indian constitution gives women equality before the law and prohibits discrimination. Patel demonstrates that the women's perception of themselves constructed through their understanding of Hindu culture and law is far more powerful than any perception of themselves as subjects with rights. Their understanding of Hindu law is based on ancient texts and symbols molded through the process of colonialism, not on legislative enactments or constitutional guarantees. To these women, legal rights are simply inconceivable in the form in which they are presented by the postcolonial state.

Legal scholars studying women's position in personal laws within the Muslim world have tended to approach the issue through interpretation of the Islamic texts, but the network Women Living under Muslim Laws has adopted a more pluralistic approach, deconstructing the myth of a single homogeneous Muslim world and a single definition of Muslim womanhood. They have documented the multiplicity and diversity of women's situations and experiences within each Muslim country and community. They encourage women to question the laws and identities imposed on them and to analyze the source of customs and laws (Shirkat Gah/WLUML, 1996: 7).

In Pakistan, Shirkat Gah, a nongovernmental organization working on women's legal issues, has developed an analysis of the complexity of women's engagement with the various normative orders, which reveals that state law and religious tenets form only part of the picture. The laws applicable to Pakistan and the customs practiced there are the outcome of historical experience in which colonialism has had a substantial impact on statutory law. They combine with local power structures (notably feudalism and tribalism) and cultural specificity (a broadly south Asian culture, with Islam as the majority faith) to produce the "living law," the rules that actually "govern women's lives and determine the space within which they strategise for their survival" (Shirkat Gah/WLUML, 1996: 6).

The diversity in practices across the country is staggering, and this is seen as a practical strength, a way of shifting the ideology that holds customary laws to be natural and immutable. It also offers a way of understanding the interaction between custom and religion. Although Islam is the country's state religion, communities maintain practices that contradict religious tenets but serve to maintain patriarchal control over women (Shirkat Gah/WLUML, 1996: 6). In this analysis, state law exists within this diversity but does not have primacy.

Feminist legal analysis is now beginning to take account of the plurality of law. Current studies recognize the plurality of normative orders that affect women's lives. They provide an understanding of the way in which "nonstate" normative orders, such as customary laws and practices and religious personal codes, interact with state law, but they avoid favoring either or setting up false dichotomies between tradition and modernity. This scholarship, based in the South, extends the scope of feminist legal scholarship.

See Also

COLONIALISM AND POSTCOLONIALISM; FAMILY LAW; FAMILY LAW: CASE STUDY—INDIA; FUNDAMENTALISM AND PUBLIC POLICY; KINSHIP; LAW: FEMINIST CRITIQUES; THIRD WORLD WOMEN: SELECTED RESOURCES

References and Further Reading

Bentzon, Agnete W., et al. 1998. *Pursuing grounded theory in law: South–North experiences in developing women's law.* Oslo: Tano Aschehoug AS.

Chanock, Martin. 1991. Paradigms, policies, and property: A review of customary law of the land tenure. In K. Mann and R. Roberts, eds., *Law in colonial Africa.* Portsmouth: Heinemann.

Dahl, Tove S. 1987. *Women's law: An introduction to feminist jurisprudence.* Oslo: Norwegian University Press.

Dengu-Zvogbu, Kebokile, et al. 1994. *Inheritance in Zimbabwe: Law, customs and practices.* Harare: Women and Law in Southern Africa Research Trust.

Griffiths, John. 1986. What is legal pluralism? *Journal of Legal Pluralism* 24: 1–55.

Kapur, Ratna, and Brenda Cossman. 1996. *Subversive sites: Feminist engagements with law in India.* New Delhi: Sage.

Manji, Ambreena. 1999. Imagining women's "legal world": Towards a feminist theory of legal pluralism in Africa. *Social and Legal Studies* 8(1): 435–455.

Mehra, Madhu. 1998. Exploring the boundaries of law, gender and social reform. *Feminist Legal Studies* 6(1): 59–83.

Merry, Sally E. 1988. Legal pluralism. *Law and Society Review* 22(5): 869–896.

Mwaka, Beatrice Odonga. 1999. Widowhood and property among the Baganda of Uganda: Uncovering the passive victim. Doctoral thesis, University of Warwick.

Patel, Reena. 2000. Labour and land rights of women in rural India with particular reference to western Orissa. Doctoral thesis, University of Warwick.

Shirkat Gah/WLUML. 1996. *Women, law and society: An action manual.* Lahore: Shirkat Gah.

Stewart, Ann. 1996. Should women give up on the state? The African experience. In Shirin Rai and Geraldine Lievesley, eds., *Women and the state: International perspectives.* London: Taylor and Francis.

Washbrook, David. 1987. Law, state and agrarian society in colonial Africa. In Yash Ghai et al., eds., *Political economy of law: A third world reader.* New Delhi: Oxford University Press.

Ann Stewart

PHALLOCENTRISM

Phallocentrism is the belief that the phallus or penis is a major symbol of male power, and feminists' use of the term extends the analysis provided through the term *sexism.* Phallocentrism includes the view that assumptions about the supposed innateness of heterosexuality are crucial to behavioral, attitudinal, and institutional sexism. It goes further than the analysis of heterosexism by focusing on sexual power and its relationship to heterosexuality. In this analysis, "heterosexuality" in its institutional form indicates considerably more than sexual preference, for the use of phallocentric definitions of "sex" positions women as subordinate and passive objects to male sexual subjectivity in its narrowly penile and penetrational form. For example, an indication of the prevalence of this view lies in the range of expletives and insults based on the penetrational use or misuse of women's genitals by men. Phallocentrism also makes "the lesbian" vanish from epistemological sight except as rejection by men, for "the lesbian" is outside of a symbolic economy based on the penis and what it penetrates.

A critique of phallocentrism has been central to a wide range of feminist discussions of heterosexual sex from the early days of the present women's movement. It has also underpinned lesbian feminist theorizations of institutional heterosexuality and lesbian oppression (Frye, 1983). In addition, it has been crucial to analyses of power within patriarchal society that have seen rape as the archetypal instance of the "force and the threat of force" that constitutes women's oppression as distinct from women's inequality and exploitation (Brownmiller, 1975). Lacanian ideas about "the phallus" see this as having a *symbolic* role in signifying binary gender, particularly in language, whereas analyses of phallocentrism are concerned with phallocentric *behavior,* specifically the threatened and actual use of the penis as a weapon against women.

See Also

ANDROCENTRISM; HETEROSEXISM; PSYCHOANALYSIS; RAPE; SEXISM

References and Further Reading

Brownmiller, Susan. 1975. *Against our will.* London: Secker and Warburg.

Frye, Marilyn. 1983. *The politics of reality: Essays in feminist theory.* New York: Crossing.

Wittig, Monique. 1992. *The straight mind.* London: Harvester Wheatsheaf.

Liz Stanley

PHARMACEUTICALS

A pharmaceutical product, or medicine, is a chemical substance used to treat illness. Pharmaceuticals originated in the herbs and potions used for centuries for healing. Modern pharmacy, however, is relatively recent. Chemical innovations in the late nineteenth century led to the synthesis of products for pain and fever, and the discovery of the germ-killing property of sulphanilamides and penicillin in the 1930s brought effective cures for many infectious diseases.

Pharmaceuticals have greatly enhanced the ability to cure disease and alleviate discomfort. However, they can also cause unwanted effects and should be used only when potential benefits outweigh risks.

Lack of access to needed medicines remains a pressing problem for more than half the people living in developing countries, especially those living in poverty, most of whom are women and children. The World Health Organization (WHO) introduced the concept of "essential drugs" in 1977, a limited list of drugs judged to be effective, acceptably safe, affordable, and able to meet the large majority of people's health needs. National policies based on essential drugs can help ensure that needed drugs are made available, while avoiding waste of resources on ineffective, harmful, or needlessly expensive products. The WHO Essential Drugs list contains about 270 drugs; in contrast, roughly 100,000 types of drugs are marketed worldwide, and more than 40,000 are on the market in (for example) India alone.

To gain a competitive edge in this saturated market, companies promote their products aggressively. Positive messages about medicines' curative powers not only lead to increased sales of specific medicines but reinforce the view that there is "a pill for every ill" and that medicines are the solution to life's problems. This is particularly evident in the promotion of medicines for women, such as tranquilizers and antidepressants for emotional problems and hormones for many aspects of women's reproductive lives, from menstruation to contraception, infertility, pregnancy, meno-pause, and postmenopause.

Drugs and Women's Reproductive Health

Oral contraceptives were first introduced in the 1960s and were hailed as liberating, freeing women from the fear of unwanted pregnancy. In her book *The Doctors' Case against the Pill* (1969), however, Barbara Seaman argued that women were not warned about potential dangers such as blood clots, heart attacks, strokes, and depression. Her work led to U.S. congressional hearings calling for package inserts and better testing. She also created a model for a feminist assessment of pharmaceuticals based on individual women's experiences as well as the medical literature.

Since the mid-1970s, most contraceptive research has been funded publicly, because the industry has shied away from the high costs of the research and of potential product-liability claims. Funding has largely been directed toward long-acting methods for women that are administered by a health worker, such as intrauterine devices (IUDs) and hormonal injectables and implants. Feminists have argued that population policies have shaped contraceptive development and led to an emphasis on high effectiveness rather than long-term safety or control by the user.

Unnecessary drug use in pregnancy has led to tragic results. The best-known example is thalidomide, used from 1958 to 1961, which resulted in the birth of more than 10,000 severely deformed babies and awakened the world to the need for stronger controls on drug licensing and use during pregnancy. Another tragedy—less extreme, but on a larger scale—was that of diethylstilbestrol (DES), a synthetic estrogen prescribed to millions of pregnant women to prevent miscarriage, a use for which it was ineffective. Prenatal DES exposure has led to reproductive problems in women and men and a rare form of cancer in women.

High-dose estrogen-progestogen (EP) drugs are sold in many Asian and Latin American countries without adequate warnings of risks of birth defects. EP drugs are often used, ineffectively, by women trying to abort. Their other uses, for menstrual problems and pregnancy tests, are medically unjustified. Mira Shiva was a leading activist in an Indian national network that succeeded in getting EP drugs banned in 1986 after six years of legal battles.

Use of medicines in pregnancy is common worldwide. A recent study of nearly 15,000 pregnant women in 22 countries found that 86 percent took drugs during pregnancy, with an average of 2.9 drugs per woman (de Jong-van den Berg, 1995). Although some of these drugs were needed, many were not.

The marketing of hormones for menopause is an example of a highly profitable medicalization of a stage of women's lives. Germaine Greer (1991) has argued that negative attitudes toward older women make it possible to turn menopause into a medical event, and Sandra Coney (1992) has described how marketing of hormones exploits women's fears of aging. Premarin, an estrogen product used during and after menopause, was the most frequently prescribed drug in the United States in 1992 (Chetley, 1993). Long-term use has been promoted to prevent osteoporosis and, until recently, heart disease. The evidence that hormones prevent heart disease is, according to some physicians, scanty and inconclusive, and the balance of benefits versus risks for prevention of osteoporotic fractures is questionable. Exercise and calcium have been suggested as effective alternatives.

Drugs and Women's Emotional Health

Drugs can offer temporary treatment of symptoms of emotional distress such as anxiety, insomnia, and depression. They do not address the causes of these problems, which are often social. European and North American studies show that women are prescribed two to three times as many tranquilizers as men. Women receive more than two-thirds of antidepressant prescriptions in the United States (Boston Women's Health Book Collective, 1992). In Canada, elderly women living alone are most likely to use mood-modifying drugs (Harding, 1986).

One risk of these drugs is dependency. One study found that 92 percent of benzodiazepine tranquilizers sold by German and Swiss companies in their countries of origin had warnings about dependency, but only 6 percent of the drugs sold by the same companies in Chile, Mexico, Peru, the Philippines, and Thailand included warnings (Hennke and Krusi, 1994). Lack of access to independent information about drugs, including information on adverse effects, is a problem everywhere but is most acute in third world countries.

The women's health movement has contributed greatly to critical assessment of drugs marketed for women. The book *Our Bodies, Our Selves* (1971) by the Boston Women's Health Book Collective encouraged women to question medical authority. DES Action groups, started by exposed women, combined support and information with effective lobbying for better health care. International networks such as Health Action International, which addresses drug issues from a users' perspective, ISIS (an international women's health network), and the Women's Global Network for Reproductive Rights have enabled groups from different regions to work together. Feminist researchers have studied women's experiences with drugs and the way social attitudes toward women have shaped health care.

Globally, many of women's most pressing health problems can be solved without medicines through measures to overcome poverty, to ensure access to clean water and sanitation, and to improve women's status in society.

See Also

CONTRACEPTIVES: DEVELOPMENT; ESTROGEN; HORMONES; MENOPAUSE; MENSTRUATION; MENTAL HEALTH, *I and II*; REPRODUCTIVE TECHNOLOGIES

References and Further Reading

Boston Women's Health Book Collective. 1992. *The new our bodies, our selves: A book by and for women.* New York: Touchstone. (See also *Our bodies ourselves for the new century*. 1998. New York: Simon and Schuster.)

Chetley, Andrew. 1993. *Problem drugs*, 177. Amsterdam: Health Action International.

Coney, Sandra. 1992. The exploitation of fear. In Peter Davis, ed., *For health or profit? Medicine, the pharmaceutical industry, and the state in New Zealand*, 179–207. Auckland: Oxford University Press.

de Jong-van den Berg, Lolkje. 1995. Current use of drugs during pregnancy in Europe. In Barbara Mintzes and Joleith Keler, eds., *DES: A drug that knows no boundaries*, 21–26. Report of the 4th European DES Symposium. Utrecht, Netherlands: DES Action.

Greer, Germaine. 1991. *The change: Women, ageing, and the menopause.* London: Hamish Hamilton.

Harding, J. 1986. Mood-modifiers and elderly women in Canada: The medicalization of poverty. In Kathy McDonnell, ed., *Adverse effects: Women and the pharmaceutical industry*, 51–86. Penang: IOCU.

Hennke, Gudrun, and Viviane Krusi. 1994. *Abhangigkeit auf Rezept: Die Vermarktung von Benzodiazepinen in der Dritten Welt.* Bielefield, Germany: BUKO Pharma-kampagne.

Seaman, Barbara. 1969. *The doctor's case against the pill.* New York: Dell.

Barbara Mintzes

PHILANTHROPY

Philanthropy is a fundamental human impulse: giving and volunteering time, money, and a broad range of other resources. People of all economic means and cultures develop lifetime habits of donation and service to a wide range of causes—aiding family members and those less fortunate, sustaining communities and cultures, and working for systemic social change. In many countries, more extensive government support for human services, cultural organizations, and even social change has meant fewer traditions of "organized" private philanthropy—although both public and private philanthropy in many countries at various stages of economic development are becoming increasingly common.

With its history of laissez-faire capitalism—lacking the governmental support networks common to many other nations—it is the United States that has evolved the most institutionalized history of philanthropy: giving by individuals, churches, community agencies, and formally organized family, public, and private foundations that is driven, at least in part, by federal income tax exemptions for contributions made to organizations certified "charitable" or "nonprofit" by state government offices.

Like most institutionalized activity, however, philanthropy has not benefited women and men equally, even though many early philanthropic and charitable efforts in the United States were launched by women to benefit needy women and children (for example, Jane Addams's Hull House, one of the first settlement houses in the United States). Since the early 1970s in the United States, women and some men working in foundations and women's and girls' organizations have lobbied for increased funding for women and girls. Key organizations that evolved from their efforts include Women and Philanthropy (formerly Women and Foundations/Corporate Philanthropy) and the Women's Funding Network (formerly the National Network of Women's Funds). Working in coalition, these and other organizations constitute a "women's funding movement" whose goal has been to increase the amount of money available to support women's and girls' needs, programs, and organizations.

At least one major advance has been growth in the number and size of women's funds, foundations organized to target support to the needs of women and girls. By early 2000, there were more than 150 women's funds worldwide. In the United States and Canada, a sample of 58 funds that belong to the Women's Funding Network reported $125.3 million in net assets for 1998 and, for the same time period, $45.1 million raised and $15.9 million given away in grants.

Women's funds and foundations, like many women's organizations, also have modeled important commitments to diversity—in the case of the women's funds, their work to democratize donors and achieve greater racial and ethnic diversity on their boards and staffs. Over the years, their experiments with less hierarchical structures and grantee-driven grant awards have brought necessary innovations to organized philanthropy. They are getting more ambitious. The Ms. Foundation for Women, for example, one of the largest women's funds in the United States with an endowment of over $15 million, gave away $2.6 million in grants in fiscal year 1999.

Reliable research on women and philanthropy is slim, both in the United States and internationally. Many perceptions of women as donors are based on stereotypes about gender that ask the wrong questions, often generating wrong answers. A survey of available research indicates that, once variables such as age, level of income, number of dependents, and health are taken into account, few discernible differences between men and women donors remain.

Some differences do exist. Women still have less wealth than men, earn less, and have to spend more than men on day-to-day expenses. Yet many women do have significant wealth and disposable income—and they give and give generously. According to projections by the U.S. Internal Revenue Service based on estate tax returns in 1992, women constitute 35 percent of U.S. wealthholders (defined as estates of $600,000 and higher), with over $1.8 trillion combined net worth. They are not as wealthy as men, obviously, but they are catching up: top female wealthholders in the United States (defined as estates of $1 million and higher) increased 20 percent from 1992 to 1995—their combined net worth grew over 27 percent. Top male wealthholders increased only 8 percent during the same period. The evidence suggests that women and men give for many of the same reasons. Yet many women and men still do *not* give—or do not give generously—to women's funds and other women's organizations.

Considering needs that have been documented over a broad range of areas that donors donate to and funders fund, money reaching women and girls is still woefully inadequate. In 1998, for example, there was only 0.5 percent (five-tenths of 1 percent) increase in the percentage of total grants awarded to women and girls in the United States since 1994 (less than $629 million out of $9.8 billion reported by 1,009 of the largest foundations tracked by the Foundation Center). Although the dollar amounts of support reaching women and girls have increased—indeed, more than doubled (114 percent) since 1994—these figures still constitute a very small portion of the total dollars given away by all U.S. foundations, projected to be more than $22.8 billion in 1999. Many funders in the United States still label grants to women and girls "special interest" funding and prefer to make "universal" or "generic" grants. This phenomenon is not nearly so pervasive in countries outside the United States, where international women's organizing efforts have convinced many international and national funding agencies that funding women's and girls' priorities changes families and changes communities.

This lack of funding reaching women and girls in the United States persists despite the fact that women in U.S. foundations and corporate funding programs in 1998 constituted 67 percent of full-time paid program officers and more than 51 percent of foundation chief executive officers (twice as many since 1982). Although philanthropy itself is becoming a "feminized" profession, numerous reports have documented over a period of more than two decades that minimal philanthropic resources actually reach women and girls and their organizations and programs in the United States, especially organizations serving women and girls of color.

Effective, efficient philanthropy dictates that those most in need receive the largest portion of available resources, that those organizations most imaginatively working to ameliorate social, economic, and personal needs and preserve cultural heritages—as defined by foundations and donors themselves—receive the most sustained support. This has not happened, nor is there much evidence that the situation is improving in the United States. So key questions for researchers, philanthropy professionals, donors, and activists—all those concerned with gender parity—include Why so little? What will it take for the funding that reaches women and girls to achieve parity with the funding that reaches men and boys?

See Also

MONEY; NONGOVERNMENTAL ORGANIZATIONS (NGOS); WOMEN'S CENTERS; WOMEN'S STUDIES: FUNDING; WOMEN'S STUDIES: RESEARCH CENTERS AND INSTITUTES

References and Further Reading

Badgett, M. V. Lee, and Nancy Cunningham. 1998. *Creating communities: Giving and volunteering by gay, lesbian, bisexual, and transgender people.* New York: Working Group on Funding Lesbian and Gay Issues/Institute for Gay and Lesbian Strategic Studies.

Capek, Mary Ellen S. 1998. *Women and philanthropy: Old stereotypes, new challenges: A monograph series.* Vol. 1, *Women as donors: Stereotypes, common sense, and challenges.* Vol. 2, *Foundation support for women and girls: "Special Interest" funding or effective philanthropy?* Vol. 3, *The women's funding movement: Accomplishments and challenges.* Battle Creek, Mich.: W. K. Kellogg Foundation. Available at <www.wfnet.org>.

Castle, Ann. 1999. *Women in philanthropy: A bibliography and resource list.* Available at <www.hamilton.edu/html/personal/acastle>.

Covington, Sally. 1997. *Moving a public policy agenda: The strategic philanthropy of conservative foundations.* Washington, D.C.: National Committee on Responsive Philanthropy.

Havens, John. 1994. *Giving behavior by income and gender: Do men give more?* Boston: Social Welfare Research Institute, Boston College.

Hodgkinson, Virginia A., and Murray S. Weitzman. 1996. *Giving and volunteering in the United States: Findings from a national survey.* Washington, D.C.: Independent Sector.

Kaplan, Ann E., ed. 1999. *Giving USA 1999.* New York: AAFRC Trust for Philanthropy.

Odendahl, Teresa. 1990. *Charity begins at home: Generosity and self-interest among the philanthropic elite.* New York: Basic Books.

Ostrander, Susan A. 1995. *Money for change: Social movement philanthropy at Haymarket People's Fund.* Philadelphia: Temple University Press.

Ostrander, Susan A., and Joan M. Fisher. 1995. Women giving money/women raising money: What difference for philanthropy? In Dwight Burlingame, ed., *Taking fundraising seriously: Cultures of giving.* San Francisco: Jossey-Bass.

Ostrander, Susan A., and P. G. Schervish. 1990. Giving and getting: Philanthropy as social relation. In J. Van Till and Associates, eds., *Critical issues in American philanthropy: Strengthening theory and practice.* San Francisco: Jossey-Bass.

Parker-Sawyer, Paula, and Cheryl Hall-Russell. 1997. African American women's philanthropy: A tradition of sharing. *Women's Philanthropy Institute News* (July): 3–4.

Schervish, Paul G. Major donors, major motives: The people and purposes behind major gifts. In Dwight F. Burlingame and James M. Hidge III, eds., *Major gifts: New directions for philanthropic fundraising.* San Francisco: Jossey-Bass.

Von Schlegell, Abbie J., and Joan M. Fisher, eds. 1993. *Women as donors, women as philanthropists.* San Francisco: Jossey-Bass.

Mary Eden Capek

PHILOSOPHY

Philosophy is often thought of as a "universal" area of study, one that addresses fundamental questions about the human condition, knowledge, ethics, and politics. Gender would seem irrelevant to the study of philosophy, and questions about gender have remained largely invisible in most "mainstream" philosophy courses. But much of philosophy has assumed and is addressed to a male subject. Many women studying philosophy came to contend that much of what male philosophers had written about women was riddled with sexism and misogyny and that many philosophical theories excluded women. Some philosophical systems consign women to household, family, and reproduction, and for this reason they are seen as incapable of citizenship, rationality, or moral agency. One of the fundamental tasks of feminist philosophical writing has been the critique of the supposed "universality" of philosophical theories.

The first task undertaken by feminist philosophers consisted of documenting the many forms of misogyny in philosophical writing. In addition, feminist philosophical work has investigated the ways in which this misogyny affects the substance of philosophical theories. One response to this misogyny has been attempts to include women in philosophical theories. But while it may often be important to stress that women, too, are capable of rationality or virtue, feminists argure that this strategy of inclusion does not address certain fundamental issues. First, it may not be possible to include women while leaving the rest of a theory intact, since gender may be an inherent characteristic of the theory. Second, feminists have wanted to examine critically those philosophical systems that have excluded women. Are there, for example, senses in which some ideals of rationality or virtue can themselves be seen as masculine, as encapsulating norms of masculinity and concerning themselves only with the sorts of issues that have been held to be typical of the life of a man? Feminists working in philosophy not only have tried to analyze its sexist and exclusionary nature but also have asked how it might change if the perspectives and concerns of women were taken seriously. There has been, for example, considerable philosophical debate about whether women's ethical perspectives tend to be different from those of men.

Ideas of female difference or women's perspectives are as potentially problematic within philosophy as they are in other areas of study. Insisting on women's difference may run the risk of lapsing into old stereotypes of women. Writing as if there is only one women's perspective may run the risk of a new kind of false universalism that fails to recognize differences among women. How can the ways in which women's perspectives might change philosophy be understood without assuming the existence of an unproblematical female voice? How can the nature of feminist philosophy itself be theorized, given that feminist inquiry addresses issues that are of general human interest and relevance and should not simply be the concern of women?

See Also

EPISTEMOLOGY

References and Further Reading

Gatens, Moira. 1991. *Feminism and philosophy.* Cambridge: Polity.

Grimshaw, Jean. 1986. *Feminist philosophers: Women's perspectives on philosophical traditions.* Brighton, U.K.: Wheatsheaf.

Lloyd, Genevieve. 1993. *The man of reason: Male and female in western philosophy.* 2nd ed. London: Methuen.

Jean Grimshaw

PHILOSOPHY OF SCIENCE

See SCIENCE: FEMINIST PHILOSOPHY.

PHOTOGRAPHY

With the invention of photography by Joseph Nicéphore Niepce in 1826, a medium was developed that literally changed our view of the world. Unlike other visual arts that reflect the individual imagination and technical ability, photography always portrays the outer reality, in that the superficial appearance is projected by the lens onto film and fixed there.

The invention of photography ushered in what may be called the "optical age": Today photography is indispensable to medicine, science, and many industries. It is a central component of journalism and is responsible for the development of the film, video, and television forms of mass media. Nearly 90 percent of the pictures with which the media inundate us originate as photographs, and this medium has become entrenched in political, social, and cultural life, used or accepted by almost everybody.

Photography documents both the macro- and the microcosm, enabling the presentation of the social life as well as certifying individual history. Photography also gives the general public a feeling of being informed about world issues and affairs, even if individuals have no influence over the pictures they see.

No other artistic medium, feminists argue, has produced as many variations of damaging, aggressive gender role stereotypes as photography has, through the "male gaze." However, because photography is often considered marginal to the art world, it is also a medium that has always been open to women, as well as dependent on photographic productions of the "female view." As both an instrument of power and a means of resistance, photography has been used and developed by women since it was invented.

Because the work of female photographers is so varied, no clear definition of a specific female aesthetics can be stated. In many outstanding forms we find images that meet the classical criteria of the ruling (male) view, as well as the criteria of (male-dominated) aesthetics in the arts and media. However, the female pioneers and their contemporaries in photography often worked in opposition to the trends of their day. These works were often discussed and analyzed in social fringe groups and subjected to social critical analysis that both respected and esteemed works which did not meet the standard genre presentations.

Nineteenth Century

Emilie Bieber (1810–1884) was the first woman in Germany to open her own studio, which she did shortly after the invention of photography. Like her contemporaries, she engaged mainly in portrait photography, a style much appreciated by the middle class as a democratic means of portraiture.

In Great Britain, upper-class women explored the creative elements of photography. For example, Julia Margaret Cameron (1815–1879), a well-traveled Scot, produced a series of internationally renowned portraits and successfully exhibited her work in London. Cameron used an unconventional technique to portray the "soul" of friends, artists, and scientists. Although photography in the Victorian era allowed only for brief exposure times and small plate forms, she forced her models to gaze at a certain spot for seven minutes. By photographing in close-up and using this long exposure time, Cameron managed to catched a relaxed expression on her subjects' faces and also gave a visionary cast to them, because of the slight blurring that occurred with this process.

In Europe, owing to the *carte de visite* (postcard) boom, technical development and industrialism were being explored. In addition to portraits, city views, architecture, and landscapes of foreign countries were the most important motifs. Alexandrine Tinne (1835–1869, the Netherlands), the first photojournalist, became famous for her pictures of Den Haag and her series about the life of the Tuareg in the Sahara. Maria Natalia Linsen (1844–1919, Finland) created, with her clear form language, architecture photography in Scandinavia and is renowned for this today.

The most important aesthetic inventions were achieved by female photographers in the United States at the end of the nineteenth century. For example, Gertrude Kasebier (1852–1934) began taking photographs at age 36, after studying portrait painting. In her portrait photography, Kasebier achieved impressionistic compositions by using certain angles of light and an intentionally dim focus. She photographed artists, mothers and children, and Native Americans and usually gave her works ironically detached titles.

Early to Middle Twentieth Century

In the 1900s, American photographers specialized in documentary photography, reaching a milestone in the development of photojournalism with their independent pictures. Dorothea Lange (1895–1965) was one of the groundbreaking documentary photographers. After academic studies and photographic training at Columbia University in New York, she started with portrait photography in her own studio in 1919. She soon changed to a more documentary style, however, in 1934 shooting a series of photographs on the living conditions of migrant farmworkers. From 1935 to 1942 she worked for the Farm Security Administration to document the specific problems of the U.S. rural population. These images have since been reprinted in more than ten thousand newspapers. From 1953 on, Lange published various photographic commentaries in *Life* magazine, as well as designing the photography book *The Country Woman,* which demonstrates the influence of a new pragmatism combined with a subtly detailed form of portrayal.

Imogen Cunningham (1883–1976) influenced the photographic history of the twentieth century with her experimental and painstakingly composed work. A scholarship allowed her to study photochemistry in Germany, and in 1910 she opened her studio in Seattle, Washington. In 1915, Cunningham published a series of male nude photographs, the first woman to do so. She shot her now-legendary close-ups of plants and blossoms in the late 1920s while she was at home looking after her children. In the 1930s, Cunningham began dedicating herself to documentary photography, although one of her most interesting works is the portrait series of people over the age of 90, which she published when she was 87.

In the 1940s, the most serious work came from Europe and was carried predominantly by women. For example, Gisele Freund (1912–) studied sociology and art history in her native Germany before fleeing to Paris in 1932. Four years later, she graduated from the Sorbonne with the first dissertation ever to be written about photography. To finance her photography, Freund worked as a photojournalist, portraying famous authors and intellectuals. *Time* and *Paris Match* published her work until she had to flee the Nazis again in 1942. She began working for *Life* in South America, and when World War II ended she traveled throughout the world for the photographers' organization Magnum. In 1945, Freund began focusing on portraits, creating sensitive studies of such noted women as Colette and Virginia Woolf. Her depiction of Eva Perón, who let herself be photographed in all her finery without thought of the political ramifications, became internationally famous.

Margaret Bourke-White (1904–1971) studied photography at Columbia University, specializing in architectural and industrial photography. In 1931, Bourke-White opened her own studio, and from 1936 to 1957 she photographed for *Life,* winning international acclaim with her aggressive photojournalism. In addition to war and catastrophes, she photographed social and cultural events and was the first western photographer to travel to Russia. After World War II, Bourke-White documented the Nazi concentration camp at Buchenwald in Germany, Mohandas Ghandhi's nonviolent resistance in India, and apartheid in South Africa. Known for her derring-do, Bourke-White survived a series of risky adventures to get a "good story," which led to her renown as a master of photographic reporting whose accomplishments set a new standard for coming generations of photographers.

Diane Arbus (1923–1971) worked as a fashion photographer with her husband before becoming inspired by the Viennese photographer Lisette Model to engage herself with social fringe groups. Arbus's works show the lives of people with deformities, insane people, dwarves, and transvestites with unflinching honesty and without sentimentality, showing self-assured Americans pictures of the "imperfect" among them. Arbus's presentations of the metropolitan subculture garnered so much criticism—not just of her work, but of her character and her gender—that she took her own life. A year later, the Museum of Modern Art mounted an extensive retrospective of her work, and at the same time her work was exhibited at the Biennale in Venice; she was the first American photographer ever to be exhibited there.

Late Twentieth Century

Since the 1950s, the number of female photographers has risen enormously. More than four hundred are named in international publications, and those who have yet to be "discovered" number even more. Research on today's women photographers is hardly developed. The profile of female photographers has changed enormously in the last few decades—in addition to "classical" photographers, other female artists work increasingly with the more contemporary medium.

Valie Export (1940–) worked in her native Austria as a model and actress before switching to photography. She started by incorporating photos into a series of performances. Her demonstrative photo sequences analyze the female body and place it in the contexts of landscapes or city views. With posterlike productions of classical works of art, Export reinterprets stereotypical images of women, underscoring the significance of female functions in our culture. Ignoring the technical sophistication that the medium of photography offers today, Export presents her picture series primarily on placards, offering both a feminist critique and a deliberate rejection of the demand for beauty not only in the images portrayed but also in the means of portrayal.

Also working today are a group of feminist photographers who have since the 1970s focused on creating a new, self-determined image of womanliness in contrast with male ideals of femininity. The German photographer Frederike Pezold (1945–), for example, uses photo sequences and films to explore her own nudity without any erotic implications. In her "Film Stills" series, Cindy Sherman (United States, b. 1954) reproduces clichéd women in contemporary popular culture by dressing herself up and creating room-size installations, thereby making caricatures of the identity changes that women must go through to keep up with current ideals of womanhood.

The most recent generation of female photographers are tackling issues of technical possibilities and the extremities of the medium, as they analyze, in the context of postmodern discussion, virtual reality and simulation, which have established themselves as an illustrative medium.

See Also

AESTHETICS: FEMINIST; FINE ARTS: OVERVIEW; FINE ARTS: CRITICISM AND ART HISTORY; FINE ARTS: POLITICS OF REPRESENTATION

References and Further Reading

Arbus, Diane. 1972. *An aperture monograph.* New York: Aperture (reissued 1988).

Callahan, Sean. 1972. *The photographs of Margaret Bourke-White.* New York: New York Graphic Society.

Cruz, Amanda, ed. 2000. *Cindy Sherman: Retrospective.* 2nd ed. New York: Thames and Hudson.

Cunningham, Imogen. 1998. *Imogen Cunningham: On the body* (text by Richard Lorenz). New York: Bulfinch.

Elliot, Georg. 1998. *Restless spirit: The life and work of Dorothea Lange.* New York: Viking/Penguin.

Freund, Gisele. 1974. *The world in my camera.* Trans. June Guicharnaud. New York.

Gernsheim, Helmst. 1948. *J. M. C.—Her life and photographic work.* London.

Prammer, Anita. 1989. *Valie Export.* Vienna.

Sontag, Susan. 1977. *On photography.* New York: Farrar Straus Giroux.

Tucker, Anne, ed. 1975. *The woman's eye.* New York: Knopf.

Edith Almhofer

PHOTOTHERAPY

Phototherapy refers to the use of photographic representations in different therapeutic contexts to promote self-awareness and healing.

The Use of Photographs as Tools in Therapy

In the 1970s, therapists in the United States and Canada started to use photographs as counseling tools (Fryear and Krauss, 1983; Weiser, 1993). Working from differing theoretical frameworks, they used photographs as metaphors as a route to the unconscious. The personal meanings that an individual finds in a photograph are a projective process and mirror the inner map she (we will assume a woman here) is using unconsciously. A therapist, using a nonjudgmental approach with skillful listening and open-ended questions, can enable the client to make conscious and then reflect on her value systems and belief structures using photographs as the catalyst. Found photographs, often selected for their ambiguity, are particularly useful when a group is working together with the aim of respecting differences. Photographs taken by the client may offer up insights into thoughts and feelings that are of deep personal concern. Family albums have provided a rich resource for autobiographical storytelling and an exploration of family systems, how it was to be part of this family and how these early experiences continue to affect the individual.

Domestic Photography: The Family Album

Personal images are collected in the family album. Analysis shows it to be an ideological construct, carefully framed and edited to maintain the mythology of the happy family (Holland and Spence 1991; Spence, 1986). Bound within the codes of commemorative convention, the recurrent themes are success, celebration, domestic harmony, and togetherness, which often prompt nostalgia in the viewer. Yet these photographs also provide a rich surface of slippery meanings and a potential route into deeper personal memories (Kuhn, 1995).

Reenactment Phototherapy

Drawing on cultural theory and therapeutic skills, Rosy Martin (the present author) and Jo Spence challenged the paucity of the existing visual representations of their lives by reconstructing and creating images of their identities (Martin, 1991a, 1991b, 1997; Martin and Spence, 1988; Spence, 1986, 1991, 1995). They worked together, in evolving the practice, alternating the roles of therapist and client. They started from an issue, which was linked to a potent memory, unearthed and explored through counseling; they then made it visual, using carefully selected clothes and props. The scenario was reenacted, with the protagonist role-playing different power positions, for example mother and daughter. The photographer-therapist offered a nurturing gaze to the protagonist, of giving permission, support, and reflection. By embodying the issues to be worked through, within the safety and containment of the therapeutic relationship, the protagonist was able to reexperience a previously disavowed trauma, shift her perceptions and feelings to reach a cathartic release, and realize a transformation. As these shifts take place within the session, the body may be seen as the scene of cultural inscriptions, rather than essentially containing them.

By reenacting and mapping out various familial and institutional gazes, a complex network of fragmented selves constructed out of the needs, views, projections, and attributions of others was made visible. This shows what it is to be subjected to and subject of the discourses within society and challenges any notion that subjectivity is fixed.

Photographs are understood to be specific choices, frozen moments, pieces of paper that simultaneously signify truth. Through this constructive contradiction an individual can learn to put aside notions of ever picturing the authentic "real me." The objectification of photography provides the necessary distancing for finding new perspectives on old painful memories, with the support of the nonjudgmental witnessing and challenge provided by the phototherapist. Moving the photographs around and creating new narratives disrupts any sense of closure. New stories may be told, new possibilities envisaged. Counseling using the images created enables the client to articulate and work through her personal history. Reenactment phototherapy makes visible the self as process and offers models for change.

How Phototherapy Relates to Women

Martin and Spence selected images from the process of phototherapy to make exhibitions. Shown as a complex interweaving of narrative fragments, this work produced a resonance of recognition in the viewer by reactivating a personal or collective memory. Working from the specifics and minutiae of personal histories, located in time, place, and culture, they emphasized the social and psychic construction of identities within the drama of the everyday. Issues addressed included gender, sexuality, family dynamics, class, aging, shame, power or powerlessness, health and disease, bereavement, grief, and loss (Martin, 1995, 1997, 1999; Spence, 1986, 1995).

Phototherapy provides women with a way to look behind the "screen memories" at the simplifications and myths of others; to explore, reflect upon, and tell their own stories, from their own point of view. This is of particular value to women who have experienced systematic cultural and historical silencing. Breaking the taboos of family and social secrets enables women to move beyond the paralysis of shame and disavowal, to articulate their experiences and ultimately reach self-acceptance. This work prompts the development of a critical consciousness that links individual and collective memories, the personal and the political, and that bridges the divisions between public and private domains.

See Also

AUTOBIOGRAPHY; CRITICAL AND CULTURAL THEORY; DIARIES AND JOURNALS; DISEASE; FEMINISM: CULTURAL; FINE ARTS: POLITICS OF REPRESENTATION; GENDER CONSTRUCTIONS IN THE FAMILY; IMAGES OF WOMEN; PHOTOGRAPHY; PSYCHOANALYSIS; PSYCHOLOGY: SOCIAL

References and Further Reading

Berman, Linda. 1993. *Beyond the smile: The therapeutic use of the photograph.* London: Routledge.

Fryear, Jerry, and David Krauss, eds. 1983. *Phototherapy in mental health.* Springfield, Ill.: Thomas.

Holland, Patricia, and Jo Spence, eds. 1991. *Family snaps: The meanings of domestic photography.* London: Virago.

Kuhn, Annette. 1995. *Family secrets.* London: Verso.

Martin, Rosy. 1991a. Unwind the ties that bind. In Patricia Holland and Jo Spence, eds., *Family snaps: The meanings of domestic photography,* 209–221. London: Virago.

———. 1991b. Dirty linen. *Ten8* 2(1): 34–50.

———. 1995. Memento mori manifest: A rite of inheritance. In Jo Spence and Joan Solomon, eds., *What can a woman do with a camera?,* 67–74. London: Scarlet Press.

———. 1997. Looking and reflecting: Returning the gaze, reenacting memories and imagining the future through phototherapy. In Susan Hogan, ed., *Feminist approaches to art therapy,* 150–176. London: Routledge.

———. 1999. Too close to home. *N. Paradoxa: International Feminist Art Journal* 3: 73–80.

———, and Jo Spence. 1988. Phototherapy—psychic realism as a healing art? *Ten8,* no. 30: 2–17.

Spence, Jo. 1986. *Putting myself in the picture.* London: Camden Press.

———. 1991a. Soap, family album work and hope. In Patricia Holland and Jo Spence, eds., *Family snaps: The meanings of domestic photography,* 200–207. London: Virago.

———. 1991b. Shame-work: Thoughts on family snaps and fractured identities. In Patricia Holland and Jo Spence, eds., *Family snaps: The meanings of domestic photography,* 226–236. London: Virago.

———. 1995. *Cultural sniping* London: Routledge.

Weiser, Judy. 1993. *Phototherapeutic techniques: Exploring the secrets of personal snapshots and family albums.* San Francisco: Jossey-Bass.

<www.phototherapy-centre.com>

<www.var.ndirect.co.uk/outrageous>

Rosy Martin

PHYSICAL EDUCATION

See EDUCATION: PHYSICAL.

PHYSICAL FITNESS

See EXERCISE AND FITNESS.

PHYSICAL SCIENCES

Physical sciences, including astronomy, physics, and geology, are known for the low percentage of women working in these fields. Women have always participated in these sciences, although their contributions have often not been recognized, and they were excluded from scientific institutions. Nowadays, women are an important part of the scientific establishment all over the world. Their numbers vary enormously among countries because of cultural differences within science and society. Feminist researchers have developed several theories of science that could make the discipline open to women.

Participation and Exclusion: A History

From the beginning, women have contributed to the development of the physical sciences, such as astronomy, physics, physical chemistry, and geology. The earliest myths from Egypt, Mesopotamia, and China tell of goddesses and heroines who invent tools, develop agriculture, and study medicine and astronomy. Encyclopedias with biographies of learned women, which appeared in Europe from the fourteenth to the beginning of the nineteenth century, also demonstrate this. Margaret Alic (1986), a North American biologist, wrote a wide-ranging book in which she recovers the presence of women within the history of science. She draws attention to the work of such women scientists as Hildegard von Bingen (1098–1179), a German abbess who wrote on natural history, medicine, cosmology, and cosmogeny. Alic also shows that although learned women had always been present in history, the scientific woman, who dedicated herself to the study of the natural sciences, was a product of the scientific revolution in the seventeenth century. Margaret Cavendish (1623–1673), Duchess of Newcastle (England), wrote on theoretical and experimental natural philosophy. The French Marquise Emilie du Châtelet (1706–1749) popularized Isaac Newton's and Gottfried Wilhelm Leibniz's work and wrote on light and heat.

Despite the above-mentioned examples, the overall participation of women has been limited. Through the ages the physical sciences have been male-dominated. Social and educational pressures and prejudices systematically hindered the entry of women into the world of learning. Until the admittance of women to the universities, which began in the middle of the nineteenth century, women were absent from the institutions of science. Before this, talented women received private tuition from their fathers or brothers or studied within female study circles. For their studies, they often used popularizations. When women were first admitted to the universities, they were most attracted to the biomedical and physical sciences.

Women's contributions to science varied from conducting experiments, developing theories, and writing popularizations to the organization of the famous salons in eighteenth-century France. Madame du Châtelet, for example, was a famous organizer of these salons. These female scientists were, with a few exceptions, from the upper classes and had sufficient resources to pursue their studies. Their work was often not recognized. As geology was becoming a science in the early nineteenth century, a number of women became involved. They were, however, never credited for their work as collectors and excavators. A famous example of the struggle of scientific women in the past is Marie Curie (1867–1934), who worked on radioactivity and was awarded two Nobel Prizes. The German Maria Goeppert-Mayer (1906–1972) won the Nobel Prize in 1963 for her work on the nuclear shell model.

Present Participation across Cultures

Currently, all over the world large numbers of women participate in the institutions of the physical sciences, in universities, governmental laboratories, and industrial research and development divisions. In general, more women work in the geosciences than in physics and astronomy. Large differences exist in the percentage of women present in the physical sciences across countries and cultures. In the early 1990s, in the northwestern part of Europe, North America, Australia, New Zealand, and some Asian countries such as Japan, Korea, and Taiwan, the proportion of women working in university physics departments was less than 10 percent. By contrast, in Latin America, southern and eastern Europe, Thailand, Philippines, China, and the former Soviet Union, percentages ranged from 17 to 34 percent. A similar trend in cultural differences can be seen in the percentage of female members of the International Astronomical Union (IAU).

In some countries, women's participation in the physical sciences is expected to increase because of the growing number of female students in the field. This is true, for example, in India and southern Europe, but not, however, in most countries in the northwestern part of Europe, where the percentage of female students is stable at a low level. The underrepresentation of women in the physical sciences is not just a problem of few being accepted for study; many women leave the field immediately after acquiring the doctoral degree.

Cultural Differences Related to Exclusion and Participation

Little research has been done to explain the cultural differences in the participation of women in the physical sciences. In a special issue of *Science* focused on women in science, women in the field offer various possible explanations (Benditt, 1994). They report differences in work ethics, attitudes toward the integration of work and family, educational practices, the status of the physical sciences in the country, and the existence of a female tradition in science.

In cultures where the extended family can provide child care, as is often the case in southern Europe and Latin America, women express the feeling that they have more opportunities to combine work and child rearing than women in countries where child care is unavailable or expensive. The difficulty of integrating family life with a career in science is the reason why many women in northern Europe and North America cease scientific work after receiving their doctorate. This usually occurs when women are in their thirties, an age when it is expected that a scientist will invest most of her time in her career. This coincides with the age at which many women want to have children. The work ethics in northern Europe and North America prescribe total dedication to the job, which further complicates the attempt to combine family life and a scientific career.

Education also affects the participation of women in the physical sciences between cultures. All-girl schools seem to give women more opportunities to pursue a career in the physical sciences. Some 58 percent of the female members of the British Institute of Physics, for example, had attended girls' schools through age 16. This is very high compared with the national average of 13 percent. Obligatory mathematics and physics in high school also prevent women from leaving the field early. In the former communist countries of eastern Europe, for example, the educational policies required girls and boys to study mathematics and physics through secondary school. This gave all students the chance to see whether they were good at science. It is striking that both these practices are common in countries where the percentage of women in the physical sciences is high.

In countries with a high percentage of women in the physical sciences, the status of these sciences is often lower than in countries with a much lower percentage of women in physical sciences. Some of the countries with a high number of women in these fields are still undergoing economic development. In these countries, the scientific establishment dates to recent times, when society was more open to women's participation. This contrasts with the countries where science and technology became established when women were not allowed in professions for which higher education was required, as in northern Europe. Science in countries still developing is not as closely integrated into the production of goods and services as it is in Europe, Japan, and the United States. It is regarded more as a cultural activity. In India, for example, engineering is much more lucrative and prestigious than science. Indian women are relatively well represented in physics but not in engineering.

Some women experience their position in the physical sciences as difficult and lonely. They feel they have to fight harder than men to be accepted as an expert by their colleagues and customers. In countries where the percentage of women is very low, they often are the only women in the laboratory. Others, however, experience no difference from their male colleagues. Women living in countries with a female tradition in the physical sciences, such as France and Italy, say they feel encouraged by their forerunners Marie Curie and Laura Bassi (1711–1778), an eighteenth-century physics professor in Italy. Not only female scientists in the past but also role models in the present are an important support to women. The absence of role models in the educational or professional environment makes it very hard for women to succeed in this male-dominated field.

Although there are large differences among cultures regarding the percentage of women in the physical sciences, women's difficulty in rising to the higher ranks is a common problem. Even in countries with a high percentage of women in these fields—Portugal, Turkey, and the Philippines, for example—women have difficulty becoming full professors or laboratory directors. This problem is not unique to the physical sciences. The glass ceiling is present in all professions all over the world. The situation in academia is most grave in northern Europe. There the proportion of female full professors was below 5 percent in the early 1990s and has been static for the past 60 years, whereas in the United States it was 14 percent and has increased by 60 percent over the past 15 years. The existence of the "old boys'" network, sex discrimination, and opposition to affirmative action programs have all been proposed as explanations for these figures.

Feminist Analysis of the Physical Sciences

European and North American feminists' discussion about women's position in the physical sciences has long focused on why so few women participate in the physical sciences and how this could be changed. As mentioned earlier, the participation of women in the physical sciences differs strongly between regions and cultures, as the conditions women work in also differ. Feminist analysis, however, has concentrated mostly on the situation in Europe and North America. Sue Rosser (1987) differentiates between five types of feminist analysis of the sciences. The first is educational transformation in teaching practices and the curriculum of science courses. Much research has been done on the development and evaluation of more "girl-friendly" science courses for secondary education, courses that are more contextual and geared to girls' perception of their environment. For girls between the ages of 10 and 15, many extracurricular projects have been realized since the 1980s to expand their knowledge, practical skills, and interests in the physical sciences. The reason for the low participation of women in physics and mathematics is also sought in innate differences in mathematical abilities between women and men. Feminist researchers often argue that these studies examine biological differences at a level where culture already intervened. From birth on, boys and girls get different messages from parents, teachers, and peers about their abilities and expectations.

The second approach is the recovery of the achievements of women in science throughout history. The aforementioned book by Margaret Alic is an example of this approach. At the university level, some women's studies courses pay attention to the history of women in science and a feminist analysis of scientific methodologies.

A third approach is the study of women's limited access to the institutions of science. In this case, women's absence from the physical sciences is an employment issue; affirmative action programs are often discussed as an appropriate remedy to fight the underrepresentation of women in the physical sciences.

The feminist critique of science is the fourth approach. This involves an analysis of how science has defined the nature of women and results in the critique that the scientific method is in essence biased, with patriarchal values. Nowadays this applies more to the biomedical sciences than to the physical sciences, but when the natural sciences were less specialized and more connected to philosophy, this also held for the physical sciences. Evelyn Fox Keller (1985), a physicist and philosopher of science, illustrates this for the seventeenth century. In the physical sciences, this approach involves an analysis of the masculinist nature of science, which perhaps is responsible for women's historical absence from science, because sex and gender are often equated. The basic assumption is that science is a gendered institution and that its results are colored by the culture in which it is produced. The culture of science gives highest priority to "masculine" values such as objectivity, abstractness, detachment, and control over nature.

Feminists differ in their views on how this could be changed. These different positions are all possible feminist theories of science, which is the fifth approach Rosser distinguishes. One can opt for a feminine science, which values connectedness, involvement, contextuality, and ecological sustainability. Feminists who do this often argue that women, because of their history and socialization, can change the masculinity of science. Sandra Harding (1986), a philosopher of science, calls this "feminist standpoint theory." Female scientists in the physical sciences often hold a position that Harding calls "feminist empiricism." They recognize that traditional science has been male-biased but insist on the existing scientific method for describing reality and doing better science. The biologist and philosopher of science Donna Haraway (1988) used both the constructedness of science and the wish to describe reality in the best possible way to arrive at the concept of situated knowledge. Feminist analysis of the construction of gender in contemporary physics, for example, is done on high-energy physics and space flight (Keller, 1992; Lykke and Braidotti, 1996; Traweek, 1988).

See Also

ENGINEERING; MATHEMATICS; SCIENCE: FEMINISM AND SCIENCE STUDIES; SCIENCE: FEMINIST PHILOSOPHY; SCIENCE: TECHNOLOGICAL AND SCIENTIFIC RESEARCH

References and Further Reading

Alic, Margaret. 1986. *Hypatia's heritage: A history of women in science from antiquity through the nineteenth century.* London: Women's Press.

Benditt, John, ed. 1993. Women in science '93: Gender and the culture of science. *Science* 260: 383–430.

———. 1994. Women in science '94: Comparisons across cultures. *Science* 263: 1467–1496.

Haraway, Donna. 1988. Situated knowledges: The science question in feminism and the privilege of partial perspective. *Feminist Studies* 14(3): 575–599.

Harding, Sandra. 1986. *The science question in feminism.* Ithaca, N.Y.: Cornell University Press.

Keller, Evelyn Fox. 1985. *Reflections on gender and science.* New Haven, Conn.: Yale University Press.

———. 1992. *Secrets of life, secrets of death.* New York.

Lykke, Nina, and Rosi Braidotti, eds. 1996. *Between monsters, goddesses and cyborgs: Feminist confrontations with science, medicine and cyberspace.* London: Zed.

Rosser, Sue V. 1987. Feminist scholarship in the sciences: Where are we now and when can we expect a theoretical breakthrough? *Hypatia* 2(3): 5–17.

Traweek, Sharon. 1988. *Beamtimes and lifetimes: The world of high-energy physicists.* Cambridge, Mass.: Harvard University Press.

Renée Heller

PHYSICAL STRENGTH

Physical differences between men and women, particularly differences in physical strength and musculature, have traditionally been put forward as "natural" justifications for gender inequalities in society (Ussher, 1997). In 1898, one "expert" claimed: "In view of his superior power of making movements and applying physical force, the male must inevitably assume control... there has never been a moment in the history of society when the law of might, tempered by sexual affinity, did not prevail" (Thomas, quoted in Ussher, 1992). Equally, female reproduction has traditionally been considered a physical weakness. For example, in nineteenth-century England many male educationalists argued vociferously that women's reproductive powers would be severely affected by the process of education, while also stating that menstruation led to inherent weakness and instability (Sayers, 1982). Thus, in 1896, Herbert Spencer protested that the reason many educated woman were not bearing children "may be reasonably attributed to the overtaxing of their brains—an overtaxing which produces a serious reaction on the physique." Therefore, women should neither think nor work.

This emphasis on men's physical strength and women's weakness was used in the late twentieth century as an explanation for apparent sex differences in performance and achievement. For example, M. G. Wardle and colleages claimed that "women have significantly smaller capacities to perform physical work and to perform specific work activities than do men" (1986: 118). The supposed weakening effects of reproduction have continued with (unsubstantiated) claims that menstruation and premenstrual syndrome make women labile, unstable, and unable to perform (Ussher, 1996).

Feminist critics have disputed the importance of physical strength and musculature as underlying reasons for sex differences in achievement and work performance. The misogynistic edicts of the nineteenth-century educationalists have been effectively contradicted by successive generations of women who have risen to prominence in a range of professions. And while women may on average be smaller or have less physical strength than men, this is a disadvantage only in a working environment designed (literally) for men. In a review of anthrometric factors in performance, L. Perival and K. Quinkert (1986) concluded that although "significant differences exist between man and women with regard to size, strength and flexibility," this leads to problems for women only if equipment, tasks, jobs, or working environments are designed "on the basis of male anthropometric data."

Even the "fact" of women's lesser strength and stamina is challenged by evidence across cultures that women carry out a substantial amount of physical work requiring endurance and stamina. Moreover, with the advent of science and technology, sex differences in physical strength become irrelevant in the world of work.

See Also

ANATOMY; AUTOMATION; EVOLUTION; MENSTRUATION; PREMENSTRUAL SYNDROME (PMS); REPRODUCTION: OVERVIEW; WORK: OCCUPATIONAL SEGREGATION

References and Further Reading

Perival, L., and K. Quinkert. 1986. Anthropomorphic factors. In M. Baker, ed., *Sex differences in human performance.* London: John Wiley.

Sayers, J. 1982. *Biological politics: Feminist and anti-feminist perspectives.* London: Tavistock.

Ussher, Jane M. 1997. *Fantasies of femininity: Reframing and the boundaries of "sex."* London: Penguin.

———. 1996. Premenstrual syndrome: Reconciling disciplinary divide through the adoption of a material-discursive epistemological standpoint. *Annual Review of Sex Research* 7: 218–252.

Wardle, M. G., M. R. Gloss, and D. S. Gloss, III. 1986. Response differences. In M. Baker, ed., *Sex differences in human performance.* London: Wiley.

Jane M. Ussher

PHYSIOLOGY

Scientific accounts of physiological differences between the sexes have a long history of being employed to justify sexual and racial inequality. From the classical period until the nineteenth century, male physiology was viewed as the true form of human nature, whereas female physiology was seen as a deviation from it.

Aristotle (384–322 B.C.E.) theorized that the female resulted from a defect in heat during conception and argued that this accounted for numerous physiological differences between women and men. Woman's imperfection, Aristotle tells us, results in her being smaller and less muscular, and possessing a smaller brain, which causes her to be more deceptive, jealous, querulous, despondent, and void of shame. Indeed, Aristotle labels the female character as "a sort of natural deficiency."

This conception of woman as an imperfectly developed man remained influential well into the eighteenth century. Physiological theory was used as a basis for concluding that a woman was less rational and moral, and that her natural role was as a wife and mother. Although physiological theories began to shift in the eighteenth century to a model of female and male bodies as opposites, the same conclusions concerning woman's abilities remained prevalent in both science and social theory. Darwin, for example, in developing his theory of evolution, argued that physiological sexual differences increase as animals evolve. This gradual differentiation resulted in two distinct sexes that became increasingly specialized in form and function. Darwin held that the female will be less complex than the male and thus less evolved. This means that men will be taller, heavier, stronger, and more courageous, pugnacious, and energetic than women and will have a more inventive genius. Despite the shift in theory, the conception of men as the superior sex remained startlingly constant.

Such justification of sexual differences went hand in hand with a justification of racial differences. Darwin posited "higher" and "lower" species, arguing that there could be no gap between apes and humans. Supposedly "primitive" cultures were seen as filling in these gaps, being more perfect than apes but less evolved than "civilized" humans. Such a conception was used, for example, in the United States by some supporters of white women's suffrage to argue that "civilized" white women were superior to black males and thus more worthy of the vote.

Such debates continued in the twentieth century. The century began with controversy over higher education for women, with outcries that education would permanently damage women's reproductive capacities. It closed with debates about the significance of brain lateralization, premenstrual syndrome (PMS), and the widespread belief that females have superior verbal ability and are more emotional, whereas males excel in visual-spatial and mathematical abilities and are more agressive. Such theories are used to argue that males are better suited for certain roles—for example, as scientists, soldiers, and politicians—and women are better parents and caregivers.

Given this history, contemporary feminist scholars have carefully evaluated studies purporting to document sex differences. Feminist scientists such as Anne Fausto-Sterling and Ruth Bleier have consistently shown that sex differences are small and often statistically insignificant, and that studies that record sex differences have simply presupposed that such differences are purely the result of innate structures, such as hormones or brain configurations. Currently accepted theories of biology question the idea that a purely biological explanation could be provided for any trait or behavior, because development is subject to generic regulatory information, external environmental influences, and random variations. Despite such critiques, numerous scientists and much of the popular press continue to insist on biological sex differences.

See Also

ANATOMY; NATURE-NURTURE DEBATE; REPRODUCTIVE PHYSIOLOGY; SCIENCE: FEMINIST PHILOSOPHY; SEXISM

References and Further Readings

Bleier, Ruth. 1984. *Science and gender: A critique of biology and its theories on women.* New York: Pergamon.

Fausto-Sterling, Anne. 1985. *Myths of gender: Biological theories about women and men.* New York: Basic Books.

———. 2000. *Sexing the body: Gender politics and the construction of sexuality.* New York: Basic Books.

Hubbard, Ruth. 1990. *The politics of women's biology.* New Brunswick, N.J.: Rutgers University Press.

Schiebinger, Londa. 1993. *Nature's body: Gender in the making of modern science.* Boston: Beacon.

Tavris, Carol. 1992. *The mismeasure of woman.* New York: Simon and Schuster.

Tuana, Nancy. 1993. *The less noble sex: Scientific, religious, and philosophical conceptions of woman's nature.* Bloomington: Indiana University Press.

Nancy Tuana

THE PILL

Historical Background

The oral contraceptive now known as "the Pill" was a brainchild of Margaret Sanger, founder of Planned Parenthood, popularizer of the diaphragm, and an indomitable fighter for women's rights. When she was in her late eighties, Sanger was introduced to Gregory Pincus, a reproductive scientist from Massachusetts. She personally raised the money to get Pincus and his collaborators, Min-Chueh Chang and John Rock, started on research for a universal contraceptive.

At first, Pincus hoped to develop products for both men and women; he tested experimental hormones on male mental patients at Worcester State Hospital. His trials conducted with women—female residents of housing projects in Rio Piedras, Puerto Rico—began in 1956 and culminated in approval of Enovid, the first oral contraceptive, in 1960. Thirty-nine years later, the filmmakers Erna Buffie and Elise Swerhone released a documentary, *The Pill* (produced by the National Film Board of Canada), in which some of the participants from Puerto Rico reported that they had no idea they were involved in an experiment. "The point," said one, "was not to have a lot of kids." Three of the women had died, but none had been autopsied.

Since then, the popularity of the Pill has varied, but at the end of the twentieth century 78.5 million women worldwide, including 10 million in the United States, were taking it. Oral contraceptives (OCs) are effective, convenient, and usually reversible, and they were at first greeted enthusiastically by feminists such as Clare Boothe Luce, who told the *Los Angeles Times,* "Modern woman is at last free, as a man is free, to dispose of her own body, to earn her living, to pursue the improvement of her mind, to try a successful career." With time and experience, however, some patients found reason to question the Pill's safety. Many observers also suspected that drug manufacturers and population controllers had denied or trivialized adverse reactions and had concealed the systemic nature of the Pill's action—although this action was stated clearly in the the 1992 edition of the *Merck Manual:* "In addition to affecting the female genital tract, the metabolic activities of synthetic hormonal components of OCs [oral contraceptives] affect nearly every other organ system."

Second-Wave Feminism and Informed Consent

The Pill had a dual effect on the development of second-wave feminism. First (as Clare Booth Luce's comment suggests), it expanded the view of women's potential; then, about a decade later, it was an impetus for a militant branch of the women's movement that emphasized full disclosure and informed consent, expressed in such slogans as "It's *my* body" and "Taking our bodies back!"

"Health feminism" seems to have first announced itself as a powerful political force in January 1970, when a young Barnard graduate, Alice Wolfson, and her colleagues at what would later become the National Women's Health Network repeatedly disrupted U.S. Senate hearings on the Pill, demanding to know why no patients were testifying, why women were serving as "guinea pigs," and why there was no Pill for men. (For an account, see *Science,* issue of 11 August 1995.) This civil disobedience was covered daily by worldwide print and television reporters; and even after the hearings concluded, in March 1970, the protest continued with sit-ins at several government offices, including the Food and Drug Administration (FDA) and the office of the secretary of Health, Education, and Welfare (HEW, now Health and Human Services, or HHS). In July of that year, despite opposition from organized medicine and the drug industry, the activists got what they wanted: prescriptions for the Pill would be accompanied by a warning noting the increased risk of cardiovascular disease, deep-vein thrombosis, pulmonary embolism, and ischemic stroke. The warning proved to be very beneficial: morbidity and mortality figures soon dropped as patients with existing blood clots and other predisposing factors avoided the Pill, and women who chose it learned to recognize early signs of trouble. In fact, by the late 1970s (after feminists had again overcome legal challenges by the drug industry), such warnings were extended to all estrogen products—and eventually similar warnings accompanied other prescription drugs as well as most gynecologic and medical treatments. There was also a more general but nevertheless dramatic effect: the medical professions became more welcoming to women, with far less of the secrecy, obfuscation, and condescension that women patients had perceived for centuries.

In 1988, under pressure from the FDA, the last of the high-dose oral contraceptives were withdrawn from the market in the United States. By then, it was clear that the original versions of the Pill had contained up to 10 times the dose of hormones required for contraception. What was not clear, however, was how much safer the lower-dose products would be. Studies published at the beginning of the twenty-first century (in, for example, *Lancet* and *Journal of the American Medical Association, JAMA*) indicate that some risks persist even with the new Pills, but that adverse effects occur less frequently. Excess mortality rates are down to half or less of what they once were. However, there is a growing body of evidence that what are called third-generation progestins, such as desogestrel and gestodene, increase the risk of blood clots as compared with the second-generation product, levonorgestrel.

Revised FDA Labeling on Oral Contraceptives

In July 2000 the FDA proposed an updated version of labeling (for providers and patients) on oral contraceptives:

- Information to prescribers should include a warning about the increased risk of serious cardiovascular side effects in women who take the Pill and smoke. Patients should be informed that these contraceptives do *not* protect against HIV or other sexually transmitted diseases.
- Labeling should explain mode of action, efficacy, and indications.
- Labeling should state that although "the chance of becoming pregnant during the first year of use is 0.1 percent, . . . typical pregnancy rates are estimated to be 5 percent."
- Labeling should mention the potential for using the Pill within 72 hours after unprotected intercourse to reduce the risk of pregnancy.
- Contraindications should be listed. The increased risk of cardiovascular disease, deep-vein thrombosis, pulmonary embolism, and ischemic stroke must still be indicated.
- The risk of breast cancer may be slightly increased among current and recent users. This risk diminishes over time after discontinuation until, by ten years after cessation, the increased risk disappears. The relationship between OCs and cervical cancer remains unclear.
- Drug interactions should be listed, and the potential for OCs to alter laboratory tests should be stated.

- Patients should be instructed on correct use, including when to begin taking the Pill and what to do if a dose is omitted. A list of medications known to lessen the effectivness of oral contraceptives should be included.

Conclusion

In her doctoral thesis for the History of Science Department at Harvard University—published in 1998 as *On the Pill*—Elizabeth Siegel Watkins wrote:

> For historians of the 1950s and 1960s, the pill serves as a barometer of changes in attitudes toward science, technology, and medicine. At the same time that eager acceptance of the pill gave way to caution and concern, trust and confidence in medical research and its products also yielded to questioning and uncertainty. . . . Although not as well organized nor as powerful as the established medical profession and the pharmaceutical industry, health feminists were determined to take on these male-dominated institutions and their traditional assumptions and practices. In the decades to follow, the interests of feminists, female patients, physicians, drug manufacturers, and government officials would clash many times. . . . However, . . . the matter of informed consent, as articulated in the controversy over the safety of oral contraceptives, would remain central. . . . *The Doctors' Case Against the Pill* inspired feminists to vocalize the shared perception that the medical profession was "condescending, paternalistic, judgmental, and noninformative."

The work Watkins mentions, *The Doctors' Case Against the Pill,* itself has a significant history. In 1996, twenty-seven years after it was first published, *JAMA* reviewed it and found it to be "a strange book and not particularly recommended . . . for either the public or the profession" (Levinson, 1996). The reviewer, an endoscopic surgeon in California, had, as it turned out, been disciplined by the Medical Board of California in 1995 for "overprescribing or misprescribing drugs" (Wolfe, 2000), but *JAMA* did not reveal either this information or the fact that Ethicon, which financed Levinson's endoscopy center, was a division of Johnson and Johnson, the world's largest manufacturer of oral contraceptives—a connection that might have called Levinson's objectivity into question ("The Pill," 1998). For feminists involved in women's health issues, this may be seen as an example of how reluctant organized medicine can be to acknowledge its shortcomings.

See Also

ABORTION; CONTRACEPTION; CONTRACEPTIVES: DEVELOPMENT; ESTROGEN; FETUS; NORPLANT; REPRODUCTION: OVERVIEW; REPRODUCTIVE HEALTH; REPRODUCTIVE RIGHTS; REPRODUCTIVE TECHNOLOGIES

References and Further Reading

Boston Women's Health Book Collective. 1998. *Our bodies, ourselves for the new century.* New York: Simon and Schuster.

Cohn, Victor. 1969. Ley urges complete data to users on Pill's side effects. *Washington Post* (22 December): A-1.

Dickey, Richard P. 2000. *Managing contraceptive pill patients.* Millennium ed. Dallas, Tex.: Emis.

Ehrenreich, Barbara, and Deirdre English. 1973. *Witches, midwives, and nurses: A history of women healers.* New York: Feminist Press at City University of New York.

FDA issues draft guidance on oral contraceptives labeling. 2000. *Reuters Medical News* (11 July).

Flanders, Laura. 1997. *Real majority, media minority: The cost of sidelining women in reporting.* Monroe, Me.: Common Courage.

Gillum, Leslie Allison, et al. 2000. Ischemic stroke risk with oral contraceptives: A meta-analysis. *Journal of the American Medical Association* 284(1: 5 July): 72–78.

Grant, Linda. 1994. *Sexing the millennium.* New York: Grove.

Hatcher, Robert A. 1998. *Contraceptive technology.* 17th ed. New York: Irvington.

Holmes, Helen B., Betty B. Hoskins, and Michael Gross, eds. 1980. *Birth control and controlling birth: Women-centered perspectives.* Clifton, N. J.: Humana.

Levinson, Carl J. 1996. Review of "The doctors' case against the pill." *Journal of the American Medical Association* (10 July).

Merck and Company. 1992. *The Merck manual.* 16th ed. Rahway, N. J.: Author.

National Black Women's Health Project. 1998. *Our bodies, our voices, our choices: National Black Women's Health Project.* Introduction by Julia Scott. Washington, D. C.: Author.

Null, Gary, and Barbara Seaman. 2000. *For women only! Your guide to health empowerment.* New York: Seven Stories.

Parrott, Roxanne Louiselle, and Celeste Michelle Condit, eds. 1996. *Evaluating women's health messages: A resource book.* Newbury Park, Calif.: Sage.

The Pill—25 years ago and today. 1998. *Journal of the American Medical Association* (13 May): 1443–1444.

Ruzek, Sheryl Burt. 1978. *The women's health movement: Feminist alternatives to medical control.* New York: Praeger.

Seaman, Barbara. 1969. *The doctors' case against the Pill.* New York: Wyden. (Revised edition, 1980, New York: Doubleday. Twenty-fifth anniversary edition, 1995, Alameda, Calif.: Hunter House.)

———. 1972. *Free and female.* New York: Coward McCann.

———. 2000. The Pill and I: 40 years on, the relationship remains wary. *New York Times* (25 June, Section 15—Women's Health, A Special Section): 19. On-line: <http:www.nytimes.com/library/national/science/health/062500hth-women-pill.html>

———, with Gideon Seaman. 1977 *Women and the crisis in sex hormones.* New York: Rawson.

———, and Susan Wood. 2000. Role of advocacy groups in research on women's health. In Marlene B. Goldman and Maureen C. Hatch, eds., *Women and health.* New York: Academic.

Seidegard, Janeric, et al. 2000. Oral contraceptives alter plasma levels of predisolone. *Clinical Pharmacology and Therapeutics* (April): 373–381.

Skegg, David, et al. 2000. Oral contraceptive users at higher risk of fatal pulmonary embolism. With commentary by Dr. Neil R. Poulter. *Lancet* (17 June): 2133–2134.

Watkins, Elizabeth Siegel. 1998. *On the Pill: A social history of oral contraceptives 1950–1970.* Baltimore, Md.: Johns Hopkins University Press.

Weisman, Carol S. 1998. *Women's health care: Activist traditions and institutional change.* Baltimore, Md.: Johns Hopkins University Press.

Wolfe, Sidney. 2000. Questionable doctors disciplined by state and federal governments. *Volume for California and Hawaii* 194.

Wolfson, Alice J. 1998. Clenched fist, open heart. In Rachel Blau DuPlessis and Ann Snitow, eds., *The feminist memoir project.* New York: Three Rivers/Crown.

Videos

Cambridge Documentary Films. 1974. *Taking our bodies back/Women's health movement.* Available from Cambridge Documentary Films, Inc., Cambridge, Mass. 02139-0004.

National Film Board of Canada. 1999. *The Pill: The untold story of the drug that changed the world.* Order from: National Film Board of Canada, P.O. Box 6100, Station Centre-Ville, Montreal, Quebec H3C 3H5.

Internet Resources

Boston Women's Health Book Collective, Boston, Mass.: <http://www.ourbodiesourselves.org>

National Women's Health Network, Washington, D.C.: <http://www.womenshealthnetwork.org>

Barbara Seaman
Laura Eldridge

PLAGIARISM IN SCIENCE

Plagiarism is the presentation of another's work as one's own. Although many use the term to describe verbatim duplication of written material, plagiarism encompasses any appropriation of another's ideas, data, methodology, and words without proper citation or reference. It is a serious offense in most countries to take credit for another's accomplishments.

In the United States plagiarism is a crime if the work is legally protected or copyrighted; otherwise, plagiarism is a tort, or civil wrong, if one can show that damage occurred. Usually ideas are not protected by law. In science, plagiarism is considered unethical, and all work, including ideas, is considered protected.

Acts of plagiarism are particularly harmful in science because they erode the trust that must be maintained in the scientific community. Scientists judge one another's work prior to, or as a condition of, publication and funding in a process called peer review. Reviewers have access to unpublished and privileged information and are entrusted with others' ideas and data. In addition, researchers share unpublished work with others in collaboration, as servants of public funds to advance science. Mistrust among scientists hinders intellectual exchange and, potentially, research advances.

Furthermore, careers are compromised when work is plagiarized. The importance of scientists' work is often measured by the number of times their work is cited in the literature; thus omissions of reference or credit can have far-reaching effects. Plagiarism can also compromise economic benefits. France currently shares patent royalties from the AIDS blood test with the United States, despite findings that U.S. scientists misappropriated the work of French scientists (Fox, 1994). Plagiarism also falsifies history. A written account of the events leading to the discovery of DNA structure minimized the contributions of Rosalind Franklin, and although the account appeared after her death and had no effect on her career, it misrepresented this important historical event (Sayre, 1975). Similarly, many contributions of women to science have gone unrecognized (Bleier, 1986).

Plagiarism is one of three instances of *scientific misconduct,* a broader term used to encompass unethical or unprofessional behavior by scientists. Other instances include fabrication and falsification of work. Approximately half of the scientific misconduct cases reported to the U.S. National Science Foundation (NSF) have involved some form of plagiarism (Buzzelli, 1993).

Scientists have been found guilty of plagiarism irrespective of career status, gender, or race. Many speculate that plagiarism is a result of the pressure to publish, produce results, or obtain research funding at any cost (Hackett, 1994). Most scientific communities are reluctant to see plagiarism as a problem and often believe that only inexperienced researchers attempt to deceive (LaFollette, 1992). Robert Bell (1992) argues that scientific misconduct has more potential to occur with senior scientists because of the greater power they hold. Given that most women in science have subordinate roles, a woman's work is more likely to be misappropriated (Bleier, 1986).

Researchers whose work is plagiarized or who raise suspicions of plagiarism often suffer (LaFollette, 1992). In a case in which a senior researcher plagiarized work by a junior researcher, the university that employed both of them did not renew the contract of the junior researcher who was the victim (*Science,* 1993, 262: 23). Such retaliation often discourages people who suspect plagiarism from coming forward. Ironically, keeping quiet about suspected misconduct is itself scientific misconduct, according to the NSF.

A fundamental issue of plagiarism is originality. Scientists must first prove they are the originators of the work in question before they can exercise control. Another issue is the assumption that the offender intended to deceive (LaFollette, 1992). Honest mistakes and sloppiness are not usually considered misconduct.

See Also

ETHICS: SCIENTIFIC; INVENTORS; SCIENTIFIC SEXISM AND RACISM

References and Further Reading

Bell, Robert. 1992. *Impure science; Fraud, compromise, and political influence in scientific research.* New York: Wiley.

Bleier, Ruth, ed. 1986. *Feminist approaches to science.* New York: Pergamon.

Buzzelli, Donald E. 1993. The definition of misconduct in science: A view from NSF. *Science* 259: 584–585, 647–648.

Fox, Mary Frank. 1994. Scientific misconduct and editorial and peer review processes. *Journal of Higher Education* 65(3): 289–309.

Hackett, Edward J. 1994. A social control perspective on scientific misconduct. *Journal of Higher Education* 65(3): 243–260.

LaFollette, Marcel Chotkowski. 1992. *Stealing into print: Fraud, plagiarism, and misconduct in scientific publishing.* Berkeley: University of California Press.

Sayre, Anne. 1975. *Rosalind Franklin and DNA.* New York: Norton.

D. Rae Barnhisel

PLASTIC SURGERY

See COSMETIC SURGERY.

PLAY

See GENDERED PLAY.

POETRY

See also LITERATURE.

POETRY: Overview

Poetry is both the most ancient of the literary arts and the most intense, characterized by its use of heightened formalized diction.

The Relevance of Power Imbalance

Mainstream commentary on and analysis of poetic forms and conventions almost always reflect androcentric and ethnocentric values and judgments, so that women's poetry, even within a dominant culture, becomes marginalized or is extinguished altogether. Women's poetry written in so-called minority languages has even less chance of reaching a wide audience. In addition, traditional ways of looking at literature produce both prescriptive and proscriptive discourse about what constitutes "great" poetry, and all this discourse, too, is almost always both androcentric and ethnocentric. The consequences of androcentric language dominance have been serious for women as the underclass of both poets and audience. The final inequity is the invisibility and inaudibility of poetry contributed by lower-class, working-class, or poor women, whose forms may be partly or even exclusively oral (for example, songs, chants, and dirges) and whose authorship may be collective, collaborative, or anonymous.

The relationship of a poem written by a woman to the prevailing system of power has implications on several levels. The very existence of a poem by a woman depends to some degree on how much that poem is valued by those in power, and for what reasons. For a poem to be valued requires more than essential "artistic worth"; it requires that the poem be understood. Just as the English-speaking world tends not to understand poetry in other languages, so a male-dominated society tends not to understand the poetry of women. It is not in the interest of those in power to understand the language of the relatively powerless; the process is usually the reverse. Furthermore, there are reasons other than pure aesthetic pleasure for the reading of poetry. A poem may be included in the school curriculum if the authorities consider it suitable; a poem may please a reader because it is one the reader easily relates to or identifies with. It is worth noting that the relatively powerless find it easier to identify with the relatively powerful rather than with themselves, a phenomenon identified by feminist theorists as self-oppression. Instances of the powerful identifying with the powerless—and therefore the less glamorous—are rarer. Again, a poem may be read because it profits the reader in terms of passing examinations or acquiring a job. Obviously, knowing a poem in the language of the powerful is likely to be more profitable than knowing a poem in the language of the powerless.

Because a woman's poem exists between her writing of it and someone's reading of it, the identity of the reader is of some consequence. The identities offered to women and men differ in the degree of power attached to them by virtue of gender alone. It is arguable that a male-dominated society produces a male-dominated literary tradition and a male-dominated literary tradition produces a male-dominated reader of a woman's poem.

Feminist theory has clarified the crucial significance of these power imbalances for women, whereas traditional teaching and scholarship, by appealing to concepts such as "universality," have ignored or derided them. The retrieval and recording of this material, which is potentially vast, will involve new forms of literary research, from fieldwork to archival reclassification.

Problems in Defining the Canon

Combing the world's literature for women poets is a relatively new activity, initiated by feminist concerns. It is a task that can be stopped even before it is started, however, by such essentialist questions as: Who is defined as a poet? What constitutes female identity? And what precisely is "women's poetry"? A more useful starting point is that because human beings have become culturally dimorphic, a woman's culture and experience are understood to be altogether different from those of a man. Therefore, for all practical purposes, a poem may be discussed within the parameters of women's poetry if it fulfills two or more of the following criteria: (1) it was written by a woman, (2) its ideal reader is a woman, (3) it is concerned with women, and (4) its center of consciousness is a woman's.

Reading and valuing women's poetry that is already established in the conventional canon of a particular language tradition inevitably involves examining what the androcentric view has found notable or acceptable about such work, together with a revaluation that takes account of feminist theoretical concerns. Moreover, establishing or developing a feminist canon involves both reclaiming poetry that has been discarded, scorned, or censored, and supporting and consolidating—through publication, teaching, research, and translation—poetry that is continually being written by women. In this way a feminist understanding of women's poetry becomes proactive rather than merely reactive. It is reactive, for example, simply to scan publishers' poetry catalogs for titles by women, arduous and important though that scanning is.

The expedience that allows poetry in general to be subdivided by the political geography of imperialism into, for example, the language cultures called English, French, and Spanish (one language, many lands), but also, for example, into African, Indian, and Chinese (one land, many languages), is often applied to poetry by women, thus extending the problems of imperialism, nationalism, and colonization into an area where relative cultural powerlessness is already a central issue. This is not to say that women's poetry should never be categorized; new categorizations concomitant with women's culture and experience, rather than the old androcentric ones, are necessary. This may be a slow process of subversion and change, as developing new categories presents similar problems to the process that women poets have always been engaged in, that of feminizing the language.

Necessary, too, is the prioritization of translation, which is the surest way to reduce entrenched ethnocentricity and to make the experience, sensibility, and perspective of women available to each other, however imperfectly.

Contextualization and Evaluation

Because of the power imbalance between the cultures of women and men, and between the cultures disposed according to the prevailing geopolitical order, poetry belonging to dominant cultures has enjoyed the best chance of survival. This poetry is not necessarily either the best (in aesthetic terms), or the most representative (in sociopolitical terms), or the most worthy (in ethical terms), or the most useful (in polemical terms). The test of time is a questionable test. The effect of any established literary canon on poetry in general, and on lyric poetry in particular, given its highly referential nature, cannot be overestimated, as words and literary conventions develop from a historical context and mean not only what the poet would like them to mean, but also what they are perceived to mean. And not just the meaning, but the judgments about the value of any particular poetry, depend on the perspective from which it is viewed. Nearly always the perspective based on the dominant cultural tradition prevails. Western second-wave feminism made clear that a patriarchal literary context was inadequate for evaluating the work of women poets. An appropriate context for the reading of women's poetry is being established by the development of a substantial body of women's poetry from many languages, which is forming its own canon and traditions.

Feminist analysis has shown that a purely literary evaluation cannot exist, and that the struggles for canonicity, for the establishment of an appropriate literary context, for the meanings of words, and for the inculcation of identities are all different forms of the same power struggle.

This is not to say that the tools of traditional, patriarchal scholarship cannot be applied to women's poetry, or that the poetry of men is a waste of time, but these pursuits should be undertaken with the conscious knowledge that women's poetry, either self-consciously or implicitly, stands always in oblique relation to the patriarchal norms.

Radical Questioning of the Nature of Poetry

Poetry has no utilitarian functions, but fundamental to its ethical and aesthetic functions is that it should tell the truth. It is the case, however, that telling the truth is very often an extremely dangerous thing to do, particularly when the truth is unflattering to those who hold power. It is understandable, therefore, if poets have tried hard not to think too hard or too long about the relationship of a poem—*their* poem—to the prevailing power systems. The realities of survival (dissidence can mean imprisonment or even death), of patronage (not saying the right things can mean starvation, as well as insignificance and invisibility), or of subsidy and publication (not being published can mean never being read) intensify the dreadful irony that the poet whose vocation is truth telling must do her best to make her craft seem as harmless as possible and to make her truth sound as pleasant as she can. A woman poet's work is thus produced by the most precarious means and is always under threat of extinction, as the extent to which she is tolerated may well measure the extent to which she holds back from telling the truth.

Yet, given the low status of poetry in large tracts of the modern world, any precautions against poets would appear redundant, although it may be that this low status is precisely the result of a fairly efficacious censorship, which does not seem like censorship at all. If there appears to be in most countries a negligible market for poetry by women, then superficially it may seem "democratic" that such poetry should not be published; but conflation of democracy with mass marketing in the early twenty-first century is particularly pernicious. There are, after all, myriad ways in which markets are manipulated to suit those in power. And, of course, there are many instances of direct and brutal censorship suffered by women poets under different regimes, whether straightforwardly militaristic or more ideologically based. That the brutality of the treatment has often been in direct proportion to the respect accorded poetry merely compounds the irony.

Poets and poetry are usually in the forefront of any rebellion, revolution, or movement for change, but become marginalized again with the onset of conformity. This is largely because poets, given the very nature of their craft (a poem exists in process, not in definition) question the rigid allegiances and identifications on offer. Later, however, when new allegiances have been formed, this questioning becomes less welcome. So it has been in the West, for example, where poetry was vital to the first upsurge of second-wave feminism. As the popular demand for women's poetry becomes less urgent, however, it becomes correspondingly even more urgent that feminist scholarship continues to build and promote the canon of women's work.

The radical questioning of gender identities and of notions of "otherness" has been one of the major contributions of women's poetry. Equally significant, though perhaps less obvious, have been the fundamental changes in the very conventions governing poetry. These include, for example, the use of mixed genres; an altered perspective on what constitutes the "epic" and the "heroic"; and, in lyric poetry, a reordering of the relationships between the "silent" woman addressed (who more often than not is no longer silent), the reader of the poem, and the poet. Experiment and innovation are characteristic of nearly all women's poetry, from the very formal to the most polemical, from the subverting of grammatical genders to the restructuring of myth and fable, from the creation of female archetypes to the exploration of hidden etymologies, from the joint work and collaboration with other women to the point of anonymity to the direct speech of personal experience. For women poets, of necessity, the personal has always been poetic, and the poetic has always been political.

See Also

POETRY: FEMINIST THEORY AND CRITICISM

References and Further Reading

Ashfield, Andrew, ed. 1995. *Romantic women poets 1770–1838: An anthology.* Manchester, U.K.: Manchester University Press.

Bernikow, Louise, ed. 1974. *The world split open: Women poets 1552–1950.* New York: Vintage.

Bogin, Meg, ed. 1976. *The women troubadours.* London: Paddington.

DeJean, Joan. 1989. *Fictions of Sappho 1546–1937.* Chicago: University of Chicago Press.

De Lotbinière-Harwood, Susanne. 1991. *Re-belle et infidèle: La traduction comme pratique de réécriture au féminin (The body bilingual: Translation as a rewriting in the feminine).* Montreal: Les éditions du remue-ménage; Toronto: Women's Press.

Linthwaite, Illona, ed. 1987. *Ain't I a woman! Poems by black and white women.* London: Virago.

Lonsdale, Roger. 1989. *Eighteenth-century women poets: An Oxford anthology.* Oxford: Oxford University Press.

Manushi (Madhu Kishwar, ed). 1991. *Women Bhakta poets.* New Delhi: Manushi.

Ostriker, Alicia Suskin. 1986. *Stealing the language: The emergence of women's poetry in America.* London: Women's Press.

<www.york.ac.uk/services/library/subjects/womenint.htm>—Women's Studies information sources at York University

<www.inform.umd.edu/EdRes/Topic/WomensStudies>—University of Maryland at College Park

<women-www.uia.ac.be/women/server/info_roa.html>—Women's Studies Roadmap Information

Gillian Hanscombe
Suniti Namjoshi

POETRY: Feminist Theory and Criticism

This article covers the discussion of poems and poets or, more generally, the genre of poetry. Criticism and theory are often linked together, but it is worth being clear about the difference between them. "Criticism" includes any discussion: from reviews of new collections to articles exploring poems' interpretation, poets' biographies, or the reception of their work. "Theories" about poetry attempt to do the same thing on a larger, more ambitious scale: constructing generalizations or hypotheses about the production or reading of poetry, then applying them to particular groups of poems or poets. One example of a feminist theory applied to poetry is Jane Dowson's use of Sandra Gilbert and Susan Gubar's concept of "the female affiliation complex" (*Feminist Review,* 1999: 7). Gilbert and Gubar develop this term to describe the woman writer's ambivalent and oscillating relationship to her male and female literary traditions. Dowson uses this idea to explain strained relations between women poets and the resultant lack of mutual support or patronage between emerging and established poets.

Not all discussion of the writings of women poets is "feminist"; it is quite possible for critics to examine the world of women poets' without having any interest in feminist politics or modes of analysis. Many assume that a feminist approach implies a narrow perspective and dissociate themselves from it on this account. However, contemporary feminist approaches are enriched by their absorption of ideas from analyses of class, race and ethnicity, and other areas of cultural critique.

Most published criticism and theory about poetry is on the work of Anglo-American poets (including African-American and black British); this is because of the wealth and consequent dominance of both academic institutions and publishing corporations in these parts of the world. Although it is possible to find anthologies of women poets from many parts of the world, it is less easy to find much published discussion of their poetry, even in the case of Nobel Prize–winning poet Wislawa Szymborska.

Triggered by women's liberation movements that surfaced in the late 1960s, initial feminist critical work in the area of poetry was concerned with the retrieval and rediscovery of poets from previous centuries. New attention focused on, for example, the Greek poet Sappho and others, such as eighteenth-century British poets and African-American blues singers and writers who were acclaimed during their lifetimes but had been ignored by more recent literary critics. During the same period, many anthologies of contemporary women's poetry were published, articulating feminist anger at, and analysis of, women's lives within a patriarchal system. The introductions to these anthologies form a useful record of critics' emerging ideas about the viability of searching for a separate female poetic tradition, or the existence of distinctive features in the work of women poets. Bernikow (1974) and Rumens (1987) are especially interesting in this respect.

Early academic studies tended to concentrate on individual poets, drawing attention to the sexism underlying the neglect, dismissal, or misreading of their work by previous (male) critics. Often such analyses would open up new, neglected aspects of the poems and approach them from original perspectives. Twentieth-century North American poets (especially Emily Dickinson, Sylvia Plath, and Anne Sexton) formed the subject for several books in which the struggle for female poetic identity was cited as a central preoccupation. British and other European studies paid more attention to the weight of centuries of poetic tradition, and expressed skepticism about the possibility of separating women from men poets. Montefiore (1987) exemplifies this adherence to a traditional evaluative aesthetic, while also making use of theories proposed by the French psychoanalytic philosophers Luce Irigaray and Julia Kristeva in her search for some specifically female or feminine quality in the work of women poets.

Several well-known poets—Audre Lorde and Adrienne Rich, for example—have also written influential criticism about the practice of poetry and the work of other poets, as well as about politics and aesthetics. Rich's essay "When We Dead Awaken: Writing as Re-Vision" (1979) recorded her own slow progress toward a more authentic poetic voice, whereas Lorde's essays (1984) insist on the crucial role played by language (and therefore poetry) in struggles to overcome the oppressive power of sexist and racist institutions. Poets' own critical writings are particularly valuable for their insights into the practice—as opposed to the critique—of poetry. Examples include Boland (1996) and Gluck (1999).

Poetry criticism and theory in the 1990s demonstrated a number of developments and preoccupations. Attempts were made to broaden definitions of "theory," after criticism that feminists had accepted a narrowly western philosophical and cerebral version of the term that excluded spiritual or creative practices of conceptualizing and generalizing. Recent critical work tends to acknowledge the importance of the specific historical, cultural, and geographical contexts of individual writers: political and class positions, sexual and ethnic identities, and the particular traditions, myths, and histories each poet has inherited. There have been attempts to expand the tools available to critics so that they are better equipped to respond to poetry that operates within oral traditions, where the published poem represents only a small part of the poet's achievement. Such tools include analysis of the use of body, voice, and audience and have been borrowed from performance studies, just as ideas and terminology from anthropology, postcolonial studies, and psychoanalysis have also enriched feminist literary analysis. Rose (1991) is an important example of the latter. Attention has also focused on the work of "experimental" poets who are often allied with a poststructuralist interest in language itself, rather than its representational capacity. Critique of this style of theoretically informed writing is pursued with particular enthusiasm in North America. The political agenda of this type of poetry is not immediately apparent, which perhaps makes it less appealing to less prosperous countries. In parts of the world where women are still struggling to secure the basic human rights of safety, health care, and education, poetry's potential to communicate experience, stir emotions, and move people to action remains its most valued quality. There has, so far, been little academic feminist analysis of this aspect of poetry's impact.

See Also

LESBIAN WRITING: POETRY; LITERARY THEORY AND CRITICISM; POETRY: OVERVIEW

References and Further Reading

Bernikow, Louise, ed. 1974. *The world split open: Women poets 1552–1950.* New York: Vintage.

Bertram, Vicki, ed. 1997. *Kicking daffodils: Essays on twentieth-century women poets.* Edinburgh: University Press.

Boland, Eavan. 1995. *Object lessons: The life of the woman and the poet in our time.* Manchester, U.K.: Carcanet.

Feminist Review 1999. Special issue on contemporary women poets, no. 62.

Gluck, Louise. 1999. *Proofs and theories.* Manchester, U.K.: Carcanet.

Keller, Lynn, and Cristanne Miller, eds. 1994. *Feminist measures: Soundings in poetry and theory.* Ann Arbor: University of Michigan.

Lorde, Audre. 1984. *Sister outsider: Essays and speeches.* Freedom, Calif.: Crossing.

Montefiore, Jan. 1987. *Feminism and poetry: Language, experience, identity in women's writing.* London: Pandora.

Rich, Adrienne. 1979. *On lies, secrets and silence: Selected prose 1966–1978.* New York: Norton.

Rose, Jaqueline. 1991. *The haunting of Sylvia Plath.* London: Virago.

Rumens, Carol. 1987. *Making for the open: Post-feminist poetry 1964–1984.* London: Chatto and Windus.

Vicki Bertram

POETRY: Lesbian

See LESBIAN CONTEMPORARY POETRY.

POLICE AND LAW ENFORCEMENT

See LAW ENFORCEMENT.

POLITICAL ASYLUM

Women constitute the majority of the world's refugee population. According to estimates published by the United Nations High Commissioner for Refugees, over two-thirds of the 19 million refugees worldwide are female.

Becoming a refugee is a traumatic experience for men and women alike; the loss not only of home, family, and income but also of a sense of identity and belonging can be devastating. But women refugees often experience social, economic, emotional, and legal problems in addition to those encountered by male refugees. These may include the loss of the traditional breadwinner and the consequent responsibility of providing for and nuturing dependent relatives in unfamiliar, often hostile surroundings, as well as exposure to rape, sexual harassment, and enforced prostitution with concomitant social ostracism (Martin, 1991).

Since the early 1980s, there has been a growing awareness of and attention to the particular socioeconomic and emotional difficulties faced by refugee women, but less attention has been paid to the distinctive legal problems these women encounter. These problems have had far-reaching consequences and have sometimes resulted in insurmountable obstacles for women seeking to flee persecution and secure refuge for themselves and their families. International refugee law does not address the particular problems and experiences of women (Bhabha and Shutter, 1994). The main international instruments governing the treatment of refugees are the United Nations Convention relating to the Status of Refugees (1951, often referred to as the Geneva Convention) and its Protocol (1967). The Convention defines a refugee as a person who "owing to a well-founded fear of being persecuted for reasons of race, religion, nationality, membership of a particular social group or political opinion, is outside the country of his [*sic*] nationality and is unable or unwilling to avail himself of the protection of that country." Gender is not expressly recognized as a ground of persecution in this definition. This may not be a problem for women refugees (and there are many) who flee "traditional persecution," such as torture and imprisonment, because of their religion or political opinion. It does, however, create difficulties for women whose fears arise out of what has recently come to be termed "gender persecution," that is, persecution arising out of forms of protest or ill-treatment specific to women (*Cornell International Law Journal,* 1993).

Four main categories of such persecution can be identified. The first category includes women persecuted through association with political opposition, either as relatives of activists or as activists themselves but with a gender-specific contribution (cooking or shopping for guerrillas, for example). The second category includes women persecuted for transgressing cultural norms, such as those who refuse to conform to Islamic dress and behavior codes or to agree to female circumcision. Both of these categories of opposition have often been held by decision makers to be "purely personal" rather than "political," a distinction that deprives these women of refugee protection.

Just as certain forms of protest have been considered personal matters, so certain forms of ill treatment have been deemed "private," thus not warranting international protection. This has included the third category, women whose persecution arises out of the systematic failure of governments to protect them from nongovernmental persecutors—battering husbands, for example. Victims of organized rape by government forces, the fourth category, have also been excluded from refugee protection by such reasoning (*Campos-Guardado v. INS,* 1987).

A dual process has thus governed much refugee decision making. On the one hand, ill treatment in the "private" or domestic sphere has frequently been considered too trivial (or too prevalent) to warrant protection; on the other hand, there has been a tendency to ignore the political nature of nontraditional forms of protest and to redefine persecution against women as mere personal conflict.

In 1993, the Canadian authorities, responding to considerable public pressure, formulated the trend-setting *Guidelines for the Treatment of Women Refugees Fearing Gender-Related Persecution.* These provide the most detailed governmental analysis to date of the range of situations giving rise to women's claims for asylum and the special considerations that apply. Several positive decisions on gender-related persecution have emanated from the Canadian authorities since. In the United States, too, growing recognition of gender-based asylum claims has resulted in the publication of guidelines specifically addressing these issues. Draft guidelines for women's asylum claims are currently being considered by the United States Immigration and Naturalization Service. No such developments have taken place yet in European countries.

See Also

DOMESTIC VIOLENCE; FEMALE CIRCUMCISION AND GENITAL MUTILATION; HUMAN RIGHTS; IMMIGRATION; RAPE; VEILING

References and Further Reading

Bhabha, Jacqueline, and Sue Shutter. 1994. *Women's movement: Women under immigration, nationality and refugee law,* 229–257. Stoke-on-Trent, U.K.: Trentham Books.

Campos-Guardado v. INS, 809 F.2d 285 (5th Cir. 1987).

Cornell International Law Journal. 1993. 26(3): 505–672. Special Issue on Refugees).

Hathaway, James C. 1991. *The law of refugee status.* Vancouver, B.C.: Butterworths.

Martin, Susan Forbes. 1991. *Refugee women.* London: Zed.

Jacqueline Bhabha

POLITICAL ECONOMY

Political economy developed as a set of theories in the eighteenth century in an attempt to establish a scientific understanding of the nature of society. The most notable early political economist was Adam Smith, who favored free market exchange and propounded, in his immensely influential book *The Wealth of Nations,* what today is called rational choice or rational exchange theory. This provided the foundation of modern economic theory, with its underlying concern with rationality and equilibrium. It is ironic that the influential part of Smith's work encouraged a simplistic, mechanistic approach to the economy, whereas Smith had broad interests akin to what later developed into the discipline of sociology. Later generations of economists abstracted the economic ideas from their broader context, launching classical economics on the narrowly focused path it still takes today.

After Smith, political economy continued, but on the periphery of what came to be the mainstream of economic thought, until the 1960s, when there was something of a resurgence as part of Marxist critique propounded by the New Left. Political economy threw out a challenge to classical economics emphasizing the propensity of economic theory to mask the fact that the market economy is more effectively understood in terms of capitalist interests rather than the rational choice of individual actors. Marxist and socialist feminists noted that this was particularly so with respect to female actors. The New Left male political economists often acknowledged gender as a basis of power distribution and the gender-biased construction of economic knowledge. However, they saw this as less important than class and failed to really address the issue. It was left to feminist writers, particularly socialist feminists, to develop their own form of economic critique. This has some points in common with New Left political economy but is essentially a separate feminist economics.

Because political economy gives a central place to the organization of the division of labor for the production of value, New Left political economy provided stimulation for feminist theory, particularly concerning the nature and contribution of domestic labor to the production of value. There were two extreme positions. On the political economy side, the most extreme view was that only manufacturing work produced surplus value, whereas on the feminist side it was suggested that women's domestic labor was effectively exploited by individual men and by capitalists and that wages for housework should be paid. No consensus was reached, but insight was gained from the debate. Another source of feminist insights came from the debates about the complexities of the role of the state and the range of interests that it can serve.

Feminist economists have called for greater recognition of the domestic economy because women's association with private unpaid work and men's association with public paid work are crucial for accounting for women's inferior economic position in all nations. They also suggest that the state can play a crucial role in facilitating greater economic equality. Although these are insights to which political economy has made a valuable contribution, feminist writers have largely abandoned direct interchange with political economy, maintaining that the very terms of economic debate, be they Marxist or conservative, remain essentially framed by masculinist thought. Feminists are developing their own feminist political economy.

See Also

ECONOMICS: FEMINIST CRITIQUES; PRIVATIZATION; WELFARE

Reference and Further Reading

Beasley, Christine. 1994. *Sexual economyths.* Sydney: Allen and Unwin.

Lois Bryson

POLITICAL ECONOMY: Households

See HOUSEHOLDS: POLITICAL ECONOMY.

POLITICAL EDUCATION

See EDUCATION: POLITICAL.

POLITICAL LEADERSHIP

The concept of political leadership has two constitutive parts. One is about politics and the other is about leadership. The term *politics* is often used as synonymous with the allocation and distribution of power in the public sphere of life, such as parties, elections, and established government structures. Feminists disagree with such a narrow definition of politics, because it excludes a whole world of noninstitutionalized activism, including women's associations, self-help projects, and protest movements.

Leadership means different things to different people. Some believe that leadership comes naturally with specific personal attributes and traits. Most other definitions reflect the assumption that leadership is not a trait, but a process of influencing and mobilizing followers. A feminist perspective on leadership is concerned less with power over others and more with nonhierarchical forms of cooperation. The leader, according to Helen Astin and Carole Leland (1991: 11), is someone who manages to empower and mobilize others toward a collective effort to improve the quality of life. Furthermore, they make a distinction between positional leaders, such as heads of organizations, and nonpositional leaders, for example, writers or researchers who provide the knowledge central to social change. Sadako Ogata of Japan, the United Nations High Commissioner for Refugees, on the one hand, is a positional leader. The U.S. feminist scholar Naomi Wolf, on the other hand, is a nonpositional leader. When women leaders appeal to moral values in pursuing higher ideals, such as justice, equality, peace, and antiracism, they are engaged in transformational leadership. Another major type of leadership is transactional leadership, which operates on the basis of exchange between the leader and the follower, for example, an exchange of jobs for votes.

Political leadership is manifest at different levels in the structure of society. The highest forms of political leadership are often considered the domain of men, but they have never been a uniquely male privilege. This holds true for the past as well as for the present. Although the lives of women leaders have often been rubbed out of official history, evidence remains that women acceded to the throne and ruled (Morgan, 1984). During the rise of great dynasties in Egypt, Kush, and Ethiopia, a number of African women became heads of state. The fame of the Ethiopian queen of Sheba, Makeda (around 900 B.C.), who organized an extensive trade network and ruled an enormous empire, is legendary. The same holds true for the warrior queen Cleopatra (around 50 B.C.), an Egyptian nationalist, who seems to be remembered less for her political cleverness than for her extraordinary beauty. With her study *The Forgotten Queens of the Islam,* Fatima Mernissi (1993) challenged the widespread belief that Benazir Bhutto, who became prime minister of Pakistan in 1988, was the first woman to govern a Muslim state. Mernissi looks back through 15 centuries of Islam and uncovers the lives and stories of more than a dozen queens, including Sultana Radiyya, who reigned in Delhi (thirteenth century); the island queens, who ruled the Maldives and Indonesia; and the Arab queens of Egypt and the Shi'ite Dynasty of Yemen.

With respect to contemporary women heads of state, the intriguing question is, Who and where are they? The first woman to be elected national chief executive in modern history was Sirimavo Bandaranaike, who became prime minister of Sri Lanka in 1960. Since then, a growing number of women have become prime minister or head of state in India (Indira Gandhi, 1966), Israel (Golda Meir, 1970), Argentina (Isabel Perón, 1974), Great Britain (Margaret Thatcher, 1979), Norway (Gro Harlem Brundtland, 1986), the Philippines (Corazon Aquino, 1986), Pakistan (Benazir Bhutto, 1988), Nicaragua (Violetta Barrios de Chamorro, 1990), Turkey (Tansu Çiller, 1993), Liberia (Ruth Perry, 1996), Guyana (Janet Jagan, 1997), and New Zealand (Helen Clark, 1999).

How to Become a Leader

The conditions under which countries select female heads are largely determined by two not mutually exclusive factors: family connections and merit. Some women clearly follow in the footsteps of assassinated husbands or fathers, Khaleda Zia from Bangladesh (1991) being a case in point. Although such women were politicized within their family surroundings, they had no previous political record or experience to speak of. In a way, this was an advantage, because it put them above existing party quarrels in an environment of demoralized politics, thus enabling them to present themselves as honest, trustworthy women who stood for certain principles (Jahan, 1987). Others get elected primarily on the basis of party membership and political merit. Absent among the countries with female national heads is the United States, the presidency of which has been white and male. The first woman candidate actually to run for the presidency, Shirley Chisholm (1972), an African-American, was (according to some observers) discounted by the press and public opinion on gender and racial grounds.

It remains a matter of some controversy to explain why, universally, fewer women than men are in leadership positions. There are those who believe that the female personality is less suited for leadership roles. They attribute to women lack of sufficient ambition and fear of success. Others seek environmental explanations. All over the world women face obstacles such as lack of money, patronage contacts, or access to the relevant networks, as well as the double workload of work and household and odd working hours. Furthermore, prejudice against women still prevails. Traditional public perceptions that childbearing and child rearing roles of women conflict with simultaneous participation in high-level political functions continue to present a significant obstacle. Another barrier has to do with a lack of previous political experience. Political leadership in class-based, ethnic, religious, or other community organizations, often a prelude to party leadership, is male-dominated. The vast majority of black politicians in the United States, for example, got their start in the church and in community organizations, which largely exclude women from leadership positions. Furthermore, women who do achieve leadership positions in oppositional movements discover that, once the organizations have achieved their goals, women have to struggle to maintain these positions.

The nature of the political system forms an important factor in determining the chances of women to become national leaders (Whicker and Areson, 1993). The presidential system, which relies more directly on popular election, works to the disadvantage of women. Women experience difficulty in securing campaign funding. Political action committees are more likely to support those perceived as proven winners or as likely to win, typically white males. Women fare better in the parliamentary system, which elects its prime minister from among fellow party members. By increasing the numbers of women in parliament, the chances for women to become national leaders might increase, too. In Europe, the need for equal numbers of men and women in the elected bodies has been recognized by the European Parliament. Numbers increased during the 1990s, but the results vary from one country to another. In Sweden, women are more than 40 percent of members of parliament (1998). In the Netherlands, and in Germany, about one-third of the members of parliament are women (1998). In Italy, however, less than 12 percent are women (1996) and in France, with 10.5 percent, even less (1997).

With respect to party leadership, there has been some progress since the 1980s in the United States and in Europe. Women reach leadership positions in some cases as representatives of the women's section within the party and in some cases as representatives of an all-women's party. It must be noted, however, that where women hold leadership positions there is a strong tendency for them to be clustered around women's issues, such as health, education, welfare, and consumer affairs.

Female Qualities?

Arguably, the number of women leaders in politics is relevant, but equally important is the question of the quality of their leadership. One would like to believe that women political leaders are more peaceful. There is, however, no hard evidence for this. Moreover, Margaret Thatcher's war in the Falkland Islands, Golda Meir's stand against Palestinian demands for liberation, and the upsurge of Turkish military action against the Kurds, under Tansu Çiller's rule, are serious warnings against simplistic generalizations about the nature of women's leadership at the highest political levels of national or international arenas.

It may well be the case that some feminists have unrealistically high expectations when they believe that all women leaders should give active and visible support for the women's cause. Disappointment follows when it appears that women leaders are "just" politicians. Apart from a few exceptions, the majority among the women prime ministers and state leaders have been silent on the issue of women's emancipation. It is also interesting that women leaders take precautions in their public appearance so as not to offend the religious or cultural sentiments of the majority. This holds true for countries such as Pakistan and Bangladesh, with respect to their Muslim majorities, but western countries have their own versions as well. In England, Margaret Thatcher made sure to convey how she enjoyed bringing her husband, Dennis, his morning tea. And recall Hillary Clinton, in many feminists' eyes a better candidate for presidency than her husband Bill, apologizing profusely during the election campaign when a statement about not planning to stay home baking cookies was taken as an offense against housewives.

Activism and Revolutions

Across times and countries anticolonial, national liberation, revolutionary, and ethnic minority struggles produced their own women leaders. Nzingha, a seventeenth-century queen of Ndongo (Angola), who dressed in male clothes and insisted on being called "king," devoted almost her entire life to the struggle against Portuguese imperialism. The French Revolution (1789) had Olympe de Gouges, leader of street demonstrations, who is probably best remembered for her work on the Declaration of the Rights of Women (1791). Also in the late 1700s, Gabriela Silang, from the Philippines, carried on the leadership of a rebellion against the Spanish occupiers. Her name lives on in the Filipina women's organization Gabriela, founded in 1984. Another remarkable leader, Queen Yaa Asantewa of the Ashanti (Ghana), initiated the war against the British (late nineteenth century) with the immortal words, addressed to the male chiefs: "If you the men of Ashanti will not go forward, then we... the women will fight the white men" (Van Sertima, 1984: 10). A Russian immigrant to the United States, Emma Goldman, who was deported back to Russia in 1919, will be remembered as the United States' most famous anarchist. Clara Zetkin, a leader in the decades surrounding the Russian October Revolution, made the organization of German proletarian women her life's task. The Guatemalan activist Rigoberta Menchú, a young peasant woman, received the Nobel Prize for Peace (1993) for her defense of the rights of indigenous communities.

Political leadership can be a dangerous undertaking, in particular when oppositional ideas or activities are involved. The human rights activist Angela Davis, a former member of the Black Panther Party and the Communist Party, was jailed, falsely charged with murder, and later acquitted (1972). Rosa Luxemburg (1871–1919), cofounder of the German Communist Party, was an internationalist who, in the face of rising German fascism, fiercely resisted the self-determination of national minorities. She was shot and thrown into a river by German soldiers. Aung San Suu Kyi, a human rights activist and leader of Burma's National League for Democracy, was detained in 1989 by the ruling military junta and has remained under house arrest ever since, a prisoner of conscience. In South Africa Winnie Mandela defied banishment orders, had her house fire-bombed, and was generally subjected to nonstop persecution during a period of more than 30 years of antiapartheid struggle.

Throughout history, the women's movement and women's organizations have been a fertile ground for leadership development. First-wave leaders include the British suffragist Emmeline Pankhurst, cofounder of the Women's Social and Political Union (1903), and Elizabeth Cady Stanton and Susan B. Anthony, late-nineteenth-century activists in the U.S. suffrage movement. Feminists of the second wave often challenged hierarchies and leadership claims. This did not prevent the media, however, from helping to push some women to the level of individual "stardom." A case in point is Camille Paglia in the United States. Likewise, the Egyptian Nawal El-Saadawi, a pioneering feminist activist, comes to mind as a feminist leader in the Arab world. Many other past and present women leaders remain anonymous or tend to be forgotten. Who, for example, would remember, today, that the reference to the equal rights of men and women in the first paragraph of the United Nations charter was included not because of North American or European women, but because the Inter-American Commission of Women (initiated in 1930), with representatives from Brazil, Mexico, and the Dominican Republic, insisted that it be there (Jaquette, 1994: 3)?

See Also

COMMUNITY POLITICS; EMANCIPATION AND LIBERATION MOVEMENTS; EMPOWERMENT; EQUAL OPPORTUNITIES; GOVERNMENT; LEADERSHIP; POLITICAL PARTICIPATION; POLITICAL REPRESENTATION

References and Further Reading

Astin, Helen S., and Carole Leland. 1991. *A cross-generational study of leaders and social change.* San Francisco: Jossey-Bass.

Berkovitch, N. 1999. The emergence and transformation of the international women's movement. In J. Boli and G. M. Thomas, eds., *Constructing world culture,* 100–126. Stanford, Calif.: Stanford University Press.

Council of Women World Leaders. 1999. *Establishing the vision.* First annual report. Cambridge, Mass.: Harvard University Press.

Genovese, Michael A., ed. 1993. *Women as national leaders.* Newbury Park, Calif.: Sage.

Jahan, Rounaq. 1987. Women in south Asian politics. *Third World Quarterly* 9(3): 848–870.

Jaquette, Jane S. 1994. Introduction: From transition to participation—Women's movement and democratic politics. In Jane Jaquette, ed., *The women's movement in Latin America,* 1–11. Boulder, Col.: Westview.

Karam, Azza, ed. 1998. *Women in parliament: Beyond numbers.* Stockholm: International IDEA.

Mernissi, Fatima. 1993. *The forgotten queens of the Islam.* Cambridge: Polity.

Morgan, Robin, ed. 1984. *Sisterhood is global.* New York: Anchor.

Nelson, Barbara J., and Najma Chowdhury, eds. 1994. *Women and politics worldwide.* New Haven, Conn.: Yale University Press.

Van Sertima, Ivan, ed. 1984. *Black women in antiquity.* New Brunswick, N.J.: Transaction.

Whicker, Marcia Lynn, and Todd W. Areson. 1993. The maleness of the American presidency. In Lois Lovelace Duke, ed., *Women in politics,* 165–175. Englewood Cliffs, N.J.: Prentice-Hall.

Philomena Essed

POLITICAL PARTICIPATION

Debates about women's political participation not only ask why and in what ways women have been excluded from full participation in the formal institutions of politics, but also explore the extent to which women have nonetheless been active in informal, movement-based politics. The juxtaposition of these two concerns raises the conceptual issue of the scope of "the political" itself and the forms of action deemed political. The slogan "the personal is political," which arose to challenge orthodox definitions of the political, acted as a rallying cry for a whole generation of feminists and is often perceived to be the key statement of second-wave feminism. The claim implicit in this statement is that women *are* political actors, where the political is held to include all power-structured relations from the interpersonal to the international.

Historically, women have been excluded from participation in the formal institutions of politics by states limiting citizenship in various ways that privilege the hegemonic form of masculinity at that time. Thus at differing periods the performance of military duty, property ownership, and the capacity for rationality have all been deemed preconditions for the granting of full participation rights. Under these conditions most women have been structurally excluded from formal political participation.

In response to this state of affairs, feminist campaigns have taken two distinct forms: the first seeking to increase women's participation within those formal institutional politics as they currently exist, the second seeking to extend the definition of the political in such a way as to reveal women's extensive existing forms of political participation outside the formal institutions. These strategies have tended to relate closely to the liberal and radical strands of the feminist movement, respectively. The former was dominant in the campaigns for women's right to vote (see also the writings of Mary Wollstonecraft on the issue of rationality and political participation), and the latter during the 1960s and 1970s when this right had been secured but women's status little improved. During the 1980s, there was a revival of interest within feminist writings for the earlier concern to increase women's participation within the formal institutions of politics, narrowly defined.

"The Personal Is Political": Extending the Boundaries of the Political

Nineteenth-century European and American feminists campaigned for the right to vote and also the right to stand in elections. In so doing, they concentrated on formal equality before the law within the institutions of mainstream party politics. These goals are now largely realized within western liberal democracies (women securing the franchise between 1893 in New Zealand and 1975 in Portugal). Women are now entering the corridors of power as state actors and participating in state-based politics, although the barriers to their entry have proved to be rather more intransigent than those advocating formal equality before the law might have hoped.

But to concentrate on these forms of political participation alone is felt by many feminists to reproduce those masculine assumptions that have worked to obscure much of women's political participation for centuries. Many women typically organize outside of state structures in such things as women's peace movements (examples include the lobbies of women peace activists at the first and second Hague Conferences in 1899 and 1907 and the numerous women's antinuclear groups that existed throughout the 1980s, such as Greenham Common in the United Kingdom, Comiso in Italy, Hunruck in West Germany, Seneca and Puget Sound in the United States, and Pine Gap in Australia) and ecology movements (see Mies and Shiva, 1993). Many of their activities are concentrated below the level of the state and are often geared toward agitating against oppressive state structures and policies (notable examples being groups such as the Mothers of the Plaza de Mayo in Argentina and Mothers of El Salvador organizing to bear witness to brutal regimes that had made their children "disappear"). Women have also tended to be involved in issues and movements that cut across state boundaries (for discussion of women as transnational actors, see Peterson and Runyan, 1993). Women's political participation in third world countries can be seen most clearly during anticolonial struggles. Although this mobilization was structurally constrained by patriarchal norms, it also allowed women to make political space for critique.

During the peak of the second-wave movements a large number of protest strategies were adopted, generally spontaneous action such as gatherings with singing and impromptu speeches. But there were also a large number of well-organized campaigns of sit-ins, marches, and demonstrations. Examples of these are the "Reclaim the Night" actions in England and West Germany in 1977, and in Italy in 1978. In Italy, certain rape cases so incensed women that well over 30 percent of Italian women participated in some form of protest. In West Germany, France, and Italy more than a half million women (in each country) marched in favor of abortion. In addition, women initiated and staged activities that were intended to maximize publicity, such as the act of laying a wreath at the monument of the unknown soldier in Paris—a wreath for his unknown wife. There were also numerous acts of civil disobedience. For example, on two occasions in the 1970s in Iceland over 90 percent of all adult women went on strike (including homemakers who refused to mind children, cook dinner, and so on), and in 1972, 300 French women, among them Simone de Beauvoir, signed an open letter and published it in a daily paper containing the confession "I have aborted" at a time when such an act was illegal and punishable by law. Yet perhaps the most common form of protest at this time were actions of the written word. The large number of journals, newspapers, magazines, and books of women's issues is an important manifestation of women's political participation over this period.

All these forms of political protest were "movement events" working outside the formal mechanisms of party politics. For during the rise of second-wave feminism, throughout the 1960s and 1970s many feminists became cynical about mainstream party politics and argued that women's energies should not be devoted to existing political institutions and electoral politics. The political participation that was advocated during this period by many within the women's movement was direct participation in women's autonomous organizations. These organizations aspired to be open to all, nonhierarchical, and informal. Issues of participatory democracy became central, with great attention paid to organizational practice (see Pateman, 1970). The explicit goal of a radical equality of participation for all women was pursued via mechanisms of rotating responsibilities, avoiding all hierarchies, validating personal experience as a mode of political expression. Thus women's political participation throughout the 1970s and 1980s was characterized largely by the extraparliamentary activity of radical and socialist groups. Seeking no collaboration with government, these feminist groups repudiated the idea that change could be orchestrated from within formal arenas of political power and purposely stayed away.

However, for many the experiences of the radical participatory democracy of the women's movement became paradoxical (see Phillips, 1991). Although claiming to be open to all, women's groups were said to be largely unrepresentative. The absence of formal structures often worked to create an insularity that left many women feeling excluded and silenced (see Freeman, 1984). The emphasis on participation was too demanding for those who were juggling many other demands on their time, particularly those from a working-class background, and the lack of representative structures raised serious questions of accountability. The 1980s were also the years of structural adjustment policies and declining state welfare in many third world countries. Women's efforts in many cases were directed toward strategies of survival rather than what might formally be called political participation. Perhaps because of these developments, there has been a notable shift of focus back toward the more conventional forms of political participation for many women. By the 1980s, feminists again became more centrally concerned with the importance of mainstream politics, working to increase the number of women present within parties and legislatures and to pursue policies in the interests of women.

"Feminizing the Mainstream": Entering the Corridors of Power

Women's attempts to gain greater participation in government, as legislators or as administrators, have had varying degrees of success. Women's representation is strongest in Scandinavia, where feminists have led the way in advocating women's participation in existing party structures as a means of pursuing women's interests. For example, in Norway no cabinet since May 1986 has included less than 40 percent women, and by May 1991 half the major political parties had elected a woman as leader.

Various strategies have been adopted for increasing the number of women in the legislature, ranging from the purely rhetorical encouragement of women to enter into the system as it is, through positive action such as training, to positive discrimination and the adoption of quotas (Lovenduski and Norris, 1993). Party ideology is a significant factor in determining which, if any, of these strategies are adopted. Social democratic and Green parties are far more likely to justify positive discrimination, while parties of the right and center are more likely to rely on rhetorical strategies.

The quota policies for women in political institutions of the Soviet Union and eastern Europe did allow 33 percent representation rates for women. However, the value of such representation in a largely nondemocratic political system was questionable. After the collapse of the system, there has been a sharp decline in women's representation.

Throughout the 1980s, all liberal democracies have witnessed some strategies for increasing the number of women participating in electoral politics. Party reforms, including new systems of candidate selection, new means of policy making, and new structures of government (such as ministries for women) have been adopted. It has been suggested that the most significant factor influencing women's success in entering national politics is the electoral system itself, specifically the operation of proportional representation, multimember constituencies, and party lists (see Norris, 1995). There are, however, other views emerging from experiences in nonwestern countries.

Reasons for advocating such increased participation vary. There are three predominant arguments forwarded for advocating women's increased participation in formal politics. One implies that numerically equal representation of women and men in legislatures is itself a sign of parity, regardless of the beliefs of those present or the policies enacted. A second holds that women need to enter formal politics to work for women's interests. Thus it is not presence alone, but the decisions made and policies formulated that matter. A third position is that women should enter into positions of power because they will do politics differently, thereby improving the nature of the public sphere. Which of these three positions one adopts will depend on whether one is arguing for women's equality with, or their difference from, men. This debate is central within feminist discourse, often serving to distinguish the liberal from the radical-cultural feminists. For example, "women representing women" was a slogan in Norway, where the rhetoric of difference was adopted to imply that women politicians would broaden the scope of decision making, bringing new issues and values to the political agenda, and might even bring a different set of priorities. Although this belief is still present, and strong in some countries (such as Italy and Norway), it is not dominant in many (particularly Britain and the United States). Empirical research into whether women's presence does bring a different form of politics is only now becoming possible (see McBride Stetson and Mazur, 1995).

See Also

POLITICAL LEADERSHIP; POLITICAL PARTIES; POLITICAL REPRESENTATION; POLITICS AND THE STATE, *specific entries*

References and Further Reading

Afkhami, Mahnaz, and Erika Friedl, eds. 1997. *Muslim women and the politics of participation.* Syracuse, N.Y.: Syracuse University Press.

Afshar, Haleh, ed. 1996. *Women and politics in the third world.* London: Routledge.

Bashevkin, Sylvia, ed. 1985. *Women and politics in western Europe.* London: Frank Cass.

Conway, Margaret, Gertrude Steuernagel, and David Ahern, eds. 1997. *Women and political participation: Cultural change in the political arena.* Washington, D.C.: CQ Press.

Corrin, Chris. 1999. *Feminist perspectives on politics.* London: Longman.

Lovenduski, Joni, and Pippa Norris. 1993. *Gender and party politics.* London: Sage.

McBride Stetson, Dorothy, and Amy Mazur. 1995. *Comparative state feminism.* Newbury Park, Calif.: Sage.

Mies, Maria, and Vandana Shiva. 1993. *Ecofeminism.* London: Zed.

Norris, Pippa. 1995. *Political recruitment: Gender, race and class in the British Parliament.* Cambridge: Cambridge University Press.

Pateman, Carole. 1970. *Participation and democratic theory.* Cambridge: Cambridge University Press.

Peterson, V. Spike, and Anne Sisson Runyan. 1993. *Global gender issues.* Boulder, Col.: Westview.

Phillips, Anne. 1991. *Engendering democracy.* Cambridge: Polity.

Rodriguez, Victoria. 1998. *Women's participation in Mexican political life.* Boulder, Col.: Westview.

Ruschemeyer, Marilyn, ed. 1998. *Women in the politics of post-communist Eastern Europe.* New York: Sharpe.

Sinha, Niroj, ed. 2000. *Women in Indian politics.* New Delhi: Gyan.

Judith Squires

POLITICAL PARTIES

Modern political parties tend to be defined in terms of their relationship to government, traditionally an almost exclusively male activity. According to a recent definition, a political party is "an institution that (a) seeks influence in a state, often by attempting to occupy positions in government, and (b) usually consists of more than a single interest in the society and so to some degree attempts to 'aggregate interests'" (Ware, 1996: 5.) Parties vary greatly in their organization, ideology, size, and policies, and in the extent of their political significance. Some states are built around a single party (as in China), others feature parties active only at election times (as in Canada), and still others are governed by coalitions of numerous parties (as in Switzerland and Italy). Parties are crucial gatekeepers to government office, one of the main channels of political mobilization in a society, and a major source of public policy. Although voters choose candidates, they do so only after political parties have limited the options. Electoral systems are subject to government policy, but candidate selection rules are made within political parties. Because voters express party preferences; the resulting male-dominated government representation is the result of party decisions. Parties, not voters, determine the composition of elected assemblies. Moreover, parties often determine who is awarded appointed offices of various kinds, not only at the cabinet level but also in state committees and organizations, including women's organizations. For example, in both Chile and France, party standing rather than experience in the women's movement is the factor determining which women are appointed to the "state feminist" bodies. (Jenson, 1990; Mateau, 1996).

The feminization of political parties is therefore important to the representation of women, whether considered in terms of their presence in legislatures and governments or in terms of their interests and perspectives. For much of their history, however, political parties have been effective barriers to women's presence in elected office, a pattern well described by Najma Chowdhury and Barbara Nelson in 1994. Drawing on evidence from 43 countries, they report that women have been more likely to get power when political parties were dormant or in disarray during a major regime event. When parties were reestablished, women lost ground. Such evidence may account for the fact that women are typically less likely than men to be members of political parties, and prefer informal and ad hoc political activity.

But feminists cannot ignore political parties. Although parties may be the main barriers to women, they are also the key to increasing women's levels of representation. The evidence of the 1980s and 1990s indicates that women make lasting political gains only when their voices are heard within their party. In the wake of the feminist movements of the 1970s, women demanded and secured party reforms with varying degrees of success. In some countries this led to the appearance of new issues in party programs, new systems of candidate selection, new means of policy making, and the establishment of new structures of government such as ministries for women, equal opportunity ombudspersons, and publicly funded women's committees. In response to pressure from women activists, members, and voters, gender issues became explicit. These efforts had significant and lasting effects on party politics. Gradually, campaigns for equality gained support and parties began to respond. But the momentum built by wide-ranging movements in support of equal rights would not have been enough to secure changes in party policies. Political parties moved on women's issues when they came under effective electoral pressure. In Greece, for example, particular parties took up women's issues when women's organizations became their affiliates. (Cram, 1994). In the United States, the strong association of feminist movements with the Democratic Party explains a gender gap in voting whereby women are more likely than men to favor Democrats (Young, 1996).

Once a party committed itself formally to the principle of gender equality in one sphere, then party women were able to use this commitment in their arguments for increased representation. Sweden is a good example of women-centered party reform. Sweden has a widespread egalitarian ethos, and several features of its electoral system favor women, but these factors cannot by themselves account for the increase in women's representation at all levels of the system since the 1960s. There, women made new claims on the party system. Four identifiable strategies were pursued within parties. First, women's issues were brought to the political agenda. Prominent party women, supported by women's organizations and networks, raised issues of sex equality in the parties. Often they began with demands for policies to secure sex equality in employment, but the implications of equality for child care, reproductive rights, and family policies were also raised. Second, seeking to avoid accusations of sectionalism, they sought to transform women's issues into universal issues. Third, women used a dual strategy of working both within women's networks and in male-dominated areas of the party. Finally, women paid close attention to the rules of the game. As they sought to transform gender relations in politics from within, they were careful to affirm their commitment to their parties (Sainsbury, 1993).

Parties have developed strategies to promote women internally into decision-making positions, both within the organization and externally into elected assemblies and public appointments. Generally parties have been more radical, determined, and imaginative in devising policies to bring women into internal positions than in nominating women as candidates for elected office. The process tends to continue inexorably to candidate selection as, under pressure from women's advocates, research, awareness training, and selection criteria, changes are made to bring more women into the recruitment pool. The most effective action has been the introduction of quotas, which are (typically temporary) measures designed to overcome imbalances between men and women within the party. Party quotas are normally voluntary, both because they are not guaranteed by legislation and because they are often not adequately backed by internal sanctions when targets are not met. Because political parties are themselves voluntary organizations, there are inevitable limitations on what can be done to implement controversial policies. Nevertheless, where political will has been present, political parties have been very effective in the implementation of quotas of women representatives. Although it is difficult to determine their exact effect, the evidence suggests that quotas do help to improve the representation of women. In 1992, quotas were used by at least 56 political parties in 34 countries, according to the Inter-Parliamentary Union. The three countries with the highest levels of women's representation in 1997—Norway, Denmark, and Sweden—all have parties that have used voluntary quotas of some kind.

These examples show how party politics have been the setting for strategies to increase women's representation. They imply that the concentration of women's political activity in informal and social movement activities has important disadvantages in that it has distanced women from crucial institutions of representation, mobilization, and policy making. In order to transform patriarchal government, feminists must first transform party politics. Examples both from established party systems and from systems in transition show that such strategies meet with considerable resistance but are eventually successful.

See Also

AFFIRMATIVE ACTION; CITIZENSHIP; EQUAL OPPORTUNITIES; ORGANIZATIONAL THEORY; POLITICAL LEADERSHIP; POLITICAL PARTICIPATION; POLITICAL REPRESENTATION; POLITICS AND THE STATE: OVERVIEW

References and Further Reading

Cram, Laura. 1994. Women's political participation in Greece since the fall of the colonels: From democratic struggle to incorporation by the party-state? *Democratisation* 1(2).

Jenson, Jane. 1990. Representations of difference: The varieties of French feminism. *New Left Review* 180.

Matear, Ann. 1996. Desde la protesta a la propuesta: Gender politics in transition in Chile. *Democratisation* 3(3).

Nelson, Barbara J., and Najma Chowdhury. 1994. *Women and politics worldwide.* New Haven, Conn., and London: Yale University Press.

Sainsbury, Diane. 1993. The politics of increased women's representation: The Swedish case. In Joni Lovenduski and Pippa Norris, eds., *Gender and party politics.* London: Sage.

Skjeie, Hege. 1993. Ending the male political hegemony: The Norwegian experience. In Joni Lovenduski and Pippa Norris, eds., *Gender and party politics.* London: Sage.

Ware, Alan. 1996. Political parties and party systems. Oxford: Oxford University Press.

Young, Lisa. 1996. Women's movements and political parties: A Canadian-American comparison. *Party Politics* 2(2).

Joni Lovenduski

POLITICAL REPRESENTATION

Since 1788, when women first gained the right to stand for election in the United States, women's right to vote and be elected has slowly been recognized throughout the sovereign states of the world. Only a handful of countries, including Kuwait and the United Arab Emirates, continue to refuse women the right to vote and stand for election. Yet active participation in national parliaments by women is still notoriously low; the percentage of women in national parliaments globally rose from 3 percent in 1945 to only 11.6 percent in 1995. As of December 1999 the world average for the percentage of women in national parliaments was 13.1 percent. The rate of change in women's electoral success has therefore not been as great as many people had expected, given that legal restrictions have largely been removed. As Joni Lovenduski notes, "Although women are more than one half of citizens in most democracies and despite the widespread passage of legislation guaranteeing equal citizenship, women are nowhere the political equal of men in terms of political representation" (1999: 192).

There is then a general underrepresentation of women, accompanied by a slow but clear rise in the proportion of women elected to national office. Within these two trends, however, there are interesting variations. The comparative percentage of women in government internationally is proving increasingly intriguing. If one looks at the average figures for regions, one finds that the Nordic countries have achieved the high of 38.9 percent women in their governing bodies and the Arab states maintain their low of 3.6 percent, but the majority of regions (including the Americas, Europe, Asia, the Pacific, and sub-Saharan Africa) have very consistent proportions of women in government, ranging between 10.9 percent and 15.9 percent only (see <www.ipu.org/wmne/world.htm> for current information). Comparisons between individual countries reveal significant, and often surprising, differences: Sweden, for example, has 42.7 percent of women in its national legislature; France, 10.9 percent; Vietnam, 26.0 percent; and Egypt, 2.0 percent. Research is now being carried out to explain these variations, which do not seem to be as clearly related to employment practices, social structures, or cultural values as many scholars had predicted.

It is now widely accepted that one of the most significant factors explaining cross-cultural differences in the representation of women is the electoral system. Research indicates that electoral systems with a high number of seats in multimember constituencies facilitate the entry of women (Lovenduski and Norris, 1993: 312). But there are other significant factors too: Lovenduski notes that the high levels of women's representation in Norway can be accounted for not only in terms of its electoral system (which is based on proportional representation and party lists) but also in terms of its political culture (which values social equality) and its "politically sophisticated women's movement" (Lovenduski, 1999: 196).

In the context of these data the rather conventional issue of the number of women in the national legislature has now become a subject of greater theoretical interest to feminists than it was throughout the 1960s and 1970s. Whereas the persistent underrepresentation of women was previously thought by many feminists to be an issue of limited interest (there being many more radical issues of structural importance to address), it is now recognized to be a significant and complex issue in its own right. As Anne Phillips notes, "Politics appears to be more of an independent variable than might have been expected and substantial political equalities look possible even in the absence of thoroughgoing social or economic reform" (1991: 19).

Throughout the 1980s and 1990s, women campaigned for increased representation, working within political parties for both party and electoral reforms. Attention was focused on three main areas: the selection process (resulting in new policies for candidate selection, notably all-women shortlists and quotas policies), the policy formation process (resulting in new structures of government, notably the creation of ministries for women), and the electoral system (resulting in new voting systems, notably multimember constituencies and party lists). For example, in France, women successfully lobbied for a "parity bill" which amends Article 3 of the constitution to "encourage equal access for women and men to political life and elected posts." In the United Kingdom, the Labour Party adopted a policy of all-women shortlists in half of all marginal seats prior to the last election. In Germany, all the major parties now run gender quotas; the Social Democrats reserve 40 percent of party posts and nominations for women. In Russia, an all-female party, Women of Russia, contested the last election (but failed to win a seat). In India, there is a National Council for Women that advocates policy for women and an entire ministry for women that manages such policies.

Although there has long been a widespread acceptance that women have been conventionally less politically active in formal politics than men, extensive research into what is called the "gender gap" is only now emerging. The gender gap measures differences between not only participation rates of men as compared with women but also differences of voting patterns and political preferences and styles. The notion that women are inherently more conservative than men in their voting behavior, based on cross-national studies in European countries in the 1950s and 1960s, is increasingly undermined by new evidence that indicates a shift toward preference for parties of the Left among women, particularly younger women. Recent research uncovers two clear trends: widespread cross-national variations in women's voting behavior, and a clear generation gap, with younger women more likely to vote for parties of the Left than men and older women more likely to vote for parties of the Right (Norris, 2000a, b). Both patterns undermine the idea of a commonality of political experience and policy preference among women and highlight the significance of differences between them.

Accompanying the growing awareness that the differences between women's experiences of political representation are as great as their commonality is the realization that there are several distinct reasons for being concerned about their underrepresentation. Concern about the underrepresentation of women and proposals to increase their representation are motivated by a number of distinct issues. Phillips has categorized these as fourfold: the argument about role models, the argument concerning justice, the argument concerning women's interests, and the argument concerning the revitalization of democracy (Phillips, 1995: 62–63; 1998: 229–238). The first is based on the belief that the existence of women representatives will encourage others to gain the confidence that they too can aspire to this role. The second implies that numerically equal representation of women and men in legislatures is itself a sign of parity, regardless of the beliefs of those present or the policies enacted. The third holds that women need to enter formal politics to work for women's interests. Thus it is not presence alone, but the decisions made and policies formulated that matter. And the fourth proposes that women should enter into positions of power because they will do politics differently, thereby improving the nature of the public sphere.

The arguments about role models and justice appeal to concerns about the just distribution of social resources: the unequal distribution of positions of political power indicates that there are structural barriers to entry operating to deny particular social groups access to these scarce resources. As Phillips points out, these approaches depict politics as simply one profession among many and women's claim to political equality as nothing more than an equal-opportunities claim to an interesting job (1998: 230–231). In contrast, the argument from women's interests focuses directly on the function of representative democracy, claiming that women share common experiences that give them specific needs and interests. Here, political representatives are viewed as mandated delegates rather than well-paid employees. Critics of this approach argue that there is too strong a presumption of homogeneity among women and there are too few mechanisms for accountability to the female electorate. The fourth argument for women's increased representation proposes that female representatives will actually participate in the political process differently; that is, they will be less beholden to party agendas and more engaged in a radical reworking of the political system itself (Phillips, 1998: 237–239). On this basis, the argument for the fair representation of women is simultaneously an argument for a more participatory form of democracy.

Finally, in considering the political representation of women, it is worth noting that there has been no clear unchanging conception of what it is that "representatives" are required to represent. Political systems can be constructed so as to represent beliefs, interests, or identities. The representation of beliefs generates a conception of ideological representation that involves collective representation via parties, whereas the representation of interests involves representatives acting as spokespeople for interest groups and new social movements and generates a model of interest-group pluralism. The representation of identities entails representatives reflecting the social composition of the electorate in terms of presence, requiring representatives to speak for social groups of which they are a part, sharing common experiences, and therefore holding common commitments and values. This understanding of representation gives rise to proposals for quota policies or reserved places for oppressed social groups, and works with a notion of "microcosmic" as opposed to "principle-agent" representation (Pitkin, 1967). Debate about the political representation of women inevitably focuses attention on the differences between these two conceptions of representation and highlights the need to distinguish between them.

See Also

COMMUNITY POLITICS; EQUAL OPPORTUNITIES; GOVERNMENT LEADERSHIP; POLITICAL LEADERSHIP; POLITICAL PARTICIPATION

Reference and Further Reading

Darcy, R., Susan Welch, and Janet Clark, eds. 1994. *Women, elections and representation.* Lincoln: University of Nebraska Press.

Githens, Marianne, Pippa Norris, and Joni Lovenduski, eds. 1994. *Different roles, different voices: Women and politics in the United States and Europe.* New York: HarperCollins.

Inter-Parliamentary Union: <www.ipu.org/wmn-e/world.htm>

Jharta, Bhawana. 1996. *Women and politics in India.* Columbia, Mo.: South Asia Books.

Lovenduski, Joni. 1999. Sexing political behaviour. In Sylvia Walby, ed., *New agendas for women.* Basingstoke: Macmillan.

———, and Pippa Norris, eds. 1993. *Gender and party politics.* London: Sage.

Norris, Pippa. 2000a. Gender gap: Old challenges, new approaches. In Susan Carroll, ed., *Women and American politics: Agenda setting for the 21st century.* Oxford: Oxford University Press.

———. 2000b. Women's representation and electoral systems. In Richard Rose, ed., *The encyclopedia of electoral systems.* Washington, D.C.: CQ Press.

Phillips, Anne. 1991. *Engendering democracy.* Cambridge: Polity.

———. 1995. *The politics of presence.* Oxford: Clarendon.

———, ed. 1998. *Feminism and politics.* Oxford: Oxford University Press.

Pitkin, Hannah. 1967. *The concept of representation.* Berkeley: University of California Press.

Rai, Shirin. 1997. Gender and representation: Women in the Indian parliament, 1991–1996. In A. M. Goetz, ed., *Getting institutions right for women in development.* London: Sage.

Judith Squires

POLITICS AND THE STATE: Overview

Both politics and the state are about the setting, challenging, and shifting of boundaries. Women have participated in political activities and movements as well as in initiating conversations and debates challenging the nature of politics and state in changing contexts and different arenas. Women's writings in the area of politics and the state focus on different aspects: the public and private spheres of politics, the vexed question of what constitutes "women" and therefore "women's interests" in the context of the politics of difference, the meanings and operations of citizenship rights for women, and the engagements between women and institutions of power such as the state. These feminist perspectives build on, and are framed by, different ideological positions: liberalism, Marxism, and postmodernism. These have emerged in and through engagements with different socioeconomic contexts, from colonialism to globalization. Discourses, structures, and agency have all been scrutinized by feminists in their critiques of mainstream views of politics and the state, as well as their sketching out of alternatives to these.

Politics

Traditionally, politics has meant "the art and science of government." The flexibility of this rather narrow definition of politics has been provided by arguments about what counts as government. Is government confined to what we recognize as the state, or does it also include religious institutions, workers' associations, property, and even the family? The answer that women and feminists gave to this question was in the affirmative. By insisting that experience was an important starting point of knowledge, they sought to contextualize the basis of politics itself (Scott and Butler, 1992). They added to the analysis of politics their insights, which involved stretching the boundaries as well as the definitions of terms and of organization. Feminists have insisted that gender, as social construction of sex, is reflected in the political roles women and men are able to perform, and indeed frames the very definition of politics and, by default, what does not constitute politics. Women's participation in politics has taken many forms—struggles for political voice and citizenship rights through the suffrage movements; anticolonialist and nationalist movements; in peace, civil rights, and environmental movements; and movements to enhance women's rights and human rights. These struggles have taken place at different levels—local, national, and global, at the level of movement, of organization, and of representation (Basu, 1995; Jayawardena, 1989).

Women's Writings and Feminist Writings: The Public and Private Spheres of Politics

Perhaps one of the most enduring contribution of women's activism and feminist theorizing is the challenging of the boundaries between the public and the private as defining (and defining out) politics. By expanding the definition of politics to encompass both the public and the private spheres, indeed, by asserting that the two were mutually constitutive, feminists were able to show how women, far from being absent from the political sphere, were very much present as an "absence"—that their exclusion from the public was necessary for the private and the public to be dominated by masculine interests and power. As Carol Pateman has pointed out, this absence goes unnoticed because "the separation of the private and public is presented in liberal theory as if it applied to all individuals in the same way" (1983: 283).

Within the orthodox Marxist framework, the mutually constitutive nature of the public and private was recognized and historically contextualized. It was argued that property relations and the need for their regulation underpin the growing divide between the public and the private and of women's position in the arena of public production and reproduction (Engels, 1972). However, the focus of much of Marxist literature and politics remained on actors—men and women—rather than on the nature of what constituted the public and the private, and whether and how men and women were differently situated within these realms. The equality position argued for women to be made part of the public political sphere through their participation in the public productive sphere of work. This understanding of the politics of gender had a tremendous impact not only on feminist debates but on the lives of millions of women worldwide as communist states emerged after World Wars I and II. While the Marxist position proved attractive to many feminists, as we shall see below, it also placed strains upon feminists.

Colonial and postcolonial understandings of politics provided further insights in this debate. Nationalist movements' engagement with modernity took the form of "complex interrelationships of contest and collusion between indigenous patriarchal norms, and those held by [colonial] administrators... visible in the colonial regulation of agrarian relations" (Sangari and Vaid, 1989: 7). In India, for example, as a consequence of the nationalist marking of a series of binary opposites between male versus female, inner versus outer, public versus private, and material versus spiritual at the beginning of the nineteenth century, there emerged a process of the formation of the private sphere as an indigenist alternative to western materialism (Sangari and Vaid, 1989: 10). For women who participated in nationalist movements, this newly emerging discourse of the public–private divide posed significant problems. Issues of authenticity and of loyalty forced choices on women that they did not wish to make. As the struggle against colonial regimes ended, many women found themselves struggling against hegemonic nationalist discourses that not only drew particular boundaries around them but, in many cases, divided women along boundaries of caste, religion, and ethnicity.

The Politics of Interests

Debates about the public and private spheres have been critical for women's engagements with regimes and structures of power. From this distinction of the public and the private emerge, in different contexts, the visualization of politics itself, its primary actors, and a concern with contestation of interests that need to be seen as separate from the particular interests of groups within society. Two separate but linked questions have been addressed in the feminist literature on politics of interest. First, how can marginalized groups such as women access the sphere of politics? Women's movements have historically insisted on greater participation in politics both outside and inside state institutions—within civil society as well as through representation of their interests via representative institutions—as means of addressing this question. Second, what interests can be legitimately insisted upon, and are women's interests legitimate? Feminists have argued that women's participation in an expanded envisioning of politics can come about only when the politics of the home is recognized to be part of the wider equation. Legitimacy of interests has posed questions for feminists even as they have argued that it is the masculinist understanding of politics that has sought to impose a metainterest narrative on politics that is actually a defense of continued dominance of men in politics.

The first of these questions has been that of defining women's interests, which can then be represented within the political system. Articulation and representation of interests require development of both political consciousness and political activism based on a new group consciousness. Women's struggles have recognized this by emphasizing "consciousness raising" and participative styles of politics from the start—consciousness that "the personal is political" and that women have shared histories within patriarchal societies that might take different forms but have enough in common for women to recognize each other as marginalized within their own boundaries and across borders (Phillips, 1991).

Theoretically, feminists have argued that women's interests are historically located, and culturally specific, that they can reflect but are not reducible to specific situations of women's lives, and that they are both politically and discursively constructed (Jonasdottir and Jones, 1988; Young, 1990). They have distinguished between practical—short-term, immediate, and urgent—and strategic interests—long-term, structural, and deep—to argue that sometimes women have to make political judgments about the costs attached to changes they wish to bring about, and that women make these judgments taking into account their specific contexts and constraints as well as the potential strength that can be derived from, at times, bargaining with patriarchy (Molyneux, 1998). Feminist scholars have also argued that articulating women's interests in terms of general interests of a just society can be an effective way of giving them greater salience in wider political debates and policies (Dietz, 1992). This would be an effective way of "mainstreaming gender" in politics—as opposed to adding gendered analysis to existing paradigms of power.

The Politics of Difference

Differences among women on grounds of class, race, ethnicity, religion, sexuality, and disability among others have prompted the question. How can a disparate group of women recognize themselves in the category of "woman," whose interests can then be represented in the political arena? Does consciousness raising about the patriarchal structures that frame politics also need to result in the construction of recognizable similarities among women? This was important for the alternative envisionings of politics that women were engaged in.

There were those who suggested that women's maternal roles allowed them access to particular ways of thinking about politics—a maternalist view of politics based not on the external world of men, but on the internal world of women that was not available to men—as preservers and defenders of life, family, and in particular children. The female vision of society was therefore shaped by the prerogatives of the *oikos,* or community (Elsthian, 1981: 372). However, as postcolonial feminist historians have argued, it was precisely such a valuation of the feminine social role that resulted in the particular recovery of the past by both the colonial and the nationalist male elites. Privileging of the narrative of motherhood, of the familial role, is also a privileging of certain motherhoods, and the erasure of others. Class and racial privilege allow for different motherhoods to be constructed and performed in political discourse of nationalism as it took up the role of "inventing tradition" (Sangari and Vaid, 1989). This process also excludes "other" conceptions of motherhood such as lesbian mothers as a threat to the constructed authenticity of these invented traditions. When women have been characterized in terms of motherhood, they have been spoken of as the reproducers of nations and ethnicities, as bearers of cultural norms, as makers of traditions, of embodying the past and future of nations. Their participation has often legitimized movements without necessarily resulting in women's political visibility, much less representative parity for them (Anthias and Yuval-Davis, 1990; Stacey, 1983).

Postmodernism contributed to the debates on difference by insisting that configurations of power were more diffuse and diverse than the modernist framework allows. There is a rejection of coherent structures of modernist society and theory that allow for diversity to be recognized, acknowledged, and able to destabilize the certain boundaries of politics, state, art and literature, social relations, and indeed "the body politic" itself (Lovell, 2000; Marchand and Parpart, 1995). Some southern feminists have found postmodernism helpful in understanding the discursive power that surrounds them and makes "real" the reading of or by themselves "under western eyes" (Mohanty, 1994). Others have built on earlier readings of Marxist and socialist texts and, while rejecting "identity politics," have favored coalition politics as well as the politics of "rooting and shifting," or transversal politics (hooks, 1991; Yuval-Davis, 1997).

The Politics of Presence: Citizenship

Interests need to be articulated through participation and then representation in the arena of politics. The argument about presence, as Anna Jonasdottir and Kathleen Jones (1988) have pointed out, concerns both the *form* of politics and its *content.* The question of form includes the demand to be among the decision makers, the demand for participation, and the demand for a share in control over public affairs. In terms of content, it includes being able to articulate the needs, wishes, and demands of various groups of women. The question of form was not in the first instance about women's insistence on being part of government together with men. Rather, it was an insistence on an equality of citizenship, which would provide women the same rights as men within the national state as agendas of welfare and of development took shape. Recently, however, citizenship debates have become prominent in the context of the impact on welfare states and southern states of globalization, restructuring and structural adjustment as well as democratization (Lister, 1997). The interest in citizenship has also been prompted by the shift in women's movements, in the 1980s, from the earlier insistence on direct participation to a recognition of the importance of representative politics and the consequences of women's exclusion from it (Lovenduski and Norris, 1993; McBride, Stetson, and Mazur, 1995; Rai, 2000). It is here that politics—public and private, practical and strategic—begins to formalize within the contours of the state.

State and Politics

In the 1970s, feminists began to engage with theories of the state, as opposed to politics. There were several reasons for this shift, many of them mirroring the shift in the study of citizenship. Traditional political theory has defined state as a "set of political institutions whose specific concern is with the organization of domination, in the name of the common interest, within a delimited territory." Max Weber in his work *Politics as a Vocation* gave a modern definition of the state as an organization with a territory, a monopoly of violence, and legitimacy to be able to use that violence. Together with Marxists and socialists, feminists have sought to move beyond this description of a neutral, organizing agency. Some have questioned the liberal presumptions of the state as a means of overcoming the state of nature and the establishment of the patriarchal state, others have attempted to use class analysis to understand how women's position within the family and wage labor regimes is regulated by the capitalist state, and still others have analyzed the state in parallel with their analysis of the law that systematizes male power (MacKinnon, 1983; Pateman, 1983). Political responses to theorizing about the state have also been varied. Although some, such as Judith Allen (1990), posed the challenging question, Does feminism need a theory of the state? (Pringle and Watson, 1994), others have seen the state as a potentially legitimate agency of the politics of change (Eisenstein, 1979). In Australia and Canada, femocrats engaged with the state bureaucracy to be able to influence policy making within state bodies in the interests of women outside. In many third world states, too, women have chosen to engage with the state after a period of maintaining suspicious distance. This shift has come about particularly in tandem with the process of democratization in many countries, such as South Africa, and in others owing to a realization of the need to shake up consolidated privilege within state structures in order to make them sensitive to growing gender demands, as in India. Women have also analyzed state power in the context of communist states to show how class-based understanding of gender relations has not translated into policies that speak to strategic interests of women. Studies of states' interests in controlling the reproductive capacity of women in many communist states have demonstrated this clearly (Davin, 1992).

The question of engagement with the state cannot be seen in terms of binary opposites. Indeed, a position of "in and against" the state that allows for a mobilization of women's interests and their articulation within the space of civil society and, in parallel, allows for an engagement with the policy-making machinery of the state is needed (Rai, 1996). In the context of globalization, the state debate has become increasingly important as the response of the state to globalizing pressures has become critical to the lives of women (Marchand and Runyan, 2000).

Politics beyond Borders

Increasingly, feminist engagement with politics has moved to encompass relations between states. International relations was a male bastion until Cynthia Enloe's book *Bananas, Beaches and Bases* (1987) showed how gendered the space of international relations, war, military, and militarization actually was. Since then a formidable body of literature has developed within the field that sheds light on both the state or political and discursive power that underlies the business among men across borders (Pettman, 1997).

In terms of participation and strategizing by women, globalization is also creating a need to cross borders. This is because the pressures of structural adjustment are leading to similar pressures of state welfare packages, migration both within and across national borders, environmental pressures that need a global response, and fracturing of states that has resulted in physical and psychological harm to women. Global social movements, issues of global governance, and international political economy are all new arenas of contestation over the meanings and the nature of politics where feminists, scholars, and activists are taking their positions, intervening, and mobilizing (Cohen and Rai, 2000).

See Also

CITIZENSHIP; DEMOCRACY; FEMOCRAT; GOVERNMENT; MILITARY; NATION AND NATIONALISM; POLITICAL

PARTICIPATION; POLITICAL REPRESENTATION; POWER; SOCIAL MOVEMENTS

References and Further Reading

Anthias, Floya, and Nira Yuval-Davis. 1990. *Woman-nation-state,* London: Routledge.

Basu, Amrita, ed. 1995. *The challenge of local feminisms,* Oxford: Oxford University Press.

Bethke, Jean. 1981. *Public man private woman: Women in social and political thought.* Princeton, N. J.: Princeton University Press.

Cohen, Robin, and Shirin M. Rai, eds., 2000. *Global social movements.* London and New York: Althone/Transaction .

Dietz, Mary. 1992. Context is all. In Chantal Mouffe, ed., *Dimensions of radical philosophy.* London: Verso.

Engels, Fredrich. 1972. *Family, private property and the state.* New York: International.

Enloe, Cynthia. 1987. *Bananas, beaches and bases: Making feminist sense of international politics.* London: University of California Press.

hooks, bell, and Corne. 1991. *Breaking bread: Insurgent black intellectual life.* Boston: South End.

Jayawardena, Kumari. 1989. *Feminism and nationalism in the Third World.* London: Zed.

Jonasdottir, Anna, and Kathleen Jones, eds., 1988. *The political interest of gender: Developing theory and research with a feminist perspective.* London: Sage.

Lister, Ruth. 1997. *Feminist citizenship.* Basingstoke, U.K.: Macmillan.

Lovell, Terry. 2000. Thinking feminism with and against Bourdieu. *Feminist Theory* 1(1): 11–32.

Lovenduski, Joni, and Pippa Norris, eds. 1993. *Gender and party politics.* London: Sage.

MacKinnon, Catharine. 1989. *Toward a feminist theory of the state.* Cambridge, Mass.: Harvard University Press.

Marchand, Marianne, and Jane Parpart, eds. 1995. *Feminism/postmodernism/development.* London: Routledge.

———, and Anne Sisson Runyan. 2000. *Gender and global restructuring: Sightings, sites and resistances.* London: Routledge.

McBride Stetson, D., and A. Mazur. 1995. *Comparative state feminism.* London: Sage.

Mies, Maria, and Vandana Shiva. 1993. *Ecofeminism.* London: Zed.

Mohanty, Chandra Talpade, ed. 1994. *Third World women and the politics of feminism.* Bloomington: Indiana University Press.

Molyneux, Maxine. 1998. Analysing women's movements. *Development and Change* 29: 219–245.

Pateman, Carol. 1983. *The sexual contract.* Cambridge: Polity.

Pettman, Jan Jindy. 1997. *Worlding women.* London: Routledge.

Phillips, Anne. 1991. *Engendering democracy.* Cambridge: Polity.

Pringle, Rosemary, and Sophie Watson. 1992. Women's interests and the post-structuralist state. In Michele Barrett and Anne Phillips, eds., *Destabilising theory, contemporary feminist debates.* Cambridge: Polity.

Rai, Shirin M., and Geraldine Lievesley, eds. 1996. *Women and the state: International perspectives.* London: Taylor and Francis.

———. 2000. *International perspectives on gender and democratisation.* Basingstoke, U.K.: Macmillan.

Sangari, Kumkum, and Sudesh Vaid, eds. 1989. *Recasting women: Essays in colonial history.* New Delhi: Kali for Women.

Scott, Joan W., and Judith Butler, eds. 1992. *Feminists theorize the political.* London: Routledge.

Stacey, Judith. 1983. *Patriarchy and the socialist revolution in China.* Berkeley: University of California Press.

Young, Iris Marion. 1990. *Justice and the politics of difference.* Princeton, N.J.: Princeton University Press.

Shirin M. Rai

POLITICS AND THE STATE: Australia, New Zealand, and the Pacific Islands

The countries and territories of the South Pacific are geographically and culturally diverse. The largest and most populous country in the region is Australia, with a population of 19 million. Australia is also the most developed nation in the area, along with its smaller neighbor, New Zealand (population of 3.6 million). The other 22 countries and territories of the South Pacific are scattered across 30 million square kilometers of ocean and are often small enough to be referred to as "micro-states."

The Pacific Islands are divided into three major groups: (1) Melanesia (in the west) comprises Fiji, New Caledonia, Papua New Guinea, the Solomon Islands, and Vanuatu; (2) Polynesia (in the southeast) comprises American Samoa, the Cook Islands, Niue, Pitcairn, Tokelau, Tonga, Tuvalu, Wallis and Futuna, Samoa, and French Polynesia; (3) Micronesia (in the north) consists of the Federated States of Micronesia, Guam, Kiribati, the Marshall Islands, Nauru, the Northern Mariana Islands, and Palau.

In addition, Australia has a small indigenous population (2 percent in 1996), of which the Torres Strait Islanders are regarded as Melanesian. New Zealand/Aotearoa has a much larger indigenous population, reflected in its official biculturalism. New Zealand Maori make up 14.5 percent of the population (in 1996). When we add the South Pacific Islanders we find that almost 20 percent of the New Zealand population is Polynesian and Auckland is the largest Polynesian city in the world.

Australia and New Zealand

New Zealand was the first country in the world to give women the vote for its national parliament (1893) and Australia the first to allow women both to vote and to stand for election at the national level (1902). In both countries there were women's suffrage movements that saw the vote as the key to increasing women's influence on national life, particularly in areas such as temperance, purity, and child protection. These traditions have been continued in New Zealand by the long-standing National Council of Women and the Maori Women's Welfare League. In 1938, a New Zealand Labour government established what at the time was the most advanced welfare state in the world. In general, the structures of the New Zealand Labour Party were relatively favorable to women, with an absence of the Irish Catholic machine politics or formalized factions of Australian labor and with affiliated trade unions exercising less power.

In the 1990s, union membership was falling rapidly in Australasia, and by 1998 only about 25 percent of the New Zealand workforce and 28 percent of Australian workforce were union members. With the contraction of union coverage outside the public sector came increasing feminization, particularly evident in New Zealand, where women constituted 57 percent of remaining unionists. In these unfavorable circumstances women were achieving leadership positions, as secretary of the New Zealand Council of Trade Unions and president of the Australian Council of Trade Unions.

New Zealand women have been strong performers at the local government level, constituting 31 percent of elected local government officials in 1998 and more than 25 percent of mayors. The mayor of Auckland, Dame Catherine Tizard, was appointed governor-general in 1990. The comparable figures for Australia indicate that in 1997 women constituted 24 percent of elected officials and 15 percent of mayors. The Australian figures were highly variable between states, with women constituting, for example, 27 percent of mayors in South Australia.

As parliamentary candidates, New Zealand women suffered from an unfavorable electoral system—Westminster-style single-member constituencies. Despite this, they achieved 21 percent of the seats in the unicameral national parliament in 1993. With the introduction of the Mixed Member Proportional (MMP) electoral system in 1996, the proportion of women in parliament rose to 29 percent—but while women held 45 percent of the new party list seats, they held only 15 percent of constituency seats.

In 1997, National's Jenny Shipley became the first woman prime minister in New Zealand, after a party-room coup. The leader of the opposition, Labour's Helen Clark, won the 1999 election, becoming the second woman prime minister and the first to lead her party to victory. It had been an interesting contest in which both major parties were headed by women, as was one of the minor parties, the Greens, that was to end up with the balance of power. Clark's new Cabinet had 7 women members (35 percent), and there were 11 in the new ministry (44 percent), including 2 Maori women.

As noted above, the Australian Labor Party did not take a lead in promoting women's rights, as did labor and social democratic parties elsewhere, and women's parliamentary representation in Australia tended to lag behind comparable countries. The impetus had to come from outside the party system, and it was organizations such as the Women's Electoral Lobby in the 1970s that pressured Australian governments to develop "femocrat" strategies—specialized machinery within government for gender analysis of policy and program delivery (Sawer, 1990).

For a time Australia led the world in its institutionalized recognition that no government activity could be assumed to be gender neutral in its effects. This meant locating women's policy units in the main policy coordinating areas of government where they would have access to all cabinet submissions and cabinet processes. Femocrats also provided internal advocacy for a wide range of government-funded women's services, often delivered by organizational hybrids that combined feminist collectivism with the compromises required by government accountability. In the 1990s, Australia slipped back from the kind of leadership role it played earlier, although one advantage of its federal political structure was that momentum could be sustained somewhere in the system.

Comparable machinery was not established in New Zealand until after the election of the Lange Labour government in 1984, and it took the form of a Ministry of Women's Affairs rather than following the Australian model (Sawer, 1998). It was a pioneering organization in both its commitment to feminist ideas about process and its commitment to biculturalism. The Maori Women's Secretariat ensures that attention is paid to the specific needs of Maori women, and in the 1990s it was particularly active in promoting Maori women's enterprises. New Zealand ministers and officials meet regularly with their Australian counterparts at ministerial and women's advisers' meetings.

After patchy results from voluntary affirmative action programs, the Australian Labor Party finally adopted a binding target in 1994 whereby women would be 35 percent of all parliamentary parties by 2002, with the sanction of reopening preselections. In another important development, an Australian EMILY's List was launched in 1996—a feminist fundraising organization designed to assist endorsed Labor women candidates who make feminist commitments. Women are now being preselected for safe seats, and the conservative parties have also been making progress, although preferring training and mentoring for women candidates rather than quotas.

Most of Australia's parliaments are bicameral, and women have tended to do much better in chambers elected by proportional representation (PR), although Labor quotas are now blurring this effect. Certainly, PR has been essential to the success of the minor parties that have facilitated women's political leadership—for example, four of the six federal leaders of the Australian Democrats have been women. At the federal level, women constituted 22 percent of the lower house and 29 percent of the Senate (elected by PR) in November 1999. The proportion of women in state parliaments is roughly similar, and after the 1999 state election in Victoria women constituted 44 percent of the new Labor Cabinet, a record high in Australia.

The Pacific Islands

Excluding Australia and New Zealand, the South Pacific had a total population estimated at around seven million in 1996, or just 0.1 percent of the world's population. Most Pacific Island economies are struggling, with agriculture and fishing still the staple economic activities despite the rapid increase of tourism in many areas.

Many Pacific Island nations have complicated colonial histories with the United Kingdom, the United States, Germany, France, Australia, and New Zealand. Although most of the colonial regimes have ended, the United States retains a significant presence in Micronesia, including Guam and the Northern Mariana Islands, and also retains American Samoa in Polynesia. Palau, the Federated States of Micronesia, and the Marshall Islands are independent countries tied to the United States by foreign aid and defense compacts. France retains Wallis and Futuna, New Caledonia, and French Polynesia as overseas territories. The Cook Islands and Niue remain as self-governing countries in free association with New Zealand, and Tokelau is a tiny, non-self-governing New Zealand territory. Although their political and constitutional structures vary, every Pacific Island nation now practices some form of democracy; often traditional authority structures, such as chiefly systems, are embedded in more recently acquired constitutions.

Although adult suffrage is now universal in the Pacific, women have generally been reluctant to stand in national elections. In 1998, there were 745 parliamentary seats contestable throughout the region (excluding Australia and New Zealand). Of these, only 21 (that is, 2.8 percent) were held by women (Drage, 1998). Polynesian and Micronesian countries (with 3.8 percent of available seats held by women) fared better than Melanesian nations, where women occupied only 1.5 percent of available seats. In Micronesia, Guam has long been exceptional, with votes for women in 1931 and a critical mass (33 percent) of women in parliament in the late 1980s and early 1990s. This changed with the 1998 election, when women's representation fell to 13 percent.

Women enjoyed considerable power and influence in traditional Polynesian cultures, and indeed Polynesian women were pioneers of full political rights under the Pitcairn constitution of 1838, the first in the world to enshrine universal suffrage. Maori women gained the suffrage along with Pakeha women in New Zealand in 1893, and women such as Te Puea Herangi exercised important leadership roles in Maori cultural revival. In Tonga, Queen Salote reigned as the constitutional monarch from 1918 until her death in 1965, and women have held the status of nobles in Tonga and chiefs (Matai) in Samoa.

The very low percentage of women in politics throughout Melanesia has been ascribed by some to the cultural traditions of the area, which also inhibit women's access to educational opportunities. Elizabeth Cox and Louis Aitsi (1988) suggest it is the robust traditions of village life, including marriage practices constructing wives as objects of exchange, that prevent or constrain women's political activity. In Papua New Guinea, the largest and most populous Pacific Island country, women have been largely absent from parliament despite a constitutional commitment to "equal participation by women citizens in all political, economic, social and religious activities."

Of the Pacific Island women who have secured election to parliament so far, many have been women of high traditional status, affiliated by kinship or marriage to politically influential men (Drage, 1995). In Tuvalu's parliament, for example, the lone woman member in 1998 was married to the prime minister. Women may give priority to issues of race or colonialism, as with action over French nuclear testing in French Polynesia or the Kanak struggle for decolonization in New Caledonia. In New Zealand and Australia, indigenous women's primary political identity also tends to be race based. Penelope Meleisea (1994) suggests that the main obstacles to women's political participation throughout the Pacific Islands derive from the interplay of traditional and current political systems and the legacies of ongoing struggles against colonialism.

The Beijing Conference (the Fourth United Nations [UN] World Conference on Women) was an important catalyst in the mobilization of Pacific women in the 1990s. The long-established Pacific Women's Resource Bureau of the South Pacific Commission held conferences across the region to develop a Pacific Platform for Action (PPA), which was then endorsed by Pacific Island governments and taken to Beijing in 1995. The global and the local met with the increased celebration of International Women's Day across the Pacific and the highlighting of global/local feminist issues such as violence against women.

An associated development has been the creation of a Women in Politics movement across the Pacific. This movement has been supported by the UN Development Fund for Women (UNIFEM) and by aid money from Australia and New Zealand. It effectively began in 1995, following a congress organized by the Manila-based Center for Asia-Pacific Women in Politics, which decided to establish a Women in Politics in the Pacific Centre (WIPPAC) in the UNIFEM office in Suva. The goal was to hold a series of Women in Politics conferences to promote networking and training in the region. Women in Politics groups have now been established in a number of Pacific Island countries, building on existing networks such as National Councils of Women (Drage, 1998).

The workshops run by Women in Politics groups have had an immediate impact, in terms of increased number of women candidates and increased lobbying of all candidates for women's policy commitments. Successes at the local government level in Fiji in 1996 were followed by a breakthrough in the 1999 parliamentary election when eight women were elected, taking the proportion of women in parliament from 3 to 11 percent. In the new government there were three women ministers, one serving also as deputy prime minister. In elections held in Papua New Guinea in 1997, two women were elected—the first since 1982—while in the Solomon Islands and Kiribati one woman succeeded in each case.

Related initiatives have encouraged ratification of CEDAW (the UN Convention on Elimination of All Forms of Discrimination against Women) in the region. Australia and New Zealand were relatively early ratifiers and in 1991 cosponsored a CEDAW seminar in the Cook Islands. Subsequently, Samoa acceded in 1992, Papua New Guinea, Fiji and Vanuatu in 1995, and Tuvalu in 1999. Periodic reporting to UN and regional bodies constitutes a useful form of leverage for governmental and nongovernmental women's organizations and for the development of national plans of action. Fiji's 1997 constitution explicitly requires international law such as CEDAW to be taken into account by courts, and its Ministry for Women and Culture (headed by a woman minister) launched a 10-year Women's Plan of Action in 1998.

Reports from the Triennial Conference of Pacific Women in 1997 indicate that, despite progress, success across the region in increasing women in decision making or establishing ongoing services for women is highly variable. Some governments have indifferent or even hostile attitudes. A government representative from Tonga reported that the ratification of CEDAW was not even on the Tongan government's agenda and that a recent report on employment in Tonga had, on the contrary, recommended the establishment of a Men's Unit. A government representative from Palau claimed that the incidence of domestic violence was low, contrary to the nongovernment representative's report that it was one of the greatest problems facing Palau women, along with drug and alcohol abuse and the sex industry (SPC, 1997).

The women of the French territories of Wallis and Futuna, French Polynesia, and New Caledonia were unable to participate in the development of the PPA or send representatives to the Beijing conference: the French delegation represented France and its territories. In 1998, the Pacific Women's Resource Bureau organized a meeting of women from the French-speaking territories to address the concern they felt at exclusion from regional activities to advance the status of women.

There is no clear evidence of any trend common to Pacific Island countries and territories. While government and nongovernment women's organizations in Kiribati were organizing radio programs, cabinet briefings, trainer training, and the extension of services to women on outer islands, in the Federated States of Micronesia few programs were being prepared or implemented. Problems across the region in implementing CEDAW and PPA initiatives include a lack of cooperation between government and nongovernment agencies, inadequate resources, language difficulties (especially in the French territories), and disunity and fragmentation among women.

Despite these difficulties, Pacific women at the 1997 Triennial Conference noted that their participation in the Beijing conference and its local initiatives had renewed their determination to work together on women's issues. Indeed, international movements for women—operating through the UN in particular—have been especially influential in supporting Pacific Island women. They have also been useful in holding governments to account, as happened when the Australian government reported to CEDAW in 1997.

See Also

FEMINISM: AUSTRALIA AND NEW ZEALAND

References

Cox, Elizabeth, and Louis Aitsi. 1988. Papua New Guinea. In Taiamoni Tongamoa, ed., *Pacific women: Roles and status of women in Pacific Societies.* Suva: Institute of Pacific Studies, University of the South Pacific.

Drage, Jean. 1995. The exception, not the rule: A comparative analysis of women's political activity in Pacific Island Countries. *Pacific Studies,* 18(4): 61–93.

———. 1998. Women and politics in the Pacific: A layered approach to increasing the numbers. Paper presented to the Pacific Islands Political Science Conference, University of Canterbury.

Meleisea, Penelope Schoeffel. 1994. Women and political leadership in the Pacific Islands. In Caroline Daley and Melanie Nolan, eds., *Suffrage and beyond: International feminist perspectives.* New York: New York University Press.

Pacific Congress of Women in Politics. 1997. *Women's voices and destiny: The political landscape of the future. Proceedings of the 2nd Pacific Congress of Women in Politics. November 17–21 1996.* Korolevu: Women in Politics Pacific Center and the United Nations Development Fund for Women (UNIFEM-Fiji).

Sawer, Marian. 1998. Femocrats and ecorats: Women's policy machinery in Australia, Canada and New Zealand. In Carol Miller and Shahra Razavi, eds., *Missionaries and mandarins: Feminist engagement with development institutions.* London: Intermediate Technology.

———. 1990. *Sisters in suits: Women and public policy in Australia.* London: Allen and Unwin.

South Pacific Commission. 1997. *Seventh Triennial Conference of Pacific Women. Joint Regional Meeting of Government Representatives and Representatives of Non-Government Organisations on Women's Affairs in the Pacific.* Noumea: South Pacific Commission.

Wormald, Eileen. 1994. Rhetoric, reality, and a dilemma: Women and politics in Papua New Guinea. In Barbara J. Nelson and Najma Chowdhury, eds., *Women and politics worldwide.* New Haven, Conn.: Yale University Press.

Marian Sawer
Heather Brook

POLITICS AND THE STATE: Caribbean

The Caribbean is made up principally of the Hispanic Caribbean, the French Caribbean, and the British Caribbean, and, to a lesser degree, areas of Dutch and U.S. influence. The people of the region are divided by their specific colonial and subsequent linguistic histories. Nonetheless, the area consists of people of a variety of racial and ethnic origins who are bound together by similar broad experiences of slavery and colonialism. These experiences, along with differing patterns of economic development, have affected the Caribbean's inhabitants in a variety of political, social, economic, and cultural fashions. Relations with the outside world also have played a major role in the development of the Caribbean. This has produced a region that encompasses areas of substantial wealth, such as the Caymans or the Virgin Islands, and pockets of deep poverty, such as Haiti and the Dominican Republic.

Although many of the Caribbean nations shared similar patterns of historical development, efforts to unite territories into federal systems had little relative success. Each of the nations of the region developed different patterns of government, language, and society. In addition, relations with external powers such as the United States have either aided or slowed efforts toward democracy and civil rights. With the end of the cold war, however, democracy has become the norm for most of the region, with the notable exception of Cuba.

Most of the Caribbean states theoretically agree that women should have rights equal to those of men. Although women participate in the social, political, and economic development of these states, however, their contributions are not fully recognized. In 1994–1996, Cuba had the largest percentage of women in parliament, with some 22 percent, and several other states, including Grenada and Guyana, had around 20 percent female representation in the legislature. Most of the former British colonies, however, such as Barbados, Jamaica, and Trinidad and Tobago, had legislatures in which women comprised about 10 percent of the members. This also was true of many of the larger, former Spanish colonies including the Dominican Republic (11 percent), although election law changes are boosting this number. Of the larger Caribbean states, Haiti had the lowest female representation in parliament, with only some 3.6 of the seats held by women.

It is the women in many of the Caribbean societies who bear the major responsibility for the family. Often they are the sole means of financial support or the head of the household. These factors, when combined with lingering gender discrimination, have limited the full involvement of women in politics. Gender discrimination has its roots in the continuing ideology of both males and females, which does not allow them to vote for women, as they believe that women are not able to represent them adequately, and they assume that women's domestic roles as mothers and wives will be given priority.

Part of this is the result of female-centered families in these nations. Under this type of system, women dominate the domestic features of the home but usually play a minor role outside of home life. There also are persistent conceptions that women are not knowledgeable enough to manage the politics and the economy of a country. Part of this male chauvinism was the result of Caribbean practices such as *su-su,* a system in which women in a community pooled money and resources to establish rudimentary social protections against poverty and disease. Although the system was a brilliant example of community and female resourcefulness, many males and those in the upper classes looked down on the practice. These factors led to a continuing deep dichotomy between the guarantees of civil rights and the de facto gender divisions that exist within the societies.

Race and Gender

Afro-Caribbean women are the largest ethnic group in the Caribbean region, but they are not the majority in every territory; therefore, Caribbean women often object to the broad generalizations of race to which they are subject. Although there are similarities from nation to nation, one cannot disregard the cultural, social, economic, and political variations that exist between them. Caribbean women do not constitute a class nor do they act as one, either in their own territory or regionally. The main variations within each nation remain based on race and class, and women within each country have developed strong affiliations based on these two factors. Differences in race and class have affected women's approaches to politics and their accessibility to that process. There is greater participation in government in most of these states, so that in 1997 some 30 percent of all government jobs in Barbados were held by women and even in Haiti some 22 percent of local and national posts were occupied by females.

There still exist in the Caribbean colonial and neocolonial "dependency" relations. For example, several of the French territories, including Guadeloupe and Martinique, remain subject to direct colonial control, whereas the former British colonies of Jamaica and Trinidad remain dependent on European-dominated organizations such as the World Bank and the International Monetary Fund (IMF), even though the nations are nominally free of direct colonial oversight. These international organizations continue to control most aspects of the economies of Caribbean nations and often dictate political and economic policy to the ruling governments.

When slavery was legal, Caribbean women were prevented from marrying, and the legal codes gave them little control over their own lives or that of their children. The division of labor that existed under slavery was based not on sex but on race, color, and class. This legacy continues to haunt Caribbean women in contemporary societies. From the very beginning of slavery, there was a class divide between the white women—who represented the slave-owner—and the slave women. In addition, there was another class of women, known as "mulatto" or "colored," which emerged as the result of miscegenation between slave women and owners. This created an even greater rift between whites and Afro-Caribbeans, as the mulattos were often given preferential treatment and position within the society. After the abolition of slavery in the British colonies, the continued need for cheap labor led to the immigration of indentured servants from India. This led to the emergence of a fourth group of women within the society, Indo-Caribbeans. Added to these groups, there remained pockets of the native peoples of the region, including members of the Arawak and Carib tribes.

This combination of five major groups of women in the islands, living and working in close proximity with each other—although from different social and psychological histories—had a significant impact on the social structure of the region. In areas such as British Guiana (Guyana) and Trinidad, where there were a large number of indentured workers, Indian women played a major role in the disturbances on the plantation fields and the efforts toward independence (Momsen, 1993). In general, Afro- and Indo-Caribbean women account for some 80 percent of the female population of the region.

Historical Development

Women from all of the groups played major roles in the struggle for increased autonomy and eventual political independence in the British areas of the Caribbean. Although all women in Jamaica were barred from formal politics in the nineteenth century, they never accepted a passive role. Indo-Caribbean women fought to end the indenture system (which was not abolished until 1917). Although they did not have the right to vote, Caribbean women were heavily involved in mass politics and protest movements. Women were very much involved in the Morant Bay Rebellion in Jamaica in 1865, even though later accounts emphasized only the role of the male leaders of the rebellion and women were eventually erased from the popular myth of the event. Better known is the legendary "Nanny" of the Maroons, who resisted the British army during the same period.

An examination of women's participation in the disturbances of the 1930s in St. Vincent (1935), Trinidad and Tobago (1937), and Jamaica (1938) suggests not only that women played a major role in these uprisings, but that they were motivated by the burden of responsibility for the social and economic welfare of themselves and their families in the matriarchal societies (Greene, 1993). In most of the territories, women's first exposure to organized mass movements was through church groups and community associations such as the Lady Musgrave Self-Help Society of Jamaica and the Trinidad Home Industries and Women's Self-Help. Similar self-help groups in British Guiana and Barbados "catered primarily to the needs of white women and highly 'coloured' ladies often from the top echelons of society" (Reddock, 1991). Indeed, throughout the Caribbean, women from the middle and upper classes initially led the struggle for suffrage and basic rights. Middle- and upper-class women, mainly teachers, clerks, and even landowners, agitated for the right to vote in Jamaica as early as 1918 (Vassell, 1993).

By the 1920s, however, Afro-Caribbean women began to organize to promote their own interests. Two prominent examples of this trend in the British colonies were Amy Baily's Jamaica's Women's Club and the Coterie of Social Workers, led by Audrey Jeffers of Trinidad. This involvement in community and religious organizations set the stage for later participation by women in politics. Mary Knibb became the first Jamaican women elected to municipal office on that island, and Audrey Jeffers became the first woman to do the same on Trinidad and Tobago. Later, during World War II, women became a more visible presence in Caribbean politics and the women of British Guiana even endeavored to develop their own political party.

In Barbados, women began pressing for greater involvement in the political process as early as 1951, when that country polled its first universal adult suffrage. That year, Barbados elected its first woman, Ernie Bourne Senior, to the House of the Assembly. Since that time, the Senate has averaged six women members per session. In 1995, the Dover Accord conference in Barbados endorsed the quota system for women's participation political parties and government. This proposal was supported by the United Nations and was a major issue at the 1995 World Conference on Women in Beijing. That same year, Barbados elected a woman, Billie Miller, as deputy prime minister. The women's movement on the island was further aided by the appointment of Dame Nita Barrow as governor-general. In office, Barrow was important in the promotion of primary health care programs.

Women of color in the Spanish areas of the Caribbean began to undertake political action as early as 1807. During the Napoleonic Wars, the capture of the Spanish monarchs Carlos IV and Ferdinand VII by the French led to widespread opposition to French rule in the Caribbean. Women in these territories cut their hair to demonstrate their opposition to the French. During the struggles for Cuban independence in the late 1800s, women participated in the armed struggle and distinguished themselves in the revolution of 1895 to 1898. By 1847, there were 47 women's revolutionary clubs and the oppression of women was recognized by the resistance in a published letter to the world.

Following Cuban independence, women began to work to gain suffrage. In 1917, women were allowed to own property and, in the 1920s, several women's congresses were held to promote rights and suffrage. By the 1930s, coeducational schools were common and there was increased funding for women's education. Women continued to be politically active during the 1930s and 1940s and participated in protest marches and, later, in the armed struggle against the dictatorial regimes that governed Cuba. Women were prominent in both of Fidel Castro's efforts (1953 and 1959) to overthrow the Batista regime in Cuba. Haydee Santamaria was a notable leader in both fights.

After Castro and the communists took power, there was a concentrated effort to improve gender equity. For example, Castro formed the Federation of Cuban Women (FMC), which endeavored to improve literacy among women and retrain domestic workers. By the 1970s, Cuba had become the most gender-equal society in the Caribbean. Eventually, Cuban women would occupy some 27 percent of the nation's political posts and an amazing 65 percent of its professional and technical workforce, including 50 percent of the nation's medical doctors. Since the end of the cold war, however, the place of women in Cuban society has deteriorated. Women's representation in parliament has decreased to about 22.8 percent, and the state has become increasingly more conservative. One of the main radical feminist groups in Cuba, Magen, was dissolved, and the FMC has become increasingly conservative and slow to react to problems, such as the growth in Cuba's sex trade as tourism increases in the nation. Meanwhile, Cuban women are largely restricted to expressing their interests through state-affiliated organizations.

Although the women's political movement was slow to mature in the Dominican Republic, the nation now has one of the most progressive political policies on gender. This country became the first Caribbean nation to enact a law requiring a minimum percentage of candidates for political parties to be female. The Dominican law requires that at least 25 percent of a party's candidates for office in both local and national elections be female.

Current Issues

On many of the islands, women remain excluded from activities outside of the domestic sphere as a result of historical and cultural gender discrimination. For example, until the 1980s, in Grenada, women were not allowed to sit on juries until they were 35 years old (although men could at age 21). On the Francophone islands, such as Guadeloupe, Haiti, and Martinique, women remain excluded from participation in political activities. In addition, they have little control over economic or social issues (including matters of reproductive health, such as contraception and abortion). Many scholars note that Caribbean women's economic contributions remain in the domestic sphere and racial and class differences prevent concerted political action.

Female participation in the political process through voting has become widespread and common. Women remain underrepresented, however, in key decision-making and executive levels in government or in any of the major political parties in the region. Influence—in the form of numbers at the ballot box—has yet to be translated into influence within the political system itself. Roberta Clarke explains this dichotomy by asserting that "women in the Caribbean do not perceive themselves as a group with separate and distinct interests from those of men and they do not appear to vote cognizant of their power to advance their interests as women" (Clarke, 1986). In addition, women in states such as Haiti have focused their attention and political resources on issues such as overall democracy and efforts to end political violence.

Women's place in the states and in the politics of the Caribbean is dependent on the fundamental issues of the nature of power, the relations of women to men, and the nature of politics itself. Caribbean women are entitled to equal participation within all aspects of their societies. Often, however, their efforts to achieve political influence have been discouraged or, at the very least, ignored.

See Also

COLONIALISM AND POSTCOLONIALISM; DEMOCRACY; DEVELOPMENT: CENTRAL AND SOUTH AMERICA AND THE CARIBBEAN; HOUSEHOLDS AND FAMILIES: CARIBBEAN; IMPERIALISM; POLITICAL LEADERSHIP; POLITICAL PARTICIPATION; POLITICAL REPRESENTATION; POLITICS AND THE STATE: OVERVIEW; REVOLUTIONS

References and Further Reading

Bishop, Maurice. 1983. *Maurice Bishop speaks: The Grenada revolution, 1979–83.* New York: Pathfinder.

Brasileiro, Ana Maria, ed. 1996. *Building democracy with women.* New York: UNIFEM.

Clarke, Roberta. 1986. Women's organizations, women's interests. *Social and Economic Studies* 35(3): 110–123.

Espin, Vilma. 1991. *Cuban women confront the future.* Melbourne: Ocean Press.

Greene, J. Edward, ed. 1993. Race, class, and gender. In *The future of the Caribbean.* Kingston, Jamaica: Institute of Social and Economic Research, University of the West Indies.

Hart, Keith, ed. 1989. *Women and the sexual division of labor in the Caribbean.* Kingston, Jamaica: University of the West Indies.

Manley, Michael. 1974. *The politics of change: A Jamaican testament.* London: Andre Deutsch.

Mohammaed, Patricia, and Catherine Shepard, ed. 1988. *Gender in Caribbean development.* Kingston, Jamaica: University of the West Indies.

Momsen, Janet. 1993. *Women and change in the Caribbean.* London: James Currey.

Reddock, Rhoda, 1991. Feminism and feminist thought: An historical overview. In Patricia Mohamed and Catherine Shepard, eds., *Gender in Caribbean development.* Kingston, Jamaica: University of the West Indies.

———. 1994. *Women and politics in Trinidad and Tobago.* Kingston, Jamaica: Ian Randle.

Shepherd, Vevene, Barbara Bailey, and Bridgette Brereton. 1995. *Engendering history.* Kingston, Jamaica: Ian Randle.

Vassell, Lennette. 1993. *The Jamaican Federation of Women and Politics, 1944–1950.* Unpublished paper, University of the West Indies, Kingston, Jamaica.

Gerlin Bean

POLITICS AND THE STATE: Central and South America

The legacies of conquest as well as societal diversity make relations between women and the state complex in Central and South America. Enlightenment ideas about (male) public and (female) private spheres, as well as Hispanic notions of male and female behavior (*machismo* and *marianismo,* respectively), in combination with varied indigenous patterns, have resulted in hybrid interactions between gender and the state. The region is therefore diverse at national and subnational levels, with women facing specific histories of political marginalization and restricting social relations. States have been very engaged in planning and promoting national progress, activities that often reproduce and reinforce strongly differentiated positions for women and men.

Linked to hierarchical family and domestic relations, patriarchy has been an important conceptual tool in the region, especially in understanding social relations in rural areas during the nineteenth century. The male patriarch's control over his family and household workers was absolute, for example, on Brazilian sugar estates, and persisted for decades despite numerous social changes. Patriarchy has increasingly been linked to public political realms, spaces characterized by male monopolies over political power and women's exclusion through formal and informal means. But patriarchy is seen to be constantly challenged and resisted by women in diverse and innovative ways, in both the past and the present day. Women's activities in the private and public spheres—*casa* (house) and *calle* (street) in Spanish-speaking areas—can undermine patriarchal relations, although women have also at times been complicit with patriarchy, especially when class and racial differences between women restrict or prevent broad coalitions. Women's active participation in the social movements of the late nineteenth century challenged their traditional roles. Anarchist, socialist, and rural movements saw women's active participation in demands for full employment and civil rights, while our growing knowledge about earlier (largely indigenous) women's uprisings against the colonizers reveals their presence and, sometimes, their leading role. Elite women are also known to have participated in early discussions of democracy, liberalism and a secular state, female education, and political rights from the late colonial period in the eighteenth century, peaking during the social turmoil of the late nineteenth century. Upper-class women often had access to, and informal influence over, male state-makers' agendas due to family and social connections, and their literary and journalistic writings.

States Picturing Women

States' gender ideologies are increasingly a research focus, revealing assumptions in apparently neutral state decisions on suffrage or development programs. For example, in the Mexican Revolution, women were seen as "taming" men, providing order and stability to society, a factor that complicated the later struggle for female suffrage, as women were perceived as conservative and as a threat to the ongoing revolution; suffrage was finally gained in 1955. In Argentina under Juan and Eva Perón, women were not supposed to fight against men, as feminism was "antinationalist," and the granting of suffrage depended on the large-scale mobilization of women in state-organized "feminine" groups in 1947.

Family and civil law often consolidate discrimination against women in Latin America. Male power and assumptions of control over their families and women are seen in laws requiring women to gain husbands' permission to work outside the home (under the *patria potesta* law, which was widespread until recently). In many countries (for example, Chile, Paraguay, Argentina), divorce is available only in exceptional circumstances. In countries with a clearer separation of church and state, reform of family law occurred earlier. Divorce was legal early in the twentieth century in Ecuador and Uruguay, countries where women won the vote earlier, in 1929 and 1932, respectively. Although large numbers of poorer and rural women do not marry formally, such family and divorce legislation influences male attitudes to their wives' property, work, and children.

Yet the Catholic Church retains great influence over the family and reproduction. Although contraception is often legal, its uptake varies with class, ethnicity, and location (urban areas are better provisioned). Abortion is either severely restricted or illegal in South and Central American countries; this results annually in thousands of illegal abortions and many maternal deaths. One Chilean woman commented, "Women don't want to talk about abortion because it's against the teachings of the church and also it's against the law, but nearly all women have abortions."

State development programs often treat women as mothers and as passive recipients of aid and assistance, rather than as active participants in work, politics, and society. Although women are generally seen in their maternal role (for example, for food aid or health programs), recent work has highlighted the subtle variations in maternal programs, varying according to the family ideology of the government party, the race or ethnicity of women involved (white women are favored, black and indigenous women are discriminated against), and the symbolism of motherhood in particular countries. Mother figures have become icons for the nation, as in Mexico (the Virgin of Guadalupe) and in Cuba (the heroic "Mother of Cuba," Mariana Grajales). Such icons contribute to nationally specific ideologies regarding motherhood, which in turn influence policy on women.

Dramatic political change, such as under communist Cuba (1959–) or Nicaragua (1979–1991), has had contradictory and uneven effects on women. The family law introduced in Cuba in the 1970s was designed to reallocate domestic work on a more equal basis between women and men, although it has not often been enforced. Assistance with shopping and child care for working parents turned out to be assistance to women in their double burden of home and wage work. State campaigns to retrain female prostitutes and against sexist advertising tackled other dimensions of women's rights. In Nicaragua, women's organizations were strengthened and given a voice in government, although state policies were oriented toward women's basic needs rather than their gender-specific interests. As with left-wing organizations throughout the region, women's issues and interests were perceived in Cuba and Nicaragua as secondary to the "primary" issue of class.

Women in Protest

In other countries of the region, recent relations between the state and women in the region have been shaped by the military regimes of the 1970s and early 1980s, and subsequent "democratization" and the 1980s economic crisis. Women under military regimes were expected to conform to an idealized womanhood, being feminine, maternal, and apolitical. Feminist actions were suppressed under military governments; for example, celebrations of International Women's Day were broken up by soldiers. Women's participation in pro-democracy movements took military regimes by surprise, especially when it was realized that they were commonly in women-only groups. Women of different classes and ethnic groups called for the return of "disappeared" sons, daughters, and husbands, transforming a traditional mothering role into an effective political lever on the state. The Mothers of the Plaza de Mayo in Argentina are perhaps the best known of these human rights groups. The Mothers chose to remain a women-only group in order to negotiate better through their mothering role, yet were the only openly politically active group in the country at a time of great political repression, and were instrumental in the military's downfall. In Argentina, Chile, and Central America, women initially gained the church's support for their human rights activities, but their growing questioning of traditional female roles alienated the church. The "motherist" groups in Central and South America challenged both society's view of older women and their own identities and political roles by reconceptualizing their own priorities and interests.

The restrictive political situation shaped the characteristics of South and Central American women's movements, as much as the women's movement affected their countries' regimes. This mutual influence can be seen in the emphasis placed on public and private patriarchy by the popular women's movement, and by numerous successful campaigns against the state. Slogans such as "democracy in the country and democracy in the home" became widespread as they reflected women's view that authoritarian governments relied on powers similar to men in patriarchal families. Not only feminists but also peasant and low-income urban women from diverse countries developed analyses of the state and their position in it. Female political activists who experienced sexual violence during arrest linked it with their specific situation as women, and with the issue of domestic violence by husbands and brothers. Female-specific experiences led women to question and challenge their traditional submissive roles, and to make connections between male power and their own lives. On the return to democracy, women's groups pressured politicians to introduce measures to deal with domestic violence (for example, Peru, Ecuador). In Peru, a police precinct staffed by female officers was set up to deal with women's claims, which on its first day received complaints from almost two thousand women. In Ecuador, domestic violence is now the center of a major public debate about appropriate policies and the direction of social change. In Argentina on the return of civilian rule, the Mothers of the Disappeared pushed through legislation to prosecute members of the military regime, making this the first country to do so.

Under civilian government, however, women's struggles were far from over. The economic crisis of the 1980s prompted various women's actions against the state, such as housewives' groups protesting price increases and demanding housewives' insurance, and women organizing traditional politics, thereby disadvantaging them with the return of the male-dominated parties. In Peru, two feminist candidates stood in the general election but were not elected, although the Peruvian women's movement was one of the largest in the region. In certain countries, women's popular momentum carried them to political office, as in Brazil, where feminists and popular women's groups entered the decision-making process in São Paulo municipality. Elsewhere, the United Nations (UN) International Decade for Women prompted governments to create women's issues departments and ratify the UN Convention on the Elimination of All Forms of Discrimination Against Women. Yet debt-reduced budgets and lack of political will often meant the marginalization or abandonment of "femocracies." Owing to political parties' continued male influence, gender issues are rarely debated or implemented.

Women's presence in government and formal political posts remains limited. Violeta Chamorro was president of Nicaragua, basing her campaign on her maternal role in a country divided by violent civil war. Her emphasis on motherhood contrasted sharply with ex-president Daniel Ortega's horse-riding masculine image. Female vice-presidents were found in Costa Rica and Honduras, but these countries have more than one vice-president. Women generally make up a small minority in the cabinet, with the highest rates of participation found in Guatemala (23 percent of cabinet members) and the Dominican Republic (14 percent). In parliaments, women are found in larger numbers in chambers of deputies than as senators, as for example in Bolivia, where women make up 3.7 percent of senators, but 7.7 percent of deputies. In 1991, Argentina introduced a quota law requiring parties to make women 30 percent of voting lists, in alternate positions with men; subsequent elections resulted in women winning 13.2 percent of seats. Generally, women make up under 8 percent of parliamentarians in bicameral systems, exceeded only in Colombia and the Dominican Republic (over 11 percent).

Some writers argue that women's recent mobilization was prompted by economic and political circumstances: economic crisis and the restriction of political activities under military regimes. They argue that women act on the basis of their traditional role, which is to provide for members of their household, and a "female consciousness," both of which take them from a restricted to an expanded sphere of activities. Neighborhood organizations, such as those demanding provision of services including water, roads, and electricity, are often given as examples of how women's "community management" role takes them into negotiation with municipal and national government over resources. Others argue that domestic burdens, *machista* attitudes, and marginalization in new social movements prompted women to question gender roles and identify strategic interests. Although women began their activism from within traditional roles such as mothering and resource provision, their participation in such movements provided a space for discussion and renegotiation regarding both public and private roles. The opportunity for women to discuss and act together, often for the first time in their lives, was crucial for the emergence of criticism of prevailing roles for women and the power of men. Such interpretations have been strengthened by recent work highlighting the provisional and multiple nature of women's identities, in which gender is not a fixed relationship but one created through constant social interaction.

The transformation of women's consciousness and expression of priorities also brings them closer to the demands and practices of the region's feminists. Although working-class and "popular" (low-income) women often declare themselves to be against feminism, owing to its association with the middle class, these same women often spend much time criticizing *machismo* and their marginalization from formal politics. As a result, feminist and popular women's organizations are increasingly converging, sharing activities, priorities, and attitudes. Despite tensions, boundaries between popular women's and feminist movements are fluid and mixed, with new ways of "doing politics." In both popular women's groups and feminist organizations, political practice reflects women's daily lives and new, less formal and less hierarchical types of organization. Popular women's organizations at times criticize feminist groups for relying upon other women's domestic labor (in the home) and for racism, whereas feminists criticize popular women's organizations for their slow recognition of women's strategic interests.

In addition to the work done by popular women's movements, female parliamentarians, and feminists, there has also been extensive female participation in guerrilla movements in Latin America. Whether in extremist Maoist movements such as the Shining Path in Peru or in the armies of national liberation in Central America, women have actively engaged in armed struggles. Liberation movements in Nicaragua and El Salvador had women in central leadership positions as well as among the rank and file, although their contributions did not guarantee full political and social rights in the new regimes. A very different struggle was fought by Rigoberta Menchú from Guatemala, whose work brought that country's human rights abuses to the attention of the world and won her the Nobel Peace Prize in 1992. As an indigenous woman from Guatemala's marginalized ethnic population, Rigoberta Menchú fought against both racial and gender discrimination.

The women's movement in Latin America thus comprises diverse streams, in which rural indigenous women are struggling for land and political voice, at times in coalition with urban low-income women or middle-class women's resource centers. Rural, often indigenous, women have been active in recent years negotiating with the state and political organizations over their status and rights. In many agrarian reforms women were disqualified from grants of land, and the political organizations set up to represent reform beneficiaries marginalized them. Women from Honduras, Peru, and Bolivia, for example, were active from the 1970s in actions supporting peasant confederations, yet did not receive political recognition from their male counterparts. In response, women-only peasant groups, such as those in Bolivia and southern Peru, were formed where women, often monolingual in local languages, could debate their position and set priorities. In a parallel move in Paraguay in the 1980s, peasant women organized their first public demonstration to demand land and democracy.

With many governments' recent market-oriented reforms, women's work and political position are changing rapidly, resulting in the further blurring of boundaries between public and private spheres. In the early 1990s, governments were dismantling public employment, welfare provision, and labor legislation in many countries. These changes meant that women's lives were experiencing yet more transformation, as work opportunities and political struggles shifted. As legislative controls were removed, women's rights often declined, although disempowerment in one sphere did not prevent activism in another. In recent government "work creation" programs, as in Peru, women appeared to develop new identities and renegotiate their domestic position, although such work was temporary and low-paid. In the newly domesticated manufacturing process, women's home-based role was rearticulated to accommodate economic and familial relations in new ways unfavorable to women. Women in the transnational company factories of the region had few employment rights.

Yet international linkages between women provide some of the necessary resources and support for women's constant struggles in the political arena. Seven regional feminist conferences have now been held, the most recent in Chile in 1996, drawing ever larger numbers of diverse women together to debate their commonalities and differences. Other international networks include one for homeworkers struggling for full employment rights, and a network among lesbians fighting legal and social discrimination. While the recent political history of South and Central America is generally one of male political power and female marginalization, the existence and dynamism of international and national groups comprising diverse women suggest that female challenges to masculine arenas of power will continue in the future.

See Also

DEVELOPMENT: CENTRAL AND SOUTH AMERICA AND THE CARIBBEAN; FEMINISM: CENTRAL AND SOUTH AMERICA; VIOLENCE: CENTRAL AND SOUTH AMERICA; WOMEN'S STUDIES: CENTRAL AND SOUTH AMERICA

References and Further Reading

Alvarez, S. 1990. *Engendering democracy in Brazil.* Princeton, N.J.: Princeton University Press.

Craske, N. 1999. *Women and politics in Latin America.* Cambridge: Polity.

Dore, E., ed. 1997. *Gender politics in Latin America: Debates and theory in practice.* New York: Monthly Review.

Dore, E., and M. Molyneux, eds. 2000. *The hidden histories of gender and the state in Latin America.* Durham, N.C.: Duke University Press.

Escobar, A., and S. Alvarez, eds. 1992. *The making of social movements in Latin America.* Boulder, Col.: Westview.

Jaquette, J., ed. 1989. *The women's movement in Latin America: Feminism and the transition to democracy.* London: Unwin Hyman.

Lavrin, A. 1995. *Women, feminism and social change in Argentina, Chile and Uruguay, 1890–1940.* Lincoln: University of Nebraska Press.

McGee, Deutsch, S. 1991. Gender and sociopolitical change in twentieth-century Latin America. *Hispanic American Historical Review* 71(2): 259.

Menchú, Rigoberta. 1983. *I... Rigoberta Menchú: An Indian woman in Guatemala.* Trans. A. Wright. London: Verso.

Radcliffe, S. A., and Westwood, S., eds. 1993. *Viva: Women and popular protest in Latin America.* London: Routledge.

Valdes, T., and E. Gomariz. 1995. *Latin American women: Comparative figures.* Madrid, Chile: FLACSO/Instituto de la Mujer (Spain).

Sarah A. Radcliffe

POLITICS AND THE STATE: Commonwealth of Independent States

The first part of this article covers the period from 1917 to 1991 and focuses geographically on the country known as the Union of Soviet Socialist Republics (the USSR).

History

Russia, the USSR's historical predecessor, was built by absorbing the territories tangibly different in terms of ethnicity and socioeconomic development. Thus Poland, Finland, and the Baltic states annexed in the course of the expansion to the west were far more developed than the regions populated by the ethnic Russians themselves. On its move to the south, the Russian Empire absorbed the Caucasus, the Transcaucasian area, and Central Asia, with dominating feudal and semifeudal institutions and with a part of the population adhering to pagan beliefs and a nomadic way of life (including tribes of the Kirghiz, Kazakhs, and Turkmens).

Generally, more than one hundred major and minor ethnic groups existed within the Russian Empire. The crisis of 1917 led to its dissolution, but only Finland, Poland, and three Baltic states gained political independence. The other territories were forced into a new empire, which was now called the USSR. Formally, it appeared on the map in December 1922. Partition of the world undertaken by Hitler in the second half of the 1930s initiated new territorial claims of the USSR. It again occupied the Baltic states and took part in the new partition of Poland. Fifteen Soviet republics found themselves as parts of the country: Russia itself, the Ukraine, Byelorussia, Moldavia, three Baltic states, Georgia, Armenia, Azerbaijan, and five Central Asian states. This arrangement existed up to the formal dissolution of the Soviet Union in December 1991.

Soviet social policies, including those relating to women, to a minimal degree took into consideration existing ethnocultural and socioeconomic distances between the various parts of the country. Communist ideology, according to its principles, ignores any gender and ethnic differences. As a result, "Soviet" women are examined here as objects of the state influence in the USSR. As for women's reactions and women's positions in family and society, there were some differences between the republics and the parts of Russia itself (Buckley, 1997; Pilkington, 1992; Tokhtakhodzhaeva, 1994). Long-standing gaps in female employment rates and fertility rates between the Baltic and Slavic republics, on one hand, and the Transcaucasian (especially in Central Asian), on the other, should be mentioned in this respect.

As a result of disintegration processes launched by perestroika, the former Soviet republics, one by one, proclaimed their political independence in 1991–1992. Later, the Commonwealth of Independent States (CIS) was created, having been, despite the initial intentions of its makers, more a political union than an economic and military one. All the former Soviet republics gradually joined the CIS, with the exception of the three Baltic states. The second part of this article focuses on the situation in Russia.

State Policy

The essence of the Soviet state's policy on the whole population including women has been the supremacy of decrees over laws. This was stipulated by the absence of the civil society, which made it possible to ignore the constitution or to manipulate its progressive articles in favor of needs and ambitions of every new leader. During the period from 1917 until the late 1990s, all the changes in the women's social positions were introduced from the top but not initiated by women themselves. This is strikingly different from the situation in western Europe and the United States, where all the civil rights of women were gained through their long and persistent struggles.

At least five periods in the policies on women in the former Soviet Union may be examined: Lenin's dictatorship (1917–1924), Joseph Stalin's regime (1924–1953), Nikitu Khrushchev's thaw (1953–1964), Brezhnev's stagnation (1964–1985), and the perestroika of Mikhail Gorbachev (1985–1991). The postrevolutionary period was a romantic impulse toward the establishment of the new order of things on the egalitarian basis. Men and women were proclaimed as equal social individuals; the Soviet legislation granted women the following basic rights: to vote, to divorce, to have an abortion, to be employed, to have equal pay, and to be entitled to maternity leaves.

These laws, however, could not be grounded easily in the predominantly peasant Russian society. Most of the people shared patriarchal norms and values. Gender identity of men and women was strongly attached to gender division of roles prescribed by the Domostroi (a guide setting down rules on domestic affairs, first published with the imprimatur of the Russian Orthodox Church in the sixteenth century). The peasant mode of life with community values and its rigid gender subordination contributed greatly to the realization of communist ideologies and social practices.

Lenin clearly understood that liberal rights for women could not become a reality without adequate material grounds. His last articles and papers, written in 1922–1923, proclaimed the necessity of public catering, kindergartens, nurseries, and children's custody on a state level. He stressed that without mass involvement of women in the revolutionary construction communism would not be built. So-called *zhenotdels* (women's sections attached to the party committees of all levels) were created. They provided work and educational opportunities for women and recruited volunteers among women into the party and public activities at factories and collective farms. These units could also release to some extent women's burden of housekeeping and maternity obligations, providing, for example, child care facilities. However, the solution of specifically women's problems was always looked upon in the light of global working-class interests. According to the communist doctrine, all structural antagonisms were abolished within socialist society, that is, those between classes, between various ethnic groups composing the Soviet Union, and between men and women as well.

Lenin regarded gender division as a harmful theoretical delusion taken from the bourgeois feminist movement. His views were actively disseminated by women working-class leaders. Thus one of the books edited by Klara Zetkin declared in 1929: "Despite some points of contiguity and even similarity of demands concerning absence of women's rights, between the two movements—bourgeois and proletariat—there exists the core opposition. Class contradictions between the exploiters and the exploited are stronger than the feeling of women's solidarity to which the feminists are appealing."

The idea of socialist economies' construction at any human cost predetermined the state policy on women during the Stalinist period. Women were considered as a large labor resource submitted to the ambitious party projects of forced collectivization of agriculture and massive industrialization. Family as a social institution has become one of the major ideological obstacles to the fulfillment of these economic programs. According to the communist doctrine, kinship relations and emotional links had to fade away for the sake of working-class solidarity. Building up of social infrastructures (services, retail trade, public catering, entertainment places, and so on) was lagging far behind the creation of plants, factories, mines, and railways. The idea of the Stalinist regime was that these facilities should be reduced to an absolute minimum: workers needed only a place to sleep and enough food to sustain themselves. As a result, while contributing their labor power to the grandiose projects under the threat of extreme sanctions, women also had to bear children, raise them, and fulfill the domestic chores with very little help from the state or from their own husbands.

Another consequence of this neglect of social services was that jobs provided for women, either town dwellers or peasant women driven to the cities by industrialization, were narrowed down to work usually considered "male" in the West—construction, railways, or metalworking. This is the true meaning of early "feminization" of such branches, presented to the world as a proof of real emancipation and abolition of the gender labor division under socialism.

The cost of the social experiments aimed at building up social economies turned out to be very high. Millions of people died of starvation and massive displacement. As early as the mid-1930s, Stalin realized the threat of depopulation and found the family to be very useful for the creation of new lives. In 1936, abortions were abolished and sanctions against divorce (large fees) were introduced. Later on, massive losses of the population resulting from World War II and the unprecedented scale of purges laid the way for the gradual U-turn in the ideology on marriage and family. New, heavier sanctions against divorce appeared, with a necessary judicial process and fees affordable only for the most well-off. Being deeply preoccupied with the low population reproduction rates, the regime encouraged men seeking extramarital and bachelors' love affairs. The law established legal differences between the children born in wedlock and illegitimate ones. Men were released of any legal and material obligations toward the latter. Different money allowances were introduced to encourage women to have more children. Since 1944, women who gave birth to six or more children began to receive medals on a par with Heroines of Labor, ideals of the previous epoch. So the postwar period turned out, perhaps, to be the most contradictory of all in determining women's place in the Soviet society (Malysheva, 1992b: 76).

Peasant women were a particular case among the rest of the population. As a result of the mass exodus of men to the cities during industrialization, further repression, and unprecedented war losses, most of these women became the only family breadwinners. They had to perform all kinds of very hard work in the fields in order to survive. The absence of the necessary machinery or even horses exhausted them completely. It was owing to their political weakness together with physical and psychological collapse that the regime found it possible to cut the prices for agricultural products in 1956. Women as a majority of the rural population were regarded by the powers as a very tolerant and "soft" human material. Their labor was always undervalued.

The so-called residual principle of investment was used consistently by the regime. Investment in education, health, and culture was contemplated only when all economic demands connected with the state bureaucracy, the military complex, and heavy industry had been satisfied. Work of a teacher, doctor, or librarian turned out to be among the most unprestigious and low-paid in the country. Feminization of health, culture, and education became inevitable under these conditions. The Khrushchev period brought some liberal changes for women. The most important among them was legalization of abortion in 1955. It was not the result of women's struggle for their reproductive rights, but was again introduced from the top as a reaction to extremely high mortality rates among pregnant women.

Because the "women's question" has never been considered under socialism as a special issue, separate from working-class liberation, it was not taken seriously during this "thaw" period either. It was de-Stalinization of the Soviet social system that happened to be the primary concern of Khrushchev, and some gender "improvements" were merely side effects of this process.

The most tangible social contribution to the human rights of both men and women was the pension legislation in 1960 and the introduction of new passports. The latter breached the previous feudal system of residence registration and activated the territorial population's mobility. Another gender-related feature of the Khrushchev period deals with the scientific and technical progress gathering momentum on a world scale after World War II. Higher education was becoming more and more prestigious in the former Soviet Union. The rates of social mobility reached their top. Women of all sociocultural backgrounds began attending colleges and universities. Special quotas were introduced for working-class and peasant youth and for residents of the national republics, but there was no quota for women. Discrimination against them was discovered, with some delay, when the gender division in highly professional occupations became obvious. The latter were concentrated mainly in the huge military-industrial complex and in rapidly developing cosmonautics. As in western countries, these spheres were predominantly male and, best of all, financed by the state. As for women, they found themselves in the other employment world, separated from the men's: clerical jobs, and jobs in health, education, culture, and so on. As mentioned earlier, these were financed according to the residual principle.

Two main conclusions may be drawn. First, "equal pay for equal work" was not more than a constitutional declaration workable only in the very limited sector of employment. Second, purely economic foundations of the described pattern of gender labor division in the Soviet Union gave birth to rigid cultural and psychological stereotypes of "men's" and "women's" types of work. That is why doctors have been predominantly women in the former Soviet Union, though they are most often men in the West.

An irony of Soviet history is that the period of Leonid Brezhnev's stagnation was officially proclaimed "developed socialism." This definition had the direct impact on perceptions of the "women's question." The slogan "to increase female labor productivity" became the central one. Although there was a slowing down of economic growth in the country, the professional demands of women themselves remained. At the same time as this slogan was popular, there were still appeals for bigger families. Evidence has shown a slackening of population growth rates in the early 1980s. As M. Buckley wrote, "A vigorous debate ensued in which sociologists, economists, demographers, lawyers and journalists suggested how women could best combine production with reproduction" (1989: 165).

In the late 1960s and 1970s, sociological research became legitimate and many empirical surveys of women were launched. Nevertheless, this research was under the strong pressure of Marxist-Leninist theory with its economic determinism. That is why the results of this research were predetermined: "The double burden of women will be inevitably released with the development of socialist economy." A gender approach, to say nothing about feminist concepts, could never become an integral part of these methodologies. But despite it all, oppositional voices started to sound from the pages of nonacademic publicist (*samizdat*) journals. The best-known example is the publication of the Leningrad feminist-spiritual group Woman and Russia.

As with Khrushchev's coming to power, under Gorbachev the "women's question" returned to the political scene. The ambiguity of his appeals was very striking. He argued that paths into the highest levels of politics had to be open to women, and at the same time he stressed that women's duties were very different and they should be firmly rooted in the moral, spiritual, and thus private sphere. As a result, democratization reforms reduced the percentage of women at the highest levels of decision and policy making. Female membership in the old Supreme Soviet was about 33 percent, whereas in the first democratically elected congress (1989) women constituted only 15.7 percent: "Although statistically women were less represented in formal political structures, politization, in the sense of women's awareness of their exclusion and their organization, has increased. There have been two significant developments: firstly, explicit recognition of male control and secondly, action by women themselves" (Browning and Wason, 1992: 167). This action has developed into various informal women's groups and organizations with strong feminist orientations, such as the League for the Emancipation from Social Stereotypes; later it gave birth to the Independent Women's Democratic Initiative (public organization) and, in 1990, to the Moscow Center for Gender Studies (research organization) headed by A. Posadskaya.

In a new Russia, approbation of market mechanisms in the previously centrally planned economy during the presidency of Boris Yeltsin was focused mainly on the economic sphere; social programs were neglected, as is usual in Soviet history. Unawareness of the fact no social transformation is gender neutral was also typical of this period. As soon as the first redundancies from the enterprises started, women were the first to be dismissed. Ideological foundations for these actions were needed and "the postsocialist patriarchal renaissance," as A. Posadskaya put it, emerged. Later, it became universal for all practices concerning women's employment and women's social status.

The idea of women's inferiority has wider applications than the labor market. For example, the reproductive rights of women have been ignored by policy makers. Even worse, facing depopulation for the first time in Russian history and with an acute shortage of young men of call-up age, officials are fueling the ideological campaign for women's maternity as predestination. A serious practical step was taken in 1994 when abortion was excluded from the basic list of free medical services.

Although experiencing severe pressures from the top, the independent women's movement was gathering pace. The Second Women's Forum (November 1992) involved more than five hundred participants from Russia and the CIS. The forum made the women's movement socially visible regardless of political, religious, and ethnic differences among women. As a result, for the first time in Soviet history nongovernmental organizations (NGOs) have won the possibility to have their voice heard at the biggest international forums and conferences. Thus over two hundred representatives of Russian women's NGOs took part in the Fourth World Conference on Women in Beijing in September 1995.

Nevertheless, there is nothing like a unified women's movement in the country. The faction Women of Russia of the first post–Soviet State Duma elected in 1993, with its "dim" social and political preferences, did not represent women as a special part of Russia's population; moreover, the next elections in 1995 did not bring success to this political movement. Most of the existing women's groups and organizations are either absorbed in practical problems of women's survival or, if not, are deeply politically engaged but representing in this case not women's interests, but those of certain political parties and social movements.

Certain positive shifts are related to slow but steady growth in the number of researchers within academia who are working intensively on gender issues and theory. They have been contributing substantially to the change of consciousness concerning women's status through introduction of women's and gender courses into the university curricula, and publications in the academic journals, popular magazines, and newspapers. A concept of "private life" completely unfamiliar to the people who grew up under socialism is making its path to their minds. Within the framework of this concept the idea of "intimacy as democracy" creates a perspective for a new world outlook. However, the people susceptible to this are limited mainly to the most educated part of the urban centers. So, a tangible cultural and socioeconomic gap has been growing between the latter and the other part of society (especially in the countryside), which is still enormous. Its conservativeness and adherence to traditional gender roles and subordination perpetuate women's political passivity and prevent the majority of women from active citizenship.

The unpredictability of the country's future development adds to uncertainties concerning the position of women and their relation to the state in postcommunist Russia.

See Also

FEMINISM: COMMONWEALTH OF INDEPENDENT STATES

References and Further Reading

Baskakova, Marina, and Marina Malyshva, eds.. 1998. *Women's rights in Russia.* Moscow: Moscow Center for Gender Studies. (In Russian.)

Browning, Genia, and Andrew Wason. 1992. Perestroika and female politization. In David Lane, ed., *Russia in flux.* N.p.: Edward Elgar.

Buckley, Mary. 1989. *Women and ideology in the Soviet Union.* New York: Harvester Wheatsheaf.

Buckley, Mary, ed.. 1997. *Post-Soviet women: From the Baltics to Central Asia.* Cambridge: Cambridge University Press.

Kosmarskaya, Natalya. 1995. Women and ethnicity in present-day Russia: Thoughts on a given theme. In Nira Yuval-Davis et al., eds., *Crossfires: Nationalism, racism and gender in Europe,* 142–60. London: Pluto.

Malysheva, Marina. 1992a. Feminism and bolshevism: Two worlds and two ideologies. In Shirin Rai, Hilary Pilkington, and Annie Phizacklea, eds., *Women in the face of change,* 186–199. London and New York: Routledge.

———. 1992b. The politics of gender in Russia. In Allison Maggie and White Anne, eds., *Women's voice in literature and society,* 75–85. Occasional Paper no. 11. Bradford: University of Bradford.

Pilkington, Hilary. 1992. Russia and the former Soviet republics. Behind the mask of Soviet Unity: Realities of women's lives. In Cris Corrin, ed., *Superwomen and the double burden. Women's experience of change in central and eastern Europe and the former Soviet Union,* 180–235. London: Scarlet.

Posadskaya, Anastasia, ed. 1994. *Women in Russia: A new era in Russian feminism.* London: Verso.

Tokhtakhodzhaeva, Marfua. 1992/1993. Women in central Asian society. *Women Against Fundamentalism* 4: 29–31.

Voronina, Olga. 1994. Soviet women and politics: On the brink of change. In Barbara J. Nelson and Najma Chowdhury, eds., *Women and politics worldwide,* 721–737. New Haven, Conn.: Yale University Press.

Zetkin, Clara. 1984. *Selected Writings.* Ed. Philip Foner. Trans. Kai Schoenhals. New York: International.

Natalya Kosmarskaya

POLITICS AND THE STATE: East Asia

The ideological and gender character of the state are key factors in the shaping of women's political and economic roles in society. Where a state professes an ideological commitment to the liberation of women, it is likely that this will be reflected in policies and legislation facilitating the participation of women in economic and public life. The different forms of patriarchy within particular states contribute in turn to diverse manifestations of gender inequality in state structures, policy, and society. The role of women in politics, both in the formal arena of government and parties and in the broader sphere of social movements and protest, is likewise a crucial ingredient in the construction of gender issues and policy.

The impact of the state on women and the political role of women in pursuing their gender interests are explored in this article with reference to east Asia, that is, China, North and South Korea, Japan, Taiwan, and Hong Kong. Apart from their geographical proximity these states have in common a patriarchal tradition of Confucianist ethics and Buddhism, historical encounters with imperialist powers, and integration into the contemporary global division of labor. Since World War II they have been divided primarily along ideological lines, with North Korea and China in the socialist camp and Taiwan, Hong Kong, Japan, and South Korea pursuing capitalist strategies of development. Whereas China has embarked on a market-oriented program of reform since 1978, North Korea has been far more averse to any radical change.

In line with Confucianist values of filial piety and male superiority, women in East Asia have historically been subject to the "three obediences," obeying their fathers in childhood, their husbands upon marriage, and their sons once widowed. This pattern of female subordination within the family has in turn reflected a more general subordination within society and contributed toward the gendered construction of the state (Carney and O'Kelly, 1990: 113–118). In all East Asian states women are underrepresented both in formal politics and in the administration. In 1994, women in Japan and South Korea made up only 8 percent and 3 percent, respectively, of parliamentary representatives (Neft and Levine, 1997: 24). In the socialist states of China and North Korea the figures stood higher, at 21 percent and 20 percent, respectively. The statistics for China and North Korea thus suggest that the ideological commitment of the state to the liberation of women can be a significant counterforce to the ongoing influence of patriarchal values in society.

Looking more closely at China, it should be noted that this ideological commitment still has to contend with deep-seated patriarchal beliefs and attitudes. Since its early days of government in the 1930s, the Chinese Communist Party has advocated greater participation of women in political and economic life. Once it took power in 1949, it began to implement policies aimed at drawing women into the workforce and engaging them in political activity. Despite the relatively high number of female parliamentarians in China, as in other socialist states, women's interests have tended to remain subordinate to those of the party and nation. Although women have reached leadership positions within the party, they have still remained in a minority. Not only have they been consistently underrepresented in the Politburo, the highest level of party and state, but they have also tended to occupy vice-ministerial rather than ministerial positions, reflecting their overall subordinate position to men and the patriarchal nature of the state. At present there is not a single woman on the Politburo Standing Committee. So although the official ideology of the state is an important factor affecting the political status of women, contending beliefs and values regarding women's roles in the family and society also undermine its potential impact.

As well as influencing the role of women in political life, the state also can have a crucial impact on their participation in the waged economy. By ideologically advocating the right of women to work, passing legislation on equal opportunities and supporting preschool childcare, the state can encourage women to enter waged employment. There are clear differences among the East Asian states regarding their economic participation rates, which relate in part to their differing ideological imperatives. In China and North Korea, for example, 80 percent and 65 percent of women aged over 15 years were economically active in 1994 (Neft and Levine, 1997: 56–57). This is clearly linked to the explicit policies of the Chinese Communist Party to draw women into the workforce, such as ideological pressure, provision of state-run child care facilities and breast-feeding periods during work. In Japan however, only 50 percent of women were economically active (Neft and Levine, 1997: 57).

Japanese companies have pursued formal and informal policies of not employing married or childrearing women or women over 25 years old, thus barring a significant number of women from long-term employment and consigning them to temporary and insecure work as a convenient reserve army of labor (Carney and O'Kelly, 1990: 236). Despite the passing of the Equal Employment Opportunity Law in 1985, discriminatory employment practices persist. However, shortages of skilled labor may push employers to recruit more women (Brinton, 1993: 234). The failure of the state to provide any extensive child care provision coupled with the tendency for Japanese women to take on prime responsibility for childrearing and care of the elderly is reflected in the high level of female part-time employment, particularly among married women (Brinton, 1993: 136).

Not only do participation rates vary across East Asia but there are also considerable differences in male and female wages. In Hong Kong, for example, the nonagricultural wage of women was 69.5 percent that of men's (United Nations Development Program [UNDP], 1995: 36). Despite China's legal and ideological commitment to equality, the average wage of women in 1997 was 59.4 percent that of men's, barely higher than South Korea's rate of 54 percent (Neft and Levine, 1997: 71; UNDP, 1995: 36). In all East Asian states this income inequality was matched by a predominance of women in low-waged and less senior positions. In Japan and South Korea, for example, women were concentrated in the bottom echelons of occupational hierarchies (Nam, 1994: 62). Only 15.9 percent of women in Hong Kong in 1994 and a mere 4.1 percent in South Korea in 1997 were employed as administrators and managers in 1994 (Neft and Levine, 1997: 69; UNDP, 1995: 69).

Although the percentage of women in East Asia in the waged labor force has increased dramatically in the post-World War II era, this has not necessarily translated into an equally marked rise in the participation of women in the political sphere. Confucianist values, family expectations, and patriarchal attitudes toward the public roles of women have combined to constrain the political engagement of women. In Hong Kong and Taiwan, for example, women workers are pushed into employment as part of a more general family strategy to accumulate resources that are then reinvested in male offspring (Cammack, Pool, and Tordoff, 1993: 219–226; Gallin, 1990: 189–190).

With regard to globalization and in particular the Export Processing Zones, the states of East Asia, regardless of their acclaimed ideological hues, have tended to collude with capital in ensuring a supply of cheap labor. Young, unmarried women, often from the rural areas, form the bulk of the labor force in these special enclaves of foreign investment. They are employed mainly in light industrial sectors such as electronics, toys, textiles, garments, and household appliances. Working longer than average hours, pressed to do overtime, and subject on occasions to sexual harassment, these women are particularly exposed to poor health and safety conditions. A spate of work accidents and fires in factories across East Asia has put pressure on the host governments to take a more active role in the protection of these women's interests. After a fire killed 84 women workers in a joint venture toy factory in southern China in November, 1993, for example, the national and local governments introduced legislation to protect the interests of female workers and spell out more clearly the legal responsibilities of foreign investors.

As well as influencing the gender aspects in the sphere of production, the state also plays a key role in controlling reproduction and the consequences of this for women. In East Asia the family plays an integral role in maintaining social order and cohesion. Relationships within the family tend to be ordered in line with Confucianist values of hierarchy, obedience, respect for age, and male superiority. Most of the East Asian states have passed legislation banning child labor and polygamy, promoting sexual equality, and facilitating divorce. In China, for example, the 1950 Marriage Law enabled women to divorce and choose their marriage partners, prohibited child marriage and arranged marriages, and abolished the betrothal gift (Croll, 1983: 75–76). The new post-World War II Japanese constitution also gave women freedom of choice in marriage as well as equal rights to divorce, although the continuing stigma of divorce has kept rates low compared with other industrialized countries.

With regard to family planning, only China has implemented a distinct policy that seeks to limit the size of the family, underlining the ways in which state power is used to configure family relations.

The "one child per family" policy has attempted to limit the number of children. Although the policy has met with success in the urban areas, the difficulties of enforcing it in rural areas has led to some relaxation. The decollectivization of land to the household during the reform era has increased the demand for male labor and so runs contrary to the restrictive family planning policy. Since the late 1980s local regulations have permitted rural residents to have a second child when the first is a girl. One sad consequence of this policy has been an increase in female infanticide. Despite state condemnation of this abhorrent practice and the efforts of the Chinese Communist Party to improve the status of women, the resurfacing of this phenomenon in the 1980s and 1990s testifies to the extent to which women continue to be undervalued.

Having explored the various ways in which the state has impacted on women, it is essential also to consider how women have attempted to influence the state. Of concern here are the role of women's groups and movements in East Asia in raising gender issues as well as the part played by women in other mass movements such as peace campaigns, environmental groups, and trade unions. How much women can influence state policy depends to a large extent on their ability to organize, which in turn is conditioned by the development of civil society, the centrality of the patriarchal family, and the character of the political system. Here again there are some important differences among the East Asian states that are linked to the nature of their respective regimes and patriarchal traditions. In North Korea and China, the Communist Party has tended to dominate society, leaving little room for any bottom-up, voluntary activity. Women's interests are thus articulated and represented by one mass organization sponsored by the state in China, the All-China Women's Federation. The spread of the market in post-Mao China has served, however, to open up spaces where women have begun to organize themselves (Howell, 1996). Given that the All-China Women's Federation is an integral component of the political system and that the party and state are closely fused, the federation has historically tended to prioritize party policy over gender interest. Moreover, the All-China Women's Federation has begun to act more autonomously and give priority to addressing women's diverse needs (Howell, 1997). The 1995 UN fourth World Conference on Women, held in Beijing, was an important catalyst in this process.

Until the recent elections, Taiwan was also an authoritarian one-party state but, unlike North Korea and China, pursued a capitalist path of development. Here, too, the lack of a vibrant civil society was reflected in the sparsity and weakness of nonstate women's groups, which was in turn reinforced by the dominance of the patriarchal household. Although Hong Kong only began to hold elections in the 1990s, the sphere of voluntary organizations, including women's groups, has been more pronounced than in neighboring China. In Japan, too, women have had more space to organize campaigns and groups than in the one-party regimes of China, Taiwan, and North Korea.

Given the political constraints on voluntary, bottom-up activity in the one-party states of East Asia, it is not too surprising to find that a grassroots feminist movement has grown up more rapidly in Japan, Hong Kong, and South Korea than in China or North Korea. These groups have raised a range of issues such as the quest for compensation for "comfort women" exploited by the Japanese army in World War II, improved employment conditions for women factory workers, and an end to sex tourism by Japanese males. For example, in South Korea the *minjung* feminist movement campaigned intensively on the issue of comfort women, lobbying the government to increase its efforts to seek reparations from Japan for the survivors of this prostitution (Louie, 1995: 424). In Hong Kong, the Association for the Advancement of Feminism has campaigned on sexual abuse, sexual discrimination, women's rights, and sexist language in children's textbooks. In Japan, feminist groups have lobbied government on issues such as the sex industry, violence against women, and discriminatory employment practices.

Women are also evident in other political movements such as the peace movement, union struggles, and environmental campaigns. For example, one of the main leaders in the 1989 Student Democracy Movement in China was Chai Ling, who was forced to escape the country. Women in Japan have campaigned vociferously against nuclear power. In South Korea, Hong Kong, and Japan, women activists have played a crucial role in protecting the rights of female workers.

To conclude, women in East Asia have both affected state policies and borne the consequences of the state construction of gender issues. Influenced by Confucianism, patriarchy, colonialism, and contemporary globalization, women in East Asia have been pushed increasingly onto the political stage. Although the representation of women in formal politics leaves much to be desired, the increasing participation of women in the nonformal arena of movements, campaigns, and voluntary groups could provide the training ground for a more active formal role later on.

See Also

DEVELOPMENT: CHINA; DEVELOPMENT: JAPAN; FEMINISM: CHINA; FEMINISM: JAPAN; WOMEN'S STUDIES: EAST ASIA

References and Further Reading

Brinton, M. C. 1993. *Women and the economic miracle: Gender and work in postwar Japan.* Berkeley: University of California Press.

Cammack, P., D. Pool, and W. Tordoff. 1993. *Third world politics: A comparative introduction.* New York: Macmillan.

Carney, L. S., and G. O'Kelly. 1990. Women's work and women's place in the Japanese economic miracle. In K. Ward, ed., *Women workers and global restructuring,* 113–148. Ithaca, N.Y.: ILR Press, Cornell University.

Croll, E. 1983. *Chinese women since Mao.* London: Zed.

Gallin, R. S. 1990. Women and the export industry in Taiwan. In K. Ward, ed., *Women workers and global restructuring,* 179–192. Ithaca, N.Y.: ILR Press, Cornell University.

Howell, J. 1996. The struggle for survival: Prospects for the All-China Women's Federation. *World Development* 24.

———. 1997. Post-Beijing reflections: Creating ripples, but not waves in China. *Women's Studies International Forum* 20 (2): 235–252.

Louie, M. C. Y. 1995. *Minjung* feminism: Korean women's movement for gender and class liberation. *Women's Studies International Forum* 18 (4): 417–430.

Nam, J. L. 1994. Women's role in export dependence and state control of labour unions in South Korea. *Women's Studies International Forum* 17 (1): 57–67.

Neft, Naomi, and Ann D. Levine. 1997. Where women stand. In *Evaluation and report on the state of women in 140 countries, 1997–1998.* New York: Random House.

UNICEF. 1995. *The progress of nations 1995.* New York: Author.

United Nations Development Program. 1995. *Human development report 1995.* New York: Oxford University Press.

Jude Howell

POLITICS AND THE STATE: Eastern Europe

The communist party-states that ruled in eastern Europe between roughly 1945 and 1989—the German Democratic Republic (GDR), Poland, Hungary, Czechoslovakia, Romania, Bulgaria, Yugoslavia, and Albania—claimed that they had resolved the "woman question" with the emancipation of women under socialism. Although the reality fell far short of the promise, these states did achieve impressive levels of gender equity in education and employment. They also provided women with widespread access to abortion, legalized divorce, and a range of social welfare benefits. Many of these gains came under threat in the dual economic and political transitions that took place after the 1980s throughout the region, but that has not significantly mobilized women to enter politics.

All of the communist party-states maintained national legislatures, which had, on average, around 30 percent female representation. This average dropped to only 10 percent in founding democratic elections. The decline was most pronounced in 1990 in Romania, Albania, and Macedonia, where women's share of legislative seats dropped to around 3 percent. Despite a general upward trajectory since the fall of communism (Macedonia and Romania have doubled the number of women they elect), eastern European legislatures still lag behind many of the western parliaments. Eastern European women also are noticeably underrepresented among political executives, party and chamber leaders, and (with the partial exception of Poland and Hungary) local governments.

The bulk of scholarly attention regarding women and politics in eastern Europe has focused on the lack of effective women's political organization and the absence of a second-wave feminist movement. For a variety of historical and sociocultural reasons, women in eastern Europe have experienced emancipation as a process handed down from above. There have been significant constraints on the development of feminist consciousness and political movements. That legacy continues to shape women's political participation at the turn of the twenty-first century.

The Precommunist Legacy

In the nineteenth century, many of the western nations developed so-called first-wave feminist movements. Women came together to demand that the state extend full citizenship rights (particularly the franchise but often a range of other social and economic rights) to women. Eastern Europe during this period was still heavily influenced and often directly controlled by foreign and decidedly undemocratic powers. Where the struggle against national oppression was most central—for example, Poland, Czech lands, and Slovenia—radical women subordinated their interests to the cause of nation building. Elsewhere, particularly in the southern-tier Balkan region (Albania, Romania, Bulgaria, and parts of Yugoslavia), women lacked the resources necessary to organize. Prior to World War II, women in the Balkans (with the exception of Slovenia) were less educated and less literature than women in most of Europe. Particularly in Albania and the Muslim enclaves of Yugoslavia, gender roles remained highly traditional until World War II. Women produced large families, lived in multigeneration families, and were subject to the will of clan patriarchs.

By the turn of the century, upper-class women in Poland, the German lands, and Hungary had begun to form women's associations, such as literary circles and charitable associations. Some of these groups allied themselves with the women's liberation movements of the day. They called for female franchise and expanded educational and occupational opportunities for women, arguing that educated citizenship would help women in their role as mothers. Women's rights were framed in terms of family and social needs. There was no eastern European equivalent of the Anglo-American or Scandinavian radical suffragist or even the Russian emancipated woman. Such a development would have been impossible in light of the excessive influence exerted by foreign powers, limitations on civil society, and the conservative values of predominately agrarian societies in the region.

At the end of World War I, Allied victors contrived a set of new east European states from the territorial remains of the vanquished Hapsburg, Ottoman, and Prussian empires. The resolution of the statehood question might have provided the space in which a women's movement could develop. All of the new states were set up as democratic republics or constitutional monarchies; in 1919, women were granted the right to vote in Czechoslovakia, Poland, and Germany. Democracy, however, did not last long in eastern Europe. All of the new states (with the exception of Czechoslovakia) fell quickly to rightist authoritarian regimes that restricted citizen participation. Women in Hungary and the Balkans did not receive the vote until after World War II, and, even then, it was handed down rather than won through a long and organized struggle. This pattern of emancipation from above continued when the communists took over.

The Legacy of Directive Emancipation

The Soviet Union liberated eastern Europe (with the exception of Yugoslavia and Albania) from fascist rule and used this as a pretext to encourage and, in some cases, directly install Stalinist regimes. Adoption of the Stalinist model brought with it a high degree of ideological uniformity in the satellite states. With regard to women, this meant the Engelsian view that women's emancipation comes through participation in the productive labor force and a socialization of "women's work." The state would provide day care centers, canteens, prepackaged foods, and a range of social welfare benefits. All of this would allow women, in the words of Engels, to focus on household duties only to a minor degree. In turn, women's interests would become like those of other social groups (workers, peasants, young people). Like those groups, women were given official interest organizations within the party-state bureaucracy. They also were guaranteed representation in elected legislatures.

In practice, political representation was little more than democratic window dressing. Quotas in single-candidate races ensured that women would sit in parliament, but the legislatures themselves held little real power, primarily serving to rubber-stamp decisions made elsewhere. Women in these marginal legislatures were excluded from leadership positions and sometimes referred to pejoratively as "milkmaid politicians."

Emancipation was very often reduced to the duty of paid labor force participation. Yet women were disproportionately concentrated in low-skill and low-wage jobs and had difficulty moving into management positions. Women missed far more days of work than men, owing to maternity leave and days off to care for sick children. As a result, the very policies that were intended to liberate women became a liability. Economic stagnation under central planning led to inadequate and insufficiently available social services, although this varied across the region. In places such as the GDR, the state was able to make good on many of its social welfare commitments to women. Women in the poorer Balkan nations, however, frequently had to supplement the family income with unpaid labor, such as growing and canning food and sewing clothes; research shows that even women in the more generous welfare states worried about the low quality of and restricted access to child care.

Women suffered under an extreme form of the dual burden—working full days, having babies, and doing the bulk of the cooking, cleaning, and child care. The burden tripled when the expectation for women, like all socialist citizens, to engage in political activity was factored in. The result was that eastern European women lacked leisure time and suffered disproportionately from exhaustion and depression. This was particularly severe for lower-class and minority women; studies conducted in Poland and Hungary in the early 1980s indicated that single mothers were particularly likely to be poor. Official women's organizations were widely seen as out of touch with these issues, but alternative forms of political organization were prohibited.

In a sense, directive emancipation may be seen as part of a broader Leninist condescension. Just as the Communist Party knew what was best for workers; it also knew what would emancipate women. The direct input of women in designing policies on women's issues was, for all practical purposes, unnecessary. In a classic instance of this thinking, the Hungarian Socialist Worker's Party suspended the activities of the official women's organization for a brief period after 1956, claiming that the woman question had been resolved.

It has been argued by some feminists that directive emancipation failed to liberate women, because it was never really designed to do so. Rather, women formed a "reserve army" of labor that could be readily mobilized to help with socialist construction (industrialization). When the state's needs changed—when extensive development strategies were exhausted and birthrates began to decline—women were demobilized through extended maternity leaves and protective legislation. Nicolai Ceaucescu's radical pronatalist policies in Romania are an extreme case. For example, women were routinely subjected to workplace pelvic examinations to prevent them from terminating unwanted pregnancies.

In fact, the communists' economistic approach to women's liberation actually tended to reinforce traditional gender roles. The dual worker-mother role was enshrined in legislation, but there was no equivalent transformation of men's roles in the family and home. Even in places such as Yugoslavia and Albania, where women had actively fought in the communist resistance to fascism, the assumption was that, once the war was over, women would return to their natural place. Despite the formal ideological commitment to women's equality, women's demands were easily reduced to consumer interests and accorded low priority in the communist systems.

Postcommunist Eastern Europe

The practice of directive emancipation and the excessive control of the state over society prevented the development of a second-wave feminist movement of the type that transformed women's political involvement in the United States and western Europe. Civil society had been severely curtailed in communist Poland and Hungary; it was virtually nonexistent in Bulgaria, Albania, Romania, and post-1968 Czechoslovakia. Where opposition to communist rule did emerge, as with the Solidarity movement in Poland, women participated in roughly equal numbers with men. Women, however, rarely held leadership positions, and women's issues were subordinated to broader concerns about human rights and national oppression.

Dissident activities in Poland, Hungary, and Czechoslovakia were explicitly antipolitical and treated private life as a sphere of genuine social interaction, protected from and subversive to the totalitarian state. Women had an important role in these movements: they maintained the home, raised children in the national culture, and provided material and emotional support for persecuted men. This was political mobilization of a sort, but, unlike the activities of women in the contemporary Latin American transitions to democracy, it did not prepare women to exert themselves in a pluralist and competitive political landscape.

When democratic transition came, women were distrustful of politics and skeptical of feminism. The feminist language of gender equality and sisterhood had been coopted by the communists, and many women were tired of being "emancipated" in that way. Because women had only a limited role in bringing down communist rule, they were largely absent from the leadership of new political parties, and they were left out of the roundtable negotiations that established democratic political institutions. In the GDR, women did make a successful last-moment bid to be included in roundtable talks, but they were rapidly pushed to the sidelines of debate.

Traditionalism and patriarchal attitudes had never been uprooted by the communist experiment with directive emancipation. Indeed, social opposition to communism emerged, at least in part, from a critique of the communist system's effect on society, particularly its role in creating a crisis of family life. It is little surprise, then, that nationalism and market consumerism have emerged as the dominant ideological alternatives in the vacuum left by the demise of communism. The nationalist movements, in conjunction with freshly legitimated traditional churches, seek to redefine women's social roles, from "worker-mother" to "mother of the nation." Clear evidence of this can be found in the debates surrounding new, more restrictive abortion legislation.

Marketization, for its part, has been accompanied by a commodification of women's bodies—as witnessed in the explosion of pornography, sex trade, mail-order bride services, and cosmetic surgery—and a rollback of the welfare state. The loss of social welfare benefits has a painful impact on women, who are the majority of welfare clients and employees. The platforms of new political parties, however, often tell women that these concerns must wait until after the market transition has been achieved.

The universal solution offered to women by the new market ideology is not much different from the promises of emancipation made by the communists. Women will be relieved of the double burden through the ability to purchase household conveniences. As with the communist project, there is no fundamental reevaluation of gender roles. The affluence promised by marketization will solve the problems of women, problems primarily seen as consumer demands. In turn, once women are relieved of the necessity of work outside the home, numerous social ills (high divorce rates, single motherhood, broken families, and declining birthrates) will be mended.

The man who can afford to keep his wife at home may have become the emblem of the market revolution but, for most women, retreat into the private sphere is a luxury that they and their families can scarcely afford. Women can, however, retreat from the burden of political activity, and several studies conclude that this is precisely what they have done. The disappearance of women in politics is explained as part of a dual process in which women voluntarily withdraw from public life and are pushed from it by voters who are "allergic to feminism."

It is difficult to empirically verify whether women have indeed withdrawn from political life, but papers presented in 1999 at a conference on women's representation in the postcommunist systems suggest that voter backlash is not as widespread as we might expect. There is certainly ample evidence in some of the postcommunist countries that voters regard "being male" as a qualification for office, but there is no clear evidence that voters carry these sexist attitudes into the ballot box any more than western voters do. Electoral results from Hungary, Poland, Germany, the Czech Republic, and Slovakia reveal that when women are placed in winnable candidacies, they fare about as well as their male counterparts. In Hungary's elections of 1998, for example, women were roughly 9 percent of the strong candidate pool (candidates with a mathematical chance of entering the legislature) and ultimately won slightly over 8 percent of the seats.

As in the established democracies, the chief barrier to women's participation appears to be the nomination phase. There are probably many reasons why party gatekeepers are reluctant to recruit women. In the poorest countries (for example, Albania, Romania, and Macedonia), women may lack the kinds of resources and attributes party gatekeepers find attractive. The prevalence of traditional gender role expectations may lead party gatekeepers to view women as "risky" candidates, whether or not they actually lose votes; and political parties vary in the degree to which they have an ideological commitment to women's equality. New Left Green parties are explicitly committed to gender equality, but these parties are usually marginal. Reformed (and not-so-reformed) communist parties are formally committed to women's representation and, in some instances, have adopted quotas for female representation on the party lists. Rightist and nationalist parties, by contrast, take a more traditional view of appropriate social roles for women. The success of conservative and nationalist groups in founding elections helps to explain the initial decline in female representation; the renaissance of the Left may help to explain the upward trend in female recruitment over the postcommunist period.

Perhaps the most powerful explanation of discrimination against women in the nomination stage has to do with the lack of organized feminist movements in the region. Women's groups within and outside the parties are weak, and the few women in leadership positions do not want to be labeled as feminists. As a result, parties do not feel pressure to balance their tickets with women, even when they have the opportunity to do so. In the West, second-wave feminist movements transformed and expanded women's access to political power. Perhaps the mobilization of women around traditional values in eastern Europe will lead to a growing feminist consciousness and something like a feminist movement. Women involved in local politics in Hungary and Poland, for example, may begin to work their way up in their parties and to view themselves as women's representatives. The curtailment of abortion and social welfare rights—rights that women took for granted because they never fought for them—may provide a catalyst for women's organization. To date, however, explicitly feminist organizations have little popular support (outside the efforts of western feminists) and little impact on public policy.

See Also

COMMUNISM; FEMINISM: COMMONWEALTH OF INDEPENDENT STATES; FEMINISM: EASTERN EUROPE; HOUSEHOLDS AND FAMILIES: CENTRAL AND EASTERN EUROPE; MARXISM; POLITICS AND THE STATE: COMMONWEALTH OF INDEPENDENT STATES; SOCIALISM; WOMEN'S STUDIES: CENTRAL AND EASTERN EUROPE

References and Further Reading

Einhorn, Barbara. 1993. *Cinderella goes to market: Citizenship, gender, and women's movements in east central Europe.* London: Verso.

Funk, Nanette, and Magda Mueller, eds. 1993. *Gender politics and postcommunism.* New York: Routledge.

Renne, Tanya. 1997. *Ana's land: Sisterhood in eastern Europe.* Boulder, Col.: Westview.

Rueschemeyer, Marilyn, ed. 1996. *Women in the politics of postcommunist eastern Europe.* Armonk, N.Y.: Sharpe.

Waylen, Georgina. 1994. Women and democratization: Conceptualizing gender relations in transition politics. *World Politics* 46(3): 327–354.

Wolchik, Sharon L., and Alfred G. Meyer, eds. 1985. *Women, state and party in eastern Europe.* Durham, N.C.: Duke University Press.

Women's political representation in eastern Europe: Ten years after the fall. 1999. Papers presented at International Conference, Bergen, Norway.

Kathleen Montgomery

POLITICS AND THE STATE: Middle East and North Africa

The *Middle East,* a term originally given to the area making up British military presence during World War II, is a vast area. Although this was never clearly delineated, it is generally assumed that the Middle East includes all Arab states—Yemen, Oman, Saudi Arabia, Kuwait, Bahrain, United Arab Emirates, Qatar, Iraq, Syria, Lebanon, Palestinian National Authority, Jordan, Egypt, Libya, Morocco, Tunisia, Algeria, and Sudan—as well as Israel, Iran, and Turkey. Among the peoples of the Middle East are those who remain "stateless." These include the Palestinians (who at the turn of the twenty-first century have yet to have their own state as such, but do have a National Authority), the Kurds (dispersed all over the region with large numbers in Turkey and Iraq), and the Sahrawis (in the western Sahara). Stateless peoples are also an important feature of conflicts in the region as well as resultant dynamics of globalization, which are elaborated below.

Straddling parts of the African and Asian continents, the Middle East is home to an area of tremendous cultural, political, social, and economic diversity. Among the aspects that most countries have in common are ancient civilizations, a history of colonialism, and—one of its most enduring legacies—both inter- and intrastate conflicts. Colonialism also led to a large body of the "knowledge" that existed for a long time on the Middle East. Partly as a result of this knowledge, the Middle East also became known, in popular western imagination, as "the Orient," the East—with often conflicting stereotypes, passed off as typical characteristics of the "Oriental other." Among these were gendered notions such as violence, poverty, ignorance, and cunning, mixed with exoticism, mysteriousness, lust, and appeal. Colonialism was also the era when a certain kind of feminist consciousness was born, in tandem with a strong sense of national consciousness.

The Birth of a Feminist Consciousness

Contemporary records of women's political participation in the early twentieth century will cite nationalist movements as significant moments of mobilization. As with many other nationalist movements elsewhere, women of the Middle East both assumed and were promised equality of rights as a result of their participation in these struggles. In most of the ensuing nationalist struggles, however, a constant factor was the low priority given to women's demands—often by the women activists themselves. The national question consistently superseded the women's question. Hence, in most countries, total equality did not materialize postindependence. These movements did, however, constitute modern women's demands for specific rights and opportunities, such as education, suffrage, and employment.

The middle of the twentieth century witnessed a number of different events: the independence of some countries after the end of World War II, the declaration of the state of Israel and ensuing Arab-Israeli wars, a move on the part of Turkey to a closer rapport with emerging NATO countries, and nationalist politicians emerging as authoritarian leaders in Syria, Iraq, Egypt, Iran, and Turkey. By the 1960s, many Middle Eastern countries were experimenting with various forms of socialism and socialist policies, in tandem with intensive industrialization policies and land reforms. Apart from other major repercussions, one of the noteworthy features of such developments is that Middle Eastern women were drawn into the labor market in increasing numbers. This economic involvement was not so much a feminist awareness on the part of socialist regimes as an economic necessity (more people were needed to turn the wheels of economic modernization) that formed the basis for what later came to be referred to as "state feminism." The latter is therefore a feature of political expediency mixed with economic necessity and is above all controlled by regimes that tend toward authoritarianism. State feminism still flourishes in many parts of the Middle East, largely as a result of the fact that many regimes will often employ feminist rhetoric (equality in representation, development, and decision-making power) when it suits their needs.

Equality between the Sexes

Most Middle Eastern countries have enshrined equality between the sexes in their respective constitutions (with the exception of some Arab Gulf countries, some of whom do not have a constitution). Yet what is available in law has not been made available in practice. Equal pay laws are also in existence, a feature few people in the western world are aware of and some western countries have yet to achieve themselves. The labor markets of most Middle Eastern countries are full of women and men—a fact belabored by some right-wing religious groups in the mid-1980s in particular. Moreover, there is an increasing tendency in most of the universities in the region to have a larger number of female students enrolled than males, and faculty and staff in many of these universities, more often than not, are tending toward an almost 50:50 male-female breakdown. Other professional women (for example, doctors, lawyers, engineers, and entrepreneurs) are also an increasing feature of the Middle Eastern landscape, as are the multitudes of women active within civil society. In fact, nongovernmental organizations are teeming with women activists, working on a range of empowerment issues—from education and health to environment and elections, and from income-generating projects to national campaigns for democracy and human rights.

Nevertheless, figures still point to high rates of illiteracy: as of 1990 women in many Middle Eastern countries had a range of 51 to 75 percent illiteracy, with 26 to 50 percent in the relatively better conditions of countries such as Iran, Turkey, Syria, Jordan, and Libya. Even more disturbing, figures for poverty rates tend to be almost unavailable for most of the countries, and where available point to levels that range from 26 to 75 percent of women living below the poverty lines (Seager, 1997: 26–28).

The Political Is Important

Despite the fact that by the 1970s most Middle Eastern women had achieved the right to vote, be educated, and work, their overall social and economic standing, although undoubtedly improving in relative terms, does not reflect general well-being. In addition, figures indicate that as far as parliamentary representation is concerned, Middle Eastern women are nowhere near the 30 percent threshold advocated by the United Nations in its Human Development Report of 1995. Indeed, in countries such as Kuwait, women are still not entitled to vote, and in most Arab countries, the regional rate of parliamentary representation is among the lowest in the world (at 3 percent). In only three Middle Eastern countries have women arrived at top decision-making posts: Prime Minister Golda Meir in Israel in the 1970s, Prime Minister Tansu Ciller in Turkey in the 1990s, and one of Iran's current vice-presidents (as of this writing), Dr. Masooreh Ebtekar, appointed in August 1997. In addition, Middle Eastern states appear to be divided in equal numbers between those who have signed and ratified the Convention for the Elimination of All Forms of Discrimination Against Women (CEDAW) and those who have neither signed nor ratified it.

Many scholars and activists alike point out that those women who have "arrived" at positions of political decision making (for example, as members of political parties and parliaments, ministers, and judges), have done so largely as a result of state support. Despite the low overall figures for women's access to institutional state politics, many of the rights women have today tend to be largely as a result of moves undertaken by the state. Activists are quick to point out that because women have yet to form strong political constituencies in the region, the reliance on the state for support and promotion has not diminished.

Women's lack of equal political clout has a great deal to do with the quantity and quality of women already in leadership positions, with class differences among women, and with broader political considerations. Most Middle Eastern women are united in their complaint that the cultures of their respective countries remain very male-dominated and, as such, are not conducive to women's public roles. Among the many consequences of this is the fact that few women feel encouraged to run for public offices, and those who do find it very difficult to muster all the relevant resources. In some countries, this also means that many of the women who "make it" to these positions can be appointed rather than elected.

The low number of women in political positions also means that few of them are encouraged to take political risks for women's issues, and in fact, many of them fear—rightly, as it turns out—marginalization and isolation from their male colleagues were they to do so. It is indeed the case that many within the general Middle Eastern electorate are not attracted by women politicians, especially if the latter's message revolves around the often scoffed at (and least understood) "women's issues." These are some of the reasons why activists tend to criticize politicians as "token" women and to see them as unrepresentative of women's interests. Indeed, some studies emphasize that most of the women politicians (and some of the most vocal activists) tend to be from the middle or upper classes. These class differences are not much different from the situation in the early parts of the twentieth century.

Moreover, many activists point out—and some women politicians themselves readily admit—that women who achieve political prominence are not always as experienced and capable as their male colleagues. In addition to this, few governments in the Middle East are prepared to invest in state-funded training and enhancement programs for their women (and sometimes even for the men) politicians. In other words, women politicians can often be disadvantaged by a number of factors: male-dominated culture, lack of sufficient political expertise, lack of access to enough resources, and lack of a dependable constituency.

Broader factors relating to women's political participation in the Middle East revolve around the region's generally lackluster record in democracy and human rights. Few countries in the Middle East are fully democratic as regards free and fair elections for overall leadership and state legislatures and the major human rights of their citizens. In fact, most states tend to control and dominate their citizens in some form or another. This often leads many women in the region to be simultaneously part of women's groups and human rights' and other organizations, maintaining that increased overall democratization is a prerequisite for any improvement in women's status.

The nondemocratic structures in many Middle Eastern countries (in particular countries like Iran, Turkey, Egypt, and Algeria) have also raised serious questions regarding state legitimacy. Few countries in the region feel completely legitimate in the eyes of their citizens (this is particularly true of several Arab countries). This factor, combined with a broader disillusion with liberalism and socialism as ideologies capable of engendering political, social, and economic change, led to the emergence of Islamic movements of opposition. These movements were given a boost by the success of the Iranian revolution in 1979, and many of them became particularly popular in the mid-1980s. Some of these movements persist today—although they are less widespread—in the form of Islamist groups and organizations. The later are very diverse and are also referred to as followers of "political Islam," or groups that espouse Islamic slogans for political ends and, to all intents and purposes, function as political parties of opposition. Islamist groups have fared differently. In Algeria, the Islamic Salvation Front's almost certain electoral victory was denied by the military intervention to cancel these elections in 1992. On the other hand, the Lebanese and Jordanian Islamists (Hezbullah and the Muslim Brotherhood, respectively) managed to get a few of their members elected to parliament. In Turkey, the Welfare Party was elected with six million votes at the end of 1995 and came to power as part of a short-lived coalition, which was brought down through the military's intervention.

Some Middle Eastern women felt that the traditional and vague notions of "woman's place" (primarily in the home as a wife and mother) that some Islamists touted threatened to end all the rights women had acquired over the years. Accordingly, these women organized and lobbied against Islamist parties and Islamisms with unrelenting energy. Other women, however, were attracted by the message of alternative activism, prospects of change, and religious purity that some Islamists espoused, and joined these movements. Whether the women were with them or against them, however, the results were a catalyst for increased feminist activism, including the creation of new alliances within each country as well as across the Middle East. The Beijing World Women's Conference in 1995, for instance, was a forum where anti-Islamist and pro-Islamist women from across the Middle East were able to both form and cement alliances, as well as vigorously demonstrate their respective standpoints.

The Effect of Globalization

Globalization has manifested itself for women in the region in a number of ways. On one hand, the technological revolution has meant that some Middle Eastern women are able to fine-tune and benefit from networking with their sisters within and outside of the region. This form of activity also enables more women to gain access to possible opportunities to improve their skills and enhance their exposure to stronger constituencies. On the other hand, access to technology is perhaps one of the most important factors that discriminate against women from different backgrounds. In short, few women actually have access to technology, and the gap between the "haves" and the "have nots" increases the gap between different women and further disadvantages (and silences) the poorer ones.

The globalization of the economic markets is also having a direct impact on many women in the Middle East. Some small businesses in several Middle Eastern countries are being forced out as a result of severe competition from outside the region. In addition, policies of the International Monetary Fund and the World Bank encouraging privatization mean that more public enterprises are becoming privately owned. In both instances, women are losing out: as small business owners and as employees subject to privatized businesses, many of whose owners either prefer not to hire women or can afford to ignore stipulations for hours, wages, and maternity-leave previously afforded by public enterprises.

Another feature of globalization has to do with mobility: both the movement abroad of women from the Middle East and the influx of other women to the Middle East. With respect to the former, a large number of women currently live in the diaspora, as a result of either voluntary migration or involuntary movements of people such as refugees (for example, Palestinians, Kurds, and Iranians). Although this tends to be seen primarily in terms of a "brain drain"—when it is noted at all—this is also an untapped potential resource in terms of information exchange and networking. As for the influx of women to the Middle East, the main source of this is Asian women (for example, from Sri Lanka, the Philippines, and South Korea) who come to the region largely as domestics. The lack of attention to these women and the lack of services provided by their employers are serious enough, but for the various Middle Eastern women's movements to ignore their presence is an indictment of these organizations' objectives, programs, and respect for human rights.

Women in the Middle East confront a number of changing realities and consequent challenges. History and recent developments indicate that Middle Eastern women, in their diversity and versatility, have managed to cope and develop newer strategies.

See Also

DEMOCRACY; DEVELOPMENT: MIDDLE EAST AND THE ARAB REGION; ECONOMY AND DEVELOPMENT: OVERVIEW; ECONOMY: GLOBAL RESTRUCTURING; ISLAM; POLITICAL LEADERSHIP; POLITICAL PARTICIPATION; POLITICS AND THE STATE: OVERVIEW; POVERTY

References and Further Reading

Afkhami, Mahnaz, and Erika Friedl, eds. 1994. *In the eye of the storm: Women in post-revolutionary Iran.* London: Tauris.

———. 1997. *Muslim women and the politics of participation: Implementing the Beijing platform for action.* Syracuse, N.Y.: Syracuse University Press.

Ahmad, Leila. 1992. *Women and gender in Islam: Historical roots of a modern debate.* New Haven, Conn.: Yale University Press.

Bodman, Herbert L., and Nayereh Tohidi, eds. 1998. *Women in Muslim societies: Diversity within unity.* Boulder, Col.: Lynne Rienner.

Chatt, Dawn, and Annika Rabo, eds. 1997. *Organizing women: Formal and informal women's groups in the Middle East.* New York: Berg.

Göcek, Fatma M., and Shiva Balaghi, eds. 1994. *Reconstructing gender in the Middle East: Tradition, identity and power.* New York: Colombia University Press.

Kandiyoti, Deniz, ed. 1991. *Women, Islam and the state.* London: Macmillan.

Karam, Azza. 1998. *Women, Islamisms and state: Contemporary feminisms in Egypt.* London: Macmillan.

———, ed. 1998. *Women in Parliament: Beyond numbers.* Stockholm: International IDEA.

Keddie, Nikki R., and Beth Baron, eds. 1991. *Women in Middle Eastern history: Shifting boundaries in sex and gender.* New Haven, Conn.: Yale University Press.

Khoury, Nabil M., and Valentine Moghadam, eds. 1995. *Gender and development in the Arab world: Women's economic participation, patterns and policies.* London: Zed.

Mernissi, Fatima. 1991. *Women and Islam: An historical and theological enquiry.* Oxford: Basil Blackwell.

Moghadam, Valentine, ed. 1994. *Gender and national identity: Women and politics in Muslim societies.* London: Zed.

Seager, Joni. 1997. *The state of women in the world atlas.* London: Penguin.

Tucker, Judith, ed. 1993. *Arab women: New boundaries, old frontiers.* Bloomington: Indiana University Press.

United Nations human development report. 1995. Oxford: Oxford University Press.

Azza Karam

POLITICS AND THE STATE: North America

Many people have heard of Jeannette Rankin, the first women elected to the U.S. Congress. Far fewer have heard of Alice Paul, a suffragist who rejected the Democratic Party and launched the National Woman's Party, dedicated to promoting the Equal Rights Amendment. A Quaker, Alice Paul was born into an intellectual family; over the years, she earned a Ph.D. in sociology as well as a degree in law. Paul represented the incredible energy of American women at the turn of the twentieth century. She was a pivotal factor in women's securing passage of the Nineteenth Amendment in 1920, giving women the right to vote. In 1923 she introduced the Equal Rights Amendment (ERA) (Barker-Benfield, 1998). Her tactics were militant and highly visible, whether she was picketing outside the White House or fasting in jail.

When the National American Woman Suffrage Association (NAWSA) objected to her tactics, Alice Paul broke from both the NAWSA and the Democratic Party to form the National Woman's Party in 1916. Her strategy was to force Democratic candidates to support the Nineteenth Amendment. The Nineteenth Amendment was passed in 1920, and Alice Paul went on to fight for the ERA and died in 1977—shortly before it was clear that the ERA would die.

Elective Office

Alice Paul was tough and cynical. She would not be surprised that 80 years after women earned the right to vote, women would still be dramatically underrepresented in the U.S. national legislature. Throughout much of the twentieth century, women have been successful in gaining the same civil rights as men, such as the right to an education, the right to vote, and the right for equal pay in the workplace. But those rights have not translated into equal representation.

At the turn of the twenty-first century, nine women—or 9 percent—sit in the 100-person U.S. Senate; and 56 women—or 12.9 percent—sat in the US House of Representatives, the highest percentage ever achieved (Center for the American Woman and Politics, 2000). In addition, two women served as delegates to the House from the Virgin Islands and Washington, D.C. At this rate, it will take 240 years for women to reach parity with men. African-American women have had an even more difficult time. Thirteen—or 2.4 percent—black women are in the U.S. Congress. Latinas hold less than 1 percent of elected offices in the U.S. Congress.

The executive level of federal government has had a total of 22 women in cabinet or cabinet-level appointments. The first woman appointed to a presidential cabinet was Frances Perkins, selected in 1933 by President Franklin D. Roosevelt to head the Department of Labor. In 1997, Patricia Harris became the first black woman and Aida Alvarez became the first Hispanic woman to hold cabinet-level positions. Women have never held the presidency or vice presidency. Twenty-one women have sought the presidency; 12 of these sought the nomination of a major party. None has ever achieved the nomination of a major party.

While Canadian women have a similar electoral history, Canadian voters have elected more women proportionally than U.S. voters. They achieved the right to vote in federal elections in 1918 and elected one of the most famous women in Canadian history, Agnes Macphail, as the first woman member of parliament. She later went on to establish the Elizabeth Fry Society, an advocacy group for incarcerated women. In 2000, in the House of Commons, 60—or 20 percent—of the 295-seat parliament were women (Status of Women, 2000). In the Senate, 32—or 32 percent—of the 100 senators were women. In 1993, Kim Campbell became the first woman prime minister of Canada. As of this writing, three women out of nine people sat on the Canadian Supreme Court. Nine women were appointed to the federal cabinet—25 percent—of the 37-member cabinet.

In the United States, women have cut their political teeth in state legislatures, not just recently but since the Nineteenth Amendment was passed. After 1920, women's interest in voting and participating in the political system was immense; they quickly obtained 15 percent of the seats in the state legislators in the 1920s. The Democratic and Republican parties moved just as quickly to absorb women into their political parties before the National Woman's Party could attract too many candidates.

The male-dominated political parties discovered that women could be absorbed into their systems and were not united enough to pose a threat to their dominance. This initial surge of women elected to state legislatures was not sustained, and that trend was reflected around the nation; the number of women legislators nationwide declined in the 1930s, and rebounded slightly in the 1940s (McCormick and McCormick, 1994). The post–World War II period was not kind to women. In addition to the absorption power of the political parties, women had to struggle against a governmental structure that raised major barriers to their being involved in politics. A good example is Texas. Molly Ivins has pointed out that women in Texas were not permitted to serve on juries until 1954. As late as 1969, married women did not have full property rights. And until 1972, a man could murder his wife and her lover and get away with justifiable homicide (Ivins, 1991: 115). It wasn't until the feminist movement in the 1970s that women began making a comeback around the nation.

For many years women have obtained a higher percentage of statewide elective and state legislatures than the national level. In 2000, 1,669—or 22.5 percent—of state legislators in the United States were women, as compared with 12 percent in the U.S. Congress. Six out of the 10 states with the highest percentages of women state legislators are in the west. By 1991, women of color made up 13 percent of women state legislators, with blacks accounting for 5.2 percent and Latinas accounting for less than 1 percent.

By 2000, 91 women held 28 percent of all statewide elective executive offices. Three were governors—in Arizona, New Hampshire, and New Jersey—and 19 were lieutenant governors. In 11 states, women held at least one-half of the statewide elective executive positions.

In Canada, universal suffrage was granted to women at different times in each of the provinces. Women got the right to vote in Quebec's provincial elections in 1940, but Montreal did not grant universal suffrage until 1970. As of 1997, only 15 percent of Quebec's parliament was women. Ontario had 19 women among its 130 members of parliament, about 15 percent.

Women are equally involved in municipal politics. It is less competitive, costs less, does not require relocation, and is a stepping-stone to other levels (Crow, 1997: 435). In 1999, women's officeholding at the municipal level had tripled since 1970. As of 1997, women constituted approximately 15 percent of municipally elected representatives (Crow, 1997: 442). In 1999, of the 228 mayors of U.S. cities with populations over 100,000, 45—or 20 percent—were women (Center for the American Woman and Politics, 2000).

In Canada, the Canadian Advisory Council on the Status of Women (1988) found that the percentage of female officeholders in municipal politics increased from 7 percent in 1981 to 19 percent in 1988. By the year 2000, women made up 22.4 percent of all councilors in Quebec's 1,300 municipalities.

There are many barriers to electing women of any color to elective office. The first and foremost is the lack of financial resources. This is the single most important consideration regarding whether a woman will run for elective office at any level (Carroll and Strimling, 1983: 8–9). Another important barrier to electing women is incumbency. Almost all elected officials on any level of government win when running for reelection (Crow, 1997: 437).

There are other obvious barriers to elective office—such as ethnicity and gender (Takash, 1997: 425). Child-rearing responsibilities are another reason women give to decline or delay running for office. Many women run for office after their children are older. Carroll reported that women legislators, unlike men, were over 40 years old. These barriers, particularly the financial one, are even greater for blacks and Latinas, who have a lower per capita income than white women (Takash, 1997: 412).

Those who do get elected are from states in which political participation is not seen as being as desirable as other occupations. Research has demonstrated that there is a relationship between female representation and factors such as the size of the districts, amount of compensation, and the degree of professionalization of the legislature. An examination of 10 states that were leaders in the proportion of women in the legislatures concluded that these states had much smaller districts, compensation was lower, and, in general, the legislatures were less professional (McCormick and

McCormick, 1994). They were states in which men were not as attracted to public office because other professions paid better.

Women legislators vote differently from men and, as their numbers grow, the agendas of legislatures change. Surveys of legislators in 12 states demonstrate that women legislators are more likely to list among their priority bills legislation relating to children, the family, or women (Welch and Thomas, 1991). The gender gap among legislators is similar to the gender gap among voters.

Women and men make different choices of political candidates. On the national level, more women than men voted for President Bill Clinton than his opponent in both 1992 and 1996. In the U.S. House of Representatives, women more often than men voted for the Democratic candidate. And, in most cases, women supported women candidates at a greater rate than men.

Male and female views on public policy issues are different. North American women express more concern than men about preserving the peace, attending to the needs of others, protecting the economic well-being of their families, and protecting the environment (Kelber, 1994: 197). Women act on their views by voting for men and women who support those views, and women are more likely to vote for other women.

Governmental Policies and Women

The federal government led the states to equality for women in many areas of life. The U.S. Congress passed the Equal Pay Act of 1963, the Civil Rights Act of 1964, Title IX of the Education Amendments in 1972 requiring equal treatment in educational programs and activities, and the Equal Employment Opportunity Act giving the Equal Employment Opportunities Commission power to take legal action to enforce its rulings; and (in 1972) it voted to send the Equal Rights Amendment to the states for ratification. The high point was 1993. With an increased number of women in Congress, 30 bills on women's issues were passed during its first year; the previous record of any year was five (Center for American Woman and Politics, 2000).

The presidents played a crucial role. In 1961, President John Kennedy created the President's Commission on the Status of Women. In 1965, President Lyndon Johnson signed an Executive Order 11246 requiring federal agencies and federal contractors to take "affirmative action" in overcoming employment discrimination. In 1981, President Ronald Reagan appointed the first woman, Sandra Day O'Connor, to the U.S. Supreme Court; and in 1992, President Clinton appointed the second woman, Ruth Bader Ginsberg. The U.S. Civil Service Commission eliminated height and weight requirements in 1973, and the U.S. Office of Federal Contract Compliance issued guidelines prohibiting sex discrimination in employment.

The federal judiciary has played a vital role. In 1973 the U.S. Supreme Court established a woman's right to abortion in *Roe* v. *Wade*. This canceled antiabortion laws in 46 states. The first sexual harassment suit was won in 1977 before the U.S. Court of Appeals for the District of Columbia.

Then came the backlash and the harsh cutbacks in an era of devolution, during which the federal government sought to pass to the states many of the functions it had assumed. What the federal government giveth, it taketh away. In 1977, Congress passed the Hyde Amendment, eliminating federal funding for poor women's abortions. In 1982, ratification efforts for an Equal Rights Amendment failed—Congress had insisted on a time limit. By 1995, only 13 states provided public funding for abortions. President Jimmy Carter changed the Commission on the Status of Women to the President's Advisory Committee for Women in 1980. President Reagan abolished it in 1985. In 1990, President George Bush vetoed the Family Leave Act, although in 1993, President Clinton signed it into law.

The Omnibus Budget Reconciliation Act (OBRA) of 1981 restricted state payments to welfare recipients. In addition, OBRA reduced supports to women on welfare. OBRA also attacked social security, adversely affecting women. OBRA phased in reductions through highly technical changes in future benefits. Sporadically employed recipients were gradually phased out and most of the basic minimum recipients had been women. OBRA also ceased payments to children at the age of 16 rather than 18. Student benefits were phased out.

The Family Support Act of 1988 signaled the end of welfare that had allowed women to remain home with their children; rather, they were expected to work. The biggest setback was in 1996 when Congress passed and President Clinton signed the Personal Responsibility and Work Opportunity Reconciliation Act (PRWORA), P.L. 104–193, which placed a five-year lifetime limit on welfare payments to the poor, most of whom were women and children.

It was the end of the twentieth century and, instead of celebrating support for women and children, the federal government took that support away. The assault on social legislation was quite successful. Millions of women were forced off welfare and into low-paying jobs or dependency on relatives. Women are still fighting for "paid parental leave, family benefits, child care and health care services that are routinely provided in generous terms by Nordic and other European governments" (Kelber, 1994: 209).

The Canadian government adopted a devolution strategy similar to that of the United States, which meant that Canadian women experienced similar setbacks in the 1980s and 1990s. In 1970, the federal government had created the Royal Commission on the Status of Women, and in 1973, the Women's Program was created as part of the office of the secretary of state, with millions of dollars dedicated to women's groups to better the life of Canadian women. Canada did create a Minister of Women's Equality. The overall budget for the Women's Program in 1996–1997 was $8 million, a reduction of $5 million since 1989. The National Action Committee on the Status of Women was forced to lay off all but two staff members in 1998.

In 1985, Parliament repealed the Canada Assistance Plan Act and introduced the Canada Health and Social Transfer with "concomitant cuts to social services, loss of entitlement to social assistance, increase in women's unpaid caregiving workload, loss of women's good jobs in the caregiving sector and amendments to the employment insurance scheme which resulted in fewer women being eligible to receive benefits" (Day and Brodsky, 1999: 121). This increased women's poverty. In 1967, one third of single women were living in poverty; by 1995, 56 percent of single women were living in poverty.

What does the future hold? Some countries have had far more success in electing a greater proportion of women to government positions. The Scandinavian countries have more than 30 percent representation by women; Norway has a female-dominated executive branch. U.S. and Canadian women have a long way to go. They must recapture the energy of the social movements from the early part of the twentieth century, in which women coalesced around issues affecting women and aggressively sought public office. It was Jeannette Rankin, the first woman elected to Congress, in 1917, who introduced the first social legislation affecting women and children, the Maternity and Infancy Protection Act in 1921 (Kelber, 1994: 206). It was women legislators who passed the most bills concerning women in the U.S. Congress in 1993.

Several strategies have been suggested. Electoral reforms could offset the bias against women in elections. One way to achieve parity would be proportional representation, in which the percentage of the popular vote for a party determines the number of seats that party will receive. Australia uses this in part of its electoral process. In Australia, the Lower House has winner-take-all elections—8 percent of the representatives are women; in the Senate, representatives are elected on a proportional basis—23 percent of the representatives are women.

A structure that could be put in place is a reconstitution of the U.S. Commission on the Status of Women. Another strategy, from Iowa, is to establish gender-balanced state appointments as much as possible. Because of the persistence of women legislators from both major parties, Iowa has been quite successful in finding equal numbers of men and women to fill boards and commissions. In Canada, the Status of Women commission recommended amending the Canadian Human Rights Act (CHRA) to include adding social condition to the list of prohibited grounds of discrimination. In addition, the Status of Women commission recommended that CHRA also recognize group disadvantage so that women can be recognized as a group under the law.

At the start of the new millennium, women still had a long way to go.

See Also

POLITICAL LEADERSHIP; POLITICAL PARTICIPATION; POLITICAL PARTIES; POLITICAL REPRESENTATION; POLITICS AND THE STATE: OVERVIEW; PRO-CHOICE MOVEMENT

References and Further Reading

Barker-Benfield, G. J., and Catherine Clinton. 1998. *Portraits of American women from settlement to the present.* New York: Oxford University Press.

Carroll, Susan J., Debra L. Dodson, and Ruth B. Mandel. 1991. *The impact of women in public office.* Rutgers, N.J.: Center for the American Woman and Politics.

Carroll, Susan, and Wendy Strimling. 1983. *Women's routes to elective office: A comparison with men's.* New Brunswick, N.J.: Center for the American Woman and Politics.

Center for the American Woman and Politics, 2000. <www.cawp.rutgers.edu>.

Crow, Barbara A. 1997. Relative privilege? Reconsidering white women's participation in municipal politics. In Cathy J. Cohen, Kathleen B. Jones, and Joan C. Toronto, eds., *Women transforming politics: An alternative reader,* 435–447. New York: New York University Press.

Day, Shelagh, and Gwen Brodsky. 1999. Women's economic inequality and the Canadian Human Rights Act: Status of women. *Women and the Canadian Human Rights Act: A collection of policy research reports.* <www.swc-cfc.gc.ca/publish/research/chra-e.html>.

Ivins, Molly. 1991. *Molly Ivins can't say that, can she?* New York: Random House.

Kelber, Min, ed. 1994. *Women and government: New ways to political power.* Westport, Conn.: Praeger.

McCormick, R. P., and K. C. McCormick. 1994. *Equality deferred: Women candidates for the New Jersey Assembly 1920–1993.* Rutgers, N.J.: Center for the American Woman and Politics.

Status of Women. 1988. *Facts concerning numbers and percentages of women parliamentarians in the House of Commons and Senate.* Ottawa, Canada: Status of Women.

Status of Women. 2000. *Women parliamentarians in the House of Commons and Senate.* Ottawa, Canada: Status of Women.

Takash, Paule Cruz. 1997. Breaking barriers to representation: Chicana/Latina elected officials in California. In Cathy J. Cohen, Kathleen B. Jones, and Joan C. Toronto, eds., *Women transforming politics: An alternative reader,* 412–434. New York: New York University Press.

Thebaud, Françoise. 1994. *A history of women: Toward a cultural identity in the twentieth century.* Cambridge, Mass.: Harvard University Press.

Welch, S., and S. Thomas. 1991. Do women in public office make a difference. In *Gender and policymaking: Studies of women in public office, II.* New Brunswick, N.J.: Center for the American Woman and Politics.

Lynne A. Weikart

POLITICS AND THE STATE: South Asia I

As a region, south Asia comprises a diversity of religions, castes, classes, ethnicities, political institutions, and constitutional structures. Women's relation to the state in each of the countries of Bangladesh, India, Nepal, Pakistan, and Sri Lanka has been structured by and negotiated within some or all of these, to varying extents, in each specific context. Furthermore, each of these factors takes on a particular form, meaning, and significance within each state. This particularity of expression, however, is founded on a shared history of social, cultural, religious, and political institutions including the period of colonial rule (with the exception of Nepal, which was not under colonial rule at any time). Colonial rule began in the early eighteenth century with the successive arrival and settlement of Portuguese, Dutch, French, and British rulers in both the Indian subcontinent and Sri Lanka. Colonial rule ended in the British-Indian subcontinent in 1947 and in Sri Lanka in 1948. The end of colonialism also provides, in each case, a departure point for each state to engage independently with religion, caste, class, ethnicity, political institutions, and constitutional structures. In the postcolonial era, therefore, the question of identity within each state has been significant. In addition, high levels of poverty and slow rates of economic growth have marked the experience of these states. The increasing marginalization and exclusion of the majority of the population from the benefits of growth that has been achieved has led to the area's characterization as "third world" or "developing." When we look at south Asia today, it is thus as a mix of shared commonalties, as well as specific identities.

The legacy of colonial rule has to a great extent structured the state's terrain. In a developmental context, the postcolonial state has been characterized by challenges that reveal fundamental tensions. At the same time, the state has also provided, through these challenges, the opportunity for growth and the definition of issues, by forcing the reevaluation and discussion of starting positions. As Shirin Rai (1996) has argued, the features of the postcolonial state make it open to negotiation by women. The rhetoric of change, coexistent with the relative autonomy of state institutions from dominant social classes, can create spaces for struggles. Furthermore, the relative ineffectiveness of state institutions to enforce laws forces women to engage with those who do have the power to affect their lives, in locations that may be outside the institutional framework of the state. This in turn draws the state into a position of defining or redefining itself and asserting or reasserting its position (Rai, 1996).

The various processes that characterize women's engagement with the postcolonial state have been reflexive. Every challenge thrown up by women has simultaneously been a challenge *for* the state to further define itself. Likewise, every attempt toward the redefinition of the state has affected definitions of women. For example, the protests of Pakistani women over the promulgation of "Islamic" criminal laws during the early 1980s forced the military regime of the day to reconsider its "Islamization" program in 1984. On the other hand, it was very clear, through promulgated directives and policies, that the state's attempt to forge a new identity based on religion and culture was formulated primarily on the redefinition of the roles, rights, and status of Pakistani women (Ali, 2000). The meaning of secularism as one of the defining traits of the Indian state was brought into severe contestation in the now well-known case of Shah Bano. In this instance, the claim of Shah Bano, a Muslim divorcee, for maintenance from her ex-husband, opened up the shaky ground on which secularism was founded in India. By the time this case had drawn to a close in the Supreme Court, it had exposed the deep fractures within Indian democracy and the highly gendered nature of the principles of secularism and constitutionalism in India.

Nationalist Struggles and Women's Mobilization

The significance of the state for women's movements in south Asia is derived from the history of colonial rule and subsequent independence. When the focus for mobilization and popular movements was first established in the region, the concept of the state and the project for its independent existence were of key significance. This provided the foundation for a commonality of interests among and within various groups. In the particular case of women, the project of creating the state itself relied to a great extent on the prior assumption of certain interests as women's interests. Thus the incorporation of women within freedom movements depended largely on their ability to influence the direction and nature of the movement, as was expressed often by Mohandas Gandhi (Jayawardena, 1986). The nationalist and subsequent independence movements provided, for the first time, the opportunity for significant numbers of women to engage in political activity and interact with the state (the colonial ruler, at this point). It was for the creation of the independent state that the phenomenal and active participation of women occurred. For women, as well as men, the struggle for independence signified a commitment to establish their interests, their needs, their aspirations, their identities: their state. Thus women in India figured in staggeringly high proportions in the various agitations against British rule from the middle of the nineteenth century. The invaluable contribution of women to the freedom movement in India was explicitly acknowledged and discussed by leaders such as Gandhi and Jawaharlal Nehru (Jayawardena, 1986: 95–99).

In the debates on social reform that informed the nationalist discussions from the early nineteenth century, women figured not only as participants, but also as subjects of debate (Uberoi, 1996). Most of the areas under discussion appertained to women's lives. Prevailing Hindu practices such as child marriage, prohibition of widows' remarriage, *sati* (the practice of burning a widow on her husband's funeral pyre), the propertyless status of Hindu women, and polygamy were denounced by the reformers as barbaric. Greater education for women was advocated by both Hindu and Muslim nationalist leaders as a necessary measure to redeem the society. As the precursor to the independence movements in the country, the reform movement established the foundational terms within which self-rule could thereafter be argued. For women, the significance of the process of creating an independent state lay, therefore, not only in the arena for their mass involvement but also in the embodiment of the struggle for the legitimacy of independence.

Prior to the creation of Pakistan, Muslim women participated in three kinds of movements: the movement to spread education, the Khilafat movement to support the Khilafat in Turkey, and the movement for the creation of Pakistan (Ali, 2000). In the eastern part of the subcontinent, women in Bangladesh at this time were active in the demand for greater education for girls, increased mobility for women, and the relaxation of *purdah* (Jahan, 1999). In the 1960s, when the demand for a separate state called Bangladesh was being made, it was with the vital cooperation of women that liberation from Pakistan was achieved. Women played a key role in the war of 1971, joining and supporting the freedom fighters toward ultimate victory.

It was expected that women's participation in freedom movements would ultimately lead to shaping their articulated interests within the state. However, as has been the experience after most other independence movements, even though women had been an integral part of the processes that led to the inception of the state, they were not necessarily a part of its project and design thereafter. The defining character of women's involvement, rooted in *their* interests, is at best only alluded to within the overarching "national" interests. At the same time, there is, of necessity, a very definite contribution of women by *numbers*. Women are part of the movement and kept within its boundaries by promises and expectations created for them as future citizens; at the same time, there is very little chance for this involvement to become a *women's movement*.

The role of women in the nationalist movements in south Asia was predicated on the acceptance of existing patriarchal relations in society and framed within dominant notions of the roles of women. As a result, women had no basis for challenging the existing social, religious, cultural, and familial structures which defined their position as subordinate. The upper- and middle-class interests within the nationalist movements, reflected in the movement for women's education and the resulting growth of women's education, contributed to the effective socializing of women into traditionally accepted roles (Jayawardena, 1986). The apparent disjuncture between the larger patriarchal framework within which women's involvement was constituted and the broader objective of self-determination as a state constitutes a key aspect of women's engagement with the state thereafter. It determines the subsequent relationships charted between women as a group and the state. Whereas the state then becomes the target and focus of mobilization, the issues thrown up by women's movements represent a challenge to the state itself to reexamine its position. Thus, the challenges posed to women's movements by religion, ethnicity, class, and caste reflect a challenge to the state to account for caste, class, religion, and ethnicity in its constitution.

Constitutions and Identities

In India, the process of constitution building opened up the issue of how women were to figure henceforth within the state. Ranging from debates regarding the representation of women in politics and political institutions (Rai and Sharma, 2000) to reform of the traditional Hindu law to better the position of women, a number of questions were part of the platform for the inclusion of women on the agenda of establishing a new state. Notwithstanding a small improvement on the question of Hindu law, the issue of increasing women's political participation through establishing quotas or reserving seats in government for women was subject to dissent from various quarters, including certain women's groups (Rai and Sharma, 2000). However, the commitment to the establishment of a state on the principles of liberalism and democracy, with a clear objective of social reform, ensured crucial constitutional guarantees for women. The Fundamental Right to Equality (Article 14, Constitution of India, 1950) explicitly prohibits discrimination based on sex, among other forms of discrimination. The goal of a Uniform Civil Code to replace personal laws on the basis of religion, which were often discriminatory against women, was also explicitly stated (Article 44, Constitution of India, 1950). In the 50 years since the constitution was adopted, there has been, in accordance with its principles and objectives, a plethora of legislation specifically addressing the position of women in India.

The newly formed state of Bangladesh was on a similar quest to build a state on the "four pillars" of democracy, secularism, socialism, and nationalism (Jahan, 1999). Although women were granted equality in the public sphere, they were still subject to Islamic injunctions in most areas of their lives. The military coup in 1975 entrenched this religion-based gender subordination through the subsequent replacement of secularism with Islam in 1977. Mobilization and campaigns by various women's groups for the return of secularism were helped by international pressure, and the state was forced to adopt a careful position. The constitution of Bangladesh also contains provisions for affirmative action favoring women, as well as for reserving 10 percent of parliamentary seats for women.

The problem of increasing women's participation in politics remains unanswered in south Asia. The number of elected women representatives remains low in Sri Lanka even though women's suffrage was achieved in 1931 (Moore, 1990; Jayawardena, 1986; de Silva, 1982). In Bangladesh, women's votes, available since 1935, have been crucial in mobilizing support for political parties. Nevertheless, the number of women representatives has been low where the dominant patriarchal and religious ideology prevents women from taking up positions independent of male support (Jahan, 1999). Debates in India from 1993 onward regarding the reservation of women's seats in local political institutions have caused problems between the state, political parties and institutions, caste, class, and gender as they reflect gender identity, interests, and relations.

Clearly, the region presents a paradox in its accommodation of women in politics. Collectively, the countries in the region have produced more women heads of government than the rest of the world combined. Indeed, India, Bangladesh, Sri Lanka, and Pakistan have all had women elected heads of government. The apparent contradiction that this poses, in conjunction with the continued underrepresentation of women in politics, perhaps reflects the inability of the state, in its collective sense, to incorporate gender interests, reflect gender positions, and provide the space for the articulation of gender identities.

Access, Empowerments and Livelihoods: Gender, Development, and the State

The widespread and extreme poverty in most areas of the region has posed developmental questions for the postcolonial states in south Asia. One of the major challenges to the region today is the continued underachievement of the state in the provision of basic education, health services, productive resources, and livelihoods. The resulting marginalization and disempowerment of large sections of the population have increasingly raised questions regarding the strength and capacity of the state, its institutions, and its policies. Women are often the most affected, and in terms of both demographics and human development, the position of women is cause for concern. Nevertheless, the postcolonial states in south Asia, as agents of social and economic transformation, despite their questionable strength and efficiency, attempt to provide opportunities for women (Rai, 1996). The numerous campaigns by women's organizations to solve the problems of violence against women, dowry and dowry-related violence, rape, and family law in all the countries aimed to call attention to the state's commitment to social transformation. Sustained movements by rural women for land ownership, ecological protection, and access to livelihoods build on and challenge state commitment to economic transformation, and they also pressure the international donor community and multilateral agencies.

In the early twenty-first century, the state is the focus of concerted action for the promotion of gender equality by women and organizations acting both "within and against" it (Rai, 1996). Innumerable organizations are working for greater access for women to livelihoods, resources, health, and education and are reflecting willingness and ability to work with the state to promote these interests. The role of nongovernmental organizations (NGOs) in facilitating the extension of state institutions and measures may be seen as efforts toward incorporating gender within existing development policies, rather than challenging the fundamental conceptions and direction of the state.

On the other hand, redressing deep-rooted hierarchies and disturbing existing power relations to achieve gender equality have led to fundamental challenges to the state. Dominant patriarchal structures of gender subordination, reinforced by religious and cultural ideologies in Pakistan, for example, are being questioned in the legal and political frameworks that legitimize the operation of discriminatory religious and customary practices. In India, the demand for a Uniform Civil Code represents a challenge to the state such that the very meaning of equality as practiced by the state has been questioned. Challenges to the hierarchical structure of caste in India have been central to demands by landless women agricultural laborers for independent titles to property. In these and many other cases, it is the legitimacy and the foundational principles of the state that must be renegotiated.

The worldwide recognition of basic human rights has broadened the framework within which the position of women can be negotiated with the state. Adoption of the Convention for the Elimination of All Forms of Discrimination Against Women by the United Nations creates an international setting in which states must justify their role in determining women's equality. Nonratification on key aspects may be grounds for scrutiny of the state by the international community. The growing primacy accorded to human rights has in fact enabled many women and organizations to engage with the state from a stronger position (Jahan, 1999; Ali, 2000). The breadth of the human rights discourse may have the potential for proving how responsible the state is for many forms of gender inequality.

See Also

COLONIALISM AND POSTCOLONIALISM; DEVELOPMENT: SOUTH ASIA; FUNDAMENTALISM AND PUBLIC POLICY; POLITICAL LEADERSHIP; POLITICAL PARTICIPATION; POLITICAL REPRESENTATION; POLITICS AND THE STATE: OVERVIEW; POLITICS AND THE STATE: SOUTH ASIA II

References and Further Reading

Ali, Shaheen Sardar. 2000. Law, Islam and the women's movement in Pakistan. In Shirin M. Rai, ed., *International perspectives on gender and democratisation.* London: Macmillan.

Chant, Sylvia, and Cathy McIlwaine. 1998. *Three generations, 2 genders, 1 world: Women and men in a changing century.* London and New York: Zed.

De Silva, K. M. 1989. The model colony: Reflections on the transfer of power in Sri Lanka. In A. Jeyratnam Wilson and Dennis Dalton, eds., *The states of south Asia: Problems of national integration.* London: C. Hurst.

Goetz, Anne Marie. 1996. Dis/organizing gender: Women development agents in state and NGO poverty-reduction programmes in Bangladesh. In Shirin Rai and Geraldine Lievesley, ed., *Women and the state: International perspectives.* London: Taylor and Francis.

Jahan, Roushan. 1999. Men in seclusion, women in public: Rokeya's dream and women's struggles in Bangladesh. In Amrita Basu, ed., *The challenge of local feminisms: Women's movements in global perspective.* New Delhi: Kali for Women.

Jayawardena, Kumari. 1986. *Feminism and nationalism in the third world.* London and New Jersey: Zed.

Kumar, Radha. 1999. From Chipko to sati: The contemporary Indian women's movements. In Amrita Basu, ed., *The challenge of local feminisms: Women's movements in global perspective.* New Delhi: Kali for Women.

Mitra, Subrata Kumar. 1990. Between transaction and transcendence: The state and the institutionalisation of power in India. In Subrata Kumar Mitra, ed., *The postcolonial state in Asia: Dialectics of politics and culture.* Hertfordshire, U.K.: Harvester Wheatsheaf.

Momsen, Janet H., and Vivian Kinnaird, eds. 1993. *Different places, different voices: Gender and development in Africa, Asia and Latin America.* London and New York: Routledge.

Moore, Mick. 1990. Sri Lanka: The contradictions of the social democratic state. In Subrata Kumar Mitra, ed., *The postcolonial state in Asia: Dialectics of politics and culture.* Hertfordshire, U.K.: Harvester Wheatsheaf.

Rai, Shirin M. 1996. Women and the state in the third world: Some issues for debate. In Shirin Rai and Geraldine Lievesley, ed., *Women and the state: International perspectives.* London: Taylor and Francis.

———, ed., 2000. *International perspectives on gender and democratisation.* London: Macmillan.

Uberoi, Patricia. 1996. *Social reform, sexuality and the state.* New Delhi: Sage.

Reena Patel

POLITICS AND THE STATE: South Asia II

In the developing societies of south Asia, the state has played a varied and frequently ambivalent role. Where political and civil liberties have been granted by constitutions and upheld by governments, effective women's movements for equality and emancipation have emerged. In other instances, state policies have allowed the abrogation of women's rights, centering the discourse and conflicts over tradition and identity on women. New educational policies and long-term structural economic changes initiated by modernizing states have benefited many urban women, but specific development strategies have also displaced and marginalized women as economic producers and resulted in deteriorating living conditions for many rural women.

The paths toward political, social, and economic development adopted by south Asian states have diverged widely. The context within which women's issues are debated varies significantly not only as a consequence of differing modernization strategies but also because of the enormous diversity of social structure, religious belief, ethnicity, language, and custom between and within countries. At the same time, a long and common history for the subcontinent as a whole, the colonial experience, and the influence of the dominant religious traditions of Hinduism, Buddhism, and Islam serve as the common factors in understanding how gender relations have been constituted throughout the region.

Colonial Legacies

The consolidation of the British Indian empire in the subcontinent and the "crown colony" of Ceylon (Sri Lanka) created the context for the emergence of the "women's question" in the nineteenth century. The impact of colonial rule was generally negative in terms of economic rights and legal codes. Implementation of new land settlements and laws of private property eroded the economic rights and status that women had enjoyed in areas characterized by communal ownership of property. In the matrilineal communities of south India and Sri Lanka, women's entitlements under joint family ownership were undermined by the transfer of property rights to male heads of household. However, even more significant in the long run was the central role played by the colonial administration in codifying and homogenizing Hindu and Muslim law. Prior to this codification, local custom and usage frequently overruled religious law for both Hindus and Muslims. The result of British policies was a new rigidity in the enforcement of legal codes over time and across different communities and groups, as well as a crystallization of identities along religious lines. The process of codification, also brought the family and crucial areas of gender relations under the purview of the state as it emerged as the protector and enforcer of separate personal laws—a legacy that has been passed down to successor postcolonial states.

The movements for women's rights in south Asia emerged in conjunction with the nationalist struggle for independence and amid nineteenth-century campaigns for social and religious reform. Thus the political mobilization of women in the Indian subcontinent (in what are now India, Pakistan, and Bangladesh) and Sri Lanka began much earlier and was much more extensive and far-reaching than in countries like Nepal or the Maldives, which as protectorates rather than colonies had retained considerable autonomy over their internal affairs. Newly established women's organizations and groups in India and Sri Lanka joined with liberal nationalist reformers to raise the issue of emancipation of women through the extension of political and civil rights, access to education and economic opportunities, and legal reform to enhance women's status related to inheritance, marriage, and divorce. The generally progressive nature of the nationalist struggle provided a favorable impetus to movements for social equality and women's rights, but the broader goal of independence from colonial rule precluded focus on more "narrowly feminist concerns" as both divisive and unnecessary. The postcolonial political order would incorporate women into public life as full and equal citizens. Established women's organizations and many progressive leaders assumed that the social and economic disabilities that hampered the exercise of political and civil rights by women would be removed by an activist interventionist state policy of promoting development to transform the traditional society, polity, and economy along more egalitarian lines.

Pakistan

The politics of partition and communal conflict that accompanied the establishment of the separate entities of India and Pakistan in 1947 modified in significant ways the new states' social and economic agenda of transformation and nation building. In Pakistan, the questions of national identity and the location and position of Islam in the body politic acquired center stage. The legitimacy of women's rights was recognized within the context of religious law. Passage of the Muslim Personal Law of Sharia in 1948 and the Family Laws Ordinance of 1961 secured women's rights to inheritance, restricted polygamy, gave women more rights on divorce, and raised the legal age of marriage for girls from 14 to 16. However, the attempt by women's groups to incorporate a Charter of Women's Rights in the constitution of 1956 was unsuccessful. Women's status and opportunities continued to be determined by the gendered divisions of public and private spheres. Pakistani women gained access to education and jobs but their limited and differentiated induction into the public arena was accomplished without any radical alterations in previous constructions of gender. With the turn toward militarization and authoritarian politics under Zia ul Haq in 1977 the stated goals of Islamization of the "laws and social fabric" of Pakistan brought a qualitative shift from limited concessions on equality to a greater emphasis on gender differentiation. While the curtailment of political freedoms has affected both men and women, the prescribed norms of behavior, dress, and public presence that have been promoted to demarcate the Islamic Pakistani identity have been more restrictive for women and reinforced their secondary status. The policies of the government have not gone unchallenged and, although their impact on policy has been limited, the Women's Action Forum and other professional associations of women have taken a lead in generating public debate on the impact on women of conservatively interpreted Islamic law.

Bangladesh

A similar process of identity formation in Bangladesh reoriented its politics from secularism and democracy to authoritarianism and religious nationalism in the late 1970s. However, in Bangladesh, unlike Pakistan, the leaders have for the most part promoted the Islamization of the state while supporting the cause of advancement and empowerment of women. The Grameen Bank's provision of training and credit to poor rural women has gained international recognition but a variety of other nongovernmental organizations have also spawned programs that have brought dramatic improvements in women's access to literacy, health care, and employment in both rural and urban areas. The emergence of women as a constituency of claimants has generated a backlash from conservative organizations, such as the Jamaat i Islami, that simultaneously lobby the state for more coercive application of religious law and employ a vigilante approach to confronting women who are seen as transcending the bounds of social norms by appearing in *bazaars* or accepting employment outside the home.

India

The politicization of religious identities has affected the position of women in India as well. The adoption of a uniform civil code soon after Independence in 1947 was thwarted as minority members of the Constituent Assembly insisted that changes in laws pertaining to family and women be initiated by religious communities themselves rather than the state. Advocates of women's rights argued that the subordination of women to men under religious personal laws was a major source of disadvantage for women and undermined their constitutional right to nondiscrimination. The Hindu Code Bill that provided for equal matrimonial rights for Hindu women, freedom to divorce, and the right to inherit property was opposed by conservatives but was passed by the new Parliament under Jawaharlal Nehru's leadership in the mid-1950s. However, the adoption of the uniform code to replace the personal laws of minority communities continues to be controversial. With the reemergence of religious revivalism and communal politics in the 1980s, the issue of women's rights has been overshadowed by a renewed emphasis on minority rights and the state's role in ensuring respect for cultural and religious diversity.

Although communal politics has slowed progress in certain areas of legal reform, both the legacy of nationalist mobilization and the political space provided by the practice of liberal democracy in India have proved crucial for the emergence of a highly visible and articulate women's movement. The form that women's activism has taken since the 1970s emphasizes empowerment through mobilization on specific issues and with special attention to grassroots activity. Women's increasing political participation in the system is most evident not so much in electoral politics and representative assemblies (although that, too, has been increasing, particularly at the local level with the promotion of quotas for women in *panchayats* or local village councils), but in consciously pursued alternative women's politics. The urban women's movement has used its skills and resources to focus media attention on women's issues and to lobby for tougher legislation and enforcement in cases of rape and dowry-related deaths, and for banning sex determination tests, among other things. It has also demanded more gender-sensitive policies of economic development and modernization.

In rural areas women have organized spontaneously against caste and class oppression in broad-based movements as well as for gender-specific issues. Linking alcoholism with spouse abuse, women have picketed liquor shops, demonstrated against sexual harassment, and demanded land titles in their own name rather than that of husbands or so-called heads of households. Women of the Himalayan foothills made their mark as some of the earliest ecofeminists by launching the Chipko (tree hugging) movement to resist deforestation and ecological degradation. Overall, notwithstanding the setbacks due to religious polarization and communal politics, the organizational skills and activities displayed by Indian women have enhanced their self-confidence and political consciousness and ensured a high visibility of gender issues in the media and in public debate.

Sri Lanka

Sri Lankan women were the first to acquire the vote in south Asia as a result of the Donoughmore Constitutional Reform of 1931, and rates of literacy, access to services, employment, and political participation continue to be among the highest in the region. In recent years, the civil strife and ethnic violence that have marked Sri Lankan politics have affected both Tamil and Sinhalese women adversely. Many have been drawn in either as participants or as protesters. The Mothers' Front, which emerged as a powerful force for a brief period to draw attention to large-scale "disappearances" and killings that occurred during 1988–1991, epitomized a strategy of mobilization in the context of traditional feminine roles that effectively created a space for protest in a patriarchally structured society. Evocation of the vocabulary of motherhood and the right of mothers to grieve for their sons and seek justice through recourse to tears and curses gendered the discourse of human rights and dissent as much as it galvanized public opinion against a repressive and corrupt government.

Smaller States of South Asia

In the smallest and more insulated states of south Asia such as Nepal and the Maldives, the status of women continues to be low, although some change is perceptible. Nepal is a rigidly male-dominated society in virtually every aspect of life. However, variations exist between classes, castes, and ethnic groups as in other areas of south Asia. Tibeto-Nepalese women enjoy more freedom and autonomy than women in the Pahari and Newari communities. The literacy gap between males and females has been enormous, although, with the launching of the 12-year literacy program in 1990, it has narrowed in urban areas and in the upper classes. Education and status are correlated, and educated Nepali women have been gaining access to prestigious government and private sector employment.

Women in the Maldives, a predominantly Sunni Muslim island republic governed by a powerful president, have also experienced some status mobility as a consequence of improving educational opportunities. However, the slow pace of change, a highly conservative culture, and broad disparities between the upper class and the masses signify that there is a long way to go before gender equality can be realized.

In the Buddhist kingdom of Bhutan, patriarchal and matriarchal systems have coexisted for a long time, and women traditionally enjoyed high status, including access to land and other forms of property. Modernization has brought more benefits, with government encouragement for greater participation of women in political life. More women have begun to aspire to careers in medicine, teaching, and industry, but the great majority of the female labor force in Bhutan is concentrated in agriculture.

Conclusion

In general, transformations in the role and position of women in south Asia have come about largely as a consequence of industrialization, urbanization, and secularization. This is evident in the more significant gains that middle- and upper-class women have made in freeing themselves of traditional constraints in contrast to the slower emancipatory efforts of their counterparts in the less upwardly mobile castes or classes. Consciousness raising and mobilization remain key strategies for empowering women, and the varied modes of resistance and protest demonstrated by women have, in most instances, been remarkably successful in putting governments and administrators on the defensive and drawing attention to unjust laws, policies, or practices. Setbacks have been experienced as well. The disturbing characteristic of south Asian politics continues to be the centrality of religious or ethnic identity, and the articulation of gender interests has been compromised by the divergent demands of secularism and communal politics. Subject to conflicting social and political pressures, a number of women have chosen to assert their community identity and actively support policies that reinforce their subordinate position in society and within the family.

In the last few decades, states in south Asia have played a dual role in regard to gender issues. They have served as a set of institutions that both reflect and mediate the power relations present in civil society. Low levels of economic development and the specific social and historical circumstances of colonial rule created the need for postcolonial states to identify with a modernist project of economic and social transformation. However, the scope and effects of state policies were conditioned by the lack of resources and infrastructure as well as by powerful interests and retrograde social structures. South Asian feminists have sought to clarify how state policies or the lack thereof contribute to women's oppression and retard progress. The policies themselves are seen as reflective of a deeper cultural and economic level of discrimination where change is essential. With some exceptions women's groups in south Asia do not perceive the state as an institution from which women have nothing to gain. There is a keen recognition that the state provides rights and benefits worthy of protection, and women's activism in the last few decades has been directed toward gaining more visibility as citizens (or subjects in the case of Nepal and Bhutan) not only to demand better enforcement of existing laws and policies but also for additional legislation and gender-sensitive public policy to further serve their needs and interests.

See Also

COLONIALISM AND POSTCOLONIALISM; DEVELOPMENT: SOUTH ASIA; FUNDAMENTALISM AND PUBLIC POLICY; NONGOVERNMENTAL ORGANIZATIONS (NGOS); POLITICAL PARTICIPATION; POLITICAL REPRESENTATION; POLITICS AND THE STATE: OVERVIEW; POLITICS AND THE STATE: SOUTH ASIA I

References and Further Reading

Agarwal, Bina, ed. 1991. *Structures of patriarchy: State, community and household in modernising Asia.* New Delhi: Kali for Women.

Alam, S. M. Shamsul. 1993. Islam, ideology, and the state in Bangladesh. *Journal of Asian and African Studies* 28(1–2): 88–106.

Basu, Amrita, ed. 1995. *The challenge of local feminisms: Women's movements in global perspective.* Boulder, Col.: Westview.

Bhasin, Kamala, Ritu Menon, and Nighat Said Khan, eds. 1994. *Against all odds: Essays on women, religion and development from India and Pakistan.* New Delhi: Kali for Women.

Clarke, Alice, ed. 1993. *Gender and political economy: Explorations of south Asian systems.* New Delhi: Oxford University Press.

Forbes, Geraldine. 1996. Women in modern India. *The New Cambridge History of India,* Vol. 2. Cambridge: Cambridge University Press.

Hasan, Zoya, ed. 1994. *Forging identities: Gender, communities and the state.* New Delhi: Kali for Women.

Hensman, Rohini. 1992. Feminism and ethnic nationalism in Sri Lanka. *Journal of Gender Studies* 1(4): 501–506.

Jalal, Ayesha. 1991. The convenience of subservience: Women and the state in Pakistan. In Deniz Kandiyoti, ed., *Women, Islam and the state,* 77–114. London: Macmillan.

Jayawardena, Kumari, and Malathi de Alwis, eds. 1996. *Embodied violence: Communalizing women's sexuality in south Asia.* New Delhi: Kali for Women.

Jeffrey, Patricia, and Amrita Basu, eds. 1998. *Appropriating gender: Women's activism and politicized religion in south Asia.* New York: Routledge.

Kishwar, Madhu, and Ruth Vanita. 1991. *In search of answers: Indian women's voices from MANUSHI.* New Delhi: Horizon India.

Kumar, Radha. 1993. *The history of doing: An illustrated account of movements for women's rights and feminism in India, 1800–1990.* New Delhi: Kali for Women.

Sangari, Kumkum, and Sudesh Vaid. 1993. *Recasting women: Essays in colonial history.* New Delhi: Kali for Women.

Sarkar, Tanika, and Urvashi Butalia, eds. 1995. *Women and the Hindu right.* London: Zed; New Delhi: Kali for Women.

Kalpana Misra

POLITICS AND THE STATE: Southeast Asia

Women and Premodern States in Southeast Asia

The great linguistic and cultural variation across southeast Asia (comprising 11 countries, including East Timor) means that generalizations can be misleading. Nevertheless, it is commonly accepted that southeast Asian women traditionally enjoyed a relatively high status in relation to men. This is attributed to several factors, including the frequency of bilateral kinship and matrilocal residence, the custom of bride wealth, the importance of women in indigenous ritual and local economies, and the historically low level of state development. Although early political centers adapted political-religious models from India and China that accorded men a substantially higher place than women, these gender constructions had little influence beyond the upper classes. Leaders in small kinship-based village societies were normally male, but women continued to wield considerable influence because of their roles in the domestic economy and in ritual life.

From the fifteenth century several new states emerged in southeast Asia. Recurring warfare and the need for physical strength in projects such as land clearance, temple building, and canal construction helped affirm the perception that men were more valuable than women. Such views were reinforced by the world religions, all of which saw females as subordinate, and which were now reaching down to ordinary people. Theravada Buddhism was the dominant religion in Myanmar, Siam (Thailand-Laos), and Cambodia; the Vietnamese court supported Confucianism; during the sixteenth century, Islam spread through the Malay-Indonesian archipelago, while Spanish colonizers brought Christianity to the Philippines. But despite the patriarchal nature of southeast Asian states, women remained critical in the marriage and family alliances on which any ruler's authority and legitimacy were based. In numerous instances a dowager queen assumed control of the government following the death of her husband, or while her son was a minor, an indication of the general influence wielded by older women. By the eighteenth century such cases became rarer as ruling elites endorsed the view that "good" women should be secluded from public life. Although law codes and other pronouncements that sought to enforce a gender hierarchy must always be regarded as prescriptive rather than reflecting the lived reality of ordinary men and women, they stand as indisputable evidence of the state's concern to regulate gender relations.

Women and Colonial States

The arrival of Europeans as traders and colonizers in southeast Asia from the sixteenth century had far-reaching effects on relationships between women and the state, especially in the island world where European economic interests were concentrated. The European understanding of political power as a male preserve fed into trends that were steadily reducing female roles. For example, women became less evident as intermediaries in interstate negotiations, while their economic influence also declined as Chinese traders began to dominate local economies, and as cash crop agriculture and mining placed greater emphasis on capital and control of labor.

From the beginning of the nineteenth century, southeast Asia became a target for European imperialist expansion because of its strategic position between India and China and its economic resources. By the 1890s, the entire region except for Thailand was controlled by European powers—Vietnam, Laos, and Cambodia were joined together as French Indochina; Myanmar, Singapore, Malaysia, and northwestern Borneo were under the British; the Dutch created the Netherlands East Indies; and the Philippines declared itself independent of Spain in 1896 only to be taken over by the United States.

Throughout southeast Asia there was resistance to European colonization, sometimes prolonged. Those at the forefront were almost all male, but occasionally a woman (usually a leader's wife or widow) earned a place in the nationalist hagiography. However, there is little comparative work on how southeast Asian women fared under different colonial regimes. Although the lives of many were radically changed, there are obvious contrasts between the situation of women in a town like Manila, where the Spanish presence dated back to the late sixteenth century, and in more isolated areas such as Laos, where French colonization came three hundred years later.

Female political awareness remained at a low level for most of the colonial period. Although women were recruited as cheap labor in the capital-intensive plantation economies (tea, sugar, tobacco, and rubber) and processing plants, they were generally quiescent. Only in a few cases, such as the state-run tobacco factories in the Philippines, was there some politicization as women agitated for better pay and conditions. Discontent with colonialism was more clearly articulated among educated women, especially teachers. By 1877, for example, around a thousand Filipino women had received teacher training, and a number later worked with anticolonial organizations and newspapers. But the number of educated females in southeast Asia was always small, and the concerns of the average woman were focused on her family.

At the village level, traditional gender relations were further undermined as colonization "reformed" the customary laws that gave women considerable autonomy in daily life. For example, European legal systems, which assumed that men controlled property, often ignored indigenous inheritance of land and houses through the female line. In addition, women were subordinated through racial hierarchies as well as gender. In 1916, the relatively liberal U.S. administration that controlled the Philippines from 1902 gave Filipino men the right to vote. Filipino women were enfranchised only in 1937 after extensive campaigning, even though the vote had been granted to U.S. women in 1921.

The impact of the western model can be seen in the region's only noncolonized country, Siam (Thailand). Although King Mongkut (1851–1868) is often lauded as a defender of female rights, limitations on marriages between noble men and commoner women and the tightening of father–son inheritance affirmed patrilineality and protected the existing class structure. Bilateral kinship had traditionally applied in Siam, but Mongkut encouraged the formulation of upper-class genealogies that traced descent through the male line. In 1913, his grandson decreed that all Thais should for the first time take a family name, which should pass through the patriline. Subsequent enactments, intended to "modernize" Thailand by forbidding polygamy, merely removed legal protection from second wives while ignoring the widespread practice of concubinage.

Women, Nationalism, and Independence

From the late nineteenth century, nationalist movements developed across southeast Asia. Although their male leaders focused on political independence and self-government, writings by educated women also indicate a deep-seated concern with issues such as polygamy, divorce, domestic abuse, and the financial responsibilities of fathers. From these women's perspective, questioning the colonial political system also meant questioning the gender hierarchies it maintained. In some cases men also espoused radical ideas about the position of women in a future independent state. The constitution that Apolinario Mabini drew up for the new Philippine Republic in 1898 was never brought into force, but it was well before its time in affirming women's right to vote, to assume certain public offices, to obtain an education, and to practice any profession or career. Socialists in southeast Asia similarly believed that the state should take the lead in emancipating women. In 1931, the newly formed Indochinese Communist Party listed sexual equality in employment, in marriage relationships, and in inheritance among its ten goals.

For the most part, however, male nationalist leaders such as Sukarno of Indonesia urged their female supporters to set aside a women's agenda because the primary goal, which should involve both men and women working together, was independence. Indonesian women's organizations generally accepted this argument and did not demand the right to vote until 1938. Across southeast Asia other politicized women also laid aside feminist aspirations to serve the nationalist cause. Nonetheless, despite their active involvement in anticolonial movements, sometimes as fighters but more often as strike organizers, journalists, couriers, and clandestine agents, women were regarded as auxiliaries and helpers rather than partners. Such attitudes were still evident when independence movements exploded with new energy after the surrender of the Japanese, who occupied most of southeast Asia between 1942 and 1945. In Java, for example, some women joined the "bamboo spears" (anti-Dutch revolutionary units, made up primarily of young men), but there was a general feeling that they should be at home. In the male-dominated environment of revolutionary warfare, there was little talk of the specific ways in which a future independent state would address the needs of its female citizens. This was even true in Vietnam, where the Vietnam Women's Union, organized in the 1930s, played a major role in organizing resistance when the revolutionary struggle against France and later the United States was renewed in the 1950s.

Women, Politics, and the State in Contemporary Southeast Asia

World War II represents a political watershed in southeast Asia because it effectively brought colonialism to an end. Theoretically, all the newly independent states were committed to gender equality, but this goal has not been easily translated into reality. A major reason has been the fragility of regional democracy, which has severely limited the political rights of all southeast Asians, men as well as women. In countries that have experienced lengthy periods of military control, formal political power has been exclusively male. Burma, for example, has been ruled by the army or army-connected governments since 1962, as was Indonesia under General Suharto (1965–1998). Other countries, notably Laos, Cambodia, and Vietnam, have undergone many years of warfare during which political processes were completely disrupted. In the Philippines, democracy was suspended between 1972 and 1986, and even Malaysia and Singapore, the only two southeast Asian countries to have held elections regularly since independence, display an extremely low toleration for political opposition.

The effective quashing of the left wing outside the communist states has eliminated most political affiliations normally supportive of women's rights. In Indonesia, for example, the communist-linked women's organization Gerwani gained widespread support as the economy declined under Sukarno, but it was banned after the military coup of 1965. Unions everywhere have been discouraged or tightly controlled, despite recurring evidence of abuse of workers' rights, especially those of women. In their desire to encourage foreign investment through a compliant workforce, contemporary southeast Asian governments have been quite willing to ignore workplace issues like maternity leave and equal pay. In Indonesia, in May 1993, Marsinah, a factory union activist, was murdered following her involvement in strike organization.

Despite the historical prominence of southeast Asian women in local economies, a second reason for female political inactivity has been the persistence of cultural attitudes that perceive them primarily as "mothers, wives, and helpers." In Suharto's Indonesia, the State Ministry for the Role of Women actively promoted an ideology that emphasized a woman's duties as wife and mother. The socialist states are not markedly different, despite the fact that sexual equality is one of communism's basic tenets. Thus, although Laos promotes the notion of Three Goods (good citizen, good mother, good wife) and Two Duties (national defense and women's emancipation), the latter are not elaborated. Such views have implications for female political representation; in 1992, there were only 8 women in the 85-member Lao National Assembly. In neighboring Vietnam, there is a rough quota of 10 to 14 percent for women delegates to the Central Committee, but with very rare exceptions there has been no female representation on the Politburo. Since Vietnam's shift to a market economy under *doi moi* (renovation) in 1986, there has even been a decline in female political participation as the state sector has retracted. Separate women's branches in Malaysia's major political parties also help relegate females to an auxiliary position. In addition, both in Malaysia and in Indonesia Islamic parties do not favor women candidates. Even in the Christian Philippines, wives and female relatives of elected members are said to wield more informal influence than officially elected women representatives, who are frequently wives or relatives of men required to resign from the legislature following the completion of their maximum term.

Nonetheless, there have been signs of change over the last twenty years as women have become more alert to the implications of state policies. For example, most governments have tried to regulate female fertility, either encouraging educated women to have more children, as in Singapore, or, more commonly, promoting birth control. But in Laos between 1975 and 1988 the communist government, which favored population growth, proscribed contraception. The Lao Women's Union successfully lobbied to have this ban lifted because of its damaging effects on women's health and wellbeing. The Vietnam Women's Union, though also part of the state structure, has similarly campaigned to protect women's rights in matters such as land allocation and inheritance.

Throughout the region there is little doubt that greater political acumen has been fostered by the increase in nongovernmental organizations (NGOs), which have blossomed since the 1980s. Through these associations, women otherwise excluded from the political process have acquired knowledge and organizational skills, an important factor in societies where men are preferred as leaders. The impact of NGOs is especially evident in Thailand, where numerous groups have helped train and educate women for government. The results are particularly impressive at the local level; in 1998, around 2.5 percent of Thailand's village heads were female and women made up well over 8 percent of elected municipal representatives. In the Philippines a unique development has been the emergence of militant nuns, whose example and leadership contributed to the downfall of President Ferdinand Marcos in 1986. As of the spring of 2000, the current chairperson of the umbrella organization GABRIELA (General Assembly Binding Women for Reforms, Integrity, Equality, Leadership, and Action) was a nun.

The increased availability of tertiary education for women is another factor contributing to greater political awareness, as female students have been caught up in prodemocracy protests like those in Thailand in 1973 and 1992, in Burma in 1988, and in Indonesia in 1998. Educated women can also provide a rallying point for those who desire change, even when they obtain leadership positions through their male connections, because there is a tendency to see women as less venal than men and as more likely to govern in the people's interest. In local politics women perform well, and in the Philippines several successful mayors have been women. Although leadership at higher echelons of government is more difficult, public expectations have helped propel some women onto the national stage. Corazon Aquino, widow of the assassinated senator Benigno Aquino and president of the Philippines from 1986 to 1992, had few political skills and achieved little in the way of reform, but her personal integrity stood in contrast to the corruption that had become a hallmark of Philippine politics. In Indonesia, similar attitudes help account for the support given to the daughter of Sukarno, Megawati, in the 1999 elections. Undoubtedly the most inspiring leadership has been that of Aung San Suu Kyi, recipient of the 1991 Nobel Peace Prize. The daughter of Burma's famous nationalist leader, she assumed leadership of the prodemocracy movement in 1988 but has been under house arrest or close government surveillance since 1990. Suu Kyi is clearly conscious of the potential for an enhanced female role in politics, and she has publicly appealed for Burmese women to give her their support.

At the beginning of the twenty-first century, it is evident that southeast Asian women are better educated, more concerned, and more willing than ever before to become involved in political affairs. Yet, despite encouraging signs at the local level, only in Vietnam's Central Committee and in the Philippine senate has female representation in any southeast Asian national government risen above 10 percent. It is estimated that another 25 percent representation would be necessary for any meaningful political participation to occur. Nor can it be assumed that those who do gain positions of political influence will be willing to stand as advocates of women's issues at the risk of alienating their male colleagues or the male electorate. Nonetheless, the resilience and pragmatism of southeast Asian women and their undoubted influence in the community provide good reason for optimism regarding the expansion of their political presence.

See Also

ANCIENT NATION-STATES: WOMEN'S ROLES; COLONIALISM AND POSTCOLONIALISM; EDUCATION: SOUTHEAST ASIA; HOUSEHOLDS AND FAMILIES: SOUTHEAST ASIA; NONGOVERNMENTAL ORGANIZATIONS (NGOS); POLITICAL LEADERSHIP; POLITICAL PARTICIPATION

References and Further Reading

Andaya, Barbara Watson, ed. 2000. *Other pasts: Women, gender and history in early modern southeast Asia.* Honolulu: Center for South-East Asian Studies, University of Hawai'i.

Barry, Kathleen, ed. 1996. *Vietnam's women in transition.* New York: St. Martin's.

Connell, R.W. 1990. The state, gender and sexual politics: Theory and appraisal. *Theory and Society, 19*(5): 507–544.

Dancz, Virginia. 1987. *Women and party politics in peninsular Malaysia.* Singapore: Oxford University Press.

Ebiota, Elizabeth Uy. 1992. *The political economy of gender: Women and the sexual division of labour in the Philippines.* London: Zed.

Ireson, Carol. 1996. *Field, forest and family: Women's work and power in rural Laos.* Boulder, Col.: Westview.

Mi Mi Khaing. 1994. *The world of Burmese women.* London: Zed.

Ramusack, Barbara N., and Sharon Sievers. 1999. *Women in Asia: Restoring women to history.* Bloomington and Indianapolis: Indiana University Press.

Roces, Mina. 1998. *Women, power and kinship politics: Female power in postwar Philippines.* Westport, Conn., and London: Praeger.

Sears, Laurie J., ed. 1996. *Fantasizing the feminine in Indonesia,* Durham, N.C.: Duke University Press.

Tantiwiramanond, Darunee, and Sashi Ranjan Pandey. 1991. *By women, for women: A study of women's organizations in Thailand.* Singapore: Institute for South-East Asian Studies.

Wong, Aline K., and Leong Wai Kum. 1993. *Singapore women: Three decades of change.* Singapore: Times Academic.

Barbara Watson Andaya

POLITICS AND THE STATE: Southern Africa

Women in southern Africa have been significant participants in politics and have historically tried to influence the state in a variety of ways. Women's relationships with the state have been mediated by age, class, religion, ethnic, and social characteristics.

History of the Region

A wide range of centralized states existed in southern Africa in the precolonial period, including the Mutapa state of Zimbabwe, the Zulu state in South Africa, the Swazi, the Sotho state in present-day Lesotho, and the Ndebele state founded by Mzilikazi. Some of these states had relatively centralized political authority and were militaristic.

In the centralized states, women of the ruling families and the monarchy were included in the economic, social, and political systems of power. They were involved in marriages that were politically advantageous and were able to influence those systems in different ways. For example, the Swazi Indlovukati (the queen mother) exercises considerable power, as she is part of the Swazi monarchy and rules with the king. Her village is the ritual capital of the nation and her powers check and complement those of the king. She is important in determining succession to the throne, and can counsel the king and act as regent in his absence. In the Mutapa state, the first wife of the Mutapa advocated the interests of the Portuguese and had much influence over relations between the Mutapa and the Portuguese. Thus mothers, wives, and sisters of kings had opportunities to influence the decisions of monarchs and to take part directly and indirectly in state affairs.

Age was a mediating factor in this influence, however, as it was the older women who could amass and wield influence as sisters and mothers of kings or heirs to thrones. Given the practice of exogamy for political purposes, the wives of kings could—in some instances—be considered outsiders, so it was sometimes prudent to curtail their influence as their loyalties could be multiple (especially if their sons were not yet eligible to succeed their fathers or were not eligible at all). Thus, even among royal women, the exigencies of exogamous marriage determined their relationships to kings—whether agnatic (by birth) or affinal (by marriage)—and the degree of their influence on affairs of state. In addition, the pedigree and class of a royal wife could determine whether her sons could succeed to their father's throne, because women born of lowly families or descended from conquered peoples could be regarded with suspicion or as too inferior to produce kings.

Women from the commoner classes—especially those from conquered peoples—did not have much direct influence on the affairs of state and politics. In this respect, they were similarly placed with the men of their classes. In the Ndebele state, men and women from conquered peoples, *amahole,* were looked down on and subjected to discrimination and political marginalization, because they were not of Nguni extraction. In the militaristic states such as the Zulu and Ndebele, however, common men had some opportunity to distinguish themselves through military service, thus earning themselves social recognition and political influence through their military abilities. Such men also could earn some wealth through the spoils of war with other peoples. Unless they were mediums of powerful territorial spirits, common women had very limited political roles. In a few instances, they could improve their social and political positions through marrying into the royal and courtly families.

It is clear that women of different classes, ages, and ethnic origins had differing degrees of political influence and participation in the states of precolonial southern Africa. All they did have in common was their gender. Even royal women could not be sovereigns and succeed to power as women. They did not serve in the military, so they could not access economic power through the spoils of war. They could not marry multiple spouses and command large pools of adult labor. Thus their political and economic power and the avenues to it were limited relative to those of men.

Colonialism and the Ruling Classes

As colonialism destroyed these states in the eighteenth and nineteenth centuries, a process of decomposition and recomposition of different women's situations occurred. Royal women lost their high status and political power as kingdoms such as that of the Zulu, Sotho, Swazi, and Ndebele were destroyed and new political entities emerged under colonial control. The royal and ruling-class women, like their men, came under the control of different types of colonial administrations. New classes were created as the colonials and the missionaries brought in school-based education, administration, and religion for chosen groups of natives. The people who were most attracted to the new systems of the colonials were the previously dispossessed classes, who saw opportunities opening up to allow them to become emancipated from the power of the old ruling classes. The previous ruling classes were not eager to subjugate themselves under the new colonial administration, so most of them resisted the education and religion of the colonials.

Although the new colonial order appeared to offer new opportunities to those previously disadvantaged, its patriarchal orientation continued to privilege whites, men, older people, and some ethnic groups over others, while creating new forms of political identity that used patriarchy as the major organizing principle. Among the Shona of Zimbabwe—who had not been subject to centralized political authority in their kin-based societies—the creation of colonial states that usurped the lineage authority over the labor, sexuality, and everyday activities of the black colonized, was a significant factor in reducing the political influence of black women in the patrilineages. In southern Africa, the interpretations of customary law by the colonial states constructed the colonized women as perpetual minors and dependents of men even in those areas where the women had exercised considerable autonomy in the precolonial societies. For example, the major productive roles played by women in agriculture and in pastoralist activities especially in the relatively nonmilitaristic uncentralized societies, such as the Shona in Zimbabwe and the Tswana in Botswana, gave women a lot of political influence from the household level to the chiefdom.

Under colonial rule, the women from the previous ruling classes and old societies lost the most political, social, and economic power, as centralized state control of the polities and economies of the region was strengthened under colonial domination. Whereas the women from the commoner classes were relatively disempowered even prior to colonial rule in comparison with those from the uncentralized chiefdoms, as the colonial states became established, the disempowerment of most black women was effected. The most disempowered were those women whose peoples had their land appropriated early in the colonizing process and those who did not have access to school-based education and training in the colonial system. Those peoples who were near mission stations and schools got a head start over their compatriots in the education stakes.

Patriarchy in Colonial Societies

Like the majority of the centralized precolonial political systems, the colonial systems turned out to be strongly patrilineal, thus relegating the majority of black women to roles secondary to those of men with respect to property, education, and political power. The missionaries favored the education of men and preferred to prepare black women for marriage to black men who had converted to Christianity and were catechists and lay preachers or were in colonial service as police officers, court interpreters, teachers, nurses, and clerks. Only a few women from relatively educated families became teachers, nurses, and social workers. It is these women who made up a section of the emerging black middle classes under colonialism.

The bulk of the black populations had limited political space in the colonial order, which was dominated by the settlers. The blacks did not have the franchise and were not proportionally represented in colonial parliaments. They were confined mainly to advisory politics at local and national levels and often could not take part in overt and direct political activity to influence the state. They had to find less overt ways of politically influencing events in their own countries. The relatively older women of the nascent middle classes obtained their political experience through welfare activities, organizing religious and secular women's clubs, and through teachers', nurses', and other civic, professional, pressure, and interest groups. They campaigned for better education, housing, and health facilities for black people.

Younger women often found themselves frustrated by the docile politics of the 1960s and early 1970s, as they began to question these politics, most of which focused on individual self-improvement under the control of the relatively older women. They joined the more radical political parties and liberation movements in countries such as Zimbabwe, Namibia, Angola, South Africa, and Mozambique, where independence had not been achieved through diplomatic means. Among these women can be counted Winnie Mandela and Lilian Ngoyi of South Africa; Josina Machel of Mozambique; Ruth Chinamano, Jane Ngwenya, and Teurai Ropa of Zimbabwe; and Rose Chibambo of Malawi, to name a few. National liberation movements from the 1960s onward helped to mobilize women in anticolonial struggles in new ways.

In those countries where armed struggles took place, young women volunteered for the liberation armies in Mozambique, Angola, Zimbabwe, Namibia, and South Africa. This enhanced their political visibility in their countries. Older peasant women also found themselves radicalized by their roles as organizers of the welfare of guerrilla armies in the villages in rural areas and mothers of the young men and women who were in the guerrilla armies. They provided intelligence, buried the dead, and looked after the wounded and the active combatants in rural areas. Together with the men in the liberation movements, they took part in the struggles for freedom for the colonized peoples, thus engaging the colonial state on a political level in ways that the white women of the settler populations did not. The participation of young, black, predominantly peasant women in liberation armies also helped to mobilize black civilian working-class and middle-class urban women to join the political parties that were operating openly or clandestinely in the colonized countries.

Independence and Emerging Women's Issues

By the time independence was attained by southern African states, women had undergone varied political experiences depending on their age, class, and race. They pushed themselves forward so that they could move into central roles as members of parliament, ministers, and civil servants. They were able to vote, associate, and move as they willed, and became legal majors in most southern African countries. The visibility of black women was enhanced by the institutionalization of the women's movement globally. Black women made more gender-focused demands on the postcolonial states, which they expected to be more receptive to their needs—needs that had been ignored or overlooked by the colonial states. Class, race, age, and ethnicity differentiated the political roles and expectations of women in the postcolonial period in southern Africa.

National liberation struggles had been informed by nationalistic ideologies that were grounded in male-focused realities and aspirations. The male dominance of the postcolonial states immediately became a problem for black women, who resented the customary laws, colonial legislation, and social practices that presupposed the subordination of women socially, politically, and economically. In Zimbabwe, Angola, Mozambique, South Africa, and Namibia, women's organizations campaigned vigorously to repeal colonial legislation regarding the family and to subordinate customary laws that were against women's interests to the general laws and constitutions of their countries. In these countries, women pushed for increased representation in organs of the state and society. Politically, the participation of the black peasant and working-class women in struggles for national liberation enabled them to press successfully for rights to education, health, and other social services that had been denied to them by the colonial governments in Namibia, Zimbabwe, South Africa, Angola, and Mozambique. In countries where monarchies still dominated the political processes, as they did in Swaziland and Lesotho to some extent, women were not able to force radical changes in the state's relationship to them.

The demands of national reconstruction in a climate dominated by economic austerity, structural adjustment programs, and the hardening of class alliances across racial boundaries also fractured the popular alignments within the liberation movements as they became ruling parties after independence. During this period, black middle-class women with education, marketable skills, and wealth fared better than other classes of women and were able to press for marriage, succession, and labor legislation that favored literate and numerate people with money to pursue justice in the legal systems. In addition, younger women supported and sponsored legislation and social changes that loosened the grip of older people. This was done through legislation on legal ages of majority, as in Zimbabwe. Politically, women's loyalties to the states and their struggles against those states have been informed by their position in the postcolonial societies with regard to age, class, race, and ethnicity. Many white women have felt threatened and disempowered by black women and the black majority, while older black women feel threatened by the displacement of family elders by the state when dealing with younger women.

Traditionally in southern Africa, older women have often acquired power through control over young women. Because young women often have better education and marketable skills, they are able to champion the rights of young, affluent urban women. In countries such as Zimbabwe, Namibia, and South Africa grassroots political activists are older peasant and working-class women. These societies favor educated officeholders who are often young, and, as a result, older women often feel unrecognized. This sometimes shakes their loyalty to their states. Where the states have adopted tough economic policies, the political consequences have realigned women and fractured the gender solidarities that may exist among women, as affluent women lose the support of poorer women, and poor women feel betrayed and abandoned by the women of the ruling parties who sit in parliaments and are state functionaries.

Economically privileged white women are less negatively affected racially by structural adjustment programs, so their political activity remains largely antagonistic to the postcolonial state, individualized and muted. Black women of poorer classes continue to be ambivalent in relation to the state, because of their support for ruling parties that led the struggles for national liberation. These same parties are the ones that control the state machineries and implement economic austerity programs that cut back on public sector employment and health, education, housing, and other social amenities required by the poorest women. This is the case in Zimbabwe and Namibia. In South Africa, the poorer classes are beginning to be restless, because of the slow pace of reform of the apartheid system, which has resulted in very little economic change for the benefit of the black majority.

Ethnicity and Women's Politics

Ethnically, the diversity of southern Africa also has created issues for women's politics, because women's loyalties may, at times, be structured along the lines of ethnicity. The colonial structures of privilege and disadvantage favored some ethnic groups over others, segmented labor markets, and changed occupations in ways that have had significant economic effects. In Zimbabwe and South Africa, agriculture and mining were traditionally considered jobs for immigrants, who were looked down on. Thus the wives and children of such immigrants have found themselves affected negatively by these practices, which have locked them into poorly paid, often hazardous jobs and separated them from the mainstream of gender and class politics until recently.

The ethnic divides also have manifested themselves in the liberation movements and national politics, necessitating painstaking "balancing" of political arithmetic and placing women in ambivalent positions as wives, mothers, and citizens. For example, women may count doubly in statistics if they belong to ethnic groups that need representation. In a cabinet, a minority woman may be used to satisfy gender and ethnic interests simultaneously. In southern Africa, women may marry men of different ethnic affiliations, thus finding themselves in different camps from those of their husbands and children. In most southern African countries, it is difficult for women to confer citizenship on their children if the fathers of those children are foreigners. Thus women who might have spent long periods of time in exile and married foreign men may find that their children are designated as stateless, because of these practices. This has alienated thousands of women of the middle and working classes, because some of the poorer women are married to immigrant men from all over southern Africa, whereas middle-class women are married to men from all over the African, European, and American continents. This struggle over citizenship and gender culminated in the Unity Dow case in Botswana: Unity Dow, a motswanan woman married to a foreign man, challenged the court ruling that made her children foreigners. She won her case. This was a test case for most of the ex-colonies of Britain in southern Africa, and it empowered women's organizations in the region to challenge these practices regarding citizenship.

Ethnicity also divides women in countries such as Zimbabwe, South Africa, and Namibia, where some ethnic groups dominate the state machineries in ways that alienate the ethnic minorities. Some women from minorities such as the Ndebele in Zimbabwe feel stronger loyalty to their ethnic groups than to the state, which they see as the architect of their problems. Significant sections of the rural population, particularly women from the Ndebele areas of the country, harbor hostility toward the state and toward Shona people because of their dominance. Thus, ethnic differences alienate women of the dominated peoples from the state in ways that destabilize the potential solidarity of women and their gender agenda.

The state's interaction with women on a political level is characterized and mediated by crosscutting loyalties in southern Africa. The challenge for the women's groups has been to navigate these divides safely, to recognize them, to neutralize them where this is desirable, and to accommodate them where possible in the attempt to craft a workable gender agenda and to advance the interests of diverse groups of women to their satisfaction. In this endeavor, women try to use the state machineries. At times, they succeed in this process, as has indeed been the case in South Africa, Zimbabwe, Namibia, and Mozambique, with regard to electing women to office and providing social services. At other times, the efforts of the women's groups have mixed results, as states prove resistant to change. This has been the case with respect to repealing customary and citizenship laws, and opening up political and economic opportunities to poorer and needy women and men.

See Also

COLONIALISM AND POSTCOLONIALISM; POLITICAL LEADERSHIP; POLITICAL PARTICIPATION; POLITICAL REPRESENTATION; POLITICS AND THE STATE: OVERVIEW

References and Further Reading

Gaidzanwa, R. B. 1992. Bourgeois theories of gender and feminism and their shortcomings with reference to southern African countries. In R. Meena, ed., *Gender in southern Africa: Conceptual and theoretical issues.* Harare: SAPES.

Kuper, H. 1947. *An African aristocracy.* Oxford: Oxford University Press.

Mudenge, S. G. I. 1988. *A political history of Munhumutapa.* Harare: Zimbabwe Publishing House.

Rudo Gaidzanwa

POLITICS AND THE STATE: Sub-Saharan Africa

The forms that women's political participation have taken are partly related to the specific nature of the state and the historical transformations that it has undergone. Although African societies have a strong indigenous state tradition, the foundations of current state systems are closely associated with the changes brought about by colonialism. In general, these changes have been detrimental to most African women and have resulted in their marginalization from formal politics.

Political Roles in Precolonial Societies

The basis for the authority of female offices in many precolonial societies lay in women's responsibility for their own affairs. The phrase "dual-sex system" (Okonjo, 1976) describes the system among the Igbo in southeastern Nigeria in which a female leader, the *omu,* was responsible for women's affairs, such as the supervision of market traders. A male leader, the *obi,* was responsible for male affairs and the overall community. In this system, unlike most other monarchical systems, the omu derived her status from her achievements and not from any attachment or relationship to the obi.

Women in political office have not always been responsible only for women's affairs, however. In some cases, women were responsible for the well-being of a community and its lands. Among the Asante in Ghana, the queen mother represented the matrilineage, not women's interests (Lebeuf, 1963). In other instances, such as among the Sherbro and Mende of Sierra Leone, women acted as chiefs in the same way as men (Strobel, 1982).

In most of the monarchical systems, one or two women exercised joint sovereignty with the king. This was the case, for example, among the Bamileke in South Cameroon and in eastern Africa, in the region of the Great Lakes. In all these systems the women belonged to a very restricted group drawn from a privileged social class. The woman who filled the chief role always belonged to the generation senior to that of the king. Her position in the royal lineage was just as important as the kinship relation between her and the king. In general, she was regarded as his "mother" and acted as his guide. Almost everywhere it was she who chose the second woman who would share power with the king (Lebeuf, 1963).

Colonialism and Its Effects

Changes during the colonial period reduced women's effective participation in politics. Colonial administrative changes undermined preexisting structures of female authority. The 1929 Igbo Women's War in Nigeria was the result of women's conviction that they were to be taxed by the colonial authorities. Reforms introduced after an investigation into the British administration in Igboland seriously weakened women's outlets for collective action. For example, their collectively applied sanction for administering justice to men who broke the customary law with regard to women, known as "sitting on a man," was outlawed (Van Allen, 1972). The British also undermined the dual-sex political structure of precolonial times by giving salaries to the male obi and dismissing the female omu (Okonjo, 1976).

Colonialism not only affected preexisting systems of female authority. It also influenced the formation of state systems, in a number of ways that worked against women. First, colonial administrations were set up in order to accumulate capital, and this situation set in motion certain processes of class formation. The growth of state structures has been part of the process of entrenching a ruling class that has been almost exclusively male. It is this ruling class that has had the greatest access to public goods. Second, women's exclusion took place through the continuous use of social control techniques that inevitably restricted their physical and social mobility. Since women were seen as central to the reproduction of labor and the maintenance of the economic bases of traditional society, they were prevented from migrating to urban centers in eastern, central, and southern Africa. Third, state intervention into land tenure and usage systems in rural areas left women tied to the land but more deprived of control over its resources. One of the major effects of colonial bureaucracies on women was to leave them unable to accumulate resources (Chazan, 1989).

Resistance to colonial oppression did not necessarily include resistance to male dominance. Nationalist movements that developed after World War II were characterized by their predominantly male leadership. Women were nevertheless mobilized and active in these struggles. In Nigeria organizations of market women were key supporters of the political parties during the elections. However, they limited their political activities to demands related to market activities and continually underestimated their own more general political strength. Consequently, the political impact they had once exercised declined with time (Mba, 1982). Women in other west African countries, such as Sierra Leone, were able to institutionalize their participation both during and after the nationalist period (Hafkin and Bay, 1976).

In more violent circumstances—such as Mau Mau, the armed peasant insurrection of the 1940s and 1950s in Kenya—women have also been active, as freedom fighters, couriers, and mainstays of their communities. The form of these contributions, however, was essentially traditional, and the innovative changes that women contributed were generally not built upon, either before or after Mau Mau. Women were engaged in political leadership during the struggle but did not achieve leadership positions in corresponding numbers afterward (Strobel, 1982).

New Issues

The creation of new arenas of decision making, such as the formation of contemporary state systems in Africa, raises a number of issues having to do with women's representation in politics. The first issue concerns the extent of female involvement in policy positions. The exclusion of women that characterized the colonial period has continued, with few exceptions, since independence. In Zambia, although women are represented at all levels of the party system, their numbers are too low relative to those of their male counterparts to help integrate women's interests into development strategies. This example indicates a pattern of female incorporation into the political system followed by segregation. The situation in Nigeria illustrates a different pattern: one of exclusion rather than unequal incorporation. Military rulers pursued a policy of deliberate neglect of females until recently. The composition of army-led public bodies was exclusively male and effectively prevented women from sharing formal power (Chazan, 1989).

The second issue concerning women's representation in politics is about to decision makers. Consistently, women appear to have very few avenues of approach to leadership at the national level. In Tanzania, high female party membership did not effectively lead to political influence after independence. In Zambia and Nigeria, female participation in central government is low, and similar patterns appear to exist at local levels as well (Chazan, 1989).

The third issue concerns women's organizations. The political effectiveness of these has been limited. Since Kenya's independence, a nominally autonomous national women's organization, Maendeleo ya Wanawake (Women's Progress), has been largely uncritical of the male leadership of the party and government. Leaders of the organization have been coopted through their connections as wives and kin of male national leaders, thus weakening the earlier grassroots base of Maendeleo. In Tanzania, Umoja wa Wanawake wa Tanzania (National Women's Organisation of Tanzania) is officially part of the ruling party. The problem here is not co-option but inefficiency and ineffectiveness (Strobel, 1982). Elsewhere, major women's organizations, such as the National Council of Women's Societies in Nigeria and the Women's Brigade in Zambia, have been periodically consulted by politicians. However, such organizations have become dependent on formal state support and have thus been unable to act effectively as representatives of women's demands or interests. This development seems to have prompted the founding of organizations, such as Women in Nigeria (WIN), with a more explicitly radical political agenda (Chazan, 1989).

Continuing Marginalization

Explanations for the marginalization of women from formal politics vary. One approach attributes it to the personal inclinations of rulers. Military rulers, for example, are viewed as being particularly unwilling to place women in leadership positions. Exceptions to this pattern are due to the personal preferences of particular individuals. A second approach claims that poor access to education and low female participation in wage employment have blocked women's political participation. A third approach emphasizes that the nature of the state and not the specificity of regimes underpins poor participation rates. This approach also highlights the preference of many women for nonformal political activity.

The state frequently plays a major role in perpetuating social, economic, and ideological processes that subordinate women. Women are often treated as the dependents of men in legal and administrative procedures rather than as persons in their own right. Social and legal adulthood for women is contingent upon marriage, and even then authority over the woman is still exercised by a man (if not the father, then the husband). In personal law, matters such as inheritance and custody of children after divorce generally favor the male line of the family. The head of the household is almost invariably held to be male; it is he who is legally responsible for tax payments and who is generally the recipient of tax benefits. Female-headed households are rarely recognized in legal terms. Through legal and administrative procedures, the state frequently upholds patriarchal family forms in which women do not have the same access to resources as men.

The existence of multiple legal systems—the received laws based on the law of the former colonial states; "customary" laws whose colonial development did not always reflect custom; and religious laws, such as Muslim laws operating in places like Gambia, Senegal, Mali, and northern Nigeria—raises a number of issues. The status of women in society inevitably becomes a contested domain in which divergent discourses may be evident in state, religious, and customary constructions of the appropriate roles of women and men and the ways in which families and households should function. Despite at times competing interests between the state and religious forces, accommodation and alliance may be evident in the maintenance by both of patriarchal forms of control over women.

Nature and Aims of Analytical Studies

Studies of women and the state (see Parpart and Staudt, 1989) have tended to focus less on the relationship between women and the aggregation of public institutions than on the impact of the state and its policies on women. This focus reflects the awareness of the state's central role in the extraction and distribution of resources and its role in structuring social relations.

The first element of such analyses focuses on the content of state policies. State systems tend to be used for regulatory purposes in ways that are contrary to women's needs and interests. Legislation regarding access to land has imposed a variety of constraints on women. Attempts to regulate trading activities and small-scale manufacturing have placed additional obstacles in the path of women's economic advancement. Women have also suffered from neglect in distributional policies. They are generally not targeted for crucial educational and training programs, nor is their work, whether in rural or urban areas, regarded as worthy of state support. Furthermore, the structural adjustment programs of the 1980s generally have been accompanied by cuts in health and social services, areas traditionally regarded as "women's work." These cuts have impeded any attempts to eradicate gender-based divisions of labor.

The second dimension of these analyses is concerned with the effect of these official policies on gender relations. Consistently, the combination of neglect and discrimination is viewed as hindering women's economic prospects. In the rural areas, not only do women perform different tasks from men, but there is a growing differentiation between women's and men's crops. In the urban areas, trading, marketing, and wage employment are gendered. Women are found predominantly in undervalued occupations in which problematic patterns of work and social exchange are institutionalized.

Political crises have accompanied the economic decline of many African economies. It is against this background that coercive control over women has been exercised by the state, as, for example, in the cleanup campaigns that have taken place in countries such as Zimbabwe and Nigeria (see Afshar, 1987). The experiences of African women highlight some of the negative consequences of many recent policy initiatives, such as structural adjustment policies. Such initiatives have acted to perpetuate the subordinate condition of African women. Interpretations of the causes and implications of these findings vary considerably. Some insist that male domination, via the state, lies at the root of the problem, whereas others stress the importance of the dynamic interaction between men, women, resources, values, the market, and the state.

See Also

COLONIALISM AND POSTCOLONIALISM; POLITICAL LEADERSHIP; POLITICAL PARTICIPATION; POLITICAL REPRESENTATION

Reference and Further Reading

Afshar, Haleh, ed. 1987. *Women, state and ideology.* London: Macmillan.

Chazan, Naomi. 1989. Gender perspectives on African states. In Jane Parpart and Kathleen Staudt, eds., *Women and the state in Africa,* 185–201. Boulder, Col., and London: Lynne Rienner.

Hafkin, Nancy, and Edna Bay, eds. 1976. *Women in Africa: Studies in social and economic change.* Stanford, Calif.: Stanford University Press.

Lebeuf, Annie. 1963. The role of women in the political organization of African societies. In Denise Paulme, ed., *Women of tropical Africa*, 93–119. Berkeley: University of California Press.

Mba, Nina. 1982. *Nigerian women mobilised: Women's political activity in southern Nigeria, 1900–1965*. Berkeley: Institute of International Studies, University of California, Berkeley.

Okonjo, Kamene. 1976. The dual-sex political system in operation: Igbo women and community politics in midwestern Nigeria. In Nancy Hafkin and Edna Bay, eds., *Women in Africa: Studies in social and economic change*, 45–58. Stanford, Calif. Stanford University Press.

Parpart, Jane, and Kathleen Staudt, eds. 1989. *Women and the state in Africa.* Boulder Col., and London: Lynne Rienner.

Strobel, Margaret. 1982. African women. *Signs: Journal of Women in Culture and Society* 8(1): 109–131.

Van Allen, Judith. 1972. "Sitting on a man": Colonialism and the lost political institutions of Igbo women. *Canadian Journal of African Studies* 6(2): 165–181.

Charmaine Pereira

POLITICS AND THE STATE: Western Europe

The relationship between women, politics, and the state is multidirectional and complex. In western Europe, however, women have been collectively and deliberately engaging with public politics and the state for well over a century. In so doing, they have influenced state policies directly or indirectly affecting women, and, to varying degrees, they also have modified the political process. The nature of women's encounter with politics and the state has differed between regions and even between countries. And, of course, it has differed according to characteristics of the women themselves, for example, class, ethnic identity, religion, or age.

Background

The modern (nation) state first emerged in western Europe. This was a protracted process but, according to some accounts, by carving out a public political sphere—from which women were excluded—this process deprived certain women of the political influence they had wielded in earlier times as members of powerful families. Although by no means the sole or original cause of women's generally subordinate status, by the early nineteenth century, the modern state reinforced that status through its policies and patriarchal assumptions. Thus, women lost legal "personhood" and property rights on marriage. At the same time, the state declined to intervene when a husband physically assaulted his wife, and it was almost impossible for women to instigate divorce. Legislation in the nineteenth century tended to strengthen prohibitions against abortion. Women were barred from a range of occupations and from the burgeoning professions, while new systems of secondary education excluded or made inferior provision for girls.

In these circumstances, early feminists soon demanded that the new, masculine arguments for the expansion of political rights be extended to women. Feminist movements in the nineteenth century demanded the vote, but this did not preclude and was often seen as instrumental to realizing other improvements in women's status. Not surprisingly, these movements tended to be overwhelmingly middle- or upper-class. Evans (1977) has argued, more specifically, that "[F]eminism, like liberalism itself... was above all a creed of the Protestant middle classes." Certainly the strength, boldness, and characteristic emphases of the movement varied from country to country. Organized feminism emerged first in Britain, where the daring of its militant "suffragettes" became legendary, but was most successful in Scandinavia. European women won the vote first in Finland (1906) and Norway (1913). (The last European countries to enfranchise women were Switzerland, in 1971, and Liechtenstein, in 1985, although the vote that women briefly won in Portugal and Spain in the 1920s was swiftly snatched away under military rule and not restored until the mid-1970s.) Partly as a consequence of feminist mobilization, by the early twentieth century there had also been real, if often limited, improvements in married women's status and in educational and employment opportunities for women in a number of countries. In Scandinavia, some reforms preceded the emergence of feminism in the 1870s; for example, Swedish women acquired the right to inherit property in 1845 (the reasons are disputed but may include women's relatively high status prior to industrialization).

Although enfranchisement opened the way for women to participate more fully in "mainstream" politics, the immediate sequel was generally disappointing. In many cases, feminist activism actually fragmented and declined. In the following decades, it was overwhelmed, in a number of countries, by political turmoil, fascist dictatorship, or invasion. (Sweden was once more something of an exception, relatively unaffected by these political trends and with feminist organizational continuity provided by the rights-oriented Frederika Bremer Association and women's involvement in the Social Democratic Party.) Where women were able to exercise the vote, they were observed to participate less often than men, and to be more likely to support conservative parties, especially where these were closely linked to the Catholic church. Nonetheless, Joni Lovenduski (1996) argues that state policies affecting women—for example, in the spheres of education and health—at least by the 1940s often suggested that male politicians did recognize women's potential voting power.

Participation

In much of western Europe, the so-called second wave of feminism—in some cases more properly seen as a first wave and, in the case of Italy, more like a third or fourth wave—stimulated women's greater political participation. Incidentally, among the complex factors underlying this second wave were changes in women's expectations triggered by postwar state policies, especially the expansion of women's access to higher education. Variations in the political impact of second-wave feminism in part reflected its character. Vibrant movements in Italy and Denmark contrasted with quiescence in Austria and Switzerland. But also significant was the particular blend of radical-separatist, socialist, and liberal-reformist strands. Radical feminism—influential, for example, in Britain and West Germany—discouraged participation in state institutions and conventional political processes; liberal and traditional socialist feminism—as in Italy or Sweden—was more conducive to it.

From the 1960s, rates of women's political participation and representation began to climb. Besides feminist influences, the pace of change was shaped by the political context. Clearly one precondition for effective participation was the existence of a broadly liberal democratic system; in its absence—as in Greece, Portugal, and Spain until the mid-1970s—women's political progress was inevitably delayed. But, within liberal democracies, two further factors were of special significance. First was the type of electoral system—with multimember districts and party lists most favorable to women's participation. Second was the party system, including changes over time in party alignments. Generally speaking, it did not prove an effective strategy for women to form their own party, although a partial exception is Iceland's Women's Alliance Party, formed in 1982, which won 5.5 percent of the vote and 5 percent of national seats in 1983. Despite women's high membership rates in conservative and religiously based parties, their political promotion depended more on the strength and attitude of parties of the left, including, more recently, Green parties. A third factor sustaining women's political participation was, of course, levels of social provision, associated with the expansion of the welfare state, that allowed them the necessary time and resources.

Scandinavia led the way, with women already constituting over 30 percent of members of pariliment in Norway and Finland by the mid-1980s. By the mid-1990s, they were over 40 percent in Sweden, and at or just above the quarter-way mark in Austria, Germany, and the Netherlands. They were still around 6 percent in Portugal, Greece, and, most remarkably, France. Women formed approximately half the membership of ruling cabinets in Norway and Sweden, with countries such as Austria and the Netherlands again creeping up. There were three women prime ministers (Britain, Norway, and Portugal) and two women presidents (Iceland and Ireland). Parallel with this growth in women's political representation within individual European countries has been their increasing numbers, since the introduction of direct elections in 1979, within the European Parliament. By no means have all these women seen themselves as feminist or even sympathised with a broadly feminist agenda. Where they have reached a "critical mass" (say 25 to 30 percent), however, and especially in conjunction with feminist pressures from without, women politicians have helped to make both the content and the style of policy making rather more "woman-friendly."

Women's participation in political institutions and arenas outside these representative channels, such as the judiciary and media, also has grown. In the important sphere of state bureaucracy, real progress has been slow. The state has emerged as one of the chief employers of women, nationally and at regional and local levels, but the proportion of women in the highest ranks everywhere has remained small. Nonetheless, a significant policy role has been played by those bureaucrats, generally women, known as "state feminists" or "femocrats," who have feminist sympathies or, at the least, have been made responsible for sex equality programs—for example, in the Netherlands, France, and within relevant directorates of the European Commission.

State Policies and Women

As Joni Lovenduski (1986) has written, "European state structures were established on the assumption that women were controlled rather than for the purposes of such control." Until recently, state policies were rarely about women as such, and even now issues of women's rights remain marginal to the political agenda. Rather, women have been affected by policies primarily concerned with matters such as economic growth, national security, population levels, and political stability. The content of these policies varied considerably from country to country, however, influenced by factors such as the level of economic development, predominant culture (place of religion), political ideology (including attitudes to state intervention), degree of internal political unity, and (perceived) external threats. Early feminist mobilization contributed to some expansion in women's rights, but it can be argued that at least as valuable for women were the changes in their position and opportunities associated with the expansion of the welfare state, in the wake of World War II. Beginning in Britain, this process spread unevenly, developing furthest under a combination of sustained economic growth and left-wing governments; it has only really begun to have an impact on the Mediterranean region quite recently. With the partial exception of Sweden (where women were more extensively involved in the labor movement, which helped to secure it), moreover, the welfare state inherited and, in some ways, further institutionalized the assumption of women's economic dependence and primary maternal role. Even so, and this is perhaps more evident to feminists, as its provisions have come under attack from the 1980s, the welfare state did provide women with new resources, not least those deriving from expanded educational opportunities and employment in its burgeoning service sector.

Partly as a consequence of direct pressure from second-wave feminist organizations and women politicians—but at least as much due to the gradual feminist-influenced shift in public attitudes—state policies from the 1970s revealed a greater sensitivity to issues of sex equality. Gradual changes occurred in policies concerning equal pay, employment opportunity, income and social security (which, for present purposes, can be classed as economic rights issues), contraception and abortion, rape and domestic violence. These are not, of course, questions on which all women, or even all feminists, are united: women have been fiercely divided in particular over abortion, with Catholic women, for example, playing a central role in prolonging the ban in the Republic of Ireland, while feminists have been divided over which issue areas should be given priority.

Taking first the area of economic rights, an important influence on national policy has been the growth and elaboration from the 1960s of the European Union (EU, formerly European Community). Countries within or anticipating inclusion in the EU have been under pressure to conform with its equal employment law, developing out of provisions in the original Treaty of Rome, as outlined in a series of directives on pay (1975), equal treatment (1976), and social security (1978). From the late 1960s to the mid-1980s, most western European states passed equal opportunities legislation of some kind, and established agencies, government ministries, or bureaus to oversee or at least monitor implementation. Generally, governments were more willing to combat negative discrimination against women than to promote positive discrimination in the form of affirmative action. Overall, too, results of such policies were disappointing, as reflected in the continuing gap between male and female rates of pay and the low number of cases brought under antidiscrimination laws. There also has been striking variation in the extent to which such policies have been accompanied by measures, such as paid parental leave and publicly subsidized day care for children, which make employment equality for women a real possibility. This is less because of feminist influence than political support for state intervention in employment and "family policy," and is one respect in which not only Scandinavia but France has been to the fore.

Abortion can be taken here to represent the second set of issues, centering on women's physical integrity and autonomy. In countries including West Germany, France, and Italy, this was the cause around which second-wave feminism initially mobilized. Conversely, in Sweden, where abortion law had been progressively liberalized from the 1930s, its virtual absence coincided with a very limited radical feminist presence. Demands for women's "right to choose" faced most resistance where the church—especially the Catholic church—retained significant political influence. Given the issue's propensity to evoke seemingly intransigent "lifestyle" confrontations, party leaders generally sought to avoid or defer it where they could. However, most western European states had liberalized their abortion laws by the mid-1980s, although in Spain and Portugal these reforms were very limited. In Germany, conservative fears that East Germany's liberal laws would prevail on reunification in 1989 threatened West German reforms already achieved. The outstanding exception, as noted above, was Ireland.

The modest gains so far described have been threatened by global recession and government measures in response, to varying degrees colored by the precepts of New Right thinking. The consequences of restructuring are felt everywhere, even in Sweden, where women have been affected, for example, by privatization and withdrawal of state support for local authorities, with their consequences for job security and child care provision. Restructuring and cutbacks in public expenditure, moreover, emphasize the differences among women. For some, changes in the law and in public attitudes made the last 15 years a period of increased freedom and opportunity, but for many life is now more arduous and insecure. In these circumstances, the near universal decline of second-wave feminism, as an autonomous movement, must be a cause for concern.

Feminist Understanding of the State

Feminists, whether activists or scholars, have inevitably reflected on this developing relationship between women and the state. First-wave feminists, deprived of the vote, tended to take as given that women's political participation was desirable and would have beneficial policy consequences. In the late 1960s, both radical and nonaligned socialist feminists began with a deep mistrust of the state, as demonstrated when they established their own women's refuges, or—as in Italy and France—their own abortion services. But in time even these feminists found themselves engaging with the state, demanding funding and changes in policy. In the 1970s, a feminist literature emerged, highly critical of what was seen as the patriarchal, capitalist welfare state. But women's actual experience in dealing with the state, together with developments in Marxist—and post-Marxist—theory encouraged more sophisticated understanding, which recognized the state itself as a site of struggle, made up of multiple and potentially conflicting arenas.

As part of this discussion, the difference between states was increasingly acknowledged. In fact, feminists' hostility toward the state had been much more evident in Britain and Germany than in Scandinavia, say, or the Netherlands, reflecting in part their different experiences. Scandinavian feminist academics first questioned the conventional wisdom about the patriarchal state, suggesting it might be better for women to depend on the state than on individual men, and raising the possibility of a woman-friendly state. Beyond this, there have been attempts to distinguish between different kinds of European state in terms of their implications for women. The work of Esping-Anderson, who divided capitalist welfare states into three categories—social democratic, conservative-corporatist, and liberal—has been criticized for failing to take gender properly into account. Jane Lewis (1993) suggests an alternative typology based on the extent to which state policies incorporate a "male breadwinner" model, whereas Gisela Kaplan (1992) divides western European states into four groups: Scandinavia; conservative countries (Germany, Austria, and Switzerland); "creative traditional" countries (France and the Netherlands), where conservative elements have been offset by a tradition of dissent; and the "radical" countries of southern Europe, where recent left-inclined governments have promoted relatively enlightened policies but without the resources to implement them effectively. None of these schemes is entirely satisfactory, however—even the notion of a Scandinavian model has been questioned (by Arnlaug Leira)—and more work is clearly needed.

There also is a more pragmatic debate among feminists, especially those who already have some purchase in state processes and institutions, as to the best strategies for securing change. The achievements of different forms of "state feminism" have been scrutinized and the merits and demerits of "mainstreaming" women-related issues, within both EU and national government bodies, is a subject of growing concern. What is clear is that feminists increasingly recognize the centrality of the state for their project.

See Also

DEVELOPMENT: WESTERN EUROPE; POLITICAL REPRESENTATION

References and Further Reading

Evans, Richard. 1977. *The feminists.* London: Croom-Helm.

Kaplan, Gisela. 1992. *Contemporary western European feminism.* London: Allen and Unwin.

Lewis, Jane, ed. 1993. *Women, work and the family in Europe.* Aldershot: Edward Elgar.

Lovenduski, Joni. 1986. *Women and European politics.* Brighton: Harvester.

Stetson, Dorothy McBride, and Amy G. Mazur, eds. 1995. *Comparative state feminism.* London: Sage.

Ward, Anna, Jeanne Gregory, and Nira Yural-Davis, eds. 1992. *Women and citizenship in Europe.* London: Trentham.

Vicky Randall

POLLUTION

Pollution is an umbrella term that encompasses a wide array of assaults on the environment. Broadly defined, it is best understood as the introduction of substances into the natural environment that cannot readily be assimilated or rendered harmless by normal biological processes (Crump, 1991; Rodda, 1991). Pollution is usually categorized into one of three types, although there is considerable crossover or transfer among the three: air pollution (gas, chemical, and particulate emissions), maritime and freshwater pollution (runoff and dumping of chemical, industrial, biological, and sewage effluents), and land pollution (dumping and disposal of wastes of all kinds). Because the planetary ecosystem is maintained by large-scale circulatory processes such as the hydrological cycle, air circulation systems, and ocean currents, pollution released in one place is seldom contained:

typically, pollutants are circulated over wide areas (even globally) and throughout large ecosystems.

Sources and Effects of Pollution

Natural processes such as volcanic eruptions and erosion produce pollution, sometimes quite acutely, but the primary environmental concern today is with anthropogenic, or human-produced, pollution. Since the industrial revolution, human activities have produced pollution at a dramatically accelerating pace, and the pollution produced is increasingly toxic and persistent. Human-made substances of extreme toxicity, such as pesticides, plastics, synthetic chemical products, and radioactive wastes, account for more and more of the pollutants that are being released into the environment.

Pollutants undermine the integrity and health of animals, humans, and ecosystems. Over much of the globe, oceans and waterways have become dumping grounds, in many places just breathing is a health hazard, and wastelands of extreme and chronic toxicity dot the global landscape. However, specific knowledge of the effects of pollutants typically lags far behind our capacity to produce and release them; controls over pollution lag even farther behind. This gap is due to several factors. Whereas some pollutants act acutely and dramatically, others act slowly and almost imperceptibly; in some cases, the effects of pollutants may not be manifest for years or decades. The materials produced by chemical industries are of particular concern. Literally thousands of synthetic compounds have been introduced and accepted into ordinary life with little understanding or monitoring of their potential environmental effects. The long-term effects of slow-acting pollutants are often noticed only if someone is looking for them. In general, there is much less commitment to examining the pollutant effects of new substances than there is to their initial production and dissemination. Many of the materials, products, and processes that produce pollutants have become thoroughly integrated into modern lifestyles and economies (this includes plastics, chemicals, and cars, among other things); it is difficult to achieve consensus on the implementation of pollution control if such control is seen to necessitate sharp reductions or elimination of these materials. Powerful forces are also at work in undermining the efficacy of pollution control: industries, governments, and armed forces typically have vested interests and profits in economic activities that pollute, whereas pollution control, in contrast, is often perceived as an impediment to the conduct of their business.

Feminist Analysis

Feminist perspectives and the work of women have made significant contributions to our understanding of environmental issues and of pollution. Feminists have been particularly active in reframing the ways in which environmental relations in general, and pollution in particular, are understood. Women's studies scholars, especially in the sciences, have documented the extent to which the ideological underpinnings of modern western science are environmentally destructive (see, for example, Harding, 1986). Indeed, feminists argue, the conduct of western "industrialized" science, and the widespread reliance on scientific rationality, is responsible for much of the egregious environmental damage we now face (see, for example, Shiva, 1989). Recent feminist scholarship further challenges the prevailing paradigm of environmental understanding, which frames environmental problems as disruptions in physical systems. If environmental problems are framed as physical phenomena, then feminist, humanistic, and cultural analysis is marginalized. It is clear to feminists that the environmental crisis is not just a crisis of physical ecosystems; it is, rather, a crisis of culture. Feminist environmental analysis refocuses attention on "agency"—the institutions, behaviors, and norms that produce our dominant "culture of pollution" (Seager, 1993). Because these institutions, behaviors, and norms are gendered, a feminist analysis of gender, power, and agency is held to be crucial to understanding the current environmental crisis. Everywhere, armed forces and multinational corporations rank at the top of the list of agents of environmental destruction; armed forces are especially powerful and are responsible for a disproportionate share of global pollution of all kinds.

At the same time, many women activists and scholars have forged a vision of recasting human relations to the environment with an "ecofeminist" sensibility. Although there is a considerable range of ecofeminist thought, most ecofeminists share a core understanding that the earth is a living entity, that the web of life is interconnected, that all life is dependent on the health and integrity of the whole, and that degradation of the environment is the product of a cultural imbalance (see, for example, Caldecott and Leland, 1983; Diamond and Orenstein, 1990).

Women activists and scholars have been instrumental in focusing attention on the differential impacts of pollution. The effects of exposure to pollution cannot be generalized across a population; they will vary considerably with age, class, race, nationality, gender, geographic location, and social location. Feminists are particularly active in exploring the ways in which the health impacts of pollution are different for men and for women. Whether in Vietnam, India, or Canada, women often experience distinctive—or singular—health problems from exposure to environmental pollutants. The timing, prevalence, and rate of particular cancers (especially breast cancer), reproductive disorders, and chronic health impairments are typically different in women and in their male counterparts. Until women started organizing around these issues in the 1980s, the impacts of pollution on women's health were ignored by mainstream environmental organizations, by official health-monitoring organizations, and by the biomedical research establishment; questions about women's health and pollution, until recently, were not examined, not taken seriously, and not followed up. In consequence, women's health has suffered and the opportunity for early detection of pernicious environmental degradation was, in many cases, forfeited. Women community activists and researchers in the medical and environmental fields are increasingly effective in raising these issues and insisting that women's experiences of pollution be viewed separately from more generalized studies.

Divergent Experiences of Environmental Toxins

The fact that men and women often do not experience the effects of pollution in the same way can be attributed to three factors: economics, biology, and gender roles. The effects of environmental degradation are pushed down the socioeconomic ladder and felt more acutely at the bottom, by those who cannot afford the means to buffer themselves from environmental deterioration; everywhere in the world, women are disproportionately clustered at the bottom of the socioeconomic ladder. Biological differences between women and men, including important differences in hormonal structure, mean that women and men are susceptible to different health effects from exposure to toxins and other pollutants; for example, the globally escalating rate of incidence of breast cancer in women is undoubtedly due, in part, to exposure to industrial pollutants, especially to the synthetic organochlorines that are ubiquitous in industrialized countries. Everywhere in the world, women do different work, in different places, and they fill social roles different from men's. Women everywhere have primary responsibility for meeting the daily needs of their families. This often means that women are in the front lines of exposure to toxins in the environment. Because of their social location (which also often has a real locational correlate), women are much more likely than their male counterparts to have early and prolonged exposure to waterborne pollutants, pollutants in the food chain, and household pollutants, including indoor air pollution.

Except for dramatic pollution incidents, such as oil spills or chemical factory explosions, the effects of pollution are often subtle and only slowly apparent; deterioration in environmental quality more typically shows up in small ways in the ordinary, lived environment. Because of women's social location as managers of the ordinary domestic environment, they are also typically the first to notice the effects of pollution. As a result, everywhere in the world, women are now in the forefront of grassroots environmental organizing; to an astonishing extent, women are the leaders in community-based environmental activism.

Challenging and Changing the World of Policy

Women are less represented in the "official" channels of environmental assessment, organizing, and policy making. They are grievously underrepresented in the environmental sciences, in government agencies with environmental responsibility, and in the large international environmentalist organizations. However, a number of women who have been able to speak from positions of legitimated authority have made significant contributions to our understanding of pollution. Rosalie Bertell, an American now living in Canada, and Alice Stewart, of England, have both challenged the nuclear establishment and have conducted research into the health effects of exposure to radioactive materials; both researchers have compiled compelling evidence to support their conclusions that exposure to low levels of nuclear radiation, even officially designated acceptable levels, is extremely dangerous. Rachel Carson alerted the world to the dangers of pesticide pollution in 1962. In her book *Silent Spring,* she wrote, "What we have to face is not an occasional dose of poison which has accidentally got into some article of food, but a consistent and continuous poisoning of the whole human environment." When *Silent Spring* was published, the chemical industry attacked Carson with great vehemence and misogyny. However, the clarity of her argument and the strength of her evidence eventually led to the banning of DDT and dozens of other pesticides in the United States and in many other industrialized nations. (The pesticide industry, however, continues in the third world to produce and sell products that are banned in the wealthier industrialized countries.) Carson died of cancer in 1964, but the importance and prescience of her work remain undiminished.

See Also

ECOFEMINISM; ENDOCRINE DISRUPTION; NATURAL RESOURCES; POLLUTION: CHEMICAL; SCIENCE: OVERVIEW; TOXICOLOGY

References and Further Reading

Caldecott, Leonie, and Stephanie Leland, eds. 1983. *Reclaim the earth.* London: Women's Press.

Carson, Rachel. 1962. *Silent spring.* Boston: Houghton Mifflin.

Crump, Andy. 1991. *Dictionary of environment and development.* London: Earthscan.
Diamond, Irene, and Gloria Orenstein, eds. 1990. *Reweaving the world: The emergence of ecofeminism.* San Francisco: Sierra Club.
Harding, Sandra. 1986. *The science question in feminism.* Ithaca, N.Y.: Cornell University Press.
Rodda, Annabel. 1991. *Women and the environment.* London: Zed.
Seager, Joni. 1993. *Earth follies: Coming to feminist terms with the global environmental crisis.* New York: Routledge; London: Earthscan.
———. 1995. *The new state of the Earth atlas.* London: Penguin; New York: Simon and Schuster.
Shiva, Vandana. 1989. *Staying alive: Women, ecology, and development.* London: Zed.

Joni Seager

POLLUTION: Chemical

Chemical pollution occurs when humans use, produce, or dispose of chemicals that cause harm to humans and other living organisms (that is, toxic, or hazardous, chemicals). A chemical may cause harm immediately (an acute poison), after a longer period of exposure (a chronic poison), or even in the next generation (a transgenerational poison). Harm may be caused by extraordinarily small amounts of certain chemicals, such as dioxin (2,3,7,8 tetrachlorodibenzo-*p*-dioxin), which is perhaps the most toxic single chemical known. The harm may be temporary, permanent, or fatal, and different chemicals harm different systems in the body in different ways (for example, by damaging the immune system or causing an imbalance in sex hormones). Because people differ in their genetic makeup and histories of exposure to toxic chemicals, certain people are particularly susceptible to harm from particular toxic chemicals.

Exposure to combinations of toxic chemicals may cause more and different kinds of harm than would be expected from knowledge of the individual chemicals. People who are nutritionally deprived or who are ill, old, or young may experience more severe toxic effects. The toxic effects of most commercial chemicals are poorly studied or understood.

"Persistent chemicals" remain toxic in the environment (for example in water, air, or soil) for months, years, or decades, and over time some of these toxics accumulate in high concentrations in humans and other organisms who eat polluted animals or plants, a process called bioaccumulation. All humans now carry some amounts of human-made, persistent, bioaccumulative toxic chemicals in their bodies, particularly in their fats—in breast milk, for example. Many of these chemicals, such as DDT and chlordane, are chlorinated. It is almost impossible to "clean up" pollution of many chemicals. For example, incineration does not destroy toxic metals at all, and incineration of chlorinated chemicals produces even more toxic chlorinated chemicals (Costner and Thornton, 1990.)

Females are susceptible to certain types of harm—breast cancer and endometriosis, for example—because of their biology. (Endometriosis is a painful condition in which bits of the tissue that line the uterus escape the uterus and become implanted on the outside of the ovaries, the fallopian tubes, the uterus, or its supporting muscles.) Hormone-disrupting chemicals are suspected of contributing to these two diseases (Colborn et al., 1996).

Women in low-income occupations are often exposed to toxic chemicals, for example, while preparing pesticide-sprayed flowers for export or working in agricultural fields where pesticides and chemical fertilizers are used or factories using solvents.

Fetuses receive certain toxic chemicals (such as alcohol and polychlorinated biphenyls, or PCBs) from their mother through the placenta and the umbilical cord; some toxic chemicals are passed to the infant through breast-feeding. Fetuses can be highly sensitive to particular toxic chemicals at particular periods during their development, and the harm may not be discovered until adulthood. Female children of women who took the synthetic estrogen called DES (diethylstilbesterol) to prevent miscarriage, for example, experienced cancer of the vagina at increased rates when they reached adulthood (Colborn et al., 1996).

Industrialized countries mostly "regulate" chemical pollution by estimating "safe" or "tolerable" amounts of human-caused toxic chemicals and then, on the basis of this "risk assessment," permitting the use of those chemicals. It is impossible, however, to estimate "safe" or "insignificant" amounts of toxic pollution, because so many toxic chemicals are causing so many types of harm. A more sensible approach is to examine and implement options for the least possible use of toxic chemicals.

Research on the human consequences of toxic exposure has focused primarily on adult males' occupational exposure. Medical research focuses primarily on cures of toxic effects rather than on preventing exposure. Little attention is paid in medical training to environmental causes (including toxic chemicals) of ill health, and the medical profession is largely ignorant of the effects of chemical pollution.

Rachel Carson (1962) raised the world's consciousness regarding all types of chemical pollution when she wrote about the effects of pesticides in *Silent Spring.* Lois Gibbs raised the issue of chemical waste dumps through her neighborhood campaign in Love Canal, New York, in the late 1970s. Theo Colborn was the first to bring scientists together from throughout the world to share their knowledge about endocrine-disrupting chemicals (Colborn et al., 1996).

Women throughout the world lead campaigns to reduce and eliminate the use of toxic chemicals, incineration, landfilling, and international trade in toxic chemicals. They provide the primary impetus for attention to effects of toxic chemicals on children and women.

See Also

CANCER; ECOFEMINISM; ECOSYSTEM; ENDOCRINE DISRUPTION; ENVIRONMENT: OVERVIEW; ESTROGEN; HORMONES; TOXICOLOGY

References and Further Readings

Carson, Rachel. 1962. *Silent spring.* Boston: Houghton Mifflin.

Colborn, Theo, Dianne Dumanoski, and John Peterson Myers. 1996. *Our stolen future.* New York: Dutton.

Costner, Pat, and Joe Thornton. 1990. *Playing with fire.* Washington, D.C.: Greenpeace USA.

Environmental Research Foundation. *RACHEL's Health and Environment Weekly.* P.O. Box 5036, Annapolis, Maryland 21403.

Mary Hallie O'Brien

POLYGYNY AND POLYANDRY

Many societies practice some form of polygamy, or plural spouses. There are two major forms, but the first is by far the most common, that is polgyny, or plural wives. Up to 70 percent of the societies in the world permit polygyny, although most members practice monogamy. Polygyny is allowed in tribes, chiefdoms, and state societies primarily in Africa, Asia, and the Americas. The second form, polyandry, plural husbands, is much more restricted, occurring in only 0.5 percent of all societies, primarily Tibet, southern India, and one area in Indonesia. The main form of polyandry is fraternal, where brothers share a wife, though nonfraternal polyandry used to exist among the Nayars of central Kerala.

Polygyny often, but not always, accompanies patrilineal rules of organization, that is, those in which identity, the control of most resources, political authority, and reputation pass through males to their children. In societies in which patrilineages have access to wealth, a man with several wives has advantages over another. There may include a strong labor force to cultivate expanding properties and a fighting force. Polygyny also expands the number of persons involved in alliances, through the marriages of numerous children. For example, the ruling Saudi dynasty consolidated state control through multiple marriages.

Women in patrilineal societies are disadvantaged first by structural principles of patrilocal residence after marriage that separate them from their natal home and patriline and consolidate male control of resources. Women are also disadvantaged by polygyny, which permits a second wife for reasons of infertility, power alliances, dissatisfaction with the wife, or love of another. In the event of her husband's death, a wife may be required to live as a second wife with her husband's brother (levirate). Yet the rights of plural spouses and resource control are denied to women. Another major disadvantage is that divorce is typically easier for husbands, and custody of children is eventually granted to men, since children are members of their father's descent group.

In ranked and stratified patrilineal societies, women are confronted by a contradiction in which powerful or rich families are polygynous, work can be shared, and the women benefit from the family's status, power, and leisure. Wives are usually ranked and may compete or cooperate with each other. They control their sons and sometimes cooperate to control the husband (Aswad, 1974).

Writers have revealed the stresses of polygyny (Abu-Lughod, 1986), and many feminists have struggled to dismantle or change laws on polygyny and divorce (Badran, 1993). Some Islamic liberals press the Islamic ruling that wives should be treated equally or polygyny disallowed, and several Muslim states have restrictions or bans on polygyny.

It should be noted that the causes, classes, distribution, and religions in polygynous societies vary (White and Burton, 1988). It does not occur, for example, in the most populous Muslim country, Indonesia (Hale, 1995).

Polyandry does not usually increase women's power in the same way that polygyny does for men. In Tibet, a wife is married to a set of brothers, joins their household, and is limited in her choices, this custom occurs where female infanticide is practiced. Levine (1988) suggests that Tibetan families emphasize sharing and solidarity of brothers as a symbolic ideal.

See Also

FAMILY: RELIGIOUS AND LEGAL SYSTEMS; HOUSEHOLDS AND FAMILIES: OVERVIEW; MARRIAGE: OVERVIEW; MORMONS

References and Further Reading

Abu-Lughold, L. 1986. *Veiled sentiments.* Los Angeles: University of California Press.

Altman, I., J. Ginat, and R. B. Yeazall. 1997. *Polygamous families in contemporary society.* Cambridge: Cambridge University Press.

Aswad, B. 1974. *Land control and social strategies.* Ann Arbor: Museum of Anthropology, University of Michigan.

Badran, M. 1993. Independent women: More than a century of feminism in Egypt. In Judith Tucker, ed., *Arab women.* Washington, D.C.: Georgetown University.

Effah, K. B. 1999. A reformulation of the polygyny-fertility hypothesis. *Journal of Comparative Family Studies* 30(3): 381–408.

Hale, S. 1995. Gender and economy, Islam and polygamy: A question of causality. *Feminine Economics* 1(2): 67–76.

Klomegah, R. 1997. Socioeconomic characteristics of Ghanaian women in polygynous marriages. *Journal of Comparative Families Studies* 28 (Spring): 73–88.

Levine, N. 1988. *The dynamics of polyandry.* Chicago: University of Chicago Press.

Mencher, Joan. 1965. The Nayars of south Malagar. In M. N. Nimkoff, ed., *Comparative family systems,* 163–191. New York: Houghton Mifflin.

Schneider, D., and K. Gough, eds. 1961. *Matrilineal kinship.* Berkeley: University of California Press.

White, D., and M.Burton, 1988. Causes of polygyny: Ecology, economy, kinship, and warfare. *American Anthropologist* 30: 871–887.

Barbara C. Aswad

POPULAR CULTURE

Feminist perspectives on popular culture are largely concerned with the ways in which gender relations are constructed within the media of mass communication (press, radio, TV and video, and the cinema and music industries). Some commentators emphasize the economic or psychological power of these media over their audiences, whereas others stress consumers' role in selectively using the information and images offered to them.

In some nonwestern contexts, of course, popular culture may have quite other meanings: it may refer to traditional cultural practices of "the people" that are at odds with the influx of popular culture that accompanies economic and cultural modernization. Popular culture in both senses is addressed in the essays collected by Kamla Bhasin and Bina Agarwal in *Women and Media* (1987). However, the term *popular culture,* as it has been used in modern western critical discourses, implies the existence of another, opposing body of "high culture." Consequently, feminist discussions become entangled in arguments about the relative value of these supposedly distinct kinds of cultural production, some defending and others attacking their potential for promoting social change. A further context for discussing women's cultural participation is the debate about how effective feminist interventions in patriarchal culture can be, or whether women should instead pursue forms of cultural separatism.

Feminists who hold the mass media largely responsible for society's negative and exploitative attitudes toward women tend to characterize the media as driven only by commercial greed, and as invariably false and corrupt. This has been a strong tradition in U.S. feminism from Betty Friedan's *The Feminine Mystique* (1963) to Susan Faludi's *Backlash* (1991) and Naomi Wolf's *The Beauty Myth* (1990). In this view, popular culture's representations of femininity are inimical to the feminist goals of women's well-being and freedom. This view attributes great power to the media and tends to view media consumers as compliant and uncritical.

It is common to recognize the mass media's immense powers of persuasion and censorship. Any feminism concerned with women's subjective sense of themselves must confront this issue, which affects more and more of the world as economic "restructuring" extends the global range of electronic media. A discussion of women's participation as consumers of popular culture through the mass media requires an understanding not only of what the media say but of how they address and construct their audiences, how they circulate meanings, and how various audiences use these cultural meanings.

Feminists wary of dismissing popular culture as evil, or even as "mere entertainment," have asked why so many women actively enjoy those genres that address themselves specifically to women, such as women's magazines, romantic fiction, television soap operas, and advertising directed to women. In her classic study of romantic and gothic fiction and soap operas, *Loving with a Vengeance* (1982), Tania Modleski argued that these forms offer pleasures designed to compensate for women's social powerlessness. Janice Radway focused her study, *Reading the Romance* (1984), on the audience rather than the texts of popular culture, and found that women had practical reasons (such as taking time out from housework) as well as desires for escape and fantasy. Janice Winship, in *Inside Women's Magazines* (1987), examined commercial factors but also made valuable observations about the ways in which ordinary women readers could obtain a sense of identity and value by entering the world of the magazine, which addressed them as readers and made them part of a community with shared interests.

These studies and others like them became very influential in the 1980s, when the study of popular cultural forms was developing, not only within women's studies but among other radical scholars looking at cultural representation and youth subcultures, working-class groups, and ethnic minorities. This movement became known as "cultural studies." Its practitioners insist on the validity of ordinary people's tastes and choices, and question the assumption that only an educated and critical perspective could escape the lures and lies of popular culture. Equal attention is paid to the constitution of various audiences and what they do with the cultural artifacts they consume, and to the texts of popular culture and the ideologies they express.

Within this broad framework, feminist cultural studies also explores the ways women might choose genres other than those traditionally marked feminine—sports programs, for example. There is widespread wariness about invoking "women in general," and a renewed feminist concern with differences among female audiences. A recent example of the interest in socially marginalized audiences finding their pleasures by reading between the lines of mainstream culture is the anthology of essays on "popular culture's romance with lesbianism," *The Good, the Bad and the Gorgeous* (Hamer and Budge, 1994). Culture industries themselves are certainly alert to the advantage of targeting identifiable minority audiences, as Ellen McCracken shows in her book *Decoding Women's Magazines* (1993).

In the 1990s the grounds of debate shifted as postmodernism questioned the opposition between popular culture and official or high culture as a construction of modernist discourse. Boundaries between the two fields are regularly crossed and blurred in cultural production and criticism. In recognition of this, for cultural critics such as Meaghan Morris (1988), everyday life has become their object of attention.

See Also

ADVERTISING; COMMODITY CULTURE; CONSUMERISM; CULTURAL STUDIES; CULTURE, *all entries;* GIRLS' SUBCULTURES; MAGAZINES; MEDIA; RADIO; SUBCULTURES: GIRLS'; TELEVISION; VIDEO; YOUTH CULTURE

References and Further Reading

Bhasin, Kamla, and Bina Agarwal, eds. 1987. *Women and media.* New Delhi: Kali for Women.

Craik, Jennifer. 1992. Cooking up cultural studies. In Cheris Kramerae and Dale Spender, eds., *The knowledge explosion.* New York: Teachers College Press.

Faludi, Susan. 1991. *Backlash: The undeclared war against American women.* New York: Crown.

Friedan, Betty. 1963. *The feminine mystique.* New York: Norton.

Hamer, Diane, and Belinda Budge, eds. 1994. *The good, the bad and the gorgeous.* London: Pandora.

McCracken, Ellen. 1993. *Decoding women's magazines.* New York: St. Martin's.

Modleski, Tania. 1982. *Loving with a vengeance: Man-produced fantasies for women.* New York: Methuen.

Morris, Meaghan. 1988. Things to do with shopping centres. In Susan Sheridan, ed., *Grafts: Feminist cultural criticism,* 193–225. London: Verso.

Radway, Janice. 1984. *Reading the romance: Women, patriarchy and popular culture.* Chapel Hill: University of North Carolina Press.

Winship, Janice. 1987. *Inside women's magazines.* London: Pandora.

Wolf, Naomi. 1990. *The beauty myth.* London: Virago.

Susan Sheridan

POPULATION: Overview

A population is the total number of individuals in a defined space. The size of a population during a certain period is defined by the number of births, the number of deaths, the number of immigrants, and the number of emigrants. A human population is often characterized by its rates of growth and decline and by its composition in terms of age, ethnic origin, language, or religion.

Global Trends

The human population in the world grew slowly until the industrial revolution. It accelerated steadily in the twentieth century, from 1.6 billion in 1900 to 6.1 billion in 2000. The United Nations estimates that the world population could reach 10.8 billion persons by 2150 and ultimately stabilize at nearly 11 billion around 2200.

Population growth rates vary considerably among the regions of the world. Ninety-seven percent of the world population increase takes place in the less-developed regions. The highest growth rates are found in Africa and Asia, the lowest in Europe. Asia will be the home of the majority of the people in the world during the twenty-first century. A high proportion of the population is below the age of 15 in many parts of the world. In other regions, the proportion of the aged is rapidly raising.

Global migration is increasing. The increase of refugees especially is perceived as a major challenge in international politics. Humanity is also involved in a gigantic urbanization process. In 2000 there were 48 metropolitan areas in the world with five million or more inhabitants; 60 percent of the world's population was living in urban areas. This large-scale, rapid urbanization creates problems of social organization that are unprecedented in human history.

The massive global population growth increases the stresses on ecosystems, on water resources, and on the sensitive layer of air surrounding the globe. It adds to deforestation and soil degradation and makes sustainable development an even more difficult challenge for humanity. Even in the wake of human progress, globally the gaps between rich and poor have also been increasing, internationally as well as within nations. One-fifth of the world's population goes hungry every night. One-quarter of the world's population lacks access to safe drinking water. One-third of the world's population lives in a state of abject poverty. Migration on a large scale may increase as more people compete over the use of scarce resources. Many will be forced to search aggressively for better opportunities elsewhere in order to survive and create better lives for their families.

Women and men live under different social and cultural conditions everywhere in the world. Slightly more than half the children born into the world are male, but in populations where females and males are treated relatively equally, there are about 106 females for every 100 males. Generally, child mortality rates up to age five are lower for girls than for boys. Also, life expectancy for women is higher than for men. The world average life expectancy was 66.3 years for women and 62.1 years for men in 1990–1995.

However, in many countries statistics reveal a reversal of these relationships between women and men. In China and southwest Asia, for example, there are only 94 females for every 100 males. This is an effect of real discrimination that favors males over females: indeed, in the late 1990s more than 100 million women were "missing" in the world population, because they died from malnutrition, neglect, or other causes during early childhood.

Childbirth is a common cause of death for adult women in many countries. The highest numbers of deaths related to pregnancy and childbirth are found in Asia and Africa. Bangladesh, India, and Pakistan account for 28 percent of the world's births and 46 percent of its maternal deaths. An African woman is 180 times more likely to die from pregnancy complications than a western European woman.

Among the oldest of the old, women dominate. In 1998, there were 132 million people in the world who were over 80 years old, with 190 women per 100 men. Among people surviving past their one-hundredth birthday, there were 386 women per 100 men.

Control of Women's Fertility

Women's ability to conceive and bear children is the focus of most discourses on population issues, be they pronatalist or antinatalist. Fertility is partly biologically defined—but only partly. The control of fertility is tightly meshed with economy, social structure, and culture. The social regulation of the fertility of individuals is accomplished by means of cultural constraints on the behavior of individuals and is also a result of conscious and goal-directed regulation by society. The family is just one of many influences on choices about fertility; larger ethnic, religious, and political communities also exert an influence on the present and future composition of their groups in terms of size, age, sex, and dominance. Social elites tend to attempt to control the fertility behavior of the masses in the society—national or global—which they aspire to control.

The management of fertility as both a personal and a social practice is firmly anchored in economic interests—a combination of the need to raise offspring and the control of ownership and maintenance of property. An implicit objective of codes defining sexual morality has often been to control women's sexual behavior and fertility. This objective is partly a manifestation of patriarchal dominance: the fidelity required of wives and the chastity of unmarried girls form the two major building blocks of sexual morality in many societies. Social management of fertility is also a manifestation of the need for maintaining a workforce compatible with the prevailing economic conditions.

The knowledge about the arts, crafts, and skills that humanity needs to manage its reproduction has grown tremendously during the past three decades. In the mid-twentieth century, the first industrially manufactured oral contraceptives were introduced on the market. For the first time in history, a technological product based on advances in biochemistry was to be distributed as a drug to be consumed by millions of healthy individuals in many countries of the world. The introduction of oral contraceptives on the global market took place at a time when the rate of global population growth was adopted by the industrialized countries as a major concern on the agenda of international politics.

Long before the invention of modern contraceptive technology, fertility control was practiced and achieved by many means. Social norms prescribing late marriages or long lactation of infants combined with abstention from coitus are known from many parts of the world as means of regulating the pressure of population on available resources. Coitus interruptus, the use of contraceptives made from herbs or material from animal bodies, abortion, and the practice of infanticide have served to prevent and space pregnancies and to ensure the survival of families, tribes, and nations. When the methods of control of reproduction have allowed for a distinction between male and female offspring, males traditionally have been valued over females.

Each society has its own rules about who may conceive children and under what circumstances, about how pregnant women should conduct themselves, about the proper process of birth, and about how children should be reared. The extended family system ensured that knowledge and control of "family planning" could be traded through generations of men and women. It asserted family interests against religious and secular power. In modern society, where the small nuclear family is the most common family unit, secular and religious institutional control over fertility management has gained in influence.

Population Politics

Uncontrolled population growth was perhaps the first ecological problem of global scope that was identified as a task for international collaboration. In international politics of the late twentieth century, the less-developed regions of the world came to be regarded as the ones where population growth rates were to be suppressed. At the same time, many groups and nations, in which fertility is perceived as low, pursued pronatalist policies and promoted childbearing and child rearing. France and Japan are two countries in which reports on low natality raised fears that the domestic population might diminish in global importance. One example of the ambiguity in population politics is the social conflict over women's right to abortion in the United States, a nation strongly committed to reducing population growth worldwide.

Modern-day concerns over global population developments are part of the continual human struggle over access to resources. Throughout history the growth of population has been associated with prosperity and strength. Control of population growth and the selection of population groups for growth or decline in numbers is at the core of the politics of families, clans, communities, and states. To obtain food for the group one perceives as one's own and to manage the fertility of the group have always been two of the most important functions of adulthood. The group may be the family, the tribe, or the nation. Its members want it to survive and grow, if necessary at the expense of other groups, and its collective fertility is highly valued.

Population control draws on ideas about the superiority and the inferiority of specific groups. A wide array of political measures have been used for controlling population developments worldwide. At times, eugenic objectives have dominated; at other times, population control measures have been motivated by wishes to alleviate suffering and to provide women and families with the means to regulate their own fertility. In the twentieth century, the political means have ranged from ethnic cleansing in central Europe in the 1930s and 1940s and in Rwanda and in the former Yugoslavia in the 1990s to peaceful programs emphasizing sex education, the distribution of contraceptives, and the provision of financial and other support to families with the desirable number of children.

During the early decades of the twentieth century conflicts over women's and families' rights to control their fertility accompanied the rise to power of new social groups in many countries. Radical social welfare ideologies included the advocacy of birth control, a position that was often in conflict both with religious communities and with the social, including the medical, establishment. The birth-control movement was allied to the eugenics movement but also to that of liberal and radical social reforms and had a strong flavor of social engineering aimed at creating better societies. Some of its concrete objectives were (1) to abolish prohibitions against the distribution and use of contraceptives, (2) to provide sex education, and (3) to enable access to contraceptives and abortion assistance, all with the aim of helping couples and individuals to control their fertility.

After World War II, the birth-control movement in the industrialized countries expanded into international family-planning policies. Its goals were transformed into population politics, which were introduced as planned parenthood, family planning, and sex education. Since then, fertility-control programs with the fecund poor as the target groups have been instituted both nationally and internationally. The initiators mostly belonged to the rich nations' dominating bourgeois strata, where fertility was low, voluntarily or involuntarily.

The global family-planning movement during the late twentieth century was clearly devoted to the improvement and dissemination of modern medical and biomedical contraceptive technology—primarily oral contraceptives and intrauterine devices (IUD)—produced by the pharmaceutical industry. Sterilization on a large scale has also been part of family-planning programs in many third world countries. Early abortion, a principal factor in reducing fertility in many countries, has been rejected in many national and nearly all international population-control programs.

Bringing down global birthrates was designated as a medical or public health task—even though ordinary medical and public health considerations often were excluded. Despite the lack of general public health services in the family-planning programs, these were interpreted as necessary public health campaigns and acquired an assured popular support in industrialized countries as well as among the elites in countries with high population growth. The programs for population control in third world countries tended to be constructed with benchmarks and targets expressed in terms of numbers of family-planning centers and clients, of performed sterilizations, and of distributed pills and IUDs. The family-planning movement escaped official condemnation and censure by rejecting or avoiding religiously taboo but otherwise effective means of birth prevention. By concentrating on new, scientific methods of contraception, it respected the prohibitions attached to the old ones.

The prime target groups for family-planning programs have been women, often selected so that single women were excluded and women professing certain religious faiths were offered only selected methods. In many family-planning programs, the problem of women's and couples' motivation for family planning was reduced to a technological issue, namely, the distribution of a technical device that would be received by women. Women, who did not quickly accept family planning, were often held to be too simple to understand the benefits of using contraception and were said to have cultural values that ought to be changed. Yet, improved education, especially for girls and women, has been shown to be one crucial factor in reducing birthrates, perhaps as crucial as women's and men's access to effective contraceptive technology.

According to United Nations statistics from the 1990s, the most common contraceptive methods were female sterilization, IUDs, hormonal pills, and condoms (in that order). New product development in the decades since oral contraceptives went on the market have included a variety of subcutaneous hormone implants, several models of intravaginal rings that would release steroid hormones, barrier contraceptives with improved spermicides, menses inducers (that is, early abortifacients), and injectable contraceptives. With the advent of HIV/AIDS as a global pandemic, condom use is promoted in order to prevent the spreading of sexually transmitted disease as well as the conception of unwanted children.

Family-planning programs and increasing use of contraceptives have dramatically reduced birthrates in industrial and developing countries. In developing countries, fertility has declined by about one-third since the 1960s. About one-third of the married women in developing countries were using modern methods of family planning at the end of the twentieth century. One explicit international political goal is to reduce fertility in developing countries to 3.2 children per woman in the years 2000–2005. There was increasing consensus that in order to achieve sustained decline in fertility, education and improvements in mothers' and children's health and women's status are as necessary as the availability of family-planning services and contraceptives.

Evaluations of family-planning programs tend to view the risks and the successes of these programs almost strictly in terms of whether or not they have prevented unintended pregnancies. But other risks are continuously involved in the methods used to prevent pregnancy. The hazards of contraceptive technologies can be well known only when a large number of individuals have been exposed to the technology for many years. For example, the social benefits of new technologies such as oral contraceptives and IUDs initially were deemed so worthwhile that they were aggressively distributed without long-term testing for safety—or without much regard for the adverse effects the technologies may have in exposed individuals. The subsequently documented health risks have not been negligible. Oral contraceptives have been shown to increase the risks of cardiovascular disease, in particular the risk of venous thromboembolism, myocardial infarction, and stroke. They have also been linked to the development of certain types of cancer, among them breast cancer, cervical cancer, and endometrial cancer. These cancers are major causes of morbidity and mortality among women. Their toll is rising in many countries. IUDs may cause more or less constant small bleeding, pelvic inflammatory disease (PID), tubal infertility, septic abortion, and uterine perforation. Barrier methods (condom, diaphragm, cervical cap, and sponge) provide less effective contraception than IUDs and oral contraceptives, but they protect against many sexually transmitted infections.

Three international conferences on population have been organized by the United Nations, in 1974 in Bucharest, in 1984 in Mexico City, and in 1994 in Cairo. The United Nations Population Fund under the leadership of Nafis Sadiq of Pakistan and the International Conference on Population and Development in Cairo in 1994 emphasized three cornerstones of population- and development-related programs: (1) to advance gender equality and equity and the empowerment of women, (2) to eliminate all kinds of violence against women, and (3) to ensure women's ability to control their own fertility. The challenge for policy makers is not only to provide comprehensive family-planning services and reproductive health services but also to ensure that policies and services enable women to make free choices on their own. Moreover, during the 1990s the United Nations High Commissioner for Refugees, Sadako Ogata of Japan, repeatedly called for measures that would protect displaced women and girls against sexual violence during warfare and communal conflicts.

Nongovernmental organizations with women in leading roles such as Health Action International, Development Alternatives with Women for a New Era (DAWN), National Women's Health Network in the United States, and International Women's Health Coalition have voiced women's concerns with regard to population policies and struggled for the empowerment of women with regard to their own health.

Women's Studies of Population Issues

Women have played key roles in the advancement of family planning in many countries. In the United States, Margaret Sanger pioneered the birth-control movement in the early decades of the twentieth century. In Sweden, Elise Ottosen-Jensen was the pioneer. Midwives, nurses, and women doctors around the world assist women and men in family-planning choices.

The subject of population control and family planning has attracted many women scholars. Female scholars have drawn attention to how population policies often have a gender bias and implicitly exert power over women. The demographer Ester Boserup has written extensively on women's living condition in developing countries. Feminist authors such as Germaine Greer and Barbara Seaman have contributed to women's awareness of the biases in family-planning policies. Women's studies have helped build a consensus regarding the need for population policies that emphasize the education and empowerment of women as high-priority strategies to achieve a balanced global population growth.

See Also

AGING; CENSUS; CONTRACEPTION; DEMOGRAPHY; FAMILY PLANNING; LIFE EXPECTANCY; MIGRATION; POPULATION: CHINESE CASE STUDY; POPULATION CONTROL; REPRODUCTIVE RIGHTS

References and Further Reading

Boserup, Ester. 1990. *Economic and demographic relationships in development.* Baltimore: Johns Hopkins University Press.

Greer, Germaine. 1985. *Sex and destiny: The politics of human fertility.* London: Picador.

Palmlund, Ingar. 1995. Risk evaluation of medical technology in global population control. In E. B. Gallagher and J. S. Subedi, eds., *Global perspectives on health care.* Englewood Cliffs, N.J.: Prentice Hall.

Reining, Priscilla, and Irene Tinker, eds. 1975. *Population: dynamics, ethics, and policy,* Washington D.C.: American Association for the Advancement of Science.

Sadik, Nafis. 1990. *The state of the world population, 1990.* New York: United Nations Population Fund.

Sen, Gita, Adrienne Germain, and Lincoln C. Chen, eds. 1994. *Population policies reconsidered: Health, empowerment, and rights.* Boston: Harvard University Press.

United Nations Development Program. 1995. *Human development report, 1995.* New York: Author.

Ingar Palmlund

POPULATION: Chinese Case Study

China is by far the world's most populous nation. At the end of 1998, its population topped 1.248 billion, more than one-fifth of the world's total. Population growth in China has fluctuated with changes in the country's social and political environment, with women, the main constituents in human reproduction and the upbringing of children, playing an important role in stabilizing the quantity and improving the quality of life.

Growth Periods

There have been two peak periods of growth since the People's Republic of China was founded in 1949. The first was in the early 1950s, when the country was recovering from decades of war and social turmoil and the population grew from a rough estimate of some 450 million in 1949 to 646.53 million in 1957. The second, in the mid-1960s, followed economic recovery from the destructive effects of the Great Leap Forward of the late 1950s and the natural disasters in the early 1960s. In 1965, the annual natural growth rate hit 28.38 per thousand, and China's population reached 924.20 million.

Many factors have contributed to a rapid growth of the population of China. First, since the founding of the People's Republic of China in 1949, improved living standards and health services have led to a drop in China's overall mortality rate, from 2 percent in 1949 to 0.65 percent in the late 1990s; the morality rate for newborns has likewise fallen dramatically, from 20 to 25 percent to 3.3 percent. The average life expectancy for Chinese rose in the last 35 years of the twentieth century to nearly 71 years. Second, for a long time the government wavered in its family planning policy introduced as far back as the mid-1950s. In his heart, Mao Zedong favored a large population. "The more people, the more strength," was the chairman's favorite saying. Third, the desire of the average family to have at least one male descendant has driven women to give birth to more children.

The Desirability of Sons

The feudal idea of regarding men as superior to women had been instilled in the Chinese people's minds for more than two thousand years. The expression "Mothers become noble for the sake of their sons" shows how important it was for a woman to give birth to sons. This idea developed for two main reasons. First, China has been predominantly an agricultural and paternal society. Families need boys and men, who are often physically stronger than girls and women, to do farmwork. Second, elder people depended on their descendants to take care of them. Women were not considered dependable because if they were married they would belong to the families of their husbands. "A married daughter is spilled water," as the saying goes. Only sons could provide for and attend the parents.

This mentality still persists, although the law gives daughters and sons the same legal status. The elder care system is not yet sufficient. Most old people would rather live alone than go to elder care centers.

Planned Growth

It was not until the early 1970s that Chairman Mao realized the consequences of excessive population growth and pointed out that "mankind must control itself and realize a planned growth." In 1973, the leading group for family planning was set up under the state council responsible for managing the country's family planning. In 1979, at the Second Session of the Fifth National People's Congress, it was advocated that "couples with only one child would be rewarded." The mothers of just one child would get extra maternity leave and extra money each month fas long as the child was under 14 years of age.

From the early 1970s to 1998, the average fertility rate of Chinese women fell from 6.0 to 1.8, marking a significant sociological change, as traditionally families in China had always been large. By the United Nations' standards, China became a country with a low fertility rate. The "family planning" policy has resulted in an estimated 300 million fewer births, a number that was more than the total population of the United States at the end of the twentieth century. China's economic success in the last two decades would have been less impressive, if not impossible, if it had implemented any other population policy.

Prospects of Women

These achievements cannot be separated from changes in women's training and expectations, changes that have come primarily from the government's focus on family planning and equality of both sexes, women's increased roles in education, and women's more global perspectives.

In the old days, females were not allowed to go to school, and very few females were literate. But since the founding of the People's Republic of China in 1949, women have enjoyed equal rights to education. Women also have taken up more responsibilities as educators. In 1996, 42.9 percent of the teachers were females. Among the family members, mothers usually spend much more time with young children. They teach their children basic scientific knowledge. Some mothers even learn new knowledge with their children when they take them to amateur classes and when the children need help with subjects in grade school.

China's illiterate population at the end of the twentieth century was only 12 percent, compared with 60 percent 50 years earlier, and the percentage of both women and men receiving higher education also increased considerably. In 1996, there were 1,101,000 female students in institutions of higher learning, compared with 207,000 in 1978.

Also, since China began to open itself to the outside world in 1978, women have more global perspectives. More and more women believe that having fewer children is essential to an easier and happier life. It is good for the world, the country, and themselves. Fewer and fewer people are concerned about having a daughter or a son. They believe that as long as they foster their children wholeheartedly, daughters can have a great future, too. Women now have higher expectations for both themselves and their children and would rather live harder lives in order to send their daughters to school. The government has set up a financial aid program entitled Mothers Project, to coordinate the Hope Project for students from poor families.

The change of women's ideas about their life possibilities has helped improve their social and family positions. First, with increased knowledge, women have participated in more social and economic activities. Their financial situation has become more equal to that of men. At the time of the fourth national population census in 1990, employment of females over 15 years of age was 72.93 percent, an increase of 2.87 percent from 1982. Increasingly, their work time is better paid. Women have started to use more social services to help improve the quality of their own life. These services have saved mothers from complex household chores and provided them with more time and energy to work, entertain, excercise, or gain knowledge as they please. Almost all the children in the cities go to nursery schools, and more nursery schools have also been set up in the rural areas. Elder care centers have decreased the worry of people having nobody to take care of them when they are old. This means that sons are not considered as indispensable. Home services also have been used pervasively. Maids help wash dishes; baby sitters help take care of children and do housework. Because most of these social services are provided by women, they give women more job opportunities.

Second, increased knowledge has enabled more women to acquire higher political and academic ranks. According to statistics of the fourth national population census of 1990, 57.07 percent more women got high ranks than in 1982, 18 percent over the increase rate of males. Therefore, women are able to use their power to give greater help to females. For example, the staff members in the All-China Women's Federation centers all over the country devote themselves to protecting women's rights, raising women's social position, and carrying out the "family planning" policy. These women must have certain levels of education according to the nature of their jobs. Moreover, of the more than 100,000 heads of the neighborhood committees, about 62 percent are females. They play an important role in protecting the stability and unity of the society.

Third, with better knowledge about marriage and reproduction, women are able to enjoy a healthier marital life and raise healthier children. Many premarriage classes and child-raising classes can be accessed anywhere. Women do not need to suffer from too many pregnancies and unwanted births. However, it should be noted that it is primarily women who are undertaking the responsibilities of contraception and birth control.

Minority Groups

Minority ethnic groups were discriminated against in old China, and their populations have been increasing very slowly, with some groups even having negative growth rates, as a result of poverty and poor medical services. The People's Republic of China has introduced special policies for minority groups to accelerate their development. For example, couples with a minority background are exempt from the general "one child" policy; they are allowed to have two children. As a result, the growth rate of minority group populations has exceeded that of the Han group (the largest ethnic population) or the nation as a whole. In 1953, the population of all 55 minority groups was 35 million, or 6 percent of the total Chinese population. By 1995, minority groups had a population of more than 100 million, or 9 percent of the national total.

The overall gains seem obvious. However, owing to insufficient government control, social services, and education, unsatisfactory conditions still exist. Nonregistration and abortion of some female infants, illegal adoption and killing of girls, generally higher mortality rate of female infants than males, and lower education of females are sad facts, especially in the poorer areas.

China still has many population-related problems. Educational opportunities should still be increased. The improvement of rural women's social and family position should be regarded as a critical issue. The recognition of the value of women's work, both within and outside families, needs to be improved.

Despite its decrease in birthrates, China still faces stern challenges. Every year, 20 million babies are born into the country. It is predicted by experts that China's population will not start to decrease until the middle of the twenty-first century, when the population will have reached a peak of 1.6 billion. Despite its widely acclaimed success stories of the last two decades of the twentieth century, the country is still lagging far behind the world average in many social and economic development indices. In real terms, then, China certainly has a long way to go yet in stabilizing its population growth and improving the quality of life of its citizens for a sustainable development.

See Also

DEVELOPMENT: CHINA; FAMILY PLANNING; HOUSEHOLDS AND FAMILIES: EAST ASIA; POLITICS AND THE STATE: EAST ASIA; POPULATION: OVERVIEW; POPULATION CONTROL

References and Further Reading

Beckman, Ashley, Abbe Goncharsky, Carrie Mitchell, Krystal Redden, Nick Spiliotis, and Valerie Vulevich. 1999. *Social problems of children in China.* <www.tulane.edu/~rouxbee/children/china6.heml>

Cordahi, Cherif. *Population: Rapid economic changes affect role of women in China.* 1999. <www.iisd.ca/cairo/ips005.html>

Department of Statistics on Population and Employment of the State Statistical Bureau. 1997. *China population statistics Yearbook—1997.* Beijing: China Statistics Publishing House.

Gu, Baochang, and Zhenming, Xie. 1999. *The effect of family planning on women's lives.* <www.fhi.org/en/wsp/wsfinal/fctshts/wsfct7>

Information Office of the State Council of the People's Republic of China. 1994. *The situation of Chinese women.* <www.chinanews.org/WhitePapers/SituationOfWomenE.html>

———. 1995. *White paper: Family planning in China.* (Available on the Internet.)

The population of China towards the 21st century. 1994. Beijing: China Statistics Publishing House.

Xinhua News Agency. 1997. *White paper on women and children.* (Available on the Internet.)

Weisi Zhao

POPULATION CONTROL

Since World War II, advocates of population control have exerted a powerful influence on the field of international development and have shaped the organization of many national family planning programs. The philosophy of population control is often described as resting on four basic assumptions:

1. Rapid population growth is a primary cause of problems related to development in the third world—problems such as hunger, poverty, political instability, and environmental degradation.
2. People must be persuaded—or in some cases forced—to have fewer children, even without any concurrent change in gender relations or any fundamental improvement of the impoverished conditions in which they live.
3. Family planning services should be aimed at women, and can be delivered even in the absence of a basic health care system.
4. In both the development and the promotion of contraceptive technologies, efficacy in preventing pregnancy should take precedence over health, safety, and ethical concerns.

From Malthus to Ehrlich

The ideological roots of population control go back to Thomas Malthus, a British clergyman turned economist who wrote in the late 1700s and early 1800s. He warned that human populations would outstrip food supplies unless restrained by preventive checks such as the poverty, famine, and pestilence brought on by overpopulation. By associating poverty directly with population growth, he encouraged a view of poverty as a "natural" human condition which, he claimed, had no direct relation to forms of government or to the unequal division of property (Malthus, 1914). He used this logic to argue against welfare measures for the poor that would improve their chance of survival.

Contrary to Malthus's predictions, food production has kept well ahead of population growth; he did not foresee the technological revolutions that would occur in both agriculture and industry. Nor did he adequately acknowledge the capacity of people to limit family size through later marriage and the use of birth control. His own native country, England, experienced a demographic transition to low birthrates, not as a result of famine, war, or disease but because of changing economic conditions and improvements in living standards.

Yet today many neo-Malthusians, as his ideological descendants are called, still claim that the world—especially the third world—is caught in a race between exploding human populations and diminishing resources. This view pervades the mainstream environmental movement in the United States and has been popularized by authors such as Paul and Anne Ehrlich. In *The Population Explosion* (1990), Ehrlich and Ehrlich blame almost every major environmental ill on overpopulation and claim that nature will solve the problem through massive famine and AIDS if humanity does not put in place a "gentler" population control program of its own.

Many international agencies also blame population growth for poverty and environmental degradation. For example, in 1993 the U.S. Agency for International Development (USAID) identified population as a key "strategic threat" which "drives environmental damage" as well as "consumes all other economic gains."

On the other side of the debate are scholars who point out that the resurgent fear of population comes at a time when populations are actually declining all over the world; they argue that poverty and environmental degradation have far more to do with inequalities in income and power between and within countries than they do with population pressures. According to statistics reported by the United Nations, in 1960 one-fifth of the world's people who lived in the developed world had 30 times the income of the poorest one-fifth; by 1995 they had 82 times as much. New estimates indicate that the world's 225 richest people have a combined wealth of U.S.$1 trillion, equivalent to the annual income of the poorest 47 percent of the world's people. Exacerbated by the debt crisis, the flow of wealth has been from the developing world (the "South") to the developed world (the "North"), not the other way around. Moreover, the industrialized nations, with only 22 percent of the world's population, consume the vast majority of its natural resources (UNDP, 1998).

The biologist Barry Commoner (1991) maintains that inappropriate technologies are more important than population in determining environmental quality. He points to the critical shift from more environmentally benign technologies to more harmful ones—for example, from natural products to synthetics—that occurred in the post-World War II period. The environmental scientist Patricia Hynes (1999) argues that the neo-Malthusian view of the population paradigm leaves out the critical role of the military and transnational corporations in environmental degradation. Hynes also notes that the neo-Malthusian view fails to differentiate between people who actively improve their environment, through reforestation and sustainable agriculture, for example, and those who destroy it.

A new generation of research is challenging the simple correlation between population growth and environmental destruction. A study of the semiarid Machakos District in Kenya found that although the district's population increased fivefold in the period 1930–1990, the environment had improved by the end of that same period, as a result of new technologies and farming systems, which include terracing and the protection of trees (Tiffen et al., 1994).

A number of New Right economists have also challenged the neo-Malthusian paradigm. They believe that under a free-market system, temporary shortages of resources will spur the development of new technologies to find them. They tend to minimize environmental constraints and to identify restrictions on private enterprise, rather than social and economic inequalities, as the real obstacle to development (Simon and Kahn, 1984).

The Politics of Family Planning

Many critics of population control believe that rapid population growth is more a symptom than a cause of poverty. They maintain that meeting people's basic needs for food, health care (including birth control), education, and employment is the most effective and most ethical path toward a decline in fertility, since this approach would diminish people's motivation for having many children as a way of providing labor and old-age security (Sen, 1994). Furthermore, in order for women to exercise meaningful control over their fertility, they need more economic and political power within the family and community, and daughters must be as highly valued as sons (Correa, 1994).

By contrast, most population control programs have focused narrowly on family planning as the most efficient means to drive down birthrates, thus ignoring the need to address economic and gender inequalities. Moreover, the way family planning programs have been developed and organized often has been detrimental to women's health and violated basic human rights (Bandarage, 1997).

In India, for example, through the use of incentives and disincentives, the government has pressured poor women to be sterilized (Ravindran, 1993). In Indonesia the national family planning program has used local authority figures, from the police to village headmen, to "persuade" women to get IUDs or Norplant inserted, often without offering proper counseling, medical screening, follow-up care, or other options for contraception. In the case of Norplant, many women have been denied access to early removal because of the government's insistence on rigid demographic targets (Hartmann, 1995). Other countries use social marketing programs in which, for example, the birth control pill is widely advertised and sold over the counter without any medical supervision.

In many countries population control has been a higher bureaucratic and budgetary priority than basic health care, because of pressure from international agencies, especially USAID and the World Bank. In Bangladesh in the 1990s, for example, population control absorbed one-third of the annual health budget; in Indonesia there were twice as many family planning clinics as primary health care centers by 1994. In the 1980s the World Bank made the implementation of population control policies a condition of structural adjustment loans in a number of African countries, at the same time that it forced governments to reduce public health expenditures (Hartmann, 1995).

The neglect of health care not only threatens people's general well-being but undermines the quality of family planning services because basic medical standards cannot be ensured. Many family planning programs have failed to include prevention and treatment of sexually transmitted diseases such as HIV/AIDS. Barrier contraceptives, such as the condom, have not received nearly the same attention as higher-technology methods aimed at women and deemed more effective at reducing birthrates.

By the end of the twentieth century, the international women's health movement, as well as feminist reformers within population agencies, had pushed governments and international agencies to move away from family planning programs based on population control to a reproductive health approach that meets a broad range of women's needs (Dixon-Mueller, 1993; Sen et al., 1994). The International Conference on Population and Development, held in Cairo in September 1994, called for the empowerment of women and endorsed a reproductive health agenda. While the Cairo Plan of Action has encouraged family planning reforms, many of its commitments have not yet been translated into actual changes in policies or programs. Resistance to this plan of action comes not only from advocates of population control but also from the Vatican and from religious fundamentalists opposed to abortion, contraception, and sexuality education.

See Also

CONTRACEPTION; ECONOMY; GLOBAL RESTRUCTURING; ENVIRONMENT: OVERVIEW; ETHICS: MEDICAL; FAMILY PLANNING; NORPLANT; THE PILL; POPULATION: OVERVIEW; POVERTY; REPRODUCTIVE HEALTH

References and Further Readings

Bandarage, Asoka. 1997. *Women, population, and global crisis.* London: Zed.

Commoner, Barry. 1991. Rapid population growth and environmental stress, *International Journal of Health Services* 21(2): 199–227.

Correa, Sonia. 1994. *Population and reproductive rights: Feminist perspectives from the South.* London: Zed.

Dixon-Mueller, Ruth. 1993. *Population policy and women's rights: Transforming reproductive choice.* Westport, Conn.: Praeger.

Ehrlich, Paul R., and Anne H. Ehrlich. 1990. *The population explosion.* New York: Simon and Schuster.

Hartmann, Betsy. 1995. *Reproductive rights and wrongs.* Boston: South End.

Hynes, H. Patricia. 1999. Taking population out of the equation: Reformulating I-PAT. In Jael Silliman and Ynestra King, eds., *Dangerous intersections: Feminist perspectives on population, environment, and development.* Boston: South End.

Malthus, Thomas. 1914. *An essay on population,* Vol. 2. New York: Dutton.

Ravindran, Sundari. 1993. The politics of women, population, and development in India. *Reproductive Health Matters* 1: 26–38.

Ross, Eric B. 1998. *The Malthus factor: Poverty, politics and population in capitalist global crisis.* London: Zed.

Sen, Amartya. 1994. Population: Delusion and reality. *New York Review of Books* 22 (September).

Sen, Gita, Adrienne Germain, and Lincoln C. Chen, eds. 1994. *Population policies reconsidered: Health, empowerment, and rights.* Cambridge, Mass.: Harvard University Press.

Simon, Julian, and Herman Kahn. 1984. *The resourceful earth.* Oxford: Blackwell.

Tiffen, Mary, Michael Mortimer, and Francis Gichuki. 1994. *More people, less erosion: Environmental recovery in Kenya.* London: Overseas Development Institute and Wiley.

United Nations Development Program. 1998. *Human development report 1998,* 29–30. New York: Oxford University Press.

U.S. Agency for International Development. 1993. *USAID strategy papers.* Draft, LPA Revision, 5 October. Washington D.C.: United Nations Development Program.

Web Sites

Committee on Women, Population, and the Environment: <www.cwpe.org>

Women's Environment and Development Organization: <www.wedo.org>

Women's Gobal Network for Reproductive Rights: <office@wgnrr.>

Betsy Hartmann

PORNOGRAPHY IN ART AND LITERATURE

Although sexual representations, in both sacred and secular venues, can be traced in many cultures from the earliest times, the concept of pornography is a modern one. Originally, the word pornography meant a description of prostitutes and prostitution. The *Oxford English Dictionary* defined pornography in 1909 in this manner and also suggested something approaching its contemporary meaning: "the expression or suggestion of obscene or unchaste subjects in literature and art."

Linda Williams (1989) argues that pornography is a genre that should be taught, understood, and appreciated. Many feminists would agree that generic pornography, whether in art or literature, high or low culture, is, as Linda Nochlin (1988) observed, about women and by and for men. Two areas of feminist concern have arisen from this. Some—for example, Andrea Dworkin, Patricia Hill Collins, Gail Dines, Catharine MacKinnon, Diana Russell, Joan Hoff, Susan Griffin, Audre Lorde, and Susanne Kappeler—argue that pornography is not about morality or free speech but about sexualized and racialized power. In this view, pornography is a form of representation that eroticizes misogyny, racism, inequality, slavery, objectification, and violence, while simultaneously hindering women's capacity to resist. Pornography negates what Audre Lorde (1984) calls "the erotic . . . the sensual—those physical, emotional, and psychic expressions" of shared passion that unify the spiritual, sexual, and political. The pornographic instead installs a sexual intimacy based in a subject-object relation, with a masculine subject (usually played by a male) dominating a wholly accessible feminine object (again, a role that, although usually played by females, can be assumed by males, especially males who are socially subordinated by race, class, age, and so on). Some sexualized images of women are meant to arouse hatred as well as desire—for example, the exotic, often racially "other" femme fatale in the popular and high arts as well as the unchaste "phallic" women, for example, in the late-nineteenth-century paintings of Franz von Stuck. One also can locate an early form of pornographic depiction in the lethal stereotypes of witches as naked, lustful, obscene hags in works by sixteenth-century German artists.

Susanne Kappeler (1986) points to a "pornographic structure of representation" that undergirds acceptable art and literature and that, like pornography, usurps "female subjectivity and experience." Analyses of art and literature by Kate Millett, Susan Gubar, and Mira Schor locate themes of misogyny, degradation, objectification, fragmentation, and abuse of women in celebrated works including those of Henry Miller, Norman Mailer, René Magritte, and David Salle. Women artists can reproduce the same structures. In 1981, Asian feminists protested that the English photographer Mary Ellen Mark's pictures of prostitutes in Bombay were voyeuristic, objectifying, and colonizing.

A different feminist position argues that pornography can be a vehicle for the subversion of mainstream class and sexual politics and an affirmation of alternative sexual identities and cultures. Lynne Hunt (1993), although deliberately making no judgment on modern pornography, notes that in early modern Europe pornography was most often a vehicle for using the shock of sex to criticize religious and political authorities, and was associated with free-thinking and heresy, science and natural philosophy, and attacks on absolutist political authority. Writing in 1969, the critic and novelist Susan Sontag (1982), influenced by her enthusiasm for French literary pornography, including Pauline Réage's (Dominique Aury's) *Story of O,* describes the "pornographic imagination" as one that marks the artist as "a freelance explorer of spiritual dangers," one who violates taboos in service of both mystical transcendence and rebellious transgression against the boundaries of the status quo.

Some feminists continue to find evidence of a subversive character in pornography. Constance Penley and Laura Kipnis claim that pornography represents a lower class sensibility and aesthetic. Others stress that one means of ensuring female subordination has been by denying, silencing, and containing female sexual subjectivity, by imposing a virgin-whore dichotomy, and by obliterating a female erotic culture, both lesbian and heterosexual, based in sexual autonomy. Hence, some (Kathy Myers, Amber Hollibaugh, Paula Webster, Susie Bright, and Lisa Henderson) argue that the embrace of the "bad girl" identity and the generation of women's pornography would tap into both subversive and transformative forces. The English writer Angela Carter (1978) calls for a "moral pornographer" who would upend male-dominated pornography's vision of near-total female acquiescence and would "use pornography as a critique of current relations between the sexes." Lesbians, in particular, argue that sexual depiction is necessary to name and claim lesbian existence. In her introduction to a book by the English photographer Della Grace, which includes some scene of lesbian sadomasochism, U.S. novelist Sara Schulman (1991) writes, "Current anti-pornography laws and pervasive anti-sex moralism have been used to declare entire lives obscene"; hence, "the mere assertion by invisible and repressed peoples that they live, love and feel requires a continued courage and arrogance."

Women writers have been prosecuted or socially disavowed for writing openly about sexual subjects. The English novelist Radclyffe Hall's novel of lesbian love, *The Well of Loneliness* (1928), was prosecuted as obscene, as was the U.S. film star Mae West's play *Sex* (1926). Although never actually charged in a court of law, Kate Chopin's *The Awakening* (U.S., 1899) was met with such social disapproval that it foreclosed her writing career. The Urdu writer Ismat Chughtai was taken to court in Lahore for writing pornography in her lesbian short story "The Quilt" (1942); after two years, the charges were dropped, because of the lack of obscene words in the story.

Some of the more prominent female writers who employ sexually explicit themes include, from France: Anaïs Nin, Pauline Réage (Dominique Aury), Emmanuelle Arsan, Collette, Violette Leduc, Monique Wittig, and Helene Cixous; from the United States: Dorothy Allison; from Argentina: Alicia Steimbers; from Cuba: Mayra Montero; from Uruguay: Christina Peri Rossi; from Mexico: Maria Luisa Mendoza, Sara Levi Calderon, and Rosa María Roffiel; and, from Brazil: Hilda Hilst. Fiction writers who address pornography as an agent of violence and inequality include Alice Walker and Andrea Dworkin from the United States and Simona Vinci from Italy.

The female nude is at the centerpiece of both elite art and pornography. Yet, when women such as the U.S. artist Judy Chicago from the late 1960s onward used "cunt" forms as metaphors for women's sexuality and experience, many critics, both male and female, patriarchal and feminist, reacted with outrage, issuing a gamut of charges. Right-wing critics in the U.S. Congress denounced Chicago's *The Dinner Party* (1979) as "ceramic 3-D pornography," while some feminist critics in the

United States and Europe decried it as "essentialist," reducing women to sexual biology. Defending Chicago's work, Mira Schor (1994) notes that the vulviform images on the plates of *The Dinner Party* "threatened the Western aesthetic conventions that privilege images of the female body as fetishistic objects for male spectatorial pleasure but prohibit direct representation of the female genitalia," especially such representations by feminist-identified artists. Chicago, along with other U.S. artists—Niki de Sainte Phalle, Louise Bourgeois, Carolee Schneeman, Hanna Wilke, Ida Applebroog, and Ana Mendieta—represent the female and male body in and on their own terms in order to reclaim it from pornographic constructions and the demands of male-identified desire. Schneeman, Wilke, Joan Semmel, and the filmmaker Barbara Hammer refuse the designation of obscenity for old women's bodies and imagine older women as sexual subjects. Other U.S. women artists, generally identified with postmodernism—for example, Cindy Sherman, Lisa Yuskavage, and Sue Williams—use irony in images that destabilize traditional female identities. Nevertheless, some feminist critics aver that these images of women as bimbos, whores, victims, and nymphets actually work to reiterate and confirm patriarchal and pornographic stereotypes.

The challenge to feminist writers and artists is to transcend false opposites, refuse the structure of the demonized, objectified, silenced other, claim and name the sexual self, and evolve forms of communication and representation that enact intersubjectivity and, in Lorde's sense, the erotic.

See Also

CENSORSHIP; EROTICA; FINE ARTS: POLITICS OF REPRESENTATION; GAZE; PORNOGRAPHY AND VIOLENCE

References and Further Reading

Carter, Angela. 1978. *The Sadeian woman and the ideology of pornography.* New York: Pantheon.

Cornell, Drucilla, ed. 2000. *Feminism and pornography.* New York: Oxford University Press.

Dines, Gail, Robert Jensen, and Ann Russo. 1998. *Pornography: The production and consumption of inequality.* New York: Routledge.

Gubar, Susan, and Joan Hoff, eds. 1989. *For adult users only: The dilemma of violent pornography.* Bloomington: Indiana University Press.

Hunt, Lynn, ed. 1993. *The invention of pornography: Obscenity and the origins of modernity, 1500–1800.* New York: Zone.

Jones, Amelia. 1996. The "sexual politics" of *The Dinner Party:* A critical context. In Amelia Jones, ed., *Sexual politics: Judy Chicago's Dinner Party in feminist art history.* Berkeley: University of California Press.

Kappeler, Susanne. 1986. *The pornography of representation.* Cambridge, U.K.: Polity.

Kipnis, Laura. 1996. *Bound and gagged: Pornography and the politics of fantasy in America.* New York: Grove.

Lorde, Audre. 1984. *Sister outsider.* Trumansburg, N.Y.: Crossing.

Nochlin, Linda. 1988. *Women, art, and power and other essays.* New York: Harper and Row.

Schor, Mira. 1994. Backlash and appropriation. In Norma Broude and Mary D. Garrard, eds., *The power of feminist art: The American movement of the 1970s, history and impact.* New York: Abrams.

Schulman, Sarah. 1991. Della Grace: Photos on the margin of the lesbian community. *Love bites: Photographs by Della Grace.* London: GMP Editions.

Sontag, Susan. 1982. The pornographic imagination. *The Susan Sontag reader.* New York: Farrar/Straus/Giroux.

Williams, Linda. 1989. *Hard core: Power, pleasure, and the "frenzy of the visible."* Berkeley: University of California Press.

Jane Caputi

PORNOGRAPHY AND VIOLENCE

Feminists in the United States and Britain began to focus critically on the multibillion-dollar pornography industry in the 1970s within the context of increased knowledge about the pervasiveness of violence against women and its legitimation in social, economic, and political institutions (Lederer, 1980). Pornography was an obvious target of feminist scrutiny because it was a growing industry and because it seemed clear in its intent to engender a culture of sexual subordination and violence: it had an explicit ideology of sexism and male supremacy, and it abused women through its production and use. Antipornography and antirape groups initially took the title of Robin Morgan's essay "Theory and Practice: Pornography and Rape" (1980) as a leading slogan. From the mid- to late 1970s, grassroots feminist antipornography groups in the United States, such as Women Against Violence Against Women, Women Against Violence in Pornography and Media (WAVPM), and Women Against Pornography, led tours of pornography districts, picketed porn films, conducted slide show discussions on pornography and sexism, and led protest marches through pornography districts such as Times Square in New York City (Dines, Jensen, and Russo, 1998; Lederer 1980; Russell 1993).

Feminists fighting the pornography industry define it as a major institution of male domination and white supremacy. The focus is on pornography produced and consumed by heterosexual men that harms women in a multitude of ways—through its ideologies, its processes of production and consumption, and its mass distribution. In contrast to the moralistic perspective on pornography, the salient issue for feminists has been not the sexual explicitness of pornography or its public availability but, rather, its sexism, misogyny, and racism; the structure and dynamics of eroticized inequality; and the sexual abuse and violence that occur through its production, consumption, and distribution (Dworkin, 1988, 1989, 1997; Itzin, 1992).

Almost since the inception of the feminist fight against pornography, a vocal contingent of anticensorship and sex-radical feminists have challenged the politics of this analysis (Snitow, Stansell, and Thompson, 1983). Although they agree that some pornography may be sexist, misogynist, and racist, they believe that the genre of pornography also contains important possibilities for sexual exploration and expression. This analysis arises within a theoretical paradigm of sexual repression that challenges the sexual double standard, the homophobic silencing of lesbian and gay sexual expression, and state control over women's sexual and reproductive rights (Vance, 1986). By defining pornography as merely representations and images of sexual practices, they emphasize issues of individual interpretation and private use. And by maintaining a complete distinction between images and realities, they evade discussion of the specific harms that arise from the production and consumption of pornography and the generalized social inequality that it legitimates and promotes (Burstyn, 1985).

Production of Pornography

The production of pornography often involves coercion and violence against the women used in it. Women's decisions to participate in the pornography industry are not typically made in a context of economic opportunity and social freedom. Poverty, racism, and limited economic and educational opportunities often influence women's decisions to become involved in the pornography industry (Barry, 1979; Dworkin, 1988; Teish, 1980). Given the structure of the economy, pornography may appear lucrative to women who are unable to obtain jobs that pay a living wage, especially when they have children to support. Some young women get involved in pornography, as in prostitution, because they have run away from abusive homes, and pimps and pornographers offer them food, shelter, and promises of love and stability (Barry, 1979; Giobbe, 1993). Some women are used in pornographic magazines and films as children and adolescents (Silbert and Pines, 1984); some young women who have been sexually abused get involved in pornography because they have been conditioned to believe that their value lies in the commodification of their sexuality or they feel that being in pornography allows them to exercise control over their sexuality. A growing number of women and children are photographed and videotaped by their husbands, boyfriends, or relatives without their consent and sometimes without their knowledge (Gaines, 1992). Women involved in the production of pornography are vulnerable to sexual harassment, abuse, violence, and sometimes murder, and the pornography is often a documentation of the harassment, abuse, rape, and torture they are experiencing (Bogdanovich, 1984; Dworkin, 1988, 1989; Lovelace, 1980). The stigma placed on women in the sex industry means that women who report sexual coercion, abuse, or rape are not believed and are likely to experience further abuse by the police and the criminal justice system (Delacoste and Alexander, 1987).

Consumption of Pornography

Some consumers of pornography use it to harass, intimidate, humiliate, and silence women (Lederer and Delgado, 1995; MacKinnon, 1987; Public Hearings, 1983; Russell, 1993). In education and employment the public presence of pornography can significantly undermine women's efforts toward gender equality and mutual respect. Pornography contributes to the creation of hostile and intimidating environments that may result in poor job or academic performance, may prompt women to leave jobs or schools, and in general may undermine women's initiative and confidence. This use of pornography has been evident in fields with histories and traditions of male domination and female exclusion, where the display of pornographic pictures and cartoons sends a message to the few women working in these areas that they do not belong and are not welcome. Men sometimes use pornography in the home to intimidate and coerce women and children into sexual activity or as a way of minimizing and distorting women's sense of self-worth, confidence, sexual identity, and equality within these relationships. Sexual abusers may use pornography in child sexual abuse and in indoctrinating young women into a life of prostitution.

Pornography has functioned as a method to motivate, orchestrate, justify, and guide sexual abuse and violence against women. Evidence exists that serial murderers and sex offenders whose victims are women are often consumers of pornography (see, for example, Wyre, 1992); the specific types of pornography they consume often correlate with the particular methods of sexual torture and murder they adopt. Some rape survivors report that the men who raped them referred to pornography as a part of the rape (Public Hearings, 1983; Silbert and Pines, 1984). Research studies show that pornography helps to create a context in which the male subjects consider violence against women acceptable, natural, and normal and that it contributes to the prevalence of violence against women (Donnerstein and Malamuth, 1984; MacKinnon, 1987; Russell, 1993).

Mass Distribution, Ideology, and Inequality

The ideology of pornography is male domination and female inferiority (Dworkin, 1989; Kappeler, 1986); in general, it presents men's sexual objectification, coercion, abuse, and violence as entertainment. Pornography links men's sexual arousal to women's sexual subordination. To neutralize the explicit powerlessness of women, the pornography says that the women desire sexual submission and abuse. Women's resistance to sexual subordination, when shown, is presented as pretense or sexual ignorance (Dworkin, 1989). In pornography, polarized power differences in combination with various levels of coercion and pain are linked to the consumer's sexual arousal and pleasure. Pornography is not creative or original in its exploitation of historical and social power dynamics; rather, it takes already existing inequalities and presents them as sexy and entertaining. It targets women differently depending on, for instance, status and occupation; race, color, and ethnicity; and size, shape, and age. Some pornography presents young, prepubescent women as the most sexually enticing and attractive erotic objects for adult men's consumption. The younger a woman is or appears, the more virginal, vulnerable, and powerless she is, and thus the sexier (that is, sexually enticing and available) she is believed to be. There is extensive illegal marketing of children in the United States and around the world (Burgess, 1984; Tate, 1992). In legal pornography, incest and adult–child sexual relations are also common themes of fictional stories and cartoons. There are pornographic paperback book series with titles such as *Spread Daughter Spread* or *Daughters Hot for Dogs* or *Daddy's Naughty Daughters. Hustler* has had a regularly featured cartoon called "Chester the Molester," whose main character, Chester, regularly "seduces" or is "seduced by" young girls. Magazines like *19 and Bound, Young Love* ("261 Sexy Young Things"), and *Eager Naked Daughter,* which use models who are over the age of 18 (as indicated on their front covers), portray the women as much younger. The pornographic stories place the young women in control of the sexual activity, which neutralizes for the reader the power imbalance of age and status.

Pornography makes racism sexy and entertaining, thereby legitimating, nourishing, and reinforcing racist stereotypes, bigotry, and mistreatment (Russell, 1993). Like other mainstream media, heterosexual pornography, which is geared to the white male population, rarely includes women of color and, when it does, differentiates women racially. Luisah Teish (1980) points out that "while white women are pictured as pillow-soft pussy willows, the stereotype of the Black 'dominatrix' portrays the Black woman as ugly, sadistic, and animalistic, undeserving of human affection" (also see Collins, 1990).

Pornography capitalizes on racism, bigotry, torture, and murder by making them sexually arousing and entertaining (Gardner, 1980; Lederer and Delgado, 1995; Walker, 1980). The eroticization of black women's skin in pornography contributes to the racist history and stereotype that black women exist for the sexual use of men, especially white men, and to the myth that they are always sexually available (Dworkin, 1989). Pornography consistently presents black men as oversexed or bestial in their sexuality, which cannot be understood separate from the ever-present societal myth that it is predominantly black men who rape or want to rape white women (Davis, 1981).

Anti-Semitism is another common staple of contemporary pornography. Following in the tradition of Nazi pornography, which Hitler used to fuel his genocidal war, contemporary propaganda makes entertainment out of the Nazis' sexual torture and murder of Jewish women. Pornography also was used to fuel the Korean and Vietnam wars by presenting Asian women in racist and misogynistic ways (Langelan, 1981), and contemporary pornography participates in the international slave traffic in Asian women. Some pornography feeds on the fears and bigotry of whites regarding Asian women and men. (For example, such titles as *Oriental Fetishes, Geisha Girls, Asian Suck Mistress, Slant-Eyed Savages, and Slut from Shanghai* focus on Asian women, and *Oriental Cock, Japanese Sadist Dungeon,* and *Jap Sadist's Virgin Captives* focus on Asian men.) This propaganda helps lay the foundation for continued bigotry, discrimination, and violence against people of color.

The mass distribution of pornographic magazines, books, videos, and computer programs perpetuates sexual abuse and discrimination in the real world of social inequality because it socially legitimates sexual and racialized harassment and abuse as a form of sexual pleasure and entertainment. It creates an environment in which men (and women) have difficulty believing women who speak out about rape, battery, child sexual abuse, and sexual harassment. The messages in pornography about women's pleasure in submission and pain contribute to the fact that men believe that victims of sexual assault derive sexual pleasure from the experience. Both men and women may assume that the women consented to the sex (assault) or in some way were responsible for the sexual experience (assault), especially in the cases of women of color, poor women, and prostitutes (Baldwin, 1984; Itzin, 1992). By placing the inequality and bigotry in a sexual and entertainment arena, pornography serves to protect its makers and consumers from sustained public scrutiny by relying on individual rights to speech and consumption to stave off criticism.

In the early 1980s, Catharine MacKinnon and Andrea Dworkin proposed a novel feminist legal perspective on pornography that defined it as an active *practice* of subordination, rather than as isolated sexual images or speech, and thereby defined pornography as a form of sex discrimination against women. This perspective became the basis on which a model civil rights ordinance was written that would make it possible for individuals harmed through the processes of pornography's production, consumption, and distribution to seek legal redress for the harms of coercion, force, assault, and generalized subordination (Baldwin, 1984; Dworkin, 1988; Itzin, 1992; Dines, Jensen and Russo, 1998). Although this legislation has not been adopted, it represents a major shift in framework for understanding the subordination of women involved in how pornography is produced, consumed, and distributed.

See Also

ABUSE; CENSORSHIP; IMAGES OF WOMEN: OVERVIEW; LAW: FEMINIST CRITIQUES; PORNOGRAPHY IN ART AND LITERATURE; PROSTITUTION; RAPE; SEXUAL SLAVERY

Reference and Further Reading

Baldwin, Margaret. 1984. The sexuality of inequality: The Minneapolis Pornography Ordinance. *Law and Inequality* 2: 635–636.

Barry, Kathleen. 1979. *Female sexual slavery.* New York: Prentice Hall.

Bogdanovich, Peter. 1984. *The killing of the unicorn: Dorothy Stratten (1960–1980).* New York: Morrow.

Burgess, Ann. 1984. *Child pornography and sex rings.* Lexington, Mass.: Heath.

Burstyn, Varda, ed. 1985. *Women against censorship.* Vancouver: Douglas and McIntyre.

Collins, Patricia Hill. 1990. *Black feminist thought.* New York: Routledge.

Davis, Angela. 1981. *Women, race, and class.* New York: Random House.

Delacoste, Frédérique, and Priscilla Alexander, eds. 1987. *Sex work: Writings by women in the sex industry.* San Francisco: Cleis.

Dines, Gail, Robert Jensen, and Ann Russo. 1998. *Pornography: The production and consumption of inequality.* New York: Routledge.

Donnerstein, Edward, and Neil Malamuth, eds. 1984. *Pornography and sexual aggression.* New York: Academic.

Dworkin, Andrea. 1988. *Letters from a war zone: Writings 1976–1989.* New York: Dutton.

———. 1997. *Life and death: Unapologetic writings on the continuing war against women.* New York: Free Press.

———. 1989. *Pornography: Men possessing women.* New York: Dutton.

Gaines, Judith. 1992. Home-video sex sells; unwilling stars cry foul. *Boston Globe* (17 May): 1, 26.

Gardner, Tracey. 1980. Racism in pornography and the women's movement. In Laura Lederer, ed., *Take back the night,* 105–114. New York: Morrow.

Giobbe, Evelina. 1993. Surviving commercial sexual exploitation. In Diana Russell, ed., *Making violence sexy,* 37–42. New York: Teachers College Press.

I Spy Productions. 1993. Pornography and capitalism: The UK pornography industry. In Catherine Itzin, ed., *Pornography,* 76–87. Oxford: Oxford University Press.

Itzin, Catherine, ed. 1992. *Pornography: Women, violence and civil liberties.* Oxford: Oxford University Press.

Kappeler, Susanne. 1986. *The pornography of representation.* Minneapolis: University of Minnesota Press.

Langelan, Marty. 1981. The political economy of pornography. *Aegis* (Autumn).

Lederer, Laura, ed. 1980. *Take back the night: Women on pornography.* New York: Morrow.

———, and Richard Delgado, eds. 1995. *The price we pay: The case against racist speech, hate propaganda, and pornography.* New York: Hill and Wang.

Lovelace, Linda. 1980. *Ordeal.* New York: Berkeley.

MacKinnon, Catharine. 1987. *Feminism unmodified: Discourses on life and law.* Cambridge, Mass. Harvard University Press.

Morgan, Robin. 1980. Theory and practice: Pornography and rape. In Laura Lederer, ed., *Take back the night,* 134–140. New York: Morrow.

Public Hearings on Ordinances to Add Pornography As Discrimination Against Women. 1983. Government Operations Committee (Minneapolis, Minnesota, City Council, 12–13 Dec). Published as *Pornography and sexual violence: Evidence of the links.* 1998. London: Everywoman.

Russell, Diana, ed. 1993. *Making violence sexy: Feminist views on pornography.* New York: Teachers College Press.

Silbert, Mimi H., and Ayala M. Pines. 1984. Pornography and the sexual abuse of women. *Sex Roles* 10(11/12): 857–868.

Snitow, Ann, Christine Stansell, and Sharon Thompson, eds. 1983. *Powers of desire: The politics of sexuality.* New York: Monthly Review.

Strossen, Nadine. 1995. *Defending pornography.* New York: Scribner.

Tate, Tim. 1992. The child pornography industry: International trade in child sexual abuse. In Catherine Itzin, ed., *Pornography,* 203–216. Oxford: Oxford University Press.

Teish, Luisah. 1980. A quiet subversion. In Laura Lederer, ed., *Take back the night,* 115–118. New York: Morrow.

Vance, Carole, ed. 1986. *Pleasure and danger: Exploring female sexuality.* Boston: Routledge Kegan Paul.

Walker, Alice. 1980. Coming apart. In Laura Lederer, ed., *Take back the night,* 95–104. New York: Morrow.

Wyre, Ray. 1992. Pornography and sexual violence. In Catherine Itzin, ed., *Pornography,* 236–247. Oxford: Oxford University Press.

Ann Russo

POSTCOLONIALISM: Theory and Criticism

Postcolonial theory and *postcolonial criticism,* both very broad and widely used terms, have come to refer to anything from critical analysis of texts produced in former British colonies to the exegesis of any excanonical aesthetic text, usually literary, produced since 1945. More specifically, the terms refer to a branch of theory and criticism directed at the appreciation and analysis of literature produced in the wake of European decolonization, particularly narratives from India and Pakistan since 1947, Britain's former African colonies since 1956, south Cyprus and Malta from 1960, the Persian Gulf and Singapore since 1971, and, at various points since the mid-1960s, Morocco, Tunisia, Algeria, and the former French Indochina.

Postcolonial and Post-Colonial

This article uses the spelling *postcolonial,* but a distinction is often made between *postcolonial* theory and criticism and *post-colonial* theory and criticism. *Postcolonial* is used to designate an amorphous set of discursive practices, akin to postmodernism. *Post-colonial* designates a more specific and "historically" located set of cultural practices. Even this second perspective is divided between those who believe that *post-colonial* refers only to the period after the colonies became independent, and those who argue that it is best used to designate the totality of practices, in all their rich diversity, that characterize the societies of the postcolonial world from the moment of their colonization to the present day, since colonization does not cease with the mere fact of political independence and continues in a neocolonial mode to be active in many societies.

It is clear that postcolonial theory existed for a long time before that name was used to describe it. Once colonized peoples had cause to reflect on and express the tension that ensued from this problematic and contested, but eventually vibrant and powerful, mixture of imperial language and local experience, postcolonial *theory* and *criticism* came into being. The terms generally designate discussion about experience of various kinds: migration, slavery, suppression, resistance, representation, difference, race, gender, place, and responses to the influential discourses of imperial Europe such as history, philosophy, and linguistics, and the fundamental experiences of speaking and writing by which all these come into being.

Women and Postcolonialism

Many women have been attracted to postcolonial theory and criticism because of the parallels between the recently decolonized nation and the situation of women within patriarchal culture. In a number of ways, both take the perspective of a socially marginalized subgroup in their relationship to the dominant culture, and this shared perspective manifests itself in narratives.

Fictions of countercolonial resistance often draw upon the many different indigenous local and hybrid processes of self-determination to defy, erode, and sometimes supplant the prodigious power of imperial cultural knowledge. Consequently, groups of people who are marginalized, whether sexually or racially, often have access to a number of different subject positions, each imbued with its own historicity and each a potentially adversarial and revolutionary agency relative to the dominant mode that holds it in captivity. The fiction of Ntozake Shange, the journalism of Mirta Vidal, and the poetry of Viola Correa, for example, highlight the impossibility of constructing a narrative or discourse that is heterogeneous, multiple, and differential enough to offer fair representation to multiple subject positions. Perhaps the best known of postcolonial theorists, Edward Said (1983), argues that ultimately the tragedy of any postcolonial question lies in the constitutive limitation imposed on any attempt to deal with relationships that are polarized, radically uneven, and remembered differently. The spheres, the sites of intensity, the agenda, and the constituencies in the metropolitan and excolonized worlds, argues Said, overlap only partially.

Postcolonial Women's Narratives

A number of postcolonial women writers, including Nawal El-Sadaawi, Gloria Anzaldúa, Aihwa Ong, and perhaps more famously, Toni Morrison, Nadine Gordimer, and Maxine Hong Kingston testify in their narratives to an ex-centric relationship to their cultures that reveals itself in subversive writing strategies such as critiques of heterosexism, postcolonial imperialism, and male phallic economies. As a consequence, many critics and theorists of postcolonial narratives, especially nonwhite women writers such as Gayatri Chakravorty Spivak (1990) and Trinh T. Minh-ha (1989), attempt to reach a self-critical appraisal of the extent to which white feelings remain central, a refusal to countenance postcolonial imperialism, and a refusal to speak for the third world, coupled with an effort to provide space in which third world voices can be heard. The concern of these and other critics with "otherness" and "difference" and the process of acknowledging "different histories," testifying to a profound shift in the intellectual climate of the academic establishment, has been very important in attempting to delegitimize the built-in Eurocentric, dominant male gaze of Orientalism.

Cultural Relativism

Despite this progress, postcolonial literary theory and criticism is beset by a number of difficulties and debates. In the attempt to avoid a Eurocentric critique, much postcolonial theory and criticism falls into the trap of a cultural relativism that refrains from criticizing oppressive social and sexual relations when they occur in cultures "other" than the critic's own and that focuses solely on describing or defending existing local traditions and cultures. Each culture is then regarded as "acceptable" in its own terms, and no common ground between them is offered. This kind of criticism and theory can easily end up appearing fragmentary rather than all-embracing; instead of trying to understand, evaluate, compare, and choose, the critic refrains from judgment and condones indiscriminately. Edward Said, among other postmodern theorists, has pointed out that apparently claims to "eternal" and "universal" truth often reflect many of the characteristics of the social setting from which they arise. Therefore unless power relations (deriving from personality, race, class, gender, and so on) are explicitly acknowledged, the knowledge gained from studying the narratives of another culture will necessarily be distorted (1983). When gender is at issue, this difficulty becomes especially pertinent, as the feminist critic Sara Suleri has remarked: "The claim to authenticity—only a black can speak for a black; only a postcolonial subcontinental feminist can . . . —points to the great difficulty posited by the 'authenticity' of female racial voices in the great game that claims to be the first narrative of what the ethnically constructed woman is deemed to want" (1992).

See Also

COLONIALISM AND POSTCOLONIALISM; CRITICAL AND CULTURAL THEORY; EUROCENTRISM; MULTICULTURALISM

References and Further Reading

Ashcroft, Bill, Gareth Griffiths, and Helen Tiffin, eds. 1995. *The post-colonial studies reader.* London: Routledge.

Ghandi, Leela. 1998. *Postcolonial theory.* New York: Columbia University Press.

JanMohamed, Abdul. 1983. *Manichaen aesthetics: The politics of literature in colonial Africa.* Amherst: University of Massachusetts Press.

Minh-ha, Trinh T. 1989. *Women, native, other.* Bloomington: Indiana University Press.

Quayson, Ato. 1999. *Postcolonialism: Theory, practice, or process?* Oxford: Blackwell.

Ramazanoğlu, Caroline. 1989. *Feminism and the contradictions of oppression.* London: Routledge.

Said, Edward. 1983. *The world, the text, the critic.* Cambridge, Mass: Harvard University Press.

Spivak, Gayatri Chakravorty. 1990. *The post-colonial critic: Interviews, strategies, dialogues.* Ed. Sarah Harasym. London: Routledge.

Suleri, Sara. 1992. Women skin deep: Feminism and the postcolonial condition. *Critical Inquiry* 18(4: Summer) 756–769.

Ailbhe Smythe

POSTFEMINISM

Feminism may be the only human rights movement that periodically gets celebrated for committing suicide. We have yet to read about the advent of "postenvironmentalism," much less hear the media applaud the "post–civil rights" era. Yet in modern times, whenever women have taken a step or two forward in challenging social and economic inequities, the media have made haste to declare feminism dead. Before the movement's aims are even achieved, the postmortem is issued—and women are charged with being their own movement's willing executioners.

Promoters of this ethic maintain that women would be better off disavowing allegiance to a movement that champions their rights. Feminism—like braces, pimples, or taxes—is something to hurry up and get behind you as quickly as possible. The fact that feminism was created and embraced by masses of women is replaced by the accusation that feminism was rudely foisted upon unwilling damsels—

and women won't feel whole and "feminine" again until they have shed the burden and become "postfeminist."

The term *postfeminism* is bewildering, and for good reason. It's often put forth in flattering terms—"You women are postfeminist now; you're too sophisticated for that old feminist claptrap"—as if being postfeminist were somehow a more evolved state than being a woman who believes equality and independence are worth fighting for. Postfeminism's flattery works as sugarcoating, making its poison pill go down smoothly. The compliments serve to mask the insult—the culture intends to bury feminism, not praise it.

The American media have classified as "postfeminist" a slew of celebrities—Camille Paglia, Madonna, Sharon Stone, Calista Flockhart's character Ally McBeal—who are known for a certain glamourous narcissism and bad-girl sexiness, but not for any meaningful challenge to their gender's second-class status. These women are celebrated for their outspokenness, their "feisty spirit," but they tend to be self-proclaimed "individualists" with little interest in feminism's core conviction, sisterhood. In this way they appear to be feminist without having to do the heavy lifting of political analysis—an appealing deal to women who are fearful of the hostility and rejection that come with asserting an authentic feminist position.

With its duplicitous message of faux liberation, postfeminism is very much the offspring of modern American advertising. The famous slogan for Virginia Slims cigarettes could be postfeminism's anthem: "You've Come a Long Way, Baby." Given postfeminism's origins in advertising, it's not surprising that it flourishes in consumer-saturated cultures. The word *postfeminism* has near cliché status in the United States, Canada, and the United Kingdom, but it is virtually unknown in third world countries. A *commercial* response to the women's movement, postfeminism offers women an adman's Faustian pact: the promise of "powerful" sex appeal and "choices" you buy with your very own credit card, in exchange for genuine power and self-determined choices for all women.

The term *postfeminism* made its first appearance in the United States in 1919, not coincidentally on the verge of American women's suffrage and the consumer culture's ascendancy. In *The Grounding of Modern Feminism* (1987), the historian Nancy Cott recounts how a group of women writers in America in 1919 produced a journal in which they renounced gender analysis and dubbed their stance "postfeminist." In the 1920s the media went a step further: women want to be flappers, not suffragists, the press held. They would rather look fetching in beaded clingy outfits than wear fuddy-duddy bonnets and march for the vote. Women didn't want to be liberated; they just wanted to have fun.

In the 1980s, the dawn of the Reagan era after the second wave of the American women's movement in the 1960s and 1970s, postfeminism returned, this time with an insidious and clever gloss that matched the insidious and clever evolution of consumer marketing. Now, women were told, they could be postfeminist *because* they were liberated. They were free to be sex objects without losing any of their power. In fact, they could *gain* power by marketing their bodies. They could bare their breasts on a magazine cover and be hailed as emancipated, as the topless Sharon Stone was in 1993 in an issue of *Vanity Fair,* which extolled her as one of the "powerful women" of the "postfeminist era." As the U.S. newspaper columnist Debbie M. Price wrote dubiously of the *Vanity Fair* cover, "Feminists burned their bras and so now, postfeminists bare their breasts?"

The earliest reference to "postfeminism" in the 1980s (according to Lexis-Nexis, the largest electronic news database) came, not surprisingly, from *Time* magazine—a publication notably devoted to issuing obituaries on the women's movement. In an article in 1983, J. D. Reed saluted the arrival of "postfeminist" literature with the giddy declaration, "The waiting is over." (Who exactly was waiting?) Unfortunately for *Time,* the examples the magazine offered hardly proved the point: Mary Gordon, Maxine Hong Kingston, Alice Walker, and Toni Morrison, all writers whose work is nothing if not feminist. Undaunted, though, the media kept on beating the drum for postfeminism and—with major assists from the advertising, publishing, movie, television, fashion, and beauty industries—eventually willed it into a virtual reality.

The "dawn of postfeminism in advertising," as the columnist Barbara Lippert (1987) observed in *The Record,* could be dated to the fall of 1984, when the feminist model for Charlie perfume returned to a strapless gown and an eagerness to wed and Anne Klein II aired TV ads in which a postfeminist glam gal appeared in various ritzy locales and was approached by women hungry to know the secret of her celebrity. Her answer was always the same: "Anne Klein II." As Lippert observed, "Implicit here, of course, is that true confidence begins with great wool separates."

Such is the message now drummed into women from all cultural outlets. Feminist-minded TV heroines such as the police partners in *Cagney and Lacy* and the journalist Mary Richards in the *Mary Tyler Moore Show*—women who sought a fair shake and serious engagement in a public world—have been replaced by the postfeminist-minded girl-lawyer in *Ally McBeal,* the catty nymphets of *Sex and the City,* and the ditsy lingerie hawker of *Veronica's Closet,* women who are shown with "careers" and economic power but use these gains primarily to shop, obsess about their weight, and whine about loser guys. They have their best-selling counterparts in popular fiction—Bridget Jones, with her incessant calorie counting and boy troubles—and popular music—the Spice Girls or Alanis Morissette, whose feminism seems to involve little more than lyrics trashing bad dates.

Inevitably, a lot of women saturated by these images have taken up the mantra themselves. "It's important not to feel bullied into dressing down," said one young woman in 1999, in a feature in *The New York Times* about how many young female artists are dolling up. A young sculptor partial to see-through skirts explained that as a member of the postfeminist generation, she is now free to make "girlie art." *Esquire* magazine was only too happy to feature on its cover what it called "'do-me' feminists"—postfemmes who were happy to assume cheesecake poses and roll their eyes at feminism. The young writer Katie Roiphe assured the magazine that date rape is a figment of an overheated feminist imagination, while another young woman exclaimed, "A lot of us just want to go spray paint and make out with our boyfriends and not worry about oppression."

In a culture driven by cover stories, it's not surprising that some young American women embrace postfeminism—in hopes that they will be granted poster-girl status by a world that recognizes little else. And in an era chilly to political analysis and activism, these young women may well feel that their only path to power is to exercise their sexuality.

In a perverse twist, the same U.S. media that invented postfeminism now blame feminism for its conception. In a cover story in 1998 entitled "Is Feminism Dead?"—illustrated with a picture of Ally McBeal—*Time* charged that *feminism* "is wed to the culture of celebrity and self-obsession" and has given birth to a pack of "post-feminist" and "self-absorbed girls." If the postfeminist girl didn't exist, in other words, they'd have to invent her...and then blame her, like everything else, on feminism.

See Also

COMMODITY CULTURE; CONSERVATISM; FEMININITY; FEMINISM: OVERVIEW; FEMINISM: LIBERAL NORTH AMERICAN; FEMINISM: SECOND-WAVE BRITISH; FEMINISM: SECOND-WAVE NORTH AMERICAN

References and Further Reading

Bellafante, Ginia. 1998. Is feminism dead? *Time* (June 29): 54.

Cott, Nancy F. 1987. *The grounding of modern feminism.* New Haven, Conn.: Yale University Press.

Faludi, Susan. 1991. *Backlash: The undeclared war against American women.* New York: Crown.

Friend, Tad. 1994. Yes, feminist women who like sex. *Esquire* (Feb.): 48.

Hayt, Elizabeth. 1999. The artist is a glamour puss. *New York Times* (18 April): section 9, 1.

Lippert, Barbara. 1987. Designer re-tailors an image. *Record* (6 Sept): Lifestyle, 8.

Price, Debbie M. 1993. Is naked aggression a sign of feminist power? *Des Moines Register* 2.

Reed, J. D. 1983. Postfeminism: Playing for keeps. *Time* 60.

Sessums, Kevin. 1993. Wild thing! *Vanity Fair* (cover story).

Susan Faludi

POSTMODERN FEMINISM

See FEMINISM: POSTMODERN.

POSTMODERNISM AND DEVELOPMENT

The postmodern critique, with its attention to difference and discourse, and its attack on the universalizing truths of Enlightenment thinking, has much to offer those who are critical of development theory and practice. Some scholars have drawn on this perspective to challenge the assumption that modernization is necessarily possible or desirable. They have questioned the belief that developing world growth and westernization and modernization are synonymous and that western political social and economic institutions and practices (whether liberal or socialist) hold the answers to development problems in the developed "North" and the developing "South." This debate has influenced thinking (and practice) about gender and development as well.

Postmodernism is not easily encapsulated in one phrase or idea, as it is actually an amalgam of often intentionally ambiguous and fluid ideas. For our purposes, the central tenet of postmodernist thought is its fundamental critique of modernist assumptions about the world, particularly the belief that rational thought and technological innovation can guarantee progress and enlightenment to humanity. This critique throws doubt on the ability of thinkers from the West either to understand the world or to prescribe solutions for it. The grand theories of the past, whether liberal or Marxist, are no longer seen as "truths" but are seen rather as privileged discourses that deny or silence competing dissident voices.

The critique of universality has led to a focus on local, specific voices and knowledge, with an emphasis on difference and multiple identities. The individual subject is no longer seen as a consistent, predictable basis for understanding society and social change. This fluid, unpredictable world requires new ways of thinking about power and social change. Michel Foucault's critique of established notions of power and his focus on the relational nature of power and its link to knowledge and discourse provide an important new perspective. Foucault argues that the ability to control knowledge and meaning, not only through writing, but also through disciplinary and professional institutions and in social relations, is the key to understanding and exercising power relations in society.

Feminists have responded to postmodern ideas in a number of ways. Feminists working within liberal and Marxist traditions have generally opposed postmodern critiques, particularly the attack on modernity and the universality of western thought. Standpoint feminists have objected to the attack on the centrality and consistency of the subject (person), arguing that it should be no surprise that the subject no longer counts just as women and other marginalized groups start to find their voice. Feminists of all persuasions worry about the political implications of focusing on difference and multiple identities, arguing that this undermines the global feminist project. A growing number of feminists find postmodernist thinking useful, however, particularly the attention to difference, to multiple identities, and to the role of language and discourse in constructions of gender hierarchies and inequalities. Although few feminists argue for a wholesale adoption of postmodernism, scholars such as Nancy Fraser and Linda Nicholson believe that these two approaches complement each other. Postmodernists offer sophisticated and persuasive critiques of western universalism, while feminists add a concern for building alliances and mobilizing political action despite difference.

How does this debate touch on development theory and practice, especially the issue of gender and development? Postmodernist conceptions of power and knowledge, particularly the role of discourse in the construction of power and knowledge systems (Foucault, 1980), have inspired critiques of mainstream development, as well as alternative perspectives, such as the dependency literature emerging from Latin America and other parts of the developing world. Scholars such as Arturo Escobar, James Ferguson, and Jonathan Crush argue that development discourse has been (and largely continues to be) embedded in the ethnocentric and destructive colonial (and postcolonial) discourses designed to perpetuate colonial hierarchies rather than to change them. It has defined people from the "South" as the "other," embodying all the negative characteristics (primitive, backward, and so forth) supposedly no longer found in "modern" societies of the "North." These scholars acknowledged the contribution of dependency critiques, which blamed mainstream development practice for underdevelopment rather than development. Although this is an important and still evolving debate, however, it has done little to undermine the links among development, modernity, and the West.

In contrast, scholars drawing on postmodernist perspectives challenge the universal pretensions of modernity, and the Eurocentric certainty of both liberal and Marxist development studies. They point out that the discourse and practices of development have often exaggerated western claims to knowledge, dismissed and silenced knowledge from the "South" and perpetuated dependence on northern "expertise." They call for a new approach to development, one that acknowledges differences, searches out previously silenced voices and knowledge, and recognizes the need to welcome multiple interpretations and "solutions" to developmental problems. Whereas some scholars argue for a synthesis of post-Marxist and postmodern approaches (Schuurman, 1993), all celebrate postmodernism's emphasis on openness, fluidity, multiple identities, and discourses.

This critique has led to an emphasis on the local, on the need to avoid top-down methods, and on the benefits of participatory approaches to development that emphasize equality, listening to others, and respect for indigenous knowledge and practices (Chambers, 1997). The current pace of change, fueled by globalization and new knowledge-based technologies, is destabilizing easy explanations of the world, especially those embedded in notions of western-defined modernity. Postmodernist explanations of the world may not provide answers, but they do offer a way to think about the complex world we live in.

How have these postmodernist approaches to development influenced the theory and practice of gender and development? Both liberal- and Marxist-inspired thinking about women's development have been embedded in modernist assumptions. The women in development (WID) approach sought greater equity between women and men, but left western gender stereotypes largely unchallenged. Although the gender and development (GAD) approach pays more attention to the roles assigned to women and men and their impact on gender relations (the relations between women and men), and to the impact of global inequalities, it remains tied to a modernist model of development.

Postmodernist feminist thinking, along with feminist writings on the environment, science, and political economy, offers some alternative ways of thinking about women or gender and development. Variously identified as empowerment approaches, participatory empowerment, and alternative approaches to development, these new perspectives are still being constructed by scholars, activists, and practitioners. They are united in their concern to eliminate top-down approaches to development, to encourage empowerment of marginalized groups, and to do so through participatory project design and implementation. Although rarely self-conscious about postmodernist influences, this position is clearly influenced by postmodern critiques of universal definitions of modernity, of the importance of language and discourse, the need to pay attention to local knowledge, and the importance of a participatory, inclusive approach to both defining development and implementing development plans. Much of the work in this vein is exploratory and experimental. The participatory rural appraisal (PRA) method of Robert Chambers (1997), in particular, with its emphasis on participation and partnership, is being applied to gender equality problems around the world. While this methodology has its limitations—it is largely unconscious of its underlying theoretical assumptions—it remains an important advance over previous more top-down approaches. More attention to the implications of both postmodernist and political economy perspectives to this methodology or approach offers a way forward. However this works out, there can be no doubt that postmodernist critiques have provided, and continue to provide, important new ways of understanding development for women and men.

See Also

COMMUNITY POLITICS; DEVELOPMENT: OVERVIEW; ECONOMY: OVERVIEW; MODERNISM; POSTMODERNISM: FEMINIST CRITIQUES

References and Further Reading

Braidotti, Rosi, Ewa Charkiewicz, Sabine Hausler, and Saskia Wieringa, eds. 1994. *Women, the environment and sustainable development: Towards a theoretical synthesis.* London: Zed.

Chambers, Robert. 1997. *Whose reality counts? Putting the last first.* London: Intermediate Technology.

Crush, Jonathan, ed. 1995. *Power of development.* New York: Routledge.

Escobar, Arturo. 1995. *Encountering development: The making and unmaking of the third world.* Princeton, N.J.: Princeton University Press.

Ferguson, James. 1991. *The anti-politics machine.* Minneapolis: Minnesota University Press.

Foucault, Michel. 1980. *Power/knowledge: Selected interviews and other writings, 1972–1977.* Trans. C. Gordon. New York: Harvester.

Hekman, Susan, ed. 1996. *Feminist interpretations of Michel Foucault.* University Park: Pennsylvania State University Press.

Kabeer, Naila. 1995. *Reversed realities: Gender hierarchies in development thought.* London: Verso.

Marchand, Marianne, and Jane Parpart, eds. 1995. *Feminism/postmodernism/development.* London: Routledge.

Moser, Caroline. 1993. *Gender planning and development: Theory, practice and training.* London: Routledge.

Nicholson, Linda, ed. 1990. *Feminism/postmodernism.* London: Routledge.

Parpart, Jane. 1993. Who is the "other?" A postmodern critique of women and development theory and practice. *Development and Change* 24(3): 439–464.

Rowlands, Jo. 1997. *Questioning empowerment: Working with women in Honduras.* Oxford: Oxfam.

Schuurman, Frans, ed. 1993. *Beyond the impasse: New directions in development theory.* London: Zed.

Jane L. Parpart

POSTMODERNISM: Feminist Critiques

Postmodernism refers to several groups of thinkers associated with various theoretical approaches:

1. *Poststructuralism* examines how texts are bound up in systems of power that legitimate the subject.
2. *Deconstruction* is an approach to literary criticism that interprets texts according to what is implied—philosophically, socially, or politically—by the way language is used.
3. *Semiotics* examines linguistic signs and symbols.
4. The *new ethnography* uses the methods of ethnography—cultural anthropology—to examine popular culture; feminists apply the new ethnography to romantic fiction, soap opera, and women's magazines, for example.
5. The *linguistic turn* is an approach to history.

Terminology

These theories sometimes overlap and sometimes conflict, but they all have to do with issues of *discourse*—a term meaning systems of linguistic representation through which power sustains itself. Feminists see the dominant discourse as *patriarchal,* that is, governed by men (Gamble, 1999).

Three contemporary French writers—Jacques Lacan (a psychoanalyst), Michel Foucault (a historian), and Jacques

Derrida (a philosopher) represent the "reigning academic elite" in postmodernism (Christian, 1988: 69); their work draws on Nietzsche, Freud, de Man, and de Sade. For at least some theorists, postmodernism emphasiszes the death of the social, the impossibility of the self, and the end of history. Feminist postmodernists often claim that postmodernism, although white, male, and eurocentric, is theoretically superior to feminism and to all liberation struggles.

The U.S. Marxist feminist Nancy Hartsock suggests that some feminist critics turned to postmodernism as a reaction against the white, middle-class perspective that dominated, and limited, literary theory. In contrast, other feminist critics find it ironic that any feminist theorist would turn to the work of male, European academics to redress wrongs which were originally pointed out by women of color. These feminist theorists argue that postmodern theorizing can itself be understood as a reaction by those who had dominated to the sense that "the ground has begun to shift under their feet" (Mascia-Lees, Sharpe, and Cohen, 1989: 16). Hartsock herself discusses the work of progressive theorists, such as Kum Kum Sangari, Fredric Jameson, Donna Haraway, Gloria Anzaldúa, Audre Lorde, Patricia Hill Collins, and Eduardo Galeano, who work outside of postmodernism and try "to expose and clarify the theoretical bases of political change, alliance, and solidarity" (1990: 24).

Barbara Christian discusses the control of the literary scene and the new literary theory from "upper-middle-class institutions" (1988: 71–73), noting that postmodern theoretical language "surfaced, interestingly enough, just when the literature of peoples of color, black women, Latin Americans, and Africans began to move to 'the center.'" She analyzes popular postmodernist terms—*minority discourse, center, periphery, text*—and concludes that what is occurring when they are used is a substitution of disembodied, alienating, egocentric western philosophy for literature, so that the centrality of western male texts is maintained. Thus mind is superior to matter, and the political self has no authority: "The literature of blacks, women of South America and Africa, and so forth as overtly 'political' literature was being preempted by a new Western concept which proclaimed that reality does not exist, that everything is relative." French feminists and others, "eager to enter the halls of power," perpetuate the restrictive tendencies of a theory that has nothing to do with variety, individual experience, or the politics of liberation.

Two additional popular postmodernist terms are *the "other"* and *difference,* both referring to a dominant culture's view of other peoples and cultures. Politically, it might appear that such language would be aligned with feminist concerns; however, the African-American feminist bell hooks asks what it means when discourse about "otherness" is produced mainly by whites. hooks is "amazed by the complete absence of references to work by black women in contemporary critical works claiming to address in an inclusive way issues of gender, race, feminism, postcolonialism, etc." and is concerned that "critiques of identity politics not serve as the new chic way to silence students from marginal groups" (1991: 174–176). hooks also finds that terms such as *other* and *difference* are replacing more forthright words such as *oppression, exploitation,* and *domination*; and the English cultural critic Suzanne Moore notes, similarly: "Flesh, blood, power—these have become the really dirty words" (1988: 190).

Feminism and Postmodernism

For feminist critics like Sheila Jeffreys and Judith Newton, feminism and postmodernism represent different attitudes. Newton, for example, holds that the emotions emphasized by postmodernists do not describe either feminists' anger or their sense of strength. The U.S. feminists Mascia-Lees, Sharpe, and Cohen argue that the postmodern sense of helplessness and disillusionment is "an experience of tremendous loss of mastery in traditionally dominant groups (1989: 14–15). The Canadian feminist Angela Miles (1996) describes the transformative power, energy, urgency, and risk-taking of a multicentered feminist radicalism that sustains diverse women affirming and asserting themselves, their confrontations, and their global visions.

Jeffreys, an English lesbian, criticizes postmodern queer theorists such as Judith Butler and Eve Sedgwick, who accept gender roles, majority heterosexuality, and male supremicist ideas about the mind-body split. According to Jeffreys (1994), queer theory glamorizes femininity but despises the female body, lesbians, and radical feminist theories of sexuality. Thus lesbians are required to be silent about lesbian theory, culture, and difference and must celebrate the clever diversity of the dominant (male) cultural theory.

From a phenomenological perspective (phenomenology is the study of consciousness and self-awareness), Marnia Lazreg criticizes traditional colonialist humanism and also the new antihumanism of Derrida and western feminists. In her analysis of writing on women in Algeria, she finds it ironic that postcolonial, Derridean, Foucaultian feminists objectify and simplify the voices, knowledge, and lives of women rather than challenging the prevailing subject-object paradigm: "Difference is seen as mere division. The danger of this undeveloped view lies in its verging on *indifference.* In this sense, *anything* can be said about women from other cultures as long as it appears to document their differentness from 'us'" (1988: 100). Lazreg also criticizes postcolonial feminist discourse in which women evolve "in nonhistorical time" with "virtually no history" (86).

With regard to history, the U.S. feminist Kathleen Barry wants to "comprehend women as acting *historical* subjects" and sees the type of deconstuctionism currently popular in history and biography as another version of individualism in the United States: "Histories become valuable only to the extent that they reveal differences." But by rejecting commonalities and emphasizing difference, postmodernism neglects "the real ideological problems that, for instance, living under U.S. liberalism poses for U.S. feminists who must transcend and refuse liberalism if they are to find valid connections between their movement and those of women in other parts of the world." According to Barry, deconstruction theory is a "complex relativism" that prefers absence to presence: "Meaning comes from the play of difference instead of from action, situation, and events." She criticizes feminist postmodernists such as Chris Weedon and Joan Scott who disregard writing by radical feminists and materialist French feminists (Christine Delphy, for one): "Feminist deconstructionists are ideologically using a deliberately depoliticized theory to silence feminism as a critique while falsely representing it as *the* French feminist theory" (1990: 92, 95, 99–100).

Suzanne Moore analyzes a "new kind of gender tourism" in the work of Roland Barthes and Jean Baudrillard "whereby male theorists are able to take package trips into the world of femininity" (1988: 167)—the same might, then, be said of tourism into the experiences of blacks and gays. Mascia-Lees, Sharpe, and Cohen also make this point, with regard to the postmodern anthropologist who "locates the 'other' in himself. It is as if, finding the 'exotic' closed off to him, the anthropologist constructs himself as the exotic" (1989: 26). For Moore, male theorists essentialize the feminine (that is, consider it as innate) and impersonate it, never acknowledging actual women, their differences, or their desires. Also, postmodernists seem unaware of feminist theories of male power, sexual politics, and the gendered construction of sexuality—theories that challenge the universal truth of the male narrative and reveal the relation of power to knowledge and language: "Many of the so-called thinkers of postmodernism remain unaware of or truly indifferent to the voices of real women.... Indeed why should they [become aware] when they have neatly managed to step into the space of the 'other' without ever having to talk to a single woman?" (1988: 174).

The west African literary critic Abena Busia describes a "double silencing of the African woman—her presumed silence and the acceptance of her silencing" (1989–1990: 99), even in studies of liberation such as those by Homi Bhabha and Gayatri Spivak when they seem to perpetuate a notion that all colonial subjects are male. In contrast to some postmodernists' pronouncements about the impossibility of subjectivity and commonality, Busia asserts: "In unmasking the dispossessions of the silences of fiction and the fictions of silence, we (re)construct self-understanding. . . . We women signify: we have many modes of (re)dress" (1989–1990: 104).

See Also

CREATIVITY; CRITICAL AND CULTURAL THEORY; DIFFERENCE, *I and II;* ESSENTIALISM; FEMINISM: POSTMODERN; POSTCOLONIALISM: THEORY AND CRITICISM; POSTFEMINISM; POSTMODERNISM AND DEVELOPMENT; POSTMODERNISM: LITERARY THEORY; QUEER THEORY

References and Further Reading

Barry, Kathleen. 1990. The new historical synthesis: Women's biography. *Journal of Women's History* 1(3): 75–105.

Brodribb, Somer. 1992. *Nothing mat(t)ers: A feminist critique of postmodernism.* North Melbourne, Victoria, Australia: Spinifex.

Busia, Abena. 1989–1990. Silencing Sycorax: On African colonial discourse and the unvoiced female. *Cultural Critique* 14(Winter): 81–104.

Christian, Barbara. 1988. The race for theory. *Feminist Studies* 14(1): 67–80.

Gamble, Sarah, ed. 1999. *The Routledge critical dictionary of feminism and postfeminism.* New York: Routledge. (Originally published 1999. Cambridge: Icon.)

Hartsock, Nancy. 1987. Rethinking modernism: Minority versus majority theories. *Cultural Critique* 7(Fall): 187–206.

———. 1989–1990. Postmodernism and political change: Issues for feminist theory. *Cultural Critique* 14: 15–33.

Hoff, Joan. 1994. Gender as a postmodern category of paralysis. *Women's Studies International Forum* 17(4): 443–447.

hooks, bell. 1991. Essentialism and experience. *American Literary History* 3(1): 172–183. (Review of Diana Fuss. 1989. *Essentially speaking: Feminism, nature, and difference.* New York: Routledge.)

Irigaray, Luce. 1974, 1985. Any theory of the "subject" has always been appropriated by the "masculine." In *Speculum of the other woman,* 133–146. Trans. Gillian Gill. Ithaca, N.Y.: Cornell University Press.

Jeffreys, Sheila. 1994. The queer disappearance of lesbians: Sexuality in the academe. *Women's Studies International Forum* 17(5): 459–472.

Klein, Renate, and Diane Bell, eds. 1996. Radical feminists "interrogate" postmodernism. In *Radically speaking: Femi-*

nism reclaimed, sec. 3. North Melbourne, Victoria, Australia: Spinifex.

Lazreg, Marnia. 1988. Feminism and difference: The perils of writing as a woman on women in Algeria. *Feminist Studies* 14(1): 81–107.

Mascia-Lees, Frances R., Patricia Sharpe, and Colleen Ballerino Cohen. 1989. The postmodernist turn in anthropology: Cautions from a feminist perspective. *Signs: Journal of Women in Culture and Society* 16(2): 7–33.

Miles, Angela. 1996. Nonintegrative antiessentialist reductionisms. In *Integrative feminisms: Building global visions, 1960s–1990s,* chap. 5. New York: Routledge.

Moore, Suzanne. 1988. Getting a bit of the other—The pimps of postmodernism. In Rowena Chapman and Jonathan Rutherford, eds., *Male order: Unwrapping masculinity,* 165–192. London: Lawrence and Wishart.

O'Brien, Mary. 1984. Between critique and community. *Women's Review of Books* 1(7): 9–11. (Review of Nancy Hartsock. 1983. *Money, sex, and power: Toward a feminist historical materialism.* New York: Longman.)

Spretnak, Charlene. 1991. The disembodied worldview of deconstructive postmodernism; and Appendix B. In *States of grace: The recovery of meaning in the postmodern age,* 121–127; 245–261. San Francisco, Calif.: Harper.

Weigman, Robyn. 2000. Postmodernism. In Bonnie Zimmerman, ed., *Lesbian histories and cultures.* New York: Garland.

Somer Brodribb

POSTMODERNISM: Literary Theory

Literary theory, often referred to as "critical theory" or sometimes simply as "theory," is not easy to define, since it is neither a genre nor an identifiable body of texts. Originally, "critical theory" referred to Frankfurt school and post–Frankfurt school thought (Max Horkheimer, Theodor Adorno, Herbert Marcuse, Jürgen Habermas), but the term is now widely used to describe any critical theoretical approach to philosophy or literature. Jonathan Culler (2000) defines literary theory as "the systematic account of the nature of literature and of the methods for analysing it . . . an unbounded group of writings about everything under the sun." Broadly speaking, theory is engaged in subjecting widely held commonsense assumptions to scrutiny, and in a literary context, this involves destabilizing the concepts of meaning, interpretation, textuality, and authorship that are taken for granted. Literary theory, therefore, can be described as the interpretation of interpretation, challenging us to think about what we do when we read.

Feminist theory is one of many different theoretical approaches or schools (others are formalism, structuralism and poststructuralism, Marxist theory, psychoanalytic theory, postcolonial theory, and queer theory). Feminist theory should be differentiated from feminist criticism, since the latter engages specifically in the analysis of literary texts, whereas, according to one recent anthology, feminist theory analyzes the conditions that shape women's lives and explores cultural understandings of what it means to be a woman (Jackson and Jones, 1998). While literary theory deals with issues of representation and interpretation, feminist literary theory focuses more narrowly on constructions of femininity and feminine sexuality in a literary context. In the 1970s, a number of critics analyzed "forgotten" women writers and the representation of women in literary texts, an area of study known as gynocriticism; notable figures in this field include Ellen Moers, Elaine Showalter, Sandra Gilbert, and Susan Gubar.

If theory in general challenges common assumptions and seeks to change the way we perceive the world, which makes it, many claim, an intrinsically political exercise, feminist theory is engaged in the same process in the specific contexts of gender, sex, and sexuality. Twentieth-century feminist theory (and indeed feminism in general) is often broken down into first, second, and third waves. The first wave refers to early-twentieth-century feminists and includes such key figures as Virginia Woolf and Simone de Beauvoir. Second-wave feminists include North Americans such as Kate Millett, Betty Friedan, and Shulamith Firestone. The declared overthrow of patriarchy was the hallmark of much radical feminism of the 1970s, although many of today's feminist theorists consider this naive and totalizing. The third wave refers to the French feminist theorists who emerged in the wake of poststructuralism, such as Hélène Cixous, Luce Irigaray, and Julia Kristeva, although the relationship of this group to both feminism and poststructuralism is by no means straightforward. The drawing of such lines (for example, Anglo-American feminist or French feminist) is problematic, since it does not take connections and crossovers into account, and in the past nonwestern feminisms have been excluded, an imbalance that a number of contemporary feminist theorists are now attempting to redress. Although feminist theory has always interacted with other theoretical inquiries, contemporary feminist theory is particularly conscious of issues such as class, race, and sexuality, and it has been influential in and influenced by postcolonial theory, gender studies, and queer theory.

The radical separatism that characterized many second-wave feminists and gynocritics is less prominent among today's feminists, many of whom adopt a deconstructive approach toward the monolithic conceptualizations of patriarchy and of the subject, which earlier writers, such as Millett, took for granted. This destabilizing of identity categories is a feature of postmodern theory, another area that is difficult to define. Postmodernism may be characterized as an orientation that emphasizes pluralism, eclecticism, and hybridity. Jean François Lyotard has called it "a war on totality" involving a sustained critique of the foundationalism and essentialism that have characterized much post-Enlightenment thinking.

The relationship between feminist theory and postmodern theory is often uneasy. Although some feminists affirm the possibility of a postmodern feminism, others have produced postmodern accounts of the female subject and subjectivity in general as constructed, parodic, and "performative." The problem seems to lie in what has been dubbed postmodernism's "anemic" engagement with social criticism: although the rejection of foundationalism and essentialism may be regarded as a political enterprise in itself, it effectively precludes the subject as a stable ground from which gender, racial, and sexual biases may be contested. Some feminists regard postmodernism's emphasis on multiplicity, heterogeneity, and parodic subversion as dangerously fragmentary, preventing the formulation of a global feminist enterprise. However, others embrace the political potential of postmodernism's rejection of oppressive metanarratives of gender and the ethno-heterocentricity that marked earlier discourses, claiming that the marginal, unstable identities described by postmodernists are already a feature of feminism (Waugh, 1989). It is important not to construct a monolith out of postmodernism itself, and its own multiplicity and heterogeneity should be recognized. Some versions of postmodernism, and specifically postmodern feminism, do not require the complete abandonment of the subject or of agency, retaining these as structuring, contingent fictions and "performative" categories that provide sites of parodic subversion.

Feminism's uneasy relationship with postmodern theory is a symptom of a continuing ambivalence regarding theory in general. Whereas some feminist theorists argue that it is important to take up the master's tools where they lie, others altogether reject theoretical discourse as masculinist and patriarchal and advocate instead the practice of feminine writing. Such formulations have been regarded by some as naive, utopian, and ethnocentric—thus many contemporary feminist theorists choose to situate themselves in a dynamic and interrogative relationship to the other theories, which influence and are influenced by their own.

See Also

LITERARY THEORY AND CRITICISM; LITERATURE: OVERVIEW

References and Further Reading

Culler, Jonathan. 2000. *Literary theory: A very short introduction.* New York and London: Oxford University Press.

Flax, Jane. 1990. *Thinking fragments: Psychoanalysis, feminism and postmodernism in the contemporary West.* Los Angeles: University of California Press.

Hutcheon, Linda. 1990. *A poetics of postmodernism: History, theory, fiction.* New York and London: Routledge.

Jackson, Stevi, and Jackie Jones. 1998. *Contemporary feminist theories.* New York: New York University Press.

McClintock, Anne. 1994. *Imperial leather: Race, gender, and sexuality in the imperial context.* New York and London: Routledge.

Suleiri, Sara. 1992. Woman skin deep: Feminism and the postcolonial condition. *Critical Inquiry* 18(Summer): 69–75.

Warhol, Robyn R., and Diane Price Herndl, eds. 1993. *Feminisms: An anthology of literary theory and criticism.* Princeton, N.J.: Rutgers University Press.

Waugh, Patricia. 1989. *Feminine fictions. Revisiting the postmodern.* New York and London: Routledge.

Sara Salih

POSTPARTUM PERIOD

See BREASTFEEDING; MATERNAL HEALTH AND MORBIDITY; PREGNANCY AND BIRTH.

POVERTY

The point at which material inequalities shade into poverty will always be a subject of debate. Despite this, there have been a number of attempts by administrators, economists, and sociologists to count the poor and enumerate their characteristics. This article deals with two of the most influential attempts and argues that they camouflage deprivations borne by women. It then outlines the causes of female poverty and indicates the social and economic changes needed to produce fairer outcomes.

Political upheavals and acute food shortages can produce mass starvation and destitution. Disasters such as the events of 1994 in Rwanda represent that endpoint of poverty where, for whatever reason, there are not enough resources to keep people alive. Poverty, however, also can be manifest in chronic illness, homelessness, unemployment, and debt. Poverty can deny people access to schools, transport, legal support, and medical facilities. Whatever the case, poverty operates to undermine people's energy and influence.

Poverty has particular and unequal implications for women. In many nonindustrial countries, women experience the sharpest consequences of poverty. Higher morbidity, mortality, and malnutrition rates have been recorded among female versus male populations, and girl children may be abandoned or left to die (Seager and Olson, 1986). Women also constitute a disproportionate number of the poor in industrialized countries. In Australia, for example, Bettina Cass reworked the figures of the Australian Royal Commission of Inquiry into Poverty (1975) to show that households headed by a woman are five times as likely to be poor as those headed by a man. Poverty, she says, "wears a female face" (Cass, 1985: 83). When racism combines with sexism, these effects are amplified. Thus 90 percent of sole-parent Aboriginal women in Australia have been estimated to have income significantly below the official poverty line (Goodall and Huggins, 1992).

Women's vulnerability to poverty has been masked by official figures, competing definitions, and academic debates. Of particular importance here are the attempts by many western nations to construct a "poverty line" that measures the extent of poverty and classifies its characteristics. These efforts became increasingly detailed over the last two decades of the twentieth century as a result of revolutions in computer technology and the entry of economists into the field of poverty research. The data are generally produced for political purposes: evaluating a government's social security policies and monitoring the effects of economic change are prime examples. These attempts to define and measure poverty are, broadly, of two kinds. Both, in different ways and to different extents, obscure women's disproportionate risk of poverty.

The first follows what is called an "absolute" approach to poverty. It argues that poverty occurs when a person does not have enough income to purchase the nutrients, clothing, housing, and other items needed for physical health and energy. It is called an absolute approach because poverty is related to a fixed notion of biological need. Ironically, this kind of measure can ignore the poverty present in many nonindustrial countries by arguing that subsistence farmers or gatherer-hunters are not "poor," provided they produce or procure enough food to maintain themselves.

The biological norm employed in the absolute approach is, in fact, an "average" male, and women, unless pregnant or breast-feeding, are said to need fewer calories than men. This approach often is used to suggest that poverty in western nations has decreased as general living standards have improved. Seebhom Rowntree's famous studies of poverty in York, England, for example, maintained that poverty in Britain had steadily decreased over the first half of the twentieth century. Because of this focus on apparent historical improvement, the enduring differences between men and women have been ignored.

In contrast, "relative" measures of poverty maintain that poverty cannot be judged in relation to fixed notions of physical need. Its advocates argue that poverty must be assessed in relation to the social and economic standards prevailing in a particular country at a particular time. Accordingly, as standards of living rise, so do the benchmarks that determine the extent of poverty. Thus as countries industrialize, access to income, primary education, and basic healthcare may replace or complement the starker indices of malnutrition and premature death as the main indices of poverty. Similarly, as industrial countries become more affluent, the ability to buy fresh food, obtain preventive health care, and participate in postcompulsory education begin to appear in poverty calculations. In both instances, many low-income families can be considered poor even though they are better housed and fed than their counterparts were some decades before.

Relative measures provide a more promising approach than absolute indicators because they widen our understanding of poverty, prompt each nation to look at its own patterns of inequality, and allow for international as well as national comparisons. However, despite their focus on relativities and their widened definition of poverty (which, it is worth noting, includes many of the traditional concerns and responsibilities of women), relative measures have joined with their absolute counterparts to camouflage the relationship between gender and poverty. There are a number of reasons for this.

First, at a technical level both approaches almost invariably use households rather than individuals as the basis from which poverty lines are calculated. Consequently, the financial arrangements *within* households are not investigated. It is assumed that the household is a single unit, from and in which all members benefit equally. This masks the deprivations experienced by women in nonpoor households and hides the fact that many women in poor households are poorer than men, precisely because income is not shared fairly (Edwards, 1982).

Second, both absolute and relative definitions of poverty ignore important questions relating to the *risk* of poverty. They thus ignore the fact that some nations and some people have less secure futures than others. A run of poor harvests, for example, has a greater impact on standards of living in subsistence economies than economic downturns in industrialized countries with a wide manufacturing and resource base. This failure to take the prevalence of risk into account (which arguably owes much to the fact that definitions of poverty were evolved in twentieth-century Europe) means that future insecurities have not become part of mainstream poverty calculations. As a result, the fact that females carry a greater risk of poverty both through their life cycle and in times of economic reversal is not brought to attention.

Third, both relative and absolute approaches to poverty have been conceptualized in terms of "class," to the exclusion of gender. Mainstream poverty research has concentrated on patterns of employment and income distribution between rich and poor households while neglecting how these same factors differentiate between men and women. It is then the workforce standing of the male head of the household that determines a family's economic status and its risk of poverty. (Female-headed households are often identified as a separate and distinct category, as a deviation from the norm.) The ways in which class and gender intersect to place particular families at risk and to differentially affect men and women go unrecognized.

It therefore has been left to feminist researchers to document and explain the female face of poverty. Feminists argue that women's vulnerability to poverty is a consequence of several interlocking factors. These include: women's economic dependency on men; women's responsibilities for caring and domestic labor; and the behaviors and attitudes expected of the "good" woman. The dominant assumption that females are (and should be) economically dependent on males, and subordinated to them, has implications for women both within and outside conjugal relationships. Those within traditional relationships may be left without adequate income when they depend on male partners with overall control of household finances (Edwards, 1982). Women outside such relationships simply may be left with negligible resources. This explains the disproportionate risk of poverty carried by women as sole parents, widows, and poorly paid income earners, and in old age. The socially endorsed practice of the self-immolation of widows stands as one extreme example of a societal "solution" to the economic predicament of such women. More generally, male control of the distribution of resources effected by a country's social security, taxation, and employment systems has ensured that these systems place women, particularly as mothers, part-time workers, and unpaid domestic laborers, at greater risk of poverty than men.

Women's responsibilities for caring and domestic labor influence and delimit their involvement and standing in the field of economic production. In both industrial and nonindustrial societies, women's connection with the labor force is likely to be disrupted and poorly paid, secondary to their caring work in the home and to their obligations to provide services "which accrue no, or at best very little, financial reward" (Cass, 1985: 73). The gendered division of labor also has distinct implications for women in countries that are experiencing, or have experienced, major economic or political change. In a number of developing countries, women's responsibilities for children have combined with the feminization of agriculture to leave them with less access to cash resources than men and susceptible to any food shortages caused by poor harvests (Geisler, 1992; Rogers, 1980). In postcolonial countries, indigenous women have experienced profound dislocation, leaving them worse off than they were prior to invasion in both absolute and relative terms. Aboriginal woman in Australia, for example, have been forced to exchange their "preinvasion security, independence and relative autonomy as harvesters of staple foods" for "hidden unemployment and the insecurity of casual work and welfare in the capitalist economy" (Goodall and Huggins, 1992: 406–407).

Finally, as the providers of care, women are expected to be altruistic, to put themselves after others, and to do without so that male partners and children can be more adequately provided for. Both historical and contemporary accounts show how this has affected women, particularly in poor households and in periods of war or depression (Harris, 1992). In such circumstances, women may restrict or forgo their own food, health care, and income. Research on expenditure patterns in Zambia shows that women are significantly more likely than men to use their income for family needs; furthermore, the more women take financial responsibility, the more men tend to withdraw from support—without, however, losing their status and rights as head of household (Geisler, 1992).

The need to provide for children, coupled with dependence on government benefits, has far-reaching effects on women's lives. In Australia sole parents have been imprisoned for welfare fraud because they infringed social security rules in their attempts to augment a meager income and meet minimum household expenditures. It also should be noted that the privacy of the domestic arena and the very act of caring for vulnerable others reduces women's capacity to bargain for better conditions for themselves. There is no union to protect the interests of women as mothers and domestic laborers.

Taken together, these factors suggest that women's vulnerability to poverty is caused by an enduring and asymmetrical relationship between economic productivity and caring labor. Caring labor is subordinate to economic production, and the women who carry responsibility for it are rendered dependent on men or on public income security systems. Welfare, in its turn, is subordinated to the commanding heights of the economy. Consequently, the social security benefits on which many women are forced to rely often fall well below official poverty lines, are subject to fluctuations depending on the state of the economy, and are almost invariably lower than minimum wage levels.

Women are not only disproportionately the victims of poverty. They also are its managers. The effects of poverty are experienced and reproduced particularly (although not solely) within the home. Women in poor households have to learn to be skilled and thrifty administrators, a task that adds enormously to their obligations as domestic laborers. In this role they have been, and remain, subject to the policing activities of the officials of the state's welfare apparatus. This scrutiny is often undertaken by other females. Women as social workers and welfare officers observe, judge, and instruct their poorer sisters.

Adequate solutions to female poverty demand changes of at least three kinds. In the first and most immediate instance, social security and public welfare systems need to ensure that the financial support available to women and children is raised to decent levels, well above prevailing poverty lines. Second, the responsibilities for paid and unpaid work need to be equally shared between men and women. Third, and most radically, the importance of caring labor, and its relationship with economic production, requires fundamental reevaluation.

See Also

ECONOMY: WELFARE AND THE ECONOMY; FOOD, HUNGER, AND FAMINE; WORK: PATTERNS

References and Further Reading

Cass, Bettina. 1985. The changing face of poverty in Australia: 1972–1982. *Australian Feminist Studies* 1 (Summer): 67–91.

Edwards, Meridith. 1982. Women, children and family poverty: Causes and cures. *Australian Quarterly* 54(3: Spring): 252–259.

Geisler, G. 1992. Who is losing out? Structural adjustment, gender, and the agricultural sector in Zambia. *Journal of Modern African Studies* 30(1): 113–129.

Gelpi, Barbara, ed. 1986. *Women and poverty.* Chicago: University of Chicago Press.

Goldberg, Gertrude, and Eleanor Kremen, eds. 1990. *The feminization of poverty: Only in America?* New York: Greenwood.

Goodall, Heather, and Jackie Huggins. 1992. Aboriginal women are everywhere. In Kay Saunders and Raymond Evans, eds., *Gender relations in Australia: Domination and negotiation,* 398–424. Sydney: Harcourt Brace Jovanovich.

Harris, Patricia. 1992. Penny pinching activities: Managing poverty under the eye of the welfare. In Kay Saunders and Raymond Evans, eds., *Gender relations in Australia: Domination and negotiation,* 287–302. Sydney: Harcourt Brace Jovanovich.

Lavinas, L. 1996. *As mulheres no universo da pobrezo: o caso Brasileiro* (Women in the universe of poverty: The Brazilian case). *Estudos-Feministas* 4(2): 464–479.

Muniz, P. 1996. *La reproduction de la pobreza* (The reproduction of poverty). *Demos* 9: 20–22.

Nordquist, Joan. 1987. *The feminization of poverty.* Santa Cruz, Calif.: Reference and Research Series.

Peeke, L. J. 1997. Toward a social geography of the city: Race and dimensions of urban poverty in women's lives. *Journal of Urban Affairs* 4(2): 464–479.

Rogers, Barbara. 1980. *The domestication of women: Discrimination in developing countries.* London: Tavistock.

Seager, Jani, and Ann Olson. 1986. *Women in the world: An international atlas.* London: Pan.

Patricia Harris

POWER

Although feminists have disagreed on the question of who exercises power or how it is distributed, they have largely agreed on what it is: power means domination. Though some attention has been given to the "empowerment" of women, power has mostly been seen in negative terms as "power over." Key debates have concerned the underlying bases of power, and whether power should be understood as dispersed among all men or concentrated in the hands of an elite. What connections could be drawn between the power of the state and the experience of power in face-to-face relations? The relationship between gender and other axes of inequality, such as class, race, and sexuality, also has been discussed. Feminists have engaged with just about every theoretical framework available, from the sociology and political science to semiotics and linguistic theory. Many have been attracted to Michel Foucault's work and ideas. Feminists increasingly have thought about power in relational terms, acknowledging its productive—and potentially positive, as well as repressive—dimensions, and the discursive practices through which the subjects and objects of power are constituted.

In commonsense terms, power involves the capacity of A to make B do something that B would not otherwise do. Although force or coercion may be important elements, power usually refers to a complex balance in which "the ability to impose a definition of the situation, to set the terms in which events are understood and issues discussed, to formulate ideals and define morality" (Connell, 1987: 107) is an important element. Social scientists have drawn up typologies of power that have been adapted by feminists to describe the variety of ways in which men dominate or exploit women. It can be readily shown, for example, that men have had a near monopoly of authority, force, and coercion, while women have been largely restricted to "weaker" forms of power, such as influence and manipulation. Power itself was assumed to rest on access to resources, especially economic ones. To this, feminists added sexual power—which, it was argued, men exercised as men, and not as a byproduct of other forms of power.

In liberal political theory, power is intimately linked with authority. For social contract theorists, the authority of the state rests on the consent of the people, who have ceded their individual sovereignty in return for the preservation of certain common interests. The state ideally is meant to act as a neutral umpire, exercising legitimate power over its subjects in the interests of social order, with power spread widely enough to ensure that everyone's interests are represented. This treatment of power as resting on consent has played a central part in western political thought throughout the modern era. But, as C. Pateman (1988) has pointed out, women have had no part in this contract. Beneath the social contract lay a sexual contract in which men controlled women. This rested on a distinction between the public and private realms and the confinement of women to the private sphere. Liberal theorists have been forced to confront the awkward questions of why women were excluded from the public sphere and why they would freely "choose" to submit to men in the realm of the private. This has led to struggles to gain equal access to the public sphere in which sex discrimination and equal opportunity legislation have been very important. In addition, it has led to struggles for equality in the private sphere and attempts to redefine the relation between the two.

Because it was clear that power is not evenly spread, even among men, much empirical work has been devoted to mapping the concentrations of power that actually exist. Summarizing these accounts, Stephen Lukes (1974) identified "three dimensions" of power. These move from situations of observable behavior and overt conflict to more complex ideological means, whereby groups are able to control the agenda of politics and to shape subjectivities. In a manner that has struck a chord with many feminists, Lukes asks, "Is it not the supreme and most insidious exercise of power to prevent people from having grievances by shaping their perceptions, cognitions and preferences in such a way that they accept their role in the existing order of things... either because they can see or imagine no alternative... or because they see it as natural and unchangeable... or because they value it as divinely ordained?" (1974: 24). Lukes argues that the greatest source of power in any society is the capacity of a select few to influence the manner in which others construct and view their world, and that this will not emerge from a concentration on political institutions and decision making.

Many feminists have simply asserted that an elite of white, heterosexual, middle-class men exercises power over everyone else. Those looking for a more nuanced position turned to Marxist accounts of the state. Here, the state is not regarded as even potentially a neutral umpire but as controlled by the ruling class, which uses power to dominate and exploit another class that lacks power. But it is difficult to avoid the fact that, in Marxism, the capitalist state and class relations inevitably are prioritized over gender relations. Even those who treated "capitalism" and "patriarchy" as analytically separate saw the two systems integrated by the "capitalist" state. Unwilling to claim that women are a class, Marxist-feminists treated the power of men and the subordination of women as effects of imperatives outside the direct relationship between the two. Even in the more sophisticated versions, which emphasized the ideological importance of patriarchy for capitalism, gender relations were effectively subordinated to those of class. Some radical feminists were willing to treat gender divisions as analogous to Marxist class divisions, and they argued not only that the state is in the hands of men but that it systematically pursues "male interests" (MacKinnon, 1987). Where Marxist feminist accounts ultimately subordinated gender to class, the latter could be criticized for overemphasizing the unity of "male" power, at the same time trivializing the differences among women organized, most obviously, around race, class, and sexuality. Poststructuralist feminists attempted to take the debate forward, stressing the importance of discursive strategies in constituting "interests" at the political level.

They argued that the state should be seen not as an institution but as a set of arenas in which "interests" are articulated; any coherence is likely to be partial and temporary, a historical product rather than a structural given. Dissatisfied with all these attempts to theorize about the state, some questioned whether feminism needed a theory of the state at all, for top-down theories do not account for the specificity of women's experience of oppression or the multiplicity of sites in which it takes place (Allen, 1990).

All of these approaches take as their reference point western forms of the state. As Shirin Rai observes, "questions such as whether the post-colonial state poses any particular problems for women, whether women in the developing world can relate such a West-centred debate to their own lives, and whether an analysis of developing world states by feminists might throw up questions for feminists theorizing and debating the state, have not been asked" (Rai, 1996: 7–8). The colonial powers refashioned gender relations within colonized countries through the exercise not only of material but of discursive power. Women have frequently been caught between their "modernizing" practices and the reassertion of "traditional" national, religious, and ethnic identities. As Rai observes, this profoundly "problematizes" the relation between state and civil society and the question of how feminists should relate to either. Feminists in the developing world see the postcolonial state as of critical importance in women's lives, both public and private. On the one hand, women are removed from the state, which is unable to make the kind of welfare provision characteristic of western states. On the other, they are routinely aware of the state's corruption and violence. The Indian women's movement, for example, has been concerned since the 1970s with police brutality: rape, murder, and beatings in police custody continue to be a common feature of state operations (Rai, 1996: 17). At the same time, civil society is also a coercive and masculinist space, so it is not as if women can look to one to oppose the other. Thus, Rai argues, women must necessarily choose to work "in and around" the state, finding in the tensions within it the possibility of political action. It is also clear that the juridical-legislative dimension of the state, based on a distinction between public and private, imprisons many women within male-dominated households. This has implications for the ways in which migrant women—in particular, servants and sex workers—may be treated by an immigration law that ties them into a potentially dangerous relationship with their employer (Phizaclea, 1996).

Whereas some feminists have been preoccupied with the state, others have focused on the operations of power in everyday cultural and social life. Ethnographic studies have traced the subtle discursive interactions through which oppression often works, drawing attention to relations between women as well as between women and men. Romero (1992), for example, identified some of the racial dimensions of this, noting, for example, in her study of domestic service, the ways in which feelings might be trivialized or ignored. Employers often behave in front of their domestic servants as if the servants are literally not there. Women of color are most likely to be treated in this way, and may be obliged to provide their white employers with the additional privilege of having their feelings noticed and considered important.

There also has been a continuing debate about language and power. Dale Spender (1980) famously argued that men control language and that women's silence, alienation, and oppression are a consequence of this. Others drew on linguistic theory and semiotics to argue that language is a vehicle for discourses and ideology (Cameron, 1985). Unhappy with the idea that men simply control language, many feminists emphasized the ways in which social organization is structured by ideologies—that is, sets of representations that construct power relations without needing to resort to obvious coercion. They also turned to psychoanalysis to explain how the ideology of masculinity and femininity constructs men and women as appropriate patriarchal subjects in capitalist society, and why these subjectivities remain so embedded and difficult to question or change (Mitchell, 1975). But theories of ideology were also shown to have their limitations. As M. Gatens has pointed out, such theories are committed to a form of humanism that puts the emphasis on the way in which a human animal is socially produced as a masculine or feminine subject and obscures the ways in which power takes hold of the body rather than merely conditioning the mind (Gatens, 1996: 66–67). As feminists contemplated the difficulty of entering the public sphere without denying their own corporeal specificity, it became clear that it was not "masculinity" as such, but the male body and its culturally determined powers and capacities on which the liberal body politic is modeled (Pateman, 1988). Feminists have become increasingly concerned with the operations of power at this microlevel of bodies and their capacities. Theorists of difference understand the body not as a biological constant but as a historical product, and emphasize the productiveness of power as positive capacity as well as a site of subordination and inequality.

For feminists disillusioned with theories of the state and of ideology, Foucault's alternative account of power was promising. Like them, he was concerned less with the state than with the local and intimate operations of power, with the body as the site of power and the locus of domination, and with the discursive practices that produce and sustain hegemonic power (Diamond and Quinby, 1988). For Foucault, power comes from below and is at its most subtle when it operates through pleasure. He rejected the notion that power originates at the pinnacle of the social hierarchy and filters down. While premodern power could strike only superficially and from afar, modern forms of power circulate throughout the entire social body, down even to the tiniest and apparently most trivial extremities. Foucault was concerned with the "polymorphous" character of power relations and the "biopolitics" that connect and consolidate these relations through "complex mechanisms and devices of excitation and incitement" (Foucault, 1980: 48).

For Foucault, there is no binary opposition between ruler and ruled, whether that be understood in class or gender terms, for it circulates through all of us. He asks how power installs itself and produces real material effects, including the creation of particular kinds of subjects who in turn act as a channel for the flow of power itself. Rather than being merely coercive, "power produces; it produces reality; it produces domains of objects and rituals of truth" (Foucault, 1979: 194). Power should not be understood, therefore, purely in terms of domination, for the subject that power has constituted becomes part of the actual mechanisms of power. It becomes a vehicle of the power that has actually constituted it as such. Power produces subjects just as much as or even more than subjects reproduce it.

Feminists have been able to readily apply Foucault's account of disciplinary practices to the oppression of women. They have argued that modern women are kept in line not only or predominantly through the direct control of husbands or fathers but through internalizing the "male gaze," constituting their own subjectivities in relation to prescribed notions of femininity. Practices relating to diet, exercise, bodily shape, and adornment have been perceived as new forms of patriarchal power. They also have taken up Foucault's notion of resistance as essentially dispersed, mobile, local, and heterogeneous, finding in it the potential for a new radical politics.

Feminists have remained, however, rather wary of Foucault. They may be right to be so, because his approach does decenter conflict and is—at very least—ambivalent about resistance, seeing it as an essential part of the exercise of power. Although Foucault does acknowledge domination, he also argues that everyone is subjected to disciplinary controls and that this may be enabling as well as constraining. Some feminists have attacked him for ignoring gender, or for denying women agency just when they were on the point of achieving it (Hartsock, 1990; Sawicki, 1991). But, as D. Cooper observes (1995: 14), even those who agree with Foucault have interpreted him rather selectively, reading him as a theorist of domination and resistance and ignoring the wider implications of his account of power as productive. This retains an attachment to the basic underlying structures of power, which remains closer to Lukes's analysis of ideology than to Foucault's work. How, for example, can one show that decisions are being made contrary to people's interests, when they appear unaware that this is the case? Lukes argued that these are examples of "false consciousness," and went on to construct a counterfactual situation to reveal what people would want if their material conditions were less oppressive. Yet, this is to assume that interests precede power, that people have certain, definable interests that power can repress but not truly eradicate.

This raises several important questions for feminists. How do we identify when power is about domination? On what grounds is it possible to say that women are "brainwashed" if, for example, they do not accept feminist definitions of what their "real" interests or "true consciousness" might be? And are there forms of power that might be acceptable and even desirable? As Hindess observes, people exercise mutual influence and control over one another's conduct in all social interactions, and it may not be helpful to treat this as an exercise of power at all (Hindess, 1996: 82). Parents and educators constantly attempt to manipulate the thoughts and desires of others, not in order to dominate them but ultimately to promote their independence. This moves us onto tricky ground, for it begs the question of precisely how to distinguish between "power to" and "power over." A strength of feminism has been that it demonstrates that what is claimed to be "power to"—a natural complementarity or a purely functional division of labor—is in fact "power over." At the same time, always to identify power with domination may be to locate oneself permanently in a position of powerlessness.

Some theorists have suggested that the need to see all forms of power as "power over" is to be motivated by the spirit of "ressentiment." Nietzsche used this term to refer to the revenge of the weak, who need to recriminate and to distribute blame, to impute wrongs, and to find sinners. They appeal for acknowledgment and rectification on the basis of the truth of their weakness and see their powerlessness as a proof of goodness. The concept has been taken up by a number of feminists (Brown, 1995; Tapper, 1993), who are concerned with the ways in which powerful women continue to identify injustice at ever deeper and more concealed levels and to present themselves as helpless victims. This makes it look as if "power over" is the only kind of power. Not only may it allow us to be co-opted into new forms of surveillance (for example, regarding equal opportunity), but it may also blind us to the possibilities of other, positive, active forms of the will to power. Although power may be oppressive, entailing domination or the control of another's actions, it also may involve the creation and use of new forms of knowledge and discipline, or the reallocation of resources. Cooper notes, "Power conceptualized in this way highlights the importance of an ethics—a framework that helps us to explore both ways of deploying as well as engaging with, power" (1995: 27). Wendy Brown calls for an "engagement in political struggles in which there are no trump cards such as 'morality' or 'truth,'" where we can "contest domination with the strength of an alternative vision of collective life, rather than through moral reproach" (1995: 47–48). This also will have a bearing on race and class in a postcolonial and postindustrial era.

See Also

FAMILY: POWER RELATIONS AND POWER STRUCTURES; LANGUAGE

References and Further Reading

Allen, J. 1990. Does Feminism Need a Theory of the State? In S. Watson, ed., *Playing the state*, 21–38. London: Verso.

Bartky, S. 1988. Foucault, feminism and the modernization of patriarchal power. In I. Diamond and L. Quinby, eds., *Feminism and Foucault*. Boston: Northeastern University Press.

Brown, W. 1995. *States of injury: Freedom and power in late modernity.* Princeton, N.J.: Princeton University Press.

Butler, J. 1990. *Gender trouble: Feminism and the subversion of identity.* London: Routledge.

Cameron, D. 1985. *Feminism and linguistic theory.* London: Macmillan.

Connell, R. W. 1987. *Gender and power.* Cambridge: Polity.

Cooper, D. 1995. *Power in struggle: Feminism, sexuality and the state.* Buckingham: Open University Press.

Diamond, I. and L. Quinby, eds. 1988. *Feminism and Foucault.* Boston: Northeastern University Press.

Foucault, M. 1979. *Discipline and punish.* New York: Vintage.

Foucault, M. 1980. *The history of sexuality.* Vol. 1, *An introduction.* New York: Vintage.

Gatens, M. 1996. *Imaginary bodies: Ethics, power and corporeality.* London: Routledge.

Hartsock, N. 1990. Foucault on power. In L. Nicholson, ed., *Feminism/postmodernism.* London: Routledge.

Hindess, B. 1996. *Discourses of power: From Hobbes to Foucault.* Oxford: Blackwell.

Lukes, S. 1974. *Power: A radical view.* London: Macmillan.

MacKinnon, C. 1987. *Feminism unmodified: Discourses on life and law.* Cambridge, Mass.: Harvard University Press.

Mitchell, J. 1975. *Psychoanalysis and feminism.* New York: Vintage.

Pateman, C. 1988. *The sexual contract.* Cambridge: Polity.

Phizaclea, A. 1996. Women, migration, and the state. In S. M. Rai and G. Lievesley, eds., *Women and the state: International perspectives*, 163–173. London: Taylor and Francis.

Rai, S. M. 1996. Women and the state in the third world: Some issues for debate. In S. M. Rai and G. Lievesley, eds., *Women and the state: International perspectives*, 5–22. London: Taylor and Francis.

Rai, S. M., and G. Lievesley, eds. 1996. *Women and the state: International perspectives.* London: Taylor and Francis.

Romero, M. 1992. *Maid in the U.S.A.* New York: Routledge.

Sawicki, J. 1991. *Disciplining Foucault.* New York: Routledge.

Spender, D. 1980. *Man made language.* London: Routledge.

Tapper, M. 1993. Ressentiment and power. In P. Patton, ed., *Nietzsche, feminism, and political theory*, 130–143. London: Routledge.

Rosemary Pringle

PRAYER

Human beings, in different times and places, have expressed their deepest religious feelings through prayer. Prayer is the humble surrendering of oneself to the author of one's faith. Through prayer, believers communicate with the divine or deities. This article describes prayer and its purpose. It also discusses the role of prayer in women's spirituality and identifies types of prayers.

Prayer is commonly described as conversation with God. Buddhists call it contemplation. Prayer, which is present in all religions, is a way of life for most believers. It is the believer's way of responding to his or her relationship with the one who is worshiped. Prayers are the thoughts, words, and expressions of a prayerful life. Prayers can be spontaneous or formal, as in liturgical prayers. Prayers can be verbal or nonverbal (silent meditation). Prayers can be practiced in personal or communal ways.

To pray is to be open and sensitive to the presence of the divine in one's daily life. In the Judeo-Christian tradition prayer serves as the direct link between the creator and the human creatures. Christian prayer, for example, is a prayer addressed to the triune God. Christians use the Lord's Prayer, which Jesus taught to his disciples (Matthew 6:9–15).

At times, they also use the prayers of saints and spiritual leaders. People's posture in prayer varies according to their traditions. Some kneel while praying, others stand or sit. At times those who pray use aids for praying such as icons and prayer knots (Greek Orthodox), prayer wheels (Buddhists), prayer books and rosaries (Roman Catholics), mantras (Hindus and Buddhists), and so on. In many traditions, one can find the elements of praise, thanksgiving, confession, petition, and intercession in prayer.

The basic purpose of prayer is to call the believer into constant communion with the divine. It is not to tell God what to do. It means being aware of and open to the will of God and God's purpose for one's life and the whole of creation. Prayer serves as a way of centering oneself and entering into a deep relationship with oneself, God, and others.

The Role of Prayer in Women's Spirituality

Prayer has been central to the spiritual life of women. Women and men in the early church gathered to pray and break bread together. Some women, such as the Spanish mystic St. Teresa of Avila, wrote about their practice of prayer. Women spiritual leaders and the indigenous peoples in Asia prayed to the spirits and to Mother Earth, emphasizing the interrelatedness of all creation.

In the experiences of women living in the "two-thirds world" (Asia, Africa, and Latin America), prayer takes on various roles in women's spirituality:

1. Prayer as a way of seeking and working for peace. For example, women in the Middle East prayed publicly to stop the war in the Gulf region. There are women marching for peace in war-torn countries. Their work for peace is itself a prayer.
2. Prayer as a protest, as an act of resistance, against violation of human rights. For example, the mothers of the disappeared in Chile, the Philippines, and Argentina kept prayer vigils in town plazas, churches, and marketplace. They prayed for their loved ones, to keep their memories alive.
3. Prayer as a source of strength to sustain the struggle for justice and peace. Women in the two-thirds world pray for strength and courage in the midst of difficult social and political situations. Christian women activists often pray for strength and guidance as they commit themselves to work with the poor. They gather in small prayer groups, study the Bible, and reflect on their life experiences.
4. Prayer as a necessary component of practicing theology. Women theologians from Asia, Africa, and Latin America realize the need for prayer in their practicing of theology. Sr. Virginia Fabella (1993) of the Philippines noted that, for women theologians, both committed action and silent contemplation are necessary for genuine theological reflection.
5. Prayer as a sign and gift of solidarity and sisterhood. Women pray with one another to express common concerns. Prayer, then, becomes a communal act and witness.
6. Prayer in celebration of life and death, beginnings and endings. Women pray during significant turning points, changing seasons, and rhythms of life. Women pray for rain, to celebrate the harvest, or at baptisms and funerals.
7. Prayer as a way to express compassion for all peoples, unity with all beings, and healing of the earth.

Types of Prayers

There are different types of prayers as practiced by women:

1. Breath prayer: silently praying while being mindful of one's breathing. It also means saying a prayer in one breath.
2. Embodied prayer: prayer using body movements, gestures, or liturgical dance.
3. Oral and written prayers: recited by individuals or by groups.
4. One-sentence prayer (Orthodox tradition): using the prayer "Lord Jesus Christ, have pity on me."
5. Contemplative prayer or prayer in silence.
6. Prayer in the form of songs and chants, litanies, and poems; prayer expressed in batik painting or pottery.
7. Praying and speaking in tongues, as with the Pentecostal communities.
8. Living prayer: doing any kind of work in love and service to others.

People discover different forms of prayer, not only to deepen their communion with God but also to contribute to world peace, justice, and the healing of the earth. Through prayer, personal or communal, women find strength, guidance, and solidarity. Prayer, therefore, is central to women's spirituality. Prayer is communion with the divine. It is the humble surrendering and responding to the divine presence and power within and beyond oneself.

See Also

DEITY; FAITH; MYSTICISM; RELIGION: OVERVIEW; SPIRITUALITY: OVERVIEW

References and Further Reading

Carmody, Denise Lardner, and John Tully Carmody. 1990. *Prayer in world religions.* Maryknoll, N.Y.: Orbis.

Fabella, Virginia. 1993. *Beyond bonding: Third world women's theological journey.* Manila: Institute of Women's Studies.

Peers, E. Allison, ed. and trans. 1964. *The way of perfection by St. Teresa of Avila.* New York: Doubleday.

Rev. Elizabeth S. Tapia

PREGNANCY AND BIRTH

Pregnancy and birth are in principle natural, healthy events in a woman's life. These processes need to be carefully supervised by a midwife or a doctor in order to detect any possible complications; however, if no complications arise, this article argues that medical intervention is undesirable. Therefore, an obstetric care provider who considers pregnancy and birth as basically normal events in a woman's life usually provides the best chances for an uncomplicated pregnancy and a spontaneous delivery. Usually an independent midwife best meets these requirements. By profession she approaches a woman who is pregnant or in labor as healthy, especially if the delivery takes place at home.

In order to guarantee the safety of mother and child, it is indispensable that a midwife is capable of detecting complications that might occur. At the same time she should be in a position in which she can refer the woman to an obstetrician in a hospital, if this proves necessary. This is the ideal situation that provides maximum safety for mother and child: they benefit from the achievements of medical science if necessary, but the natural, spontaneous course of pregnancy and birth is not disturbed by medical intervention if there is no need for it. Moreover, this is the least expensive course of action: no costs are incurred for the hospitalization if there is no need to go there.

Control of Pregnancy and Birth

When a woman is about two to three months pregnant, it is desirable that she starts seeing a midwife, family doctor, or gynecologist who can control and guide her pregnancy, birth, and the lying-in period. At this time, the risk of a miscarriage is no longer actual, and the womb can be felt on the outside by the midwife or doctor above the pubic bone. Usually a blood sample is taken in order to check blood type and the presence of antibodies for several infectious diseases. From this time on, controls should take place on a regular basis to check blood pressure, weight, growth and position of the baby, and the possible development of anemia and other inconveniences. In some countries many more routine examinations are done, such as ultrasounds, regular vaginal examinations, or more elaborate blood tests. These are mostly unnecessary. Only a specific medical indication justifies undertaking them.

During the delivery, four stages are distinguished. The first stage is the dilation period, in which contractions of the uterus cause the cervix to efface and dilate. This period can last from one to more than twenty-four hours, depending on the force of the contractions and on whether the woman has given birth before.

When the cervix is fully dilated, the second stage begins, in which the uterus starts to push the baby through the pelvis and the vagina, and the woman usually feels like pushing as well. The most natural way to do this is in a vertical position; sitting, standing, squatting, or kneeling. Only if medical intervention is necessary (for example, in case of a vacuum extraction) can a lying position be required. When the baby is born, it is desirable for the mother to immediately hold the child and keep it with her as much as possible.

In the third stage, the placenta (or afterbirth) is expelled. The first few hours after the placenta is delivered are called the fourth stage.

During all these stages the woman will be examined by the midwife, family doctor, or gynecologist to check the progress of the birth and the condition of mother and child.

The condition of the baby is checked by listening to the heartbeat from time to time, especially during the second stage. This can be done with a simple wooden stethoscope, or with ultrasound. If no complications are expected, continuous monitoring is not necessary.

The Obstetric Care Provider

Whether a woman will be seen by a midwife, a family doctor, or a gynecologist depends on various factors. The same goes for the place where the birth takes place: at home or in the hospital.

In many countries, especially in the third world, poor people are compelled to turn to a midwife, and give birth at home. Their financial situation gives them no choice, and very often a doctor or a hospital is not even available. This can be a favorable situation if no complications arise and if the midwife is well trained or experienced. In Indonesia, for instance, and in some African countries, such as Burkina Faso, the indigenous midwives work in a relatively safe way. However, in case of complications, quick referral to a hospital should be possible. If this is not the case, a dangerous situation can arise for mother and child.

People who can afford to usually choose the most expensive care: a hospital-based gynecologist. As explained above, the greatest extent of medicalization does not guarantee the greatest safety and definitely not the best experience for mother and child. Especially if no complications are expected, the hospital setting can do more harm than good because of its alienating and medicalizing effect. On the other hand, if the circumstances for a home birth are not favorable, a hospital birth is sometimes the best option.

In an increasing number of western countries, women are in the privileged situation that the choice of a midwife or a home birth is no longer determined by one's financial situation. Most women choose a midwife because she takes care not only of the physical aspects of pregnancy and birth, but also of the well-being of mother and child. She makes sure that a woman in labor feels at ease and retains her independence.

Home Birth

In western countries women are increasingly aware of the advantages of home birth, and in Great Britain, Italy, and Denmark, midwives are promoting home births as a viable alternative to hospital births. In the Netherlands, for instance, home birth is very safe because pregnant women are screened by well-trained, independent midwives during pregnancy and birth. As long as everything is normal, a woman can give birth at home. If complications arise, she is referred to the gynecologist in the hospital.

In other western countries, like Denmark, the United Kingdom, Canada, Italy, and parts of the United States, more and more midwives are starting to work independently and the possibilities of a safe home birth are increasing.

If the delivery takes place at home, the woman's own environment contributes to her feeling of security. This raises the level of the hormone oxytocin, which is responsible for stimulating the contraction of the uterus. At the same time, the low level of stress in the home situation enhances the production of pain-relieving hormones that are produced by the woman in labor: the so-called *endorphins.* In general, therefore, a home birth under favorable conditions provides the best chances for a spontaneous birth without the necessity of pain relief.

Unwanted Pregnancy

If a woman has an unwanted pregnancy, it is extremely important that she see a doctor or midwife as soon as possible, preferably immediately after she is aware of her situation. The various options—abortion, adoption, keeping the child—can then be explored, and counseling should be available as well. A doctor or midwife is bound by professional confidentiality, so all information should be kept private, even in the case of a teenage pregnancy.

See Also

ABORTION; CHILDBIRTH; FERTILITY AND FERTILITY TREATMENT; FETUS; GYNECOLOGY; MATERNAL HEALTH AND MORBIDITY; MIDWIVES; MOTHERHOOD; OBSTETRICS; REPRODUCTIVE HEALTH

Beatrijs Smulders
Mariël Croon

PREJUDICE

See DISCRIMINATION; HETEROPHOBIA AND HOMOPHOBIA; MISOGYNY; RACISM AND XENOPHOBIA; SEXISM.

PREMENSTRUAL SYNDROME (PMS)

PMS is a medical term used to describe the cyclic occurrence of a wide range of distressing physical, psychological, or behavioral symptoms in the final week of the fertile menstrual cycle which resolve with the next menses. Symptoms commonly include but are not limited to bloating, breast tenderness, depression, excessive anger or irritability, excessive fatigue, difficulty concentrating, and food cravings. Although symptoms can begin as early as ovulation (midcycle), central to the definition of PMS is that symptoms disappear after menses. Thus, it is the timing, duration, and severity of symptoms, rather than the symptoms per se, that distinguish PMS as a distinct medical disorder, separate from other physical or psychological problems. In its worst form, PMS results in significant interference with daily activities and personal relationships and the consequent need for medical intervention. Because of the preponderance of debilitating emotional symptoms, severe PMS (which affects less than 10 percent of childbearing women in western countries) is considered a chronic mental disorder and has been used as a legal defense in court trials of women accused of violent crimes.

In western countries the sensationalization of PMS by the mass media has helped support a popular perception that all women suffer from "raging hormones" once a month and thus are unable to function effectively in highly skilled careers such as surgeons, airline pilots, or political leaders. In fact, however, the majority of childbearing women do not experience severe PMS, but instead report mild to moderate symptoms premenstrually which are self-managed with home remedies, diet, exercise, and other symptom-specific therapies (Harrison, 1985). Cross-cultural studies have shown that the types of symptoms vary widely by country and ethnic group, suggesting there is a strong sociocultural component to the type and severity of symptoms. Other explanatory factors may include nutritional status and patterns of fertility and contraception.

Physiology vs. Psychology

The cause of PMS is unknown and at the end of the 1990s there was still no way to diagnose it by physical examination, blood test, or X ray. Most medical experts support the idea of a hormonal trigger for the entrainment of symptoms to the menstrual cycle. The antidepressant drug fluoxetine, which blocks the breakdown of the brain chemical seratonin, has been shown to be more effective than placebos (sugar pills) in treating PMS, suggesting that PMS may be related to a biochemical disorder in the brain.

At the same time, there is much evidence to suggest that most women have been socialized to have negative expectations about menstruation, thus leading to self-fulfilling prophecies of negative mood and psychological distress. Women seeking costly medical treatment for PMS may have certain expectations about the origin, nature, and course of their symptoms. Studies suggest that approximately 50 percent of women who seek medical treatment for PMS fail to demonstrate cycle-entrained changes when prospective symptom charting is performed. Other studies have demonstrated marked differences in self-esteem, guilt about anger, and stress levels in patients who seek medical help for symptoms compared with women with the same degree of symptom severity who do not perceive the symptoms as distressing.

The diagnosis of PMS relies heavily on the assessment of self-reported symptoms charted daily across the menstrual cycle. Feminist scholars have challenged the practice of tracking only negative symptoms in making the diagnosis of PMS, arguing that women should also chart symptoms of health and well-being to heighten awareness of positive changes across the menstrual cycle (Chrisler et al., 1994).

Managing PMS

Education about the nature of premenstrual changes provides reassurance to women that they are not "going crazy" and validates the legitimacy of their health problem. Keeping a menstrual-symptom diary can be therapeutic and empowering for the woman who feels out of control and at the mercy of her symptoms. Additionally, such a diary can often document the influence of social and family rhythms, such as weekly patterns in work, medication use, and lifestyle behaviors—including the effects of binge drinking, which can be easily mistaken for menstrual cycle effects.

It may be necessary for the woman to undertake realistic strategies for carrying out specific lifestyle changes, especially if they require considerable renegotiation of family, professional, and social roles. In some cases where family functioning has been maintained at the expense of the woman's health, the initiation of long-term change may require family counseling, support groups, or other psychosocial interventions by a skilled mental health professional. Such strategies may be unrealistic for poor women or in cultures where women's roles are dictated by religion and tradition.

See Also

CURSE; DEPRESSION; HORMONES; MENSTRUATION; MENTAL HEALTH *I and II;* REPRODUCTIVE HEALTH; STRESS

References and Further Reading

Chrisler, Joan, Ingrid Johnston, Nicole Champagne, and Kathleen Preston. 1994. Menstrual joy: The construct and its consequences. *Psychology of Women Quarterly* 18: 375–387.

Golub, Sharon, ed. 1983. Lifting the curse on menstruation: A feminist appraisal of the influence of menstruation on women's lives. *Women and Health* 8 (2/3), special issue.

Harrison, Michelle. 1985. *Self-help for premenstrual syndrome.* New York: Random House.

Taylor, Diana, and Nancy Woods, eds. 1991. *Menstruation, health, and illness.* New York: Hemisphere.

Nancy King Reame

PRESCHOOL EDUCATION

See EDUCATION: PRESCHOOL.

PRESS: Feminist Alternatives

Today's diverse and expanding array of feminist news and information sources—print, broadcast, and on-line—have their roots in global feminism of the 1970s and feminist concerns that the mainstream media of the era were not serving women's needs. These concerns grew out of feminists' widespread assumption that mainstream media possess the power both to perpetuate women's secondary social status and to help advance women toward fuller social participation, depending on the kind of messages and images of women they circulate.

Media as Agenda Setter

Media researchers have shown that the news media perform an important agenda-setting role in society by legitimizing serious issues for public debate and in conferring status on particular leaders and organizations. Research also demonstrates that social movements have needed the new media in their formative and later stages to mobilize and maintain membership and to keep their agendas before the general public (Kielbowicz and Scherer, 1986). Feminist leaders throughout the world have needed the mainstream media's attention to move new ideas about women's problems and experiences into traditional male domains of discourse and policy making, including legislatures, courts, schools, religious organizations, and other social institutions. They want the media to make visible women's legal and other successes brought about through organized feminist campaigns, and, in general, to expand women's voices in every facet of public life.

Media Treatment of Women

Through the 1970s, both local and world news routinely ignored the effects of feminist leaders, much as they had long ignored women's concerns and accomplishments in general. One content analysis of mainstream international wire services in the late 1970s showed that only 1.5 percent of the stories analyzed contained news about women (Gallagher, 1981). Even when the news did cover women's activities, the coverage tended to trivialize those activities or emphasize women's sexuality and traditional roles over their accomplishments (Ceclemans and Fauconnier, 1979; Tuchman et al., 1978). Development news emerged as an innovative news format in third world nations during the 1970s, emphasizing changes in economic, political, and social institutions rather than discrete news events. Although this more historical and process-oriented news format, with its emphasis on everyday citizens' lives, might have incorporated gender issues, it too ignored women, much as development processes themselves had done for more than a decade (Anand, 1983; Byerly, 1995).

Early Feminist News Alternatives

Consequently, feminist news alternatives began to emerge on several fronts in the 1970s. One generator was the first meeting associated with the United Nations (UN) Decade for Women, held in Mexico City in 1975. This event created the historical occasion for feminists of different philosophies and backgrounds to refine their cross-cultural feminist critiques of the media and, subsequently, to develop strategies for media intervention and change. Delegates attending the official UN convention that year articulated the "women and media" concerns in the *World Plan of Action,* and later, in the *Forward Looking Strategies* report. These documents set forth a global feminist media critique, the main tenets being that the news and other media throughout the world had systematically (1) underrepresented women in news and other media, (2) stereotyped women as sex objects and inferior to men, and (3) denied women access to news and other media professions. The last point reflected feminists' shared belief that more female reporters with progressive perspectives on women would help to change the content of new professions (Byerly, 1995).

This three-part critique would also serve as the rationale for UN agencies' sponsorship of a series of programs to create an academic literature on women and the media, as well as to sponsor new forms of women-controlled media. The UN Decade for Women documents also recognized that if communications media operated in the service of women, they held enormous potential to remove prevailing attitudes underlying women's inequality and to promote women's fuller integration into their communities around the world.

Subsequently, the UN Educational, Scientific, and Cultural Organization (UNESCO) funded both regional and cross-cultural studies to analyze women's treatment by the mainstream media. This research created an international baseline literature, including Ceulemans and Fauconnier's *Mass Media: The Image, Role and Social Conditions of Women* (1979), Gallagher's *Unequal Opportunities: The Case of Women and the Media* (1981), and Cuthbert's *Women and Media Decision-Making in the Caribbean* (1981). This UN-funded research complemented emerging independent academic research documenting women's marginalization by the news and entertainment media around the world.

UNESCO and its sister entity, the UN Fund for Population Agency (UNFPA), created the Women' Feature Service project in 1978 to expand news about women in five regions of the developing world: the Caribbean, Latin America, Africa, the Middle East, and south Asia. Project funding ended in 1983; however, two of the projects have continued operating as women-controlled news services to the present time. Depthnews Women's Service, part of the Manila-based Press Foundation of Asia, is the smaller of the two operations, producing occasional stories about women in the Philippines and south Asia.

Recent Developments in Women's News

The second and larger of the two agencies retains the original name Women's Feature Service (WFS). WFS, which emphasizes women's conditions and activities in the developing nations of the "South," separated from its parent agency, Inter Press Service of Rome, in 1990. After establishing new headquarters in New Delhi, India, WFS has set up a regional bureau in San Jose, Costa Rica, to oversee news production in the Latin American region. That office broke away from WFS in 1999 and formed an independent agency, Servicio de Noticias de la Mujer (SEM).

Like other agency personnel, WFS's full- and part-time journalists are all female, most of them nationals in the nations they cover. The agency produces 250 to 300 stories a year on health care, education, laws, religious customs, war, family, employment, and other matters affecting women's lives for its varied clientele—both mainstream and alternative print media and governmental and nongovernmental organizations. Feature stories are distributed electronically through the Internet, as well as regular mail. WFS treats women's experiences and analyses as central to stories, emphasizes female sources of varied social status, and explores not only women's problems but also their efforts to solve them (Byerly, 1995; Byerly, in press). In these ways, WFS redefines development news, incorporating gender in ways that this news format traditionally has not incorporated it. Since 1993, WFS had added audio and video news, research, and technical reports to its news services.

There are numerous other international women's news sources available on a regular basis today, some of them with roots in the 1970s and some of them more recent.

A group of three women began the independent, quarterly news magazine called *Isis International* in 1974 in Rome. Today the Isis organization publishes a monthly newsletter, *Women Envision,* and a quarterly magazine, *Women in Action.* The Isis organization also maintains a resource center and library in Manila that houses books, journals from all over the world, feature films, documentaries, and audiotapes related to women's culture and politics. Isis publications circulate worldwide on a subscription basis (Isis, 1993). The web sie is <www.peg,apc.org./~isis.html>.

Mujer/Fempress, a monthly news magazine that circulates in published form in all of Latin America, began in Santiago, Chile, in 1981. Since late 1997, the magazine is also available in Spanish on the World Wide Web at <www .fempress.cl>. The publication is a project of Fempress, a women's news network with regular correspondents in fourteen nations. Fempress also produces a 20-minute radio program, available on cassette. Fempress's goal is to help unite women around common problems and aspirations so they can work together.

Asimita newsmagazine was established by two women journalists in Kathmandu, Nepal, in 1988. Monthly circulation is 6,000, with special-interest editions increasing to 15,000. *Asimita* serves primarily educated women living in Nepal and northern India, with content focusing on women's property rights, legal rights, and other practical issues. However, in an effort to reach neoliterate and semiliterate rural women, the editors created a second bimonthly publication, *Sachari. Aisimita* can be reached at its Web site address: <www.peg.org/~women/asimita.html>.

The 1990s witnessed an explosion of feminist on-line news sources from all regions of the world—in fact, too many to catalog and describe in detail. Following is a partial listing of sites on the World Wide Web that provide access to multiple feminist news sources.

- The Web site for "Magazines and Newsletters on the Web," a woman-focused service, is available through the University of Wisconsin library system. The site provides links to *Agenda,* a South African feminist journal; *AnaLize,* a Romanian journal of feminist studies; *Ariadne Newsletter,* a women's studies resource from the Austrian National Library; *Adantis,* a women's studies journal from Nova Scotia, Canada; *Auf,* from Germany; and *AVIVA,* an international monthly Web zine, among many others (<www .library.wisc.edu/libraries/Women's-Studies/mag.htm>).
- The San Francisco–based Institute for Global Communication's "Womensnet" page is a veritable feast of links to feminist organizations and publications around the world, on subjects including women and technology, violence, activism, economics, health, and women's studies. The site is <www.igc.org/igc/gateway>.
- The Women in Development Network (WIDNET) provides links to news and information about women's progress in Africa (<www.focusintl.com/widnet.htm>).
- The Women's International Net, a New York-based Web zine, publishes several times a month with articles from writers in both developed and developing nations. (E-mail address: winmagazine@mail.digi-net.com).
- The Network of East-West Women provides links to feminist publications and organizations related to women in Eastern Europe and the former Soviet States. The site is (<www.neww.org/publications.htm>).

The importance of regularly published on-line international feminist news should not be underestimated in this era of corporate globalization, which has seen the concentration of media ownership and the resulting control of all major communications media by fewer and fewer rich, powerful men (UNCTAD, 1996). Employment for women in news reporting has risen unevenly from nation to nation over nearly three decades of global feminism, with women today constituting less than 50 percent of media workforces. Most significant is that women fill less than 12 percent of the decision-making positions across all media (Gallagher, 1995). On-line news allows educated women—who arguably have the greatest potential to affect social policy—the possibility of staying informed and in touch with one another regularly through on-line feminist networks. The imperative now is for these women of more privileged position to find ways of extending feminist news and information into populations of women with limited literacy and technology access. Although a few feminist news organizations are already taking these steps, there is a clear and present need for others to follow suit so that women of varied socioeconomic status can benefit from feminist analyses and the political organization that flows from them.

See Also

MEDIA: ALTERNATIVE; MEDIA: MAINSTREAM

References and Further Reading

Anand, Anita. 1983. Rethinking women and development. In Isis International and Information Service, ed., *Women in development: A resource guide for organizations and action, 5–11.* Geneva: Isis.

Byerly, Carolyn M. 1995. News, consciousness and social participation: The role of Women's Feature Service in world news. In Angharad N. Valdivia, ed., *Feminism, multiculturalism, and the media,* 101–118. Thousand Oaks, Calif.: Sage.

———. in press. Women's Feature Service. In Elizabeth Burt, ed., *Historical dictionary of women's press organizations.* Westport, Conn.: Greenwood.

Ceulemans, Mieke, and Guido Fauconnier. 1979. *Mass media: The image, role, and social conditions of women.* Paris: UNESCO.

Cottingham, Jane. 1989. Isis: A decade of international networking. In Ramona R. Rush and Donna Allen, eds., *Communication at the crossroads: The gender gap connection,* 238–250. Norwood, N.J.: Ablex.

Cuthbert, Marlene. 1981. *Women and media decision-making in the Caribbean.* Kingston, Jamaica: Caribbean Institute of Mass Communications, University of the West Indies.

Gallagher, Margaret. 1995. *An unfinished story: Gender patterns in media employment.* Paris: UNESCO.

———. 1981. *Unequal opportunities: The case of women and the media.* Paris: UNESCO.

Isis International. 1993. *Let our silenced voices be heard: The traffic in Asian women.* Quezon City, Philippines: Isis.

Joseph, Ammu, and Kalpana Sharma. 1994. *Whose news: The media and women's issues.* New Delhi: Sage.

Kielbowicz, Richard, and Clifford Scherer. 1986. The role of the press in the dynamics of social movements. *Research in Social Movements, Conflict and Change* 9: 71–96.

Riaño, Pilar R. 1994. *Women in grassroots communication: Furthering social change.* Thousand Oaks, Calif.: Sage.

Rush, Ramona R., and Donna Allen. 1989. *Communication at the crossroads: The gender gap connection.* Norwood, N.J.: Ablex.

Steeves, H. Leslie. 1993. Gender and mass communication in a global context. In Pamela Creedon, ed., *Women and mass communication,* 2nd. ed., 32–60. Newbury Park, N.J.: Sage.

Tuchman, Gaye. 1978. The symbolic annihilation of women by the mass media. In Gaye Tuchman, et al., eds., *Hearth and home: Images of women in the mass media.* New York: Oxford University Press.

Tuchman, Gaye, et al., eds. 1978. *Hearth and home: Images of women in the mass media.* New York: Oxford University Press.

UNCTAD. 1995. *World investment report on transnational corporations and competitiveness.* New York: United Nations Conference on Trade and Development.

UNESCO. 1987. *Women and media decision-making: The invisible barriers.* Paris: UNESCO.

Women's Feature Service, ed. 1992. *The power to change: Women in the third world redefine their environment.* New Delhi: Kali for Women.

Carolyn M. Byerly

PRIDE

See GAY PRIDE.

PRIMATOLOGY

Primatology is the study of the biology, behavior, ecology, and evolution of primates—a group of mammals that includes humans and our close relatives the monkeys, apes, and prosimians. There are many women primatologists, especially in the United States, where more than half of the members of scientific societies are female. It is unusual for a biological science to include as many women as men practitioners. Primatology is often singled out by feminists as a "female-friendly" or even a feminist science.

Scientific interest in the behavior of monkeys and apes goes back at least as far as Darwin's attempts in the nineteenth century to describe and understand communication in captive primates. In the first half of the twentieth century, psychologists in several countries studied the mental processes of captive macaques and chimpanzees, and there were a few preliminary attempts to study primates in their natural habitats. However, it was not until after World War II that concerted efforts were made to reach the remote tropical areas where nonhuman primates occur naturally and to observe their behavior in the wild. In the 1950s, scientists from Europe, the United States, and Japan simultaneously fanned out across the equatorial areas of the globe in search of field sites to study primates. Primatology is an unusual science in that it was independently invented at least twice, by the Euro-Americans and concurrently by the Japanese (who were not at first in contact with their scientific colleagues in the West).

In the 1950s and 1960s, most primatologists were men, and much of the focus of their research was on male primates. Macaques, baboons, and chimpanzees were the first species to be studied in the wild, and in these types of primates adult males are larger and often more aggressive than the adult females. Opportunistic note-taking on the part of scientists led them to take more notice of the swashbuckling males. Female primates were usually described as desirable mates for the males and as nurturing mothers for the young, but as little else. Sometimes, females were even said to be "owned" by the males in their social groups. However, some early researchers presented a different picture of female primates, one in which females played active roles in the life of their social groups. They described females as choosing mates, determining daily travel routes, defending territories, and protecting themselves and their young from predators, as well as carrying and nursing their infants—"dual career mothers," according to Jeanne Altmann (1980).

There were always some women primatologists, and many of these early women fieldworkers became key role models for the next generation. The work of Jane Goodall, Dian Fossey, and Birute Galdikas in studying chimpanzees, gorillas, and orangutans has been particularly influential in drawing younger women into the science of primatology. *National Geographic*'s coverage of the long-term field studies of these three women reached around the world and into the hearts and minds of many young people who grew up to become primatologists in their own right.

In the 1970s, three significant trends emerged: (1) women began to make up substantial proportions of professional primatologists in North America and Europe (but not in Japan), (2) the second wave of the women's movement began exhorting scientists to address questions of interest to women, and (3) primatologists began to bring female monkeys and apes onto center stage in their descriptions of primate social life. Donna Haraway's extensive history of primatology in her book *Primate Visions* (1989) describes how this science, like many others, came to be criticized by feminists in the 1970s, and how primatology responded in the 1980s. Unlike many other scientists, primatologists reacted quickly and effectively to criticisms of androcentric ("male") bias by largely eliminating sexist language, by developing an awareness of the permeating variable of sex differences, and by building a strong focus on female as well as male primates.

After the publication of Haraway's book, many feminist theorists singled out primatology as a science in which the feminist perspective has been a transformative agent. Surprisingly, few primatologists identify themselves as feminists or feel that their science has been influenced by the feminist critique. It is difficult and controversial to determine exactly what would constitute a feminist science, but if a feminist science is defined in terms of features such as reflexivity, gender awareness, cooperation with nature, humanitarian applications of science, and greater inclusiveness of formerly marginalized groups, then it can be argued that primatology has increasingly exhibited these features over the past 25 years. Furthermore, primatologists have extensively used what Londa Schiebinger (1999) refers to as "tools of gender analysis"—that is, devices for designing women-friendly research along feminist lines. For example, primatologists have warned of the dangers of extrapolating from one group (males) to another (females), called for better representational sampling of age and sex classes, and reset priorities to increase research on issues of interest to women, and have begun to provide a more complete picture of the roles of females in primate societies.

Why then would many primatologists deny that they are feminists or that they have been influenced by the feminist critique of science? There are several possible reasons. First is the concern that primatology not be perceived as a "feminized" science because of the widespread belief that feminized sciences become devalued in the minds of the scientific community, the public at large, and possible recruits. Second is a desire on the part of many scientists to distance themselves from anything perceived as political, feminism being a body of theory and a social movement with strong political connotations. Third is the fact that many primatologists hold an idealized view of science as a realm that is pure and objective, whereas most feminists hold a view of science as being contextual and subject to sociocultural influences, as are all other human enterprises. Finally, many primatologists argue that they changed their practices in the past 25 years not because of feminism but because it is good science—scientifically correct—to flesh out the picture of female primates, to consider questions from a female as well as a male perspective, and to research issues of concern to women as well as men. Thus the goals of feminist theorists and primatologists would seem to dovetail in this respect, as both groups agree that such changes have resulted in a better, more inclusive science.

See Also

ARCHAEOLOGY; BIOLOGICAL DETERMINISM; BIOLOGY; EVOLUTION; NATURE–NURTURE DEBATE; SCIENCE: FEMINIST PHILOSOPHY

References and Further Reading

Altmann, Jeanne. 1980. *Baboon mothers and infants.* Cambridge, Mass.: Harvard University Press.

Asquith, Pamela. 1991. Primate research groups in Japan: Orientations and East-West differences. In L. M. Fedigan and P. J. Asquith, eds., *The monkeys of Arashiyama: Thirty-five years of research in Japan and the West,* 81–98. New York: State University of New York Press.

Fedigan, Linda. 1997. Is primatology a feminist science? In L. Hager, ed., *Women in human evolution,* 56–75. London: Routledge.

———. 1994. Science and the successful female. Why there are so many women primatologists. *American Anthropologist* 96: 529–540.

Haraway, Donna. 1989. *Primate visions: Gender, race and nature in the world of modern science.* New York: Routledge.

Montgomery, Sarah. 1991. *Walking with the great apes.* Boston: Houghton Mifflin.

Schiebinger, Londa. 1999. *Has feminism changed science?* Cambridge, Mass.: Harvard University Press.

Linda Marie Fedigan

PRISONS

See CRIME AND PUNISHMENT.

PRIVATIZATION

The term *privatization* is most commonly used today to denote the transfer of responsibilities from the public or state sector to the private or market sphere. This transfer has been a significant policy trend over the past two or so decades in western capitalist societies and during the 1990s in the formerly state socialist societies.

Globally, privatization forms one element of an ascendant economic conservatism that favors the market, private profitability, a minimal state, and individual self-reliance (Ernst, 2000). These tenets are supported by much recent mainstream economic theory and by global economic organizations such as the Organization for Economic Cooperation and Development. This economic approach rejects the expectation of a gradually expanding public sector and welfare state, a trend that was recognizable in most industrialized societies in the post–World War II era. In the most extreme application of privatization policy, the private market is accepted as the appropriate source of even the most basic societal services, such as water supply, power generation, and prisons. Formerly "public" tasks that have been increasingly devolved to private business include child care, care for the aged, pensions, education, and health services, as well as a host of general maintenance tasks with respect to public buildings and enterprises, such as cleaning, laundry, waste disposal, and building upkeep.

While the rhetoric of the free market is widespread, the degree of actual privatization varies from country to country. The United Kingdom in the 1980s undertook a concerted program of selling state services—including telecommunications, water, electricity, public housing, and jails—to the private sector. However, even those countries accepted as most committed to the welfare state, such as the Scandinavian countries, have moved in a similar direction, though less speedily and with less enthusiasm. In former socialist societies the trend to the privatization of state enterprises and property has a particularly dramatic quality because these societies had, throughout their history, displayed such a strong commitment to state ownership and service provision.

The economic liberal position that underpins privatization involves the view that the state has become a drain on society's financial resources, which can no longer be sustained, and that only strengthening the commercial and business sectors will ensure prosperity, good management, and fair distribution. Historically, this conservatizing trend represents an ideological shift that can be identified as a reaction to the success of New Left politics during the 1960s and 1970s. At this time women and a range of minority groups made some gains toward greater equality, largely with support from the state. Privatization is associated with reducing the state and a reassertion of conservative politics, in the form of the New Right, in reaction against earlier successes of New Left politics (Bryson, 1992).

Feminists are concerned that the trend to economic liberalism, with its emphasis on privatization and a retreat from state intervention, is likely to disadvantage women generally and doubly disadvantage certain groups of women. Insofar as the changes imply the reprivatization of caring activities, it is women within families who once more will bear the major responsibility for care for the aged and those with disabilities. This particularly affects women's lives when appropriate privatized or market services are not available or cannot be afforded. Privatization will be keenly felt therefore by poorer women and by women from groups overlooked by the market, which are likely to include women from certain ethnic minorities and those from rural or isolated areas. Collective services have not always catered well for these groups either, but the principle of equal treatment is embedded in collective services. This is not a principle underpinning privatized services.

Privatization can have multiple effects in relation to women and caring. Not only may caring revert to an exclusively family responsibility, but these responsibilities in turn interfere with women's income-earning activities, which are vital for achieving greater gender equality. On top of this, moves away from the collective provision of caring services will result in reduced employment opportunities in a sector of the public service where women have predominated and where the jobs have generally had better pay and conditions than many available to women in the private sector.

Increases in gender equality within contemporary welfare states have been facilitated by state activity and by women's movement into the public realm. The reduction of state activities promoted by trends to privatization therefore poses a threat to these gains. This is particularly so in relation to the privatization of caring service, because this may lead to an accentuation of women's traditional family responsibilities at the expense of their newly won roles in the workforce and the public arena more generally.

See Also

CAREGIVERS; POVERTY

References and Further Reading

Bryson, Lois. 1992. *Welfare and the state: Who benefits?* London: Macmillan.

Ernst, John. 2000. The post-welfare state? The political economy of the new social policy. In Wendy Weeks and Marjorie Quinn, eds., *Issues facing Australian families: Human services respond,* 55–65. Melbourne: Longman.

Lois Bryson

PRO-CHOICE MOVEMENT

Abortion has been debated and regulated in a number of different ways for most of human history. The movement for safe and legal abortion, in contrast, is rather recent. Not until the mid-twentieth century, when abortion became a matter for public debate, did a reproductive rights movement fully emerge. While the movement has enjoyed considerable success in many nations, including the United States, women's reproductive health and abortion rights advocates continue to face enormous repression around the world.

The Early Struggle

By the 1950s, all 48 of the United States had laws and penalties governing abortions. However, feminists around the globe began to view reproductive liberty as essential to their economic and political parity. Meanwhile, during the 1950s, many of the communist states of the eastern bloc passed legislation to permit abortions. As the women's movement blossomed worldwide in the 1960s, women began to discuss their abortion experiences, legal and otherwise, for the first time (Lader, 1973). As more women entered the labor force, they sought greater control over their reproductive lives. Demand for abortion, along with other contraceptive choices, increased. Still, the movement to remove the legal barriers to legitimate abortions was some time off. What the movement needed was a catalyst.

Between 1967 and 1987, a powerful wave of movements favoring the reform of restrictive abortion policies washed over western democracies. The reasons for the movement are linked to global fears regarding overpopulation, the advancing status of women in many countries, the improved safety of the procedure, and a general climate of reform and protest. In the United States, it was not until the highly publicized case of Sherri Finkbine followed by the German measles epidemic of 1966 that the liberalizing abortion reform movement began, of all places, in the medical community.

In 1962, Sherri Finkbine, 29-year-old mother of four and respected member of her Arizona community, discovered that, as a result of having taken the European drug thalidomide for morning sickness, she was carrying a severely deformed fetus. Finkbine appealed to her hospital's therapeutic committee, which initially granted her request for an abortion. However, the local chapter of the American Medical Association (AMA) delayed her procedure. Finkbine ultimately flew to Sweden for the procedure, but the international publicity challenged the legitimacy of abortion policies worldwide.

Four years later, a second event made the abortion issue more public still. In San Francisco, a German measles epidemic broke out in 1966. It was estimated that most pregnant women with the disease would deliver badly deformed babies. The rate of abortions among the infected women skyrocketed. Their experience in attending to pregnant women during the epidemic convinced a powerful contingent of doctors to press for easier access to abortion. In response to the tragic consequences of the epidemic, the public scrutiny of the state's rigorous abortion restrictions, and the influence of the pro-abortion rights physicians' lobby, the California legislature passed its abortion reform bill in 1967. The newly elected governor, Ronald Reagan, signed the bill into law, setting into motion a nationwide abortion rights reform movement led initially by doctors.

The Feminists Step In

Moderate U.S. feminists joined physicians in the fight for abortion rights in 1967—the same year that British feminists won national liberalization of their abortion law. The National Organization for Women in the United States officially embraced abortion reform with its Bill of Rights, which claimed the "right of women to control their own reproductive lives." But it was not long after the physicians' abortion rights movement took hold and moderate feminists joined their ranks that radical feminists became dissatisfied with the temperate nature of the changes.

Responding to the inadequacies of the reform efforts, radical feminists formed their own alternative organizations. These groups shifted the debate from reform of abortion statutes, which might allow some restrictions to stand, to their outright repeal. Groups such as New York's Redstockings and the Chicago Women's Liberation Union radicalized the abortion movement through street theater, picketing American Medical Association conferences, and "burying" traditional womanhood at Arlington National Cemetery. In addition, the radicals performed abortion speak-outs, where women injured by illegal abortions would tell their stories and claim the right to abortion "on demand." The Chicago-based group established an underground abortion clinic in 1969.

At the same time, a burst of medical information and services sprang up to provide women with alternative services to those provided by the "regular" doctors. *The Birth Control Handbook* and the famous *Our Bodies, Ourselves* provided women with alternative medical information. In effect, radical women were attempting to shift control of abortion away from the medical profession back to women and their alternative health care providers, who were predominantly women.

The effect of the radicals' involvement was tremendous. Their vocal tactics and alternative abortion services provided a catalyst for change, but at the same time created a strain in the women's movement between the radicals, who demanded abortion access for all women, and the mainstream organizations that sought the "right to choose." In 1969, radicals and moderates convened at a national conference on abortion law in Chicago. At that conference, abortion-rights advocates formed the National Association to Repeal Abortion Laws (NARAL), which supported the total repeal of abortion laws at that time. The momentum for repeal accelerated in 1969 when Planned Parenthood reversed its historic opposition to abortion and embraced the repeal effort. The Commission on Population Growth lent its support to the cause shortly thereafter, in 1972.

By 1973, as a result of the abortion rights movement, the United States was a patchwork quilt of abortion laws. Hawaii, Alaska, New York, and Washington had repealed their laws altogether, while a number of other states provided limited access to abortion; still others prohibited the procedure altogether. In response, feminist organizations demanded that all women, regardless of their state of residence, have access to a full range of reproductive options. Hence, the push for a national solution was an effort to formalize and equalize women's access to abortion across state lines. Not only would the Supreme Court's intervention make abortion law more consistent nationwide and grant a fundamental right to privacy (which extended to abortion); it would revolutionize abortion politics by catapulting it into the national limelight. Practically speaking, the high court's landmark 1973 ruling in *Roe* v. *Wade* overturned 49 state abortion laws and established abortion as part of a woman's fundamental right to privacy. Ironically, it was not until after *Roe* granted all U.S. women the freedom of abortion that the feminist movement truly unified radical and moderate feminists around abortion rights. These efforts proved necessary: by the mid-1970s the Court began to limit the *Roe* decision by upholding a range of restrictions on abortion, such as limits on public funding, mandatory waiting periods, fetal viability tests, and parental involvement laws. The pro-abortion rights movement continued to defend women's need for safe and legal abortion.

Roe v. *Wade* was heralded as the ultimate expression of women's progress by the groups who fought for reproductive liberty. For those opposed to abortion, *Roe* signaled an affront to moral principles. *Roe* set into motion a powerful antiabortion backlash movement that identifies abortion as a grave example of the erosion of Christian values in the United States. The rise of this countermovement in response to *Roe* v. *Wade* has kept the abortion issue alive in the United States.

Outside the United States

Perhaps the most dramatic success of the pro-choice movement has been in promoting its agenda in international organizations, especially the United Nations (UN). Some 189 nations around the globe allow abortion. Of these, 120 countries permit abortion in order to preserve the mental health of women, while 83 allow the practice in response to rape or incest, and 76 allow it if there is the potential for birth defects. In 52 nations, abortion on demand is permitted.

The United Nations has promoted family planning as a human right. The UN Population Commission reaffirms "the right of all couples and individuals to decide freely on if and when to have children, but also the right to attain the highest standard of sexual and reproductive health and the right to make reproductive decisions free from discrimination, violence and coercion." Through organizations such as the World Health Organization (WHO), the UN distributes funds for family planning and provides support for reproductive rights (UN, Population Commission, 1996). As a result of UN involvement, over thirty nations have begun reexaminations of their reproductive laws.

The UN estimates that there are 25 million legal abortions each year (1996). This figure does not include the illegal or underground abortions that may add 20 million. As a result of unsafe abortion practices, an estimated 70,000 women die each year (UN, Population Commission, 1996). The legality of abortion does not necessarily guarantee women's access to safe abortions. For example, abortion has been legal in Russia since 1956, but economic constraints have led to the proliferation of unsanitary and unsafe clinics. Despite support from international organizations such as the UN and nongovernmental organizations (NGOs), such as the International Planned Parenthood Federation (IPPF), pro-choice movements in many nations continue to face obstacles based on religious, cultural, or economic constraints. In Egypt, despite government support, at least 18 percent of women have little or no access to family planning.

Studies of three nations, Ireland, Greece, and China, demonstrate the range of governmental policy on abortion and the relative success and failure of pro-choice movements. In many nations, government support or cooperation with the established churches has prevented action on reproductive rights. Pro-choice movements in nations such as Iran have found that the strength of religious taboos on abortion prevent government action. Another example is Ireland, where abortion has been illegal since 1869. The pro-choice movement in the nation worked unsuccessfully to prevent an amendment to the constitution in 1983 that guarantees the right to life for the unborn from the moment of conception. In 1992, however, pro-choice advocates were able to pass a new referendum that allowed travel and advertising for abortions.

The United States has also applied pressure to NGOs and individual nations that receive U.S. foreign aid to prevent the promotion or even the discussion of abortion in family planning. This "gag" order applies even to those groups that operate completely outside of the United States. Pro-choice groups in the United States and international groups such as the IPPF have had little success in overturning this U.S. policy.

Greece is among the nations where the pro-choice movement has had success. For example, in 1986, the nation passed one of the most liberal abortion laws in western Europe. Greece allows abortion on demand during the first 12 weeks of pregnancy and abortion in the case of rape or for medical reasons up to 24 weeks. All abortions are covered by health insurance and are free.

In China, abortion is also granted on demand, and has been used extensively to combat the nation's chronic overpopulation problems. However, feminists and pro-choice advocates have condemned the government's use of abortion in cases where the procedure was unwanted by the mother. Women's groups condemn the cultural traditions that devalue girl children and often lead to abortions in order to ensure that a boy child is born in order to carry on the family lineage.

As Ireland, Greece, and China demonstrate, the challenges for the international pro-choice movement are wide-ranging. Successes in some nations need to be emulated in others. In addition, opposition to certain types of family planning by the United States and other nations has to be overcome. However, the increasing endorsement of family planning and reproductive rights by the UN and NGOs increases the likelihood that the main goals of the pro-choice movement will be internalized by governments around the world.

See Also

ABORTION; FETUS; HEALTH CHALLENGES; INTERNATIONAL ORGANIZATIONS AND AGENCIES; REPRODUCTION: OVERVIEW; REPRODUCTIVE RIGHTS; RU 486

References and Further Reading

Craig, Barbara Hinkson, and David M. O'Brien. 1993. *Abortion and American politics.* New York: Chatham House.

Critchlow, Donald T. 1999. *Intended consequences: Birth control, abortion, and the federal government in modern America.* New York: Oxford University Press.

Francome, Colin. 1984. *Abortion freedom: A worldwide movement.* London: George Allen and Unwin.

Glendon, Mary Ann. 1987. *Abortion and divorce in western law.* Cambridge, Mass.: Harvard University Press.
Goggin, Malcolm, ed. 1993. *Understanding the new politics of abortion.* London: Sage.
Gordon, Linda. 1990. *Woman's body, woman's right.* 2nd ed. New York: Penguin.
Lader, Larence. 1973. *Abortion II: Making the revolution.* Boston: Beacon.
Luker Kristin. 1984. *Abortion and the politics of motherhood.* Berkeley, Calif.: University of California Press.
Petchesky, Rosalind. 1984. *Abortion and womens' choice: The state, sexuality, and reproductive freedom.* New York: 1998 Summit Books.
Staggenborg, Suzanne. 1991. *The pro-choice movement: Organization and activism in the abortion conflict.* New York: Oxford University Press.
Tatalovich, Raymond. 1997. *The politics of abortion in the United States and Canada: A comparative study.* Armonk, N.Y.: Sharpe.
United Nations. 1999. *World Abortion Policies, 1999.* New York: Author.

Melody Rose

PROFESSIONAL SOCIETIES

Women's professional societies and feminist professional societies in the natural sciences, social sciences, physical sciences, behavioral sciences, health and life sciences, and technology and engineering have played an important role in both early and contemporary women's movements throughout the world.

Often organized to counter the exclusion of women from areas of study, and to provide women with opportunities to utilize their professional skills, women's professional societies have filled a number of other functions, including providing support for women in historically male-dominated professions, monitoring the status of women in professions, lobbying professional bodies as well as government representatives to improve the status of women in the professions as well as the wider society, and providing a network for women in professions as well as a forum for women to develop leadership skills. In some professions (such as psychology) women's professional societies have also challenged the profession's view of women, while encouraging more feminist approaches to women within a profession.

In this article, the evolution of women's professional societies and the functions they fill are outlined. The formation of women's professional societies is discussed, and an overview of the range of women's professional societies currently in existence and the relationship of women's professional societies to other forms of women's organizations are addressed.

Background

The emergence of women's professional societies is best understood in relation to women's struggles to gain entry into higher education and to put their education to use in professional employment. In North America women began entering colleges and universities in the first half of the 1800s. Women were initially granted access to higher education so they could better contribute to the moral development of children, and, by extension, society. Throughout the world women's organizations were founded to raise public interest in the issue of women and education. For example, in the United States, Catherine Beecher established the American Women's Educational Association in 1852 (Rosenberg, 1982). With the aim of promoting women's access to medical education, Maude Abbott organized the Association for the Professional Education for Women in the late 1800s in Montreal (Gillett, 1990)

By the late 1800s women were increasingly attending college. As women completed college in the United States and Canada, they found it difficult to gain access to further training or employment in their professions. Professional organizations formed during this time (such as the Association of Collegiate Alumnae, or ACA), often met the dual goals of offering encouragement to young women wanting to go to college as well as expanding opportunities for women college graduates (Rosenberg, 1982). The ACA and similar groups such as the Canadian Federation of University Women (founded 1919), the Indian Federation of University Women's Associations (founded 1921), the International Federation of University Women (founded 1919), the New Zealand Federation of University Women (founded 1921), and the more recently founded Japanese Association of University Women (founded 1946) provide financial support for women seeking a university education and also encourage women who have obtained university training to utilize their education in order to advance the interests of women in society.

Women's professional associations fill numerous mandates. For example, in addition to assisting women university graduates in reentering the workforce and obtaining further education, the Association Suisse des Femmes Universitaires (founded 1924) also represents the interests of women to the federal government, assists members in developing professional contacts, and fosters the international exchange of ideas. Some associations of university women also conduct research (for example, the Federacion Argentina de Mujeres Universitarias and the Uganda Association of University Women), represent the interests of women to government (for example, the South African Association of University Women), and disseminate information about study and career opportunities (for example, Vereniging Van Vrouwen Met Academische Opleiding, founded in 1918). Additional associations of university women exist in Sri Lanka, Turkey, Russia, and elsewhere in the world.

At the end of the nineteenth century and the beginning of the twentieth century, many women who obtained a college education subsequently found it difficult to obtain employment in their chosen professions. Many women became involved in social reform work, which afforded them employment opportunities as well as opportunities to improve the health and welfare of women. However, as more women obtained college education, there was a trend away from reform work and toward professionalism (Rosenberg, 1982). This was accompanied by a concurrent growth in autonomous professional associations for women.

Teachers were among the first group of professional women to organize autonomous women's professional organizations. For example, the New Zealand Educational Institute-Women's Network (NZEI) was founded in 1883. Still in existence, it seeks to improve the status of women teachers, their working conditions, and their salaries. It also promotes access to child care for working teachers, offers counseling and support for victims of sexual harassment, provides professional training, and encourages affirmative action programs to enhance women's employment opportunities in senior teaching and administrative jobs.

Women in the medical profession were among the earliest groups to develop autonomous professional societies. For example, in the United States, the Medical Women's National Association (MWNA) founded in 1915, urged the inclusion of women in the Army Medical Reserve Corps. In addition, the MWNA provided care for civilian war victims through an overseas branch known as the American Women's Hospitals. The Medical Women's International Association (MWIA), founded in 1919, brings together women involved with or interested in medicine from 70 countries. In addition to encouraging women to enter the field of medicine and related sciences, the MWIA provides women with an opportunity to exchange information about medical problems with worldwide implications and secures members' support in international health matters. In addition, the MWIA helps women in developing countries obtain funds for research and travel.

Formation of Professional Societies

The formation of women's professional societies is a fluid process that occurs over time. It reflects both wider social patterns (for example, changing attitudes toward women's work and labor shortages in professions, which may in turn lead to increased tolerance of women in a profession) as well as the flexibility or rigidity of existing professional societies. Many women's professional societies have begun as informal task forces, caucuses, or divisions within larger professional associations. Sometimes women's professional groups within larger professional societies are short-lived (for example, the women's section of the American Pharmaceutical Association, A.Ph.A., which was founded in 1913 and disbanded in 1922), and in other instances these professional societies within larger societies are relatively enduring. The professions of pharmacy and psychology help illustrate the processes characteristic of the formation of women's professional societies.

In the United States, by World War I, the number of women is schools of pharmacy had grown large enough to encourage the formation of sororities for women in pharmacy, such as Lambda Kappa Sigma (founded in 1917–1918) and Kappa Epsilon, founded in 1921. Although these sororities survived, the women's section of the A.Ph.A. (as noted above) was disbanded in 1922 as more women entered the profession. The pharmaceutical profession had been exemplary in its treatment of women, and a women's section within the A.Ph.A. was deemed unnecessary because women ceased to be viewed as anomalous within the profession (Stieb et al., 1990).

In some instances informal task forces representing the professional interests of women become formal divisions within larger professional societies. In other instances efforts to advance the status of women in a profession may result in the development of an autonomous women's professional organization. A review of women's professional societies in psychology in the United States provides many insights into the dynamics of the formation of women's professional societies.

The American Psychological Association (APA) began in 1892. Women constituted 14.2 percent of the APA's new members between 1892 and 1921. By the 1930s about one-third of the APA's members were women, a trend that has continued. Between 1892 and 1921, two women became presidents of the APA, but no women held the presidency between 1922 and 1970. Most women psychologists who managed to obtain academic positions in the early part of the twentieth century were concentrated in two specialty areas: educational psychology and child psychology. The concentration of women in these two specialties and their inability to secure positions in the leadership of the APA prompted a group of women and men to form the American Association of Applied Psychology in 1937. Women represented a greater proportion of members in this organization and held more elected positions and appointments than they had in the APA (Walsh, 1985).

Despite these important successes, a lack of willingness to appoint women to the Emergency Committee (which was to coordinate the contributions of psychologists to the war effort) provided the impetus for women psychologists to form another professional society, the National Council of Women Psychologists (NCWP), in 1941. The NCWP's aims included furthering the work of women psychologists in the war effort and promoting psychology as a science and profession with respect to women's contributions. By 1943 just under 20 percent of qualified women psychologists in the United States had joined the NCWP. In 1946 the organization expanded to include women psychologists from other countries, and the name changed to the International Council of Women Psychologists (I-NCWP). The I-NCWP engaged in a number of activities including sponsoring a newsletter that listed the accomplishments of women psychologists, as well as a series of workshops at the APA meetings between 1946 and 1949 on topics such as the role of women psychologists. Although many of its activities clearly promoted women psychologists, the I-NCWP was careful not to engage in any activities that could be viewed as militant. For example, although in 1953 a committee on the status of women in psychology was formed within the I-NCWP, the committee made every effort to focus on what women psychologists were doing in the field, rather than on the fact that women psychologists were not receiving equal treatment (Walsh, 1985).

Many members of the I-NCWP were ambivalent about belonging to a single-sex organization and questioned the effectiveness of separation as a strategy, as opposed to integration. Members of the I-NCWP had little if any influence on the APA, and their membership in the I-NCWP could in fact be quite damaging to their careers. Eventually the I-NCWP leadership decided that the best way to raise awareness of women's issues in psychology would be to become a division of the APA. When the I-NCWP approached the APA about obtaining APA-division status in 1948, the I-NCWP was told that no group limited to one sex could become an APA division. In efforts to appease the APA, the I-NCWP voted to allow men to join, and, with a few male members, formally applied for division status in 1958. The APA voted to postpone the I-NCWP's request. The I-NCWP members were told that their group, which consisted mostly of women, was a women's group and thus ineligible for division status. Still committed to affiliating with the APA, the I-NCWP voted to delete the word *women* from its name. Despite these efforts, which some claim marked the end of the original purpose of the I-NCWP, the APA again rejected the I-NCWPO's request to become a division (this time on the grounds that it was inappropriate for an international organization to be a division of a national origination). In the meantime, with "women" deleted from the name of the organization, the I-NCWP attracted considerably more male members, and by 1968 a majority of the organization's leadership was actually male (Walsh, 1985).

After four years of protests, and the formation of a task force on the status of women in psychology in 1971 (which later became the permanent Committee on Women in the APA), in 1972 the APA accepted a petition to begin a division on the psychology of women (Division 35). The goals of Division 35 included the promotion of research and study of women and the integration of the results into current psychological theory (Walsh, 1985).

The existence of Division 35 of the APA owes much to both the social climate of the times and the efforts of another group, the Association for Women in Psychology (AWP). The AWP was founded during the APA conference of 1969 after several sessions erupted into intense debates about sexual practices at the conference, sexism within the APA, discrimination in both academic and professional psychology, and the role of psychology in women's oppression. Several actions were taken at the conference, including the development and circulation of several petitions addressing various aspects of women's position in psychology, the APA, and society. As tensions mounted, the AWP was founded (Tiefer, 1991).

Unlike members of the I-NCWP, the founders of the AWP did not fear militancy and were not concerned with threatening other members of their profession. The AWP was formed to encourage feminist psychological research and theory on women and women's issues, as well as to expand women's role in psychology. The organization's statement of purpose clearly stated that the AWP was interested in changing sex roles in society from a research, education, and professional standpoint. In addition, the goals of maximizing professional opportunities for women and enhancing the effectiveness of women psychologists were clearly set forth in the AWP's statement of purpose. Unlike the I-NCWP, the AWP contained in its bylaws a commitment to taking action in order to effect equal treatment of women in the profession, as well as in the wider society. From its beginning the AWP has had annual conferences and has maintained a presence at annual APA conferences as well. With the formation of the women's division of the APA, AWP members considered—and rejected—the possibility of disbanding. AWP members decided to continue the organization in order to exert radical pressure on the APA and to promote the treatment of feminist topics that were likely to remain outside areas of interest addressed within the APA (Tiefer, 1991).

The example above suggests that autonomous women's professional associations often provide women with opportunities for greater involvement with their profession, help set the profession's agenda with respect to women, and may exert pressure to change on other professional societies. Both autonomous professional societies and women's committees within larger professional societies monitor the status of women in the professions and help create a supportive environment for women both in terms of professional advancement and more broadly in terms of women's equality. Although the AWP presents an example of a women's professional society that is explicitly feminist in purpose, many women's professional societies have an uncomfortable relationship with the term *feminism* (though their activities may be viewed as feminist).

Witz (1990) suggests that all professional projects are projects of occupational closure that are exclusionary, demarcationary, or inclusionary, or involve dual strategies of closure. A dominant group (such as doctors) may attempt to exclude women from a profession. In response, women may attempt to usurp power in the profession through an inclusionary strategy. Women's professional societies often provide a way for women to engage in inclusionary usurpation. Strategies of demarcation involve attempts to control labor in other related professions (for example, doctors' attempts to control the labor of midwives). Dual-closure strategies involve a two-way exercise of power and describe the ways in which women may resist demarcation. Women's professional societies may fill one or more of the functions outlined by Witz. In addition, many professional associations also engage in a range of activist activities, often in collaboration with community-based organizations.

Range of Women's Professional Societies

There are numerous women's professional associations in the sciences, social sciences, technology, and engineering throughout the world. For example, several counties have societies for women in science and engineering, including the United Kingdom (the Association of Women in Science and Engineering), the United States (Association of women in Science and the Society for Women in Engineering, SWE), New Zealand (Association of Women in Science), Canada (the Canadian Association of Women in Science and the Society for Canadian Women in Science and Technology), South Africa (South African Women in Science and Engineering), Australia (Women in Science and Engineering Network), and Ireland (Women in Technology and Science). The Association of Women Engineers in Mali acts as a network for women engineers and provides support for women engineers' professional endeavors. The German Association of Women Engineers is similar. The International Network of Women in Technology represents women of diverse backgrounds, positions, and disciplines working for technology organizations, in academia, and in governmental agencies.

Among the professional associations representing women's interests as autonomous societies are the Association for Women in Computing, the Association for Women Geoscientists, the Association for Women in Science, the Association for Women in Mathematics, the Association for Women Veterinarians, the Association for Women Geoscientists, Women in Aerospace, Women in Energy, Women in Entomology, the Society of Women Engineers, and the Society of Women Geographers. Although many of these organizations are located in North America, several women's professional societies are international in focus, including the International Association of Women Philosophers (which operates in three languages and represents women in 15 countries) and the International Women's Anthropology Conference, which represents women sociologists and anthropologists teaching and conducting research on topics such as women and development, feminism, and the international women's movement.

As was the case with the APA women's division, often women attempt to both provide support for one another and reform their professions from within an existing professional society. Among the professions with women's caucuses, committees, or divisions representing women's concerns within a larger professional society are anthropology, geography, immunology, astronomy, chemistry, economics, mathematics, public health, physics, physiology, and statistics. As was the case with psychology, in some instances these professions may also have an autonomous women's professional society.

Unlike several women's professional societies founded before the 1970s, many women's professional societies founded more recently have an explicit commitment to feminism. For example, Sociologists for Women in Society (SWS) is dedicated to improving the professional opportunities for women sociologists, as well as exploring the contributions that sociology can, does, and should make to investigating and improving the status of women in society. In addition to acting as a watchdog of the American Sociological Association to ensure that women's professional needs are addressed, SWS publishes the journal *Gender and Society.* Often the publication of a journal by a professional society signals its commitment to both investigating the effects of work in that profession on women and using the resources of the profession to improve women's status in society. Both professional societies and caucuses of larger professional societies publish journals. For example, the Society for the Advancement of Women's Health Research (SAWHR) publishes the *Journal of Women's Health,* and the APA women's division publishes the *Psychology of Women Quarterly.*

Links to Other Women's Organizations

The line between professional societies and activist organizations is often blurred. Some organizations represent the interests of women in a given profession as well as support community-based projects that directly serve women. This is particularly true of feminist and women's studies associations, which are generally open to women professionals and activists in any profession engaged in feminist research or committed to feminist change.

Unions often have their own women's committees that work with other women's organizations to stimulate feminist change. Unions whose members are largely women (such as many teaching unions) may have one association that acts as both a union and a professional association. When a union and a professional society exist within a single profession (for example, nursing), members of both groups may join around particular issues, such as staffing levels in workplaces. Occasionally, organizations (such as the Union of Women's Work Committees in Israel) may attempt to provide a forum for communication and exchange of information among women professionals and workers, in addition to promoting advancement of women in the workplace.

See Also

EDUCATION: ADULT AND CONTINUING; ENGINEERING; FEMINISM: NINETEENTH CENTURY; PSYCHOLOGY: OVERVIEW

References and Further Reading

Barrett, Jacqueline K., ed. 1993. *Encyclopedia of women's associations worldwide.* London: Gale Research.

Bauchum, Rosalind G. 1985. *The black business and professional women: Selected references of achievement.* Monticello, Ill.: Vance Bibliographies.

Brecher, Deborah, and Lippitt, Jill, eds. 1994. *The national women's information exchange national directory.* New York: Avon.

Gillett, Margaret. 1990. The heart of the matter: Maude E. Abbott, 1869–1940. In Marianne Gosztonyi Ainley, ed., *Despite the odds: Essays on Canadian women and science,* 179–194. Montreal: Vehicule.

Glazer, Penina Migdal, and Miriam Slater. 1986. *Unequal colleagues: The entrance of women into the professions, 1890–1940.* London: Rutgers University Press.

O'Malley, Grace. 1982. *A woman's yellow pages: 570+ organizations concerned with women's issues.* Washington, D.C.: Federation of Organizations for Professional Women.

Rosenberg, Rosalind. 1982. *Beyond separate sphere: The intellectual roots of modern feminism.* New Haven, Conn.: Yale University Press.

Russell, John T., ed. 1995. *National trade and professional associations of the United States and Canada and labor unions.* Washington, D.C.: Columbia.

Stieb, Ernst W., Gail C. Coulas, Joyce A. Fergusen, Robert J. Clark, and Roy W. Hornosty. 1990. Women in Ontario pharmacy, 1867–1927. In Marianne Gosztonyi Ainley, ed., *Despite the odds: Essays on Canadian women and science,* 121–133. Montreal: Vehicule.

Thurn, Linda, ed. 1996. *Encyclopedia of associations: International organizations.* New York: Gale Research.

Tiefer, Leonore. 1991. A brief history of the Association of Women in Psychology: 1969–1991. *Psychology of Women Quarterly,* 15: 635–649.

Walsh, Mary Roth. 1985. Academic professional women organizing for change: The struggle in psychology. *Journal of Social Issues,* 41(4): 17–28.

Witz, Anne. 1990. Patriarchy and professions: The gendered politics of occupational closure. *Sociology,* 24(4): 675–690.

Ellen Balka

PRO-LIFE MOVEMENT

See ABORTION REPRODUCTIVE RIGHTS.

PROPERTY

See FAMILY: PROPERTY RELATIONS.

PROSTITUTION

Prostitution can be defined as the provision of sexual services in exchange for material gains. Like any other form of exchange, prostitution is governed by a set of social relations.

The long history of prostitution has produced both diversity and inconsistency in these relations, and thus a variety of forms of prostitution. Despite this, the historical forms of prostitution do exhibit a clear relationship with the state as a regulator. The changing class position of women in prostitution is directly related to the changing regimes of regulation.

In ancient India and Babylon, practices of prostitution were closely connected with religious rituals. Devadasi (temple prostitutes) in India and women affiliated with Babylonian temples possessed social prestige and privileges through their dedicated status and skills. Devadasi had access to religious goals in a context where salvation was otherwise misogynic (women needed to be reborn as men before undertaking the quest for salvation). The Devadasi have gradually lost many of their traditional rights and are now forced to work as common prostitutes within highly commercialized and exploitative relations.

Nonreligious prostitutes in east Asian societies such as China, Japan, Korea, and Vietnam were socially respected as artists, providing music, poetry, and dance as well as sexual services to men of the ruling aristocracy and the court. They could acquire significant privileges and some social influence. In western Europe, similar forms of prostitution existed in royal and aristocratic circles, although courtesans were replaced by demimondaines with the advent of capitalism and the emergence of the bourgeoisie, and many of the categories of prostitutes affiliated with the monarchy and aristocracy have gradually disappeared. Side by side with courtesanery, "common" prostitution also existed and provided a place for men dislocated from their kin to satisfy sexual needs, a place for dislocated women to be sheltered in the absence of other possibilities such as marriage or cloister, and a source of income for municipalities.

Until the nineteenth century, prostitution in many countries was regulated under various forms of licensing. However, the spread of syphilis and other venereal diseases led gradually to tighter control and eventually to the labeling of women in prostitution as a source of moral and physical infection. Prostitutes became singled out as a deviant subspecies of the female sex. Attempting to advance women's rights, the Social Purity movement in the nineteenth century and early twentieth century in England, the Netherlands, the United States, and Japan sought to pressure governments to abolish prostitution on the basis of promiscuity as vice, the exploitation of prostitutes as fallen women, and the trafficking in women as slavery.

The view of prostitution as promiscuity has reinforced the stigmatization of women in prostitution, and in the process their voices were also silenced. At present, unable to abolish the institution of prostitution along the lines advocated by the Social Purity movement, many governments have focused on the rehabilitation of prostitutes as individuals and the criminalization of the practice of prostitution as an income-earning activity. Criminalization has mainly affected women while leaving clients, pimps, and owners of sex enterprises relatively untouched.

Two Contemporary Feminist Views of Prostitution

Contemporary feminist political thought on prostitution is polarized between advocacy of abolition of prostitution and support for regulation of the practice. The mainstream view continues to be dominated by moral concern over female sexual slavery. Prostitution is viewed as the epitome of the principle of women's oppression and hence as something that should be abolished. In this regard, there is little deviation from the main line of argument advanced by the Social Purity movement in the last century. The antiprostitution lobby today supports the International Convention for the Suppression of the Traffic in Women and Persons and the Exploitation of the Prostitution of Others (1949). This lobby's main concern is how to develop legal instruments that would make the Convention more effective in penalizing sex syndicates. Alliances with prostitutes are created insofar as women in prostitution are regarded as or claim themselves to be victims. Women in prostitution as actors with their own social world and agendas that may conflict with the feminist project still remain removed from mainstream feminist political thought.

However, this view has also been challenged by other perspectives that are more grounded in the reality of the lives of women in prostitution. Over the last two decades, women in prostitution in many countries have been trying to make their voices heard. They point to the complexity of sexual transaction today and its strong links with the service sector. Their views and factual evidence suggest that labor relations in the sex industry today may range from slavery to legally sanctioned sex work such as masseuses, porno models, and escorts, with considerable mobility between occupations and with each category of worker trying to maintain a separate identity to avoid the social stigma entailed in the sex industry.

The plurality of relations of power and production in the sex industry has also produced a diverse consciousness among women in prostitution. Depending on their location, women in prostitution have emphasized women's autonomous choice, women's survival needs, or victimization and exploitation. Their views are reflected in the proprostitute lobby, working closely with groups that oppose the stigmatization of sexual identities and advocate the freedom of sexual choices, or with groups that try to gain the recognition of domestic work as work, or with groups that lend support to victims of trafficking.

Driven by pragmatic concerns over the conditions of women in prostitution, the proprostitute lobby makes a distinction between prostitution as a capitalist-patriarchal institution and prostitutes as individuals. It aims at the introduction or improvement of existing regulation on prostitution so as to maximize the protection of women from exploitation and victimization by clients, pimps, owners of commercial sex enterprises, and the state. It advocates the view that the process of capital accumulation in prostitution today hinges on the stigmatization of prostitutes by the law and society at large. Stigmatization fosters and enhances the relation of domination and dependency between women in prostitution and their employers. Such a relation minimizes the effects of the wage system as a redistributive measure and permits the use of force to discipline women in prostitution in order to intensify their productivity. Legal persecution limits the space for resistance by women in prostitution or discounts resistance where space has been created. As such, it benefits men as pimps and as sex-capitalists rather than women.

Unresolved conflicts about prostitution within feminism have led to divisive political practices. Conceptual clarity is required to provide adequate answers to questions relating to power and domination, accumulation and exploitation. An analysis of prostitution through the lens of sexual labor as a concept may shed more light on the ongoing controversies.

Sexual Labor

Sexual labor is the utilization of the sexual elements of the body as an instrument of labor. It may take the form of biological sex for bodily pleasure or procreation. Social relations governing sexual labor are historically and socially specific and are linked to social interpretation of biological differences. The dynamics of sexual labor may be best explored through the concept of the apparatus of sexuality developed by Michel Foucault, who wrote a three-volume history of sexuality. In his view, sexuality is managed socially by mechanisms of power and knowledge that are embedded in discourses on biological sex, such as religion, law, pedagogy, and medicine. Such discourses create sexualized bodies and sexual identities which are differentiated and through which social power is exercised. Foucault's view can be extended to include the link between the constitution of the sexual subject through discourse and the active role of discourse in the transformation of sexuality into sexual labor.

Sexuality as a history of ideas about sex cannot be disconnected from concrete practices of the utilization of sexual labor. Whereas wage labor in production has been considered as productive, the productivity of sexual services for the purpose of reproduction under wage relations has been concealed by cognitive and institutional structures governing sexuality. Discursive constitutions of sexual subjects are stratified along polarized lines of normality and deviancy, both sexual and asexual. The "valorization" of female sexuality finds its expression through this polarization, which in turn facilitates the use of sexual labor.

Thus in feudal societies under hierarchized polygamy the link between female sexuality and motherhood may be applicable only to the wife of the first order and not to the lower-ranking wives. The absence of this link facilitates the access to the body of the lower-ranking wife merely as biological reproducer or wet nurse. Similarly, it is sometimes said, the absence of the family among slaves consciously brought about by planters in the Caribbean in the nineteenth century, legitimized the creation of "stud farms" for the biological reproduction of new slaves. Also, the sale of sexual labor among a certain class of women may be glorified as an erotic art or debased as moral and hygienic pollution.

Traditionally, the category of labor that is purely sexual and essential to human life and to society has been confined to kinship or patron-client relations. Sexual labor became dislocated from such relations and available under wage relations through wider processes of socioeconomic changes that disrupt traditional mediating structures. Accumulation of capital from sexual labor could become intensified under capitalism by the very denial of its existence. Therefore, sexual labor must be analytically placed within the historical process that has incorporated both men and women into the wage-labor force. This process is both gendered and sexualized in the sense that men and women have been incorporated in waged production on different terms, and some women are incorporated as reproducers using mainly sexual labor.

In various periods and contexts since the beginning of capitalism, organized forms of women's sexual labor have been critical to the maintenance of civilian and military labor forces. Women's sexual labor has been formally provided in prisons, on colonial plantations, in industrial settings. More recently, colonial historical records in Indonesia and Kenya show that such labor is provided implicitly through military "rest and recreation" agreements between national governments as in the case of Thailand and the Philippines. The types of work women performed did not change substantially, but the disintegration of the preindustrial locus of reproductive activities and the related commodification of sexual labor created a class of reproducers performing social and sexual tasks with minimal recognition and reward.

Historical examples of the use of sexual labor show that the management of biological sex as a source of life is conducted through the manipulation of female sexuality, with sexual norms selectively applied to increase the supply of sexual labor or to cut the costs of its maintenance. On the basis of race and class, selective emphasis is given to different dimensions of sexual labor (biological sex, procreation, maintenance through domestic work). These dimensions are kept deliberately separated and not allowed to coalesce. The division between various socially constructed sexual identities denies women who provide sexual labor both the significance of that labor and the intimacy and social significance of marriage and motherhood.

Forms of sexual labor do respond to technological innovation. Innovation in reproductive technology now allows sexual labor in biological reproduction to take the form of surrogate motherhood based on monetary exchange rather than through slavery and indenture. Similarly, innovation in the field of transport and communication technology enables the formation of a proliferation of forms of sexual labor for pleasure, ranging from sex-package tours and the provision of pornographic materials to escort services, eros centers, sex therapy centers, and telephone sex lines. Technology may help firms to disintegrate these dimensions to the point of the total absence of bodily contact in sexual labor for pleasure (as in the case of both traditional and technologically advanced forms of pornography). It can also help to integrate different dimensions of sexuality into one single product such as sex-package tours, commonly known as sex tourism.

Sex Tourism

Sex tourism represents the convergence of prostitution with the international tourist industry, known since the late 1970s. The currently expanding tourism industry in a number of third world countries arose through a combination of factors, including the entry of leisure into the international division of labor fostered by postwar economic growth in the West, the emergence of long-distance leisure travel induced by innovation in air transport and information technology and an enormous surplus of facilities that could not be absorbed by the expansion of commerce and government activities alone, and the international promotion of tourism as a means for poorer countries to earn foreign exchange.

Sex tourism in particular has been facilitated by the specific structure of the tourist industry as well as by the nature of its products. As an "experience good"—that is, a service to be consumed at the place of destination rather than the place of purchase—tourism is marked by an unpredictable demand structure and an industrial structure skewed toward the control and interests of tourist-generating countries. To maximize earnings, intensive efforts are made by governments and firms in countries of destination to encourage visitors to spend money locally and to manipulate demand through the promotion of culturally constructed notions about "nature," including the "nature" of women, which have a dynamic function in attracting tourists. Combined with promotional campaigns at an international level, these efforts have created a symbiotic relationship between tourism and advertising and a new playground "culture" in which "sand, sea, sun, and sex" are the main elements.

Against this background, sex tourism must be understood as part and parcel of the broader incursion of capital into the domain of sexuality and eroticism. Apart from formalizing the place of sexual labor in the existing international division of labor, this incursion has also initiated a new process of sexual subjugation. Through the construction of new sexual and erotic categories, this incursion is able to conceal the intensification of accumulation from sexual labor while at the same time providing a seemingly more progressive sexual morality to consumers.

The reality of prostitution and sex tourism today confronts the ethics of labor and the ethics of sexuality at the deepest level. The industrial production of sexual services and eroticism implies that a continuous supply of sexual labor must be ensured. This has led directly to an increase in the use of violence to locate and control sexual labor. In this respect, plurality of sexual choice and recognition of prostitution as a practice that confronts both patriarchal ideology and economic dependence may not be considered adequate responses. The border of sexual ethics extends beyond the question of individual choices regarding practice or consumption. It includes the process of sexual domination that precedes the availability of such sexual choices. It is therefore important to keep in mind that ceasing to judge prostitution does not imply ceasing to impose ethical boundaries on the use of sexual labor.

See Also

ECONOMY: INFORMAL; SEXUAL SLAVERY; TRAFFICKING

References and Further Reading

Barry, K. 1984. *International feminism: Networking against female sexual slavery.* New York: International Women's Tribune Center.

Bell, L., ed. 1987. *Good girls, bad girls: Sex trade workers and feminists face to face.* Toronto: Women's Press.

Enloe, C. 1990. *Bananas, beaches and bases: Making feminist sense of international politics.* Berkeley: University of California Press.

Foucault, M. 1980. *The history of sexuality.* Vol. 1, *An introduction.* New York: Vintage.

Lerner, G. 1986. *The creation of patriarchy.* New York: Oxford University Press.

Lim, L. L., ed. 1998. *The sex sector: The economic and social bases of prostitution in southeast Asia.* International Labour Office, Geneva.

Phongpaichit, P., Piriyarangsen and Tacrat, N. 1998. *Guns, girls, gambling, ganja.* Chiengmai: Silkworm.

Truong, T. D. 1990. *Sex, money and morality: Prostitution and tourism in southeast Asia.* London: Zed.

Truong, T. D., and V. O. del Rosario. 1994. Captive outsiders: Trafficked sex workers and mail-order brides in the European Union. In J. Wiersma, ed., *Insiders and outsiders: On the making of Europe II.* Kampen: Pharos.

Warren, J. F. 1993. *Ah ku and karayuki-san: Prostitution in Singapore.* Singapore: Oxford University Press.

Thanh-Dam Truong

PSYCHIATRY

Psychiatry is the study and treatment of mental disorder. Behavior viewed as "unwell" is modified by using psychotropic drugs (biological psychiatry) or by using therapies based on increasing self-awareness through insight and counseling from a therapist or altering relational and social factors (psychosocial therapies). Psychiatrists are routinely involved in using normative models of behavior and evaluating competing definitions of aberrant or maladaptive behavior. Thus psychiatry—like all disciplines that propose and defend a socially constructed model of normality—has an important function in determining gender roles and contributes to psychosocial definitions of the "mentally healthy woman." In the past, for example, psychiatry was the site of the medicalization of homosexuality. Women face difficulties that arise from the masculinist model of dominant teachings in psychiatry in developed countries. Normative views of behavior are fundamentally masculinist, whether applied to patient or therapist (Russell, 1995).

Women as Patients and Consumers

Beginning with the early studies of hysteria, women have been the favored subjects of psychiatric scrutiny. Women are the major consumers of mental health services, both directly, as patients, and indirectly, as the major providers of home-based (or community) care of the mentally ill. The latter model is increasingly popular in developed nations as a means of minimizing hospitalization and other medical costs.

That more women seek mental health services reflects socialization processes (Ehrenreich and English, 1978) that encourage women to seek help from health care professionals for themselves and their families. Women are also more expressive and less inhibited than men in disclosing their distress and more sensitive to contextual factors such as relational disturbances. Finally, women are most vulnerable to psychiatric disorder during the postpartum period (reflecting hormonal and psychosocial factors) and most vulnerable to depression when caring at home for preschool children. Thus they are positioned to receive more medication and attract more diagnoses than men. Women consume more psychotropic medications (prescription drugs) while men consume more alcohol and illicit drugs. These basically social differences in gender role behavior contribute to an overrepresentation of women as consumers of mental health services. Similarly, women's acting out of personal distress is more likely to take the form of some sort of somatization and hence to attract the attention of health care services. Men are more apt to express their distress in risky and aggressive behavior and are more likely to kill or injure themselves or others or to be treated as "criminal" rather than as unwell. Finally, sexual and physical abuse and domestic violence contribute enormously to women's distress and relate to institutionalized mores of male violence.

Women as Psychiatrists

Psychiatry is one of the more popular medical specialties for women doctors, who generally enter those areas of medicine to which they seem more "naturally" suited, namely pediatrics, family medicine, and counseling. These choices are determined by a number of factors: women manifest a more affiliative and humanitarian orientation and hence are more attracted to the direct-care areas of medicine; also, there is greater resistance to the entry of women into traditionally masculine fields, such as orthopedic surgery and high-technology medicine. Although at least half of all premedical students are women, only 10 percent of medical specialists, professors, and senior administrators are women. The majority of women in medicine are involved in direct clinical care; this is the "glass ceiling" observed in women's career paths within many professional fields.

Increasingly there is a strong demand for female practitioners, especially by female consumers, and to a lesser extent among men as well. This reflects skepticism within the community about polypharmacy and high-technology medicine and the expectation that women doctors will be less inclined to rely on those interventions. It also reflects concerns about sexual exploitation of female patients by male practitioners. Psychiatry seems destined to become a (numerically) female-dominated profession, but the status of psychiatry is threatened with decline owing to the large number of nonmedical therapists whose work overlaps considerably.

Like women careerists generally, women psychiatrists bear the burdens of role strain and the "double shift" (that is, doing most of the domestic work in addition to wage work) while remaining a minority group within the profession itself. Women do more of the "emotional housekeeping" at work, where they offer support and advice to students and junior staff, and more of the political housework that is necessary to ensure equitable conditions for women. These extra roles mean less time to devote to research, and hence fewer publications and research grants—and promotions are based primarily on research achievements. Women earn less money and work fewer hours in the earlier years of their careers when child care responsibilities are maximal; but, with an average of less than two children and a life expectancy of 80 years (in developed countries), childbearing is highly overrated as the major obstacle to upward mobility for women. The rhetoric of women's role as caregivers disguises the abdication of family responsibilities by their male counterparts. Over a lifetime, women doctors work only slightly fewer hours than their male peers, and many factors other than childbearing maintain women's status as a minority group within the profession. Women psychiatrists have a suicide rate four times higher than women in the general population. This may relate to their greater sophistication in methods of self-destruction, but it suggests also that the traditionally male-dominated institutions can be somewhat toxic to women.

Negative stereotypes about female professionals are entrenched; women cannot transcend the body, hence they are depicted as efficacious in their traditional roles as either mother figures or sexual beings, rather than by virtue of intellectual power or professional status. These stereotypes are perpetuated by images in the mass media and exemplified by Hollywood's female psychiatrists, who are invariably depicted as highly sexualized. The idea of women as powerful in the public arena is one that destabilizes a social system based on male dominance (Betterton, 1987); hence the status of professional women is degraded by media images through sexualization.

How Psychiatry Has Dealt with Women

While psychiatry seems to have a single system of values and to make an objective distinction between "health" and "disorder," feminists have increasingly argued that normative models of psychiatry have been masculinist; that is, the ideal character is constructed as independent, autonomous, self-directed, and adventurous—all stereotypically masculine attributes. By contrast, stereotypically feminine attributes are reported as neurotic; the relational, emotionally expressive, other-directed character is regarded as nonnormative (Jordan et al., 1991). Psychiatric diagnoses perpetuate notions of women as intrinsically mad or unstable, so that, for example, to classify premenstrual syndrome (PMS) as a mental disorder means that between 40 and 100 percent of women could be considered mad at least part of the time (Russell, 1995).

The normative character in psychiatry—in addition to being male—is implicitly English-speaking, heterosexual, and middle-class, in other words, western. Not only are attributes such as autonomy and individuality at odds with female values; they are not applicable to nonwestern cultures (Gunew and Yeatman, 1993). Feminism generally has begun to address the diversity of women—non-English-speaking, lesbian, and so on—but contemporary psychiatry has been slow to incorporate this recent feminist work (Chodorow, 1989; Penfold and Walker, 1983; Russell, 1995; Ussher, 1991).

The female condition is both medicalized and pathologized; for example, battered wives may be regarded as masochistic and alcoholic wives as codependant. Thankfully the "schizophrenogenic" mother (the mother who supposedly caused schizophrenia in her offspring) has disappeared, but family systems theories still focus on "enmeshed" mothers, and psychodynamic models feature pathogenic mothers who are intrusive, engulfing, or nonattuned with respect to their offspring. This is so despite a growing literature that identifies sexual abuse of women and children by men as a background to adult psychiatric disturbance. Traditional psychoanalytic models of femaleness as derivative of maleness are beginning to yield to more women-centered models (Quadrio, 1995) and to acknowledge the importance of lesbian sexuality (Falco, 1991).

Psychiatry espouses a biopsychosocial model of disorder that acknowledges an interplay between biological, psychological, and social dimensions. The psychology from which this derives is research-based, with a tradition of empiricism or positivism that perpetuates the subjectivity-objectivity paradigm with little acknowledgment of feminist critiques of this gender dichotomy. Those critiques have exposed scientific objectivity as a masculinist concept and one that disguises the inevitable observer bias in any investigation.

Currently, psychotherapies in the developed world are heavily influenced by economic rationalism and exploding national health budgets, with a push for briefer, cheaper therapies. Psychotherapists favor behavioral cognitive interventions (in which there is considerable overlap with the practice of psychologists), and biogenetic models that rely upon the prescription of drugs—an intervention still monopolized by psychiatry. The psychodynamic therapies, of longer duration and less symptom-focused, are receiving less support, because of their expense, their unproven effectiveness, and intense debate about the theoretical (phallocentric) premises of psychoanalytic theory. These evolutions seem inevitably to be leading psychiatry into the field of medicalized, drug-based therapies, leaving the psychosocial therapies increasingly in the hands of nonmedical professionals.

See Also

PSYCHOANALYSIS; PSYCHOLOGY: OVERVIEW; PSYCHOLOGY, COGNITIVE; PSYCHOLOGY: NEUROSCIENCE AND BRAIN RESEARCH; PSYCHOLOGY: PERSONALITY RESEARCH; PSYCHOLOGY: PSYCHOMETRICS; PSYCHOLOGY: SOCIAL; SCIENCE: FEMINIST CRITIQUES

References

Betterton, Rosemary. 1987. *Looking on: Images of femininity in the visual arts and media.* London: Pandora.

Chodorow, Nancy. 1989. *Feminism and psychoanalytic theory.* London: Yale University Press.

Ehrenreich, Barbara, and Deirdre English. 1978. *For her own good: 150 years of the experts' advice to women.* London: Pluto.

Falco, Kristine. 1991. *Psychotherapy with lesbian clients.* New York: Brunner/Mazel.

Gunew, Sneja, and Anna Yeatman. 1993. *Feminism and the politics of difference.* Sydney: Allen & Unwin.

Jordan, Judith, Alexandra Kaplan, Jean Baker Miller, Irene Stiver, and Janet Surrey. 1991. *Women's growth in connection: Writings from the stone centre.* New York: Guilford.

Penfold, Susan, and Gillian Walker. 1983. *Women and the psychiatric paradox.* London: Eden.

Quadrio, Carolyn. 1994. Woman-centred perspectives on female psychosexuality. *Australian and New Zealand Journal and Psychiatry* 28: 478–487.

Russell, Denise. 1995. *Women, madness and medicine.* Cambridge: Polity.

Ussher, Jane. 1991. *Women's madness: misogyny or mental illness?* Hertfordshire: Harvester Wheatsheaf.

Carolyn Quadrio

PSYCHOANALYSIS

Psychoanalysis, which was developed by Sigmund Freud (1859–1939), is both a theory of human psychology and a form of psychotherapy. Theoretically, psychoanalysis is based on Freudian concepts such as the unconscious; the id, ego, and superego; sexuality; repression; and the oedipus complex. As a therapeutic method, it involves free association, interpretation of dreams, and phenomena such as resistance and transference. Psychoanalysis, though it has always drawn criticism, has become part of western culture, not only in psychology but in literature, drama, art, history, social science, and so on. Critiques of psychoanalysis take various forms: for example, some critics address its scientific status while others—and feminists have often been among these—use psychoanalytic insights as a tool to examine and reevaluate other fields of thought.

Although in the popular imagination feminism and psychoanalysis are sworn enemies, and many feminists continue to be hostile to Freud, serious feminist engagement with psychoanalysis began with post-1970 feminism in the work of Juliet Mitchell, Luce Irigaray, Dorothy Dinnerstein, and Nancy Chodorow. In particular, feminists in philosophy—who will be the focus of this article—used psychoanalytic theory to understand what they perceived as the masculinism of philosophy and its attempt to exclude the feminine. Since psychoanalysis is specifically concerned with issues such as the formation of masculine and feminine identity at the unconscious level, it provides a framework for arguing that rationality and knowledge are always unconsciously gendered, thus challenging the self-proclaimed neutrality and universality of philosophy, a claim which feminists have increasingly seen as suspect.

Trends in Psychoanalytic Feminism

It is interesting to compare psychoanalytic approaches to literary theory and to philosophy. Because psychoanalysis looks at the effects of desire in language, psychoanalysis and literary criticism are allies in a way that psychoanalysis and philosophy are not. Whereas psychoanalysis has given literary criticism a new lease of life, it has tended to destabilize traditional philosophy.

Psychoanalytic criticism examines texts to identify literary and rhetorical strategies analogous to psychic mechanisms. It considers relationships between author and text, and between reader and text; and it often extrapolates from textual strategies to strategies of the culture in general. There are five main approaches (Wright, 1984):

1. Psychobiography or psychocritique analyzes the author or the characters.
2. Reader-response theory (as the term implies) analyzes the reader, or the relationship between reader and writing.
3. Analysis of psyche as text starts from Jacques Lacan's assumption that psychic and linguistic mechanisms are analogous.
4. Analysis of the text as psyche starts from Jacques Derrida's assumption that textual and psychic mechanisms are analogous.
5. Ideological analysis, an approach inspired by Michel Foucault, sees psychoanalysis as a discourse producing effects of power, both positive and negative.

Feminist work in analytic philosophy has tended to remain within psychobiography or psychocritique, although this approach is vulnerable to the charge of reductivism. In early studies, the analysand—the subject of analysis whose psyche or psychopathology was up for scrutiny—could be an individual philosopher (Plato, Descartes, and Hobbes were typical examples), a philosophical system, or western culture overall. Today, there is probably general acceptance of Naomi Scheman's definition (1993: 7) of the analysand as the "normative philosophical subject," that is, the rational subject of knowledge.

Feminist English-language philosophy relies on the strand of psychoanalytic theory known as object-relations theory, which differs from both classical Freudianism and poststructuralist psychoanalysis. Whereas classical Freudianism focused primarily on the conflict between instinctual drives and the frustrations of external reality, object-relations theory focuses more on the child's relations with real or fantasized "others." It thus provides a more intersubjective and socially oriented account of psychic reality. Similarly, whereas Lacanian theory stresses the internal splitting and division of the self, object-relations theory is more likely to stress the integration of different parts of the self in healthy development, with "splitting" as a mark of pathology; the child's social and familial environment assists or impedes psychic integration. Object-relations theory plays down drives in favor of social reality; this makes it readily accessible to feminist theory, which already has a predominantly social orientation. It is argued, for example, that the sexual division of labor, both within the family and also between public and private worlds, creates a pathogenic environment, reproducing the distortions of masculinity and femininity which have been the target of feminist critiques (Chodorow, 1978).

In the continental tradition, psychoanalytic critique has been more far-reaching. There was a convergence between the feminist critique of philosophical claims and the structuralist and poststructuralist critiques of the primacy accorded to consciousness. Feminism argued that there is no ultimate ground or "anchoring" for knowledge; similarly, psychoanalysis claimed that complete self-possession or self-awareness is impossible, since the subject is dependent on structures which are outside conscious control and are not entirely knowable. For feminists in the continental tradition, the aim is to rethink subjectivity, given the hypothesis of the unconscious, which displaces the centrality of consciousness.

In continental philosophy, Lacan's reading of Freud has dominated; but there is also a flourishing French tradition of psychoanalysts with an interdisciplinary orientation, who are acquainted with Nietzsche, Hegel, Heidegger, the phenomenologists, surrealism, structural linguistics, and structural anthropology (Roudinesco, 1986). Unlike object-relations theory, French psychoanalysis has retained and developed Freud's controversial notion of the death drive, remains suspicious of the Americans' stress on the integration of the ego, and is much more likely to emphasize the decentered subject.

Structuralism and poststructuralism have made it clear that there is more than one way to read Freud: there is the Enlightenment Freud, committed to science and rational mastery; there is also a more deconstructive Freud, whose drive theory introduces a permanent threat of destabilization to the constructions of the rational ego. Feminist theorists in the continental tradition have been more interested in the deconstructive Freud, since they perceive the constructions of the rational ego as hostile to the feminine. While this has produced some powerful theoretical work, the links to feminism as a social movement remain on the whole more tenuous and less programmatic than for more ego-oriented philosophy.

Theoretical Issues in Psychoanalytic Feminism

Two levels of theoretical problems can be identified in the encounter between feminism, psychoanalysis, and philosophy. On the first level are feminist (though not necessarily philosophical) objections to the use of psychoanalytic theory as such. Here we can distinguish four types of argument.

First, it can be held that psychoanalytic theory is organized around male desire (represented by the centrality of the phallus) and that its central concepts, implicitly or explicitly, maintain women as inferior. This argument is associated with the view that psychoanalysis is inevitably prescriptive rather than primarily descriptive. Psychoanalytic feminists accept that psychoanalytic theory is often phallocentric; however, masculine bias may also be seen not as a reason for rejecting psychoanalysis *in toto,* but rather as a reason for rethinking its concepts (Brennan, 1992; Flax, 1990; Kofman, 1980; Schneider, 1980). Even in his own lifetime, Freud's account of women's psychosexuality was challenged by women analysts.

The second argument at this level is that psychoanalytic theory (particularly in the work of French feminists) equates the feminine with the irrational, so that a celebration of the feminine in effect promotes irrationality. However, it is not so much that objectivity and rationality are thrown out (which would be self-defeating) as that they are displaced. Psychoanalytic feminists have discussed issues such as objectivity as a mechanism of defence (involving splitting, or the attempt to distance oneself from unacceptable or unbearable feelings by projecting them elsewhere) and the consequences of this, especially for women (Keller, 1985).

A third argument is that it is reductive to read a philosophical text in terms of the hypothetical psychopathology of its author, who may be long-dead. This argument has been generally accepted and has led to more sophisticated textual readings.

The fourth and perhaps most telling objection is that major tenets of Freudian theory, such as the oedipus complex, were presented as though they were universal and ahistorical data, rather than hypotheses generated in a particular social, cultural, and historical era. In response to this critique of ethnocentrism, there has been an attempt to distinguish between the content of unconscious fantasies, which may be culturally specific, and the inevitability of certain types of mental processes occurring during children's development and socialization. These processes have greater claim to universality, and it seems legitimate to accept them provisionally as cross-cultural, although the distinction between form and content is not always easy to make in psychoanalytic theory, so that the problem of universality remains controversial.

We now turn to the second level, where the arguments taking place within the three-way debate between feminism, philosophy, and psychoanalysis are more conceptual. At this level, central issues include the status of psychoanalytic theory and the limits of philosophy.

Freud's account of the mind (and its elaboration in subsequent and not always mutually compatible theories) provides a critique of its own constructions. Psychoanalytic theory explicitly recognizes that all theory, itself included, has unconscious determinants. For example, one problem of psychoanalytic theory has to do with the representation of drives and the way in which fantasies, images, and words become attached to somatic (bodily) impulses. Since no correspondence can ever be established between a drive and its representation (there is no possible position from which the drive can be observed; one can observe only the representation), it is argued that representations have a structuring effect on drives (Irigaray, 1974). Arguments of this type have major implications for theoretical formulations in psychoanalysis, which are claimed to produce as well as derive from the objects which are their field of study. This gives a passionate edge to theoretical arguments.

It also means that questions about the status of psychoanalytic concepts can be raised without necessarily implying a complete rejection of psychoanalytic findings. Such questions are major philosophical issues in contemporary feminist theory. For example, Judith Butler (1990), drawing on Foucault, analyzes the "power effects" of psychoanalytic discourse. According to Butler, psychoanalytic theory maintains the irreducibility of the binary (and heterosexist) structure of gender as though this were fundamental. It accepts that masculine and feminine identities are constructions, but it continues to build on the bedrock of the castration complex, which divides human beings into men and women. In so doing it takes culture to be nature. In Butler's view, the sexual binary reinforces male primacy and makes heterosexuality normative. She puts forward an alternative account of the construction of gender designed to allow for the possibility of multiplicity where previously there had only been a hierarchical dualism.

Feminists in more activist traditions such as socialist feminism are also concerned that psychoanalytic feminism, with its emphasis on unconscious determinants, does away with any useful notion of agency; they are concerned about its apparent lack of strong social orientation. At the same time, they accept that materialist theory has no adequate account of subjectivity and that psychoanalysis might be a source of indispensable insights here (Sayers, 1986).

If we draw an analogy between psyche and text, the mental operations described by psychoanalysis—projection, introjection, identification, splitting, repression, disavowal, unconscious fantasy, and so on—are identified in the text of the culture at large (following a precedent set by Freud, who thought that social phenomena could be described in psychoanalytic terms). They are seen as functions of a text, a discourse, or a culture in general, so that a whole culture, or subsections of it, may be said to be projecting (for example, projecting men's gender-specific fears onto women), splitting, or disavowing (for example, disavowing the debt to the mother, or the bodily origins of language). This leads to an analysis of the unconscious fantasies of a whole culture, a task undertaken by many feminists who do not define themselves as philosophers but who use psychoanalytic premises. Outstanding studies include work by Parveen Adams, Teresa Brennan, Elisabeth Bronfen, Teresa De Lauretis, Jane Gallop, Mary Jacobus, Rosalind Krauss, Griselda Pollock, Ellie Ragland-Sullivan, Jacqueline Rose, and Kaja Silverman (Wright, 1992). There are particularly incisive analyses in metapsychological theory, literary theory, film theory, and art criticism. If one accepts Michèle Le Doeuff's argument that the traffic between philosophy and the wider culture is not all one-way—that philosophy clarifies culture but also is influenced by it—then the boundaries between what is philosophically relevant and what is not become debatable.

Feminists are interested in psychoanalysis because of a felt necessity for change. They take from psychoanalysis the recognition that intellectual understanding does not in itself effect unconscious transformation, for which the shifts of desire in transference are necessary. Such transformations are evidently subject neither to conscious decision nor to the exercise of will, reason, or force. This indicates the dilemmas with which psychoanalysis confronts the feminist project.

See Also

POSTMODERNISM: FEMINIST CRITIQUES; POSTMODERNISM: LITERARY THEORY; PSYCHOLOGY: OVERVIEW; PSYCHIATRY

References and Further Reading

Brennan, T., ed. 1989. *Between feminism and psychoanalysis.* New York and London: Routledge.

Braidotti, R. 1991. *Patterns of dissonance: A study of women in contemporary philosophy.* Trans. E. Guild. New York: Routledge; Cambridge, England: Polity.

Butler, J. 1990. *Gender trouble: Feminism and the subversion of identity.* New York and London: Routledge.

Chodorow, N. 1978. *The reproduction of mothering: Psychoanalysis and the sociology of gender.* Berkeley: University of California Press.

Flax, J. 1990. *Thinking fragments: Psychoanalysis, feminism, and postmodernism in the contemporary West.* Berkeley: University of California Press.

Irigaray, L. 1974, 1985. *Speculum of the other woman.* Trans. G. C. Gill. Ithaca, N.Y.: Cornell University Press.

Keller, E. F. 1985. *Reflections on gender and science.* New Haven, Conn.: Yale University Press.

Kofman, S. 1980, 1985. *The enigma of woman: Woman in Freud's writing.* Trans. C. Porter. Ithaca, N.Y.: Cornell University Press.

Le Doeuff, M. 1989, 1991. *Hipparchia's choice: An essay concerning women, philosophy, etc.* Cambridge, Mass., and Oxford: Blackwell.

Mitchell, J. 1974. *Psychoanalysis and feminism.* London: Allen Lane; New York: Pantheon.

Mitchell, J. 2000. *Mad men and madness: Reclaiming hysteria and the effects of sibling relations on the human condition.* London: Allen Lane.

Roudinesco, E. 1986. *Jacques Lacan and Co.: A history of psychoanalysis in France 1925–1985.* Trans. J. Mehlman. Chicago, Ill.: University of Chicago Press. (Also published 1990. London: Free Association.)

Sayers, J. 1986. *Sexual contradictions: Psychology, psychoanalysis, and feminism.* New York and London: Tavistock.

Scheman, N. 1993. *Engenderings: Constructions of knowledge, authority, and privilege.* New York and London: Routledge.

Schneider, M. 1980. *La parole et l'inceste.* Paris: Aubier-Montagne.

Wright, E. 1984. *Psychoanalytic criticism: Theory in practice.* New York and London: Methuen.

Wright, E., ed. 1992. *Feminism and psychoanalysis: A critical dictionary.* Cambridge, Mass., and Oxford: Blackwell.

Margaret Whitford

PSYCHOLOGY: Overview

"Psychology" refers both to an academic discipline and to a profession practiced outside the academy, and psychologists are at work in many countries. Thus, the knowledge and practices of psychology vary widely, as do the roles and images of women in psychology. This article is an overview of different branches of psychology and how they have historically dealt with women, femininity, and gender. Major themes of feminists' work in psychology are outlined.

Psychologies exist in every culture under different guises. This discussion is limited to work called "psychology" by its practitioners, which originated in late-nineteenth-century European medicine and universities. The number of people with formal training in psychology increased dramatically following World War II. During this period, English-language publications predominated in the world psychological literature, as did North American and western European perspectives. Since the mid-1970s, however, work by psychologists with different interests and priorities has become more prominent.

Overview of Psychology: Discipline and Profession

As an academic discipline, psychology is defined as the systematic study (often the *scientific* study) of the behavior, emotions, and motivations of individuals. Psychology as a profession is usually regarded as the use of systematic psychological knowledge to assess, evaluate, test, or diagnose individuals or to offer them counseling or therapeutic services. Both branches of psychology are themselves composed of several more specialized branches.

Academic psychology in most countries, is divided by research traditions and institutional histories into several subfields. These include perception, learning, cognition (often collectively termed "experimental" psychology), comparative and physiological psychology, development (childhood, adolescence, aging), social psychology (including organizational behavior, group dynamics, and intergroup relations), personality psychology, abnormal psychology, psychometrics, individual differences, and general psychology. During the last two decades of the twentieth century, other subfields emerged as well: the psychology of women, cross-cultural psychology, health psychology, environmental psychology, and cognitive science.

Research in some subfields of psychology (intergroup relations, organizational psychology) merges with sociology. Research in others (learning, memory, physiological and comparative psychology) merges with biology under names such as cognitive neuroscience, behavioral neurobiology, evolutionary psychology, and sociobiology. Psychology's distinctive focus is said to be the experiences and actions of the individual.

Many academic psychologists consider themselves scientists, although the importance of this self-identity differs greatly from subfield to subfield and from country to country. Scientific psychologists' stated aim is to discover fundamental principles of human behavior, true in all times and places. For many, the methodological ideal is the laboratory experiment, in which behavior can be observed under controlled conditions. Outside the laboratory, questionnaires, surveys, and scales are widely used. Data that can be treated as discrete units, counted, and analyzed statistically are preferred in most cases, although methods for treating qualitative data are recognized. Outside North America and Britain, and outside the academy, psychologists seem less concerned to make their discipline "scientific" in this sense. Most seek systematic knowledge through research, however.

As professionals in settings outside the academy, psychologists use disciplinary-based and practice-based knowledge to assess, evaluate, test, and diagnose individuals in schools, workplaces, the military, prisons, and hospitals, and to provide mental health services. In most countries, the professional practice of psychology is regulated by law, and a license or other certification is required.

The branches of professional psychology (sometimes called "applied" psychology) are usually identified by institutional setting where the work is done and by the functions psychologists are trained to perform. These include school, community, counseling, testing, industrial-organizational, and clinical psychology. In some countries psychologists are the only professionals certified to administer and interpret psychological tests used for personnel selection and evaluation and for educational placement and to provide vocational and guidance counseling. Clinical psychologists (who usually have a Ph.D., Psy.D., or a Master's degree) offer individualized psychotherapy for persons in psychological distress, as do other professionals providing mental health services, including psychiatrists (who have M.D. degrees) and psychiatric social workers.

Psychology as a field is configured differently in different countries, and the relationship between the state and the practitioner, applied and basic research, and academic and professional spheres varies accordingly. Overviews of the organization, functions, and contents of psychology in different countries, written by psychologists in those countries, can be found in Sexton & Hogan (1992).

Women in Psychology

Since its beginnings in the late nineteenth century, women have been involved in all branches of psychology, as both critics and contributors. From the 1970s to 2000, however, the proportion of advanced students in psychology who are women has increased very rapidly in many countries.

Overall, the proportions of women in academic psychology continue to be lowest in laboratory-based, equipment-dependent fields, those considered to be the most scientific. Women are represented in higher proportions in stereotypically "feminine" fields and in semi-"applied" research areas (such as education), which traditionally were regarded by many academic scientific psychologists as lower in prestige.

In professional psychology, women were and are better represented in branches such as educational, school, and counseling psychology, where the master's degree is often the highest degree required to practice as a psychologist. In branches requiring a higher academic degree, the proportions of women have been increasing during the last two decades of the twentieth century. In most countries, the faculties at universities where professional psychologists are trained continue to be composed primarily of men, however. The gender of the clients or patients with whom professional psychologists work varies with the setting.

Images of Women in Traditional (Prefeminist) Psychological Research, Theory, and Practice

In the various branches of academic psychology prior to 1970, researchers either ignored women altogether or were primarily concerned with a single question: Do women differ from men? In this research psychologists would typically make conclusions about "women" and "men" from studies of relatively small and homogeneous samples of subjects. "Sex differences" were treated as a research topic within the subfield of academic psychology called "individual differences," which also included "race differences."

In the 1930s to the 1950s, psychologists in personality psychology and psychometrics developed questionnaires and projective tests for assessing "masculinity-femininity," which was conceptualized as if it were a cluster of traits inside an individual. Most of the items on M–F scales were personality traits, attitudes, and preferences, and they were very often class- and culture-related. One of the older M–F scales, part of the Minnesota Multiphasic Personality Inventory (MMPI), continues to be widely used in translation in several countries around the world.

Professional psychologists working in applied settings frequently used (and use) such measures to assess, select, diagnose, and counsel individuals in various school and work settings. Psychotherapists tried to help individuals change to fit the images of "normal" masculinity or femininity defined both by these tests and by prevailing psychoanalytic theories, particularly those of Freud.

Feminists and Psychology, 1970–Present

Beginning in the early 1970s, feminists in many countries began to critique and challenge the ways psychology traditionally dealt with women (for example, Burman, 1990). They began to enter the field in greater numbers, and in academic psychology began asking different research questions and using a wider range of methods. The new research questions were shaped partly by how the women's movement in their countries engaged with political questions, and partly by the state of psychology in the academic subfield or branch of professional practice where they worked.

In the Netherlands, for example, a women's movement encompassing many perspectives and a psychology constituted by a rich array of theoretical and methodological traditions have allowed feminists to develop psychological knowledge relevant to feminist politics using resources from psychology and other academic disciplines and from the women's movement (Hermsen and van Lenning, 1991). By contrast, in the United States, the predominance of "scientific" approaches within psychology and of liberalism within the women's movement has meant that much of the work by feminists has retained closer ties to the concepts, methods, and practices of mainstream psychology, with less connection to developments in feminist theory in Europe, Australia, New Zealand, and elsewhere (Denmark and Paludi, 1993; Matlin, 1993).

Working in different countries and from different theoretical perspectives, some feminists in academic psychology have critiqued psychology's traditional views of (and silences concerning) women and have reconceptualized some of its questions and methods. Drawing on work in interdiciplinary feminist theory, a few are challenging psychology's core theoretical and methodological commitment to a social notion of the "individual," rethinking it terms of power and thoroughly social conceptions of subjectivity (for example, Hollway, 1989).

Beginning in the early 1970s, feminists also critiqued psychology as a profession. Some documented the physical and mental abuse of women by psychology and other mental health professions. Others proposed new conceptions of "mental health" and its treatment and analyzed its relation to state-sponsored violence (Kitzinger and Perkins, 1993; Lykes, 1993; Ussher and Nicholson, 1992). Feminists also critiqued psychoanalytic theory, a central theoretical framework in many fields of professional psychology (Sayers, 1986), and developed alternative theories of women's development. As a result, psychology as a profession now addresses important topics it previously ignored (such as rape and other violence against women, AIDS, and women's reproductive health; see Matlin, 1993).

Some of this new work has been published in books, some in English-language journals founded since the 1970s by feminist psychologists, for example, *Women and Therapy, Sex Roles: A Journal of Research, Psychology of Women Quarterly, Feminism and Psychology,* and *European Journal of Women's Studies.* (This and other work is cited in *New Literature on Women: A Bibliography,* a quarterly published in Swedish and English by Göteborg University Library.)

Emerging Trends in Psychology Around the World That Are Relevant to Women's Studies

The subject matter of psychology as a discipline is obviously important for feminism and for women's studies. But feminists inside and outside academic psychology have observed that where psychology defines itself as a science (in a narrow sense), it has been difficult for feminists to make fundamental changes in its contents or methods (Stacey and Thorne, 1985). In this kind of psychology women continue to be treated as objects of knowledge rather than as speaking subjects. In women's studies, then, "psychology" often means some form of psychoanalytic theory or qualitative "sociological" research—*not* research-based knowledge from mainstream, traditional academic psychology.

In the last two decades of the twentieth century, however, the conception of psychology as a "science" in a narrow sense was seriously challenged by feminists and by others. In a related development, the predominance of U.S. psychology in international psychology is also being challenged (Sexton and Hogan, 1992). These trends suggest that during early years of the twenty-first century, the work of feminist psychologists, from many countries, and from all branches of psychology, may become more fully integrated into the interdisciplinary enterprise of women's studies and into the diverse political projects of feminism.

See Also

PSYCHIATRY; PSYCHOANALYSIS; PSYCHOLOGY: COGNITIVE; PSYCHOLOGY: SOCIAL; PSYCHOLOGY: NEUROSCIENCE AND BRAIN RESEARCH; PSYCHOLOGY: PSYCHOPATHOLOGY AND PSYCHOTHERAPY; SCIENCE: OVERVIEW

References and Further Reading

Burman, Erica, ed. 1990. *Feminists and psychological practice.* London: Sage.

Gilligan, Carol. 1993. *In a different voice: Psychological theory and women's development.* 2nd ed. Cambridge, Mass.: Harvard University Press.

Hermsen, Joke J., and Alkeline van Lenning. 1991. *Sharing the difference: Feminist debates in Holland.* Trans. Anne Lavelle. London: Routledge.

Hollway, Wendy. 1989. *Subjectivity and method in psychology: Gender, meaning and science.* London: Sage.

Kitzinger, Celia, and Rachel Perkins. 1993. *Changing our minds: Lesbian feminism and psychology.* New York: New York University Press.

Lykes, M. Brinton. 1993. Human rights and mental health among Latin American women in situations of state-sponsored violence. *Psychology of Women Quarterly* 17(4): 525–544.

Matlin, Margaret W. 1993. *The psychology of women.* 2nd ed. New York: Harcourt, Brace, Jovanovich.

Sayers, Janet. 1986. *Sexual contradictions: Psychology, psychoanalysis and feminism.* London: Tavistock.

Sexton, Virginia Staudt, and John D. Hogan, eds. 1992. *International Psychology: Views from around the World.* Lincoln: University of Nebraska Press.

Stacey, Judith, and Barrie Thorne. 1985. The missing feminist revolution in sociology. *Social Problems* 32: 301–316.

Tiefer, Leonore. 1994. *Sex is not a natural act and other essays.* Boulder, Col.: Westview.

Ussher, Jane, and Paula Nicolson. 1992. *Gender issues in clinical psychology.* London: Routledge.

Wilkinson, Sue, and Celia Kitzinger, eds. 1993. *Heterosexuality: A feminism and psychology reader.* London: Sage.

Mary Brown Parlee

PSYCHOLOGY: Cognitive

Cognitive psychology incorporates many different aspects of how an individual learns, stores, and utilizes information. Cognitive psychologists are interested not only in specialized knowledge, such as how to operate an answering machine or how to play a game, but in knowledge in general. Consider the idea of how an individual is able to put together words to create meaningful sentences. Or what is it that allows a person to remember how to ride a bike? All these activities involve knowledge of one form or another. Most individuals have vast amounts of information that they have learned over time. The questions cognitive psychology focuses on include how we retrieve this information, how it is stored, and, ultimately, how it is used.

Knowledge is stored in the form of mental representations that symbolize external objects or relationships. These mental representations are based on our perception of the external world. Perception does not, however, give us direct knowledge of the world. Our perceptions are determined as much by the way our mind works as by what is really out there (Martindale, 1991). There have been three dominant paradigms, or schools of thought, in twentieth-century U. S. psychology: structuralism, behaviorism, and cognitive psychology.

A primary method used by structuralists was introspection, that is, the attempts to observe one's mental processes as they occur. Because it depends on how theorist's are trained (usually to observe whatever they expect to find) it is seen as significant but unreliable and lacking in supportive empirical evidence (Martindale, 1991). Behaviorism was highly critical of introspection and argues that any observer can objectively measure behavior that can be seen. Therefore, unlike private mental events, behavior is public. Explanations about simplified mental events as the result of behavior were highlighted in Pavlov's conditioning experiments with dogs. New and more challenging questions were identified when more complex processes needed understanding. Language acquisition was one such process that needed more in-depth research. These more complicated processes led to the development of cognitive psychology.

Cognitive psychology represents a return to the historical subject matter of psychology in that it asks questions concerning the nature of the mind. The behaviorist is interested in behavior for its own sake, whereas the cognitive psychologist is interested in behavior only to the extent that it tells something about the mind (Martindale, 1991). The desire to understand the inner working of the mind is an important motivation for the study of cognitive psychology. Many of the issues we face come from the inability to effectively deal with the cognitive demands made on us. These issues are becoming more complicated, given the technological revolution, the information explosion, and the age of the Internet.

Cognitive psychology emerged in the two decades between 1950 and 1970 (Anderson, 1995). The first research was on human performance and was given a great boost during World War II. Practical information was badly needed to train soldiers to use sophisticated equipment and to deal with problems such as the breakdown of attention. After the war, psychologists developed ideas regarding perception and attention. The concept of information processing became the dominant viewpoint. In addition, the concept of artificial intelligence as it relates to computers was developed. Although the direct influence on cognitive psychology was minimal, it did lead to many new concepts that could be applied to psychological theories focused on how the mind works. The most important was the liberation of many theorists from inhibitions and misconceptions about analyzing our own intelligence. Last, analysis of the structure of language, headed by Noam Chomsky in the 1950s, helped to enable cognitive psychologists to explain the complexities of learning to talk.

The study of cognitive psychology encompasses a vast amount of information, most of which cannot be adequately explained in this article. It is important to note, however, that included in the study of the way the mind works are topic areas such as perception, attention, performance, meaning-based knowledge representations, memory (including encoding, storage, retention and retrieval), problem solving, development of expertise, reasoning, decision making, language structure, comprehension, and individual differences. Each topic, whether alone or in conjunction with other topics, could be the focus of countless books or articles. Of practical interest to many individuals is how cognitive theories have shaped psychology, and, therefore, made significant contributions to the development of clinical interventions. As a way to apply cognitive theory, psychotherapy that targets cognition is the focus of this article. Common clinical issues for women include depression, anxiety, eating disorders, substance abuse, posttraumatic stress, marital conflict, and parenting. Treatment plans that target maladaptive cognitions have been implemented for the conditions mentioned above and more. The principles of cognitive change have received considerable empirical validation and have become central to cognitive and cognitive-behavioral therapy.

As women have become a more visible in the world of employment, their roles have multiplied. Wearing many different hats has improved the quality and meaning of life for many women. Along with a more fulfilling life comes more pressure, more stress, and, in some cases, an increased vulnerability to internal and external forces that can lead to depression, anxiety, and even worse. Many times, women internalize the negative messages all around them and turn these messages into tightly held beliefs that will govern their daily lives. Cognitive therapy is one type of intervention that has provided many individuals with symptom relief, education about their situation or condition, coping tools, and relapse-prevention strategies.

The principle of cognitive therapy is that individuals develop and maintain beliefs about themselves as they mature. Individuals view themselves, the world, and the future in light of these beliefs. The beliefs organize themselves around important themes in a person's life and are reflected in the self-talk in which individuals engage. For example, a woman may have the deep-seated belief that she is incompetent. This may be reflected in statements she makes about herself as a friend, spouse, mother, employee, and so on. Often, these self-statements may be categorized around the need to be perfect or the need to obtain approval by others (Beck, Rush, Shaw, and Emery, 1979).

The goal of cognitive therapy is to change the beliefs that the individual holds about herself. A part of the therapy process will be to get the individual to see how she talks to herself (self-statements) around the themes identified and how she, in that process, attributes responsibility to positive and negative events (Martindale, 1991). The primary goal, however, remains the changing of the individual's basic beliefs rather than just changing the self-statements associated with those beliefs. One way to change the connections between self-statements and beliefs is the identification and modification of dysfunctional and distorted assumptions the client makes about herself.

According to Beck et al. (1979), there are a variety of cognitive distortions common in individuals who are depressed and anxious. These include overgeneralizing (if something is true in one case, it applies in all cases), selective abstraction (focus on negative only), catastrophizing (always think the worst will happen), dichotomous thinking (everything is seen as all good or all bad), and personalization (attention is always focused on the self, and all misfortune is attributed to the self). Cognitive therapy works to correct these types of maladaptive assumptions and in their place, to provide coping strategies that will improve daily functioning overall.

The process of change in cognitive therapy initially involves the use of behavioral strategies to increase activities, especially those that give an individual a sense of mastery or pleasure. The cognitive procedures include: (1) identification of dysfunctional and distorted cognitions and realization that they produce negative feelings and maladaptive behaviors; (2) self-monitoring of negative thoughts, or self-talk; (3) identification of the relationship of thoughts to underlying beliefs and to feelings; (4) identification of alternative (functional and nondistorted) thinking patterns; and (5) hypothesis testing regarding the validity of the person's basic assumptions about self, world, and future (Craighead, Craighead, Kazdin, and Mahoney, 1994).

Cognitive therapy is an intensive collaborative endeavor of the therapist and client as a team, in order to agree on the definition of the cognitive distortions that require modification. Clients learn to identify explicitly the thoughts, assumptions, and beliefs that they hold about themselves, the world, and the future, and then to collect data to test the validity of those cognitions (Craighead et al., 1994). Thus, the therapist is teaching the client to be her own therapist. Strategies to undo distorted thinking are made available in session (to learn and then practice) and, ultimately, the client is encouraged to experiment out in the world with her new way of thinking.

See Also

MENTAL HEALTH; PSYCHIATRY; PSYCHOLOGY: OVERVIEW; PSYCHOLOGY: NEUROSCIENCE AND BRAIN RESEARCH; PSYCHOLOGY: PSYCHOMETRICS; PSYCHOLOGY: SOCIAL; PSYCHOLOGY: PSYCHOPATHOLOGY AND PSYCHOTHERAPY; SCIENCE: FEMINIST CRITIQUES; STRESS

References and Further Reading

Anderson, J. R. 1995. *Cognitive psychology and its implications.* New York: Freeman.

Beck, A. T., A. J. Rush, B. F. Shaw, and G. Emery. 1979. *Cognitive therapy of depression.* New York: Guilford.

Craighead, L. W., W. E. Craighead, A. E. Kazdin, and M. J. Mahoney. 1994. *Cognitive and behavioral interventions: An empirical approach to mental health problems.* Needham Heights, Mass.: Allyn and Bacon.

Martindale, C. 1991. *Cognitive psychology: A neural-network approach.* Belmont, Calif.: Wadsworth.

Gloria Pedroza

PSYCHOLOGY: Developmental

Developmental psychology is the psychological discipline that studies the lifelong process of human change. Change is considered to be any qualitative or quantitative modification in structure or function. Examples would be a child's babbling turning to speaking, moving from adolescence to adulthood, or changing from concrete to abstract thinking. G. S. Hall first described this area of study around the beginning of the twentieth century. Hall envisioned this study to consider the entire life span of humans, although it has historically focused most specifically on child development. In order to clarify this field of study, several subdisciplines have been advanced, such as gerontology (the study of aging) and adolescent psychology, so that it does encompass the totality of the human life span.

Psychological Development

Psychological development is understood to encompass the changes in psychic (mind) structures, the growing capacity for complex intrapsychic life together with the ability for thought and fantasy, and the emergence of psychopathology (Tyson and Tyson, 1990). The most famous psychologist in this area is Sigmund Freud, who proposed psychosexual stages to identify maturational points for the human psyche. Freud considered that an individual progressed through stages and that the impetus for the movement through stages was biological maturity. The first stage in Freud's model is the oral stage (0–1 year), in which the infant's libidinal or pleasure (eros) drive is satisfied by stimulation of the mouth through sucking. This stage gives way to the anal stage (1–3 years), when the child is stimulated by the tension and discharge states of bladder and bowels. Freud suggested that emotions such as anxiety and guilt emerge in this stage as the child attempts to navigate in the world from a more verbal and mobile position. The child may be subjected to a chorus of "No's" from her caregivers, as well as conflicts between her desires and those of her caregivers. Freud argued that the successful movement through these stages led to the development of an intact internal psychological structure and an ability to manage the conflicts of life in a healthy manner.

The most controversial—from a feminist perspective—of Freud's stages is the third, infant genital or phallic (3–5 years). The child is aware of her own genital area and obtains elemental pleasure from this erotogenic zone. Freud termed the conflict of this period oedipal, and focused his writing on the boy's ability to deal with a conflict between his love for his mother and his fear of his father (castration anxiety). The proper resolution of this period would see the boy identifying with his father and maintaining a loving relationship with his mother. Because of the outcome of this conflict, Freud suggested that the superego developed during this stage and the boy was able to develop a conscience or moral sense. Freud attempted to develop the concept of penis envy as a parallel notion of women's development. Freud initially believed that all women had a repressed wish to possess a penis. This wish defined the conflict for women during this developmental period. This characterization of women has been vigorously criticized, and today few take this idea seriously (Greenberg, 1991). Eventually, Freud admitted that he did not know how to explain females' experience of this period. Freud wanted to develop a unified theory of psychological development but was aware of the contradictions his model posed for girls. Freud eventually concluded that the strength and persistence of a girl's attachment to her mother was a developmental difference between the sexes. Freud deemed this difference to be a developmental failure (Gilligan, 1993). Freud seemed unable to conceive of a different theory, so his limited theoretical model began a "problem" in women's development. From the earliest periods of theorizing about psychological development women's tendency to define their sense of self in relation to others was seen as abnormal against the template of male dominance.

Freud's psychosexual development ended with the genital stage (starting in adolescence) and did not account for further development through the life span. Erik Erikson was among the first to suggest additional stages and developmental conflicts throughout the life span. Erikson, in contrast to Freud, considered that not only drives are important to human development, but also the individual's interpretation of those drives. Erikson was somewhat more focused on a person's interaction with others (1963). Erikson's idea was that a human life was successful if initial trust in self and others was achieved early in the life cycle (infancy) and if one's sense of the life lived was good just as it was (old age). Erikson attempted to theorize about the differences between male and female development. He suggested that there were substantial differences in how women's egos were structured and function, but he did not see this as a developmental problem. Although Erikson's theory does attempt to explain female development, he continues to view male development as the norm. Here again separation is seen as good development and attachments (social relations) are seen as developmental handicaps.

Women Theorists and Attachment Theory

It is important to note that influential early twentieth-century female theorists such as Anna Freud and Margaret Mahler also saw individuation or separation as a critical component in successful development. For Margaret Mahler, a critical period of early childhood development was the period she described as individuation-separation. During this period, the infant individuates, which means she develops an intrapsychic sense of "I am" or a sense of being. The infant also separates, and Mahler viewed this as developing an internal sense of separateness from the mother or a clear psychological representation of self as different from other people. For Mahler, this stage allows the human infant to begin to view herself as a distinct individual but an individual who also exists in relationship with others. It has been established through brain-scanning technology that both intimate relationships with the mother and separation from her are critical to normal development (Schore, 1994). This mother–child interaction depends on both individuals. The mother provides emotional support and containment for the child and the child performs behaviors (social releasers) such as crying or clinging that evoke the care behavior of the mother.

The interactional pattern between mother (caregiver) and infant has been the focus of much research over the past 50 years. John Bowlby—and others, such as Melanie Klein and David Winnicott—suggested that relationships play a critical role in psychological development. Bowlby saw attachment as biologically based, because the human infant requires protection to survive within the environment. Bowlby also suggested that attachment is a human need that exists across the life span, and, therefore, relationships can be best understood in terms of attachment. Much of the current research concerning attachment patterns is focused on how children form relationships and how these patterns of secure or insecure attachment predispose the child to healthy or abnormal patterns of adult relationships. Mary Ainsworth, a colleague of Bowlby, developed a research methodology—the "strange situation"—for observing the behavior of young children toward strangers who enter a room as well as the children's reactions to their mothers' leaving and returning. From these observations, Ainsworth was able to categorize several styles of secure (normal) and insecure (problematic) attachment. Within this body of work, women's relational or attachment patterns are not viewed as "pathological" because of their sex. They are viewed as pathological only if they reflect insecure patterns. These insecure patterns are the same for both men and women. As the importance of attachment theory continues to grow, women's innate tendencies may become the "norm" from which deviance is seen as leading to psychopathology.

Cognitive Development

Another important milestone in developmental psychology was the work of Jean Piaget. Piaget had a more cognitive focus and suggested that mental development occurred through a series of stages. Each stage is marked by the acquisition of a new cognitive capacity and the accommodation of this capacity causes disequilibrium and emotional vulnerability. Piaget was also interested in how a child develops a moral sense. He observed how children played games and followed rules and suggested that moral development advances through the mutual give-and-take within a game or a peer relation. Piaget considered the moral development of girls to be less than boys because of girls' tendency to make exceptions, foster innovations, and display tolerance toward rules. Piaget found this disturbing and equated normal moral development with the development demonstrated by boys. Here again, patterns of female behavior that should be seen as strengths that foster relational play are labeled as "substandard" against the template of male-dominated theories. Perhaps even more condescending to women was the work of Lawrence Kohlberg, who posited six stages of moral judgment that developed from childhood through adulthood. Kohlberg called this a unified theory of development, even though none of his test subjects were women. He suggested that women's moral development is adequate for life within the home, but inadequate unless they enter traditional male activity (Gilligan, 1993).

Life Span and Women's Perspectives

The process of psychological development involves the integration of a complex array of biological, behavioral and psychological components. Change and flexibility that allow the individual to take in and react to the ever-changing demands of her world mark this process throughout the life span. The history of this developmental theory can be seen as attempting to understand and describe the course of psychological development by emphasizing male development. This emphasis has viewed the male as normal and, by comparison, the female as abnormal, when she demonstrates different qualities and characteristics. As the emphasis of research changes to explore the critical contributions and unique attributes of women, their development will be seen from a more "normal" perspective and the deviations from male development then become nothing other than different. As Carol Gilligan suggests, once there is a focus on the lives of women, theorists will begin to "encompass the experiences of both sexes" (1993: 23). This should lead to a more intricate and satisfying understanding of human psychological development.

See Also

LIFE CYCLE; PSYCHIATRY, PSYCHOLOGY: COGNITIVE; PSYCHOLOGY: OVERVIEW; PSYCHOLOGY: SOCIAL; PSYCHOPATHOLOGY AND PSYCHOTHERAPY

References and Further Reading

Bowlby, J. 1958. The nature of a child's tie to his mother. *International Journal of Psycho-Analysis* 39: 350–375.

Cassidy, J., and Shaver, P. R., eds. 1999. *Handbook of attachment: Theory, research, and clinical applications.* New York: Guilford.

Developmental psychology. <www.mental help.net>.

Erikson, E. 1963. *Childhood and society.* New York: Norton.

Freud, S. 1905. *Three essays on the theory of sexuality.* Vol. VII. In J. Strachey, ed. and trans. (1961), *The standard edition of the complete psychological works of Sigmund Freud,* 7 and 125. London: Hogarth.

Gilligan, C. 1993. *In a different voice: Psychological theory and women's development.* Cambridge, Mass.: Harvard University Press.

Greenberg, J. 1991. *Oedipus and beyond.* Cambridge, Mass.: Harvard University Press.

Piaget, J. 1965. *The moral development of the child.* New York: Free Press.

Psychology resources. <www.cambridge.edu/psychology.html>.

Schore, A. N. 1994. *Affect regulation and the origin of the self.* Hillsdale, N.J.: Erlbaum.

Siegel, D. J. 1999. *The developing mind: Toward a neurobiology of interpersonal experience.* New York: Guilford.

Tyson, P., and R. L. Tyson. 1990. *Psychoanalytic theories of development.* New Haven, Conn.: Yale University Press.

Joan E. Huebl

PSYCHOLOGY: Neuroscience and Brain Research

Neuroscience is the study of brain function and the underlying neural structures that govern behavior. Neuropsychology is a discipline within physiological psychology that is specifically interested in identifying and understanding the interrelationships between neurological processes and behavior. Among the major areas that are the focus of ongoing research are cognition, memory, and affect or emotions.

Research in this area is a new and emerging discipline. Scientifically based studies of how the female brain affects women's behavior do not yet exist outside the male paradigms that have defined scientific research throughout history. There is some valid evidence from primate research (Allman, 2000) that estrogen has a protective effect on the brain's hippocampal neurons and serotonergic systems (both of which are involved in the body's stress responses and survival rates), but the data have not yet been extrapolated to human social contexts in any meaningful way. The evolutionary biologist Alison Jolly (1997) suggests that building bridges between biology, anthropology, and women's studies will be necessary before the female brain and female intelligence can be properly understood.

Brain and Mind

Two terms that often give rise to some confusion within this field are *brain* and *mind.* Although William James equated the brain with the mind, more recent research has suggested that these are separate ideas. The brain is made up of central nervous structures within the skull. The brain exists, physically, and can be subjected to rigorous scientific study. In contrast, the mind has long been understood as a metaphysical construct or hypothesis. It is thought to encompass the infinite interactions within the brain that are explanations for psychological data and mental processes. These processes are generally studied by psychologists as perception and cognition.

In *Project for a Scientific Psychology (1895),* Sigmund Freud started out to explain mental processes in terms of the physiological events taking place in the brain. He soon discovered that neuroscience at the end of the nineteenth century was not sophisticated enough to prove or disprove his ideas. Freud believed that the mind was an integral part of the body and used the term *mind* to refer to all the conscious and unconscious mental experiences of a human being. Even though many mental processes can be traced through neuronal activity in the brain, these events do not provide adequate explanations of mental phenomena. For example, being able to determine that the *hippocampus* is critical to long-term memory and to watch this area being activated through Positron-emission tomography (PET) scanning cannot tell the observer anything about the content of the memory.

Mental processes take on their own uniqueness that arises from the structure or pattern of an individual human's brain. Although each component part is necessary to the process, the whole cannot be fully explained as the sum of the parts. As the Nobel laureate Roger Sperry suggests, "A mental process is like a wheel rolling downhill—the rolling is determined by the 'overall system properties' of the wheel, not by the atoms and molecules of which it is made" (quoted in Hunt, 1993). It is the human mind that makes each individual unique with her own memories, thoughts, and patterns of cognition. Researchers and theorists remain hard at work on the "mind–brain" problem, searching for more definitive descriptions of how the mind is related to the brain.

Brain Structure

The brain is a highly complex system of interconnected and specialized structures. The "primitive" brain or hindbrain controls the physiological condition of the body—for example, heart rate, temperature, or breathing—through the medulla oblongata. States of arousal or alertness, commonly known as "fight or flight reflexes," are also mediated through this portion of the brain (reticular formation and raphe system). One of the largest structures in this area of the brain is the cerebellum, which plays a role in controlling movement as well as the speed and skill of acquiring language and cognition. These systems lie at the base of the skull and at the top of the spinal column.

The "higher" structures or forebrain are the largest portion of the human brain. Some of these structures are cerebral cortex, limbic system, hypothalamus, thalamus, and hippocampus. These structures are involved in more sophisticated processing functions such as thinking, reasoning, or perceiving. These structures are known to play a role in memory and sensory input. For example, the limbic system is specifically thought to be linked intricately to emotional and motivational behavior. This structure appears to integrate a wide range of processes such as the interpretation of social experiences, the assessment of meaning, and the regulation of emotions.

The brain functions through its intricate interconnectivity. There are over one hundred billion neurons within the human brain that are collectively over two million miles long (Siegel, 1999). Each neuron has, on average, 10,000 connections that link it to other neurons. When these numbers are considered, there are thought to be over one million billion connections within the human brain, making it the most complex structure known to humans (Green et al., 1998). And it is within these intricate connections that the human mind exists.

It is known that the brain develops as a result of interactional experiences. Experiences will shape the activity of the brain throughout life because the brain remains extremely flexible. It is thought, however, that early life experiences are critical for organizing how brain structures evolve. At birth, the brain is the most undifferentiated organ in the human body. The brain components differentiate through environmental influence. The brain develops by pruning (parcellation) connections that are not stimulated. It can be argued, therefore, that rich and stimulating early experiences will contribute to more complex development. This appears to be particularly relevant, for instance, to the development of emotional awareness and interpersonal relationship abilities (Schore, 1994).

Women's Brain

Within the human brain there are several structural differences between men and women. The corpus callusum, a band of tissue that allows the two hemispheres of the brain to communicate, is generally larger in women than in men. The anterior commisure—another, more primitive, connection between the hemispheres—is also larger. This area is thought to link the unconscious areas of the hemispheres. These structures may be one reason women are more aware of emotions, because they provide a larger bandwidth for women to communicate information between the emotional right hemisphere and the logical and linguistic left hemisphere. These larger connections also may facilitate women's ability to use more emotion in their speech and thinking (Carter, 1999). This also may account for the different way in which women and men approach problems. Women appear to utilize both hemispheres of their brain in problem solving, which may suggest that women take a broader view of life.

Several portions of the hypothalamus differ in size between men and women. One portion of the medial preoptic nucleus is two to three times larger in males than in females. This area is thought to be responsible for male-typical sexual behavior. The presence of testosterone, a male hormone or androgen, is critical for the development of the hypothalamus. But how testosterone effects the hypothalamus is very surprising. After testosterone enters a neuron, it is converted to estradiol, the female hormone or estrogen. Unless testosterone is converted to estradiol within a neuron, it will not have a male organizing effect, for example, the long-lasting effect of a hormone that is present during a critical early developmental period, on the hypothalamus. Women who were exposed to elevated testosterone levels during prenatal development tend to spend more time than most other girls playing with traditional "boys' toys" (Kalat, 1995), and show evidence of larger than normal medial preoptic nucleii.

Women tend to retain their brain tissue longer and in greater quantities than do men. Men lose tissue in the frontal and temporal lobes, brain areas that are known to affect thinking and feeling. Women tend to lose tissue in the hippocampus and parietal areas that are associated with memory and visuospatial abilities (Carter, 1999).

When groups of women and men are compared on cognitive tasks, women demonstrate several abilities that differ from men's. Women score better than men on some language tasks and develop language at a faster rate. Women score better than men do on tests that measure social judgment, empathy, and cooperation. Typically women are better at generating ideas. Women also have a much lower rate of developmental dysphasia (disruption of speech caused by brain irregularities).

Women are faster than men on activities involving fine motor control (Kimura, 1999). Although men are better than women at spatial skills such as image rotation and targeting, women show greater skills at recalling positions of objects in an array and at remembering landmarks along a route. They also are superior in their ability to make rapid comparisons, a process known as perceptual speed. As would be expected, women are generally better than men at interpreting facial and body expressions. These differences are thought to be the result of both genetic and endocrine processes.

The intricacies of how and why female and male brains evolve in different manners has not yet been fully explored. It should be noted that these are simple differences, but nevertheless they are differences that definitely seem to have an impact on the ways women and men think and how they perceive information.

See Also

BIOLOGICAL DETERMINISM; DIFFERENCE I; DIFFERENCE II; ESSENTIALISM; MENTAL HEALTH I; MENTAL HEALTH II; PSYCHOLOGY: COGNITIVE; PSYCHOLOGY: OVERVIEW; PSYCHOLOGY: PSYCHOMETRICS

References and Further Reading

Allman, John. 2000. *Evolving brains.* New York: Scientific American Library.

Carter, R. 1999. *Mapping the mind.* Berkeley: University of California Press.

Green, T., S. F. Nememann, and J. E. Gusella. 1998. Molecular neurobiology and genetics: Investigation of neural function and dysfunction. *Neuron* 20: 427–444.

Hunt, M. 1993. *The story of psychology.* New York: Doubleday.

Jolly, Allison. 1997. Social intelligence and sexual reproduction: Evolutionary strategies. In Mary Ellen Morbeck, Alison Galloway, and Adrienne L. Zihlman, eds., *The evolving female: A life-history perspective,* 262–269. Princeton, N.J.: Princeton University Press.

Kalat, J. W. 1995. *Biological psychology.* 5th ed. Pacific Grove, Calif.: Brooks/Cole.

Kimura, D. 1999. *Sex and cognition.* Cambridge, Mass.: MIT Press.

Schore, A. N. 1994. *Affect regulation and the origin of the self.* Hillsdale, N.J.: Erlbaum.

Siegel, D. J. 1999. *The developing mind: Toward a neurobiology of interpersonal experience.* New York: Guilford.

Joan E. Huebl

PSYCHOLOGY: Personality Research

Personality refers to the patterns of behaviors, feelings, thoughts, and goals that characterize individual persons. An important goal of personality research is to identify ways to describe characteristic patterns. These characteristic patterns can be used to portray how people respond to situations and to examine whether there are continuities over time in how people behave, think, and feel.

The belief that there are stable patterns of actions, emotions, and motives that are different for men and women is common in many societies. At one time it was believed that differences between men's and women's personalities could be characterized along a single unipolar dimension referred to as masculinity–femininity. For example, in industrialized societies men were believed to be independent and competitive, and women were believed to be gentle and helpful to others. Revisions to this model have emphasized that masculinity and femininity are not opposites. Rather, masculinity and femininity are separate and independent dimensions, and an individual's position on one dimension does not necessarily predict the opposite level on the other dimension. For example, in one combination, known as androgyny, men and women can be both highly masculine and highly feminine, as reflected in characteristics such as independence, autonomy, nurturance, and consideration (Bem, 1974).

There is further complexity to the notions of masculinity and femininity. Researchers have proposed that it is not even sufficient to characterize differences between men and women as occurring along two dimensions. There is evidence that masculinity and femininity are multilayered, and individuals' positions on the different layers can vary (Koestner and Aubé, 1995; Spence, 1993). Three layers that are often distinguished are people's traits, their behaviors, and their interests. So, for example, a woman could be very independent (a masculine trait) in the occupation of dietician (a feminine interest) while deciding which investments to make with her earnings (masculine behavior). Moreover, the differences between men and women are not constant across situations; differences between men and women are conditional on the roles and situations in which individuals find themselves (Deaux and Major, 1987).

Contemporary personality researchers have reframed masculinity and femininity as the broader terms known as *agency* and *communion* (see, for example, Helgeson, 1994), which fit better into contemporary theories concerning the organization of interpersonal behavior (Moskowitz, 1994; Wiggins, 1991). In this model, dominant–submissive qualities (the agentic dimension) are independent from agreeable–quarrelsome qualities (the communal dimension).

There are a variety of theories to explain sex differences in personality. One set of theories based on evolutionary arguments proposes that sex differences in behavior are innate and based on inherited characteristics. Through evolution, male and female mammals, including humans, have evolved different adaptive strategies to meet the challenges posed by different ecological niches (see Buss and Kenrick, 1998).

Alternative theories have argued for the learned basis of sex differences. One theory of learned differences (Eagly, 1987; Eagly et al., in press) emphasizes the different expectations that societies have for men and women (gender roles). In many societies, gender roles are conditioned on the functions of men as income earners and women as caretakers. Consequently, men are often assertive and independent in response to expectations about their work roles, whereas women display nurturant and agreeable behaviors that facilitate caring for others. Personality differences between men and women are then not innate (that is, a function of different biologies) but rather a function of the different roles that men and women typically occupy. To the extent that men and women occupy similar roles, their behavior should be more similar. For example, Moskowitz and her associates (1994) compared the behavior of men and women in similar social roles at work. When men and women were in supervisory roles, their behavior was similarly dominant. When men and women were in the role of supervisee, their behavior was similarly submissive.

There are trends within industrialized countries (for example, more women in the workplace, women entering professions traditionally occupied by men) that suggest that women's and men's behavior, at least in workplace roles, may become more similar over time. Women are describing themselves as more agentic then they described themselves in previous decades.

See Also

ANDROGYNY; DIFFERENCE I; DIFFERENCE II; ESSENTIALISM; FEMININITY; MASCULINITY; NATURE-NURTURE DEBATE; PSYCHOLOGY: SOCIAL

References and Further Reading

Bem, Sandra Lipsitz. 1974. The measurement of psychological androgyny. *Journal of Consulting and Clinical Psychology* 42(2): 155–162.

Buss, David M., and Douglas T. Kenrick. 1998. Evolutionary social psychology. In Daniel T. Gilbert, Susan T. Fiske, and Gordon Lindzey, eds., *The handbook of social psychology,* Vol. 2, 982–1026. Boston: McGraw-Hill.

Deaux, Kay, and Brenda Major. 1987. Putting gender into context: An interactive model of gender-related behavior. *Psychological Review* 94(3): 369–389.

Eagly, Alice H. 1987. *Sex differences in social behavior: A social-role interpretation.* Hillsdale, N.J.: Erlbaum.

———, Wendy Wood, and Amanda Diekman. In press. Social role theory of sex differences and similarities: A current appraisal. In T. Eckes and H. M. Trautner, eds. *The developmental social psychology of gender.* Mahwah, N.J.: Erlbaum.

Helgeson, Vicki S. 1994. Relation of agency and communion to well-being: Evidence and potential explanations. *Psychological Bulletin* 116(3): 412–428.

Koestner, Richard, and Jennifer Aubé. 1995. A multifactorial approach to the study of gender characteristics. *Journal of Personality* 63(3): 681–710.

Moskowitz, D. S. 1994. Cross-situational generality and the interpersonal circumplex. *Journal of Personality and Social Psychology* 66(5): 921–933.

———, Eun Jung Suh, and Julie Desaulniers. 1994. Situational influences on gender differences in agency and communion. *Journal of Personality and Social Psychology* 66(4): 753–761.

Spence, Janet. 1993. Gender-related traits and gender ideology. *Journal of Personality and Social Psychology* 64(4): 624–635.

Wiggins, Jerry S. 1991. Agency and communion as conceptual coordinates for the understanding and measurement of interpersonal behavior. In William M. Grove and Dante Cicchetti, eds., *Thinking clearly about psychology,* 89–113. Minneapolis: University of Minnesota Press.

Debbie S. Moskowitz

PSYCHOLOGY: Psychometrics

Psychometrics is the measurement of psychological characteristics such as intelligence, aptitude, and anxiety. The relationship between psychometrics and gender was ambiguous from the beginning (Ryan, 1999). Using a scientific theory that assumed brain size was related to intelligence and precise measurements of brain size and cranial volume, phrenologists concluded that since females had smaller brains than males, females were different from males and less intelligent. The gender "differences" model had arrived.

Long after phrenology was discredited, the legacy of this first gender "differences" model has continued to color research in this area (Ryan, 1999). When Louis Terman, an early proponent of intelligence testing, attempted to standardize a U.S. version of the Stanford-Binet IQ (intelligence quotient) in 1916, he found that females scored higher than males (Mercer, 1989). Concluding that these gender differences were an error, Terman addressed this issue in the 1937 revision of the test. By eliminating several verbal items that favored females and replacing them with nonverbal items that were easier for males, the differences between males and females in test performance were reduced. Although ethnic differences were already recognized, Terman also found differences in IQ based on soioeconomic status and geographical location. Nevertheless, no efforts were made to balance the test items; these differences in IQ scores were considered genuine differences in performance.

Psychometrics continues to be fundamentally grounded by the notion that the inferences from a single interpretation of test results—whether the test is an aptitude battery, intelligence test, or anxiety measure—are valid. That the meaning and the use of tests may vary substantially by social class, gender, ethnicity, and interactions among these characteristics and others remains unacknowledged. Instead, within context of test bias, the single interpretation is warranted by the application of different technical procedures. Although these procedures are mathematically complex, there are limitations. The procedures cannot address issues of fairness and tend to maintain the status quo. For example, while women do score substantially lower on the mathematics portion of the Scholastic Aptitude Test (SAT), performance on the SAT-M underpredicts females' performance in college math courses in comparison with men, in spite of the fact that the SAT is one of the most technically sound tests available (Wainer and Steinberg, 1992).

The consequences of a single interpretation of the SAT-M test results are significant. Women receive fewer scholarships than men, are less likely to be admitted to highly regarded universities, and pursue careers involving mathematics and science less often (Linn and Kessel, 1996; Willingham and Cole, 1997).

Several remedies are proposed. First, recognize that gender "differences" are not fixed; instead, differences are located within the context of power and resources (Tavris, 1993). Second, acknowledge the position of values and social relations within the psychometric tradition; this makes multiple or alternative interpretations of test results and use possible. Third, the presence of women in testing has expanded the study of gender and psychometrics. Recruiting people of diverse backgrounds to work in psychometrics is essential for continued progress (Madaus, 1994).

See Also

EXAMINATIONS AND ASSESSMENT; EXPERIMENTS ON WOMEN; PSYCHOLOGY: NEUROSCIENCE AND BRAIN RESEARCH; SCIENCE: TECHNOLOGICAL AND SCIENTIFIC RESEARCH

References and Further Reading

Linn, Marcia, and Catherine Kessel. 1996. Participation in mathematics courses and careers: Climate, grades, and entrance exams. *Educational measurement: Issues and practices.*

Madaus, George. 1994. A technological and historical consideration of equity issues associated with proposals to change the nation's testing policy. *Harvard Educational Review* 64(1): 76–95.

Mercer, Jane. 1989. Alternative paradigms for assessment in a pluralistic society. In James A. Banks and Cherry McGee Banks, eds., *Multicultural education: Issues and perspectives,* 289–303. Boston: Allyn and Bacon.

Ryan, K. E. 1999. Revisiting gender and achievement. *Educational Researcher* 28(5): 30–32.

Tavris, Carol. 1993. The mismeasure of woman. *Feminism and Psychology* 3(2): 149–68.

Wainer, Howard, and Linda Steinberg. 1992. Sex differences in performance on the mathematics section of the Scholastic Aptitude Test: A bidirectional validity study. *Harvard Educational Review* 62: 323–26.

Willingham, W., and N. Cole. 1997. *Gender and fair assessment.* Mahwah, N.J.: Erlbaum.

Katherine Ryan

PSYCHOLOGY: Psychopathology and Psychotherapy

The modern fields of clinical psychology and psychiatry have their roots in the late nineteenth and early twentieth century. Psychiatry was developed by the medical profession in the service of administering the newly founded mental hospitals in the late 1900s. The province of its practitioners was inpatient diagnosis and treatment. Psychology, on the other hand, owes its existence to the development of standardized assessment techniques, particularly those used to assess the intellectual capacities of newly arrived immigrants to Ellis Island in New York City at the end of the nineteenth century and extending to the evaluation of military personnel during the two world wars. In their own way, each was involved from inception in defining and discovering the presence of psychological deficits or pathology. Social work, the third major profession involved with the practice of psychotherapy, had a different beginning, although at the same historical moment, and can also trace its origins in the United States to the settlement of early immigrants.

No one theorist or practitioner is more responsible for the emphasis on psychopathology in these fields than Sigmund Freud. As a physician, he conceptualized psychological problems according to a medical model or model of pathology. Such a model is based on the assumption that there is an underlying disease process that can be diagnosed successfully by the presence of particular clusters of symptoms. Psychological illness then is analogous to physical illness and problems are seen as symptomatic of an underlying pathology that must be diagnosed and then treated or cured.

Since Freud's time, several models not based in disease or pathology have influenced ideas about psychotherapeutic treatment, including the humanist, the behavioral or behavioral-cognitive, and the family systems approaches. Perhaps none has been as critical of the psychoanalytic approach as feminist psychology, particularly in its early years in the late 1960s and early 1970s.

Beginnings of Feminist Psychology

With the rebirth of feminism in the United States and western Europe, women began to enter academic disciplines from which they had previously been excluded—clinical psychology and psychiatry prominent among them. Chesler (1972), in her groundbreaking critique of the masculine bias in these fields, estimated that, during the decade of the 1960s, 88 percent of all psychiatrists and clinical psychologists were men and the overwhelming majority of clients and patients were women. As a result, both theory and practice tended to define male psychology as the norm and, as a result, to misconstrue and pathologize women's psychology.

The feminist psychologists and psychiatrists entering these fields produced the most extensive and profound critique of the theory and practice of psychotherapy in its history. One of the most important studies was that of Broverman and her colleagues, who conducted a study in which psychiatrists, psychologists, and social workers were asked to select the qualities that they believed described a healthy adult, an adult male, and an adult female. Male and female clinicians alike described the adult male much as they described the healthy adult. Their description of the adult female was nearly opposite. In the eyes of these therapists, then, it was seemingly impossible to be both a healthy adult and an adult female.

This study and many others began to reveal the profound and previously invisible gender bias in the theory and practice of psychotherapy. Other major issues that were examined for their bias included the prevalent belief, introduced by Freud, that women experienced two kinds of orgasm. The results of research by Masters and Johnson established empirically that this was erroneous. The widely held belief that female psychology was inherently masochistic and hysterical—so that, for example, women who were raped or otherwise abused either benefited from or were even psychologically complicit in their own abuse—were exposed as erroneous and damaging to the very population that psychotherapy was supposed to be serving. The widespread use of medication, hospitalization, and even electroconvulsive shock therapy on women who did not conform to gender role expectations was also exposed and documented.

For the first time, systematic studies of the prevalence of rape, battering, and incest were conducted. Feminist theorists and practitioners began to develop models that named and made visible the previously invisible abuses to which girls and women were subjected and to develop appropriate treatment programs at professional and grassroots levels. These programs included rape crisis centers, shelters for battered women, and treatment programs for survivors of physical and sexual abuse.

Perhaps the earliest attempt by feminists to develop a positive, nonsexist model of personality resulted in the idea of the androgynous individual who supposedly combined stereotypical feminine and masculine qualities. This model was soon rejected for many reasons, prominent among which was its overly simple embracing of stereotypic masculine and feminine qualities, as if they did not change in different contexts and situations. It was nevertheless the first of several important steps that have led to the current conceptualization of a complex and culturally contextualized psychology.

Feminist Psychology in Practice

In these early years, the first groups of feminist therapists began to meet and to form collectives to develop and practice an alternative to contemporary mainstream approaches. This alternative developed into feminist therapy based on the feminist principle that the personal is political. This meant that psychological problems were to be viewed within the larger societal context and with a particular focus on power differentials in women's lives and in the psychotherapy relationship as a microcosm. Lack of access to financial and decision-making resources inside and outside the family was identified as one of the sources of psychological distress, particularly the various expressions of depression. The other crucial tenet of feminist therapy was that women's stories were to be believed; when they reported being wounded or abused, it was not to be attributed to fantasy or desire as was the current prevalent practice among many psychotherapists. In this way, not only could appropriate treatment be developed and offered, but, for the first time, accurate information on the prevalence of abuse could be gathered.

Certain approaches and techniques were developed and favored as being congruent with these principles and findings. The consciousness-raising group, which itself had been based on the "speak bitterness" groups of the Chinese revolution, in which formerly oppressed individuals would meet to tell their stories and express their feelings about their prior circumstances, was taken as an early model for feminist therapy. Group therapy was seen as a way to balance the extreme power differential in individual therapy and to permit each woman to have access to the similar experiences of the other group members both for support and for the essential feminist process of identifying the gender-based sources of women's problems. That is, what had previously appeared to be individual pathology was being revealed to be a function of female status and socialization.

Other specific techniques introduced by early feminist practitioners and typically used within the context of group treatment included assertiveness training and behaviorally oriented preorgasmic women's groups which were highly successful in treating a problem in 10 weeks that had previously been thought to require years of psychotherapy. As feminist therapy developed, these issues would come to be treated within the fuller context of each individual's life circumstances.

Contributions of Feminist Psychology

Feminist therapy called for opening the boundary around the individual to allow the real experiences of women in society to become visible and the real sources of pain to be discovered. One prevalent model, for example, called for sociotherapy rather than psychotherapy, as a way of including the full social context in the therapeutic focus. From its inception, feminist psychology has located much of the sources of psychopathology in the social environment rather than inside the individual, considering it a myth that an individual can exist separately from the social context. In addition to demonstrating the social construction of gender and how it increases the probability that certain psychological problems and issues will be associated with femininity and others with masculinity, feminist psychology has also been the first major psychological approach to include in its focus the full complement of sociocultural influences that intersect and interact to create what has come to be thought of in western society as individual identity. These include, but are not limited to, race, ethnicity, sexual orientation, class, age, and presence or absence of disability.

A strong tenet of feminist therapy has been, for many practitioners, a resistance to labeling women's problems as pathology, and for others as redefining what gets labeled as pathology, where the sources lie, and who is empowered to do this labeling. Feminist therapy calls for models based in strength and not weakness or pathology for women. This principle has had several important ramifications, including the development of nonpathological models of human functioning and ongoing organized attempts by feminist psychiatrists and psychologists to influence the content of the *Diagnostic and Statistical Manual* of the American Psychiatric Association.

Feminist psychotherapy practice developed in response to the urgency of fair and effective treatment for women. Only then were theorists and practitioners able to begin to formulate developmental and personality theory grounded in women's real experience. Many of these approaches attempted to reconcile aspects of feminist theory with psychoanalytic principles. Jean Baker Miller (1976) offered a psychoanalytically based treatment model for women. Nancy Chodorow (1978), using object relations theory, carefully traced the effects of women's mothering on the development of masculinity and femininity in children. Carol Gilligan (1982) introduced a model of moral development also based in gender difference. The Stone Center's theorists and practitioners have continued to extend the work of these theorists in what is known as the self-in-relation model of female psychology. This model holds that female psychology is strongly grounded in relationships and characterized by relational concerns.

Feminist theorists have continued to investigate and propose treatment paradigms for the all too ordinary disorders that are significantly more prevalent in girls and women, including eating disorders, agoraphobia, and depression. In recent years there has been more focus on girls and adolescents, highlighting issues of self-esteem and resilience, particularly in the difficult years of adolescence. Several theorists have noted the centrality of appearance and other physical concerns in girls' and women's psychology.

Another important developmental and personality theory, self-in-context, has been proposed by Ellyn Kaschak (1992), who considers the idea of a consistent individual self that is so central to western psychology to be a cultural construct. The psychological self, in this approach, is multiply determined by a combination of complex influences including genetics, biology, individual experience, and societal variables. Furthermore, the combination of qualities that come to be known as the self vary somewhat with the perceived or real demands of any situation. The sources of what appeared to be psychopathology or disorders are revealed to be quite orderly results of the real and ordinary experiences of women's lives.

These theories have also expanded the analysis of women's issues to issues of gender, eventually addressing specific problems of masculinity and men's issues as well. In recent times, there has also been a growing body of literature on male psychology by feminist writers and by profeminist male writers.

In addition to its impact on individual and group therapy, feminist therapy has, in recent years, had a profound influence on the practice of family therapy. Prior to the introduction of feminist thought, even the most systemic approaches to family processes failed to consider the profound influence of gender both inside and outside the family. Currently there is a growing body of theory and practice that engages with gender as a basic dynamic and organizing principle in family life.

Feminist practitioners have also been in the forefront of the organized critique of the *Diagnostic and Statistical Manual (DSM)* of the American Psychiatric Association, the current version of which is known as *DSM-IV.* Feminists and other critics have asserted and demonstrated the value-based biases of those in the professions who have the power to define from their perspective what is considered a psychological disorder. It has been demonstrated repeatedly that this is not a scientific process, but a subjective and value-laden one. Unfortunately, such individual values were left unchallenged and came to influence the entire field.

Feminist Psychology and Diagnosis

There are currently two major schools of thought among feminist psychotherapists regarding the use of diagnosis. One advocates the development of more careful and accurate diagnosis that takes into consideration the social context of the individual being diagnosed. The other calls for the elimination of diagnosis as a legitimate aspect of a feminist psychology not based in a disease model or an epistemology that can divide human experience neatly into discrete categories or taxonomies.

With regard to this issue, a major development in the field has been the identification of childhood trauma and other traumas as the source of many of the psychological symptoms that have been previously defined in such categories of pathology as hysteria, masochism, and borderline personality disorder. The contemporary diagnosis of post-traumatic stress disorder (PTSD), originally introduced to describe the experiences of returning Vietnam War veterans and later applied to women's experience of sexual abuse and violence, has become accepted as a more accurate description of the aftereffects of traumatic experience ranging from childhood sexual abuse to military experience. This diagnostic category has become the subject of extensive research and application by feminist and nonfeminist theorists and practitioners alike.

Feminist Psychology and the Therapeutic Setting

Feminist psychologists and psychotherapists have also been active in highlighting abuses of the therapeutic relationship, in particular the damaging effect of sexual relations between male therapists and female clients. As a result, the professional ethical codes have been revised to prohibit this violation explicitly. Many feminist therapists continue to be active in developing ethical codes that are protective of the rights of clients. Members of the Feminist Therapy Institute, an organization of feminist therapists, have been particularly active in this struggle, as well as in the controversies surrounding *DSM*. This group has written extensively about ethics in psychotherapy and has published its own ethical code.

Feminist theory and practice respects diverse identities, as well as the full complexity of influences on women's psychology. There has, thus, been an emphasis on such meaningful sociopsychological experiences as ethnicity, race, sexual orientation, aging, and disability as they affect each individual. In addition, as feminist theory is based in actual lived experience, feminist theory and practice continue to engage new issues as they become relevant in the real lives of women and men, girls and boys.

Feminist therapy is currently practiced internationally and is no longer confined to the United States or western Europe. It is the psychotherapy approach that has been most clearly associated with multicultural concerns and utilizes a complex model that includes the multiple sociocultural influences on diverse populations. Both formal organizations of practitioners and graduate and training programs for feminist therapists have been and are continuing to be developed.

See Also

PSYCHIATRY; PSYCHOLOGY: OVERVIEW; PSYCHOLOGY: COGNITIVE; PSYCHOLOGY: NEUROSCIENCE AND BRAIN RESEARCH; PSYCHOLOGY: PERSONALITY RESEARCH; PSYCHOLOGY: SOCIAL; SCIENCE: FEMINIST CRITIQUES; SEXUALITY: PSYCHOLOGY OF SEXUALITY IN CROSS-CULTURAL PERSPECTIVES

References and Further Reading

Adleman, J. and G. Enguidanos, eds. 1995. *Racism in the lives of women: Testimony, theory, and guides to antiracist practice.* New York: Haworth.

Brown, L. and M. P. P. Root, eds. 1990. *Diversity and complexity in feminist therapy.* New York: Harrington Park.

Chesler, Phyllis. 1972. *Women and madness.* New York: Doubleday.

Chesler, P., E. D. Rothblum, and E. Cole, eds. 1995. *Feminist foremothers: Women's studies, psychology and mental health.* New York: Haworth.

Chodorow, Nancy. 1978. *The reproduction of mothering: Psychoanalysis and the sociology of gender.* Berkeley: University of California Press.

Comas-Diaz, L., and B. Greene, eds. 1994. *Women of color: Integrating ethnic and gender identities in psychotherapy.* New York: Guilford.

Eichenbaum, L. and S. Orbach. 1983. *Understanding women: A feminist psychoanalytic approach.* New York: Basic Books.

Gilligan, Carol. 1982. *In a different voice.* Cambridge, Mass.: Harvard University Press.

Herman, Judith. 1992. *Trauma and recovery: The aftermath of violence.* New York: Basic Books.

Kaschak, Ellyn. 1992. *Engendered lives: A new psychology of women's experience.* Basic Books: New York.

Lerman, H., and N. Porter, eds. 1990. *Feminist ethics in psychotherapy.* New York: Springer.

Lips, Hilary M. 1999. *A new psychology of women: Gender, culture, and ethnicity.* California: Mayfield.

Luepnitz, D. A. 1988. *The family interpreted: Feminist theory in clinical practice.* New York: Basic Books.

Miller, Jean Baker. 1976. *Toward a new psychology of women.* Boston: Beacon.

Walters, M., B. Carter, P. Papp, and O. Silverstein. 1988. *The invisible web: Gender patterns in family relationships.* New York: Guilford.

Ellyn Kaschak

PSYCHOLOGY: Sexuality

See SEXUALITY: PSYCHOLOGY OF SEXUALITY IN CROSS-CULTURAL PERSPECTIVES; SEXUALITY: PSYCHOLOGY OF SEXUALITY IN THE UNITED STATES.

PSYCHOLOGY: Social

The study of women in social psychology has focused on the social context in which women develop, behave, and relate. The major themes in the study of the social environment of women are gender-role socialization, gender stereotyping, attitudes toward women, and the changing experiences of women in the areas of home life and work life. In addition to including women in the content of psychological studies, feminist critique of psychology has also initiated a process of social construction for developing a women-inclusive psychology.

Research findings from both social learning and behavior genetics theories concur that there is a lack of evidence for any strong relationship between parental behavior and children's gender attributes. Meta-analysis of studies on parents' differential socialization of boys and girls found little evidence of direct effects on sex-typed cognitive and social characteristics. Within-sex variations are generally far greater than between-sex differences. On the other hand, the society's gender-roles expectations, and in particular parents' gender-role stereotypes, affect others' perception of children's ability and performance. These beliefs, in turn, have an impact on the subsequent development of children's abilities, self-concept, and interests. In most patriarchal societies across the world, masculine attributes are associated with instrumentality, power, and success, and are valued more than feminine attributes, which are associated with expressiveness and emotionality.

Gender-role orientations are originally studied in terms of masculinity versus femininity. This dichotomy is reconceptualized as multiple dimensions including masculinity, femininity, and androgyny (Bem, 1974). More recent research found the concept of androgyny as a simple combination of masculinity and femininity to be flawed philosophically as well as methodologically. Even Sandra Bem herself now argues against the concept (1993). Alternative models to conceptualize the combination of different gender-related characteristics include gender-role transcendence or instrumentality-expressiveness.

While there are more individual variations in terms of gender-role identities, gender stereotypes tend to be more homogeneous within cultures. Gender stereotypes are composed of the characteristics that people associate with the typical male and the typical female, as well as the ways that he or she should behave. Children at an early age are able to differentiate between male and female characteristics. Cross-cultural studies have consistently found that the male stereotype is associated with a competency-strength cluster of characteristics, whereas the female stereotype is associated with a warmth-expressiveness cluster of characteristics. The male stereotype is generally given more favorable ratings than the female stereotype. The degree of gender-stereotype differentiation among children varies across different nations (Williams and Best, 1990).

Women's self-esteem is, to a large extent, affected by society's attitudes toward women as members of the female gender. Measures of attitudes toward women have utilized rating scales depicting attitudes toward women's rights, changing roles of women, and gender equality (Spence et al., 1974). Positive attitudes toward women are also found to be related to other social attitudes, such as modernity values in developing countries, and to more sympathetic attitudes toward rape victims in both western and Asian societies.

Attitudes toward women and women's own self-perceptions are factors affecting women's entry into and advancement in the workforce. As more women become employed outside the home in developed and developing countries, the societal transition from traditional divisions of labor poses new challenges to women. At the subjective level, stereotypes about the ability and aspirations of women are manifested in the form of prejudice and discrimination against women entering traditionally male-dominated fields. Women's own aspirations are likewise restricted by these stereotypic expectations. On the objective level, women's roles have expanded without a corresponding redefinition of gender roles. Although more women are entering the workforce, the traditional gender imbalance in domestic labor is still evident across different societies, with wives taking primary responsibility for the majority of household tasks. The burden of women's dual roles has often been cited as a source of potential stress. However, existing research results do not provide a simple answer as to whether this is the case. Nevertheless, women's changing expectations of redefined gender roles are a possible source of conflicts in marital and social relationships.

Feminist perspectives in social psychology not only have enriched the understanding of gender within society as a whole but also have changed the self-definition of psychology itself as a discipline. Efforts are made to explain women's relationship to the discipline and to incorporate women, women's perspective, and women's work into mainstream psychology.

See Also

ANDROGYNY; CHILD DEVELOPMENT; DIVISION OF LABOR; DOMESTIC LABOR; FEMININITY; IMAGES OF WOMEN: OVERVIEW; MASCULINITY; PSYCHOLOGY: PERSONALITY RESEARCH; SEXISM; SOCIALIZATION FOR COMPLEMENTARITY

References and Further Reading

Bem, Sandra L. 1993. *The lenses of gender: Transforming the debate on sexual inequality.* New Haven, Conn.: Yale University Press.

———. 1974. The measurement of psychological androgyny. *Journal of Consulting and Clinical Psychology* 42: 155–62.

Bohan, Janis S., ed. 1992. *Seldom seen, rarely heard: Women's place in psychology.* Boulder, Col.: Westview.

Frieze, Irene H., and Maureen C. McHugh, eds. 1997. Measuring beliefs about appropriate roles for women and men. [special issue]. *Psychology of Women Quarterly 21*(1).

Oskamp, Stuart, and Mark Costanzo, eds. 1993. *Gender issues in contemporary society.* Newbury Park, Calif.: Sage.

Spence, Janet T., Robert Helmreich, and Joy Stapp. 1974. The personal attributes questionnaire: A measure of sex role stereotypes and masculinity-femininity. *JSAS Catalog of Selected Documents in Psychology* 4(43): ms. no. 617.

Twenge, Jean M. 1997. Changes in masculine and feminine traits over time: A meta-analysis. *Sex Roles* 36: 305–325.

Williams, John E., and Deborah L. Best. 1990. *Measuring sex stereotypes: A multination study.* Rev. ed. Newbury Park, Calif.: Sage.

Fanny Mui-ching Cheung

PUBERTY

See ADOLESCENCE; SEXUALITY: ADOLESCENT SEXUALITY.

PUBLISHING

"To publish" means to make content available to the public. In contrast to content circulated only via oral traditions, material that is published involves not only the literary art of content creation but also the industrial and trade crafts of manufacturing, marketing, distributing, and storing the content. The publishing industry requires access to capital, labor, property, bricks-and-mortar warehouses, distribution channels, bandwidth, education, and literacy. In societies where literacy is not widespread, or where it is denied to segments of the population, or where it is criminalized (as happens to women in some parts of the world), publishing contributes little to daily living. In societies where literacy is nearly universal, or where access to information drives the economy, publishing is an essential activity.

Those with the power to decide what gets published and what remains unrecorded, silent, private, restricted, or off limits are the publishers. The publishers usually represent the social power structure and, arguably, published history is, in the main, the recorded history of the world's patriarchies. The content of most publications throughout recorded history has concerned laws and government, sacred texts and religion, contracts and trade, science and industry, and (relatively recently) entertainment and leisure.

History of the Publishing Industry

Publishing predates the common era, with early content recorded on stone tablets, wood carvings, pottery, papyrus, parchment, silk, and other textiles. Establishing timelines and locales for the earliest publications and earliest libraries is the work of archeologists. The medieval scribes who lettered manuscripts by hand in monastaries, universities, and guilds set the pattern for publishing's modern era, which usually is identified as starting with the work of Johannes Gutenberg (c. 1398–1468) in Mainz, Germany. Earlier printed books are designated as incunabula.

Gutenberg and his colleagues used metalworking techniques to create movable type. These machine-created type fonts were designed to resemble the hand lettering of professional scribes, but when the metal letters were assembled into words, spaces, lines, columns, and pages, they could be used on a printing press to reproduce multiple copies of a single text, which previously had to be produced one copy at a time. The new technology was used primarily in the service of religion and government, and Gutenberg is best remembered for his edition of the Judeo-Christian Bible, which he or his associates published c. 1450–1456, called the

Bible of 42 Lines, or more commonly the *Gutenberg Bible.* Several copies survive in rare book collections. The introduction of publishing to the western hemisphere is attributed to the American colonial printer Stephen Day (1594–1668) in Cambridge, Massachusetts, who is remembered for his *Bay Psalm Book* (1640), again a religious work. Newer editions of the Bible and other sacred texts of the world's religions continue to be best-sellers today (Association of American Publishers, 2000; Bookwire, 1999).

Gutenberg, Day, Aldus Manutius (1450–1515), William Caslon (1692–1766), and other early modern publishers identified their profession as "printer." These early publishers also performed tasks that precede and follow the actual printing process, tasks that today are assigned to writers, editors, literary agents, typesetters, and proofreaders before a book is printed, and to bookbinders, booksellers, and book distributors afterward. The process that combined printing, publishing, and bookselling remained the prevailing model until the nineteenth century, at which time those activities began to diverge into separate industries. The division of labor in publishing continues to be subject to frequent reorganization, and today's writers often perform the tasks of writer, editor, agent, typesetter, proofreader, indexer, and book publicist combined. Today's multinational publishers often control all the same activities as did their sixteenth-century counterparts, with ownership shares in paper mills added for good measure.

The growth of the publishing industry during the years 1500 to 2000 contributed in complex ways to the expansion of scholarship, education, science, libraries, literacy, and linguistic diversity. The Canadian educator and media theorist Herbert Marshall McLuhan (1911–1980) linked the development of the printing press to the transformation of the modern world into a unified global village. His landmark study *The Gutenberg Galaxy* (McLuhan, 1962) carries the unfortunate subtitle *The Making of Typographic Man,* however, reminding us that twentieth-century media scholarship continues to be as androcentric as the earlier varieties.

With the rise of the novel and other new literary genres in the eighteenth century, publishing became a medium of entertainment for those who had economic means, leisure time, the ability to read, and access to private or lending libraries. When lower-priced softcover books were introduced in the mid-twentieth century, publishing became a medium of mass culture. Today's mass-market paperbound book with its crowded pages, high-acid-content paper stock, glued-on paper covers, and trim size designed to fit convenience stores' sale racks—continues to be a relatively affordable consumer product. With the expansion of electronic technology in the 1960s and 1970s, publishing was finally able to shift from the hot-metal typesetting and letterpress printing processes that had remained substantially unchanged since Gutenberg's era. Technological developments of the late twentieth century include computer-created photocomposition ("cold type"); desktop publishing; optical character recognition (OCR); voice recognition; scanning and imaging software; machine-readable markup languages like SGML (standard generalized markup language), HTML (hypertext markup language), and XML (extensible markup language); machine-readable indentifiers like the ISBN (international standard book number), ISSN (international standard serial number), and DOI (digital object identifier); photo-offset printing; print-on-demand; digitized content; and online publication.

Even with the proliferation of Internet postings and electronic document delivery, the printed book (that unique combination of words and images inked onto large sheets of paper that are then folded, gathered, and bound between covers) continues to be the archetypal symbol of the publishing industry. Digital content may be posted on-line and transmitted to readers in nonpaper formats (for example, disk, fiche, film, tape, and file transfer protocols), but "publication" still is considered to occur when an ink-and-paper version is released for public distribution. Paper, printing, and binding (ppb) continue to be core components of the publisher's cost of doing business.

The Publishing Industry Today

Seven hundred years after Gutenberg's birth, publishers by and large have stopped calling themselves "printers" and have started identifying themselves variously as the knowledge industry, the information industry, and the copyright industry. Today's publishing industry comprises the creation, production, manufacturing, sale, and distribution of books, journals, newspapers, magazines, advertising, music, videos, databases, software, and digital content posted on the Internet.

The publishing industry today has global reach. Industry gatherings are international events, with important book fairs taking place each year in Frankfurt, Bologna, London, Jerusalem, Cairo, New Delhi, Tokyo, Guadalajara, São Paulo, Chicago, and upward of 50 other cities (Bookwire, 1999). Industry concerns, as reflected in the agendas of its local, regional, and international gatherings, include:

- Ownership of intellectual property and works in the public domain; copyright treaties for literary and other works; and protection of copyrighted material against infringement, piracy, and expanding definitions of fair use (Her Majesty's Stationery Office, 1998, U.S. Library of Congress, 2000: World Intellectual Property Organization, 2000).

- Improving technologies for digitizing, producing, selling, distributing, and archiving content cost effectively.
- Reducing censorship and promoting freedom of the press, literacy, and education.
- Expanding markets for the sale of published materials and the licensing of distribution, translation, and subsidiary rights.

Organizations that include publishing as part of their operations today include governments, universities, professional societies, religious organizations, and for-profit corporations ranging from multinationals through small presses run by individual people. In the for-profit sector, organizational concerns focus on profit margins, which often lead to mergers and consolidations among imprints, corporate divisions, booksellers, and book distributors. In the professional, scholarly, and educational sectors, organizational concerns usually focus on expanding the distribution of research results, scholarly journals, textbooks, and content through traditional means and through newer forms of distance learning and the Internet.

Women and the Publishing Industry

Because publishing has always represented and furthered the needs of social power structures, and because (arguably) those power structures have been mostly patriarchal, the narratives, writings, and records of women have only recently been deemed worthy of discovery, reconstruction, and publication (DeLamotte et al., 1997). If Gutenberg's sister, wife, mother, or daughter used the family printing press, for example, history does not seem to have taken note. When women did manage to get their content published, they created some of the important milestones of the women's movement, including *A Vindication of the Rights of Woman* (1792) by Mary Wollstonecraft (1759–1797), the suffragist journalism of Elizabeth Cady Stanton (1815–1902) and Susan B. Anthony (1820–1906), and *The Feminine Mystique* by Betty Friedan, to name just a few.

Worldwide in the twenty-first century, out of the 30,000 publishing houses in 180 countries, only 600 or so identify women's studies books and journals as components of their product line, with the United States and Canada accounting for about half that total (Bookwire, 1999). Publishers who offer women's studies material as part of their list include university presses (for example, Indiana University Press, Open University Press, and the Feminist Press at the City University of New York) and divisions of larger organizations (for example, Routledge, Beacon, and HarperCollins), but publishing houses independently owned and directed by women are considered the pioneers of this genre. Notable names among these independents are Aunt Lute Books, Cleis Press, Firebrand Books, Naiad Press, Seal Press, Spinifex Press, Spinsters Ink, Virago Press, Volcano Press, and Women's Press.

Periodicals that publish scholarship about women are an essential element of women's studies as an emerging and maturing academic discipline. Notable journal titles include *Signs: Journal of Women in Culture and Society, International Journal of Women's Studies, NWSA Journal* (from the National Women's Studies Association in the United States), *Feminist Studies, Women's Studies International Quarterly, Gender and Society, Women and Health,* and *Psychology of Women Quarterly.* Guides to the literature include *Feminist Collections: A Quarterly Review of Women's Studies Resources* and *Feminist Periodicals: A Current Listing of Contents,* both of which originate on-line with the University of Wisconsin System Women's Studies Librarian.

Careers in publishing are a popular choice among women. "Glass ceilings" and other barriers to access, advancement, decision making, and pay equity continue to be pervasive problems, however (Women in Publishing, 1995), and female members of most professional societies within the industry often find themselves starting women's caucuses to increase visibility and voice. In preparation for International Women's Day on 8 March 2000, the director-general of UNESCO issued a public reminder to directors and editors-in-chief of news media that it would be appropriate to allow women journalists to report on the events of that day. Without such reminders, women's absence from or underrepresentation in positions of power continues unabated (Rakow, 1992).

Women book buyers are an important target market for the publishing industry, as well as for the advertiser-supported consumer magazine industry. In the United States, for example, approximately $25 billion worth of books are sold annually (Association of American Publishers, 2000). Of that total, about $1.5 billion falls within the mass-market paperback sector, with about half those sales ($800 million) accounted for by women's genre fiction. Not surprisingly, religious books continue to be an important sector of the industry as well (Bookwire, 1999).

By far the largest sector of the publishing industry today focuses on education, scholarship, science, medicine, technology, and professional training (Bookwire, 1999). Sexism and structural biases against women are pervasive in this sector of the industry, affecting textbook content (Rosser and Potter, 1991), the organization of the academic diciplines

(Spender, 1981), and the scholarly practice known as "publish or perish."

"Publish or Perish"

In contrast to commercial sectors of the economy, advancement and success in academic careers usually depend on factors that are not always measured directly by money. University communities sometimes debate the importance of teaching students versus the importance of research and publication, but decisions about faculty promotions, salaries, and awarding of tenure all are based primarily on the frequency with which academics publish the results of their research and the frequency with which that published scholarship is then cited by others (Carrigan, 1990; Henon, 1990). Commonly referred to as "publish or perish," this practice creates multiple barriers that prevent women's equitable participation in academic communities (Schneider, 1998). Among common obstacles are:

- Family versus work: The years when women's parenting responsibilities are greatest are the same years when publishing counts most toward career advancement.
- Research and writing hours versus teaching and administrative hours: Career hours for research and writing are awarded disproportionately to men, and career tasks that interfere with research and writing (teaching and administrative work) are assigned disproportionately to women. Research grants, clerical support, and graduate assistants also are awarded more frequently to men than to women.
- Authorship conventions: Research and scholarship mostly are team efforts, and journal articles in particular often are the result of collaborative research and writing. It is not uncommon for "senior" authorship to be awarded to the scholar with the most name recognition and support (usually male), leaving the junior scholar (often female) with less visiblity ("et alia") at a time when visibility is the key to success. When journal style guides require that authors identify themselves by first initial and last name rather than by full first and last names, the result almost always is the presumption of male authorship.
- Peer review: Written work must undergo a process of peer review before it is published. At its best, the peer review process ensures that only accurate scholarship is published. At its worst, peer review ensures that only submissions from members of "old boy networks" and the protégés they mentor are accepted for publication. The readers and editors who serve on peer review boards are those who have mastered the art of publishing. As the women's studies sector of academe expands and matures, it will be interesting to see whether "old girl networks" develop the same exclusionary practices or whether women scholars are able to achieve more inclusivity among colleagues.
- Citation indexes: Also important to how scholarly merit is judged is the frequency with which one's published work is cited by others as a research source. In the same way as peer review, this practice perpetuates the privileges of those who have long publication histories and raises barriers to those awaiting publication.
- Scholarly discourse: The standards for written language, it is held, have been set by patriarchal tradition (Penelope, 1990). These standards render women invisible, with sexism so deeply entrenched in language that style guides attempting to prescribe "nonsexist" writing usually result in circumlocutions, awkward prose, and errors of grammar.

As has been true throughout recorded history, the greatest barrier to the publication of scholarship by and about women continues to be the fact that scholarship by and about men occupies the center of the page, leaving room for women only at the margins. Contemporary searches of publication databases and published literature still retrieve only content about men unless the searcher adds the modifier "women and" to the keywords. The growth of feminist publishing during the second half of the twentieth century gave us a start toward undoing "male" as the default setting in publishing. That trend needs to continue.

See Also

BOOKSHOPS; COMMUNICATIONS: OVERVIEW; FICTION; LIBRARIES; LITERACY; MAGAZINES; MEDIA: OVERVIEW; PRESS: FEMINIST ALTERNATIVES; PUBLISHING: FEMINIST PUBLISHING IN THE WESTERN WORLD; PUBLISHING: FEMINIST PUBLISHING IN THE THIRD WORLD

References and Further Reading

Association of American Publishers. 2000. <www.publishers.org> Industry Statistics.

Bookwire. 1999. <www.bookwire.com>. Inside the Book Business. Includes links to the *Book Industry Study Group, Literary Market Place,* and *Publishers Weekly* Web sites.

Carrigan, Dennis P. 1990. The political economy of scholarly communication and the American system of higher education. *Journal of Academic Librarianship* (6): 332–337.

DeLamotte, Eugenia C., Natania Meeker, and Jean F. O'Barr, eds. 1997. *Women imagine change: A global anthology of women's resistance.* New York: Routledge.

Henon, Alain L. 1990. Publish *and* perish. *Serials Librarian* 17 (3–4): 35–41.

Her Majesty's Stationery Office. 1998. <www.hmso.gov.uk> Crown Copyright in the Information Age: A Consultation Document on Access to Public Sector Information.

McLuhan, Marshall. 1962. *The Gutenberg galaxy: The making of typographic man.* Toronto: University of Toronto Press.

Penelope, Julia. 1990. *Speaking freely: Unlearning the lies of the fathers' tongues* (Athene Series). New York: Teachers College Press.

Rakow, Lana F. 1992. What's a nice feminist like you doing in journalism and mass communication? In Cheris Kramerae and Dale Spender, eds., *The knowledge explosion: Generations of feminist scholarship* (Athene Series, 191–199). New York: Teachers College Press.

Rosser, Sue V., and Ellen Potter. 1991. Sexism in textbooks. In Sue V. Rosser, *Female-friendly science: Applying women's studies methods and theories to attract students* (Athene Series). New York: Teachers College Press.

Schneider, Alison. 1998. Why don't women publish as much as men? *Chronicle of Higher Education* 45 (3): A14ff.

Spender, Dale, ed. 1981. *Men's studies modified: The impact of feminism on the academic disciplines* (Athene Series). New York: Pergamon.

U.S. Library of Congress. 2000. <www.loc.gov> Copyright Office. See also Center for the Book in the Library of Congress <lcweb.loc.gov/loc/cfbook>.

Women in Publishing. 1995. <www.cyberiacafe.net/wip/greysuits.html>. Still Grey Suits at the Top.

World Intellectual Property Organization. 2000. <www.wipo.int>. International Protection of Copyright and Neighboring Rights.

Faye Zucker

PUBLISHING: Feminist Publishing in the Third World

Feminist or women's publishing has a relatively recent history in countries of the "South," otherwise known as the third world. This is not because women have not written or been published, but more because publishing in southern countries has historically been hampered by a lack of resources, and feminist publishing is no exception. In most countries shortages of paper are common, technology is expensive, and professional training is unavailable. When more basic constraints such as a lack of literacy, education, and buying power are added to these, the status of publishing suffers considerably, and women's writing and publishing are further marginalized.

The history of women's publishing in southern countries, as elsewhere in the world, is directly linked to the growth of women's movements. Such movements have helped to create a hospitable environment and a receptive readership. Ursula Owen, one of the founders of Virago, the pioneering British feminist house, noted in 1988 that "when we started in 1973, we already knew there was an audience, because we came out of the women's movement. And in a sense, we were created by that audience—we're a result of history." While the origins of northern and southern feminist publishers may have been similar, the trajectories they have followed are different and are closely related to the political, social, and economic contexts out of which they have grown. The emphasis in countries of the South has been less on straightforward commercial publishing (and therefore less on what are known as "trade" books) but more on helping to develop writing skills, and on making interventions in literacy and education, and also, to some extent, in the more "conventional" types of publishing.

Feminist publishing in the South is also closely related to the growth of a relatively new discipline: women's studies. With the setting up of women's studies courses and research institutes, activists and academics, many of them women, began to generate a fair amount of material. Because such material was, by and large, critical of the patriarchies embedded in the more "acceptable" academic disciplines, it did not find a ready place in most publishers' lists. It was thus left to feminist publishers and women's groups to take on the task of publishing it. Unfortunately, because this history is not documented at all, it is difficult to put dates and times on the formation of publishing enterprises. But it would not be wrong to say that it was in the late 1970s or early 1980s that efforts began to be made to put together publishing ventures that would focus on the works of women.

One of the early pioneers was a Nigerian writer, Flora Nwapa. Concerned about the absence of women writing in mainstream publishing, Nwapa set up two small imprints, Flora Nwapa and Co. and Tana Press, the former to publish mainly her own writing and the latter to do books for children. Before her untimely death, Nwapa had begun to speak of her commitment to both feminism and the publishing of feminist books, an ideal that she was not able to realize. Another early publisher was a South African, Dinah Lefakanu, who set up a feminist publishing house, Sritti ya Sechaba, which won a feminist writing-publishing award. Although this press does not exist anymore, it holds an important place in the history of feminist publishing.

At a later stage these women were joined by others. In 1984, two women, Urvashi Butalia and Ritu Menon, set up a feminist publishing house in India, Kali for Women. This was followed, in 1986, by a small imprint, Cuarto Propio, set up by Marisol Vera in Chile. In 1990, Layla Chaouni, a Moroccan, set up a small, independent publishing house, Le Fennec, to publish books in Arabic and French. Over the years, Chaouni came to turn her attention increasingly to women's books, and today gender forms a substantial part of her list. Four years later, in Vanuatu in the Pacific, Grace Mera Molisa started publishing her own writing from her living room. Over time, through contact with feminist publishers in other countries, Molisa became interested in books on and by women and started planning her own list of Pacific writers.

If these were some of the pioneering individuals, there were also, in these and other parts of the world, activist groups who began to produce books about women. The production and dissemination of knowledge has always been a central part of women's activism and it is for this reason that many publishers of books and pamphlets on women are not publishing houses in the formal sense of the term. Instead, they are often women's groups who have produced books and pamphlets and have put together autobiographies, biographies, essays, and research works. Together with the work of feminist publishers, it is this body of knowledge that has, in recent years, transformed our understanding of the world and brought many key ideas to center stage. Material produced by such "publishers" forms the bedrock of women's movements in southern countries.

Thus, in Latin America, the work of Cuarto Propio supplemented that of a number of women's groups such as Flora Tristan (1979) in Peru, Isis International (1984) in Chile, and CIPAF (Research Center for Women's Action) set up in the Dominican Republic in 1980, as well as that of DEMAC in Mexico and GREMCU in Uruguay, all of whom were later joined by Feminaria in Argentina in 1987. All these groups were already beginning to publish books and pamphlets on and by women, although Curato Propio remained the only "real" publishing house.

Among the early publishers in Africa were a number of groups, mainly membership organizations, that took on the twin tasks of encouraging women's writing and publishing. One of the most successful groups in this regard was Zimbabwe Women Writers (ZWW), which was set up in response to a need expressed at a writing workshop in 1990. From its modest beginnings, the ZWW by the turn of the century had more than 90 branches all over the country. Here, young, aspiring women writers are taught writing skills and encouraged to publish with ZWW. Roughly around the same time, another group, the Zimbabwe Women's Resource Center and Network (ZWCRN) was set up as a documentation center that also publishes bibliographies, reports, and discussion papers from meetings and conferences. Zimbabwe is perhaps the most lively country where women's publishing in Africa is concerned and women's groups such as the ones mentioned above, as well as others, publish subsidized books that cater largely to a niche audience. Among the mainstream houses, perhaps the only one to specifically start a women's list was Baobab, which also published some key books on women. More recently, the Zimbabwean pioneers have been joined by others: in 1995, five years after the setting up of ZWW, the Uganda Women Writers Association set up a similar group, Femwrite. Also a membership organization, Femwrite publishes writing by its members and works toward bringing out materials with the aim of removing illiteracy. It was in Uganda, too, that another group, Isis-Wicce, took on some publishing to supplement its other activities with women. A similar but smaller group is Sister Namibia, which focuses mainly on bringing out a magazine with writings by women but has plans to publish books as well. In the northern part of Africa, Le Fennec was joined in the mid-1980s by a small publishing collective, Nour, in Egypt. After bringing out some excellent books in Arabic, the Nour collective split and while one arm of the group has moved away from books, the other one continues to locate and publish women writers from the Arab world.

In Asia, the first publishing house to be set up to publish books on women was Kali for Women in India (1984). Kali's focus on southern writers and on both academic and trade books has proved to be a successful mix, and today it publishes some 12 to 15 titles a year. Shortly after Kali was set up, three women's groups in Pakistan (Simorgh, ASR, and Shirkat Gah) took up the task of publishing different kinds of books by women. Between them, they produce fiction, research studies, reports, primers, and pamphlets. In India, Kali was followed by a women's bookstore in Bangalore (Streelekha), and later by a small women's imprint (Stree), based in Calcutta. Earlier, in the Philippines, the 1970s had seen the setting up of women's studies centers and courses and a small group, the Women's Resource and Research Center (WRRC), began to publish books for such courses. Genderpress, a Thai feminist house, was set up in 1992, following in the footsteps of a smaller imprint, Tigress Press, which focused mainly on bringing out women's diaries. In Singapore, AWARE, a group set up in the 1980s, and CAW (Committee on Asian Women), continue to bring out the occasional book on women.

When placed against the mainstream publishing industry, this handful of houses and groups does not seem to add up to much. But there is little doubt that their contribution has been significant. The production and dissemination of knowledge by and about women has been one of the key ways in which feminist writers and publishers have intervened in the debate on women. It is such knowledge that has brought about a major change in the way women are perceived the world over. Gender studies, queer theory, women's studies, or what we might call writing from the margins, are all a result of feminist publishing.

Although some of these groups were not publishers in the recognized sense, there is no denying that they brought out excellent publications on and by women. The limitations of their size, coupled with a lack of resources and minimal knowledge of the technicalities of publishing, meant that many of these books (with the exception of those brought out by the "real" publishers) did not make it into the market and circulated mainly within alternative networks. Nonetheless, they made—and continue to make—a major contribution to the creation of feminist knowledge.

In the initial days, many feminist and women's publishers faced a fair amount of skepticism in the market: Were there enough subjects or authors to sustain them? Did they really believe they could continue to publish on such a "limited" theme indefinitely? Was there a market for women's books? Most of these doubts were proved groundless, and the threat, when it came, was from a different quarter altogether. There has been no dearth of writers, publishers, or readers for women's books. Indeed, in the heady days of the mid-1980s, when feminist publishing in the "North" was at its peak, it was agreed at the First International Feminist Book Fair in London (1984) that the two new growth areas were women's books and floppy disks. No sooner had feminist publishers created a market, however, the large, mainstream houses—ever ready to seize on a new opportunity—moved in. With them came all the things women writers, hitherto cast into the shade, had been looking for: stability, acceptability, a mythical objectivity, a presence alongside other, more "respected" writers, financial security, a wider reach, and so on.

As more and more authors begin to move to the larger houses, feminist publishers are faced with a peculiar situation: this very "flight" marks the success of their efforts to find a place in the sun for women writers, but they see, too, how this "success" has helped to strengthen the structures they set out to fight, mainly the market and the mainstream. The irony is that feminist publishers, whose rationale was to open up the world of publishing and writing to women, cannot now argue against greater choice, or indeed against exercising it to claim the better option, which is what many women writers continue to do. Some feminist publishers in the North and South have been forced to sell out, or to be taken over by larger conglomerates. In countries of the South, there is a further imbalance: many of the mainstream publishers are large, multinational conglomerates, or subsidiaries of old colonial houses. Small, independent publishers or women's groups taking on the publishing of women's works can hardly hope to compete with their reach and power and to simultaneously address the issue of confronting multiple patriarchies.

For feminist publishers in the South, therefore, the challenges are manifold: they must continue to survive in difficult situations and they must maintain a distinct identity, while at the same time attempting to influence and open up the mainstream. Because many of them have their roots in women's movements, and draw a large number of their readers, too, from this constituency, they cannot easily go entirely commercial. As long as they remain connected with women's movements, they must turn their attention to the more pressing issues of literacy and education in their countries in which they have a key role to play. At the same time, although it is not easy to maintain this precarious balance between retaining a sense of social purpose and attempting to influence the mainstream, southern publishers perhaps have more cause for hope than publishers in the North, precisely because they come out of a different situation. If they are able to continue to inform their politics with their practice, and vice versa, and to focus on areas which are not so "attractive" to the mainstream but which are nonetheless important, they can still continue to make a major contribution to the world of knowledge. If the knowledge generated by feminist and women's publishers in southern countries can circulate not only within other countries of the South but also to the North, then a further process of transformation will have begun. To some extent, because of the international nature of the women's movement, this is an option feminist publishers have been able to explore, and it would not be wrong to say that there has been relatively more exchange between feminist publishers of the North and South than there has been in many other areas of publishing. Whether this will remain as more and more northern houses are sold to larger conglomerates is another question.

See Also

BOOKSHOPS; LITERACY; LITERATURE: OVERVIEW; PUBLISHING; PUBLISHING: FEMINIST PUBLISHING IN THE WESTERN WORLD; WOMEN'S MOVEMENT: OVERVIEW; WOMEN'S STUDIES: OVERVIEW

References and Further Reading

Altbach, Philip G., and Hyaeweol Choi. 1993. *Bibliography on publishing and book development in the third world, 1980–1993*. Westport, Conn.: Ablex.

Urvashi Butalia

PUBLISHING: Feminist Publishing in the Western World

> For many of us, the women's presses have literally made possible our art, our movement, our lives. (Clausen, 1976)

In order to communicate their ideas with one another, the women's movements became print movements out of necessity. In the nineteenth century, print was the only way to disseminate information to large numbers of women. Women could not rely on men to do this for them, as coverage of women's issues in mainstream publications was distorted and trivializing. This was no less true in the women's movements of the twentieth century.

Beginnings of Feminist Publishing

The upsurge of publishing by and for women in the 1970s had a rich past in the nineteenth century, particularly in the United States. Many of the early feminists (they called themselves "strong-minded women") were also important editors and publishers, and, starting in the 1850s, there were a number of periodicals founded and run by them. Among these were *The Lily,* Amelia Bloomer's temperance and women's rights journal, published from 1849 to 1858; *The Genesis of Liberty,* edited by Elizabeth Aldrich, published from 1851 to 1853; *The Pioneer and Woman's Advocate,* edited by Anna Spencer, published from 1852 to 1853; *The Una,* edited by Paulina Wright Davis, published from 1853 to 1855; *The Sybil,* edited by Dr. Lydia Hasbrouck, published from 1856 to 1864; and *The Woman's Advocate,* edited by Anne McDowell, published from 1855 to 1858. These periodicals were followed by others, perhaps the most important of which was *The Revolution,* published from 1868 to 1871, and edited by Susan B. Anthony, Elizabeth Cady Stanton, and Parker Pillsbury.

These periodicals, as major sources of information and a connecting link to feminists of the nineteenth century, were very influential in the development of the women's rights movement, but the issues they dealt with were not restricted to women's rights alone. Of major concern, too, were temperance (not surprising in an age when women were economically dependent on men and drink could ruin them and their families) and abolition. The women who founded them were mainly from the middle and upper classes, were actively engaged in political and social reform and were interested in bettering the lot of women in general, not just women of their class.

The push for social reform abated somewhat after the Civil War and Reconstruction in the United States, but it never disappeared entirely. The push for women's suffrage brought new publications, among them *The Women's Rights,* which was published in the 1920s. But once women gained the right to vote, activity virtually ceased until the feminist movement of the 1970s brought a resurgence of interest in women's rights. Many journals and newspapers as well as a feminist publishing house, the Feminist Press, sprang to life in 1970.

The Women-in-Print Movement

This part of the feminist "revolution" became known as the women-in-print movement. It was composed of women who felt so strongly about the need to record and preserve women's words that they dedicated all their time, energy, and often meager resources to this end. They bought used Multilith offset presses and put them in their basements, they rebuilt old barns to house their equipment, they quit well-paid jobs to work for $2.00 an hour, or kept their jobs and spent evenings and weekends setting type, running presses, editing manuscripts—whatever it took to put women's words down on paper and distribute them to a hungry and enthusiastic audience.

The 1970s and 1980s witnessed the birth of over 50 feminist book publishers. These were independent, women-owned publishers who were producing books for and about women, many of them combined with women-owned and women-operated print shops. Many, including the Feminist Press, are still going strong. And some, like Persephone Press, charged onto the landscape in 1976, only to burn out in 1984.

Much of what became the women-in-print movement took shape in the middle of a Nebraska prairie under the hot August sun in 1976. June Arnold and Parke Bowman, her partner in Daughters, Inc. (Plainfield, Vermont, 1973), conceived of the idea of a national conference and decided to have it in the geographical center of the United States, so women from each coast would have an equal distance to travel. One hundred and twenty-seven women representing 73 groups—feminist newspapers, journals and magazines, bookstores, book publishers, printers, and distributors—came to this conference at a camp outside Omaha. The concept was to "share skills and problems, get to know each other and strengthen our political network of feminist communication."

This conference proved to be an inspiration to those who had plunged into the third wave of feminism with enthusiasm, dedication, and a large dose of idealism; many were convinced that if women owned newspapers, magazines, publishing companies, and print shops, as well as distribution companies and bookstores, their words could not be suppressed.

June Arnold was one of the movement's visionaries, with "dreams of building a feminist literature in which the power of women's words can reshape the language and the culture in which they are written." Among other groundbreaking titles published by Daughters was Rita Mae Brown's *Rubyfruit Jungle.*

Naiad Press was established in 1972 by Andya Marchant (better known as Sarah Aldridge). The original goal was to publish lesbian fiction, which it has continued to do, putting out over 25 books a year.

Some of the more significant feminist publishers to emerge in the 1970s were Lollipop Power, in North Carolina, producing feminist children's books; Diana Press, which started in Baltimore and later moved to Oakland, California, to merge with the Woman's Press Collective, publishing the works of Judy Grahn, Elsa Gidlow, and Pat Parker, among others; Alice James in Boston, publishing women's poetry; Seal Press, founded in 1976 by Barbara Wilson and Rachel daSilva, which started out with a capital investment of $125 doing poetry chapbooks on a small letterpress. They brought the issue of battered women into print for perhaps the first time, and helped create the lesbian detective genre. Seal became a successful company with over 135 titles in print and grossing close to $1 million a year. Down There Press, founded in 1975 by Joni Blank, is dedicated to the liberation of women's sexuality. In 1976, New Victoria Publishers in Lebanon, New Hampshire, founded by Claudia Lamperti and Beth Dingman, also began publishing lesbian fiction. In 1978, Spinsters, Ink was founded by Maureen Brady and Judith McDaniel.

The movement continued to flower during the 1980s, as more presses came into being, including Cleis Press, founded by Felice Newman and Fredérique Delacoste in 1980; Kitchen Table, Women of Color Press, founded by Barbara Smith, Audre Lorde, Cherrie Moraga, and Hattie Gossett in 1981; Firebrand Press, founded by Nancy Bereano in 1984; and Papier Mâché Press, founded by Sandra Martz in 1984. Of the 64 women-owned and -operated publishing companies with a feminist perspective that were founded between 1970 and 1991, 21 were still publishing in 1999.

There were two more women-in-print conferences, bringing together book, newspaper, and magazine publishers, and bookstore owners, who provided the all-important outlet for the sale of all this printed material. The second, held in Washington, D.C., in 1981, was organized by the staff of *off our backs,* a newspaper. It was attended by 250 women representing about half of the over 400 lesbian-feminist bookstores, magazines, newspapers, printers, and publishers. Although there is a general impression that the women's movement was made up of middle-class white women, in a self-identified census at the conference, there were 25 women of color and 70 who considered themselves born into working-class families. One of the accomplishments of that conference was the collection of $1,300 (by passing the hat) to help support the creation of Kitchen Table Press.

The third women-in-print conference was held in Berkeley, California, in 1985; it brought together 205 women "to promote and strengthen feminist publishing and feminist women in the print and publishing trades."

The networks that were set up in the early 1970s continued through the next 30 years. Carol Seajay's *Feminist Bookstore News,* a bimonthly publication that grew out of the first women-in-print conference in 1976, kept everyone informed as to the news of feminist bookstores and publishers.

It is important to note that these feminist presses could more accurately be known as lesbian-feminist presses. Over 90 percent of the women who founded and continue to run these presses are lesbians. "Lesbian publishers have kept women's ideas in circulation; they have helped to disperse new theoretical insights to new audiences of women, particularly insights about multiple interlocking oppressions (the basis of identity politics), and they have provided women with the self-help, spiritual, activist, and imaginative literatures necessary for them to sustain themselves and their political movements."

The importance of feminist publishers should not be underestimated. Not only have they brought to the world celebrated writers such as Dorothy Allison, Audre Lorde, Jane Rule, Pat Parker, Rita Mae Brown, and Sarah Schulman, but the feminist presses since the 1970s have been responsible for bringing to general consciousness the issues of abortion and reproductive freedom; women's bodies and self-image; stereotypes of women; women's health; equal rights; ecofeminism; spirituality; violence against women; and disabilities. They have published philosophers, storytellers, poets, social critics, sex workers, and adventurers. "Healing, in one form or another, was the major form of independent women's book publishing in the seventies: healing (and preventing) disease; healing psychological and emotional trauma; curing society of its poisonous attitude toward the female majority. This healing took place on practical and mythical levels, both of which were explored in depth in feminist publishing" (Armstrong, 1981).

Worldwide Feminist Publishing

Feminist publishing houses began in the 1970s in Canada, Great Britain, and Germany, and somewhat later in Australia, as well. Some were imprints of larger, male-run publishing houses, but some, particularly in Canada and Germany, were entirely women-owned and -operated.

Most of the Canadian presses paralleled those in the United States, with Press Gang originating in 1975, along with the Women's Press of Canada (1972), Second Story (1988), Sister Vision, and Gynergy.

Germany also boasts a number of feminist presses, including Frauenoffensive Verlagsgesellschaft (1974) in Munich and Orlanda Frauenverlag (1974) in Berlin.

In an attempt to communicate and share experiences, Carol Spelling helped to organize the first International Feminist Bookfair in London in 1984. Feminist publishing houses and women involved in publishing came together from all over the world to network, support, and encourage each other, and to raise the image of feminist publishing. The fair was so successful that it repeated itself every two years: in Oslo (1986), Montreal (1988), Barcelona (1990), Amsterdam (1992), and Melbourne, Australia (1994). Unfortunately, after Melbourne, no one could muster the energy or support to carry on.

In the 1970s and 1980s feminist presses seemed to be everywhere in Britain, and many still survive. Chief among these are Virago (though now part of the Little, Brown group), founded in 1973, which started by publishing the works of neglected women writers; the Women's Press, with its flatiron logo, founded in 1977; and Onlywoman. Ireland has Attic Press (1984), and Spinifex Press (1991) is a major feminist publisher in Australia.

The Future of Feminist Publishing

The 1990s were a time of consolidation of large publishers, distributors, and the growth of megabookstores. Although feminist publishers continued to emerge, including Third Side and Rising Tide Press, these trends had a very adverse effect on all small independents. Feminist publishers, who did so much to raise the awareness of women and men, suffered as a result of this push toward larger, more impersonal stores and demand for bigger discounts.

It is interesting to note that in many instances, the same women who founded these presses still managed them in the late 1990s. Now the goals of these dedicated women, who learned the workings of offset presses, living on meager if any wages, in order to bring the words of women into being, have to a great degree been accomplished.

In the 1990s, gay, lesbian, and transgender issues came to the forefront, superseding the traditional "feminist" issues.

The growing pervasiveness of the Internet has the potential to totally change the way we communicate ideas, leaving the future of feminist publishing quite unpredictable.

See Also

BOOKSHOPS; COMMUNICATIONS: OVERVIEW; INFORMATION REVOLUTION; JOURNALISM; MEDIA: ALTERNATIVE; PUBLISHING; PUBLISHING: FEMINIST PUBLISHING IN THE THIRD WORLD

References and Further Reading

Armstrong, David. 1981. *A trumpet to arms: Alternative media in America.* Boston: South End.

Rakow, Lana, and Cheris Kramarae. 1990. *The revolution in words: Righting women 1868–1871.* London and New York: Routledge.

Russo, Ann, and Cheris Kramarae. 1991. *The radical women's press of the 1850s.* London and New York: Routledge.

Beth Dingman